Mason and McCall Smith's

LAW AND
MEDICAL ETHICS

Seventh Edition

JK MASON CBE MD LLD
FRCPath FRCP(Edin) FRSE

*Regius Professor (Emeritus) of Forensic Medicine
at the University of Edinburgh*

GT LAURIE LLB PhD

Professor of Medical Jurisprudence at the University of Edinburgh

with a chapter by
M AZIZ LLB PhD

*Barrister at Law
Lecturer in Law at the University of Siena*

OXFORD
UNIVERSITY PRESS

OXFORD

UNIVERSITY PRESS

Great Clarendon Street, Oxford OX2 6DP

Oxford University Press is a department of the University of Oxford.
If furthers the University's objective of excellence in research, scholarship,
and education by publishing worldwide in

Oxford New York

Auckland Cape Town Dar es Salaam Hong Kong Karachi
Kuala Lumpur Madrid Melbourne Mexico City Nairobi
New Delhi Shanghai Taipei Toronto

With offices in

Argentina Austria Brazil Chile Czech Republic France Greece
Guatemala Hungary Italy Japan Poland Portugal Singapore
South Korea Switzerland Thailand Turkey Ukraine Vietnam

Oxford is a registered trade mark of Oxford University Press
in the UK and in certain other countries

Published in the United States
by Oxford University Press Inc., New York

Sixth edition 2002
Seventh edition 2006

British Library Cataloguing in Publication Data

Data available

Library of Congress Cataloging in Publication Data

Data available

Typeset in Minion by RefineCatch Limited, Bungay, Suffolk
Printed in Great Britain
on acid-free paper by
Ashford Colour Press Limited, Gosport, Hampshire
ISBN 0–19–928239–0   978–0–19–928239–5

1 3 5 7 9 10 8 6 4 2

PREFACE

Can it really be only three years since we last wrote a Preface to *Law and Medical Ethics*? It scarcely seems possible, yet so much has happened in the meantime both to the book itself and to its subject matter. The fact that a 7th edition has been called for is, in itself, an indication of the continuous, and apparently relentless, expansion of medical law as the framework of ethical medical practice—to such an extent that it is becoming increasingly difficult to write a generalised account of the subject within a book of manageable size.

As regards the book itself, the most significant change has been the loss of Professor Sandy McCall Smith as a co-author due to his overwhelming commitments in other fields. Although his retiral results from wholly felicitous circumstances, it has been a sad moment for the survivors and we are very pleased to have been able to retain his foundation connection with the book within its title. As a knock-on effect, we have been forced into an apology for the clear falsehood contained in the preface to the 6th edition; the senior author is, indeed, still with us but .... (*we did tell you so ...* RAAMcCS, GTL). On a fresher note, we are happy to welcome Dr Miriam Aziz as a contributor. Her chapter (chapter 3) is to be appreciated not only for its own sake but also as an indication of the trend towards considering the European, rather than the pure Anglophone, dimension that we are hoping to develop.

The sheer volume of material available has also dictated some fundamental adjustments to the contents of the book. We have decided to concentrate on those aspects of medical law which have a clear ethical component. As a result, we have eliminated the sections on sex law—where the legal problems of gender dysphoria have now been virtually solved—and on the criminal aspects of mental disorder. At the same time, political developments in the United Kingdom left us in a particularly unfortunate situation as Bills became either Acts or waste paper with the dissolution of Parliament; we hope that our readers will appreciate our difficulties, especially in relations to chapters 12 and 20. Along with all other authors in this field, we must also regret having missed the moving targets set by the appeal courts in some instances; the case of *R (on the application of Burke) v General Medical Council*, to which we refer at several points, is a case particularly in point. Despite the additional fact that nothing could stop the expansion of the remaining sections, we hope that the book will still retain its particular place in the relevant literature.

It will be noted that we have changed publishers and it is a pleasure to be associated with such a prestigious organisation as the Oxford University Press. Considering that the authors have been separated by some 7,000 miles, it has not been an easy production and we are most grateful to the publishers, and most particularly Ms Fiona Kinnear, for their understanding, forbearance and willingness to bend the fast-track rules when necessary.

We must also acknowledge with deep gratitude the contribution of our research assistant, Mr Geoff Pradella, whose services were made available through a generous contribution from the AHRC Research Centre for Studies in Intellectual Property and Technology Law at the University of Edinburgh. His prodigious appetite for work has pulled us out of the water on numerous occasions when others would have happily abandoned the task.

Other colleagues and friends have helped us out on particular points very readily whenever they have been asked. These include Dr Sharon Cowan, Dr Derek Chiswick, Ms Hilary Patrick, Dr Parker Hood, Mrs Elspeth Reid and Mme Joelle Godard. We thank them very sincerely for their friendly co-operation—and add a special word of thanks to Mrs Nadine Eriksson-Smith for frequent and invaluable technical assistance.

Finally we should say that we believe the law to be accurate as at March 2005.

JKM
GTL
May 2005
Edinburgh and Buenos Aires

CONTENTS

TABLE OF CASES

TABLE OF STATUTES

Please note that all references are to paragraph order. Legislation for the United Kingdom is covered first, followed by foreign legislation.

TABLE OF EUROPEAN AND INTERNATIONAL INSTRUMENTS

All Tabling is to paragraph number

PROPOSALS

RECOMMENDATIONS

REGULATIONS

TABLE OF STATUTORY INSTRUMENTS (UK)

All Tabling is to paragraph number

1

MEDICAL ETHICS AND MEDICAL PRACTICE

1.1 This book is concerned with a vital debate which has captured the imagination of people throughout the world—that is, as to how we should deal with the remarkable advances in medicine and human biology that bid fair to change the way in which we see ourselves as human beings. But the debate is also concerned with the more day-to-day issues of the role of law in medical practice and with the moral and legal contours of the doctor/patient relationship. It has an academic side to it—bioethics and medical law are recognised components of the curricula of many universities and colleges—but it also involves legislators, national bioethics commissions or committees and, increasingly, the public itself. It is, of course, inevitable that such an issue should give rise to a burgeoning literature consisting of both general and specialised material.[1]

1.2 The importance and intensity of the public moral conversation about bioethics and medical law are explained in part by the very nature of their subject matter. This is an area of concern which touches upon people's most intimate interests. It deals with matters of human reproduction and human mortality—or sex and death—both of which have traditionally involved our religious convictions and have provoked intense emotions. In addressing these issues, the debate raises many fundamental questions. What is it to be a person? What is the value of human life? How, if at all, should we attempt to influence the future biology of the species through the use of new (genetic) knowledge?

1.3 There is no shortage of conviction on any of these issues. Most major religious traditions have firm views on such matters and are frequently prepared to assert them as being valid for all. Those who approach the subject from the viewpoint of individual freedom, or of human rights, will argue just as vigorously that issues of this sort lie clearly within the confines of individual moral action. The antagonism

---

[1] The literature on bioethics is now greater than its counterpart in any other area of applied ethics. Constraints of space prevent more than a few examples of the genre but, of the general works available, T L Beauchamp and J F Childress *Principles of Biomedical Ethics* (5th edn, 2001) has established itself as a classic. Other well-known works include J Harris *The Value of Life* (1985), a thought-provoking work by a philosopher who has made a major contribution to the subject. A useful starting point for many readers will be the various compilations which have been made, including J Harris (ed) *Bioethics* (2001) and P Singer and H Kuhse (eds) *A Companion to Bioethics* (2001).

between these two positions is sometimes intense and it often seems as if there is little prospect of common ground. Yet, in so far as we have to live in a community, we are obliged to identify what is permissible and what is not—and this implies the involvement of the law. So we do need, for example, a law concerning artificial reproduction because, unless the law pronounces on the issue, society can be seen to be endorsing a non-interventionist approach which allows for unrestricted freedom of choice. In some cases, this may be what society actually wants but, in others, it will not represent the communal position, which also deserves protection. To take another example, the possibility of embryo stem cell research requires a legal response unless the human embryo is to be considered as a mere artefact. In fact, there are very few people who would argue for no regulation of such a form of research; the majority of supporters of a liberal attitude to this issue would accept that *some* level of regulation is vital in this area even if it is only in respect of the type of research permitted and the period during which it can be carried out. In other respects the law has steadfastly resisted pressure to facilitate or endorse individual choice about the most critical of life events. Euthanasia and physician assisted suicide, for example, remain prohibited in the vast majority of jurisdictions despite numerous challenges before the courts and attempts to introduce enabling legislation.

1.4   Inevitably, then, the law is drawn into the debate and this is especially so when there is a conflict of individual interests. A dispute involving the parents and hospital authorities or social workers as to the medical treatment of a child provides an example. Such an issue arose in dramatic form in the conjoined twins case decided by the Court of Appeal in England in 2000. The courts were clearly uncomfortable about being embroiled in this tragic matter but, ultimately, the judges had to reach a decision.[2] The law cannot avoid taking a view in such cases; the alternative is an irrational and inconsistent approach to their solution. In a liberal society, however, the legislature and courts may seek to limit legal intervention in medically-related matters. Such a society may take a positivist stance and view the function of the law as being that of the neutral adjudicator—a role in which the moral content of legal decisions is kept to a minimum. This concept of the legal role has proved largely unrealistic in the area with which we are concerned. Medical law is catalysed by moral issues. The debate on embryonic stem cell research, for example, is essentially an exposition of different moral views; yet, in practice, it becomes one concerning what the law should be. It is pointless to attempt to disengage the moral from the legal dispute—when we talk about legal rules, we are inevitably drawn into a discussion of moral rules.

1.5   Thus, we often find ourselves engaged in debating not what the law is but what it should be. This requires us to engage in moral evaluation and this, in turn, raises the question of how we are to identify what is right. More specifically, we are confronted

---

[2] *Re A (children) (conjoined twins: surgical separation)* [2000] 4 All ER 961, (2000) 57 BMLR 1. Fully discussed below at para 16.48 et seq.

with a need to identify an ethical basis for the practice of medicine and its regulation by the law. And this is no easy task, living, as we do, in a pluralist, secular age.

A BASIS FOR MEDICAL ETHICS

1.6　There is a plethora of theories on hand that are designed to help us decide what is morally right. These range from authoritarian, revelatory theories at one extreme to subtly nuanced visions of existential ethics at the other. In between these options— each of which, in its own way, discourages meaningful moral debate—there is a range of categories to which moral responses might be allocated. Of course there is always the possibility of eclecticism; morality, it seems, is sometimes not so much a maze as a smorgasbord.

RELIGIOUS THEORIES

1.7　Many accounts of medical ethics are strangely silent as to the importance of religious theories of medical ethics—the element of surprise stemming from the fact that medicine and religion have been intertwined from the earliest times, when priests were also recognised as physicians. As a direct result, religious theories historically constitute a major element of thinking in medical ethics and their influence continues to be felt in all corners of the subject. The common feature of such theories is a vision of man as involved in a dialogue with a divine creator, or possibly a spiritual force, as to the way in which the human body should be treated. This vision may manifest itself in an insistence on ritualistic practices, for example, in relation to burial. Such examples should not, however, be dismissed as an exercise of power based on superstitious reverence—many religious practices, especially those of orthodox Judaism, are, in fact, based on sound principles of public health. It may, on the other hand, be expressed at a higher level of abstraction, fashioning a view of the sanctity of human life which is capable of resolving a whole raft of practical issues. The Judaeo-Christian religious tradition has had the greatest impact in the Western world and is one which continues to influence much of the contemporary debate.

1.8　Religiously-based medical ethics have a clear sense of fundamental values. In the Christian tradition, these include not only a belief that human life is a divine gift which cannot be disposed of by mortals but also a strong attachment to the importance of monogamous, enduring marriage. These values are translated into practical rules in the shape of an antipathy to euthanasia and abortion—an antipathy that amounts to prohibition in orthodox Roman Catholic thinking—and of a belief that various forms of intervention in human reproduction are morally wrong. Inherent in many of these traditions is a strong sense of the *natural*, which proposes a teleology for man. In the light of this, it is often seen as wrong to interfere with the manifest destiny which has been prepared for humanity. This may result in the rejection of an everyday medical issue such as sterilisation just as much as it might lead to a blanket refusal to contemplate interference in the genetic endowment of mankind.

1.9   It would be wrong to assume that those who approach medical ethics from a religious viewpoint are uncritical and authoritarian in their moral thinking. Indeed, many of the more sensitive contributions to the literature of medical ethics have been made by those who approach the subject from this background. And sometimes it is only such a voice which will raise awkward, and yet very important, questions. The debate on euthanasia provides an instance of this in the form of the serious and persistent questioning provided by John Keown.[3] An historic example is the Protestant theologian, Paul Ramsey, whose work anticipated many of the questions which have since become the staple of contemporary debate in medical ethics.[4]

THE CURRENTS OF MEDICAL ETHICS

1.10   Ethical discourse is concerned with the search for justification for our actions. An ethical dilemma arises when two or more courses of conduct may be justifiable in any given set of circumstances, possibly resulting in diametrically opposed outcomes. How, then, do we know what is the 'right' thing to do? Various means may be employed to argue for an ethical resolution to a dilemma and morality is but one such means. Morality may be individual or communal, in that it reflects a core set of values by which individuals or communities abide. As we discuss below, morality may even be a simple question of intuition and, on this criterion alone, it is difficult to argue that an individual's personal value system is 'wrong'. Ethics, on the other hand— while they may be informed by moral debate and argument—usually operate within an established framework of values which serves as a reference from which to conduct the debate about the rightness or wrongness of an action. Thus, for example, Beauchamp and Childress have long championed the utility of 'principlism' as a way to this end.[5] In brief, they hold that ethically appropriate conduct is determined by reference to four key principles which must be taken into account when reflecting on one's behaviour towards others. These are:

   (i)   the principle of respect for individual autonomy (i.e.—individuals must be respected as independent moral agents with the 'right' to choose how to live their own lives),

   (ii) the principle of beneficence (i.e.—one should strive to do good where possible),

   (iii) the principle of non-maleficence (i.e.—one should avoid doing harm to others), and

   (iv) the principle of justice (i.e.—people should be treated fairly, although this does not necessarily equate with treating everyone equally).

---

[3] In particular by way of *Euthanasia Examined* (revised 1997) and *Euthanasia, Ethics and Public Policy* (2002). See the discussion of euthanasia, chapter 17, below.

[4] See e.g. P Ramsey *The Patient as Person* (1970).   [5] N 1 above.

While principlism is by no means universally accepted as the lingua franca of ethics,[6] it does, nonetheless, provide a very good example of how ethical discourse requires reflection and justification of our actions by reference to accepted values and mores.

1.11   At a broader level of abstraction, contemporary medical ethics can be seen as a tapestry in which an array of philosophical theories interweave with one another. The two strands of deontological and utilitarian thought are, however, particularly evident. Deontological theories focus on the rightness or wrongness of an act in itself. They are not so much concerned with the consequences which that act will have; rather, they are concerned with identifying those features of the act which mark it as morally acceptable or otherwise. The classical exposition of such a theory is that by Kant, who stressed that every person must be treated as an end in him- or herself, rather than as a means to an end. Thus, the essential message of Kantian moral teaching is that we should not use others but should respect their integrity as individuals. Many modern theories of autonomy find their roots in this background and, as we shall see later, autonomy has come to be associated closely with the liberal individualism which has exerted a massive influence on the philosophical climate surrounding medico-legal debate in the last few decades. An irony, however, is that many Kantians emphasise that the core message of their philosophy concerns the *obligations* that we owe to others while, at the same time, many contemporary conceptions of autonomy insist on the atomistic *rights* of individuals to decide for themselves, all the while ignoring the impact of those decisions on the broader community.

1.12   Critics of deontological theories of morality, particularly of those in the Kantian mould, often stress what is seen as a rigidity of approach. The 'strict' Kantian does not give sufficient weight, it is said, either to human intuitions as to what is right at the time or to the virtues. An alternative, and more flexible, approach might be one which was more sensitive to the human feelings involved in any moral dilemma and one which also paid more attention to the consequences which flow from our actions. One such approach is that adopted by utilitarianism, a philosophy which has played a major role in the medical debate and which is regarded by many as underpinning modern ethical medicine.

1.13   Utilitarians are accustomed to being misrepresented by those who believe that utilitarianism is a philosophical theory which started, and ended, with the work of Jeremy Bentham. Classic utilitarianism of the Benthamite school held that the test of the morality of an action was the extent to which it promoted good consequences (pleasure) or bad (pain). The utilitarian measure of good is, therefore, the maximisation of happiness, although modern utilitarians, in particular, would stress that this does not necessarily lead to unrestricted hedonism. Modern utilitarianism acknowledges the importance of rules in identifying moral goals and, in this way, prevents the happiness of the many from overshadowing the rights of the few. Preference

---

[6] For an excellent collection of papers on the 'virtues' and 'vices' of principlism, see J Savulescu et al. 'Festschrift Edition of the Journal of Medical Ethics in Honour of Raanan Gillon' (2003) 29(5) J Med Ethics.

utilitarianism, a further modification of the classical theory, allows for the judging of the good of individuals according to their own values, a position perhaps best expressed in modern bioethics through the work of Peter Singer.[7]

1.14   Liberal individualism leans towards a utilitarian or consequentialist approach, in that it measures the effect of a decision on individuals. To the liberal individualist, the good which society should pursue is the fulfilment of the individual. The ideal society is, then, one in which each person makes his own decisions as far as is possible and 'creates himself'. In this way, the individual exercises and enhances his autonomy—how autonomy is used is not a major concern to the liberal individualist, so long as it is not used in a way which restricts others from exercising their own autonomy.

1.15   This is the near antithesis of the last variation on ethical theory that we propose to mention—that is the communtarian ethos which is gaining ground as something of a counterweight to the almost relentlessly increasing reliance on personal autonomy as the cornerstone of both medical ethics and medical law. Communitarianism visualises the community as the integral unit in which autonomy is expressed not so much on an egocentric base but, rather, as a state that is modified by a sharing of values with those of the group in which the individual operates; put in practical terms, the rightness or wrongness of an action is to be judged by the goodness or badness of its effect not on an individual per se but on persons as interdependent units of society—in short, it recognises John Donne's aphorism that no man is an island.[8] The critic will, immediately, ask what is a community?—and the simple answer is that group of persons who are significantly affected by an action or a decision. The application of community ethics to medicine is illustrated in Glover's consideration of abortion.[9] Accepting that there should be as few unwanted children as is possible, he points out that there are large and relevant moral differences between prevention of conception and abortion. These include the side-effects not only on the doctors and nurses concerned but also potentially on society as a whole by way, for example, of 'undermining the general reluctance to kill'. In some senses, a well-tuned concept of communitarian ethics can draw on elements of deontological *and* utilitarian thinking whereby the emphasis is both on the obligations that we owe to those around us as well as on the consequences of our individual decisions.[10]

1.16   We have to admit to our, at least, partial adherence to community ethics. Nevertheless, a book such as this must recognise the undoubted fact that autonomy is by far the most significant value to have influenced the evolution of contemporary medical law. The concept which has dominated the control of medical practice more than any other in the last half-century is the insistence that individuals should have control

---

[7] Singer's contribution to contemporary applied ethics has been considerable. In the field of bioethics, he is associated with challenges to the traditional sanctity of human life view; on which, see his *Rethinking Life and Death* (1994).

[8] For a wide-ranging exposition, see M Daly (ed) *Communitarianism: A New Public Ethics* (1994).

[9] J Glover *Causing Death and Saving Lives* (reprinted 1986), p 142.

[10] For an interesting defence of communitarianism against principlism see D Callahan 'Principlism and Communitarianism' (2003) 29 J Med Ethics 287.

over their own bodies, should make their own decisions relating to their medical treatment and should not be hindered in their search for self-fulfilment. The acknowledgment of autonomy has served to discredit medical paternalism in almost all its forms and has led to the promotion of the patient from the recipient of treatment to being a partner in a therapeutic project—and this change has been reflected in the development of the legal and political regimes by which medical treatment is regulated.

1.17   In one sense, the philosophical apotheosis of autonomy has brought liberation. It has enhanced the freedom of those whose vulnerability, physical or mental, may have exposed them to insensitive treatment or even to exploitation; it has imparted dignity to the lives of those who might, otherwise, have felt themselves to be powerless in the face of the articulate and the professional. Yet, from another view, the acceptance of a particularly-individualistic sense of autonomy as the benchmark of the good has led us to ignore other values, and this may have negative effects.[11] The communitarian approach tells us that, even if self-fulfilment does shine through the development and the exercise of autonomy, there is a social dimension to life which is potentially equally enriching. Autonomy must be qualified by the legitimate interests and expectations of others, as well as by economic constraints. In the medical context, the claims of autonomy must be moderated so as to accommodate the sensitivities of others, including those of the doctor—who is, after all, also an autonomous agent.[12] It may be that respect for individual autonomy points in the direction of allowing voluntary euthanasia—but another moral agent has to administer the drug that ends life, and that person may be affected by the task. There are also the interests of others in being protected against involuntary euthanasia; it is possible that, in providing such protection, we may have to deny self-determination to those who are truly volunteers.[13] Personal autonomy must also be measured against the needs of society as a whole. In an ideal world, a sick person should be able to demand the treatment of his or her choice. A moment's reflection, however, is enough to show us that this is an impossible goal. Society itself demands a just distribution of resources and this cannot be achieved in an ambience of unrestricted 'rights'—put another way, we can only realise our autonomy within the framework provided by society.[14]

---

[11] The conflict between individual autonomy and, say, society's interest in the preservation of life is illustrated in the Israeli Patient's Rights Act 1996 which allows for non-consensual treatment in certain circumstances. See M L Gross 'Treating Competent Patients by Force: The Limits and Lessons of Israel's Patient's Rights Act' (2005) 31 J Med Ethics 29—'there are no grounds for respecting a patient's less-than-informed refusal of treatment'.

[12] Discussed in G M Stirrat and R Gill 'Autonomy in Medical Ethics after O'Neill' (2005) 31 J Med Ethics 127.

[13] This was the basis of the decision of the House of Lords in R (on the application of Pretty) v DPP [2002] 1 AC 800, [2002] 1 All ER 1 (see para 17.54 below) that Article 8 of the European Convention on Human Rights is not infringed by the Suicide Act 1961, s 2.

[14] See A V Campbell 'Dependency: the foundational value in medical ethics' in K V M Fulford and G J M Gillett (eds) Medicine and Moral Reasoning (1994).

1.18   Even so, the concept of rights has many proponents and, like autonomy, rights theory plays an important part in contemporary moral debate. Yet the language of rights may also become unduly assertive and combative and may hinder, rather than promote, moral consensus.[15] This is not to decry the importance of rights. Many of the central moral positions defended in this book can be couched in terms of rights. Once again, however, rights-talk is peculiarly suited to an individualistic moral tradition and conflicts of rights tend to lead to moral impasse. Most discussion centres on the rights of the patient—but has the doctor no rights when choosing treatment in accordance with his Hippocratic principles and his training? The law, itself, is prepared to recognise this as a de facto situation. The one-time Master of the Rolls, Lord Donaldson, expressed this unequivocally when he said:

> [I cannot, at present, conceive of any circumstances] in which the court should ever require a medical practitioner to adopt a course of treatment which in the bona fide clinical judgment of that practitioner is contraindicated as not being in the best interests of the patient.[16]

In the same passage, Lord Donaldson described the fundamental duty of the doctor as being to treat the patient in accordance with his own clinical judgment—which opens the way to an alternative dialogue through the language of obligations. The way to a satisfactory doctor/patient relationship is not through the confrontational profession of rights but, rather, through a realisation of the obligations incumbent upon each side to work towards the ideal.[17]

AUTONOMY AND PATERNALISM

1.19   The paternalist acts for the benefit of another, or in the other's best interests, without the specific consent of the person for whom he acts. Until a few decades ago, the practice of medicine was unquestionably paternalist—at least in parts—and many of those involved might have been surprised to discover that their practices could be considered morally objectionable. Thus, patients were often treated without adequate explanation of what was involved or significant facts about their illness were kept from them. It was, for example, common not to pass on information if it was thought that the knowledge would cause distress, and psychiatric patients could be subjected to treatments without any concern as to their views or preferences. Such practices are

---

[15] In the view of some philosophers, rights can be reduced to principles which form the real content of morality. For a sceptical view, see R Frey *Rights, Killing and Suffering* (1983); to be contrasted with L W Sumner *The Moral Foundation of Rights* (1987) and with the outstanding contribution of K Cronin *Rights and Christian Ethics* (1992).

[16] For a useful discussion in depth, see H Teff *Reasonable Care* (1994) and, in particular, his discussion of medical models in ch 3.

[17] In *Re J (a minor) (wardship: medical treatment)* [1992] 2 FLR 165 at 172, (1992) 9 BMLR 10 at 17.

now largely regarded as unethical in modern Western medicine,[18] and are consequently rare. Yet examples still occur and have surfaced, for instance, in disclosures of the unauthorised retention of tissues from paediatric post-mortems examinations. Certainly, a proportion of the pathologists involved in these practices did not ask for the permission of the parents, but at least some of these failed to do so because they wished to protect the parents from distressing facts. To quote from the President of the Royal College of Pathologists:

No one ever had enthusiasm for discussing the detailed autopsy process with recently bereaved relatives, and it was always more comfortable to draw a veil over it. But that veil meant that relatives did not know what was going on . . . Strip away [the extraneous factors] and there remains the inescapable and uncomfortable fact that in the past post-mortem organ retention has been a prime example of professional paternalism.[19]

Even so, while an unqualified rejection of paternalism in medicine might satisfy some proponents of autonomy, it would undoubtedly, at the same time, cause avoidable harm. Paternalism is acceptable in principle—and, indeed, necessary in practice— where the person who is the object of such action is incapable of making his or her own decision.[20] An intervention in such a case will be justifiable if the disabling condition is either permanent or cannot be expected to lift in time for the person in question to decide for him or herself. The advantages of any intervention must, however, significantly outweigh the disadvantages which would otherwise accrue and the intervention itself must carry a reasonable prospect of success. This is essentially a test of reasonableness, which involves a careful assessment of motives for action and a balancing of interests. To achieve this balance, it may be necessary to take into account not only the patient's past views—when these are knowable—but also to consider what are likely to be his or her future views.

1.20   The principal subjects of medical paternalism are likely to be children, the psychiatrically ill, and the unconscious. The medical treatment of children who are too young to make up their own minds provides a common and clear case of justified medical paternalism. Indeed, at times, the medical professional is called upon to protect the interests of a child against the wishes of his or her parents as to the appropriateness, or otherwise, of medical treatment.[21] Notwithstanding, the paternalist must take into account in this context the fact that capacity increases with growing maturity; caution must, therefore, be exercised in acting paternalistically towards teenagers. Paternalism in relation to the psychiatrically ill may be justified on the grounds that there is a mental disability which incapacitates the patient to the extent

[18] Compare a Western view: R J Sullivan, L W Menapace and R M White 'Truth-telling and Patient Diagnoses' (2001) 27 J Med Ethics 192 with: D F-C Tsai 'Ancient Chinese Medical Ethics and the Four Principles of Biomedical Ethics' (1999) 25 J Med Ethics 315. Generally, see S Bok *Lying: Moral Choice in Public and Private Life* (1999).

[19] J Lilleyman 'From the President' (2001) Bull R Coll Path No 114, p 2.

[20] For a detailed account of paternalism in all its forms, see E Buchanan and D W Brock *Deciding for Others: The Ethics of Surrogate Decision Making* (1990).

[21] Consider, for example, the treatment of children of Jehovah's Witnesses.

that he or she cannot understand that treatment may be required; it is, then, reasonable to assume that the patient will endorse what has been done once recovery has occurred. This latter justification—the appeal to subsequent approbation—may also be invoked in the treatment of the unconscious. The anticipated agreement may well be forthcoming in the majority of cases, but the treatment of those who are unconscious after an attempt at suicide may be more difficult to justify. The doctor who treats such a person is clearly acting paternalistically and might argue either that the attempt at suicide could have resulted from a mental illness (and could, therefore, be treatable without consent), or that the patient will later endorse the treatment. But what about the case where the patient has made it clear in advance that suicide is what he or she wants and is the result of rational consideration?[22] In practice, such patients are often treated, although it is difficult to fit that into the category of justified paternalism.

1.21   As in all areas of medical practice, room must remain for clinical discretion to be exercised by the doctor. There will be cases where minor acts of paternalism aimed at preventing distress to those who are anxious will be the ethically right thing to do. The law might be expected to recognise this at the same time that it recognises and protects the right of individual autonomy. In short, paternalism and autonomy are not mutually exclusive: the task of medical ethics and of medical law is to balance the two in a way which enhances individual dignity and autonomy but which does not inhibit the exercise of discretion in the marginal case.

INTUITIONS, EXPERIENCE AND MORALITY

1.22   There are grounds, then, for doubting the practicality or effectiveness of applying a broad deontological brush to medical ethics. Each case is unique, and its individual features may change with each consultation. In supporting this approach, some moral philosophers have stressed the importance of imagination as a means of navigating our way through the moral landscape.[23] This moral imagination may, to an extent, rely on metaphors rather than on rules—which, in turn, points to a role, even if a circumscribed one, for moral intuitions. Intuition may have a limited appeal as a basis for moral philosophy but it should not be wholly discounted and this, for the reasons given above, is especially so in the field of health care.[24] Intuitions may point in the direction of a value which may not always be articulated formally but which may none the less be very important.

1.23   Our own view is that medical ethics are perhaps not best served by a rigid attachment to an undiluted vision of patient autonomy—but neither were they well served

---

[22] We will see later that there is also a hazard that the patient's life may be reprieved but only in a disabled state.

[23] See M Johnson *Moral Imagination: Implications of Cognitive Science for Ethics* (1993); L May, M Friedman and A Clark (eds) *Mind and Morals: Essays on Ethics and Cognitive Science* (1996).

[24] For expression of this view, see T B Brewin 'How Much Ethics Is Needed to Make a Good Doctor?' (1993) 341 Lancet 161. Also G Gillett 'Euthanasia, Letting Die and the Pause' (1988) 14 J Med Ethics 61.

by the paternalistic philosophy of the past. What is required is an openness to the complexity of moral decisions, and an awareness of the sensitive, contextual nature of the doctor-patient relationship. An understanding of the demands of this relationship is not necessarily something that philosophers can teach or lawyers prescribe. The insights of cognitive science, and of psychology in general, increasingly recommend a model of moral reasoning which gives a large role to learned moral responses. These moral abilities—if one may call them that—are acquired through education within a particular ethos and through hands-on experience in dealing with people and their suffering. There is all the difference in the world between, say, the experienced nurse who has spent years working in a hospice setting and the lay person who approaches the issue of end-of-life decisions from an entirely theoretical perspective. A moral response which discounts the validity of the insights of the former would be unlikely to be helpful. Those involved in caring for patients are moral beings who must be encouraged to develop and express their sense of the moral demands of a particular situation. There is not necessarily one right answer to the dilemmas which they encounter, and this should perhaps be recognised more extensively than it is today. There may be two, or even more, right answers depending on the people involved and the circumstances. The crucial point is that the particular 'answer' that is eventually pursued can be justified within a recognised and accepted moral framework. A moral straitjacket is hardly helpful. Having said which, we should, perhaps go on to examine the practical environment in which health carers set about their work.

THE HIPPOCRATIC INFLUENCE

1.24 For the origins of our current medical practice—with its emphasis on the one-to-one relationship between doctor and patient within the confines of the home, surgery or hospital—we must look to Greece where, even by 500 BC, the originally strong influence of the priest/physician had waned; a predominantly religious discipline had been taken over by the philosophers who, through the processes of logical thought, observation and deduction, transformed the concepts of medicine. Inevitably, this led to the formation of schools involving the close association of practitioners, paternalism and the elements of the 'closed shop'; a code of intra-professional conduct evolved, heralding the dawn of what has become known as medical etiquette. In addition, the new concepts dictated that the physician went to the patient rather than that the patient to the temple. A standard of practice relevant to the new ideals was required and has survived as the Hippocratic Oath.[25]

1.25 While Hippocrates remains the most famous figure in Greek philosophical medicine, he was not alone and it is probable that the Oath predates his own school. It therefore indicates a prevailing ethos rather than a professorial edict and it is still regarded as the fundamental governance of the medical profession. Much of the preamble relates to medical etiquette and is clearly outmoded—very few ageing

---

[25] See Appendix A.

medical professors now anticipate social security by way of the generosity of their students! This, however, is not our concern here—and it is to be distinguished clearly from medical ethics. As to the latter, the Oath lays down a number of guidelines. First, it implies the need for co-ordinated instruction and registration of doctors—the public is to be protected, so far as is possible, from the dabbler or the charlatan. Secondly, it is clearly stated that a doctor is there for the benefit of his patients—to the best of his ability he must do them good and he must do nothing which he knows will cause harm. This is reflected in modern times in the principles of beneficence and non-maleficence articulated above. Thirdly, euthanasia and abortion are proscribed; the reference to lithotomy probably prohibits mutilating operations (castration) but has been taken by many to imply the limitation of one's practice to that in which one has expertise. Fourthly, the nature of the doctor-patient relationship is outlined and an undertaking is given not to take advantage of that relationship. Finally, the Oath expresses the doctrine of medical confidentiality.

1.26   In fact, the Hippocratic Oath did not become an integral part of ethical teaching until well into the Christian era; it lapsed with the decline of Greek civilisation and was restored with the evolution of university medical schools. It is doubtful if any British medical school now requires a reiteration of the Oath at graduation—although most Scottish universities require assent by students to a modified version—but, avowed or not, all doctors would admit to its persuasive influence. The language of the Oath is, however, archaic and a modernised version was introduced by the World Medical Association as the Declaration of Geneva. This was last amended at Stockholm in 1994[26] and provides the basis for several national and international codes.[27]

1.27   We have seen that Greek medicine was essentially a private matter and, indeed, its mode of practice was scarcely attuned to the needs of public health. For the origins of this, we must turn to the Judaeo-Christian influence which, certainly in the Israeli tradition, expressed itself most powerfully in accepting that the rights of the individual must sometimes be sacrificed for the good of the community—there was strong emphasis, for example, on the isolation of infectious cases, including those of venereal disease, the regulation of sewage disposal and the like—and the principles of public health medicine were born. As we have already noted, the fact that medicine was dominated by religion turned out to be mutually advantageous. Much of this attitude passed to the Christians, who were also forced into the group lifestyle, and were fortified by the concepts of equality, charity and devotion to the less fortunate— concepts which should still underlie the ethical practice of medicine in Christian countries. It is unsurprising that, during the Dark Ages, medicine was virtually kept alive in the monasteries which provided the template for the voluntary hospitals of later years.

---

[26] See Appendix B.
[27] Including the International Code of Medical Ethics which was first amended at Venice in 1983.

THE ORGANISATION OF MODERN MEDICINE

1.28   Probably the single most important feature which distinguishes 'modern medicine' is the importance attached to experimentation and research[28] and it was this change in emphasis which dictated most urgently that medical practice should be subject to central control.

1.29   The age of medical research can be said to have begun with the Renaissance and, since that time, the practice of medicine has become increasingly scientifically based. New dimensions are, thus, introduced and new dilemmas posed. It is obvious that scientific medicine cannot improve without extensive research while, on the other hand, that process tends to turn medical practice into a series of problem-solving exercises—a diversion which, even now, stimulates, at the same time, some of medicine's severest critics and its admirers.

1.30   Perhaps the first practical effect of the scientific approach was to convince doctors that they have an expertise worth preserving and, as early as the sixteenth century, we find the establishment of the Royal College of Physicians of London, together with a general tightening of the rules governing the practice of surgery. The early Royal Colleges had considerable powers of examination and registration. The latter function has now gone and the major purpose of the colleges—which now represent some eight specialities with additional faculties—is to maintain a standard of excellence among specialised practitioners—a matter of current importance to which we return below.

1.31   As organisation proceeded, fortune began increasingly to depend upon fame, and fame in its turn upon academic superiority over one's colleagues—from all accounts, British medicine in the eighteenth and early nineteenth centuries was not the happiest of professions. Even so, it was not so much medical ethics, as they are understood today, that were found wanting but, rather, medical etiquette. Something had to be done to ensure the status of the profession and this need was first met by the formation of the British Medical Association (BMA) in 1832. In so far as the BMA is, today, a non-affiliated registered trade union,[29] its primary function has traditionally been the protection of doctors' interests. Clearly, such an interested party could not satisfy the public need for control of a profession with such power and it was largely due to the lobby of the BMA itself that the General Medical Council (GMC) was established by

---

[28] For a recent monograph which eloquently analyses this, see R Tallis *Hippocratic Oaths: Medicine and its Discontents* (2004).

[29] Trade Union and Labour Relations (Consolidation) Act 1992. The distinction between a trade organisation and a regulatory body such as the GMC has recently been emphasised in *General Medical Council v Cox* (2002) *The Times*, 16 April, in which it was held that the GMC was not a trade organisation for the purposes of the Disability Discrimination Act 1995, s 13.

the Medical Act 1858.[30] The current statutory regulation of the medical profession is found in the Medical Act 1983 which, recently, has been substantially amended.[31]

1.32   There is no doubt that the number of high profile, individual instances of alleged misconduct that were exposed at the end of the twentieth century caused considerable public disquiet. How far this was fanned by the increasingly aggressive news media or was dictated by political expediency remains open for argument.[32] The fact remains that sufficient evidence accrued to provide solid grounds for review—and revision—of the existing system for control of the medical profession.[33] The consequence has been that, while the GMC remains the governing body of the medical profession,[34] its most significant public function from now on will be encapsulated in ensuring that medical professionals are up to date and fit to practise.[35] Given that the function of the National Health Service is now a major topic in the mind of the electorate, it is unsurprising that the profession's leaders have been under intense pressure to accept

[30] The General Medical Council at present consists of 35 members of which 19 are elected by the medical profession (elected members must form a majority of the Council). The Academy of Medical Royal Colleges and the Council of Heads of Medical Schools each nominate one member and there are 14 lay members nominated by an independent commission. The President is elected by the Council which is responsible for the strategic management of the delivery of its statutory functions. There are, of course, a large number of persons working with or on behalf of the Council who are recruited through open selection or appointment.

[31] Medical Act 1983 (Amendment) Order 2002 (SI 2002/3135). Discipline within the National Health Service is additionally regulated within a complex framework of disciplinary committees: see National Health Service (Service Committees and Tribunal) Regulations 1992, SI 1992/664. Incompetence by hospital practitioners is investigated under the terms of Ministry of Health Circular HM(61)112(1961) as amended by HC(90)9(1990). Personal misconduct is dealt with by a system of internal inquiry but the distinction may be difficult to make: *Skidmore v Dartford and Gravesham NHS Trust* [2003] 3 All ER 292, HL. The actions of a disciplinary inquiry are subject to judicial review and to scrutiny under the Human Rights Act 1998: *R (on the application of Mahfouz) v Professional Conduct Committee of the General Medical Council* [2004] Lloyd's Rep Med 377, (2004) 80 BMLR 113. As we write, the system is being overhauled—particularly with a view to streamlining the investigative procedures: Z Kmietowicz 'New Suspension Procedures Aim to Cut NHS Disciplinary Bill' (2005) 330 BMJ 437.

[32] For a cynical appraisal, see T Jackson 'Gods and Monsters' (2001) 322 BMJ 371.

[33] Aside from regular reports of individual errors, a number of major incidents were disclosed which resulted in public investigations. Among these are to be included the standards of paediatric cardiac surgery at Bristol: *Report of the Public Inquiry into Children's Heart Surgery at Bristol Royal Infirmary 1984–1995* (Cm 5207, 2001) www.bristol-inquiry.org.uk; the retention of organs at Alder Hey Hospital: *The Royal Liverpool Children's Inquiry Report* (HC12, 2001) www.rlcinquiry.org.uk; the retention of organs in Scotland: *Final Report of the Independent Review Group on Retention of Organs at Post-mortem* (Scottish Exec, 2001) www.show.scot.nhs.uk/scotorgrev/Final%20Report/ropm-00.htm. Note also that the restyled GMC, itself, came under savage attack in what was, essentially, an investigation into a mass murder: Dame Janet Smith *The Shipman Inquiry* 5th Report, *Safeguarding Patients: Lessons from the Past—Proposals for the Future* (2004) (Cm 6394).

[34] The increasing status afforded to 'alternative medicine' is to be noted. These practitioners have their own controlling bodies: see, for example, Osteopaths Act 1993; Chiropractors Act 1994. A practitioner of any form of alternative medicine will be judged by the standards of that particular art but must recognise that he is practising alongside orthodox medicine: *Shakoor v Situ* [2000] 4 All ER 181, (2001) 57 BMLR 178.

[35] A function that was allowed by statute only as recently as 1995 by way of the Medical (Professional Performance) Act 1995.

the dictates of the ruling political party; nevertheless, they now express themselves as well satisfied with the proposed changes.[36]

1.33 Maintaining the official register of medical practitioners remains a basic function of the GMC. The purpose of the register has, until now, been to protect the public from those who have not undergone recognised training; unlike the practise of dentistry, no specific offence lies in an unqualified person practising medicine in the United Kingdom—the offence has always been that of pretending to be a registered medical practitioner[37] or of usurping functions which are statutorily limited to registered practitioners—such as prescribing 'prescription only' medicines. Registration does not, however, provide a positive entitlement to practise; an additional licence to practise is now required. This is granted on first registration but, thereafter, is subject to revalidation—a procedure whereby the practitioner's continuing fitness to practise is evaluated. The process of revalidation is still under review.[38] One technical result is that one must now read 'registered practitioner with a licence to practise' wherever the words 'registered practitioner' arise in a legal sense.

1.34 The disciplinary function of the GMC has, perhaps, always been its activity which has occasioned the most interest and, here, the Amendment Order 2002 has caused a sea change in attitude.[39] The overriding factor is now the doctor's fitness to practise and misconduct is but one possible cause of unfitness; the changing emphasis is exemplified by the relevant title in the Medical Act 1983 being altered from 'Professional Conduct and Fitness to Practise' to 'Fitness to Practise and Medical Ethics'. As a result, the traditional Professional Conduct Committee has been abolished along with those others that are currently operative—only the Education Committee survives (see below). The power to co-opt committee members is a prominent feature of the new regulations. Some or all of the members of Committees may be persons who are not members of the Council[40]—which suggests that there will be increasing lay-person control at all levels—and, indeed, a member of the Council will not be allowed to sit on several committees, including the most significant Fitness to Practise Panels.[41]

---

[36] Even so, a leading article in the BMJ has it that 'the independence of the medical profession in the United Kingdom is under unprecedented attack through these government proposals': D P Gray 'Deprofessionalising Doctors?' (2002) 324 BMJ 627. For a general academic review, see R Tallis *Hippocratic Oaths: Medicine and Its Discontents* (2004).

[37] Medical Act 1983, s 49. The Council has occasionally lapsed in this respect. An example is that of an unqualified person from overseas who managed to obtain registration with the GMC; he received £450,000 in salary from the NHS before being detected through the vigilance of a pharmacist: J Ironside 'Five Year Sentence for Fake General Practitioner' (1992) 304 BMJ 1652. It will, in future, be a similar offence to hold a licence to practise (Medical Act 1983, s 49A inserted by the 2002 Order).

[38] And has, in fact, been put on hold pending consideration of the *Shipman Report*, n 33 above: GMC News, issue 28, February 2005, p 1.

[39] Major modification of the Medical Act by way of an Order in Council is empowered by Health Act 1999, s 60.

[40] Medical Act 1983, Sch 1, Article 25(2A) inserted by 2002 Order.

[41] Medical Act 1983 (Amendment) Order 2000, SI 2000/1803, Article 4. It appears, at the time of writing, that the extensive changes to the disciplinary powers of the GMC that were negotiated are to be considered inadequate before they were implemented. For one side of the argument, see R Smith 'The GMC: Expediency before Principle' (2005) 330 BMJ 1.

1.35　　We make no attempt here to consider in detail the administrative law concerning medical practice.[42] Indeed, such is the speed with which new codes and regulations appear, that it would be a fruitless task.[43] Suffice it to say that a doctor's fitness to practise can be questioned before a Fitness to Practise Panel on the grounds of misconduct, deficient professional performance, a conviction for, or caution following, a criminal offence, his or her mental or physical health and, finally, a determination by any body responsible for the regulation of the health or social care professions in the United Kingdom that his or her fitness to practise is impaired.[44] The doctor whose fitness to practise is found to be impaired may be subject to erasure from the register (except in a 'health case'),[45] to suspension for up to 12 months, to conditional registration in accordance with the Panel's directions for up to three years or, in the case of misconduct, criminal conviction or of a determination by another body, to reprimand. Any of these restrictions can be imposed when an original suspension order is reviewed and, in the case of indefinite suspension, the doctor may request a review not more often than every two years. An appeal against a decision of the Fitness to Practise Panel is available to the High Court in England and Wales, the Court of Session in Scotland and the High Court in Northern Ireland.[46] Finally, it is to be noted that the name of a doctor that has been erased can be restored to the Register but not within five years of erasure; subsequently, applications for restoration can be made yearly.

1.36　　The effect of the transfer of the existing appellate function of the Privy Council to the High Court and its equivalents in Scotland and Northern Ireland will be watched with interest. Even as things stand, the attitude of the Privy Council has been changing over the years. Traditionally, the Council has been reluctant to alter the view of the

---

[42]　For that, the reader is referred to the seminal work by J Montgomery *Health Care Law* (3rd edn, 2005). It is to be noted that the conduct of the GMC is open to judicial review both as to its 'advice' (*Colman v General Medical Council* [1989] 1 Med LR 23, QBD; sub nom *R v General Medical Council, ex p Colman* (1989) 4 BMLR 33, CA) and as to the actions of its Committees (*R v General Medical Council, ex p Gee* [1987] 1 All ER 1204, CA). While exercising a judicial power, the GMC is not part of the judicial system of the state: *General Medical Council v BBC* [1998] 3 All ER 426, (1998) 43 BMLR 143.

[43]　Witness the National Health Service Reform and Health Care Professions Act 2002 altering the composition and powers of the Commission for Health Improvement (CHI) at the same time as CHI, itself, was being merged with part of the Audit Commission to form the new Commission for Healthcare Audit and Inspection (CHAI) (Department of Health *Delivering the NHS Plan* (April 2002)) www.doh.gov.uk/about/nhsplan/index.htm.

[44]　Medical Act 1983, s 35C(1). An interim suspension order can be imposed for a period of up to 18 months in the event that it is considered that protection of the public is a matter of urgency (s 41A). The relationship between the GMC and the newly constituted National Clinical Assessment Authority (see para 1.43 below) (www.ucaa.nhs.uk), which is intended to advise employers on doctors' efficiency, is still uncertain: S Dewar and B Finlayson 'Dealing with Poor Clinical Performance' (2001) 322 BMJ 66.

[45]　Suspension in a 'health case' can only become indefinite if the original suspension has been in force for at least two years (s 35D(6) inserted by 2002 Order). For limitations of application, see *Raji v General Medical Council* [2003] 1 WLR 1052, [2003] Lloyds Rep Med 280.

[46]　National Health Service Reform and Health Care Professions Act 2002, s 29. Judgments on appeal from decisions related to health and performance are no longer limited to points of law (a limitation that the Privy Council found frustrating: *Hall v General Medical Council* [2001] UKPC 46, (2001) 65 BMLR 53).

facts taken by the disciplinary committee.[47] Times, however, have changed, perhaps particularly with the advent of the Human Rights Act 1998. Indeed, it is only the availability of an appeal to an independent tribunal that saves the disciplinary function of the GMC and its equivalents from incompatibility with the 1998 Act.[48] As a result, there has been something of a steady flow of cases in which the findings of the committees of the GMC have been modified on appeal[49] and it is to be expected that the High Court, being closer to the 'coal-face', may be even more interventionist in the future.

1.37   The future must, however, be indefinite as one of the most far reaching recent legislative actions has been the establishment of a Council for Healthcare Regulatory Excellence,[50] the main function of which is to promote the interests of patients and other members of the public by way of overseeing the performance of the individual professional 'regulatory bodies'[51]—in common parlance, to dictate their policies. A regulatory body must comply with any directions given by the new Council[52] which will have the power to investigate complaints as to the regulatory bodies' exercise of their functions. The Council has, however, a major proactive role in that it scrutinises the disciplinary decisions of the regulators, considers them, if necessary, in a case meeting and, finally, may appeal some decisions to the High Court if it is considered that their leniency was incompatible with adequate protection of the public.[53] It was expected that the last option would be limited to 'extreme cases';[54] nevertheless, seven

[47] *Libman v General Medical Council* [1972] AC 217, [1972] 1 All ER 798.

[48] *Preiss v General Dental Council* [2001] 1 WLR 1926, [2001] Lloyd's Rep Med 491. For a similar Scottish decision, see *Tehrani v United Kingdom Central Council for Nursing, Midwifery and Health Visiting* 2001 SC 581, 2001 SLT 879.

[49] *Krippendorf v General Medical Council* [2001] 1 WLR 1054, (2001) 59 BMLR 81 (wrong assessment tests—Professional Performance); *Bijl v General Medical Council* (2001) 65 BMLR 10 (unnecessarily draconian penalty—PCC); *Manzur v General Medical Council* (2001) 64 BMLR 68 (disproportionate penalty for fraud—PCC); *Srirangalingham v General Medical Council* (2002) 65 BMLR 65, [2002] Lloyd's Rep Med 77 (inappropriate suspension—PCC); *Hossain v General Medical Council* (2001) 65 BMLR 1, [2002] Lloyd's Rep Med 64 (unreasonable erasure—PCC); *Mateu-Lopez v General Medical Council* 2003 WL 21491880 (erasure disproportionate—PCC). Other reported cases in which the GMC's findings were quashed include: *Silver v GMC* [2003] Lloyd's Rep Med 333; *Misra v GMC* (2003) 72 BMLR 108; *Raji v GMC*, n 45 above. On the other hand, the Privy Council have decreed that the reputation of the whole profession can, at times, take precedence over the interests of an individual member: *Gosai v General Medical Council* (2004) 75 BMLR 52. See also *Sadler v GMC* [2003] 1 WLR 2259, [2004] Lloyd's Rep Med 44 (seriously deficient performance confirmed).

[50] Renamed very shortly after establishment as the Council for the Regulation of Health Care Professionals (CRHP) by way of National Health Service Reform and Health Care Professions Act 2002, s 25. For early assessment, see S Dewar and B Finlayson 'Regulating the Regulators' (2002) 324 BMJ 378.

[51] Currently, the General Medical, Dental, Optical, Osteopathic and Chiropractic Councils, the Nursing and Midwifery Council, the Health Professions Council and the Royal Pharmaceutical Societies of Great Britain and Northern Ireland.

[52] Although it may be that changes to the rules of the regulatory bodies will only be made with the agreement of both Houses of Parliament.

[53] Section 29 of the 2002 Act.

[54] C Dyer 'New Council Takes GMC to High Court for Undue Leniency' (2004) 328 BMJ 541.

cases, one of which was later withdrawn, were referred in the first year of the Council's operation.[55]

1.38   The GMC—together with its cousins—is, it seems, in something of a cleft stick. On the one hand, more appeals against the sanctions imposed on doctors are succeeding while, on the other, the CRHP is clearly determined to ensure a high level of 'sentencing'. It is fortunate that the same High Court will now be hearing appeals from either side—which means that the same standards should apply. At the same time, we feel it would be unfortunate if the current emphasis on performance were to lead to the maintenance of standards of conduct of the profession assuming a relatively small part of the Council's remit. So far as this book is concerned, one of the most important roles of the GMC has been to fill the gap in constraining such actions as are not actionable at law yet which would not be expected of the ethical practitioner. For example, the law on medical confidentiality is in many ways unclear, but few doctors would have wished to tangle with the GMC on the issue of professional secrecy. There is nothing criminal in adultery; yet the public cannot expect family relationships to be destroyed as a result of the doctor's privilege to enter the bedroom.

1.39   It is, therefore, interesting and encouraging to find that the Council for the Regulation of Health Care Professionals (CRHP) is certainly not losing sight of this. Three of the more high profile cases that have been referred to the High Court have concerned sexual relationships with patients[56] and another with a paediatric nurse's interest in pornography.[57] Although the impression gained from the High Court judgments could be seen as relatively sympathetic to the professionals involved, much of their reasoning has been criticised in the Court of Appeal; as a result, we feel that CRHP is increasingly likely to use its powers to the full and that the High Court will respond accordingly.

1.40   This is no place to discuss the Court of Appeal's ruling in the combined cases of *Ruscillo* and *Truscott*[58] in detail—no doubt it will have been analysed by many commentators before this book reaches the printer. Basically, the Court held that the protection of the public was the paramount concern—a sentiment with which few would want to quarrel. A feeling remains, however, that, as a recent leading article in the *British Medical Journal* put it: the purpose of section 29 'is to address public concern that at times too much regard might be paid to the profession and its members in the process of self regulation'[59]—and the two concepts are by no means interchangeable. The Court of Appeal has, however, clarified two major concerns.

---

[55] Five from the GMC and two from the Nursing and Midwifery Council. These derived from 213 cases which were considered, of which 15 were investigated at case meetings of Council members: Council for Healthcare Regulatory Excellence *Annual Report 2003–2004*.

[56] *Council for the Regulation of Health Care Professionals v General Medical Council and Ruscillo* [2004] 1 WLR 2068, [2004] Lloyd's Rep Med 365; same *and Solanke* [2004] 1 WLR 2432, [2004] Lloyd's Rep Med 377; same *and Leeper* (unreported).

[57] *Council for the Regulation of Health Care Professionals v Nursing and Midwifery Council and Truscott* [2004] EWHC 585, (2004) *The Times*, 8 April.

[58] *Ruscillo v Council for the Regulation of Health Care Professionals and the General Medical Council, CRHP v Nursing and Midwifery Council and Truscott* [2005] 1 WLR 717, [2005] Lloyd's Rep Med 65.

[59] A Samanta and J Samanta 'Referring GMC Decisions to the High Court' (2005) 330 BMJ 103.

1.41   First, it has, throughout, interpreted section 29 in a purposive sense and has laid down that the remit of CRHP is not confined to sentencing—the Council is also entitled to refer an acquittal by the regulatory authority to the High Court. The logic of this is unassailable once the former power is imposed—a wrong conclusion that conduct is not professional misconduct is just as important for the protection of the public as is too lenient a penalty.[60] Second, as a corollary to this, the law now accepts that this places doctors in double jeopardy.[61] Lord Phillips quoted Collins J in *Truscott*:

There is an element of double jeopardy of which account must be taken. It is of less importance in the context of s.29 of the 2002 Act because the emphasis is on the protection of the public rather than of the individual concerned (at para 29)

and went on to say:

Considerations of double jeopardy must take second place when a case has been referred as necessary for the protection of the public.[62]

All of which is unashamedly public policy—but which, nevertheless, gives rise to some doubts as to the accused's position in respect of Article 6 of the European Convention on Human Rights.

1.42   The introduction of Part 2 of the 2002 Act was described as 'facing the medical profession with its greatest assault in 150 years',[63] a statement which may carry a ring of hyperbole. The Council for the Regulation of Health Care Professionals is characterised as an independent body. Nevertheless, at least a bare majority of its members are appointed by a devolved Parliament or by the Secretary of State, albeit through a Special Health Authority; one would surely need rosy spectacles of the deepest hue not to see this as raising the spectre of overt political control of the health care professions.

1.43   Supervisory regulation of the 'regulators' seems to be a major feature of modern governance and is currently moving out of the administrative sphere into that of clinical health care.[64] The most significant reorganisation in this respect is the Health-care Commission, which is a synonym for the Commission for Healthcare Audit and Inspection,[65] and which is responsible for improving the quality, effectiveness and efficiency of health care in the widest sense; to this end, it has extensive inspectorate and investigative powers. The obvious possibility of duplication of effort by the large number of organisations with similar powers of inspection has been recognised by a

---

[60] N 58 above at para 45.

[61] In view of the extensive powers given to the High Court, this might legitimately be regarded as treble jeopardy.

[62] N 58 above at para 42.

[63] Chairman of the Academy of Medical Royal Colleges quoted in (2002) BMA news, 16 March, p 1.

[64] K Walshe 'The Rise of Regulation in the NHS' (2002) 324 BMJ 967.

[65] Established under the Health and Social Care (Community Health and Standards) Act 2003, s 41. It incorporates the former Commission for Health Improvement, the Mental Health Act Commission and the National Care Standards Commission which covered the private sector of medicine. CHAI works very closely with the Commission for Social Care Inspection.

concordat agreed between nine current inspecting bodies, including the Academy of Medical Royal Colleges. The National Institute for Clinical Excellence,[66] which provides information on what is the best practice and, significantly, on the effective use of available resources (see chapter 11 below), has an equivalently powerful influence on the coal-face provision of treatment. Other significant controllers of the profession include the National Clinical Assessment Authority,[67] which provides a service to NHS bodies who are concerned at the performance of individual doctors. Medical education has not been neglected. Undergraduate education and examination and the supervision of those undertaking their year of provisional registration remain within the ambit of the Education Committee and, currently, postgraduate education is still controlled by the Specialist Training Authority of the Royal Medical Colleges.[68] A new Postgraduate Medical Education and Training Board is, however, in the process of formation; one suspects that its establishment will deprive individual qualifications such as Membership or Fellowship of the Colleges of any real meaning.

1.44   On the other side of the coin one must also note the regulatory arrangements that are specifically directed to public participation in health care delivery. The most important of these appeared to be the Commission for Patient and Public Involvement in Health but this was disbanded within six months of its inception.[69] Since a prominent component of the Commission's remit included advising and monitoring the success of Patients' Forums which were established for each NHS Trust or Primary Care Trust[70] in England under s 15 of the same Act, one wonders what is to become of these very significant bodies. In any event, Health Authorities, Primary Care Trusts and NHS Trusts are under a general duty to involve and to consult with the public on any aspect of the services they provide while, at the same time, the Secretary of State must now make arrangements for the provision of an independent Advocacy Service which will assist the public in making complaints under procedures operated by a health service body.[71]

1.45   A main purpose of this long and arguably incomplete survey of recent legislation is to emphasise the burden of regulation thereby imposed on the pattern of medical practice. While it would be premature to attempt to praise or criticise the function of the various bodies, it would, at the same time, be idle to deny that the plethora of regulation could give rise to a wave of political control not only of health administration

---

[66] National Institute for Clinical Excellence (Establishment and Constitution) Order 1999, SI 1999/220 and 1999/2219.

[67] National Clinical Assessment Authority (Establishment and Constitution) Order 2000, SI 2000/2961.

[68] Post-graduate training for general practitioners is similarly controlled by the Joint Committee on Postgraduate Training for General Practice: General and Specialist Medical Practice (Education, Training and Qualifications) Order 2003 (SI 2003/1250, art 3).

[69] S Lister 'Reid Scraps Patients' Agency Six Months On' (2004) *The Times*, 1 July, p 2.

[70] Primary Care Trusts were established by the Health Act 1999, s 2 which inserts s 16A into the National Health Service Act 1977.

[71] Health and Social Care Act 2001, ss 11 and 12. Community Health Councils are now abolished (2002 Act, s 22) by reason of increased powers of scrutiny of the health services that is given to local authorities in the Heath and Social Care Act 2001, ss 7–10.

but also of clinical practice—and, while the needs and aspirations of the public must have priority, comparable legislation designed to protect the independence and integrity of the medical profession is conspicuous in its absence. Doctor/patient relationships are changing in a changing world and this shift is not confined to the United Kingdom.[72] We can only hope that the change will be for the better.

1.46   A major criticism of the GMC has been that it has very little power to institute disciplinary proceedings itself; effectively, the Council has been able to act only by way of information received—a little understood fact which has resulted in some grossly unfair criticism of its efficiency. Very often, the only likely informants will be fellow doctors—for example, in the important circumstances when treatment of doubtful validity is being provided.[73] Most professional men and women are inherently unwilling to denounce their colleagues and this reticence was severely criticised in the Bristol inquiry.[74] Even so, the distinction between disparaging the skill of another doctor, which the GMC would regard adversely, and informing of behaviour which raises a question of patients' well-being, which is rightly approved,[75] may be tenuous and it is the uncertainty of the dividing line that often separates those who have an equal understanding of the problems at issue. In practice, a large proportion of reports of dubious behaviour on the part of doctors stems from outraged nursing staff.[76] Many such protests are based on grounds of conscience, these being related especially to life or death decisions, and the probability is that the great majority are motivated by the genuine belief that they are protecting the public against undisclosed violations of the moral, professional and criminal codes. An employee who discloses in good faith, inter alia, that the health or safety of an individual has been, is being or is likely to be endangered is now protected from recrimination by the Employment Rights Act 1996, ss 43A–J[77]—protection of the individual is, of necessity, subject to a number of qualifying conditions which include following a prescribed procedure. Clearly, the practice of what is popularly known as 'whistle blowing' is open to abuse or misconception; nevertheless, the great majority would now approve the spirit of the regulations,

[72] See N Edwards, M J Kornacki and J Silversin 'Unhappy Doctors: What Are the Causes and What Can be Done?' (2002) 324 BMJ 835.

[73] R Smith 'Doctors, Unethical Treatment, and Turning a Blind Eye' (1989) 298 BMJ 1125. See also criticism of the management of a case of doubtful practice associated with advertising: A B Kay 'Alternative Allergy and the General Medical Council' (1993) 306 BMJ 122; R Smith 'GMC in the Dock Again' (1993) 306 BMJ 82.

[74] N 33 above.

[75] General Medical Council Good Medical Practice (1998) para 24. See also Appendix C.

[76] A survey of community nurses indicated that only some 61% would certainly have reported a general practitioner whose performance was thought to put patients at risk: J Burrows 'Telling Tales and Saving Lives: Whistleblowing—the Role of Professional Colleagues in Protecting Patients from Dangerous Doctors' (2001) 9 Med L Rev 110. Interestingly, as many would have been more likely to report fellow nurses than report doctors. Very clear guidance is now provided in the new Nursing and Midwifery Council Code of Professional Conduct (2002), section 8 (www.nmc-uk.org/cms/conduct/Publications/Code%20of%20professional%20conduct.pds).

[77] Inserted by Pubic Interest Disclosure Act 1998, s 1.

particularly having regard to the fact that the reasonableness of the disclosure will be judged specifically on a 'need to know' basis—that is, on the identity of the person to whom the disclosure is made. Not only is frankness in the investigation of both ethical and clinical error to the advantage of the patient[78] but it is also important that the spectre of 'closed ranks' does not undermine the public's faith in the health care professions.[79]

PUBLIC RELATIONS

1.47   The importance of the overall relationship between the medical profession and the public cannot be overstated. The growing primacy of the cult of patient autonomy and patient choice has carried with it a parallel claim to a right to personal assessment of one's doctor's expertise and quality—aided by a surfeit of 'league tables' and mortality records. This has added a new dimension to the GMC's traditional attitudes to advertising by the medical profession. Time was when, for example, a doctor discussing medical matters of public interest on the radio had to do so anonymously for fear of disciplinary action on the part of the GMC. There is little doubt that such restrictions were based on a fear of competitive doctors 'touting' for patients; the advent of the National Health Service virtually eliminated any need for them and the antipathy of the GMC was steadily relaxed.

1.48   Solution of the matter was, however, catalysed by the reference of the GMC's ban to the Monopolies and Mergers Commission who held that the rule forbidding advertising in the press by general practitioners was against the public interest.[80] At the same time, the Commission, fearing exploitation, declined to extend its recommendations to advertising to the general public by specialists. This rule has now been relaxed, subject to the proviso that information about specialist services should include advice that patients cannot usually be seen or treated by specialists, either in the NHS or private practice, without a referral, usually from a general practitioner.[81] The recommendations of the MMC have now been accepted by the GMC,[82] whose advice currently reads:

---

[78] This is the purpose behind the National Patient Safety Agency (National Patient Safety Agency (Establishment and Constitution) Order 2001, SI 2001/1743), the function of which is to set up a system for mandatory reporting and collation of incidents and 'near-misses' on a national scale. The Agency will also take responsibility for overseeing research ethics committees: Department of Health *Reconfiguring the Department of Health's Arm's Length Bodies* (2004).

[79] The case of Dr Chapman, whose allegation of wrongful dismissal for questioning a colleague's research was rejected after eight years' investigation, is in point: H Spencer ' "Never again" says NHS whistleblower' (1997) 314 BMJ 623.

[80] Interestingly, the Court of Appeal subsequently upheld that the recommendation did not render the GMC's position unreasonable (*Colman* para 1.35 above).

[81] GMC *Good Medical Practice* (1998), para 46.

[82] The history of the GMC's change of attitude was outlined in D H Irvine 'The Advertising of Doctors' Services' (1991) 17 J Med Ethics 35.

If you publish or broadcast information about services you provide, the information must be factual and verifiable . . . The information you publish must not make claims about the quality of your services nor compare your services with those your colleagues provide. It must not, in any way, offer guarantees of cures, nor exploit patients' vulnerability or lack of medical knowledge.[83]

1.49 The GMC's general opposition to elitism on the part of 'specialists' has been overtaken and overruled by the Council of Europe.[84] As a result, a Specialist Register, referring to 53 medical specialties, is now held and constitutes the benchmark for those claiming a particular expertise and who have qualified for a Certificate of Completion of Specialist Training conferred by the Specialist Training Authority.[85] Thus, the traditional secrecy surrounding specialism no longer exists.

LEGAL INTERVENTION IN MEDICINE

1.50 The early twenty-first century picture of medical practice is one of rapidly advancing technology which is effected in a strongly research-orientated environment and which exists within an increasingly hedonistic and materialistic society. Society, for its part, demands more and more esoteric methodology, and personal involvement in medical care is encouraged at all levels. The law, however, moves more slowly than either medicine or public mores. Thus, the general rules of doctoring are being developed within a moral framework which is constantly being restructured by contemporary society while, at the same time, doctors frequently find themselves operating in an atmosphere of legal uncertainty. All of this promotes confrontation within the triangular relationship of medicine, society and the law;[86] a major purpose of medical jurisprudence as it evolves is to break down the barriers of latent hostility.

1.51 Whether the law has a right to impose morality is a well-known and controversial issue in jurisprudence but, for present purposes, we argue that the public conscience, as embodied in the law, provides a useful guide to medical ethics. As Hoffmann LJ once put it persuasively:

I would expect medical ethics to be formed by the law rather than the reverse.[87]

This, however, is not to say that the law should dictate to the profession and, particularly, not that it should dictate by means of restrictive statute. Effectively, we are merely pointing out that medicine must operate within broadly stated legal

[83] N 81 above, paras 44–45.

[84] Directive 93/16/EEC (OJ No L 165, 7.7.1993), Title II and III.

[85] European Specialist Medical Qualifications Order 1995, SI 1995/3208. A number of additions and amendments to the list of specialties have since been effected but these are generally of a semantic nature.

[86] Lord Woolf, now Lord Chief Justice, identified 5 main areas of dissatisfaction involving all three parties in 'Clinical Negligence: What is the Solution? How Can We Provide Justice for Doctors and Patients?' (2000) 4 Med L Internat 133.

[87] In *Airedale NHS Trust v Bland* [1993] 1 All ER 821 at 858, (1993) 12 BMLR 64 at 103.

rules—such as those embodied in the common law—and, as Lord Scarman classically indicated,[88] the law must be flexible in the absence of parliamentary direction.

1.52   The crucial question, then, is that of determining the *extent* to which medical decisions should be the object of legal scrutiny and control. At one extreme there are those who hold that the medical profession should be left to regulate itself and that it alone should decide what is acceptable conduct. According to this view, intervention by the law is too blunt a way of tackling the delicate ethical dilemmas which doctors have to face: the individual must confront and resolve the day-to-day ethical issues of medical practice—and it is a truism that no two patients present precisely the same problems in diagnosis and management.

1.53   The contrary view, often expressed just as firmly, denies that there is any reason why doctors alone should regulate their relationship with their patients. In this view, reserving to the medical profession the right to decide on issues, say, of life and death is an improper derogation from an area of legitimate public concern and an encroachment by clinicians into what is, properly, social policy. According to the proponents of this opinion, the law, even if it is an imperfect and often inaccessible weapon, is at least one means of controlling the health care professions in the interests of the community as a whole. In the event, modern conditions are such that the courts cannot avoid involvement in decisions that are essentially matters of medical ethics rather than law; as a result, they are increasingly prepared 'to adopt a more proactive approach to resolving conflicts as to more traditional medical issues'.[89] The reasons for this are several and, in many ways, indeterminate. We suggest, however, that it is in large part due to the rise of the culture of rights and the impact this has had on the non-acceptability of paternalistic practices. In essence, there have been fundamental adjustments in the doctor/patient relationship—and the relationship between law and medicine is also changing.

1.54   We will see as we go through the various problem areas discussed in this book that the relationship between the law and medicine had, over the years, effectively settled into a classical domestic state in which mutual trust was, occasionally, interspersed with outbursts of disaffection. Certainly, the law has, traditionally, been content to allow doctors as free a hand in carrying out their duties as is possible. Nonetheless, as Lord Woolf has cogently pointed out in a non-judicial capacity,[90] times change—including as to the distribution of domestic chores—and can change rapidly if the conditions are ripe. Thus, we have Lord Brandon holding, some 15 years ago:

... [T]he lawfulness of a doctor operating on, or giving treatment to, an adult patient disabled from giving consent will depend not on any approval or sanction of a court but on the question whether the operation or other treatment is in the best interests of the patient concerned.[91]

---

[88] In *Gillick v West Norfolk and Wisbech Area Health Authority* [1986] AC 112, [1985] 3 All ER 402, HL.
[89] Lord Woolf 'Are the Courts Excessively Deferential to the Medical Profession?' (2001) 9 Med L Rev 1.
[90] N 89 above.
[91] *Re F* [1990] 2 AC 1 at 56, sub nom *F v West Berkshire Health Authority* (1989) 4 BMLR 1 at 8, HL.

By 2000, however, the Court of Appeal was unanimously limiting the powers of the doctor beyond matters of clinical judgment and, at the same time delineating the relative powers and responsibilities of the doctors and the judges:

[I]n determining the welfare of the patient, the Bolam[92] test [of the acceptability of a doctor's actions] is applied only at the onset to ensure that the treatment proposed is recognised as proper by a responsible medical opinion skilled in delivering that particular treatment . . . In deciding what is best for the disabled patient the judge must have regard for the patient's welfare as the paramount consideration. That embraces issues far wider than the medical . . . In my opinion Bolam has no contribution to make to this second and determinative stage of the judicial decision.[93]

In effect, this retreat from Bolam is but part of a steady shift of judicial and societal concern away from the duties of the medical profession and its relocation under the umbrella of patients' rights[94]—though whether or not this serves to harmonise doctor/patient relationships is open to discussion. We return to the issue later in this chapter.

1.55   It has to be said, however, that the courts are also willing to recognise their position in relation to the legislature in face of the speed of evolution of modern technology— as Lord Browne-Wilkinson put it: 'Existing law may not provide an acceptable answer to the new legal questions [raised by the ability to sustain life artificially].'[95] He went on to question whether judges should seek to develop new law to meet a wholly new situation and to suggest that it was a matter which required society, through the democratic expression of its views in Parliament, to reach its decisions on the underlying moral and practical problems and then reflect those decisions in legislation— and, in this, he was strongly supported by Lord Mustill.[96] In other words, the House of Lords, at least, is anxious that society, as the third point in the triangle of policy decision-makers, should take its full share of responsibility for the ethico-legal directions we are following. Numerous examples of reforming legislative initiatives have emerged since the previous edition of this text only three years ago. Notable measures include the passing of the far-reaching Human Tissue Act 2004, due to come into force in April 2006, and the implementation of the European Clinical Trials Directive

---

[92] *Bolam v Friern Hospital Management Committee* [1957] 2 All ER 118, (1957) 1 BMLR 1. We discuss the *Bolam* test, which judges the propriety of a doctor's action by way of the standards of the medical profession itself, in detail in chapter 9 below. Both the Lord Chief Justice of England (nn 86 and 89) and the Lord Chancellor (Lord Irvine of Lairg 'The Patient, the Doctor, their Lawyers and the Judge: Rights and Duties' (1999) 7 Med L Rev 255) see its modification as central to the development of a medical jurisprudence.

[93] *Re SL (adult patient) (medical treatment)* [2001] Fam 15, (2000) 55 BMLR 105 at 119 per Thorpe LJ.

[94] See, in particular, the seminal case of *Chester v Afshar* [2004] 4 All ER 587, HL (para 9.95 below). We have discussed the implications of the case in K Mason and D Brodie '*Bolam, Bolam*—Wherefore Art Thou, *Bolam*?' (2005) 9 Edin LR 398.

[95] In *Airedale NHS Trust v Bland* [1993] 1 All ER 821 at 878, (1993) 12 BMLR 64 at 124.

[96] (1993) 12 BMLR 64 at 135.

in May 2004, which the British government took as an opportunity to undertake sweeping regulatory reforms of the conduct of research in the United Kingdom.[97]

1.56   The fact that the courts are prepared to assist doctors in coming to their ethical decisions—and have shown this by the steadily extended use of their declaratory powers[98]—is laudable and helpful. But it does not compensate in toto for the fact that doctors often still have to work in a 'legal vacuum' in which, without such pre-emptive assistance, they may be uncertain as to whether or not they face the prospect of a civil action or, again in the words of Lord Mustill, they take the risk of having to validate their conduct after the event in the context of a trial for murder. For these reasons, some may see it as preferable to have certain general rules set out clearly by way of statute and we have, in fact, concrete examples of the benign effect of legislative involvement in medical issues. It is through statute, for example, that a framework was established in an attempt to address the legal uncertainties of the new reproductive technologies.[99] Yet, while the basic legislation itself went far to dispel many such uncertainties, it has taken many court decisions in the wake of the statute to clarify the position further—and the process continues today with reforms of the Act now being considered (see chapter 4).

1.57   The use of regulatory frameworks varies according to the jurisdiction. The common British approach is for Parliament to state its general aims and to demit their refinement to officially appointed Authorities on which the profession and the public are adequately represented.[100] This approach serves to circumvent one of the most cogent arguments against introducing legal rules into human affairs—which is, that once rules acquire a specific meaning, they allow little room for manoeuvre and can turn out to be more restrictive than was originally intended by the framer of the rule. An effect of this can be to distort people's behaviour through the fear of litigation or prosecution. One may then be concerned, not with doing what one feels to be right, but with what one feels to be the legally safest thing to do. It is arguable that just such a problem has arisen in the shadow of the Data Protection Act 1998 which tightly controls the processing of individuals' personal data. Although many of the fears expressed have been found to be ungrounded, a culture of caution has grown up

---

[97] Directive 2001/20/EC of the European Parliament and of the Council of 4 April 2001 on the implementation of good clinical practice in the conduct of clinical trials on medical products for human use, implemented in the UK by the Medicines for Human Use (Clinical Trials) Regulations 2004 (SI 2004/1031).

[98] See, for example, Practice Note (Family Division: Incapacitated Adults: Declaratory Proceedings) [2002] 1 All ER 794, [2002] 1 WLR 325.

[99] Human Fertilisation and Embryology Act 1990.

[100] E.g. the Human Fertilisation and Embryology Authority established under the 1990 Act and, now, the Human Tissue Authority under the Human Tissue Act 2004. There are plans to merge the functions of these two authorities under one body to be known as the Regulatory Authority for Fertility and Tissue (RAFT), see Department of Health *Reconfiguring the Department of Health's Arm's Length Bodies* (2004); the opposition is such, however, that this may not happen.

around the operation of the Act in respect of uses of patient data for research purposes; many researchers have abandoned their plans for fear of contravening the
Act.[101]

1.58   Doctors in the United Kingdom may be particularly fortunate in this respect as,
notwithstanding the subtle changes of direction that we have discussed, the courts
remain inherently reluctant to interfere in clinical matters. While they will accept the
absolute right of a patient to refuse treatment,[102] they will, at the same time, refuse to
dictate to doctors what treatment they should give.[103] Indeed, the fear could be that, if
anything, the pendulum has swung too far in favour of therapeutic immunity.[104]

1.59   Moreover, one must question whether the adversarial system is the right route to
follow if there is to be a decision in the event of disagreement between doctor and
patient or, more often, between doctor and surrogate decision-maker. The concept of
winners and losers provides an uneasy foundation for the solution of sensitive and
complex ethico-legal problems but one looks in vain for a suitable alternative. Certainly, the vision of a bed-side consultation, as evidenced in Re B,[105] has its attractions
but it would be ingenuous in the extreme to suppose that it could take the place—or
even partly take the place—of a full court hearing in every similar case. The resolution
of allegations of medical negligence is a particular source of societal dissatisfaction
with the legal process; it is, however, a problem of completely different nature and one
that is considered in detail in chapter 9 below.

THE DOCTOR'S POSITION

1.60   There is no doubt, either, that the intrusion of the law into the doctor/patient relationship, essential as it may be in some instances, leads to a subtle but important
change in the nature of the relationship. Trust and respect are more likely to flourish
in one which is governed by morality rather than by legal rules and the injection of
formality and excessive caution between doctor and patient cannot be in the patient's
interest if it means that each sees the other as a potential adversary.

1.61   Where, then, does the doctor stand today in relation to society? To some extent, and
perhaps increasingly, he is a servant of the public, a public which is, moreover,

---

[101] See Faculty of Public Health of the Royal Colleges of Physicians of the United Kingdom *The Impact of Data Protection on Public Health Research* (2004) available at: www.fpmh.org.uk.

[102] *Re T (adult: refusal of medical treatment)* [1992] 4 All ER 649, (1992) 9 BMLR 46.

[103] *Re J (a minor) (wardship: medical treatment)* [1992] 2 FLR 165, (1992) 9 BMLR 10.

[104] Though the case of *R (on the application of Burke) v General Medical Council* [2005] QB 424 (2004) 79 BMLR 126 suggests a shift in judicial opinion. For comment see J K Mason and G T Laurie 'Personal Autonomy and the Right to Treatment: A Note on *R (on the application of Burke) v General Medical Council*' (2005) 9 Edin LR 123. *Burke* has, however, since been successfully appealed: [2005] EWCA Civ 1003.

[105] *Re B (adult: refusal of medical treatment), sub nom Ms B v An NHS Hospital Trust* [2002] EWHC 429, (2002) 65 BMLR 149.

widely—though not always well—informed on medical matters. The competent patient's inalienable rights to understand his treatment and to accept or refuse it are now well established and society is encouraged to distrust professional paternalism. The talk today is of 'producers and consumers' and the ambience of the supermarket is one that introduces its own stresses and strains.

1.62   It is, moreover, in many ways extraordinary that the provision of a national health service, which one would have thought should, above all other services, be free of bias, has, in recent years, become perhaps the main political issue that determines the voters' intentions in the United Kingdom.[106] As a result, more and more extravagant claims—and, more significantly, promises—are made with little regard for the fallibility and limitations of those who must implement them. Like it or not, only one person can be the best thoracic surgeon in Startown; the rest can only carry on doing their personal best which no amount of 'hype' or sanction can improve.

1.63   Unless the humanity of both health carers and patients is appreciated by both sides and is not exploited in the political arena, the resulting disappointment, again on both sides, may well lead to a relationship of conflict—or of mutual suspicion—which is in the interests of neither doctor nor patient. What is needed is one of mutual understanding in which doctors acknowledge the interests of patients and patients, for their part, reciprocate this respect while appreciating the pressures, both physical and mental, under which a health carer must work. The public has also to understand the broader issues in medicine. The profession must experiment and research if it is to improve its art and many would hold that a slight loss of autonomy on the part of patients is a small price to pay for a useful advance in therapeutic skills. The profession must also teach, or there will be no doctors to serve future generations; some loss of confidentiality can be looked upon as a return for the best treatment and the best investigative facilities. Clearly, these opposing attitudes cannot be reconciled so long as they are polarised or if the claims of one party are accepted to the exclusion of the other.[107] A middle way, based on respect and trust,[108] must be found and this is the function of medical jurisprudence which we attempt to express in the chapters which follow.

---

[106] The Chairman of the BMA believes the NHS has become 'the Punch and Judy show of British politics': L Eaton 'Politicians Must Stop Exploiting Patients' (2002) 325 BMJ 6.

[107] Do documents such as *Your Guide to the NHS* (2001) (www.nhs.uk/nhsguide/start.htm) assist in this or do they serve to amplify the potential for conflict? Certainly, the 2001 Guide is a marked improvement on its predecessor, *The Patient's Charter*, in that it also emphasises patients' responsibilities. Going a stage further, should the conditions set out in such guides be legally enforceable? See M H W Silver 'Patients' Rights in England and the United States of America' (1997) 23 J Med Ethics 213.

[108] For the importance of trust, see O O'Neill *Autonomy and Trust in Bioethics* (2002).

2

PUBLIC HEALTH AND THE STATE/PATIENT RELATIONSHIP

2.1 Medical practice encompasses more than a simple, private doctor/patient relationship. The State has a basic duty to protect its citizens from harm and we, ourselves, have comparable obligations to each other as members of our particular community. Inevitably, these duties include protection from disease and, as a consequence, the medical profession must be heavily involved in what can be loosely termed public health. In so far as public bodies are now involved, the doctor's private relationships are subtly altered and we have to consider how these alterations affect our concepts of medical ethics as a whole.[1]

2.2 Public health measures tend to fall into two overlapping categories: health promotion and/or disease prevention and control. There is, for example, much that we can do to ensure or promote our own health for the sake of ourselves and our significant others. We can eat more healthily, take exercise and avoid alcohol and drugs. But when our state of health becomes beyond our control, and most particularly, if our state of *ill* health becomes a threat to others, then the time for individual action has passed and it may be necessary for government to step in to institute measures to protect the community, even when this might entail threats to the rights of the immediately-affected individual. The important relationship, then, is no longer that between doctor and patient but rather that between patient and state. The role of the law in this sphere is to police the boundaries of this relationship and to ensure that every reasonable justification is offered to support state action that encroaches on individual rights. Even so, as we shall see, the health interests of the community can sometimes be so strong—or the threat to its health so great—that even compulsory action against the bodily integrity and freedoms of individuals can be defended.

2.3 A word of caution is, however, needed. This description of (coercive) public health measures should not be taken as a form of unqualified utilitarianism whereby the

---

[1] For a classic treatment of the issues, see M R Brazier and J Harris, 'Public Health and Private Lives' (1996) 4 Med L Rev 171.

public good will always trump individual freedoms. The modern, ethically-sound public health system is not to be characterised by such an unreconstructed and crude approach. Rather, firstly, robust health protection programmes should always require the state to justify every measure and intervention; secondly, the interventions should be minimal and 'necessary' in the circumstances—that is, no other reasonable means are available to achieve the same ends; and, thirdly, there should be full respect for other individual rights that are not implicated in the immediate health threat—for example, state agencies must remain bound by data protection measures which ensure that patient personal information will be used on a strict need-to-know basis.[2]

2.4   Health promotion programmes that are aimed at improving the health of individuals can be yet more controversial. While it may be legitimate for the state to educate and encourage the public in good health practices, the prospect of coercive measures in this field is controversial and politically charged. To what extent, for example, is it justifiable for a government to require the wearing of seat belts or to ban smoking in public places? And what about state action aimed to promote the future health of children? The European Commission recently issued a warning to the food industry about advertising 'junk food' to children, the threat being that the Union will legislate if the industry does not self-regulate to stop advertising and to improve labelling.[3] For many, such interventions represent questionable exercises of paternalism by the 'nanny state', but their legitimacy turns largely on our perspective on the issue: is one's own health simply a matter of individual choice or do we owe a responsibility to ourselves and to others to ensure that we remain as healthy as possible? The communitarian will undoubtedly favour the latter; the libertarian will tend towards the former to the extent that we can or should be held responsible for our own ill-health. This, however, might have significant implications as to access to health care in the face of scarce resources—is the smoker less entitled to coronary by-pass surgery than is the non-smoker? We return to discuss this and similar sensitive issues in chapter 11. For now, we need only note that States take more interest in their public's health than ever before[4] and this means that, when set against the unprecedented rise in popularity of the cult of autonomy in recent years, the tensions inherent within public health law are, perhaps, now more acute than ever before.

---

[2] See, for example, Health Protection Agency *Safeguarding the Confidentiality of Patient Information while Protecting Public Health* (2004), available at www.hpa.org.uk/confidentiality/default.htm.

[3] BBC News, 'EU takes aim at junk food adverts', available at www.bbc.co.uk/2/hi/business/4190313.stm.

[4] See, for example, the recent plans of the UK government: Department of Health, 'Choosing Health: Making Healthier Choices Easier' (2004), available at www.dh.gov.uk.

HANDLING HEALTH THREATS TO THE COMMUNITY

2.5   HIV/AIDS emerged in the United Kingdom in 1981.[5] The virus attacks the human immune system leaving the individual exposed to any number of opportunistic diseases. Forty million people worldwide are currently living with the virus and infection rates continue to grow. The hysteria which met the advent of the disease has calmed somewhat as a result of public education campaigns and the development of anti-retroviral drugs which can slow the progress of the disease, but significant public health issues remain, in particular, over access to those drugs, most especially in developing countries.[6] HIV/AIDS has come to represent the paradigm pandemic affecting humanity on a global scale: its spread has been greatly facilitated by modern air travel,[7] the absence of a cure makes the prospect of infection particularly significant, and early ignorance and misunderstanding about the disease and its pattern of spread led to calls for draconian measures to be taken against affected groups (and in some cases against groups that were thought to be at 'high risk').[8] But the viruses of hepatitis are more easily spread than HIV and constitute a potentially far greater threat to global health—it is estimated that there are currently some 350 million people who are chronically infected.

2.6   In fact, although HIV/AIDS has tended to dominate headlines and capture the public attention, the assault on global health comes on a number of fronts. Tuberculosis (TB), for example, has long been considered the stuff by which to carry off the heroines in nineteenth century novels, but the infection is increasing dramatically and is, now, the no. 1 killer among infectious diseases on a worldwide basis; the prospect of transfer of viruses to humans from other species (zoonoses) has been highlighted by the recent SARS[9] scare and by the prospect of xenotransplantation using animal organs;[10] and 'bioterrorism'—or the deliberate release of biological agents—has become the obsession of national security agencies in recent years.[11]

2.7   All such health risks threaten us as a community—a global community—and not merely as individuals. Responsive State agencies exist in most jurisdictions but the

---

[5] Human Immunodeficiency Virus (HIV) is a virus that attacks the immune system leaving it incapable of dealing with further assault. Acquired Immune Deficiency Syndrome (AIDS) refers to a state when the individual's immune system is compromised beyond a certain degree. There is international disagreement about the point at which AIDS should be diagnosed. Indeed, recent trends are away from the use of the term altogether.

[6] See, Commission on Intellectual Property Rights, *Integrating Intellectual Property Rights and Development Policy* (2002), chapter 2.

[7] 'Patient 0'—the first confirmed case of the infection—was, in fact, an airline steward.

[8] G J Annas, 'Detention of HIV Positive Haitians at Guatanamo—Human Rights and Medical Care' (1993) 329 New Eng J Med 589.

[9] SARS (Sever Acute Respiratory Syndrome) is thought to have been transmitted to human from birds after the mutation of a strain of avian influenza.

[10] We discuss this further in chapter 14.

[11] See, for example, the instances of deliberate release of anthrax in light of the terrorist attacks on the USA on 11 September 2001.

response cannot simply be at a local level given the nature of the beast. International efforts and coordination are essential to an effective defensive strategy. For this reason, the World Health Organization is currently revising its International Health Regulations—the first time in over half a century—in response to these increasing hazards.[12]

2.8   British regulations are similarly rooted in the past,[13] and many feel are in drastic need of reform.[14] The legal combatant provisions within the UK remain divided along jurisdictional lines, which, of course, are of little consequence to infectious diseases that know no respect for man-made boundaries. Agencies with responsibilities for various aspects of public health proliferate and, generally, are operationally jurisdiction-specific.[15] Furthermore, a worrying conclusion of a 2003 report was that:

In relation to the particular function of the surveillance and control of communicable disease there is at present no one individual or body unambiguously responsible and accountable for this function—*no-one is in charge.*[16]

2.9   This has since been addressed to some extent by the creation, in the same year, of the Health Protection Agency (HPA)[17] which has as its core remit the anticipation, identification and rapid response to infection disease threats and other health dangers. The body was initially established for England and Wales only, but it is due to merge with the National Radiological Protection Board (NRPB) in 2005 to become a UK-wide agency. Notwithstanding, the legal basis for the authority to intervene in the name of public health remains grounded in 'old law' and it to a consideration of these provisions that we now turn.[18]

---

[12] L O Gostin 'International Infectious Disease Law: Revision of the World Health Organization's International Health Regulations' (2004) 291 J Amer Med Ass 2623. European Union responses include Decision No. 2119/1998/EC of the European Parliament and of the Council of 24 September 1998 setting up a network for the epidemiological surveillance and control of communicable diseases in the Community (Official Journal L268, 03.10.1998 p 0001–0007).

[13] The original measures began in the nineteenth century with the Infectious Disease (Notification) Act 1889 and are now covered by the Public Health (Control of Disease) Act 1984. The Scottish legal position is found in the Public Health (Scotland) Act 1945. Secondary legislation currently governs the notification of several infectious diseases.

[14] W W Holland and S Stewart *Public Health: The Vision and the Challenge* (1998).

[15] See, for example, the Health Development Agency which has powers extending only to England, while the constraints of the new Heath Protection Scotland organisation are evident in its very name; see, similarly, the Public Health Institute of Scotland which combined with the Health Education Board for Scotland in 2003 to become a special health board, *Health Scotland*.

[16] S Monaghan, D Huws and M Navarro *The Case for a New UK Health of the People Act* (Nuffield Trust: 2003), p 23.

[17] See now the Health Protection Agency Act 2004 which incorporates the functions of the National Radiological Protection Board within the HPA.

[18] Monaghan points out that the current framework was established in the nineteenth century with 'no reasoned reform since 1945', see S Monaghan *The State of Communicable Disease Law* (2002).

HEALTH PROTECTION: THE LAW

2.10 Effective health protection for the community depends on a number of crucial factors. These include early detection, rapid and effective intervention and control, and on-going surveillance of the situation. Central to these, in turn, is the proper flow of information between those responsible for implementing the public health agenda; categorisation of diseases as 'notifiable' is essential to this process. A notifiable disease is one which a registered medical practitioner is legally bound to report to the relevant authorities. Failure to do so can result in summary conviction and fine. The Public Health (Control of Disease) Act 1984 for England and Wales defines five diseases as notifiable: cholera, plague, relapsing fever, smallpox and typhus.[19] This is clearly antiquated and the Public Health (Infectious Diseases) Regulations 1988 added 24 more, including the A, B, and C strains of the hepatitis virus.[20] The Secretary of State also has powers to make such regulations as are needed to respond to a immediate disease threat.[21] Interestingly, HIV infection is not notifiable in the United Kingdom. The reasoning behind this decision reveals one of the fundamental tensions associated with notification of diseases—that is that its compulsory nature effectively *requires* practitioners to breach patient confidentiality. Concern with HIV infection has traditionally related not to the nature of the disease itself but, rather, to the social stigma that has surrounded it. The fear was that patients would perceive a forced breach of their confidentiality as a significant threat to their interests and would not return for care; in turn, other infected persons might refuse to come forward—thus, health authorities would be left with no effective means by which to monitor the disease. We see, then, that this policy was justified on both private *and* public grounds. It is to be hoped, however, that it has become less valid as the public has becomes more educated and less reactionary towards the disease.[22] Even so, the case of HIV illustrates the sensitivity of the situation when a new disease emerges and we are uncertain as to what we are dealing with.

2.11 This having been said, specific legislation for HIV/AIDS was introduced in the guise of the AIDS (Control) Act 1987 which requires regular reporting by a health authority on the incidence of HIV/AIDS within its area.[23] Moreover, specific powers of detention were established in the 1988 Regulations whereby a Justice of the Peace can order continued detention of a person with AIDS if he has reason to believe that he or she will fail to take proper precautions as to the spread of the disease on release.[24] These measures operate over and above those that can be applied in respect of other diseases, and which include initial detention in hospital by order of a Justice

---

[19] Public Health (Control of Disease) Act 1984, s 10.

[20] SI 1988/1546.   [21] N 19, above, 1984 Act, s 13.

[22] The *medical* case for not making HIV notifiable simply does not exist given that other infectious diseases such hepatitis, mumps and measles must all be reported.

[23] This is not the same as notification which requires the reporting of the name, age, sex and residence of each affected person.

[24] N 20, above, 1988 Regulations s 5.

on the application by a health authority in the light of relevant medical evidence.[25] Similarly, compulsory medical examination can be ordered prior to, or during, such detention.[26] Local Authorities also have power to enter premises to investigate possible violations of the law; normally, this should be with 24 hours notice, but a Justice can authorise earlier entry as a matter of urgency and with the use of force, if necessary.

2.12   We can, however, also find balance in the law. As regards personal privacy, for example, the 1988 Regulations provide:

> Any certificate, or copy, and any accompanying or related document, shall be sent in such a manner that its contents cannot be read during transmission; and the information contained therein shall not be divulged to any person except: (a) so far as is necessary for compliance with the requirements of any enactment (including these Regulations), or (b) for the purposes of such action as any proper officer considers reasonably necessary for preventing the spread of disease.[27]

2.13   Just how well these, and other measures, are suited to respond to new threats to public health is debatable.[28] A report on the English public health regime was published by the Department of Health in 2002,[29] and a similar consultation was undertaken by the Scottish Executive in the same year;[30] both recommended a review of the law on infection control. This has not yet been undertaken. From what studies do exist,[31] however, there is strong evidence that the system is creaking under the weight of new challenges that could never have been envisaged when it was first established. Not least among these is the standard of human rights compatibility to which all public laws are now subject. It is far from clear how well our public health systems would withstand close scrutiny from this aspect.

PUBLIC HEALTH AND THE CRIMINAL LAW

2.14   Discussion of the state's protection of public health would be incomplete without mention of the role of the criminal law. The criminal justice system is society's most overt commitment to the protection of its citizens and much of its success is built on its deterrent effect—that is, the power of the system to influence individual behaviour through the threat of criminal sanction. In most circumstances, however, disease transmission is not a matter of choice; it is not, therefore, something that can rightly be subject to deterrence. But this is not true of all diseases and, in particular, of sexually transmitted diseases which require unique circumstances for their transmission—circumstances which can be brought about, or avoided, through individual

---

[25] N 19, above, 1984 Act, s 38.   [26] *Ibid*, s 35.

[27] Public Health (Infectious Diseases) Regulations 1988, s 12.

[28] For a discussion in the context of the SARS virus, see V Howes and K Tinline 'Bird Flu (SARS): How to Control an Epidemic' (2004) 154 New LJ 254.

[29] Department of Health, *Getting Ahead of the Curve: A Strategy for Combating Infectious Diseases* (2002).

[30] Scottish Executive *Health Protection in Scotland: A Consultation Paper* (2002).

[31] See n 16, above.

action. It is, therefore, meaningful to consider whether the criminal law has a role to play in encouraging people to behave responsibly when it comes to sexual matters.

2.15   The landmark in the English jurisprudence was established as long ago as 1888 with the decision in *R v Clarence*[32] in which a husband with gonorrhoea infected his wife in the knowledge, and his wife's ignorance, that he had the condition. Clarence was prosecuted—and convicted—under ss 20 and 47 of the Offences Against the Person Act 1861 (inflicting grievous bodily harm and actual bodily harm respectively). There was no suggestion that he intended to infect his wife and it was accepted that she would not have consented to sexual intercourse if she had known the truth. His convictions were, however, reversed on appeal, largely on the grounds that (i) successful prosecution depends on some direct and intentional wounding to the body of the victim and these are not present in the case of reckless infection; and (ii) consent of a wife to sexual intercourse was a given; the only factors that would vitiate it would be fraud as to the nature of the act in question or as to the identity of the actor and neither applied in the instant case. This unrealistic precedent stood for more than a century and distorted the jurisprudence as a result. However, as we will see below, it has recently—and thankfully—been overturned.[33]

2.16   There have been a number of attempts in Commonwealth jurisdictions to circumvent the evidential difficulties left by *Clarence*,[34] but the case law has led to inconsistent results. The first successful prosecution for reckless transmission of HIV in the United Kingdom is to be found in the unreported Scottish case of *Kelly v HM Advocate*[35] where the relative flexibility of Scots law allowed for a charge of 'culpably and recklessly engaging in sexual intercourse to the danger of a woman's health and life'. More recently, however, the essential legal issues have been laid out in *R v Dica* and this now represents the current legal position in England and Wales.[36] This case involved the prosecution of an HIV positive defendant for allegedly having infected two partners with the condition. The charge was under s 20 of the Offences Against the Person Act 1861, a route which, as we have seen, has caused logical and doctrinal problems because (i) there is no 'assault' on the victim in the sense of physical violence to the victim's body, and (ii) authority suggested that consent to such an 'assault' was irrelevant for criminal purposes.[37] But here the court held that so long as all the other elements of a s 20 offence were present, infection with disease could constitute a crime. Moreover, consent is only irrelevant in circumstances where there

---

[32] (1889) 22 QBD 23.

[33] The 'given' as to intramarital consent to sexual intercourse was rejected in *R v R* [1992] 1 AC 599, [1991] 4 All ER 481. For Scotland, see *Stallard v H M Advocate* 1989 SCCR 248, 1989 SLT 469.

[34] The New South Wales Crimes Act 1900, as amended, now includes an offence of causing grievous bodily disease at s 36. The moral obligations are, of course, a distinct matter: see R Bennett, H Draper and L Frith 'Ignorance is Bliss? HIV and Moral Duties and Legal Duties to Forewarn' (2000) 26 J Med Ethics 9.

[35] (2001) High Court of Justiciary, Glasgow, 23 February.

[36] [2004] 3 WLR 213, [2004] 3 All ER 593.

[37] *Clarence*, para 2.15 above and *R v Brown* [1994] 1 AC 212, [1993] 2 ALL ER 75.

is actual intention to harm. In cases involving recklessness, however, the consent of the victim to running the risk of infection could be a complete defence. The central issue is not consent to sexual intercourse but rather consent to run a known risk by engaging in unprotected sexual intercourse. This requires some degree of knowledge about the presence and nature of the risk involved; but, given the general prevalence of knowledge about sexually transmitted diseases in society, this state of knowledge may be all-but-assumed in the majority of cases. This is a clear message about personal responsibility and to that extent it is a very modern ruling that reflects a particular view of the society in which we want to live. It does, however, beg the question of where the line is to be drawn between intention and recklessness of conduct.[38] This is largely a question of the judgment of the criminal prosecution services which carry a heavy burden in deciding which messages to send to the community for adjudication.

HEALTH PROMOTION: THE ISSUES

2.17   As we have already discussed, the modern 'cult of the individual' has resulted in extremely unfavourable reactions to paternalistic behaviour. Yet, we have also noted that states now take more interest in the health of their citizens than ever before. On one level this may simply be sound investment, for what is a State without its healthy people? More sceptically, it may be a largely economic policy designed to avoid longer-term, greater, costs dealing with a chronically ill population. Either way, governments spend vast sums trying to persuade or gently coerce their citizens into healthier lifestyles. Moreover, as the reach of public health programmes extends ever further into our private lives, the subtlety with which those programmes are promoted increases: it is surely no accident that the latest British government white paper on public health is entitled *Choosing Health: Making Healthier Choice Easier*.[39] Facilitating choice is certainly more palatable than manipulating behaviour, but to the extent that choice is predicated on information, one of the biggest challenges for governments is in ensuring that *mis*information does not become the primary driver for citizens' behaviour. As a recent consultation document poignantly stated:

The recent BSE enquiry and MMR controversy have highlighted the need for health protection agencies to pay as much attention to assessing public perceptions about risk and communicating with people about them as they do investigating hazards and controlling exposures.[40]

2.18   The so-called MMR controversy related to the perceived risks associated with the measles, mumps and rubella vaccine which was introduced in the UK in 1988. A fear

---

[38] On the effect of consent in the context of contact sports, see *R v Barnes* [2004] All ER (D) 338.
[39] Department of Health *Choosing Health: Making Healthier Choices Easier* (2004) Cm 6374.
[40] Scottish Executive *Health Protection in Scotland: A Consultation Paper* (2002), para 23.

developed that the vaccine was a cause of autism in children who received it.[41] This provoked a crisis of confidence among British parents, many of whom began to refuse the vaccine for their children. Matters came to a head—in the courts at least—with the case of *Re C (welfare of child: immunisation)*[42] in which two estranged fathers sought court orders to ensure that their children were inoculated with the vaccine despite the fact that, in each case, the mother was the primary carer and disagreed with the father's position. The Court of Appeal confirmed the trial judge's approach, which was to consider the best interests of the children, first, from the medical and, then, from a non-medical perspective.[43] Sedley LJ stated that such an approach could admit a variety of possibilities, including support for a parental view that medical intervention was not appropriate. In the instant cases, however, the scientific evidence relied upon by the mothers to demonstrate the dangers of the vaccine was held to be untenable. In contrast, the effectiveness of the vaccine was shown to be high and side effects were rare.[44] Orders were issued that the children should be vaccinated.

2.19   The decision may be contrasted with that of the Irish Supreme Court in *North Western Health Board v W(H)*[45] in which the court considered an action brought by a local health board against parents who had refused a 'heel prick' test for their son—a simple blood test aimed at screening for some treatable conditions, including phenyl-ketonuria (PKU).[46] It is a routine practice in respect of all newborns. The parents resisted, however, because of the 'assault' on their son that the prick would represent. The Supreme Court upheld the right of the parents to refuse, relying on the Irish constitutional right to 'family autonomy' which, it was held, should be protected against undue interference by the State. As in the English courts, the notion of the child's best interests was a central consideration; the difference came in how, and by whom, these were to be determined.[47]

2.20   Each of these cases demonstrates important points—such as the extent of parental rights over their children—to which we shall return in due course. For present purposes, they also illustrate that there is no clear line between health promotion and health protection measures. However, it is the extent to which any given measure can

---

[41] The original paper which sparked the controversy was A Wakefield et al 'Ileal-lymphoid-nodular Hyperplasia, Non-specific Colitis, and Pervasive Development Disorder in Children' (1998) 351 The Lancet 637. Evidence to the contrary includes K M Madsen et al 'A Population-Based Study of Measles, Mumps and Rubella Vaccination and Autism' (2002) 347 New Eng J Med 1477; H Honda, Y Shimizu and M Rutter 'No Effect of MMR Withdrawal on the Incidence of Autism: A Total Population Study' (2005) 46 J Child Psychol Psychiat 572.

[42] [2003] 2 FLR 1095 (CA).

[43] See also, *Re B (a child)(immunisation)* [2003] 2 FCR 156 (CA)—medical evidence must be 'clear and persuasive'.

[44] For commentary, see K O'Donnell '*Re C (Welfare of Child: Immunisation)* Room to Refuse? Immunisation, Welfare and the Role of Parental Decision-Making' (2004) 16 CFLQ 213.

[45] [2001] IESC 70, 8 November.

[46] PKU is a debilitating brain condition which—if detected early—can be avoided by simply dietary changes; otherwise, affected victims can suffer profound disability.

[47] For commentary see, G Laurie 'Better to Hesitate at the Threshold of Compulsion: PKU Testing and the concept of Family Autonomy in Eire' (2002) 28 J Med Ethics 136.

be classified under the latter heading—at least at the community level—that determines the degree of paternalistic or coercive state interference that is involved.
Whether or not it is justified must, then, be argued on the particularities of the case.

THE DARKER SIDES OF MEDICINE

2.21   Society, also, occasionally demands questionable practices from its doctors. The
extreme of the medico-ethical problems of the late twentieth century related to what
are described as cruel, inhuman or degrading treatments or punishments. Political
violence is all around us and the doctor cannot wholly dissociate himself from this; an
international attempt to define his position is to be found in the Declaration of
Tokyo,[48] which shows well the difficulties of drafting ethical codes of an academic
nature—definitions of principle can only be interpreted in the mind of the individual.
Who is to define a degrading procedure? Is it self-evident that the well-being of an
indiscriminate terrorist bomber is as valuable as is that of his potential victim?
Granted that unethical biological measures are used in detention and interrogation,[49]
could it not be that a doctor's presence, although disapproving, might be to the
benefit of the subject? And, one might ask, by what right can the doctor command
complete clinical independence when, in some circumstances, he may be ignorant of
the widespread effect his decision may have on others? The motivation of the Declaration of Tokyo is impeccable in condemning the excesses of politically-motivated
punishment and torture, but it fails in its general purpose because it was drafted with
that rather narrow end in view.

2.22   There has always been something of an armed truce between the medical profession
and the police as to confidentiality. The anxiety engendered here has been summed up:
'Although doctors in general wish to co-operate with the police, they must be sure that
any information divulged *in confidence* will not be used in court unless they are aware
at the time of interview that that information might be so used.'[50]

2.23   The professional relationship between doctors and the police in England and
Wales is, to a large extent, dictated by the Police and Criminal Evidence Act 1984. The
major contentions involved in its drafting centred not only on confidentiality but
also on those associated with intimate body searches. The controversy exemplifies
the difficulties exposed when relying on individual conscience as a guide to ethical
medical practice. As regards confidentiality, the BMA—and other interested groups—
succeeded in protecting medical records from the powers of police search by way of

---

[48] See Appendix C. It is to be noted that the spirit of the Declaration of Tokyo is also expressed in the
United Nations Declaration of Human Rights, art. 5 and, domestically, in the Human Rights Act 1998, Sch 1,
Article 3; the European Convention on which it is based allows for no derogation.

[49] For which there is considerable evidence: D Summerfield 'Fighting "Terrorism" with Torture' (2003)
326 BMJ 773.

[50] The problem is discussed further in chapter 8 below.

having them classified as excluded material.[51] The doctor, however, remains the holder of the records and is, therefore, at liberty to disclose them if he so wishes;[52] on the other hand, in the absence of a court order, he may withhold them even in the face of serious crime.[53] Quite clearly, the law and the professions will, when possible, take a pragmatic approach which includes consideration of the community's interests.[54] As to searches, the leadership of the BMA agreed with those politicians who regarded the legal permit to make searches as 'an oppressive and objectionable new statutory power [which was] a serious affront to a person's liberty'.[55] Many others, including ourselves, would consider drug peddling, with its potential catastrophic effect on people of all ages, as being a crime which merits draconian preventive methods. In the event, the 1984 Act retained the legal right of the authorities to ask for an intimate search (s 55) and/or for the taking of an intimate sample (s 62) but stipulated that the latter must be performed by a medical practitioner or, now, a registered nurse.[56] So far as we know, these provisions of the 1984 Act have not been challenged in the European Court of Human Rights.[57]

2.24   The small cadre of police surgeons, or forensic medical examiners, comes into closest contact with the police[58] but it is, perhaps, the prison medical service which most magnifies and brings into focus many of the problems associated with codified ethics. Given a normal population, is it possible to apply to it normal methods? One would have hoped that this would be so, but there is little doubt that prison doctors are under considerable stress which results, in summary, from attempting to answer the question: are they there to serve the prisoners or the prison?[59] Smith, in an

---

[51] Police and Criminal Evidence Act 1984, ss 11, 12.

[52] *R v Singleton* [1995] 1 Cr App R 431, [1995] Crim LR 236. Section 29 of the Data Protection Act 1998 permits the use or disclosure of 'personal data' for the purposes of prevention or detection of crime or the prosecution or apprehension of offenders without observing the normal formalities of the Act (such as informing the subject of any such use or disclosure).

[53] *R v Cardiff Crown Court, ex p Kellam* (1993) 16 BMLR 76. It is to be noted that Evans LJ made this ruling 'with considerable reluctance'.

[54] In the Scottish High Court case of *HM Adv v Kelly* (2001)—an unreported case of reckless exposure to HIV infection—the police were allowed to breach the anonymity and confidentiality of a research project involving prisoners in order to trace the strain of virus involved. Discussed in J Chalmers 'The Criminalisation of HIV Transmission' (2002) 26 J Med Ethics 160; also S M Bird and A J Leigh Brown 'Criminalisation of HIV Transmission: Implications for Public Health in Scotland' (2001), 323 BMJ 1174.

[55] W Russell 'Intimate Body Searches—for Stilettos, Explosive Devices, et al' (1983) 286 BMJ 733.

[56] S 62(9) as amended by the Criminal Justice and Police Act 2001, s 80. There have been a number of amendments to the 1984 Act which include increased powers of the police to retain samples and records in certain circumstances even if the donor was acquitted. These have survived a challenge by way of the European Convention on Human Rights: *R (on the application of S) v Chief Constable of South Yorkshire* [2004] 4 All ER 193, HL. Comparable powers are available in Scotland by way of the Criminal Procedure (Scotland) Act 1995, ss 18 and 19 or by obtaining a Sheriff warrant. Further amendments, similar to those in England, are contained in the Criminal Justice (Scotland) Act 2003, Part 8.

[57] The vexed problem of searches by transsexuals has now been resolved—the sex of a constable is that of the reassignment sex: *A v Chief Constable of West Yorkshire Police* [2004] 3 All ER 145, HL.

[58] For a critical editorial comment, see The Lancet 'Three-faced Practice: Doctors and Police Custody' (1993) 341 Lancet 1245.

[59] R Smith 'Prison Doctors: Ethics, Invisibility, and Quality' (1984) 288 BMJ 781.

early in-depth study, believed that those in the service who regard their problems as exaggerated delude themselves; there was no reason to suppose that conditions have changed greatly[60] and the frequent allusions to prisoners made in this book—particularly as to consent to examination and treatment—testify to the strength of this view. The number and proportion of mentally disordered prisoners has increased steadily over the years and is swelled by those who find themselves unable to live in the community by virtue of mental illness.[61] It is not at all uncommon for such persons to end up in prison where access to psychiatric care may be inadequate and, at the same time, transfer to a psychiatric hospital is very difficult in practical terms. This may have tragic consequences—as was demonstrated in a study from New Zealand which showed that the prison suicide rate escalated by some 500 per cent when arrangements for such transfer deteriorated.[62] This has clear implications as to human rights and in respect of the prison authorities' duty of care towards mentally disordered inmates. While the courts are reluctant to extend the task of an already overburdened service still further, it is clear that there is a certain minimal level of care that prisons must meet. In *Kirkham v Chief Constable of the Greater Manchester Police*,[63] liability was imposed on the police for failing to inform a remand centre that a prisoner being transferred to their care was a suicide risk. By contrast, the Court of Appeal in *Knight v Home Office*[64] took the view that a prison hospital could not be expected to meet the same standard of care as a psychiatric hospital in the treatment of a potentially suicidal prisoner. However, the European Court of Human Rights, while admitting that the assessment of the minimum level of severity necessary to demonstrate ill-treatment is a relative exercise, has now decided that inadequate psychiatric care can constitute degrading treatment under Article 3 of the Convention[65]—which must be a matter of concern to the UK authorities. The limitations placed on prison authorities are an inevitable consequence of the overcrowded conditions. It is undesirable enough to house ordinary offenders in such conditions;[66] it is unconscionable to treat in this way those who may only be there because of mental illness. It must be a matter for general satisfaction that the present government has announced a positive policy

---

[60] J Reed and M Lyne 'The Quality of Health Care in Prison: Results of a Year's Programme of Semi-structured Inspections' (1997) 315 BMJ 1420.

[61] P Stephenson 'Mentally Ill Offenders are being Wrongly Held in Prisons' (2004) 328 BMJ 1095.

[62] K Skegg and B Cox 'Impact of Psychiatric Services on Prison Suicide' (1997) 338 Lancet 1436.

[63] [1990] 2 QB 283, [1990] 3 All ER 246. Liability cannot be avoided by a claim that the suicidal act of the deceased amounted to a novus actus interveniens: *Reeves v Metropolitan Police Comr* [1998] 2 All ER 381, (1998) 41 BMLR 54, CA. At the same time, the obligation on the police to prevent a prisoner taking his own life arises only if they knew, or ought to have known, that he presented a suicide risk: *Orange v Chief Constable of West Yorkshire Police* [2002] QB 347, [2001] 3 WLR 736, CA.

[64] [1990] 3 All ER 237, (1989) 4 BMLR 85.

[65] *Keenan v United Kingdom* (2001) 33 EHRR 913.

[66] At least, the appalling practice of 'slopping out' has now been branded as in breach of Articles 3 and 8: *Napier v The Scottish Ministers* (2004) *The Times*, 13 May.

designed to empower and improve co-operation between the prison medical service and the NHS.[67]

THE IMPACT OF HUMAN RIGHTS ON MEDICAL LAW

2.25 We have already noted that rights discourse is not without its problems, and in some circumstances the assertion of 'patients' rights' may be antithetical to the establishment and maintenance of a healthy and productive therapeutic relationship. Nonetheless, the relatively young discipline of medical law has emerged against a background of universal human rights, as embodied in a wide range of international treaties, covenants, agreements and laws.[68] Taken together, these measures endorse a particular view of the world which has as its central focus the primacy of the human being, and flowing from this are a number of direct and collateral rights which, it is declared, all human beings are possessed of. In the health care context, it is frequently asserted that these include:

- The right to be respected and treated with dignity
- The right to the highest attainable standard of physical and mental health and associated right to health care
- The right to consent and to refuse medical interventions
- The right not to be subjected to medical or scientific experimentation without consent
- The right to equality under the law
- The right to protection against arbitrary interference with privacy or with the family
- The right to enjoy the benefits of scientific progress and its application
- The protection of the rights of vulnerable persons

2.26 This list reflects an impressive array of rights when seen together, although it is important to note that not all are of the same genre. Rights of non-interference (*negative rights*), such as the right to consent and refuse and the right to protection of

---

[67] National Health Service Reform and Health Care Professions Act 2002, s 23. Also published is the Recommendation of the Council of Europe on *Ethical and Organisational Aspects of Health Care in Prison*, Recommendation R(98)7 which sees the prison medical officer as doubling as clinician and public health officer (paras 22–25).

[68] For example, the Universal Declaration of Human Rights (10 December 1948), the Convention for the Protection of Human Rights and Fundamental Freedoms (4 November 1950), the European Social Charter (18 October 1961), the UN Convention on the Elimination of All Forms of Racial Discrimination (21 December 1965), the International Covenant on Civil and Political Rights and the International Covenant on Economic, Social and Cultural Rights (16 December 1966), the Convention for the Protection of Individuals with regard to Automatic Processing of Personal Data (28 January 1981), the UN Convention on the Rights of the Child (20 November 1989), and the Universal Declaration on the Human Genome and Human Rights (UNESCO, 11 November 1997).

one's privacy, rank alongside rights of entitlement (*positive rights*), such as the right to the highest attainable standard of health. The difference between such categories of right is more than a mere matter of classification. The consequences of giving effect to positive rights are generally thought to be more far-reaching than respecting negative rights, especially in economic terms, and this has a direct correlation to the likelihood of such rights being respected or protected by states in practice. The rhetoric of rights has been a powerful motivator for international bodies, including the Council of Europe, to produce instruments such as the *Convention on Human Rights and Biomedicine.*[69] Nonetheless, many states, including the United Kingdom, do little more than pay lip-service to these measures,[70] and continue to implement domestic laws in flagrant breach of their provisions.[71] The problem is that instruments such as the Council of Europe Convention represent an ideal of circumstances. They are ethically justified and contain sound principles and provisions (at least from a Western perspective); but the lawyer who is concerned with turning rights into realities may see them as largely vapid documents that contain little more than aspirations. States which agree to their provisions and sign up to their terms rarely do so with a view to making substantive changes in domestic law. Either it is argued that laws are adequate as they stand, or reservations are taken if the consequences of signing are too great yet, at the same time, political expediency dictates a show of commitment. Moreover, not only is there a substantial lack of *volonté* to be bound by their terms, but also there is a pitiful lack of effective mechanisms to ensure enforcement by aberrant states.

2.27   None of which is to decry the usefulness of these instruments—indeed, they certainly have an intrinsic value in that they can influence to a large extent the form of further developments and can guide a path through the ethical and legal mire that must be negotiated if further measures are to be instituted. Additional assistance can be obtained from other quarters. For example, in 1993, the Director-General of UNESCO created the International Bioethics Committee (IBC) to respond to the major concerns raised by the progress made in the life and health sciences, but, as the first chair of the Committee (Noelle LeNoir) stated:

The International Bioethics Committee is to be designed first and foremost as a forum for the exchange of ideas and debate. It will also incite concrete action to be taken in the field. Far from setting itself up as an inspection authority, its basic task will be to facilitate understanding of the upheavals in progress.

---

[69] Council of Europe Convention for the Protection of Human Rights and Dignity of the Human Being with Regard to the Application of Biology and Medicine: Convention on Human Rights and Biomedicine (1997). This has since been joined by the Additional Protection on the Prohibition of Cloning Human Beings (1998), the Additional Protocol on Organs and Tissues of Human Origin (2002), and the Additional Protocol on Biomedical Research (2005).

[70] Only 19 of the 46 member states of the Council of Europe had ratified this Convention by January 2005, Steering Committee on Bioethics (2005: CDBI/INF(2005) 3. The UK was not one of them—and remains so.

[71] For example, the UK passed the Human Fertilisation and Embryology (Research Purposes) Regulations 2001, SI 2001/188 widening the circumstances in which human embryos can be created for research purposes in clear contravention of Article 18(2) of the Council of Europe Convention.

2.28   The IBC has been particularly active in the last few years[72] and UNESCO made its Bioethics Programme a principal priority in 2002. The IBC's most ambitious project by far is currently underway in the guise of the development of a Declaration on Universal Norms on Bioethics.[73] UNESCO sees its role as a leading standard-setter in this field, and the current draft of the instrument (January 2005) states among its aims '[the provision of] a universal framework of fundamental principles and basic procedures designed to guide States in the formulation of their legislation and their policies in the field of bioethics . . .'.[74] The commitment is 'to promote respect for human dignity and the protection of human rights . . .', and indeed the obligation to respect the 'inherent dignity of the human person' has pride of place as the first of the Declaration's general principles. But therein lie many of the problems and challenges that such a project faces. It is said, for example, that Japanese culture does not recognise a notion of 'human dignity'; in what sense, then, can this truly be a Universal instrument? Moreover, the term 'human dignity' itself begs the question of what exactly this means and who enjoys it. It is telling that the draft makes no specific mention of the position of the human embryo, is this a 'person' within the terms of the instrument? The omission is undoubtedly nothing more than political expediency because there are few issues that give rise to instantaneous global disagreement than the question of the moral (and legal) status of the embryo; the reality is that truly sensitive issues often remain unaddressed because the greatest challenge for the drafters of such instruments is to reach consensus. The current draft of the Declaration is a considerably watered-down version of the original report of the IBC on the possibility of a universal agreement on bioethics which contemplated, inter alia, issues as broadranging as abortion, euthanasia and intellectual property rights.[75] None of these is considered in the present draft. It may be for the best. One need only consider the machinations at the United Nations in the attempt to elaborate an International Convention Against the Reproductive Cloning of Human Beings[76] to understand how fraught the international political process can be.[77]

2.29   At the present time, then, the most effective impetus for change remains the implementation of laws at the national level, and this is most clearly demonstrated by the passing of the Human Rights Act 1998 which incorporated the Articles of the

---

[72] See, for example, the Universal Declaration on the Human Genome and Human Rights (1997) and the International Declaration on Human Genetic Data (2003).

[73] The progress of the process of the instrument can be tracked at the UNESCO Bioethics website: http://portal.unesco.org.

[74] International Bioethics Committee *Elaboration of the Declaration on Universal Norms on Bioethics: Fourth Outline of a Text* (December 2004), Article 3.

[75] International Bioethics Committee *Report of the IBC on the Possibility of Elaborating a Universal Instrument on Bioethics* (June 2003: SHS/EST/02/CIB–9/5 (rev.3)).

[76] The General Assembly of the United Nations (UN) established an Ad Hoc Committee to address the issue in 2001 (Resolution 56/93 of 12 December 2001). The debate and the various standpoints can be seen here: www.un.org/law/cloning/.

[77] G J Annas and R M Isasi 'Arbitage, Bioethics and Cloning: The ABCs of Gestating a United Nations Cloning Convention' (2004) 35 Case Western Reserve J Int Law 397.

European Convention on Human Rights (ECHR, 1950) into UK domestic law in October 2000.

THE HUMAN RIGHTS ACT 1998

2.30   The terms of the Human Rights Act protect our citizens against the acts or omissions of a public authority that contravene their rights, and the institutions of the NHS are paradigm examples of such authorities.[78] Other examples include the Human Fertilisation and Embryology Authority and similar statute-based bodies. Moreover, it is easy to envisage how the Articles of the ECHR might have a significant influence on patient rights and the practice of medical law. Key provisions of the Convention embody rights that affect areas at the core of the discipline. These include Article 2 (the right to life), Article 3 (the prohibition on torture, and cruel and inhuman treatment), Article 5 (the right to liberty of the person), Article 8 (the right to respect for private and family life), Article 9 (the right to freedom of thought, conscience and religion), Article 10 (freedom of expression, especially where this is likely to conflict with other rights such as those to privacy), Article 12 (the right to marry and found a family), and Article 14 (the prohibition on discrimination in the protection or exercise of these rights). Throughout this book we examine the jurisprudence to date and assess the ways in which the recognition of these rights has, or has not, changed this area of the law. It is salutary, however, to note that initial predictions of wide-sweeping changes have not been borne out in practice.[79] It has been established, for example, that the right to life does not imply a correlative right to die,[80] that the withdrawal of feeding and hydration from severely incapacitated patients precipitating their death can still be justified in their best interests,[81] and that so-called dangerous persons can continue to be subjected to a medical control system which can do nothing for them by way of treatment.[82] In some areas the courts have declared that the Convention rights add nothing to domestic law,[83] while in others the change has simply been a shift in argumentation from an interest- to a rights-based

---

[78] See generally, J Wadham and H Mountfield *Blackstone's Guide to the Human Rights Act 1998* (1999).

[79] See, for example, British Medical Association *The Medical Profession and Human Rights* (2001). Cf, G T Laurie 'Medical Law and Human Rights: Passing the Parcel Back to the Profession?' in A Boyle et al (eds) *Human Rights and Scots Law: Comparative Perspectives on the Incorporation of the ECHR* (2002).

[80] *R (on the application of Pretty) v DPP* [2002] 1 AC 800, [2002] 1 All ER 1; confirmed in the European Court of Human Rights as *Pretty v United Kingdom* (Application 2346/02) [2002] 2 FCR 97, [2002] 2 FLR 45.

[81] *NHS Trust A v M, NHS Trust B v H* [2001] 1 All ER 801, (2000) 58 BMLR 87 and more recently, *NHS Trust v I* [2003] EWHC 2243 (Fam).

[82] *A v The Scottish Ministers* 2001 SC 1, confirmed by the Privy Council at 2001 SLT 1331.

[83] *Re Wyatt (a child)(medical treatment: parents' consent)* [2004] Fam Law 866.

approach, leaving the outcome largely unaltered.[84] And, in the background, we have the European Court of Human Rights in Strasbourg which, inter alia, continues steadfastly to refuse to extend protection of the Convention to the fetus.[85]

2.31   At the same time, this is not to imply that the 1998 Act has had no influence whatsoever. Indeed quite the contrary is true, particularly in the realm of judicial review where procedural safeguards have been subjected to very close scrutiny and, in many cases, have been strengthened as a result.[86] Notably, the European Court of Human Rights has taken a stand in favour of the rights of parents who disagree with the medical assessment of their child and on the proper course of action to be taken. In *Glass v United Kingdom*,[87] the Court held not only that a decision to treat a child against his parents' wishes constituted an interference with his right to respect for private life under Article 8(1), but that the failure to seek court authority for the action in the face of dispute meant that there was insufficient justification for the treatment. Procedurally, then, the message is clear: court involvement in contested cases is mandatory if patients' rights are to be fully protected. Although this does not give parents a 'right' to have their every wish respected, it does limit the authority of health care professionals to manage a case on their uncontested view as to what are the patient's best interests.[88] At the same time, we must remember that human rights protection is not limited to patients. Professionals, too, can claim procedural safeguards, especially when their professional conduct is under scrutiny.[89]

2.32   Ultimately, the overall impact of human rights discourse on the discipline of medical law will turn on the willingness of the courts to adopt an openness towards an *ethos* of human rights. There is little prospect of significant change if they assume a narrow, legalistic interpretative approach to the individual rights contained in the Convention and consider themselves constrained by existing domestic and European case law. The better option is to take a step backwards and to consider the bigger

[84]   See *Campbell v Mirror Group Newspapers Ltd* [2004] 2 WLR 1232 which concerned an alleged breach of the medical confidentiality of the supermodel Naomi Campbell by publication of details of her addiction therapy. Lord Hope remarked in the House of Lords that, while the language of the action had now changed from a balance of public interests to a balance of Article rights, he doubted whether 'the centre of gravity has shifted', *ibid*, para 86ff.

[85]   *Vo v France* [2004] 2 FCR 577. For commentary, see J K Mason 'What's In a Name? The Vagaries of *Vo v France*' (2005) 16 CFLQ 97.

[86]   See, for example, *R (Wilkinson) v RMO, Broadmoor Hospital Authority* [2002] 1 WLR 419, (2001) 65 BMLR 15 (procedural requirements regarding forced treatment of detained persons). Several other decisions relating to the treatment of the mentally ill are discussed in chapter 20.

[87]   *Glass v United Kingdom* [2004] 1 FCR 553, [2004] 1 FLR 1019. For commentary, see R Huxtable and K Forbes '*Glass v UK*: Maternal Instinct v Medical Opinion' (2004) 16 CFLQ 339.

[88]   Other examples of the courts contemplating procedural safeguards include *D v An NHS Trust (medical treatment: consent: termination)* [2004] 1 FLR 1110 (concerning the legitimacy of proceeding with an abortion involving an incompetent adult woman) and *R (on the application of Khan) v Secretary of State for Health* [2003] 4 All ER 1239 (patient death potentially at the hand of State agents must be investigated promptly and publicly to ascertain the true cause).

[89]   See, for example, *Threlfall v General Optical Council* [2004] All ER (D) 416 (QB) (breach of Article 6 because inadequate reasons given by GOC for finding of serious professional misconduct); cf *Abu-Romia v General Medical Council* [2003] EWHC 2515.

picture—that is, to take into account the *values* that are more fundamental than the *particular* rights that are articulated in the Convention and the 1998 Act and which underpin these instruments. This calls for a more holistic approach to the role of giving effect to human rights. Values such as respect for human dignity and self-determination then emerge as principles that guide the interpretation of individual rights.[90] But this too raises questions as to *how* such values will be used to interpret the Convention rights. Medical lawyers spend much of their time calling for the courts to take responsibility away from the medical profession and to assume it themselves; on the other hand, many fear that the system will 'lead to a major shift in power from the Executive and Legislature to the Judiciary'.[91] It is possible to discern the beginnings of such a shift. The case of *R (on the application of Burke) v General Medical Council and Others*[92] is an apposite, if somewhat extreme, example. Here Munby J wholeheartedly embraced the language and fundamental values of human rights discourse, lauding the importance of human dignity and autonomy in upholding the right of the patient to insist that he would not be deprived of artificial hydration and nutrition when he became too debilitated to consent or refuse on his own behalf. It was stated as a matter of principle that not only is the patient, rather than the health care team, best placed to decide in advance what is in his or her own best interests, but that this view is determinative of those interests. This was so in the instant case irrespective of the attendant resource implications that continued interventions would incur. The ruling comes worryingly close to the rhetoric of a right to care which would, quite simply, be unsustainable under any system. The case is currently on appeal but its relevance for present purposes lies in its illustrative force as to the inherent dangers of rights discourse. It represents a highly individualistic, pseudo-deontological approach to patients' rights that makes autonomy the trump card and which ignores the wider impact of the decision.

2.33   The role of rights need not, however, be so partial. Few rights under the European Convention are absolute; most provide for justifiable interferences, usually in the name of the wider community. While 'autonomy' per se is not explicitly mentioned in the Convention, it is now widely accepted that it forms part of the penumbra of rights enjoying protection, most notably as part of the respect due to private and family life under Article 8(1). Article 8(2), however, provides for legitimate interferences with private and family life when this is 'necessary in accordance with the law' and in the furtherance of certain interests that include public safety, the economic well-being of the country, the protection of health and morals, or the protection of the rights of others. It is in the search for a just balance of such considerations that the character and richness of human rights in the UK will develop. Our concern in

---

[90] See D Beyleveld and R Brownsword *Human Dignity in Bioethics and Biolaw* (2001).

[91] See, Sir Nicholas Lyall 'Whither Strasbourg? Why Britain Should Think Long and Hard Before Incorporating the European Convention on Human Rights' [1997] EHRLR 132 at 136.

[92] *R (on the application of Burke) v General Medical Council and Others* (2004) 79 BMLR 126.

the sphere of medical law is that disproportionate weight will be accorded to overly-individualistic notions of autonomy, as demonstrated by *Burke*, when this need not be so. Autonomy is undoubtedly a most important consideration but it remains no more than one value in the family of values that underpins and informs this discipline.

3

HEALTH RIGHTS AND OBLIGATIONS IN THE EUROPEAN UNION

INTRODUCTION

3.1 The evolution and implementation of policies of bioethics and health have traditionally been the responsibility of the nation state. The last quarter of the twentieth century, however, saw a gradual shift towards globalisation of bioethical concepts and a resulting movement away from the predominance of single state governance of the discipline. There have been two main consequences. First, those to whom a given principle is directed are not now confined within national borders and, second, those who shape the policies of bioethical practice are no longer drawn from a parochial pool but, rather, from a society that is relatively unconcerned with political boundaries. This is particularly evident within the European Union (EU) where bioethical issues have developed which, broadly speaking, fall into four separate, but inter-related, themes:

- mobility—e.g. the cross border access to health care by EU citizens and the mobility of health care professionals;

- the development of new technologies—especially in the fields of biotechnology and medical devices;

- the liberalisation of trade within the internal market;

- the extension of public health legislation in such fields as the control of the use of tobacco as well as in the management of medical emergencies, such as the recent outbreak of the severe acute respiratory syndrome (SARS).

3.2 Given the economic basis on which the process of European integration is grounded, it is understandable that the discipline of bioethics in the EU is being driven and shaped predominantly by market forces and is, thereby, being framed in terms of the market, rights and values of a European market for health. Thus, for example, health is viewed as an economic priority[1] and EU policies are designed to

---

[1] 'Health is a productive factor in a competitive economy . . . improving the population's health must become an economic priority': The EU's Public Health Commissioner, Markos Kyprianou, 28 January 2005 reported on www.euractiv.com.

achieve European integration anchored in what is referred to as the 'European Social Model'.[2]

3.3   The following section serves as an introductory analysis, not of EU health policy as a whole[3] but, rather of examples of those elements of that policy which contain a significant 'rights' dimension.

HEALTH CARE POLICY IN THE EUROPEAN UNION

3.4   None of the bioethical issues itemised in the chapters of this book can still be regarded as being within the sole prerogative of individual States of the Union. Health policy has also evolved as a EU policy in its own right which is designed to 'complement national policies improving public health, preventing human illness and diseases'.[4] We must now look to a health policy that is based on a wider jurisdiction which has been framed in terms of inalienable rights embedded in a national and increasingly, a supranational constitutional framework. As a result, different countries have articulated a rights based approach to formal access to health care in a number of different ways—and not only do constitutional arrangements differ but so do values and attitudes regarding bioethics.[5]

3.5   The example of the right to human dignity that is contained in the German Basic Law[6] provides a useful example of the extent to which a country's past can frame the parameters of reasoning in constitutional terms. There, the paramount protection accorded to human dignity, together with the responses to biotechnological issues from within academic circles and throughout society as a whole, are underwritten by the experience of National Socialism. This also explains the restrictive response to medical research[7] as well as the regulation of animal experimentation[8] and embryo research[9]—a reaction that is in direct contrast to the position adopted in other EU member states, notably the United Kingdom.[10] This is but one example of the

---

[2] See COM (2004) 29 final *Delivering Lisbon: Reforms for the Enlarged Union*. In 2000, expenditure on health accounted for 27% of all social protection expenditure in the then 15 EU member states, the second largest item after retirement and survivor's pensions (Statistical Annex to the Draft *Joint Report on Social Inclusion, 2003* SEC (2003) 1425).

[3] For which see T Hervey and J McHale. *European Health Law* (2004). Also B Toebes 'The Right to Health' in A Eide, C Krause and C Rosas (eds) *Economic, Cultural and Social Rights* (2001) 16.

[4] See COM (2000) 285 final in conjunction with the public health programmes which are set out in article 152(4) of the Treaty establishing the European Community.

[5] T Hervey 'The Right to Health in EU Law' in T Hervey and J Kenner *Economic and Social Rights under the EU Charter of Fundamental Rights* (2003) 193–222.

[6] Article 1(1) of the Basic Law.   [7] *Arzneimittelgesetz* of 19. 10. 1994 BGBl. I, 3018 at 3040.

[8] See the *Tierschutzgesetz* of 18. 8. 1986 BGBl. I, 1319.

[9] *Embryonenschutzgesetz* of 13. 12. 1990, BGBl. I, 2746.

[10] For the position in other EU member states, see L Matthiesen-Guyader (ed) *Survey on Opinion of National Ethics Committees or Similar Bodies, Public Debate and National Legislation in Relation to Human*

different legal arrangements, cultural attitudes and values regarding bioethical issues that exist in EU member states. Others include the liberal legal and cultural approaches to the 'right to die' to be found in the Netherlands,[11] Belgium[12] and, latterly, France where legislation concerning the right to allow to die, or 'laissez mourir', was enacted by the French Senate in April 2005 after a lengthy and heated discussions across the country as a whole.[13] Even so, the legislation has nowhere been enacted in terms of the 'right to die' but, rather, in the context of the depenalisation of euthanasia, this being achieved through amendments to the respective criminal codes. The evolution of the French legislation has not only highlighted the complex and diverse approaches to medical treatment at the end of life to be found both within and outside France but it has also underlined the diverse relationships that exist between the church and the state throughout the Union. In the case of Italy, for instance, the Catholic Church is particularly influential in the context of bioethical issues and remains influential in the making and implementation of policy.[14] Three factors explain the particularly strong relationship between church and state in Italy. First, the historical and cultural heritage of catholicism in Italy is an integral element of national identity; second, the ecclesiastical authorities are particularly influential among those with public power (e.g. administrators at both regional and national levels of policy making, Parliament and the courts); and, third, the legal status of the church is such that it retains considerable privileges,[15] notwithstanding the secularisation of society as a whole. Even if it is arguable that catholicism provides a sort of 'shared legacy' across many of the EU member states, it is clear that the influence which this legacy exerts on matters of bioethics differs markedly. Generally speaking, it would be erroneous to view the legacy of the relationship between church and state in a non-differentiated manner given the presence of particular historical and socio/ political, as well as institutional and extra-institutional, markers.

3.6   At the same time, EU citizens themselves have benefited from the diverse

Embryonic Stem Cell Research and Use in EU Member States (European Commission, Directorate General Research, Directorate E, Biotechnology, Agriculture and Food, Brussels, July 2004), reproduced at http://europa.eu.int/comm/research/biosociety/pdf/mb_states_230804.pdf.

[11] The Law of 12 April 2001, which entered into force on 1 April 2002, amending articles 293 and 294 of the Dutch Penal Code.

[12] The Law on Euthanasia, or *La loi relative à l'euthanasie*, adopted on 16 May 2002 which entered into force on 20 September 2002 and which exculpates doctors from prosecution under the penal code in the event of having satisfied the conditions set out in the *loi*.

[13] *Le Monde* (2005) 13 April, p 1.

[14] See L Diotallevi *Religione, Chiesa e Modernizzazione: Il Caso Italiano* (1999).

[15] According to the Italian constitution, catholicism is not a state religion. However, the Catholic Church retains some privileges which not available to other faiths due to the special concordatarian (i.e. international) status. Thus, for example, classes of catholic religious instruction are given in public schools by teachers remunerated by the state (but selected by the bishops), catholic priests are given permission to serve in public hospitals, in the Army and in prisons and public funding of churches and charitable associations is generously provided. The lack of equal treatment poses considerable limitations. Moreover, the attitude of civil authorities has been shown to be discriminatory towards other religious communities. See M Ventura *La laicità dell'Unione Europea. Diritti, mercato, religione* (2001). C Cardia, *Ordinamenti religiosi e ordinamenti dello Stato* (2003).

approaches to bioethical issues to be found in the member states. As the case of the 14-year-old Irish citizen who sought to travel to the UK to seek an abortion shows,[16] EU citizens have, to some extent, relied on their rights under EU law to seek help in another EU state which provides treatment which is unavailable in their own because of the restrictive laws informed by particular moral or religious values.[17] Pragmatism is another strong motivator to encourage citizens to travel to other EU member states where the treatment is of better quality and/or where the waiting lists are shorter. Indeed, the UK Department of Health has increasingly sought to encourage general practitioners to send patients to continental Europe in order to cut waiting lists.[18] The tightening of legislation concerning access to fertility treatment in Italy was partly inspired by the desire to limit the likelihood of 'medical tourism' by EU citizens who targeted Italy given the hitherto liberal approach enshrined in the Italian legislation.[19] EU citizens have, however, not only relied on their rights; they have also accessed other EU health care systems by cutting across EU law altogether by seeking private treatment, thereby avoiding the legal and administrative mazes which endanger the realisation of their EU rights, particularly as regards fertility treatment, dental procedures and hip replacements. Interpretations concerning cross border access to health care differ within the EU, no more so than at the coal face of legal and administrative practice which lacks uniformity, coherence and consistency.[20]

3.7   Access to health care is not explicitly mentioned in the EC Treaty but derives from the freedom of movement provisions contained in the Treaty and the principle of equal treatment. While there had been some Community activity in this field since the later 1970s, it was not until the Treaty of Maastricht[21] that it was recognised as an explicit EU policy (or what is referred to in EU parlance as a 'competence'),[22] though it has since then also arisen in other fields of competence.[23] The case law which has

---

[16] Case-C 159/90 *Society for the Protection of Unborn Children v Grogan and others* [1990] ECR I-4685, (1991) 9 BMLR 100. See also *Open Door Counselling and Dublin Wellwoman Centre v Ireland* (1993) 15 EHRR 244, (1994) 18 BMLR 1.

[17] The ground-breaking UK case of Mrs Blood who obtained permission to be posthumously impregnated with her husband's sperm in Belgium is in point (see para 3.22 below)

[18] See further para 3.20 below.

[19] See the *Legge 19 Febbraio 2004, n 40 'Norme in Materia di Procreazione Medicalmente Assistita'*, pubblicata nella Gazzetta Ufficiale n 45 del 24 Febbraio 2004. See P Crosignani 'Italy Approves Controversial Legislation on Fertility Treatment' (2004) 328 BMJ 9.

[20] See M Aziz *The Impact of Human Rights on National Legal Cultures* (2004) at chapter 4.

[21] Article 152.

[22] See V G Hatzopoulos 'Killing National Health and Insurance Systems but Healing Patients? The European Market for Health Care Services after the Judgments of the ECJ in Vanbraekel and Peerbooms' (2002) 39 Common Market L Rev 683; T K Hervey 'Community and National Competence in Health After Tobacco Advertising' (2001) 38 Common Market L Rev 1421; G Tridimas and T Tridimas 'The European Court of Justice and the Annulment of the Tobacco Advertisment Directive: Friend of National Sovereignty or Foe of Public Health?' (2002) 14 European J Law Econom 171.

[23] See, for example, the Race Directive: Directive 2000/43 [2000] OJ L180/22 which involves harmonisation in the area of health.

evolved in this area[24] has tended to regard health as a mere 'by-product' or 'flanking policy'. In other words, it is not health policy per se that can be seen as having been comprehensively Europeanised but, rather, that Europeanisation has occurred on a sectoral basis, despite the several policy statements which give a contrary impression.[25] Moreover, it has occurred in such a way as to cut across—and, some might even say, bypass—traditional methods of policy-making and implementation, and has employed different forms of leverage, such as research funding. The European Commission's ethical guidelines that apply to the funding of research projects involving the derivation of stem cells from human embryos is a case in point[26] and has been framed in the context of what has been referred to as 'responsible science'.[27] The ethical dimension of the so-called 6th Framework Programme is even more evident when one considers the actual wording of Decision 1513/2002 EC of the European Parliament and of the Council, which provides, in recital 17, that:

Research activities carried out within the sixth framework programme should respect fundamental ethical principles, including those which are reflected in Article 6 of the Treaty on European Union and in the Charter of Fundamental Rights of the European Union.

3.8   Further examples of EU legislation include (the list is not exhaustive):

- the directive concerning medical devices incorporating derivatives of human blood and plasma;[28]

- the directive on the approximation of the laws, regulations and administrative provisions of the Member States relating to the implementation of good clinical practice in the conduct of clinical trials on medicinal products for human use;[29]

- the directive on setting standards of quality and safety for the donation, procurement, testing, processing, storage and distribution of human tissues and cells;[30]

[24] See Case C-238/82 *Duphar BV and Others v the Netherlands State* [1984] ECR 523; Case C-158/96 *Kohll v Union des Caisses de Maladie* [1998] ECR I-1931; Case C-120/95 *Decker* [1998] ECR I-1831 and more recently cases C-368/98 *Vanbraekel* and C-157/99 *Geraets-Smits v Stichting Ziekenfonds, Peerbooms v Stichting CZ Groep Zorgverzekeringen* [2001] ECR I-5363. See also the Irish cases at para 3.6 above.

[25] Thus the Laeken Declaration includes better health care as being part of the expectations of EU citizens. It also refers to the need of intensifying co-operation on health matters. See the Laeken Declaration on the Future of the European Union available at http://european-convention.eu.int/pdf/LKNEN.pdf.

[26] See *Procedural Modalities for Research Activities involving Banked or Isolated Human Embryonic Stem Cells in Culture to be Funded under Council Decision 2002/834/EC.* Also ethical guidelines set out for researchers applying for European Commission funding set out in http://europa.eu.int/comm/research/science-society/ethics/rules_en.html.

See also Directive 98/44/EC on the legal protection of biotechnological inventions which provides, inter alia, that processes for cloning human beings and uses of human embryos for industrial or commercial purposes are deemed to be unpatentable. See also Directive 98/79/EC concerning *in vitro* diagnostic medical devices.

[27] See the so-called 'Science and Society Action Plan' detailed in COM (2001) 714 final.

[28] Modifying Directive 93/42/EEC of 14 June 1993 concerning medical devices.

[29] Directive 2001/20/EC of the European Parliament and of the Council of 4 April 2001.

[30] Directive 2004/23/EC of the European Parliament and of the Council of 31 March 2004.

- pharmaceutical legislation;[31]
- the 'e-Health' initiatives which cover health cards, integrated care records, evidence based decisions, clinical excellence, health portals and telemedicine;[32]
- the Communication from the Commission to the Council, the European Parliament, the Economic and Social Committee and the Committee of the Regions on the Future of Health Care and Care for the Elderly, guaranteeing accessibility, quality and financial viability.[33]

The regulation of tobacco products is a further example of the many faces of EU health care policy which is linked to public health concerns as well as to the achievement of the internal market.[34] Health also arises in a plethora of other EU policy spheres such as trade and development. Thus, for example, the European Commission has been proactive in calling for changes to the World Trade Organization (WTO) patent rules, so as to ensure that the poorest countries can have access to generic drugs. In particular, the EU has formulated several proposals to the Trade Related aspects of Intellectual Property Rights (TRIPS) agreement to enable poor countries which do not have the capacity produce drugs, to gain access to essential medicines; this was done by proposing a new paragraph in the TRIPS agreement, so that a foreign supplier can provide medicines on the basis of a compulsory licence issued to a developing country in order to address serious public health needs. Health has also arisen in the context of EU environmental policy.[35] Ever since the Commission Paper on Food Safety published in 1999, EU health policy has also been developed under the aegis of consumer protection[36] and in particular regarding food labelling relating to nutritional and functional claims. In addition, Community actions on food safety and nutrition are complemented by EU regulations which establish general principles of food law and establish the European Food Safety Authority (EFSA).[37] Furthermore, the Commission is responsible for an array of public health campaigns such as a EU

[31] Regulation (EC) No 726/2004 of the European Parliament and of the Council of 31 March 2004 laying down Community procedures for the authorisation and supervision of medicinal products for human and veterinary use and establishing a European Medicines Agency; Directive 2004/27/EC of the European Parliament and of the Council of 31 March 2004 amending Directive 2001/83/EC on the Community code relating to medicinal products for human use; Directive 2004/28/EC of the European Parliament and of the Council of 31 March 2004 amending Directive 2001/82/EC on the Community code relating to veterinary medicinal products; Directive 2004/24/EC of the European Parliament and of the Council of 31 March 2004 amending, as regards traditional herbal medicinal products, Directive 2001/83/EC on the Community code relating to medicinal products for human use. Note that on the 2nd of June 2003, the Health Council adopted a political agreement on the proposal for regulations modifying Council Regulation 2309/93 on the centralised procedure and the EMEA and on the proposal modifying Directive 2001/83/EC establishing a Community code on medicinal products for human use.

[32] See the website of the Irish Presidency: www.eu2004.ie.   [33] COM (2001) 723 final.

[34] See, for example, the Tobacco Products Consolidation Directive 2001/37/EC which is aimed at the elimination of national differences regarding the manufacture, presentation and sale of tobacco products. See also Directive 2003/33/EC as well as the 'Television without Frontiers' Directive 89/552 EEC which prohibits all television which advertises the promotion of cigarettes.

[35] See the *European Environment and Health Action Plan 2004–2010* COM (2004) 461 final.

[36] COM (1999) 719 final.   [37] Regulation (EC) No. 178/2002.

anti-smoking campaign,[38] nutrition and physical activity,[39] as well as childhood obesity projects. No mention is made throughout EU policy initiatives and legislation of the 'right to health' as is contained in the EU Charter of Fundamental Rights although such policies undoubtedly have implications regarding the rights of EU citizens.

3.9   In sum, the 'rights' dimension of EU health care policy has arisen in a variety of policy contexts. Many of these have been taken up in legislation and have been enforced by the European Court of Justice. Other provisions—such as those devoted to discrimination (racial, ethnic, sex),[40] equal treatment for EU migrants, the co-ordination of social security entitlements and the impact of free movement of services and entitlements to health care in the context of the internal market[41]—are anchored in the Charter of Fundamental Rights. Health care policy in the EU provides a useful case study of the challenge posed by European rights to the legal norms and mores of the member states. Questions of health have customarily been regarded as being within the exclusive competence of the member states, but the word 'exclusive' is misleading as it ignores the 'pooling' of sovereignty[42] which arises as a consequence of EU membership.

RIGHTS AND ACCESS TO HEALTH CARE IN THE EUROPEAN UNION

3.10   The purpose of this section is to outline the legal framework for the rights dimension of health care policy in the EU.[43]

3.11   Although European Union law contains elements of international law, it cannot be understood exclusively in such terms. This is particularly so given that Community law has priority over national legal provisions,[44] that Community law prevails when it

---

[38] With a budget of 72 million euros: see European Commission MEMO/05/68.

[39] Nutrition and Physical Activity under the Public Health Action Programme (2003–2008), whereby the Community finances projects aimed at collecting data on obesity, nutrition and physical activity. See the Core Report, Eurodiet: Nutrition and Diet for Healthy Lifestyles in Europe: Science and Policy Implications (The European Commission, DG Health, reproduced at http://eurodiet.med.uoc.gr).

[40] For example, article 13 EC taken in conjunction with article 3 of the anti-racism directive which includes the prohibition of discrimination in relation to social protection, health care, housing and education (Directive 2000/43 [2000] OJ L180/22). See M Bell *Anti-Discrimination Law and the EU* (2002).

[41] A P van der Mei 'Cross-Border Access to Medical Care within the European Union-Some Reflections on the Judgments in *Decker* and *Kohll*' (1998) 5 Maastricht J European Comp Law 277. See also A P van der Mei *Free Movement of Persons within the European Community. Cross-Border Access to Public Benefits* (2002).

[42] See generally N MacCormick *Questioning Sovereignty: Law, State and Nation in the European Common-wealth* (1999).

[43] This section is drawn from M Aziz *The Impact of European Rights on National Legal Cultures* (2004), pp 113–127.

[44] Case C-6/64 *Costa v ENEL* [1964] ECR 585.

conflicts with national law,[45] and, that damages can be obtained for its non-implementation.[46] Thus, unlike International Law, European Community law creates rights upon which individuals can rely directly.[47]

3.12 The language of rights in connection to health care policy in the EU must be qualified from the outset. It is arguably more appropriate to speak in terms of interests which may give rise to a duty unless it is counteracted by conflicting considerations[48]—put another way, it is preferable to speak of rights to health care in terms of obligations on behalf of those who are entrusted by the state to provide it, due allowance being made for the tension underlying the allocation of finite resources in the face of infinite demand. Even so, the inclusion of rights to health care in constitutions does little to clarify the need for this distinction. Indeed, it goes some way towards encouraging the view that health care rights include justiciable public rights as well as the rights of members of the medical profession to practice in EU member states.[49] This tendency is, to some extent, mirrored in EU legislation.

3.13 The EC Treaties refer to maintaining a 'high level of social protection, the raising of the standard of living and quality of life'[50] as well as a high level of health protection.[51] A system of co-ordination of national social security systems, developed under the aegis of Regulations 1408/71 and 574/72, facilitates the free movement of workers. In particular, workers have the right to medical treatment,[52] EU citizens have the right to emergency treatment[53] and patients can obtain prior authorisation to be treated in member states other than that in which they are ordinarily resident.[54] Article 35 of the EU Charter of Fundamental rights provides a right to health care in the sense that: 'Everyone has the right of access to preventative health care and the right to benefit from medical treatment under the conditions established by national laws and practices'. Two main legal implications stem from this provision. First, it is the foundation of the individual entitlements of EU citizens to both medical treatment and to preventative health care. Second, it is the basis for what is referred to as 'mainstreaming'[55] which is to say that it creates an obligation on the EU institutions in the context of Community policies and activities of the Union.

3.14 Whilst EU member states retain a firm hold over matters of health on the basis of the principle of subsidiarity,[56] their competence, like their sovereignty, is not absolute.

---

[45] *Factortame Ltd v Secretary of State for Transport (No. 2)* [1991] AC 603. See also cases C-46/93 and C-48/93, *Brasserie du Pêcheur SA v Germany, R v Secretary of State for Transport, ex p Factortame Ltd* [1996] ECR I-1029.

[46] Case C-6/90 and Case C-9/90 *Francovich and others v Italy* [1992] IRLR 84.

[47] Case C-26/62 *Van Gend en Loos v Nederlandse Administratie der Belastingen* [1963] ECR 1.

[48] See J Raz *The Morality of Freedom* (1986) at p 166.

[49] See Council Directive 93/16/EEC of 5 April 1993 to facilitate the free movement of doctors and the mutual recognition of their diplomas, certificates and other evidence of formal qualifications [Official Journal L 165 of 07.07.1993] as amended by a host of legislative acts.

[50] See article 2 EC Treaty.   [51] See article 3 of the EC Treaty read in conjunction with article 152.

[52] Through use of the E106 form.   [53] Through use of the E111 form.

[54] Through the use of the E112 form.

[55] See article 152(1) EC and CHARTE 4473/00 CONVENT 49.   [56] See article 152(2) EC.

It has been qualified and/or pooled, notably by the European Court of Justice which has developed a principled approach to interpretation which may be summarised as: while European Community law does not detract from the powers of the member states to organise their social security systems, member states must, nevertheless, comply with Community law when exercising their powers.[57] The requirement for prior authorisation of treatment in another member state constitutes a restriction of the freedom to provide services as contained in the Treaty. Restrictions can, however, be objectively justified on the basis of the protection of the financial balance of the system or on grounds of public health—though in practice this burden of proof, as yet, has been rebutted time and time again, and has never been successfully discharged, before the European Court of Justice.

3.15   Inevitably, the provision of health care varies widely across the Union.[58] Three sources of finance are available—out of pocket payments, voluntary (or private) insurance premiums and compulsory (or public) contributions through insurance or taxation. Three methods of the provision of health care must also be distinguished— reimbursement, benefits in kind and, lastly, ownership and management of providers. 'Administrative fragmentation'[59] is accentuated across EU member states. In Germany, for example, the provision of health care is distributed at Federal and State level and through the courts, the insurance funds and their organisations and the doctors' organisations. The German example is also notable for the absence of centralised control. In the case of Spain, it is the regions which are responsible for the provision of health care but it is the Department of Health which determines the overall health budget. Experiences differ markedly as regards implementation of health care policy, particularly between the regions of the north and south of Spain, a situation which, in some member states, including the United Kingdom, may also arise in relation to the area in which a person lives.[60] This diversity will be further amplified as a result of enlargement of the Union which will bring with it a population with a varying range of health profiles and different systems of health care, not to mention levels of resources.[61] The gap is particularly affected by the effect of simultaneous transition to a market economy which has created considerable fiscal problems. In fact, two basic

---

[57] A further analogy is to be found in the field of education where similar principles have been developed. See Case C-9/74 *Casagrande* [1974] ECR 773 at 12. See also Case C-293/83 *Gravier* [1985] ECR 293 at 19.

[58] The European Observatory on Health Care Systems (EOHCS) is a useful source of information about the health care systems in Europe. See www.observatory.dk.

[59] As in the case of the United Kingdom's National Health Service and in particular, the presence of Health Authorities, Primary Care Trusts and NHS Trusts. See the National Health Service and Community Care Act 1990 which established District Health Authorities as purchasers of health services on behalf of the local population. See also the Health Act 1999, s 2 which inserted s 16A into the National Health Service Act 1977. See further the latest proposals by the Department of Health for so-called 'foundation hospitals' which would enable them to be relatively free from central control. See *The Observer*, 2 March 2003 at p 8, 'Split as NHS trusts bid for new freedom'.

[60] For the problems of 'post-coding' in the UK, see chapter 11 below.

[61] See B Merkel and K Kärkkäinen 'Public Health Aspects of Accession' (2002) 8 Eurohealth 3.

health indicators—infant mortality and life expectancy[62]—reveal that most candidate countries lag well behind the original EU member states.[63]

3.16   Public health profiles already differ greatly across the Union. Thus, for example, the survival rates for cancer of the bladder reveal substantial variations among the EU member states, with five year survival rates ranging from 78 per cent in Austria to 47 per cent in Poland and Estonia.[64] Life expectancy is significantly lower in the new member states given the high rates of cardiovascular disease and cancer—especially lung cancer—associated with high rates of tobacco and alcohol consumption and low levels of physical exercise.[65] The communist legacy in the new member states of the Union is such that their health care systems suffer from chronic under-funding; the combination of the difficulties involved in the transition to market economies and associated corruption means that access to health care is not equal.[66] This has fuelled fears among the wealthier EU members that citizens of the new member states will over-exercise the right to freedom of movement in order to indulge in 'medical tourism', which not only has budgetary implications but also raises the possibility of destabilising the administration of existing national systems of social welfare.

3.17   Added to the internal markers of differentiation, we have the impact of Community law which has consequences for the financing of health care systems at a number of levels. Here, too, the courts' decisions concerning cross border access to health care have complemented the EU regulations and the prior authorisation procedure.[67]

[62] M Bobak and M Marmot 'East-West mortality divide and its potential explanations: proposed research agenda' (1996) 312 BMJ 421.

[63] Indeed, the level of spending on health in absolute and percentage terms is significantly less than in the EU Health's share of the GDP. The average for the candidate countries has been estimated at 4.5% (although there is considerable variation) whilst the EU average is approximately 8%. What is even more worrying is that the former is in fact decreasing, whilst the latter shows an increase.

[64] EUROCARE 3—Survival of cancer patients in Europe; see www.eurocare.it.

[65] See B Merkel and K Kärkkäinen 'Public Health Aspects of Accession' (2002) 8 Eurohealth 3 and also COM (2004) 301 final pp 17 et seq.

[66] C Lawson and J Nemec 'The Political Economy of Slovak and Czech Health Policy: 1989–2000' (2003) 24 Internat Political Sci Rev 219.

[67] Such as E112 which is based on article 22 of Regulation 1408/71 which entitles patients to benefits in kind as well as cash benefits. See also E109 which applies to those working abroad for a short period, E110 which applies to those working in international transport and E111 which provides temporary but emergency medical care for those who are abroad for a short while, such as tourists and business people.

CROSS BORDER ACCESS TO HEALTH CARE
IN THE EUROPEAN UNION

3.18   In *Kohll*[68] and *Decker*,[69] individuals were able to obtain medical treatment in a EU member state other than where they were resident.[70] In *Kohll*, the Court held that the need to obtain prior authorisation from an institution of the State for treatment in another member state constituted a restriction on the freedom to provide services within the meaning of articles 59 and 60 (now 49 and 50) of the Treaty. The court rejected arguments advanced by the defendants that expenditure control and the 'genuine and actual risk' of upsetting the financial balance of the social security system provided an objective justification.

3.19   In *Decker*, a Luxembourg national purchased a pair of spectacles with corrective lenses from an optician in Belgium on a prescription from an ophthalmologist in Luxembourg but was refused reimbursement from his insurers on the grounds that he did not obtain prior authorisation. He argued that this was contrary to articles 30 and 36 of the EC Treaty—that is, an unjustifiable barrier to the free movement of goods. The Court held that social security and the conditions concerning the right or duty to be insured with a social security scheme—as well as the conditions for entitlement of benefits—were matters for each member state but that they must comply with Community law. It rejected an objective justification based on the grounds of public health and ensuring the quality of medical products. The Court referred to the general system concerning the recognition of professional education and training and to the fact that the spectacles were purchased on prescription from an ophthalmologist, which guaranteed the protection of public health. Thus, the quality argument was rejected and articles 30 and 36 EC Treaty were held to preclude national rules requiring prior authorisation from a social security service for the purchase of any medical product abroad, a position which has been upheld in later case law.[71]

3.20   The issues that arise as a consequence of these cases include, inter alia, the idea of 'medical tourism' by EU citizens seeking the most favourable services, the

---

[68]   Case C-158/96 *Kohll v Union des Caisses de Maladie* [1998] ECR I-1931.

[69]   Case C-120/95 *Decker v Caisse de Maladie des Employés Privés* [1998] ECR I-1831.

[70]   See article 22(1)(c) Regulation (EEC) No. 1408/71 which allows EU citizens to go to another member state to receive medical treatment and to obtain reimbursement of the costs at the rates applicable there. Note that this covers public health insurance schemes only. See also Regulation (EEC) 574/72.

[71]   See Case C-368/98 *Vanbraekel* [2001] ECR I-5382 in which a Belgian social security institution wrongly refused permission to an insured person to seek medical treatment abroad. See also Case C-157/99 *Smits/ Peerbooms* [2001] ECR I-5509. See also Case C-56/01 *Inizan v Caisse Primaire d'Assurance Maladie des Hautes- de- Seine* [2003] ECR I-12403. See generally M Fuchs 'Free Movement of Services and Social Security-Quo Vadis?' (2002) 8 European L J 536.

See also cases C-385/99 *Müller-Fauré* and C-385/99 *Van Riet* in which standard procedures for obtaining reimbursement for costs of treatment abroad were not followed. Thus, reimbursement was not granted on the basis that the treatment concerned care which was non-urgent (*Müller-Fauré*) or treatment which could have been provided in the country of insurance (*Van Riet*).

protectionism of the medical establishment[72] as regards the labour market and so on.[73] The problem of medical tourism is an example of 'social dumping' whereby individuals seek enhanced social protection across borders. It remains one of the customary objections that are raised vis-à-vis individuals realising their social citizenship in a state of which they are not a national. However, practice shows that few patients seek such treatment. It is currently estimated that some 2 per cent of the insured population in the EU actually opt for cross border care,[74] and this despite the encouragement by some national member state governments which, as we have already noted, have adopted policies to send patients abroad in order to reduce waiting lists.[75] The impact of the right to cross border health care in the EU on the sovereignty and on the resources of member states is, at best, slight, if one takes the frequency of the realisation of these rights as the indicator. However, this may be because, in practice, patients have been faced with considerable administrative hurdles when attempting to exercise their right to cross border access to health care, both once they are in another EU member state for treatment and when they return to their state of origin. In other words, each stage of the process brings not only benefits, but also respective burdens.[76]

3.21   A more significant impact is also discernible if one considers the way in which rational decision-making has been subjected to the forces of Europeanisation. It is here that the distinction drawn at the outset of this section must be reiterated—that is to say that it is more appropriate to speak of rights to health in terms of obligations on behalf of those who are entrusted by the state in providing it. Thus, EC law constrains—and, indeed, prevents—the evolution of any policy which denies reasonable access to readily available resources to EU citizens.

3.22   In *Blood*,[77] an English woman resident in the UK was held not to be precluded from travelling to Belgium for fertility treatment by way of insemination with her husband's posthumous sperm.[78] The Human Fertilisation and Embryology Authority

---

[72] See an article in *The Independent*, 13 February 2003 at p 3 entitled, 'GMC [the General Medical Council] "biased" against foreign doctors' in which the results of an independent inquiry into Britain's system for disciplining doctors are reported. According to the report, National Health Service (NHS) doctors trained overseas are more than three times as likely to be found guilty of a disciplinary offence than UK trained colleagues despite attracting the same volume of complaints. Doctors from overseas were more likely to be found guilty and get harsher sentences.

[73] See generally A S Paulus, S Evers et al 'Cross Border Health Care: An Analysis of Recent ECJ Rulings' (2002) 14 European J Law Econom 61.

[74] W Palm, J Nickless, H Lewalle and A Coheur *Implications of Recent Jurisprudence on the Co-Ordination of Health Care Protection Systems* (2000).

[75] Para 3.20 above. See also 'EU backs health care plans', 21 August 2002 reported at www.news.bbc.co.uk/2/hi/health/1511180.stm.

[76] See H Hermans 'Access to Health Care and Health Service in the European Union: Regulation 1408/71 and the E111 Process' in R Leidl (ed) *Health Care and its Financing in the Single European Market* (1998). It remains to be seen to what extent these administrative barriers might be circumvented by the introduction of the so-called European health card.

[77] *R v Human Fertilisation and Embryology Authority, ex p Blood* [1997] 2 All ER 687, (1996) 35 BMLR 1. The case is discussed in greater detail in para 4.13 below.

[78] The main provisions on medical treatment are to be found in Title III, Chapter 1 of Regulation (EEC) No. 1408/71—OJ L 28 30.1.1997.

(HFEA) originally refused to release the sperm so that she could be treated in Belgium to be treated there; the Court of Appeal, however, held this to be contrary to EC law and in particular to Articles 59 and 60 (freedom to obtain services). The Authority were unaware of the EC law nexus of the case, electing instead to draw from principles of private international law by maintaining that the plaintiff did not have adequate 'connecting factors' to link her to Belgium.[79]

3.23   The *Blood* case also illustrates the link between health policy and the achievement of the internal market. The so-called 'Tobacco Advertising case'[80] in which the European Court of Justice annulled Directive 98/43 (prohibiting the advertising and sponsorship of tobacco products)[81] on the grounds that it did not fall within the scope of the internal market is a further case in point. The health and the internal market implications of the directive are inseparable elements. Indeed, health is regarded not as a policy in its own right but in terms of the removal of barriers to trade and the distortion of competition which arise as a consequence of differing national laws regarding the restrictions on the advertising and sponsorship of tobacco products.[82] The case highlights the limits of the elastic nature of EU competences,[83] the extent to which health policy is scattered across a host of EU policies as well as the predominant nature and tenor of the values and principles which inform decisions of the ECJ, namely, the market and economic integration.

3.24   Health has customarily been viewed as remaining within the exclusive competence of the member states albeit in the context of particular policies. Moreover, it establishes a duty for public authority officials not only to be aware of the impact but also one to demonstrate this awareness. The former duty is dependent on both knowledge and understanding of the Treaty basis regarding matters of health[84] as well as the jurisprudence of the European Court of Justice which has been pivotal in the development of cross border access to health care by EU citizens. It has been said that knowledge of the European law and its concomitant impact on national law amongst public authority officials in the current EU member states is extremely poor. The case law of the European Court of Justice demonstrates that this also applies to other actors too, such as the health care civil servants, the medical profession and hospital

---

[79] The Authority was also, however, intent on trying to prevent the creation of a precedent as regards access to gametes where express, written consent has not be given by the donor.

[80] C-376/98 *Germany v Parliament and Council (Tobacco Advertising)* [2000] ECR I-8419.

[81] Directive 98/43/EC of the European Parliament and of the Council of 6 July 1998 on the approximation of the laws, regulations and administrative provisions of the Member States relating to the advertising and sponsorship of tobacco products (OJ 1992 L213, p 9).

[82] In particular, the Court held that articles 57(2), 66 and 100a of the EC Treaty did not constitute an appropriate legal basis for the adoption of the directive and annulled it. See also Case C-491/01 *British American Tobacco (Investments) Limited and Imperial Tobacco v Secretary of State for Health*, decision of 10 December 2002 (unreported). See www.eu.int/en/cp0299en.htm.

[83] See G de Búrca and B de Witte 'The Delimitation of Powers between the EU and its Member States' in A Amull and D Wincott (eds) *Accountability and Legitimacy in the European Union* (2002) 201–222.

[84] Introduced by the Treaty of Maastricht through article 129 EC, now amended and renumbered to article 152 EC.

administrators. However, it is difficult to draw assumptions concerning individual member states as knowledge concerning access to health care services across borders varies. For example, 'Euregios',[85] include health service arrangements as part of their activities.[86] Indeed, some of the regions have even gone as far as to enact measures to ease the administrative burden on patients.[87] It is also not difficult to assume that the level of knowledge in the new member states will be lower than in the old although, in fact, some of the medical professionals in the new member states, as in Slovenia, have had the experience of cross border health care for over 50 years.[88] In some of the new member states, many of the medical professionals have undergone part of their training in the old EU states making them more aware of the possibility of cross border health care.[89]

3.25   *Kohll* and *Decker*, which were joined cases, were pivotal as part of the evolutionary process of the development of mobility of EU citizens for medical treatment. The European Court of Justice has arguably undertaken to rush in where policy makers at both the national and the supranational level have feared to tread. Notwithstanding, the ECJ has at least adopted a approach which reveals a degree of coherence, clarity and consistency, all of which are notably absent in the complexity and confusion which underpins EU health policy. Thus, for example, in *Vanbraekel* and *Geraets-Smits/Peerbooms*,[90] two applicants, who were insured under a Dutch social-insurance scheme for persons whose income is below a certain level, received medical treatment outside the Netherlands without obtaining prior authorisation from the fund. The question referred to the ECJ was whether the need to obtain prior authorisation in the circumstances contravened articles 49 and 50 (previously articles 59 and 60). The Court held that the authorisation requirement was a restriction of the freedom to provide and to receive services but that, in the case at hand, it could be objectively justified in the interests of maintaining a balanced medical and hospital service that was available to all and of preventing a social security system becoming seriously undermined—thus confirming *Kohll* and *Decker*. The Court rejected arguments

---

[85] Which are border regions of EU member states which benefit from a system of mutual recognition of the arrangements for the provision of health care.

[86] As in, for example, the Meuse-Rhine Region (Belgium, Germany and the Netherlands), Rhine-Waal (Germany and the Netherlands), Scheldemond (Belgium and the Netherlands) and Hainaut/Nord-Pas-de-Calais (Belgium and France) who benefit from the EU's INTERREG initiative.

[87] By simplifying the E112 procedure. Thus, in the case of Hainaut/Nord-Pas-de-Calais, the E112TF form is filled out by the hospital and is sent directly with a request for payment to the relevant institution in the member state. See A Coheur 'Integrating care in border regions: An Analysis of the Euregio projects' (2001) 7 Eurohealth 10.

[88] Arising out of the agreements with Italy enabling movement of people and services across the border. (Gorizia, Trieste and Udine Agreements between the Socialist Federal Republic of Yugoslavia and the Republic of Italy, 31 March 1955, Rome, Italy. See T Albrecht 'Opportunities and Challenges in the Provision of Cross Border Care' (2002) 8 Eurohealth 8.

[89] See J Cachia 'Human Resources in Maltese Healthcare. Solutions for Common Needs' (2002) 8 Eurohealth 17 and also S Nicholas 'Movement of Health Care Professionals. Trends and Enlargement' (2002) 8 Eurohealth 11.

[90] Cases C-368/98 *Vanbraekel* and C-157/99 *Geraets-Smits v Stichting Ziekenfonds, Peerbooms v Stichting CZ Groep Zorgverzekeringen* [2001] ECR I-5363.

advanced by the insurers, namely, that the assessment as to whether treatment should be one that is regarded as 'normal in the professional circles concerned' and whether the same or equally effective treatment could be obtained without undue delay from an establishment with which the insured person's sickness insurance fund has contractual arrangements was one in which medical professionals were obliged to take into account the findings of international medical science when deciding whether the treatment sought was 'normal'. The Court can be seen here to be laying down guidelines to national authorities in relation to their decision-making, a practice it consolidated in a subsequent decision.

3.26   In *Müller-Fauré*,[91] the plaintiff, a Dutch national, had dental treatment while on holiday in Germany over the space of a month without authorisation and applied to her Dutch insurers for reimbursement of the costs of the treatment. The Fund refused on the advice of its advisory dental officer.

3.27   In the conjoined case, Ms Van Riet's doctor requested the Amsterdam Fund's medical advisor to grant authorisation for an arthroscopy to be undertaken in Belgium as the waiting lists were shorter there. The request was rejected on the grounds that the procedure could also be performed in the Netherlands but, notwithstanding, Ms Van Riet went ahead with the procedure in Belgium. The results of the arthroscopy indicated the need for an ulnar reduction which was also carried out in Belgium. Ms Van Riet's sickness fund refused to reimburse the cost of care. The *Ziekenfondsraad* confirmed the refusal on the basis that it was not an emergency, there was no medical necessity and appropriate medical treatment was available in the Netherlands within a reasonable period (6 months).

3.28   Three questions were referred to the European Court of Justice in respect of these conjoined cases: first, are national provisions stipulating the need to obtain prior authorisation for treatment outside of the Netherlands with an institution with whom the sickness fund has not concluded an agreement contrary to the original articles 59 and 60 of the EC Treaty? Secondly, if so, does the nature of the Dutch system—which provides benefits in kind rather than reimbursement—justify an exemption? Thirdly, is it relevant that the treatment involved hospital treatment? The Court held that as regards hospital treatment, the prior authorisation requirement does not violate articles 59 and 60. Authorisation can be refused only if treatment which is the same or equally effective for the patient can be obtained without undue delay in an establishment which has an agreement with a fund. As regards non-hospital treatment, however, the prior authorisation requirement does violate articles 59 and 60 even if the system is one that provides benefits in kind.[92]

---

[91] Case C-385/99 *VG Müller-Fauré v Onderlinge Waarborgmaatschappij OZ Zorgverzekeringen UA* and *EEM van Riet v Onderlinge Waarborgmaatschappij ZAO Zorgverzekeringen*, Judgment of 13 May 2003 (unreported).

[92] This to some extent mirrors the development of principles of access to education in the context of the application of EC law rules governing freedom to provide services. Here, the European Court of Justice has drawn a distinction between public education, to which the rules on services do not apply because they are not provided 'against remuneration', and private commercial education for which the normal rules on

3.29   A variety of issues arise from the case, not of all which can be dealt with here. The implications of the decision as to state sovereignty necessitate the reconfiguration, or, in the words of the Court, 'adjustment' of both the domestic law and culture of the member states. In this context, the Court reiterated that, while the sovereignty of the member states was not undermined, they must adjust their systems of social security in order to accommodate the fundamental freedoms.[93] Although it was untenable to distinguish between medical services based on benefits in kind and reimbursement, the Court stated that member states can establish ceilings for reimbursement as long as they are based on objective, non-discriminatory and transparent criteria. It is here that the Court addresses administrative decision-making in the member states which, according to the Treaty, it is bound to respect. It held that, when assessing the issue of undue delay, national authorities are required to consider 'all of the circumstances of each specific case' which include the nature of the medical condition as well as the degree of pain and the nature of the patient's disability in relation to, for example, his or her professional activity.[94]

3.30   This is not the first time that the Court has intervened in decision-making by medical professionals and medical insurers regarding patient care. Thus, as we have already seen, the Court in *Geraets & Peerbooms*[95] held that, concerning the problem of undue delay and the necessity of the treatment, account must be taken of practices which have been 'tried and tested by international medical science' and not only national medical opinion This issue arose in a Court of Appeal decision in *R (on the application of Watts) v Bedford Primary Care Trust*,[96] a consequence of which is that PCT's in the UK may now be obliged to pay for the hospital care that patients receive in the EU. In this case, the patient was a 72-year-old pensioner suffering from osteoporosis who obtained bi-lateral hip replacements in a hospital in Lille, France which was able to perform the operation within three months as opposed to the normal waiting time which her PCT in Bedford claimed was up to 12 months. Having had the operation, the Bedfordshire PCT refused to pay the bill on the grounds that the waiting time was 'normal' for NHS patients and that, in the light of her consultant's re-assessment of her case, she had in fact been offered NHS treatment within four months. Accordingly, Mrs Watts applied for judicial review seeking reimbursement of her costs of her treatment abroad by relying on the case law of the ECJ in the context of the free movement of services. Munby J ruled that a wait of up to 12 months constituted an 'undue delay' because all such cases should be considered on their individual merits and not in the light of NHS waiting times. The Court of Appeal

services do apply. The Court does not seem to draw such a strict distinction in the cases concerning cross border access to health care—in particular, in the context of hospital services. The Treaty rules on services are applied without special regard to the public nature of hospitals. This raises the issue why education and health are treated differently. Further, and in the alternative, the recent cases on cross border access to health care may in effect overrule the older education cases. See G Davies 'Welfare as a Service' (2002) 29 Legal Issues of Economic Integration 27.

[93] N 91 above at para 102.   [94] N 91 above at para 90.   [95] N 90 above.
[96] [2004] EWCA Civ 166, (2003) 77 BMLR 26.

referred the case to the ECJ as part of the preliminary reference procedure[97] in order to clarify whether interpretation of its decisions in this area meant that patients in EU member states could effectively 'queue jump' by seeking medical treatment in other EU member states, even if this created an impact on an already strained NHS budget and possible postponement of more urgent treatment by others. Ordinarily speaking, preliminary reference procedures take up to two years to reach the ECJ. Once it has resolved the questions referred to it by the Court of Appeal, the matter will be re-heard by the Court of Appeal whilst giving effect to the answers provided by the ECJ in applying it to circumstances of the case. Thus, at the time of writing, we cannot provide a full appraisal of the implications of the case. However, it is clear that PCTs are obligated to demonstrate that decisions concerning patient requests to be treated in other EU member states must be reached in an objective and impartial manner. In particular, the criteria for the decision are not restricted to NHS waiting times as the determinant of the definition of 'undue delay'.

3.31   The decisions in the European Court of Justice have obvious implications for those with administrative power in the member states. Clearly, these persons are now constrained by the requirements of European integration. But, although there are some examples, such the *Blood* case, which indicate the impact of Europeanisation on medical decision-making, it is impossible to draw concrete conclusions as to how seriously European rights, and cross border rights to access to health care in particular, are being taken. The extent of the implementation of these rights cannot be judged by a study of the reported litigation alone.[98] It is clear, however, that the principles developed by the ECJ will eventually find their way into EU legislation in one form or another.

3.32   A recent move to exclude the health sector from draft European legislation, namely, the so-called 'Bolkenstein directive', is further to the point.[99] The directive is designed to open up the market for services in the Union including employment services. It is aimed at reducing administrative obstacles to services across the European Union, enshrining the principle that the laws applying to the service will be determined by the 'country of origin' of the company supplying the services. Hitherto, the relevant directive contained provisions, such as those concerning patient mobility and the development of health care in the Community, which included the assumption of health care costs.[100] Some member state governments, such as the UK, were extremely ill at ease with the inclusion of health care in the directive, the provisions of which were considered to be too far reaching. The decision to exclude the health sector from the Bolkenstein directive was welcomed by many. However, it is

---

[97] Article 234 EC.

[98] Even litigation does not provide a comprehensive overview of the implementation of the acquis. Despite documentation services, such as CELEX and the Commission and the Court of Justice Annual Reports on the monitoring of the application of EC law, gaps in the coverage arise, given that many of the cases of the lower courts are unreported.

[99] COM (2004) 2 final/3. See also BMJ of 12 March 2005.

[100] See the (8) of the Preamble as well as article 23 of COM (2004) 2 final/3.

highly likely that those provisions pertaining to the health sector will eventually become part of EU policy legislation, albeit it slightly modified form, and in other policy sectors, such as anti-discrimination.[101] Be that as it may, national public authority officials may be unaware of the clarity, coherence and consistency of the approach adopted by the ECJ, particularly given the difficulties in ensuring effective communication between the national and the supranational levels of implementation of this strand of EU policy. This is understandable when one bears in mind that it is perhaps more appropriate to speak of EU policies with a health dimension than EU health policy per se. The Draft European Constitution is a further case in point.

3.33   References to health matters are scattered across the Draft Treaty establishing a Constitution for Europe which was delivered to the European Council meeting in Thessaloniki on 20 June 2003 and later submitted to the President of the European Council in Rome on 18 July 2003.[102] Thus, references exist to solidarity,[103] to the 'well-being of its peoples',[104] and 'a high level of protection and improvement of quality of the environment'.[105] Article 7 incorporates the rights, freedoms and principles that have been set out in the EU Charter of Fundamental Rights. Public health matters are included as an area of shared competence alongside, inter alia, the internal market.[106] The protection and improvement of human health is included as an area of supporting, co-ordinating or complementary action.[107] However, the attempt to codify social rights in the Draft Constitutional Treaty is limited because of the competence clause which provides that the Union shall act only in so far as the Member States have conferred the competence to do so whilst respecting the principles of subsidiarity and proportionality.[108] Accordingly, the Charter will not provide rights in the traditional sense but will provide a framework for policies[109] and, by extension, rights to health care. It will, in conjunction with other forms of EU policy, have implications, not only for these rights but also for other forms of EU health care policy, such as research.

---

[101] See, for example, the inclusion of health in the anti-racism directive which includes the prohibition of discrimination in relation to social protection, health care, housing and education: Directive 2000/43 [2000] OJ L180/22.

[102] CONV 820/03. This text was revised twice (CONV 820/1/03 REV 1, CONV 820/1/03 REV 2). See also CONV 847/03, CONV 848/03.

[103] See the Union's values which are outlined in article 2 although this reference is not exclusively made to social solidarity but also to solidarity in the face of terrorist attacks and natural disasters. See the solidarity clause contained in article 42.

[104] Article 3(1).   [105] Article 3(3).

[106] Article 13(2). See also Chapter V: Areas where the Union May Take Coordinating Complementary or Supporting Action provided in Article III-179.

[107] Article 16(2). It is of interest to note that the reference to public health in the list of areas of shared competence was modified. The Praesidium's proposal to divide paragraph 4 of article 151 EC Treaty into two separate paragraphs was adopted in the final draft. See CONV 724/03 at p 75.

[108] Article I-11.

[109] See G de Búrca, 'Fundamental Rights and Citizenship' in B de Witte (ed) *Ten Reflections on the Constitutional Treaty for Europe* (2003), 11.

ETHICS IN SCIENCE AND NEW TECHNOLOGIES IN THE EUROPEAN UNION

3.34   EU policy makers have increasingly begun to embrace the merits, and indeed the necessity, of a European Research Area (ERA) which is able to both stimulate and generate innovation in research and which will place the EU on a par with the United States, competitively speaking. This is particularly so in the context of Biotechnology. The European Commission's 6th Framework Programme provides funding for research, and this is, in itself, contestable given that its implementing provisions arguably shape the ethics of research in the EU, thereby opening the door to a progressive Europeanisation of values.[110] Until the adoption of the clinical trials directive, the Union was unable to obtain a clear consensus on behalf of EU member states in agreeing to explicitly regulate medical research at the EU level. Thus, a more pragmatic and, indeed, preferred approach was to legislate by means of directives which are more implicit[111]—and this, again, is questionable in terms of democratic legitimacy. The status quo is anything but transparent, particularly given the role of committees in both the framing and the implementation of research policy.

COMMITTEES AND COMITOLOGY

3.35   Generally speaking, the EU legislative process relies on the use of committees and what is referred to as 'comitology', which refers to relatively autonomous committees and agencies[112] that are responsible for the collection and the generation of specialised information and expertise as opposed to having direct regulatory functions.[113] Their role is controversial, particularly in terms of democratic principles and accountability. Moreover, their working methods are obfuscated by the lack of transparency which pervades both national and European channels of policy making and

---

[110] See European Commission, press release, DN:IP/03/969, 9 July 2003: 'European Commission proposes strict ethical guidelines on EU funding of human embryonic stem cell research'. Note that the European Commission's proposal presents a coherent set of strict ethical guidelines that will apply to the EU funding of research projects involving the derivation of stem cells from human supernumerary embryos.

[111] See, for example Directive 98/44/EC on the legal protection of biotechnological inventions which provides that processes for cloning human beings and uses of human embryos for industrial or commercial purposes are deemed to be unpatentable. See also Directive 98/79/EC concerning *in vitro* diagnostic medical devices (including the use of human tissues) which provides that, '. . . the removal, collection and use of tissues, cells and substances of human origin shall be governed, in relation to ethics, by the principles laid down in the Convention of the Council of Europe for the protection of human rights and dignity of the human being with regard to the application of biology and medicine and by any Member States regulations on this matter'.

[112] Such as the Office for Internal Market Harmonization and the Agency for the Evaluation of Medicinal Products.

[113] See C Joeges and E Vos (eds) *EU Committees: Social Regulation; Law and Politics* (1999).

implementation. Monitoring and evaluating the development of EU health policy is altogether a 'needle in a haystack' affair, despite the attempts by the European Commission to centralise much of its decision-making through bodies such as the Agency for the Evaluation of Medicinal Products and the European Group on Ethics in Science and New Technologies. The latter has been particularly proactive in advising the Commission concerning the ethics of new technologies—this being as part of a varied selection of EU integration policies and not just those which arise in the context of EU health policy. However, just as the influence of the Group regarding the formulation of European Commission legislative initiatives involving bioethical issues should not be underestimated, neither should it be overestimated.

3.36   Briefly stated, the European Group on Ethics in Science and New Technologies, which was set up by the European Commission in December 1997, is part of the Group of Policy Advisors which advises the Commission on the ethical aspects of science and new technologies in relation to the preparation and implementation of Community legislation or policies.[114] Many of their opinions, such as the Report of the Charter on Fundamental Rights related to technical innovation—as well as those concerning issues such as, inter alia, human embryo and human stem cell research[115]—have been highly influential, though it is difficult to evaluate the full extent of this influence.[116] It is also difficult to assess the extent of their remit, given that EU policy making in this area is also generated, shaped and structured by a plethora of both institutional and extra-institutional actors. The response to stem cell research is a case in point[117] in that actors in the policy making process included not only other EU institutions,[118] but also international organisations (the Council of Europe), patient groups, the Standing Committee of European Doctors, industry (the European Medical Technology Industry Association, the European Association for Rare Disorders or 'Eurordis'), non-governmental organisations (the European Association of Tissue Banks and the European Association for Tissue Banks), religious groups etc, not to mention national ethics commissions and committees in the EU member states.[119] Such too was the response to the adoption of the EU's biotech directive, the adoption of which took approximately 10 years amidst controversial and

---

[114] The Group was set up in December 1997 to succeed the Group of Advisers on the Ethical Implications of Biotechnology (GAEIB 1991–1997).

[115] See Opinion 16 on *The Ethical Aspects of Patenting Inventions Involving Human Stem Cells*, presented on 7 May 2002, reproduced at http://europa.eu.int/comm./european_group_ethics/activities_en.htm.

[116] While the EGE Opinion on patenting human stem cells was considered for guidance by the European Patent Office in its deliberations on the validity of the so-called 'Edinburgh Patent' on cloning technolgies, the Opinion was rejected because classic concepts of patent law are misinterpreted and confused: see European Patent Office, Opposition Division, 'Edinburgh' patent (EP 0695351), July 2002, unreported. See, further, chapter 15.

[117] See www.euractiv.com which collects and collates opinions of institutional and extra-institutional actors as part of EU policy making including in the area of health. See the section on human tissues.

[118] E.g. the various Directorates General of the European Commission and the European Parliament.

[119] See, for example, a survey by a selection of ethics committees across EU on stem cell research, n 10 above.

sometimes heated debates. Indeed, the prohibition on patenting uses of embryos and cloning techniques as a response to the ethical pressure by lobbyists across national, supra- and international levels occurred through a variety of channels of decision making and policy making, not all of which were, are, nor will be immediately open to public scrutiny.

3.37   A note of caution concerning the European Group on Ethics in Science and New Technologies reminds us that the precise ambit of its influence is unclear in the context of the cut throat business of EU lobbying. The closer the aims of EU policy initiatives are connected with the achievement with the internal market, the greater the impact of market actors such as, for example, representatives of industry. The influence of the 'hidden hand' of the market is not easily discernible as part of the EU legislative process.

3.38   It is difficult to distinguish between the rhetoric and the reality of EU policy making. One cause for concern is that bodies such as the European Group on Ethics in Science and New Technologies serve the ends of EU policy makers who are increasingly being called upon to ensure that the Union is not too remote from the citizen. The impact of the Group in EU policy making reveals only part of the picture of the shaping of bioethical concerns which attach to health rights and obligations in the Union. For instance, in an opinion of the European Group on Ethics in Science and New Technologies to the European Commission referring to stem cell research,[120] the word 'values' is used consistently throughout in relation to embryo research, in terms of the 'values we live by',[121] in allocating 'appropriate moral values to the complexity of our origins as humans'[122] and in 'a system of values as embodied in a system of constitution and convention.'[123] However, the word 'values' is not referred to once in the Commission Proposal for a Council Decision on the specific programme for research, technological development and demonstration[124] which is a curious omission considering that it undoubtedly has ramifications not only for the values inherent in stem cell research in the European Union but also for those in the research policies of member states—not to mention their health care policies. Indeed, it provides the basis for the administration of values which is a subtle process and, thereby, difficult to monitor.

3.39   It is suggested that a more nuanced and altogether more sophisticated approach to monitoring the development of the health rights and obligations in the EU must be adopted in order to best evaluate the impact of Europeanisation which is multi-faceted, multi-level and, also, multi-dimensional. It is multi-faceted to the extent that the impact of these rights and obligations are part and parcel of the symbiosis

---

[120] European Group of Ethics (2002), *Opinion Number 15, Adoption of an Opinion on Ethical Aspects of Human Stem Cell Research and Use*, Paris, available at http://europa.eu.int/comm/europeangroupethics.

[121] Opinion Number 15, *ibid* n 121 at p 147.   [122] Opinion Number 15, *ibid* n 121 at p 135.

[123] Opinion Number 15, *ibid* n 121 at p 141.

[124] Proposal for a Council Decision amending decision 2002/834/EC on the specific programme for research, technological development and demonstration: Integrating and strengthening the European research area (2002–2006), COM (2003) 390 final.

between EU legislation and the diverse constitutional cultures of the member states. It is multi-level in that rights and obligations are implemented at the local, regional, national and supranational levels of law and modes of governance in the European Union. It is multi-dimensional in the sense that they arise in spheres of EU competence which often overlap in ways which are not always obvious. In order for debates concerning bioethical issues in the EU to be conducted throughout the public spheres of the Union, greater openness is required regarding both the *status quo* and the way in which norms are being generated. Currently, there is an underlying suspicion that the ethics and the legality of health rights and obligations in the EU are being generated and driven by elite actors whilst, at the same time, participation by society as a whole is excluded. Given its significance for mankind, this is troubling.

3.40   In fact, the European Commission's ethical guidelines for EU funding of stem cell research have been seriously contested, particularly as such research is illegal in some member states.[125] The moratorium on stem cell research[126] ended on 31 December 2003 after which detailed implementing provisions for the 6th Framework Programme and research were formulated.

3.41   The EU Charter of Fundamental Rights prohibits various practices possibly related to embryo research, including 'eugenic practices, in particular those aiming at the selection of persons' and the 'reproductive cloning of human beings'.[127] This 'cluster' of norms reveals a complex interplay of direct and indirect processes of Europeanisation as a part of the administration of values in the European Research Area. This also enables EU policy makers to encroach on the domain of values which is, strictly speaking, a within the competence of member states. The framing of the debate in terms of principles, as opposed to values, has enabled EU policy makers to exert more influence given that the principle of subsidiarity applies in the case of the latter. Thus, for example, in the recommendations contained in a further Report of the European Commission on stem cell research,[128] the word 'values', appears only three times.[129] By contrast, fundamental ethical principles, including inter alia, respect for human dignity, individual autonomy, justice and beneficence, freedom of research and the principle of proportionality, are referred to more frequently.[130] This is also the case regarding the European Commission's Proposal for a Council Decision on the specific programme for research, technological development and demonstration where there are no references to values but some reference to principles[131] and to

---

[125] Reported by www.eu-interactiv.com on 5 December 2003.

[126] Since stem cells can be grown to substitute dead or diseased cells in a number of organs; possible therapeutic use of stem cells arises in the context of neurodegenerative diseases such as Parkinson's disease and Huntington's chorea, myocardial infarction, stroke, paralysis, epilepsy, diabetes mellitus, leukaemia and deficiencies of the immune system.

[127] See article 3 of the Charter.   [128] See Matthiesen-Guyader, n 10 above.

[129] Matthieson-Guyader, n 10 above at p 41: '. . . the early embryo has a value and it deserves special respect, but this value can be pondered with regard to other values.' No mention is made of what these other values might be.

[130] Matthieson-Guyader, n 10 above at p 58.

'ethical rules'. Indeed, it is intriguing to note how carefully the Commission avoids the use of the word 'values'. Thus, for example, in a section entitled *The European Context*, the proposal states that:

There is a great diversity among Member States concerning the ethical acceptability of various research fields and this is reflected in the national laws, in accordance with the principle of subsidiarity. No research involving the use of human embryos or human embryonic stem cells, of any type, will be supported by Community funding to a legal entity established in a country where such research is forbidden. Participants in research projects must conform to current legislation, regulations, and ethical rules in countries where the research will be carried out.[132]

3.42   The present position regarding stem cell research is an example of what has been argued in the context of EU health policy as a whole—that is, that the generation of ethical and legal norms is being effected under the aegis of the internal market. Competitiveness and the role of industry, is stressed in the context of the 6th Framework Programme as well as in the Constitution for Europe.[133] This may be advantageous in the development of the EU's competence on the international stage but, at the same time, it allows the policy makers to be more interventionist than if the framework was dedicated solely to research per se or, indeed, to health policy.[134] The danger is, then, that the ethics—and, indeed, the legality—of research is being generated and driven by a favoured few whilst, at the same time, excluding participation by society. In such delicate and sensitive areas, we must beware of the power vested in the relatively faceless persons who make up the many committees that are scattered at all levels of the European decision-making process.

[131] COM (2003) 390 final, see n 124 above.   [132] *Ibid* at p 5.
[133] See, for example, article III-146 to 156 of the Constitution for Europe.
[134] See the decision of the European Court of Justice concerning the Tobacco Directive: *Germany v European Parliament and Council* Case C-376/98 [2000] ECR-I-8419.

4

THE MANAGEMENT OF INFERTILITY AND CHILDLESSNESS

4.1 We believe that the title of this chapter draws attention to a distinction which is of practical, as well as semantic, importance. Primary infertility is a problem of the production of gametes or of implantation of the embryo. This may be susceptible to hormone therapy—a matter which we barely consider here; ovum or sperm donation then become secondary treatments of childlessness due to unsuccessful treatment of the primary condition. Similarly, the basic in vitro fertilisation (IVF) technique is most commonly used as a treatment of childlessness due to blockage of the fallopian tubes which cannot be corrected by recanalisation therapy. This distinction between infertility and childlessness may seem narrow but it may also be significant in relation to resource allocation. Thus, it could be held that, whereas the treatment of infertility is clearly a medical matter, childlessness can be seen as a social problem which should be funded from a different source.[1] While we do not subscribe to this theory, it might serve to justify the relative scarcity of the latter facilities in the National Health Service.[2]

4.2   Some 10 per cent of marriages are said to be infertile and the couple desire children in, at least, a high proportion of these.[3] In addition, there are couples who should give special thought to producing children naturally for genetic reasons, either because one may carry a dominant deleterious gene or because both are known to bear adverse recessive characteristics (see chapter 7, below). Again, a couple may be able to conceive a child but the woman is unable to carry it for medical reasons.

---

[1] For discussion, see S Redmayne and R Klein 'Rationing in Practice: the Case of In Vitro Fertilisation' (1993) 306 BMJ 1521. The difficulties of mixing political and clinical decisions have been aired more recently in R E Ashcroft 'In vitro Fertilisation for All? (2003) 327 BMJ 511.

[2] The *Twelfth Annual Report of the Human Fertilisation and Embryology Authority* (2003) indicates that there are now 75 licensed centres offering IVF treatments, with an additional 21 providing donor insemination only. In 2000–01, 38 IVF clinics accepted both fee paying and non-fee paying patients; 30 were fully fee paying and only 6 were exclusively non-fee paying.

[3] This notional figure, which must be extremely hard to validate, has its basis in *Report of the Committee of Inquiry into Human Fertilisation and Embryology* (Dame Mary Warnock, chairman, 1984), para 2.1. It may be an underestimate in modern terms: M Freeman 'Medically Assisted Reproduction' in A Grubb (ed) *Principles of Medical Law* (2nd edn, 2004), para 10.03, suggests a possible figure of 1:6 couples.

Opportunities for the adoption of infants are now meagre and, for many years, attention has focused on the elaboration of methods designed either to substitute the gametes of one or other person or to bypass the natural process in other ways.

4.3   The legal and moral issues involved have been considered at governmental level in many countries.[4] There are considerable differences but, in general, these refer to the degree of respect to be paid to the embryo *in vitro*. Even so, there are additional procedural variations which contribute to what has been described as a 'procreative tourism' within Europe.[5] The United Kingdom is in some ways atypical in that, while the practice is tightly regulated, embryonic status is comparatively ill-protected.

THE CONTROL OF ASSISTED REPRODUCTION IN THE UNITED KINGDOM

4.4   The legal response of the United Kingdom is to be found in the Human Fertilisation and Embryology Act 1990.[6] The main thrust of the Act is to establish a Human Fertilisation and Embryology Authority (HFEA) (s 5) which is mandated to supervise and provide information and advice to the Secretary of State about embryos and about treatment services governed by the Act.[7] The Authority maintains a Licence Committee through which only three types of licence can be issued to clinics approved for the purposes of the Act—these authorise activities in the course of providing treatment services (s 13), the storage of gametes and/or embryos (s 14), and reproductive research (s 15); the activities governed and limited by the licences are detailed in Schedule 2. In respect of assisted reproductive treatment provided for the public—with which we are primarily concerned in this chapter—the Act, in broad practical terms, prohibits the use, or storage, of gametes and the creation of embryos outside the body unless the clinic is in possession of a licence to do so.[8] Thus, in

---

[4] For a précis of European attitudes, see S Goldbeck-Wood 'Europe is Divided on Embryo Regulations' (1996) 313 BMJ 512. The situation is not, however, static; Italy, for example, has, at least temporarily, moved from virtual non-regulation to having one of the most restrictive jurisdictions: F Turone 'Italy to Pass New Law on Assisted Reproduction' (2004) 328 BMJ 9.

[5] M Brazier 'Regulating the Reproduction Business ?' (1999) 7 Med L Rev 166.

[6] Hereafter 'the 1990 Act'. The Act is a complex piece of legislation and it would be superfluous to attempt a detailed analysis. A very complete commentary is to be found in R G Lee and D Morgan *Human Fertilisation and Embryology* (2001). It is, however, to be noted that the House of Commons Scientific Committee has published a report that is highly critical of the provisions of the Act and, particularly, of the role of the Authority. The report itself was, however, controversial and its likely effect is uncertain. See House of Commons Science and Technology Committee Fifth Report *Human Reproductive Technologies and the Law* (2005, HC 7). Available at www.parliament.uk/s&tcom. A consultation document will be prepared for later in 2005.

[7] For details, see L Hagger 'The Role of the Human Fertilisation and Embryology Authority' (1997) 3 Med L Internat 1.

[8] Interestingly, the licence holder, or person responsible for the clinic, is not necessarily responsible for criminal activity under the Act by a senior member of the staff: *Attorney-General's Reference (No. 2 of 2003)* [2005] 3 All ER 149, [2004] 1 WLR 2062.

general, it allows for a flexible development of reproductive art under the control of peer and lay review.[9] However, sections 3 and 4 of the Act define activities which *cannot* be licensed. These include: placing in a woman any live gametes or embryos other than those of human origin; placing a human embryo in any animal; replacement of an embryonic nucleus by a nucleus taken from a cell of any other person or embryo;[10] and, of particular significance, keeping or using an embryo after the appearance of the primitive streak—defined in the Act as equating with later than 14 days from the day the gametes were mixed but excluding any time for which the embryo was stored (s 3(4)).

4.5   Section 1 of the Act contains some important definitions, the most significant of which include, firstly, that, except where otherwise stated, an embryo means a live human embryo where fertilisation is complete;[11]—and fertilisation is not complete until the appearance of a two-cell zygote. Secondly, in so far as the Act governs the creation, keeping or use of an embryo, it applies only to an embryo outside the human body.[12]

4.6   The Authority must also prepare and maintain a Code of Practice outlining the proper conduct of activities carried on under licence (s 25). As with all such mandated codes, the code is not legally binding per se. Nevertheless, the fact that it had been disregarded would count heavily in any criminal or civil actions brought against the offending clinic. Of perhaps greater practical importance, the Licence Committee is empowered to vary, revoke or refuse to renew a licence in the light of any deviations from the provisions of the code (s 25(6)).

4.7   With that précis completed, we can go on to consider the practical applications of the Act.

---

[9] The Chairman of the Authority may not be a registered medical practitioner or directly associated with the provision of treatment services; such persons must, however, constitute at least one third but not more than one half the total membership (Sch 1, para 4). The current membership includes appointments from such varied professions as the religious ministry, the law, dentistry and broadcasting.

[10] The House of Commons Committee (n 6 above) could find no good reason for relaxing these prohibitions. The regulation of somatic cell nuclear replacement of the nucleus of an *egg* is discussed later at para 7.101.

[11] By virtue of the Human Reproductive Cloning Act 2001, it is an offence to place in a woman an embryo that has been created otherwise than by fertilisation.

[12] It will be noted that, as a result, GIFT, or gamete intra-fallopian transfer, which involves the introduction of the sperm to the ovum in their natural habitat—the fallopian tube—rather than in the Petri dish, is not subject to licensing unless either the sperm or eggs are donated. Even so, the HFEA is maintaining a watchful eye on the process which carries its own hazards. By contrast, in ZIFT, or zygote intra-fallopian transfer, the preformed zygote is placed in the tube; fertilisation is, therefore, in vitro.

INSEMINATION

4.8 Donor insemination (DI)[13] may provide a solution to male infertility, a condition which accounts for roughly 50 per cent of cases of involuntary failure to conceive. In this procedure, semen obtained from a donor is injected into the woman; this results in conception in a proportion of cases which is surprisingly low.[14] The husband's or male partner's semen may similarly be introduced into the uterus by artificial means (AIH or AIP)—a need which might arise from impotence, from inadequate formation of spermatozoa or from a hostile vaginal reaction to constituents of the semen; treated semen would be used in the last two instances.

ARTIFICIAL INSEMINATION BY THE HUSBAND OR MALE PARTNER

4.9 In general terms, both AIH and AIP lie beyond the scope of the 1990 Act. This derives from the terms of s 4(1)(b) which are that no person shall use the sperm of any man in the course of providing treatment services for a woman except in pursuance of a licence *unless* the services are being provided for the woman and the man together. The meaning is perfectly clear so long as the man and woman are husband and wife; it is less so in the event of AIP. This is because, first, the Act does not use the word 'partner' which, as a result, remains undefined and, second, because the phraseology is very similar to that used in s 28(3) which deals with paternal status and which has provoked considerable legal confusion. We return to the matter below where it will be seen that, for the purposes of the Act, it is reasonable to interpret 'together' as implying a partnership in 'an enduring family relationship'[15]—which, in turn, of course, begs the definition of 'enduring'.[16] The Act is, also, at best veiled as to its attitude to donor insemination within an unmarried partnership and, again, we return to this at para 4.26.

4.10 Finally in this context, it is to be noted that AIH has been refined in recent years by the introduction of micromanipulative techniques—in particular, those of intracytoplasmic sperm injection (ICSI) or sub-zonal insemination (SUZI). In these methods, a single spermatozoon is injected directly into an egg. The sperm can, thus, be pre-selected and the technique is a valuable adjunct to the management of male infertility

---

[13] In so far as insemination by donor will virtually always be artificial, we have adopted the modern terminology in preference to the traditional acronym AID. The same does not apply to insemination by husband or partner where we continue to use the common abbreviations.

[14] The national clinical pregnancy rate per treatment cycle has risen from 6.6% in 1991/92 to 12.1% in 1998/9: HFEA *Ninth Annual Report* (2000) Table 4.18. These figures include GIFT using donated gametes. Interestingly, the number of treatment cycles administered has more than halved between 1992 and 1999.

[15] The phrase is taken from the Human Tissue Act 2004, s 54(8) as a probable template for any future amending legislation.

[16] Twelve months is the applicable period for the purposes of the Civil Partnership Act 2004 (s 17)—but this is a retrospective assessment whereas, in the present context, it is the *future* intention of the couple which matters to a resultant child.

due to poor quality of the semen. It is, perhaps, self-evident that such sophisticated methods, which involve in vitro fertilisation,[17] must be conducted in a licensed clinic in accordance with the Act. It is to be noted that the opportunities for pre-implantation genetic selection—a technique which, itself, poses a number of moral issues (discussed further below at para 7.24)—are greatly reduced using ICSI or SUZI as compared with standard techniques; this is a matter of particular concern when the quality of the spermatozoon, which is now enjoying a non-competitive existence, is, itself, suspect. As a result, most academic embryologists have been adopting a cautious attitude to the new techniques.[18]

4.11   Leaving aside any aspects of family law which depend upon marital status, and excluding any consideration of the moral value of marriage, it is tempting to conclude that uncomplicated AIH and AIP give rise to no major legal, status or ethical problems of themselves; the procedures will only be regarded as questionable if there is objection to *any* interference with nature in this area. This, however, is something of a simplistic view as AIH can be used for reasons other than compromised fertility in the male and its morality may then be questionable. Pre-eminent among these is the use of AIH as a preliminary to selection of the sex of the conceptus and we discuss this as a separate matter below.

4.12   Otherwise, the major issue raised by AIH lies in the possibility of 'sperm banking' either as an insurance against later sterility due to treatment—e.g. radiotherapy for malignant disease—or for use by a woman after her husband's or partner's death as, for instance, when the man is in a high-risk occupation; these possibilities can, obviously, arise in combination. Legally, it could lead to complex problems in relation to probate and succession.[19] More specifically, the Human Fertilisation and Embryology Act 1990, s 28(6)(b) stated baldly that where the sperm of a man, or any embryo the creation of which was brought about with his sperm, was used after his death, he was not to be treated as the father of the child.[20] Thus, posthumous insemination not only has a general moral relevance as to the effect on the child born into a single parent family,[21] but the Act, as drafted, actually created a potential class of 'fatherless' children—a form of discrimination that was widely criticised.

---

[17] For which see para 4.43 below. The techniques can be combined with ZIFT (zygote intrafallopian transfer).

[18] See S Mayor 'Technique for Treating Infertility may be Risky' (1996) 313 BMJ 248. Moreover, the HFE Authority itself lays down stringent conditions as to training in and practice of the newer techniques: *HFEA Code of Practice* (6th edn, 2003), Part 16.

[19] Although these do not seem insuperable in the United States: *Woodward v Commissioner of Social Security* 435 Mass 536 (2002).

[20] The 1990 Act left open the related questions of the man who is reported missing but is, in fact, dead and of the woman who reasonably believes her dead partner to be alive—we think it is likely that legal paternity could be established in either case.

[21] Posthumous insemination would not be lawful in France where both the donor and the recipient must be in stable partnerships at the time consent is given—Loi no 94–564, Article 10, which supersedes the court ruling made in *Parpalaix c le CECOS* JCP 1984.II.20321. For discussion, see M Latham 'Regulating the New Reproductive Technologies: A Cross-Channel Comparison' (1998) 3 Med L Internat 89.

4.13   The problem was brought to a head in the United Kingdom in the case of Mrs Blood,[22] which is atypical in that the man concerned was dying rather than dead when the sperm was obtained. The case, however, has wide implications and merits consideration in some depth.[23] In essence, Mr Blood was the victim of meningitis. When he was in terminal coma, his wife requested, and obtained, a specimen of semen, which she hoped to use for insemination after his death.[24] Given that he was alive, removal of the specimen could have been seen as treatment for a husband and wife together and, thus, beyond the requirements of a licence; aside from the difficulty of establishing that it was in 'his best interests' that it should be done,[25] there would have been nothing to stop his wife's immediate AIH.[26] And, therein lies the rub. Somewhat ironically, the team was reluctant to proceed without authority and the imposed delay dictated storage of the specimen—and the legality of storage of gametes under licence, in turn, depends on the written consent and counselling of the donor. Neither condition could be satisfied—albeit that there was anecdotal evidence of verbal consent during life. Accordingly—and in the face of something of a public outcry[27]—the HFEA held that storage of the specimen and its future use would be unlawful; furthermore, the Authority declined to exercise its discretion to allow the gametes to be exported to another country where treatment could be given in the absence of the donor's written consent.

4.14   Mrs Blood applied for judicial review of this decision but her application was dismissed, Sir Stephen Brown P holding that the HFEA was, effectively, following the will of Parliament; more specifically, he judged that EC law did not assist the applicant. The Court of Appeal agreed with the High Court decision in so far as treatment in the United Kingdom was concerned. It did, however, conclude that, in failing to exercise its discretion to facilitate treatment abroad, the HFEA had not been properly advised as to the importance of EC law in relation to cross-border services and had

---

[22] *R v Human Fertilisation and Embryology Authority, ex p Blood* [1997] 2 All ER 687, (1997) 35 BMLR 1, CA.

[23] For a very readable account of the case, see D Morgan and R G Lee 'In the Name of the Father? *Ex Parte Blood*: Dealing with Novelty and Anomaly' (1997) 60 MLR 840. For retrospective consideration in depth, see S A M McLean 'Creating Postmortem Pregnancies: A UK Perspective' (1999) Juridical Rev 323. The less satisfactory aspects of the case are examined in S J Treece and D Savas 'More Questions than Answers? *R v Human Fertilisation and Embryology Authority, ex parte Blood, The Times* 7th February 1997' (1997) 3 Med L Internat 75.

[24] Requests for posthumous *recovery* of sperm are not all that uncommon. Something of the order of 4% of American and Canadian fertility clinics were found to have undertaken the procedure: (1997) 125 Bull Med Ethics 5. Israel has recently dispensed with the man's consent in response to the importance in Judaism of having children: J Siegel-Itzkovich 'Israel Allows Removal of Sperm from Dead Men at Wives' Request' (2003) 327 BMJ 1187

[25] It is an assault to touch a person who is incapable of consenting unless, among other possibilities, it is in his or her best interests to do so: *Re F (mental patient: sterilisation)* [1990] 2 AC 1, sub nom *F v West Berkshire Health Authority* [1989] 2 All ER 545. The law's ability to recognise best interests in an ever widening circle of circumstances is a continuing theme in this book.

[26] Accepted by Lord Woolf in the Court of Appeal [1997] 2 All ER 687 at 696, (1997) 35 BMLR at 23.

[27] Well described by P R Ferguson 'Posthumous Conception: Blood and Gametes' 1997 SLT 61.

been over-concerned with the creation of an undesirable precedent.[28] The case was, therefore, remitted to the Authority, who exercised their discretion in the light of the further evidence adduced in the Court of Appeal.[29]

4.15   In the end, then, and despite the almost palpable anxiety of the court to support Mrs Blood's quest for reproductive freedom, *Blood* did nothing to alter or to ease the effect of existing domestic law. It is to be noted that posthumous insemination has never been prohibited—indeed, Sch 3, para 2(2) of the 1990 Act allows for the relevant consent from the man prior to his death. Nevertheless, as we will see later, the 1990 Act, s 13(5) and the *Code of Practice* allow the clinics considerable leeway as to the selection of patients and, particularly, in respect of the production of fatherless children;[30] the indications are that a significant proportion of clinics disapprove the process.[31]

4.16   As a result of the *Blood* case, s 28(6) of the 1990 Act was declared, by consent, to be incompatible with the Human Rights Act 1998.[32] The Government had, meanwhile, set up a review of the consent provisions in the 1990 Act[33] which, inter alia, recommended that s 28(6) of the Act should be amended so as to allow the child to acknowledge its deceased father—albeit while retaining the existing law as to inheritance.[34] This, in turn, resulted in the Human Fertilisation and Embryology (Deceased Fathers) Act 2003, section 1 of which amends the 1990 Act so that, if a child has been carried by a woman as a result of the placing in her of an embryo or of sperm and eggs or her artificial insemination involving the use of her husband's sperm after his death, then, subject to a number of conditions, including his extant written consent, the husband's particulars can be entered as the particulars of that child's father in a

[28] This was, in fact, impossible given the ruling that the original storage was illegal in the absence of written consent.

[29] Following some minor administrative hiccups, Mrs Blood was delivered of a first son by caesarian section on 11 December 1998. It is understood that the specimen was used successfully a second time.

[30] 1990 Act, s 13(5).

[31] E Corrigan, S E Mumford and M G R Hull 'Posthumous Storage and Use of Sperm and Embryos: Survey of Opinion of Treatment Centres' (1996) 313 BMJ 24. For criticism of the practice in general, see R D Orr and M Siegler 'Is Posthumous Semen Retrieval Ethically Permissible?' (2002) 28 J Med Ethics 299. In an unusual recent case, which is also of interest as to the meaning of 'undue pressure', a clinic actually put pressure on a man to withdraw his consent to posthumous use of his sperm; the court found, with regret, that he had done so: *Centre for Reproductive Medicine v U* [2002] EWHC 36 (Fam), (2002) 65 BMLR 92, [2002] Lloyd's Rep Med 93; the decision was upheld on appeal: [2002] Lloyd's Rep Med 259. It seems that there is far less opposition in, say, the United States: S M Kerr, A Caplan, G Polin et al 'Postmortem Sperm Procurement' (1997) 157 J Urol 2154. The process is forbidden under the generally positivist legislation of Victoria: Infertility Treatment Act 1995 (Vict), s 43. The basis for national guidelines where none currently exist is analysed in A Douglass and K Daniels 'Posthumous Reproduction: A Consideration of the Medical, Ethical, Cultural, Psychosocial and Legal Perspectives in the New Zealand Context' (2002) 5 Med Law Internat 259.

[32] The case was heard in February 2003 before Mr Justice Sullivan and appears to be officially unreported: 'Blood Claims IVF Paternity Victory', 28 February http://news.bbc.co.uk/1/hi/health/2807707.stm.

[33] S A M McLean *Review of the Common Law Provisions Relating to the Removal of Gametes and of the Consent Provisions in the Human Fertilisation and Embryology Act 1990* (1998).

[34] For a comparative analysis, see R Atherton '*En Ventre sa Frigidaire*: Posthumous Children in the Succession Context' (1999) 19 LS 139.

register of live- or still-births.[35] The concession is very specifically limited to this purpose[36] and, as a result, s 28(6) is not repealed but is to be read as subject to ss28(5A—B).

4.17   Yet a further legal problem could arise were nullity of the marriage to be mooted— as it could well be in some circumstances calling for AIH. Use of the procedure does not constitute consummation of marriage and a decree of nullity can still be obtained if a woman conceives in this way; approbation might, however, preclude the granting of such a decree.[37] Any resulting children would still be regarded as legitimate on the grounds that the parents were married at the time of conception.

4.18   A somewhat bizarre application of AIH relates to long-term prisoners whose wives may wish, or need on the grounds of age, to conceive before their release. A relevant case was heard in the Court of Appeal[38] in 2001 in which it was held that the justifiable withdrawal of conjugal rights which was inherent in imprisonment could include a denial of access to artificial insemination. However, the principle of proportionality applies and it was held that exceptional circumstances could require the consequences of imprisonment to yield to the European Convention on Human Rights;[39] the policy whereby the Secretary of State judges each case on its merits was considered to be neither in breach of the Convention nor irrational or unlawful.[40] In an interesting obiter opinion, Lord Phillips thought that the starting point for exceptional circumstances could be when the founding of a family was prevented absolutely rather than delayed by a refusal to grant facilities for insemination.[41]

Primary sex selection

4.19   Public concern has been aroused in recent years by the entry into the market place of preconception sex selection of children. Most methods claiming scientific respectability depend upon altering the proportion of male- and female-bearing spermatozoa in the ejaculate and artificial insemination with the processed specimen. Opinions differ as to whether such methods are efficient and to what extent they can be relied upon but claims have been made to an accuracy of the order of 90 per cent.[42] The efficiency of the method is not, however, our main concern. What calls for analysis is the ethical position in the event that this was found to be true. Discussion is then at

---

[35] 1990 Act, s 28(5A), s 28(5I). Ss 28(5B–D) cover the cases of an unmarried couple being treated together by a licensed practitioner and the consensual use of donor sperm so as to conform with the Act as it applies to a living husband or partner.

[36] 1990 Act, s 29(3B).

[37] *REL v EL* [1949] P 211, [1949] 1 All ER 141 (see also *G v G* 1961 SLT 324).

[38] *R (on the application of Mellor) v Secretary of State for the Home Department* [2001] 3 WLR 533, (2001) 59 BMLR 1.

[39] Per Lord Phillips MR at [45]. See now Human Rights Act 1998, Sch 1, Articles 8 and 12.

[40] The Court noted that the European Commission on Human Rights had already approved this possibility in *ELH and PBH v United Kingdom* (1997) 91A D & R 61.

[41] At [68].

[42] Scottish views, in the form of media interviews, are given in S McLean and K Mason 'The Great Baby Debate . . . Viewed from Both Sides' *Sunday Herald*, 8 July 2001, p 11.

two levels—the practical and the deontological. The fact that both are highly culture-dependent—with a very evident East/West divide—deserves emphasis. Thus, at the practical level, it is probably fair to say that preconception sex selection would have, at most, a negligible effect on the distribution and status of the sexes in the United Kingdom. But this is essentially a Western view and one which might well not be true of countries in the Far East—indeed, the gender balance has become dangerously unstable in parts of India where health carers who practise a post-conception sex determination service are now liable to have their licences revoked.[43] On the ethical plane, very few, it is supposed, would oppose primary sex selection for the prophylaxis of X-linked disease.[44] Similarly, even those concerned to minimise embryonic and fetal rights would see 'sperm sorting' as being morally preferable to secondary sex selection by way of embryo selection or abortion.

4.20   Beyond this, sex selection for non-medical or social reasons has been classed as anything from 'playing God' to offering an acceptable new dimension to family planning.[45] The latter view cannot be rejected out of hand—it is difficult to see why family design should not be refined in this way when so much family planning of other sorts is practised and encouraged. This, however, presupposes that the method is perfected and, whatever proportion of choice is ultimately effected, it can never be 100 per cent. There is bound to be a residue of couples who have been to considerable expense and discomfort to select the sex of their child and who will be bitterly disappointed when their wishes are unfulfilled; thus, we foresee a possibly disastrous outcome for some 30 per cent of children currently born using this technique. It follows that, in contrast to other forms of reproductive liberty,[46] primary sex selection poses a real threat of harm to a resultant child; an equally distasteful increase in the number of 'social' abortions might also result. For these reasons alone, we advocate a legal limitation of 'gender clinics' to those licensed to undertake the practice; the potential consequences for individual children—and, perhaps, for society by way of a 'eugenic wedge'[47]—are too serious for the process to be left unsupervised.[48]

---

[43] G Mudur 'Indian Medical Authorities Act on Antenatal Sex Selection' (1999) 319 BMJ 401. The need for control is, however, questioned by B M Dickens 'Can Sex Selection Be Ethically Tolerated?' (2002) 28 J Med Ethics 335.

[44] See para 7.6 below.

[45] This seems to be the view of the Dutch Health Council—the reproductive freedom of parents should be respected: 'Sex Selection for Non-medical Reasons' (1996) 119 Bull Med Ethics 8. The process was, however, rejected as ethically unacceptable by all 16 members of the Danish Council of Ethics: (2003) 191 Bull Med Ethics 9.

[46] D McCarthy 'Why Sex Selection should be Legal' (2001) 27 J Med Ethics 302 makes a powerful case for the onus being with those who oppose sex selection to show that its restriction would be a restriction of liberty that could not reasonably be rejected.

[47] A phrase borrowed from T Marteau 'Sex Selection' (1993) 306 BMJ 1704.

[48] The Human Fertilisation and Embryology Authority has no control so long as the sperm is not stored and the process is carried out in private for the benefit of a man and woman together. However, licensed clinics are expected not to select the sex of embryos for social reasons: HFEA *Code of Practice* (2003, 6th edition) para 8.9. Interestingly, the previous ban on the use of sperm sorting techniques has now been removed—this despite the fact that the Authority recommends its legal prohibition: Z Kmietowicz 'Fertilisation Authority Recommends a Ban on Sex Selection' (2003) 327 BMJ 1123. It is notable that the

DONOR INSEMINATION

4.21   Donor insemination introduces two additional concepts into the management of infertility. First, the procedure escapes the confines of a private matter between two persons in a close emotional relationship; rather, it involves a third party whose contribution lies at the heart of the enterprise. Secondly, sperm donation inevitably results in the production of a gross excess of gametes and, consequently, to the creation of options for their storage and later use. Ideally, therefore, all forms of DI should be subject to control but, effectively, this is as impossible as is the control of natural insemination. We have seen already that the wording of s 4(1)(b) clearly excludes the need for a licence when carrying out simple AIH or AIP; whether or not DI is also excluded is, however, less obvious. The solution seems to lie in the fact that the section must be interpreted along with the meaning of treatment services which are defined in s 2(1) as 'services provided to the public or a section of the public'. It is not immediately apparent—at least to one of the authors—why an individual should not be regarded as 'a section of the public'. Nevertheless, it is widely agreed that, taken together, ss 2(1) and 4(1)(b) combine to exclude 'do-it-yourself' or 'private' inseminations from the strictures of the Act and that this is irrespective of whether the sperm used is that of a husband, a partner or a donor.

4.22   Control of a public insemination programme is, however, both desirable and possible and, to this end, the use of a man's sperm—and, conversely, the use of a woman's eggs—has been classed as one of the two *treatment services*, as defined in s 2, which are permitted only in pursuance of a licence—the other includes, broadly, any treatment which involves the creation of an embryo outside the human body and, hence, is almost entirely a matter of management of childlessness due to abnormality in the woman.[49] Ultimately, the legality and morality of donor insemination and ovum donation[50] depend on the consent of the donors to their use; consent provides the plinth on which control is based and its form is detailed in the 1990 Act, Sch 3.

4.23   In summary, so-called 'effective consent' must be in writing and can apply to the use, storage and/or disposal of gametes. Thus, gametes cannot be used or received other than in accordance with the terms of an effective consent (Sch 3, para 5) and this extends to the use of any embryo created from those gametes (Sch 3, para 6); a consent to storage of gametes—which is, itself, governed by the clinic's possession of a 'storage licence' (s 11(b))—must specify the maximum period of storage[51] and, again, this applies to any embryo so formed (Sch 3, para 8); thirdly, the person giving

Council of Europe *Convention on Human Rights and Biomedicine* (1997) specifically outlaws the use of techniques of medically assisted procreation for the purpose of choosing a child's sex other than for sound medical reasons (Article 14); the United Kingdom has not, however, yet ratified the Convention.

[49] 1990 Act, ss 1(2), 3(1)(a).   [50] See para 4.49 below.

[51] They cannot, normally, be stored for longer than ten years (1990 Act, s 14(3)). An exception may be made if the person seeking storage was under 45 years of age when the gametes were placed in storage and the other conditions laid down in regulation have been satisfied. These include the fact that the special circumstances arose after storage began (Human Fertilisation and Embryology Act (Statutory Storage Period) Regulations 1991, SI 1991/1540).

consent must specify what is to be done with the gametes or created embryos in the event that he or she dies or becomes incapacitated (Sch 3, para 2(b)). In addition, the donor must be given adequate information and must be counselled before consenting (Sch 3, para 3).

DI and the marital bond

4.24 Notwithstanding the restrictions imposed by the consent requirements, there are those who object strongly to DI on the grounds that the basis of the marriage bond is compromised by the wife's pregnancy through another man. It is supposed that the privity of marriage is invaded and that, in this respect, DI is little different from adultery. The question of whether DI constitutes adultery in legal terms was debated in the Scottish case of *MacLennan v MacLennan*,[52] where it was determined that adultery could not be held to have taken place because there was no sexual contact between the woman and the donor. This approach to the question would probably be acceptable now throughout the common law jurisdictions. DI without the consent of the husband may, however, be taken as constituting cruel and unreasonable conduct for divorce purposes. Given the consent of both parties, the acceptance of DI can be seen as the fulfilment of the perfectly legitimate desire to have a child to care for. The very fact of agreement to the process testifies to the strength of the bond between the parties—and this is confirmed by the comparatively low incidence of divorce in couples who have chosen DI. The marital bond is disturbed by the procedure only in a metaphysical sense and this disturbance is, in any event, actively sought by the couple.

4.25 This is not to recommend that DI be undertaken lightly. Ill-considered donation can lead, inter alia, to unfortunate anatomic incompatibilities between the social parents and the resulting child and to the transmission of both genetic and sexually transmitted disease; in addition, it may promote some aspects of eugenic selection that are, at least, of questionable morality.[53] Counselling as to its psychological and legal implications is an integral part of the provision of a public DI service in the United Kingdom.

Major ethical problems

4.26 It is probably fair to say that the major ethical problems associated with DI have been eliminated from the standard husband and wife or heterosexual partnership situations. It can, however, happen that a single woman requests DI or the request may come from a lesbian couple. Since there is no legal regulation of the matter, the practitioner acting in a private capacity will have to decide on ethical grounds alone whether or not to proceed in these circumstances; the doctor providing a public service will, however, be constrained by the conditions of HFEA's Code of Practice which we discuss below.

---

[52] 1958 SC 105.
[53] These risks have, of course, been recognised for some time: C L R Barratt and I D Cooke 'Risks of Donor Insemination' (1989) 299 BMJ 1178.

4.27   It is a matter of common observation that marriage and procreation are no longer seen as being inseparable. A married couple may prefer to remain childless; similarly, a single woman may have precisely the same desire for a child as her married counterpart. Many—probably, most—would hold that she should have the same access to a child as has her married counterpart. The same argument may be put forward on behalf of the homosexual woman, whether she is living by herself or with a partner. Should the experience of giving birth and raising a child be denied in either case because of the absence of a male partner? Why should society exclude the possibility of assisted conception when it allows such women to conceive by normal means and permits them to keep their children as a normal right of parenthood?[54]

4.28   Artificial insemination is not, however, a natural process and it usually involves the medical profession. Even if the principal objective of DI is to satisfy the desire for a child, thought has to be given to the child who is the end result and the paramountcy of the child's interests is a general tenet throughout the spectrum of family law. The doctor must, therefore, question whether he should play a part in the deliberate creation of a child who could be disadvantaged as compared with his peers who have fathers. Whether or not such disadvantage is real or imaginary is undecided[55] and is, perhaps, indeterminable, for there are probably proportionately as many good and bad homes regularised by church or state as there are occupied by single parents.

4.29   The 1990 Act, s 13(5) currently emphasises the importance of this particular problem by specifying consideration of 'the need of the child for a father' as one of the welfare principles to be satisfied before treatment is given under licence. HFEA's *Code of Practice*[56] lists five major factors which clinics should take into account when people seek treatment using donated gametes—and which, incidentally, appear to us to provide almost unlimited discretion as to whether or not to provide treatment. It is not without significance, however, the 'need for a father' is no longer included in para 3.14 of the Code—the emphasis in this respect is now entirely on the *woman's ability*, and that of other persons within her circle, to meet the needs of the child. More importantly, perhaps, the Chair of the Authority is on record as believing that: 'It is anachronistic for the law to include a statement about a child's need for a father'.[57]

---

[54] A comprehensive survey of lesbian claims to DI, including empirical evidence as to the effect on children of being raised in a lesbian ambience is to be found in P Baetens and A Brewaeys 'Lesbian Couples Requesting Donor Insemination: An Update of the Knowledge with Regard to Lesbian Mother Families' (2001) 7 Human Repro Update 512. Some have cast doubt on the motivation of single women seeking DI: e.g. S Jennings 'Virgin Birth Syndrome' (1991) 337 Lancet 559. For an up-to-date review of the current position, see E E Sutherland ' "Man not Included"—Single Women, Female Couples and Procreative Freedom in the UK' (2003) 15 CFLQ 155.

[55] For review, see S Golombok and J Rust 'The Warnock Report and Single Women: What About the Children?' (1986) 12 J Med Ethics 182. In general, see M B King and P Pattison 'Homosexuality and Parenthood' (1991) 303 BMJ 295. The Committee of Inquiry into Human Fertilisation and Embryology (Dame Mary Warnock, Chairman) (Cmnd 9314) (hereafter referred to as Warnock) was unable to conclude any more firmly than that it is, as a general rule, better for children to be born into a two-parent family (at para 2.11). Lady Warnock has now modified her views in this respect: M Warnock *Making Babies* (2002) at 60.

[56] HFEA *Code of Practice* (6th edn, 2003) at para 3.12.

[57] http://news.bbc.co.uk/1/hi/health/3416055.stm, 21 January 2004.

Needless to say, this impromptu statement has aroused considerable opposition. However, a thorough review of the 1990 Act is now in progress and we would hazard a guess that it will be significantly amended in this respect.[58]

4.30 Even so, professional intervention in such contentious issues is unarguably a matter of social, rather than medical, expedience; we doubt if a doctor ought to confuse his role as a therapist with that of a social worker or political economist. HFEA's *Code of Practice* undoubtedly allows the health care professional a wide margin of appreciation as to his or her choice of patients and s 38 of the 1990 Act relieves one who conscientiously objects to such procedures of a duty to act. At the same time, it has to be remembered that, while the Code has no legal force per se, it is produced pursuant to a statutory obligation; renewal of a licence would undoubtedly be prejudiced were its recommendations to be flouted (1990 Act, s 25(6)).[59]

Legal considerations

4.31 The legal position of the child born as a result of AID in the United Kingdom is now governed by the 1990 Act which repealed the Family Law Reform Act 1987, s 27 and, at the same time, resolved the anomalies previously extant between England and Wales and Scotland.

4.32 Section 28(2) covers the case of the married woman. In essence, the rule is that, when she has been inseminated with the sperm of a man other than her husband, and provided that her husband has consented, her husband will be treated as the father of the child; s 28(4) emphasises that, in these circumstances, no other person is to be treated as the father of the child and the donor is covered against withdrawal of consent by the husband by s 28(6)(a).[60] The s 28(2) rule is voided if the husband can show that he did not, in fact, consent to the procedure. The somewhat confusing terms of s 28(5) do, however, retain the common law principle of *pater est quem nuptiae demonstrant*; thus, the husband who does not consent to DI will still have to rebut that presumption by way of accepted methods of paternity testing. It is to be noted that the statutory provisions will prevail in the event of disagreement between the partners.[61] Section 29(4) preserves the somewhat archaic exclusion of hereditary titles, honours and the like from the general principles attaching to the AID child— although where the onus of proof or disproof of patrilinearity then lies or, indeed, how it can be discharged is a matter for speculation. An exception of greater practical

[58] Interestingly, the High Court of Australia has confirmed that the Infertility Treatment Act 1995, s 8 (Vic.), which limits IVF treatment to actual and de facto married women, is incompatible with the Sex Discrimination Act 1984 (Cth): *McBain v Victoria* (2000) 177 ALR 320, affd *Re McBain, ex p Australian Catholic Bishops' Conference* (2002) 188 ALR 1.

[59] The discussion is, however, more germane to those forms of assisted reproduction which depend wholly upon medical expertise. See para 4.42 below.

[60] This section also applies to inseminations done privately (or 'DIY' inseminations). There is, of course, nothing to prevent a man *claiming* paternity under the common law: *X v Y* 2002 SLT 161, Glasgow Sheriff Court. The potential advantages of this to the child were expressed in the pioneer Australian case *Re Patrick* (2002) 28 Fam LR 579.

[61] *Re CH (contact: parentage)* [1996] 1 FLR 569.

importance is that, by virtue of Sch 4, para 8, ss 27–29 of the 1990 Act do not apply for the purposes of restricting live organ transplants between persons not genetically related (Human Organ Transplants Act 1989, s 2).[62]

4.33   Section 28(3) extends the responsibilities and privileges of fatherhood to a woman's partner subject, first, to the insemination being carried out in a licensed clinic and, secondly, to their seeking treatment 'together'—a matter we have already touched upon in relation to unlicensed treatment. Despite the similarity of the wording in ss 4(1)(b) and 28(3)(a), its use in the latter carries rather more practical significance. Although it may be the result of no more than selective publicity, it is, in many ways, surprising how many of these cases result in acrimony. The question of 'fatherhood' then becomes central to the dispute and its solution may depend upon the interpretation of 'treatment together'. It is unsurprising that the matter has been debated in the courts. Does it mean 'together' in a spatial sense—i.e. that the woman and the man are physically present in the clinic?—or does it, perhaps, mean that both the woman and the man are receiving treatment?—in which case, it is reasonable to ask what 'treatment' the man is being given other than emotional support. The latter interpretation was clearly in the mind of Johnson J when he said:

> It seems plain to me that the subsection envisages a situation in which the man involved himself received medical treatment, although ... I am not sure what treatment is envisaged.[63]

4.34   This, however, seems an improbable Parliamentary intention and the question was aired more thoroughly by Wilson J in *U v W*.[64] In this bizarre case, a woman conceived and bore twins as a result of micromanipulation of her ova and the sperm of an anonymous donor, the process having failed when using the semen of her partner. U applied to have her partner declared the father of the twins by virtue of the 1990 Act, s 28(3)(a).[65] In the process of deciding the meaning of the suspect wording, Wilson J rejected the tentative interpretation offered in *Re Q* and opined:

> [W]hat has to be demonstrated is that, in the provision of treatment services with donor sperm, the doctor was responding to a request for that form of treatment made by the woman and the man as a couple, notwithstanding the absence in the man of any physical role in such treatment.[66]

4.35   In short, this judgment confirms the generally held view[67] that the purpose of the words 'treatment . . . together' is, as we have already seen, in s 4(1)(b) to exclude AIH, AIP and privately arranged DI from the restrictive terms of the 1990 Act and, in s 28(3), to ensure legal paternity of the child born to a woman and her bona fide

---

[62] The 1989 Act is now repealed other than in Scotland but, presumably, its terms will be continued in regulations to be made under the Human Tissue Act 2004.

[63] In *Re Q (parental order)* [1996] 1 FLR 369 at 371.

[64] *U v W (A-G intervening)* [1997] 2 FLR 282, (1997) 38 BMLR 54.   [65] See para 4.33 above.

[66] (1997) 38 BMLR 54 at 66. Wilson J also drew attention to the terms of the optional acknowledgment of paternity suggested in what is now Annex E of the HFEA *Code of Practice*.

[67] As expressed by Bracewell J in *Re B (parentage)* [1996] 2 FLR 15.

partner as a result of DI conducted in a licensed clinic.[68] In conferring parenthood on a man who, otherwise, has neither genetic nor legal claim to that status, s 28(3) represents a remarkable advance in legislation and it is, in many ways, surprising that the Act makes no simultaneous attempt to define a 'partner'—indeed, it does not mention the word.[69] *U v W* suggests that whether or not a couple 'qualify' for s 28(3) status is a matter to be determined on the facts[70]—although there is nothing to stop responsible bodies fixing their own arbitrary limits in other situations.[71] On the other side of the coin, the law recognises that a partnership can be broken; a couple are being 'treated together' for the purposes of s 28 if they are together at the time the treatment is provided, not at the time consent is given.[72]

4.36   The 1990 Act makes no specific mention as to the registration of the birth of the child but, again, this appears to be clarified by implication. Section 29(1) states that the treatment in law of a woman's husband as the father of a child resulting from consensual donor insemination is 'for all purposes'—and this must include the registration of births and marriages. Near absolute freedom from parental responsibility is conferred on the donor by s 28(6)(a) of the 1990 Act, which specifically excludes him from legal paternity.[73] However, freedom from responsibility and anonymity do not necessarily go hand in hand and the latter status has been the subject of vigorous debate during the preparation of this book.

4.37   As the 1990 Act was drafted, anonymity of the donor was ensured, subject to the licensing authority being obliged to keep a register of identifiable individuals who have been treated, whose gametes have been stored or used and who were, or may have been, born as a result of treatment services (s 31(2)). As a corollary to this, a person over the age of 18 years, or a person over 16 years old and intending to marry,[74] could require the licensing authority to establish whether he or she might have been born as a result of treatment services and, if so, to provide general,

---

[68] U, in fact, failed in her bid to impose paternity on W because the procedure was not carried out in a clinic licensed in the UK. The restriction was held not to constitute an infringement of the European Convention on Human Rights, Article 59. A comparison of *Blood* and *U v W* provides a nice example of the juggling which can accompany attempts to harmonise domestic and European Community law. See para 3.13.

[69] This obviously concerned the Lord Chancellor during the debate on the Bill when he referred to 'the difficulty in distinguishing partners to stable relationships from more transitory ones': Official Reports, HL, 20 March 1990, col 209–10.

[70] [1997] 3 WLR 739 at 749, (1997) 38 BMLR 54 at 66.

[71] One railway company, for example, laid down two years as a period of partnership qualifying for family rebates: *Grant v South-West Trains Ltd* [1998] All ER (EC) 193, [1998] 1 FLR 839.

[72] *Re R (parental responsibility: IVF baby)* [2003] 2 All ER 131, *sub nom Re R (a child)* (2003) 71 BMLR 157. This case, admittedly, refers to the insertion of an embryo (see para 4.49 below) but the same principles would apply to DI.

[73] It will be seen from what has already been said that the donor could, for example, be seen as the legal father if he provides a specimen for insemination of an unmarried couple by an unlicensed practitioner.

[74] One purpose of a register is to guard against the possibility of incest or of marriage within the prohibited degrees in later generations; the HFEA's *Code of Practice* dictates that, save in exceptional circumstances, no more than ten children should be fathered by one donor. The dangers, both real and imaginary, of such matings as a result of DI may well be overstated.

non-identifying information as to the donor such as, say, his ethnic type and genetic health.[75]

4.38   The terms of the 1990 Act were, however, successfully challenged in the High Court in 2002.[76] Although the QBD did not specifically consider whether there was an infringement, it was determined that the restrictions in the Act were engaged by the Human Rights Act 1998 in respect of Schedule 1, Article 8—this in so far as respect for private and family life requires that everyone should be able to establish details of their identity as individual human beings and that this includes their origins and the opportunity to understand them.[77] As a result, new regulations[78] came into force on 1 April 2005 which allow a person over the age of 18 access to the name, date and place of birth, appearance and last known address of a donor parent. However, since a change in the regulations cannot be retrospective,[79] the new facility cannot be invoked until 2023 at the earliest.

4.39   We admit to some doubts as to the advantages of abandoning the anonymity rule. Certainly, the right to discover the identity of the donor has been recognised in some countries,[80] this being based on the supposition not only that a knowledge of one's true parentage is a fundamental right but also that children have a strong psychological urge to acquire this knowledge.[81] Although the latter is now regarded as almost a proven fact, much of the evidence is, of its very nature, anecdotal and no comparable study of children born by way of adultery has been, nor can be, made. Moreover,

---

[75] Note that the restrictions apply to ovum as well as sperm donation. Personal data relating to treatments under the 1990 Act are exempt from the subject access provisions of the Data Protection Act 1998, s 7 except in so far as their disclosure is made in accordance with s 31. Disclosure can, however, be ordered by the courts in the interests of justice (s 34) and in the case of proceedings under the Congenital Disabilities (Civil Liability) Act 1976 or of comparable actions for damages in Scotland (s 35). The limited access to the records of a deceased person afforded to his or her personal representatives by the Access to Health Records Act 1990, s 3(1)(f) is unaffected.

[76] R (on the application of Rose) v Secretary of State for Health [2002] 2 FLR 962, (2003) 69 BMLR 83, per Scott Baker J at para [45].

[77] For the balance between parental anonymity and the child's desire to know, see the ECHR opinion, and particularly that of the minority, in Odièvre v France [2003] 1 FCR 621, (2004) 38 EHRR 871 and commentary by T Callus 'Tempered Hope? A Qualified Right to Know One's Genetic Origin: Odièvre v France' (2004) 67 MLR 658. This was an adoption issue, peculiar to French law.

[78] Human Fertilisation and Embryology Authority (Disclosure of Donor Information) Regulations 2004 (SI 2004/1511).

[79] 1990 Act, s 31(5).

[80] Anonymity in Europe ranges from absolute in France to a child's right to identify his or her father on reaching maturity in Sweden—right which still depends, to an extent, on parental discretion. For an interesting review of Swedish donors' attitudes, see K R Daniels, H L Ericsson and I P Burn 'The Views of Semen Donors Regarding the Swedish Insemination Act 1984' (1998) 3 Med L Internat 117. Surprisingly, opposition to lifting the veil was found as much, if not more so, among the families and doctors as among the donors. For further commentary, see C Gottlieb, O Lalos and F Lindblad 'Disclosure of Donor Insemination to the Child: The Impact of Swedish Legislation on Couples' Attitudes' (2000) 15 Human Reproduction 2052. In Germany, a need for knowledge of the truth of one's heredity is so much ingrained in the national psyche that laws provide for compulsory examinations in order to obtain the evidence from reluctant parties: §372a of the German Civil Procedure Code (ZPO).

[81] For a new look at the overall situation, see R Probert 'Families, Assisted Reproduction and the Law' (2004) 16 CFLQ 273.

there is also some evidence that hurtful psychological consequences can result from the receipt of such information.[82] The frequently drawn analogy with adoption—in which there is a statutory right to discover a true genetic relationship[83]—is flawed. In the latter situation, some bonding with the true parents may have occurred; there is, at least in the 'stranger' process, no necessary genetic affiliation with either adopting parent; and, pragmatically, disclosure of status is almost certain once the child requires to see his or her birth certificate. The *need* for the DI child to have the same discovery rights as the adoptee is, therefore, by no means self-evident.

4.40   Very few of us ever question our paternity and still fewer will doubt their maternity—for the same regulations apply to ovum donation[84] as to sperm donation; it seems to us that the almost inevitable result of regulating for a few to question their parentage will be to encourage the majority to do so. It is doubtful if the statutory creation of children anxiously awaiting their eighteenth birthday in order to exorcise an implanted suspicion can be to the overall benefit of family relationships.[85] Occasionally—and particularly in the event of the reason for DI lying in a genetic abnormality in a woman's husband or partner—disclosure of true parentage may be highly desirable; such situations are, however, better met by good counselling within a responsible family environment.[86]

4.41   Finally, there is always the possibility that the supply of suitable semen specimens will be compromised even further than is currently the case[87]—and the prospect of semen specimens being imported from abroad is less than appealing. But it will be for the next edition of this book to assess this hypothetical.

THE INFERTILE OR CHILDLESS WOMAN

4.42   Childlessness due to abnormalities in the man is, as we have seen, largely a matter of the defective formation of spermatozoa. A woman may also suffer from primary infertility. In addition, however, she may be beset by anatomical problems which prevent her having children by natural means—of which, blockage of the fallopian tubes is the most common. The proportion of cases due to anatomical abnormality

---

[82] A J Turner and A Coyle 'What Does It Mean to be a Donor Offspring? The Identity Experiences of Adults Conceived by Donor Insemination and the Implications for Counselling and Therapy' (2000) 15 Human Reproduction 2041.

[83] Adoption Act 1976, s 51; Adoption (Scotland) Act 1978, s 45(5).

[84] See para 4.49 below.

[85] Much the same concerns are expressed by J Harris 'Assisted Reproductive Technological Blunders' (2003) 29 J Med Ethics 205.

[86] For a novel approach to the dilemma, see S Wilson 'Identity, Genealogy and the Social Family: the Case of Donor Insemination' (1997) 11 Int J Law Pol Fam 270.

[87] The evidence from Sweden is, in our view, equivocal. Very many opinions have been expressed as to the likely effect of the new regulations. For an interesting lay view, see J Hjul 'Society Must Realise that No Anonymity Means No Donors' (2004) *Sunday Times*, 25 January, p 21.

and to infertility resulting from faulty ovum production is about equal. We do not, here, discuss the purely medical treatment of the latter; its incidental legal and ethical significance is noted briefly below.[88] However, when hormonal treatment has failed, the anovular woman is in the same position as the azoospermic man and may be able to parent a child by way of gamete replacement; ovum donation is a practical routine procedure despite the fact that ova are far more scarce and are more difficult to handle than are spermatozoa. Even so, it is, perhaps fortunately, still impossible to develop a full-term fetus in a laboratory environment. Ovum donation is, therefore, pointless without, at the same time, providing a womb. Both may be contributed by the same woman or they may be available independently. It is these features that underlie the majority of the legal and moral problems which complicate the treatment of the infertile woman. By contrast, childlessness due to various anatomic or physiological abnormalities must be treated according to its specific cause; the nature of the available procedures will become apparent as the chapter progresses.

IN VITRO FERTILISATION (IVF)

4.43   Many modern reproductive techniques involve the fertilisation of the ovum in laboratory—or in vitro—conditions and the subsequent transfer of the embryo[89] from the petri dish to the uterus. Strictly speaking, therefore, IVF and embryo transfer (ET) are technical terms applicable to a number of specific treatment regimes. Nevertheless, popular usage generally equates IVF with the particular treatment for childlessness due to blockage of the fallopian tubes and it is in that sense that we use the term in this section.

4.44   Standard IVF treatment involves collection of ova from the wife's abdomen, fertilisation of these with her husband's sperm in the laboratory and transfer of the resulting embryo to her uterus; the treatment is, therefore, essentially one designed to bypass diseased fallopian tubes. The actual collection of ova is now relatively simple through a laparoscope; the treatment cycle does, however, involve complex hormonal priming to ensure superovulation. This is important to the process as an excess of subsequent embryos is needed so that a choice can be made so as to ensure that the embryos inserted are normal. A significant collateral advantage is that unused ova can be made available for ovum donation—a process known as 'egg-sharing' to which we return at para 4.49.

4.45   The mean live birth rate depends to an extent on the size and expertise of the

---

[88] See para 4.76.

[89] The *First Report of the Voluntary Licensing Authority for Human In Vitro Fertilisation and Embryology* (1986) p 8, recommended the use of the term pre-embryo to distinguish the organism before differentiation into fetal and placental cells has occurred. There is, thus, physiological justification for this. We, however, prefer not to use the term as, despite protestations to the contrary, it smacks of an attempt to make a moral distinction between the pre-embryo and the embryo—which we suggest is spurious and unnecessary. The interjection of pre-embryo as a stage in development is also inconsistent with the definition of an embryo as a two-cell zygote given in the 1990 Act, s 1(1).

treatment centre but is currently in the order of 21 per cent of treatment cycles; clinical pregnancy rates vary from 9.5 per cent when one embryo is transferred to 26 per cent when two are implanted.[90] Thus, while IVF may well be the optional treatment for one of the commonest female causes of childlessness, the expectations of success are relatively low—an important point to be made when counselling child-less couples. The pregnancy and live birth rates following IVF show no significant differences when related to the underlying reason for the treatment.[91]

4.46   The rationale of the process corresponds closely to that of AIH and, as such, presents no problems in the field of family law. The genetic and natural parentage of the resulting infant are not disputed. All that has occurred is that a technique has been substituted for a natural process; if any would protest that this is in some way immoral, they would, at the same time, have to contend that the surgical treatment of any disease is similarly immoral. It is, however, apparent that IVF, by definition, involves the creation of an embryo outside the human body. It is a fundamental premise of the 1990 Act that it is unlawful for an unlicensed person to do so; accordingly, IVF therapy can only be undertaken by a licensed practitioner. There is, of course, no technical reason why the sperm must be those of the husband or partner and, in the event of combined male infertility and an impassable female genital tract, donor semen could be used in the same way. In such circumstances, the legal problems and solutions would be comparable to those of DI, which have been discussed above.

4.47   All of which clearly depends on there being no error. Standards in UK fertility clinics are very high but, humanity being what it is, occasional mistakes must be made; again, it is in the nature of things that any such errors are likely to be discovered only in exceptional circumstances. Such an instance arose in *Leeds Teaching Hospital NHS Trust v A*.[92] Here, a white couple—Mr and Mrs A—were undergoing IVF treatment together. When twins were born, it was apparent that they were of mixed race and it was established that the sperm used had been provided by a Mr B who was also being treated with his wife. The issue of fatherhood was settled mainly on the basis of the consent requirements in s 28 of the 1990 Act. Clearly, Mr A did not consent to Mr B's sperm being used; he was, therefore, not the legal father by virtue of s 28(2). Section 28(3) was found not to apply to married couples despite some cogent arguments to the contrary; even if it did, the 'fundamental error' vitiated the whole concept of 'treatment together' for the purposes of the 1990 Act.[93] Furthermore, s 28(6), which excludes parenthood in the case of a consenting donor, could not be

[90] There is no significant difference in pregnancy or birth rates when either 2 or 3 embryos are implanted but the triplet rate is unacceptably high in the latter event. As a result, the HFEA has limited the number of embryos inserted to 2 per cycle save in the case of a woman over 40 years of age using her own eggs when three may be used (*Code of Practice* (2003), paras 8.20–8.22).

[91] The report of the House of Commons Science and Technology Committee (n 6 above) commented, at para 297, on the relatively poor results of IVF in the UK across Europe as measured by the number of embryos required to produce a live birth but was unable to explain it.

[92] [2003] 1 FLR 1091, (2003) 71 BMLR 168.   [93] Per Butler Sloss P at [37].

applied because Mr B did not consent to the use of his sperm. In the end, then, Mr B remained the legal father of the twins by virtue of their genetic relationship. The court also considered the human rights dimension of the case with particular reference to the rights and interests of the children. They would remain within a loving and stable home and their rights could be met by appropriate family or adoption orders—and these would be proportionate to the undoubted potential infringement of their rights to respect for their family life with Mr and Mrs A.

4.48   In our view, the main interest of *Leeds v A* lies in its value as a precedent. There is no doubt that it is an atypical case. Despite the fact that such a situation could arise within the terms of s 28 of the 1990 Act, there was no doubt that Mr A was *not* the father of the twins but all the parties were agreed that they should remain with the family into which they were born.[94] In relation to the question of a child's right to know his or her genetic origins,[95] Butler Sloss P emphasised that it was not a 'sperm donor' case and that to refuse to recognise Mr B as the twins' biological father would be to distort the truth which, some day, the twins would have to learn. Significantly, she said that, had she been compelled to do so, it would have been possible 'so to construe s 28(3) as to squeeze it into the present situation'.[96] There may come a time when the solution reached in the *Leeds* case is not in the best interests of the children. It may not be binding and the case is another good example of the importance of the particularities of individual cases in the evolution of medical law.[97]

OVUM AND EMBRYO DONATION

4.49   An alternative scenario is that the ovum is donated by another woman. The need might arise as being the only way in which a woman with, say, abdominal adhesions could have children and it might be desirable in the event of a potential mother carrying an X-linked genetic disease (see chapter 7); about 16 per cent of childlessness for female reasons is due to ovarian failure and the ovaries may be destroyed during, say, treatment for cancer. The procedure is, then, that the donated egg is fertilised by the husband's semen and the embryo then transferred to the wife's womb. The process can, therefore, be looked upon as the female variant of DI. The obvious practical difference is that, whereas spermatozoa are plentiful and easily harvested, ova are scarce and their recovery involves some discomfort and inconvenience to the donor. Thus, the donor must be stimulated hormonally in order to coincide with the

---

[94] It has been suggested that any adversarial litigation following a laboratory error would be based on a 'wrongful birth' action (chapter 6 below): M Ford and D Morgan '*Leeds Teaching Hospitals NHS Trust v A*— Addressing a Misconception' (2003) 15 CFLQ 199.

[95] See para 4.38 above. The device of giving legal parentage to the genetic father and legal responsibility to the social father is applauded in A Bainham 'Whose Sperm Is It Anyway?' [2003] CLJ 566.

[96] At [58].

[97] The happy conclusion in *Leeds General Hospital* can be compared with a Californian case in which a woman who received wrong embryos was awarded $1m in damages and yet may lose her baby to the true parents. The mistake was, however, deliberately concealed. Source: C Ayres 'Mother Wins $1m for IVF Mix-up but May Lose Son' (2004) *The Times*, 5 August, p 3.

recipient's optimal menstrual state and, in many cases, a laparoscopy will be required. The difficulties, then, associated with ovum donation lie not only in the technique but, also, in finding the donors—the process is such that pure altruism generally provides not more than a fraction of the overall requirement. Ova may be obtained from women in the course of other surgery—in particular, during sterilisation. There is, however, some concern lest their consent may be flawed in that a measure of coercion in the form, say, of free treatment is often used; the International Federation of Gynecology and Obstetrics has, in fact, declared that the process is unethical.[98] Nevertheless, centres in the United Kingdom may still pursue such arrangements provided that very strict criteria as to counselling, management and consent are met. The HFEA has also accepted, without great enthusiasm, the more common practice of 'egg sharing'—in which women who are, themselves, undergoing infertility treatment involving ovarian stimulation donate a proportion of their surplus ova for others to use. Very stringent requirements as to consent are imposed—including a double consent by the egg provider both as an IVF patient and a donor and consent by her male partner. In addition, special counselling as to the implications must be provided and agreements have to be reached as to the allocation of the eggs harvested and as to the settlement of costs—which may include redistribution of the expenses involved in the donor's own IVF treatment.[99] The Authority's hesitance to becoming involved is easy to understand—but, currently, the demand for eggs greatly outstrips their availability and 'egg-sharing' is a near essential component of satisfactory treatment services.

4.50   The difficulties associated with ovum donation or the delayed use of the patient's own ova are compounded by the fact that, in contrast to the storage of spermatozoa and early embryos, cryopreservation of ova is not proven to be entirely risk free in respect of induced chromosomal abnormality;[100] the HFEA has, however, sanctioned the use of stored ova in strictly controlled conditions.[101] An alternative, presently experimental, approach to the preservation of a woman's procreative capacity is to remove, store and, later, graft a portion of ovarian tissue; however, clinics will not be able to use oocytes obtained from frozen ovarian tissue in treatment until HFEA is better convinced of the safety of the method.[102]

---

[98] *Recommendations on Ethical Issues in Obstetrics and Gynecology* (1997) 133 Bull Med Ethics 8. See also the restrictions in Canada under the Assisted Human Reproduction Act 2004. The main problem is that of the woman developing the ovarian hyper-stimulation syndrome including the formation of ovarian cysts and the so-far unproven risks of more serious sequelae. See L Bernier and D Grégoirs 'Reproductive and Therapeutic Cloning, Germline Therapy, and Purchase of Gametes and Embryos: Comments on Canadian Legislation Governing Reproduction Technologies' (2004) 30 J Med Ethics 527.

[99] HFEA *Code of Practice* (2003), Appendix A. Currently, direct payments of more than £15 (plus reasonable expenses) for straightforward gamete donation are disallowed.

[100] Though it has to be noted that IVF using frozen embryos results in significantly lower live birth rates than when using fresh embryos: 17% as against 29% (HFEA *IVF National Data Statistics* 1 April 2000–31 March 2001).

[101] In particular frozen eggs are not to be mixed with fresh eggs in any configuration. Currently, 21 clinics are licensed to store frozen human eggs.

[102] HFEA *Code of Practice* (2003), Appendix H.

4.51   Once fertilisation by the husband or partner and implantation of a donated ovum has been achieved, however, the natural—though not the genetic—parentage will be reasonably clear. It is difficult to see any circumstances in which motherhood would be challenged[103] and, in a patrilineal society, there are fewer objections to an admixture of ovum-derived genes in the family than to those which arise as a result of DI. In any event, the matter is put beyond legal doubt by s 27(1) of the 1990 Act which holds that a woman who carries a child as a result of the placing in her of an embryo or of sperm and eggs, and no other woman, is to be treated as the mother of the child.

4.52   But what of the similar wife with an infertile husband or partner (or, of course, the infertile, single woman who wants a child)? Such a combination could, theoretically, arise in about one in every 400 marriages or partnerships seeking children. Such a state can be managed by embryo donation whereby an embryo preformed from donated ovum and donated sperm is implanted in the infertile woman. The resultant complications then lie somewhere between those of in vitro fertilisation and those surrounding surrogate motherhood and are best discussed under that heading below. Even so, it is emotionally, morally and legally important to distinguish unrelated embryo transfer of this type from surrogate motherhood—the intense relationship between mother and fetus occurs in both but, in normal circumstances, does not progress to that between mother and child in the latter procedure. Once again, the 1990 Act has cleared the legal air; by virtue of ss 27 and 28, the child born of embryo donation is, for all purposes, the child of the carrying mother and her consenting husband or partner.

THE AVAILABILITY OF IVF

4.53   We have discussed some of the moral issues surrounding assisted reproduction under the heading of donor insemination. Very much the same principles apply in the case of the infertile wife. There is, however, one major, and obvious, difference—while DI is a relatively simple process, IVF and its counterparts are both cost- and manpower-intensive. Problems of resource allocation are, thus, superimposed on those of ethical practice.[104] The response to the question of whether the effort applied to the alleviation of childlessness is well- or mis-directed is such a personal matter that specific discussion would be invidious; the general principles of resource allocation are outlined in chapter 11 below. In point of fact, the government now aims to provide three free cycles of IVF to interfile couples on a national basis but it is unlikely to come to pass for several years[105]—indeed, it is doubtful if the Health Service will be

---

[103] See *Ampthill Peerage* [1977] AC 547, HL, per Lord Simon at 577.

[104] For a very controversial and critical early review of the cost-effectiveness of the IVF programme, see M G Wagner and P A St Clair 'Are In Vitro Fertilisation and Embryo Transfer of Benefit to All?' (1989) 2 Lancet 1027.

[105] National Institute for Clinical Excellence *Fertility: Assessment and Treatment for People with Fertility Problems* accessible at www.nice.org.uk. See also R E Ashcroft 'In Vitro Fertilisation for All?' (2003) 327 BMJ 511; J R McMillan 'NICE, the Draft Fertility Guideline and Dodging the Big Question' (2003) 29 J Med Ethics 313.

able to provide more than one cycle.[106] We are, however, here concerned with the broader question of whether, an in what circumstances, IVF should be available to fertile couples. This involves a consideration of the motives behind the request—and these are many and varied.[107]

4.54   Simplistically, one could classify the possible reasons into medical and non-medical, although we will see that this is not the easy division that might be supposed. In essence, the ethics of embryo selection mirror those of sperm selection which we have discussed above save for the fact that we are now dealing with an organism which, *of itself,* has the potential for human development; put at its lowest level, the human embryo is deserving of *some* respect and protection in law.[108] There may be good medical reasons, mainly in relation to the carriage of abnormal recessive genes, which the likely majority of persons would see as justifying appropriate intervention on behalf of otherwise fertile couples; indeed, IVF combined with preimplantation genetic diagnosis (PGD), may offer the *correct* management.[109]

4.55   Rather more uncertainty surrounds the extension of pre-implantation diagnosis into the realm of therapy—currently into therapy for an existing child that suffers from genetic disability; this involves the production of an embryo that is not only genetically but also tissue-type compatible with the disabled child so that, following its birth, its umbilical stem cells can be used to supply a normal gene for its affected elder sibling. The HFEA agreed to provide licences for this process on a case by case basis in 2001. This policy was, however, challenged by way of judicial review of a case intended to benefit a child suffering from the genetic disease of β-thalassaemia; the application was successful.[110] In essence Kay J held that the purpose of the 1990 Act was to protect the in vitro embryo and that, accordingly, tissue typing came within the constraints of s 3. Furthermore, a licence to provide treatment services was provided for the purpose of 'assisting women to carry children'—and this did not cover the purpose of the proposed procedure which, of itself, would not affect the carrying of the subsequent child.

4.56   The 'Hashmi case' then went to appeal[111] which was allowed. The basis for the unanimous decision can be summed up in the words of Lord Phillips. The Master of the Rolls agreed that it would be strange if the law prohibited the practical application of research designed to detect the presence of genetic abnormalities in embryos before implantation which Parliament had approved; he then went on to say:

---

[106] The cost per cycle is estimated as £2771 and the total cost to the NHS for full implementation would be around £85m per annum: BBC News http://news.bbc.co.uk/1/hi/health/3516941.stm.

[107] An early, but still authoritative, review is to be found in K Dawson and P Singer 'Should Fertile People Have Access to In Vitro Fertilisation?' (1990) 300 BMJ 167.

[108] Warnock Committee at para 11.17. See para 4.65 below for further discussion.

[109] For an excellent review of the advantages and shortcomings of PGD, see J R Botkin 'Ethical Issues and Practical Problems in Preimplantation Genetic Diagnosis' (1998) 26 J L Med & Ethics 17. A PGD National Service for Scotland will be introduced in April 2005.

[110] *R (on the application of Quintavalle on behalf of Comment on Reproductive Ethics) v Human Fertilisation and Embryology Authority* [2003] 2 All ER 105, (2003) 70 BMLR 236, QBD.

[111] *R (on the application of Quintavalle) v Human Fertilisation and Embryology Authority* [2003] 3 All ER 257, (2003) 73 BMLR 116, CA, affirmed [2005] 2 All ER 555, (2005) 83 BMLR 143, HL.

[I]f the impediment to bearing a child is concern that it may be born with a hereditary defect, treatment which enables women to become pregnant and to bear children in the confidence that they will not be suffering from such defects can properly be described as 'for the purpose of assisting women to carry children'.[112]

Which, of course, deals with PGD. As to tissue typing, he added:

No evidence suggests that the wish of a woman to bear a child in order to provide a source of stem cells for a sick or dying sibling was anticipated at [the time the Act was passed]. Such a wish is now the reality,[113]

and the only difference between activities that were already regularly licensed and tissue typing was the nature of the 'desired characteristics' of the embryo. Lord Phillips concluded that IVF treatment that includes PGD constituted 'treatment for the purpose of assisting women to bear children' irrespective of the purpose of the PGD.

4.57   The 'Hashmi case' was another which generated much emotional public support and there is no doubt that the decision of the Court of Appeal was in line with current popular opinion. As indicated, however, we do have our reservations as to its general adoption. The creation of a number of embryos with the avowed intention of destroying the majority, which is inherent in the IVF process as a whole, is undoubtedly amplified by the use of this procedure. We feel, however, that it infringes more than 'respect' for the status of the embryo and can also be seen as offending the fundamental Kantian principle that a person should not be used as a means—the procedure involves the creation of a child primarily as a therapeutic tool for the benefit of its sibling and that child is undoubtedly a person.[114] Further, we are, perhaps, even more concerned with the practical possibility that the therapy does not work; attitudes to the new arrival, which will undoubtedly have been loving and caring at its inception, may change to those of acute disappointment—in which case, the provision of IVF cannot be said to have been in the neonate's best interests.[115] There can be few applications of the technique that merit more intensive counselling and, at the time of writing, the case is proceeding to the House of Lords. (See now n 111 above.)

4.58   Non-medical reasons are of several types, the extreme being, perhaps, that of sex

---

[112] At para [43].   [113] At para [47].

[114] It has been suggested that Kant only proscribes treating persons *solely* as a means: R Boyle and J Savulescu 'Ethics of Using Pre-implantation Genetic Diagnosis to Select a Stem Cell Donor for an Existing Person' (2001) 323 BMJ 1240. The same approach is adopted by B Mulvenna 'Pre-implantation Genetic Diagnosis, Tissue Typing and Beyond: The Legal Implications of the Hashmi Case' (2004) 6 Med Law Internat 163. The issue appears to us, however, to be no more than one of degree.

[115] Shortly after the decision, the HFEA refused a licence for similar treatment to be applied in the case of Charlie Whittaker who was suffering from Diamond-Blackfan anaemia. The reason given was that, while it was possible to ensure that an embryo was not affected by β-thalassaemia, it was not possible to test for Diamond-Blackfan disease. It might well, therefore, not be in the interests of the 'saviour sibling' to be born. Although the reasoning seems hard, it does seem to pay lip service to the fragile Kantian principles. For a rather similar argument, see D King 'Why We Should Not Permit Embryos to be Selected as Tissue Donors' (2003) Bull Med Ethics no. 190, 13. The distinction is forcibly criticised in S Sheldon and S Wilkinson 'Hashmi and Whitaker: An Unjustifiable and Misguided Distinction?' (2004) 12 Med L Rev 137.

selection as a matter of parental choice.[116] The issue arose as something of a *cause célèbre* in 2000 when a couple wished to ensure the birth of a girl, having lost their only daughter in tragic circumstances.[117] IVF as a method of sex selection is discouraged, but not wholly excluded by the HFEA.[118] In this particular instance, no clinic could be found which was willing to undertake the case and Mr and Mrs Masterton, who were later unsuccessfully treated in Italy, may yet plead their case in the European Court of Human Rights. It will, however, be seen that the case demonstrates the difficulties of categorisation. If the parents can show that they are suffering from, say, a demonstrable reactive depression as a result of their loss, selective replacement of their child *becomes* a medical treatment and the moral high ground has shifted— though perhaps not far enough to justify disregard for the interests of the resulting child. Even so, there is a tenable case for holding that we should not pass judgment in respect of a personal dilemma which affects no-one else.[119]

4.59   Other 'non-medical' reasons for 'fertile IVF treatment' include the early removal of ova and their impregnation for use in later life, thus circumventing the increased risk of chromosomal abnormalities in the child of a late pregnancy, or, secondly, the wholly hedonistic use of 'womb-leasing' for social reasons. The latter is discussed below.[120] As to the former, there are no legal objections in the United Kingdom to preserving embryos in the same way as sperm and a case for women deliberately delaying their pregnancies can be made out on grounds of social utility. There are, however, practical difficulties. The problems introduced by limitations on the storage times for embryos have been alleviated to an extent since the maximum time was raised to ten years provided the storage was for treatment purposes. Even so, there are important conditions as to the clinical status of the gamete providers which restrict the concession to genuine cases of medical need and storage cannot continue beyond the 55th birthday of the woman involved; the limit remains at five years if these conditions are not met. Secondly, the risks of pregnancy itself rise dramatically with age—the maternal mortality rate over the age of 40 is some ten times that in the case of women aged 20–24.[121] Thirdly, the pregnancy rate following embryo transfer

[116] Purely preferential reasons are criticised, inter alia, on sexist grounds. J A Robertson 'Extending Preimplantation Diagnosis: Medical and Non-medical Uses' (2003) 29 J Med Ethics 213 has pointed out that this applies only to the selection of the sex of a first child.

[117] See, for example, K Scott 'IVF Selection Still Off Limits' *Guardian*, 19 October 2000.

[118] HFEA *Code of Practice* (2001) para 9.9 says that Centres *should* not select the sex of embryos for social reasons (our emphasis). PGD for medical reasons is, of course, accepted. This restrictive attitude is not held universally: S Gottlieb 'US Doctors Say Sex Selection Acceptable for Non-medical Reasons' (2001) 323 BMJ 828. Interestingly, a Scottish survey indicated that only 8% of persons favoured giving parents the right to choose the sex of their unborn children: V Hannah 'Scots Reject Creation of Designer Children' *The Herald*, 8 November 2000.

[119] It is, of course, equally possible to argue that the deontological problem involved *is* a matter for public decision and the issue is now due for consideration.

[120] See para 4.79.   [121] Editorial Comment 'Too Old to have a Baby?' (1993) 341 Lancet 344.

deteriorates with age[122] and, finally, the indications are that older women require the implantation of more embryos than do the young in order to achieve the same implantation rate.[123]

4.60   We discuss the concept of ageism later[124] and there is no doubt that there is, at least, emotional discrimination against the old that is based on little more than societal conditioning. Have we any moral right to discriminate against an older woman in denying her access to motherhood when we would provide the facilities without qualm to her younger sister in otherwise identical circumstances? It is difficult to support such a policy when the woman herself is providing the scarce resource—the eggs—as is the case in IVF provided for the premenopausal woman. The counterargument depends, of course, on the effect on the consequent child and it is not difficult to dream up circumstances in which an 'ageing' mother could be seen as a disadvantage to a young child. Nevertheless, given that we would not consider depriving 40-year-old women of natural pregnancy, it seems paternalistic in the extreme to deny them assisted reproductive services on the grounds of age alone. It is for these reasons that we find it hard to support judicial acceptance of a health authority's decision not to purchase infertility services for women above the age of 35[125]—an age which, to one of us at least, appears to be that of golden adolescence! We might add, in parentheses, that the same may not apply to the post-menopausal woman. Quite apart from the fact that, here, we are dealing with ovum donation—and, hence, with a publicly scarce resource—treatment in this case is not that of an unfortunate abnormality but is, rather, an interference with the natural order. Paternalism is, thus, excluded from the equation and we are free to concentrate entirely on the resultant child—and with good reason when we hear of a 62-year-old Frenchwoman giving birth to a child derived from her brother's sperm.[126] None the less, the British Medical Association has declared its antagonism to an age-based limitation.[127]

---

[122] Figures are not available for the use of frozen embryos. Otherwise, this statement appears to be true only when the woman is using her own eggs. The live birth rate in the case of women aged 40–44 is then only 5.4% as opposed to 17.2% when donor eggs are used. There is a similar trend in the case of AID. See also A Templeton, J Morris and B Parslow 'Factors that Affect Outcome of In Vitro Fertilisation Treatment' (1996) 348 Lancet 1402.

[123] M G R Hull, C F Fleming, A O Hughes and A McDermott 'The Age-related Decline in Female Fecundity' (1996) 65 Fertil Steril 783. Despite all this, the Dutch are, apparently, prepared to provide IVF for older women: T Sheldon 'IVF Could be Offered to Older Women in the Netherlands' (1996) 312 BMJ 1319.

[124] See chapter 12.

[125] R v Sheffield Health Authority, ex p Seale (1994) 25 BMLR 1. It is to be noted that HFEA imposes age limits for gamete donors. In respect of treatment, gametes should not be taken from women over 35 and men over 45. Gametes must not be taken for treatment from persons below the age of 18. These limits may be relaxed when the gametes are to be used for self-treatment or in exceptional circumstances: Code of Practice (2003) paras 4.22–4.25. The intended availability of IVF through the NHS is to be limited to women under 40.

[126] C Bremner 'French Woman Aged 62 Has Brother's Baby' The Times, 21 June 2001, p 13. The procedure was carried out in California.

[127] (1994) 308 BMJ 723. There seems little limit to human ingenuity in the 'new reproductive era'; a mother has taken the Tees Health Authority to task for not providing an unmarried 17-year-old with IVF: P Wilkinson 'Mother Demands IVF for Teenager' The Times, 13 November 1999, p 3.

4.61   As in the case of DI, the question of the child's well-being raises the question of the potential mother's status—single, lesbian or of doubtful suitability. Here, in contrast to the DI situation, medical involvement in the procedure is essential if it is to be undertaken; it follows that the doctor cannot opt out of judgments, despite the fact that they involve purely social values. It is for this reason that the guidelines for assisted reproductive treatment centres included, from an early stage, the establishment, and use, of an ethical committee which has a wide remit as to the management of individual cases. No legally enforceable principles as to selection of candidates for the limited resource have been laid down, although the *Code of Practice*, as we have noted, contains a number of arguably intrusive conditions. In the only apposite case so far reported, refusal of treatment on the grounds that the patient had a history of prostitution and had been rejected as an adopter, was not considered so questionable as to provide grounds for judicial review of the decision.[128]

4.62   Nor is there, in our opinion, a great deal of help to be obtained from the 1990 Act, s 13(5). This, as noted above under DI, states that a woman shall not be provided with treatment services unless account has been taken of the welfare of any child born as a result of the treatment and of any other child who may be affected by the birth. Not only is this condition extremely wide—*any* child within the extended family might be said to be affected—but it is imprecise as to the quality and depth of account to be taken other than subtly indicating a covert disapproval of treatment outside the 'married' state. Moreover, it seems to us to have its own dangers. 'Taking account of' does not imply reaching a uniform conclusion; it is not too far-fetched to envisage 'shopping expeditions' on the part of unconventional would-be mothers to identify the most 'liberal' clinic as a source of treatment.

The legal position of the clinician

4.63   All procedures involving gamete donation carry the risk that the gametes themselves are defective and, as we have seen, this is a major justification for controlling the treatment of childlessness. Moreover, all those involving in vitro embryo transfer introduce the additional hazard that the embryo will be damaged either by the hormonal treatment required for superovulation or during manipulation and that an abnormal fetus will result. Animal experiments indicate that there is no higher incidence of abnormalities in live born neonates resulting from reimplantation than in those which are conceived normally and reports of an excess of human cases beyond the probability of chance are very rare.[129] The HFEA's Annual Report of 2000 (the last figures available) quoted 120 children born as a result of IVF, DI or

---

[128]   *R v Ethical Committee of St Mary's Hospital (Manchester), ex p H (or Harriott)* [1988] 1 FLR 512, [1988] Fam Law 165. The possibility was not foreclosed—the greater part of the argument turned on whether the Committee was purely advisory or whether it had administrative responsibility. The case was also somewhat clouded by allegations of deceit.

[129]   A disturbing report has, however, come from Australia: M Hansen, J J Kurinczuk, C Bower and S Webb 'The Risk of Major Birth Defects after Intractyoplasmic Sperm Injection and In Vitro Fertilization' (2002) 346 New Engl J Med 725. The incidence of defects is said to be twice that following normal conception.

micromanipulation having developmental defects or syndromes—an occurrence of 1.3 per cent of babies born, which does not indicate any increased risk.[130] The outcome of litigation following such a misfortune would depend largely on proof of causation. However, the ground rules are clear. Section 44 of the 1990 Act applies the Congenital Disabilities (Civil Liability) Act 1976, s 1 to infertility treatments in that, if a child resulting from embryo transfer, GIFT,[131] micromanipulation or DI is born disabled and the disability results from an act or omission in the course of the selection, or the keeping or use outside the body, of the embryo or the gametes used by a person answerable to the child, then the child's disabilities are to be regarded as damage resulting from the wrongful act of that person and actionable at the suit of the child. This does not apply if one or both parents knew of the risk of their child being born disabled; particular importance is, therefore, likely to attach to the effectiveness of their consent in respect of the information given. Interestingly, this seems to open the door to an action for 'wrongful life'.[132]

UTERINE LAVAGE

4.64   Uterine lavage represents a somewhat unusual extension of the technique of IVF through embryo transfer. In this process, a fertile woman is impregnated with semen; the resultant embryo is washed out of the uterus before implantation and is transferred to the infertile patient. While such a process might be seen as constituting an abortion, for reasons discussed below (chapter 5), it is improbable that it would be considered so in the United Kingdom. The Warnock Committee looked at the matter from the point of view of the donor and concluded (para 7.5) that the risks were such that the technique of embryo donation by lavage should not be used at that time— and it is still regarded with some scepticism. The method seems to us to be so comparable to the practice of animal husbandry that there are good policy reasons for its proscription. Nevertheless, the current British legislation clearly allows for the use of embryos formed in vivo (1990 Act, Sch 3, para 7).

THE SURPLUS EMBRYO

4.65   It is inevitable that surplus embryos will be produced whether IVF or ovum donation is being attempted. The status and disposal of such embryos have significance which is independent of the problems of successful implantation.

---

[130] The occurrence differs according to the method used—0.9% for fresh IVF and 1.4% for DI. The rates are of the same order whether IVF is 'fresh' (0.9%) or involves the use of frozen embryos (1.2%).

[131] I Kennedy and A Grubb *Medical Law* (3rd edn, 2000) p 1530 point out that GIFT may not be included by reason of the precise wording of the section. We believe that, should it be questioned, it would be decided on the basis of 'Parliamentary intention' as per *R (on the application of Quintavalle) v Secretary of State for Health* [2003] 2 AC 687, [2003] 2 All ER113, HL.

[132] See para 6.3 below.

4.66   In so far as the embryo has no legal status, the problem can be characterised as purely ethical and one which turns on the *nature* of the embryo. As already noted, the Warnock Committee (at para 11.17) recommended only that the embryo of the human species should be afforded *some* protection in law. Such prevarication indicates the measure of the moral difficulties involved but is, at the same time, unhelpful. The extreme positions can be summarised as holding either that the embryo is a full human being—in accordance with rigid theological, perhaps mainly Roman Catholic, doctrine—or, as the pure scientist might claim, it is a laboratory artefact, comparable to a culture of human tissue. The individual must, then, decide on his or her moral stance—does one stand at either extreme or can one establish a tenable intermediate position?

4.67   We have argued previously that 'humanity' is not established until implantation— this being largely on the grounds that it is only at implantation that the embryo achieves a capacity for meaningful development.[133] The acceptance of a 'specific moment' theory as to the acquisition of humanity is, however, by no means universal; an alternative approach suggested by Poplawski and Gillett[134] is to regard the process of becoming a human person as 'a progression through a series of linked developmental stages' and to attribute rights to the embryo because it represents a phase in the whole human form. The authors went on to base this moral value on the human capacity to react with others—a capacity which exists in modified form from implantation to death. We find this approach helpful, if only in a negative way, because, despite the authors' disclaimer, none of their perfectly valid analysis applies to the embryo in vitro. In the absence of implantation, there is no continuum and there is no human interaction; moreover, no moral value can be attributed to the embryo by virtue of its potential for personhood—for no such potential exists in the medium of the petri dish.[135]

4.68   Acceptance of this premise also solves one's moral problems as to embryonic research which, when well done, must be valuable to the community as a whole. Nevertheless, this conclusion cannot be accepted without qualification—at the very least, the embryo must be accorded the respect due to any living human tissue. It could be replied that, in logic, there is no need to control laboratory interference with a research object that one believes has no human status; but there *is* public disquiet over scientific involvement in the reproductive process and, on these grounds alone, it must be contained within a controlling framework. Most importantly, the morality of the argument rests upon the limitations of current technology. It is clear that our

[133] J K Mason *Medico-legal Aspects of Reproduction and Parenthood* (2nd edn, 1998) at 234. For the argument based on 'ensoulment', see N M Ford *When Did I Begin?* (1988) at 56, 171. Perhaps 'humanity' and 'ensoulment' are different expressions of the same thing.

[134] N Poplawski and G Gillett 'Ethics and Embryos' (1991) 17 J Med Ethics 62.

[135] However, even if one concludes that the unimplanted surplus embryo has no moral value *of itself*, it could be that we should accord it *some* value on the grounds that it has considerable moral importance for others. This approach is sometimes referred to as 'transitivity of respect'—on which, see M A Warren *Moral Status* (1997) p 170.

formula would be inadequate should technology advance to the state of being able to 'grow' fetuses to full term in vitro; were this to happen, we would be confronted with the production of non-humanised human beings, which would be intolerable.

4.69   But, whenever one considers technical limitation as representing a barrier on the theoretical 'slippery slope', one inevitably asks: 'for how long will we be able to do so?'[136] For the present, the interests of the embryo/fetus are protected from encroachment by the 1990 Act, s 3(3)(a) which, in essence, makes it a criminal offence, punishable by up to ten years' imprisonment, to keep or use an embryo in vitro that is more than 14 days old—excluding any time spent in suspended animation while frozen. Even so, this specific time limit can be attacked, mainly on the grounds that a 13-day embryo is no less alive than is one of 15 days' gestation and that it is entitled to the same respect—as is the embryo formed at fertilisation.[137] The counter-argument is that *some* controlled embryonic research is essential if the attack on genetic disease—which may well be the most important single factor dictating morbidity in humans—is to be carried on in a scientifically acceptable way.

4.70   Given that the undeveloped in vitro embryo merits a certain, albeit unspecified, respect, its management presents a dilemma of which there are three major elements. The first is that of the use of and, indeed, the production of embryos for research purposes; this highly emotive issue is discussed in chapter 19. The second is closely related and concerns the pre-implantation selection of embryos as potential neonatal therapeutic agents. We have discussed the possibility of creating siblings with the aim of providing donor cells above at para 4.55. Although this raises formidable ethical issues, we have seen that they can be solved—at least at the legal level.

4.71   The third main problem derived from embryonal status relates to the practical problems surrounding the disposal of those that are surplus to immediate therapeutic needs. As already mentioned, overproduction of embryos is inherent in the treatment of infertility by IVF; it is impossible to guarantee receptive wombs for those which remain unused in the individual case and, in many instances involving defective embryos, it could be wrong to attempt to implant them all. It follows that any new legislation that attempted to criminalise the necessary destruction of embryos would, at the same time, effectively shut the door on this form of treatment. In practice, the United Kingdom stands virtually alone within Europe in that current legislation allows for the production of embryos for the express purpose of research. Within this protective envelope, the disposal of gametes and embryos depends almost entirely on the consent and, hence, the decision of those donating the gametes. It follows that whether or not an embryo can be used for treatment or research or whether it is to be

---

[136] It has been reported that competent researchers anticipate the availability of artificial wombs within a few years: R McKie 'Men Redundant? Now We Don't Need Women Either' *Observer*, 10 February 2002.

[137] Much of the argument was developed in the early days when IVF was being introduced. See T Inglesias 'In vitro Fertilisation: The Major Issues' (1984) 10 J Med Ethics 32. The same issue contains a contrary view from a moralist: G R Dunstan 'The Moral Status of the Human Embryo: A Tradition Recalled' (1984) 10 J Med Ethics 38. See also M Lockwood (ed) *Moral Dilemmas in Modern Medicine* (1985) ch 1; and the philosophical argument in A Holland 'A Fortnight of My Life is Missing' (1990) 7 J Appl Philos 25.

destroyed at a certain time or in certain circumstances—e.g. on the death of the donor—depends upon the agreed consent of the two progenitors (1990 Act, Sch 3, para 6). The 1990 Act, however, makes no provision for the condition most likely to cause difficulty—that is, when there is disagreement between the two parties concerned. The need for some such form of legislation was foreshadowed in two significant American cases, the first of which arose in Tennessee in 1989. Here, a married couple who had provided stored embryos were divorced before the latter could be used. The father asked that they be destroyed while the mother wished to become pregnant by them. The judge at first instance ruled that the embryos were human beings—with all the rights attending that status—and that their fate should, therefore, be decided on the principle of their best interests; this meant that they should be implanted. This decision was reversed by the State Supreme Court, which held that the man's interest in not reproducing outweighed those of his spouse in procreating.[138] In a more recent case, the New York Court of Appeal came down firmly in favour of the enforceability of a valid preconception contract[139]—but this assumes, firstly, that there is a contract and, secondly, that it is unambiguous. Similar cases were bound to arise in the United Kingdom and this has recently come to pass.

4.72   The case of *Evans and Hadley*[140] is complex and was subject to a particularly thorough examination by Wall J. There is insufficient space in a book of this type for a full analysis[141] and, in the end, the issue was, essentially, a matter of statute law with very little ethical component. In essence, the case concerned two couples who had stored embryos which they had not used successfully before they parted. The women were anxious to become pregnant but both male gamete donors withdrew their consents to storage and subsequent use of the embryos which, in effect, meant that they should be allowed to die. Amongst other pleas, Ms Evans and Mrs Hadley sought injunctions requiring restoration of their partners' consent, declarations that they could be lawfully treated during an extended period of storage and, uniquely, a declaration that the restrictions imposed by the 1990 Act were incompatible with the Human Rights Act 1998 by way, particularly, of Articles 8 and 12 of the European Convention. Additionally, Articles 2 and 8 were pleaded in respect of the embryos themselves.

4.73   The first and second pleas were disposed of on the grounds of the statutory requirements as to consent. Consent had been given to the use of the embryos for treatment of the donors 'together'; treatment together was provided when the

---

[138] *Davis v Davis* 842 SW 2d 588 (Tenn Sup Ct, 1992). The case was, however, clouded by the fact that Mrs Davis now only wanted to donate the embryos; the court recognised that the issue would have been closer had she still wanted to become pregnant.

[139] *Kass v Kass* 696 NE 2d 174 (NY, 1998) where the issue turned very much on the interpretation of the couple's instructions—an example of how difficult the drafting of 'advance directives' of all sorts can be.

[140] *Evans v Amicus Healthcare Ltd, Hadley v Midland Fertility Services Ltd* [2003] 4 All ER 903, (2003) 75 BMLR 115.

[141] One of us has attempted this elsewhere: J K Mason 'Discord and Disposal of Embryos' (2004) 8 Edin LR 84.

embryos were transferred into the woman[142] and, by this time, the couples were no longer together. Thus, there was no effective consent either to storage or use of the embryos by either of the women on their own and, accordingly, the clinic could not store or use the embryos lawfully.[143] Wall J found the human rights aspects of the case to be far more demanding—particularly those governed by Article 8 of the Convention. In the end, he decided that the provisions of the 1990 Act, Sch 3 do interfere with the right to respect for a person's private life but that any infringement applies equally to each gamete donor. Moreover, the court considered that the provisions of the 1990 Act, based as it was on consent of the parties and the interests of the unborn child, were proportionate to the restrictions they imposed. A possible infringement of the rights of the embryo to life was dismissed fairly peremptorily, largely on the grounds that it is illogical to attribute a right to life to the embryo when no such right attaches to the fetus.[144] An appeal by Ms Evans was, predictably, rejected.[145] Thorpe LJ summed up:

> To dilute [the requirement for bilateral consent to implantation] in the interests of proportionality, in order to meet Ms Evans's otherwise intractable biological handicap, by making the withdrawal of the man's consent relevant but inconclusive, would create new and even more intractable difficulties of arbitrariness and inconsistency . . . The sympathy and concern which anyone felt for Ms Evans was not enough to render the legislative scheme of Schedule 3 disproportionate.

4.74   *Evans and Hadley* was a generally unpopular decision but there is no doubt that it was the correct legal result given the fact that it reflected the unarguable will of Parliament. Nonetheless, this still leaves open the question of whether a law framed some 15 years ago remains good law. Our main concern lies in the fact that, in this particular area, it is founded on the principle of equality between the gamete donors. Yet it is undeniable that mammalian reproduction is not gender neutral—within the spectrum of assisted reproduction, it is far more difficult for the woman to produce eggs than for the man to produce sperm, the woman must carry the embryo from implantation to birth and it is she who will nurse the neonate. It is because of this disparity of biological contribution that we have suggested in previous editions of this book that, in the event of discord, British legislation should allow for 'a right of management' (akin to a property claim) to be vested in the person for whom the embryos were intended—that is, the proposed woman recipient.[146] This solution,

---

[142] See also *Re R (a child)* [2003] 2 All ER 131, (2003) 71 BMLR 157 which disposes of the argument that insertion of the embryo is merely consequential to the *mixing* of the sperm and eggs.

[143] 1990 Act, Sch 3, para 6(3).

[144] It is arguable that this is paralogic in so far as the absence of fetal rights derives from a possible conflict of interests between the fetus and its mother; no such conflict exists between the embryo in vitro and its progenitors (see also para 4.66). It is, however, clear that a limitation on embryonic rights exists *throughout* the IVF programme.

[145] *Evans v Amicus Healthcare Ltd* [2004] 3 All ER 1025, [2004] 3 WLR 681. Leave to appeal to the House of Lords was refused but it understood that the case is being taken to the European Court of Human Rights.

[146] We discuss this further in chapter 15.

admittedly, ignores the man's interest in his genetic survival and it opens the door to imposing unwanted financial obligations on him in the future.[147] The former seems a relatively small price to pay for the advantage to women, many of whom, like Ms Evans, will have no more gametes to provide.[148] The latter can be dealt with by legislation—there seems little reason why a man who wishes to opt out of an arrangement should not be granted the same legal immunity as that accorded the anonymous sperm donor.[149] A major review of the 1990 Act is now being undertaken—it may well be appropriate for Parliament to consider incorporating the lessons learned from *Evans and Hadley*.

4.75   In passing, it is to be noted that the power of both gamete donors to decide the fate of the embryo is limited by statute even when they are in accord—stored gametes must be destroyed at the end of ten years and embryos must be allowed to perish after five years' preservation (1990 Act, ss 14(3) and (4)) unless they are to be used for treatment in the special circumstances outlined in para 4.59. This, at least, sets a limit to the difficulties in estate planning and the like that are inherent within a permitted policy of indefinite preservation of embryos.[150]

THE SURPLUS FETUS

4.76   The management of both infertility and childlessness due to abnormalities in the female provokes the particular problem of multiple pregnancies. Hormone treatment of primary infertility can be over-successful and result in pregnancies involving anything up to sextuplets—and, occasionally, beyond. As to childlessness, the chances of in vitro fertilisation ending in a live birth are improved by the insertion of 2–3 embryos and more than one of these then implants in about 27 per cent of those transfers that result in pregnancy.[151] Few people can afford to bring up several children of the same age at the same time. Moreover, the common scenario of high order pregnancies which lead to live birth is that the infants are of very low birthweight; they occupy the facilities of a neonatal intensive care unit to a disproportionate extent; the parents face the spectre of their children dying one by one over a period of weeks

---

[147] By way of the Child Support Act 1991.

[148] A Mrs Grant of Inverness was in the same position and her embryos were destroyed on the instructions of her former husband. It seems that, at least, women will now have to be informed before unilateral action can be taken: F Gibb 'Woman Who Lost IVF Embryos Wins Change in the Law' (2003) *The Times*, 20 May, p 2.

[149] 1990 Act, s 28(6).

[150] Despite its antiquity, H Brown, M Dent, L M Dyer et al 'Legal Rights and Issues Surrounding Conception, Pregnancy, and Birth' (1986) 39 Vanderbilt LR 597 remains one of the best reviews of the many legal problems introduced by artificial reproductive methods. The relatively academic problems of succession of 'twin embryos' that are implanted at different times are settled by the elimination of 'storage time' from the age of an embryo (1990 Act, s 3(4)).

[151] HFEA *IVF National Data Statistics* (2000–2001).

and those that survive may well be brain damaged as a result of prematurity.[152] It is largely in order to circumvent this prospect that the current United Kingdom Code of Practice now decrees that no more than two eggs or embryos are to be transferred in any one cycle; as an exception to the rule, women over the age of 40 may be implanted with no more than three embryos when using their own embryos.[153] Nevertheless, even triplets[154] may be an unwelcome result of a successful treatment and evidence has been adduced that a multiple pregnancy rate of over 40 per cent arises when more eggs are used in the GIFT process.[155] Moreover, the superfetation of hormone therapy is hard to control. Thus, the clinician may well be faced with the option of pregnancy reduction in utero.

4.77   This process, which is carried out at or earlier than the twelfth week of pregnancy, is generally known as selective reduction of pregnancy, but it has been pointed out that, as the individual fetal characteristics are unknown at the time, there is no 'selection' other than that dictated by operative convenience. We prefer the suggested alternative of reduction of multifetal pregnancy[156]—a description which serves to distinguish the process from the truly selective termination that may be used, say, when one fetus of twins is found to be compromised. The legality of the practice depends upon additions to the Abortion Act 1967 arising from the 1990 Act, s 37(5); its morality is inseparable from that of abortion.[157]

---

[152] In a particularly publicised case, a woman conceived octuplets through a series of adventures and misadventures. She decided to maintain her pregnancy and all eight were stillborn at 19 weeks: Leading Article 'The Death of Babies' *Daily Telegraph*, 4 October 1996, p 25. At much the same time, a furore erupted when a woman carrying twins elected to have one of them aborted: C Dyer 'Selective Abortions Hit the Headlines' (1996) 313 BMJ 380; J Woods 'Mother's Dilemma over the Right to Choose Life' *Scotsman*, 6 August 1996.

[153] HFEA *Code of Practice* (6th edn, 2003), paras. 8.20–8.21. The Authority's right to limit practice in such a way has been upheld in the Court of Appeal: *R (on the application of Assisted Reproduction and Gynaecology Centre) v Human Fertilisation and Embryology Authority* [2002] Lloyd's Rep Med 148.

[154] Triplets may, of course, arise from two embryos by the chance of individual twinning. Some 5% of clinical pregnancies derived from the transfer of three embryos will result in a triple pregnancy. In *Thompson v Sheffield Fertility Clinic* (QBD, unreported, 24 November 2000), three embryos were inserted into a woman who had requested that only two be used. She was delivered of triplets and accepted an award of £20,000 for loss of amenity. See C Dyer 'Triplets' Parents Win Fight to Damages for Extra Child' (2000) 321 BMJ 1306. The case is of additional interest in that it may represent the exception for the birth of a healthy child in breach of contract which was left open as a possibility by the House of Lords in *McFarlane v Tayside Health Board* [2000] 2 AC 59, [1999] 4 All ER 961 (see para 6.20 et seq).

[155] *Sixth Report of the Interim Licensing Authority* (1991) p 15. Up-to-date figures are hard to come by as GIFT is currently not controlled under the 1990 Act.

[156] R L Berkowitz and L Lynch 'Selective Reduction: An Unfortunate Misnomer' (1990) 75 Obstet Gynecol 873.

[157] See para 5.61 et seq.

SURROGATE MOTHERHOOD

4.78 Surrogate motherhood requires the active co-operation of an otherwise uninvolved woman in the process of pregnancy and birth. It thus introduces a third party into the reproductive process.

4.79 At its simplest, and as the term is most commonly used, the infertile woman and her husband arrange with another woman that she will carry a child conceived by donor insemination with the husband's semen and will surrender it to its genetic father after birth. The alternative, which also concludes with the return of the infant to its genetic parents, is that an embryo which is created in vitro from the gametes of a husband and wife is then implanted in the uterus of a 'surrogate'. There are several reasons for separating the two processes, which are often described as partial or complete surrogacy; we find it easier to refer to the latter technique more descriptively as 'womb-leasing'.[158] We return to this subject below but, for the present, we limit discussion to partial surrogacy which depends on the relatively easily achieved impregnation of a fertile woman. The process, as defined, is akin to a pre-emptive adoption with the advantage that the 'adopted' baby shares half its genes with its 'adopting' parents. Since the practical possibility of following the normal process of adoption is decreasing steadily, there is much to be said, theoretically, in favour of surrogate motherhood as a treatment for the woman who is irrevocably childless— indeed, it is the *only* treatment for one who is childless by virtue of being both sterile and without a functional uterus. Yet the great majority of commentators and, possibly, the medical profession as a whole, still shy away from accepting it as a means of satisfying an urge to parenthood—why?[159] The reason was summarised many years ago in the classic words of Winslade:[160] 'The practice has a potential for economic exploitation, moral confusion and psychological harm to the surrogate mothers, the prospective adoptive parents and the children.' This view crystallises the debate which has surrounded surrogacy since it first came to the attention of British courts some 25 years ago.

STATUTE LAW AND SURROGACY

4.80 Prior to 1990, the only way by which the prospective social parents—the 'commissioning couple'—could achieve their aim was through the medium of adoption and, as we have noted, it is quite reasonable to regard a surrogacy arrangement as a form of adoption—albeit pre-arranged. The terms of the Adoption Act 1976 thus have at least an indirect bearing on surrogacy.[161]

---

[158] The technical term 'in vitro fertilisation surrogacy' is also used.

[159] An opposing view was expressed by I Craft 'Surrogacy' (1992) 47 Brit J Hosp Med 728.

[160] W J Winslade 'Surrogate Mothers: Private Right or Public Wrong?' (1981) 7 J Med Ethics 153.

[161] And also, of course, the Adoption (Scotland) Act 1978. However, for ease of writing, we will refer here only to the 1976 Act.

4.81   The significant parts of the Adoption Acts for present purposes relate to the prohibition of commercialism within the process—effectively banning 'baby selling' and the private placement of infants.[162] From the very beginning, therefore, there was a real probability that surrogate motherhood which involved any form of monetary transaction was illegal.[163] However, the rigid prohibition of commercialisation within adoption derives from a fear of exploitation of the women concerned and, from this aspect, there is much to be said for the view that surrogate motherhood and adoption are distinct, albeit closely linked, processes.[164] In the first place, the surrogate mother is not pregnant, nor has she an existing child which she has to abandon at the time the proposition is put to her. Moreover, she is under no pregnancy-related economic pressure. True, it was pointed out[165] that, at least in the 1980s, 40 per cent of volunteer surrogate mothers in the United States were unemployed or were in receipt of welfare;[166] surrogacy might, therefore, be one response to economic need—but the element of urgency that is a hallmark of adoption is still lacking. The nature of any proposed payment is also different in the two cases. In one it is a matter of purchase of an existing commodity for sale; in the other it is a matter of expenses coupled with payment for services rendered.[167] In the absence of specific legislation, the legality of surrogacy associated with exchange of money depends upon the acceptance of this distinction.

4.82   We will see later that harmony between the statutory provisions of the Adoption Acts and the practicalities of surrogacy has been virtually achieved with the introduction of the parental order; it is, nevertheless, interesting to see how the courts struggled with the problem when it presented—*Re an adoption application (surrogacy)*[168] concerned just such a case which was a remarkably amateurish affair. The principals met casually, the surrogate being motivated by a desire to help a childless couple, and she was impregnated naturally. A fee of £10,000 was agreed. All the principals, the judge said later, were supremely happy. They were also inexperienced and it was not for a further two and a half years that the de facto 'parents' applied for an adoption order. The issue was simply whether or not this would be valid following the 'payment or reward'.[169] In summary, Latey J held that a surrogacy arrangement would not

---

[162] Adoption Act 1976, s 57.

[163] In the first American test, the court agreed on the fundamental right to include a third party in a pregnancy arrangement but excluded the right to carry a child for payment: *Doe v Kelly* 307 NW 2d 438 (Mich, 1981).

[164] I M Mady 'Surrogate Mothers: The Legal Issues' (1981) 7 Am J Law Med 323; I Davies 'Contracts to Bear Children' (1985) 11 J Med Ethics 61. The great majority of citations in this area result from the surge in interest in surrogacy in the 1980s. The dust has now settled and there is very little recent research.

[165] P Parker 'Motivation of Surrogate Mothers: Initial Findings' (1983) 140 Am J Psychiat 117.

[166] M Freeman, in a powerful exposure of the 'exploitation' theory, pointed out that a similar result would probably obtain were a matched sample of applications for a factory job to be considered: 'Is Surrogacy Exploitative?' in S A M McLean (ed) *Legal Issues in Human Reproduction* (1989) ch 7.

[167] R Macklin 'Is There Anything Wrong With Surrogate Motherhood? An Ethical Analysis' (1988) 16 Law Med Hlth Care 57. For a strongly opposing view, see B Cohen 'Surrogate Mothers: Whose Baby Is It?' (1984) 10 Am J Law Med 243.

[168] [1987] Fam 81, [1987] 2 All ER 826.   [169] Adoption Act 1976, s 57(1).

contravene the Adoption Act so long as the payments made did not constitute an element of profit or financial reward; he thought that the payments in the instant case did no more than compensate for the inconveniences of pregnancy. More significantly, he showed his faith in the commissioning parents by stating that, if necessary, he would apply his powers to allow some profit and reward[170] retrospectively in the interests of the child. An adoption order was made. This relatively courageous decision has been followed without qualm.[171]

4.83   The problem was not considered in Scotland until considerably later in the comparable case of *C v S*,[172] which provided something of an antithesis. The surrogate, who was unemployed, received £8,000 in expenses but then regretted her decision to give up the child. A parental order (for which, see para 4.85 below) was, therefore, unavailable on the grounds of lack of consent by the legal mother and the commissioning couple sought to adopt the child a year after its birth. The sheriff, while holding that consent to adoption was being withheld unreasonably, none the less refused an adoption order because he considered the monetary transaction breached the terms of the statute;[173] a custody order was granted in lieu. On appeal to the Court of Session, however, it was held that the money had been paid in the expectation of a parental order rather than of adoption; the Act had, accordingly, not been contravened and an adoption order was substituted. While it is unclear to us why a provision for unreasonable withdrawal of consent should be available in respect of an adoption order but not of a parental order, *C v S* serves, at least, to harmonise policy as to the authorisation of 'reasonable' payments in respect of surrogacy on both sides of the Border.[174]

4.84   None the less, outside the United States, there appears to be a consensus which condemns the blatant commercialisation of child-bearing by way of intermediate, profit-making agencies and it was this which prompted the first relevant United Kingdom statute in the form of the Surrogacy Arrangements Act 1985.[175] The main purpose of the Act is to prohibit the making of a surrogacy arrangement on a commercial basis.[176] The principals involved are expressly excused from criminal liability (s 2(2)); moreover, payments made to or for the benefit of the surrogate are not regarded as being made on a commercial basis (s 2(3)). On the face of it, this hurried

---

[170] *Ibid*, s 57(3).

[171] *Re Q (parental order)* [1996] 1 FLR 369. The sum of £8,280 was authorised retrospectively.

[172] 1996 SLT 1387, sub nom *C and C v GS* 1996 SCLR 837.

[173] Adoption (Scotland) Act 1978, ss 24(2) and 51.

[174] Although this decision may seem a trifle contrived, it was clearly motivated by the best interests of the child. It is probable that an adoption order could, in any case, have been granted on these grounds alone: L Edwards and A Griffiths *Family Law* (1997) p 174.

[175] This aspect has been the subject of legislation in many jurisdictions. In Australia, see Infertility Treatment Act 1995 (Victoria); Family Relationships Act Amendment Act 1988 (South Australia); Surrogate Parenthood Act 1988 (Queensland); Surrogacy Contracts Act 1993 (Tasmania).

[176] Advertising by way of newspapers, periodicals and telecommunications is proscribed in s 3, the criminal liability resting on the proprietor, editor, publisher etc. I Kennedy and A Grubb *Medical Law* (3rd edn, 2000) believe that the Act also criminalises the woman who advertises herself (at 1383).

and somewhat ill-prepared measure is broadly acceptable. It removes the financially motivated entrepreneur from the scene and, at the same time, is at pains to exclude any suggestion of a criminal ancestry for the resulting children. Some aspects are, however, open to criticism. It does not involve non-commercial agencies who can, and do, operate without regulation; we will see later (at para 4.106) that this is a concession of, at best, doubtful value. By contrast, it appears to preclude the involvement of a remunerated professional lawyer in the making of a surrogacy arrangement; there is nothing in the Act to prevent the principals drawing up an understanding but it seems that it must be an amateur affair. For ideologists who disapprove of the idea of an experienced agency, it is worth noting that break-down of surrogacy arrangements is far less common in those clinics which require the intervention of professional expertise.[177] The doctor who merely assists in a pre-arranged surrogacy, however, commits no offence even if he or she is paid for the service.[178] The British Medical Association, while still regarding surrogacy as a reproductive option of last resort 'in cases where it is impossible or highly undesirable for medical reasons for the intended mother to carry a child herself', has recognised the widespread public acceptance of surrogacy and has softened its attitude to medical participation in the procedure.[179] The HFEA also allows for surrogacy to be initiated in licensed clinics subject to a similar medical restriction.[180]

4.85   Even so, a system which depends upon the vagaries of the courts cannot be satisfactory and some formula must be evolved if the commissioning couple is to have a legal right to receive the child—for the surrogate, at least in the United Kingdom, is clearly its legal mother[181] irrespective of whether or not it is the product of her own ovum and, if she is married and conception was via consensual donor insemination, her husband is its father (1990 Act, ss 27 and 28); moreover, neither can simply surrender their parental duties.[182] The 1990 Act, s 30 now offers an alternative to adoption by which the court may make a parental order which provides for a child carried by a surrogate to be treated in law as the child of the commissioning couple, provided that the gametes of one or both have been involved and that they are married and have attained the age of 18. This is subject to the consent of the surrogate and, where

---

[177] See P R Brinsden, T C Appleton, E Murray et al 'Treatment by In Vitro Fertilisation with Surrogacy: Experience of One British Centre' (2000) 320 BMJ 924.

[178] I Kennedy and A Grubb *Medical Law* (3rd edn, 2000), p 1381. A minor difficulty as to confidentiality has been eradicated in the Human Fertilisation and Embryology (Disclosure of Information) Act 1992.

[179] BMA *Changing Conceptions of Motherhood—the Practice of Surrogacy in Britain* (1996). At least two surrogacies have been funded through the NHS: 'NHS Pays for Sister's Surrogacy' *The Times*, 10 April 1996, p 11. For the evolution of medical attitudes, see L Foxcroft 'Surrogacy—Warnock and After' (1997) 2 Med L Internat 337.

[180] *Code of Practice* (2003), para 3.17. The courts have, however, disallowed the funding of a surrogacy as part of the damages for negligence resulting in a woman's childlessness: *Briody v St Helens and Knowsley Area Health Authority* [2001] 2 FLR 1094, (2001) 62 BMLR 1, CA.

[181] The interesting thought has been mooted that it might be to the child's advantage to be aware of its wider kinship and that there is no absolute reason why a child should not have two 'mothers': J Wallbank 'Too Many Mothers? Surrogacy, Kinship and the Welfare of the Child' (2002) 10 Med L Rev 271.

[182] Children Act 1989, s 2(9).

applicable, the father of the child—including a man who is the father by virtue of the 1990 Act, s 28—if they can be found;[183] moreover, the agreement of the woman who carried the child is ineffective if made less than six weeks after the child's birth. The application must be made within six months of the birth and the child must be living with the commissioning couple. Applications are heard in private and a guardian ad litem is appointed to watch over the child's interests. It is a stipulation that no money, other than reasonable expenses, has been given to the surrogate other than that authorised by the court.[184] It is exceptional for a parental order to be refused if these conditions are fulfilled.[185]

4.86   The question of consent to a parental order leads to consideration of the validity of any contract made between a commissioning couple and the surrogate and to the last piece in the current jigsaw of statutory control of surrogacy in the United Kingdom. Section 36 of the 1990 Act inserts section 1A into the Surrogacy Arrangements Act 1985, by virtue of which no surrogacy arrangement is enforceable by or against any of the persons making it. In so legislating, the United Kingdom Parliament has followed the majority trend of those countries that have addressed the subject; whether it is the correct approach is open to argument. Undoubtedly, it is the nature of the contract which poses the greatest complications for surrogate motherhood. Non-commercial surrogacy is not illegal in the United Kingdom and is not, therefore, a practice which is fundamentally against public policy. To introduce deliberately the uncertainties of a breakable agreement seems to do little more than reflect an ambivalence in a Parliament which, while unable to follow the German model in outlawing the prac-tice,[186] seems determined to oblate any signs of approval—surrogacy is to be seen as a form of legal liberty. A surrogate arrangement is clearly a difficult contract to draw up—it must allow for changes of heart on either side, illness in the surrogate, abnormalities in the resultant child and other imponderables, some of which, such as an abortion within the terms of the Abortion Act 1967, can be seen as basic rights.[187] The current law, however, is entirely negative. Rather than, in effect, hiding the issues, we feel it would be better to grasp the nettle and lay down positively what a surrogacy arrangement could *not* include—for example, a contract to pay an unreasonable sum of money, an undertaking not to accept a therapeutic abortion and the like.

[183] For some of the difficulties, see *Re Q (parental order)* [1996] 1 FLR 369.

[184] Parental Orders (Human Fertilisation and Embryology) Regulations 1994, SI 1994/2767; Parental Orders (Human Fertilisation and Embryology) (Scotland) Regulations 1994, SI 1994/2804. For analysis, see A Grubb 'Surrogate Arrangements and Parental Orders' (1995) 3 Med L Rev 204; K McK Norrie 'The Parental Orders (Human Fertilisation and Embryology) (Scotland) Regulations 1994' (1995) Fam LB 13–3. The first 'order' was, in fact, made pre-emptively: *Re W (minors) (surrogacy)* [1991] 1 FLR 385.

[185] S M Cretney and J M Masson *Principles of Family Law* (6th edn, 1997) p 947. The very great advan-tages of the parental order system are illustrated by the parallel US cases: *Doe v Doe* 710 A 2d 1297 (Conn, 1998) and *Doe v Roe* 717 A 2d 706 (Conn, 1998), the gist of which was to apply parental rights in the best interests of a child who had been accepted into a family.

[186] Embryonenschutzgesetz (Embryo Protection Act) 1990, s 1(1)(vii).

[187] Nevertheless, it can be done; the judicial decision at first instance in the celebrated American case of *Re Baby M* 525 A 2d 1128 (NJ, 1987) was largely based on the law of contract (see para 4.94 below).

4.87   Surrogacy contracts can certainly provide cautionary tales. In *W and B v H (child abduction: surrogacy)*,[188] a British woman entered into a legally binding contract to act as a surrogate in California. The discovery shortly after she was implanted with an egg from an anonymous donor, fertilised by W, that she was carrying twins led to a dispute. She then issued civil proceedings in California, resulting in an order declaring that W and B should have custody of the children at birth, and that the surrogate mother did not have any parental responsibility or rights. She returned to England, changed her mind about the surrogacy, and resolved to keep the children. When she refused to give up the children at birth, the Californian couple brought abduction proceedings under the Hague Convention on the Civil Aspects of Child Abduction 1980. The judge at first instance decided that, since the children had no permanent home, they could not be abducted and the surrogate was allowed to keep them. The commissioning couple then appealed under the inherent jurisdiction of the court[189] which, then, ordered the summary removal of the children to California— California being the most convenient jurisdiction for the determination on the merits of the future of the twins. The words of Hedley J, who presided at both hearings, deserve repetition as a warning to those who believe that any advance in reproductive technology must, ispo facto, be advantageous:

> This case is a tribute to the scientific skills of those involved but its outcome, its cost in terms of human unhappiness let alone its future implications for these children, may serve to caution against an imbalance between our scientific and ethical capacities . . . What it will mean to these children as they grow up and try to unravel and come to terms with their origins, no one can say. Much more sad is the fact, as I suspect, that no one has ever considered it.[190]

4.88   Given our present de facto position, there is much to be said for the encouragement of non-contractual memoranda of understanding which can be available in the event of later disagreement—a point to which we return below (para 4.110).

The British cases

4.89   The development of judicial attitudes can be traced through a brief review of what are, by now, well-known cases. The earliest example, *A v C*,[191] arose in 1978—some time before 'assisted reproduction' became widely acceptable. The gist is that an unmarried couple arranged for a prostitute's friend to be inseminated on the under-standing that the resultant child was returned to them; a fee of £3,000 was involved. The mother changed her mind and the father applied for access; this was granted in the child's best interests. Nevertheless, on appeal, Ormrod LJ described the agreement as 'pernicious and void' and the father as being 'a constant reminder of the whole

---

[188] [2002] 1 FLR 1008.

[189] *W v H (child abduction: surrogacy)* [2002] 2 FLR 252, [2002] Fam Law 501.

[190] [2002] 1 FLR 1008, para [1].

[191] (1984) 14 Fam Law 241, [1985] FLR 445. Commentators at the time saw the case as of interest from the DI aspect only.

sordid story'; the Court of Appeal unanimously reversed the decision and decreed that the father should not be allowed to see his son.

4.90   *Re C (a minor)*[192] was the first case to be fully covered but was, essentially, a matter of wardship. An American couple arranged a surrogacy in England through a commercial agency. As soon as the child was born, the local authority obtained a place of safety order under the Children and Young Persons Act 1969, s 28, in the belief that it would be abandoned by its mother; the genetic father then initiated wardship proceedings. Latey J refused to discuss the rights and wrongs of surrogacy and concentrated solely on the welfare of the child—how she had been born was irrelevant. On these grounds, he considered that no one was better equipped than the commissioning couple to care for her; accordingly, he gave them care and control while, at the same time, continuing the wardship—even so, permission was given for the baby to live outside the jurisdiction. For present purposes, the most important aspect of the case is that the judge rejected suggestions that the commissioning couple were unfit parents because they had entertained a commercial surrogacy arrangement.

4.91   Surrogacy itself, and particularly the relationship between that process and adoption, was more directly considered in *Re an adoption application (surrogacy)*.[193] The facts and the outcome—including the liberal stance of the trial judge—have been discussed above.[194] *Re P (minors) (wardship: surrogacy)*[195] was heard contemporaneously with the adoption case. In this instance, the surrogate declined to hand over the twins she had conceived by a married professional man. The children were made wards of court and were allowed to stay with their natural mother; the court action was essentially a matter of custody. By the time the case came to be heard, the twins had been with their natural mother for five months and the judge was strongly influenced by the degree of maternal bonding that had already arisen. Accordingly, he found 'nothing to outweigh the advantages to these children of preserving the link to the mother to whom they are bonded, and who has exercised a satisfactory degree of maternal care'. Once again, it is to be noted that there was no criticism of either the commissioning parents or of the surrogate for having entered into a surrogacy agreement.[196]

4.92   One further case merits mention—*Re W*[197]—in which, as noted above, the judge was prepared to pre-empt the law in order to ensure bonding of 'womb-leased' twins with their genetic parents. Following this, there was a comparative dearth of new cases

---

[192] [1985] FLR 846.   [193] [1987] Fam 81, [1987] 2 All ER 826.

[194] See para 4.82. A similar attitude to the rules governing both payment and maternal objection was followed in *Re AW (adoption application)* [1993] 1 FLR 62 and *Re MW (adoption: surrogacy)* [1995] 2 FLR 789, [1995] Fam Law 665. In both cases, the welfare of the child was the determining factor although the decision must have been difficult in the former.

[195] [1987] 2 FLR 421.

[196] For contemporary discussion of these cases see J Montgomery 'Constructing a Family—After a Surrogate Birth' (1986) 49 MLR 635; S P de Cruz 'Surrogacy, Adoption and Custody: A Case Study' (1988) 18 Fam Law 100.

[197] *Re W (minors) (surrogacy)* [1991] 1 FLR 385.

until the leading Scottish case of *C v S*[198] which has been discussed already.[199] The marked change in reportage probably does no more than reflect the fact that surrogacy is now so well established that cases are now no longer regarded as meriting report unless there are special circumstances. Even so, there are sporadic newspaper reports of examples which have had a less than happy ending.[200]

The American scene

4.93   Comparative American law is, perhaps, now becoming less important as the United Kingdom and Europe develop their own medical jurisprudence. Surrogacy is, however, far more common in the United States and, as a result, there are lessons still to be learnt from across the Atlantic. It is, however, also true that cases come to public notice only when there is conflict and reported cases should be considered on the understanding that, as in the UK, the great majority of arrangements proceed smoothly; cases such as that of *Re Baby M*[201] are instructive but not necessarily typical.

4.94   In that case, the surrogate, who had agreed to a fee of $10,000, refused to relinquish her child and, in fact, absconded with it contrary to a court order. When the matter came to trial, the judge was concerned to limit the issues to those of strict law and, in this respect, he rejected any relevance of the adoption laws. He concluded, on the one hand, that a valid contract had been made and broken and, on the other, that the state's interest in the welfare of its children dictated that the child be adopted by the commissioning couple. The Supreme Court of New Jersey, however, had no hesitation in overturning this decision—and doing so forcibly.[202] The surrogacy contract was found to be against public policy and, as such, invalid; both the termination of the mother's parental rights and the adoption order were voided. None the less, the Supreme Court could find nothing in law against voluntary, non-commercial surrogacy, provided that the arrangement did not include any clause binding on the surrogate to surrender her baby. As a result, the court was able to dissociate the contractual aspects of surrogacy and the 'best interests' of the child and followed the lower court in awarding custody to the commissioning parents.[203]

4.95   A contrast is to be seen in the Californian case of *Johnson v Calvert*.[204] Here, the surrogate was paid $10,000 to carry the embryo of a commissioning couple. After gestating for six months, she changed her mind as to handing over the child and the

---

[198] 1996 SLT 1387, sub nom *C and C v GS* 1996 SCLR 837.   [199] See para 4.83 above.

[200] In one, the surrogate was thought to be acting on behalf of two families at the same time: C Dyer 'Surrogate Mother Refuses to Give Up Baby' (1997) 314 BMJ 250. In the other, there were allegations that the surrogate had fabricated an abortion in order to keep the child: D Kennedy 'Minister Hints at Change in the Law' *The Times*, 16 May 1997, p 2. See also *W v H*, n 189 above.

[201] 525 A 2d 1128 (NJ, 1987).   [202] 537 A 2d 1227 (NJ Sup Ct, 1988).

[203] See G P Smith 'The Case of Baby M: Love's Labor Lost' (1988) 16 Law Med Hlth Care 121.

[204] 851 P 2d 776 (Cal, 1993) discussed by A Grubb 'Surrogate Contract: Parentage' (1994) 2 Med L Rev 239. See also G Annas 'Using Genes to Define Motherhood: The California Solution' (1992) 326 New Engl J Med 417 discussing the decision in the lower court. Others may, however, feel as strongly as to the importance of the genetic affiliation: D R Bromham 'Surrogacy: The Evolution of Opinion' (1992) 47 Brit J Hosp Med 767.

court was asked to decide on its parentage. The trial court held that a surrogate contract was both legal and enforceable and that the commissioning couple were the child's genetic, biological and natural parents; no parental rights attached to the surrogate. This disposition was upheld on appeal. In dismissing a further appeal, the Supreme Court of California held that it was the intention of the parties at the time of making the arrangement which decided the issue when there were conflicting grounds on which parentage could be established—in the present case, the surrogate had done no more than 'facilitate' the procreation of the commissioning couple's child.[205] The court further stated that surrogate contracts did not violate any existing public policy as to adoption; any payments in the former were, effectively, made for services rendered and not as compensation for the transfer of parental rights.[206] Needless to say, this opinion has been severely criticised as fundamentally misunderstanding the biological realities of the surrogate's contribution.[207]

4.96   The significance of the apparent inconsistency between *Re Baby M* and *Johnson v Calvert* is explained to some extent by *Re Marriage of Moschetta*.[208] Here, the 'parents' of a year-old child, born by standard surrogacy, separated and the surrogate then claimed legal parentage. The Court of Appeal was, then, able to distinguish the case from *Johnson* because there was no conflict as to maternity—the surrogate was both the genetic and the gestational mother and was to be regarded as such. It is, however, to be noted that the court distinguished the definition of status from the allocation of custody—the latter was governed by the best interests of the child.

Australia

4.97   In view of that country's leading position in the early development of medical jurisprudence, it is surprising that a surrogacy case was not litigated in Australia until 1998. *Re Evelyn*[209] was an interfamilial, altruistic case that 'went wrong' and resulted, ultimately, in a residency dispute in the Full Court of the Family Court. The final decision was in favour of the surrogate mother, a conclusion based largely, but not entirely, on the assumption that the child's best long-term interests lay in preservation of her natural bonding with her biological mother—this despite the fact that she had lived with the commissioning couple for the first year of her life. Both the trial judge

---

[205] The concept of intention was carried a stage further in *In the Marriage of Buzzanca* (1998) 72 Cal Rptr 2d 280 (CA) where a separated couple who had used both a surrogate and a donated embryo were declared the legal parents on the grounds that they initiated the pregnancy. This approach is embedded in statute in several of the United States—e.g. Florida, Virginia and New Hampshire.

[206] The situation as to commercialism of surrogacy in the United States is hard to unravel. It seems that, while *Johnson v Calvert* clears the way in California, at least five states have passed statutes restricting the practice: R A Charo 'Legislative Approaches to Surrogate Motherhood' (1988) 16 Law Med Hlth Care 96.

[207] R B Oxman 'California's Experiment in Surrogacy' (1993) 341 Lancet 1468.

[208] 30 Cal Rptr 2d 893 (1994), discussed in detail by A Grubb 'Surrogate Contract: Parentage' (1995) 3 Med L Rev 219.

[209] (1998) FLC 92. The case is examined in depth in M Otlowski '*Re Evelyn*—Reflections on Australia's First Litigated Surrogacy Case' (1998) 7 Med L Rev 38. The author points out that, despite the varying, but generally antipathetic, attitudes to surrogacy shown by the States' legislatures, non-commercial surrogacy arrangements are acceptable in Australia save in Queensland.

and the Full Court also considered that the ambience of the surrogate's family was preferable for the child. Nevertheless, some residual determinative rights were granted to the commissioning couple.[210]

The cases assessed

4.98   The British cases indicate that the public, as represented by its judiciary, are sympathetic to surrogate motherhood—an attitude which probably derives more from the *fait accompli* nature of the proceedings than from any basic empathy with the practice. It can be taken that no future decisions will be driven by antagonism. Accordingly, it is very unlikely that a parental order will be withheld in the event of application by the commissioning parents and consent on the part of the surrogate and the legal father—if there is one. While it would always be possible for the court to override agreement by the parties, it is difficult to see how the motivation of the couple and their almost inevitable material status could be irrelevant to the child's 'best interests'—which is not to say that economic advantage will always take precedence.[211] In so far as it is possible to apply pre-1990 standards to the present day conditions, the indications are that the prime factor in the court's thinking in the event of disagreement between the parties would be the extent of family bonding—we suspect that much would depend on where, and for how long, the child was living at the time of adjudication. It would, however, be impossible to generalise. The most important common feature would lie in the search for the child's best interests; it is this which would determine the direction and method of disposal of each case and it has to be remembered that what constitutes best interests is determined by an individual judge. There is no indication of what would result if the commissioning couple were to refuse to accept the infant; the precise details of each case would, again, be all-important, but it is difficult to see, in general, an alternative to intervention by the local authority by way of care proceedings. The position of the surrogate's husband under the terms of the 1990 Act, s 28(2) might then be problematical.

4.99   While there is no evidence on the point, we fancy that much the same approach would be taken whether the surrogate had incubated her own egg, that of the commissioning woman or one donated. This, however, might well not be the case in the United States where, judging from the Californian cases, major significance would be attributed to genetic status. As Grubb has put it:

Infertile couples who seek surrogacy linked with IVF treatment can be reasonably certain they will come out of the arrangement . . . as the child's parents. By contrast, couples who resort to traditional surrogacy . . . will have no such reassurance.[212]

---

[210] Wallbank, n 181 above, reiterates that, since a variety of factors were taken into consideration, the case does not establish a legal precedent—particularly as to the sharing of long-term care.

[211] See e.g. *Re P (minors) (wardship: surrogacy)* [1987] 2 FLR 421.

[212] (1995) 3 Med L Rev 219 at 221. Other cases tend to support this view: eg *Soos v Superior Court of Arizona* 896 P 2d 1356 (Ariz, 1994), *Belsito v Clark* 644 NE 2d 769 (Ohio, 1994)—though the latter case is far less convincing.

THE MORALITY OF SURROGATE MOTHERHOOD

4.100   What, then, is so special about the morality of surrogacy? Clearly, the most important new factor lies in the inclusion of a third party to procreation—and in such a way as to provoke not only serious moral but also important socio-political questions—and the latter are, by definition, gender-based. Stripped to its essentials, surrogacy can be viewed from this perspective as being one way of exploiting women for the benefit of men[213]—a matter to which we have alluded above. The alternative is to see the outlawing of the practice as downright paternalism which denies a woman a chance to use her body as she pleases. It seems fair to say that the feminist movement is divided in its approach;[214] the argument is one which we will not take further here save to note the difficulties that arise from generalising in personal and individual affairs.

4.101   The second major concern lies in the suggestion that surrogacy is 'baby-selling'.[215] It is possible, however, to maintain that a baby is 'sold' only if persons with no genetic association purchase an infant that is already in being. It seems more logical to regard any monetary transaction in respect of surrogacy as payment for gestational expertise and, as the British cases indicate, the critical distinction lies between reasonable recompense and inducement to gestate.[216] The great majority of assisted reproduction is centred on private health care and, even within a public health service, there is indirect payment for obstetric expertise. Looked at in this way, either both surrogacy and embryo transfer are 'baby purchasing' or neither is—and there is no suggestion that sophisticated reproductive techniques are immoral on this score.[217] Thirdly, it is widely believed that surrogacy must have an ill-effect on children in general or on the individual resultant child. The former, represented by a fear that children may become 'objects for barter', is valid only so long as surrogacy itself is categorised as objectionable; the premise disappears once it is regarded as a legitimate treatment for childlessness. Any effect on the individual child by way of confusion as to parentage is comparable to that which we have discussed in relation to other forms of assisted reproduction. Whether or not there is a detriment seems to us to be unproven but if there is, it should not be insurmountable—certainly no more than in other examples

---

[213] G J Annas 'Fairy Tales Surrogate Mothers Tell' (1988) 16 Law Med Hlth Care 27.

[214] L B Andrews 'Surrogate Motherhood: The Challenge for Feminists' (1988) 16 Law Med Hlth Care 72 and, by the same author: 'Beyond Doctrinal Boundaries: A Legal Framework for Surrogate Motherhood' (1995) 81 Va L Rev 2343. For a more recent analysis of the extensive literature, see E Jackson *Regulating Reproduction* (2001), pp 291 et seq.

[215] So far as is known, only Israel positively encourages a commercial element in surrogacy arrangements: D A Frankel 'Legal Regulation of Surrogate Motherhood in Israel' (2001) 20 Med Law 605.

[216] The court in *Johnson v Calvert* 851 P 2d 776 (Cal, 1993) considered many of these points and rejected the suggestion that surrogacy arrangements violated public policy. For further debate, see A van Niekerk and L van Zyl 'Commercial Surrogacy and the Commodification of Children: An Ethical Perspective' (1995) 14 Med Law 163.

[217] M Freeman 'Does Surrogacy Have a Future after Brazier?' (1999) 7 Med L Rev 1 suggests that remuneration is inevitable and is better in the open rather than underground.

of the unconventional family.[218] Even so, there is little doubt that the provisions of the 1990 Act, s 13(5)—discussed above[219]—are likely to discourage professional implication in surrogacy outside licensed clinics.

4.102   In favour of surrogacy, it must be remembered that, as already noted, it *is* a treatment for some forms of childlessness. Such cases may be rare, yet to encourage treatment by way of ovum donation for the woman who is childless because of ovarian inadequacy and, at the same time, to forbid surrogacy for the one who has no uterus, smacks of unfair discrimination.

4.103   Surrogacy could, however, be used for purely selfish reasons—for example, a desire to have a child without interference with a career—although the prospect may be given exaggerated importance.[220] Such hedonistic womb-leasing is so comparable to nineteenth-century wet-nursing that 'full' surrogacy as a whole has become suspect. This is unfortunate because there are, in fact, far more conditions in which IVF-linked surrogacy would be the preferred treatment of childlessness than there are those in which standard surrogacy would be indicated. Abnormality of the uterus or other causes of persistent miscarriage are commoner than loss of both uterus and ovaries; moreover, womb-leasing is the logical answer to an inability to carry, rather than to conceive, a baby—say, by virtue of heart disease, diabetes and the like. The other, and obvious, important difference is that, in womb-leasing, the commissioning couple are the genetic parents. Thus, one would imagine that the surrogate, having no such relationship to her fetus, would be less exposed to psychological trauma on surrendering it; the receiving parents are in precisely the same end position as natural coital parents; and the child suffers no 'genetic insecurity'. Certainly, womb-leasing involves the use of high-grade technology—but even this serves to remove some of the intuitive distaste provoked by standard surrogacy. Neither the Warnock Committee nor the resultant legislation have distinguished between partial and full surrogacy; we feel, however, that the better practice lies in favour of clearly separating the two.[221]

4.104   There is, however, one aspect of womb-leasing that merits special attention—that is, the use of intrafamilial surrogates. Not only does this seriously disturb familial relationships but the procedure opens the door to emotional coercion. It appears to be a practice which should be made unlawful—as it is in many jurisdictions—although not everyone would agree.[222]

---

[218] It has been pointed out that, to be a parent, one must have some, but not necessarily all, of the defining features of parenthood: L van Zyl and A van Niekerk 'Interpretations, Perspectives and Intentions in Surrogate Motherhood' (2000) 26 J Med Ethics 404.

[219] See para 4.15.

[220] Since both the HFEA and the BMA regard surrogacy as a last resort to be used only on medical grounds, it is unlikely that the procedure would be carried out by practitioners responsible to the GMC.

[221] Theoretically, womb-leasing should be the preferred surrogacy method for those of the Jewish faith as 'jewishness' is transferred through the female line. In fact, current Israeli law states that surrogacy is legal in that country only if the ovum does not come from the surrogate: R H B Fishman 'Surrogate Motherhood Becomes Legal in Israel' (1996) 347 Lancet 756.

[222] In response to an English case involving a post-menopausal woman acting on behalf of her childless daughter, Lady Warnock is reported as saying 'It is a wonderful idea': D Kennedy 'Surrogacy Attempt Divides Experts' *The Times*, 3 July 1995, p 8. The baby was successfully delivered by caesarian section.

THE FUTURE

4.105 The one thing that this rather extensive analysis has shown is that, despite its widespread public acceptance, both the ethics and the law relating to surrogacy are still in an uncertain state and that the latter, at least, has been applied in piecemeal fashion. Many would say that it is right that customs so private as reproductive choice should be allowed to evolve by way of public opinion as represented by the common law. We have seen, however, that the United Kingdom has opted for statutory regulation and there is a good argument, to which we subscribe, for harmony across the board.

4.106 At present, while IVF-associated surrogacy clearly lies within the framework of the Human Fertilisation and Embryology Act 1990, standard surrogacy does not do so unless it involves donor insemination that is provided *as a public service* (ss 2 and 4). That being so, DI in the context of surrogacy is lawful only if performed privately or under cover of a licence—and we have seen that the involvement of licensed clinics as, as best, not encouraged by the HFEA.[223] This leaves an unsatisfactory dichotomy, the solution of which is central to the repute of the process. Most people would now agree with the minority of the Warnock Committee[224] that it should remain available as a treatment option.[225] Nevertheless, most would also agree that it must be controlled.[226] It was against this background that the Brazier Review Team was set up in 1997, intending to ensure that the law continued to meet public concerns.[227]

4.107 Briefly,[228] the team recommended, first, that payments to surrogate mothers should cover only genuine expenses associated with the pregnancy and that additional payments should be prohibited in order to prevent surrogacy arrangements being entered into for financial benefit; reasonable expenses should be defined by the Ministers. Second, it was recommended that agencies to oversee surrogacy arrangements should be established and registered by Health Departments which would be required to operate within a Code of Practice; an advisory code would be drawn up to provide guidance for the registered agencies and also for those acting in a private capacity. Thirdly, current legislation dealing with surrogacy should be repealed and replaced by a consolidated Surrogacy Act which addressed the whole subject rather than specific aspects. In this respect, it was recommended that surrogacy arrangements should remain unenforceable, that the ban on commercial agencies and advertising should

---

[223] Less than one-third of licensed clinics will provide a surrogacy service (Brazier, n 227 below at para 6.9)

[224] Cmnd 9314, n 55 above, 'Expression of Dissent A'.

[225] So far as we know, in the English-speaking world, only Queensland has criminalised the procedure in all its forms: Surrogate Parenthood Act 1988 (Qd).

[226] For an appraisal of the early attitudes, see D Morgan 'Who to Be or Not to Be: The Surrogacy Story' (1986) 49 MLR 358. The possibility that regulation offends against the Human Rights Act 1998 is discussed by J Ramsey 'Regulating Surrogacy—A Contravention of Human Rights?' (2000) 5 Med L Internat 45. The author concludes that it is unlikely to be so held and we agree.

[227] M Brazier (Chairman) *Surrogacy: Review for Health Ministers of Current Arrangements for Payment and Regulation* (1998, Cm 4068).

[228] For a very detailed critique see Freeman, n 217 above.

remain in force and that the prohibition should include the operation of unregistered agencies.

4.108   These proposals were carefully researched and have much to commend them; nevertheless, we would take issue with some of them. Prominent in this respect is the question of payment—the rejection of which is central to the Brazier position. The concepts of provision of a service and recompense for that service are so closely linked that, save in unusual circumstances, the majority of persons would expect them to go hand in hand. Given that the demand for surrogates will not abate and given that private surrogacy arrangements are not prohibited, we have to agree with Freeman[229] that the effect of prohibiting paid arrangements in the registered field must be to force the process onto the 'back-streets', which would be to overturn the whole purpose of regulation. Of perhaps more immediate concern, as we have already intimated, it would take a very great deal of argument to convince us that payments to a surrogate mother are any less moral than payments to an IVF clinician. We support the case for reasonable payments provided these are determined by an overall authority.

4.109   As to the status of the regulatory authority, we prefer a policy of centralisation rather than regionalisation if for no reason other than to avoid the possibility of availability by 'post-code'. The concept of a State Surrogacy Board has been mooted for some time.[230] This, we feel, would involve the establishment of yet another, and probably superfluous, quango. It is certainly true that surrogate motherhood introduces problems additional to those involved in the provision of a treatment for childlessness; nevertheless, it is central to our view of surrogacy that, at base, it is precisely that and we remain unconvinced that the responsibility for its regulation is not best invested in a distinct Committee of HFEA or of such a conglomerate authority as arises from the ashes of the next Governmental reappraisal.[231]

4.110   Finally, we are unrepentant in our antipathy to declaring all surrogacy arrangements unenforceable. Very little attention is paid by commentators to the situation in which the commissioning couple wish to avoid their responsibilities and it is this that, in our opinion, constitutes the main potential mischief attached to surrogate motherhood; as we have already stated, it seems to be far preferable to establish the specific *conditions* of an arrangement that are unenforceable rather than its whole.[232]

4.111   Overall, we feel strongly that the procedure should be unlawful unless it is

---

[229] N 217 above.   [230] P Singer and D Wells *The Reproduction Revolution* (1984) at p 118.

[231] It is, for instance, suggested that HFEA should be combined with the Human Tissue Authority (for which see chapter 14) under such a heading as the Regulatory Agency for Fertility and Tissues—a policy for which we can see little logical justification.

[232] A relatively minor recommendation of the Brazier team was that judges should be unable to authorise otherwise impermissible payments. There will always be exceptional circumstances and the adoption and surrogacy procedures are so close to one another that it should not be possible to play one off against the other. Similarly, there seems no reason why it should not be possible to overrule an unreasonable objection to a parental order such as can be done in relation to an adoption order.

undertaken for a bona fide medical reason, other options having been considered and properly rejected. Effectively, then, we are making a plea for medicalising surrogacy—thus emphasising our view that surrogacy is the treatment of choice for a specific group of causes of childlessness and is, therefore, comparable to any other 'treatment services' provided under cover of the 1990 Act.

5

THE CONTROL OF FERTILITY

5.1   There are few areas of medical jurisprudence that illustrate more forcefully the potential conflict of moral values than does that of the control of fertility. This is, to a large extent, a by-product of modern medical expertise. It is hard to see that fertility control as represented by the prevention of unwanted conception is ethically unacceptable per se. Wastage of gametes, which, of themselves, are incapable of further development, occurs in nature on a vast scale; only the ultra-conservative ethicist who perceives sexual intercourse and procreation as a unitary function can object to, say, barrier methods of contraception—and only the purist who sees any interference with the human body as unethical unless it be for therapeutic purposes will condemn, say, ligation of the fallopian tubes as being fundamentally wrong. Modern fertility control, however, involves more than numerical limitation of the family. It also includes control of the nature of the family and this may encompass anything from selection of the sex of one's children to manipulation of the family's genetic pool. It is in this field, in particular, that the seeds of ethical conflict are sown.[1]

5.2   On the one hand, we have the fundamental bioethical principle of autonomy (see chapter 1) which, as we argue throughout this book, is acquiring ever-increasing importance not only in the ethical control of medical practice but also in its legal regulation. It is possible to regard *any* restriction of an adult's lifestyle as an invasion of that autonomy and many would see reproductive choice as one of its major components. On the other hand, given that quantitative and qualitative choice of one's offspring must involve rejection of some forms of future life, fertility control confronts both the ethical and legal acceptance of personal autonomy with the essentially communitarian principle that human life should be preserved whenever this is possible. Both ethics and the law must, therefore, compromise and, clearly, the result of that compromise will depend upon how one resolves the age-old question of when does human life begin?

---

[1] For a very full consideration of modern reproductive medicine, see J A Robertson 'Procreative Liberty in the Era of Genomics' (2003) 29 Amer J Law Med 439.

THE CONCEPT OF PERSONHOOD

5.3   The value that we place on human life is intimately linked with respect for personhood but what constitutes personhood is a matter of moral supposition and not one of scientific fact. The conservative view, as exemplified, particularly, by the Roman Catholic Church, lies at one extreme; this holds that personhood, and its consequent right to protection, exists from the moment of conception—put another way, that the zygote formed from the union of male and female gametes is a 'person'.[2] We suggest that there are comparatively few who would support this view; there are, in fact, relatively good reasons, based, inter alia, on the totipotential capacity of the early embryonic cells, for regarding the pre-implantation blastocyst as being, also, pre-embryonic. We will see, however, that personhood may be one thing and human life another; hence, it is possible to argue that, while the zygote may not be a person, there is no logical alternative to regarding it as the first stage in human life—and we return to this aspect below at para 5.5. At the other end of the scale, there are those who would equate personhood with intellect and with the power to make decisions.[3] We reject such an extreme, if for no reason other than an intuitive distaste for its natural consequence which would be to deprive even infants of a right to be valued as persons.

5.4   Many attempts are made to define the point at which the embryo or fetus is morally entitled to, at least, consideration. Within these brackets, for example, the Jewish rabbinical law sets the time as when pregnancy is recognisable externally;[4] the early Christian moralists were attracted to the evidence of life exhibited by quickening —or perceptible fetal movement;[5] and there is a widely accepted tendency to accord additional protection to the fetus when it is capable of being born alive. The def-initional complications of 'viability' are discussed later.[6] At this point, we would only remark on the well appreciated fact that the limits of viability in terms of gestation periods will be steadily lowered to their physiological baseline as improved neonatal medicine becomes more widely available. Perhaps as an indirect consequence of this, the law, in its search for certainty, draws a bright line at birth. There is no legal personhood in a fetus but a neonate has all the legal attributes and rights to protection

---

[2] The senior author was very influenced by a short, but most sympathetic, early monograph: J Poole *The Cross of Unknowing: Dilemmas of a Catholic Doctor* (1989). The book is probably now out of print.

[3] M Tooley 'A Defense of Abortion and Infanticide' in J Feinberg (ed) *The Problem of Abortion* (1973) and H Kuhse and P Singer *Should the Baby Live?* (1985), in particular, ch 6. A valuable modern discussion of 'personhood' from a rather different aspect is to be found in M Ford 'The Personhood Paradox and the "Right to Die" ' (2005) 13 Med L Rev 80.

[4] A Steinberg 'Induced Abortion in Jewish Law' (1980) 1 Int J Law Med 187.

[5] See G R Dunstan 'The Moral Status of the Human Embryo: A Tradition Recalled' (1984) 10 J Med Ethics 38 for a comprehensive review.

[6] At para 5.91. A Peterfy 'Fetal Viability as a Threshold to Personhood' (1995) 16 J Leg Med 607 provides a most interesting overview.

of a 'reasonable creature in being'—and this distinction, as we will see, leads to some anomalous conclusions insofar as it excludes a moral dimension.[7]

5.5   As to the latter, an alternative approach, which we endorse, can be couched in terms of potential—a human 'organism'[8] acquires humanity when it has the potential to become a human being. On this basis, the pre-implantation embryo has no potential and implantation, itself, represents the critical moral watershed in human development.[9] This discussion has, however, already shown us that, whatever point we may choose as the marker for the acquisition of humanity, it represents no more than a convenient fare-stage in the continuum of early human development; an embryo in the process of implantation is the same embryo once it has become embedded and a fetus *in utero* is the same fetus whether or not it could survive after parturition. That is, until we revert to the beginning of the journey. Left to themselves, gametes can only die. The only absolute in the saga is that 'life' as it is generally understood begins with the formation of the zygote; on this view, the conservative Roman Catholic view represents the only tenable option—the difficulty is that it is also the least practical solution to the question.

5.6   At the same time, however, this concept of a continuum provides an opportunity to create a comparative, albeit arguably false, morality when faced with the inherent conflict within fertility control that was posed at the beginning of this chapter. There being no potential 'life' in gametes, contraception stands as the morally most acceptable form of fertility control[10] and a form of 'quality' control that depends on gamete selection will attract less criticism than will one that depends on destruction of embryos. By the same token, embryocide is less subject to objection than is feticide in the form of abortion while abortion itself becomes progressively less acceptable as fetal maturity increases. Finally—and, perhaps, fortunately—the law steps in; a 'reasonable' being does not have to be a 'rational' being and, subject to the vagaries of legal and medical necessity (for which, see chapter 16), neonaticide remains unlawful killing irrespective of the opposing philosophical attractions. We discuss these possible procedures and distinctions in the following paragraphs and chapters.

5.7   We are, however, still left with something of a moral lacuna. The legalist may well say that the fetus, not being a person, has no rights. But we would say that, while this may be true for the fetus *qua* fetus, it does not mean to say that it has no legally protected interests. These are demonstrated in at least two contexts:

---

[7] But even this provides no absolute certainty—a fetus in the process of being born is not legally 'born' and requires the specific statutory protection of the Infant Life (Preservation) Act 1929—which does not run to Scotland.

[8] In the important case *Attorney-General's Reference (No. 3 of 1994)* [1998] AC 245, [1997] 3 All ER 936, Lord Mustill was unable to define the status of the fetus and referred to it as 'a unique organism' at AC 256, All ER 943; for further discussion, see para 5.8 below.

[9] This comes very close to the comparable theological position based on 'ensoulment': see N M Ford *When Did I Begin ?* (1988)

[10] Subject to the possible rejoinder 'abstinence excepted'.

- legally controlled abortion—which, as we will discuss, is a criminal act save when the provisions of the legislation are satisfied and which, thereby, implies, self-evidently, that the fetus has a legally recognised interest in remaining alive; and

- harm to the fetus *before* birth can be actionable *after* birth despite the fact that there is no recognisable offence of feticide.

5.8 On this last point, it has been established that injury to the fetus is injury to a person if the fetus is subsequently born alive,[11] but this is essentially protection of the neonate and recognition of the fetus of *itself* has been steadfastly opposed. An opportunity arose in *Attorney-General's Reference (No. 3 of 1994)*,[12]—a case of fetal injury resulting from an attack on its mother—but the House of Lords' only conces- sion was to override the Court of Appeal in accepting that the fetus was more than an adjunct of its mother but then declined to elaborate on what it was in moral terms.[13] More recently, an almost perfect case for a full analysis of fetal status presented to the European Court of Human Rights.[14] The result was unsatisfactory but most of the problems associated with the definition or 'personhood' that we have discussed above were addressed as the case progressed through the French courts; it is, therefore worth considering in some detail as a form of envoi.

The case of Mrs Vo

5.9 Mrs Vo attended an ante-natal clinic at approximately 21 weeks' gestation. Following a series of extraordinary administrative mishaps, the obstetrician negligently perfor- ated the amniotic sac and this resulted in the death of the fetus; Mrs Vo raised actions under both the civil and the criminal law but it is the latter with which we are mainly concerned, the charge against the doctor being that of unintentional homicide. The passage through the courts was turbulent—the main basis for the action lying in Article 16 of the French civil code which provides:

The law secures the primacy of the person . . . and guarantees the respect of every human being from the beginning of life.

The court noted that the terms 'embryo' and 'human embryo' were undefined in the law and that there was no legal rule to determine the position of the fetus in law. A number of definitions attempted by members of parliament were, however, quoted. The following[15] expresses the general tenor:

---

[11] E.g. *Burton v Islington Health Authority, de Martell v Merton and Sutton Health Authority* [1993] QB 204, [1992] 3 All ER 833; *Hamilton v Fife Health Board* 1993 SLT 624. For discussion see A Whitfield 'Common Law Duties to Unborn Children' (1993) 1 Med L Rev 28.

[12] N 8 above.

[13] For discussion of the case, see M Seneviratne 'Pre-natal Injury and Transferred Malice: The Invented Other' (1996) 59 MLR 884. Also J K Mason 'A Lords' Eye View of Fetal Status' (1999) 3 Edin LR 246.

[14] *Vo v France* (2005) 10 EHRR 12, (2004) 79 BMLR 71. We have discussed this case at length in J K Mason 'What's in a Name?—The Vagaries of *Vo v France*' (2005) 17 CFLQ 97.

[15] Attributed to Professor J-F Mattéi.

It is not yet known with precision when the zygote becomes an embryo and the embryo a f(o)etus, the only indisputable fact being that the life process starts with impregnation.

Faced with such legal indecision, the court resorted to basic science and declared that a fetus of 21 weeks' gestation was not viable, was not, therefore, a 'human person' and that, accordingly, the offence of unintentional homicide of a 21-week-old fetus was not made out—in short, there was no such offence as feticide.

5.10   The Cour d'Appel, however, reverted to the concept of 'the beginning of life' and also to the truism that viability is an indefinite and uncertain concept[16]—it was, in fact, held to be devoid of all legal effect and that 'elementary common sense', inter alia, dictated that negligence leading to the death of a 20- to 24-week-old fetus should be classified as unintentional homicide. The Cour de Cassation, by contrast, almost inevitably decided that the criminal law provisions must be strictly construed and that the fetus was not a person in law.

5.11   The issue then went to the European Court of Human Rights whose decision was eagerly awaited. In the event, however, the majority of the Court reverted to the standard practice[17] and addressed the case in terms of abortion law; having done so, it ruled that it had no competence to decide on matters which were essentially the prerogative of individual legislatures. Clearly, the cynic might well say that it is but another example of the refusal of judiciaries to come to terms with the problem of fetal rights. It seems to us that there is no insuperable difficulty in harmonising the concept of feticide—of which *Vo* was an undoubted example[18]—with therapeutic abortion, nor does the acceptance of the former threaten the rights of the pregnant woman as to the latter. Rather, acknowledging an offence of feticide serves only to protect the interests of the woman who *wants* to maintain her pregnancy.[19]

CONTRACEPTION

5.12   We have seen that there are few moral objections that can be levelled against contraception. Certainly it is possible that the use of contraceptives increases casual sexual activity but, other than in connection with children (for which, see para 5.15 below), we are not, here, concerned with sexual mores. In our view, the important feature in

---

[16] For which see para 5.94 below.

[17] We discuss the historic attitude of the European Court of Human Rights towards fetal status in G T Laurie 'Medical Law and Human Rights: Passing the Parcel Back to the Profession' in A Boyle et al (eds) *Human Rights and Scots Law* (2002).

[18] The minority opinions in the case are especially useful and concede that the Court could and should have done better.

[19] But this is, admittedly, the easy case. The reluctance of the ECHR and other judicial fora to address the fetal question directly may largely be born of the fear of establishing precedents that cannot then be controlled and which might open dangerous floodgates in the realm of maternal/fetal conflict in circumstances where the woman does *not* want to remain pregnant.

the present context is that, while contraception may inhibit the production of a life that would otherwise materialise, it does not involve the *destruction* of human *life* in any of its forms. Problems of a physical nature, however, arise with many forms of contraception which should, therefore, not be undertaken—and, certainly, not imposed—lightly. For these reasons, we believe a short consideration of the complications to be essential to the discussion.

5.13   Oral hormonally-based contraception has been greatly refined over the years but there is no doubt that compounds with a high oestrogen content will predispose to intravascular thrombosis;[20] as with any form of hormonal contraceptive, progestogens increase the liability to cardiovascular disease when combined with smoking.[21] Although the evidence is ambiguous, the probability is that the risk of venous thrombosis following the use of the newer, or 'third generation', progestogen pills is rather higher that when using the earlier preparations.[22] The courts have also attempted to resolve the issue. It was accepted in a major class action,[23] brought on behalf of seven women who had died from thrombotic disease, accepted that the risk from third generation contraceptives was some 1.7 times that of the second generation; it had been, however, agreed that the action would fail if the increased risk was less than x2—the issue cannot be said to be settled as yet. Against this background, it must be remembered that, on a worldwide scale, the risk of death associated with pregnancy is several hundred times that of death associated with contraception. We should also mention that 'depot' preparations may cause menstrual disturbances;[24] and a possible

[20] So far as we are aware, contraceptives have been blamed for death in only one reported case litigated on the point: *Coker v Richmond, Twickenham and Roehampton Area Health Authority* [1996] 7 Med LR 58; the action failed on the grounds that the risks had been properly explained—which probably accounts for the dearth of reports. Similarly, an allegation that a second generation contraceptive was responsible for a tragic case of brain stem stroke, failed on its facts and on the grounds of causation—an association between the drug and the event could not be shown on the balance of probability: *Vadera v Shaw* (1999) 45 BMLR 162, CA. The case, which has considerable significance in relation to statistical evidence, is discussed by R Goldberg 'The Contraceptive Pill, Negligence and Causation: Views on *Vadera v Shaw*' (2000) 8 Med L Rev 316.

[21] Smoking *per se* is a potent cause of cardiovascular disease in both sexes.

[22] J M Kemmeren, A Algra and D E Grobbee 'Third Generation Oral Contraceptives and Risk of Venous Thrombosis: Meta-analysis' (2001) 323 BMJ 131. The annual death rate due to idiopathic venous thromboembolism in users of contraceptives in general is of the order of 1:100,000: L Parkin, D C G Skegg, M Wilson et al 'Oral Contraceptives and Fatal Pulmonary Embolism' (2000) 355 Lancet 2133. The uncertainty of the situation was emphasised by J O Drife 'The Third Generation Pill Controversy ("Continued")' (2001) 323 BMJ 119. Other national medical organisations may be more cautious: T Sheldon 'Dutch GP's Warned against New Contraceptive Pill' (2002) 324 BMJ 869.

[23] *X, Y, Z and others v Schering Health Care and others* (2002) 70 BMLR 88. The report contains a mass of statistical detail and is reviewed in D C G Skegg 'Oral Contraceptives, Venous Thromboembolism, and the Courts' (2002) 325 BMJ 504. Thromboembolism has also been in the courts in relation to airline travel: *Deep Vein Thrombosis and Air Travel Group Litigation, Re* (2004) 76 BMLR 38, CA—causation was not pursued but it would have been interesting to know how many of the 55 claimants were women 'on the pill'.

[24] D R Bromham 'Contraceptive Implants' (1996) 312 BMJ 1555; *Blyth v Bloomsbury Health Authority* [1993] 4 Med LR 151, discussed at para 10.121 below. Insertion and removal also requires expertise and may be a source of litigation: J Roberts 'Women in US Sue Makers of Norplant' (1994) 309 BMJ 145.

association between contraceptive therapy and an increased incidence of carcinoma of the breast or cervix is still debated.[25]

5.14   The very effective interceptive methods are also suspect in that, although any such association is certainly not a simple one, they may cause pelvic inflammation and permanent infertility. The formulation of IUDs is, however, changing—in particular, the customary copper base is being replaced by physiological progestogens; the latter are effective for at least 7 years and have the additional advantage of significantly reducing the menstrual flow, while the reputation of the former is being re-established.[26] In general, IUDs offer rather better protection against pregnancy than do depot hormonal contraceptives. These are, however, mainly aspects of clinical medicine; they are introduced here only to emphasise that non-surgical contraception also has its pitfalls and cannot be imposed without forethought.

CONTRACEPTION AND MINORS

5.15   The main legal and ethical issues of contraception relate to their provision for minors; although this was once a burning issue, it has now lost its urgency and the historic case of *Gillick*[27] is probably best discussed under 'Consent' (see chapter 10). Nevertheless, the dilemma confronting the doctor who is consulted by a female minor requesting contraceptive advice and treatment still merits consideration.

5.16   The problem is essentially that of deciding whether the physician should do anything which might facilitate her engaging in sexual activity. If the patient is, say, aged 14 or 15, he may well be of the view that that is too young an age for sexual intercourse. This disapproval may rightly be based on the view that sexual activity at such an age may lead to emotional trauma and a risk of disease—including iatrogenic disease—rather than on social or moral grounds. On the other hand, a refusal to prescribe contraceptives may ultimately be more damaging to the patient in that sexual activity may result in pregnancy—and giving birth to a child or abortion at such an age are likely to be severely disruptive of the patient's life.

5.17   Even so, a decision to provide contraception to a minor poses a number of additional ethical and legal dilemmas for the doctor, including whether he can proceed without the consent of the parents (which we discuss in chapter 10), the nature and extent of his obligation of confidence to the minor (which we explore in chapter 8), and whether he attracts any criminal liability as being a party to an offence of sexual intercourse with a minor.

---

[25] J O Drife 'The Contraceptive Pill and Breast Cancer in Young Women' (1989) 298 BMJ 1269. For a succinct analysis of the whole field, see A Szarewski and J Guiilebaud 'Contraception' (1991) 302 BMJ 1224.

[26] Useful recent reviews include J A Fortney, P J Feldblum and E G Raymond 'Intrauterine Devices: The Optimal Long-term Contraceptive Method?' (1999) 44 J Reproduct Med 269; D Hubacher, R Lara-Ricalde, D J Taylor et al (2001) 345 New Engl J Med 561. Note that the Court of Appeal in *Re S (adult patient: sterilisation)* [2001] 3 Fam 15, [2000] 3 WLR 1288 preferred the use of the Mirena coil to sterilisation (see para 5.55 below).

[27] *Gillick v West Norfolk and Wisbech Area Health Authority* [1984] QB 581, [1984] 1 All ER 365; on appeal [1986] AC 112, [1985] 1 All ER 830, CA; revsd [1986] AC 112, [1985] 3 All ER 402, HL.

5.18   All these issues were considered in *Gillick*, a controversial case that resulted from the publication of a circular by the Department of Health stating that practitioners could, in strictly limited circumstances, discuss and apply family planning measures to minors without the express consent of their parents; Mrs Gillick sought, inter alia, to have the instruction declared unlawful. In the absence of any binding authority, the trial judge relied heavily on the common law and on the Canadian case of *Johnston*[28] and concluded that a person below the age of 16 was capable of consent to contraceptive therapy provided she was of sufficient mental maturity to understand the implications. The Court of Appeal, however, concentrated on the duties and rights of parents, which they considered to be inseparable. The trial judge's decision was overturned unanimously. The Authority, strongly backed by the BMA, then appealed to the House of Lords which reverted to what might be loosely termed the 'mature minor' principle—and has come to be known as '*Gillick*-competence'—and decided against Mrs Gillick by a majority of 3:2.

5.19   We return to *Gillick* in chapter 10. For the present we need only note the overall tenor of the judgment as expressed by Lord Scarman:

If the law should impose upon the process of growing up fixed limits where nature knew only a continuous process, the price would be artificiality and a lack of realism in an area where the law must be sensitive to human development and social change.[29]

5.20   The thrust of the case is, however, to be found in Lord Fraser's speech, in which he said that the doctor would be justified in proceeding with contraceptive advice without the parents' consent or even knowledge provided that he or she was satisfied that:

(i)   the girl would, although under 16, understand the advice;

(ii) she could not be persuaded to inform her parents or to allow the doctor to inform the parents that she was seeking contraceptive advice;

(iii) she was very likely to have sexual intercourse with or without contraceptive treatment;

(iv) unless she received contraceptive advice or treatment her physical or mental health or both were likely to suffer; and

(v)   her best interests required the doctor to give her contraceptive advice, treatment or both without parental consent.[30]

Lord Fraser emphasised that the judgment was not to be regarded as a licence for doctors to disregard the wishes of parents whenever they found it convenient to do so and he pointed out that any doctor who behaved in such a way would be failing to discharge his professional responsibilities and would be expected to be disciplined by his own professional body accordingly.

5.21   The House also considered the second question posed and, despite one dissenting

---

[28] *Johnston v Wellesley Hospital* (1970) 17 DLR (3d) 139.   [29] [1985] 3 All ER 402 at 421.
[30] *Ibid* at 413.

opinion, ruled that it was unlikely that a doctor giving contraceptive advice to a female minor would be committing an offence under the then relevant Sexual Offences Act 1956, s 28. The discussion is, however, now of academic interest only as the matter is now solved by recent statute. A person is not guilty of aiding, abetting or counselling the commission of offences associated with childhood sexuality if he or she acts for what are, essentially, medical reasons and not for the purpose of encouraging the activity or the child's participation in it[31]—and it is difficult to conceive of a doctor falling foul of the latter conditions.

5.22   The medical response to the House of Lords decision in *Gillick* was generally one of relief. Yet it is possible that it was something of a Pyrrhic victory; in the event of a complaint being laid, it may be very much harder for a doctor to show that he or she conformed to all five of Lord Fraser's conditions than merely to convince his peers that he was following his reasonable medical judgment. The doctor undoubtedly has a difficult task in assessing whether or not his young patient has sufficient understanding and intelligence for him to treat her with equanimity. The GMC's guidelines now state that the doctor who considers that the patient lacks capacity to give consent to treatment or disclosure, and who has failed to persuade the patient to allow the involvement of an appropriate third party, may disclose relevant information to an appropriate person or authority if it is essential to do so in the patient's medical interests. This, however, is subject to the incapax having been told of the intention.[32]

5.23   The narrowness of the decision in *Gillick* cannot be overlooked—it is noteworthy that, on a simple head count, more judges supported the complainer than opposed her throughout the legal process. Moreover, in view of the current concern at the upsurge in sexually transmitted disease among the young,[33] the words of Lord Templeman, albeit of 20 years ago, still merit preservation: 'There are many things which a girl under 16 needs to practise, but sex is not one of them.'[34] Having said which, it must be admitted that the sexual connotations of *Gillick* are now relegated to history; the lasting importance of the case is that, by extrapolation, it changed the entire face of adolescent medical treatment.

POST COITAL CONTRACEPTION

5.24   Certain types of contraception are designed to—or, in practice, do—work after the embryo has formed.[35] These are referred to as interceptive methods—or emergency

---

[31] Sexual Offences Act 2003, s 73.

[32] General Medical Council *Confidentiality: Protecting and Providing Information* (2004) para 28. See also General Medical Council *Seeking Patients' Consent: The Ethical Considerations* (1998) para 23.

[33] A useful recent review is to be found in J Tripp and R Viner 'Sexual Health, Contraception and Teenage Pregnancy' (2005) 330 BMJ 590.

[34] [1985] 3 All ER 402 at 432.

[35] On the face of things, this is a contradiction in terms in that conception has already occurred. One should be thinking, rather, of contragestational methods but the terminology is now in general use. The moralist might hold that, irrespective of the legal situation, interceptive 'contraception' is less acceptable than a truly contraceptive method which prevents fertilisation of the ovum (see para 5.1 above).

contraception—of which the intrauterine device and the misnamed 'morning after' pill are prime examples.[36] Such methods are, essentially, designed to prevent implantation and the question has arisen as to whether they offend against the Offences Against the Person Act 1861 (see para 5.61 below). Much of the discussion turns on the interpretation of the word 'miscarriage' and whether or not this relates only to the displacement of the implanted embryo. For our part, we find it illogical to suggest that there can be miscarriage in the absence of true carriage. In any event, the use of an IUD must surely be morally preferable to the legal destruction of an implanted human fetus and it is a matter for satisfaction that the issue has now been put beyond doubt. It is currently legal for a pharmacist to dispense 'emergency contraception' without a doctor's prescription[37] and an application for judicial review of the relevant order has been dismissed on the grounds that we have outlined above— interceptive methods of control of pregnancy, it was said, were plainly excluded from the operation of the 1861 Act.[38]

5.25   We do, however, see a clear legal distinction between interception and the use of displanting methods that are specifically designed to displace the implanted embryo—the technique that is euphemistically termed 'menstrual extraction' is a common example of the latter while an IUD may be used for both purposes, its intended function being largely a matter of timing. These techniques come squarely within the definition of abortion and we return to them at para 5.88 below.

STERILISATION

5.26   The aim of sterilisation is to end the patient's reproductive capability. A number of surgical procedures may be used to achieve this. In males, the most common method is vasectomy, in which the vas deferens is cut and tied. Sterilisation in females is usually achieved by division or clipping of the fallopian tubes, which carry the ova between the ovary and the womb.[39] An important feature of both operations from the legal and ethical standpoint is that they are generally intended to be irreversible;

---

[36] It has been pointed out that the term 'morning after' implies a spurious sense of urgency; in fact, emergency hormonal contraception need only be instituted within 72 hours of sexual intercourse and current evidence is that this is an over-cautious estimate: A M C Webb 'Emergency Contraception' (2003) 326 BMJ 775.

[37] As a result of relatively intense lobbying, the Prescription Only Medicine (Human Use) Amendment (No 3) Order 2000 (SI 2000/3231) came into force in January 2001. 'Over the counter' emergency contraception is available in the United States in Washington, California, New Mexico, Alaska and Hawaii.

[38] *R (on the application of Smeaton) v Secretary of State for Health and others* [2002] 2 FLR 146, (2002) 66 BMLR 59. This provides an exhaustive review of the relevant literature.

[39] Reviews of the literature indicate that vasectomy is the more successful and less expensive of the two procedures. Nevertheless, sterilisations involving the woman are more common than are those performed on men: N W Hendrix, S P Chauhan and J C Morrison 'Sterilization and its Consequences' (1999) 54 Obst Gynec Survey 766. Tubal ligation is also frequently complicated by ectopic pregnancy: C Westhoff and A Davis 'Tubal Sterilization: Focus on the US Experience' (2000) 73 Fertil Steril 913.

although it may be possible to repair the operation, prospective attempts to allow for reversibility are likely to result in procedures which fail in their primary purpose. Modern microsurgery has improved on this position—a development which may account for some of the apparently disparate court decisions that have been taken;[40] nevertheless, it is generally held that sterilisation will, or at least may well, bring a basic human function to an end.[41]

5.27   Ethical objections to sterilisation usually focus on this aspect of irreversible interference with the ability to reproduce. Those who object on these grounds would argue that such interference is unjustified, in that the individual may later undergo a change of mind and may wish to return to a position which is probably now closed. They would also stress that the decision to sterilise is one which is taken in the midst of subtle social and personal pressures; the likelihood of the decision being entirely free is, thereby, diminished—yet it is one that cannot easily be retracted.[42] The objection of the Catholic Church is more direct. In Catholic teaching, sterilisation is a mutilation of the body which leads to the deprivation of a natural function and which must, therefore, be rejected unless it is carried out for strictly therapeutic purposes— that is, where it is necessary for the physical health of the patient; the performance of hysterectomy in the treatment of excessive menstrual bleeding, for example, is admissible.[43] The secular counterpart lies in the concept of maim; although, historically, this refers to injuries which limit a man's capacity for military service, the courts might well take exception, say, to castration on non-therapeutic grounds.[44] In so far as it is possible to identify a lay consensus on the matter, it is that sterilisation is an acceptable method of contraception provided that the person undergoing the operation is adequately informed of the implications. Very strong objections may be voiced, however, when there is any question as to the reality of the patient's consent and we return to the subject below.[45]

5.28   The legality of contraceptive sterilisation in the United Kingdom is now beyond doubt.[46] It is also clear that the decision is personal to the individual concerned—the

[40] See para 6.6 below.

[41] Current methods also allow for reversal of vasectomy—a success rate of up to 40% successful pregnancies is claimed. See A K Banergee and A Simpson 'Reversing Vasectomy' (1992) 304 BMJ 1130.

[42] See an excellent letter: E Tuddenham 'Sterilise in Haste: Repent at Leisure and at Great Expense' (2000) 321 BMJ 962.

[43] For a sensitive view from a Catholic clinician of this and other dilemmas, see Poole, n 2 above; 'Time for the Vatican to Bend' (1992) 339 Lancet 1340. On a world scale, the attitude of orthodox Islam is just as rigid: D A R Verkuyl 'Two World Religions and Family Planning' (1993) 342 Lancet 473. The growing debate between modern medical ethics and orthodox Catholicism is well illustrated by D M Cowdin and J F Tuohey 'Sterilization, Catholic Health Care, and the Legitimate Autonomy of Culture' (1998) 4 Christ Bioeth 14; J E Smith 'Sterilizations Reconsidered?' (1998) 4 Christ Bioeth 45.

[44] This raises the general question of self-inflicted injury, for which, see R v Brown, discussed at para 15.1 below.

[45] See paras 5.29 et seq.

[46] Many jurisdictions impose a legal age limit. The situation in the United Kingdom would be governed by the general rules as to consent (see chapter 10). Age would be of particular importance depending on whether the operation was regarded as medical treatment or a medical procedure (see para 10.27).

doctor owes a duty of care to the patient, not to his or her spouse or partner, and it has been held that the courts would never grant an injunction to stop sterilisation or vasectomy.[47] On the other hand, the very term 'family planning' implies a shared responsibility and it is good practice for the doctor to *encourage* patients to discuss such matters with their partners. On purely practical grounds, the surgeon may wish to avoid involvement in divorce proceedings and the like. *Bravery*[48] is no longer an acceptable authority but Lord Evershed MR may still be regarded as correct in saying:

It would not be difficult ... to construct in imagination a case of grave cruelty on a wife founded on the progressive hurt to her health caused by an operation for sterilisation undergone by her husband in disregard of, or contrary to, the wife's wishes or natural instincts.[49]

—and the alternative proposition would also apply. As to consent, the British Medical Association now regards the routine search for a partner's agreement as being inappropriate—the decision to be sterilised is one for the individual patient.[50]

NON-CONSENSUAL STERILISATION

5.29   If consensual sterilisation raises ethical misgivings, then non-consensual sterilisation can be seen as a minefield of powerful objection. Neither legislatures nor courts can totally disregard the ghost of the eugenic movement which flourished in the first half of the twentieth century and led to legislative measures in several jurisdictions that provided for the sterilisation of mentally handicapped persons, those suffering from certain forms of genetically transmissible diseases and even criminal recidivists.[51] Eugenics on a national scale can, however, now be relegated to history and we are concerned here only with the management of individual cases.[52]

5.30   The root problem of non-consensual sterilisation lies in the fact that it raises starkly the subject of what has been named the basic human right to reproduce—to which we return for general discussion below.[53] The phrase seems to have originated in the American case of *Skinner v Oklahoma*[54]—which, in fact, concerned the punitive

---

[47] *Paton v British Pregnancy Advisory Service Trustees* [1979] QB 276 at 280, [1978] 2 All ER 987 at 990 per Sir George Baker P.

[48] *Bravery v Bravery* [1954] 3 All ER 59, [1954] 1 WLR 1169, CA.

[49] [1954] 3 All ER 59 at 62, [1954] 1 WLR 1169 at 1173.

[50] BMA Ethics Department *Medical Ethics To-day* (2nd edn, 2004) at 235.

[51] Some 12,500 operations were performed in the United States between 1907 and 1963: Annotation 'Validity of Statutes Authorizing Asexualization or Sterilization of Criminals or Mental Defectives' 53 ALR 3d 960 (1973). Comparative later developments in Europe are discussed by A N Sofair and J C Kaldjian 'Eugenic Sterilization and a Qualified Nazi Analogy: The United States and Germany, 1930–1945' (2000) 132 Ann Intern Med 312.

[52] The result of a long line of early decisions in the United States can be summarised by *Re Hayes* 608 P 2d 635 (Wash, 1980) in which it was laid down that the courts could authorise sterilisation in the absence of consent so long as, inter alia, the subject was incapable of forming a judgment, was physically capable of procreation, was likely to engage in sexual activity and there was no reasonable alternative to sterilisation.

[53] See para 5.39 et seq.   [54] 316 US 535 (1942).

sterilisation of a man—and has, since, come into common usage throughout the English-speaking world. In the United Kingdom, the concept was first articulated in the very significant case *Re D (a minor)*.[55] The minor in this case was an 11-year-old girl who suffered from a rare condition known as Sotos syndrome. Her IQ was roughly 80, a rating which need not necessarily make it impossible for the person in question to cope reasonably well in everyday life or even to marry and raise a child. There was medical evidence to the effect that her condition showed some signs of improvement and that this improvement could continue.

5.31   In her judgment in this case, Heilbron J was strongly influenced by the evidence given to the court to the effect that sterilisation was not always appropriate in such cases and that a decision to sterilise was beyond the clinical judgment of a single doctor dealing with the case. Also to be taken into account was the irreversibility of the operation and the significance of carrying it out on so young a person:

> A review of the whole of the evidence leads me to the conclusion that in a case of a child of 11 years of age, where the evidence shows that her mental and physical condition and attainments have already improved, and where her future prospects are as yet unpredictable, where the evidence also shows that she is unable as yet to understand and appreciate the implications of this operation and could not give valid or informed consent, that the likelihood is that in later years she will be able to make her own choice, where, I believe, the frustration and resentment of realising (as she would one day) what happened could be devastating, an operation of this nature is, in my view contra-indicated.[56]

5.32   Heilbron J raised the concept of the 'basic human right of a woman to reproduce' and concluded that it would be a violation of that right if a girl were sterilised without her consent for non-therapeutic reasons. *Re D* remained the English authority for more than a decade and was quoted with approval in the Canadian case of *Re Eve*.[57] *Eve* is an important case because, among other reasons, the Supreme Court of Canada took several years to deliberate and, in so doing, canvassed a large number of opinions; moreover, by the time the trial had gone through all its stages, virtually every variant had been supported in the judgments.

5.33   Eve was a mentally disabled adult whose mother asked that she be sterilised, a major plank supporting the request being that, in the event of Eve becoming pregnant, neither she nor her mother would be able to care for the baby. The Supreme Court was in no doubts as to its having a parens patriae jurisdiction through which to authorise sterilisation should the need arise. That power was, however, limited by the principle of its being exercised in the best interests of the girl. In the light of this, the judgment was deeply concerned to distinguish between therapeutic and non-therapeutic reasons for sterilisation; La Forest J concluded:

> The grave intrusion on a person's rights and the certain physical damage that ensues from non-therapeutic sterilization without consent . . . have persuaded me that it can never safely

---

[55] [1976] Fam 185, [1976] 1 All ER 326.   [56] [1976] Fam 185 at 196, [1976] 1 All ER 326 at 335.
[57] (1986) 31 DLR (4th) 1.

be determined that such a procedure is in the best interests of that person . . . [I conclude that non-therapeutic sterilization] should never be authorised . . . under the *parens patriae* jurisdiction.[58]

He appreciated that there could be difficulty in drawing a line between a therapeutic and a non-therapeutic operation, but was content to emphasise that: 'the utmost caution must be exercised commensurate with the severity of the procedure'. In essence, it was this problem which provoked the apparent conflict between the court in *Eve* and that involved in the comparable English case of *Re B*,[59] which was the first of its kind to reach the House of Lords.

5.34 It is unfortunate from the comparative aspect that *Re B* concerned a girl aged 17—she would, therefore, shortly have passed out of the English wardship jurisdiction and it was considered that there was no parens patriae authority on which to fall back in the case of an adult such as was available to the Canadian courts.[60] A speedy decision was, thus, dictated, and there is no doubt that Lord Hailsham LC, on it being suggested that the girl's progress could well be observed for a year, laid open his defences when he said: 'We shall be no wiser in twelve months than we are now.'[61] A massive literature built up around the case and we refer here only to those aspects of it that we regard as essential to the understanding of the seminal decision.

5.35 B was a mentally disabled epileptic with a mental age of five to six years. She had never conceived and was not pregnant but, absent being fully institutionalised, she was in danger of becoming so. Medical opinion—which, in contrast to that given in *Re D*,[62] was scarcely challenged—was that she would either have to be maintained on hormonal contraceptives for the rest of her reproductive life or her fallopian tubes could be occluded—and the court accepted this as being an irreversible procedure; it was common ground that any pregnancy that occurred would have to be terminated.

5.36 In authorising sterilisation, the House of Lords upheld the decisions of both the court of first instance and the Court of Appeal. The basic principle involved was the welfare of the girl; Lord Oliver, in particular, emphasised that there was no question of a eugenic motive, no consideration was paid to the convenience of those caring for the ward and no general principle of public policy was involved. Lord Hailsham LC made some specific comments aimed, in the main, at explaining any apparent variances from other relevant decisions. With particular reference to *Eve*, he said:

---

[58] The extant case at the time, *Re K and Public Trustee* (1985) 19 DLR (4th) 255, in which the main therapeutic ground for sterilisation was a phobic aversion to blood which would be accentuated with the onset of the menses, was regarded as 'at best, dangerously close to the limits of the permissible'—this despite the fact that an Appeal Court judge in *Re K* thought that the case should never have come to the court (per Anderson JA at 277). See also the later New Zealand case *Re X* [1991] 2 NZLR 365.

[59] *Re B (a minor) (wardship: sterilisation)* [1988] AC 199, [1987] 2 All ER 206, HL.

[60] See G T Laurie '*Parens Patriae* Jurisdiction in the Medico-legal Context: The Vagaries of Judicial Activism' (1999) 3 Edin LR 96.

[61] [1987] 2 All ER 206 at 212. The interesting point has been made that, since the procedure is prophylactic in nature, there can be no such thing as an 'emergency' sterilisation. See G B Little 'Comparing German and English Law on Non-consensual Sterilisation: A Difference in Approach' (1997) 5 Med L Rev 269.

[62] [1976] Fam 185, [1976] 1 All ER 328.

[The] conclusion that the procedure of sterilisation should 'never be considered for non-therapeutic purposes' is totally unconvincing and in startling contradiction to the welfare principle . . . [The] distinction [drawn] between 'therapeutic' and 'non-therapeutic' purposes of this operation in relation to the facts of the present case . . . [is] irrelevant . . .[63]

Lord Oliver also found, in effect, that there was no logic in distinguishing preventive medicine from therapy directed to the ward's interest and we would certainly agree with this. It is, however, possible to argue that 'non-therapeutic' in terms of La Forest J's judgment in *Eve* referred only to treatment designed for the benefit of others. If this be so, *Eve* and *Re B* are not greatly in conflict.[64]

5.37   The *Re B* decision was widely criticised in the British academic literature.[65] We wonder, however, whether sufficient attention was paid to the *medical* aspects of the case. There is no doubt that pregnancy *is* contraindicated in some mentally disabled patients or that B was one of them—medically speaking, *Re B* and *Re D* are poles apart. We suggest that the major conceptual difference between *Eve* and *Re B* is that the former generalises on the basis of principle, whereas the latter is determined to particularise on the facts—and we see no objection to the latter line of thinking so long as it is accepted as such.[66]

5.38   Lord Hailsham, however, also addressed the question of rights and it is this issue that so occupied the commentators at the time and has done so ever since. He said: 'The right [of a woman to reproduce] is only such when reproduction is the result of informed choice of which the ward in the present case is incapable'[67] and, again:

To talk of the 'basic right' to reproduce of an individual who is not capable of knowing the causal connection between intercourse and childbirth . . . [or who] is unable to form any maternal instincts or to care for a child, appears to me wholly to part company with reality.[68]

5.39   The concept of a right to reproduce is one which deserves discussion in depth but which, again, we cannot provide in the space available; suffice it to say that the existence of an absolute right is by no means certain. Simplistically, it is difficult to envisage a right that requires the co-operation of another person who is under no obligation to provide it; moreover, an absolute right to reproduce would entail access by right to all means of assisted reproduction including surrogate motherhood by

---

[63] *Re B* [1987] 2 All ER 206 at 213.

[64] K McK Norrie 'Sterilisation of the Mentally Disabled in English and Canadian Law' (1989) 38 Int & Comp LQ 387.

[65] See e.g. M Freeman 'For Her Own Good' (1987) 84 LS Gaz 949; S P de Cruz 'Sterilization, Wardship and Human Rights' (1988) 18 Fam Law 6; R Lee and D Morgan 'Sterilisation and Mental Handicap: Sapping the Strength of the State?' (1988) 15 J Law & Soc 229; J Montgomery 'Rhetoric and "Welfare" ' (1989) 9 OJL Stud 395—a particularly trenchant attack. It is fair to remark that the decision in *Eve* has not been applauded everywhere in Canada: see M A Shone 'Mental Health—Sterilization of Mentally Retarded Persons' (1987) 66 Can BR 635.

[66] We discuss this matter in general in J K Mason 'Particularity in Medical Law' in Z Bankowski (ed) *The Universal and the Particular in Legal Reasoning* (2005, in press).

[67] [1987] 2 All ER 206 at 213.   [68] *Ibid* at 213.

way of womb-leasing—and this is clearly untenable.[69] Grubb and Pearl[70] argued very convincingly that the only such right currently recognised in English law is the right to choose whether or not to reproduce—this being grounded in the principle of individual autonomy.[71] If this be so, it is not difficult to accept the courts' assumption of that right on behalf of a subject who is unable to make a rational choice.

5.40   An alternative approach is to regard the 'right' as one to retain the capacity to reproduce.[72] While this is still subject to the individual's ability to choose, its acceptance makes it harder to justify court interference with that right. In our view, the resolution of the dilemma rests upon the definition of reproduction which, surely, cannot be limited and impersonalised to the single aspect of giving birth—it must include an element of after-care;[73] some mentally handicapped persons may not be able to supply this, although some can—it is, again, a question of degree and a matter of the individual medical status.[74] Moreover, the practical significance of this limited definition disappears when, as in *Re B*, it is acknowledged that any pregnancy would have to be subject to therapeutic abortion.

5.41   A final criticism of *Re B* has been based on the suggestion that it, and others like it, are sex discriminatory—'Would the court', asked Freeman,[75] 'have sterilised a boy of 17?' The answer is certainly 'no'—and has been shown later to be so[76]—but this only proves the rule. Unfair it may be, but it is a fact of life that reproduction can have no immediately adverse medical effect on a man. The only bases for intentional, non-consensual, non-therapeutic sterilisation of a man would be punitive or eugenic, which is what all would agree should be avoided; the fact that decisions such as *Re B* are gender-based actually contributes to their justification.

5.42   Two very similar wardship cases were reported shortly after *Re B*.[77] In both, sterilisation was approved at first instance and neither was appealed. Significantly, however, medical evidence was given at both hearings to the effect that the proposed operation

---

[69] Per Hale LJ in *Briody v St Helens and Knowsley AHA* [2002] 2 WLR 394 at 404–405, [2001] 2 FLR 1094 at 1104.

[70] A Grubb and D Pearl 'Sterilisation and the Courts' (1987) 46 C LJ 439. See also Nicholson CJ in the Australian case *Re Jane* (1989) FLC 92–007. The reasoning in this case was very similar to that in *Re B*.

[71] Reproductive autonomy has been re-examined extensively by E Jackson *Regulating Reproduction* (2001), especially chapter 1.

[72] As originally proposed by S A M McLean and T D Campbell 'Sterilisation' in S A M McLean (ed) *Legal Issues in Medicine* (1981).

[73] For a remarkably prophetic discussion, see J A Robertson 'Procreative Liberty and the Control of Conception, Pregnancy, and Childbirth' (1983) 69 Va L Rev 405; A Thomas 'For Her Own Good—A Reply' (1987) 84 LSG 1196.

[74] See L Appleby and C Dickens 'Mothering Skills of Women with Mental Illness' (1993) 306 BMJ 348.

[75] (1987) LS Gaz R 949.

[76] *Re A (Medical Treatment: Male Sterilisation)* [2000] 1 FLR 549, (2000) 53 BMLR 66, [2000] Lloyd's Rep Med 87. This is an odd decision as males with Down's syndrome are characteristically sterile.

[77] *Re M (a minor) (wardship: sterilization)* [1988] 2 FLR 497, [1988] Fam Law 434; *Re P (a minor) (wardship: sterilization)* [1989] 1 FLR 182, [1989] Fam Law 102.

was reversible[78]—in up to 75 per cent of cases, according to the gynaecologists in *Re M* who, in disclaiming the emotive overtones of 'sterilisation', preferred to regard the operation as contraceptive in nature. We suspect that this greatly influenced the judges because the evidence in favour of early sterilisation was less than fully agreed in both cases. Perhaps the most interesting feature of both *Re M* and *Re P* is that they can well be regarded as sterilisations which were authorised on social grounds for the benefit of the wards—a matter of protecting their lifestyles—with a strong hint of regard for the benefit of their carers; the decisions are certainly open to criticism.[79]

5.43   Thus far, we have been dealing only with minors concerning whom there was no doubt, at the time, of the courts' authority under the wardship jurisdiction. The problem of the adult who was incapable of consent to treatment was yet to come and was first addressed by Wood J in *T v T*,[80] a case which involved an adult incompetent who was found to be pregnant; medical opinion was consistent that the pregnancy should be terminated under the terms of the Abortion Act 1967 and there was an additional application from the subject's mother for leave to sterilise her at the time of the termination. In the course of a wide-ranging determination, which had to be made in the absence of precedent, Wood J fell back on the expedient of an anticipatory declaration that the performance of the two operations would not be unlawful[81]—a solution which was later approved in the House of Lords in the important case *Re F*.[82]

5.44   In the end, *Re F* was concerned very largely with court procedure. Nevertheless, it forms the basis for the 'best interests' test which is now such an integral part of British medical jurisprudence; it, therefore, still merits consideration in some detail. The conditions of *Re B* were, effectively, duplicated save that F was now beyond the protection of wardship. The trial judge, Scott Baker J, was prepared to see all treatment for physical conditions that was given to mental patients in good faith and in their best interests as lying within the exceptions to the law of battery which had been created so as to allow for the exigencies of everyday life.[83] His declaration that the operation would not be unlawful was upheld by the Court of Appeal where Lord Donaldson MR, likewise, saw nothing incongruous in doctors and others who had a caring responsibility being required to act in the interests of an adult who was unable to exercise a right of choice.[84] The Master of the Rolls was, understandably, reluctant to accept that serious medical treatment could be subsumed under the umbrella of actions acceptable in everyday life and preferred the formula of it falling 'within

---

[78] It was said, in somewhat unusual phraseology: 'The situation to-day is that the operation is not irreversible although it is the current *ethical* practice to tell the patients that it is an irreversible operation' [our emphasis] (per Eastham J, *Re P* [1989] 1 FLR 182 at 189).

[79] E.g. M Brazier *Medicine, Patients and the Law* (3rd edn, 2003) at 276.

[80] [1988] Fam 52, [1988] 1 All ER 613. Discussed in depth by J E S Fortin 'Sterilisation, the Mentally Ill and Consent to Treatment' (1988) 51 MLR 634.

[81] RSC Ord 15, r 16.

[82] *Re F (mental patient: sterilisation)* [1990] 2 AC 1, *sub nom F v West Berkshire Health Authority* [1989] 2 All ER 545.

[83] *Collins v Wilcock* [1984] 3 All ER 374 at 378, [1984] 1 WLR 1172 at 1177, per Goff LJ.

[84] [1990] 2 AC 1 at 18.

generally acceptable standards'. Neill LJ, approaching the problem from principle, concluded that the performance of a necessary, albeit serious, operation, including an operation for sterilisation, on a patient who could not consent would not be a trespass to the person or otherwise unlawful.[85] The court was, however, unanimous as to the need for approval of the High Court before a non-consensual sterilisation operation was undertaken.

5.45   The correctness of the decision to sterilise was not challenged in the House of Lords, which was, rather, concerned with the resolution of questions of law and of legal procedure. The House, inter alia, confirmed that the parens patriae jurisdiction no longer existed in England, and that, if it were to be recreated, it would be for the legislature to do so. Their Lordships also ruled that the procedure by way of declaration was appropriate and satisfactory in cases of the kind, the court having no power to consent to the operation. Undoubtedly, however, the most important aspect of the decision for our purposes was to the effect that the common law provides that a doctor can lawfully give surgical or medical treatment to adult patients who are incapable of consenting—provided that the operation or other treatment is in their best interests; it would be in their best interests if, but only if, it was carried out in order to save their lives or to ensure improvement, or prevent deterioration, in their physical or mental health[86]—a rather curious juxtaposition of the major emergency with mild palliation. The House went even further in indicating that it might be the common law *duty* of the doctor to provide treatment in the case of adults suffering from mental disability who were in the care of a guardian or who were detained in mental hospitals.[87] Logically, this authority would also apply to sterilisation but six reasons were given for distinguishing that operation—including its general irreversibility which would almost certainly deprive the woman of 'what was widely, and rightly, regarded as one of the fundamental rights of a woman, the right to bear a child'.[88]

5.46   At the same time, however, the House of Lords held[89] that whether the 'best interests' test had been met would be judged on *Bolam*[90] principles. The application of a test for negligence to a question of clinical practice can be criticised[91] and it seemed at the time that, having made a bid for judicial supervision, the court, in so stating, effectively handed back control of the decisions to the doctors. The matter has, however, now been resolved and, although it is jumping ahead in time, it should be noted here that the current Practice Direction makes it clear that sterilisation of a person who cannot consent to the operation is one of two types of case that will require the prior sanction of a High Court judge in virtually every instance.[92]

---

[85] *Ibid* at 32.   [86] Per Lord Brandon [1990] 2 AC 1 at 55.

[87] Per Lord Brandon [1990] 2 AC 1 at 56.   [88] [1990] 2 AC 1 at 55, 56.

[89] [1990] 2 AC 1 per Lord Bridge at 52, Lord Brandon at 66–68, Lord Goff at 78.

[90] *Bolam v Friern Hospital Management Committee* [1957] 2 All ER 118, [1957] 1 WLR 582.

[91] D Ogbourne and R Ward 'Sterilization, the Mentally Incompetent and the Courts' (1989) 18 Anglo-Am L Rev 230.

[92] *Practice Note (Official Solicitor: Declaratory Proceedings: Medical and Welfare Decisions for Adults who Lack Capacity)* [2001] 2 FCR 158, (2002) 65 BMLR 72; it is to be emphasised that this note deals only with

5.47   The precedent set by *Re F* is that decisions of this nature will continue to be made on a case-to-case basis and it is because the details of each case differ, and because only the doctors in clinical charge of a case can possess all the facts, that we approve the process; calls for specific legislation should, we believe, be resisted because it would, inevitably, lead to generalisation in an area where the welfare of the individual is paramount. With that in mind, it is useful to follow the fate of some of the cases that have been decided since *Re F.*

5.48   Two cases were heard in 1992. *Re HG*[93] was another which was heard in something of a hurry due to the imminence of the subject's 18th birthday. The girl was an epileptic who suffered from an unspecified chromosomal abnormality; there was no dispute that pregnancy would be disastrous for her and that long-term hormonal contraception was contraindicated. In making the order, the deputy judge said:

> [My conclusion is that] a sufficiently overwhelming case has been established to justify interference with the fundamental right of a woman to bear a child. I am certainly satisfied that it would be cruel to expose [her] to an unacceptable risk of pregnancy and that that should be obviated by sterilisation in her interests.[94]

5.49   The adult patient in *Re W*[95] was also an epileptic who, again, was at small risk of becoming pregnant. Nevertheless, sterilisation was held to be in her best interests and a declaration was granted. A feature of the case was the reliance on *Bolam* as a measure of 'best interests'; the decision was, thus, dominated by medical, rather than judicial, opinion—an aspect that came in for some criticism.[96]

5.50   The *Practice Note*[97] relevant at the time, however, specifically advised that a declaration in favour of non-consensual sterilisation should be granted only if there was a real danger rather than a mere chance of pregnancy resulting—and this was reflected in *Re LC*.[98] *LC* seems to have been the first case since *Re D* in which sterilisation was refused in the face of medical opinion. The danger to the woman was, however, not so much that of pregnancy as of sexual assault—and the latter risk was present irrespective of her fertility. One notable feature was that the care afforded her was exceptional, and this, of itself, was thought to provide good grounds for not imposing the risks of a surgical intervention.

5.51   There was, then, a hiatus in reported cases until 1998, when two further cases

---

adults. The other situation is the discontinuation of nutrition and hydration of a person in a vegetative state (see chapter 16). For Scotland, see Adults with Incapacity (Specified Medical Treatments) (Scotland) Regulations 2002, Sch 1 (SSI 2002/275).

   [93] *Re HG (specific issue order: sterilisation)* [1993] 1 FLR 587, (1992) 16 BMLR 50.

   [94] *Ibid* at 592. This case had some administrative significance in indicating that declarations can be made as specific issue orders under the Children Act 1989, s 8 although an appeal to the inherent jurisdiction of the court is the preferred route.

   [95] *Re W (Mental patient: sterilisation)* [1993] 1 FLR 381, [1993] Fam Law 208.

   [96] See I Kennedy 'Commentary' (1993) 1 Med L Rev 234.

   [97] *Practice Note (Official Solicitor: Sterilisation)* [1993] 3 All ER 222, [1993] 2 FLR 222.

   [98] *Re LC (Medical treatment: sterilisation)* [1997] 2 FLR 258, [1997] Fam Law 604 (judgment in the case was given in October 1993).

were heard. In the first of these,[99] Johnson J found the circumstances to be indistinguishable from those in *Re LC* in that the risk of pregnancy was speculative rather than real. This aspect of the case was independent of any 'right to reproduce' which, it was agreed, was irrelevant in *Re B* terms.[100] The freedom from risk, however, was, again, due to the care expended by the woman's parents; it is probably this factor which mainly caused the judge to reach his conclusion and to follow *Re LC* 'with reluctance'. Thus, it seemed that a group of cases were being separated which depended on the immediacy of the risk of pregnancy. This was confirmed from the other side of the coin in *Re X*,[101] in which the woman concerned actually wanted to have a baby—sterilisation was authorised when it was agreed that she would have been incapable of looking after it.

5.52   All the cases thus far discussed have been related to the incompetent's way of life or, put another way, to her social best interests. At the same time, however, a line of cases was developing which referred to the subject's medical interests. The solution of some such cases will be obvious—clearly, for example, it would not be necessary to obtain court approval before undertaking a hysterectomy in the treatment of carcinoma of the uterus despite the fact that the patient would be rendered infertile as a secondary effect. Rather more difficulty arises when the disability is associated with menstrual excess—a very real problem in the case of the incompetent who may well be confused and disturbed even by normal periods. Sterilisation is, however, a high price to pay for treating what may well have been, in ordinary circumstances, a comparatively simple menstrual disorder or, even, no more than a 'phobia'. In the first such case to come before the British courts, *Re E*,[102] concerning a 17-year-old, Sir Stephen Brown held that no formal consent of the court was necessary and that the parents were in a position to give a valid consent: 'A clear distinction is to be made between an operation to be performed for a genuine therapeutic reason and one to achieve sterilisation.'[103] Sir Stephen's easy assurance in the face of the difficulties encountered in Australia (see n 109 below) is a little difficult to accept. Nevertheless, in a second case, *Re GF*,[104] which concerned a 29-year-old woman, the President confirmed his opinion and declined to grant a declaration of lawfulness on the grounds that it was unnecessary when an operation was designed to improve the health of the patient. He did, however, lay down the conditions under which no application to the court was needed. These were that two doctors agreed: first, that the operation was necessary for therapeutic purposes; secondly, that it was in the patient's best interests; and, thirdly, that no practicable less intrusive treatment was available.

---

[99] *Re S (Medical Treatment: Adult Sterilisation)* [1998] 1 FLR 944, [1998] Fam Law 325.

[100] [1988] AC 199, [1987] 2 FLR 314. See para 5.36 above for dicta of Lord Oliver and Lord Hailsham in that case. Johnson J did not, however, feel the same way about the House of Lords' somewhat cavalier attitude to the risks of surgical operation.

[101] *Re X (Adult Patient: Sterilisation)* [1998] 2 FLR 1124, [1998] Fam Law 737.

[102] *Re E (a minor) (medical treatment)* [1991] 2 FLR 585, (1992) 7 BMLR 117.

[103] (1992) 7 BMLR 117 at 119.

[104] [1992] 1 FLR 293, [1993] 4 Med LR 77, sub nom *F v F* (1992) 7 BMLR 135.

5.53   It was probably this last condition that brought a third case to the Family
Court—that of Re Z [105] which involved a 19-year-old woman with Down's syndrome.
There was essentially no dispute as to the facts that Z suffered from painful and
excessive periods and that a pregnancy would be disastrous; however, the experts
disagreed as to how these conditions were to be managed—was it to be by way of the
insertion of a Mirena intra-uterine device (see para 5.14 above) or by hysterectomy?
Bennett J, relying on Lord Goff in Re F,[106] clarified the position of experts vis-à-vis the
court:

> Experts are what they are—experts. They must be listened to with respect, but their opinions
> must be weighed and judged by the court.[107]

In the end, Bennett J concluded that Z's best interests were served by hysterectomy, the risks of which were offset by the certainty that it would eliminate her
periods and would, at the same time, protect her totally from pregnancy; the use of a
coil was unacceptably uncertain on both counts.

5.54   The problem of treatment of menstrual 'phobias' has also arisen in Scotland,
where it provided a part basis for the only reported case so far in which sterilisation of
an incapax has been opposed. In L, Petitioner,[108] it was held in the Outer House of the
Court of Session that sterilisation of an autistic woman would not be justified by the
avoidance of pregnancy alone—other methods of contraception were available
although, as we have discussed above at para 5.13 et seq, these had their inbuilt risks.
The fact that these would not prevent menstruation, with which she was unable to
cope, tipped the balance in favour of sterilisation by way of partial hysterectomy.[109] It
is to be noted that sterilisation of an incapax in Scotland, other than when there is
disease of the reproductive organs, is now statutorily subject to the approval of the
Court of Session.[110]

5.55   In England, the various threads of 'social' and therapeutic sterilisation have now
been drawn together in Re S[111]—the first relevant case to reach the Court of Appeal
since Re F. Here, the conditions and the problems were very similar to those in Re Z
save that the risks of pregnancy were rather more proximate in the latter—indeed,
Wall J at first instance confirmed that the only reason a declaration was sought was
that alternative methods of treatment were available and had been advocated. Wall J,

---

[105] Re Z (medical treatment: hysterectomy) [2000] 1 FLR 523, (1999) 53 BMLR 53.

[106] [1990] 2 AC 1 at 80.   [107] (2000) 53 BMLR 53 at 64.

[108] 1996 SCLR 538. Other, unopposed, sterilisation applications have been granted: A Ward 'Tutors to
Adults: Developments' 1992 SLT 325.

[109] The 'menstrual case' has been especially well considered in Australia. See, in particular, Secretary,
Department of Health and Community Services (N T) v J W B and S M B (Marion's Case) (1992) 175 CLR 218,
(1992) 66 ALJR 300. The case is thoroughly explored by N Cica 'Sterilising the Intellectually Disabled' (1993)
1 Med L Rev 186. For later cases, see Re L and M (Sarah's Case) (1993) 17 Fam LR 357 and P v P (1994) 19
Fam LR 1.

[110] Adults with Incapacity (Specified Medical Treatments) (Scotland) Regulations 2002, Sch 1 (SSI
2002/275).

[111] In re S (adult patient: sterilisation) [2000] 1 FLR 465, [2000] Fam Law 322, revs'd [2001] 3 Fam 15,
[2000] 3 WLR 1288.

in fact, regarded S's menstrual problems as more important than the risk of pregnancy and followed Bennett J in *Re Z* in concluding that S's best interests lay in a subtotal hysterectomy rather than in the insertion of a coil which, of itself, did not require court approval. Having declared the hysterectomy to be lawful, he then adopted the rather innovative strategy of leaving the choice of treatments to S's mother and her medical advisers in consultation.

5.56   In the event, the Court of Appeal was highly, and perhaps unfairly, critical of this decision, pointing out that the judge had run contrary to unanimous medical opinion; the declaration in favour of hysterectomy was reversed in favour of the insertion of a coil with the option of a further hearing should this not prove an effective remedy. The details of the individual case are not, however, as important as are the wider implications as to the relationship between the *Bolam* test[112] and the 'best interests' test. As Thorpe LJ put it: 'There can be no doubt that the speeches in *Re F* determine that the *Bolam* test is relevant to the judgment of the adult patient's best interests when a dispute arises as to the advisability of medical treatment'. There can, however, be a number of courses which might be followed by responsible doctors; the function of the *Bolam* test is, therefore, of a preliminary nature, doing no more than to establish the propriety of the options on offer. By contrast, there can be only one '*best* interest'—a phrase which the court considered to be synonymous with the patient's welfare—and it is the function of the doctor or of the court to establish this as the paramount precondition to providing treatment for the incompetent. Moreover, the welfare of the patient will be decided on more than medical grounds—ethical, social, moral and welfare considerations must also be weighed in the balance.[113] The *Bolam* test, thus, has no place in the second or determinative phase of what is, effectively, a two-stage test for the lawfulness of non-voluntary treatment. It will be seen in chapter 9 that *Bolam* is coming under increasing attack as a modern legal principle; in our view, *Re S* provides a particularly strong barrier to any extension of its application. A final and important comment on *Re S* is to note that the Court of Appeal was unanimous in holding that any interpretation of Sir Stephen Brown's ruling on the need for involvement of the courts in cases such as these[114] should 'incline towards the strict and avoid the liberal'—a form of words which carries a ring of euphemism!

5.57   However, one of the most significant features to be extracted from the cases throughout the Anglophone jurisdictions is their pragmatic acceptance that non-therapeutic or social considerations—which we are happy to see as aspects of preventive or holistic medicine—can properly be prayed in aid of the incompetent minor. The words of Pashman J in the influential American case of *Re Grady* provide a suitable coda to the discussion:

[112] Discussed in detail at para 9.21. In brief: The doctor is not negligent if he follows a course which would be regarded as acceptable by a responsible body of medical opinion.

[113] Per Butler-Sloss P at 3 WLR 1288, 1296. The President also noted that she had expressed similar views in *Re A*, n 76 above.

[114] N 104 above.

[She] should have the opportunity to lead a life as rewarding as her condition will permit. Courts should cautiously but resolutely help her achieve the fullness of that opportunity. If she can have a richer and more active life, only if the risk of pregnancy is permanently eliminated, then sterilisation may be in her best interests [and] it should not be denied to her.[115]

TERMINATION OF PREGNANCY

5.58   We have included the legal termination of pregnancy, or legal abortion,[116] within this chapter because it is logical to do so—the control of pregnancy *is* an aspect of the control of fertility. This not to imply, however, that it should, as a consequence, be regarded as a facet of family planning—at best, it should be seen in that context as *failed* family planning. One's attitude must, of course, depend on how far one accepts the concept of existing rights of the fetus in the reproductive process which we have outlined in para 5.5 above—and this forms a main basis of the discussion that follows.

5.59   As is only too well known, the abortion debate is one that is centred on ethics. Any legal argument is, essentially, confined to how, and to what extent, the ethics should be constrained by the law. The passing of the Abortion Act 1967 did, however, exercise a profound and direct influence on the medical ethos. Once the Act was accepted by doctors, the profession abrogated a main tenet of its Hippocratic conscience—as recently as 1994, the Declaration of Geneva, as amended in Stockholm, was advising: 'I will maintain the utmost respect for human life from its beginning'.[117] The Declaration of Oslo, however, while retaining this moral principle, modified it to accord with modern attitudes: 'Diversity of response to this situation [the conflict of vital interests of the mother with vital interests of the child] results from the diversity of attitudes towards the life of the unborn child. This is a matter of individual conviction and conscience.'[118] This ethical watershed has spilled over to influence the attitudes of and towards doctors in relation to all aspects of life and death. Modern medicine now shows no embarrassment in toying with the concept of the wanted and the unwanted.

5.60   In the wider context, however, attitudes to abortion depend almost entirely on where the holder stands in respect of, on the one hand, the fetal interest in life and, on

---

[115] *In the matter of Lee Ann Grady* 426 A 2d 467 (NJ, 1981) at 486.

[116] It is of interest that the Abortion Act 1967 started as the Medical Termination of Pregnancy Bill and many would wish that it had remained so. 'Abortion', in our view, has traditional ties with criminality and, so far as is possible, we avoid the term in the present context. Abortion is, however, so firmly equated in the public mind with the legal termination of pregnancy that it would be perverse not to use the former expression as shorthand; the two terms can be regarded as synonymous so far as this book is concerned.

[117] There is, however, a subtle change of wording from the original 'from the time of conception'. See Appendix B.

[118] World Medical Association (as amended 1983).

the other, a woman's right to control her own body[119] and it is this which perpetuates a near intractable moral conflict. The trial of strength has been waged at a relatively low key in Britain.[120] Passion has, however, run high in the United States, where the protagonists have not been above resorting to serious crime in order to advance their cause;[121] moreover, the issue has been debated at an overtly political level. The political significance has been no less important nearer to home in the European Union, where it bid fair to forestall the reunification of Germany. We return to these examples later; meanwhile, we look briefly at the development of legal abortion in the United Kingdom.

THE EVOLUTION OF THE LAW ON ABORTION

5.61   The evolution of legislation to decriminalise abortion is so well known as to merit only brief description. The fundamental law in England and Wales lies in the Offences Against the Person Act 1861, ss 58 and 59. The Act proscribes procuring the miscarriage of a woman by a third party, self-induced miscarriage, attempted procurement of miscarriage and supplying the means to do so—it is to be noted that the word 'abortion' appears only in the marginal note to the sections.[122] The Act makes no distinction between criminal and therapeutic activity and, despite frequent scrutiny, these sections have not been repealed. The proscription prior to 1967 was so strong that, in addition to being punished by the courts, a doctor involved in a termination of pregnancy was very likely to have his name erased from the medical register. Although the extent of the activity has never been established satisfactorily, there is no doubt that, as a result, a large number of illegal abortions were performed in varying conditions by persons of varying skill.

5.62   The first statutory variation is to be found in the Infant Life (Preservation) Act 1929, which introduced the offence of child destruction or causing the death of a child capable of being born alive before it has an existence independent of its mother. The offence was not committed, however, if the act was done in good faith for the purpose only of preserving the mother's life. This meagre concession to the needs of therapy was still highly restrictive both as to reason and as to time—effectively, it served only to decriminalise feticide in the event of an impacted labour. It was left to the case of

[119] The absolute nature of such a right is seldom questioned. The view that it is, in fact, restricted by correlative duties has been put by H V McLachlan 'Bodies, Rights and Abortion' (1997) 23 J Med Ethics 176.

[120] At the moment of writing, however, it cannot be excluded as a political issue in the forthcoming general election. A classic comment is in S Jenkins 'An Election Dominated by Holy Rows? May the Good Lord Spare Us' (2005) *The Times*, 23 March, p 19.

[121] See Lancet 'This Is a Deadly Game' (1993) 342 Lancet 939—and the legal battle continues: F Charatan 'US Judges Rule in Favour of Abortion "Hit list" ' (2001) 322 Brit Med J 818. For an excellent study of the development of the conflict in the US, see L H Tribe *Abortion: The Clash of Absolutes* (1992).

[122] The distinction, if any, between 'miscarriage' and 'abortion' is of academic interest in relation to pre-implantation methods of contraception (see para 5.24 above). Some writers believe the terms to be interchangeable: see, e.g. I J Keown ' "Miscarriage": a Medico-legal Analysis' [1984] Crim LR 604.

R v Bourne[123] to temper the legal influence on medical practice in the field. Mr Bourne performed an abortion, with no attempt at secrecy, on a 15-year-old girl who was pregnant following a particularly unpleasant rape.[124] Although Mr Bourne was indicted under the Offences Against the Person Act 1861, the trial judge, Macnaghten J, took the opportunity to link the 1861 and 1929 statutes and ruled that, in a case brought under the 1861 Act, the burden rested on the Crown to satisfy the jury that the defendant did not procure the miscarriage of the girl in good faith for the purpose only of preserving her life: the word 'unlawful' in the 1861 Act 'imports the meaning expressed by the proviso in section 1(1) of the Infant Life (Preservation) Act 1929'.[125] The summing-up essentially recognised that a woman's life depended upon her physical and mental health and that an abortion was not illegal if it was performed because these were in jeopardy[126]—and Mr Bourne was acquitted. The law and the medical profession then lived in harmony for many years; the *Bourne* decision was undoubtedly stretched to the limits of interpretation by many doctors but the authorities turned a sympathetic eye.

5.63   But it is never a good thing for any section of the public, no matter how well intentioned, to flirt with illegality; moreover, there was still no authority for termination of the pregnancy in the event of probable handicap of the potential neonate. The situation was resolved when the Abortion Act was put into law in 1967; despite repeated attack, it remained unchanged until 1990.

5.64   It is interesting to compare the historic attitudes in England with those prevailing in Scotland where procuring a woman's miscarriage has always been a common law offence but undefined by statute. The whole subject, including a review of the 1967 Act, occupies less than three pages in *Gordon*.[127] The difference in concern lies in the emphasis laid in Scots law on 'evil intent' as a measure of criminality; there is little doubt that Mr Bourne would have been unlikely to provoke a test case in Scotland. It is, in fact, arguable that there was no need to extend the Act to Scotland; its inclusion was only justified in that it removed any doubt as to the limits of therapeutic abortion in that country where, in effect, a policy similar to that recognised in *Bourne* had been openly followed for decades.

The Abortion Act 1967

5.65   The Abortion Act 1967[128] was significantly amended by the Human Fertilisation and Embryology Act 1990, s 37.[129] In summary, it now states that a person shall not be

---

123   [1939] 1 KB 687, [1938] 3 All ER 615.

124   There is a particularly instructive review of the trial and its ambience in B Brookes and P Roth '*Rex v Bourne* and the medicalization of abortion' in M Clark and C Crawford (eds) *Legal Medicine in History* (1994) ch 13.

125   [1939] 1 KB 687 at 691, [1938] 3 All ER 615 at 617.

126   [1939] 1 KB 687 at 694, [1938] 3 All ER 615 at 619. The Australian courts have also interpreted the word 'unlawful' as indicating that there must be a 'lawful' reason for termination of pregnancy. See para 5.83 below.

127   G H Gordon *The Criminal Law of Scotland* (3rd edn, 2001) ch 28.

128   Hereafter 'the 1967 Act'.   129   Hereafter 'the 1990 Act'.

guilty of an offence under the law of abortion when termination is performed by a registered medical practitioner and two registered medical practitioners have formed the opinion in good faith that the continuance of the pregnancy would involve risk, greater than if the pregnancy were terminated, of injury to the physical or mental health of the pregnant woman or any existing children of her family (s 1(1)(a)); these therapeutic and social grounds, which accounted for 177,286 or 97 per cent of all abortions in England and Wales in 2003, are subject to the pregnancy not having exceeded its twenty-fourth week. The remaining justifications are now free of such temporal restriction. They are that there is a risk of grave permanent injury to the physical or mental health of the pregnant woman (s 1(1)(b)); that the continuance of the pregnancy would involve risk to the life of the pregnant woman greater than if the pregnancy were terminated (s 1(1)(c))—accounting together for 2355 cases in England and Wales in 2003; and, finally, that there is a substantial risk that, if the child were born, it would suffer from such physical or mental abnormalities as to be severely handicapped (s 1(1)(d))—1 per cent of the total in 2003.[130] Subsections (b) and (c) are, additionally, not restricted by requiring the opinion of two registered medical practitioners; single practitioners may operate on their own initiative in such circumstances.[131] Termination under the Act may be carried out in National Health Service hospitals or in places approved for the purpose by the Minister or the Secretary of State (s 1(3)). It is this clause which legalises abortions performed privately and for a fee. The demand for termination is, however, so great that, since 1981, a compromise position has been achieved whereby the private sector acts as an agency for the NHS. The advent of medical methods for the termination of pregnancy has dictated a change in the location rules, which are now relaxed for this purpose.[132]

5.66   As noted above, the vast majority of legal terminations are performed under s 1(1)(a) of the 1967 Act for minor therapeutic or social reasons. It is arguable that the risks of an abortion to the health of a woman are always less than those of a full-term pregnancy—particularly if the termination is carried out in the first trimester.[133] Equally, it is obvious that the mental health of a woman who is carrying an unwanted pregnancy must suffer more damage if she is forced to carry her fetus than it would is she were relieved of her burden. It can also be argued that simple economics dictate that a *risk* to the well-being of any existing members of the family is occasioned by the advent of another mouth to feed. The indications are, therefore, that it is impossible for a doctor to perform an abortion in Great Britain[134] that can be shown to have been

[130] Abortion Statistics, England and Wales, 2003—Government Statistical Service Bulletin 2004/14. These figures do not include slightly under 10,000 abortions performed on non-residents of E & W in 2003.

[131] It is to be noted that s 1(1)(b) contains no comparative element—there simply has to be a risk.

[132] Section 1(3A), inserted by the 1990 Act, s 37(3). 16% of terminations in 2003 involved the use of antiprogestcrones—the highest recorded proportion following a very steady increase over the years.

[133] Abortion methods are becoming increasingly safe but complication rates still increase with the period of gestation.

[134] The Abortion Act 1967 does not extend to Northern Ireland, where the Infant Life (Preservation) Act 1929 is preserved in the Criminal Justice Act (Northern Ireland) 1945, s 25; conditions as to the latter are unaffected by the Human Fertilisation and Embryology Act 1990, s 37 (see 'Northern Ireland' below).

unlawful provided that all the administrative conditions are met.[135] As a corollary, the doctor who applies the letter of the law must always be acting in good faith—indeed, possibly the only way in which a termination can be carried out in *bad* faith is when it is done without the woman's consent.[136]

5.67   Apparently paradoxically, this also applies when considering terminations under s 1(1)(d)—the 'fetal abnormality' ground—which one might have thought was there for the benefit of the fetus who may, otherwise, be born in a handicapped condition.[137] Apart from anything else, the prospect of a disabled child is likely to affect a woman's mental health more than if she terminated the pregnancy; from the woman's aspect, there is, therefore, no absolute need for sub-section (d)—other than, perhaps, to take advantage of the concession as to the length of gestation. More specifically, the sub-section is, again, open-ended in its phraseology.[138] What is a substantial risk? What is a serious handicap? Neither is defined and each can be interpreted on a wholly subjective basis.[139] As a result, it will be difficult, if not impossible, to demonstrate that a decision to terminate the pregnancy was not taken in good faith. At the time of writing, a pastor has succeeded in obtaining access to judicial review of a termination performed because the fetus had a cleft palate; she received no sympathy from either the police or the medical profession and the CPS has refused to take action on the grounds that the decision had been taken in good faith.[140] As a result of all this, it is hardly surprising that we have been able to find only one conviction under the Act[141] and this appears to have arisen mainly because of the way the operation was performed.

5.68   Nor is it remarkable that the medical profession as a whole tends to look on the Act as a success and resists any attempt to stiffen its conditions. Occasionally, however,

---

The Channel Islands have adopted legislation which is similar to, although rather more strict than, that of Great Britain—e.g. Termination of Pregnancy (Jersey) Law 1997.

[135] One could, in fact, apply much the same reasoning to s 1(1)(c) though we fancy that this section is intended to cover terminations once the life-threatening condition has arisen—most commonly in late pregnancy when the dangerous toxaemias of pregnancy may arise and the risks associated with termination are, correspondingly, greater.

[136] And, even then, the charge would be under the Offences Against the Person Act 1861 rather than under the 1967 Act. See C Dyer 'Gynaecologist Acquitted in Hysterectomy Case' (1996) 312 BMJ 11.

[137] We discuss the question of 'wrongful life' in the following chapter. In fact, the sub-section is probably intended for the protection of the woman who may have to rear a disabled child; fetal 'rights' are not involved. And, in fact, there are relatively few circumstances in which death, rather than a life with disability, would be in the interests of the neonate—see S Sheldon and S Wilkinson 'Termination of Pregnancy for Reason of Foetal Disability: Are there Grounds for a Special Exception in Law?' (2001) 9 Med L Rev 85.

[138] See, in particular D Morgan 'Abortion: The Unexamined Ground' [1990] Crim LR 687.

[139] For a full discussion, see E Wicks, M Wyldes and M Kilby 'Late Termination of Pregnancy for Fetal Abnormality: Medical and Legal Perspectives' (2004) 12 Med L Rev 285. The problem also vexes the professionals: Royal College of Obstetricians and Gynaecologists *Termination of Pregnancy for Fetal Abnormality* (1996).

[140] R Gledhill 'Curate Loses Legal Challenge over "Cleft-palate" Abortion' (2005) *The Times*, 17 March, p 14. It is remarkable how consistently the authorities will avoid reconsidering some of the more uncertain aspects of the statute.

[141] *R v Smith (John)* [1974] 1 All ER 376, [1973] 1 WLR 1510, CA.

issues arise which strain the constancy even of the medical establishment—abortion on the basis of fetal sex selection provides such an example. The problem being put to him, Dr John Dawson, spokesman on medical ethics for the British Medical Association at the time, is reported as saying:

To terminate a pregnancy solely on the grounds of the sex of the foetus is an abuse of medical skills. It is unethical and I believe the GMC should take a serious view . . . [of] a doctor who undertakes that sort of work.[142]

Which may well be so—the issue is of a different dimension from pre-conception selection which we have discussed above[143] or, indeed, pre-implantation selection (see para 7.24); nevertheless, it is difficult to see it as illegal. The 1967 Act, at s 1(2), specifically states that, in making a determination as to the risk of injury to the woman's or her existing children's health, 'account may be taken of the pregnant woman's actual or reasonably foreseeable environment'. Given the right ethnic ambience—most particularly within Asian and Muslim cultures—there can be no doubt that the birth of a female child could affect a woman's mental health and, possibly, her physical well-being, and there is nothing in the Act which limits such risks to those directly associated with the condition of pregnancy.[144] Even a person with a Western background may be mentally disturbed by the thought of a third male (or female) child and, while gender-led abortion may not constitute a major problem in our society, it serves to illustrate how wide is the facility for termination within the wording of the 1967 Act.

5.69   The availability of lawful termination has been further extended by s 37(4) of the 1990 Act, which amends s 5(1) of the 1967 Act so as to read:

No offence under the Infant Life (Preservation) Act 1929 shall be committed by a registered medical practitioner who terminates a pregnancy in accordance with the provisions of this Act.

The criminal associations with 'viability' of the fetus[145] and the living abortus (to which we refer briefly below at para 5.98) are, therefore, now almost, although not quite, entirely dispelled.

5.70   There are still some who regard abortion in Great Britain as being unreasonably restricted as compared with other jurisdictions;[146] even so, the scope of the Abortion Act 1967 probably exceeds that envisaged by its originators. The number of

---

[142] 'Babies of Wrong Sex Aborted, Claims Report' *The Scotsman*, 4 January 1988, p 2. It has to be acknowledged, however, that a case can be made for sex selection based on the concept of procreative autonomy: J Savulescu 'Sex Selection: The Case For' (1999) 171 Med J Austral 373.

[143] See para 4.19.

[144] Similar views were expressed by D Morgan 'Foetal Sex Identification, Abortion and the Law' (1988) 18 Fam Law 355.

[145] See para 5.94 below. For review of attitudes to late terminations, see J Savulescu 'Is Current Practice around Late Termination of Pregnancy Eugenic and Discriminatory?' (2001) 27 J Med Ethics 165.

[146] For a very complete review, see P de Cruz *Comparative Healthcare Law* (2001), chapter 13. It has been suggested that some 42% of the British public would support availability of abortion without any reason other than the woman's choice: J Wise 'British Public Supports Legal Abortion for All' (1997) 314 BMJ 627.

terminations carried out in England and Wales rose relentlessly until 1990, when 186,912 abortions were performed on women resident in England and Wales. There was then a steady decrease until a sharp rise occurred in 1996 and, since then, the upward trend has resumed, reaching an all-time high of 190,660 in 2003; the crude abortion rate among residents in England and Wales in the age group 15–44 years is now 16.6/1,000 women. The figures for Scotland show less of a trend and tend to oscillate around the 12,000 per annum mark. The rate is as high as that in England only in Tayside.

5.71   The number of terminations provided for non-resident women in England and Wales in 2003–9,078[147]—represented 4.5 per cent of the total. This shows a marked decline from the peak in 1973 when 33.8 per cent of legal abortions were for patients from overseas. Clearly, there have been policy changes in other countries in the intervening years and it is worth considering some of these briefly.

THE COMPARATIVE POSITION

Northern Ireland

5.72   We have, thus far, spoken only in terms of Great Britain as far as domestic law is concerned. The position in Northern Ireland is particularly sensitive, due to its close association with the Republic of Ireland.[148] As a result, the Abortion Act 1967 does not run to the Province, where the law is still governed by the 1861 Act; this has, however, been modified by some important court decisions. In *Re K (a minor)*,[149] it was held that the law lay in the 1861 Act as modified by the charge to the jury in *R v Bourne*;[150] termination of a 13-week pregnancy in a severely handicapped ward of court was authorised. Again, in *Re A*,[151] the court used the reasoning in *Bourne* to apply the Criminal Justice Act (Northern Ireland) 1945, s 25 to the 1861 Act; a termination was held to be in the handicapped woman's best interests. It will be seen, below, that a very similar situation—albeit one that could be regarded as confusing—exists in New South Wales, where a particularly liberal approach to abortion has evolved. Thus, it may well be that the potential exists for homologation of abortion practice through-out the component parts of the United Kingdom. However, such a potential has not yet been realised; 1,318 women from Northern Ireland obtained terminations in England and Wales during 2003.

The Republic of Ireland

5.73   The Republic of Ireland, along with Germany within the European Union, confers a constitutional right to life on the fetus while, at the same time, paying due regard to

---

[147]   97% were under s 1(1)(a) of the 1967 Act.

[148]   The position is still under review: D Payne 'Abortion in Northern Ireland to be Reviewed' (2001) 322 Brit Med J 1507.

[149]   *Re K (a minor), Northern Health and Social Services Board v F and G* (1991) 2 Med LR 371.

[150]   [1939] 1 KB 687, [1938] 3 All ER 615.

[151]   *Re A (Northern Health and Social Services Board v AMNH)* (1991) 2 Med L Rev 274.

the equal right to life of the mother.[152] The definitive law on abortion is derived from the UK's Offences Against the Person Act 1861 which is incorporated in the Health (Family Planning) Act 1979. As a consequence, a maternal/fetal conflict of interests may arise and, in recent years, this potential has been considered by both the European Court of Justice (ECJ) and the European Court of Human Rights (ECtHR). The results indicate a slow but significant erosion of the previously rigid position.

5.74   In 1991, the Irish High Court sought a ruling from the ECJ on the legality of prohibiting the distribution of information relating to the availability of abortion facilities for Irish citizens in the United Kingdom; the answer was that, as a matter of morality, the Irish government was entitled to follow its own public policy.[153] The following year, the Supreme Court of Ireland extended the grounds on which a termination was permissible from circumstances in which there was an inevitable or immediate risk to the life of the mother to those where there was a real and substantial risk to her life—represented in the instant case by the possibility of suicide. In obiter remarks, however, the court indicated that the right of an unborn child to life would, were the conflict to arise, take precedence over the right of the mother to travel.[154]

5.75   Later in the year, the twin problems of providing information and arranging travel to another jurisdiction were again aired, this time before the European Court of Human Rights[155] when an injunction of the Supreme Court restraining such counselling was challenged. On this occasion, while agreeing that the purpose of the injunction was to protect the national morality, the European Court decided that the degree of restraint imposed was disproportionate to the aim pursued. Accordingly, Article 10 (freedom of expression) of the European Convention on Human Rights was infringed. Two national referenda supported this view and, as a result, the Regulation of Information Act 1995 was passed and held to be constitutional; the injunctions against the provision of information concerning the availability of abortion in Great Britain were subsequently lifted. A further rape-associated case, very similar to that involving X, arose in 1997; here it was confirmed that a 'suicide risk' came within the definition of a substantial risk to the mother's life, by reason of which an abortion carried out in Ireland would not be unlawful; by the same token, the girl concerned could leave the country in order to have the termination.[156]

5.76   Abortion law in the Irish Republic is, therefore, still in an evolutionary phase and a further amendment to the Constitution intended to embody a proposed Protection of Human Life in Pregnancy Act 2002 is still debated.[157] The Act cannot, however,

---

[152] Irish Constitution, Article 40.3.3.

[153] *Society for the Protection of Unborn Children Ireland Ltd v Grogan* [1991] 3 CMLR 849, (1992) 9 BMLR 100.

[154] *A-G v X* [1992] 2 CMLR 277, (1994) 15 BMLR 104.

[155] *Open Door Counselling and Dublin Well Woman v Ireland* (1993) 15 EHRR 244, (1994) 18 BMLR 1.

[156] *A and B v Eastern Health Board* [1998] 1 IR 464. An interesting feature of the case is that the Health Board applied for, and obtained, authority to arrange a termination against the wishes of the 13-year-old girl's parents.

[157] In fact, the referendum came down to a decision as to whether the threat of suicide would justify a termination. The vote was so close that it can have no effect of itself.

come into force unless it is approved in a further referendum. Meantime, the practical effect of the current situation is of some interest. 3,650 Irish women had terminations in Great Britain in 1982; by 2003, this figure had risen to 6,320.[158]

The United States

5.77   Although the transatlantic experience now has little relevance to the United Kingdom, the United States remains one of the few jurisdictions where abortion remains an active political issue. It is, therefore, worth taking a brief look at its development.

5.78   Prior to 1973, abortion law was solely a matter of individual state concern. In that year, however, the Supreme Court was called upon to determine the relationship between state abortion laws and a woman's rights under the US Constitution. It did so in the historic twin decisions of *Roe v Wade*[159] and *Doe v Bolton*.[160] The effect of these well-known cases can be summarised thus: it is an invasion of a woman's constitutional right to privacy to limit her access to abortion by statute—and this applies also to schoolchildren, although their parents may still be informed of the circumstances;[161] the expression 'to preserve the life' of a woman, which defined the grounds for a legal termination in several States, was declared unconstitutionally vague, although 'to preserve the life or health' is acceptable. It was suggested at the time the decisions were reached that health is inclusive of convenience and that this effectively allows for abortion on demand—and although the Supreme Court specifically stated that there was no such absolute constitutional right, there is no doubt that the result of *Roe* is that abortion during the first trimester is an inalienable prerogative of the American woman and is grounded in the right to individual privacy. To confirm the essential nature of privacy, the court also ruled that an appeal on the grounds that wholly liberal laws were invalid—because they deprived unborn children of the right to life—was not available to an individual. Nevertheless, the court did give some weight to the rights of the developing fetus. In the first trimester, the question of termination was to be decided solely between the woman and her physician; during the second trimester, the State could intervene by reason of its interest in the health of the mother, no such interest being vested in the fetus—interference of this type could include stating where, and by whom, an abortion could be done. After 'viability', which the court assessed as somewhere between the twenty-fourth and twenty-eighth week of pregnancy, it was agreed that the State had a compelling interest in the health of the fetus and could, therefore, constitutionally intervene on its behalf excepting when the conditions threatened the life or health of the mother.

5.79   The decision in *Roe v Wade*, which has resulted in about one quarter of pregnancies in the United States ending in legal termination,[162] has been a subject of controversy

---

[158] An interesting attempt to reverse the process and claim that deportation of a pregnant woman offended Article 40.3.3 in so far as neonatal care was inferior in her country to that in Ireland was unsuccessful. The Article, it was said, was relevant to abortion, not to fetal and neonatal health: *Baby O v Minister for Justice, Equality and Law Reform* [2002] 2 IR 169.

[159] 93 S Ct 705 (1973).   [160] 93 S Ct 739 (1973).   [161] *HL v Matheson* 101 S Ct 1164 (1981).

[162] Estimated in 2000.

ever since it was made.[163] Aside from the moral issues involved, the most practical objection is that the trimester rule, which rests upon fluctuating medical expertise and medical technology, is unreliable. This was well put by O'Connor J:

The lines drawn [in *Roe*] have now become 'blurred' . . . The state can no longer rely on a 'bright line' that separates permissible from impermissible regulation. . . . Rather, the State must continuously and conscientiously study contemporary medical and scientific literature in order to determine whether the effect of a particular regulation is to depart from accepted medical practice.[164]

5.80   There are, however, additional reasons why we should dissociate American attitudes and British thinking in this area. Fundamentally, and despite the emotions it engenders, abortion in the United States is not so much a philosophical issue as it is one of constitutional law.[165] Moreover, the subject has become highly politicised and the composition of the Supreme Court is subject to political adjustment. Thus, the Supreme Court firmly repelled a major attack on *Roe* which was mounted in the mid-1980s[166] but a change in personnel encouraged a further sally towards the end of the decade.[167] This was rather more successful in that, although the court was unwilling to overturn the principles laid down in *Roe*, it upheld a Missouri statute which certainly limited the availability of abortion; the implication is that other States may be able to introduce similar restrictions. The central issue in *Webster* turned on the State's right to restrict the reasons for which pregnancies could be terminated at public expense and, in fact, it had been held for some time[168] that federal funding in the form of 'Medicaid' was available for abortions only in limited circumstances—such as preserving the life of the mother or terminating pregnancies resulting from rape or incest.

5.81   The struggle continued and, in 1992, the Supreme Court was again asked to pronounce on the legality of a State statute—in this case, the Abortion Control Act of Pennsylvania, which created a number of obstacles in the way of abortion 'on demand'.[169] The issue, here, as in many of the United States cases, was not so much related to a maternal/fetal conflict as to one involving, on the one hand, the woman's

---

[163] It is poignant to find that 'Ms Roe' has been converted to the 'pro-life' cause and that, in fact, she never obtained her own termination: N McCorvey 'My Legal Fight Helped Start a Generation of Child Slaughter and That Makes Me Weep' *Daily Telegraph*, 20 January 1998, p 4.

[164] In *Akron v Akron Center for Reproductive Health* 462 US 416 (1983) at 455–456.

[165] See I Loveland 'Abortion and the US Supreme Court' (1992) 142 NLJ 974.

[166] *American College of Obstetricians and Gynaecologists v Thornburgh* 476 US 747 (1986).

[167] *Webster v Reproductive Health Services* 109 S Ct 3040 (1989). For extensive and critical discussion, see W Dellinger and G B Sperling 'Abortion and the Supreme Court: The Retreat from *Roe v Wade*' (1989) 138 U Penn LR 83 and related papers. In J Bopp and R E Coleson 'What Does *Webster* Mean' (1989) 138 U Penn LR 157, the authors maintain, inter alia, that 'the trimester scheme may be considered *defacto* and *sub silentia* overruled'.

[168] *Harris v McRae* 100 S Ct 2671 (1980).

[169] *Planned Parenthood of Southeastern Pennsylvania v Casey* 112 S Ct 2791 (1992). See A Charo 'Undue Burden of Abortion' (1992) 340 Lancet 44.

right to bodily privacy and, on the other, the State's interest in the protection of life and a preference for childbirth over abortion.[170] Put simply, *Casey* introduced an 'undue burden' test—which meant that the State was empowered to impose financial, medical or emotional barriers to abortion provided that these did not become a substantial obstacle, or undue burden, to choosing to terminate a pregnancy; the basic premise of the woman's liberty of conscience and bodily integrity was, in this way, upheld. Even so, some fetal rights were maintained, in that States could restrict abortion of the 'viable' fetus save in relation to a medical emergency threatening the mother. As might be expected, this decision was by the barest of majorities and powerful dissenting opinions were handed down—including a rejection of the whole concept of a fundamental women's liberty to choose abortion. The opinion has been said to please no lobby[171] and there is every indication that the abortion debate will continue in the United States in an atmosphere of increasing acrimony and increasing subservience to political exigency.[172]

The Commonwealth

5.82   Turning to the Commonwealth, the most interesting, and hard fought, abortion battles have been waged in Canada where, until the last 20 or so years, the law was not outstandingly liberal. Control of legal terminations was vested in hospital abortion committees under the Criminal Code 1971, s 251; in the long-running case of *R v Morgentaler*,[173] however, the Supreme Court held that this section violated the security and liberty of the pregnant woman. The Chief Justice expressed his reasons for this conclusion as follows:

Forcing a woman, by threat of criminal sanction, to carry a fetus to term unless she meets certain criteria unrelated to her own priorities and aspirations, is a profound interference with a woman's body and thus a violation of security of the person.[174]

In parallel litigation, the Canadian Charter of Rights and Freedom, Article 7 of which guarantees the 'right to life, liberty and security of the person', was held to be inapplicable to the fetus.[175] Those opposed to abortion gained a surprise victory in

---

[170] However, the government is not required to finance the latter simply because it prefers, and supports, the former: *Rust v Sullivan* 111 S Ct 1759 (1991).

[171] See Loveland n 165 above. It was severely criticised in the dissents in *Stenberg v Carhart*, n 172 below.

[172] More recently, the problem of the control of the method of abortion—in the form of 'partial birth abortion'—has been before Congress. A Bill to ban the method was introduced in 1995, passed, vetoed by President Clinton, reintroduced and, eventually, passed as the Partial Birth Abortion Ban Act 2001. Meantime, the Supreme Court, by a 5:4 majority, had deemed a State statute which constrained the use of the method to be unconstitutional: *Stenberg v Carhart* (2000) 530 US 914. The Act is currently under challenge in New York and California. For early commentary, see G J Annas 'Partial-birth Abortion, Congress, and the Constitution' (1998) 339 New Engl J Med 279 and G J Annas ' "Partial-birth" Abortion and the Supreme Court' (2001) 344 New Engl J Med 152.

[173] [1988] 1 SCR 30.

[174] *Ibid* at 56, per Dickson CJ. For discussion of this decision, see M L McConnell 'Abortion and Human Rights: An Important Canadian Decision' (1989) 38 ICLQ 905.

[175] *Borowski v A-G of Canada* (1987) 39 DLR (4th) 731 (Sask, CA).

Tremblay v Daigle[176]—in which a father gained an interlocutory injunction to prevent the abortion of his child; the decision rested on the Provincial Charter of Rights and the case was held under the civil law jurisdiction of Quebec. The breach was, however, short-lived, the full Supreme Court of Canada reversing the decision unanimously.[177] It is to be noted that neither the Supreme Court of the United States nor that of Canada will allow of 'trade-off' or balancing act between fetal and maternal rights to life or health—it is the latter which are to be safeguarded.

5.83   The innate tendency towards liberal abortion law is also demonstrated in Australia where, other than in South Australia, the Northern Territories and Western Australia, which have enabling statutes, the basic law corresponds to that in the Offences Against the Person Act 1861. Several landmark judicial interpretations of the word 'unlawful' in relation to medical practice have resulted in a very wide availability of terminations.[178] The so-called 'Kirby ruling'[179] suggests that, in the same way as we see the position in Great Britain, it would be very difficult to establish that any termination performed by a medical practitioner was unlawful. However, two doctors were charged in 1998 with procuring abortion in contravention of the Criminal Code of Western Australia. The result was the rapid passage of the Acts Amendment (Abortion) Act 1998 (WA) which established the most liberal legislative control of abortion in Australia. While the lawfulness of the procedure was wholly medicalised,[180] the grounds included what is virtually abortion on request up to the twentieth week of pregnancy. Interestingly, termination after the twentieth week is rather more restricted than it is in other Australian jurisdictions.[181]

The German experience

5.84   The history of German legislation is instructive in that it was developed in the ambience of constitutional drama resulting from reunification of the country.[182] Here, abortion legislation was isolated at the time as the only exception to the general reunification formula that Western institutional and legislative experience should be

---

[176] (1989) 59 DLR (4th) 609.   [177] (1990) 62 DLR (4th) 634.

[178] Originating with *R v Davidson* [1969] VR 667 which introduced the concepts of necessity and proportionality of termination of pregnancy to offset potential harm; *R v Wald* (1972) 3 DCR (NSW) 25 in which the social and economic effects of pregnancy were taken into consideration; for a 'Code jurisdiction', see *Veivers v Connolly* [1995] 2 Qd R 326.

[179] *CES v Superclinics (Australia) Pty Ltd* (1995) 38 NSWLR 47 per Kirby AC-J. For commentary, see K Petersen 'Medical Negligence and Wrongful Birth Actions: Australian Developments' (1997) 23 J Med Ethics 319. The same author provided a very useful comparison of abortion laws in 'Abortion Laws: Comparative and Feminist Perspectives in Australia, England and the United States' (1996) 2 Med Law Internat 77.

[180] By amendments to the Health Act 1911, s 334 (WA).

[181] An outstanding overview of the Australian scene is to be found in N Cica 'Abortion Law in Australia' *Australian Parliamentary Library Research Paper 1 1998–99* at www.aph.gov.au/library/pubs/rp/1998–99/99rp01.htm.

[182] Some member States of the EU—e.g. Denmark—have very liberal abortion laws and the impression is that, with the recent increase in membership of the Union, this will apply to the majority—especially when termination is sought in the first 12 weeks of pregnancy. A helpful review of the original States' legislation is to be found in P de Cruz *Comparative Healthcare Law* (2001).

extended to the East.[183] In brief, the existing situation was that, whereas abortion during the first 12 weeks of pregnancy was controlled solely by the free choice of the pregnant woman in the East, abortion was illegal in the West save in specific circumstances dependent, in large part, on 'stage of the fetus' provisions—a situation analogous to that in Britain with 'general hardship' substituted for s 1(1)(a) in the 1967 Act. Approximately 33 per cent of pregnancies were terminated in East Germany but, very interestingly, abortions were at least as frequent in the West. Controversy, therefore, rested on a purely ideological base. The resulting conflict was undoubtedly influenced by an increasingly wide perception of abortion as a potentially dangerous piece of social engineering rather than as a woman's right.[184]

5.85   Following a pre-arranged free vote in the Bundestag two years after reunification, the federal parliament duly passed a law under which a pregnant woman could choose to have an abortion in the first three months of pregnancy provided she had undergone social counselling at least three days before the termination was carried out.[185] The Constitutional Court then declared that the legislation was contrary to the Basic Law in that, in particular, it failed to meet the minimum standards for the protection of unborn human life as set out in the Constitution; these could only be satisfied if the state placed a fundamental legal duty on the woman to carry her fetus to term.[186] As an interim measure, procedures were laid down which, if followed, would render consensual abortion within the first three months of pregnancy still illegal but not subject to criminal sanction.[187] The court's decision was founded on the premise that abortion offends against that part of the German Constitution which 'guarantees the right to life and freedom from bodily harm'—a right which extends, even if in modified form, to the fetus. These provisional measures continued in force until 1996, when a new law came into effect.[188] Abortion now remains illegal, but no criminal sanctions will be applied if it is performed within specified limits. Abortion is freely available on request in the first 12 weeks of pregnancy provided the woman has been counselled by her own doctor and by staff from an independent counselling centre. In providing this counselling, the doctor must give priority to the protection of the fetus. Abortion is available after 12 weeks' gestation when the life or the health of the woman is threatened or if the fetus suffers from a serious defect.

---

[183] Treaty on German Unity (31 August 1990), Article 31 *Family and Women*, para 4, Bundesgesetzblatt (BGbl) II, 1990, p 885.

[184] E Kolinsky 'Women in the New Germany' in G Smith et al (eds) *Developments in German Politics* (1992) ch 14.

[185] A Tuffs 'Germany: Abortion, the Woman's Choice' (1992) 340 Lancet 43.

[186] H Karcher 'Abortion Law Diluted Again in Germany' (1993) 306 BMJ 1566; A Tuffs 'Germany: Illegality of Abortion' (1993) 341 Lancet 1467.

[187] For a controversial appraisal of the situation, see A Simon 'A Right to Life for the Unborn? The Current Debate on Abortion in Germany' (2000) 25 J Med Philos 220. Other 'compromises' were introduced—e.g. an illegal abortion could not be funded from statutory medical insurance but the woman could, subsequently, enjoy the social welfare and unemployment benefits. See the very full commentary by D van Zyl Smit 'Reconciling the Irreconcilable? Recent Developments in the German Law on Abortion' (1994) 2 Med L Rev 302.

[188] Schwangeren-und Familienhilfänderungsgesetz (1995).

5.86   Compromise, albeit an imperfect solution, depolarises attitudes and fosters less violent confrontation.[189] The German experience, however, reinforces the view that, in the context of abortion, it dictates some acknowledgment of fetal rights and, here, one senses a wind of change blowing against a well-established screen in several jurisdictions.[190]

SOME SPECIAL ASPECTS OF FETAL STATUS AND TERMINATION OF PREGNANCY

5.87   We have considered fetal status in terms of a continuum at para 5.5 above. There are, however, points in fetal development which have special legal implications. The first of these is at the very beginning of fetal life.

5.88   So-called interceptive methods of contraception have been discussed within that section at para 5.24 above. They are to be contrasted with other procedures, in particular menstrual extraction and late insertion of intrauterine devices, are performed not for contraceptive purposes but, at least partly, because a pregnancy might exist and before a definitive diagnosis can be made. In our view, menstrual extraction, which deals with the termination of a problematical implantation, is probably unlawful from two aspects. In the first place it is difficult to see why it is not using an instrument with the intention to procure the miscarriage of a woman 'whether or not she be with child' and, accordingly, transgresses the Offences Against the Person Act 1861, s 58. In addition, it cannot be rendered legal under the terms of the 1967 Act which is concerned with the assessment of an established pregnancy and, in the circumstances, it is impossible to comply with the regulations as to certification.[191] Nevertheless, as we have already suggested, displanting 'contraception' is among those forms of 'after the fact' action to prevent the birth of an unwanted baby which are less likely to offend the public conscience than is frank fetal destruction; it seems illogical that they could be equally liable to censure under the 1861 Act.

5.89   The same considerations apply to the late insertion of an IUD but, so far as we know, only one apposite prosecution has succeeded; the case did, however, concern the insertion of an IUD into a woman who was certainly pregnant.[192] Rather more help can be gained from an unreported case[193] which involved a charge under the

[189] But cannot eliminate it—see the dogged opposition from the Bavarian Government. A rather more restrictive Bavarian Act was passed in 1996 but was found to be unconstitutional as it conflicted with the Federal law.

[190] The European Court of Human Rights has steadfastly refused to pronounce on fetal 'personhood'. Nevertheless, the court held in *Bruggemann and Scheuten v Federal Republic of Germany* [1977] 3 EHRR 113 that not every aspect of the regulation of termination of pregnancy constitutes an interference with a woman's private life. The State had not done so by prohibiting abortion on demand.

[191] SI 1968/390.

[192] *R v Price* [1969] 1 QB 541, [1968] 2 All ER 282. The conviction was quashed on the grounds of a misdirection.

[193] *R v Dhingra* (1991) *Daily Telegraph*, 25 January, p 5. The case was quoted with approval in *Smeaton*, n 38 above but it is to be noted that *Smeaton* was not concerned with mechanical displanting methods.

Offences Against the Person Act 1861, s 58 against a doctor who fitted a contraceptive coil to his secretary some 11 days after they had had intercourse. The judge, having heard gynaecological evidence that implantation would not have occurred, withdrew the case from the jury on the grounds that the woman could not have been pregnant 'in the true sense of the word'. He is also reported as saying: 'Only at the completion of implantation does the embryo become a fetus. At this stage, she can be regarded as pregnant.'[194] Thus, the question of what would be the result if an IUD were to be fitted after the eleventh day following intercourse still remains open. It seems unlikely that a prosecution would succeed—the difficulty of proving intent would be almost insurmountable. Whatever may be the true situation in England and Wales, it is apparent that a prosecution in these circumstances for the common law crime of abortion could not succeed in Scotland, where proof of pregnancy is essential to a successful prosecution for that offence. None the less, the possibility of a prosecution for attempted abortion remains open.[195]

5.90   Consideration of early termination techniques must now include 'medical' abortion. There has been surprisingly little overt opposition to the method in Britain[196]—although, by contrast, the introduction of mifepristone in France resulted in pressure sufficient to force the manufacturers to withdraw the product until the government, as a major shareholder, insisted on the resumption of research and clinical evaluation. Emotional accusations such as 'the launching of chemical warfare against unborn children' were met by emollient attempts to recategorise the process as 'contragestation' rather than abortion.[197] Semantics cannot, however, disguise the fact that the treatment is clearly abortifacient; it can, therefore, be administered only within the terms of the 1967 Act.[198] We view the introduction of 'medical abortion' with some concern as, in the same way as the 'morning after pill', it will inevitably come to be regarded as a safe form of contraceptive back-up. The result must be to blur the ethical distinction, which we regard as essential, between contraception and abortion; while the two processes may be comparable in that they both *prevent* new life, it is only abortion that can be seen as *taking* life.

---

[194] He may have been attentive to the terms of the Human Fertilisation and Embryology Act 1990, s 2(3) which states that '*For the purposes of this Act*, a woman is not to be treated as carrying a child until the embryo has become implanted.' The emphasis is added but the wording could be persuasive in other branches of the law.

[195] *Docherty v Brown* 1996 SLT 325.

[196] Some 29,000 terminations using antiprogesterones (16% of the total) were carried out in England and Wales in 2003 (Statistical Bulletin, 2004).

[197] A whole issue of Law, Medicine and Health Care was devoted to the subject. R Macklin 'Antiprogestin Drugs: Ethical Issues' (1992) 20 Law Med Hlth Care 215 is of particular interest.

[198] The way is now cleared for medicinal abortion by the Abortion Act 1967, s 1(3A) (inserted by Human Fertilisation and Embryology Act 1990, 37(3)) which extends the types of premises in which a legal abortion can be performed.

Viability

5.91　Elsewhere in the context of fetal life, the law's main concern with gestational age lies in the concept of viability. This is not only a matter of United Kingdom jurisprudence; viability is universally regarded as an important milestone—and we have seen to what an extent it worried the French courts in the case of Mrs Vo. It merits more than cursory consideration

5.92　Viability is something of a legal fiction, originating in the United States, that is designed to define some point at which the state accepts a compelling interest to protect the lives of its unborn citizens. Conceptually, therefore, viability is a term of American constitutional law and it probably has no place in English law[199] which generally refers, in the present context, to 'capability of being born alive'. 'Live birth' itself, however, remained undefined until the seminal case of *C v S*.[200] and this led to some interpretative confusion. A still-born child is one that did not at any time after being completely expelled from its mother breathe or show any other sign of life[201]— from which it follows that, from the Registrar's point of view, the neonate need only have managed one breath, which may well have been unproductive, to have been 'born alive'.[202] Definitions intended for statistical use are not, however, necessarily the same as those to be applied in practice. Thus, on the one hand, the statutory definition has considerable relevance to the investigation of infanticide or child murder. Very different issues are, however raised in relation to abortion which, as we have said, attracts moral overtones in addition to those of criminality. As Sir John Donaldson MR said in *C v S*,[203] the interpretation of the statutory words 'capable of being born alive' is a matter for the courts—and he contented himself with holding that, in respect of the 1929 Act, a fetus that would be incapable ever of breathing either naturally or with the aid of a ventilator was *not* capable of being born alive.

5.93　This is a negative conclusion and the obverse decision was reached in *Rance*,[204] which, like its closely analogous case *Gregory*,[205] was a matter of 'wrongful birth' (see chapter 6). There it was held that a child was born alive if, after its birth, it existed as a live child, that is to say was breathing and living through the use of its own lungs alone. From the point of view of the law of homicide, therefore, the meaning of being born alive remains as it was decided more than a century ago.[206] 'Live birth' is clearly

---

[199] K McK Norrie 'Abortion in Great Britain: One Act, Two Laws' [1985] Crim LR 475.

[200] [1988] QB 135, [1987] 1 All ER 1230.

[201] Births and Deaths Registration Act 1953, s 41; Registration of Births, Deaths and Marriages (Scotland) Act 1965, s 56. It must also be of 24 weeks' or more gestation: Still-Birth (Definition) Act 1992, s 1.

[202] 'Any other sign of life' might also include a feebly beating heart. This was the view of the World Health Organisation quoted in *C v S* [1988] QB 135 at 142, [1987] 1 All ER 1230 at 1236.

[203] At QB 151, All ER 1242.

[204] *Rance v Mid-Downs Health Authority* [1991] 1 QB 587, [1991] 1 All ER 801.

[205] *Gregory v Pembrokeshire Health Authority* [1989] 1 Med LR 81.

[206] *R v Handley* (1874) 13 Cox CC 79.

defined by the capacity to breathe and the confusing phrase 'any other sign of life' is, correspondingly, irrelevant in this context.[207]

5.94   Thus, the concepts of American viability and British live birth are, now, congruent but both have their difficulties. In the first place, both depend upon the medical support available; secondly, the diagnosis can only be made after the event—a matter of importance in relation to the living abortus (see below). The case of Mrs Rance also demonstrates vividly the practical difficulties and, hence, the unsatisfactory state of the law prior to 1990. Her child was known to be physically abnormal but, by the time the diagnosis was established, the gynaecologists were unable to terminate the pregnancy for fear of transgressing the Infant Life (Preservation) Act 1929. The possibility of the doctor being accused of child destruction under the 1929 Act by way of aborting a 'child capable of being born alive' has now been removed[208] but it is arguable that it has been replaced by additional technical problems and by moral considerations which are, if anything, exaggerated by the 1990 amendments to the 1967 Act.

5.95   Those who support the interests of the fetus have always been concerned to prevent the abortion, or feticide, of those capable of a free existence by lowering the fetal age beyond which termination is impermissible so as to keep in step with the increasing medical capacity to lower the age of 'viability'. They can be said to have succeeded to an extent by having this set at 24 weeks for the relatively slight medical and social reasons described in s 1(1)(a) of the 1967 Act.[209] The offset is that it may be difficult, particularly in the face of human error, to make a prognosis of serious neonatal handicap within that timescale. Accordingly, the 1990 Act removed the pre-existing 28 weeks' legal limit and imposed no other time restrictions on abortions performed by reason of fetal abnormality. Similar de-restriction applies in the event of risk or grave injury to the pregnant woman—and such conditions are likely to arise particularly in late gestation. The *need* for late abortion thus remains and the Act is silent as to what is to be done with a live abortus. It has to be remembered that a living abortus is a creature in being; to kill such a being or to allow it to die without good reason may be murder or manslaughter—and s 37(4) of the 1990 Act absolves the gynaecologist of child destruction only.

5.96   One practical solution is to ensure that no mature abortus is given the opportunity to live. Not only may this involve the use of feticidal methods which are, at the same time, relatively dangerous to the pregnant woman but such methods may also be repugnant to all associated with the procedure—it is difficult to visualise a process which offends the Hippocratic and intuitive conscience more than the

---

[207] But it may still have significance in some circumstances. Based on the *C v S* definition, a case can be made out for the disabled Siamese twin in the well-known case of *Re A (children) (conjoined twins: surgical separation)* [2001] Fam 147, [2000] 4 All ER 961 having been stillborn despite the apparent evidence of life. See J K Mason 'Conjoined Twins: A Diagnostic Conundrum' (2001) 5 Edin LR 226.

[208] 1990 Act, s 37(4).

[209] In passing, s 37 of the 1990 Act brings the law, as well as the practice, of abortion in Scotland into line with that of England.

dismemberment of a relatively well-formed fetus.[210] This is precisely the situation the 'pro-life'[211] parliamentary lobby sought to avoid and a clause designed to ensure that reasonable steps were taken to assist a mature abortus to live was introduced at a late stage in the debate on the 1990 Bill.[212] The motion was defeated, largely as a result of advice that doctors carrying out terminations after the twenty-fourth week of pregnancy 'would make every conceivable effort . . . to make sure the baby was capable of living . . . a normal and independent existence'.[213] Lord Ennals quoted a letter from 20 gynaecologists:

> If the fetus is mature enough to have a reasonable chance of survival with intensive care, all possible steps are taken to optimise the recovery of both mother and fetus. Delivery then is usually by Caesarean section.[214]

5.97   If, then, late and deliberate termination is the prerogative of the maverick, why was the medical profession as a whole so antipathetic to the proposed clause? The answer must lie in the number of complex issues that the proposal raises. What distinction, if any, is made between the normal and handicapped fetus? Could the doctor be required to use a process which might result in a damaged neonate and possible litigation?[215] Is it right to subject a woman to an invasive procedure on behalf of the fetus and would she, in fact, consent?—a matter to which we return in chapter 10. Above all, how is the doctor to dispose of his or her new patient?

The living abortus

5.98   The gynaecologist is certainly in a difficult position. On the one hand, he or she has effectively contracted to relieve a woman of her fetus. On the other, there is now an infant who, on any interpretation, is entitled to a birth certificate and, if necessary, a certificate as to the cause of death.[216] Considerations as to the proper use of limited resources must also colour any decision-making. The principles of selective non-treatment of a disabled neonate (see chapter 16) might well apply but, otherwise, we can see no theoretical objection to the view that failure to attempt to sustain a living infant could result in a charge of manslaughter or, in Scotland, of culpable homicide.

5.99   Legal precedents are slender in Great Britain and, what few there are, are inconsistent. In one case, an area health authority inquiry concluded that allowing an

---

[210] The House of Lords approved the action of the BBC when it prohibited an election broadcast that showed abortions in practice: *R (ProLife Alliance) v British Broadcasting Corporation* [2004] 1 AC 185. The furore surrounding 'partial birth' terminations has been noted at n 172 above.

[211] It has been pointed out that the wide use of this term is unfortunate in that it implies that the opponents are 'anti-life': S McLean 'Emotional Extremes Miss the Heart of Abortion Dilemma' (2004) *Scotland on Sunday*, 25 April.

[212] Such a condition has been declared unconstitutional in the United States: *Colautti v Franklin* 439 US 379 (1979); *American College of Obstetricians and Gynecologists Pennsylvania Section v Thornburgh* 106 S Ct 2169 (1986).

[213] Official Reports (Lords) vol 522, col 1043, 18 October 1990, per Lord Walton at 1050.

[214] *Ibid* at 1052.

[215] For discussion, see R P S Jansen 'Unfinished Feticide' (1990) 6 J Med Ethics 61.

[216] See Lord Wells-Pestell HL Official Reports (5th series) col 776 (12 December 1974).

aborted fetus to die was an action which was fully within the law. In another, where an infant lived for 36 hours after having been aborted at 23 weeks, the coroner found that death was due to prematurity and that there was no culpability on the part of the medical staff. So far as we know, only one coroner, faced with such circumstances, has brought in a conclusion of death due to want of attention at birth to a premature infant;[217] no further action seems to have been taken. One prosecution is known to have been mounted by the DPP against a doctor who was alleged to have left a living abortus to die in the sluice-room; the magistrates took the unprecedented step of deciding there was no case to answer.[218] There was a further instance of a supposedly 21-week-old fetus, breathing and with a heart beat, being left to die without assistance for three hours; neither the birth nor the death were registered and the body was incinerated. In the absence of a cadaver, the coroner applied to the Home Office for authority to hold an inquest but this was refused for reasons which were not given publicly.[219] The dearth of more recent reports suggests, either, that gynaecologists are ever more inclined to avoid the possibility, or that the law is now content with a pragmatic reaction to an insoluble dilemma.[220]

5.100　　In principle, we find it illogical to distinguish in legal terms between abandonment of the newborn infant and abandonment of the living abortus. The coroners' courts are, however, apparently happy to maintain a non-confrontational approach. It was reported in 1996 that a normal infant, wrongly suspected of having severe physical abnormality and aborted at 27 weeks, survived for 45 minutes without active resuscitation. The coroner recorded a verdict of death due to legal termination.[221] The fact that this surprisingly innovative finding went uncontested confirms our view that further similarly grounded actions against the doctor are unlikely.[222]

5.101　　There is, in fact, no certainty that all women seeking a termination of pregnancy also seek the destruction of their fetus—indeed, the longer a woman has carried her fetus, the more likely it is that she would wish to preserve it. McLean, while insisting on the woman's right to control her whole pregnancy, has enlarged this concept and has suggested that attitudes might, with advantage, be overturned and that women might be given encouragement and the *opportunity* to undergo late, and salvageable, abortions.[223] There are considerable health hazards, in respect of both the woman and the fetus underlying such a policy. Indeed, one might go further and encourage

---

[217]　Inquest on Infant Campbell, Stoke-on-Trent, 19 October 1983.

[218]　*R v Hamilton* (1983) *The Times*, 16 September.

[219]　Reported by M Fletcher, *The Times*, 25 February 1988, p 2. The case was raised in Parliament on a motion for the adjournment: Official Reports (HC), 8 June 1989, vol 154, col 460.

[220]　Even so, an investigative journalist reported six relevant and recent cases in which a living abortus was allowed to die: S-K Templeton and L Rogers 'Babies that Live after Abortions Are Left to Die' (2004) *Sunday Times*, 20 June, p 1.3.

[221]　(1996) 119 Bull Med Ethics 4.

[222]　It is fair to say that this view has been regarded as unduly complacent: Wicks et al, n 139 above.

[223]　S A M McLean 'Women, Rights and Reproduction' in S A M McLean (ed) *Legal Issues in Human Reproduction* (1989) see the same author 'Abortion Law: Is Consensual Reform Possible?' (1990) 17 J Law & Soc 106.

women to go to term; there is no reason why surviving neonates of either category should not be regarded as parentless infants and offered for adoption on that basis.

OTHER PEOPLE'S RIGHTS

5.102 The rights of those who, of necessity, participate in terminations of pregnancy receive comparatively little attention in the abortion debate as compared with that devoted to the woman and her fetus. Yet they are of very considerable communitarian importance.

Conscientious objection

5.103 The Abortion Act 1967, s 4 excuses the conscientious objector from participating in treatment by abortion unless that treatment is directed towards the saving of life or of preventing grave permanent injury to the health of the mother. But, while this would seem to be perfectly clear, the doctor's situation is not uncomplicated. An unfortunate result of the 1967 Act is that some discrimination must arise against doctors, and especially those seeking to become gynaecologists, who are unable to accept its wide terms.[224] It is to be noted that, while a doctor may, in general, refuse to take part in the abortion procedure, he remains under an obligation to advise. Such advice is subject to the normal rules of medical negligence and the conscientious objector's only recourse is, therefore, to refer his patient to another practitioner, a practice which is only marginally compatible with a strong conscience and which must damage the essential bond of trust between doctor and patient.[225] The facts that the woman may well be unaware of her practitioner's attitude and that a second referral inevitably delays the termination provide one of the most powerful arguments put forward by those who would demedicalise early abortion.[226] It is often forgotten that a doctor's objection to abortion may be Hippocratic rather than, say, religious in origin; whatever its basis, however, the doctor's conscience does not, as we have seen, absolve him or her from treating a woman when the continuation of the pregnancy is life-threatening and there is, of course, no right to conscience in treating the *results* of a legal abortion. These considerations apply equally to the nursing staff and other health care workers.

The nursing staff and others involved

5.104 The role of the nurse in therapy of all sorts is becoming more significant; this is exemplified in the sphere of abortion by the widespread use of prostaglandin infusions for induction of premature labour. Nurses have so great a part to play in this process that some doubt was raised as to whether they were, in fact, thus guilty of performing illegal abortions in the sense that they were not 'registered medical

---

[224] J Warden 'Abortion and Conscience' (1990) 301 BMJ 1013.

[225] *Barr v Matthews* (2000) 52 BMLR 217 provides an interesting commentary, including the option of adoption. Alliott J approved an arrangement whereby a conscientious objector immediately referred a termination case to a colleague.

[226] For a major argument on these lines, see S McLean *Old Law, New Medicine* (1999), chapter 4.

practitioners' as required by the 1967 Act; the Royal College of Nursing accordingly sought a declaration to the effect that the advice in a departmental circular[227] stating that, irrespective of the precise action taken, an abortion was legal provided that it was initiated by and was the responsibility of a registered medical practitioner, was wrong in law. The complexities were such that the Royal College lost its case in the High Court, won it in the Court of Appeal and, finally, lost it in the House of Lords.[228] Effectively, therefore, abortion, no matter how it is performed, is a team effort and is no different in this respect from any other form of treatment. It is, nevertheless, interesting that, in total, five out of nine judges involved took the view of the nurses.

5.105   We believe that, in general, the sensibilities of the nursing staff are inadequately recognised within the abortion debate. The damage that conscientious objection causes to their career prospects may well be greater than that sustained by doctors—a doctor does not *have* to practise gynaecology but, as Lord Denning emphasised, nurses are expected to be mobile throughout the hospital system.[229] Moreover, current methods of termination beyond the twelfth week of pregnancy involve the nursing staff in an uncompromising way—whether it be in the delivery of what is comparable to a premature birth or in counting the fragmented parts of a formed fetus;[230] there can be no doubts as to their *rights* to special consideration even if these are not always respected.

5.106   Valid conscientious objection within the terms of the Abortion Act 1967, s 4 is, however, limited by a proximity test—that is, that it covers only those involved in the therapeutic team effort. The case of Mrs Janaway, who regarded herself as having been unfairly dismissed following her refusal to type a letter referring a patient for termination of pregnancy, was considered so important that it was taken to the House of Lords.[231] In the event, Mrs Janaway failed at every step, essentially on the grounds that participation in treatment, as applied to s 4, referred to actual participation in treatment administered in a hospital or other approved place; the suggestion in the Court of Appeal that the conscience clause applied to activities which would have been criminal absent the 1967 Act was rejected in the House of Lords—and, at any rate, a typist could not be held to be an accessory in the criminal sense. Mrs Janaway was clearly well distanced from the actual treatment but one can only guess whether others more closely involved—e.g. hospital porters—would be similarly excluded; the

[227] CMO (80) (2).

[228] *Royal College of Nursing of the United Kingdom v Department of Health and Social Security* [1981] AC 800, [1981] 1 All ER 545, HL.

[229] [1981] AC 800 at 804–805, [1981] 1 All ER 545 at 555.

[230] See R J Lilford and N Johnson 'Surgical Abortion at Twenty Weeks: Is Morality Determined Solely by the Outcome? (1989) 15 J Med Ethics 82. J Glover *Causing Death and Saving Lives* (reprinted 1986) p 142 points to the effects on the health carers as providing a major moral distinction between, say, contraception and abortion.

[231] *R v Salford Health Authority, ex p Janaway* [1989] AC 537, CA; affd sub nom *Janaway v Salford Area Health Authority* [1989] AC 537, [1988] 3 All ER 1079, HL.

dividing line might be fine.[232] The advent of medical termination raises the unusual position of the conscientiously objecting pharmacist who is asked to fill the necessary prescriptions; in our view, the proximity test would be satisfied, although much depends on how the relationship between the pharmaceutical and medical professions is viewed.[233]

The father

5.107 The anomalous position of the father in the right to life debate also falls to be considered. It is clear from current worldwide decisions that, in so far as abortion is concerned, he has, for practical purposes, *no* rights. It seems incongruous that this should be so, irrespective of the reason for the abortion, and that it should apply even in cases which do not relate to the health of the mother; a father could not, for example, save the existence of a *potentially* haemophiliac son. Morally speaking, it seems that the anxious father should, ideally, be entitled to a hearing. Even so, this would surely be as far as one could go—it would not be possible to support any legal right to the unacceptable consequences that might attend acceptance of his wishes.

5.108 The English position was established in *Paton*,[234] where it was clearly laid down that a husband cannot by injunction prevent his wife from undergoing a lawful abortion. The decision was upheld by the European Commission on Human Rights; the Commission was, however, clearly worried by the possible complication of fetal 'viability'—the matter was not decided and it remains an area of potential doubt.[235] It was clarified no further in *C v S*,[236] in which the unmarried father's locus standi was firmly rejected—and the decision was not appealed—but in which the main thrust of the hearing was to establish that the fetus in question was *not* viable. Any possibility that a Scottish fetus might be able to petition through its tutor—i.e. its father—for interdict of any threatened harm has now been excluded. In *Kelly v Kelly*,[237] the Inner House of the Court of Session agreed that the remedy of interdict would be available to prevent damage being caused to a person which, if it occurred, would sound in damages to that person. However, a review of the extensive Commonwealth decisions supported the view that the fetus had no rights for the protection of which the remedy of interdict might be invoked. It followed, therefore, that the

---

[232] It is interesting that, whereas the 'conscience clause' in the 1967 Act refers to participation in 'any treatment' authorised by the Act, s 38 of the Human Fertilisation and Embryology Act 1990, which 'governs' abortion by way of s 37, refers to participation in 'any activity' governed by the Act. The latter is, arguably, open to wider interpretation.

[233] For analysis, see B D Weinstein 'Do Pharmacists Have a Right to Refuse to Fill Prescriptions for Abortifacient Drugs?' (1992) 20 Law Med Hlth Care 220. This is from the American view, where the matter is not addressed by statute—but the principles remain the same.

[234] *Paton v British Pregnancy Advisory Service Trustees* [1979] QB 276, [1978] 2 All ER 987.

[235] *Paton v United Kingdom* (1980) 3 EHRR 408.   [236] [1988] QB 135, [1987] 1 All ER 1230.

[237] 1997 SC 285, 1997 SCLR 749.

father, as the guardian of the fetus, had no standing by which to prevent his wife's abortion.[238]

5.109   Attitudes elsewhere in the English-speaking world are diverse. The firm English stance would seem to be accepted in New Zealand but the reasoning there is based more on statute than on common law.[239] It is unlikely that an injunction to prevent a maternally-desired abortion would ever be granted in Australia but the position there is, again, complicated—this time by considerations of legality.[240] Relevant United States cases denying paternal rights to veto abortions are now very old[241] and the door seems, now, to have been closed in *Casey*.[242] It is only in Canada that paternal status has achieved a glimmer of recognition. In *Medhurst*[243] a husband was given standing to seek an injunction against abortion and in *Tremblay*[244] it was considered that a potential father had as much right to speak on behalf of the fetus as anyone; neither of these cases succeeded beyond this and they probably represent no more than the general willingness of the Canadian courts to grant a locus standi to interested parties.[245]

5.110   It is probable that this world-wide negative attitude to paternal/fetal rights will persist. Nothing can alter the fact that it is the woman who carries the fetus for nine months and whose health is mainly at risk during that time—and it is almost certainly this factor which explains the difference in legal attitudes to the father's interest in his fetus and in his in vitro embryo which we have discussed at para 4.74. An objecting father may well deserve sympathy but, in the final analysis, a woman's right to control her body must take precedence.

A doctor's duty to the fetus?

5.111   The nature of the doctor's duties in relation to the fetus itself in the context of abortion is not completely solved—we have, for example, already discussed a potential duty to maintain the life of a viable abortus. Far more legal and ethical importance attaches to the management of both the mother and the fetus when the latter is known—or should be known—to be disabled. This is, essentially, a matter of liability under the terms of the Abortion Act 1967, s 1(1)(d)—to what extent has the health professional a legally enforceable duty to offer a pregnant woman a termination and to what extent has he or she a duty to the disabled fetus to prevent its birth? We discuss these very significant problems in detail in chapter 6.

---

[238] *X v United Kingdom* (1980), application no 8416/79. By contrast, paternal rights as to the neonate have been confirmed by the ECtHR. An unmarried father can veto the adoption of his child: *Keegan v Ireland* (1994), application no 16969/90, (1994) 18 EHRR 342.

[239] *Wall v Livingston* [1982] 1 NZLR 734, NZCA. The code of decision-making is laid down in the Contraception, Sterilisation, and Abortion Act 1977.

[240] *A-G of Queensland (ex rel Kerr) v T* (1983) 46 ALR 275 indicates the difficulties.

[241] *Coe v Gerstein* 41 L Ed 2d 68 (1973); *Doe v Doe* 314 NE 2d 128 (Mass, 1974); *Planned Parenthood of Missouri v Danforth* 428 US 52 (1976).

[242] *Planned Parenthood of SE Pennsylvaia v Casey* 112 S Ct 2791 (1992).

[243] *Medhurst v Medhurst* (1984) 9 DLR (4th) 252.   [244] *Tremblay v Daigle* (1989) 59 DLR (4th) 609.

[245] See also *Re Simms and H* (1980) 106 DLR (3d) 435.

5.112   For the present, we refer only to the somewhat unusual correlate of whether a doctor has a duty *to the fetus* to ensure that the abortion is carried out in a satisfactory manner. In the Canadian case of *Cherry v Borsman*,[246] a negligently performed abortion, followed by a remarkably lax follow-up, resulted in a severely disabled neonate. It was held and confirmed on appeal that, insofar as a negligently performed abortion can cause foreseeable harm to the fetus, the practitioner owed a duty to the fetus to prevent that harm; accordingly, causation being inferred, he was liable to the neonate in negligence.

5.113   The case, for which we know of no equivalent, raises some interesting points. Certainly, the inference that the doctor caused the injuries is justified. His intention, however, was to kill the fetus—or, at least, prevent her survival. Given that the law considers the greatest injury to be death, it is a little difficult to see how mitigating that injury can be tortious. The court in *Cherry* appears to have been anxious that the disabled neonate should be recompensed. We cannot disagree with that aim; we do, however, feel that it would have been achieved more logically by way of an action for wrongful life—and we return to the case under that heading at para 6.56 below. Meantime, the dilemma remains unresolved—what is the extent of the abortionist's duty to the fetus? or, put another way, is there, in fact, a duty to the fetus to kill it in the most effective way?[247]

ABORTION AND THE INCOMPETENT

5.114   We have no reason to believe that termination of pregnancy in the mentally incapacitated or minors is to be regarded as different from any other aspect of medical treatment; the principles involved are, therefore, best considered within the whole spectrum of consent which is addressed in chapter 10. In respect of minors, the courts will, in the event of conflict, always put the interests of a young mother above those of her fetus—indeed, they *must* do so.[248]

5.115   Specific problems as to confidentiality—and particularly in respect of parental rights and duties—are, however, likely to arise in the unique context of under-age pregnancy. These have caused particular concern in the United States, where there

---

[246] (1990) 75 DLR (4th) 668, aff'd (1992) 94 DLR (4th) 587, BCCA.

[247] And, remembering that s 1(1)(d) is there for the benefit of the mother rather than the fetus, would the fetus' condition make any difference? For an interesting discussion, see J Gillott 'Screening for Disability: a Eugenic Pursuit?' (2001) 27, supp.II J Med Ethics 21 and J Wyatt 'Medical Paternalism and the Fetus', idem, p 15.

[248] Children Act 1989, s 1(1). See the specific criticism of an expert witness in *Re B (wardship: abortion)* [1991] 2 FLR 426 at 431 per Hollis J.

have been a number of conflicting decisions;[249] the matter has now probably been put beyond dispute in *Casey*,[250] where the need for parental consent was confirmed.

5.116   In Britain, the concept of the 'understanding child' has gone unchallenged since it was first mooted by Butler-Sloss J in 1982.[251] There can, however, be no doubt that to perform an operation without parental permission on a child too young to under-stand the issues—and, hence, to give a valid consent—would constitute an assault. In practice, absent strongly held religious views, it must be very rare for the parents of an unmarried girl below the age of 16 not to consent to termination of pregnancy[252] but the question remains—*must* the parents be informed prior to legal termination of a minor's pregnancy? The Abortion Act itself makes no distinctions as to age[253] groups but it is probably reasonable to assume that the majority of children who are old enough to *become* pregnant are also old enough to understand the consequences; the conditions laid down in *Gillick*[254] would, then, apply. Thus, although the knowledge and agreement of the parents are clearly desirable, it is likely that a doctor who has made reasonable efforts to induce his patient to confide in her parents and is still faced with an adamant refusal of consent to disclosure and who goes on to terminate a minor's pregnancy would be secure from action in the courts or before the General Medical Council. The trend in medical, legal and societal attitudes towards children's rights over the last two decades gives added support to this view.

5.117   Almost certainly, many abortions are carried out on the mentally handicapped under the twin cover of good medical practice and legal necessity; authority for termination of pregnancy has probably also been obtained in camera on more than one occasion.[255] Abortion is to be distinguished from, say, sterilisation in that the former is governed by statute which gives sufficient protection to doctors provided they comply with its terms; a formal declaration of lawfulness by the High Court, is not, therefore, needed.[256] Although a supposed 'right to procreate' is violated by both non-consensual abortion and non-consensual sterilisation, the former does not create the same conditions of permanence as does the latter; the routine involvement of the

---

[249] In *Re T W* 551 So 2d 1186 (Fla, 1989), the court was unable to discern a compelling state interest in overriding a minor's right to privacy only when abortion was concerned. In *Hodgson v Minnesota* 110 S Ct 2926 (1990) and *Ohio v Akron Center for Reproductive Health* 110 S Ct 2972 (1990), the Supreme Court held that only one parent need be notified. In both cases, however, it was noted that a judicial process to bypass parental consent was sufficient protection for the minor.

[250] *Planned Parenthood of Southeastern Pennsyvania v Casey* 112 S Ct 2791 (1992). The importance of the judicial bypass was re-emphasised.

[251] *Re P (a minor)* [1986] 1 FLR 272, (1982) 80 LGR 301.

[252] For a case in which a mother opposed a termination for her 12-year-old daughter, see *Re B (wardship: abortion)* [1991] 2 FLR 426.

[253] In 2003, 1171 legal terminations were carried out on girls aged less than 15.

[254] *Gillick v West Norfolk and Wisbech Area Health Authority* [1986] AC 112, [1985] 3 All ER 402, HL. The position in Scotland would be covered by the Age of Legal Capacity (Scotland) Act 1991, s 2(4). See chapter 10 for a full discussion.

[255] F Gibb 'Judge Orders Abortion on Woman, Aged 25' *The Times*, 28 May 1987, p 1 records the surprise of a judge when his decision was publicised.

[256] *Re SG (adult mental patient: abortion)* [1991] 2 FLR 329, sub nom *Re SG (a patient)* (1992) 6 BMLR 95; superseding *Re X* (1987) *The Times*, 4 June.

High Court would serve no useful purpose in an uncontested case involving termination of pregnancy.

REDUCTION OF MULTIPLE PREGNANCY AND SELECTIVE REDUCTION

5.118   The need for a reduction in the number of fetuses carried at one time has been discussed in chapter 4 at para 4.76. Original doubts as to the legality of the process were based mainly on terminological grounds—first on whether the phrase 'termination of pregnancy' in the 1967 Act relates to the pregnancy as a whole and, if this strict interpretation is inappropriate, whether individualised feticide in situ can be regarded as an abortion.[257] Whatever the solution of this interesting academic argument may be, the situation has now been resolved in practice—both selective reduction and reduction of multiple pregnancy in utero are legal when the requirements of the Abortion Act 1967, as amended, are fulfilled in relation to the individual fetus.[258]

5.119   Given that account may be taken of the woman's actual or reasonably foreseeable environment, there is no legal difficulty in justifying pregnancy reduction on the grounds that continuance of a multiple pregnancy would involve a risk of injury to the mental health of the pregnant woman greater than if it was reduced.[259] It might be equally appropriate to plead risk to the physical or mental health of the existing family—particularly if the intended remaining fetus or fetuses were regarded as 'existing children of the family'. Selective destruction of an abnormal fetus is, of course, justified under the serious handicap clause of the 1967 Act. Whether there is tort liability in the event of damage to a surviving fetus is arguable; the probability is that the doctor would not be liable in the absence of negligence in the operation.[260]

5.120   It scarcely needs emphasising that all the foregoing relates to legal justification—the morality of the procedure is open to question.[261] There is, clearly, a marked difference between reducing a twin pregnancy and reducing one involving sextuplets. To say that both are wrong in that they offend against the principle of respect for human life is to ignore the equally valid argument that ensuring the death of all six fetuses by inaction is, equally, disrespectful; the death of all octuplets following refusal of fetal reduction in an, at the time, *cause célèbre* provides an extreme example.[262] The subject opens up the age-old question of whether it is permissible to use unacceptable means to achieve a desirable end—at which point, one can only retire behind the defence that each case must be judged on its particular merits.

---

[257] For somewhat opposing views, see J Keown 'Selective Reduction of Multiple Pregnancy' (1987) 137 NLJ 1165; D P T Price 'Selective Reduction and Feticide: The Parameters of Abortion' [1988] Crim LR 199.

[258] Human Fertilisation and Embryology Act 1990, s 37(5) adding to the 1967 Act, s 5(2).

[259] R L Berkowitz 'From Twin to Singleton' (1996) 313 BMJ 373. See below for the moral justification.

[260] M Brazier 'A Legal Commentary' (1990) 16 J Med Ethics 68 in discussion of Jansen (1990) 6 J Med Ethics 61.

[261] Conservative Roman Catholic opinion remains implacably opposed to the process, which is regarded as 'embryonicide' rather than abortion. See the Official Statement of the Centre of Bioethics, Catholic University of the Sacred Heart, Rome 'Against So-called Embryo Reduction' (1997) 127 Bull Med Ethics 8.

[262] See para 4.76 above.

6

CIVIL AND CRIMINAL LIABILITY IN REPRODUCTIVE MEDICINE

6.1   It will be appreciated from what has gone before that the medical control of reproduction requires considerable expertise. Moreover, it is not without risk, not only to
the prospective parents but, perhaps especially, to the resultant child. Risks to the
former by virtue of the necessary hormonal and invasive techniques employed—at
least in the case of the mother—have already been noted. For the purposes of this
chapter, however, we are concerned with parental 'risk' only in the sense that their
child was originally unwanted or, better, uncovenanted.[1] This situation commonly
results from a failed sterilisation of either the man or the woman involved and is
generally known as a 'wrongful pregnancy'.[2] A variation in which a multiple, or
excessively multiple, birth is unwanted is a specific hazard of *in vitro* fertilisation and
has been discussed under that heading.

6.2   It is also, perhaps unfortunately, true that many parents who want a child do not, at
the same time, want the responsibilities of caring for one that is disabled. Certainly,
save in exceptional circumstances, very few would actively seek a child that most
people would regard as disabled;[3] fortunately, however, there are many who would
happily adopt such a child. Some couples will have no anticipation of a disabled child;
others, whether by virtue of age or family history may be well aware of a potential risk.

---

[1] The expression 'uncovenanted' was used by Kennedy J in *Richardson v LRC Products Ltd* (2001) 59 BMLR
185; [2000] Lloyd's Rep Med 280 to describe such a situation. In Scots law, the word has been used to describe
not so much an unexpected happening as one which was not contemplated by the parties concerned. It is,
therefore, apt to describe the results of a failed sterilisation. We believe that it is preferable to use the
expression in place of the more commonly used, but distasteful term 'unwanted pregnancy'. This may also be
inaccurate—it is a tribute to human nature that the child has come to be greatly loved in nearly all the
reported cases.

[2] Many writers use the term 'wrongful conception' rather than 'wrongful pregnancy'. We prefer the latter
on the grounds that no damage is sustained by conception; the potential for damage arises only at implantation. Again, we deprecate the term 'wrongful' and would prefer to use 'uncovenanted'—the former is,
however, in such popular use that a change would only be confusing.

[3] Some years ago, a deaf lesbian couple created a stir in deliberately attempting to create a deaf child who
would fit into their milieu: N Levy 'Deafness, Culture and Choice' (2002) 28 J Med Ethics 284. The ethical
arguments for and against such a choice are wide ranging: see the companion article K W Anstey 'Are
Attempts to Have Impaired Children Justifiable?' (2002) 28 J Med Ethics 286.

In either case, the actual birth of a disabled child may derive from inadequate ante-natal care—often associated with genetic counselling or its lack[4]—and result in what is popularly known as a 'wrongful birth'. It goes without saying that the categories may overlap; a wrongful pregnancy, for example, can also result in a disabled child.

6.3   The initiative in commencing legal proceedings lies with the parents or parent in all the instances so far discussed. Occasionally, however, an action may be raised on behalf of the disabled neonate him- or herself. The neonate who has been injured *in utero* may, of course, seek an action in negligence against the person he or she regards as responsible for that injury; this may or may not be available and we consider the jurisprudential quality of such an action at the end of this chapter. In the present context, however, neonatal risk is almost entirely that of congenital disease, as a result of which—and depending on its severity—the complainant may plead, effectively, that he or she would be better dead than alive and that he or she is alive only because of mismanagement of his or her gestation. Such a 'wrongful life' action is, therefore, one of a very distinct nature. Wrongful birth and wrongful life actions may be, and often are, raised simultaneously but there is no overlap; they are based on different premises and will be analysed separately. As suggested above, this chapter also pro-vides a convenient place in which to review the predominantly legal aspects of fetal injury and of feticide in the form of fetal manslaughter or murder. Finally, we will take the opportunity to overview the status of the fetus by way of considering the particular legal responsibilities of the mother to her child *in utero*.

6.4   All these legal actions involve a form of negligence. We explore the nature and content of the negligence action—including that of criminal negligence—extensively in chapter 9; for present purposes, a brief introduction will assist the unfamiliar reader in the discussion that follows. An action in negligence is premised on the notion of a duty of care. That is, it must be shown that the defender to the action—for us, the health care professional – had a duty to provide a certain level of care to his or her patient; the action will be successful if it can be established that this standard of care was not provided and, importantly, that this breach of duty of care caused a recognisable form of harm to the claimant. The benchmark standard in all cases is that of *reasonable care*, which can only be determined in light of all of the circum-stances in a given case. While all doctors—and other health carers such as nurses and midwives—will owe a duty to patients for whom they accept responsibility, the more problematic issue is as to the nature and extent of that duty. Here, we confine discussion to professional duties as they relate to reproductive choice and care.

---

[4] For a discussion of which, see chapter 7 paras 7.10–7.13.

THE UNCOVENANTED CHILD—THE ACTION FOR WRONGFUL PREGNANCY

6.5   Before discussing the nature of the duty of care in the action for wrongful pregnancy, we must first consider to whom the duty is owed. Clearly, if a man or woman seeks sterilisation independently, the doctor's duty of care is limited to that man or woman. By contrast, the doctor owes a duty to both partners if they come to him together seeking a limitation of fertility that is of benefit to both. It follows from either premise that the doctor cannot be held liable to a potential present or future sexual partner of his patient of whom he has no knowledge. While this seems to be a relatively simple proposition, it has been the subject of extensive argument in the Court of Appeal. Here, it was confirmed that a woman who became pregnant by a man who had been told three years previously that he need take no contraceptive precautions had no cause of action against those who had given the advice.[5]

6.6   Given, however, that a duty of care has been established, liability for a pregnancy resulting from an unsuccessful sterilisation will not be imposed unless it can be established that the surgeon failed in his or her duty. Such failure can, in turn, be attributable either to incompetent clinical expertise or, and more controversially, to inadequate explanation of the inherent shortcomings of the procedure—in particular, as to the possibility that conception might still occur after the operation due purely to the vagaries of nature.

6.7   As to what constitutes a breach of duty of care, we need, here, only remark that the jurisprudnce is largely governed by the *Bolam*[6] principle, under which it is held that a doctor's action will not be held to be negligent if it conforms to a practice which would have been adopted by a responsible body of medical opinion. As a result, it has long been supposed that a judge presented with two divergent expert opinions as to what was the correct procedure to adopt cannot simply choose which to accept. A distinction has to be made, however, between preferring an opinion—as in the House of Lords case of *Maynard*[7]—and preferring an interpretation of the facts. This was neatly explained in *Fallows v Randle*.[8] In this case of failed female sterilisation, the rings occluding the fallopian tubes had either been placed negligently or had slipped off through no one's fault. In preferring the former sequence of events, Stuart Smith LJ had this to say:

[The *Bolam* principle] has no application when what the judge has to decide is, on balance,

---

[5] *Goodwill v British Pregnancy Advisory Service* [1996] 2 All ER 161, (1996) 31 BMLR 83.
[6] *Bolam v Friern Hospital Management Committee* [1957] 2 All ER 118, [1957] 1 WLR 582.
[7] *Maynard v West Midlands Regional Health Authority* [1985] 1 All ER 635, [1984] 1 WLR 634, HL.
[8] (1997) 8 Med LR 160.

which of the explanations [of failure] is to be preferred. This is a question of fact which the judge has to decide on the ordinary basis of a balance of probabilities.[9]

6.8 We suspect that the majority of actions based on the negligent *performance* of a sterilising operation will generally be of this relatively simple type and that liability may well be acknowledged prior to any hearing. An exception might lie when the patient has insisted on a modified operation in the anticipation of reversal at some time in the future—but such cases must be rare.[10] A relatively specific aspect of negligent sterilisation in women is, however, to be found in a failure to diagnose pregnancy at the time of the operation. Error as to missed diagnosis then tends to be piled upon error, each resulting in therapeutic delay; consequently, either the patient finds herself no longer able, often on moral grounds, to consent to an abortion or the opportunity for a lawful termination is lost due to the lapse of time.

THE UNDIAGNOSED PREGNANCY

6.9 Several such cases are of importance in tracing the development of liability for 'wrongful pregnancy' in the United Kingdom and are discussed in greater detail below. Typical of these was *Scuriaga v Powell*[11] in which a healthy child was born following a negligently performed termination. Although there was no claim for damages in respect of the child's upbringing, Watkins J, at first instance, foreshadowed future developments in saying:

Surely no one in these days would argue [that damages were irrecoverable] if the child was born defective or diseased. The fact that the child born is healthy cannot give rise to a different conclusion save as to a measure of damages

and this view was supported in the Court of Appeal.

6.10 In *Venner*,[12] a gynaecologist who accepted the patient's word that she could not be pregnant at the time of the operation was held to be not negligent on the grounds that other practitioners would have omitted a precautionary curettage in similar circumstances. Other defendants have not been so fortunate. In the virtually identical case of *Allen v Bloomsbury Health Authority*,[13] the authority admitted liability and the only matter in issue was the quantum of damages. In a still later case, damages of over

---

[9] *Ibid* at 165. Moreover, two techniques may each pass the *Bolam* test for professional acceptability but it is for the court to decide which is in the patient's best interests: *Re S (adult patient: sterilisation)* [2001] 3 Fam 15, [2000] 3 WLR 1288, CA.

[10] As exemplified in the very early twin Canadian cases of *Doiron v Orr* (1978) 86 DLR (3d) 719 and *Cataford v Moreau* (1978) 114 DLR (3d) 585. Liability for a subsequent pregnancy was not imposed in the former in which the operation had been modified; the surgeon was found to have been negligent in the latter where there were no such extenuating conditions.

[11] (1979) 123 Sol Jo 406. In 2001, a Mrs Nicholls received £10,000 in an out of court settlement when a twin pregnancy was missed at termination; the second child was born healthy—O Wright '10,000 for mother who gave birth after abortion' (2001) *The Times*, 23 November, p 14.

[12] *Venner v North East Essex Area Health Authority* (1987) *The Times*, 21 February.

[13] [1993] 1 All ER 651, (1993) 13 BMLR 47.

£88,000, which included an element to cover private schooling, were awarded against a gynaecologist who failed to explain to a patient that she might be pregnant at the time of her sterilisation.[14] Interestingly, a diagnostic partial dilatation and curettage was actually performed but, again, no warning was given that the nature of the procedure was not such as to ensure the dislodgement of any fetus that was present. In fact, the patient was several weeks pregnant at the time and did not appreciate the fact until the fifteenth week of gestation—at which point she was unwilling to consent to a termination. Fortunately, the child was healthy. The most recent case of *Groom v Selby*[15] is very comparable but, at the same time, raises some unique features; it is considered separately below at para 6.29.

STERILISATION AND INFORMATION DISCLOSURE

6.11   It will have been noted that the majority of these 'missed pregnancy' cases were founded largely on a failure of communication between doctor and patient. They lead us naturally to the more common actions in both negligence and in contract which have been based entirely on the grounds of inadequate provision of warning of the possibility of failure of the sterilisation operation. In such cases, the supposed deficit has proved to be no more than a matter of misunderstanding—in effect, providing good examples of the distinction to be made between consent that is based on information and that which is based on understanding of the information to which we refer at para 10.110 below. Thus, in the interesting case of *Thake v Maurice*,[16] the issue turned eventually on the definition of the word 'irreversible'—the defendant claiming that it implied no more than that the procedure could not be reversed by surgery while the plaintiff contended that it represented a contract[17] to provide absolute sterility which was beyond recall by natural processes. After something of a *volte face* between the trial court and the Court of Appeal as to breach of contract—which was accepted in the trial court—it was held that the surgeon had been negligent in his failure to warn of the possibility of natural reversal of vasectomy. A rather similar case turned on the interpretation of the words on the form signifying consent to operation which stated: 'We understand that this means we can have no children' and which the plaintiffs contended amounted to a representation that the operation was foolproof; the trial judge, however, held that the words merely acknowledged that the intended effect of the operation was that the couple should not have more children and found for the defendants.[18] Such semantic difficulties had been foreseen in the important

---

[14] *Crouchman v Burke* (1998) 40 BMLR 163.

[15] [2002] Lloyd's Rep Med 1, (2002) 64 BMLR 47, CA.

[16] [1986] QB 644, [1984] 2 All ER 513; revsd [1986] QB 644, [1986] 1 All ER 497. It was later said of the trial stage of this case: 'I, for my part, think that . . . the less we say about that decision, the better' (per Slade LJ in *Eyre v Measday* [1986] 1 All ER 488 at 492).

[17] Mr Thake was, in fact, a private patient.

[18] *Worster v City and Hackney Health Authority* (1987) *The Times*, 22 June. As a further hurdle, the plaintiffs may have to convince the court that they would have continued contraceptive methods if they had been informed of a risk: *Newell v Goldenberg* [1995] 6 Med LR 371.

Australian case of *F v R*[19] when King CJ specifically drew attention to the need not only to warn of the possible complications of surgery but also of the risk of failure as to the intended end result. There have been further English cases involving much the same issues[20]—one of which concerned a woman who became pregnant while her husband was producing persistently negative seminal specimens[21]—but these are better discussed together under the heading of consent to treatment.[22]

6.12   Thus far, we have accepted that a surgeon and/or his or her employers can be liable in the event of a wrongful pregnancy. What we have not broached is the *extent* of that liability and it is here that we run into considerable analytical difficulty which has been highlighted in a succession of relatively recent cases. Even so, we must return to the older examples if only on the grounds that one cannot see where a principle should go without an idea of where it came from.[23]

THE EXTENT OF LIABILITY FOR FAILED STERILISATION

6.13   Damages following a wrongful pregnancy can be sought under two main heads. First, there are those that derive from the pregnancy itself including damages for the pain and suffering of gestation and childbirth together with recompense for loss of earnings or additional expenses resulting from pregnancy and its convalescence—the bases of what can be loosely referred to as 'the mother's claim'. So far as we know, such damages have never been denied in any jurisdiction.[24] Second, and far more controversial, is the claim for the upkeep of the resulting child until maturity—and it is here that the law has followed a course of sine-wave appearance over the last two decades. Put at its simplest, the questions to be resolved are whether damages for the upkeep of an uncovenanted child should ever be awarded and, if so, whether the condition of the child or its mother should affect the quantum.

6.14   On the face of things, the issue is reasonably clear. A surgeon owes a duty of care to a couple. He has failed in that duty and, as a result, the very circumstance his

---

[19]   (1983) 33 SASR 189, SC.

[20]   E.g. *Eyre v Measday* [1986] 1 All ER 488, CA; *Gold v Haringey Health Authority* [1986] 1 FLR 125, revsd [1988] QB 481, [1987] 2 All ER 888.

[21]   *Stobie v Central Birmingham Health Authority* (1994) 22 BMLR 135. The case drew attention to the fact that the common law interpretation of paternity may be challenged by way of laboratory tests. The phenomenon is said to occur in about 1:80,000 cases—see J C Smith, D Cranston, T O'Brien et al 'Fatherhood without Apparent Spermatozoa after Vasectomy' (1994) 344 Lancet 30.

[22]   See chapter 10 below. It is possible to discern an incremental shift towards judicial reliance on the patients' understanding rather than on what the surgeon said: *Gowten v Wolverhampton Health Authority* [1994] 5 Med LR 432; *Lybert v Warrington Health Authority* (1995) 25 BMLR 91, [1996] 7 Med LR 71. The importance of proximity in such cases scarcely needs emphasis. By no stretch of the imagination could the Department of Health or its advisers be regarded as being sufficiently proximate to members of the public to be responsible for providing advice on sterilisation: *Danns v Department of Health* (1995) 25 BMLR 121.

[23]   Quoting from Lord Mustill in *Attorney-General's Reference (No. 3 of 1994)* [1998] AC 245 at 256, [1997] 3 All ER 936 at 944.

[24]   This policy of 'limited recovery' has been adopted by thirty of the some forty-nine United States which recognise a wrongful pregnancy action: *Emerson v Magendantz* 689 A 2d 409 (RI, 1997).

intervention was intended to avert has, in fact, occurred; ergo, the couple are entitled to restitution.[25] The fact that a child—and, particularly, a healthy child—is involved, however, introduces complications which are more of a moral than a legal nature; in essence, objection to *any* award in such a context is based on the view that a child is a blessing and that the gift of a child should never be regarded as a matter for compensation. The question was first fully addressed many years ago by the court in *Doiron v Orr*; the judge stated that he would have been prepared to award damages for mental anguish caused to the plaintiff, but was adamant in his refusal to accept that there could be liability for the cost of bringing up an unwanted child:

> I find this approach to a matter of this kind which deals with human life, the happiness of the child, the effect upon its thinking, upon its mind when it realised that there has been a case of this kind, that it is an unwanted mistake and that its rearing is being paid for by someone other than its parents, is just simply grotesque.[26]

6.15   Such rejection concentrates on the effect which an award might have on the child; in other cases, the focus has been more on the entitlement of the *parents* to damages. Basically, there are four possibilities in the solution of actions for wrongful pregnancy: damages should never be awarded; damages should always be awarded; the blessing of parenthood should be offset against the economic loss and the damages adjusted accordingly; and, finally, a distinction should be made between healthy and disabled children and damages awarded only for the *extra* costs involved in the upkeep of the latter.

6.16   Actions for wrongful pregnancy originated in America where the courts have taken a less than uniform approach to the problem since the index suit of *Custodio v Bauer*.[27] There are certainly several cases in which redress has been refused, the view having, again, been that parents cannot be held to have been damaged by the blessing of children.[28] Elsewhere, a middle view has prevailed, the assumption being that it is illogical to suppose that a benefit—that of parenthood—can derive from failure to provide proper medical care.[29] In still other instances, damages have been awarded not only in respect of the pain and suffering involved in an unwanted pregnancy but also to offset the cost of rearing the child to maturity.[30] In summary, while it is probably

---

[25] See, for example Waller LJ in *Rees v Darlington Memorial Hospital NHS Trust* [2002] 2 All ER 177, (2002) 65 BMLR 117 at para 44 quoting previous concurrence.

[26] (1978) 86 DLR (3d) 719 at 722, per Garett J.   [27] 251 Cal Rep 2d 303 (1967).

[28] *Terrell v Garcia* 496 SW 2d 124 (Tx, 1973); *Public Health Trust v Brown* 388 So 2d 1084 (Fla, 1980); *Sutkin v Beck* 629 SW 2d 131 (Tx, 1982).

[29] *Kingsbury v Smith* 422 A 2d 1003 (NH, 1982); *Ochs v Borelli* 445 A 2d 883 (Conn, 1982).

[30] *Lovelace Medical Center v Mendez* 805 P 2d 603 (NM, 1991). This policy has, however, been adopted in only two States. The offset rule was followed in *Sherlock v Stillwater Clinic* 260 NW 2d 169 (Min, 1977); *Burke v Rivo* 551 NE 2d 1 (Mass, 1990). This 'balancing' approach was criticised in *Public Health Trust v Brown*, n 28 above: see J H Scheid 'Benefits vs. Burdens: The Limitation of Damages in Wrongful Birth' (1984–5) 23 J Fam Law 57. For a comparative review, see A Stewart 'Damages for the Birth of a Child' (1995) J Law Soc Scot 298. The argument for full recovery in the US has been put forcibly by P Baugher 'Fundamental Protection of a Fundamental Right: Recovery of Child-rearing Damages for Wrongful Pregnancy' (2000) 75 Wash L Rev 1205.

true to say that the majority of states has allowed recovery for all losses excluding those attributable to bringing up a healthy child,[31] it is, nevertheless, possible to extract virtually any 'solution' to the problems involved by a judicious selection of opinions within the various US jurisdictions—and, wherever one looks, it is generally possible to find a powerful dissenting voice.[32] It is fair to say that the United Kingdom courts could derive little precedental assistance from the United States' experience.

6.17 Even so, the validity of the wrongful pregnancy action was upheld in *Udale v Bloomsbury Area Health Authority*[33] in which damages were given for pain and suffering along with loss of earnings following a negligently performed operation; at the same time, an award in respect of the cost of bringing up the child was firmly rejected. In his judgment, Jupp J reiterated that the joy of having the child and the benefits it brought in terms of love should be set off against the inconvenience and financial disadvantages resulting from its birth—'It is an assumption of our culture', he suggested, 'that the coming of a child into the world is an occasion for rejoicing'.[34]

6.18 The Court of Appeal criticised this view in the later case of *Emeh v Kensington and Chelsea and Westminster Area Health Authority*;[35] in addition, there was a strong rejection of the trial judge's view that the plaintiff's refusal of abortion was so unreasonable as to eclipse the defendant's wrongdoing.[36] Equally significantly, however, the Court of Appeal awarded damages for the cost of rearing the child and rejected the policy objections voiced in *Udale*. Thus, despite the somewhat unsatisfactory nature of the case, the stage was set for *Emeh* to be established as the leading case in England and the practice of allowing damages for the upkeep of an uncovenanted, albeit healthy, child was followed in a succession of cases—and these included special damages for the costs associated with any defect and, conspicuously, for the costs of private education when that seemed appropriate.[37] None of these cases was taken to

[31] *Cockrum v Baumgartner* 447 NE 2d 385 (Ill, 1992). Our latest research indicated 35 cases in which compensation for the birth of a healthy child was refused as against 14 in which it was allowed. Interestingly, however, the proportion of the latter seems to increase in the more recent cases. The problem of the unhealthy child depends very much on the doctor's expected anticipation of such an outcome: e.g. *Williams v University of Chicago Hospitals* 688 NE 2d 130 (Ill, 1997).

[32] A jurisprudence was also building up within the Commonwealth. See the intense debate in *CES v Superclinics (Australia) Pty Ltd* (1995) 38 NSWLR 47 where the concept of 'offset' was well described by Kirby A-CJ at 77.

[33] [1983] 2 All ER 522, [1983] 1 WLR 1098. Similar sentiments were expressed in an unreported negligence case, *Jones v Berkshire Area Health Authority*, first quoted in *Gold v Haringey Health Authority* [1986] 1 FLR 125; revsd [1988] QB 481, [1987] 2 All ER 888.

[34] At All ER 531, WLR 1109.

[35] (1983) *The Times*, 3 January; revsd [1985] QB 1012, [1984] 3 All ER 1044, CA.

[36] More recently, see *Crouchman v Burke*, n 14 above, where a woman who would have had an early termination refused one at 15 weeks 'for understandable reasons' (per Langley J at 176). It is now doubtful if a different approach would be adopted to an *early* abortion. For early discussion of the relationship between abortion and wrongful pregnancy, see K McK Norrie 'Damages for the Birth of a Child' 1985 SLT 69; A Grubb 'Damages for "Wrongful Conception" ' (1985) 44 CLJ 30. We have discussed the problem in the light of later cases in J K Mason 'Unwanted Pregnancy: A Case of Retroversion?' (2000) 4 Edin LR 191.

[37] *Benarr v Kettering Health Authority* [1988] NLJR 179; *Robinson v Salford Health Authority* (1992) 3 Med LR 270; *Allen v Bloomsbury Health Authority* [1993] 1 All ER 651, (1993) 13 BMLR 47; *Crouchman v Burke*, n 14 above.

appeal. Indeed, the only remaining difficulty appeared to lie in the relationship between the two heads of damage—were they distinct or did one flow from the other? The Court of Appeal later held that a wrongful pregnancy is a personal injury which cannot be separated from its consequences.[38]

6.19   Meantime, Scottish policy was evolving independently. Earlier reports are, for the most part, concerned with procedural matters and do not deal with the substantive legal arguments or their outcomes.[39] Two unreported cases,[40] both based on lack of warning of the risk of failure rather than on operative negligence, caught the attention of the media. Both were settled out of court; but the substantial sum of £50,000 was offered in compensation in *Lindsay*,[41] suggesting that the Scottish courts might well recognise the unexpected birth of a healthy child as a suitable matter for 'damages'. This was confirmed in *Allan v Greater Glasgow Health Board*,[42] in which the court explicitly accepted that there were no grounds—of principle or of policy—to prevent an award of damages for the upbringing of a child born in such circumstances. There is, of course, much force in the argument that such compensation amounts to a rejection of a fundamental value in our society—that of family love. On the other hand, it is implicit that the patient undergoing consensual, non-therapeutic sterilisation does not want any more children and that this may be for economic reasons. That being so, it is hard to refute the words of Peter Pain J: 'Every baby has a belly to be filled and a body to be clothed.'[43]

The *McFarlane* case and its immediate outcome

6.20   The relatively still waters of cross-border consensus were, however, to be rudely disturbed when this fundamental contradiction was addressed by the entire gamut of appeal courts in *McFarlane v Tayside Health Board*.[44] Here, at first instance, the Lord Ordinary in the Outer House of the Court of Session held that a normal pregnancy culminating in a healthy child was a natural event which could not be regarded as an injury—hence, it could not form a basis for damages. He also decided that the joys of the child's existence wholly compensated the financial cost of its upbringing— he rejected the concept of 'off-set', or a balancing of some benefit against some

---

[38]   *Walkin v South Manchester Health Authority* [1995] 4 All ER 132, (1995) 25 BMLR 108. Which meant, in passing, that actions for wrongful pregnancy would be subject to the Limitation Act 1980, s 11—followed in *Godfrey v Gloucestershire Royal Infirmary NHS Trust* [2003] EWHC 549 (QB). Interestingly, the British Columbia Court of Appeal took the opposite view in the same year in a case of wrongful birth: *Arndt v Smith* [1996] 7 Med LR 108, (1995) 126 DLR (4th) 705.

[39]   *Smith, Petitioner* 1985 SLT 461; *Jones v Lanarkshire Health Board* 1990 SLT 19, 1989 SCLR 542, aff'd 1991 SLT 714, 1991 SCLR 806; *Teece v Ayrshire and Arran Health Board* 1990 SLT 512.

[40]   *Pollock v Lanarkshire Health Board* (1987) *The Times*, 6 January; *Lindsay v Greater Glasgow Health Board* (1990) *The Scotsman*, 14 March.

[41]   N 40 above.

[42]   (1993) 17 BMLR 135, 1998 SLT 580, OH. The court found, however, that there had been no negligence in this case. See also *Cameron v Greater Glasgow Health Board* 1993 GWD 6–433 (Lexis transcript available), in which damages of £40,000 were agreed; again, however, the action was unsuccessful.

[43]   In *Thake v Maurice* [1984] 2 All ER 513 at 526, [1985] 2 WLR 215 at 230.

[44]   1997 SLT 211 (1996) *The Times*, 11 November.

disadvantage, in that it involved placing a specific value on the life of the child, which he regarded as unacceptable. This decision, which was, in the circumstances, surprising, was reversed in the Inner House, where the Lord Justice-Clerk declined to discuss the relationship of pregnancy to personal injury and, rather, addressed the problem in terms of the basic principles of Scots law.[45] Injuria, or the wrongdoing, coincided with the damnum, or interference with a person's legal interests, when Mrs McFarlane conceived. Damnum was manifested, firstly, in the adverse effects of pregnancy and childbirth on her bodily integrity and, secondly, in the pecuniary interests of both parents. An obligation to make reparation arises when there is concurrence of injuria and damnum—and these conditions were satisfied in the instant case once the pregnancy was established.[46] The Inner House rejected the proposition that the blessing of a child was an overriding benefit, pointing out that the couple were relying on sterilisation in order to avoid the additional expenditure which the birth of another child would entail and, having decided the issue by way of principle, went on to conclude that there was no overriding consideration of public policy which the awarding of damages would contravene.

6.21 Most commentators then assumed that equilibrium between English and Scots law had been re-established but *McFarlane* was appealed to the House of Lords,[47] presumably so as to ensure that this was so. While the House decided by a 4:1 majority that the 'mother's claim' in respect of pain and suffering due to pregnancy and childbirth should stand, the main appeal related to reparation for the costs of bringing up a healthy child was, somewhat surprisingly, upheld unanimously.

6.22 The reasoning behind the rejection of the latter claim, which undoubtedly represents a U-turn in the development of the jurisprudence, has never been easy to unravel, given that the defender's duty of care to the pursuers was admitted and acknowledged by way of the 'mother's' claim; each of the five Lords of Appeal gave different reasons for his decision and there is neither the space nor, perhaps, the need to explore these in detail here.[48] In summary, Lord Slynn concluded that it would be neither just nor reasonable to impose on the doctor liability for the upkeep of a child until maturity and this is the theme which is adopted most often in the post-*McFarlane* cases; Lord Steyn took refuge in some rather tenuous concepts of distributive justice; Lord Hope thought that, since the benefits associated with a healthy child were incalculable, it was illogical to attempt an assessment of the net economic loss sustained by the child's parents; Lord Clyde was struck by the disproportion between the damages available when based on the full costs of upbringing and the surgeon's

---

[45] *McFarlane and McFarlane v Tayside Health Board* 1998 SC 389 at 393, 1998 SLT 307 at 310.

[46] Reiterated by Lord McCluskey 1998 SC 389 at 398 who went so far as to hold that the right of a married couple to have sexual relations with each other without any likelihood that those relations will result in a pregnancy is a right that the law recognises. The House specifically held that the deliberate continuation of the pregnancy did not affect the chain of causation: cf Slade LJ in *Emeh v Kensington and Chelsea and Westminster Health Authority*, n 35 above.

[47] *McFarlane v Tayside Health Board* [2000] AC 59, 2000 SC 1, HL.

[48] One of us has analysed the case in greater detail elsewhere: see Mason, n 36 above.

culpability; while Lord Millett eventually returned to the reasoning in the index English case[49] in holding that the law must accept the birth of a healthy baby as a blessing, not a detriment.[50]

6.23   We find none of the arguments based on the value of a child to be entirely satisfactory—rather, the problem is simply that of whether or not two persons should be compensated if their financial resources are diverted as a result of the negligence of the agent engaged to avert that outcome.[51] Moreover, the House in *McFarlane* deliberately left open the possibility of recompense for the upkeep of an unexpected *disabled* child—since this was, apparently, still available by way of existing precedent, the resulting doubt had to be settled with some urgency. Efforts both to circumvent the decision and to clarify the situation were, therefore, to be expected.

6.24   Attempts to undermine the 'healthy child = no maintenance' rule were disposed of summarily. In *Richardson v LRC Products Ltd*[52]—a burst condom case brought under the Consumer Protection Act 1987, s 3—it was clearly held that the rule applied whether the claim was laid in negligence or in breach of a statutory duty. *Greenfield v Irwin (a firm)*[53] was a further case of missed pregnancy rather than failed sterilisation; otherwise, the conditions were very similar to those in *McFarlane*. The plaintiff, however, sought to distinguish her case on the grounds that her loss was consequent on the physical injury of the pregnancy rather than on negligent advice; she also rather ingeniously attempted to demonstrate a difference between expenditure on a child and loss of earnings due to caring for that child. The Court of Appeal found both distinctions to be irrelevant; the suggestion that failure to provide financial support would contravene the Human Rights Act 1998, Sch 1, art 8—respect for family life—was also dismissed.

6.25   By contrast, attempts to entrench the possible exception for disabled children firmly within the law have, in general, been successful. Unfortunately, the underlying reasoning has been misapplied in that the great majority of cases in which this aspect of *McFarlane* has been argued have been, in fact, instances of wrongful birth. As has been indicated at paras 6.1 and 6.2, these have a wholly different foundation; accordingly, they are considered later in this chapter.[54]

---

[49] *Udale v BloomsburyArea Health Authority*, n 33 above.

[50] Although the matter was discussed in depth only by a minority of the House, a refusal to terminate the pregnancy was very firmly regarded as not constituting a *novus actus interveniens*. The circumstances surrounding 'wrongful pregnancy' are such that a termination would be lawful under the Abortion Act 1976 irrespective of the health of the fetus (see chapter 5 for discussion).

[51] The decision was, in general, badly received by academic lawyers—e.g. E Cameron-Perry 'Return of the Burden of the Blessing' (1999) 149 NLJ 1887; J Thomson 'Abandoning the Law of Delict?' 2000 SLT 43; O Radley-Gardner 'Wrongful Birth Revisited' (2002) 118 LQR 11.

[52] N 1 above. Attempts to substitute breach of contract for negligence have been summarily dismissed— e.g. *Reynolds v Health First Medical Group* [2000] Lloyd's Rep Med 240.

[53] [2001] 1 WLR 1279, sub nom *Greenfield v Flather and others* (2001) 59 BMLR 43.

[54] A fact which was particularly noted by Brooke LJ in *Parkinson v St James and Seacroft University Hospital NHS Trust* [2002] QB 266, [2001] 3 All ER 97 at [48]. For a fuller consideration of the post-*McFarlane* cases, see J K Mason 'Wrongful Pregnancy, Wrongful Birth and Wrongful Terminology' (2002) 6 Edin LR 46; L C H Hoyano 'Misconceptions about Wrongful Conception' (2002) 65 MLR 883.

6.26   The only acceptable comparator in our view is *Parkinson v St James and Seacroft University Hospital NHS Trust*.[55] Here, a woman gave birth to a disabled child following an admittedly negligent sterilisation operation. Brooke LJ pointed out that parents in a similar position had been able to recover damages for some 15 years following *Emeh*[56] and that both the 'fair, just and reasonable' test and the principles of distributive justice would be satisfied if the award was limited to the special costs associated with the disability. He was supported in a powerful speech by Hale LJ who was, incidentally, the first female judge to express a view on the *McFarlane* judgment. Hale LJ started from the premise that to cause a woman to become pregnant against her will was an invasion of her bodily integrity; she then listed an impressive catalogue of the consequences of pregnancy which, she insisted, retained an invasive nature despite the fact that they derived from a natural process. She could find nothing unusual or contrary to legal principle in awarding damages in such a case on the grounds that that the caring role—and, hence, the interference with the woman's personal autonomy—persists throughout childhood. Admitting damages limited to the restitution of costs beyond those involved in bringing up a normal child gave no offence to those with disability and simply acknowledged that the costs in the event of disability were greater than in the case of normality—put another way, the 'deemed equilibrium' between the benefits derived from and the costs of maintaining an uncovenanted healthy child that underpins the *McFarlane* decision is distorted to an extent that is determined by the degree of disability in an unhealthy child.[57]

6.27   In our view, however, the importance of Lady Hale's opinion is that her arguments based on bodily invasion can be applied almost verbatim to the birth of an uncovenanted *normal* child and, somewhat paradoxically, this leads one to question the logic of the *Parkinson* decision. It was, in fact, agreed that the child's disability was in no way attributable to a breach of duty on the defendant's part; that being the case, why is liability apportioned in *Parkinson* but not in *McFarlane*? The feeling remains that one or other decision must be wrong.[58] In the event, the tenor of the *Parkinson* judgment leaves a strong impression of dissatisfaction with *McFarlane*[59] and the

---

[55] N 54 above. It is to be noted that, even so, the child's disability in *Parkinson* (autism) only became apparent during infancy as opposed to at birth. *Taylor v Shropshire Health Authority* [1998] Lloyd's Rep Med 395 is a comparable case which pre-dated *McFarlane*; the nature of the disability is uncertain but it was present at birth and, presumably, it was not detected *in utero*. Full expenses were allowed subject to a very modest 'offset' for any associated joy and comfort; in fact, had *Taylor* gone to appeal, the case might have provided a better test of the *McFarlane* exception than *Parkinson*.

[56] N 35 above.

[57] It is important to note that the apparently attractive concept of 'deemed equilibrium' was rejected in *Rees*, n 74 below in both the concurring and dissenting judgments. We do not think that this affects the practical value of Hale LJ's exposition.

[58] Such a lack of a causal link between the doctor's negligence and the child's disability was emphasised in what seems to have been the most recent apposite US appeal case: *Simmerer v Dabbas* 733 NE 2d 1169 (Ohio, 2000).

[59] Described by both Gummow and Kirby JJ as a 'rebellion' in *Cattanach v Melchior*, transcript, 11 February 2003, p 23. See also Lord Scott in *Rees v Darlington Memorial NHS Trust* [2003] 4 All ER 987 at para [143].

decision in the Court of Appeal in that case has not been appealed to the House of Lords. Thus, the extent to which compensation for the unexpected birth of a disabled child is available is not entirely settled—and we will see in the light of later litigation that this may have significant implications.

6.28   Hale LJ's innovative recognition of the invasive nature of the negligence involved in cases of unwanted pregnancy was further expressed in *Groom v Selby*[60] which was tried at first instance before, and at appeal after, the Court of Appeal hearing in *Parkinson*. *Groom* is an unusual case which almost defies classification and is, therefore, somewhat parenthetic to the present discussion. However, it reflects an important aspect of the reaction to *McFarlane*.

6.29   In brief, *Groom* was an instance of the not unusual condition, reverted to briefly above,[61] in which a sterilisation is carried out in the presence of an unnoticed pregnancy. Ms Groom later consulted her general practitioner who negligently failed to diagnose her pregnancy until her fetus was so far developed as to make a termination personally unacceptable; a normal infant was born, albeit three weeks prematurely. Thus far, then, the case was an example of an action for wrongful pregnancy of the 'missed' variety. However, some three weeks after birth, the child developed meningitis due to infection by salmonella organisms derived from her mother's birth canal; as a result, she was left with a prognostically uncertain degree of brain damage. *Groom*, therefore, raises an interesting variation on the wrongful pregnancy theme— was the child normal at birth and, thus, subject to the *McFarlane* rule, or was she born disabled as a consequence of negligence during the process of birth? At first instance, Clark J found that 'Megan is not and never has been a healthy child', a proposition that was, in our view justifiably, contested on appeal. Nevertheless, the Court of Appeal upheld the judgment. Brooke LJ summarised the position:

[The] birth of a premature child who suffered salmonella meningitis though exposure to a bacterium during the normal processes of birth was a foreseeable consequence of Dr Selby's failure to advise the claimant that, although she had been sterilised, she was in fact pregnant.[62]

At first glance, this seems harsh but acceptable in that a fetus is not 'born alive' until it is completely extruded from the mother; the infant's 'injury' here was clearly sustained during the birth process. Brooke LJ, however, went a stage further and considered that, although the child was apparently healthy at birth 'it should not stand in the way of our doing justice, in a case like the present, in which a child's enduring handicaps, caused by the normal incidents of intra-uterine development and birth, were triggered within the first month of her life' and he went on to say that the longer the period before the disability is triggered off, the more difficult it may be to establish a right to recover compensation. Whether it is right to undermine the *McFarlane* rule in such indefinite terms remains to be established.

---

[60] (2002) 64 BMLR 47, [2002] Lloyd's Rep Med 1, CA at [31].
[61] At para [6.9].   [62] At para [24].

6.30   During the course of her judgment in *Groom*, Hale LJ repeated her view that the costs of bringing up a child who has been born as a result of another's negligence are not 'pure' economic loss but, rather, economic loss consequent upon the invasion of a woman's bodily integrity. Her concept of unavoidable responsibility imposed by motherhood was, again, applied when she extended the potential *McFarlane* exception from disability in the resultant child to disability in its mother.[63] In *Rees*, as a result of a negligently performed sterilisation operation, a healthy child was born to a woman who was severely visually handicapped. Hale LJ could see no essential difference between compensating for the extra costs of bringing up a disabled child vis-à-vis his or her normal counterpart—as in *Parkinson*—and compensating a woman for the extra costs in supporting a normal child that were dictated by her own disability— thus continuing and extending the concept of a *persisting* injury that she developed in *Parkinson*. Hale LJ thought that this did no more than put the mother in the same position as her 'able bodied fellows' who, by contrast, had no *need* for additional help in attending to a child's basic needs. Walker LJ, while rejecting the argument based on a 'deemed equilibrium' between the advantages and disadvantages of an uncovenanted normal child, nevertheless agreed that the circumstances of the case were not covered by *McFarlane* and represented a legitimate extension of *Parkinson*. Waller LJ, however, in a dissenting judgment, pointed to the unfairness of compensating a woman by virtue of her physical disability when other mothers in as great a need could not benefit. While many may have considerable intuitive sympathy for the majority in *Rees*, it has to be admitted that the decision raises its own problems. We have, for example, suggested that the courts are well able to judge the additional costs associated with disability in a child; it is, pace Lady Hale's disclaimer, far less easy to assess the *costs* resulting from a degree of disability in its mother. Moreover, we must ask what constitutes disability? and what is so special about physical disability? Presumably, *Rees* would extend quite naturally to mental handicap and, if so, why not to life's other challenges, including that of economic hardship? Waller LJ found these to be good reasons for dissenting in *Rees*. At the same time, he reminded us that the House in *McFarlane* recognised that a claim for damages for bringing up a healthy child born as a result of the negligence of a surgeon would succeed under the normal rules of tort[64] and there is little doubt that a case that was decided to the contrary on what were, largely, moral principles, provides a less than satisfactory base from which to explore its various implications.

Wrongful pregnancy in Australia

6.31   Precisely this point was taken up in the important case of *Cattanach v Melchior*[65] which was heard in the High Court of Australia shortly after *McFarlane* was decided

---

[63] *Rees v Darlington Memorial Hospital NHS Trust* [2002] 2 All ER 177, (2002) 65 BMLR 117.

[64] At para [44]. See also Thomson, n 51 above, for similar criticism.

[65] (2003) 199 ALR 131. Our detailed assessment of the case is available electronically in J K Mason 'A Turn-up Down Under; *McFarlane* in the Light of *Catanach*' (2004) 1 SCRIPT-ed, at www.law.ed.ac.uk/ahrb/script-ed/docs/mason.asp.

in the House of Lords. The circumstances in *Cattanach* were comparable to those in *McFarlane* save that the former involved a negligent female sterilisation. Holmes J's comment at first instance set the scene:

[W]ere there a single, distinct line of reasoning to be discerned from either [*McFarlane* or *CES*[66]] I should follow it. However given the divergence of approach, I can see no alternative but to distil from those decisions the reasoning which appeals to me as sound[67]

and she awarded $A105,249 for the costs of raising a normal but uncovenanted child.[68] An appeal to the Supreme Court of Queensland was then dismissed and the case was finally heard by a seven-judge panel in the High Court where the deliberations were confined to the single issue of whether or not a court could award damages which require a doctor who is responsible for the negligent birth of an unintended child to bear the cost of raising and maintaining that child.

6.32   The judgment in *Cattanach* is very long and detailed and, in so far as the result depended on a narrowly split decision, the arguments provide an interesting contrast to those deployed in the unanimous decision in *McFarlane* This is, however, no place to consider them in detail. In essence, they rested on whether the Court should be governed by moral or legal principles—that is, is it wrong that the addition of a much loved, albeit unsought, child to a family should be regarded as a compensatable damage or should the legal principles of tort law be maintained in the face of such moral considerations.

6.33   In the end, the Court divided 4:3 in favour of legal principle and, thus, rejected the *McFarlane* rule. The case for allowing the appeal can be summarised in the conclusion to the speech of Heydon J who put it thus:

The various assumptions underlying the law relating to children and the duties on parents created by the law would be negated if parents could sue to recover the costs of rearing unplanned children. That possibility would tend to damage the natural love and mutual confidence which the law seeks to foster between parent and child. It would permit conduct inconsistent with a parental duty to treat the child with the utmost affection, with infinite tenderness, and with unstinting forgiveness in all circumstances because these goals are contradicted by legal proceedings based on the premise that the child's birth was a painful and a highly inconvenient mistake. It would permit conduct inconsistent with the duty to nurture children.[69]

6.34   The case for the majority was put most forcibly by Kirby J who was highly critical of the *McFarlane* decision, of which he said: '. . . [T]he diverse opinions illustrate what can happen when judges embark upon the "quicksands" of public policy, at least when doing so leads them away from basic legal principle'.[70] And, to summarise his

---

[66] *CES v Superclinics (Australia) Pty Ltd* (1995) 38 NSWLR 47—a similar case in the NSW Court of Appeal that ended as something of a contrived compromise and which was widely quoted in *McFarlane*. Leave to appeal to the High Court was given in *CES* but the case was settled prior to the hearing.

[67] *Melchior v Cattanach* [2000] QSC 285 at para [50].

[68] Relying in the main on the case of *Perre v Apand Pty Ltd* (1999) 73 ALJR 1190.

[69] Para [404].   [70] At para [158].

position:[71] 'Neither the invocation of Scripture nor the invention of a fictitious oracle on the Underground[72] ... authorises a court of law to depart from the ordinary principles governing the recovery of damages for the tort of negligence'.

6.35 It is to be noted that, while the most common denominator in the House of Lords decisions lies in an appeal to justice, fairness and reasonableness based on *Caparo* principles,[73] *Caparo* currently forms no part of the Australian jurisprudence; it is, therefore, at least possible to see *McFarlane* and *Cattanach* as not being incompatible, at least in precedental terms. Nonetheless, most would have seen two of the highest courts in the Commonwealth as being on a collision course and one wondered if there might be an opportunity to resolve the differences should the House of Lords have occasion to review its position.

The status quo in the United Kingdom

6.36 This arose when Ms Rees' case was further appealed to a bench of seven judges in the House of Lords.[74] Unfortunately, the House did not analyse *Cattanach* in depth, the general feeling being that the arguments had already been fully rehearsed. At the same time, the decision in *McFarlane* was confirmed unanimously; this, however, was not as a result of further consideration but, rather, on the grounds that it would be improper to reverse a House of Lords' decision within the short period of 4 years.[75] *Rees*, however, remains a most important case in its own right and, in the event, the House allowed the appeal by a majority of 4:3. Given the narrow majority, it is unsurprising their Lordships' reasons were, again, diverse.[76] The argument rested on whether, on the one hand, it was disability in either the child or the parent which dictated exceptional costs in bringing up the child—and, hence, attracted recompense—or whether the overriding factor was *normality* in the resultant child. In the event, the latter view held sway.

6.37 Perhaps the most interesting aspect of *Rees* lies in the fact that *McFarlane* was accepted as representing an exception to the normal rules of tort by both the majority and minority—thus renewing concern that justice was, at least, not being seen to be done. Lord Bingham's response,[77] which was followed by the majority, was to make a conventional award of £15,000 to all victims of a negligent sterilisation in recognition of the affront to a woman's autonomy imposed by an unwanted pregnancy. Lord Bingham was adamant that this was in no way compensatory but it is difficult to

---

[71] At para [151].

[72] An allusion to Lord Steyn's commuter on the Underground as an assessor of distributive justice in *McFarlane* at AC 59 at 62, SLT 154 at 165.

[73] *Caparo Industries plc v Dickman* [1990] 2 AC 605, [1990] 1 All ER 568.

[74] *Rees v Darlington Memorial Hospital NHS Trust* [2004] AC 309, [2003] 4 All ER 987.

[75] See Lord Bingham at para [7]. Even so, the possibility was open: *Practice Statement (Judicial Precedent)* [1966] 1WLR 1234. The cases quoted, however, indicated that even 11 years could be too short an interval.

[76] For a brief appraisal, see C Dixon 'An Unconventional Gloss on Unintended Children' (2003) 153 NLJ 1732. One of us has examined the case in detail: J K Mason 'From Dundee to Darlington: An end to the *McFarlane* Line?' [2004] JR 365.

[77] At para [8].

accept this at face value and, clearly, other members of the House—including those who supported the measure—were in some doubt. Lord Steyn, indeed, went so far as to question the power of the courts to make such an award—to do so, he maintained, should be the prerogative of Parliament. For our part, we would prefer to see the 'conventional award' as recognition of a new head of damages—that is, a breach of autonomy or interference with the right to plan one's life as one wishes. This, we believe, would harmonise the apparent conflict between the Inner House of the Court of Session and the House of Lords in *McFarlane* and would be widely recognised as being a fair solution to an intense moral and legal dilemma.

6.38   Nevertheless, it does not represent the law as it stands at the time of writing which is that the *McFarlane* rule—there should be no compensation for the costs of upkeep of a healthy, uncovenanted child—stands, and it is to be emphasised that it is the state of health of the child that determines the issue.[78] The rule is modified in that a conventional award is proffered in recognition of the wrong done to a woman's autonomy by denying her the chance to exercise a reproductive choice. The persistence of the Court of Appeal ruling in *Parkinson*, however, means that recompense in tort is available for the excess costs imposed by any disability in the resultant child. Lord Bingham indicated that he would give the conventional award to *all* victims of wrongful pregnancy and this leaves some doubt as to the outcome should another case like that of Mrs Parkinson arise—will both damages for the excess costs of upbringing and the conventional award be given or will one replace the other? To that limited extent, the law in relation to wrongful pregnancy remains uncertain. Were it to be reconsidered, we suspect that the overriding consideration would be to align the decision with that which has evolved from the cases of wrongful birth to which we now turn.

REPRODUCTIVE COUNSELLING AND NEGLIGENCE—THE ACTION FOR WRONGFUL BIRTH

6.39   The parents of an afflicted child may choose to raise an action in negligence against a doctor or genetic counsellor who has failed either to advise them of the risk of illness in their children or to carry out, and interpret correctly, appropriate diagnostic procedures which would have disclosed abnormality in the fetus. The doctor or genetic counsellor owes them a duty of care in which he or she has been found

---

[78] This was foreseen in *AD v East Kent Community NHS Trust* [2003] 3 All ER 1167, (2003) 70 BMLR 230, CA which was heard before *Rees* went to the House of Lords. Here a woman who was detained under the Mental Heath Act 1983 was delivered of a healthy child as a result of supposed negligent supervision. The case is complicated in that the child's grandmother voluntarily undertook charge of the infant. In the end, *McFarlane*, rather than *Rees* at CA level was applied in so far as no 'extra costs' were involved.

wanting; the parents may contend that, as a result, they have been deprived of the opportunity to terminate the pregnancy and they are now burdened with a sick or handicapped child. Such an action, brought by and on behalf of the parents, is generally known as one for 'wrongful birth'. Damages may be sought in respect of the distress occasioned by the parents in respect of the existence of the defect in their child and for the extra costs which are entailed in bringing up the child. It should be noted that many of the cases that follow involve instances of genetic disease which has been misdiagnosed or has gone undetected. We refer the reader to the first section of chapter 7 for a detailed account of the nature of genetic disease and testing. For present purposes, however, we are less concerned with the *medical* cause of harm— that is, whether the child suffers from a genetic or non-genetic disease—and more concerned with whether the courts consider that the costs of raising an unhealthy child is a *legal* harm when those costs are incurred because of mismanagement of prenatal care.

6.40   The courts in the United States, which can, again, be seen as the pathfinders in this area, experienced something of a roller-coaster ride on their early journey to recognising a legitimate claim for damages for the birth of a handicapped child. In one of the first cases, *Becker v Schwartz*,[79] the New York Court of Appeals allowed a parental claim for damages in respect of the cost of the institutional care of a child suffering from Down's syndrome. The negligence in question was the failure of the doctor to recommend amniocentesis to a 37-year-old mother who, by virtue of her age, had a relatively high risk of bearing a handicapped child. Later, however, the courts found difficulty as to the conflict of interests. On the one hand, there was the question of public policy which should, in theory, favour birth over abortion.[80] On the other, the woman's prerogative to control her own body, and the consequent acceptability of abortion, have been increasingly recognised. The general rule that has now emerged is that such claims will succeed.[81] Even so, the causation problem remains. In *Noccash*,[82] for example, widely based damages were awarded for the birth of an infant with Tay-Sachs disease but costs concerned with the child's funeral were disallowed on the grounds that the fatality was the result of hereditary factors rather than of the defendant's negligence. Other difficulties relate to the fact that pregnancy has been actually sought in these cases. Should the damages awarded then reflect the full costs of rearing a defective child or should they be limited to the difference in financial burden posed by a normal and a handicapped infant? Should they extend to compensation for emotional distress? These questions seem to be very finely balanced in the

[79] 386 NE 2d 807 (NY, 1978).

[80] But this argument has been used in the main to counter claims for wrongful life (see para 6.47 below).

[81] For a major list of relevant cases, see *Siemieniec v Lutheran General Hospital* 512 NE 2d 691 (Ill, 1987). These early actions are discussed in P M A Beaumont 'Wrongful Life and Wrongful Birth' in S A M McLean *Contemporary Issues in Law, Medicine and Ethics* (1996) ch 6.

[82] *Noccash v Burger* 290 SE 2d 825 (Va, 1982).

American courts[83] and, while, as has been noted, they will accept a wrongful birth action in principle in most cases, some state legislatures have enacted laws stating clearly their preference for denying such causes of action.[84]

6.41   Comparable cases have appeared relatively recently in the United Kingdom but the courts have shown no reluctance to allow the action—indeed, we suspect that many cases are settled out of court;[85] the early case of *Salih*,[86] involving the congenital rubella syndrome, is apposite in this connection in that liability was admitted without question. In *Gregory v Pembrokeshire Health Authority*[87] the trial judge found that the doctors' neglect to inform of the failure of an amniocentesis was a breach of the duty of care; the action failed, however, on grounds of causation, the plaintiff being unable to convince the court, or the Court of Appeal, that she would have had a second investigation had she been offered one, far less that she would have aborted her child. In *Anderson v Forth Valley Health Board*,[88] a couple sought damages in respect of the alleged negligence of a health board which led to their two sons being born suffering from muscular dystrophy. The pursuers averred that, had they been referred for genetic counselling and testing, the genetic disorder carried by the wife would have been discovered and the couple would have chosen to terminate both pregnancies. As it was, no tests were ever offered or carried out, despite the fact that the hospital had been informed of a history of X-linked Duchenne muscular dystrophy among the male members of the wife's family. The children's condition only came to light when one of the boys injured himself in a fall. After a very comprehensive review of the case law, Lord Nimmo Smith held that he could see 'no good reason' not to treat the pursuers as having suffered personal injuries 'in the conventional sense' and he accordingly awarded damages under the heads of both solatium—injury to the feelings—and patrimonial loss. *Anderson* was followed shortly afterwards in England in *Nunnerley v Warrington Health Authority*[89]—a case involving admittedly defective

---

[83]   The only cases discovered which have refused the claim in toto are: *Azzolino v Dingfelder* 337 SE 2d 528 (NC, 1985), *Atlanta Obstetrics and Gynecology Group v Abelson* 398 SE 2d 557 (Ga, 1990) and *Grubbs v Barbourville Family Health Center* 120 SW 3d 682 (Ky, 2003). The latter is a significantly recent decision by the Supreme Court of Kentucky; the action failed on grounds of causation and of a fear of reintroducing eugenics into the law.

[84]   As an example, consider this provision from the Utah Code Ann para 78–11–24: '[a] cause of action shall not arise, and damages shall not be awarded, on behalf of any person, based on a claim that but for the act or omission of another, a person would not have been permitted to have been born alive but would have been aborted.' Other States imposing some limitation include Idaho, Minnesota, Missouri, North Dakota, Pennsylvania and Georgia.

[85]   For general discussion of the liability of genetic counsellors, see M L Lupton 'The Impact of Genetics on Society: The Law's Response' (1991) 10 Med Law 55. The status of the wrongful birth action on both sides of the Atlantic has recently been reviewed in depth by R Scott 'Prenatal Screening, Autonomy and Reasons: The Relationship between the Law of Abortion and Wrongful Birth' (2003) 11 Med LR 265.

[86]   *Salih v Enfield Health Authority* [1990] 1 Med LR 333; on appeal (1991) 7 BMLR 1, CA. It is to be noted that, while the trial judge awarded damages which included the basic costs of maintaining a child, the Court of Appeal held that the family had been spared the cost of a normal child and this head of damages was extinguished.

[87]   [1989] 1 Med LR 81.   [88]   (1998) 44 BMLR 108, 1998 SLT 588.

[89]   [2000] Lloyd's Rep Med 170.

genetic counselling; here, the parents were held to be entitled to full compensation for the upkeep of their child up to and beyond his eighteenth birthday.

6.42 The decision of the Scottish courts in *McLelland v Greater Glasgow Health Board*[90] should, also, be noted as to the matter of damages for solatium. In this case, a father was, for the first time, awarded damages for the shock and distress he suffered as the result of the birth of a son suffering from Down's syndrome—as in *Anderson*, the hospital had been made aware of a family history suggestive of genetic disease but had failed to offer an amniocentesis. This ruling was unprecedented because it is normally only the mother of the child who will receive damages for pain and suffering. The closest analagous authority we can find in England is *Newell v Goldenberg*,[91] in which a couple were awarded £500 for the anxiety and distress suffered when they discovered that Mrs Newell had become pregnant following the failure of her husband's vasectomy. Normally, the plaintiff must prove an element of psychiatric disturbance or illness in order to recover damages for personal injury in the form of 'nervous shock'. In *McLelland*, however, Lord MacFadyen was persuaded that this criterion goes only to the question of the existence of a duty of care; once liability is admitted the question becomes whether or not there has been material prejudice to a pursuer's interest that is recognised by law. The father had suffered—and would suffer further—shock and distress which he would not have done had the management of the case not been negligent. Accordingly, his claim to solatium was sound.[92]

6.43 So far, so good, but the United Kingdom courts' attitudes were to be markedly affected by the House of Lords' ruling in *McFarlane v Tayside Health Board*[93] which has already been discussed in some detail. It will be remembered that, while the House rejected the concept of compensation for the undesired normal child, it left open the position were such a child to be born disabled—thus raising the possibility that the well-established action for wrongful birth might no longer be available or, at best, might only be available in a modified form.[94] This resulted in a rash of cases anxious to settle the matter. This could be unfortunate as the two actions—wrongful pregnancy and wrongful birth—are distinct both in concept and practice; to argue the latter in terms of the former might well confuse the jurisprudence. It is not inappropriate, therefore, to recapitulate some pointers as to the nature of the distinction.

---

[90] 1999 SC 305, 1999 SLT 543.   [91] [1995] 6 Med LR 371.

[92] The McLellands, in fact, fell into the *McFarlane* trap (see para 6.23 above) between the Outer and the Inner Houses. Solatium was still awarded but the 'ordinary' costs of maintaining their child were deducted from the previously awarded full costs at the appeal which was heard after *McFarlane: McLelland v Greater Glasgow Health Board* 2001 SLT 446. The opinions are both interesting and innovative; in particular, Lord Morison, dissenting, gave good reasons for considering the two cases distinct—an analysis with which we would clearly agree.

[93] 2000 SC (HL) 1, [2000] 2 AC 59.

[94] When one applies the reasoning of the individual Lords of Appeal in *McFarlane*, it becomes apparent that that might well have been the case: J K Mason 'Wrongful Pregnancy, Wrongful Birth and Wrongful Terminology' (2002) 6 Edin LR 46. For further analysis of the proposition, see G Hughes-Jones 'Commentary on *Taylor v Shropshire HA*' [2000] Lloyd's Rep Med 107.

6.44   These include the fact that, although the Health Trust may well be involved in both, the individual defender is likely to be different in the two cases. The surgeon will be accused of negligence in the wrongful pregnancy case while, in wrongful birth, responsibility will probably shift to the obstetrician or, even more likely, to the laboratory or the genetic counsellor. A more important difference is that, in the former case, the woman did not want a child whereas in the latter, save in exceptional circumstances—as in *Greenfield*[95]—she wanted a child but not one that was disabled. Thirdly, it is at least arguable that an action for personal injury cannot survive within the context of one for wrongful birth for the pregnancy has been willingly accepted.[96] And, fourthly, there can be no question of failure to minimise one's losses or of *novus actus interveniens* by way of refused termination in wrongful birth[97] because the action is founded on the denial to the woman of the opportunity to invoke that intervention. The specific situation that ante-natal care was designed to avoid has arisen and we are as close to a recognisable plea of *res ipsa loquitur* as we can get.[98]

WRONGFUL BIRTH FOLLOWING *MCFARLANE*

6.45   There is little to be gained by a detailed description of the several relevant cases although each introduced some individual observations which should be recorded. It can be said in general that the pattern developed in *Rand*[99] has been widely accepted and, as a result, the underlying validity of the wrongful birth action has been fully upheld. The extent of the available damages has, however, been modified in the light of *McFarlane* in that the costs of rearing a healthy child must, now, be deducted from the gross costs of caring for one who is disabled.[100]

6.46   *Rand*, a Down's syndrome case, was followed closely by *Hardman v Amin*[101] which involved a child suffering from the congenital rubella syndrome. *McFarlane* was analysed in detail in both and no difficulty in basing the costs derived on the degree of

[95] *Greenfield v Irwin (a firm)* [2001] 1 FLR 899. An unusual case of missed pregnancy in which the woman would have opted for termination despite the fact that her child was normal; the judge had, therefore, to follow *McFarlane*.

[96] Nevertheless, Henriques J applied the opinion in the Court of Appeal in the wrongful pregnancy case of *Walkin v South Manchester Health Authority* [1994] 1 WLR 1543 per Auld LJ at 1552 in the wrongful birth case of *Hardman v Amin* (2000) 59 BMLR 58 at 64 and concluded that both constituted personal injuries.

[97] Although the House in *McFarlane* specifically rejected such a failure as constituting a *novus actus*—the defence has, effectively, not been available since the trial judge in *Emeh*, n 35 above, was overruled in the Court of Appeal. Interestingly, a failure to initiate emergency post-coital contraception was so construed in *Richardson v LRC Products Ltd* (2000) 59 BMLR 185 per Kennedy J at 194.

[98] An interesting contrast is shown in the Supreme Court of Illinois: *Siemieniec v Lutheran General Hospital* 512 NE 2d 691 (Ill, 1987) (haemophiliac child—liability for extra costs of disabled child allowed); *Williams v University of Chicago Hospitals* 688 NE 2d 130 (Ill, 1997) (child with attention deficit hyperactivity disorder—liability disallowed).

[99] *Rand v East Dorset Health Authority* [2000] Lloyd's Rep Med 181, (2000) 56 BMLR 39.

[100] T Weir 'The Unwanted Child' (2002) 6 Edin LR feared that this might result in the courts 'finding' disability where none exists; we doubt if this would arise in cases of wrongful birth though might be possible in the event of wrongful pregnancy.

[101] [2000] Lloyd's Rep Med 498, (2000) 59 BMLR 58.

disability *per se* was evidenced in either; the only rather surprising difference lay in the fact that, whereas the quantum in *Rand* was related to the parents' means and, hence, their economic loss, Henriques J in *Harman* preferred an assessment made on the basis of the child's needs; the latter is, surely, to be supported.[102] Interestingly, both courts agreed that the mere existence of the Abortion Act 1967 establishes a relationship between the medical advisers and the patient and is sufficient, of itself, to impose liability for the consequences of failure to warn of the likelihood of fetal disability. Finally, we draw attention to the last, and fully confirmatory, apposite case—*Lee v Taunton and Somerset NHS Trust* [103]—the main thrust of which, in our view, was to define the extent of the health carers' liability in cases of wrongful birth. As Toulson J put it, the needs of a severely disabled child should be uppermost in everyone's thoughts when investigating the possibility of fetal abnormality; as a consequence, the authorities cannot plead injustice and unreasonableness when a heavy penalty is imposed—the problem which so exercised the minds of the Lords of Appeal in *McFarlane*.[104]

WRONGFUL (OR DIMINISHED) LIFE ACTIONS

6.47   The basis of a parental claim for 'wrongful birth' may be clear enough, but it could well be argued that it is misplaced. The parents of a disabled child may be exposed to both emotional and financial hardship but it is the child who suffers from the disablement. This is not to deny that many disabled children, particularly those whose disability is confined to learning disorder, may have happy and contented lives; nevertheless, the potential for suffering is always present. The disabled neonate whose existence results from health-care negligence can, therefore, legitimately argue that he or she would not be exposed to an impaired existence were it not for that negligence—and that, consequently, he or she is entitled to compensation in tort. An action so based is commonly known as one for wrongful life.

6.48   The purist could, of course, dismiss such an action as being flawed from the start. The function of tort law, it may be said, is to restore the victim of negligence, so far as is possible, to the position he or she would have occupied absent that negligence—and there can be no cause of action in this particular instance in so far as it is impossible to restore someone to the state of pre-existence; moreover, when assessing the difference between an existence an non-existence, we have no known comparator. While we have much sympathy with the logic of such a view, it seems to represent an unduly

---

[102] As it was in the still later case of *Lee v Taunton and Somerset NHS Trust* [2001] 1 FLR 419, [2001] Fam Law 103 (see below).

[103] N 102 above. The availability of a claim based on defective counselling has been confirmed yet more recently: *Enright v Kwun* [2003] EWHC 1000 (2003) *The Times*, 20 May.

[104] Applying the well-known principle laid down in *Caparo Industries plc v Dickman* [1990] 2 AC 605.

formalistic way of disposing of what can be seen as a matter of justice.[105] The action for wrongful life faces some barely superable hurdles but it deserves closer consideration.

6.49   Perhaps the main hurdle lies in a complex of emotions that can be summed up as distaste. Put brutally, the neonate is saying that death is preferable to a sub-standard life—a claim that not only disturbs the public conscience but is one which is particularly offensive to those concerned for the interests of the disabled and to those who object to the basic concept of therapeutic abortion. It is also potentially offensive to those who might be living with the particular disability. The underlying, and, perhaps, more tangible, arguments can best be distilled from the seminal UK case of *McKay v Essex Area Health Authority.*[106]

6.50   In this classic case, the mother of the handicapped child had been in contact with the virus of German measles and had consulted her doctor. A blood sample was taken but this was mislaid. A second sample of blood was taken and the mother was informed that neither she nor the infant had been infected with rubella; however, the infant girl was found to be severely handicapped when she was born. The plaintiffs – who included both the mother and the child—alleged that there was negligence on the part of the defendants in that they either failed to carry out the necessary tests on the blood samples or failed to interpret them correctly. A number of claims were made as a result of this alleged negligence, including one by the child for damages in respect of entry into a life of distress and suffering. While recognising that there was no reason why a mother in such circumstances may not be able to claim in respect of the negligent failure to advise her of her right to choose abortion—that is, to raise an action for wrongful birth—the court was not prepared to recognise any claim by a child to damages for wrongful life.

6.51   The initial analysis was in terms of the duty of the doctor. The doctor clearly owes a duty to the fetus not to do anything to injure it, but what duty is owed to a fetus which has been damaged by some agency for which the doctor can bear no responsibility— in this case by the rubella virus?[107] The only duty which the court could see would be an alleged duty to abort the fetus and the question then to be considered was whether

---

[105] The arguments against allowing an action for wrongful life have been rejected comprehensively by Mason P in the New South Wales Court of Appeal in *Harriton (by her tutor) v Stephens and other cases* [2004] NSWCA 93. This dissenting opinion merits attention at every stage in the following discussion.

[106] [1982] QB 1166, [1982] 2 All ER 771, CA. The Law Commission had considered the merits of the wrongful life action prior to this Court of Appeal decision in its Report on Injuries to Unborn Children, Law Com No. 60, and had come to the conclusion that it should not be allowed. The Congenital Disabilities (Civil Liability) Act 1976 was enacted as a result and s 1(2)(b) is said to exclude the right of a child to sue in such circumstances. A good argument can, in fact, be made out that wrongful life actions are not excluded. It can also be argued that such actions are still available at common law: J E S Fortin 'Is the "Wrongful Life" Action Really Dead?' [1987] J Soc Welfare Law 306. See also the commentary on the US case of *Cowe v Forum Group Inc* 575 NE 2d 630 (Ind, 1991): A Grubb [1993] 1 Med L Rev 262. In any event, the infant plaintiff in *McKay* was born before 22 July 1976 and did not come within the ambit of the Act; the issue of the wrongful life action was, therefore, open to the court.

[107] For this reason, the doctor's liability was rejected in the US case of *Wilson v Knenzi* 751 SW 2d 741 (Mo, 1988).

there could ever be a legal obligation to terminate a person's existence.[108] As to 'wrongful life', it was held that an *obligation* to abort:

[W]ould mean regarding the life of a handicapped child as not only less valuable than the life of a normal child, but so much less valuable that it was not worth preserving, and it would even mean that a doctor would be obliged to pay damages to a child infected with rubella before birth who was in fact born with some mercifully trivial abnormality. These are the consequences of the necessary basic assumption that a child has a right to be born whole or not at all, not to be born unless it can be born perfect or 'normal', whatever that may mean.[109]

6.52 Having declined to find a duty basis of the claim, the court also cavilled at the difficulties of assessing damages in such a case. Here, the impossibility-of-comparison argument was seen as a strong one: how could a court compare the value of a flawed life with non-existence or, indeed, with any 'after life' which an aborted child was experiencing?—the court declined to undertake any judgment on the conflicting views of theologians and philosophers on the latter aspect. Even having accepted this conceptual difficulty, Stephenson LJ was, somewhat ironically, of the opinion that it was better to be born maimed than not to be born at all except, possibly, in the most extreme cases of mental and physical disability—which provokes the questions: 'what is extremity?' and 'by what right do the courts take the view that existence is always to be preferred to non-existence?' The decision is, surely, one which should be left to the handicapped child by way of an objective substituted judgment—that is, given the degree of disability, what would the individual child have thought?[110] Although the matter has not been tested directly, it is very probable that a Scottish court would follow the ruling in *McKay*.[111]

WRONGFUL LIFE IN PERSPECTIVE

6.53 As might be expected, *McKay* was by no means the first such case to be considered in a common law jurisdiction and the history of the wrongful life action can, again, be traced through the United States courts. In *Gleitman v Cosgrove*,[112] the plaintiff was born deaf, mute and nearly blind as a result of his mother's exposure to German measles during pregnancy. The Supreme Court of New Jersey dismissed the plaintiff's claim for damages against the doctors who were alleged to have told the mother that there was no risk of German measles harming her child. The basis for dismissal was

---

[108] Ackner LJ's reference at QB 1188, to 'a person . . . *in utero*' is interesting in other contexts (see para 5.4). His suggestion that what was an unacceptable duty of care would arise by way of advice to the mother is, in our view, difficult to reconcile with a corresponding duty *to the mother* to advise her of the possible effects of rubella infection. See Mason P in *Harriton*, n 105 above at [109] *et seq*.

[109] [1982] 2 All ER 777 at 781, per Stephenson LJ.

[110] This was clearly in the mind of counsel for the plaintiffs in a reference to *Re B (a minor) (wardship: medical treatment)* [1990] 3 All ER 927, [1981] 1 WLR 1421 (see para 16.26).

[111] *Anderson v Forth Valley Health Board* 1998 SLT 588 at 604, per Lord Nimmo Smith, referring to Lord Osborne in *P's Curator Bonis v Criminal Injuries Compensation Board* 1997 SLT 1180, (1997) 44 BMLR 70.

[112] 296 NYS 2d 687 (1967). The seminal article is H Teff 'The Action for "Wrongful Life" in England and the United States' (1985) 34 ICLQ 423.

that its acceptance would amount to a statement that it was better not to be born at all than to be born handicapped; it was logically impossible, the court felt, to weigh the value of a handicapped life against non-existence. As it was expressed:

It is basic to the human condition to seek life and to hold on to it however heavily burdened. If Jeffrey [the plaintiff] could have been asked as to whether his life should be snuffed out before his full term of gestation could run its course, our felt intuition of human nature tells us he would almost surely choose life with defects against no life at all 'For the living there is hope, but for the dead there is none . . .'

6.54   A year later, the claim of a child similarly damaged by its mother's illness was rejected on the grounds that to allow a claim based on failure to abort the plaintiff would be the antithesis of the principles of the law of tort, which is directed towards the protection of the plaintiff against wrongs. The greatest wrong, it was pointed out by the court, is to cause another person's death.[113] In other cases, the courts have chosen to reject the claims of handicapped children on the grounds that it is impossible to assess the child's damages.[114]

6.55   There is no indication that the courts, in refusing the children's claims, have intended to limit compensation for this type of negligence. Actions by the parents for emotional shock, expenses incurred in rearing a defective child and the like have been successful and the trend has been—as explained in *Robak*[115]—to focus on the family as the true object of the claim. This was emphasised in *Prokanik v Cillo*,[116] which was a rare instance of a wrongful life action being accepted; a main reason for so doing was that the parents were time-barred and could not sue on their own behalf. In line with other common law jurisdictions, the American courts will, where it is possible, allow the neonate a suit for prenatal injury while denying one for wrongful life.[117]

6.56   To our knowledge, there is only one straightforward instance of a wrongful life action being allowed in full in the United States.[118] This case was effectively over-turned by the Supreme Court of California in *Turpin*,[119] when it adopted the principle of allowing the suit to proceed and accepting a claim to special damages—i.e. those incurred as a result of the congenital defects—but not to general damages; the basis for the latter restriction lay in the still insoluble problem of comparing an impaired existence with not being born at all. Any movement towards acceptance of the suit has, however, been arrested and there is now a definite trend in favour of rejecting

---

[113] *Stewart v Long Island College Hospital* 296 NYS 2d 41 (1968).

[114] E.g. *Dumer v St Michael's Hospital* 233 NW 2d 372 (Wis, 1975); *Blake v Cruz* 698 P 2d 315 (Idaho, 1984); *Smith v Cote* 513 A 2d 341 (NH, 1986); *Cowe v Forum Group Inc* 575 NE 2d 630 (Ind, 1991). There is no evidence that the widespread antipathy to the wrongful life action has diminished as is implicit in, for example, the currently unfinalised Kentucky case *Bogan v Altman and McGuire, PSC* (2001).

[115] *Robak v United States* 658 F 2d 471 (1981).

[116] 478 A 2d 755 (NJ, 1984). A similar option has been left open more recently: *Viccaro v Milunsky* 551 NE 2d 8 (Mass, 1990).

[117] E.g., *Cowe v Forum Group Inc* 575 NE 2d 630 (Ind, 1991).

[118] *Curlender v Bio-Science Laboratories* 165 Cal Rptr 477 (1980).

[119] *Turpin v Sortini* 182 Cal Rptr 377 (1982). Also followed in *Harbeson v Parke-Davis Inc* 656 P 2d 483 (Wash, 1983).

such claims in toto.[120] When the plaintiff in *Bruggeman v Schimke*[121] averred that actions for wrongful life were being increasingly recognised, the court replied that this was simply not true and that any theory sustaining a legal right to be dead rather than to be alive with deficiencies was one completely contrary to the laws of the state.

6.57   The depth of antipathy to the wrongful life action is exemplified in the Canadian case of *Cherry v Borsman* which was heard in the British Columbia Court of Appeal.[122] Here, a continuing pregnancy following a negligently performed abortion resulted in a severely disabled neonate who, subsequently, brought an action against the obstetrician. We have discussed the case already in chapter 5. The interesting feature for present purposes, however, is that, while the action was raised in negligence, the defendant sought to categorise the action as one for wrongful life— presumably assuming that it would be disallowed on the grounds of precedent. Indeed, as the trial judge said, the admission of negligent post-operative care and the fact that the woman would have had a second abortion had she been aware of her continuing pregnancy: 'do set up a wrongful life action [and], in fact … almost encourage such an action'.[123] Even so, both the Supreme Court and the court of Appeal were able to set this aside and to confine the issue to that of negligently causing the neonate's injuries; the issue of the validity of an action for wrongful life was determinedly avoided.[124]

6.58   In practical terms, children who fail in an action for wrongful life are unlikely to be wholly abandoned by the law since an action by the mother for wrongful birth will always be available. We have, however, seen that the effect of *McFarlane* is that recompense will be available only for the *extra* costs imposed by rearing a child that is disabled and, to that extent, the child itself may be indirectly disadvantaged. Moreover, the recompense will be awarded to the mother and is not there to compensate the child for its suffering. There is, therefore, no absolute guarantee that the child will benefit under the existing jurisprudence.[125] These are undoubtedly the considerations which led the French courts to counter the trend and become the first European jurisdiction to allow an action for wrongful life.[126]

---

[120] E.g. *Ellis v Sherman* 515 A 2d 1327 (Pa, 1986); *Proffitt v Bartolo* 412 NW 2d 232 (Mich, 1987); *Cowe v Forum Group Inc* 575 NE 2d 630 (Ind, 1991); *Hester v Dwivedi* 733 NE 2d 1161 (Ohio, 2000).

[121] 718 P 2d 635 (Kan, 1986).   [122] (1992) 94 DLR (4th) 487, BCCA.   [123] At 679.

[124] No case has yet succeeded in Australia—see P Watson 'Wrongful Life Actions in Australia' (2002) 26 MULR 736. The recent Court of Appeal case of *Harriton and others*, n 105 above, also failed despite the strong dissent by Mason P. The action has also been rejected at first hand in the Roman-Dutch jurisdiction of South Africa: *Friedman v Glickson* 1996 (1) SA 1134, where the coincident claim for wrongful birth was upheld.

[125] We have also noted the increasing concern of both the United States courts and the state legislatures to express their preference for birth over abortion—and this to the extent that not only wrongful life but also wrongful birth actions may be rejected. For evidence of this from state legislatures see n 84 above. Also, *Azzolino v Dingfelder* 337 SE 2d 528 (NC, 1985). For a seminal review, see E H Morreim 'The Concept of Harm Reconceived: A Different Look at Wrongful Life' (1988) 7 Law & Philos 3.

[126] We have found only one previous jurisdiction that has accepted the infant plaintiff's cause when confronted with the problem de novo: *Zeitzoff v Katz* [1986] 40(2) PD 85 (Supreme Court of Israel). See J Levi 'Wrongful Life Decision in Israel' (1987) 6 Med Law 373; A Shapira ' "Wrongful Life" Lawsuits for Faulty Genetic Counselling: Should the Impaired Newborn Be Entitled to Sue?' (1998) 24 J Med Ethics 369.

Wrongful life in Europe

6.59   In what, for ease of reference, we will refer to here as the *Perruche* case,[127] the familiar scenario arose in which a handicapped child was born following the negligent failure to interpret correctly a pregnant woman's positive tests for rubella antibodies; had she been correctly counselled, she would certainly have terminated the pregnancy. In an action for breach of contract brought on behalf of the parents, the court of first instance found against both the physician and the laboratory; innovatively, however, it also found them liable to the child for the loss caused by his handicap.[128] The Cour d'Appel then followed precedent and, while confirming the decision in favour of Mme Perruche, overturned that in favour of the child on the grounds of causation[129]—the arguments being similar to those rehearsed in *McKay*. The case then went through a series of appeals and was eventually referred to full chamber of the Cour de Cassation who held that causation in the child's case was demonstrated by the mother having been prevented from exercising her freedom to proceed to a termination of the pregnancy in order to avoid the birth of a handicapped child; the harm resulting to the child from such handicap was caused by that negligence and he could claim compensation for it. The court was, in addition, anxious to ensure that the child himself was compensated because there was no guarantee that his parents would always support him.[130] This very unusual case[131] not only disturbed the accepted medical jurisprudence in this area but also caused something of a political uproar in France. At heart, the public rejection of the *Perruche* judgment was based on revulsion at the concept of being compensated for being born and came, in the main, from three sources. It was attacked by the anti-abortion lobby by virtue of the stress laid on the woman's right to choose a termination of pregnancy. Disabled support groups protested that it devalued the lives of the imperfect—criticism was especially loud in the case of two allied Down's syndrome decisions.[132] Most powerfully, the medical profession rebelled and, indeed, went on strike at the thought of being compelled to be always right in their pre-natal screening.

6.60   The furore was sufficient to force the government into emergency legislation. As a result, one cannot, in France, treat the mere fact of being born as constituting damage.

---

[127] *X c Mutuelle d'Assurance du Corps Sanitaire Français et a* (2000) JCP 2293. The case is discussed in detail, and the decision disapproved, by T Callus ' "Wrongful Life" a la Francaise' (2001) 5 Med Law Internat 117. It is carefully analysed, and again disapproved, by T Weir 'The Unwanted Child' (2002) 6 Edin LR 244 where the German position is also considered. An extensive review of the Anglo-French situation is to be found in A Morris and S Saintier 'To Be or Not To Be: Is that the Question? Wrongful Life and Misconceptions' (2003) 11 Med LR 167.

[128] Tribunal de Grande Instance, Evry, 13 January 1992.

[129] Casse Civ. 1, 26 March 1996, Bull. Civ, 1996.1.156.

[130] See also Mason P in *Harriton*, n 105 above, at [141].

[131] A similar judgment was handed down in 2001 in the case of *L*, a child with Down's syndrome. See M Spriggs and J Savulescu 'The Perruche Judgment and the "Right not to be Born" ' (2002) 28 J Med Ethics 63.

[132] A third untraced case has been reported as a news item: http://news.bbc.co.uk/hi/english/world/europe/newsid_1752000/1752556.stm. Since persons with Down's syndrome are not suffering and are probably perfectly happy in their own environment, this particular resentment can be well appreciated.

The parents of a child born with handicap which remained undiagnosed during pregnancy due to a *serious* professional fault can claim compensation for harm suffered by them personally but not for expenses attributable to the child's being handicapped—these will be covered through the social services.[133] Thus, the French government has gone one stage further than the House of Lords in *McFarlane* and has outlawed damages for the upbringing of an uncovenanted child whether that child be healthy or disabled. Moreover, not only is an action for wrongful life no longer available but neither is one for wrongful birth. So, in the end, the ruling of the Cour de Cassation had an effect opposite to that which was intended—but we still wonder if that should be a matter for universal rejoicing. Indeed, it was only a matter of some two years before the matter was again raised—this time in the Netherlands.[134]

6.61   In what we will call, again for ease of reference, the *Molenaar* case,[135] a midwife failed to heed indications for diagnostic amniocentesis and a child was born suffering from an unspecified chromosomal abnormality which resulted in severe physical defects and pain. Here, the Court of Appeal in The Hague followed the French courts and awarded damages not only to the parents on the basis of a wrongful birth claim but also to the child in respect of non-pecuniary damage. The court's reasoning as to the latter took two lines. First, it was proposed that the midwife had a contractual obligation to the pregnant woman and that the unborn child could be considered to be party to that contract.[136] In our view, it is unlikely that such an extended interpretation would be accepted in the United Kingdom[137] and The Hague court was, itself, clearly hesitant on the point. In the alternative, it was held that the health authority was under a legal obligation to look after the interests of the fetus as an independent entity. Here, the court relied to an extent on the *nascituras* principle—that is, that a child *in utero* can be regarded as being alive if it is in his or her interests to do so. The element of causation necessary for a successful action in negligence was supplied by the fact that the birth of the child could have been prevented; the child's suffering was, as a result, a direct consequence of a negligent medical error.

6.62   The difficulty with both these last points lies in the fact that they require that the court should say to the plaintiff: 'Yes, it would be better had you not been born.' This judgment, however sympathetic to the motives behind it, would seriously compromise the value of human life which the courts are more usually called upon to endorse. The disabled should be helped and, if possible, compensated for the suffering which their lives may entail, but the moral basis for such compensation should be the desire

---

[133] Law adopted by the French Senate on 19 February 2002. We are indebted to Weir, n 127 above, for the translation on which this précis is based.

[134] *X v Y*, The Hague, Court of Appeals, 26 March 2003.

[135] T Sheldon 'Court Awards Damages to a Disabled Child for Having Been Born' (2002) 326 BMJ 784. See also H F L Nys and J C J Dute 'A Wrongful Existence in the Netherlands' (2004) 30 J Med Ethics 393.

[136] As had previously been accepted in the unreported 'Baby Joost' case of 8 September 2000. However, this argument was unanimously rejected in Australia in *Harriton*, n 105 above.

[137] It is not unlike the concept of transferred malice which was rejected in *Attorney-General's Reference (No. 3 of 1994)* [1998] AC 245, HL.

to make life more comfortable and bearable—not the notion that they should not be in existence at all.

6.63   As a result, *Molenaar* was appealed to the Dutch Supreme Court which considered the case so thoroughly that its decision has only just been released as we go to press. In the event, the Supreme Court upheld the appeal court and have awarded damages for 'material and emotional damage' both to the parents and to the child—the latter's emotional damage being attributable to the fact that she was born. All the costs of the child's upbringing were awarded together with those resulting from the mother's psychiatric treatment which was necessitated by the birth. To obviate some of the inevitable criticism, it was emphasised that the damages were based exclusively on the fact that 'the midwife made a serious mistake with regard to the fundamental rights of the parents'.[138] It remains to be seen whether public pressure will be sufficient to draw the legislature into the argument as happened in France.

WRONGFUL LIFE RECONSIDERED

6.64   While we fully appreciate the sensitivities of those who regard the wrongful life action as generally contrary to human dignity and, in particular to the interests of the disabled, we feel, intuitively, that it is wrong to accept an action for wrongful birth and, at the same time, reject one for wrongful life. We suggest that many of the conceptual difficulties associated with the latter would be largely dissipated if, first, the Abortion Act 1967, s 1(1)(d)—the 'eugenic clause'—were accepted as having been drafted in the fetal, rather than the maternal, interest.[139] The 'right' of the handicapped fetus to abortion is then comparable to the defective neonate's 'right' to refuse treatment (see paras 16.38 et seq); failure to respond to the interests of either, albeit necessarily expressed by proxy, then falls into the ambit of consent-based negligence (see chapter 9)—in effect, the fetus is saying: 'but for the negligent advice given to me through my parents, I would not have chosen a disadvantaged condition; I now have to be disadvantaged and, therefore, I am entitled to compensation.' Secondly, we favour abandoning the principle of 'wrongful life' in favour of 'diminished life'; we can then look not at a comparison, whether it be between the neonate's current existence and non-existence or with normality, but, rather at the actual suffering that has been caused. There would have been no suffering in the event of an abortion, there was no abortion as a result of negligence, and it follows that the negligence has produced suffering which should be compensated according to its degree. This carries the practical advantage that the courts can understand and accommodate this form of damage, which allows for a distinction to be made between serious and slight

---

[138] We should emphasise that this synopsis is based not on the transcript but on a short appraisal by T Sheldon 'Dutch Supreme Court backs damages for child for having been born' (2005) 330 BMJ 747.

[139] For discussion, see J K Mason *Medico-Legal Aspects of Reproduction and Parenthood* (2nd edn, 1998) pp 157–158. It is noteworthy that Stephenson LJ adopted this view in *McKay* (at All ER 780). But, having done so, why disallow 'wrongful life' actions on the grounds that they would encourage abortion?

defect.[140] Thus, while the legal and philosophical arguments in favour of rejecting the wrongful life action are powerful, they can be challenged.

6.65   Even so, the apparently insurmountable hurdle on the road to acceptance is posed by causation—it is undeniable that, save in exceptional circumstances, such as direct injury,[141] no *person* has caused the disabilities. Yet, in an age when compensation for injury is so widely available, it is difficult to see why the faulty genetic counsellor should be thus protected and intuition, again, urges that equity is, thereby, thwarted—suffering, if not the cause of the suffering, has been created by the negligence and to suffer is to be injured. We have attempted to resolve the impasse by suggesting that, while the genetic counsellor has not caused the disability, he or she has allowed the disabled fetus to survive in the face of a duty to prevent this; accordingly, he or she is liable to the disabled neonate.[142] While this formula will not satisfy every criticism of the wrongful life action, it would, if accepted, ensure that justice was seen to be done. It is also reflected in the reasoning of both the French and the Dutch courts outlined above.

6.66   Before leaving the topic of wrongful life, it should be noted that a comparable action in negligence will be available if the problem of causation can be evaded. Such a situation arises in what is known as the 'preconception tort'. As is clear from the phrase itself, the child may, in such an action, claim that there was negligence prior to his or her conception and that this negligence has resulted in he or she being born disabled. An example of such a claim is provided by the American case of *Yeager v Bloomington Obstetrics and Gynecology, Inc.*[143] This concerned a child born suffering from brain damage due to haemolytic disease of the newborn which occurred because the hospital negligently failed to treat rhesus immunisation of the mother during a previous pregnancy; the court held it to be reasonably foreseeable that subsequent children would be injured as a result. Such a claim would also be competent in English law provided that, at the time of conception, the parents were not aware of the risk that their child would be born disabled. This exemption does not apply if, in an action by the child against its father, it is established that the father knew of the risk while the mother did not.[144]

---

[140] See also Ackner LJ in *McKay* (at All ER 786): 'Subsection (2)(b) [of the 1976 Act] is so worded as to import the assumption that, but for the occurrence giving rise to a disabled birth, the child would have been born normal and healthy, not that it would not have been born at all'—and that, having disposed of the phrase 'wrongful life', appeared to be acceptable.

[141] As in *Cherry v Borsman*, n 122 above. Nearer to home, section 1A of the Congenital Disabilities (Civil Liability) Act 1976 (inserted by way of the Human Fertilisation and Embryology Act 1990, s 44) allows for an action by a disabled infant when the disability is attributable to wrongful acts or omissions—including embryo selection—arising during the provision of treatment for infertility. This seems indistinguishable from an action for wrongful life, in which case it is accepted that the difficulties of assessment of damages and the like are solvable difficulties.

[142] J K Mason 'Wrongful Life: The Problem of Causation' (2004) 6 Med Law Internat 149. This is, essentially, the argument put forward by Mason P in *Harriton*, n 105 above.

[143] 585 NE 2d 696 (Ind, 1992). For earlier examples, see *Lazevnick v General Hospital of Monro County Inc* 499 F Supp 146 (Md, 1980); *Jorgensen v Meade-Johnson Laboratories* 483 F 2d 237 (1973); *Renslow v Mennonite Hospital* 367 NE 2d 1250 (Ill, 1977).

[144] Congenital Disabilities (Civil Liability) Act 1976, s 1(4).

6.67   The concept of the preconception tort also draws attention to its counterpart in the field of human rights—that of intergenerational justice[145] which suggests that we have a duty to future generations not to harm their prospective parents: 'The present generations have the responsibility of ensuring that the needs and interests of future generations are fully safeguarded'.[146] The issue has also been addressed in the European Court of Human Rights where it was strongly indicated that the State may well have a positive obligation to protect the quality of life of those who have yet to be conceived.[147] The subject is, however, large and is, perhaps, only peripheral to the current topic. Nonetheless, it serves to remind us that there is a public as well as a private interest in the health of our future children whether it be genetically or environmentally determined.

WRONGFUL INJURY TO THE FETUS

6.68   This discussion of wrongful life also reminds us that the fetus per se receives surprisingly little legal protection. We have seen in chapter 5 how the law takes a pragmatic view of fetal status and legal personhood—the generally accepted threshold for the emergence of rights is birth. Thus the fetus—as opposed to the child—has no rights as such. It does not follow, however, that that those who harm the fetus necessarily enjoy immunity from liability, and we explore this more fully in this section.

6.69   Any protection provided to the fetus by the Offences Against the Person Act 1861, ss 58 and 59 is no more than derivative of the primary offence which is unlawfully procuring the miscarriage of a woman; feticide is no more than its, generally, inevitable correlate.[148] Otherwise, the only direct protection of fetal life *in utero* is provided by the Infant Life (Preservation) Act 1929 which defines the offence of child destruction or 'destroying the life of a child capable of being born alive'.[149]

6.70   Despite this paucity of statutory protection, it is perfectly clear that the fetus has a general, and strong, interest in not being injured by the wrongful act of a third party. This was first clearly recognised at common law in Canada and in Australia in two important decisions, *Duval v Seguin*[150] and *Watt v Rama*.[151] The almost universally accepted limitation on this, however, is that, although fetal interests may be

---

[145]   Discussed briefly in S McLean and J K Mason *Legal and Ethical Aspects of Healthcare* (2003), p 124.

[146]   UNESCO *Declaration of the Responsibilities of the Present Generations towards Future Generations* (1997), Article 1.

[147]   *LCB v UK* (1999) 27 EHRR 212. The case concerned the effect of radiation on future generations rather than genetics but the issues are similar. In the event, the case failed because the government had insufficient knowledge of the potential risk.

[148]   We have discussed the case of Mrs Vo in chapter 5 above.

[149]   The 1929 Act does not run to Scotland although it is very probable that an offence comparable to child destruction exists. But the Canadian courts still deny such protection: see *R v Sullivan* (1991) 63 CCC (3d) 97.

[150]   (1973) 40 DLR (3d) 666.   [151]   [1972] VR 353.

established while in utero—or even before conception—they cannot be realised unless the fetus is born alive and attains an existence separate from that of its mother;[152] moreover, the legal concept of a separate existence is still further limited in England and Wales in the Congenital Disabilities (Civil Liability) Act 1976, under which the neonate must survive for 48 hours before being able to recover damages in negligence.

6.71 The principle is unequivocal. 'There can be no doubt, in my view', said Sir George Baker,[153] 'that in England and Wales the foetus has no right of action, no right at all, until birth' and the same is equally true in Scotland—Scots law recognises no right of the fetus to continue to exist in its mother's womb.[154] From Canada, we have: 'There is no existing basis in law which justifies a conclusion that foetuses are legal persons',[155] from which it follows that a stillbirth cannot benefit. No suit for wrongful fetal death is recognisable in the United Kingdom[156] and we are left with an apparent paradox—as Pace[157] has put it: 'Liability is incurred for negligent injury to the foetus but not—or, at least, not necessarily—for its deliberate destruction.'

6.72 There is, however, evidence that some jurisdictions are moving towards the recognition of such suits. Thus, in the United States, we read in very similar vein:

To deny a stillborn recovery for fatal injuries during gestation while allowing such recovery for a child born alive would make it more profitable for the defendant to kill the plaintiff than to scratch him.[158]

The tone in this case, and in others that have both preceded it and followed it, indicates not so much a shift in jurisprudential reasoning as a search for punitive sanctions against the person who negligently destroys the child in utero—another form of expression of an intrinsic concern for the status of the fetus.[159]

---

[152] An exception probably lies in the criminal law of California, where an offence of feticide has been established: *People v Davis* 872 P 2d 591 (Cal, 1994). The courts in other states seem to be resisting such a move: e.g. *State v Green* 781 P 2d 678 (Kan, 1987). Closer to home, the constitutional rights of the fetus to life that pertains in the Republic of Ireland and in Germany has been discussed at para 5.73 above.

[153] *Paton v British Pregnancy Advisory Service Trustees* [1979] QB 276 at 279, [1978] 2 All ER 987 at 989.

[154] *Kelly v Kelly* 1997 SC 285, 1997 SCLR 749, per Cullen LJ-C.

[155] *Borowski v A-G of Canada and Minister of Finance of Canada* (1984) 4 DLR (4th) 112 at 131, per Matheson J. See also *Winnipeg Child and Family Services (Northwest Area) v G(DF)* (1997) 3 SCR 925.

[156] Damages have been given for a stillbirth resulting from negligent treatment: *Bagley v North Herts Health Authority* [1986] NLJ Rep 1014. These were, however, to the mother; damages in respect of bereavement under the Fatal Accidents Act 1976 were expressly disallowed on the grounds that the negligence had caused the child to die in utero. The court was, however, at pains to ensure adequate compensation notwithstanding. See also *Grieve v Salford Health Authority* [1991] 2 Med LR 295, where only the quantum of damages for negligence leading to stillbirth was considered.

[157] P J Pace 'Civil Liability for Pre-natal Injury' (1977) 40 MLR 141.

[158] *Amadio v Levin* 501 A 2d 1085 (Pa, 1985).

[159] It seems that, while 'wrongful fetal death' statutes are in place throughout the US, judicial interpretation varies—an action for wrongful death was dismissed in *Milton v Cary Medical Center* 538 A 2d 252 (Me, 1988) and, in general, most States operate a 'viability' limitation with recovery available only to the viable fetus. For further discussion, see A Peterfy 'Fetal Viability as a Threshold to Personhood' (1995) 16 J Leg Med 187.

6.73   There are some signs that the United Kingdom courts are also anxious to invest the fetus with as positive an identity as is possible within current legal constraints. In general terms, we have the Master of the Rolls stressing the right of an adult to refuse life-saving treatment but, at the same time, acknowledging that there might well be an exception to the rule were a viable fetus to be involved[160]—this was, however, an obiter statement that has been put to the test and rejected.[161] In England, it has been held that, subject as always to it being born alive, the fetus has common law rights irrespective of the Congenital Disabilities (Civil Liability) Act 1976[162] and, in Australia, this has been extended to an acceptance of a child's right to sue its mother for negligent injury in utero.[163] The trial judge in that case said:

I would hold that an injury to an infant suffered during . . . its journey through life between conception and parturition is not injury to a person devoid of personality other than that of the mother-to-be. Nicole's personality was identifiable and recognisable.

6.74   A similar trend has been evidenced in Scotland, where a fetus has been recognised as a person when criminally injured under the Road Traffic Act 1972,[164] while an extension of the statutory 'person' beyond a being 'with legal personality' has been approved under the Damages (Scotland) Act 1976:[165]

It is perfectly common in ordinary speech to refer to a child in the womb as 'he', 'she', 'him' or 'her' . . . it was this child who sustained injuries to his person and who died in consequence of personal injuries sustained by him.[166]

But, despite the evident tone of judicial concern, all these later examples still depend upon the fetus being born alive and it can be said with confidence that there is no civil action available to the fetus in the United Kingdom for its negligent death.[167]

Feticide

6.75   Having considered the problems of negligent injury to the fetus, we should briefly consider its criminal counterpart insofar as this also is of major significance to the analysis of judicial attitudes to fetal status. The most important case within this

---

[160] *Re T (adult: refusal of medical treatment)* [1992] 4 All ER 649 at 653, (1992) 9 BMLR 46 at 50.

[161] *Re MB (adult: medical treatment)* [1997] 2 FCR 541, (1997) 38 BMLR 175 and *St George's Healthcare NHS Trust v S* [1998] 3 All ER 673. The problem of the enforced caesarian operation is dealt with at some length below in paras 10.65 et seq.

[162] *Burton v Islington Health Authority, de Martell v Merton and Sutton Health Authority* [1993] QB 204, [1992] 3 All ER 833.

[163] Reported by D Brahams 'Australian Mother Sued by Child Injured in Utero' (1991) 338 Lancet 687. This being a road traffic accident, there seems no reason why such an action should not be available in England under the 1976 Act s 2 (see para 6.78 below).

[164] *McCluskey v HM Advocate* 1998 SCCR 629, [1989] RTR 182. The importance of subsequent live birth was acknowledged in the Sheriff Court in *HM Advocate v McDougall* 1994 Crim LB 12–13.

[165] *Hamilton v Fife Health Board* 1993 SLT 624. The 1976 Act must now be read in conjunction with the Damages (Scotland) Act 1993.

[166] *Ibid* Lord McCluskey at 629.

[167] A Whitfield 'Common Law Duties to Unborn Children' (1993) 1 Med L Rev 28.

limited framework is that contained in *A-G's Reference (No. 3 of 1994)*.[168] In essence, this reference concerned the stabbing of a pregnant woman who gave birth to a severely premature baby two weeks later; it transpired that, contrary to what had been supposed, the fetus had been injured in the assault and the resulting infant died 120 days after birth. The attacker was charged with murder and the trial judge directed an acquittal on the grounds that neither a conviction for murder nor for manslaughter was possible under the existing law. The Attorney-General then sought a ruling from the Court of Appeal, asking whether the crimes of murder or manslaughter could be committed where unlawful injury was deliberately inflicted to a child in utero or to a mother carrying a child in utero, where the child was born alive and died having existed independently of the mother, the injuries in utero having caused or made a substantial contribution to the death; the court was also asked whether the fact that the child's death was caused solely as a consequence of injury to the *mother* could remove any liability for murder or manslaughter in those circumstances.

6.76   We are concerned here not with the niceties of the criminal law but, rather, with those aspects of the judgment which relate to the legal status of the fetus. In this respect, Lord Taylor LCJ developed a two-stage argument. First, it was held that, in the eyes of the law, the unborn fetus is deemed to be part of the mother—an intention to cause serious harm to the fetus is, therefore, an intention to cause severe injury to a part of the mother; and, secondly, this being the case, malice directed at the mother can be transferred to the fetus once it is born.[169]

6.77   This decision was greeted by many lay commentators as another step towards the recognition of a fetal right to life. In fact, it is nothing of the kind, in so far as it deprives the fetus of any individual personality it may have enjoyed previously. The concept of an intention directed towards a child capable of becoming a person in being was summarily rejected—as Lord Taylor put it:

An intention to cause serious bodily injury to the foetus is an intention to cause serious bodily injury to a part of the mother just as an intention to injure her arm or her leg would be so viewed,[170]

thus glossing over several differences, including the not unimportant fact that an arm is incapable of developing into an individual human being. And, in fact, the House of Lords would have nothing to do with that view when the case was referred to them,[171] Lord Mustill believing it to be wholly unfounded in fact.[172] Pointing to the truism that mother and fetus were unique human beings once the latter was born, his Lordship emphasised that the maternal-fetal relationship was one of bond, not of identity. In effect, the fetus was neither a 'person' nor an adjunct of its mother—it was a unique organism. Unfortunately, the House never defined the nature of that unique

---

[168] [1996] QB 581, [1996] 2 All ER 10, CA.

[169] For an analysis of this decision, see M Seneviratne 'Pre-natal Injury and Transferred Malice: The Invented Other' (1996) 59 MLR 884.

[170] [1996] 2 All ER 10 at 18.

[171] *A-G's Reference (No. 3 of 1994)* [1998] AC 245, [1997] 3 All ER 936, HL.   [172] *Ibid* at AC 255.

organism save in the negative sense that it is not, legally speaking, a person in being while in utero—it was confirmed yet again that there is no offence of feticide and there never has been.[173] At the same time:

> For the foetus, life lies in the future, not the past. It is not sensible to say that [the foetus] cannot ever be harmed or that nothing can be done to it which can ever be dangerous . . . It may also carry with it the effects of things done to it before birth which, after birth, may prove to be harmful.[174]

Thus, the fetus remains a person-in-waiting—or a thing which will, in due course, become something; *A-G's Reference (No. 3 of 1994)* dispels the 'maternal appendage' theory of fetal existence but, in the end, it does nothing to improve the legal status of the fetus itself.[175]

MATERNAL RESPONSIBILITY FOR FETAL WELL-BEING

6.78   Maternal negligence in respect of the fetus—both tortious and criminal—merits special mention. The Law Commission considered the first of these questions and decided that an action against its mother in respect of damage resulting from her negligence during pregnancy should not be available to a child. It was felt that a claim of this type would compromise the parent-child relationship and might also be used as a weapon in matrimonial disputes. Accordingly, the English Congenital Disabilities (Civil Liability) Act 1976 excludes claims by a child against its mother except as to injuries sustained during traffic accidents; here, special policy grounds and the availability of insurance were held to justify the admissibility of such claims.[176] The issue remains open in Scotland because there is no legislation on the subject and there is no reason in law to exclude a claim by a child against its mother in respect of prenatal injuries. It is possible, however, that, as in Canada, the courts might be unsympathetic to such claims on policy grounds.

6.79   In general, discussion along these lines is related to injury to the fetus resulting from negligence as it is commonly understood. We, however, have to look a degree deeper so as to determine the extent to which the mother's duty of care towards her unborn child might be held to limit her freedom of personal behaviour during pregnancy. Interest in this aspect of the fetal-maternal relationship reached its peak

---

[173] The House did not address the question of deliberate injury to a fetus which dies following a live birth.

[174] *Ibid* at AC 271, per Lord Hope.

[175] Which is unfortunate as, in the circumstances prevailing, the mother is being deprived of a child she actively desires. For commentary, see J K Mason 'A Lords' Eye View of Fetal Status' (1999) 3 Edin LR 246; also 'What's in a Name? The Vagaries of *Vo v France*' (2005) 17 CFLQ 97.

[176] S 2. An apposite case, possibly the prototype, has been reported by C Dyer 'Boy Wins Damages after Injury in Utero' (1992) 304 BMJ 1400. See also n 163 above. Note, however, the rejection of maternal duty of care to her fetus, including while driving, in Canada: *Dobson (Litigation Guardian of) v Dobson* [1999] 2 SCR 753. The contribution of a seat-belt to injury to the fetus—or to its protection—would be an interesting discussion in many cases.

over two decades ago.[177] Major attention has since focussed on the use of alcohol and other drugs, including tobacco, on fetal morbidity and mortality and there is now virtually irrefutable evidence of their teratogenic effects.[178] The issues of responsibility and liability for any consequent negligent injury have been the subject of widespread debate.

6.80　　Scrutiny of the interplay of fetal interests and maternal lifestyle has been nowhere more intense than in the United States, where well over 6,000 children are born each year suffering from the fetal alcohol syndrome and where the occurrence of drug withdrawal symptoms in neonates has been escalating.[179] There, the state has not only a right but also a duty to protect its children under the parens patriae jurisdiction and there is strong support for the view that this extends to an interest in the well-being of the 'viable' fetus. Cases of fetal neglect that have come before the courts have been assessed both under the common law and through the federal and state legislation prohibiting child abuse and neglect; as might be expected, the outcomes have not been entirely consistent and depend, to a large extent, on how the charges were framed and on the States' attitudes to feticide.[180] The American case most widely publicised in the United Kingdom concerned Ms Stewart, who was found to have ingested amphetamines and cannabis before her infant was born brain damaged. The mother was charged in the criminal court with omitting to furnish necessary medical attendance or other remedial care; the case was dismissed on the grounds that there was no statutory basis for the charge.[181] This has been the general fate of most criminal charges.[182] A number of civil actions have, however, been officially reported; these suggest that the fetus enjoys an enhanced standing in such courts and, having been born, may be able to sue on its own behalf.[183]

[177] See e.g. E W Keiserlingck 'A Right of the Unborn Child to Pre-natal Care—the Civil Law Perspective' (1982) 13 Rev de Droit 49; P L Hallisey 'The Fetal Patient and the Unwilling Mother: A Standard for Judicial Intervention' (1983) 14 Pac LI 1065; J L Lenow 'The Fetus as a Patient: Emerging Rights as a Person' (1983) 9 Amer J Law Med 1.

[178] For review: K O Haustein 'Cigarette Smoking, Nicotine and Pregnancy' (1999) 37 Int J Clin Pharmacol Therap 417; American Academy of Pediatrics 'Fetal Alcohol Syndrome and alcohol-related neurodevelopmental disorders' (2000) 106 Pediatrics 358.

[179] For relevant data, see E J Larson 'The Effects of Maternal Substance Abuse on the Placenta and Fetus' in G B Reed (ed) *Diseases of the Fetus and Newborn* (2nd edn, 1994). The problem is, however, worldwide. Closest to home, approximately 13% of all neonatal discharges from hospital in Scotland demonstrate withdrawal symptoms due to maternal use of drugs of addiction: Scottish Executive, Written Parliamentary Answers, 2 May 2001 (Mr Malcolm Chisholm).

[180] Currently, it seems that specific punitive legislation is in place in Wisconsin, South Carolina and South Dakota but other States may be following suit.

[181] See R I Solomon 'Future Fear: Prenatal Duties Imposed by Private Parties' (1991) 17 Amer J Law Med 411.

[182] E.g. *State v Gray* 584 NE 2d 710 (Ohio, 1992); *State v Carter* 602 So 2d 995 (Fla, 1992); *Commonwealth v Kemp* 643 A 2d 705 (Pa, 1994). Successful prosecution and imprisonment appears to have been reported in only one truly apposite case: *Whitner v South Carolina* 492 SE 2d 777 (SC, Sup Ct, 1995). Routine neonatal testing for drugs has been found unreasonable on account of its penal connotations: *Ferguson et al v City of Charleston* 121 S Ct 1281 (2001).

[183] *Grodin v Grodin* 301 NW 2d 869 (Mich, 1981). See also *Re Vanessa F* 351 NYS 2d 337 (1974).

6.81   The courts in Canada have also appreciated the concept of intra-uterine child abuse and have immediately placed in care and protection neonates who have been subjected seriously to drugs or alcohol during pregnancy.[184] However, the courts will not go so far as to restrict the freedom of a woman to live her life as she would please while she is pregnant. In *Winnipeg Child and Family Services (Northwest Area) v G (DF)*[185] the Supreme Court ruled on a case involving an order which had been granted at first instance requiring that a five-month pregnant woman who was addicted to glue sniffing be detained in a health centre until the birth of her child. One of the grounds for the order was the parens patriae jurisdiction in respect of the fetus. It was argued that this inherent jurisdiction of the courts to protect the vulnerable—normally incapax adults and minors—should be extended to protect the fetus in utero. The Supreme Court refused, however, to sanction such a major change to the law. Noting that this would involve conflicts of fundamental rights and interests and difficult policy issues, the court recognised that the unique relationship which a woman has with her fetus is such that 'the court cannot make decisions for the unborn child without inevitably making decisions for the mother herself'. Such a power, if it were thought desirable, had to be introduced by the legislature.[186]

6.82   A ruling to the same effect has already been given in England in *Re F (in utero)*,[187] a case in which the local authority sought to make the fetus a ward of court so that it could be protected from its mother, who was leading a nomadic existence and who, shortly before the child was due, again went missing. The application was refused both at first instance and in the Court of Appeal on the grounds that, until the child was actually born, there would be an inherent incompatibility between any projected exercise of the wardship jurisdiction and the rights and welfare of the mother. Relying heavily on *Paton*,[188] the Court of Appeal first concluded that the fetus had no individual personality and that, therefore, there could be no jurisdiction in wardship; and, secondly, it was made clear that, in practice, it would be impossible to follow the principle of the paramountcy of the child's welfare in wardship if that conflicted with the liberty and legal interests of the mother.

6.83   The preferred course of action in such cases is to make the child a ward of court on its birth. The authority for this is the decision of the House of Lords in *D (a minor) v Berkshire County Council*,[189] in which the court upheld a decision to make a care order

---

[184] *Re Children's Aid Society of Kenora and JL* (1982) 134 DLR (3d) 249; *Re Superintendent of Family and Child Service and McDonald* (1982) 135 DLR (3d) 330.

[185] [1997] 2 SCR 925. See, also, an earlier case, *Re Baby R* (1989) 53 DLR (4th) 69—powers to interfere with the rights of women must be given by specific legislation.

[186] For a wide-ranging review of the whole field, see R Scott 'Maternal Duties to the Unborn? Soundings from the Law of Tort' (2000) 8 Med L Rev 1.

[187] [1988] Fam 122, [1988] 2 All ER 193. Other Commonwealth jurisdictions have attempted rather similar protection of the viable fetus: *In the matter of Baby P (an unborn child)* [1995] NZFLR 577. The absence of fetal/maternal conflict was a feature of this case in which the mother was taken into care in the interests of the fetus.

[188] *Paton v British Pregnancy Advisory Service Trustees* [1979] QB 276, [1978] 2 All ER 987.

[189] [1987] AC 317, [1987] 1 All ER 20, HL.

in respect of a child born prematurely and suffering from drug dependency. The House held that the words: '[The child's] proper development is being avoidably prevented or neglected' in the Children and Young Persons Act 1969, s 1(2)(a) referred to a continuing, rather than an instant, situation. Thus, while the court would not go so far as to make a fetus a ward of court, conditions both before birth and in the hypothetical future could be taken into account when assessing a neonate's need for care and control, the important point being that there is a genuine continuum. The decision caused considerable concern; first, on the grounds that its application to family law might be extended to the criminal field and, secondly, because it denied the drug addicted mother the right to prove her capacity for motherhood. For ourselves, we see *D (a minor)* as yet another case that was decided on its own facts; there is no reason to suppose that a similar decision would be taken in every instance—only that the remedy is there should it be needed in serious cases.[190]

6.84   *D (a minor)* is an example of fetal interests maturing into child rights at birth. The reasons for seeking fetal protection in *Re F* were, we feel, far less pressing; the nature of any maternal improbity differed and it is possible to explain the two decisions in that simple light.[191] None the less, *Re F* is the more significant in that it lays down a principle which is likely to be followed in the absence of parliamentary intervention. Any claims for protection vested in the fetus are strictly circumscribed. Whether or not one agrees with such a loading of the odds, there is little doubt that it has to be accepted on pragmatic grounds. There is simply no way in which the criminal law could be invoked so as to control a pregnant woman's smoking, eating or sexual habits, nor is it desirable—amongst other ill-effects, doctors would be turned into police informers. We can also foresee great difficulty in proof of causation: teratogenic effects are maximal in the first trimester of pregnancy and the further in time that the cause is removed from the visible effect, the more difficult it becomes to associate the two.

6.85   Finally, we mention the problem of the mother's duty to her full-term child—and, particularly, the dilemma associated with refusal of caesarean section when that operation is indicated in the fetus' best interests. We do so, however, only to refer the reader to chapter 10 where the subject is explored in detail. For the present, it need only be said that that, while, say, some of the United States might regard such refusal as being contrary to statutory child abuse, or even homicide, provisions,[192] there is now no way in which a surgical procedure can be forced on a mentally competent[193] woman who refuses such treatment in the United Kingdom—and this irrespective of the effect on a viable fetus.

[190] The court will certainly use its power. In *Re P (a minor) (child abuse: evidence)* [1987] 2 FLR 467, CA a place of safety order was granted on the day of a child's birth into a family which had a history of sexual abuse. For US examples involving drug abuse, see *Re Ruiz* 500 NE 2d 935 (Ohio, 1986); *In re Valerie D* 613 A 2d 748 (Conn, 1992).

[191] It is noteworthy that the Court of Appeal was unable to see any logical difference between the early and the 'viable' fetus as regards a need for protection ([1988] 2 All ER 193 at 199, per Balcombe LJ).

[192] C Marwick 'Mother Accused of Murder after Refusing Caesarian Section' (2004) 328 BMJ 663.

[193] But the definition of competence is all important—see chapters 12 and 20.

7

GENETIC INFORMATION AND THE LAW

GENETICS: THE SCIENCE AND CHALLENGES

7.1   The purpose of this introductory section is to outline the nature of genetic disease and to discuss the role of the genetic counsellor in handling personal and familial genetic information. Issues of liability arising from the mishandling of that information have been dealt with in chapter 6; here we explore the challenges posed by the—some would say 'unique'—familial nature of much genetic data.

7.2   The importance of genetically dependent diseases has risen as the control of those due to infection has increased. Currently, the proportion of childhood deaths attributable wholly or partly to genetic factors runs at about 50 per cent. And it is becoming increasingly clear, in the era following the mapping of the human genome—that is, the genetic code of the human species—that a genetic component may well operate in many illnesses and conditions, the control of which was previously thought to be independent of genetic factors. The social, ethical and legal implications which advances in genetics have for all of us expand by the day; correspondingly, genetic considerations increasingly breathe new life into the study of medical jurisprudence.

7.3   Thus, the rather tired adage that 'information is power' has been rejuvenated with the advent of the so-called 'new genetics'. Developments in genetic medicine over the last few years now mean that access to genetic information through genetic testing is relatively cheap and easy but, as a result, this has given rise to serious concerns about access to, and the use of, test results.[1] While the sensitivity of medical data is an issue of general concern which we address in the context of confidentiality in chapter 8, matters are particularly complicated in the context of genetics because of certain features that are said to be particular to genetic information.[2] First, a test result has implications not only for the individual who has been tested (the 'proband') but also for blood relatives of that person who share a common gene pool.[3] Second, this

---

[1]   See generally, G T Laurie *Genetic Privacy: A Challenge to Medico-Legal Norms* (2002).

[2]   For a good account of the range of problems which can flow from this and for recommendations on tackling them, see the work of the European Commission STRATA Group *Ethical, Legal and Social Aspects of Genetic Testing: Research, Development and Clinical Applications* (2004).

[3]   On this, see L Andrews 'Gen-Etiquette: Genetic Information, Family Relationships and Adoption' in M A Rothstein (ed) *Genetic Secrets: Protecting Privacy and Confidentiality in the Genetic Era* (1997) ch 14; R Deech 'Family Law and Genetics' (1998) 61 MLR 697; L Skene 'Patients' Rights or Family Responsibilities' (1998)

information has implications also for *future* relatives, in the sense that genetic disease passes vertically through generations and, thus, impacts directly on reproductive decisions. Third, genetic test results can disclose a likelihood of *future* ill health in persons who are currently well. Fourth, because, in most cases, testing is carried out by analysing a person's DNA, which remains unchanged throughout their life, genetic testing can be done at any stage from the cradle to the grave—and, indeed, beyond.[4] Thus, a fetus can be tested in utero for a condition such as Huntington's disease which might not manifest itself until middle age. Finally, underlying all of these factors is the perceived benefit which genetic testing can offer in the guise of predictability. This is the 'standard account' of the nature of genetic information which we will challenge in due course (see para 7.28). For present purposes, however, it is important to note that it has significance for two particular classes of subject: first, the fetus, who is often the most common subject of genetic testing and for whom the consequences can be most severe (that is, termination of pregnancy), and second, family members of an individual who has been tested for genetic disease. We will consider the respective positions of these two groups following our discussion of the nature of that disease.

TYPES OF GENETIC DISEASE

7.4 Genetic diseases are of three main types. Some are chromosomal—the structure or the number of chromosomes is altered and typical disease states arise, many of these being associated with learning disability. The classic example is Down's syndrome— technically known as trisomy-21. The occurrence of some chromosomal abnormalities in the neonate increases markedly with maternal age. Some 2 per cent of women aged 40, left to uncontrolled pregnancy, will produce a chromosomally defective child, half of these suffering from Down's syndrome; by the age of 45, the risk of trisomy-21 rises to about 4 per cent. It is possible that advanced paternal age may also be a risk factor.

7.5 The second group includes those conditions described as unifactorial in origin. Genes are positioned on chromosomes which exist in the cells in pairs, one member of each pair being derived from each parent. Unifactorial disease results from the presence of a specific abnormal gene and, since either of a pair of genes can be donated at random by either parent to their offspring, it is a simple calculation to determine the statistical probability of an infant being so endowed (see Fig. 7.1). The genes may be 'autosomal dominants'—in which case they will express themselves, in this case as a disease, when the pair of genes contains only one which is abnormal. Normal natural selection should lead to the eradication of dangerous dominant genes.

6 Med L Rev 1; and, generally, T Marteau and M Richards *The Troubled Helix: Social and Psychological Implications of the New Human Genetics* (1996).

[4] For an explanation of the range of ways in which genetic tests differ from other medical tests, see Advisory Committee on Genetic Testing *Consultation Report on Genetic Testing for Late Onset Disorders* (1997) p 10. A good review article is E W Clayton 'Ethical, Legal and Social Implications of Genomic Medicine' (2003) 349 New Engl J Med 562.

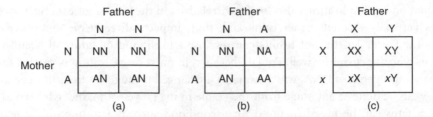

(a) The mother has an abnormal gene (A). If this is dominant, half the children will have the
     disease; if it is recessive, half the children will be carriers.
(b) Both the mother and the father have one deleterious recessive gene (A); half the children will
     be carriers and one in four will suffer from the disease.
(c) The mother is a carrier of an abnormal X-linked gene (x); half the male children will have the
     disease and half the female children will continue to carry the disease.

Fig. 7.1 Unifactorial disease

They may arise by mutation, or spontaneous change—a process which is greatly augmented by, for example, ionising radiation—or the gene may possess some special attribute. Huntington's disease, for example, persists because the symptoms associated with the responsible gene often do not appear until beyond the time when the subject has attained procreative age—a situation known as late onset genetic disease. Alternatively, the gene may be an 'autosomal recessive', in which case its expression is repressed by its normal dominant partner. Those persons possessing a single abnormal recessive gene will be 'carriers' of—and are unlikely to show any evidence of—the disease with which it is associated. Frank disease will result only if an individual inherits the same two recessive genes—which means that both parents must have been carriers or one was a carrier and the other diseased; this, incidentally, provides the genetic basis for discouraging in-breeding.

7.6   Unifactorial disease may also be 'sex-linked'—or, better, 'X-linked'. Simplistically, this implies that the abnormal gene is present on part of the X chromosome which has no counterpart on the Y chromosome, the possession of which determines maleness. An abnormal recessive X-linked gene will be suppressed in the female by the dominant normal gene on the other X chromosome; it will, however, be free to express itself when coupled in the male XY configuration. Haemophilia is a classic example of such a disease.

7.7   It almost goes without saying that this description of unifactorial disease is grossly simplified. The picture must be painted on a background of penetrance—that is, the ability of the gene to express itself. Some may be so powerful that they cause some symptoms or signs in the recessive state; other dominant genes may be virtually asymptomatic. The degree of penetrance in individuals probably depends mainly on the total genetic environment—that is, the penetrance of a gene depends, to an extent, on the company it keeps.

7.8   The result is that very few genetic diseases can be regarded as truly unifactorial. The great majority of genetic disorders result from multifactorial traits which are believed to be the result not only of the effects of one or several genes but also of a combination of genetic and environmental factors. It is, therefore, generally impossible to predict mathematically the occurrence of this commonest type of genetic disorder. Coronary heart disease, for example, is to some extent genetically determined but the occurrence of symptoms will depend upon a number of uncertain features such as the potential patient's job, diet, recreation and smoking habits or the genetic control of blood cholesterol levels. The appearance of such conditions, however, lies in the individual's unpredictable future; in respect of defects which can be demonstrated in utero, neural tube defects—spina bifida and anencephaly—are the most important multifactorial diseases.

7.9   Some form of behavioural or surgical treatment is often available for those suffering from multifactorial disease and the same is true for a few unifactorial conditions. But there is no curative treatment for most of the more serious genetic disorders,[5] the control of which then depends on prevention. As the House of Commons Science and Technology Committee pointed out:

While genetics is likely eventually to transform medicine, it may take some while before treatments based on genetic knowledge become available . . . [i]n the short term, the most widespread use of medical genetics will be, as now, in diagnosis and screening.[6]

This 'public health' objective is a central function of the genetic counsellor; its relative importance, however, poses one of the major ethical problems of modern medicine— and one which is likely to increase.[7]

GENETIC COUNSELLING AND FETAL TESTING FOR GENETIC DISEASE

7.10   Assessed as an arm of public health, the task of genetic counselling seems easy; in practice, it abounds with practical, ethical and, inevitably, legal problems; the Nuffield Council on Bioethics chose to make genetic screening the subject of its first report for just such reasons.[8] Modern genetic counselling involves more than merely quoting risks. The ideal is to avoid a directive approach but, rather, to concentrate on the psychological circumstances so that couples can be led to make decisions which are right for them rather than right for the scientists. Almost inevitably, however, the

---

[5] N A Holtzman et al 'Predictive Genetic Testing: From Basic Research to Clinical Practice' (1997) 278 Science 602.

[6] House of Commons Science and Technology Committee *Human Genetics: The Science and its Consequences* Third Report, 6 July 1995, pp 36–37, paras 71, 72. As the report makes clear, *diagnosis* is aimed at individuals; genetic *screening* is routine screening of populations, or identifiable subsets of populations (for example, men or women only, or ethnic groups at increased risk for particular diseases).

[7] While 95% of the more common genetic disease can now be tested for, the number of available cures remains very low.

[8] Nuffield Council on Bioethics *Genetic Screening: Ethical Issues* (1993).

counsellor's opinion will be sought and how this is reached depends particularly on whether the counselling is retrospective or prospective—are parents seeking advice because they already have an affected child or is the need for consultation prior to parenting based on information derived from other sources? Patient-clients who know that genetic disease might affect their family come, in the main, with a degree of preparedness and an appreciation of their future options. The role of the counsellor assumes an entirely different mantle, however, if he is privy to information of which his clients know nothing—perhaps as a result of a confidential discussion with another health care professional; the question then arises as to whether and how such information should be imparted, and we return to this below.

7.11   In assisting clients towards a particular reproductive decision, the counsellor can virtually never make a firm statement as to having or not having a further child. He can take extraneous circumstances—e.g. religious or financial status—into consideration but, in the end, he is down to speaking about probabilities. In the case of unifactorial disease, he can give accurate figures—e.g. the chances of an overtly affected child are one in four pregnancies if both the mother and father carry recessive deleterious genes. The position as to chromosomal disease is rather more complicated. In the usual circumstance, the condition is due to trisomy, in which three similar chromosomes are present in the cells rather than a pair; this is a chance occurrence which cannot be predicted mathematically. Males with trisomy-21 or Down's syndrome are commonly sterile but there is the theoretical risk that half the children of a female sufferer will also have the chromosomal defect; in practice, not only is such a pregnancy unlikely but, also, more than half of any affected fetuses would miscarry naturally. However, rather under 5 per cent of Down's syndrome patients are not trisomic but, instead, demonstrate a chromosomal abnormality known as translocation—parts of chromosome-21 are exchanged for those of another.[9] This may also occur sporadically but, once it has done so, a carrier state can develop and affect one in three children—passage to later generations is, thus, possible and its occurrence will be independent of maternal age. The counsellor must, therefore, consider each sub-type of chromosomal disorder separately.[10]

7.12   In the event of a multifactorial condition, the probabilities can only be derived in an empirical fashion. Even then, the prospects are subject to interpretation. Thus, presented with a child with spina bifida, one can say there is a 10 per cent chance that the couple will have a further child with developmental abnormality; it will sound quite different when expressed as a 90 per cent chance of a normal infant. Moreover, nine to one are acceptable odds to many; others might regard anything less than 99 to 1 as an unacceptable risk. In the end, the choice rests with the couple and this choice is a product of their ability to understand and the skill of the counsellor. But, as is so

[9] Some readers may require a more detailed explanation than we have space for. The seminal work is A E H Emery, R F Mueller and I D Young (eds) *Emery's Elements of Medical Genetics* (11th edn, 2001).

[10] The risk is 1:3 rather than the anticipated unifactorial 1:4 because a quarter of the conceptuses will be monosomic and will die in utero. The significance of translocation disease was noted in *Gregory v Pembrokeshire Health Authority* [1989] 1 Med LR 81.

often the case, the matter may not be restricted to the confines of the consulting room. In particular, the prospect of undue societal pressure to decide in favour of abortion may be considerable. We return to discuss this at paras 7.86–7.87 in light of our treatment of policy advice and guidance on the matter.

7.13   Counsellors, for their part, have several advisory options: they can dismiss the risks, they can advise sterilisation of either partner, they can put the options of artificial insemination by donor or of ovum donation, or they can arrange for a suitably controlled pregnancy coupled with the alternatives of live birth or abortion as conditions indicate.

CONTROLLED PREGNANCY

7.14   The counsellor may have advised a pregnancy or may be presented for the first time with a couple in which the wife is already pregnant. In either event, should it be felt that a risk exists, he or she now has a considerable technical armamentarium to help in closing the gap between probability and certainty. The methods may be non-invasive or invasive.

Non-invasive techniques

7.15   X-rays of the fetus are contra-indicated save in an emergency. The modern alternative is visualisation by means of ultrasound. This is now so widely used in obstetric management that testing may well be considered to be governed by implied consent alone;[11] moreover, its use in locating the placenta is an essential prerequisite to amnio-centesis, chorionic villus sampling and fetoscopy.[12] Ever-increasing technical and interpretative skills have transformed ultrasonography from a fairly crude diagnostic tool to one which is capable of demonstrating not only the sex of the baby and major external abnormalities, such as spina bifida or anencephaly, but also congenital disease of the internal organs, and minor defects such as cleft lip—indeed, the identification of Down's syndrome is often based on the appearance of relatively subtle fetal anomalies.[13] The processes of obstetric management and genetic counselling are, therefore, irrevocably entwined and it is important that the woman is aware of the implications, which are similar to those we discuss below under amniocentesis. The clinician who discovers a fetal abnormality as a by-product of management can scarcely conceal his knowledge while the woman, for her part, may be ill-prepared to receive it; the case for 'informed consent'[14] to ultrasonography is still strong. It is an

---

[11] See Lippman (1991) 17 Am J Law Med 15. It is difficult to know how seriously we should take suggestions such as ultrasound predisposing to, e.g., left-handedness: K A Salvesen, L J Vatten, S H Eik-Nes et al 'Routine ultrasonography in utero and subsequent handedness and neurological development' (1993) 307 BMJ 159—perhaps they should serve as gentle reminders.

[12] See para 7.18 et seq.

[13] Ultrasonography of the fetal neck tissues now has an 80% chance of detecting Down's syndrome: J Wise 'Nuchal Test Detects 80% of Down's Syndrome Pregnancies' (1998) 317 BMJ 368.

[14] See further chapter 10.

interesting psychological side-effect of the process that many parents regard the sonogram as their first 'baby-picture'—something which tends to endow the fetus with a recognisable personality; this, in itself, has some influence on the management decision.[15]

Maternal invasion

7.16   Fetuses with neural tube defects—spina bifida or anencephaly—secrete an excess of the protein α-fetoprotein into the amniotic fluid and some of this is transferred to the maternal circulation. Testing the maternal serum thus offers a simple and risk-free method of diagnosing abnormality in the fetus and is very acceptable to mothers. While 80–90 per cent of neural tube defective fetuses can be diagnosed in this way, the test is probably best regarded as a major indication of the need for amniocentesis. Conversely, it has been recognised for some time that a low maternal concentration of α-fetoprotein is associated with Down's syndrome in the fetus. Other maternal serum constituents—e.g. unconjugated oestriol, human chorionic gonadotrophin and the protein inhibin A—are also influenced. A very effective rate of diagnosis of Down's syndrome can be achieved by combining ultrasound and biochemical tests in the first trimester with further biochemical analyses after 14 weeks gestation—a detection rate of 85 per cent is claimed for this integrated test with, equally importantly, a low false positive rate of less than 1 per cent.[16] Most practitioners, however, probably would still wish to offer amniocentesis or chorionic villus sampling to women aged over 35 years and at, generally, higher risk. None the less, the introduction of a relatively cheap and effective test raises the possibility of extending routine testing to all pregnant women rather than to the older group alone—and the government appears to be committed to this policy.[17] This serves to draw attention to the conflict which arises between those who would hold that 'because a test is possible, testing should be implemented as a service'[18] and those who emphasise the importance of cost-effectiveness before a new policy is established—in itself, often a source of contention.[19] All those involved in the field of prenatal screening would, however, agree that the provision of a test without adequate back-up counselling as to the significance of the results is likely to

[15] D Callahan 'How Technology is Reframing the Abortion Debate' (1986) Hastings Center Rep, February, p 33.

[16] N J Wald, H C Watt and A K Hackshaw 'Integrated Screening for Down's Syndrome on the Basis of Tests Performed during the First and Second Trimesters' (1999) 341 New Engl J Med 461. There is a continuing need for evaluation of the various tests and combinations of tests available; a very useful synopsis is to be found in Z Alfirevic and J P Neilson 'Antenatal Screening for Down's Syndrome' (2004) 329 BMJ 811.

[17] Department of Health *Our Inheritance, Our Future* (2003), Cm 5791.

[18] Editorial Comment 'Screening for Fetal Malformations' (1992) 340 Lancet 1006. And see Wald et al, n 16 above.

[19] E.g. M Connor 'Biochemical Screening for Down's Syndrome' (1993) 306 BMJ 1705. The original article sparked a massive correspondence, most of which was doubtful of the justification for extended screening. There is still considerable doubt as to the scientific basis for widespread serum testing; it is suggested that the use of maternal age combined with analysis of the routine ultrasound scan has been much underrated: D T Howe, R Gornall, D Wellesley et al 'Six-year Survey of Screening for Down's Syndrome by Maternal Age and Mid-trimester Ultrasound Scans' (2000) 320 BMJ 606.

introduce as much harm as good.[20] We also question the ethical propriety of making available a plethora of tests for conditions, such as is Down's syndrome, for which no treatment or cure is available. In these circumstances, the availability of such tests can only be fully justified as facilitating an abortion decision—although the possible collateral benefit of preparing parents for a disable child could also be prayed in aid, a matter that we address further at para 7.83 below. By contrast with what is, arguably, a dubious justification, it is possible to mount a *strong* ethical argument justifying tests which will identify illnesses, such as spina bifida, that are likely to expose a child to physical suffering and major surgical interventions.

7.17   Serum tests are generally performed in the second trimester; reliance on maternal serum for diagnosis thus leads to late terminations when one is indicated, whereas the current emphasis is on identifying chromosomal abnormalities in early pregnancy.[21]

Uterine invasion

7.18   The commonest invasive techniques for prenatal diagnosis which involve the fetus or its environment are amniocentesis and chorionic villus sampling. The former is technically easier and carries a lesser risk to the pregnancy; despite the theoretical advantages of the latter, amniocentesis is still probably the more popular method of direct investigation in the United Kingdom.

7.19   A significant number of British mothers undergo amniocentesis. The process consists of needling the sac surrounding the fetus and withdrawing fluid which contains excretions and metabolites of the fetus together with representative cells; the latter can be grown in culture for chromosomal studies and to detect certain metabolic diseases; the fluid can also be used for biochemical testing. Biochemical tests can be made rapidly and can directly diagnose some rare diseases of defective metabolism of the gargoylism type. The onset of 'rhesus disease' can also be detected. But by far the most important test in the present context is that for α-fetoprotein, by means of which an efficient laboratory can now diagnose all neural tube lesions. Cell culture can indicate the presence of chromosomal disorder in some 10–20 days. In expert hands, the presence of what are termed 'inborn errors of metabolism' can be detected after some six weeks' culture.

7.20   On the face of things, therefore, amniocentesis provides very powerful means of preventing genetic disease but, at the same time, it presents both technical and ethical problems. First, a 'defensive' policy of amniocentesis for all would offer little or no benefit in terms of the proportion of positive results. In practice, it is used selectively on approximately 8 per cent of the population[22] and mainly for the diagnosis of chromosomal abnormalities, especially Down's syndrome. As has been discussed above, the maternal a-fetoprotein level and other biochemical parameters are widely

[20] We have argued this point in connection with the government's White Paper (n 17 above): S A M McLean and J K Mason 'Our Inheritance, Our Future: Their Rights?' (2005) 13 Int J Child Rights 255.

[21] See para 7.19 below.

[22] Based on data from the Simpson Memorial Maternity Pavilion, Edinburgh—A A Calder, personal communication.

used in conjunction with the mother's age to calculate a risk score on which a decision to recommend amniocentesis may be more robustly based. Having decided to test, however, it is to be noted that, even in the best hands, an adequate amount of fluid can only be obtained after about the fourteenth week of pregnancy—although the use of sophisticated ultrasonography may reduce this to 12 weeks; no fluid is obtained in some 5–10 per cent of cases and the test must then be repeated; add to this the time required for effective cell culture and it will be seen that one is close to producing a viable infant—and a consequently more hazardous operation—in the event that termination of pregnancy is indicated.[23]

7.21   These concerns can be reduced by the use of chorionic villus sampling—or removal and study of the early placental cells; used in conjunction with recombinant DNA techniques, it can revolutionise the diagnosis and management of genetic disease. Chorionic villus sampling suffers in being of no value in the identification of neural tube defects; the incidence of doubtful chromosomal analyses is some four times greater than that following amniocentesis; it is more expensive; and, currently, the risk of miscarriage following the procedure is certainly greater—occurring in some 2–3 per cent of examinations. Against this, chorionic villus sampling provides a good source of fetal DNA. Perhaps the most important practical consideration lies in the fear that early villus sampling may result in facial or limb abnormalities in an otherwise normal fetus.[24] For all these reasons, the early enthusiasm with which the procedure was greeted has waned somewhat. It is probably best reserved for those women who are at greatest risk—and, therefore, most likely to seek an early termination—or for cases where there is a single gene defect likely to require diagnosis.[25]

7.22   Amniocentesis and chorionic villus sampling together are said to carry a fetal mortality rate of up to 1 per cent; this is a not inconsiderable risk which, again, indicates the need for case selection—particularly if fertility is already low. It, too, cannot be used in a 'blanket' fashion—only specific diseases can be sought and discovered; moreover, irrespective of negligence, some false positive or false negative tests are inevitable and will increase with the complexity of the tests undertaken.

7.23   Such limitations of technique give rise to ethical, as well as practical, problems. Although modern techniques of gene marking have reduced the toll,[26] a proportion of normal male children at risk of X-linked disease are still legally aborted. Again, a raised α-fetoprotein level does not give a clear indication of the degree of neural tube defect and, although the additional use of high quality ultrasonography greatly improves the position, the routine abortion of fetuses with any detectable spinal abnormality will result in the destruction of some salvageable—and lovable—

---

[23] The Human Fertilisation and Embryology Act 1990, s 37(4) has eliminated the legal concern here; the aesthetic distaste for, and the comparative danger of, late abortions remains.

[24] H V Firth, P A Boyd, P Chamberlain et al 'Severe Limb Abnormalities after Chorionic Villus Sampling at 56–66 Days' Gestation' (1991) 337 Lancet 762.

[25] R J Lilford 'The Rise and Fall of Chorionic Villus Sampling' (1991) 303 BMJ 936.

[26] E.g. markers are already available for cystic fibrosis, Duchenne muscular dystrophy and Huntington's disease.

children. On the other hand, 10–20 per cent of 'missed' cases will have a severe defect and will require much corrective surgery. Similarly, the mere presence of the typical chromosomal abnormality does not indicate the likely severity of Down's syndrome. There are other problems of interpretation. For example, given a chromosomal abnormality, what does it mean? Certain arrangements are well known to be associated with severe disease but in others—notably the 'XYY syndrome'—the evidence is by no means clear. XYY boys are said to be prone to vicious behaviour but 'prone' is a very relative concept.[27] Should a doctor, on the one hand, recommend abortion of such a fetus as a 'precaution' or, on the other, say nothing and risk leaving the parents with an inexplicably 'difficult' child; alternatively, should he inform the parents, allow the pregnancy to run normally and possibly expose the family unnecessarily to an atmosphere of distrust? What is one to do when one of the other common aberrations of the sex chromosomes—for example Klinefelter's (XXY) or Turner's (XO) syndrome—is discovered? Such abnormalities are often, but by no means always, associated with a degree of infertility or learning disability. The variations are so many that it is impossible to generalise. The essential point is that patients who request or consent to antenatal diagnoses of this type must fully understand the extent of their consent and must be aware of the potential consequent decisions to be made.[28] Some might wish to be apprised of every item of information which has come to light, while others might require to know only of conditions which have a fully understood and significant prognosis; much subsequent searching of conscience can be avoided by preparatory discussion of the issues.

7.24 At the same time, as we have already intimated, the doctor's own motivation, prejudices and failings cannot be discounted. Much will depend upon whether, and to what extent, he sees himself as a community rather than a personal physician—and how he sees his duty to be apportioned between the woman and her progeny. We have already concluded that it is well-nigh impossible to perform an illegal therapeutic abortion in Great Britain but the clinician is still confronted with the moral problems inherent in the interpretation of 'severe handicap' in the Abortion Act 1967, s 1(1)(d)—it is, for example, even possible to construct an argument which casts doubt on the ethical justification for abortion in such a serious condition as Huntington's disease.[29] What seemed, at first sight, to be an uncomplicated and thoroughly desirable procedure presents, in the end, as a Pandora's box of moral uncertainties.

7.25 Some of the difficulties can be overcome by more direct techniques. Fetoscopy, for example, allows for direct inspection of the fetus and, thence, an assessment of the degree of abnormality; at the same time, fetoscopy carries with it a fetal mortality of about 1 per cent. Fetal blood sampling, originally developed for the diagnosis, inter alia, of haemophilia has had a relatively short life as the need for such relatively

---

[27] On the supposed link between genetics and criminality see, generally, Ciba Foundation *Genetics of Criminal and Antisocial Behaviour* (1996).

[28] An interesting survey was reported by H Statham and J Green 'Serum Screening for Down's Syndrome: Some Women's Experiences' (1993) 307 BMJ 174.

[29] S G Post 'Huntington's Disease: Prenatal Screening for Late Onset Disease' (1992) 18 J Med Ethics 75.

dangerous investigations recedes with the availability of recombinant DNA tech-niques.[30] Mention must also be made of the very different potential of in vitro fertilisation (for which see chapter 4) combined with embryo biopsy as an answer to the very high risk pregnancy and/or for those who find feticide morally unacceptable but who can tolerate embryocide. The technique of pre-implantation diagnosis involves removal and genetic analysis of single cells from eight-cell embryos, followed by selection of such embryos as are found to be normal for implantation. This immediately raises the question of the status of the surplus embryo which we discuss in detail elsewhere.[31] Aside from such moral implications, the procedure also carries with it the many difficulties associated with in vitro fertilisation of itself (see chapter 4) and it is possible to doubt whether its benefits outweigh the imposed emotional and financial costs.[32] That having been said, however, it is impossible to ignore either the speed with which this branch of science moves forward or the demand for the techniques available. The range of pre-implantation diagnoses is growing such that it is referable to an ever widening body of patient-clients. It is now possible to screen for a large number of conditions, including cystic fibrosis, Tay Sachs disease, Duchenne muscular dystrophy and even dominant disorders such as Marfan's syndrome.[33] Although, given the need for either, embryocide will be generally regarded as prefer-able to abortion, fears can be raised that the increasing availability of preimplantation genetic diagnosis may lead to a return to eugenics and increasing disrespect for the disabled—and, although the proposition seems doubtful, this is certainly an ethical dimension that must be borne in mind.[34]

7.26   But increasing sophistication to some extent only serves to underline the funda-mental moral issue of prenatal screening which is—how far is one to go in defining abnormality? Is the 'perfect baby' to be encouraged?[35] The concept of parents obtaining a termination on the grounds of, for example, the sex of the child may seem frivo-lous—or unprincipled—to many; but, as we discuss above,[36] it may be both medically defensible and legally acceptable. One can foresee more generally applicable dilemmas of conscience. Cases of Down's syndrome or of spina bifida which have not

There is also a semantic problem as to whether the words 'if the child were born it would suffer from . . .' (Abortion Act 1967, s 1(1)(d)) exclude conditions that are not present at birth—but any discussion is surely no more than academic pedantry.

[30] N M Fisk and S Bower 'Fetal Blood Sampling in Retreat' (1993) 307 BMJ 143.

[31] See chapter 4.

[32] A relatively early discussion is to be found in M Michael and S Buckle 'Screening for Genetic Disorders: Therapeutic Abortion and IVF' (1990) 16 J Med Ethics 43.

[33] And it may now be possible to extend this list to Down's syndrome: S Gottlieb 'Doctors May Be Able to Detect Down's Syndrome during IVF' (2001) 323 BMJ 67. Licences to screen for inheritable breast cancer are also being sought: M Henderson 'Gene Tests to Start Era of Baby-to-order' (2004) *The Times*, 26 June, p 1.

[34] D S King 'Preimplantation Genetic Diagnosis and the "New" Eugenics' (1999) 25 J Med Ethics 176; T S Petersen 'Just Diagnosis? Preimplantation Genetic Diagnosis and Injustices to Disabled People' (2005) 31 J Med Ethics 231.

[35] R F Chadwick 'The Perfect Baby: An Introduction' in R F Chadwick (ed) *Ethics, Reproduction and Genetic Control* (1987) p 93. See also E Yoxen *Unnatural Selection* (1986).

[36] See para 5.68.

been discovered through prenatal screening are already candidates for selective non-treatment—or neonaticide—or local authority care. Is such disposal to run parallel with an increasing prenatal diagnostic capability when, as a result, more parents reject what will be regarded as imperfect children on increasingly demanding criteria?

7.27   On the other side of the coin, it is clear that genetic counsellors should not overemphasise the interests of the state in reducing the incidence of genetic disease and, as clinicians, should not join with the scientists in welcoming the genetic issue as 'unstoppable'.[37] Rather, the aim should be to concentrate on the particular circumstances and interests of the parents in wanting a child. The Nuffield Council on Bioethics,[38] the House of Commons Science and Technology Committee[39] and the British Medical Association[40] have all stressed the importance of accepting the ethical principle that screening or testing is justifiable only if based on free and informed consent. Similarly, in the United States, the National Institutes of Health Task Force on Genetic Testing stated that '[it] is unacceptable to coerce or intimidate individuals or families regarding their decision about predictive genetic testing'.[41] An elderly couple, for example, might see a pregnancy as their last possibility and might prefer to take their chance in the ignorant way of natural parenthood—and they should be allowed to do so; a woman who has managed to conceive by assisted means may rightly refuse to take the risks involved in subsequent chorionic villus sampling or amniocentesis. A refusal to accept information must be respected just as much as must the desire to receive information. But it has to be admitted that the interests of the state may not stop here, and we return to consider them more fully at paras 7.82–7.87 below.

LEGAL AND ETHICAL RESPONSES TO THE 'FAMILIAL' NATURE OF GENETICS

7.28   We have already outlined the standard account of genetic information as 'unique', 'predictable', 'certain' and of 'utility to others' in para 7.3 above. We cannot let this account pass unchallenged, however, because of the important consequences its adoption could have for the future direction of law, policy and practice. First and foremost, we point to other examples that can be found of non-genetic information which functions in one or more of these ways and we have already mentioned some of these above at para 7.8. As the report *Genetics and Health* states:

[37] Editorial Comment 'Ethics and the Human Genome' (1991) 351 Nature, Lond 591, quoted by Clarke (1991) 335 Lancet 1145.
[38] *Genetic Screening: Ethical Issues* paras 4.6.–4.16.
[39] Third Report (1995) paras 81–105, esp paras 88, 97.
[40] BMA *The BMA's Views on Genetic Testing* (21 November 1995).
[41] N A Holtzman and M S Watson (eds) *Promoting Safe and Effective Genetic Testing in the United States* (1997).

[h]igh cholesterol levels [are] known predictors of cardiovascular disease, and high blood pressure of cerebrovascular disease risk . . . [and] . . . without recourse to genetic testing familial aggregation [is] discernible not only in the monogenetic disorders but also in a range of common disorders including heart disease, cancers and diabetes.[42]

Moreover, the term 'genetic information' covers a broad spectrum, from highly predictive monogenic disorders through susceptibility genes and on to a simple family history. Even the colour of our eyes provides a form of genetic data. However, not every class of this information is predictive of future ill health—indeed, many examples of genetic information are no more predictive than is general health information. These factors militate against the argument that genetic data are in some way different from other forms of medical data and, for these reasons, the Human Genetics Commission (HGC) has stated that 'we do not feel that all personal genetic information should be treated in the same way in every set of circumstances'.[43] None the less, the debate about how law and ethics should respond to genetic advances has proceeded in large measure on the premise that genetic information is exceptional.[44] There is certainly a general perception that genetic information is especially private,[45] and the HGC was established partly in response to this public intuition. Its 2002 report, *Inside Information*, is an attempt to address the public concerns and 'to maintain public trust and confidence that personal genetic information is properly protected'.[46]

7.29   The belief that genetic data are highly predictive is a key element underpinning the view that genetic information is somehow different, and this has led a range of persons or bodies to claim an interest in genetic test results.[47] For example, relatives might wish to know if they too will be affected by disease or, indeed, if their progeny will be so affected. Insurers have always taken family history as an index of risk into the assessment of insurance cover but, now, genetic testing offers a seemingly more accurate and more scientific means of predicting liability. Similarly, employers might harbour deep concerns about the future employability of persons likely to be struck

---

[42] See, The Nuffield Trust *Genetics and Health: Policy Issues for Genetic Science and their Implications for Health and Health Services* (2000).

[43] Human Genetics Commission *Inside Information: Balancing Interests in the Use of Personal Genetic Data* (2002), para 1.26.

[44] Cf, L O Gostin and J G Hodge Jr 'Genetic Privacy and the Law: An End to Genetics Exceptionalism' (1999) 40 Jurimetrics 21.

[45] Human Genetics Commission *Public Attitudes to Human Genetic Information* (2001).

[46] Human Genetics Commission, n 43 above, para 1.25. This report follows the HGC's consultation document *Whose Hands on Your Genes?* (2000). More recent work of the Commission includes consultations on *Paternity Testing Services* (2004) and *Genetic Testing Services supplied Direct to the Public* (2003). The current work of the HCG relates to 'Profiling Babies at Birth' and 'Genetics and Reproductive Decision-Making'. Similar consultation has been undertaken in Australia jointly by the Australian Law Reform Commission (ALRC) and the Australian Health Ethics Committee, see their comprehensive Discussion Paper *Protection of Human Genetic Information* (Paper 66, 2002) and the final report: ALRC *Essentially Yours: The Protection of Human Genetic Information in Australia* (2003).

[47] For a discussion of the (non)relationship between genetics and behaviour see, Nuffield Council on Bioethics *Genetics and Human Behaviour: The Ethical Context* (2002).

down by genetic disease, and the state itself has an undeniable interest in promoting public health by reducing the incidence of genetic disease in its citizens. In light of this range of interests, the potential for conflict over access and control of genetic information is axiomatic and it is important to recognise that the impact of a genetic test result on an individual's life might well be felt long before they experience the onset of disease. In its struggle to respond adequately to the dilemmas posed by advances in genetics, the law turns to ethics for guidance.[48] It is, therefore, apposite to consider the nature and strength of the ethical arguments which both support and refute the claims of those in each of the above categories and to assess the responses of the law in the light of this to date.

INDIVIDUAL AND FAMILY INTERESTS IN GENETIC INFORMATION

7.30   The availability of genetic information is appealing because of its perceived utility: what does it allow one to do? Even so, we consider it preferable to begin our inquiry by asking the opposite question: what does genetic information *not* allow one to do? Probably the most important single factor bearing on this debate is that few cures or successful treatments for genetic illnesses exist at present. Thus, except in rare cases, genetic information does not necessarily allow us to avoid genetic disease. This is important because it bears on the motivation of those who seek access to genetic testing or test results. Let us begin by considering the claims of the proband and his or her relatives.

7.31   In the absence of treatment or cure, *preparedness* is often cited as the justification for offering or seeking genetic testing. Adults and children can ready themselves, both psychologically and in other ways, for the onset of disease and couples contemplating a family or who have a child on the way can make a more informed reproductive choice in light of all the available facts.[49] Such justification is, however, a double-edged sword for a number of reasons. First, it is by no means clear that pre-emptive knowledge of future ill health is necessarily 'a good thing'.[50] While there are indications that this can be so,[51] there is also a growing body of evidence which suggests that adverse

---

[48]   See A Buchanan et al *From Chance to Choice: Genetics and Justice* (2000).

[49]   V English and A Sommerville 'Genetic Privacy: Orthodoxy or Oxymoron?' (1999) 25 J Med Ethics 144. Cf, T M Marteau and C Lerman 'Genetic Risk and Behavioural Change' (2001) 322 BMJ 1056.

[50]   Knowledge in this context will be relative both as to occurrence and severity of disease.

[51]   M Hietala et al 'Attitudes towards Genetic Testing among the General Population and Relatives of Patients with a Severe Genetic Disease: A Survey from Finland' (1995) 56 Amer J Hum Gen 1493; M R B Hayden 'Predictive Testing for Huntingon's Disease: Are We Ready for Widespread Community Implementation?' (1991) 40 Amer J Med Gen 515; J Brandt et al 'Presymptomatic Diagnosis of Delayed-Onset with Linked DNA Markers: The Experience with Huntington's Disease' (1989) 216 J Amer Med Ass 3108.

psychological sequelae can flow from such knowledge.[52] For example, Almqvist et al[53] found in an international study that the suicide rate among persons given a positive genetic test result for Huntington's disease was 10 times higher than the United States average.[54] The Danish Council of Bioethics has warned too of the possibility of *morbidification*:

The risk of participants in screening programmes possibly suffering from some form or other of morbidification or the notion of 'falling victim' to some inescapable 'fate' uncovered by the genetic examination in itself furnishes a basis for ensuring the provision of adequate information, counselling and follow-up in connection with such programmes.[55]

7.32   While it is important to draw a distinction between genetic *testing*, which involves an individual patient being tested in his or her own medical interests, and genetic *screening*, which involves the testing of populations for public health or research reasons, the Danish Council's observation remains valid in both contexts. It is for reasons such as these the Advisory Committee on Genetic Testing (ACGT)[56] issued a code of practice to regulate the availability of 'over-the-counter' genetic testing.[57] The committee recommended strongly that only tests which reveal carrier status for inherent recessive disorders should be made available outside the NHS genetic services.[58] This is allowable because the discovery of carrier status has no direct health implications for the proband. By contrast, however, testing for adult onset dominant conditions and X-linked disorders should only be provided in a clinical setting.[59] The importance of full and proper counselling in this context cannot be

---

[52] L Andrews *Future Perfect: Confronting Decisions about Genetics* (2001), chapter 3, esp pp 31–40. Cf, S van Dooren et al 'Psychological Distress and Breast Self-Examination Frequency in Women at Increased Risk for Hereditary or Familial Breast Cancer' (2003) 6 Community Genetics 235 and Gonzalez et al 'Short-Term Psychological Impact of Predictive Testing for Macahdo-Joseph Disease: Depression and Anxiety Levels in Individuals at Risk from the Azores' (2004) 7 Community Genetics 196.

[53] E Almqvist et al 'A Worldwide Assessment of the Frequency of Suicide, Suicide Attempts, or Psychiatric Hospitalization after Predictive Testing for Huntington Disease' (1999) 64 Amer J Hum Gen 1293. The authors surveyed 100 centres in 21 countries and gathered data on 4,527 individuals who had undergone predictive genetic testing for Huntington's disease. Of those reviewed, 1,817 people had received a positive result, of whom five had taken their own lives. This extrapolates to 138/100,000 suicides per year, compared to the United States average of 12–13/100,000 per year. See, T Bird 'Outrageous Fortune: The Risk of Suicide in Genetic Testing for Huntington Disease' (1999) 64 Amer J Hum Gen 1289.

[54] While this rate is no greater than that for the symptomatic Huntington disease population, it is significant that the survey primarily focused on the two years after test results were given. This would tend to indicate that the deaths were more directly related to the disclosure of the genetic information, rather than to some other factors, such as the onset of the disease itself.

[55] Danish Council of Ethics *Ethics and Mapping the Human Genome* (1993) p 60.

[56] The Advisory Committee on Genetic Testing was established in the UK in July 1996 with a remit to give full consideration to the ethical and social aspects of genetic testing and to advise the government accordingly. It has since been replaced by the HGC, as we discuss below.

[57] The first such test made available in the UK was for cystic fibrosis: see ACGT *First Annual Report: July 1996–December 1997* (1998).

[58] ACGT *Code of Practice for Genetic Testing Offered Commercially Direct to the Public* (1997).

[59] *Ibid*, p 12.

over-emphasised.[60] But issues move quickly in genetics and, partly in response to an unexpectedly pressing public interest in gaining access to a wider range of tests than was originally envisaged,[61] the Human Genetics Commission (HGC) issued a further consultation document in July 2002 which was aimed at a reconsideration of the position of over-the-counter genetics tests.[62] The final report, *Genes Direct*,[63] takes as it starting premise that '. . . the best way of protecting the public is through a combination of legal controls on the sale of tests and professional self-regulation of those who might supply tests'.[64] Thus, the Commission recommended stricter control of the supply of tests but it eschewed the statutory prohibition of some, or all, direct genetic tests. This was largely in recognition of the 'right' to obtain information about oneself and in the belief that the state should not intervene unless there is a risk of harm. By the same token, the Commission felt strongly that there should be more of a commitment to developing genetics services within the NHS so as to elide the possibility that the public would need to seek testing outside that context. Moreover, because of the potential impact of predictive testing, the Commission considered that most such instances should not be offered as direct tests (thereby reflecting the views of the ACGT). The *presumption* should be that such a genetic test is generally unsuitable for supply direct to the public; the onus, therefore, is on those who would seek to offer such a service to convince the regulatory authority that this is acceptable. The Commission also pointed to its 2002 recommendation for the creation of a criminal offence of non-consensual testing which, it argued, should be implemented before home testing is thought acceptable. The concern, for example, is in the testing of children for paternity[65] or other reasons when this is not in their interests. As we discuss in chapter 15, the government has now instituted such a criminal offence in the Human Tissue Act 2004.[66] A person commits an offence if he has bodily material *intending* that it be analysed without consent and that the results will be used other than for an 'excepted purpose'. As to regulation, the HGC outlined possible roles for existing or new agencies to assist in the task, including the new Medicines and Healthcare Products Regulatory Agency (MHRA)[67] which oversees European legislation that controls certain aspects of commercial genetic kits and laboratories.[68] Finally, as for

---

[60] Similar caution is urged in the Code of Practice on Genetic Paternity Testing Services (2001) issued by the Ad Hoc Group on Genetic Paternity Testing Services, available at www.dh.gov.uk.

[61] For an account of international testing practices, see Organisation for Economic Co-operation and Development *Genetic Testing: Policy Issues for the New Millennium* (2001).

[62] Human Genetics Commission *The Supply of Genetic Tests Direct to the Public* (2002).

[63] Human Genetics Commission *Genes Direct: Ensuring the Effective Oversight of Genetic Tests Supplied Directly to the Public* (2003).

[64] *Ibid*, p 7.   [65] See n 60 above and associated text.

[66] Section 45 of the Human Tissue Act 2004 and Schedule 4. The penalty extends to up to 3 years in prison, a fine, or both. The government is due to issue guidance on the offence in 2006. For general comment, see G Laurie 'DNA Theft: A New Crime in the UK' (2003) 4(8) *Nature Reviews Genetics* p 584.

[67] The Medicines and Healthcare Products Regulatory Agency (MHRA) was established on 1 April 2003 and it replaced the Medical Devices Agency (MDA) and the Medicines Control Agency (MCA).

[68] On the challenges of regulation in this field, see R Brownsword 'Regulating Human Genetics: New Dilemmas for a New Millennium' (2004) 12 Med L Rev 14.

the troublesome phenomenon of the internet and the prospect of the British public purchasing tests beyond our shores,[69] the HGC could do little more than acknowledge the potential for harm while emphasising the importance of working closely with other national and international bodies so as to improve generally the standards of regulation in the field.[70]

7.33   Knowledge of one's own genetic constitution and of possible future ill health can have profound effects on one's sense of 'self'.[71] And, while an individual who seeks out genetic testing might have prepared himself for possible bad news, can the same be said of that person's relatives who might suspect nothing as to the presence of genetic disease in their family? Eighty-five per cent of high risk couples are reported as having no knowledge of their condition. In such circumstances, information must come to these persons in ways which may raise issues of confidentiality. Even so, while the prevention of genetic disease may well be seen as admirable community medicine, there are difficulties when the principles are applied to the individual.[72] Should one impose knowledge on someone who has not sought it and who may, perhaps irrationally, be disturbed as a consequence? At what stage should this knowledge be used? It is arguable that premarital advice is preferable to prenatal warning, but to implement such a policy has implications which are scarcely acceptable. On the other hand, has a doctor a moral duty to impose counselling? Here the roles of the genetic counsellor and the health care professional assume paramount importance. The general practitioner who is in possession of familial genetic information is in a particularly difficult position; he has a general duty of care to all his patients, but a specific duty of confidentiality to the proband. What should he do? It might be asked if there is a legal duty in so far as an action might be brought were parents to discover after the birth of an abnormal child that relevant information had been available but not disclosed.[73] Yet, as we discuss in chapter 8, the practitioner might find himself facing an action for breach of confidence if disclosure was made. In legal terms, no precedent exists in the UK to guide the way in such cases.[74] We must, therefore, rely on ethical argument.

[69] For discussion see B Williams-Jones 'Where There's a Web, There's a Way: Commercial Genetic Testing and the Internet' (2003) 6 Community Genetics 46.

[70] The In Vitro Medical Device Regulations ensure that safety, quality and performance criteria are met before tests are placed on the market, see HGC Inside Information, para 7.28 above. However, these provisions do not regulate the actual testing *service* that patients might receive.

[71] M Levitt 'The Ethics and Impact on Behaviour of Knowledge About One's Own Genome' (1999) 319 BMJ 1283.

[72] For general discussion of the implications of imparting genetic knowledge, see I Pullen 'Patients, Families and Genetic Information' in E Sutherland and A McCall Smith (eds) *Family Rights* (1990) ch 3. But not everyone would see a contradiction between concern for the genetic health of the population and concern for the problems of the individual family: see e.g. R F Chadwick 'What Counts for Success in Genetic Counselling?' (1993) 19 J Med Ethics 43.

[73] G Laurie 'Obligations Arising from Genetic Information: Negligence and the Protection of Familial Interests' (1999) 11 CFLQ 109. See also R Brownsword 'An Interest in Human Dignity as the Basis for Genomic Torts' (2003) 42 Washburn Law Journal 413.

[74] There is some US authority that supports disclosure, see for example, *Safer v Estate of Pack* 677 A 2d 1188 (NJ, 1996), discussed in Laurie, n 1 above, pp 268–69. See also, K Offit et al 'The "Duty to Warn" a Patient's Family Members About Hereditary Disease Risks' (2004) 292 JAMA 1469.

A RIGHT TO KNOW AND A RIGHT NOT TO KNOW

7.34 The origin of this polemic lies in the fact that various parties have valid claims to the same information because, in essence, it relates to each of them.[75] One could, in the first instance, categorise the strength of any claim to information by straightforward reference to the degree of consanguinity: the chances of a second cousin being affected by the same genetic condition are statistically smaller than those of a first cousin and the strength of any claim by the former is correspondingly weaker. This is, however, an unsophisticated approach and unhelpful in the case of the nuclear family, where claims to the information are at their strongest. Matters are complicated by the additional problem of deciding what is the best thing to do—to disclose or not to disclose? While few would argue that the risk of genetic disease should be withheld from family members when an effective treatment or cure is available, the motivation for disclosure in the absence of treatment is, once again, called into question. If the aim is to facilitate preparedness, then the health care professional must consider the possibility that a relative might not, in fact, wish to know that he might develop a genetic disease. Yet, even if the practitioner is confident that a relative would wish to know, he must justify any disclosing action in ethical terms if he is faced with the proband's refusal to authorise release of the information. Current ethical principles are tested to their limits in such circumstances. Why, for example, should the autonomy of the relative who wants to know trump the autonomy of the proband who wishes to keep the information private? As Ngwena and Chadwick rightly state:

> . . . what has to be taken into account is the fact that respecting the autonomy of one person may have implications for the autonomy of others. As the Royal College of Physicians argue, 'Blood relatives have an interest in knowing the truth which has nothing to do with influencing their behaviour towards affected individuals in their families, but as a necessary means to finding out the truth about themselves' . . . How is the choice between the autonomy of different people made? . . . What is clear is that the decision cannot be taken *on autonomy grounds.*[76]

7.35 The ethical principle of respect for patient confidentiality assists the practitioner to a certain degree in that it constitutes one of his primary duties to the proband. Yet release of the information can be justified equally by reference to the principle of non-maleficence if he genuinely feels that harm to relatives (or even their progeny) can be averted through disclosure—neither in ethics nor law is the principle of confidentiality seen as absolute (see chapter 8).

---

[75] This has been acknowledged recently by the Supreme Court of Iceland in a judgment in which the court held that a daughter had legal standing to control the flow of information held in her deceased father's medical records because, in a certain sense, it also revealed something about her: see R Gertz 'Is it "Me" or "We"? Genetic Relations and the Meaning of "Personal Data" under the Data Protection Directive' (2004) 11 Euro J Health Law 231.

[76] C Ngwena and R Chadwick 'Genetic Diagnostic Information and the Duty of Confidentiality: Ethics and Law' (1993) 1 Med Law Internat 73 at 77.

7.36   If the avoidance of harm is, indeed, the paramount consideration, then the prospect of harming a relative who might be disturbed by unsolicited information must also be considered. For this and other reasons, we argue elsewhere that the interest or right not to know deserves recognition.[77] Moreover, the basis of this interest lies not in autonomy or confidentiality but, rather, in privacy.[78] Privacy consists of two aspects: informational privacy and spatial privacy. Informational privacy is concerned with the control of personal information and with preventing access to that information by others. An invasion of informational privacy occurs when any unauthorised disclosure of information takes place. Confidentiality is a subset of this privacy interest and is breached when confidential information which is the subject of the relationship is released to parties outside the relationship without authorisation. Informational privacy is wider than this in that it does not require a relationship to exist.

7.37   Spatial privacy protects the individual's sense of 'self'. It recognises the interest which each of us has in maintaining a sense of separateness from others. Our spatial privacy is invaded when others 'invade our space' and this includes invasion of our psychological privacy which occurs, inter alia, when unsolicited information about oneself is received. An interest in *not* knowing about oneself has been recognised by the Convention for the Protection of Human Rights and Dignity of the Human Being with regard to the Application of Biology and Medicine,[79] Article 10(2) of which states:

Everyone is entitled to know any information collected about his or her health. *However, the wishes of individuals not to be so informed shall be observed.* (Emphasis added.)

Similarly, the UNESCO Universal Declaration on the Human Genome and Human Rights[80] states in Article 5c that:

The right of every individual to decide whether *or not* to be informed of the results of genetic examination and the resulting consequences should be respected. (Emphasis added.)

7.38   However, the efficacy of grounding such a 'right' *solely* in terms of choice is doubtful.[81] The principle of respect for autonomy requires that we see the individual as a 'moral chooser'.[82] In order to choose meaningfully we require full information about the range of options available and the consequences of any particular choice. Unfortunately, this paradigm breaks down in the context of an interest in *not* knowing genetic information. Here, the choice is about knowledge itself. As Wertz and Fletcher have put it:

---

[77] Generally, Laurie, n 1 above, esp chapter 5.

[78] Cf R Andorno 'The Right Not to Know: An Autonomy-Based Approach' (2004) 30 J Med Ethics 435 and G Laurie 'Commentary' (2004) 30 J Med Ethics 439.

[79] Council of Europe *Convention for the Protection of Human Rights and Dignity of the Human Being with regard to the Application of Biology and Medicine: Convention on Human Rights and Medicine Oviedo* (1997).

[80] Adopted unanimously on 11 November 1997 in Paris at the Organisation's 29th General Conference.

[81] Cf J Husted 'Autonomy and A Right Not to Know' in R Chadwick, M Levitt and D Shickle *The Right to Know and the Right Not to Know* (1997) ch 6.

[82] This expression is borrowed from Stanley Benn, who explores the ideas of the 'moral chooser' and 'private life', inter alia, in *A Theory of Freedom* (1988).

[t]here is no way . . . to exercise the choice of not knowing, because in the very process of asking 'Do you want to know whether you are at risk . . .?' the geneticist has already made the essence of the information known.[83]

The principle of respect for patient confidentiality is similarly unhelpful in protecting the interest in not knowing. It is simply not meaningful to talk of a breach of confidence when information about the party to whom the duty is owed is disclosed *to that party*.

7.39 How then is the interest in not knowing to be protected? It is argued in more detail elsewhere that the concept of spatial privacy—which requires that a degree of respect be paid prima facie to an individual's state of separateness or, in this case, state of 'ignorance'—provides a viable mechanism.[84] Spatial privacy can be invaded legitimately, but only if good cause can be shown. The following criteria could be considered for use by any health care professional when deciding how to resolve competing claims to genetic information in the familial context:

- the availability of a therapy or cure
- the severity of the condition and the likelihood of onset
- the nature of the genetic disease
- the nature of any further testing which might be required
- the nature of the information to be disclosed
- the nature of the request (for example, testing for the individual's health or for diagnostic purposes for a relative)
- the question of whether disclosure can further a legitimate public interest
- the question of how the individual might react if offered unsolicited information (for example, whether any advance directive has been made)

7.40 A practitioner who is faced with a refusal by a proband to communicate test results to relatives when a cure or effective treatment is available would be justified in disrespecting the proband's wishes in order to protect other family members from harm. He might, however, be rightly less inclined to disclose information about a condition for which nothing can be done and which has relatively mild symptoms. This nuanced approach can be supplemented by taking a hierarchical attitude when testing families—the need to test members of the younger generation can be greatly clarified if the older generations are approached and tested first.[85] The HGC endorses such a balancing approach:

---

[83] D C Wertz and J C Fletcher 'Privacy and Disclosure in Medical Genetics Examined in an Ethic of Care' (1991) 5 Bioethics 212 at 221.

[84] Laurie, n 1 above.

[85] See B S Wilfond et al 'Cancer Genetic Susceptibility Testing: Ethical and Policy Implementations for Future Research and Clinical Practice' (1997) 25 J Law Med & Ethics 243.

Bearing in mind the principle of genetic solidarity and altruism,[86] we take the view that disclosure of sensitive personal genetic information for the benefit of family members in certain circumstances may occasionally be justified. This would arise where the patient refuses to consent to such disclosure and the benefit of disclosure substantially outweighs the patient's claim to confidentiality.

7.41   However, the HGC goes on to state that such disclosure should be subject to the provisos that '(1) an attempt has been made to persuade the patient in question to consent; (2) the benefit to those at risk is so considerable as to outweigh any distress which disclosure would cause the patient; and (3) the information is, as far as possible, anonymised and restricted to that which is strictly necessary for the communication of risk'.[87] Of course, the problem of controlling communication between family members always remains, and a particularly problematic scenario arises when members of the younger generations are tested for a genetic condition and found to be positive. This must mean that one or more parents or grandparents are also affected in some way, yet these persons may have no idea of their condition or may have chosen not to know. It can be very difficult to stem the tidal flow of information within the familial milieu.

7.42   It is in the case of children that an appreciation of these subtleties can be found among legislatures and governments. In the United States the model Genetic Privacy Act was drafted in 1995 as part of the ELSI[88] division of the Human Genome Project. This is a piece of federal legislation designed for possible adoption by individual states. The draft explains the Act's remit:

[T]he overarching premise of the Act is that no stranger should have or control identifiable DNA samples or genetic information about an individual unless that individual specifically authorizes the collection of DNA samples for the purpose of genetic analysis, authorizes the creation of that private information, and has access to and control over the dissemination of that information.

7.43   The Act gives an individual from whom a sample is taken (the 'sample source') a number of rights, including the right to determine who may collect and analyse DNA, the right to determine the purposes for which a sample can be analysed and the right to order destruction of samples. Those who collect samples have a number of corresponding duties. The Act also protects genetic information from a number of potential abuses by third parties, such as the state or employers and insurers, and we return to

---

[86] These principles remind us that: 'We all share the same basic human genome, although there are individual variations which distinguish us from other people. Most of our genetic characteristics will be present in others. This sharing of genetic constitution not only gives rise to opportunities to help others but it also highlights our common interest in the fruits of medically-based research', see HGC *Inside Information*, n 43 above, para 2.11.

[87] HGC *Inside Information*, n 43 above, para 3.68.

[88] Part of the Human Genome Project has included programmes examining the 'Ethical, Legal and Social Issues' which arise from mapping of the human genome (ELSI): www.genome.gov.

this below.[89] For present purposes we focus on the provisions of the Act which deal with testing minors for genetic conditions.

7.44   The Genetic Privacy Act provides that an individually identifiable DNA sample source shall not be taken from a minor under 16 to detect any genetic condition which, in reasonable medical judgment, does not produce signs or symptoms of disease before the age of 16 unless an effective intervention is available to delay onset or ameliorate the severity of the disease; the said intervention must be made before the age of 16 and written authorisation has to be given by the minor's representative. The rationale behind this has been explained by the authors of the Act:

There are two reasons for this prohibition on the exercise of parental discretion. First, if someone learns that the child is a carrier of a gene that disposes the child to some condition later in life, this finding may subject the child to discrimination and stigmatization by both the parents and others who may learn of this fact. Second, a child's genetic status is the *child's* private genetic information and should not be determined or disclosed unless there is some compelling reason to do so. (Emphasis added.)[90]

7.45   The Act is clearly designed to protect the spatial privacy interests of children, and recognises that these should not be invaded without due cause. Arguably, however, it is deficient in not recognising such interests for *all* persons about whom genetic information is known but who have not sought it themselves.

7.46   In the United Kingdom, the House of Commons Science and Technology Committee, in its third report, alerted the public to the range of issues and problems which flow from the availability of genetic information.[91] The Committee recommended the establishment of a Human Genetics Commission with the power, inter alia, to monitor the provision of genetic services in the United Kingdom, advise on testing and screening procedures, and prescribe the circumstances in which particular screening or diagnostic procedures are provided or proscribed. This body, which we have already mentioned, was eventually set up in 1999 whereupon it took over the responsibilities of the pre-existing Advisory Committee on Genetic Testing (ACGT), the Human Genetics Advisory Commission (HGAC), and the Advisory Group on Advances in Genetics (AGAG). Other bodies, such as the Gene Therapy Advisory Committee (GTAC), and the Genetics and Insurance Committee (GAIC) are unaffected by the establishment of the HGC and we discuss their work below.[92] The government issued a White Paper on Genetics in 2003 in which it stated its commitment to invest over £50 million pounds over three years to develop genetics

[89] See para 7.49 et seq.

[90] The Act was drafted by George Annas, Leonard Glantz and Patricia Roche of the Boston University School of Public Health. A text of the Act and the comments of the authors can be found at www.ornl.gov/TechResources/Human_Genome/resource/privacy/privacy1.html.

[91] House of Commons Science and Technology Committee *Developments in Human Genetics and Embryology* HC791, July 2002, para 13.

[92] See paras 7.56 and 7.91.

knowledge, skills and provision within the NHS.[93] It also took the opportunity to confirm its belief that the existing regulatory framework, composed in the main by these bodies, is a 'robust and proportionate regulatory framework around genetics and health'.[94]

7.47   Each of the existing bodies has produced guidelines which show great sensitivity in respect of genetic information. In particular, the ACGT strongly recommended that no pre-symptomatic testing for late onset disorders for which there are no clinical treatments should be carried out on minors under 16,[95] and this has been endorsed by the Human Genetics Commission.[96]

7.48   No specific legislation to regulate the control and use of genetic information has been introduced in the United Kingdom to date. The HGC has, however, recommended a number of specific reforms, including (i) the creation of a criminal offence of the non-consensual or deceitful obtaining and/or analysis of personal genetic information for non-medical purposes (a version of which now appears as s 45 of the Human Tissue Act 2004), (ii) the possible introduction of exemption from the notification requirements of data protection laws for clinicians who hold information about genetic relatives, (iii) stringent controls of the uses of data in genetic databases, and (iv) new legislation to address genetic discrimination. We consider aspects of these recommendations below.

OTHER PARTIES' INTERESTS IN GENETIC INFORMATION

7.49   A number of parties outside the family context profess an interest in access to genetic information. These include insurers, current and prospective employers, researchers, and the state itself. In this section, the nature of the interests at stake is considered and their respective weights in light of the interests of the proband and his relatives are assessed.[97] The important issue of protection against genetic discrimination is also addressed.

---

[93] Department of Health *Our Inheritance, Our Future: Realising the Potential of Genetics in the NHS* (Cm 5791-II, 2003).

[94] *Ibid*, para 6.54. The work of these bodies will soon have to dove-tail with that of the Human Tissue Authority (HTA), established by the Human Tissue Act 2004. In due course the HTA itself will be subsumed under the work of a new body—the Regulatory Authority for Fertility and Tissue (RAFT)—which will bring the work of HTA together with that of the Human Fertilisation and Embryology Authority. See Department of Health 'Reconfiguring the Department of Health's Arm's Length Bodies' (2004).

[95] HGC *Inside Information*, n 43 above, para 4.37.

[96] *Ibid*, para 7.6.

[97] See generally, B Godard et al 'Genetic Information and Testing in Insurance and Employment: Technical, Social and Ethical Issues' (2003) 11 Supp 2 Euro J Hum Gen S123.

INSURANCE

7.50 The forms of insurance most relevant to genetic testing are life and health insurance. Private health insurance is currently less important in the United Kingdom than in other jurisdictions because of the existence of the National Health Service. Life insurance, however, is a prerequisite for certain types of loan, including, in most cases, mortgages for the purchase of property. Most individuals also take out life insurance to protect their families in the event of their own premature death and, as we face the growing needs of an increasingly aged population, long-term care insurance is becoming a necessity. Insurance thus touches the lives of most of us and its denial can have far-reaching consequences for both individuals and families.[98]

7.51 Genetic information is clearly important to the insurance industry in order to assess the risk of providing cover at all and to determine the level of premiums if an offer of insurance is made. The nature of the interest at stake is entirely financial, and it is one that the industry may legitimately seek to protect. An insurance contract is an example of a contract *uberrima fides*: of the utmost good faith. In practice, this means that any information having a bearing on the assessment of risk should be disclosed to the insurer; otherwise, the contract can be avoided at any future time. Two possible avenues are open to the insurer in the context of genetic information. First, a request can be made that all test results be disclosed. Second, the insurer can require that the prospective insured undergo genetic testing. In respect of the first of these, it might be argued that this is no different from any other form of medical history. A genetic test result should be disclosed in the same way as one would disclose the removal of a melanoma or a family history of high blood pressure. That having been said, a concern has been expressed in many quarters that individuals might be deterred from seeking testing if it were to be the case that all test results should be disclosed. As the Science and Technology Committee commented:

We accept that the insurance industry has collectively tried to deal with genetics in a responsible way; nonetheless we are concerned there is a real danger that people could decide to decline testing, even when such testing would be advantageous to them, because of the possible insurance implications.[99]

7.52 This has been borne out by a MORI poll on public attitudes to human genetic information published in March 2001 which showed that the use of genetic information to set insurance premiums was thought to be the least appropriate of the possible uses of that information. Four out of five respondents said it should not be used for that purpose.[100]

7.53 As to insurers actively requiring prospective customers to be tested, there is a fear that the increased availability of tests will lead to the 'development and proliferation

---

[98] For an account of the respective approaches in the US and the UK, see O O'Neill 'Insurance and Genetics: The Current State of Play' (1998) 61 MLR 716.

[99] Third Report, para 7.9 above, para 242.

[100] HGC *Public Attitudes*, para 7.28, n 45 above, para 33.

of predictive genetic testing'.[101] This is to be deprecated because of the serious implications which it has for the (spatial) privacy interests of individuals required to be tested. An unacceptable degree of coercion is brought to bear in such circumstances which might vitiate any 'consent' to undergo testing.

7.54   The Council of Europe has issued a recommendation on the protection of medical data which are processed automatically;[102] genetic data are specifically included. The Council recommends that member states take steps to ensure that their laws and practices reflect certain key principles embodied in the recommendation. These provide, among other things, that medical data should, in principle, be collected only by health care professionals or their assistants and, in the context of genetic information, this should only be for preventive treatment, diagnosis or treatment of the data subject or for scientific research, judicial procedure or criminal investigation. The collection and processing of genetic data outside these categories should be permitted only for health reasons; it could be allowed in order to predict ill health, but only in the case of an overriding interest and subject to appropriate safeguards defined by law. The drafters of the recommendation make it clear in the explanatory memorandum that:

> a candidate for employment, an insurance contract or other services or activities should not be forced to undergo a genetic analysis, by making employment or the insurance dependent on such an analysis, unless such dependence is explicitly provided for by the law and the analysis is necessary for the protection of the data subject or a third party.[103]

7.55   The Nuffield Council on Bioethics has opined that those individuals with a known family history who decide to take a test and test positive should not be treated by the insurance company any differently from other family members—that is, they should still be assessed at the same level of risk as those family members who have not been tested[104]—it was reasoned that, since the industry tends to interpret family history cautiously,[105] 'there is unlikely to be a major difference in insurability between an individual with a family history of a genetic disorder and an individual who has had a positive genetic test result'. By corollary, the Council envisages that those who test negative should benefit from this result and be treated as persons with no family history. In this way the Council hopes that individuals will not be deterred from having genetic tests and also that insurers will not be adversely affected, since they can

---

[101] R Chadwick and C Ngwena 'The Human Genome Project, Predictive Testing and Insurance Contracts: Ethical and Legal Responses' (1995) 1 Res Publica 115.

[102] Council of Europe *The Protection of Medical Data*, Recommendation No (97) 5 and explanatory memorandum, 13 February 1997.

[103] *Ibid*, para 103.

[104] Nuffield Council on Bioethics *Genetic Screening: Ethical Issues* (1993) para 7.28.

[105] E.g. the Council notes that (para 7.23): 'Tables used by the insurance industry show that insurers treat 5% risk of developing Huntington's disease in the same way as a 50% risk: such individuals may be declined insurance or offered insurance at an increased premium, depending on their age at the time of application. Insurance prospects for individuals with a family history of Huntington's disease only improve when the risk is below 5%.'

continue their present practice based on family history. However, the recommendations of the Council are somewhat different in respect of population screening programmes. In such cases the majority of those taking part would not be aware of any family history of disease. The Council considers that:

[i]f insurers were to demand access to the results of population screening for polygenic or multifactorial disease (for example, for genetic predisposition to breast cancer), and premiums were increased for those who tested positive, many people would clearly be discouraged from participating in such programmes. This could have adverse consequences both for the health of individuals and for the public health,[106]

and it concludes that it is not acceptable for insurers to have access to genetic test results which arise from such programmes. Furthermore, because of the principle of free and informed consent (discussed in chapter 10), genetic testing should not be made a prerequisite for obtaining insurance. Thus, it can be seen that the Council is emphatic that genetic testing solely for the purposes of assessing insurance risk is unacceptable—and this is true both for those who have a family history and for those who do not.

7.56   In the absence of clear government guidelines or legislative intervention, the Association of British Insurers (ABI), whose representatives account for 95 per cent of insurance business in the United Kingdom, affirmed in 1997 and 1999 that insurers would not require a genetic test as a prerequisite for insurance cover.[107] A 2004 compliance report from the Association showed that member companies had been 100 per cent compliant with the Code of Practice during 2002.[108] Moreover, the Association agreed in 2001 to extend the self-imposed moratorium for a period of five years (until November 2006), and it instructed its members not to ask for any genetic test results from applicants for any insurance policies up to £500,000 for life insurance or £300,000 for other forms of insurance. Above that level, only tests approved by the Genetics and Insurance Committee (GAIC) will be taken into account.[109] This body was established by the Government in 1999 to discharge the task of approving access to certain genetic test results that are thought to have a clear actuarial significance. So far, only the test for Huntington's Disease has been approved in the context of life insurance.[110] But the House of Commons Select Committee on Science and Technology made a series of stringent recommendations in its Fifth Report in April

---

[106] *Ibid*, para 7.31.

[107] ABI Genetic Testing: Code of Practice (1999). See also, Joint Guidelines from the British Medical Association and the Association of British Insurers *Medical Information and Insurance* (2002).

[108] ABI *ABI Code of Practice on Genetic Testing: Compliance Report and Data Analysis for 2002* (2004). This is to be lauded as far as it goes, but it is important to remember that these data were generated by a questionnaire returned by members. 61 returns were received covering 99 members; the voluntary nature of the exercise raises the likelihood that non-compliant members will also be those who do not respond.

[109] HGC *Inside Information*, n 43 above, para 7.7.

[110] Department of Health, 'Committee Announces Decision on Use of Genetic Test Results for Huntington's Disease by Insurers' (13 October 2000). For an account of the work of the Committee and its remit, see Genetics and Insurance Committee, *Second Report: September 2002—December 2003* (2004).

2001,[111] including reform of the membership of GAIC and a call for the reformed body to re-examine its approval of the use of Huntington's disease test results. GAIC was reconstituted in September 2002 and spent much of its initial time reconsidering the work of its former self. The Huntington's disease decision none the less stands. Seventeen other applications for approval of use of test results are pending.[112] GAIC has now also assumed a monitoring compliance role in respect of the insurance industry's conduct and a responsibility to consider complaints from the public.

7.57   Most recently, in March 2005, the Secretary of State for Health announced an agreement with the ABI to extend the current moratorium until November 2011.[113] The terms are essentially those outlined above, and the Concordat notes that only 3 per cent of policies issued in 2004 fell within the financial limits that can trigger access to genetic data.[114] Two further encouraging features of the instrument are worthy of note: first, it confirms that genetic tests taken for research purposes need not be disclosed (which is strongly in the public interest), and second, the industry itself has committed to more transparency for customers in respect of what is done with their data and how actuarial decisions are taken. Not all parties are happy with this latest development, however. GeneWatch UK issued a swift response condemning the mere extension of the moratorium period which, it claimed, still leaves people with uncertainty about their possible future insurance cover. The organisation argues that anything short of new legislation prohibiting access to *all* genetic data—in both the insurance and employment contexts—is inadequate.[115]

7.58   This argument has been made by others. For example, Harper has argued that insurers should not be allowed to require disclosure of genetic test results within the ordinary run of life insurance policies.[116] But, even so, the problem remains of deciding whether a family history—as a form of genetic information—should also be excluded in such circumstances. The HGC has expressed reservations on this matter, and has called for further research.[117] Whether it is right that the increased costs of such a scheme should be passed on to the 'normal' population is probably a matter for Parliament to decide; ultimately, we cannot escape the fact that insurance, like most social constructs, is a cultural phenomenon. The task, then, is to match the most appropriate legal response to the way in which we wish insurance to operate within our culture. An approach that is biased towards solidarity might be an acceptable

---

[111] House of Commons Science and Technology Committee Fifth Report, *Genetics and Insurance* (2001 HC 174). See too, Government response to the report from the House of Commons Science and Technology Select Committee: Genetics and Insurance Cm 5286 (2001).

[112] These relate to Huntington's disease, early-onset Alzheimer's disease, and hereditary breast and ovarian cancer. The applications cover insurance in the fields of life, critical illness, income protection and long-term care.

[113] Department of Health Press Release, March 2005, Ref: 2005/0112: HM Government and ABI *Concordat and Moratorium on Genetics and Insurance* (2005). The Concordat is to be reviewed in 2008.

[114] *Ibid*, p 4.

[115] www.genewatch.org.

[116] P S Harper 'Insurance and Genetic Testing' (1993) 341 Lancet 224. See, now, P Harper et al 'Genetic Testing and Huntington's Disease: Issues of Employment' (2004) 3 Lancet Neurol 249.

[117] HGC *Inside Information*, n 43 above, paras 7.16–7.18.

price to pay for a gesture of support for those who, through no fault of their own, are likely to find themselves increasingly disadvantaged.[118]

EMPLOYMENT

7.59   An employer might have two contrasting reasons for seeking access to genetic information about his employees or future employees. First, there is a financial interest in not employing persons who are likely to become debilitated through disease and so affect profits through days lost. Second, he might have a genuine concern that the working environment could affect an employee's health adversely, perhaps by exacerbating an existing condition or by provoking symptoms in an otherwise asymptomatic individual.[119] This concern might relate to the person's health *in se*, and/or to the fear that compensation could be sought by an individual so affected. The propriety of permitting an employer or prospective employer access to genetic information must be addressed in each case. As with the insurance industry, access could be granted either to existing test results or a genetic test could be made a condition of the employment contract. Moreover, a request for genetic information could be made either pre- or post-employment.

7.60   Pre-employment requests for genetic information are the most effective means of reducing costs for the employer. Little expenditure is incurred in obtaining the information; the prospective employee is asked either to reveal existing knowledge or to take a relatively inexpensive test. No future expenditure need be incurred because the employer has no obligation to do so in the absence of an employment contract.

7.61   An employer who seeks genetic information from a current employee is in a very different position. Time and money may have been spent training someone who now cannot do the job, and termination of the employment contract is subject to strict requirements. All of which means that it is very much in the employer's financial interests to seek genetic information from *potential* rather than from *actual* employees. And one might argue that *future* employees can (and should) be excluded from employment if information reveals either the actual presence of, or a predisposition to, genetic disease such as is likely to pose a risk to themselves and/or others if they are employed.

7.62   This advantage of pre-employment screening was considered further by the Nuffield Council on Bioethics, which stated:

Employees would, in principle, be empowered to avoid occupations which would increase the risk of ill health and which in the long run might be life threatening. In this way they could protect the economic security of themselves and their families.[120]

---

[118] There are two basic models of insurance: mutuality and solidarity. The former provides that the contribution of individuals should approximately reflect their level of risk. The principle of solidarity, however, requires that the burden of bearing risks is spread throughout the general body of insured persons.

[119] E.g. an environment which is dense with heavy particles is very bad for individuals suffering from or prone to alpha 1-antitrypsin deficiency because this can lead to emphysema.

[120] See para 7.10 n 8, para 6.6.

7.63   A major difficulty with such an otherwise admirable approach lies in the fact that the predictive accuracy of genetic predictive information is far from assured, and the very factors which concern employers—such as the likely date of onset and degree of affliction—are unlikely to be known. Also, the sensitivity of such information and the apparent public misunderstanding which surrounds genetic information provoke the very legitimate fear that the information could be used to exclude individuals from employment, or to terminate employment, even when they are not affected by disease and are unlikely to be so for some time. The question thus arises as to whether access to genetic information is an acceptable way by which to ensure the interests of employers and of employees or job applicants.[121]

7.64   A number of bodies have recognised and appreciated the privacy implications of employer requests for genetic information.[122] Relying heavily on recommendations of the Nuffield Council, the Science and Technology Committee itself recommended that legislation to protect the privacy of genetic information be introduced and be drafted so as to prohibit employers testing for genetic conditions other than those which might put the public at direct and substantial risk. Furthermore, any genetic testing for employment purposes should be strictly limited to specific conditions relevant to the particular employment and samples provided for testing should not be examined for evidence of other conditions.[123] The European Group on Ethics has recently opined that only the present health status of employees should be considered in the employment context.[124]

7.65   The clear message here is that employers' access to genetic information must be justified on the grounds that the knowledge can have a direct bearing on the job of work to be done. In other words, it is unacceptable for an employer to seek access to another individual's genetic information simply to further his financial interests. This is especially true when that access is sought in order to identify some *future* risk when that possibility does not affect the individual's current ability to perform his or her work.

7.66   What, however, of the argument that genetic information should be revealed in order to protect the interests of employees and job applicants themselves? The Science and Technology Committee concluded that:

---

[121] It should be noted, however, that the Human Genetics Commission found no evidence that there is any systematic use of predictive genetic information in employment in the UK, see HGC *Inside Information*, n 43 above, para 8.9.

[122] See Nuffield Council on Bioethics, para 7.10 above, paras 6.20–6.23, the House of Commons Science and Technology Committee (1995), para 7.9 above, paras 231–233, and the Human Genetics Advisory Commission *The Implications of Genetic Testing for Employment* (1999).

[123] Science and Technology Committee Report quoting Memorandum (vol II) p 52.

[124] European Group on Ethics *Opinion No.18: Ethical Aspects of Genetic Testing in the Workplace* (2003). For comment see N A Holtzman 'Ethical Aspects of Genetic Testing in the Workplace' (2003) 6 Community Genetics 136.

Genetic Screening for employment purposes should be contemplated only where:

(i) there is strong evidence of a clear connection between the working environment and the development of the condition for which the screening is conducted;

(ii) the condition in question is one which seriously endangers the health of the employee; and

(iii) the condition is one for which the dangers cannot be eliminated or significantly reduced by reasonable measures taken by the employer to modify or respond to the environmental risks.[125]

Importantly, the Committee stresses that 'employees should have the right to decide whether or not to participate in such screening'. It is unclear, however, whether the recommendations are intended to extend both to current employees and job applicants. No convincing argument could be put that this should not be the case, but the Committee only mentions 'employees'. The HGC broadly agrees with this, but emphasises that employers must not demand that an individual take a genetic test as a condition of employment. There must be compelling medical or safety grounds for offering a genetic test in any other circumstances.[126] As regards future uses of personal genetic information, the HGC has recommended a voluntary undertaking by employers to inform HGC of any proposals to use genetic testing for health and safety or recruitment purposes and, also, the establishment of a joint committee to monitor developments in genetic testing in this field. All of this is reflected at the European level in the Opinion of the European Group on Ethics, viz: when, in exceptional circumstances, genetic screening is thought to be necessary to guarantee worker health, this is only acceptable if the following conditions are fulfilled:

(a) the performance of the test is necessary for guaranteeing the protection of the employee's health and safety or those of third parties,

(b) there is scientifically-proven evidence that the genetic test is valid and is the only method to obtain this information,

(c) the performance of the test does not prejudice the aim of improving conditions in the workplace,

(d) the principle of proportionality is respected regarding the motivations involved to perform the test, and

(e) the principle of non-discrimination is not violated.[127]

7.67 In contrast, the position in the United States seems to give rise to more concern. One study of 1,500 genetic counsellors and physicians found that 785 patients had

---

[125] See para 7.9 at 233. For a criticism of the Nuffield Council's recommendations, and by implications those of the Science and Technology Committee, see M A Rothstein 'Genetic Discrimination in Employment: Ethics, Policy and Comparative Law' in O Guillod and P Widmer (eds) *Human Genetic Analysis and the Protection of Personality and Privacy* (1994).

[126] HGC *Inside Information*, n 43 above, generally chapter 8. Further policy guidance is offered by the Recruitment Society *Proposal for a Code of Practice for Genetic Testing for Employers* (2000).

[127] Para 7.64 above, paras 2.11–2.12

reported having lost their jobs or insurance because of adverse reactions to genetic knowledge about them.[128] In February 2000, President Clinton signed an Executive Order which prohibits federal government agencies from obtaining genetic information from employees or job applicants and from using genetic information in hiring or promotion decisions.[129] The European Group on Ethics has pointed out that there has been far more interest in genetic testing in the employment context in the USA compared to Europe because in the former employers often contribute to health insurance as part of the employee's contractual entitlements;[130] but it also warned that US models for health insurance might start to apply in Europe.[131] At present, there is only one example that can be found of genetic screening in the workplace in Europe and this is the screening of British aircrew for the sickle cell gene (which might give rise to susceptibility to low oxygen levels at altitude). But even this was eventually abandoned. None the less interest in genetic testing remains high. A survey by the Institute of Directors in 2000 showed that 50 per cent of directors approved of genetic testing of employees with consent, while 16 per cent felt that this should be compulsory.[132] Vigilance must therefore remain the watchword.

DISCRIMINATION

7.68   Perhaps the single most important concern related to genetic information lies in the potential for discrimination that it generates.[133] This is relevant to both the employment and insurance scenarios, yet no specific legal regulation currently exists in the United Kingdom to control genetic testing or screening or the uses to which the results can be put.[134] The matter of discrimination must, therefore, be dealt with under the current anti-discrimination laws. More focused efforts have occurred in the United States, however, where, after many years of negotiation, the US Senate passed the Genetic Information Non-Discrimination Act 2003 which extended its provisions to both the insurance and employment settings.[135] The House of Representatives did not, however, act on the Bill in the 108th Congress and a new

---

[128] D Martindale 'Pink Slip in Your Genes: Evidence Builds that Employers Hire and Fire Based on Genetic Tests' (2001) January Scientific American 19.

[129] The Executive Order to Prohibit Discrimination in Federal Employment Based on Genetic Information (2000).

[130] Para 7.63, para 1.6.

[131] It has been reported recently that the German Government has drafted legislation that will permit employers to require that employees undergo genetic tests if their constitution might adversely affect their ability to do their job, see Public Health Genetics Unit, Newsletter (October 2004), available at: www.phgu.org.uk.

[132] N 124, para 1.6.1.

[133] A failed Discrimination (Genetic Information) Bill was sponsored by Anne Campbell MP in the parliamentary session 1994/95. For discussion of regulation generally, see J Black 'Regulation as Facilitation: Negotiating the Genetic Revolution' (1998) 61 MLR 621.

[134] The HGC has, nevertheless, recommended specific legislation and the government has agreed to investigate the possibilities, see para 7.76 below.

[135] S 1053, 108th Congress, 2003.

version was considered by Senate in February 2005 as the Genetic Information Non-Discrimination Act of 2005.[136] The only difference from the earlier instrument is the deletion of one tax-related provision. If passed, this would be the first federal legislation in the field, which would give comprehensive protection to US citizens beyond the state-level action which had already occurred in 40 states as of January 2005.[137] The Act would also require the establishment of a Genetic Nondiscrimination Study Commission to advise on scientific developments and possible policy responses.

7.69   Anti-discrimination law in the United Kingdom is governed by three pieces of legislation: the Sex Discrimination Act 1975, the Race Relations Act 1976 and the Disability Discrimination Act 1995. The protection afforded against discrimination by the 1975 and 1976 Acts is restricted to their precise remits—that is, sexual or racial discrimination. Since many genetic conditions are sex-linked or affect particular ethnic and racial groups, differential treatment of afflicted individuals could amount to discrimination within the terms of these Acts, probably as examples of indirect discrimination. It is not clear, however, how successful such arguments would be, there being no cases on point. More opportunities for redress lie with the Disability Discrimination Act 1995, which is the first piece of United Kingdom legislation to deal directly with discrimination against disabled people. The Act outlaws discrimination in a wide range of fields—such as employment, the provision of goods, facilities and services, the sale and let of property, education and public transport.

7.70   The Act defines 'disability' and 'disabled persons' in Pt I as follows:

1(1) Subject to the provisions of Schedule 1, a person has a disability for the purposes of this Act if he has a physical or mental impairment which has a substantial and long-term adverse effect on his ability to carry out normal day-to-day activities.
1(2) In this Act 'disabled person' means a person who has a disability.

7.71   In the context of employment, the provisions of the Act ensure that it is unlawful for an employer to treat an individual less favourably than he would treat others for a reason which relates to the individual's disability and when he cannot show that the treatment in question is justified. Discrimination can occur, inter alia, in respect of: (a) the arrangements which an employer makes for the purpose of determining to whom he should offer employment; (b) in the terms in which he offers employment; (c) his refusal to offer, or deliberate not offering of, employment; (d) his refusal to afford an employee opportunities for promotion, a transfer, training or receiving any other benefit, or his treating the employee differently in such opportunities; (e) his dismissal of an employee, or subjecting the employee to any other detriment.

7.72   These provisions could clearly go a long way to preventing discrimination against individuals based on information about their genetic constitution—note, particularly, how pre-employment discrimination is also outlawed. However, the question arises of whether the provisions of the Act extend to persons whose genome contains defective

---

[136] S 306, 110th Congress, 2005.
[137] See National Human Genome Research Institute: www.genome.gov/11510227.

genes which do, or can have, a bearing on their ability to do their job. The crucial term here is '*can have*'. Clearly, persons who are already affected by a genetic condition come within the definition of 'disabled person'. But what of a person who merely has a predisposition to ill health? A literal interpretation of s 1(1) excludes such a person for it speaks of one who '*has* a physical or mental impairment'. The section must, however, be read in conjunction with Schs 1 and 2, which allow for regulations to be made which will clarify the definitions in s 1. In particular, Sch 1, para 8 concerns 'progressive conditions'. The examples given of such conditions are cancer, multiple sclerosis, muscular dystrophy or infection with the human immunodeficiency virus. The paragraph provides that someone who suffers from such a progressive condition will be treated as 'disabled' provided that their condition results in an impairment which, at least, has (or had) an effect on their ability to carry out normal day-to-day activities, even if that effect is not a substantial adverse effect. Even so, the individual must still be in some way symptomatic, thus excluding those who have 'merely' a predisposition to disease at the relevant time. This means, by inference, that discrimination against persons in this last category is not unlawful under the Act. This disparity and the question of genetic testing were raised in the parliamentary debates but the minister in charge stated:

. . . except in a few well-publicised cases, genetic tests are not as yet a useful indicator of future actual disability. Their inclusion would open up the [Act] to large numbers of people who are clearly not, and may never become disabled . . . we cannot wander into a situation whereby, for some reason or another, potentially the entire population could claim protection under the [Act].[138]

7.73   It is certainly true that genetic tests are by no means accurate at present, but that does not mean that such tests cannot be misused by employers and others, nor that they will not be used to exclude people from jobs and other services for irrelevant and irrational reasons. Legislation designed to outlaw discrimination on the grounds of disability should cover *all* forms of discrimination, whether the disability is actual or perceived, current or future. It is arguable that the provisions of the Act as they currently stand are inadequate and are potentially prejudicial to persons likely to develop genetic conditions later in life. Moreover, matters would be scarcely improved under the proposed Equality Act, which at the time of writing had successfully passed through the House of Lords and was awaiting attention from the House of Commons (introduced 2nd March 2005).[139] Here 'disabled person' is defined as '. . . a person who is a disabled person within the meaning of the . . . 1995 Act, or *has been a disabled person* within that meaning . . .'[140] This extends the definition but still fails to address our concerns as expressed above. Notwithstanding, the Secretary of State might, with

---

138 Official Reports, HC, vol 257, col 887, 28 March 1995.

139 For more on the Equality Bill and its progress see: www.odysseustrust.org/equality.html.

140 Equality Bill 2003, cl 10(2). Note, too, that this Act would go far beyond the current legislation, outlawing discrimination on the grounds of age, gender reassignment, religion or belief or sexual orientation, as well as the current grounds of sex, race or disability.

advantage, use the powers given under the Acts to expand the definition of disability to cover the specific circumstances of asymptomatic genetic conditions.

7.74   The British position is to be contrasted with that in Australia. The Disability Discrimination Act 1992 covers disability which an individual (a) has now, (b) has had in the past (e.g. mental illness), (c) may have in the future, and (d) has imputed to her. This is eminently sensible since discriminatory practice do not need a founding in fact to exist; indeed, differential treatment founded on a factual basis might even be justified in certain circumstances. Prejudice is another matter. Moreover, these provisions were considered by the Australian Law Reform Commission to be adequate and adaptable to the genetic context; it did not, therefore, recommend the adoption of specific legislation to cover genetics.[141]

7.75   The anomalies in the current UK provisions were summed up by Baroness Jay in the House of Lords:

The paradox which is possible in the present situation is that where genetic counselling, genetic testing and identifying genetic markers is potentially one of the most exciting and liberating developments in medical science at the end of the 20th century, if it becomes the case that people feel that identifying those markers in their own personal situation will lead to discrimination, they will be less likely to take advantage of those extraordinary scientific advances which may help their own condition and in which medical science may be able to help future generations of children.[142]

7.76   While recognising the validity of arguments concerning adverse treatment of asymptomatic persons, the Human Genetics Commission has recommended separate legislation to address genetic discrimination, rather than wholesale reform of the Disability Discrimination Act (DDA).[143] It is stated that this is partly because reform of the DDA would require a significant alteration to the definition of 'disability', and because of the difficulty in defining those with a pre-symptomatic genetic condition. The Government accepted the Commission's recommendation to explore the need for such legislation in its 2003 White Paper,[144] and undertook to consider '. . . the appropriate means of addressing any concerns in this area'.[145] We question such attempts to make a 'special case' of genetics and draw attention to the recommendations of the Disability Rights Commission which, in its first review of the 1995 Act, has called for extension of the Act to those with a predisposition to genetic disease.[146] The obvious model here is the Australian experience—one which would in the end avoid the charge of genetic exceptionalism.

7.77   The fear that existing statutes will be interpreted to cover just such circumstances

---

[141] Australian Law Reform Commission *Essentially Yours* (2003), paras 9.49—9.55.

[142] Official Reports, HL, vol 564, col 1713, 13 June 1995.

[143] HGC *Inside Information*, n 43 above, paras 6.30–6.31.

[144] N 93 above, para 6.35.

[145] *Ibid*.

[146] Disability Rights Commission *Disability Equality: Making It Happen—First Review of the Disability Discrimination Act 1995* (2003), p 83. The Commission also recommended specific legislation to prohibit employers and insurers from viewing genetic data save in very restricted circumstances, *ibid*.

has led to out-of-court settlements in the United States in favour of employees. For example, the US Equal Employment Opportunity Commission (EEOC) settled its first court action in April 2001 in which it had challenged the conduct of an employer in using genetic information and requiring genetic testing of employees to handle claims for work-related injuries.[147] The Burlington Northern Santa Fe railway (BNSF) had implemented a programme of genetic testing of previously donated samples without the knowledge or consent of employees to investigate worker claims for injuries based on carpal tunnel syndrome. At least one worker had been threatened with termination of employment for refusing to submit to testing. The settlement ensures that the employer shall not directly or indirectly require its employees to submit blood for genetic tests, nor shall it analyse any blood previously obtained. The settlement was deemed to be enforceable by the relevant District Court, although the court in question was at pains to point out that it offered no ruling on the respective arguments of the parties under the Americans with Disabilities Act 1990.[148]

RESEARCH INVOLVING GENETIC MATERIAL

7.78   We lay our cards on the table at this point by admitting our full support for medical research that is ethically sound and subject to the rigorous checks and balances that we outline in chapter 18. To this extent, genetic research is no different from other forms of research in the health care sector although, once again, we find that perceptions do not always reflect this reality.[149] The Medical Research Council conducted a survey on public attitudes towards the collection of human biological samples in October 2000 which found disparate knowledge and understanding of the meaning and the goals of genetic research.[150] There was considerable evidence of negative associations with this type of work where understanding was lacking[151] and this was so despite the fact that most people continued to find general medical research to be worthy and worthwhile.[152] As the report states:

[u]nderlying these negative associations was a feeling that genetics research can make people feel vulnerable about themselves. It was believed to be about seeking to perfect the human body, for good or bad ends, and that it could induce concern about individuals' own imperfections . . . [a]longside this was a feeling expressed by a few that genetics research, if put to these sorts of uses, conflicts with the (beneficial) diversity of the human race. Though

---

[147] See also, the federal Health Insurance Portability and Accountability Act 1996 which has been interpreted as covering genetics in the workplace, see HGC *Inside Information*, N 43 above, para 6.36.

[148] United States Equal Employment Opportunity Commission, Press Release, 18 April 2001: www.eeoc.gov/press/4-18-01.html.

[149] For a discussion of trends in genetic research see B M Knoppers and R Chadwick 'Human Genetic Research: Emerging Trends in Ethics' (2005) 6 Nature Reviews Genetics 75.

[150] Medical Research Council *Public Perceptions of the Collection of Human Biological Samples* (2000).

[151] *Ibid*, para 2.2.   [152] *Ibid*, para 2.1.

it would be a good thing to attempt to eliminate genetically linked diseases and conditions, this is likely to go hand-in-hand with other developments that will make it possible to produce 'perfect' people.[153]

7.79 The Human Genetics Commission's People's Panel Quantitative Study of March 2001 revealed similar results.[154] Over one third of those surveyed considered genetics research to be 'tampering with nature' and so unethical. The response of the Human Genetics Commission, in turn, has been to recommend that all genetic research on human non-anonymised tissue samples or bodily material should be subject to independent research ethics review and that clear policies should be established by all research bodies for compliance with ethical review.[155] Whether such measures will succeed in engendering more public trust and confidence remains to be seen.[156] As O'Neill has stated: '... reported public trust in science and even in medicine has faltered *despite* successes, *despite* increased efforts to respect persons and their rights, *despite* stronger regulation to protect the environment and *despite* the fact that environmental concerns are taken far more seriously than they were a few years ago'.[157]

7.80 The balance of interests is nowhere more delicately struck than between the concern to protect individuals' rights and the public interest in furthering research.[158] Few would now deny that some compromises must be made with the former in order to accommodate the latter. Thus, for example, the HGC supports the view that it is acceptable to seek general consent to future research in cases where there will be anonymisation of data and samples involved in genetic research.[159] Repeated processes of re-consent may not only be impractical but also unnecessarily invasive. Some jurisdictions have gone further still. In Iceland, for example, the law establishing the Icelandic Health Sector Database—which is a project to create an electronic database containing anonymised details from the health records of the majority of the Icelandic people—provides only for an opt-out system,[160] that is, the legal presumption is that every citizen agrees to have his or her medical data entered onto the database unless he or she states otherwise. The justification for this is the need to obtain as much data as possible for sound epidemiological purposes.[161] However, the Icelandic

---

[153] *Ibid.*

[154] HGC *Public Attitudes*, pp 20–22. Compare A L Jack and C Womack 'Why Surgical Patients Do Not Donate Tissue for Commercial Research: Review of Records' (2003) BMJ 262.

[155] HGC *Inside Information*, paras 5.33 and 5.37.

[156] Laurie (2002), n 1 above, pp 166–67 and pp 296–98.

[157] O O'Neill Autonomy and Trust in Bioethics (2002), p 11.

[158] See generally R Tutton and O Corrigan *Genetic Databases: Socio-ethical Issues in the Collection and use of DNA* (2004). Also, sometimes there can be a very fine line between research and treatment, see M Parker et al 'Ethical Review of Research into Rare Genetic Disorders' (2004) 329 BMJ 288.

[159] HGC *Inside Information*, n 43 above, paras 5.18–5.19.

[160] Act on a Health Sector Database No 139/1998. For a history and review of the system see H Rose *The Commodification of Bioinformation: The Icelandic Health Sector Database* (2001).

[161] See H Roscam Abbing 'Central Health Database in Iceland and Patients' Rights' (1999) 6 Euro J Hlth Law 363. For a discussion of the Iceland experience and similar measures in Estonia, see Laurie (2002), n 1 above, pp 287–293.

government has been strongly criticised for failing to pay sufficient respect to its citizens and their rights by not actively seeking informed consent.[162] Indeed, most recently, the Supreme Court of Iceland has declared the enabling legislation to be unconstitutional for its failure to establish an adequate framework to protect citizens' rights, most particularly those relating to privacy.[163]

7.81   No such research proposal has been advanced in the United Kingdom, although UK Biobank[164] raises similar issues.[165] This is an ambitious long-term longitudinal study which will follow 500,000 subjects aged between 40 and 69 through various periods of good and ill health, examining genotypic and phenotypic data together with environmental factors to establish the relationships between diseases and genes and the interaction between genes and environment. The funders have been extremely sensitive to the delicacy of the issues from the very beginning and have been determined to get the legal and ethical framework 'right' for the project. Thus, in tandem with the development of the scientific protocol, an interim group of advisers worked to create a viable Ethics and Governance Framework to address the various strands of the project; from the role of patient consent to questions of feedback of results; from confidentiality concerns to commericalisation policies. A particular challenge for the group was to operate with ever-moving scientific goalposts, but the project is now at the stage of initiating Phase I Pilot Studies and a permanent Ethics and Governance Council has been established. This will act as an 'ethical mirror' to the funders and researchers involved in the project. It remains to be seen, however, whether all of these efforts will make UK Biobank and its personnel any more trustworthy to the British public.[166]

THE STATE INTEREST IN GENETIC INFORMATION

7.82   The above sections have identified many varied interests in genetic information which are held by both individuals and institutions. Two particular state concerns arise from these interests: an inclination to reduce the financial burden wherever possible and a desire to minimise or eliminate harm to its citizens. The state has a role in protecting and advancing 'the public good'—that is, the collective interests of society as a whole.

---

[162] For a comparison of the UK proposal with the Icelandic experience, see J Kaye and P Martin 'Safeguards for Research Using Large Scale DNA Collections' (2000) 321 BMJ 1146.

[163] For comment see R Gertz 'An Analysis of the Icelandic Supreme Court Judgement on the Health Sector Database Act' (2004) 1:2 SCRIPTed 290, available at: www.script-ed.org.

[164] This is a joint venture between the Wellcome Trust, the Medical Research Council and the Department of Health, see: www.ukbiobank.ac.uk.

[165] See also M A Austin, S Harding and C McElroy 'Genebanks: A Comparison of Eight Proposed International Genetic Databases' (2003) 6 Community Genetics 37.

[166] For a similar project in Scotland (but one which focuses on families and includes people of all ages) see Generation Scotland: www.generationscotland.org. For an account of the related legal and ethical issues, see G Laurie and J Gibson Generation Scotland: Legal and Ethical Aspects (2003), available at: www.law.ed.ac.uk/ahrb/publications.

To what extent, then, can the state legitimately request results of genetic tests or require genetic testing?[167]

7.83 One of the most obvious state interests in the health care setting is that of securing public health and, perhaps unsurprisingly, it has been argued that mandatory testing for genetic disorders might halt the spread of genetic disease.[168] Even if little or nothing can be done for those already afflicted, disclosure might prevent the transmission of defective genes to future persons. Set against this, however, is the potential infringement of privacy interests which such practices can represent. We have touched on this above at paras 7.34 et seq indicating that various eminent bodies have concluded that patient autonomy and the right to choose should be the overriding consideration. But, in this connection, can it then be argued that the state has a positive interest in *facilitating* individual choice? Certainly, it can adopt a more pastoral role towards individuals by providing them with information which may help them make important life decisions such as whether or not to have a child if both partners are carriers of cystic fibrosis. Not only does this make individuals more independent as moral choosers but it might also have the desired social end of curtailing the further spread of genetic disease.[169] For example, Ball et al have noted that this view is held by the Royal College of Physicians:

[the] Royal College of Physicians report suggests that as long as individuals have the right to decide for themselves whether to bear children it could be argued that such individuals should have access to the fullest possible information, including genetic, pertinent to that decision and therefore this should not be withheld.[170]

7.84 This implies that the state should seek to further its interest in facilitating choice by providing comprehensive screening programmes, a plethora of genetic tests accompanied by suitable counselling services and other support mechanisms, such as easy access to abortion. Cost implications aside, this would certainly further both individual and state interests by making free choice a market commodity. The risk of a

[167] The contrast between permissive and restrictive legislation is highlighted in B M Knoppers and R M Isasi 'Regulatory Approaches to Reproductive Genetic Testing' (2004) 19 Human Repro 2695.

[168] See S M Suter 'Whose Genes Are These Anyway?: Familial Conflicts Over Access to Genetic Information' (1993) 91 Michigan L Rev 1854 at 1897, citing H P Green and A M Capron 'Issues of Law and Public Policy in Genetic Screening' in D Bergsma (ed) *Ethical, Social and Legal Dimensions of Screening for Human Genetic Disease* (1974). See also M Shaw 'Conditional Prospective Rights of the Fetus' (1984) 5 J Leg Med 63, in which it is argued that prospective parents should face mandatory screening for certain conditions.

[169] For sound policy recommendations, see European Society of Human Genetics 'Populations Genetic Screening Programmes: Technical, Social and Ethical Issues: Recommendations of the European Society of Human Genetics' (2003) 11 Supp.2 Euro J Hum Gen S5.

[170] D Ball et al 'Predictive Testing of Adults and Children' in A Clarke (ed) *Genetic Counselling: Practice and Principles* (1994) at 77 referring to the Royal College of Physicians of London *Ethical Issues in Clinical Genetics: A Report of the Working Group of the Royal College of Physicians' Committees on Ethical Issues in Medicine and Clinical Genetics* (1991).

conflict of interests would be almost entirely eliminated if such programmes were provided free of any coercive measures.[171]

7.85   The moral basis for introducing population genetic screening programmes has been questioned when no appropriate medical intervention is possible in light of a positive result.[172] No such programmes exist in the United Kingdom for adults and the only routine screening of children relates to neonates in respect of phenyl-ketonuria, haemoglobin disorders and hypothyroidism.[173] The availability of a pleth-ora of tests for prenatal or pre-implantation genetic diagnosis has been noted above. While this can facilitate parental choices as to the continuance of a pregnancy, it still raises concern that such testing is open to abuse if parents are in any way pressurised to test for a range of conditions and to abort any affected fetuses.[174] Indeed, one has to ask whether the goal of free patient choice is possible, given the fact that, once genetic counselling has been offered and accepted, a likely chain of events has already been set up in the minds of all those involved.[175] Clarke also asks whether the objective is, itself, morally defensible—or have we, for fear of being labelled eugenists, 'fled so far from medical paternalism that we deny ethical responsibility for our professional activities'? Moreover, the whole concept of genetic counselling can be questioned, in so far as it increasingly involves the systematic selection of fetuses and, hence, approaches children as consumer objects subject to quality control.[176]

7.86   The increasing 'need' for genetic counselling can be seen as being based on the increasing number of disorders which can be diagnosed and, as Lippman has said, before long, the definition of fetal imperfection will come to mean any condition which can be diagnosed in utero. The social and economic pressures on a woman to terminate a pregnancy once an abnormality is discovered in her fetus may be such that her autonomous choice is severely prejudiced. These pressures would escalate

---

[171] However, as the Nuffield Council has pointed out (para 7.10 above at 8.11): '[i]t has been argued that the availability of prenatal screening and diagnosis, together with the termination of seriously affected pregnancies, both reflect and reinforce the negative attitudes of our society towards those with disabilities. Indeed medical genetics may add a new dimension if genetic disorder came to be seen as a matter of choice rather than fate.' See, inter alia, Advisory Committee on Genetic Testing (para 7.32 above) Annex A and the Science and Technology Committee Third Report (para 7.9 above) para 83.

[172] Nuffield Council on Bioethics (para 7.10 above) at 27. Screening for cystic fibrosis has been introduced more recently in some areas.

[173] Cf, the US Advisory Committee on Heritable Disorders and Genetic Diseases in Newborns and Children has recently recommended that all 50 states embark on a programme of extended genetic screening of children for at least 30 conditions: see C Simon Silver 'Panel Urges States to Screen Newborns for 30 Disorders' (2004) Genome News Network, available at www.genomenewsnetwork.org.

[174] J M Green et al 'Psychological Aspects of Genetic Screening of Pregnant Women and Newborns: A Systematic Review' (2004) 8 Health Technol Asess 1.

[175] See, particularly, A Clarke 'Is Non-directive Genetic Counselling Possible?' (1991) 338 Lancet 998. On genetic counselling in general, see the major reference: A Clarke *Genetic Counselling: Practice and Principles* (1994). Not only may the patient accept or reject the advice given but so may her general practitioner: G H de Bock, C J van Asperen, J M de Vries et al 'How Women with a Family History of Breast Cancer and their General Practitioners Act on Genetic Advice in General Practice: Prospective Longitudinal Study' (2001) 322 BMJ 26.

[176] See A Lippman 'Prenatal Genetic Testing and Screening: Constructing Needs and Reinforcing Inequities' (1991) 17 Am J Law Med 15.

were the somewhat bizarre suggestion adopted that the cost-efficiency of a genetic counselling service could be gauged by the number of abortions performed.[177] It is astonishing to read, for example, that the House of Commons Science and Technology Committee found that, in Edinburgh, a prenatal test for late onset Huntington's disease will not be offered to a woman who is herself afflicted unless she agrees to terminate if the test proves positive.[178] The rationale is that the child is otherwise burdened by the knowledge of its early death. Yet, such a policy betrays an underlying attitude towards those affected by such a condition and ignores the fact that they can enjoy many happy asymptomatic years of life. One thing is, however, certain: no woman can be forced to destroy her fetus. There is no legislative basis for such a suggestion which has strong overtones of positive eugenics.[179]

7.87   The prospect that parents who choose not to abort a child might come to be seen as irresponsible is deplorable.[180] We agree with the ACGT in this regard—the aims of any programme should be clearly articulated, including any public health-related agenda on the part of the state, all programmes should be subjected to strict scrutiny by the National Screening Committee and each programme should be accompanied by impartial pre- and post-testing counselling.[181] While it can be accepted that the state may have legitimate reasons for encouraging individuals to act responsibly in their use of any available genetic information, such encouragement should be offered only in the most moderate of terms. The autonomy and privacy interests of each of us require prima facie respect and this should be borne in mind whenever the introduction of a population screening programme is being considered. It is very difficult to justify any screening programme of children or adults which is unaccompanied by an effective cure or treatment. The strength of the state interest in promoting public health per se is insufficient to justify compromising the interests of individuals in receiving or not receiving genetic information about themselves.[182] The Human Genetics Commission is well aware of these issues and has undertaken to consider both the matter of prenatal testing and screening programmes as part of its work on genetics and reproductive choice.[183]

[177] For discussion, and rejection, see A Clarke 'Genetics, Ethics, and Audit' (1990) 335 Lancet 1145.

[178] House of Commons Science and Technology Committee, Third Report, para 90.

[179] D J Galton and C J Galton 'Francis Galton: and Eugenics Today' (1998) 24 J Med Ethics 99; D J Kevles 'Eugenics and Human Rights' (1999) 319 BMJ 435. See also *Emeh v Kensington and Chelsea and Westminster Area Health Authority* [1985] QB 1012 at 1024, [1984] 3 All ER 1044 at 1053, per Slade LJ, CA.

[180] M Grodin and G Laurie 'Susceptibility Genes and Neurological Disorders: Learning the Right Lessons from the Human Genome Project' (2000) 57 Arch Neurol 1569.

[181] The National Screening Committee has clear guidance: *Criteria for Appraising the Viability, Effectiveness and Appropriateness of a Screening Programme* (2003).

[182] Yet the government seems intent on introducing such programmes and even on establishing genetic profiles of all children: *Our Inheritance, Our Future* (2003), Cm 5791. The proposal is criticised by the Joint Working Party of the Human Genetics Commission and the National Screening Committee. See also McLean and Mason, n 20 above.

[183] HGC *Inside Information*, n 43 above, chapter 4.

GENE THERAPY

7.88 Advances in screening constitute only one aspect of the progress which has been made in human genetics over recent decades. Perhaps more significantly from the scientific point of view, possibilities have opened up for manipulation of the genes of existing and future individuals. This is best known as genetic engineering; inevitably, it has given rise to considerable bioethical debate.[184]

7.89 Gene therapy is one such form of genetic engineering and this may be of two types—somatic or germ-line. Somatic gene therapy is directed towards the remedying of a defect within the patient and involves the insertion of genetic material which will perform some function which the patient's own genetic material cannot achieve. Germ-line gene therapy can be visualised in two ways: the insertion of genetic material into the pre-embryo, which is pre-emptive treatment of the future being and his or her progeny, or as the insertion of a gene into the germ cells of an individual. The latter therapy has no direct bearing on the individual but is intended to ensure that any subsequent children are born with or without certain characteristics. The scientific techniques involved have spawned considerable—and emotional— debate;[185] indeed, genetic engineering is one of the few modern medical technologies in which study of the moral aspects has preceded the practical realities.

7.90 The ethical implications of somatic gene therapy were considered by the Committee on the Ethics of Gene Therapy—the Clothier Committee—which reported in 1992.[186] The Committee thought that this form of treatment was uncontroversial, if novel, and felt that it gave rise to no new ethical challenges. The Group of Advisors on Ethical Implications of Biotechnology of the European Commission similarly reported in 1994 and encouraged somatic gene therapy at a number of levels, including basic research, clinical trials and biotechnology.[187] This having been said, the group considered that, because of certain unknown risks associated with the process, research into somatic gene therapy should be restricted to serious diseases for which there is no other effective available treatment. Similar views have been expressed in the United States and in international documents concerned with the bioethics of manipulation of the human genome.[188] We can accept these assessments; the goals of

---

[184] For an informative account of gene therapy, see J Kinderlerer and D Longley 'Human Genetics: The New Panacea?' (1998) 61 MLR 603 at 614ff.

[185] See R Iredale 'Public Attitudes to Human Gene Therapy: A Pilot Study in Wales' (2003) 6 Community Genetics 139. This study shows general support for somatic gene therapy but ambivalence about germline gene therapy.

[186] Report of the Committee on the Ethics of Gene Therapy (1992).

[187] Opinion of the Group of Advisers on Ethical Implications of Biotechnology of the European Commission *The Ethical Implications of Gene Therapy* (1994).

[188] For the US position, see Report and Recommendations of the Panel to Assess the National Institutes of Health Investment in Research on Gene Therapy (1995). The Council of Europe Convention for the Protection of Human Rights and Dignity of the Human Being with regard to the Application of Biology and Medicine: Convention on Human Rights and Biomedicine states, in Article 13: 'An intervention seeking to

somatic gene therapy are identical to the goals of other forms of treatment and, provided that it does not involve undue risk to the patient or to others, it is as ethically acceptable as is drug therapy or surgical intervention. There may be a need for caution if somatic gene therapy is developed so as to combat behavioural disorders; even then, however, the ethical considerations will be similar to those which already arise from the use of psychotropic drugs or psychosurgery and which are discussed in greater detail in chapter 20.[189]

7.91   Trials involving gene therapy began in 1990 but suffered a real setback in 1999 when the first death attributable to the technique occurred.[190] None the less, it has been reported in the United States that 'in the year of the tragedy, . . . the National Institutes of Health (NIH) approved a record 91 gene transfer protocols that year, as compared with only 2 in 1990 and 51 in 1998. In 2000, that number dropped to 71, but it edged up to 73 in 2001, according to the NIH's Office of Biotechnology Activities'.[191] Twenty-one gene therapy protocols were reviewed by the UK's Gene Therapy Advisory Committee (GTAC) in 2000.[192] The GTAC also responded to the American experience by issuing stricter and clearer guidelines on making proposals to conduct gene therapy research on human subjects in its Seventh Report published in 2001.[193] By the beginning of 2004, a total of 90 gene therapy protocols had been approved by the Committee.[194] GTAC also maintains an active public engagement programme, raising awareness of its function and the promise of gene therapy more generally. The government renewed its commitment to the safe exploration of gene therapies in its 2003 White Paper on Genetics, while at the same time it sought to reassure the public that adequate safeguards are already in place in the guise of the GTAC and, on a more practical level, the Medicines and Healthcare Products Regulatory Authority which must approve all gene therapy products.[195]

7.92   The controversial nature of germ-line gene therapy—whether directed to the pre-embryo or to an individual's germ cells—rests on its capacity to change future people. Some such changes will, in themselves, be unobjectionable; it is difficult, for example, to find grounds for objection to preventive medicine which will ensure that the bearers of a serious genetically transmissible disease will not pass the condition on to their children. Such medical practice is no different from other, long-accepted, efforts to eradicate disease within the human population which, arguably, interfere with the natural order to a comparable degree.

modify the human genome may only be undertaken for preventative, diagnostic or therapeutic purposes and only if its aim is not to introduce any modification in the genome of any descendants.'

[189] M Cavazzana-Calvo, A Thrasher and F Mavilio 'The Future of Gene Therapy' (2004) 427 Nature 779.
[190] E Weiss and D Nelson 'Teen Dies Undergoing Gene Therapy' (1999) *Washington Post*, 29 September, p A1.
[191] T Ready 'Gene Therapy in Recovery Phase' (2002) 8 Nature Medicine 429.
[192] GTAC Seventh Annual Report (January 2000–December 2000) (2001).
[193] *Ibid.* This report also contains a summary of gene therapy research from 1993–2001.
[194] GTAC *Latest UK Gene Therapy Research 1993–2003* (2004). GTAC was expecting its 100th application in the course of 2004: GTAC *Tenth Annual Report: January 2003—December 2003* (2004).
[195] Genetics White Paper, para 7.46 above, para 6.12.

7.93   The difficulty that some have with any form of germ-line therapy is that of the 'slippery slope' which is encountered at a number of points in medical juris-prudence.[196] If we allow germ-line therapy in relation to, say, a seriously debilitating disease, then how are we to prevent its use to eliminate characteristics which we would not, currently, label as a defect but which may be considered undesirable? Rifkin put the problem as follows:

Once we decide to begin the process of human genetic engineering, there is really no logical place to stop. If diabetes, sickle cell anaemia, and cancer are to be cured by altering the genetic make-up of an individual, why not proceed to other 'disorders': myopia, colour-blindness, left-handedness? Indeed, what is to preclude a society from deciding that a certain skin colour is a disorder?[197]

7.94   This is a bleak view of scientific ambitions, but the concern for possible abuse that it expresses has been potent enough to cause a number of governmental or other official bodies to proscribe germ-line gene therapy. The Council of Europe was, ini-tially, sufficiently suspicious to recommend a complete ban on such practices—on the grounds of its insult to human dignity—but later modified this to allow germ cell manipulation for therapeutic purposes.[198] UNESCO has not ruled out germ-line therapies ab initio in its Universal Declaration on the Human Genome and Human Rights but, rather, prohibits 'practices which are contrary to human dignity'[199] and UNESCO's most recent effort—the draft Declaration on Universal Norms on Bioeth-ics—similarly requires that 'any decision or practice shall be made or carried out with full respect for the inherent dignity of the human person . . .'[200] An arguable case can be made that germ-line research falls into this category. The total outlawing of germ-line therapy has been recommended in Germany—and this attitude was endorsed in a statement from the medical research councils of 11 European states in 1988.

7.95   However, germ-line gene therapy is not without its supporters—as Harris has asked: is there anything really wrong in wanting to have a fine child?[201] The real difficulty lies in distinguishing between eugenically-motivated, or enhancement, germ-line manipulation on the one hand and truly therapeutic intervention on the other. It should be necessary to forbid *all* work in this area only if it is felt that the demarcation line can never be held. Unfortunately, science's bad record in keep-ing to a narrow, acceptable track lends some force to the arguments of those who would prevent such meddling altogether.[202] We agree with the Human Genome

---

[196] N Holtug 'Human Gene Therapy: Down the Slippery Slope' (1993) 7 Bioethics 402.

[197] J Rifkin *Algeny* (1983) p 232, quoted in Holtug 'Human Gene Therapy: Down the Slippery Slope' (1993) 7 Bioethics 402 at 405.

[198] Council of Europe Recommendation 934 on Genetic Engineering (1982); Recommendation 1100 on the Use of Human Embryos and Foetuses in Scientific Research (1989).

[199] See para 7.37 above, Article 11.

[200] UNESCO *Preliminary Draft Declaration on Universal Norms on* Bioethics (2005), Article 4.

[201] J Harris 'Is Gene Therapy a Form of Eugenics?' (1993) 7 Bioethics 178.

[202] For a range of informed views, see G Stock and J Campbell *Engineering the Human Germline: An Exploration of the Science and Ethics of Altering the Genes We Pass to Our Children* (2000).

Organisation's Ethics Committee (HUGO) which has called for 'widespread discussion on the appropriateness of the possible future use of gene transfer technology for enhancement and for germ-line interventions'.[203]

7.96   A final irony in the debate is revealed by this quote from Capecchi:

> ... the pressure to initiate germline gene therapy will not likely come from government or dictators with a desire to make a super race, but rather from parents who desire to improve the chances for their biological children to function effectively within our society.[204]

Thus, once again, choice may become the primary policy driver in the advancement of a new field of technology. But the irony to which we allude is this: the post-war development of human rights discourse and the renewed commitment to individualism that this represented was largely driven in response to eugenic practices, albeit at that time at the hands of states. Are eugenic practices any less offensive if they are dressed up in the guise of autonomous choice? Does *choice* bring us back to where we started?[205]

CLONING

7.97   The birth of Dolly the lamb in 1997 sparked one of the greatest furores to affect the discipline of medical law and ethics since its beginnings some 30 years ago. Dolly was the first example of an adult vertebrate cloned—that is, genetically copied—from another adult. She was created using a 'fusion' technique whereby the nucleus from an adult cell (in this case mammarian cells) was fused with an unfertilised egg from which the nucleus had been removed. This egg was then transplanted into another adult sheep for normal gestation to take place. The benefits of such a technique include the improvement of production of transgenic livestock which can be used to produce therapeutic agents involving human proteins. Most recently, the development of stem cell technology has made possible the creation of pluripotent cell lines from undifferentiated human cellular material taken from embryos and deceased fetuses.[206] The potential therapeutic benefits of this form of cloning technique such as the cultivation of replacement cells and tissues for diseased body parts have proved very attractive to researchers and governments alike,[207] leading to the rapid moral and legal acceptance of the practice in many countries.

---

[203] HUGO Ethics Committee Draft Statement on Gene Therapy Research (2001).

[204] M R Capecchi 'Human Germline Gene Therapy' in G Stock and J Campbell (eds) *Engineering the Human Germline: An Exploration of the Science and Ethics of Altering the Genes that We Pass to our Children* (2000), pp 31–32.

[205] See too A Caplan, G McGee and D Magnus 'What is Immoral About Eugenics?' (1999) 319 BMJ 1284.

[206] For an account of the science, its promise and the ethical concerns, see European Commission *Commission Staff Working Paper: Report on Human Embryonic Stem Cell Research* (2003).

[207] For a North American perspective, see Committee on Science, Engineering, and Public Policy *Scientific and Medical Aspects of Human Reproductive Cloning* (2002), and for the European position see B Gratton

7.98   These developments, however, also raise the spectre of human cloning, and it is in this regard that much of the controversy has arisen.[208] The prospect that individuals could clone themselves and have children who share precisely the same genetic make-up is, for some, to go too far. There is serious concern that the use of such a technique would alter our perception of what it means to be human. Moreover, many fear that the potential for exploitation is too great and envisage the production of human clones to be used as sources of spare parts.[209] Yet others have posited that the birth of a clone would distort beyond recognition traditional familial hierarchies and relationships.[210] While many of these fears must be unfounded, we cannot deny that the strength of the reaction to these developments dictates a very cautious approach to the future.

7.99   Initial governmental responses to the birth of Dolly were swift and unanimously condemnatory. The United Kingdom government quickly confirmed its position that any work which was designed to produce cloned human beings was unethical and illegal[211]—a matter which we address further below. In the United States, the National Bioethics Advisory Commission (NBAC) reported in June 1997 and concluded that the risks of research into human cloning involving clinical trials were too great and that legislation should be passed to prohibit research into cloning 'complete people'. As a result, the Cloning and Prohibition Bill 1997 was sent to Congress, but the Act was not introduced. Numerous cloning prohibition bills followed in its wake but no federal action has been taken. In August 2001 President Bush announced that research using federal funds to study embryonic stem cells could only be done on stem cell lines or colonies that existed prior to the date of his announcement.[212] This, in effect, precluded federal funding for research into stem cells from cloned human embryos, and one year on it was reported that only three cell lines were available to researchers.[213] Note, that this does not preclude research using private monies—and, indeed, other reports tell of actual attempted reproductive assistance through cloning in America and elsewhere.[214]

7.100   A protocol to the Council of Europe Convention on Human Rights and Biomedicine

'Survey on the National Regulations in the European Union Regarding Research on Human Embryos' (July 2002) prepared for the European Group on Ethics in Science and New Technologies to the European Commission), available at: http://europa.eu.int/comm/european_group_ethics/docs/nat_reg.pdf.

[208] A fear that gathers some substance when we read R J Boyle and J Savulescu 'Ethics of Using Preimplantation Genetic Diagnosis to Select a Stem Cell Donor for an Existing Person' (2001) 323 BMJ 1240.

[209] For a range of views and arguments see generally (1999) 25 Journal Med Ethics Issue 2.

[210] For a measured proposal, see A L Bonnicksen 'Procreation By Cloning: Crafting Anticipatory Guidelines' (1997) 25 J Law Med & Ethics 273.

[211] Official Reports, HC 26 June 1997, col 615ff.

[212] Executive Order on Embryonic Stem Cell Research (2001).

[213] J Gillis and R Weiss 'Stem Cell Research Not Yet Booming' *Washington Post* 6 August 2001, p A01. For a recent overview of the regulatory position see, R Benson Gold 'Embryonic Stem Cell Research—Old Controversy; New Debate' (2004) 7(4) The Guttmacher Report on Public Policy 4.

[214] R Dobson 'Claims of Clone Pregnancy Could Threaten US Stem Cell Research' (2002) 324 BMJ 868. See too, D Cyranoski 'Stem-Cell Research: Crunch Time for Korea's Cloners' (2004) 429 Nature (May) 12.

prohibits the cloning of human beings[215] and the UNESCO Declaration on the Human Genome and Human Rights specifically disallows cloning as being contrary to human dignity.[216] Moreover, incentives to carry out research in this field in Europe have been removed with the passing of the Directive on the Legal Protection of Biotechnological Inventions,[217] Article 6 of which expressly prohibits the granting of a patent for 'processes for cloning human beings'.[218] Most controversy has been created, however, by the United Nations attempt to ban cloning. Efforts to agree a binding legal treaty were abandoned in 2004 for lack of consensus over what, precisely, should be banned: should it be all forms of human cloning, should it be only reproductive cloning done with a view to producing a child, and, perhaps most importantly from the research perspective, should embryo stell cell research be allowed to continue? Utimately, after various proposals for compromise, it was agreed in early 2005 to produce a non-binding declaration whereby member states are called upon to prohibit '. . . all forms of human cloning inasmuch as they are incompatible with human dignity and the protection of human life'.[219] This suitably vague wording permits a range of interpretation, and doubtless this facility with be exploited to the full.

7.101   The United Kingdom voted against this Declaration. There is, indeed, a strong commitment to research in this field and the UK is a world leader. The Westminster Parliament voted in December 2000 to legalise the creation of embryos purely for research purposes, including stem cell research,[220] while, on the reproduction side, there has been considerable dispute over whether a cloned human organism is an 'embryo' for the purposes of the Human Fertilisation and Embryology Act 1990.[221] This has been resolved in favour of a purposive interpretation that brings such an organism within the definition and, therefore, within the Human Fertilisation and Embryology Authority's (HFEA) regulatory regime.[222] It is likely, therefore, that licences for cloning techniques performed to a reproductive end will not be granted— at least in the short to medium term; but the HFEA did grant the first licence in

---

[215] Additional Protocol to the Convention on Human Rights and Biomedicine on the Prohibition of Cloning Human Beings (1998).

[216] Para 7.37 above, Article 11.

[217] Directive of the European Parliament and of the Council on the Legal Protection of Biotechnological Inventions No 98/44/EC of 6 July 1998, published at OJ L213, 30 July 1998, p 13.

[218] It should also be noted that, inter alia, this article excludes processes for modifying the germ-line genetic identity of human beings from patentability. We discuss this Directive further in chapter 15.

[219] United Nations 'Legal Committee Recommends UN Declaration on Human Cloning to General Assembly' (2005, Press Release GA/L/3271).

[220] 'MPs Give Go Ahead for Embryo Research', *The Times*, 19 December 2000. The House of Lords approved this vote of the House of Commons on 22 January 2001. See now, the Human Fertilisation and Embryology (Research Purposes) Regulations 2001, SI 2001/188.

[221] *R (on the application of Quintavalle) v Secretary of State for Health* [2002] EWCA Civ 29, [2002] QB 628, (2002) 64 BMLR 72.

[222] *R (on the application of Quintavalle) v Secretary of State for Health* [2003] 2 AC 687, [2003] 2 WLR 692. We are divided here as one of us believes that this was properly a matter for the legislature: J K Mason 'Clones and Cell Nuclear Replacements: A *Quintavalle* Saga' (2003) 7 Edin LR 379.

Europe to allow therapeutic cloning to produce embryonic stem cells.[223] It is also possible, despite the ruling of the House of Lords in *Quintavalle*, to see the moral status of the 'embryo' derived from cloning as being instinctively less equivalent to that of a human being than is that of the embryo resulting from fertilisation;[224] that being so, the preference for therapeutic cloning as a source of stem cells can be justified on deontological as well as utilitarian grounds and it is far from clear how long the tide against its general introduction can be held.

7.102   In what can only be described as a surprising move—and certainly one that could scarcely have been contemplated at the time of the last edition of this book—Baroness Mary Warnock has recently expressed regret about the absolute nature of the ban on reproductive cloning which has gripped most legislatures.[225] We suspect that the days of the outright prohibition on reproductive cloning are numbered.[226]

7.103   When responding to developments which have consequences as far-reaching as do so many of those subsumed in the discipline of medical law, it is essential that a broad cross-section of views are obtained and, where possible, taken on board. The final response of the law to the advent of cloning remains to be seen—but the means by which the final end is reached can be as important as the reaching of the end itself.

---

[223] 'Scientists given cloning go-ahead', BBC News, 11 August 2004: http://news.bbc.co.uk/1/hi/health/3554474.stm. A challenge to the decision has, however, been mounted and the High Court will consider an application for judicial review, see Public Health Genetics Unit, Newsletter, No. 76, November 2004: www.phgu.org.uk.

[224] J-E Hansen 'Embryonic Stem Cell Production through Therapeutic Cloning Has Fewer Ethical Problems than Stem Cell Harvest from Surplus IVF Embryos' (2002) 28 J Med Ethics 86.

[225] M Warnock *Making Babies: Is There A Right to Have Children?* (2002), pp 102ff, 'Would the cloning of human be intrinsically wrong?'

[226] A useful overview of the current international situation is provided by S D Pattinson and T Caulfield 'Variations and Voids: The Regulation of Human Cloning Around the World' (2004) 5 BMC Med Ethics 9 available at www.biomedcentral.com/1472-6939/5/9.

8

MEDICAL CONFIDENTIALITY

THE PRINCIPLE OF CONFIDENTIALITY

8.1   A general common law duty is imposed on a doctor to respect the confidences of his patients.[1] The nature of this obligation[2]—which applies to all confidential information and not only to medical material[3]—was discussed by the House of Lords in *A-G v Guardian Newspapers Ltd (No. 2)*,[4] in which it was affirmed that there is a public interest in the protection of confidences received under notice of confidentiality or in circumstances where the reasonable person ought to know that the information was confidential. Traditionally, three elements have been needed to establish a breach of the obligation. First, the information divulged must have the necessary quality of confidence about it; secondly, that information must have been imparted in circumstances importing an obligation of confidence; and, thirdly, there must be an unauthorised use of that information;[5] there is no need in personal privacy cases to establish further detriment beyond the fact that unauthorised use has occurred.[6] All

---

[1] This chapter is concerned with confidentiality and not the converse idea of freedom of information. The Freedom of Information Act 2000 came into force on 1 January 2005 giving individuals a right of access to data held by, or on behalf of, public authorities, which include NHS bodies. Any request for access to personal data, however, is inappropriate under this Act (and should instead be sought under the Data Protection Act 1998, see below); moreover, any request for access to material containing data identifying another individual should be refused if disclosure would breach the data protection principles or the common law duty of confidence: see Information Commissioner's Office *Freedom of Information Act Awareness Guidance No. 1* (2004).

[2] The doctor-patient and priest-penitent relationships were cited as classic examples in *Stephens v Avery* [1988] Ch 449 at 455, [1988] 2 All ER 477 at 482, per Browne-Wilkinson V-C.

[3] The duty to respect confidences is to be distinguished from the (broader) notion of respecting individual privacy although the two are obviously related. Indeed, the House of Lords has confirmed that there is no common law right of privacy in the UK, see *Wainwright v Home Office* [2003] 4 All ER 969, [2003] 3 WLR 1137, HL; this is not at all the same as saying the privacy interests are not protected.

[4] [1990] AC 109, [1988] 3 All ER 545.

[5] Per Megarry J in *Coco v A N Clark (Engineers) Ltd* [1969] RPC 41 at 47, repeated with approval in *Stephens v Avery* [1988] Ch 449, [1988] 2 All ER 477.

[6] See generally R Pattenden *The Law of Professional-Client Confidentiality: Regulating the Disclosure of Confidential Personal Information* (2003), chapter 5.

these criteria would apply in a medical context where the duty of discretion has been endorsed judicially. Thus, in *Hunter v Mann*[7] the court accepted that:

... the doctor is under a duty not to [voluntarily] disclose, without the consent of the patient, information which he, the doctor, has gained in his professional capacity.

In the very significant case of *W v Egdell*,[8] which we discuss in greater detail at para 8.17 et seq, the court accepted the existence of an obligation of confidentiality between a psychiatrist and his subject, an obligation which counsel submitted was based not only on equitable grounds but also on implied contract. Most recently, the House of Lords has confirmed in *Campbell v Mirror Group Newspapers Ltd*,[9] that details of one's medical circumstances are 'obviously private' and deserving of the full protection of the law of confidence, albeit now subject to the slant afforded to the law by the Human Rights Act 1998, which we also consider further below.

8.2   Whatever may be the legal basis for the duty, its ethical content is considerable. Indeed, in the context of medical law in particular, it is difficult to dissociate the two disciplines—thus, we have Lord Coleridge CJ: 'A legal common law duty is nothing else than the enforcing by law of that which is a moral obligation without legal enforcement.'[10] We can, therefore, look not only at what the patient feels is his legal entitlement but also at the ethical requirements of the medical profession itself. Here there are a number of sources from which the doctor can seek guidance. The Hippocratic Oath[11] makes several demands which can scarcely be regarded as binding on the modern doctor; none the less, its stipulations as to professional confidentiality are still firmly endorsed. The translation cited in the *sponsio academica* at graduation ceremonials in the University of Edinburgh runs: 'Whatever things seen or heard in the course of medical practice ought not to be spoken of, I will not, save for weighty reasons, divulge'. The Declaration of Geneva (amended at Sydney [1968], Venice [1983] and Stockholm [1994])[12] imposes much the same obligation on the doctor, requiring him to 'respect the secrets which are confided in me, even after the patient has died'.

8.3   The great majority of commentators on medical ethics endorses a continued adherence to a strict principle[13] although some doubt the efficacy of an absolute rule and prefer a form of quasi-contractual obligation which, it is thought, would promote the individual patient's autonomy.[14] Most critics, however, see the concept as being

---

[7] [1974] QB 767 at 772, [1974] 2 All ER 414 at 417 per Boreham J. For a general discussion of the duty of confidentiality in the medical context, see G T Laurie *Genetic Privacy: A Challenge to Medico-Legal Norms* (2002), pp 211ff.

[8] [1990] Ch 359, [1990] 1 All ER 835.   [9] [2004] 2 AC 457, [2004] 2 All ER 995.

[10] In *R v Instan* [1893] 1 QB 450 at 453.   [11] See Appendix A.   [12] See Appendix B.

[13] E.g. J M Jacob 'Confidentiality: The Dangers of Anything Weaker than the Medical Ethic' (1982) 8 J Med Ethics 18; M H Kottow 'Medical Confidentiality: An Intransigent and Absolute Obligation' (1986) 12 J Med Ethics 117. Indeed, it is even suggested that the concept has '. . . been elevated to the status of a principle of Medical Ethics', see C Ngwena and R Chadwick 'Genetic Diagnostic Information and the Duty of Confidentiality: Ethics and Law' (1993) 1 Med L Internat 73 at 74.

[14] S J Warwick 'A Vote for No Confidence' (1989) 15 J Med Ethics 183.

something of a pretence in that bureaucracy, fired by modern administrative technology, is increasingly invasive of the principle; computerisation merely facilitates wider and faster dissemination of patient information, heightens the risk of unauthorised disclosure and generally exacerbates the problem. Certainly, patients' records must circulate fairly widely—and among professionals who are less deeply indoctrinated as to confidentiality than are their medical colleagues. Early suggestions that institutions should take over custodianship of confidences and impose an overall standard of duty on all who work in health care institutions[15] have now come to represent the position both at common law[16] and by statute.[17] Indeed, sensitivity towards patient confidentiality has probably never been greater, with health authorities and boards holding training sessions for staff at regular intervals.

8.4   Even so, the special position of the doctor is unlikely to change in the foreseeable future and he is currently bound by the authority of, and is subject to the discipline of, the General Medical Council. Subject to certain exceptions, which we discuss further later,[18] the GMC imposes a strict duty on registered medical practitioners to refrain from disclosing voluntarily to any third party information about a patient which he has learnt directly or indirectly in his professional capacity.[19] A breach of this duty will be a serious matter, exposing the doctor to a wide range of potential professional penalties. It is to be noted, however, that sanctions of this nature are purely intra-professional and it has long been questioned whether they give adequate protection to the aggrieved patient; thus, the Law Commission suggested as long ago as 1981 that the common law position should be strengthened by establishing a statutory offence of breach of confidence which would include that arising between doctor and patient; no action has ever been taken.[20]

8.5   The passing of the Data Protection Act 1998, implementing a 1995 EC Directive,[21]

[15] D L Kenny 'Confidentiality: The Confusion Continues' (1982) 8 J Med Ethics 9; M Siegler 'Confidentiality in Medicine: A Decrepit Concept' (1982) 307 New Engl J Med 1518. See also D F H Pheby 'Changing Practice on Confidentiality: A Cause for Concern' (1982) 8 J Med Ethics 12; A W Macara 'Confidentiality: A Decrepit Concept?' (1984) 77 J Roy Soc Med 577.

[16] A-G v Guardian Newspapers Ltd (No. 2), para 8.1 above imposes a duty on all those who receive confidential information in circumstances which objectively (and reasonably) import a duty of confidence. Communications in a hospital must surely be a paradigm example of this.

[17] Data Protection Act 1998. For commentary, see M Earle Data Protection in the NHS (2002).

[18] See para 8.9 et seq.

[19] General Medical Council Confidentiality: Protecting and Providing Information (2004). The advice of the British Medical Association (BMA) has no disciplinary authority but provides invaluable background to the GMC's instructions: see BMA Confidentiality and Disclosure of Health Information (1999). Other BMA guidance includes Confidentiality and People Under 16 (1994), Revised Interim Guidelines on Confidentiality for Police Surgeons in England, Wales and Northern Ireland (1998), and most recently, Taking and Using Visual and Audio Images of Patients (2004).

[20] Breach of Confidence (Cmnd 8388) para 6.1.

[21] European Directive 95/46/EC on the Protection of Individuals with Regard to the Processing of Personal Data and on the Free Movement of Such Data (Data Protection Directive). There is a general and strong European interest in the subject which is reflected elsewhere in the Council of Europe's Recommendation on the Protection of Medical Data (1997). This recommendation includes not only general principles which should guide national laws on the confidentiality of medical information, but also embraces specific

has provided further protection for medical information. It is not necessary for the purposes of this book to examine the provisions of the Directive or the Act in any great depth.[22] It is sufficient simply to note certain key features.[23] The law protects the privacy rights of individuals in respect of their personal data. 'Personal data' are defined as 'any information relating to an identified or identifiable natural person; an identifiable person is one who can be identified, directly or indirectly, in particular by reference to an identification number or to one or more factors specific to his physical, physiological, mental, economic, cultural or social identity'.[24] The law regulates the processing of such data by reference to a set of eight principles that ensure, inter alia, that data are only processed when it is fair and lawful to do so, that data are processed only so far as is necessary for the purposes for which they were obtained, that the data are accurate and kept up to date, and that they should not be transferred to any jurisdiction where there are inadequate data protection provisions.

8.6   The law makes only two attempts to categorise information into distinct groupings. These are (a) sensitive personal data, and (b) anonymous data. Both are of relevance in the health care setting. Sensitive personal data are defined as data relating to racial or ethnic origin, political opinions, religious or philosophical beliefs, trade-union membership, and the processing of data concerning health or sex life.[25] Additional protection is afforded to such data and, as we have seen elsewhere in this book, the primary point of reference is the concept of consent. In most circumstances, the data subject's specific consent to processing must be obtained. However, a wide range of alternative justifications for processing accompanies this protection, of which the following are most pertinent. For example, it is lawful to process sensitive data to protect the vital interests of the data subject or of another person where the data subject is physically or legally incapable of giving his consent.[26] Also, processing is lawful without specific consent if it is required for the purposes of preventive medicine, medical diagnosis, the provision of care or treatment or the management of health care services, and where those data are processed by a health professional subject to the obligation of professional secrecy or by another person also subject to an equivalent obligation of secrecy. Overarchingly, member states have the power to create exemptions on the basis of 'substantial public interest'.[27] What those public interests are, or may be, is discernible in large part from the general tenor of the Directive, which makes special provisions for, among others, national security,

---

recommendations relating to such matters as storage of data, their transmission across borders, and the use of data in medical research.

[22] The Data Protection Act 1998 came into force on 1 March 2000.

[23] For a guide to the Act, see R Jay and A Hamilton *Data Protection: Law and Practice* (2002).

[24] Data Protection Directive, Article 2.

[25] *Ibid*, Article 8.

[26] The Information Commissioner's Office has issued useful guidance entitled *Use and Disclosure of Health Data* (2002) in which, for example, it is stated that 'vital interests' refers to matters of life and death, *ibid*, p 4.

[27] Data Protection Directive, para 8.5 above, Article 8(4).

the investigation and prosecution of crime, legitimate journalistic activities and research.[28]

8.7   In this last regard, the law creates a number of important protections for scientific researchers using data obtained from individuals. First, there is no requirement to notify a data subject as to the identity and purposes of those who will process the data, nor of the identity of any further recipients of those data when they have not been received directly from the data subject[29]—a requirement that must, normally, be met. Moreover, member states have a discretion to waive rights of access for individuals in the context of scientific research.[30] Second, the subject access provisions of the Directive do not apply when data are anonymised, for the law is concerned solely with personal data—i.e. those from which an individual can be identified.[31] Even so, patients must still be informed when data are to be processed and the purposes to which this is likely to be put unless the research is being carried out on records that are so old that it would involve a disproportionate effort to contact patients in order to obtain their consent.

8.8   The 1998 provisions are all encompassing of identifiable personal information and, to that extent, are to be welcomed. Consent has a role to play but it does not emerge as a trump card. Indeed, some might argue that the broad and indistinct categories of justifications for processing without consent potentially weaken the protection that is afforded to informational privacy interests. The model, however, is, as always, a search for a balance and few could deny that privacy protection should sometimes bow to other interests. But the devil is in the detail of determining which interests should be weighed in the balance and how far privacy should be compromised in any given case. The example of research is particularly apt. Some member states, for example Denmark and Austria, allow research on secondary uses of patient data—that is, uses beyond those for which the data were first obtained—without the need for patient consent so long as the national data protection office gives prior approval.[32] The United Kingdom also has mechanisms for allowing research using patient data subject to rigorous review, and we discuss these below. It is to be noted with some regret, however, that a culture of caution has grown up around the workings of the Data Protection Act such that there is a widespread belief that the law now hinders research.[33] In the main, we consider this to be unfounded.

---

[28] See further in England and Wales, the Health and Social Care Act 2001, s 60, discussed further below.

[29] Data Protection Directive, para 8.5 above, Article 11(2).   [30] *Ibid*, Article 13(2).

[31] *Ibid*, Recital 26.

[32] See the reports of the European Commission Article 29 Data Protection Working Party which is charged with monitoring the Data Protection provisions throughout Europe: http://europa.eu.int/comm/internal_market/privacy/workingroup_en.htm.

[33] J Peto et al 'Data Protection, Informed Consent and Research' (2004) 328 Brit Med J 1029.

RELAXATION OF THE RULE

8.9   All the classic codes of practice imply some qualification of an absolute duty of professional secrecy. Thus, the Hippocratic Oath has it: 'All that may come to my knowledge . . . which ought not to be spread abroad, I will keep secret', which clearly indicates that there are some things which *may* be published. The Declaration of Geneva modifies this prohibition to: 'I will respect the secrets which are confided in me' and the word 'respect' is open to interpretation. The GMC, while always emphasising its strong views as to the rule dictating professional secrecy, still lists a number of specific possible exceptions to the rule which provide a sound basis for discussion.[34]

CONSENT TO PUBLISH

8.10   The first, and most easily recognisable, exception is when the patient, or his or her legal adviser, consents to a relaxation of secrecy. The situation is simple when viewed from the positive angle. A positive consent to release of information elides any obligation to secrecy owed by the person receiving that consent;[35] equally, an explicit request that information should not be disclosed is binding on the doctor save in the most exceptional circumstances—a matter which is of major concern in relation to communicable disease.[36]

Sharing information with others providing care

8.11   The position is not so clear when looked at from the negative aspect—that is, when the patient has neither consented to nor dissented from disclosure—and it may, indeed, be frankly unsatisfactory. How many patients know whether the person standing with the consultant at the hospital bedside is another doctor, a social worker or just an interested spectator? Would they have consented to their presence if they had been informed? The consultant may be responsible if, as a result, there is a breach of confidence—but this is small consolation to the patient who feels his rights have been infringed. What patient at a teaching hospital out-patient department is likely to refuse when the consultant asks: 'You don't mind these young doctors being present, do you?'—the pressures are virtually irresistible and truly autonomous consent is well-nigh impossible, yet the confidential doctor-patient relationship which began with his general practitioner has, effectively, been broken.

8.12   It is obvious that such technical breaches must be, and generally are, accepted in practice—a modern hospital cannot function except as a team effort and new doctors

---

[34] *Confidentiality*, n 19 above.   [35] *C v C* [1946] 1 All ER 562.

[36] See para 8.27 et seq below. The General Medical Council also considers a request by a patient before death to maintain confidentiality after death as an important factor in favour of a strong continuing professional duty, n 19 above, para 30.

have to be trained, the return for a technical loss of patient autonomy being access to the best diagnostic and therapeutic aids available.[37] The GMC recognises this in permitting the sharing of information with other practitioners who assume responsibility for clinical management of the patient and, to the extent that the doctor deems it necessary for the performance of their particular duties, with other health care professionals who are collaborating with the doctor in his patients' management.[38] The implication cannot, however, be taken for granted—particularly as to the particular *need* for the information to be imparted. In *Cornelius v De Taranto*,[39] for example, the question of whether consent had been given to referral of a patient to a consultant was disputed; what was clear, however, was that there was no justification for including information in the referral note that had no therapeutic relevance. It was confirmed, moreover, that it is the doctor's responsibility to ensure that those entitled to information appreciate that it is being imparted in strict professional confidence.[40] The doctor's duty is thereby restricted in a reasonable way; it is difficult to see how he can be expected to carry the onus for any subsequent actions by his associates. The guidance from the Information Commissioner's Office in respect of using and disclosing health data takes a pragmatic approach. It deems there to be implied consent to processing data for *essential* health services from patients who present for and accept care.[41] While this also applies to the administration of records and to clinical audit, it does not apply to the use of data for clinical research.

THE PATIENT'S INTERESTS

8.13 It is ethical to break confidentiality without a patient's consent when it is in his or her own interests to do so and when it is undesirable on medical grounds to seek such consent. The recipient of the information may be another health care professional as above, or a close relative or, as in a case where the doctor suspects that the patient is a victim of neglect or physical or sexual abuse, an unrelated third party[42]—but it remains the doctor's duty to make every reasonable effort to persuade the patient to allow the information to be given, and to make clear to the third party that the information is given in confidence. When these situations occur, decisions rest, by definition, on clinical judgment—a properly considered clinical decision cannot be *unethical* whether it proves right or wrong and, in the event of action being taken on the basis of breach of confidence, the fact that it was a justifiable breach would offer a complete defence both in the civil courts and before disciplinary proceedings of the

---

[37] See, now, the Code of Practice for contractors to the NHS: Department of Health, *Confidentiality and Disclosure of Information: General Medical Services, Personal Medical Services and Alternative Provider Medical Services Code of Practice* (2004).

[38] *Confidentiality*, n 19 above.   [39] (2001) 68 BMLR 62, CA   [40] *Ibid.*

[41] *Use and Disclosure of Health Data*, n 26 above.

[42] For interesting discussion of possible liability for *failure* to report suspected abuse, see *C v Cairns* [2003] Lloyd's Rep Med 90, QB. Note too, the GMC Guidance states that doctors '. . . *must* give information promptly to an appropriate responsible person or statutory agency . . .' [emphasis added] where she or he believes that a patient is a victim of neglect or abuse, n 19 above, para 29.

GMC;[43] the GMC does, however, stress the need for caution when the patient has insufficient understanding, by reason of immaturity, of what the treatment or advice being sought involves; we return to this aspect later in the chapter.[44]

THE DOCTOR IN SOCIETY

8.14   In so far as it rests on subjective definitions, the doctor's overriding duty to society represents what is arguably the most controversial permissible exception to the rule of confidentiality. Society is not homogeneous, but consists of groups amenable to almost infinite classification—regional, political, economic, by age and so on. It follows that what one person regards as a duty to society may be anathema to another. Individual doctors are bound to weigh the scales differently in any particular instance while, in general, all relative weighting must change from case to case—there is, for example, a great deal of difference in respect of confidentiality between being stung by a bee and suffering from venereal disease. While it is clear that no hard rules can be laid down, some aspects of this societal conflict are sufficiently important to merit individual consideration.

8.15   The most dramatic dilemma is posed by the possibility of violent crime. What is the doctor to do if he knows his patient has just committed rape—particularly if there is evidence that this is but one of a series of attacks on women? Perhaps even more disconcertingly, what if it becomes apparent that his patient is about to commit such an offence? Statute law is helpful here only in a negative sense—misprision of felony, other than as related to treason, is no longer an offence.[45] There is case law to the effect that the doctor need not even assist the police by answering their questions concerning his patients, although he must not give false or misleading information.[46] The obligation on the prosecution to disclose to the defence all unused material which might have some bearing on the offences charged has also caused some difficulty for police surgeons. Generally speaking, an accused gives consent to disclosure of specific information only. Other information may, however, come to light during the course of an examination; once this is in their notes, the police may feel it their duty to include it in their 'disclosure', despite the fact that there is no consent to their so doing. The police surgeon may, therefore, feel it his ethical imperative to conceal his knowledge—but the decision must, at times, be difficult to make.[47]

8.16   In the early part of the twentieth century, both medical and legal opinion was divided on the issue of disclosure of serious crime; discussion was, however, based

---

[43] On which, see chapter 1.   [44] See para 8.40 et seq.   [45] Criminal Law Act 1967, s 5(5).

[46] *Rice v Connolly* [1966] 2 QB 414, [1966] 2 All ER 649 and more recently *A Health Authority v X and others* [2001] 2 FLR 673, (2001) 61 BMLR 22. But, see the specific position in respect of acts of terrorism, discussed at para 8.58 below. The European Court of Human Rights has confirmed, in contrast, that it is not a breach of the right to respect for private life for national law to require doctors to disclose records to police authorities provided that each person in receipt of the information is under a duty to continue to respect the individual's privacy: *Z v Finland* (1997) 25 EHRR 371, (1997) 45 BMLR 107.

[47] For guidance, see British Medical Association *Revised Interim Guidelines for Police Surgeons*, n 19 above.

largely on the subject of illegal abortion, which has emotional overtones of its own. Nevertheless, it was in that context that Avory J made his well-known observation:

There are cases where the desire to preserve [the confidential relation which exists between the medical man and his patient] must be subordinated to the duty which is cast on every good citizen to assist in the investigation of serious crime,[48]

and this probably represents the foundation of the doctrine of the public interest as applied to medicine. This crystallised in the case of *W v Egdell*.[49]

8.17 Here, a prisoner in a secure hospital sought a review of his case with a view to transfer to a regional secure unit. His legal representatives secured a report from an independent consultant psychiatrist that was, in the event, unfavourable to W; as a result, the application for transfer was aborted. W was, however, due for routine review of his detention and the psychiatrist, becoming aware that his report would not be included in the patient's notes, feared that decisions would be taken on inadequate information with consequent danger to the public. He therefore sent a copy of his report to the medical director of the hospital and a further copy reached the Home Office; W brought an action in contract and in equity alleging breach of a duty of confidence. The trial judge, Scott J, considered that, in the circumstances:

The question in the present case is not whether Dr Egdell was under a duty of confidence; he plainly was. The question is as to the breadth of that duty.[50]

Attention was drawn to the advice of the GMC as to the circumstances in which exception to the rule of confidentiality is permitted. The GMC's guidelines which applied at the time were contained in the so-called '*Blue Book*'. Para 79 stated:

Rarely, cases may arise in which disclosure in the public interest may be justified, for example, a situation in which the failure to disclose appropriate information would expose the patient, or someone else, to a risk of death or serious harm.

8.18 Scott J based his conclusions on broad considerations—that a doctor in similar circumstances has a duty not only to the patient but also to the public and that the latter would require him to disclose the results of his examination to the proper authorities if, in his opinion, the public interest so required; this would be independent of the patient's instructions on the point.

8.19 The Court of Appeal unanimously confirmed the trial judge's decision to dismiss the action but did so with rather more reservation—particularly as expressed in the judgment of Bingham LJ. The concept of a private interest competing with a public interest was rejected in favour of there being a *public* interest in maintaining professional duties of confidence; the 'balancing' of interests thus fell to be carried out in

---

[48] Birmingham Assizes, 1 December 1914, reported in (1914) 78 JP 604. The judge referred to a possible moral duty in the event that the patient was not dying; his views as to strict moral duty were mainly concerned with the loss of evidence in failing to take a dying declaration from a moribund patient.

[49] [1990] Ch 359, [1990] 1 All ER 835.

[50] [1990] Ch 359 at 389, [1989] 1 All ER 1089 at 1102.

circumstances of unusual difficulty. Doubts, which we share, were cast on the applicability of the provisions of the *Blue Book* (para 78(b)) to a doctor acting in the role of an independent consultant; disclosure would have to be justified under para 78(g) and, here, it was for the court, not the doctor, to decide whether such a disclosure was or was not a breach of contract. Moreover, there was no doubt that the Mental Health Act 1983, s 76 showed a clear parliamentary intention that a restricted patient should be free to seek advice and evidence for specific purposes which was to be accepted as confidential. Only the most compelling circumstances could justify a doctor acting contrary to the patient's perceived interests in the absence of consent. Nevertheless, in the instant case, the fear of a real risk to public safety entitled a doctor to take reasonable steps to communicate the grounds of his concern to the appropriate authorities.

8.20   Looked at superficially, it is easy to view *Egdell* as a serious intrusion into the relationship of confidential trust between doctor and patient; it is equally possible to perceive the principle as emerging relatively unscathed. W's case was clearly regarded as extreme and, although we cannot exclude some concern, there is no evidence in the judgment that the courts would condone a breach of confidence on less urgent grounds. The 'danger area' seems to be better deliminated by way of independent activity on the part of doctors—as anticipated by Bingham LJ in *Egdell*. In *R v Crozier*,[51] a psychiatrist called by the accused, concerned that his opinion should be available to the court, apparently handed his report to counsel for the Crown; the now sentenced accused appealed on the grounds that the breach of confidentiality between doctor and patient had denied him the opportunity of deciding whether medical evidence would be tendered on his behalf. The Court of Appeal again thought that there was a stronger public interest in the disclosure of the psychiatrist's views than in the confidence he owed to the appellant; the psychiatrist was found to have acted responsibly and reasonably in a very difficult situation. But what if a doctor acts *un*reasonably in such circumstances? The damage to the patient is done and he will get little satisfaction from the fact that the doctor is censured; it is surely a thoroughly paternalistic practice that should be carefully restrained.

HUMAN RIGHTS AND THE ACTION FOR BREACH OF CONFIDENCE

8.21   The House of Lords has recently considered the state of the breach of confidence action post-Human Rights Act in *Campbell v Mirror Group Newspapers Ltd.*[52] Although great play was made in the House of Lords that it was the complainer's medical status that was particularly in issue, *Campbell* is not strictly within the common scenario of 'medical confidentiality' in so far as no medical practitioner was involved in its disclosure. However, the case demonstrates a number of important points which would clearly influence the courts' approach to such a breach; it, therefore, merits consideration in depth. The circumstances were that an internationally

---

[51] (1990) 8 BMLR 128.   [52] [2004] 2 AC 457, [2004] 2 All ER 995.

renowned supermodel accepted that she had previously lied publicly about her being addicted to drugs and did not seek to prevent publication of the fact. She did, however, bring an action in breach of confidence for the publication of additional details of her therapy and of photographs taken of her, covertly, in the street as she left her clinic; it was claimed that these acts interfered with her right to respect for private life (Article 8 ECHR). The defendant, in turn, argued the case for freedom of expression (Article 10 ECHR) and for the public interest in publishing the materials in order to correct the claimant's earlier untrue statements.[53] But how were these rights and freedoms to be balanced in the shadow of the Human Rights Act? Lord Hope remarked that the language of the breach of confidence action had now changed from a balance of public interests to a balance of Article rights—but he still doubted whether 'the centre of gravity has shifted'. Furthermore, he considered that the balancing exercise is essentially the same but that it is, now, 'more carefully focused and penetrating'.[54]

8.22 Even so, the focus is now notably on the underlying values that support respect for private life—values based on privacy and personal autonomy—rather than on the need for a confidential relationship, however artificially this may be constructed. Secondly, the focus of such a claim, and the test to be applied as to whether a sound cause of action arises, lies not within the conscience of the receiver of the information but, rather, on the reasonable expectation of privacy that the subject of the information might have.[55] Moreover, we now have a clearer idea of how the process of considering competing claims to control confidential information should be managed. The entire House agreed with Lord Hope that the court must, first, ask if Article 8 is engaged. If it is, then a balance of considerations, applying a proportionality test, is to be undertaken as between the respective claims under Article 8 and Article 10.

8.23 In determining whether the threshold has been crossed on Article 8, the court will ask 'was the claimant entitled to a reasonable expectation of privacy in all the circumstances?', and this can be answered in one of two ways: (i) was the matter 'obviously private', or, if it was not, (ii) 'would disclosure be highly offensive to a reasonable person'?[56] If Article 8 interests fall to be protected, then the approach to the balance with other interests is, once again, two-fold: (i) does publication pursue a legitimate aim?, and (ii) are the benefits achieved by publication proportionate to the harm to privacy?

[53] Campbell also claimed compensation for violation of the provisions of the Data Protection Act 1998, s 13, to which the defendant claimed the public interest exception under s 32.

[54] *Campbell*, para 8.21, per Lord Hope, para 86.

[55] This was already being recognised by the Court of Appeal, inter alia, in *A v B plc and C* [2003] QB 195, [2002] 2 All ER 545.

[56] In articulating this, Lord Hope borrowed from Australian and American concepts; most interestingly, the US approach requires that disclosure also must be of legitimate concern to the public, *Campbell*, para 8.21 above, para 94. He considered the Australian test from *Australian Broadcasting Corporation v Lenah Game Meats Pty Ltd* (2001) 185 ALR 1 which asks whether disclosure would '. . . give substantial offence to A, assuming that A was placed in similar circumstances and was a person of ordinary sensibilities', *ibid* paras 92–94.

8.24   Some questions arise from this. First, what is 'obviously private'? In the instant case, the majority held that the details in question, being sensitive medical details, were obviously private, and doubtless many would agree.[57] Other suggested examples include information about personal relationships and finances. Such a visceral test may at first disturb those is search of certainty, yet it reflects our intuitive responses to many privacy claims. The second (alternative) criterion places a far more problematic obstacle in the path of a claimant, requiring that disclosure be *'highly offensive'*— which, again, remains undefined. But the fundamental point is that the relevant perspective is that of the subject of the disclosure—in this case, the celebrity. The House of Lords confirmed that public figures are entitled to respect for their privacy, and that the mere fact of being a public figure—even one who has courted publicity— does not automatically create a public interest in publishing private details. None the less, it was also stated that '. . . a person's right to privacy may be limited by the public's interest in knowing about certain traits of her personality and certain aspects of her private life . . .'[58] In the final analysis the House of Lords held that Campbell's privacy had indeed been infringed. While there was a public interest in correcting the celebrity's previous lies,[59] this did not extend to the publication of the additional details about her therapy or the photographs and captions drawing attention to her problems. The balance fell in favour of the appellant because it could not be shown that the publication in question was *in the public interest.*

8.25   Despite this helpful ruling from our highest court, the common law public interest exception to the duty of confidence remains frustratingly ill-defined. *Egdell* confirms that a threat of physical harm to third parties clearly justifies a breach, as will reasonable assessments by doctors that such a threat may be founded on a person's state of health—an obvious example is the need to report a sick patient to the DVLA regarding his or her fitness to drive. Even this, however, may not be straightforward as is shown by an example reported from New Zealand. There, a bus driver underwent a triple coronary bypass operation and was subsequently certified as fit to drive by his surgeon. His general practitioner, however, asked that his licence to drive be withdrawn and, furthermore, warned his passengers of their supposed danger. The practitioner's activities resulted in a report to the Medical Practitioners' Disciplinary Committee and a finding that he was: 'guilty of professional misconduct in that he breached professional confidence in informing lay people of his patient's personal medical history'. Dr Duncan sought judicial review of this decision. The High Court accepted the propriety of breaching medical confidentiality in cases of clear public interest, but refused the application on grounds which can be summed up: 'I think a doctor who has decided to communicate should discriminate and ensure the recipient

---

[57] Lady Hale points out, however, that not all medical details will necessarily be private, *Campbell*, para 8.21 above, para 157.

[58] *Ibid* per Lord Hope, para 120, citing the Supreme Court of Canada in *Aubry v Les Editions Vice-Versa Inc.* [1998] 1 SCR 59, paras 57–58.

[59] *Ibid*, as per Lord Nicholls para 24, Lord Hope para 117, Lady Hale para 151 and Lord Carswell para 163.

is a responsible authority.'[60] Seldom can there have been a case which demonstrates the 'need to know' principle so forcibly.

8.26   Access to patient records in order to carry out internal investigations regarding the proper discharge of health care responsibilities can also be justified on this basis[61] and, beyond these specific examples, a few general parameters can be laid down. We recall the classic dictum of Lord Wilberforce in *British Steel Corporation v Granada Ltd*[62] in which he drew the crucial distinction between what is *in the public interest* and that which the *public is interested in*—journalists take note! Furthermore, a disclosure should only occur where it is *necessary* to achieve the pubic interest in question, when there is a *reasonable likelihood* that it can do so, and when the disclosure is to those persons or agencies who can further that interest. The onus of justification is placed firmly on the shoulders of the health care professional.[63]

CONFIDENTIALITY AND HIV INFECTION

8.27   The spread of the human immunodeficiency virus (HIV) has given rise to a host of problems related to confidentiality.[64] Sexually transmitted diseases are not new to the medico-legal arena, but the HIV/AIDS complex can be set apart for several reasons—prominent among which are its relatively specific sexual connotation, together with its serious association with drug addiction. Those who are found to be HIV-positive may be disadvantaged in a number of practical ways which have been noted in chapter 2 and to which we refer again below;[65] all serve to fuel the concern which many such persons harbour as to the confidentiality of their status.

8.28   Such concerns attract great sympathy, yet there are also social interests to be considered. The crucial dilemma here is whether relaxation of the confidentiality rule would lead to failure to seek advice and treatment and hence to the spread of the disease, or whether the imposition of absolute secrecy improperly denies others the opportunity to avoid the risk of exposure to infection or to take advantage of the benefits of early therapy where exposure has occurred.[66] Should a sexual partner be told of the risk if the patient himself declines to pass on the information? What is the situation if a person known to be infected is employed in circumstances in which he might expose others to the virus? The problem of confidentiality cannot, however, be settled by the balancing of conflicting private interests alone—the public health dimension has to be taken into account. HIV/AIDS is not, at present, a notifiable

---

[60] *Duncan v Medical Practitioners' Disciplinary Committee* [1986] 1 NZLR 513 at 521, per Jeffries J.

[61] *A Health Authority v X and Others* [2001] 2 FLR 673, (2001) 61 BMLT 22. Statutory obligations of disclosure are, by definition, more clear-cut, as we discuss below.

[62] [1981] AC 1096, 1168.

[63] Medical research is clearly a matter of public benefit but we discuss this as a separate aspect at para 8.53 et seq.

[64] See Pattenden, n 6 above, paras 20.28–37.   [65] See generally chapter 10.

[66] While it is probably too early to speak of a cure, supportive therapy is now very efficient.

disease as we discuss in chapter 2[67]—a dispensation which certainly helps to maintain confidentiality. Any public health 'risk' is justified on the grounds that, in the conditions of everyday social contact, HIV is transmitted only with great difficulty—if at all. As a result, it is government policy, supported by the majority of informed opinion, that any departure from the strictest anonymity in respect of HIV-related information must be subject to intense scrutiny.[68]

8.29   The English courts long ago declared their hand in weighing the balance between a strongly supported public policy in favour of freedom of the press against the need for loyalty and confidentiality with particular reference to AIDS patients' hospital records. In $X \ v \ Y$,[69] the names of two doctors being treated in hospital for AIDS were improperly disclosed; the health authority sought, and obtained, an injunction to prevent their publication by a newspaper. While holding that the health authority had not made out a case for forced disclosure of the source of the information, Rose J stated that such luck a second time was highly unlikely and that prison would be the probable consequence if the informer repeated his or her betrayal of confidence:

> The public in general and patients in particular are entitled to expect hospital records to be confidential and it is not for any individual to take it upon himself or herself to breach that confidence whether induced by a journalist or otherwise.[70]

8.30   The authority's action was not a 'cover-up' operation—the basic reasons underlying absolute confidentiality in AIDS-related cases should be applied irrespective of the patient's calling. The decision can be justified medically on the grounds that the risks of a well-counselled physician passing the disease to a patient are, at worst, slightly more than negligible.[71] This is, however, an area in which the media have been insatiable. A decade or so ago a rash of cases occurred in which the names of infected doctors were widely publicised in the press;[72] a number of letters from the health boards concerned testified to the fact that, given that the previous government policy required the boards to notify all patient contacts of such practitioners, it was virtually impossible to preserve anonymity.[73] Matters came to a head in the case of

---

[67] Under the AIDS (Control) Act 1987, health authorities must provide reports to the responsible minister. The minister can also order hospitalisation and, if necessary, detention of sufferers: Public Health (Infectious Diseases) Regulations 1988, SI 1988/1546.

[68] For an early overview of the ethical position which is still valid today, see R Gillon 'AIDS and Medical Confidentiality' (1987) 294 BMJ 1675.

[69] [1988] 2 All ER 648, (1992) 3 BMLR 1.

[70] [1988] 2 All ER 648 at 665, (1992) 3 BMLR 1 at 21, per Rose J.

[71] This is extremely rare. For example, at the turn of the century there were only two reported instances of patients being infected by health care workers during clinical procedures, and in only one of those was the transmission route clear, see F Lot, J C Seguier, S Fegueux et al 'Probable Transmission of HIV from an Orthopaedic Surgeon to a Patient in France' (1999) 130 Ann Int Med 1, and C Ciesielski, D Marianos, C Y Ou et al 'Transmission of Human Immunodeficiency Virus in a Dental Practice' (1992) 116 Ann Int Med 798.

[72] See e.g. the banner headlines in a quality newspaper: B Christie 'Hunt for AIDS Scare Patients' *Scotsman*, 27 May 1993, p 1. It seems that the doctor's name was published by the paper despite the fact that the Health Board intended to preserve anonymity.

[73] Although this information need not be given 'face to face': *AB v Tameside and Glossop Health Authority* (1997) 35 BMLR 79, [1997] 8 Med LR 91.

H (a healthcare worker) v Associated Newspapers Ltd.[74] This case was unlike any other in so far as the provisions of the Human Rights Act 1998 were in force at the time when the press sought either to name the health authority (N) for which H worked, or to disclose H's speciality and the approximate date when he became HIV positive. A fundamental tension of rights and interests therefore arose between, on the one hand, H's right to respect for his private life (Article 8) and, on the other, the right of the press to freedom of expression (Article 10). The issues were complicated by the fact that H, having received expert advice that the risks of exposure given his discipline were negligible, had challenged the existing government policy[75] that required a health authority to undertake a 'lookback exercise' to identify patients who had come into contact with HIV positive health workers. He would not, therefore, grant access to his patient records and sought injunctory relief to prevent any disclosure of his identity, discipline or the name of the health authority for which he worked. In defiance of an order that was given, the *Mail on Sunday* published a story from which clues to H's identity could be gleaned. The injunction was then varied to allow greater disclosure and a challenge was lodged in the Court of Appeal by H and N. In balancing the delicately poised issues surrounding the tensions between Articles 8 and 10, the Court of Appeal found some measure of support for both sides of the argument. First, the court reiterated the strong public interest in maintaining the confidentiality of health workers infected with HIV—to do otherwise, it was held, would simply deter others from coming forward, and this could be in no-one's interests. The injunction against naming H or N was, accordingly, upheld. However, the risk of H being thereby identified was insufficient to justify a continuing restriction on disclosure of his speciality—he was, in fact, a dentist. Such a constraint inhibited the airing of aspects of the debate which were of important public interest. Moreover, the court recognised the public interest in the new policy guidelines on recontacting patients and, with this in view, ordered that H should hand over his patient records once new guidelines were in place (although these records should not be used without his permission or that of the court).

8.31   It is interesting to note that, as a result, the government's subsequent guidance supports lookback exercises only in very rare circumstances.[76] A major factor in this decision, beyond the scientific evidence of negligible risk in most cases, was the disproportionate negative public effect that previous exercises have had by way of unduly distressing sectors of the public. And, once again, the importance of maintaining the confidentiality of those with HIV is recognised.

8.32   Anyone infected with HIV constitutes an undoubted danger to his or her sexual partner(s), although the risk of transmission depends upon the nature of the sexual activity, the frequency and diversity of exposure and the extent to which precautions

---

[74] [2002] EWCA Civ 195, (2002) 65 BMLR 132.

[75] Health Service Circular *Guidance on the Management of AIDS/HIV Infected Health Care Workers and Patient Notification* (HSC 1998/226).

[76] Department of Health *AIDS/HIV Infected Health Care Workers: Guidance on the Management of Infected Health Care Workers and Patient Notification* (2003).

are taken. Counselling of HIV cases includes such information routinely, and patients are advised as to the need to disclose their status to those whom they might have put at risk of infection. It is unsurprising that there will be some patients who are not prepared to do so nor, indeed, to inform their general practitioners; the doctor is then faced with the problem of whether or not he, himself, should inform those with 'a need to know'. The GMC has advised doctors that:

You may disclose information about a patient, whether living or dead, in order to protect a person from risk of death or serious harm. For example, you may disclose information to a known sexual contact of a patient with HIV where you have reason to think that the patient has not informed that person, and cannot be persuaded to do so. In such circumstances you should tell the patient before you make the disclosure, and you must be prepared to justify a decision to disclose information.[77]

8.33   Thus, passing information to a patient's spouse or other sexual partner in the absence of consent is allowable so long as every effort has been made to persuade the patient to do so and there is a serious and identifiable risk to a specific individual. The GMC concludes that the responsibility for any action taken is entirely that of the individual doctor—which tells us nothing as to how to construct that responsibility.

8.34   The Institute of Medical Ethics has advocated a relationship of mutual empowerment based on a balance between, on the one hand, the patient's proper power of decision-making and, on the other, the doctor's exercise of clinical skills and, most importantly, of effective communication of information.[78] The ideal is that the person at risk should be able to make an informed choice whether or not to accept the risk and that this choice will be offered by the patient. In the exceptional case where the patient frustrates this policy, the doctor should, in the Institute's view, base his decision as to whether or not to breach confidentiality on the strength of his judgment that, by maintaining confidentiality, he can encourage the infected patient to acknowledge his or her responsibility to respect the interests of others. In this respect, great importance is laid on whether or not the person at risk is also a patient of the doctor—the implication being that, in the first case, disclosure would be justified fairly easily but that confidentiality would be the better choice in the latter.

8.35   This may be a pragmatic solution, but it appears to us to be morally ambivalent. If it is medical beneficence to inform one's *patient* of a risk, it is scarcely justifiable to bask in the safety-net of confidentiality when one's duty of care is no more than indirect. A discussion based on moral principles, however, takes little account of the legal issues involved and it is arguable that a patient would have a right of action against a doctor who warned his or her spouse or other sexual partner of their potential risk. Despite the prima facie breach of confidence, a court would almost certainly balance the interests involved and hold that disclosure was justified by the intention to protect others from a possibly fatal risk. It is difficult to imagine a court

---

[77] General Medical Council *Serious Communicable Diseases* (1997), para 22.
[78] K M Boyd 'HIV Infection and AIDS: The Ethics of Medical Confidentiality' (1992) 18 J Med Ethics 173.

awarding damages to such a plaintiff but there has been no decision directly in point taken in the United Kingdom. That having been said, the health care professional would need to consider a number of unknown factors in reaching his or her decision to disclose: is there a real on-going risk of infection?—i.e., will the partners continue in risky behaviour? Is the health status of the partner known?—i.e., does he or she already have the disease? Who has been at risk from whom? Perhaps the partner transmitted the condition to the doctor's patient. The lesson is that no breach of confidence should be incurred lightly and any action to approach a third party must be justified in the clearest of terms. Doubts as to the nature and degree of risk would undoubtedly undermine the case for disclosure.

8.36   Conversely, it seems that there is a general common law duty, and a statutory duty on the doctor in some parts of the United States and Canada, to inform those at risk[79]—and the *Tarasoff* decision,[80] which we discuss in chapter 20, could be taken as a pointer. A recent Australian example reveals the complexities. In *PD v Harvey and Chen*,[81] the Supreme Court of New South Wales upheld a negligence claim by a woman (PD) against two health care professionals who had mismanaged her care and that of her HIV positive partner. The couple had attended for testing prior to their marriage and each expected that the other would be informed of their respective results. This, however, was prohibited by statute without express patient consent, and they were not told of this legal reality. PD tested negative but her partner (FH) did not—and PD was refused access to FH's results. At no point did either doctor discuss with FH the prospect of informing PD of his status. FH failed to attend a clinic and deceived PD as to his health status; she became HIV positive. The Court held that the health care professionals were negligent for not taking more steps to protect PD. Importantly, however, it was not part of the decision that either doctor should have approached PD to tell her of FH's results—to do so was expressly prohibited by statute. None the less, they could have maintained better communication between themselves as to the state of play and kept fuller records, they could have better informed FH and PD of the realities of risk, they could have pursued FH for non-attendance at the clinic, and, ultimately, they could have reported the case to the Director-General of Health who *did* have the legal authority to communicate the risk to PD without breaching confidentiality. We see, then, that compromising confidentiality was contemplated only as a last resort; the case also makes the point that much can be done in operational terms to protect third party interests.

---

[79] In a number of American states specific statutory provisions impose a duty of disclosure on HIV positive persons to disclose their status to their partners: see J W Rose 'To Tell or Not to Tell: Legislative Imposition of Partner Notification Duties for HIV Patients' (2001) 22 J Legal Med 107. For Canada see, Canadian HIV/AIDS Legal Network, *Privacy Protection and the Disclosure of Health Information: Legal Issues for People Living With HIV/AIDS in Canada* (2004), available at www.aidslaw.ca.

[80] *Tarasoff v Regents of the University of California* 529 P 2d 55 (Cal, 1974); on appeal 551 P 2d 334 (Cal, 1976). Decisions following upon this include the contrasting cases of *Brady v Hopper* 751 F 2d 329 (1984) and *Peterson v State* 671 P 2d 230 (Was, 1983).

[81] [2003] NSWSC 487.

8.37   A final curious twist to the topic emerged in the remarkable Californian case of *Reisner*.[82] A young girl had been exposed to HIV infection through the transfusion of tainted blood but neither she nor her parents were informed of this. Some years later she became intimate with a boyfriend, whom she infected with the virus. He raised a successful action for damages against the doctors for their failure to inform her, thereby subjecting him, as a foreseeable victim, to the risk of infection. This decision did not imply that the doctor had a duty to warn and it is not clear how a court might react to a similar situation in the United Kingdom where the inference of a duty to care in respect of endangered third parties is difficult to reconcile with existing notions. No duty to warn exists in the absence of a special relationship between the parties and it is difficult to see why the HIV/AIDS situation should constitute an exception to the general common law rule, in both England and Scotland, that there is no duty to rescue.[83] It is, however, possible that a doctor might even be held to have a *duty*—as opposed to mere justification—to warn (or at least protect) a third party *who was also his patient* as, in this case, the relationship could be sufficiently proximate to give rise to a duty of positive action.

8.38   It is impossible to leave the subject of confidentiality in HIV infection without mention of the specific problem of prisons—the environment could have been designed for the spread of the condition and the consequences of disclosure of a positive status could be disastrous for the individual. A policy of confidentiality exists but, clearly, it is difficult, if not impossible, to maintain so long as a positive test is associated with segregation, provision of personalised eating utensils and the like; there has also been some limited purposeful breaching of confidentiality in respect of a 'need to know' on the part of the staff.[84] Such potentials for disclosure discourage voluntary testing and counselling and serve as barriers to effective public health measures. It has been shown that a guarantee of confidentiality results in a marked increase in identified positive subjects.[85] Such evidence tends to support the general national policy on confidentiality and HIV; at the same time, it cannot be denied that more prisoners are infected than are identified. The issue is, thus, delicately balanced and is, also, closely tied to the use of preventive measures such as the issue of condoms to prisoners—a policy that is only marginally compatible with strict confidentiality; the subject is, however, beyond the compass of this book.[86]

8.39   A unique example of the possible significance of confidentiality as to HIV infection

---

[82] *Reisner v Regents of the University of California* 37 Cal Rptr 2d 518 (1995). See, too, *Garcia v Santa Rosa Health Care Corp* 925 SW 2d 372 (1996).

[83] For further discussion, see A McCall Smith 'The Duty to Rescue and the Common Law' in M Menlowe and A McCall Smith (eds) *The Duty to Rescue* (1993) p 55.

[84] M Beaupré 'Confidentiality, HIV/AIDS and Prison Health Care Services' (1994) 2 Med L Rev 149. The vexed question of the police's 'need to know' was discussed in J K Mason 'Recording HIV Status on Police Computers' (1992) 304 BMJ 995.

[85] S A M Gore and A G Bird 'No Escape: HIV Transmission in Jail' (1993) 307 BMJ 147.

[86] See *R v Secretary of State for the Home Department* (1999) *The Times*, 21 July and for a full exposition, admittedly in the context of Hepatitis C virus: *R (on the application of H) v Ashworth Hospital Authority* [2002] 1 FCR 206, (2002) 64 BMLR 124.

in the prison context was, however, provided by the Scottish case of *R v Kelly*.[87] Kelly had given a blood sample while in Glenochil prison as part of a research study into HIV prevalence in the institution. On discovering this, the prosecution sought, and received, a Sheriff warrant to gain access to confidential data from which to prove that the strain of virus with which Kelly was infected was also that contracted by his girlfriend. Serious concern has subsequently been raised as to the impact of such practices on uptake by research subjects in prisons.[88] It is not hard to see how such draconian measures in the name of one public interest may finish by thwarting another.[89]

CONFIDENTIALITY WITHIN THE FAMILY

8.40 A narrower area of societal privilege lies within the family, where the doctor may be the first to recognise the signs of violence. The police are, in general, disinclined to interfere in cases of marital violence because of the unsympathetic reception they are likely to get from both sides in so doing. But this may not always be the case, and the doctor cannot be content to watch his patient suffer physical injury and mental trauma either separately or together. In the end, however, it is clear that an adult woman of sound mind is entitled to her autonomy; she has the opportunity of reporting to the police or, often more usefully, she has access to one of the many voluntary shelters which operate. She now has considerable protection under the law.[90] All the doctor can effectively do is to advise, and in this he may be able to help by arranging for treatment of the offender—'wife battering' is markedly associated with alcoholism and neurotic symptoms in the husband or partner, although it would be more accurate today to talk of spousal abuse which can occur at the hands of either party.

8.41 The position is different in the case of child abuse. Parental autonomy must be forfeited on the grounds of impropriety while the doctor is covered, legally, by the doctrine of necessity, and, professionally, by the advice of the GMC that disclosure is justified in such circumstances.[91] By the same token, the courts recognise the fundamental importance in a social care setting of ensuring frankness from parents about what has happened to the child they have allegedly abused; it is within courts' discretion to refuse to order disclosure of reports containing parental statements to the

---

[87] *HM Adv v Kelly* (23 February 2001, unreported), HCJ. See para 2.16 above for fuller discussion.

[88] C Dyer 'Use of Confidential HIV Data Helps Convict Former Prisoner' (2001) 322 BMJ 633.

[89] In another case the wheels of the criminal justice system paid scant regard for the sensitivities of a witness in respect of his health, se C Dyer 'HIV positive witness learns of his status in courtroom' (2004) 328 Brit Med J 1334.

[90] Family Law Act 1996, Part IV, as amended and, now, in particular: Domestic Violence, Crime and Victims Act 2004; see also Matrimonial Homes (Family Protection) (Scotland) Act 1981, as amended, and the Protection from Abuse (Scotland) Act 2001.

[91] *Confidentiality*, n 19 above para 29.

police, and a range of factors have been laid down to consider when assessing such cases.[92]

8.42   In addition to legal problems, however, the doctor faces a clinical dilemma which, although less publicised, is of greater importance. The introduction of registers for infants at risk from violence and the obvious merit in nipping violence in the bud act as servo-mechanisms to one another.[93] There is a real possibility that truly accidental injuries are being misdiagnosed, with a consequent reluctance on the part of parents to seek help for fear of being 'branded';[94] children may, therefore, actually suffer despite the doctor's concern for their safety. A case misdiagnosed as child abuse will cause considerable distress for those accused;[95] but, equally, a missed case which ends in murder can bring great recrimination on the doctor. The concern of the profession as to possible actions for defamation was certainly eased by the decision that a recognised caring authority may refuse to disclose the name of an informant.[96] In the end, however, such a right to or privilege of non-disclosure depends not so much on principles of confidentiality as on what lies in the public interest[97]—or, indeed, in the child's interests.[98] Actions for libel and slander over child care proceedings continue unabated; while absolute privilege does not attach to such sensitive communications, communications between the relevant authorities, in good faith, and with a view to acting in the best interests of the child, attract qualified privilege.[99]

8.43   Confidentiality between parent and child becomes further involved at teen age. Consent to treatment is discussed in detail in chapter 10; in the present context, we are concerned only with confidentiality and, particularly, with the doctor's relationship with the family.[100] It is possible to conceive of other medical conditions which a minor might wish to conceal from his or her parents but, in practice, such conditions are likely to be limited to their sexual affairs.[101] It is trite knowledge that young persons of both sexes do have intercourse and the doctor may be confronted by requests as to contraception or abortion by young girls or for treatment of venereal

---

[92] In Re C (a minor)(care proceedings: disclosure) [1997] Fam 76.

[93] For professional guidance, see Royal College of Paediatrics and Child Health Responsibilities of Doctors in Child Protection Cases with Regard to Confidentiality (2004).

[94] D M Wheeler and C J Hobbs 'Mistakes in Diagnosing Non-accidental Injury: 10 Years' Experience' (1988) 296 BMJ 1233. The European Court of Human Rights has now held that a means of determining allegations of negligence in this respect against local authorities must be available: Z v United Kingdom [2001] 2 FLR 612, (2002) 34 EHRR 3, overturning X and others (minors) v Bedfordshire County Council [1995] 2 AC 633, [1995] 3 All ER 353.

[95] See two 'at-risk register' cases: R v Harrow London Borough Council, ex p D [1989] 3 WLR 1239; R v Hampshire County Council, ex p H [1999] 2 FLR 359.

[96] D v National Society for the Prevention of Cruelty to Children [1978] AC 171, [1977] 1 All ER 589, HL.

[97] Contrast this with the non-medical case of Interbrew SA v Financial Times Ltd [2002] 1 Lloyd's Rep 542 (public interest in discovering iniquity overrode privilege against disclosing sources).

[98] Breach of confidence might, for example, be needed in order to assist in tracing a missing child.

[99] W v Westminster City Council and others [2005] 1 FCR 39.

[100] See J Loughrey, 'Medical Information, Confidentiality and a Child's Right to Privacy' [2003] Legal Studies 510.

[101] But see the case of Emma Hendry discussed below. Inquiry into the death of Emma Jane Hendry (15 January 1998, unreported), Glasgow Sheriff Court.

disease by minors of either sex. It is therefore unsurprising that the leading case to address the question of minors' rights to confidentiality—*Gillick*[102]—should concern contraception and has, in fact, been discussed under that head.[103]

8.44 The background to the *Gillick* decision is relatively simple, yet it represents the core of the case. As we have already suggested, contraception must be seen as sociologically preferable to abortion; even so, only a few young girls are likely to consent to their parents being told they are 'on the pill' and refusal to supply is unlikely to deter those who want sexual intercourse. On this basis, the doctor who supplies contraceptives on request to a girl under the age of 16 is performing a duty to society.[104] On the other hand, most would agree that parents have a right to know what is happening to their children and should, ideally, give consent to medical treatment irrespective of the minor's capacity to understand the complexities. It is, therefore, apparent that any entitlement to consent carries with it a simultaneous entitlement to confidentiality and vice versa. The House of Lords' solution of the problem is to be found in Lord Fraser's five criteria which have been recapitulated above[105] and which can be summarised as granting a right of confidentiality to the mature minor when the exercise of that right was in her best interests. It must, however, be emphasised that, throughout the case, an obligation was firmly imposed on the doctor to attempt to persuade the girl to inform her parents or to allow him to do so—that, in itself, constituting an important qualification of the normal rules of professional secrecy. Thus, despite the case seeming to represent a victory for the autonomy of youth, reliance on *Gillick* can still lead to unease on the part of both the doctor and the patient. On the one hand, the latter cannot know the former's intentions until *after* the consultation; on the other, the doctor must be prepared to justify his decision—but to whom and in what circumstances is left unstated. The decision to respect a minor's right to confidentiality may be a delicate one, and this is particularly so when drugs are prescribed. In one Scottish Fatal Accident Inquiry concerning a 14-year-old girl's death from an overdose of tricyclic antidepressants, a doctor's decision not to inform her parents of her treatment was considered to be perfectly correct. The patient's maturity was held to be such that her desire for confidentiality in relation to her parents had to be respected.[106]

8.45 The jurisprudence concerning the position of children and the proper respect due to their autonomy as to confidences remains disputed. From one perspective, we have the paternalistic stance of the House of Lords being repeated in *Re C (disclosure)*[107]

---

[102] *Gillick v West Norfolk and Wisbech Area Health Authority* [1984] QB 581, [1984] 1 All ER 365; on appeal [1986] AC 112, [1985] 1 All ER 533, CA; revsd [1986] AC 112, [1985] 3 All ER 402, HL.

[103] See para 5.15 et seq above.

[104] Protection from criminal prosecution for a health care professional who acts to protect a child's interests in matters of sexual health or pregnancy is now secured by statute: Sexual Offences Act 2003, s 14(2) and (3) and s 73.

[105] See para 5.20.

[106] *Inquiry into the Death of Emma Jane Hendry* (15 January 1998, unreported), Glasgow Sheriff Court.

[107] [1996] 1 FLR 797.

where the court agreed that it would be lawful to respect the child's wish that her mother not be informed of certain matters during care proceedings, but then expressly noted that the importance of maintaining confidentiality may 'decline' as circumstances change. Autonomy here is relative and subject to the overriding issue of best interests. In contrast, we have Munby J in *Torbay Borough Council v News Group Newspapers*[108] supporting the right of a mature minor (almost 17) to disclose to the press the details of own teenage pregnancy, with or without parental approval. On one level these cases might seem distinguishable: the first is about maintaining and the second about ending confidentiality. At a deeper level, however, the core issue is how far we are willing to recognise emerging autonomy and whether we will go back on the deal. As we argue in the context of consent, the trend remains one of protectionism towards the child.[109]

8.46   The relationship that is longest established within the core family is that between the spouses—what are their mutual rights as to both the positive and negative aspects of confidentiality? If the treatment is for a medical condition, a married person has the same rights to confidentiality in respect of the spouse as in respect of anyone else and, since the Abortion Act 1967 refers only to medical indications, this must apply to abortion. This can be implied also on legal grounds in that, since the husband has no right of veto either in Great Britain or in the United States[110] he similarly has no right to information, and it is not hard to think of instances where disclosure of an abortion to the spouse could be construed as being malicious.

8.47   The conditions are not quite so clear, however, when treatment of an individual is not primarily based on medical considerations but, at the same time, affects the whole family—effectively, this is a matter of sterilisation. Lord Denning was in no doubt in an early, minority, opinion that the surgeon should 'approach the spouse in order to satisfy himself as to consent'.[111] Times have, however, changed and we have no doubt that this cannot now hold—certainly when the operation is in pursuit of personal procreative liberty. On the face of things, there ought to be a consensual decision, but the twenty-first-century couple is not certainly going to be together until parted by death; religious differences may prohibit agreement and there must be times when one spouse feels compelled to act for his or her individual, rather than family, reasons. It could be that unilateral action could lead to the divorce courts and the doctor might, for example, not wish to run the risk of being involved. Refusal to sterilise in the absence of consent to spousal consultation would, then, be a matter of personal

---

[108]   [2004] 2 FLR 949, [2004] Fam Law 793.

[109]   *In the Matter of X* [2002] JRC 202 the court upheld the right of the 16-year-old woman to refuse to authorise transfer of tissue from her aborted fetus to the police to determine paternity for the purposes of possible prosecution for unlawful sexual intercourse. This was so despite affidavits from the parents consenting to the procedure. None the less, the court reiterated that its inherent jurisdiction meant that the refusal could be overridden in the child's best interests; in the instance case, however, the court was not convinced that those interests would be served by dismissing the refusal.

[110]   Initially confirmed in *Paton v British Pregnancy Advisory Service Trustees* [1979] QB 276, [1978] 2 All ER 987, and in the US in *Planned Parenthood of Southeastern Pennsylvania v Casey* 112 S Ct 2791 (1992).

[111]   *Bravery v Bravery* [1954] 3 All ER 59 at 67, [1954] 1 WLR 1169 at 1177, CA.

choice—but he would, we suggest, still be under an obligation to refer the patient to another practitioner. The matter has been discussed in greater detail in chapter 5.

8.48   Finally, and as we discuss in chapter 7, the familial nature of much genetic information means that both immediate and not-so-immediate family members may have an interest in knowing, or having access to, a relative's genetic data because of the implications that it might have for their own health or life decisions. We explore this far more fully elsewhere,[112] but the most important point for present purposes is to recognise the challenge which these realities pose to the existing legal regimes for protecting patient privacy. Two examples from the data protection domain illustrate this. First, the European Commission's Article 29 Data Protection Working Group—which is charged with monitoring and recommending necessary changes to European data protection law—has specifically stated that:

To the extent that genetic data has a family dimension, it can be argued that it is 'shared' information, with family members having a right to information that may have implications for their own health and future life.[113]

But, as to the implications of this, the Group continues:

The precise legal consequences of this argument are not yet clear. At least two scenarios can be imagined. One is that other family members could also be considered 'data subjects' with all the rights that flow from this. Another option is that other family members would have a right of information of a different character, based on the fact that their personal interests may be affected. However, in both scenarios further options and conditions would have to be considered to accommodate the various conflicts that are likely to arise between the different claims of family members, either to have access to information or to keep it confidential.[114]

8.49   Data protection law is not currently drafted so as to accommodate such claims easily. Its focus on the individual as the 'data subject' perpetuates an atomistic view of how rights under the law are to be managed. Nonetheless, recognition of the possible interconnectedness of family claims through genetic data has penetrated the judicial consciousness. In late 2003, the Supreme Court of Iceland adopted a purposive approach to the Icelandic data protection law (which is essentially an adoption of the 1995 EC Directive) in respect of its application to the ambitious Icelandic Health Sector Database (HSD) project. This project—of which we say more in chapter 19—aims ultimately to link genetic data from the Icelandic people with other records, such as medical and genealogical, so as to create a powerful genetic research resource. The HSD was enabled by legislation from the Icelandic parliament (the Althing) but it has proved to be controversial from the beginning, not least because of its adoption of an opt-out scheme—that is, that all Icelanders are to be included in the project unless they expressly refuse. The case in point arose as an action to prevent transfer to the HSD of a deceased man's medical records to which his daughter laid claim. The

[112] Laurie *Genetic Privacy*, n 7 above.
[113] Article 29 Working Group, *Working Document on Genetic Data* (2004), pp 8–9.   [114] *Ibid*.

enabling legislation provided grounds for such a transfer but no opt-out was available to the relatives of deceased persons. Moreover, the provisions of the data protection law did not apply to deceased persons.[115] The Supreme Court, however, held that personal information relating to the daughter herself could be derived from that of the father because of their genetic connection. Moreover, the Court held that the enabling legislation was unconstitutional because it breached Article 71(1) of the Icelandic Constitution which states that: 'Everyone shall enjoy freedom from interference with privacy, home and family life'—a clear reflection of Article 8(1) of the European Convention on Human Rights. This was, in part, because the sheer richness of the resource increased the risk that individuals could be identified by linkage. The implications of this ruling could be far-reaching through Europe in at least two respects, namely: (i) the meaning of 'personal data' under European data protection law—do all first generation family members, living or dead, have a say in the management of each other's data? and (ii) the legality of human genetic databases—how far must researchers go in protecting personal privacy?[116]

8.50   This ruling is to be contrasted with the recent decision by the English Court of Appeal in *Durant v Financial Services Authority*.[117] While this is not a case dealing with medical information, it nonetheless lays down an important precedent about the meaning of 'personal data' in the UK.[118] Indeed, the court preferred a narrower conception of the term than had previously been thought to apply: the law protects personal data 'relating to' a data subject and this could mean, broadly, information 'having some connection with . . .' or, more narrowly, 'having reference to . . .' the subject. The court preferred the latter, stating:

> The information should have as its focus the data subject rather than some other person with whom he may have been involved or some transaction or event in which he may have figured or had an interest . . . In short, it is information that affects his privacy . . .[119]

This may leave us no further forward in the genetic context because a relative can continue to claim that the processing of a family member's data will 'affect her privacy'. By the same token, this dictum certainly gives a court a way out if it wishes to avoid the uncertainty generated by the Icelandic ruling. It has been reported that Durant has filed papers with the European Commission alleging that the UK has improperly implemented the Data Protection Directive.[120] Certainly, greater clarity in the area would be most welcome.

---

[115] This is also the case under the Data Protection Act 1998.

[116] For comment, see R Gertz, 'Is it "Me" or "We"? Genetic Relations and the Meaning of "Personal Data" under the Data Protection Directive' (2004) 11 Euro J Health Law 231.

[117] [2003] EWCA Civ 1746, [2004] IP & T 814.

[118] See, Information Commissioner's Office *The Durant Case and its Impact on the Interpretation of the Data Protection Act 1998* (2004).

[119] *Durant*, n 117 above, para 28.

[120] For comment see L Edwards 'Taking the "Personal" Out of Personal Data: *Durant v FSA* and its Impact on the Legal Regulation of CCTV' (2004) 1:2 *SCRIPTed* 377: available at www.script-ed.org.

OTHER SPECIAL GROUPS

8.51   There are many special groups which can be conceived of as raising particular problems in relation to medical confidentiality—those which spring to mind most readily are accused persons, prisoners and members of the armed forces. Accused persons are legally innocent and therefore have the same rights as any member of the public. The police surgeon must state that the result of his examination will be reported to third parties and cannot proceed if, as a result, consent to examination is refused. In the interests of justice, however, he may make, and transmit the results of, observations which need not be confined to purely visual impressions.[121] The doctor-patient relationship is complicated in respect of prisoners and confidentiality is best considered as part of the whole spectrum of prison medicine (see chapter 2). The relationship of medical officers in the armed forces to their individual patients is precisely the same as in civilian practice, with the proviso that the doctor's duty to society is accentuated when this is formulated as a duty to a fighting unit; eventually, the lives of many are dependent upon the health of individuals. There is thus a wider justification for disclosure than exists in civilian life and the serviceman has tacitly accepted this in enlisting; nevertheless, the principle of justification remains valid. Similar considerations apply, for instance, to doctors in medical charge of sports teams; the discussion has come full circle in that, basically, one's ethical standards depend upon one's definition of society.

8.52   Doctors employed by companies or other institutions to act as medical advisers on staff health also occupy a special position.[122] A workplace doctor who is employed to carry out regular examinations on staff is bound by the terms of her contract to deliver information to the employer if this might have a bearing on the employer's business.[123] Moreover, such a doctor is not under a duty of care to a job applicant when assessing suitability for employment, even although it is reasonably foreseeable that the applicant might suffer economic loss if a careless error in assessment leads to the loss of a chance of employment.[124] It must now be stated explicitly before carrying out a pre-employment medical examination, or for fitness to work, that the results of that examination may be communicated to the employer and the written consent of the examinee should be obtained in the light of that information. Likewise, in the case of examinations carried out for insurance purposes, the doctor must obtain the positive agreement of the patient to waive the normal obligations of confidentiality within a 'need to know' formula.[125] In the absence of such agreement, it is unlikely that the doctor engaged in industrial or insurance medicine could justify, on either

---

[121]   *Forrester v HM Advocate* 1952 JC 28.

[122]   All medical professionals require now to follow the Information Commissioner's Guidance, The Employment Practices Data Protection Code: Part 4 – Information About Workers' Health (2003).

[123]   *Kapfunde v Abbey National plc and Daniel* (1998) 46 BMLR 176.

[124]   *Ibid.* We explore what some of these options or conditions might be in *Genetic Privacy*, n 7, above, and chapter 7.

[125]   At the present time a moratorium is in place in respect of accessing genetic test results, except in the most limited of circumstances; this is due to be revised in 2008, see further chapter 7.

ethical or legal grounds, a breach of a patient's confidence on the grounds that he, the doctor, owed a duty as an employee to his employer.[126] As a corollary, the European Court of Justice, for its part, has held that patients cannot be required to undertake medical tests against their will, nor can these be carried out clandestinely, to further an employer's interest in maintaining a healthy workforce.[127] This would be contrary to the right to respect for private and family life. But the irony is that there is no corresponding right not to be asked questions about one's health; indeed, in X v Commissioner it was held to be legitimate for an employer to draw adverse inferences from a candidate's refusal to disclose health data. The employer could not be obliged to take the risk of recruiting an unhealthy candidate. This is something of a hollow view of privacy protection. It might well be thought that we are entitled to expect better.

FOR THE PURPOSES OF MEDICAL RESEARCH

8.53   Information may be disclosed if necessary for the purposes of a medical research project which has been approved by a recognised ethical committee.[128] The matter is included in the general discussion of medical research in chapter 19.[129] For the present, we need only note the increasingly beneficent view of the public interest in research adopted by officialdom. The Department of Health, for example, has stated that:

... when the public good that would be served by disclosure is significant, there may be grounds for disclosure [of patient information]. The key principle to apply is that of proportionality. Whilst it would not be reasonable and proportionate to disclose confidential information to a researcher where patient consent could be sought, if it is not practicable to locate a patient without unreasonable effort and the likelihood of detriment to the patient is negligible, disclosure to support the research might be proportionate.[130]

8.54   Somewhat more controversially, relaxation of the principles involved has spilled over into statute where section 60 of the Health and Social Care Act 2001 allows the Secretary of State to make provisions requiring or regulating the processing of patient medical data in their own medical interests or in the public interest, including research interests.[131] Regulations made under this Act state that:

---

[126] See, generally, Joint Guidelines from the *British Medical Association and the Association of British Insurers* (2002).

[127] Case C-404–92P *X v Commission* [1994] ECR I-4737.

[128] On the data protection position see the guidance by the Information Commissioner's Office, n 26, above, chapter 3.

[129] For a balanced discussion of the privacy issues see, W Lowrance *Learning from Experience: Privacy and the Secondary use of Data in Health Research* (2002).

[130] Department of Health *Confidentiality: NHS Code of Practice* (2003), para 34.

[131] These provisions only apply in England and Wales. The Confidentiality and Security Group for Scotland (CSAGS) produced its report of recommendations in April 2002, *Protecting Patient Confidentiality: Final Report* (2002) in which a more even balance between protecting individual rights to privacy and public interests in research is sought.

Anything done by a person that is necessary for the purpose of processing patient information in accordance with these Regulations shall be taken to be lawfully done despite any obligation of confidence owed by that person in respect of it.[132]

Inter alia, the Regulations allow confidential patient information to be processed with a view to (a) diagnosing communicable diseases and other risks to public health; (b) recognising trends in such diseases and risks; (c) controlling and preventing the spread of such diseases and risks; or (d) monitoring and managing—(i) outbreaks of communicable disease; (ii) incidents of exposure to communicable disease; (iii) the delivery, efficacy and safety of immunisation programmes; (iv) adverse reactions to vaccines and medicines; (v) risks of infection acquired from food or the environment (including water supplies); (vi) the giving of information to persons about the diagnosis of communicable disease and risks of acquiring such disease. Note how these terms cover both public health measures and research ends. While, as we have already discussed, the former, at least, can be reasonably easily justified, the extensive discretion of the Secretary of State has been criticised, in general, as giving undue preference to the ill-defined 'public interest' as compared to the individuals' private interests in confidentiality of their medical data.[133] Even so, applications for such uses of patient data are vetted by the Patient Information Advisory Group which consists of a mix of professional and lay members.[134] A similar function is performed in Scotland by the Privacy Advisory Committee[135] which is an independent ad hoc body, established in the early 1990s, to advise on these sensitive issues.[136]

8.55   Trends at common law have been, in some respects, more worrying. In *R v Department of Health, ex p Source Informatics Ltd*, the Court of Appeal was asked to rule on the legality of disclosing anonymised prescribing data to a firm that wished to sell them to pharmaceutical companies to assist in the marketing of their products.[137] Pharmacists had been asked to provide details of general practitioners prescribing habits, and all data were stripped of patient identifiers before being passed on. None the less, the Department of Health issued a policy statement to the effect that this practice was a breach of patient confidentiality in that there was no provision for obtaining patient consent, nor could this be implied from the circumstances in which the information was originally generated. The Court of Appeal held, however, that there could be no breach of confidentiality because: '[t]he concern of the law here is to protect the confider's personal privacy. That and that alone is the right at issue in this

---

[132] Health Service (Control of Patient Information) Regulations 2002, SI 2002/1438, reg 4.

[133] D Beyleveld 'How Not to Regulate in the Public Interest' (2001) 2 Genetics L Montr 5; cf, J Higgins 'Two Sides of the Fence' (2004) Health Service Journal, 7 October 2004, p 20.

[134] www.advisorybodies.doh.gov.uk/piag/.   [135] www.isdscotland.org/isd/.

[136] For a review of these functions, see J Chalmers and R Muir 'Patient Privacy and Confidentiality' (2003) 326 BMJ 725.

[137] [2000] 1 All ER 786, (2000) 52 BMLR 65. For criticism of both the trial court's ruling ([1999] 4 All ER 185, (1999) 49 BMLR 41) which was overturned, and that of the Court of Appeal, see D Beyleveld and E Histed 'Anonymisation is not Exoneration' (1999) 4 Med L Internat 69 and 'Betrayal of Confidence in the Court of Appeal' (2000) 4 Med L Internat 277.

case'.[138] In the Court's view, patient privacy was not under threat because there was no realistic possibility that patient identity could be revealed. Moreover, because the obligation of confidence binds in conscience as an equitable doctrine, and because a reasonable pharmacist's conscience 'would not be troubled by the proposed use made of patients' prescriptions',[139] such treatment of patient information was a fair use and entirely legal.

8.56   This decision represents a major challenge to the law of confidence in that it shifts the basis of the duty of confidence from the public interest to that of the fairness of use. Furthermore, in re-assessing the basis upon which a duty will arise and how far it will extend, the Court conflated the establishment of a duty with its scope despite the fact that, while the former is founded in equity in English law—where a proper role for the question of fairness might arise—the latter has traditionally been treated as being no more than a logically subsequent issue. But the position now seems to be that there is no breach of confidence where there is no unfairness to the confider in a possible use of information—and this is so even when that use is unauthorised. Put another way, the decision in *Source Informatics* indicates that the onus has shifted to the confider who feels that his or her confidence has been abused to show unfairness of use before an action will lie. Moreover, it has removed the public interest requirement from the equation, and this is particularly disturbing because it also led the court to ignore the wider and longer term impact of its decision on the generality of public interest in maintaining confidences. Arguably, the effect of *Source Informatics* is to reduce the individual's legal interest in his or her own information to no more than that of ensuring that anonymity is maintained. In so doing, other fundamental issues are ignored, including the role of consent in legitimising the uses of information, the concept of reasonable expectations of use and, ultimately, the importance of maintaining a prima facie respect for confidences.

CONFIDENTIALITY AND THE LEGAL PROCESS

8.57   Disclosure of confidential medical information as part of the legal process can be considered in two main categories—statutory and non-statutory. Statutory disclosure presents no problem to the doctor but it is, nevertheless, showing signs of encroachment on traditional values. Thus, the original requirements for reporting by the doctor of infectious disease[140] or industrial poisoning[141] are clearly directed to the good of society. More recently, however, compulsory notification has become required

---

[138] *Ibid*, at All ER 797a.   [139] *Ibid*, at All ER 796f.
[140] Public Health (Infectious Diseases) Regulations 1988, SI 1988/1546.
[141] Reporting of Injuries, Diseases and Dangerous Occurrences Regulations 1995, SI 1995/3163, as amended.

more for statistical purposes[142] or for the protection of individuals by the state.[143] The two latter examples also exemplify the increasing acceptance of state control of the medical profession itself. Despite occasional protests at 'interference', we feel that most people would accept such regulations.[144]

8.58   It is to be noted that no immunity is granted to the doctor when a statutory duty is imposed on 'a person' to provide information. Such a situation arises, for example, under the Terrorism Act 2000, s 19, which places every person under an obligation to disclose to the police information connected with acts of terrorism.[145] Opinion is divided, however, as to the working of the Road Traffic Act 1988 when, by virtue of s 172,[146] the doctor must provide on request any evidence which he has which may lead to the identification of a driver involved in an accident. The patient can scarcely expect the doctor to breach confidentiality; yet the doctor's liability under the law has been confirmed.[147]

8.59   There may, of course, be other times when the police would have an interest in access to medical records. Police engaged in the investigation of a serious arrestable offence may obtain a warrant to search for material which is likely to be relevant evidence. Under the Police and Criminal Evidence Act 1984,[148] magistrates cannot, however, issue a warrant to search for 'excluded material' which includes personal records relating to a person's physical or mental health and which are held in confidence; medical records are, therefore, excluded material. However, a constable may still apply to a judge for an order to obtain such records. Not only must the court be satisfied of the need for access, but there must have been some statutory authority passed before the 1984 Act which would have authorised such a search. The Act illustrates some of the difficulties in applying an ethical principle by way of statute. Hospital notes are clearly excluded material and can, therefore, be withheld from the police irrespective of the purpose of their search. Thus, the police cannot obtain them even though their sole purpose is, for example, to establish the whereabouts of a potential murderer at a given time[149]—as Morland J said in *R v Cardiff Crown Court, ex p Kellam*:[150]

Presumably Parliament considered that the confidentiality of records of identifiable

---

[142] Abortion Regulations 1991, SI 1991/499, as amended; Abortion (Scotland) Regulations 1991, SI 1991/460, as amended.

[143] Misuse of Drugs (Supply to Addicts) Regulations 1997, SI 1997/1001.

[144] But some powerful objections can be raised. See, in particular, M Brazier and J Harris 'Public Health and Private Lives' (1996) 4 Med L Rev 171.

[145] Exceptions such as exist do not apply to medical practitioners, see Terrorism Act 2000 (Crown Servants and Regulators) Regulations 2001, SI 2001/192.

[146] As substituted by Road Traffic Act 1991, s 21.

[147] *Hunter v Mann* [1974] QB 767, [1974] 2 All ER 414.

[148] Section 9(1). On the scope of powers of seizure, see the Criminal Justice and Police Act 2001, s 50, and on the international dimension see Crime (International Co-operation) Act 2003, s 16.

[149] *R v Cardiff Crown Court, ex p Kellam* (1993) 16 BMLR 76. The court set aside the order to produce the documents 'with considerable reluctance'.

[150] (1993) 16 BMLR 76 at 80.

individuals relating to their health should have paramountcy over the prevention and investigation of serious crime.

But one wonders if this was really in the contemplation of the legislature or of those who lobbied them so assiduously. Even so, a doctor who sees it as a public duty to co-operate with the police may produce such records[151]—provided, of course, that he is prepared to justify this later in a court of law or before his peers.

8.60   We are each of us a walking record of our own genetic constitution. A DNA sample can reveal our entire genetic make-up and DNA-based evidence has transformed criminal investigation and prosecution in the two decades since profiling was developed. The power of our genetic secrets is, indeed, so strong and potentially useful to the pursuit of the public interest in crime prevention and detection that many countries have instituted specific provisions relating both to the protection of genetic privacy and, perhaps more significantly, to legitimising the invasion of genetic privacy in the name of criminal justice. In this last regard, the United Kingdom has been by far the boldest, instituting provisions in 2004 to allow the retention of samples from people who have been detained on the suspicion of a recordable offence—samples which can be taken without the individual's consent—even when that person is never subsequently charged with an offence.[152] Such data will be entered in the National DNA Database (NDNAD), which has been in existence since 1995 and which is now the most extensive—and, thereby, most powerful—forensic database of its kind in the world. Interestingly, there is evidence of strong support for the forensic uses of data among some sections of the public;[153] others, however, point to the not-inconsiderable risks to human rights and privacy that such a collection presents.[154] Everyone wants a safer society, but not at any cost. For our part, we simply caution against blind faith in DNA technologies, and endorse the recommendations of the Human Genetics Commission regarding suitable safeguards against abuses of the system.[155] These include the establishment of an independent body to oversee the NDNAD, and strict controls on any further extensions of collection and retention powers that might threaten other public interests. Of particular interest for this book is the need to prevent police access to medical research results because of concern for the deterrent effect this might have on future research subjects.

8.61   Other than by regulations, courts of law can compel the disclosure of medical material either through the production of documents or during evidence and cross-examination.

---

[151] *R v Singleton* [1995] 1 Cr App R 431, [1995] Crim LR 236.

[152] See the Criminal Justice and Public Order Act 1994 and the Criminal Justice and Police Act 2001, s 82. Confirmed in *R (on the application of S) v Chief Constable of South Yorkshire* [2003] 1 All ER 148, [2003] Cr App R 16, CA.

[153] Human Genetics Commission *Public Attitudes to Human Genetic* Information (2001), pp 35–38.

[154] GeneWatch UK *The Police National DNA Database: Balancing Crime Detection, Human Rights and Privacy* (2005).

[155] Human Genetics Commission *Inside Information: Balancing Interests in the Use of Personal Genetic Data* (2002), chapter 9.

DISCLOSURE OF DOCUMENTS

8.62 A patient contemplating negligence proceedings against a doctor or a health authority will usually need access to his medical records so that his claim can be evaluated by his legal and medical advisers.[156] Those in possession of such records have been enjoined by the courts to act in a spirit of candour and not to resist disclosure—a course of action which might have the effect of delaying the resolution of a dispute and preventing a just outcome.[157] Failure to put one's 'cards on the table' can be met with an order for the discovery of documents under ss 33 and 34 of the Supreme Court Act 1981. Disclosure may be made to a medical expert or to the applicant's legal advisers. A plaintiff cannot engage in a general 'fishing expedition' to see whether he has a cause of action—an application must disclose the 'nature of the claim he intends to make and show not only the intention of making it but also that there is a reasonable basis for making it'.[158]

8.63 A person in possession of documents may be entitled to refuse disclosure on the grounds that it is not in the public interest to make the documents available.[159] This will rarely arise in medical negligence cases, but the court may have to consider whether disclosure should be denied when there is a public health dimension to a case.[160] This was the position in *Re HIV Haemophiliac Litigation*,[161] where the public interest in question was the confidentiality of policy documents relating to blood products policy. Similarly, in *AB v Glasgow and West of Scotland Blood Transfusion Service*,[162] the Court of Session would not order disclosure of the identity of a blood donor in an action resulting from the donation of contaminated blood—the pursuer's right to claim damages was not of such magnitude that it should take precedence over a material risk to the sufficiency of the national supply of blood for transfusion. In contrast, international co-operation between courts ordering access to relevant materials or premises has now been greatly facilitated by the adoption of a European Union Regulation; thus, in *MMR and MR Vaccine Litigation (No. 10); Sayers and others v Smithkline Beecham plc and others*[163] the British court deemed it appropriate to request an Irish court to require disclosure of material relevant to the action in respect of adverse consequences of taking vaccines produced in Ireland but administered in the United Kingdom.[164]

---

[156] For the converse situation where it was claimed (and rejected) that a patient who raises legal proceedings against his health care professional impliedly waives his right to confidentiality in the relevant medical records, see *Kadian v Richards* [2004] NSWSC 382.

[157] *Naylor v Preston Area Health Authority* [1987] 2 All ER 353, [1987] 1 WLR 958, CA.

[158] *Dunning v United Liverpool Hospitals Board of Governors* [1973] 2 All ER 454 at 460.

[159] *Re EC (disclosure of material)* [1996] 2 FLR 725, [1997] Fam Law 160.

[160] Section 35 of the Supreme Court Act 1981 allows the court to refuse access in the public interest.

[161] [1990] NLJR 1349, (1998) 41 BMLR 171. For the superiority of the public interest in food production for the NHS, see *Tillery Valley Foods Ltd v Channel Four Television Corporation* (2004) *The Times*, 21 May.

[162] 1993 SLT 36, (1989) 15 BMLR 91.

[163] [2004] All ER (D) 67.

[164] Council Regulation (EC) 1206/2001. For an example of a transatlantic dispute, see *United States of America v Philip Morris Inc* [2004] EWCA Civ 330.

8.64   Court directions may also be made for the disclosure before trial of expert medical reports which it is proposed to bring in evidence. The exception to this policy once lay in cases involving a suggestion of medical negligence—the rationale being that parties should not have to disclose experts' reports which were directed to establishing liability rather than to the prognosis and quantum of damages.[165] Largely as a result of the unsatisfactory trial in *Wilsher*,[166] alterations were made to the Rules of the Supreme Court so as to bring medical negligence cases into line with others involving personal injury—prior disclosure was to become the norm rather than the exception. In general, *all* the cards must now be put down, not just those obviously concerned with the action; the current view is that the court can deal with problems of confidentiality relating to irrelevant conditions—such as a past history of sexually transmitted disease—by limiting disclosure to the other side's medical advisers who must respect medical confidentiality except where litigation is affected.[167] The whole tenor of the medical negligence case and its management have been reformed by the Woolf Report[168] which, we suggest, should be consulted in the original—it gives a major insight as to how the wind is blowing in this area.[169]

8.65   Disclosure of documents and information is, in any case, subject to what is commonly known as 'legal professional privilege'—a doctrine designed to allow the client unfettered access to his advisers.[170] The concept is not without difficulties, of which the doctor should be aware. First, legal professional privilege is tightly defined and is likely to be overridden, whenever this is possible, in the interests of legal fairness.[171] Thus, disclosure of reports which are designed primarily for accident investigation and prevention and only secondarily for the purpose of seeking legal advice is likely to be ordered. It is clear that this gives rise to a conflict of interests. On the one hand, it could be held that the public good of preventive medicine must take second place to the threat of private litigation;[172] on the other, the imposition of professional privilege

---

[165] *Rahman v Kirklees Area Health Authority* [1980] 3 All ER 610, [1980] 1 WLR 1244, CA.

[166] *Wilsher v Essex Area Health Authority* [1987] QB 730, [1986] 3 All ER 80, CA. *America v Philip Morris Inc* [2004] EWCA Civ 330.

[167] *Dunn v British Coal Corpn* [1993] ICR 591, CA.

[168] Lord Woolf *Access to Justice* (1996), chapter 15 (www.lcd.gov.uk/civil/finalfr.htm). For further thoughts, see Lord Woolf, 'Are the Courts Excessively Deferential to the Medical Profession?' (2001) 9 Med L Rev 1.

[169] For an assessment of the effects of the reforms after three years, see Department for Constitutional Affairs, *Further Findings: A Continuing Evaluation of of the Civil Justice Reforms* (2002).

[170] For the latest authoritative pronouncements on the nature of legal professional privilege, see *Three Rivers District Council v Governor and Company of the Bank of England (No. 5)* [2004] UKHL 48. While this focuses on lawyers and banker clients the contrast is nevertheless drawn as between doctors and their patients, *ibid*, para 28ff.

[171] Professional privilege is, in a sense, a product of the adversarial system of presenting evidence and is less likely to be upheld when proceedings are more akin to inquisitorial. Classic examples of the latter are cases brought under the Children Act 1989 or in wardship proceedings: *Oxfordshire County Council v M* [1994] Fam 151.

[172] *Waugh v British Railways Board* [1980] AC 521, [1979] 2 All ER 1169. The order to disclose may extend to specific accident report forms which might well be thought to be privileged (*Lask v Gloucester Health Authority* (1985) *The Times*, 13 December). Failures, mistakes and 'near-misses' must now be reported to the

has, on occasion, been granted only reluctantly in that secrecy is inequitable to the person who suffers medical mishap.[173] Secondly, while professional privilege is there in order to allow the client to be uninhibited when approaching his legal advisers, there is no corresponding privilege to encourage a patient to be equally open in relation to his medical advisers.[174] This was demonstrated forcefully in *W v Egdell*,[175] where it was concluded that a clear and important distinction was to be made between, on the one hand, instructions given to an expert and, on the other, the expert's opinion given in response to those instructions; the former was covered by legal professional privilege, while the latter was not. We have some difficulty in understanding how a question can be subject to absolute confidentiality while the answer is not; nevertheless, the ruling given at first instance was fully supported in the Court of Appeal. Thirdly, a request for information from a solicitor is not the same as an order of the court even though the conditions—e.g. that litigation is in progress—may seem similar; medical practitioners have been found guilty of serious professional misconduct for making such a mistake in good faith but in ignorance.[176] It is worth noting that, while the legal representative may, of course, withhold any documents to which professional privilege applies, the adversary may have advantage of these if they are disclosed in error and it is not obvious that privilege has not been waived.[177] Finally, where an order is sought for the disclosure of the medical records of a non-party to a dispute—and we know of only one reported case directly in point—it will be granted only in the most exceptional of circumstances. In *A v X (Disclosure: Non-party Medical Records)*[178] the defendants sought access to the medical records of the brother of the claimant to cast doubt on his claim that the defendant's negligence had brought about psychiatric problems; the implication was that those problems were already manifest in the family. The court refused the order stating that it would only be granted when: (1) the documents for which disclosure is sought are likely to support the case of the applicant or adversely affect the case of one of the other parties to the proceedings, and (2) disclosure is *necessary* in order to dispose fairly of the claim or to save costs.[179]

8.66   The doctor in the witness box has absolute privilege and is protected against any action for breach of confidence. The authority of the Earl of Halsbury LC remains undisputed today: the immunity of the witness in court 'is settled in law and cannot

---

National Patient Safety Agency (www.npsa.org.uk). How the intended 'no blame' culture will meld with the growing taste for litigation has yet to be seen: G Watts 'Coaxing Doctors to Confess' (2001) 323 BMJ 890.

[173] *Lee v South West Thames Regional Health Authority* [1985] 2 All ER 385, [1985] 1 WLR 845, discussed also in 'Disclosure of Documents by Doctors' (1985) 290 BMJ 1973.

[174] *Three Rivers*, n 170, above.   [175] [1990] Ch 359, [1989] 1 All ER 1089.

[176] 'Medical Confidence and the Law' (1981) 283 BMJ 1062.

[177] *Pizzey v Ford Motor Co Ltd* [1994] PIQR P15, CA.   [178] [2004] EWHC 447.

[179] Cf, *S v W Primary Care Trust* [2004] EWHC 2085 where the court ordered disclosure of the records of a child despite concerns on the part of the Trust that it might damage his health interests and that early entries contained sensitive material on his mother. Disclosure was, however, only authorise to legal and medical representatives and to his maternal grandmother as carer.

be doubted'.[180] This privilege extends to pre-trial conferences and Scottish precognitions,[181] the exception being that a privileged communication must not be made maliciously.[182] Judges may go to great lengths to protect the witness but, when so ordered, the doctor is bound to answer any question which is put to him;[183] refusal to answer in the absence of the court's discretion to excuse a conscientious witness must expose the doctor to a charge of contempt—and the court will take precedence even when there is a statutory obligation of secrecy.[184] In some European countries, however, the obligation to maintain confidentiality extends to the courtroom.

PATIENT ACCESS TO MEDICAL RECORDS

8.67   It is only recently that patients' rights to see their medical records have been established on a relatively firm basis.[185] An important early development in this respect came with the Access to Medical Reports Act 1988. The reports to which the Act refers are limited to those prepared by a doctor who has clinical charge of the patient and which are intended for direct supply to the patient's employer, prospective employer or to an insurance company (s 2). Reports by doctors who have had only a casual, non-caring professional association with the patient are excluded. Such reports as are included have always been subject to the patient's consent but the applicant must now positively seek such consent and must inform him of his rights to access (s 3). The patient can see the report before it is sent and, unless he has done so, issue of the report must be delayed for three weeks (s 4). He has the right to ask the doctor to alter anything that he feels is inaccurate and he may add a dissenting statement should the doctor refuse to do so (s 5). Access may be withheld if disclosure would cause serious harm to the patient's physical or mental health—or to that of any other person—but, in those circumstances, the patient may withdraw his consent to its promulgation.[186]

8.68   Considerable concern was, however, being expressed over the storage of

---

[180] In *Watson v M'Ewan* [1905] AC 480 at 486, HL.

[181] On the position regarding pre-trial work generally, see *Raiss v Paimano* [2001] 4 Lloyd's Rep PN 341.

[182] *AB v CD* (1904) 7 F 72, per Lord Moncrief. This is the Court of Session stage of *Watson v M'Ewan*. The same applies in other Commonwealth countries. See *Hay v University of Alberta Hospital* [1991] 2 Med LR 204 (QB, Alberta), in which it was held that the plaintiff had no right to withhold consent to pre-trial discussions by the defendants with his medical attendants.

[183] The exception to this requirement being disclosure of a source of information for which special rules apply (Contempt of Court Act 1981, s 10).

[184] *Garner v Garner* (1920) 36 TLR 196.

[185] See, Department of Health *Guidance for Access to Health Records Requests under the Data Protection Act 1998* (2003).

[186] The Access to Health Records Act 1990 provided access rights to manual files subject to certain limits at the discretion of the health care professional. However, since the passing of the Data Protection Act 1998, the terms of this Act are now redundant except in so far as they relate to a deceased person (s 3(1)(f)).

information on computers[187] and it was this general development which led to further changes in perspective. The Council of Europe's Data Protection Convention (1981) required the recognition of a right of access to personal data stored in computer banks; this gave rise to the Data Protection Act 1984, which has now been replaced by the Data Protection Act 1998. Under the 1998 Act, the subject has a right to information as to the purposes for which data about him are being processed and the persons who will have access to them.[188] The protection of those about whom information is stored lies in preventing the holding of inaccurate information or of concealing the fact that information is stored at all. As a consequence, a patient has the right, subject to a fee, to be told by the 'data controller'—who could be any health caring body holding records—whether any such information is held and, if it is, to be supplied with a copy of that information.

8.69   Subsequent to the passing of the 1998 Act, further regulations were implemented which deal directly with the management of personal data in the health care context. The Data Protection (Subject Access Modification) (Health) Order 2000 restricts patients' rights over their medical data in a number of respects.[189] For example, the Order provides exceptions to the subject's access rights in the case of personal data consisting of information as to his or her physical or mental condition—which will include most information held by NHS bodies. These are: (a) again, where permitting access to the data would be likely to cause serious harm to the physical or mental health or condition of the data subject or any other person (which may include a health professional); and (b) where the request for access is made by another on behalf of the data subject, such as a parent for a child. In the latter case, access can be refused if the data subject had either provided the information in the expectation it would not be disclosed to the applicant or had indicated it should not be so disclosed, or if the data were obtained as a result of any examination or investigation to which the data subject consented on the basis that information would not be so disclosed.[190]

8.70   The European Court of Human Rights has confirmed that access to records containing personal information is, prima facie, a matter of entitlement under Article 8 of the European Convention and is part of the State's obligation to respect the private and family lives of is citizens.[191] It is not, however, an absolute right and other interests may be in play. For example, in *MG v UK*[192] the applicant sought access to social

---

[187] On the interface between disclosure provisions and data protection rights of access, see *Johnson v Medical Defence Union* [2005] 1 All ER 87.

[188] There are, of course, some exceptions to this, for example, medical research uses that do not affect the patient directly and the results do not identify her, see the Information Commissioner's Office Guidance, n 26 above, chapter 3.

[189] The Data Protection (Subject Access Modification) (Health) Order 2000, SI 2000/413.

[190] Before deciding whether these exemptions apply a data controller who is not a health professional must consult the health professional responsible for the clinical care of the data subject; or if there is more than one, the most suitable available health professional. If there is none, a health professional who has the necessary qualifications and experience to advise on the matters to which the information requested relates must be consulted.

[191] *MG v United Kingdom* [2002] 3 FCR 413.   [192] *Ibid.*

service records to confirm his suspicions of childhood abuse at the hands of his father. It was recognised by the Court that the authorities had legitimate concerns about the privacy of third parties in such a case (e.g., the siblings), and that this might be a legitimate reason to deny full access. Notwithstanding this, the absence of an appeal body to challenge a refusal of access constituted a breach of the applicant's human rights. This has now been remedied in the United Kingdom whereby the Information Commissioner's Office can hear appeals against denial of access to personal records.

8.71   It was at one time feared that patients' access to their records would lead to less frank opinions being expressed in hospital notes and to greater reliance on oral communication between health carers; the potential disadvantage to the patient is, then, evident—in the event of a change of location, his accompanying medical documents will be of less value to his new health carers than ought to be the case.[193] There is, however, no hard evidence that rights of access have affected medical practice adversely and, certainly, an impressive body of research can be quoted which stresses their practical advantages. There is even a movement towards giving patients physical possession of their records,[194] a facility made all the easier with the advent of swipe-card and biometric technologies.[195] The ownership of the intellectual property contained in a record—i.e. the copyright—is held by the person who has created the notes or his employer, and not by the subject of those notes. Moreover, the physical notes themselves are owned by the GP practice, trust or health authority. The patient is therefore unlikely ever to have a successful property claim over his or her records.[196]

THE REMEDIES

8.72   For many years the law was unclear as to the remedies for breach of confidentiality in spite of its recognition of such breaches as a proper basis for legal action. This latter was considerably clarified and its requirements set out in the House of Lords decision in *A-G v Guardian Newspapers (No. 2)*.[197] It is likely that a patient would be able to claim damages for improper disclosure of information about his health even if he suffered no financial loss as a result; this is almost implicit from *X v Y*,[198] in which it was said that 'No one has suggested that damages would be an adequate remedy in this case'—the implication being that they were there for the taking in the absence of a better solution. They might, of course, be only nominal; on the other hand, they might be considerable were it possible to show loss of society, severe injury to feelings,

---

[193] For a relatively early debate, see A P Bird and M T I Walji 'Our Patients Have Access to Their Medical Records' (1986) 292 BMJ 595; A P Ross 'The Case Against Showing Patients Their Records' (1986) 292 BMJ 578.

[194] For an example of the arguments see, M L M Gilhooly and S M McGhee 'Medical Records: Practicalities and Principles of Patient Possession' (1991) 17 J Med Ethics 138.

[195] G Eysenbach 'Recent Advances: Consumer Health Informatics' (2000) 320 BMJ 1713.

[196] In *R v Mid Glamorgan Family Health Services, ex p Martin* [1995] 1 All ER 356, [1995] 1 WLR 110, the court accepted that medical records were owned by the health authority, and a similar view was taken by the High Court of Australia in *Breen v Williams* (1996) 138 ALR 259.

[197] [1990] 1 AC 109, [1988] 3 All ER 545.   [198] [1988] 2 All ER 648, (1992) 3 BMLR 1.

job loss, interference with prospects of promotion or the like. However, a distinction has to be made between actions in contract and in tort. Thus, in the trial stage of *W v Egdell*,[199] Scott J discarded the possibility of damages for shock and distress—other than nominal—largely on the particular facts of the case but also because it was based on breach of an implied contractual term;[200] the decision had no relevance to an action in tort.

8.73 The question first came before the courts in Scotland over a century ago in two similarly named and well-known decisions, the *AB v CD* cases. In the earlier *AB v CD*,[201] the Court of Session considered an action for damages brought against a doctor who had disclosed to a church minister that the pursuer's wife had given birth to a full-term child six months after marriage. The court held that there was a duty on the part of the doctor not to reveal confidential information about his patient unless he was required to do so in court or if disclosure were 'conducive to the ends of science'—but, in that case, identification of the patient would be improper. In the second *AB v CD*,[202] the pursuer was seeking a separation from her husband. Having been examined by the defender at the suggestion of her lawyers, she was later examined by the same doctor who was then acting on behalf of her husband. The doctor disclosed to the husband certain information he had obtained in the course of his first examination and the wife argued that this constituted a breach of confidence. Once again, the court accepted that there was a duty on the part of a doctor not to disclose confidential information about his patient but stressed that not every disclosure would be actionable. As Lord Trayner pointed out,[203] some statements may be indiscreet but not actionable; there might be, for example, an actionable breach if the disclosure revealed that the patient was suffering from a disease which was a consequence of misconduct on his part.[204] In fact, disclosure of the background to the illness may be of greater importance than the disclosure of illness itself.

8.74 All of which amounts to really no more than saying that the patient is entitled to protection against defamatory statements, a protection which is hardly adequate. In both English and Scots law, the patient is not being defamed if what the doctor says is true.[205] Moreover, in England, the law of slander (spoken defamation) requires that the plaintiff should be able to prove special damage—which is, essentially, pecuniary damage—except in those limited cases of slander which are actionable per se. The protection provided by the law of defamation in cases where the doctor verbally reveals confidential information to another is, thus, unlikely to be significant.

8.75 Qualified privilege should, in the absence of malice or reckless unconcern as to the truth of the statement, be a defence against any action for breach of confidence, as it

---

[199] [1990] Ch 359, [1990] 1 All ER 835.

[200] Quoting *Bliss v South East Thames Regional Health Authority* [1987] ICR 700.

[201] (1851) 14 D 177. [202] (1904) 7 F 72. [203] (1904) 7 F 72 at 85.

[204] Scots law provides a potential remedy in the form of the *actio iniuriarum*. For comments on the possible application of this delict in cases of breach of confidence, see Scottish Law Commission, Memorandum No. 40 *Confidential Information* (1977) p 28.

[205] The doctor's most likely exposure to defamation is, of course, on an intra-professional basis.

already is in the law of defamation—qualified privilege in this context being but another expression of the 'need to know' principle. This is the ultimate determinant of ethical disclosure. The profession is not, or should not be, over-concerned with the niceties of intra-professional relationships or of communication in good faith with paramedical or other responsible groups; what really matters is irresponsible gossip— and, here, the ultimate deterrent is the power of the General Medical Council over its members (for which see chapter 1). Punitive action against a doctor is unlikely to be of material benefit to a wronged patient, but it is still a very effective preventive weapon.

8.76   More immediately effective is injunctory relief—a common remedy in this area of law—and one which has been extended considerably in recent years.[206] Given that the real fear at the core of a breach of confidence action is public disclosure of private facts, the 'gagging order' will, in many cases, be more desirable to the plaintiff than damages—and the utility of this remedy endures, as cases such as *X v Y* and *H v Associated Newspapers* demonstrate.[207] Often, however, damage has already been done because information has already been made public and, even if it is achieved, victory in a damages action can be phyrric: Ms Campbell, for example, received only £3,500 in compensation.[208]

8.77   We have seen, particularly in *X v Y*, that the courts have no great love for the 'media mole' in the hospital and, while there is deep-rooted respect for freedom of the press, there is an equally strong realisation of the need for integrity within the whole of the hospital hierarchy—and not only from those governed by professional codes of con-duct; *how* the press comes by its information may be of considerable relevance as to how the courts interpret the media's use of it. Such matters came to a head in the House of Lords in *Ashworth Hospital Authority v MGN Ltd.*[209] Here, a newspaper published an article that included verbatim extracts from the medical records of a multiple murderer detained in a secure hospital who was, at the time, engaged in a well-publicised hunger strike. The hospital applied for, and obtained, an order to the newspaper to explain how they obtained their information and to identify any employee of the hospital or intermediary who was involved in its acquisition. The newspaper appealed, largely on the basis of the Contempt of Court Act 1981, s 10 which holds that no correspondent can be compelled to disclose his sources of infor-mation unless it is established that disclosure is necessary in the interests of justice; the order, it was contended, was neither proportionate nor necessary on the facts of the case. The House held, however, that security of hospital records—and particularly those of a security hospital—was of such importance that it was essential that the source should be identified and punished in order to deter similar wrongdoing in the

---

[206] *Venables v News Group Newspapers Ltd, Thompson v News Group Newspapers Ltd* [2001] 1 All ER 908 (indefinite injunction against the entire world in respect of the identification of child killers).

[207] See *X v Y*, para 8.29 above, and *H (a healthcare worker) v Associated Newspapers*, para 8.30 above.

[208] *Campbell*, para 8.1 above.

[209] [2001] 1 All ER 991, [2001] 1 WLR 515, CA; affd [2002] UKHL 29, [2002] 1 WLR 2033, HL.

future—that was what made the order necessary, proportionate and justified. The importance of the hospital informational security as opposed to the privacy concerns of the individual was emphasised in that the fact that the subject himself had been in contact with the press was immaterial to the House's decision. And Lord Woolf could not resist pointing to the fact that the disclosure was made worse by the fact that it had been purchased by a cash payment! From our point of view, perhaps the most important aspect of *Ashworth* lies in its clear message that every member of a hospital's staff is subject to the same duty of confidentiality to the patients. By the same token, the Court of Appeal took the opportunity more recently to re-enforce the countervailing public interest of maintaining a free press, at least in terms of the procedural safeguards to be followed. *Mersey Care NHS Trust v Ackroyd*[210] arose from the same circumstances as *Ashworth* and concerned essentially the same scenario: a journalist received information from a hospital employee about the patient and the Trust sought disclosure of the source. The only essential difference was that no exchange of money took place. The trial judge merely followed *Ashworth* and gave summary judgement for the claimant and ordered disclosure of the source. The Court of Appeal allowed the appeal and held that although there is a clear public interest in the confidentiality of medical records, this alone could not be regarded as an overriding requirement in every circumstance. Each case had to be decided on its own facts, and since there was a real prospect that the defendant could defend himself in the instant case, he was, at least, entitled to a trial of fact. While this is not an automatic journalistic right, the Court did further opine that 'the subject matter argued in favour of a trial in most cases'.

CONFIDENTIALITY AND DEATH

8.78   Final reflection might, appositely, be concerned with death. The Declaration of Sydney says: 'I will respect the secrets which are confided in me, even after the patient has died.' This view is also endorsed by the GMC in its guidance to doctors:

> You still have an obligation to keep personal information confidential after a patient dies. The extent to which confidential information may be disclosed after a patient's death will depend on the circumstances.[211]

8.79   In practice, this is incapable of fulfilment as to the cause of death since a death certificate, signed by a doctor, is a public document—albeit, available only on payment of a fee for a copy. Once again, the spectre of AIDS raises its head in so far as confidentiality may, here, be as important to the bereaved family as to the deceased during life. It is certain that death certification in the United Kingdom—and probably elsewhere—is inaccurate, but this can only be compounded if doctors take it upon

---

[210] [2003] EWCA Civ 663.   [211] *Confidentiality*, n 19 above, para 30.

themselves to 'sanitise' the diagnosis so as to spare the relatives distress and, maybe, harm. A government publication[212] has suggested that certificates relating to recent deaths should be available only to those who may legitimately want them—but such measures are unlikely to achieve strict confidentiality.[213] The dilemma of conscience for doctors is acute in many types of death which carry a social stigma but, pending an alteration in the law, we find it hard to accept that doctors should be encouraged to falsify facts which are attested to be 'true to the best of my knowledge and belief'. Our major concerns here, however, are, first, with conditions discovered after death and, secondly, with the circumstances leading to death. The legal position is that, as the confidence is prima facie a personal matter, the legal duty ends with the death of the patient, although it has been suggested that 'Equity may impose a duty of confidence towards another after the death of the original confider . . . the question is not one of property . . . but of conscience'.[214] Elsewhere, as has been the case in the Netherlands, access to medical information is regarded as a personal right that is not inherited by the deceased relatives.[215] In the UK, however, as we have seen, the provisions of the Access to Health Records Act 1990 continue to apply to deceased persons.

8.80   In professional ethical terms, there can be no doubt that a post-mortem report merits the same degree of confidentiality as does the report of the clinical examination; insurance companies and the like have an obvious interest in its content but their right to disclosure is the same as the right to discovery of hospital records—in the absence of a court order, consent to disclosure from the next of kin of the deceased is essential.

8.81   But has the public any rights to details of the medical history of the dead?[216] While the principle remains irrespective of personalities, this is essentially a problem of public figures—and it is remarkable how rapidly professional ethics can be dissipated, say, in describing to the media the wounds of President Kennedy or the psychiatric history of the principals in any *cause célèbre*. The former physician to President Mitterand of France faced professional disbarment, a fine and up to one year's imprisonment for publishing his book, *Le Grand Secret*, immediately after the President's death in January 1996. The book detailed Mitterand's long battle with cancer throughout his Presidency which had been hidden from the French public. The affair caused a storm of controversy over the appropriate balance between the public's 'right to know' and the individual's 'right to privacy':[217] in the end the French courts followed up an interim injunction on sales with a permanent injunction on publication, the publishers received a hefty fine, and the author was given a four-month suspended

---

[212] Registration: A Modern Service (Cm 531).

[213] M B King 'AIDS on the Death Certificate: The Final Stigma' (1989) 298 BMJ 734.

[214] See *Morison v Moat* (1851) 9 Hare 241; affd (1852) 21 LJ Ch 248, quoted by R G Toulson and C M Phipps *Confidentiality* (1996), paras 13–17. However, any action for breach of confidence before the death of the patient could be transmitted to the executor.

[215] C Ploem 'Medical Confidentiality after a Patient's Death' (2001) 2 Med Law 215.

[216] S E Woolman 'Defaming the Dead' 1981 SLT 29.

[217] A Dorozynski 'Mitterand Book Provokes Storm in France' (1996) 312 BMJ 201.

sentence. Most recently, however, the European Court of Human Rights has declared France in breach of human rights over its reaction to the book, holding that, while the state could defend its laws imposing civil and criminal liability for breach of confidence as 'necessary in a democratic society', the continued ban on distribution of the book no longer met a 'pressing social need' and was disproportionate to the aim pursued; it was, in effect, a breach of the right to freedom of expression.[218] It is easy to say 'History will out, let it be sooner than later' but it is less easy to decide at what point revelations become history. The European Court of Human Rights, however, felt confident that the imposition of a permanent publication ban nine and a half months after the death of the French President was inappropriate.[219]

8.82   Returning to the British perspective, and as we say above, the GMC has stated that a duty of confidence persists after the patient's death; whether or not disclosure after death will be improper depends, inter alia, on whether there was any specific request to keep information confidential, whether disclosure may cause distress to, or be of benefit to, the patient's partner or family, and whether the information is already public knowledge or can be anonymised. The GMC does not specify any time limit; a practitioner must be prepared to justify and explain every disclosure. Moreover, a bark in this context carries a bite—no less a person than a former editor of the British Medical Journal has been taken to task for reporting information concerning the health of a well-known, albeit controversial, general after his death.[220]

8.83   Respect for the privacy of the dead seems reasonable—particularly when children or, especially, spouses are alive.[221] The Human Genetics Commission, for example, has endorsed the principle of respect for persons, both living and dead. It advocates something akin to a balance of factors similar to that offered by the GMC in determining when, if ever, genetic information can be derived from a deceased person: 'The seeking of DNA information for a good reason may justify the intrusion into the privacy of the dead, whereas seeking it purely for the purposes of sensational disclosure would not provide justification.'[222] The courts, for their part, may apply the principles of medical confidentiality by insisting that an order imposing anonymity in judicial proceedings should remain in force after the subject's death in cases of major sensitivity—such as those involving declarations as to the withdrawal of treatment from the incompetent.[223] Not only does this appear logical but post-mortem publicity

---

[218] *Plon (Société) v France*, Application No. 58148/00, 18 May 2004, paras 50ff.

[219] *Ibid*, para 53.   [220] S Lock and J Loudon 'A Question of Confidence' (1984) 288 BMJ 123, 125.

[221] The courts are, however, concerned for a balancing of interests between those of the bereaved and of freedom to publish. See *Re X (a minor) (wardship: restriction on publication)* [1975] Fam 47, [1975] 1 All ER 697, and more recently, at the European level, see the discussion of the rights of Mitterand's family in *Plon (Société) v France*, para 8.81 above.

[222] Human Genetics Commission *Inside Information: Balancing Interests in the Use of Personal Genetic Data* (2002), para 4.71.

[223] *Re C (adult patient: publicity)* [1996] 2 FLR 251—though this may not hold if the public interest dictates otherwise. For the balance of private and public interest and the imposition of anonymity in general, see *Re G (adult patient: publicity)* [1995] 2 FLR 528. See too, Practice Direction [2002] 1 WLR 325. Cf—the House of Lords has recently ruled that the anonymity of a dead child and the mother accused of its murder

may, in turn, raise questions as to the ethics of previous non-disclosure. It has, for example, been seriously argued that Lord Moran invited criticism not so much for his disclosures after the death of Winston Churchill[224] as for his failure to draw attention to the physical state of his patient during life. Which brings us back almost to where we started—to the dilemma of the doctor's relationship to his patient vis-à-vis society.

should not be restrained merely to protect the privacy of the surviving child who was not directly involved in the trial: *Re S (a child) (identification: restriction on publication)* [2004] 4 All ER 683.

[224] Lord Moran *Winston Churchill: The Struggle for Survival, 1944–1965* (1966).

9

LIABILITY FOR
MEDICAL INJURY

9.1 Medical negligence is more than a matter between two parties—it is also a political issue. There is concern in both medical and governmental circles over the growing incidence of personal injury actions against doctors and over the cost to the health system of compensating the victims.[1] It is pointed out that medical negligence actions are destructive of trust in a doctor-patient relationship and distort the practice of medicine in an over-cautious direction. From the doctor's point of view, the prospect of being sued in the event of making a mistake is stressful and demoralising—and, in the context of increasing emphasis on 'patient-orientated medicine', the definition of 'mistake' is ever-widening. Many of those working outside medicine may face such a prospect in the course of exercising their profession but, in the case of the doctor, the fundamentally hazardous nature of the work, combined with the demanding and fraught conditions under which it has to be performed, makes the possibility of error and subsequent legal action very strong indeed. Legal action is, thus, a very real risk for the medical practitioner and it would be surprising if litigation at this level did not seriously compromise medical morale. Funding bodies might expect to find the picture equally bleak, and the figures are alarming. Annual NHS clinical negligence expenditure rose from £1 million in 1974/75 (equivalent to £6.33 million in 2002) to £446 million in 2001/2002.[2] The costs of compensating patients jumped 400 per cent in the course of the 1970s and 750 per cent in the 1990s,[3] and the NHS Litigation Authority has reported an overall 15-fold increase in the number of claims for medical injury arising after April 1995.[4] When one adds such correlates as the fact that, for settlements up to £45,000, the cost of reaching the settlement are actually greater than the damages awarded in the majority of cases,[5] it seems that only radical

---

[1] See generally, Department of Health *Making Amends: A Consultation Paper Setting Out Proposals for Reforming the Approach to Clinical Negligence in the NHS* (2003).

[2] *Ibid*, p 60.

[3] *Ibid*, p 26. It is important also to note, however, that the costs represents a little less than 1% of the NHS annual expenditure, *ibid*.

[4] NHS Litigation Authority: www.nhsla.com. Indeed the NHSLA estimates that '. . . its total liabilities (the theoretical cost of paying all outstanding claims immediately, including those relating to incidents which have occurred but have not yet been reported to us) are £7.78 billion', *ibid*.

[5] National Audit Office *Handling Clinical Negligence Claims in England*, n 2 above.

methods can contain the flood. The reader is referred to the Department of Health's comprehensive document, *Making Amends*, for both a full account of the crisis and a discussion of various reform options both at home and abroad.[6] We return to the specific recommendations in due course.

9.2   But what greater malaise lies behind this increase in litigation? First and foremost, modern medicine is intrusive and the chances of injury are therefore increased: 10 per cent of hospital in-patient admission may result in some adverse event and some 5 per cent of the population report deleterious after-effects of medical care.[7] Secondly, the current social climate encourages expectations of cure. When these are not met, the culture of consumerism—fuelled by a press eager to disclose wrongdoing—advocates the allocation of blame and the seeking of compensation.[8] Finally, intolerance of error, and of the fact that any complex human endeavour will inevitably involve the making of mistakes, means that the public increasingly insists on accountability and, if possible, the pinning of an adverse outcome on some identifiable human agency. The public's tolerance for accidents has been greatly reduced—somebody, somewhere must be made to answer for what has happened.[9] This has created a climate which is excessively stressful for social workers, teachers and, to a marked extent, health care staff.[10]

COMPENSATION FOR INJURY

9.3   The current system comes under attack from all quarters.[11] Patients, it is argued, have great difficulty seeking compensation for negligently inflicted medical injury and may face daunting hurdles in the process of suing a doctor. Only a relatively small proportion of the victims of medical negligence bring an action for damages and, currently, 76 per cent of these fail.[12] Those claimants who do succeed may have to wait a considerable time before damages are paid; the average time from claim to payment of damages above £10,000 is now some five and half years. The current system thus seems to the patient to be flawed: he or she has suffered an injury and yet it may be difficult to recover what is seen as his or her due. Moreover, having failed to get any explanation as to what went wrong and having been offered no apology, the patient

---

[6] N 1, above. See, too, National Audit Office, *Citizen Redress: What Citizens Can Do if Things Go Wrong with Public Services*, HC 21, Session 2004–2005 (2005).

[7] Department of Health *An Organisation with a Memory* (2000).

[8] Cf, Department for Constitutional Affairs *Tackling the Compensation Culture* (2004), available at: www.dca.gov.uk.

[9] Compare the assessment in A Merry and A McCall Smith *Errors, Medicine and the Law* (2001).

[10] The situation is particularly well discussed by R Tallis *Hippocratic Oaths: Medicine and Its Discontents* (2004).

[11] Not least from the senior judiciary: Lord Woolf 'Clinical Negligence: What is the Solution? How Can We Provide Justice for Doctors and Patients?' (2000) 4 Med L Internat 133.

[12] See n 5 above.

may have felt that there was no alternative to bringing an action. Both sides—if one should talk of sides in this matter—see the current system of compensation for medical injury as being slow, traumatic and socially expensive, one from which it is often only the lawyers who profit. There must be a better way of dealing with this issue—a way which provides reasonably efficient compensation without destroying the doctor-patient relationship and without diverting health-targeted funds from hospitals and patient care into legal fees and damages.

9.4   The question of compensation for medical injury in the United Kingdom has, in fact, had a number of official airings. It was discussed many years ago as a special issue by the Royal Commission on Compensation for Personal Injury (The Pearson Commission),[13] and Lord Woolf addressed the matter in his wide-ranging investigation into the operation of the system of civil justice. He singled out medical negligence as an area for special consideration on the grounds that it was in respect of these claims that civil justice was 'failing most conspicuously'.[14] This failure was demonstrated by a variety of factors, including an unacceptable delay in the resolution of cases and a success rate which was lower than that in other personal injury litigation. The report suggested that the system could be improved by a better complaints procedure and by extending the jurisdiction of the Health Service Ombudsman to include complaints against the clinical expertise of NHS staff, both of which suggestions have been acted upon.[15] Lord Woolf was also concerned to establish what he described as a 'climate of change' that is marked by greater openness. He suggested that the GMC might explore ways of clarifying the responsibilities of the doctor in terms of candour,[16] and he also favoured the wider use of mediation schemes. Both of these elements feature in the latest proposals for reform as we shall see below.

9.5   A widely canvassed alternative to negligence actions, which commands much support,[17] is to introduce a system of no-fault compensation, which would provide for the making of awards to injured patients irrespective of the requirement of proving fault on the part of medical personnel.[18] Such a scheme has operated in New Zealand since 1974 as part of an overall no-fault compensation scheme and, even if it has had its opponents, it has now survived into its fourth decade—albeit in a scaled-down

---

[13] Cmnd 7054–1, 1978.

[14] *Access to Justice*: Final Report to the Lord Chancellor on the Civil Justice System in England and Wales (1996) 15.2. See too, Scottish Office Home Department *Access to Justice: Beyond the Year 2000* (1997). Reforms involving the whole UK were instituted in the Access to Justice Act 1999.

[15] See chapter 1.

[16] See L Beecham 'GMC approves new Ethical Guidelines' (1998) 316 BMJ 1556. For the current version of guidelines see the GMC website: www.gmc-uk.org.

[17] Although not from the Pearson Commission, n 13 above, which concluded that there were insufficient grounds for introducing no-fault compensation schemes. Cf, from a medical perspective, WJ Gaine 'No Fault Compensation Systems' (2003) 326 BMJ 997 and the ensuing 'rapid responses' available on the BMJ website: www.bmj.org.

[18] An up-to-date account of various schemes around the world is provided in *Making Amends*, n 1 above, chapter 6.

model.[19] In the medical context, however, the New Zealand claimant must still establish that the injury resulted from 'medical or surgical misadventure', a requirement which has caused difficulties in distinguishing between those conditions which result from the physiological progress of a medical condition and those which are genuinely the result of misadventure occurring in the course of treatment. A considerable body of case law is devoted to determining just when a complication following upon a medical procedure is so rare as to amount to a misadventure.[20] Thus, it will be seen that such schemes do not do away entirely with all the difficult issues of foreseeability and causation which dog the operation of conventional tort law. It is, perhaps, significant that organisations such as the British Medical Association, whose primary concern as a trade union is for the interests of the profession, have consistently supported the introduction of a no-fault based system into the United Kingdom.[21] Under the scheme proposed by the BMA, compensation would be available for medically-induced injury but would exclude those injuries which were not avoidable through the exercise of reasonable care. The concept of negligence is therefore effectively preserved, although it would undoubtedly be easier to establish; moreover, there would be no inference of 'fault' of quite the same nature as arises in a tort-based system. A no-fault system of compensation was also the preferred option in the Report of the Royal College of Physicians on the subject,[22] and most recently such a recommendation also appeared in the Report of the Royal Bristol Infirmary Inquiry.[23]

9.6   For a variety of reasons, predominantly those of cost, the government has not supported the movement and a Private Member's Bill aimed in that direction was defeated in Parliament.[24] The government's attitude has not, however, been one of total inaction and the Department of Health has encouraged discussion of ways by which to make compensation more readily available and less costly.[25] Its latest offering—the

---

[19] Criticisms included those of unacceptably low levels of compensation, high cost to the taxpayer and the removal of deterrents to safety practices in the workplace. On the last of these, see A Lewis 'No Fault Liability—Thirty Years of Experience in New Zealand' (1996) 15 Med & Law 425. The current legislation is to be found in the Injury Prevention, Rehabilitation, & Compensation Act 2001. The Act is administered by the Department of Labour: www.dol.govt.nz. The administration of accident insurance is run by the Accident Compensation Corporate: www.acc.co.nz.

[20] The issue was fully discussed by K Oliphant 'Defining "Medical Misadventure": Lessons from New Zealand' [1996] 4 Med L Rev 1. Oliphant suggested that, in a possible British scheme, medical misadventure should be equated with 'treatment error', a concept which should include errors which have occurred in spite of the exercise of reasonable skill on the practitioner's part.

[21] BMA *Report of the BMA No Fault Compensation Working Party* (1987); since when, the Representative Body has recommended a no-fault scheme annually. Most recently, see BMA *Funding No Fault Compensation for Medical Injuries* (2003) (July 2003), available at: www.bma.org.uk.

[22] *Compensation for Adverse Consequences of Medical Intervention* (1990).

[23] Royal Bristol Infirmary Inquiry, *Learning from Bristol: The Report of the Public Inquiry into Children's Heart Surgery at the Bristol Royal Infirmary 1984–1995* (2001).

[24] National Health Service (Compensation) Bill 1991. The case against no-fault compensation is summarised by B Capstick, P Edwards and D Mason 'Compensation for Medical Accidents' (1991) 302 BMJ 230.

[25] The administration of civil justice was, of course, thoroughly considered and overhauled as a result of Lord Woolf's Report *Access to Justice* (1996). The application to medical negligence is discussed further below.

consultation paper, *Making Amends*, referred to above—takes the bold step of recommending a sui generis system of care and compensation for patients harmed within the NHS; the instrument is in the form of a report from the Chief Medical Officer (CMO) and relates only to England and Wales although any new scheme would doubtless extend to Scotland. Following the government's long-standing antipathy to no fault compensation, however, this idea is, once again, being rejected as a reform option. Basically, four reasons are offered:

(1) a proper no fault system would be significantly more expensive than our current approach (costing an estimated £4 billion annually),

(2) payments to patients would have to be substantially lower than at present to keep costs within manageable boundaries,

(3) definitional problems in differentiating between harm caused by sub-standard care and that occasioned by natural progression of disease would be considerable (as has been experienced in New Zealand), and

(4) such a scheme does not address broader systemic problems, such as learning lessons from sub-standard practices.

But to us this is essentially just the same old argument about cost. No compensation scheme on its own can tackle operational matters without parallel reforms in the realms of education, training and openness (e.g. in error reporting). Likewise, problems of definition and causation are standard in any system. Indeed, the CMO's proposed alternative scheme itself seeks to exclude harm from natural disease processes. Notwithstanding, it seems that no fault compensation for medical injury will not see the light of day any time soon in the United Kingdom.

9.7   This is not to say that no-fault compensation is unknown on British shores. Indeed, three schemes currently operate. These are the Industrial Injuries Scheme, the Criminal Injuries Compensation Scheme and the Vaccine Damage Payment Scheme (see para 9.115). The first two function on a tariff system whereby claims are categorised according the nature and degree of injury sustained and set payments are made accordingly. A medical injury scheme based on this approach, however, has also been rejected by the Chief Medical Officer as too blunt an instrument to respond accurately and fairly to patients' circumstances and needs. Rather, the government seeks a far more holistic approach to the question. The proposed reforming framework is thus designed not only to ensure fair and efficient care and compensation of those injured at the hands of health care professionals; it is also aimed at addressing operational issues concerning the nature of the NHS itself and the working practices of its employees. Here the longer term aim is to reduce the overall instance of clinical error and medically-induced harm.

9.8   Limiting medical accidents—if that were possible—would, of course, simultaneously limit their costs, even if no change were made to the system of compensation or to the rules surrounding the bringing of claims. There has been a greatly increased awareness of the scale of medical accidents in recent years and this has been

accompanied by a more sophisticated approach to their understanding and prevention.[26] Studies of the occurrence of such events have concluded that the incidence of
medical errors is unacceptably high and that many of these errors are potentially
avoidable.[27] In the United Kingdom, this new approach has resulted in a number of
initiatives within the NHS, including the setting up of a National Patient Safety
Agency, the aim of which is to enable safe systems to be installed and to encourage a
system of error reporting which will assist in the avoidance of future accidents.[28] The
shift to a safety-orientated approach to medical injury requires the placing of less
emphasis on blame, in favour of an approach which encourages safer practices.[29] The
proponents of such systems believe that, in the long run, this approach will reduce the
level of patient injury and control the cost of medical error far more effectively than
will litigation or any system of punishment of those who make errors. The Chief
Medical Officer is clearly one such proponent, and key among his recommendations
are measures to reform the law to prevent disclosure of adverse event reporting
documents in court[30]—the thinking being that this will encourage more such reporting within the health system. By corollary, he also argues to place a duty of candour on
a statutory footing such that health care professionals would be required to inform
patients if they become aware of a negligent act or omission.[31]

9.9   The real substance of the reforms lies in the proposed NHS-based System of
Redress which is composed of four main elements: (1) investigation, (2) explanation,
(3) care, and (4) compensation. It would be administered by a new national body that
would build on the work of the NHS Liability Authority and which would have overall
responsibility to ensure that the elements of the system were implemented. Thus,
following a local investigation of what went wrong and why, there would be provision
of an explanation to the patient and an apology from a suitably high-ranking official
within the Trust (if appropriate). Thereafter, a 'package' of care and compensation
would be put together designed to respond to the patient's particular circumstances.
Monetary compensation would only be offered where care needs could not be met by
the NHS. This may frequently be the case in the short term; changing this would
require considerable reform and updating of the NHS's rehabilitation services; this,
however, is also recommended by the CMO.

[26] See, for example, Institute of Medicine *To Err is Human* (2000), a document which sets ambitious
targets for the reduction of the number of adverse events resulting in patient injury. This is an American
study, and rather different considerations apply in the United Kingdom. For a United Kingdom perspective,
see K G Alberti 'Medical Errors: a Common Problem' (2001) 322 BMJ 501.

[27] R M Wilson, W B Runciman, R W Gobberd et al 'The Quality in Australian Healthcare Study' (1995)
163 Med J Australia, 458. On reporting considerations, see W Runciman, A Merry and A McCall Smith
'Improving Patients' Safety by Gathering Information' (2001) 323 BMJ 298

[28] The direction of official thinking was indicated by the Department of Health document, *An Organisation with a Memory. Report of an Expert Group on Learning from Adverse Events within the NHS* (2000). The
NPSA has now set up a National Reporting and Learning System which aims to collect reports from health
professionals across England and Wales: V Katikrieddi 'National Reporting System for Medical Errors is
Launched' (2004) 328 BMJ 481.

[29] See too, Department of Health, *Building a Safer NHS for Patients: Improving Medication Safety* (2004).

[30] *Making Amends*, n 1, above, Recommendation 13.   [31] *Ibid*, Recommendation 12.

9.10   The proposed system is radically different from a negligence-based compensation scheme both in its philosophy and its practice. The focus is very much on improving patient care—both now and in the future; this is achieved in a very direct fashion and in a way that allows patients and health care professionals to cooperate towards common ends. The negligence action is, in contrast, an adversarial process, with each party pitted against the other. Its outcome, if successful for the patient, is a crude monetary payment—only then can proper care be sought. Moreover, its longer term implications for overall patient care are at best speculative and depend upon us accepting the deterrent effect of the threat of a negligence action. We, for example, question whether it is ever possible to deter negligence which, by definition, is *inadvertent* behaviour. Far more likely is the prospect of defensive medicine, which once again places the parties to the doctor-patient relationship in an adversarial stance.

9.11   But as is so often the case, the devil is in the detail of how a new scheme might work and who might benefit. The broad qualifying criteria proposed are:

(a) there were serious shortcomings in the standards of care,

(b) the harm could have been avoided, and

(c) the adverse outcome was not the result of the natural progression of illness.

We find ourselves, then, back with the same problem that beleaguers every compensation system, namely, causation. We must also ask what is meant by 'serious shortcomings' and how, if at all, this test might differ from the standard of care that prevails in the common law. On this point, the CMO is, in fact, open to suggestions from the consultation process itself. The expectation is that while an initial pilot would apply the common law test—the *Bolam* test which we discuss below—it would also examine the consequences of applying a lower threshold of 'sub-standard care'.

9.12   Other features of the proposed model include a suggested financial limit of £30,000 on the monetary compensation element of the package, and a close link between the scheme and the new NHS complaints mechanisms (discussed in chapter 1); it would then no longer be the case that investigation of a complaint should be halted pending the outcome of a compensation claim.

9.13   A parallel package is proposed in respect of families of neurologically impaired babies born under the NHS system when the impairment is birth-related and manifests itself within the first eight years of life. A combined care/compensation approach is, once again, envisioned with initial lump-sum payments up to £50,000 for costs related to adapting the home and for pain and suffering; thereafter monthly payments related to care costs would be payable up to a maximum of £100,000 a year.

9.14   The consultation paper also considers what should happen if a particular patient's case does not qualify under the framework. The expectation is that mediation should be the first port of call and that any settlement payments should be paid on a staggered, periodic basis. It is also argued that the law should be changed to rule out compensation extending to the costs of future private health care.

9.15   As a final point, it is essential to note that the reforms in question are intended to exist in parallel with the common law. There is no suggestion that we abandon negligence. Patients will be free to choose how to seek recompense for harm done. The only caveat is that a choice to take advantage of the NHS scheme will require a patient to sign a waiver indicating that no future action will be pursued in the courts on the basis of the same facts or injury. Thus, irrespective of whether these (or other) reforms are passed in the United Kingdom, we cannot escape a thorough examination of the negligence action.

THE BASIS OF MEDICAL LIABILITY

9.16   Most claims in respect of medical injury are brought in tort, that is, on the basis of a non-contractual civil wrong. The reason for this is that patients within the NHS are not in a contractual relationship with the doctor treating them. By contrast, there will be a contractual relationship in the private sector and it is, therefore, possible to bring an action for damages in contract.[32] In practice, there is very little difference between the two remedies,[33] although the law of contract may provide a remedy for an express or implied warranty given by a doctor.[34] In a Canadian case, *La Fleur v Cornelis*,[35] the court held that a plastic surgeon was bound to an express contractual warranty that he had made to the patient. This warranty arose when he was unwise enough to say: 'There will be no problem. You will be very happy'. This sort of case will be comparatively unusual and, for all practical purposes, any discussion of medical negligence can confine itself to liability under the law of torts, in which the first question to be asked is: whom do we sue?

9.17   A medical injury may have been caused to the plaintiff by any one or more of the health care personnel who have treated him. Locating negligence may be simple in some cases but, in others, the patient may have to choose the responsible party from a fairly large group, which may include a general practitioner, a hospital consultant, other hospital doctors and the nursing staff. Locating the specific act of alleged negligence which caused the injury may also involve a considerable degree of disentanglement.

9.18   The plaintiff may proceed directly against the doctor in question if an allegation is made of negligence on the part of a general practitioner. The general practitioner in the United Kingdom is solely responsible for the treatment of his patients and there can be no question of responsibility being imposed on a health authority unless the authority has intervened in the practitioner's treatment of his patient—all partners in

---

[32] *Pfizer Corporation v Ministry of Health* [1965] AC 512.

[33] For a useful discussion of the distinction between contractual and tortious remedies in this context, see M A Jones *Medical Negligence* (3rd edn, 2003) pp 56–59.

[34] An issue which arose in *Thake v Maurice* [1984] 2 All ER 513; revsd [1986] QB 644, [1986] 1 All ER 479.

[35] (1979) 28 NBR (2d) 569, NBSC; discussed by Jones, n 33 above.

a practice may, however, be liable for the actions of one of their number. The general practitioner must have approved indemnity cover,[36] which will normally be by way of membership of a medical defence society, to whom he will refer any claim against him; the society then advises him and undertakes the defence or settlement of the claim. General practitioners are not covered by the Crown indemnity which applies to hospital doctors[37] unless a claim arises in respect of work undertaken under a health authority contract. A general practitioner will be vicariously liable for the negligence of staff employed by him—nurses, receptionists etc—but not for the acts of a locum tenens or a deputising doctor who will, normally, be insured independently.[38]

9.19   The position is different if the alleged negligence occurs after the general practitioner has referred the patient for further treatment within the NHS. If the negligent act is committed by a health service employee, the patient then has the choice of proceeding either against the individual he feels has been negligent, or against the health authority or trust, or against both in a joint action. In practice, many actions are brought against the health authority or trust on the grounds of convenience. The liability of the authority or trust may be based on either of two grounds: (1) the direct duty of a hospital to care for patients; or (2) the vicarious liability of a health authority for the negligence of its employees.

9.20   There has been some doubt as to whether a hospital owes a non-delegable duty to use skill and care in treating its patients.[39] This has been addressed in some Commonwealth jurisdictions which have a somewhat different form of health care delivery to that existing in the United Kingdom. Thus, in the Australian case of *Ellis v Wallsend District Hospital*,[40] the majority held that there was a non-delegable duty in those cases where patients were permitted to go directly to the hospital for treatment and advice; no such duty would exist where the hospital merely provided services which a doctor could use to treat his own patients.[41] By contrast, the Ontario Court of Appeal has found that the hospital's duty extends no further than employing competent staff.[42] The minority view was, however, that hospitals, to a growing extent, hold out to the public that they provide medical treatment and emergency services—and that the public increasingly relies upon them to do so; Blair JA, in expressing this view, drew upon the evolution of the law in England which he thought supported the view that the hospital could be personally liable for negligent treatment in certain

---

[36] National Health Service Act 1977, s 43C inserted by Health Act 1999, s 9.

[37] See para 9.23 below.

[38] There was no vicarious liability for the negligence of a locum tenens in the Canadian case of *Rothwell v Raes* (1988) 54 DLR (4th) 193.

[39] For discussion, see A M Dugdale and K M Stanton *Professional Negligence* (3rd edn, 1998) para 22.20.

[40] (1989) 17 NSWLR 553, CA; confirmed on appeal [1990] 2 Med LR 103.

[41] The matter was also pronounced upon, obiter, by the High Court of Australia in *Commonwealth v Introvigne* (1982) 56 ALJR 749 and *Kondis v State Transport Authority* (1984) 154 CLR 672, 55 ALR 225.

[42] *Yepremian v Scarborough General Hospital* (1980) 110 DLR (3d) 513.

circumstances.[43] The English case of *Wilsher*[44] could have provided an ideal ground to decide the matter but the issue was not raised by the plaintiffs; nevertheless, the possibility clearly remains open—it was said that:

I can see no reason why, in principle, the health authority should not be [directly] liable if its organisation is at fault.[45]

9.21   The point is of some importance, particularly in respect of staff whose group or personal cover may be less comprehensive than is that of the professions, and the issue does, in fact, seem to have been decided in the ratio of *Re R (a minor) (No. 2)*. Here it was said:

Although it is customary to say that a health authority is vicariously liable for breach of duty if its responsible servants or agents fail to set up a safe system of operation in relation to what are essentially management as opposed to clinical matters, this formulation may tend to cloud the fact that in any event it has a non-delegable duty to establish a proper system of care just as much as it has a duty to engage competent staff and a duty to provide proper and safe equipment and safe premises.[46]

9.22   The discussion is, however, relatively sterile in the case of hospital doctors, the vast majority of whom are direct employees of the NHS. The health authority is, therefore, clearly liable for their negligence under the principle of vicarious liability. This provides that an employer is liable for his employee's negligent acts, provided that the employee is acting within the scope of his employment. It should be borne in mind that the employer may still be held vicariously liable even if the employee acts in direct contradiction of his employer's instructions or prohibitions.[47] The vicarious liability of hospitals throughout their hierarchy has been clearly established for half a century[48] and requires no further discussion.[49] If anything, it may be expanding. In *Godden v Kent and Medway Strategic Health Authority*[50] it was held to be an arguable ground of action that a health authority could be held vicariously liable for the acts of a general practitioner who had indecently assaulted and possibly negligently treated his patients.

9.23   The costs, especially to young doctors, of being members of a defence society have

---

[43] (1980) 110 DLR (3d) 513 at 579.

[44] *Wilsher v Essex Area Health Authority* [1987] QB 730, [1986] 3 All ER 801, CA; revsd [1988] AC 1074, [1988] 1 All ER 871, HL, discussed below at para 9.66. The case was recently applied in *Fairchild v Glenhaven Funeral Services Ltd* [2002] UKHL 22, [2003] 1 AC 32.

[45] [1987] QB 730 at 778, [1986] 3 All ER 801 at 833, per Browne-Wilkinson V-C.

[46] *Re R (a minor) (No. 2)* (1997) 33 BMLR 178 at 197, CA, per Brooke LJ—a case including inadequate hospital communications (the case is also known as *Robertson v Nottingham Health Authority*).

[47] R F V Heuston and R A Buckley *Salmond and Heuston on the Law of Torts* (21st edn, 1996), p 446.

[48] *Roe v Minister of Health; Woolley v Ministry of Health* [1954] 2 QB 66; *Hayward v Board of Management of the Royal Infirmary of Edinburgh and Macdonald v Glasgow Western Hospitals Board of Management* 1954 SC 453. For discussion, see M A Jones *Medical Negligence* (3rd edn, 2003) pp 595 et seq.

[49] It is also possible to sue the Secretary of State for policy-based operational failures in the delivery of health care, see *Re HIV Haemophiliac Litigation* (1998) 41 BMLR 171.

[50] [2004] Lloyd's Rep Med 521.

increased so dramatically that those who are working in the National Health Service have had to be subsidised by the authorities. Crown immunity has been extended to NHS doctors, dentists and community physicians since January 1990[51] and, as a result, the entire costs of negligence litigation are now borne by the Health Service itself— though there is, of course, nothing to stop a plaintiff suing an individual doctor. One consequence is that health authorities may feel obliged to settle cases on the grounds that this is the cheapest, if not the fairest, option; moreover, there is a strong suspicion that compensation for the injured may be bought at the expense of limitations in treatment facilities for other patients—but this is, perhaps, to take too pessimistic a view and, in practice, the load is now spread in that all trusts are encouraged to make use of the mutual insurance offered by the Clinical Negligence Scheme for Trusts operated by the National Health Service Litigation Authority.[52] It is to be noted that the scheme as it relates to individual doctors applies *only* to services provided within the NHS; doctors should, therefore, retain cover for any private or 'good Samaritan' work—and, indeed, for medico-legal activity. All negligence litigation involving the NHS is now handled by the NHS Litigation Authority.[53] The Authority itself reports that since its inception in 1995, 35 per cent of claims were abandoned by the claimant, 43 per cent were settled out of court, 1.5 per cent were settled in court in favour of the patient, 0.5 per cent were settled in court in favour of the NHS, and 20 per cent remain outstanding. Thus, very few medical negligence cases ever get to court. For those that do, however, the battle has only just begun.

WHAT CONSTITUTES NEGLIGENCE?

9.24   We have flirted with the legal concept of negligence in chapter 6, where we also outlined briefly the core elements of each negligence action. Once again, these are that the plaintiff must establish:

(1) that the defendant owed him a *duty of care*,

(2) that there was a *breach* of this duty of care, which amounts to a requirement to demonstrate that the standard of the treatment given by the defendant fell below the standard expected of him by the law, and

(3) *because of* this sub-standard treatment the plaintiff suffered a legally-

---

[51] See now Department of Health *NHS Indemnity—Arrangements for Clinical Negligence Claims in the NHS* (1996) Cat No 96 HR 0024.

[52] NHS (Clinical Negligence Scheme) Regulations 1996, SI 1996/251 made under National Health Service and Community Care Act 1990, s 21, as amended by SI 2004/2987.

[53] For more on which see: www.nhsla.com.

recognised harm (for example, physical injury or psychiatric illness).[54] This is otherwise known as *causation*: did the defendant's acts or omissions *cause* the plaintiff's harm?

If successful in proving all three elements, the plaintiff is entitled to monetary compensation which is supposed to place him as far as is possible back in the position he would have been in if the negligence had not occurred. Of course, when the harm is something other than financial—as it almost always is in medical cases—the recompense can only ever be a theoretical measure of what the person has lost. *Fault* remains the theoretical underpinning of the law until such time as strict liability may be imposed.

9.25   The concept of medical negligence has experienced a schism over the last 20 years. On the one hand, we have the standard line of cases in which there has been a technical failure or misadventure—in other words, those that are associated with medical treatment in one form or another. There has, however, been a rapid growth in accusations of negligence arising before treatment was started—these have become known as information disclosure cases which are based on the rights of the patient to make an informed choice as to his or her treatment. The principles underlying the tort of negligence are very similar in both situations. None the less, the latter has developed a jurisprudence of its own which is best discussed under the heading of 'consent'—for which, see chapter 10. Here, for the moment, we confine discussion to the established field of medical misadventure.

9.26   In either situation, a major difficulty for any plaintiff lies in the burden which falls upon him to prove that the defendant's negligence caused his injury. This is often a difficult burden to discharge and, indeed, suggestions have been made that the patient attempting to succeed in an action against a doctor should face a heavier burden in establishing his case than is required in any other personal injury litigation. There is an indication that this occurs in practice in so far as payment is made in some 30–40 per cent of medical cases as compared with 86 per cent in the general run;[55] the figures may, however, conceal more than a simple cause and effect phenomenon. The legal foundation for this view, which was put forward by Lawton LJ,[56] may be tenuous and it was, in fact, strongly opposed in *Ashcroft*;[57] nevertheless, it is certainly true that there has been a degree of policy-based judicial reluctance to award damages against doctors.[58] The clearest example of this has already been discussed in the context of

---

[54] Cf, *Fairlie v Perth and Kinross Healthcare NHS Trust* 2004 SLT 1200 (OH) in which it was held that averments to 'distress' on the part of a father of a young woman who accused him of abusing her after undergoing allegedly negligent psychiatric treatment were irrelevant in the absence of an identifiable psychiatric or psychological condition or illness.

[55] See M A Jones *Medical Negligence* (3rd edn, 2003) pp 275–279.

[56] In *Whitehouse v Jordan* [1980] 1 All ER 650 at 659.

[57] *Ashcroft v Mersey Regional Health Authority* [1983] 2 All ER 245 at 247, per Kilner Brown J.

[58] See, now, the Lord Chief Justice, writing extra-judicially: Lord Woolf 'Are the Courts Excessively Deferential to the Medical Profession?' (2001) 9 Med L Rev 1.

wrongful conception/birth cases in chapter 6. Beyond that realm, May LJ suggested in *Dwyer v Roderick*[59] that it would be:

to shut one's eyes to the obvious if one denied that the burden of achieving something more than the mere balance of probabilities was greater when one was investigating the complicated and sophisticated actions of a qualified and experienced [inter alia] doctor than when one was enquiring into the inattention of the driver in a simple running down action.[60]

9.27   At the same time, the courts have not been insensitive to the plaintiff's difficulties in a medical negligence case. The correctives applied have been the occasional invocation of the principle of res ipsa loquitur or, as in *Clark v MacLennan,*[61] an attempt to shift the burden of proof to the defendant. The observations of Kilner Brown J in *Ashcroft* on this point are revealing:

When an injury is caused which never should have been caused, common sense and natural justice indicate that some degree of compensation ought to be paid by someone. As the law stands, in order to obtain compensation an injured person is compelled to allege negligence against . . . a person of the highest skill and reputation.[62]

We return to res ipsa below.[63] For now, we begin with a consideration of the first element of the negligence action: is there a duty of care?

DUTY OF CARE

9.28   How do you know if your doctor owes you a duty of care? The answer, in most cases, is disarmingly simple: because he *is* your doctor. That is, an automatic legal duty of care arises if a health care professional has accepted to treat you, or a general practitioner has accepted you onto his files. A duty will also arise in the case of a private patient by virtue of his contractual relationship with his doctor (or the hospital) and, within a public national health system, the duty arises when the patent presents for treatment and is admitted. It does not follow, of course, that you are entitled to everything that you demand—but this is a question of the *standard* of care that can be expected, and we return to this below.

9.29   Duties in law can be assumed or imposed. The paradigm example of an assumed obligation (of care) is that of contract, where parties voluntarily agree to be bound to each other. As we have noted, however, this is not the legal basis for the operation of the NHS; rather, tort law dictates if and when a duty of care arises. The standard legal and policy position in respect of all duties of care in tort is to ask whether it would be fair, just and reasonable to impose such a duty in the given circumstances.[64] Furthermore, the relationship between the plaintiff and the defendant must be sufficiently

---

[59] (1983) 127 Sol Jo 806, CA.
[60] But one doubts if this would, or should, apply almost a quarter of a century later.
[61] [1983] 1 All ER 416.   [62] [1983] 2 All ER 245 at 246.   [63] See para 9.80 et seq.
[64] See, principally, *Caparo v Dickman* [1990] 2 AC 605; also, *Kent v Griffiths (No. 3)* [2001] QB 36, [2000] 2 All ER 474 and *Rees v Darlington Memorial Hospital NHS Trust* [2004] 1 AC 309, [2003] 4 All ER 987, HL.

'proximate' such that harm following the defendant's actions/omissions was 'reasonably foreseeable'.[65] This, in essence, is a question of how directly a plaintiff might be affected by the behaviour of another. The more direct the likelihood of harm, the more likely it will be that a duty of care will be imposed. This is always, however, subject to the fairness and reasonableness of creating that duty. This can be particularly problematic for relatives who claim that they have been harmed as a result of negligent care of a loved one. Thus, in *Fairlie v Perth and Kinross Healthcare NHS Trust*[66] the argument that a father was owed a duty of care by a health board in respect of the distress he suffered at being accused of abusing his daughter after she underwent allegedly negligent psychiatric treatment was rejected. The court opined that there was nothing to suggest circumstances in which it could be said that the father came at any stage into a special relationship with the attending psychiatrist such that a duty of care would arise.[67] Similarly, in *MK (a child) v Oldham NHS Trust*[68] it was held that disruption to family life occasioned from a prolonged medical and social services investigation of a child's injuries, during which time she was separated from her parents, was not a recognised head of damage in the absence of psychiatric disturbance to the child;[69] nor was there a sufficient degree of proximity between the parents and the defendants to make it fair, just and reasonable to impose a duty of care as between the parties.[70]

9.30   One thing that is unquestionable is that a public health service owes duties of care to the patients it accepts for treatment—on any analysis it is a fair and reasonable legal position. But is it possible for personnel not to accept patients and so to reject this duty? What of the over-tired houseman who is fed up dealing with the drunks who stagger into the Accident and Emergency Department on a Saturday night after a fight? Can he turn them away? Quite simply, no, he cannot. The reason he cannot do so is because the hospital is holding itself out as offering emergency services, which, self-evidently, is a public statement that it will respond to the public need, however unpleasant that may be.[71] By the same token, it does not follow that any public health care establishment must accept whosoever presents. It is arguably fair and reasonable

---

[65] See, for example, *Goodwill v British Pregnancy Advisory Service* [1996] 2 All ER 161, [1996] 7 Med LR 129, *Vowles v Evans* [2003] EWCA Civ 318, [2003] 1 WLR 1607.

[66] (2004) SLT 1200 (OH).

[67] See also, *Sion v Hampstead Health Authority* (1994) 5 Med LR 170 and our discussion of the case of *Palmer v Tees Health Authority* (1998) 45 BMLR 88 in chapter 20.

[68] [2003] Lloyd's Rep Med 1.

[69] *Reilly v Merseyside Regional Health Authority* [1995] 6 Med LR 246 and *McLoughlin v O'Brian* [1983] 1 AC 410 applied.

[70] Note: the possibility of raising a human rights challenge in Strasbourg that the domestic system provided for no adequate remedy was, however, raised by the court (the plaintiffs could not rely on the Human Rights Act 1998 because it was not in force at the relevant time). This has since been addressed by the Court of Appeal in *D v East Berkshire Community NHS Trust and others* [2004] QB 558 in which it was held that the 'fair, just and reasonable' test withstands a human rights analysis under Art. 6 ECHR (no duty of care was owed to parents wrongfully accused of child abuse).

[71] The same applies to the ambulance service where there is a legal duty to respond to a call for help, see *Kent v Griffiths* [2000] 2 WLR 1158, [2000] 2 All ER 474.

for a hospital *not* to offer emergency services and to direct patients elsewhere. The same applies to the individual doctor. Whatever one might think of moral obligations, it is no part of the law in the UK that a doctor must respond to someone in medical need when that person is not already his patient. The doctor need not then raise his hand in response to a request for medical assistance for the airline passenger who has collapsed in the flight. However, a duty of care will clearly arise should he do so and begin to examine the patient. Let us turn, then, to consider the second element of the negligence action, namely, the standard of care, where we seek out what the content of any duty entails.

THE STANDARD OF CARE: THE REASONABLY SKILFUL DOCTOR

9.31   It is apt to continue here with the theme of emergency care. The old, but still relevant, case of *Barnett v Chelsea and Kensington Hospital Management Committee*[72] has something of relevance for each element of the negligence action. As to the role of the casualty officer, the judge had this to say:

It is not, in my judgment, the case that a casualty officer must always see the caller at his department. Casualty departments are misused from time to time. If the receptionist, for example, discovers that the visitor is already attending his own doctor and merely wants a second opinion, or if the caller has a small cut which the nurse can perfectly well dress herself, then the casualty officer need not be called. However, apart from such things as this, I find the opinion of Dr. Sydney Lockett entirely acceptable. He said . . . In my view, the duty of a casualty officer is in general to see and examine all patients who come to the casualty department of the hospital.

The case concerned three workmen who suffered violent illness after drinking tea. They presented to the local cottage hospital, but the doctor was ill himself. The nurse phoned the doctor with the symptoms and he advised that the men go home and see their own doctors. In the event, one of the men died—as it turned out, from arsenic poisoning—and the action was brought by his widow. The court held that the doctor not only owed a duty of care to those who presented to his casualty unit but that, in these circumstances, he should have ensured that the patients were properly examined. Ultimately, however, as we shall see, Barnett's widow did not recover, despite there being a duty of care and despite the ruling that the requisite standard had not been met.

9.32   In this case, the standard was about examining emergency patients. But how are we to know what that standard is across the whole spectrum of medical care? There have been many judicial pronouncements by the courts on the subject. As early as 1838 we find Tindall CJ ruling that:

Every person who enters into a learned profession undertakes to bring to the exercise of it a reasonable degree of care and skill. He does not undertake, if he is an attorney, that at all

---

[72] [1968] 2 WLR 422, [1968] 3 All ER 1068.

events you shall gain your case, nor does a surgeon undertake that he will perform a cure; nor does he undertake to use the highest possible degree of skill.[73]

An echo of this is to be found in *R v Bateman*,[74] where the court explained that:

If a person holds himself out as possessing special skill and knowledge, by and on behalf of a patient, he owes a duty to the patient to use due caution in undertaking the treatment . . . The jury should not exact the highest, or very high standard, nor should they be content with a very low standard.

9.33   Thus, the doctor is not expected to be a miracle-worker guaranteeing a cure or to be a man of the very highest skill in his calling. What standard then is he expected to meet? McNair J provides us with the classic answer to this question in *Bolam v Friern Hospital Management Committee*:[75]

The test is the standard of the ordinary skilled man exercising and professing to have that special skill. A man need not possess the highest expert skill at the risk of being found negligent. It is a well-established law that it is sufficient if he exercises the ordinary skill of an ordinary man exercising that particular art.

Nevertheless, he *is* professing a particular skill and, in the further immortal words of McNair J, the test of that skill 'is not the test of the man on the top of the Clapham omnibus because [that man] has not got this special skill'.[76]

9.34   The doctor having that degree of competence expected of the ordinary skilful doctor sets the standard. He is the practitioner who follows the standard practice of his profession—or, at least, follows practices that would not be disapproved of by responsible opinion within the profession; he has a reasonably sound grasp of medical techniques and is as informed of new medical developments as the average competent doctor would expect to be. The circumstances in which a doctor treats his patient will also be taken into account. A doctor working in an emergency, with inadequate facilities and under great pressure, will not be expected by the courts to achieve the same results as a doctor who is working in ideal conditions.[77] This was alluded to by Mustill J in *Wilsher*, where he said that, if a person was forced by an emergency to do too many things at once, then the fact that he does one of them incorrectly 'should not lightly be taken as negligence'.[78]

9.35   The reasonably skilful doctor has a duty to keep himself informed of major developments in practice but this duty obviously cannot extend to the requirement that he should know all there is to be known in a particular area of medicine. In the case of *Crawford v Board of Governors of Charing Cross Hospital*[79] the plaintiff had developed

---

[73] *Lanphier v Phipos* (1838) 8 C & P 475 at 478.

[74] (1925) 94 LJKB 791 at 794, [1925] All ER Rep 45, CCA.

[75] [1957] 2 All ER 118 at 121, [1957] 1 WLR 582 at 586.

[76] A test approved by the Privy Council: *Chin Keow v Government of Malaysia* [1967] 1 WLR 813.

[77] This is in accordance with the general principle in the law of torts that errors of judgment are more excusable in an emergency: *The Metagama* 1928 SC(HL) 21; the strength of this precedent was recently confirmed in the non-medical case of *Morris v Richards* [2003] EWCA Civ 232.

[78] [1987] QB 730 at 749, [1986] 3 All ER 801 at 812.   [79] (1953) *The Times*, 8 December, CA.

brachial palsy as a result of his arm being kept in a certain position during an operation. Six months prior to the operation an article had appeared in the *Lancet*, pointing out just this danger but the anaesthetist against whom negligence was being alleged had not read the article in question. The Court of Appeal eventually found in favour of the anaesthetist, Lord Denning stating that:

it would, I think, be putting too high a burden on a medical man to say that he has to read every article appearing in the current medical press; and it would be quite wrong to suggest that a medical man is negligent because he does not at once put into operation the suggestions which some contributor or other might make in a medical journal. The time may come in a particular case when a new recommendation may be so well proved and so well known, and so well accepted that it should be adopted, but that was not so in this case.[80]

9.36　Failure to read a single article, it was said, may be excusable, while disregard of a series of warnings in the medical press could well be evidence of negligence. In view of the rapid progress currently being made in many areas of medicine, and in view of the amount of information confronting the average doctor, it is unreasonable to expect a doctor to be aware of every development in his field. At the same time, he must be reasonably up to date and must know of major developments. Hindsight is, of course, a harsh judge; yet, in a number of HIV-related cases, the courts have indicated that doctors could not have been expected to have known of a risk at a time when its significance was only just being established.[81] The practice of medicine has, however, become increasingly based on principles of scientific elucidation and report—the so-called 'evidence-based medicine'—and the pressure on doctors to keep abreast of current developments is now considerable. It is no longer possible for a doctor to coast along on the basis of long experience; such an attitude has been firmly discredited not only in medicine but in many other professions and callings.

Usual practice

9.37　The 'custom test'—the test whereby a defendant's conduct is tested against the normal usage of his profession or calling—is one that is applied in all areas of negligence law. The courts have given expression to this test in the medical context in a number of decisions. In the important Scottish case of *Hunter v Hanley*, for example, there was a clear endorsement of the custom test in Lord Clyde's dictum:

To establish liability by a doctor where deviation from normal practice is alleged, three facts require to be established. First of all it must be proved that there is a usual and normal practice; secondly it must be proved that the defender has not adopted that practice; and thirdly (and this is of crucial importance) it must be established that the course the doctor

---

[80] (1953) *The Times*, 8 December, CA.

[81] *Dwan v Farquhar* [1988] Qd R 234. In this case the risk of HIV transmission through blood transfusions was discussed in an article published in March 1983; there was no negligence in respect of a transfusion given in May of the same year. See also *H v Royal Alexandra Hospital for Children* [1990] 1 Med LR 297; M A Jones *Medical Negligence* (3rd edn, 2003) pp 225–227.

adopted is one which no professional man of ordinary skill would have taken if he had been acting with ordinary care.[82]

9.38 This attractively simple exposition of the law, however, conceals a hurdle at the outset.[83] It may, in many cases, be possible to prove that there is a 'usual and normal practice'—this is particularly so if there are guidelines covering a procedure, a ploy which is increasingly used in UK legislation[84] and which might be seen as being helpful to the plaintiff.[85] On the other hand, there will obviously be disagreement as to what is the appropriate course to follow in a number of medical scenarios. In some circumstances, the existence of two schools of thought may result in more than one option being open to a practitioner. If this is so, then what are the liability implications of choosing a course of action which a responsible body of opinion within the profession may well reject? Precisely this question arose in *Bolam*,[86] where the plaintiff had suffered fractures as a result of the administration of electro-convulsive therapy without an anaesthetic. At the time, there were two schools of thought on the subject of anaesthesia in such treatment, one holding the view that relaxant drugs should be used, the other being that this only increased the risk. In this case, the judge ruled that a doctor would not be negligent if he acted 'in accordance with the practice accepted by a responsible body of medical men skilled in that particular art'. Negligence would not be inferred merely because there was a body of opinion which took a contrary view.[87] Subsequent cases confirmed this approach. In *Maynard v West Midlands Regional Health Authority* the trial judge had preferred an alternative medical approach to that which had been chosen by the defendant, notwithstanding the fact that this latter course found support in responsible medical opinion; both the Court of Appeal and the House of Lords confirmed that this was an unsatisfactory way of attributing negligence.[88]

9.39 *Bolam* has been the object of sustained criticism from those who object to the implication that the medical profession itself determines what is an acceptable level of care.[89] Critics have persistently argued that doctors themselves should not determine

---

[82] 1955 SC 200 at 206. The rigid simplicity of Lord Clyde's definition was defended in an anonymous article, 'Medical Negligence: *Hunter v Hanley* 35 Years On' 1990 SLT 325. *Hunter* was specifically approved by Lord Scarman in *Maynard v West Midlands Regional Health Authority* [1985] 1 All ER 635, [1984] 1 WLR 634. For a useful discussion of custom in a medical context, see *E v Australian Red Cross Society* (1990–91) [1991] 2 Med LR 303.

[83] For an early, and approving, discussion of *Hunter*, see *McHardy v Dundee General Hospitals' Board of Management* 1960 SLT (Notes) 19 per Lord Cameron.

[84] B Hurwitz 'Clinical Guidelines and the Law' (1995) 311 BMJ 1517.

[85] These have not proved to be as productive of litigation as might be expected: A I Hyman, J A Brandenburg, S R Lipsitz et al 'Practice Guidelines and Malpractice Litigation: a Two-Way Street' (1995) 122 Ann Int Med 450.

[86] [1957] 2 All ER 118, [1957] 1 WLR 582.   [87] Cf, *Hucks v Cole* (1968) [1993] 4 Med LR 393.

[88] [1985] 1 All ER 635, [1984] 1 WLR 634. *Maynard* was followed in *Hughes v Waltham Forest Health Authority* [1991] 2 Med LR 155, in which the court emphasised that the fact that a surgeon's decision was criticised by other surgeons did not amount *in itself* to an indication of negligence.

[89] Particularly in the Commonwealth: *Reibl v Hughes* (1980) 114 DLR (3d) 1; *Rogers v Whittaker* (1992) 109 ALR 625, [1993] 4 Med LR 79. And see, in general, 'informed consent' in chapter 10.

whether conduct is negligent; this should be a matter for the courts. In fact, courts had on occasion made precisely this point themselves[90] and a number of judges in the English High Court have not been afraid to attack the traditional view. In *Smith v Tunbridge Wells Health Authority*,[91] an action based on failure of information disclosure, for example, the judge applied *Bolam* but, despite the existence of a competent body of opposing opinion, held that the decision not to do so was neither reasonable nor responsible. Nevertheless, there had been no high level judicial attack on the *Bolam* custom test in the Commonwealth until the High Court of Australia broke down the doors in the controversial information disclosure case of *Rogers v Whittaker*.[92]

In Australia, it has been accepted that the standard of care to be observed by a person with some special skill or competence is that of the ordinary skilled person exercising and professing that special skill. But that standard is not determined solely or even primarily by reference to the practice followed or supported by a responsible body of opinion in the relevant profession or trade.

9.40   The High Court of Australia has a reputation for creativity; would the English courts, with their rather more conservative reputation, follow suit? An answer—even if a hesitant one—came in the House of Lords decision in *Bolitho v Hackney Health Authority*,[93] a case regarded by some commentators as representing a significant nail in *Bolam*'s coffin. *Bolitho* arose out of a failure on the part of a hospital doctor to examine and intubate a child experiencing respiratory distress. Negligence derived from a failure to attend was not disputed; however, the problem of causation still remained. Expert evidence was led by the plaintiff to the effect that a reasonably competent doctor would have intubated in such circumstances. The defendant, however, had her own expert witnesses prepared to say that non-intubation was a clinically justifiable response. The defendant argued that, had she attended the child, she would not have intubated her and her failure to attend would not, therefore, have made any difference to the outcome. The House of Lords accepted the truth of this evidence. The causation issue, here, is important from the jurisprudential aspect in so far as it was made clear that, while the *Bolam* test had no relevance as to the doctor's intention, it was central to the collateral question—would she have been negligent in failing to take action? In other words, *Bolam* was attached to the question of causation when, in reality, the test is concerned only with standards of care. As a result, given that she had responsible support, the action failed on both counts. However, the particular significance of *Bolitho* lies in the House of Lords' support for the Court of Appeal's departure from the certainties of *Bolam*. Rather than accepting a 'body of opinion' simply because it was there, Lord Browne-Wilkinson held that the court must, in addition, be satisfied that the body of opinion in question rests on a logical basis:

---

[90] See Lord Irvine 'The Patient, the Doctor, their Lawyers and the Judge: Rights and Duties' (1999) 7 Med L Rev 255.

[91] [1994] 5 Med LR 334.   [92] (1992) 109 ALR 625 at 631, [1993] 4 Med LR 79 at 82.

[93] [1998] AC 232, [1997] 4 All ER 771, HL.

In particular, in cases involving, as they so often do, the weighing of risks against benefits, the judge before accepting a body of opinion as being responsible, reasonable or respectable, will need to be satisfied that, in forming their views, the experts have directed their minds to the question of comparative risks and benefits and have reached a defensible conclusion on the matter.[94]

9.41   This appears to be a clear rejection of the *Bolam* rule simpliciter,[95] but it must be read in the light of the strong caveat which Lord Browne-Wilkinson attached:

In the vast majority of cases the fact that distinguished experts in the field are of a particular opinion will demonstrate the reasonableness of that opinion . . . But if, in a rare case, it can be demonstrated that the professional opinion is not capable of withstanding logical analysis, the judge is entitled to hold that the body of opinion is not reasonable or responsible . . . I emphasise that, in my view, it will very seldom be right for a judge to reach the conclusion that views genuinely held by a competent medical expert are unreasonable.[96]

9.42   Thus, *Bolitho* undoubtedly devalues the trump card which *Bolam* presented to the medical profession, but only in limited circumstances. And, as to that, it is arguably undesirable to undermine the standard test beyond a certain point. *Bolam* provides some protection for the innovative or minority opinion. If this protection is removed, then the opinion which the cautious practitioner will wish to follow will be that which involves least risk. This may have an inhibiting effect on medical progress: after all, many advances in medicine have been made by those who have pursued an unconventional line of therapy. Such doctors may quite easily be regarded as negligent by a judge given to favouring conventional medical opinion.

9.43   In this respect, we can look to the decision in *De Freitas v O'Brien*,[97] which, rather than bolstering a conservative approach in assessing the acceptability of a body of opinion, gives comfort to the so-called 'super-specialist' who may, perforce, undertake procedures which others might regard as being inappropriate or even too risky. In this case, a spinal surgeon—said to be one out of only 11 such specialists in the country— maintained that the surgery he performed was in line with what his fellow spinal surgeons would have considered clinically justified. The plaintiffs, by contrast, claimed that run of the mill orthopaedic surgeons would not have operated in the circumstances. The Court of Appeal confirmed that the *Bolam* test did not require that the responsible body of opinion be large, thus endorsing the acceptability of acting within limits defined by a sub-speciality. One criticism of the decision in *De Freitas* is that it licenses the taking of risks. Yet, the court clearly retains its ability to declare an opinion to be unreasonable, a power which is firmly endorsed by *Bolitho*.

9.44   The Court of Appeal in *Bolitho* has been hailed as ushering in the 'new-*Bolam*'[98]

---

94 [1997] 4 All ER 771 at 778, (1998) 39 BMLR 1 at 9.

95 For an example of weighing the reasonableness and responsibleness of medical opinion post-*Bolitho*, see *M (a child) v Blackpool Victoria Hospital NHS Trust* [2003] EWHC 1744 in which an appeal on *Bolitho* terms was rejected.

96 [1997] 4 All ER 771 at 779, (1998) 39 BMLR 1 at 10.

97 (1995) 25 BMLR 51, [1995] 6 Med LR 108, CA.

98 A phrase which we would attribute to A Grubb 'Commentary' (1998) 6 Med L Rev 378.

although there were many who viewed it with a modicum of distrust.[99] It is, therefore, interesting to consider its progress since its birth—and, certainly, the case has attracted its fair share of attention. Maclean scoured the databases and unearthed 64 post-*Bolitho* medical negligence cases involving a standard of care[100] and concluded that, prior to November 2001, *Bolitho* was referred to in four cases in the Court of Appeal and in 25 at first instance.[101] There is no way in which all these cases—and those since—could be aired in a book of this size and several of them were 'consent-based' and are considered under that heading. Some do, however, merit mention—if only briefly.

9.45 *Wisniewski v Central Manchester Health Authority*[102] seems to us to be the most apposite case in that the 'logic' underlying the expert evidence was specifically considered. The case concerned a child who was born brain-damaged following 13 minutes' hypoxia during the birthing process; it was alleged that the midwife over estimated her ability and, as a result, the doctor failed to attend in appropriate time. As in *Bolitho*, negligence in relation to non-attendance was not in dispute; the problem, again, lay in causation—and in the two-stage definition of causation developed in *Bolitho* as to what would and should have happened in the absence of negligence. The establishment and the status of a 'responsible body of supporting opinion' were, therefore, of major importance and the conflict is illustrated in two quotations. Thomas J, at first instance, had this to say:

[W]here analysis of the expert evidence on the facts relating to a particular case shows that a decision made by a doctor and supported by experts cannot be justified as one that a responsible medical practitioner would have taken, then a judge should not preclude himself from reaching [a] conclusion simply because clinical judgment is involved.[103]

However, Brooke LJ said in the Court of Appeal:

[I]t is quite impossible for a court to hold that the views sincerely held by doctors of such eminence cannot logically be supported at all . . . and the views of the defendants' witnesses were views which could be logically expressed and held by responsible doctors.[104]

9.46 The clear inference is that, had the doctor survived the first hurdle as to what he would have done had he attended, *Bolam* would have prevailed and the *Bolitho* exception would not have applied. Logic is, however, a somewhat unusual criterion on which to assess what is, essentially, a matter of clinical judgment and it seems unlikely

---

[99] A most searching review is that of M Brazier and J Miola 'Bye-Bye Bolam: A Medical Litigation Revolution?' (2000) 8 Med L Rev 85. See also J Keown 'Reining In the *Bolam* Test' (1998) 57 CLJ 248, H Teff 'The Standard of Care in Medical Negligence—Moving on from *Bolam*' (1998) 18 OJLS 473.

[100] A Maclean 'Beyond *Bolam* and *Bolitho*' (2002) 5 Med L Internat 205.

[101] At the same time, there was judgment explicitly by way of the *Bolam* test in eight Court of Appeal and ten High Court cases; the author remarks that 'it would seem that *Bolam* is far from dead'.

[102] [1998] Lloyd's Rep Med 223, CA.

[103] Quoted [1998] Lloyd's Rep Med 223 at 235.

[104] [1998] Lloyd's Rep Med 223 at 237.

that the courts will be able to retain control over health care standards if they rely on 'logic' alone.

9.47   It is, therefore, useful to turn to *Marriott*,[105] where a man sustained severe intra-cranial injury allegedly aggravated by his practitioner's failure to refer him back to hospital when his condition deteriorated. The health authority called expert evidence in support of the doctor but the trial judge considered this not to be reasonably prudent and found for the plaintiff. The Court of Appeal dismissed the appeal on two main grounds. First, the court questioned the acceptability of the evidence for both sides—'it is questionable whether either had given evidence from which it was reasonable to infer that their individual approaches were shared by a responsible body of others in their profession'[106]—a statement which seems to eliminate the single maverick from the *Bolam* equation. Even so, the judge was effectively dismissing the evidence of *both* sides—the court's opinion suggests that the result might have been different had she chosen one expert's evidence in preference to the other rather than substitute her own analysis. Secondly, however, the court affirmed her entitlement to question whether an opinion was reasonably held given an analysis of the risks involved in following that opinion. On the face of things, then, *Marriott* moves the *Bolitho* test from one of logic to one of reasonableness, which is much more akin to the reasoning applied in other, non-medical standard of care decisions. Unfortunately, the situation is still not clear as, while the Court of Appeal supported the trial judge's approach, it still retained the language of 'logic'. *Marriott* does, however, open an alternative route to 'New *Bolam*'.

9.48   The final case that we select for discussion in the present context is that of *Penney v East Kent Health Authority*,[107] which concerned three women who developed cancer of the cervix following a reported negative screening test. As with all screening tests, that for potential cervical cancer inherently involves both false positive and false negative tests, the latter being estimated as occurring in between 5 per cent and 15 per cent of cases examined. It was not, therefore, argued that a false negative report indicated negligence on the part of the screener per se; the issue was confined to what should have been done, in 1993, given the agreed fact that there were abnormalities in the claimants' slides. The health authority maintained that the unusual abnormalities present were open to interpretation and disposal and that the outcome of the case should be decided on *Bolam* principles. The trial judge considered, and the Court of Appeal agreed, however, that the *fact* was that abnormal cells were present which no screener, acting with reasonable care, could have been certain were not pre-cancerous; the slides should, therefore, have been labelled at least as borderline—he found 'the *Bolam* principle ill-fitting to Mrs Penney's case'. It is not easy, however, to see why that should be so in respect of 'excusability'. Pepitt J was clearly conscious of this and

---

[105] *Marriott v West Midlands Regional Health Authority* [1999] Lloyd's Rep Med 23.
[106] Per Beldam LJ at 27. There is an interesting aside here—does it imply that there *is* a difference between the *Bolam* and the *Hunter v Hanley* tests?
[107] (2000) 55 BMLR 63, [2000] Lloyd's Rep Med 41.

further held that, in the event that he was wrong, he would revert to *Bolitho* in that, given the facts, the contention of the health authority's experts that the slides could well have been reported as negative was inconsistent with the accepted principle of 'absolute confidence' and was, consequently, illogical—a conclusion with which it is difficult to disagree.[108]

9.49　While it is unwise to generalise from a small number of selected cases, the impression gained thus far is that, while the courts are increasingly determined to see that the *Bolam* principle is not extended,[109] they still have an innate reluctance to abandon it in respect of medical opinion; there is a sense that *Bolitho*, although welcome, is being used mainly in a 'back-up' position. What is certain is that *Bolam* can no longer be regarded as impregnable.

Innovative or alternative techniques

9.50　Resort to an innovative therapeutic technique may be appropriate in certain cases but should be made with caution. Whether or not the use of such a technique could amount to negligence would depend on the extent to which its use was considered justified in the case in question. In assessing this, a court would consider evidence of previous trials of the treatment and would also, no doubt, take into consideration any dangers which it entailed. It is possible that a court would decline to endorse the use of an untried procedure if the patient was thereby exposed to considerable risk of damage.[110] Other factors which might be taken into account would be the previous response of the patient to more conventional treatment, the seriousness of the patient's condition and the attitude of the patient himself towards the novelty and risk. Thus in *Cooper v Royal United Hospital Bath NHS Trust* (2004, unreported), the Trust was held to have breached its duty of care to the claimant for abandoning a preferred course of medical care without adequately advising her as to the risks of implementing an alternative method. The standard of care to be applied in such circumstances would be expected of a doctor who is reasonably competent in the provision of *such treatment*. A doctor should not, therefore, undertake procedures which are beyond his capacity.[111]

9.51　A relevant Scottish case demonstrates the issues.[112] Here, the pursuer had suffered from abdominal pain for more than a year. In something of a last ditch attempt, her

---

[108] *Penney* was considered most recently in *Lillywhite and another v University College London Hospitals NHS Trust* [2004] EWHC 2452, [2004] All ER (D) 41.

[109] As, for example, into judging the patient's best interests: *Re S (adult patient: sterilisation)* [2001] Fam 15, [2000] 3 WLR 1288.

[110] Although, if the only alternative is serious harm or death, then the courts have endorsed the application of highly experimental techniques, see for example, *Simms v Simms, A v A* [2002] 2 WLR 1465 [2003] 1 All ER 669.

[111] In *Tomkins v Bexley Area Health Authority* [1993] 4 Med LR 235, the patient's lingual nerve was damaged in the course of an operation for the removal of wisdom teeth. Wilcox J observed: 'When fine movements and fine judgments are the order of the day, with surgery being conducted in the confined space of the mouth, a high degree of care is needed.'

[112] *Duffy v Lanarkshire Health Board* (1998, unreported).

doctor prescribed chloramphenicol as a result of which she developed aplastic anaemia from which she recovered only after receiving a bone marrow transplant. She sued her doctor in negligence on the grounds that he could have chosen another drug which was not known to carry the 1:8000 to 1:30000 risk of bone marrow dysplasia which was associated with chloramphenicol—it was claimed that the treatment given was, in effect, a 'shot in the dark'.

9.52   In the event, Lord Johnston was not prepared to hold as negligent a decision which had been carefully arrived at, the doctor having weighed up all the possibilities. Drawing from Lord Browne-Wilkinson in *Bolitho*, the Lord Ordinary held:

> Within the framework of a balanced judgment, I consider that the decision of Dr Todd can be rationally and responsibly supported . . . whatever may have been his alternatives. Furthermore, I consider that it should not be categorised even as an error of judgment . . . I am prepared to hold that, within the options reasonably available to him . . . it was a reasonable course to adopt.[113]

9.53   And what of alternative medicine? By what standard should such practitioners be judged? In *Shakoor v Situ*[114] a patient died from an 'idiosyncratic' liver reaction after taking nine doses of a traditional Chinese remedy prescribed by a herbal medicinalist. The skin condition from which the patient had been suffering could only be treated by surgery in orthodox medicine. His widow sued in negligence and the issue came down to the appropriate standard of care. The court held that an alternative medical practitioner could not be judged by the standard of orthodox medicine because he did not hold himself out as professing that 'art'; rather, he would be judged by the prevailing standard in his own 'art' subject to the caveat that it would be negligence if it could be shown that that standard itself was regarded as deficient in the United Kingdom having regard to the inherent risks involved. In the event, the negligence action failed because the court held that the practitioner had acted in accordance with the standard of care appropriate to traditional Chinese herbal medicine as properly practised in accordance with the standards required in the United Kingdom.

Misdiagnosis

9.54   A doctor is expected by the law to use the same degree of care in making a diagnosis that is required of him in all his dealings with his patients. A mistake in diagnosis will not be considered negligent if this standard of care is observed but will be treated as one of the non-culpable and inevitable hazards of practice.[115] Liability may, however, be imposed when a mistake in diagnosis is made because the doctor failed to take a

---

[113] As a postscript, Ms Duffy's claim under the Administration of Justice Act 1982, s 8 for remuneration in respect of her sister's marrow donation was also rejected (1998 SCLR 1142, 1999 SLT 906).

[114] [2001] 1 WLR 410, [2000] 4 All ER 181, 57 BMLR 178.

[115] In *Crivon v Barnet Group Hospital Management Committee* (1959) *The Times*, 19 November, the judge said of misdiagnosis: 'Unfortunate as it was that there was a wrong diagnosis, it was one of those misadventures, one of those chances, that life holds for people.' Courts—and patients—might be less inclined to take such a view today.

proper medical history,[116] failed to conduct tests which a competent practitioner would have considered appropriate, or simply failed to diagnose a condition which would have been spotted by a competent practitioner. As a minimum, the doctor must examine his patient and pay adequate attention to the patient's medical notes and to what the patient tries to tell him.[117] Telephone diagnosis or advice is hazardous, especially if the facts as related by the patient are such as to raise in the doctor's mind a suspicion that can only be allayed by proper clinical examination.[118]

9.55   One of the problems in determining whether there has been a mistake in diagnosis turns on deciding what investigative techniques need to be used in a particular case. The answer to this is doubly difficult insofar as the decision is now dictated not entirely by medical intuition; the increasing importance attached to patient choice must, inevitably, lead to a correspondingly increasing defensive attitude—and all this in the face of budgets that are stretched to the limit. In making his choice of diagnostic aids, the doctor must be guided by the *Bolam* test but it will be the 'new *Bolam*'—that is, the test that the courts will read as incorporating an element of 'patient expectation'. Ordinary laboratory tests must be used if symptoms suggest their use and, here, the situation is eased by the widespread introduction of automated 'battery' testing—the financial implications of doing several rather than a single biochemical analysis are now minimised.

9.56   The use of radiography provides a good example of the problem. Both professionals and the public are aware of the major contribution made by diagnostic radiography to the background radiation in developed countries and of the dangers to the individual of cumulative exposure. At the same time, it is widely stated that only some 1 per cent of radiographs taken of the ankle in casualty departments demonstrate a fracture and, of these, a high proportion would have healed in the absence of identification. The academic will, therefore, remember the archival words of Lord Denning with approval:

In some of the early cases, the doctor has been criticised for not having taken X-rays with the result that they have sometimes been taken unnecessarily. This case shows that the Courts do not always find that there has been negligence because a patient has not had an X-ray; it depends on the circumstances of each case.[119]

And, indeed, this may sometimes be so. In *Laskey*'s case,[120] the patient fell and it was agreed that she had sustained a fracture of the pelvis when she attended hospital.

---

[116] *Chin Keow v Government of Malaysia* [1967] 1 WLR 813 (failure to inquire as to the possibility of penicillin allergy); *Coles v Reading and District Hospital Management Committee* (1963) 107 Sol Jo 115 (failure to consider possibility of tetanus).

[117] *Giurelli v Girgis* (1980) 24 SASR 264, discussed in M A Jones *Medical Negligence* (3rd edn, 2003) p 290.

[118] *Barnett v Chelsea and Kensington Hospital Management Committee* [1969] 1 QB 428, [1968] 1 All ER 1068; *Cavan v Wilcox* (1973) 44 DLR (3d) 42. A number of 'failure to attend' cases have been discussed above.

[119] In *Braisher v Harefield and Northwood Hospital Group Management Committee* (13 July 1966, unreported), CA. See H Jellie [1966] 2 Lancet 235.

[120] *Lakey v Merton, Sutton and Wandsworth Health Authority* (1999) 40 BMLR 18, [1999] Lloyd's Rep Med 119, CA.

The casualty officer found no evidence of fracture and, since the patient had been exposed to X-irradiation on several previous occasions, he decided against X-ray examination before sending her home; the presence of fracture was, however, confirmed on re-admission. The trial judge found that the original decision was taken after conscious deliberation and was not negligent—a ruling affirmed in the Court of Appeal. This must have been a close-run decision even in 1999 and much has happened since then. We fancy that a similar result would be a rarity today.

9.57   *Langley v Campbell*[121] and *Tuffil v East Surrey Area Health Authority*[122] provide old, but still good examples of successful actions against doctors on the basis of failure to diagnose correctly the nature of the patient's complaint. In *Langley*, the patient had returned from East Africa shortly before the development of symptoms. The general practitioner failed to diagnose malaria and negligence was found, the judge accepting the evidence of a relative who said that the family had suggested such a diagnosis to the doctor. In *Tuffil*, the patient had spent many years in a tropical climate; the doctor failed to diagnose amoebic dysentery, which proved fatal. This failure to diagnose was held to be negligence on the doctor's part. The publicity given to 'exotic disease' is now such that, again, we doubt if such cases would be defensible today.[123]

9.58   In cases where a doctor is doubtful about a diagnosis, good practice may require that the patient be referred to a specialist for further consideration. It may be difficult for a doctor to know when to seek specialist advice—a fact explicitly acknowledged in the case of *Wilsher v Essex Area Health Authority*[124]—but in case of doubt, it is certainly safer for a doctor to refer the patient.[125] In *Official Solicitor v Allinson*[126] a general practitioner was found liable in negligence when a patient died from breast cancer after he had examined her and reassured her there was nothing to worry about. His negligence was demonstrated by the failure at least to review his patient's condition within a short period of time given the asymmetry and localised abnormality of the lump in her breast and, on the probable findings at review, for failing to refer her to a specialist.[127]

Negligence in treatment

9.59   The most important distinction here is that to be made between a medical mistake which the law regards as excusable[128] and a mistake which would amount to

---

121 (1975) *The Times*, 6 November.   122 (1978) *The Times*, 15 March.

123 See, for example, the general work of the Health Protection Agency (www.hpa.org.uk) and, in particular, P D Crook et al *West Nile Virus and the Threat to the UK* (2002) and the Chief Medical Officer's *West Nile Contingency Plan* (2004).

124 [1987] QB 730 at 777, [1986] 3 All ER 801 at 833.

125 It is to be noted that access to a second opinion is now a matter of patient entitlement.

126 [2004] EWHC 923.

127 For another 'failure to refer' case—this time in the context of allegation of sexual abuse—see *C v Cairns* [2003] Lloyd's Rep Med 90. Negligence was not found in the case. We refer to its more interesting confidentiality aspects in chapter 8.

128 See, for example, *E v Castro* (2003) 80 BMLR 14. For which, also see the rigid application of the *Bolam* test.

negligence.[129] In the former case, the court accepts that ordinary human fallibility precludes liability while, in the latter, the conduct of the defendant is considered to have strayed beyond the bounds of what is expected of the reasonably skilful or competent doctor.

9.60　　The issue came before the courts most classically in the case of *Whitehouse v Jordan*, which still remains the authoritative example.[130] In this case negligence was alleged on the part of an obstetrician who, it was claimed, had pulled too hard in a trial of forceps delivery and had thereby caused the plaintiff's head to become wedged, with consequent asphyxia and brain damage. The trial judge held that, although the decision to perform a trial of forceps was a reasonable one, the defendant had in fact pulled too hard and was therefore negligent. This initial finding of negligence was reversed in the Court of Appeal and, in a strongly worded judgment, Lord Denning emphasised that an error of judgment was not negligence.[131] When the matter came on appeal before the House of Lords, the views expressed by Lord Denning on the error of judgment question were rejected. An error of judgment could be negligence if it were an error which would not have been made by a reasonably competent professional man acting with ordinary care. As Lord Fraser pointed out:

The true position is that an error of judgment may, or may not, be negligent; it depends on the nature of the error. If it is one that would not have been made by a reasonably competent professional man professing to have the standard and type of skill that the defendant holds himself out as having, and acting with ordinary care, then it is negligence. If, on the other hand, it is an error that such a man, acting with ordinary care, might have made, then it is not negligence.[132]

In the event, the House of Lords held that there had not, in any case, been sufficient evidence to justify the trial judge's finding of negligence.[133]

9.61　　Gross medical mistakes will almost always result in a finding of negligence. Operating mistakes such as the removal of the wrong limb or the performance of an operation on the wrong patient are usually treated as indefensible and settled out of court; hence the paucity of decisions on such points.[134] Use of the wrong drug or, often with more serious consequences, the wrong gas during the course of an anaesthetic will frequently lead to the imposition of liability, and in some of these situations the res ipsa loquitur principle[135] may be applied.

---

[129] For discussion, see Merry and McCall Smith, n 9 above.

[130] [1981] 1 All ER 267, [1981] 1 WLR 246, HL.　　[131] [1980] 1 All ER 650 at 658, CA.

[132] [1981] 1 All ER 267 at 281, (1980) 1 BMLR 14 at 30. See a very comparable case in which the obsterician was found to have pulled on the forceps with a force beyond that which would have been used by a competent practitioner. The difficult issue of causation in cases of neonatal brain damage was also well aired: *Townsend v Worcester and District Health Authority* (1995) 23 BMLR 31.

[133] A misjudgment will also be negligent if it is in respect of something 'lying within the area where only a sound judgment measures up to the standard of reasonable competence expected': *Hendy v Milton Keynes Health Authority (No. 2)* [1992] 3 Med LR 119 at 127, per Jowitt J.

[134] An example is *Ibrahim (a minor) v Muhammad* (21 May 1984, unreported), QBD, in which a penis was partially amputated during circumcision; only the quantum of damages was in dispute.

[135] See para 9.80 below.

9.62   Many historic cases deal with items of operating equipment being left inside patients after surgery. In these, generally known as the 'swab cases', the allocation of liability is made according to the principle laid down in the locus classicus of the law on this point, the decision in *Mahon v Osborne*.[136] In this case, as in subsequent decisions, the courts have shown themselves unlikely to dictate to doctors in a hard and fast way the exact procedure that should be used towards the end of an operation in order to ensure that no foreign bodies are left in the patient. At the same time, however, it is clear that the law requires that there should be some sort of set procedures adopted in order to minimise the possibility of this occurring. Overall responsibility to see that swabs and other items are not left in the patient rests on the surgeon; he is not entitled to delegate the matter altogether to a nurse. This point was emphasised in *Mahon* by Lord Goddard, who said:

> As it is the task of the surgeon to put swabs in, so it is his task to take them out and if the evidence is that he has not used a reasonable standard of care he cannot absolve himself, if a mistake has been made, by saying, 'I relied on the nurse'.[137]

9.63   In the later case of *Urry v Bierer*[138] the Court of Appeal confirmed that the patient was entitled to expect the surgeon to do all that was reasonably necessary to ensure that all packs were removed and that this duty required more than mere reliance on the nurse's count.

THE PROBLEM OF THE NOVICE

9.64   The degree of expertise possessed by a medical practitioner obviously depends to a considerable extent on his experience and the argument has been put forward that the standard of competence of a newly qualified doctor will be less than that expected of an experienced practitioner. Although this may be the day-to-day expectation, it is not that of the law. The strict application of the *Bolam* principle[139] would lead the courts to expect the doctor to show that degree of skill which would be shown by the reasonably competent professional. This is an objective standard and it is therefore irrelevant whether the doctor has qualified the day before or ten years before the alleged incident of negligence—it should make no difference to the way in which his conduct is assessed.

9.65   The problem was considered in the case of *Wilsher v Essex Area Health Authority*.[140]

---

[136] [1939] 2 KB 14, [1939] 1 All ER 535, CA.

[137] [1939] 2 KB 14 at 47, [1939] 1 All ER 535 at 559. Scott LJ, however, qualified this by pointing out that it might be necessary to dispense with normal precautions in an emergency.

[138] (1955) *The Times*, 15 July, CA. For discussion of further swab (and forceps) cases see M A Jones *Medical Negligence* (3rd edn, 2003) pp 329–332.

[139] [1957] 2 All ER 118, [1957] 1 WLR 582.

[140] [1987] QB 730, [1986] 3 All ER 801. A lower standard of care for novices was proposed in the Australian case of *Cook v Cook* (1986) 162 CLR 376, in which it was held that an inexperienced driver might not be judged on the same standard as others. In this case, however, there were special features in the relationship between the parties.

The plaintiff had been born prematurely and had been admitted to a specialised neonatal intensive care unit. Extra oxygen was administered by junior hospital doctors, who made an error in monitoring the arterial oxygen tension. It was claimed that this could have caused the virtually blinding condition of retrolental fibroplasia which occurred. It was argued by the defendants that the standard of care expected of the junior doctor was not the same as that of his experienced counterpart. Extensive use, it was said, had to be made of recently qualified medical and nursing staff and it was unavoidable that such staff should 'learn on the job'; it would be impossible for public medicine to operate properly without such arrangements and to do otherwise would, ultimately, not be in the best interests of patients. The judgments in the Court of Appeal are not free of ambiguity. The majority of the judges maintained that the public were entitled to expect a reasonable standard of competence in their medical attendants. The decision of Mustill LJ, however, makes it clear that he, at least, was prepared to define the standard of care according to the requirements of the post. An inexperienced doctor occupying a post in a unit which offered specialised services would, accordingly, need that degree of expertise expected of a reasonably competent person occupying that post; the defendant's actual hospital rank—house officer, registrar etc—would not be relevant in the determination.

9.66   Glidewell LJ also stressed the importance of applying an objective standard which would not take account of an individual doctor's inexperience. The apparent harshness of this conclusion was, nevertheless, mitigated by his suggestion that the standard of care is very likely to be met if the novice seeks advice or consults with his more experienced colleagues when appropriate. Even so, this apparently simple solution does not answer the question which many juniors may ask—how am I to be so experienced as to know when I should be uncertain? And, if, I cannot tell this, am I to ask my seniors before I make any important decision? This question effectively forces us back to accepting a standard of care test which is based on the doctor of similar experience irrespective of the post in which he operates. Conversely, however, an experienced doctor occupying a junior post would be judged according to his actual knowledge rather than by the lower standard of the reasonably competent occupant of that post—the rationale being that, by reason of his superior expertise, he would be more able to foresee the damage likely to arise from any negligent acts or omissions.[141] It is important to bear in mind that *Wilsher* was very much concerned with specialist units and there is no certainty that the judgments are applicable, say, to the general practitioner in so far as delegation of responsibility, hierarchical organisation and the like are particular features of hospital practice.

9.67   Hospital authorities cannot, of course, rely too much upon junior employees; the principles of vicarious liability will, by themselves, prevent this. As Lord Denning said in *Jones v Manchester Corpn*:

It would be in the highest degree unjust that the hospital board, by getting inexperienced

---

[141] See *Wimpey Construction UK Ltd v Poole* [1984] 2 Lloyd's Rep 499.

doctors to perform their duties for them, without adequate supervision, should be able to throw all the responsibility on to those doctors as if they were fully experienced practitioners.[142]

Once again, this may reflect Lord Denning's particular concern for the practitioner at the coal-face and there is little doubt that delegation of responsibility to another can amount to negligence in certain circumstances. A consultant could, for example, be held to be negligent were he to delegate responsibility to a junior in the knowledge that the junior was incapable of performing his duties properly.

9.68   A junior to whom responsibility has been delegated must carry out his duties as instructed by his superior in order to avoid liability. If he chooses to depart from specific instructions, he will be placing himself in a risky position in the event of anything going wrong.[143] At the same time, there may be circumstances in which he is entitled to depart from instructions; obedience to manifestly wrong instructions might, itself, be construed as negligence in some cases.

PROTECTING PATIENTS FROM PRODUCTS

9.69   A great deal of the power of the doctor comes from his ability to prescribe medicines. The biggest difference between the psychiatrist and the psychologist, for example, lies in the authority of the former to treat his patient with drugs. But all medicinal products (and devices) carry inherent risks; and others, tragically, are just plain defective. The thalidomide scandal of the late 1950s and early 1960s[144] was among the first wake-up calls for both law and medicine as to the dangers of the 'medicalisation' of the modern age.[145] Recovery of damages for harm caused as a result of defective products in now largely dealt with under statute as a matter of products liability arising from the Consumer Protection Act 1987 (see below). But this legislation does not preclude recovery under the common law negligence action, nor does it extend to products marketed before 1 March 1988. The relevance of negligence therefore endures. None the less, under either scheme there are common and manifold difficulties. For example, given that the complex interactions between drugs, environment and the human body can take years to manifest health problems, at what point can we say that the drug is sub-standard? Even putting aside the challenge of demonstrating that the drug was the 'cause' of ill-health (see paras 9.91 et seq), how does emerging evidence of risks and harms affect the standard of care due to patients who are taking a course of treatment of a particular drug? We do not move from a state of ignorance about dangers to one of enlightenment overnight; rather, growing evidence begins to point in a particular direction—but how and when should this affect the

---

[142] [1952] 2 QB 852 at 871, [1952] 2 All ER 125 at 133, CA.

[143] *Junor v McNicol* (1959) *The Times*, 26 March, HL.

[144] See, H Teff and C Munro *Thalidomide: The Legal Aftermath* (1976).

[145] This phenomenon continues to this day, see, House of Commons Health Committee, *The Influence of the Pharmaceutical Industry*, Fourth Report of Session 2004–2005, HC 42-I (2005), especially pp 100–1.

standard of care which patients are entitled to expect? We can do no better than refer the reader to the Creutzfeldt-Jakob disease (CJD) litigation in answering these questions.

9.70 The CJD litigation takes up an entire volume of the Butterworths Medico-legal Reports and the reader is referred there for a full account.[146] Creutzfeldt-Jakob disease is an incurable degenerative brain disease caused by a transmissible agent called a prion. It is a rare condition, but it has come to the public attention in recent years largely because of instances of transmission through food and across species from cattle to humans. This litigation, however, had nothing to do with such cases. This was about human to human infection and contamination of a medicinal product. The actions related to children who were treated with Human Growth Hormone (HGH) in the period between 1959 and 1985 (and so before the passing of the Consumer Protection Act 1987). The HGH was derived from a large number of human pituitaries taken from cadavers,[147] and the allegation was that the product was contaminated with the CJD prion; it was further claimed that the duty of care to patients receiving the HGH was breached by an inadequate programme of administration of the hormone, by failures to avoid predictable risks as far as possible, and by the omission to inform parents and patients of the growing evidence of a risk in treatment.

9.71 The litigation was complicated by many factors, but two are of importance here. First, different classes of litigant were claiming different things. Class A concerned patients who had actually contracted CJD (some of whom had already died). Class B involved persons who claimed to have suffered distress at having been exposed to the risk of CJD; they had not, as yet, developed the disease, but there was no means of detecting whether they carried the prion—thus, their lives were blighted by uncertainty. The legal harms in question were, therefore, distinct—that is, Group A involved physical injury or death, while Group B related to mental injury or upset. Secondly, the long period of time involved—during which over 2,000 children received HGH—meant that peoples' circumstances were not the same in respect of what was, or was not, known about the dangers of the product. That is, some people may already have completed a course of treatment before evidence of the risks came to light; others may only have begun treatment after it was clear that there was a danger. Still others would have been receiving a course of treatment as evidence began to accumulate. Should they have been told? Should treatment have ceased and, if so, at what point?

9.72 Morland J had the unenviable task of sorting through these issues.[148] The central question for him was how do standards of care shift in light of growing medical evidence and experience, and, indeed, *when* does the shift take place? A fundamental

---

[146] (2000) 54 BMLR.

[147] An interesting tangential issue is the question of the legitimacy of the initial harvest and the possible effects on this on subsequent rights of action, see *The Creutzfeldt-Jakob Disease Litigation* (1995) 54 BMLR 1.

[148] See *CJD litigation, Plaintiffs v UK Medical Research Council* (1996) 54 BMLR 8.

principle of the law was re-iterated: a court cannot look back at events with the benefit of hindsight; standards must be judged in the light of what was known at the relevant time.[149] Evidence therefore becomes crucial. It was found, for example, that indications of risk were in the literature well before 1973, but this was not so strong as to require an overhaul of the HGH programme at that time. But letters from eminent virologists warning of the dangers emerged in late 1977 and these were not seen at that time by the central committee in charge of the programme. Moreover, responsibility for running the programme shifted from the Medical Research Council to the Department of Health on 1 July 1977 but its operation continued on the same old basis until 1980. Morland J found this date of 1 July 1977 to be significant. He held that the shift to safer production methods of HGH that took place in 1980 should have occurred earlier and that the programme should have been suspended as of 1 July 1977 to allow a thorough review.[150] That this did not happen was negligence. For people who began treatment after this date, then, recovery should be allowed. By corollary, those who began and finished treatment prior to this time would receive nothing. This legal fiction may seem to many to be arbitrary and unjust. It is certainly artificial to select a specific day as the date on which standards of care suddenly change. By the same token, it is difficult to see how a court could do otherwise when attempting to negotiate the morass of available evidence. We must bear in mind too that 'standard of care' is also an artificial construct, and, to the extent that a line must be drawn somewhere, there will always be someone who finds himself on the wrong side.

9.73   This initial ruling did not address the problem of the 'straddlers' whose treatment was on-going before and after July 1977 and who argued that they should have been told of the increased risk; moreover, it only concerned Group A patients, i.e. those who contracted the disease. In a subsequent judgment, however, Morland J held that it was not negligent to fail to apprise straddler patients of the increased risk because the finding of negligence in the litigation related to the failure to suspend the programme *for new patients*. He then went on to say that it as not in the public interest to entertain the claims of Group B in respect of psychological upset: we all receive bad news about our health at some point in our lives.[151] The Court of Appeal overturned the first aspect of this ruling and opined that it was at least arguable that a duty of care had also been breached by failing to inform patients of new knowledge about risk.[152] The litigation therefore proceeded and was ultimately resolved entirely in the realm of hypthotheticals: what would have happened if there had been no negligence and clinicians had been properly informed? Here Morland J held that it would have been the responsibility of the individual clinician to advise their patient on whether treatment should continue.[153] In this respect, however, it

---

[149] This was well established in *Roe v Minister of Health* [1954] 2 QB 66.

[150] An exception was in the case of hypoglycaemia patients who would have experienced serious ill-health if treatment was stopped.

[151] *The Creutzfeldt-Jakob Disease Litigation* (1996) 54 BMLR 79.

[152] *The CJD Litigation, Newman v Secretary of State for Health* (1997) 54 BMLR 85.

[153] *The CJD Litigation, Newman v Secretary of Health (No. 2)* (1998) 54 BMLR 95.

was also found that there would have been unanimous consensus among the specialist clinicians that treatment should be stopped. Thus, but for the negligence, treatment would have ceased. It did not and harm was the result.[154] In the end, then, the straddlers won the day.

9.74   Finally, what of Group B patients who suffered more than mere distress as a result of being told of exposure to the disease? Morland J conceded, along general tort lines, that compensation would also be payable for those who suffered such a degree of mental anguish as to amount to a psychiatric condition.[155] Damages were to be calculable on the basis that they would *not* develop the disease, but this was subject to review if things developed otherwise.[156]

9.75   We have spent some time dealing with this litigation to demonstrate a number of points:

(i)   that while inherent risks do not change over time, the same is not true of knowledge about risks,

(ii)   that the standards of care that patients can expect will also change in light of new knowledge,

(iii)   that the organic nature of human knowledge acquisition is not matched by an equally subtle legal response: lines of liability must be drawn somewhere, and

(iv)   that, occasionally, despite the odds, the negligence action can come down on the side of the patient!

PROTECTING PATIENTS FROM THEMSELVES

9.76   In certain circumstances, it is part of the duty of care of doctors and nurses to predict that patients may damage themselves as a result of their medical condition.[157] The extent of the duty to safeguard against such damage is problematical and the decisions have not all gone the same way. In *Selfe v Ilford and District Hospital Management Committee*,[158] the plaintiff had been admitted to hospital after a drug overdose. Although he had known suicidal tendencies, he was not kept under constant observation and climbed on to the hospital roof while the two nurses on duty were out of the ward; he fell and was injured. Damages of £19,000 were awarded against the hospital.

9.77   By contrast, the plaintiff in *Thorne v Northern Group Hospital Management*

---

[154] *The CJD Litigation, Straddlers Groups A and C v Secretary of State for Health* (1998) 54 BMLR 104.

[155] *The CJD Litigation, Group B Plaintiffs v Medical Research Council* (1997) 54 BMLR 92, [2000] Lloyd's Rep Med 161.

[156] *The CJD Litigation, Andrews v Secretary of State for Health (Damages Assessments)* (1998) 54 BMLR 111.

[157] For the nature and extent of the non-medical duty of care in such cases in respect of people in detention see, *Gary Smiley (through his litigation friend Raymond Smiley) v Home Office* [2004] EWHC 240, approving *Reeves v The Commissioner of Police of the Metropolis* [2000] 1 AC 360.

[158] (1970) 114 Sol Jo 935.

Committee[159] failed to win an award of damages for the death of his wife who had left a hospital in suicidal mood. In this case, the patient had slipped out of the hospital when the nurses' backs were turned, returned home and gassed herself. The court took the view that, although the degree of supervision which a hospital should exercise in relation to patients with known suicidal tendencies is higher than that to be exercised over other patients, they could not be kept under constant supervision by hospital staff. A similar view was expressed more recently by the Court of Appeal in *Dunn v South Tyneside Health Care NHS Trust*[160] where a bipolar patient on one-hourly observations evaded detection and returned home to consume large quantities of anti-asthma tablets which resulted in severe brain damage. The subsequent negligence action claimed that an observation regime at 15-minute intervals was the appropriate standard of care; moreover, had this been implemented the harm would not have resulted because the police would have been alerted sooner and would have found the patient. The action failed on both counts. The one-hour regime was a reasonable standard of care given the patient's history and mental state on detention and by reference to *Bolam* and *Bolitho*; furthermore, the Court found that it was not an established matter of 'fact' that the police would have intervened to prevent the harm even if they had been alerted earlier.

9.78   In *Hyde v Tameside Area Health Authority*[161] the Court of Appeal overturned a High Court award of substantial damages to a plaintiff who, believing he had cancer, made a suicide attempt in hospital. Not only did the court take the view that there had been no breach of duty on the part of the defendants, but Lord Denning stressed in his judgment that there were strong policy grounds why damages should not be awarded in respect of attempted suicide. Nowadays, that would probably be a minority view; the case was, in fact, discussed and doubted in *Kirkham v Chief Constable of Greater Manchester*[162] which involved an appeal to the ex turpi causa principle—which may exclude liability where the plaintiff's act is in some way wrongful. This was, however, rejected. It was held that the award of damages in respect of a suicidal death caused no affront to the public conscience and suicide was no longer a criminal matter.

9.79   Finally, in *Hay (Gill's curator bonis) v Grampian Health Board*,[163] a voluntary psychiatric patient, who was known to be a high suicide risk, hanged herself in a bathroom while two nurses were attending other patients. She suffered serious and irreversible brain damage as a result. In a negligence action against the Health Board, it was claimed that the doctrine of res ipsa loquitur applied because the patient was supposedly under a regime of close observation. We now turn to a consideration of that principle.

---

[159] (1964) 108 Sol Jo 484. A similar decision was taken in the Scottish case *Rolland v Lothian Health Board* (1981) unreported, OH, per Lord Ross.

[160] [2003] EWCA Civ 878, [2004] PIQR 150. See also the approval of *Hunter* in *McHardy v Dundee Hospitals*, n 83 above.

[161] [1981] CLY 1854, CA; (1986) 2 PN 26, CA.

[162] [1990] 2 QB 283, [1990] 3 All ER 246. Other police cases are highlighted in n 157 above.

[163] 1995 SLT 652, (1995) 25 BMLR 98.

RES IPSA LOQUITUR

9.80   Because it may be difficult in many personal injury actions to establish negligence on the part of the defendant, plaintiffs occasionally have recourse to the doctrine of res ipsa loquitur. This doctrine does not shift the onus of proof to the defendant, as is sometimes suggested; what it does achieve is to give rise to an inference of negligence on the defendant's part.[164] If the defendant cannot then rebut this inference of negligence, the plaintiff will have established his case. It follows from this that it is considerably easier for the plaintiff to succeed in his claim when res ipsa loquitur applies.

9.81   The classic case is probably that of *Cassidy v Ministry of Health*,[165] in which the plaintiff went into hospital for an operation to remedy Dupuytren's contracture of two fingers and came out with four stiff fingers. Denning LJ (as he then was) expressed the view that the plaintiff was quite entitled to say:

> I went into hospital to be cured of two stiff fingers. I have come out with four stiff fingers and my hand is useless. That should not have happened if due care had been used. Explain it if you can.[166]

9.82   The doctrine is most useful in cases where damage has occurred in an incident involving machinery or in the context of damage suffered while the plaintiff was involved in some sort of complex process. It can apply only where the plaintiff is unable to identify the precise nature of the negligence which caused his injury and where no explanation of the way in which the injury came to be inflicted has been offered by the defendant. The injury itself must be of such a kind as 'does not normally happen' in the circumstances unless there is negligence. Thus, in a case of neurological damage following difficult aortography,[167] the plea of res ipsa loquitur was rejected on the grounds that the injury sustained was of a kind recognised as an inherent risk of the procedure.

9.83   The doctrine's application in medical cases may still be particularly apt because of the difficulty that the ordinary plaintiff sometimes experiences in unravelling the cause of an injury sustained during technical procedures of which he has little understanding; indeed, he may well have been unconscious at the relevant time. It may also be seen as a potential corrective to the tendency of the medical profession to 'close ranks' when one of their number is accused of negligence. However, it is possibly of

---

[164] There has been some debate as to the precise effect of res ipsa loquitur, but the current weight of opinion favours the view outlined here: see *Ng Chun Pui v Lee Chuen Tat* [1988] RTR 298, PC. For discussion, see J Fleming *The Law of Torts* (9th edn, 1998) p 353; D Giesen *International Medical Malpractice Law* (1988) p 515.

[165] [1951] 2 KB 343, [1951] 1 All ER 574, CA.

[166] [1951] 2 KB 343 at 365, [1951] 1 All ER 574 at 588. Other medical cases in which res ipsa loquitur has applied include: *Saunders v Leeds Western Health Authority* (1984) 129 Sol Jo 225; *Cavan v Wilcox* (1973) 44 DLR (3d) 42 and *Holmes v Board of Hospital Trustees of the City of London* (1977) 81 DLR (3d) 67.

[167] *O'Malley-Williams v Board of Governors of the National Hospital for Nervous Diseases* (1975, unreported), cited in [1975] 1 BMJ 635.

less importance in a climate of increasing openness—or, in today's usage, transparency. It must also be borne in mind that the courts are generally reluctant to apply the res ipsa loquitur principle and that this is certainly evident in medical negligence cases. As Megaw LJ said:

[if one were to accept the view that negligence was inevitably proved if something went wrong and it was unexplained], few dentists, doctors and surgeons, however competent, conscientious and careful they might be, would avoid the totally unjustified and unfair stigma of professional negligence probably several times in the course of their careers.[168]

9.84   An unsuccessful attempt to raise the doctrine of res ipsa loquitur was made in *Ludlow v Swindon Health Authority*,[169] in which it was stressed that the plaintiff had to establish facts which, if unexplained, would give rise to an inference of negligence. In this case the plaintiff claimed to have regained consciousness during a caesarian section operation and to have experienced intense pain. She failed, however, to establish that the pain arose at a stage during which halothane should have been administered; there was, accordingly, no inference of negligence in the administration of the anaesthetic. Nevertheless, there are cases where the injuries sustained by the patient are of such a nature that there is an inescapable inference of negligence. In *Glass v Cambridge Health Authority*[170] the patient suffered brain damage as a result of suffering a heart attack under a general anaesthetic. The court held that this was not an event which normally would be expected to happen in the circumstances and that the onus therefore transferred to the defendant to provide an explanation of the event which was consistent with the absence of negligence.

9.85   The courts' general antipathy to res ipsa has been re-emphasised more recently. In *Ratcliffe v Plymouth and Torbay Health Authority*,[171] a case involving paraesthesia following a spinal anaesthetic, the plaintiff's appeal was based largely on the trial judge's dismissal of the maxim. In a very extensive and carefully explanatory judgment, the Court of Appeal affirmed that it could not be inferred that the untoward symptoms could not have occurred in the absence of negligence. The courts, it was said, would do medicine a considerable disservice if, because a patient suffered a grievous and unexpected outcome, a careful doctor was ordered to pay him compensation as if the doctor had been negligent:

If the untoward outcome was extremely rare, or was impossible to explain in the light of the current state of medical knowledge, the judge will be bound to exercise great care in evaluating the evidence before making such a finding, but if he does so, the prima facie inference of negligence is rebutted and the claim will fail.[172]

9.86   In effect, and as expressed by Hobhouse LJ, the court pointed out that res ipsa loquitur is no more than a convenient phrase to describe the proof of facts which are

---

[168] *Fletcher v Bench* (1973, unreported), CA cited in [1973] 4 BMJ 117.
[169] [1989] 1 Med LR 104.   [170] [1995] 6 Med LR 91.
[171] (1998) 42 BMLR 64, [1998] Lloyd's Rep Med 162, CA.   [172] Per Brooke LJ at BMLR 80.

sufficient to support an inference—based on ordinary human experience with no need for expert evidence—that a defendant was negligent and, therefore, to establish a prima facie case against him. Hobhouse LJ may, indeed, have ended the matter once and for all by pointing out that res ipsa loquitur is not a principle of law; it is an expression that should be dropped from the litigator's vocabulary and replaced by the phrase 'a prima facie case'.[173]

9.87   And, as something of a coda, we note that in *Hay (Gill's curator bonis) v Grampian Health Board*[174] the use of the res ipsa doctrine was rejected although it was held that negligence had occurred. It was stated that the doctrine can only be used in cases where no explanation for events is available. Here, there was a clear explanation of how the patient came to attempt suicide—she had been allowed to go to the bathroom unsupervised. This approach has been repeated most recently in *Smith v Sheridan*[175] where there was little doubt as to the negligence of a doctor during a forceps delivery when he gave a 'hard pull' on the child who suffered serious brain damage as a result. None the less, the court rejected the case as an example of res ipsa loquitur on the rather confusing reasoning that '. . . it is clear that the defendant must have used excessive force in delivering Jake and was thus negligent in the absence of any other explanation'. It would seem that the basis of this is that having excluded all other causes on the basis of expert argument, it was probable—perhaps a near certainty—that, despite his protestations, the obstetrician was at fault.

OPERATIONAL FAILURES

9.88   As we have discussed in earlier sections, reforms to the compensation system are as much about addressing system failures in health care delivery as they about recompensing patients harmed as a result of those failures. It is, therefore, important to point to other areas of law where such operational oversights are revealed. Two recent cases illustrate the point.

9.89   The role of the coroner in England and Wales is to carry out full and effective inquests into sudden and unexpected deaths, particularly those which give rise to a public interest. This is part of the state's obligation to its citizens and is accordingly also a matter which is subsumed under the umbrella of human rights. Thus, in *R (on the application of Davies) v HM Deputy Coroner for Birmingham*[176] it was held by the Court of Appeal that the coroner had failed in his duty on behalf of the state under Article 2 ECHR (right to life) when he did not invite the jury to consider the care offered to a prisoner. The patient had been a heroin addict who suffered withdrawal symptoms on admission to prison. He was not seen by a doctor, and the nurse who did attend wrongly assessed him as requiring no further medical assistance. He died

---

[173] *Ratcliffe* was followed in *Gray v Southampton and South West Hampshire Health Authority* (2000) 57 BMLR 148.

[174] (1995) 25 BMLR 98.   [175] [2005] EWHC 614.   [176] [2003] EWCA Civ 1739.

the next day. The coroner had failed in his duties by not instructing the jury to consider a verdict of *systemic* neglect.

9.90   Very similar circumstances were considered by the European Court of Human Rights in *McGlinchey v United Kingdom*.[177] Here, again, an asthmatic heroin addict was admitted to prison with severe withdrawal symptoms. Her weight was inaccurately assessed using scales known to be defective and the medical professional made only an impressionistic assessment of her condition. Out of duty-hours medical cover was thin and, although the patient's condition deteriorated, she was not seen by a doctor over the weekend; she died a few days later. It was argued that the standard of care had been so low as to be a breach of Article 3 ECHR (cruel and inhuman treatment), and, because causation difficulties precluded an action in negligence (see below), the claimant was left with no domestic remedy. The ECtHR upheld the complaint on both of these grounds, namely (i) that the catalogue of systemic omissions and errors demonstrated a breach of Article 3, and (ii) that the non-availability of compensation under domestic law was in violation of Article 13 ECHR (the right to an effective remedy for violation of Convention rights).

CAUSATION

9.91   As if the problems of fault were not enough, it will do the plaintiff no good to establish negligence on the part of a defendant doctor unless he is also able to prove that the damage he has suffered was caused by that negligence. Thus, Mr Barnett's widow (see *Barnett v Chelsea and Kensington Hospital Management Committee*, para 9.31 et seq above) was unable to recover damages for her husband's death from arsenic poisoning even though she proved that her husband was owed a duty of care when he attended the cottage hospital and that it was negligent for the doctor to send him away without examination. Why? Because it is the nature of arsenic poisoning that *even if* Mr Barnett had been examined he would have died anyway, there being no cure or treatment for the condition. In law, therefore, the doctor's negligence did not cause the death.

9.92   Causation issues can be particularly difficult in the medical context because there may be a variety of possible independent explanations for the occurrence of a condition. Thus, if a person brings an action for 'nervous shock', it may well be arguable that the symptoms complained of are those of a psychiatric state which existed before the claimed precipitating event.[178] Some assistance in this respect was provided to the

---

[177] (2003) 37 EHRR 41, (2003) 72 BMLR 168.
[178] For modern examples, see *Abada v Gray* (1997) 40 BMLR 116, CA (schizophrenia could not be precipitated by a road traffic injury); *Gates v McKenna* (1998) 46 BMLR 9, [1998] Lloyd's Rep Med 405

plaintiff through the Scottish case of *McGhee v National Coal Board*,[179] in which it was held that liability will be imposed if it can be established that the negligence of the defender materially increased the risk of the plaintiff being damaged in the way in question.[180]

9.93   This principle was endorsed in *Clark v MacLennan*,[181] in which it was held that, where there was a precaution which could have been taken to avoid the precise injury which occurred, the onus was then upon the defendant to establish that his failure to take this precaution did not cause the plaintiff's injury. This 'recognised risk avoidance' concept brings us very close to that of res ipsa loquitur which, as we have seen, the courts are reluctant to apply. This antipathy was demonstrated in the very comparable case of *Ashcroft v Mersey Regional Health Authority*,[182] which was heard at much the same time as *Clark*. Here, the plaintiff underwent a relatively straightforward and commonplace operation to remove granulation tissue—the result of chronic infection—from the ear; she sustained a severe paralysis of the facial nerve. Opinion was divided as to whether the surgeon had negligently pulled too hard on the nerve or whether the injury was an unfortunate accident. In the result, Kilner Brown J was, with obvious reluctance, unable to shift the burden of proof and found that, on a balance of probabilities, there was no negligence. The correctness of this view was later confirmed in *Wilsher*,[183] where the House of Lords went so far as to reverse the opinion of the Court of Appeal and to order a retrial on the grounds that the coincidence of a breach of duty and injury could not, of itself, give rise to a presumption that the injury was so caused: 'Whether we like it or not, the law . . . requires proof of fault causing damage as the basis of liability in tort.'[184]

9.94   The difficulty for the plaintiff in *Wilsher* lay in the fact there were five possible causes for the condition with which he was afflicted. One of these was medical negligence but it could not be established that this *possible* cause actually made a material contribution to the injury. It might have done so, but this fact still required to be proved by the plaintiff. The House of Lords discarded the notion that *McGhee v National Coal Board*[185] constituted an authority for transferring the onus of proof to the defendant. *McGhee* was to be distinguished from *Wilsher* in that there were several agents which could have caused the injury in the latter but only one in the former.[186]

(it was improbable that taking part in a stage hypnosis programme could precipitate schizophrenia and the possibility was unforeseeable).

[179] [1972] 3 All ER 1008, [1973] 1 WLR 1.
[180] [1972] 3 All ER 1008 at 1011, per Lord Reid, [1973] 1 WLR 1 at 4, per Lord Reid.
[181] [1983] 1 All ER 416.   [182] [1983] 2 All ER 245.
[183] *Wilsher v Essex Area Health Authority* [1988] AC 1074, [1988] 1 All ER 871, HL. For a useful summary of the complicated post-*Wilsher* landscape, see M A Jones *Medical Negligence* (3rd edn, 2003) pp 387–392; see too a discussion of the scope and effect of the important decision in *Fairchild v Glenhaven Funeral Services Ltd and others* [2003] 1 AC 32, [2002] 3 All ER 305; (2002) 67 BMLR 90, at pp 393–402.
[184] [1988] AC 1074 at 1092, [1988] 1 All ER 871 at 883, per Lord Bridge.
[185] [1972] 3 All ER 1008, [1973] 1 WLR 1.
[186] See the dissenting opinion of Browne-Wilkinson V-C in *Wilsher v Essex Area Health Authority* [1987] QB 730 at 779, [1986] 3 All ER 801 at 834. For discussion of the issue, see J Fleming 'Probabilistic Causation in the Tort Law' (1989) 68 Can BR 661.

This provided an exceptional inference as to cause and, as a result, *McGhee* positively affirmed that the onus of proving causation lies on the pursuer or plaintiff.[187]

9.95   These issues are clearly matters of legal policy and justice. Causation is not a strict technical matter which can be 'solved' by the application of quasi-mathematical formulae. Indeed, this is well reflected in two important and recent House of Lords cases. In the non-medical negligence case of *Fairchild v Glenhaven Funeral Services Ltd*[188] the claimant had suffered multiple exposures to asbestos in the course of working for various employers and could not, strictly, demonstrate *who* then had caused his disease. The court applied *Wilsher* in holding that justice demanded a modified approach to the rules of causation; thus, so long as the claimant could show, on a balance of probabilities, that the wrongdoing of each employer had materially increased the risk to the employee that he might contract the disease, then this would be enough to establish that each employer had materially contributed to it, i.e. *each* had caused his loss in legal terms. *Fairfield* was then approved—and, perhaps, expanded—by the House in *Chester v Afshar*.[189] This case involved a dispute about information disclosure and for that reason it is better discussed in chapter 10. Its relevance for present purposes is to illustrate further the House of Lords' willingness—albeit by majority only—to bend the rules of causation in the name of justice. Here a patient was not told of an inherent risk in a procedure to cure back pain. The risk materialised and the law of causation dictated that she had to prove that if she had known of the risk she would never have had the operation. But the patient did not, and could not, prove that she would *never* have the operation; she only proved that she would not have had it on the day that she did. All five of their Lordships agreed that she should therefore fail on a strict application of the law—but the majority could not accept this outcome and argued that the patient's right to self-determination demanded a remedy. All of the judgments in the case make interesting reading as to how and how far abstract notions such as 'justice' and 'policy' can and should influence the direction of the law. *Chester* is one of the clearest examples we have of this to date, but we find, as a result, that our causation rules are now in a state of flux.

9.96   It is undoubtedly the case that these recent policy-driven decisions are a direct response to the considerable difficulties that claimants can face when attempting to clear the causation hurdle. The problems are well illustrated by the lengthy and complicated litigation over pertussis vaccination. In *Loveday*[190] the court held that establishing a mere chance that the vaccine might cause brain damage in children did not discharge the obligation on the plaintiff. It is to be noted, parenthetically, that the

---

[187] As to the influence of the plaintiff's own actions on the chain of causation, see *Pidgeon v Doncaster HA* [2002] Lloyd's Rep Med 130 (unwillingness to undergo subsequent smear tests did not break chain of causation in respect of negligent error in original tests) and *Gregory v Pembrokeshire Health Authority* [1989] 1 Med LR 81 (refusal to abort damaged fetus irrelevant to wrongful birth action; the plaintiff did, however, lose her case on other grounds).

[188] [2003] 1 AC 32, [2002] 3 All ER 305.

[189] [2005] 1 AC 134, [2004] 4 All ER 587. We discuss the case in K Mason and D Brodie '*Bolam, Bolam—Wherefore Art Thou, Bolam?*' (2005) 9 Edin LR 398.

[190] *Loveday v Renton* [1990] 1 Med LR 117.

decision in *Loveday* was not the last word on pertussis vaccine; in *Best v Wellcome Foundation Ltd*,[191] the Supreme Court in Ireland awarded £2.75m to a young man who had suffered brain damage after its administration. The ground for the award was, however, that the particular batch of vaccine used was sub-standard and should not have been released on the market—future litigants will still have to prove that, on the balance of probabilities, their injuries were caused by the vaccine per se. And, in a rather similar causation problem, both the Court of Session and the House of Lords declared that a judge was not entitled to propound his own theory of a causative link between an overdose of penicillin and deafness; the weight of the evidence in *Kay* was that the causative factor was the meningitis for which the penicillin had been prescribed.[192]

9.97   An interesting look at the obverse in vaccination cases was provided by *Thomson v Blake-James*.[193] Here, a child developed post-measles encephalitis and the parents sued their general practitioner for having given negligent advice as to vaccination. The child was subject to suspected seizures which, in the practitioner's view, contraindicated vaccination; he did not, however, mention a special protocol for vaccination in such circumstances which had been issued by the DHSS and, for that and other reasons, the trial judge later found against the first practitioner. Meantime, the parents had moved and had received very similar advice, with additional explanation, from a second practitioner; when they approached a third general practitioner, they informed him they had decided against vaccination. The claims against the second and third practitioners were dismissed at first instance. On appeal, the court distinguished between general and specific advice. In so far as the vaccination could not, at any rate, be undertaken for several months, Dr Blake-James was providing the former and the court decided that failure to mention alternatives would not necessarily constitute a breach of duty in such circumstances. Moreover, the parents had received further advice from the other practitioners; Dr Blake-James's advice was not, therefore, definitive and was not the cause of the child's disability.

9.98   The increased attention paid in recent years to what might loosely be termed 'psychosomatic' diseases has led to some interesting developments in the field of causation. Repetitive strain injury (RSI)—now more specifically referred to as Prescribed Disease A4[194]—is one such condition. Medical opinion differs as to whether it is organic or psychiatric in origin or whether it results from a combination of causes. Thus, it is not surprising that litigation has led to some confusing results—ranging from large out of court settlements[195] to judicial comments such as: '[I agree] that RSI

---

[191] [1994] 5 Med LR 81, Ir SC; see D Brahamas 'Court Award for Pertussis Brain Damage' (1993) 341 Lancet 1338; C Dyer 'Man Awarded damages after Pertussis Vaccination' (1993) 306 BMJ 1365.

[192] *Kay's Tutor v Ayrshire and Arran Health Board* [1987] 2 All ER 417, 1987 SLT 577, HL.

[193] (1998) 41 BMLR 144, [1998] Lloyd's Rep Med 187, CA.

[194] Social Security (Industrial Injuries) (Prescribed Diseases) Regulations 1985, SI 1985/967, Sch 1, Pt 1. There is nothing to stop an employee suing his employers in negligence despite the fact that the condition sustained is recognised as a work hazard (for which see Social Security Contributions and Benefits Act 1992, s 108(2)).

[195] 'Revenue to Pay £79,000 to RSI Victim', *The Scotsman*, 19 January 1994, p 5.

is, in reality, meaningless . . . Its use by doctors can only serve to confuse.'[196] In what is probably the most important judicial airing of the subject,[197] the House of Lords overturned the Court of Appeal in holding that the fact that the trial judge was unwilling to accept that the plaintiff's condition was simply that of conversion hysteria was not, of itself, sufficient ground to sustain her claim in negligence; it was essential to the success of her case that she proved that her condition had been caused by repetitive movements while typing. If it was impossible to decide what was the cause of the condition from the medical evidence alone, the court was entitled to consider all the other evidence in concluding that the plaintiff had failed to prove her case.[198]

9.99   Other conditions that raise similar problems include post-traumatic stress disorder,[199] myalgic encephalomyelitis[200] and the purely psychiatric condition of so-called 'nervous shock'.[201] We believe that a full discussion of the law in this area, a proportion of which is based on policy considerations, is beyond the scope of a book of this size.

9.100   An important variation on the causation theme was re-introduced in *Hotson*.[202] Here, the plaintiff was, admittedly, negligently treated following traumatic avulsion of the head of the femur and developed avascular necrosis. However, there was a 75 per cent chance that this lesion would develop even in the event of correct diagnosis and treatment. The trial judge concluded that the matter was simply one of quantification of damages and the Court of Appeal upheld the view that the mistreatment had denied the plaintiff a 25 per cent chance of a good recovery; damages were awarded and reduced accordingly. The House of Lords, however, declined to measure statistical chances[203] and concluded that it was the original injury which caused the avascular necrosis. Lord MacKay expressed the true situation:

. . . the probable effect of delay in treatment was determined by the state of facts existing when the plaintiff was first presented at the hospital . . . If insufficient blood vessels were left intact by the fall, he had no prospect of avoiding complete avascular necrosis whereas if sufficient blood vessels were left intact . . . he would not have suffered the avascular necrosis.[204]

---

[196] *Mughal v Reuters Ltd* (1993) 16 BMLR 127 at 140, per Prosser J.

[197] *Pickford v Imperial Chemical Industries plc* [1998] 3 All ER 462, [1998] 1 WLR 1189.

[198] For a recent instance of an appeal court questioning the trial judge's finding of fact and so changing the outcome as to causation, see *Roughton v Weston Area Health Authority* [2004] EWCA Civ 1509.

[199] *Frost v Chief Constable of South Yorkshire Police* [1997] 1 All ER 540, (1996) 33 BMLR 108, CA.

[200] *Page v Smith* [1995] 2 All ER 736, (1995) 28 BMLR 133, HL.

[201] *Alcock v Chief Constable of South Yorkshire Police* [1992] 1 AC 310, (1991) 8 BMLR 37.

[202] *Hotson v East Berkshire Area Health Authority* [1987] AC 750, [1987] 2 All ER 909, HL. A similar claim was dismissed in the early Scottish case of *Kenyon v Bell* 1953 SC 125. For discussion, see D T Price 'Causation—The Lords' "Lost Chance" '(1989) 33 ICLQ 735.

[203] Statistical chances and personal chances are quite different matters: T Hill 'A Lost Chance for Compensation in the Tort of Negligence by the House of Lords' (1991) 54 MLR 511. The author regrets the fact that the House of Lords appears to leave open the possibility of future successful actions based on a *personal* loss of chance.

[204] [1987] AC 750 at 785, [1987] 2 All ER 909 at 915.

or, as put in *The Times* transcript,[205] what was meant by a chance was that if 100 people had suffered the same injury, 75 would have developed avascular necrosis and 25 would not. Thus, on the balance of probabilities, the plaintiff fell into the larger group—there being no evidence that he was one of the fortunate 25 per cent who could benefit from treatment—and, consequently, his injury could not be attributed to the negligence of the defendants. It would be different if 51 per cent of people sustaining the sort of injury which the plaintiff suffered could be treated with, say, a 20 per cent chance of success. Then, on the balance of probabilities, the plaintiff would have fallen into that group of 51 per cent, and, if a hospital negligently failed to offer him the treatment, he would have personally lost that 20 per cent chance of a successful outcome. Whether that 20 per cent loss is something which should attract compensation in the form of 20 per cent damages is left open by the decision in *Hotson*.

9.101   'Loss of a chance' has now been re-visited by the House of Lords in *Gregg v Scott*[206] where the whole percentage approach towards such cases was called into question. The facts related to what must be, sadly, a fairly common occurrence. A patient presented to his doctor with an uncomfortable lump under his left arm. The doctor diagnosed this as benign and re-assured the patient such that this was the patient's one and only visit to the GP. In truth, the lump was a malignant tumour for which aggressive treatment was required. This did not commence until some 14–15 months after the initial consult, by which time the cancer had spread to the patient's chest. It was accepted that the cursory examination of the patient by his GP was negligent;[207] the crux of the matter was whether this had caused a recognised legal harm. In the final analysis, the plaintiff argued that his 'harm' was the loss of the chance of survival for more than 10 years,[208] or put slightly differently, the loss of the chance of a more favourable outcome to his prognosis.[209] Statistical evidence[210] indicated that while the plaintiff might have had a 42 per cent chance of still being alive after 10 years if there had been no negligence, this chance was reduced to 25 per cent because of the negligence. There was, therefore, a significant drop in his statistical chances as a result of the misdiagnosis, but—crucially—at no point did he enjoy a more-than-50 per cent chance of survival beyond 10 years.[211] On a strict application of *Hotson* and the balance of probabilities test, then, the GP did not cause the alleged harm: it was not 'more probable than not' that *but for* the negligence the patient would be alive

---

[205] (1987) *The Times*, 6 July.

[206] [2005] UKHL 2, (2005) 82 BMLR 52. An even more recent apposite case is *Al Hamwi v Johnston* [2005] EWHC 206 (delay in testing for Down's syndrome would have made no difference to choice as to termination).

[207] See also para 9.31.   [208] Per Lord Hoffmann, *ibid*, para 87.

[209] Per Lord Phillips, *ibid*, para 125. Lady Hale seems to concur on this analysis, para 226. Cf, Lord Hope who denied that this was a 'loss of a chance' case, para 117.

[210] Which was seriously questioned by Lord Phillips, *ibid*, para 147 ff.

[211] The significance of the criterion of 'survival at 10 years' is that this is generally acknowledge in medical circles to amount to a 'cure'. The relevance of this to a legal concept of 'cure' was, however, rejected by Lady Hale, *ibid*, para 197.

after 10 years. Indeed, the trial judge found that he probably would not be. To put it another way, even without negligence, there would have been a 58 per cent chance that the patient would not survive the decade.

9.102   This outcome was unacceptable to Lords Nicholls and Hope. Lord Nicholls, in particular, argued forcefully that the 'all-or-nothing' approach to what would have happened but for the negligence—that is, the application of the 49/51 per cent rule from *Hotson*—was premised on a falsehood[212] and led to arbitrary and unjust outcomes: '[i]t means that a patient with a 60 per cent chance of recovery reduced to a 40 per cent prospect by medical negligence can obtain compensation. But he can obtain nothing if his prospects were reduced from 40 per cent to nil'.[213] And Lord Hope opined that the principle on which a patient's loss as a result of negligence is to be calculated—and, presumably, recompensed—is the same whether the prospects were better or worse than 50 per cent.[214]

9.103   The majority, however, rejected the appeal and did so largely to protect the integrity of legal principles. Lady Hale distinguished the House's rulings in *Fairchild* and *Chester* (above) as cases 'dealing with particular problems which could be remedied without altering the principles applicable to the great majority of personal injury cases which give rise to no real injustice or practical problem'.[215] She considered the instant case to be an invitation to introduce 'liability for the loss of a chance of a more favourable outcome', but refused to do so for the complexities involved and the consequences that this would have. Those consequences were largely summed up by Lord Phillips and Hoffmann in their view that a departure from *Hotson* would change the basis of causation from *probability* to *possibility*, i.e. that some form of recovery would be due if it was shown that it was *possible* that negligence might affect a patient's case. Not only should this be a matter for Parliament, but as Lady Hale put it: 'it would in practice always be tempting to conclude that the doctor's negligence had affected . . . [the claimant's] chances to some extent, the claimant would almost always get something. It would be a "heads you lose everything, tails I win something" situation'. And, finally, we have Lord Phillips: 'it seems to me that there is a danger, if special tests of causation are developed piecemeal to deal with perceived injustices in particular factual situations, that the coherence of our common law will be destroyed'.[216]

9.104   We have, then, in the short period since the last edition of this book, seen three significant rulings from the House of Lords that demonstrate well both the power and the dangers of policy-driven judicial activism. While a hard line was clearly taken in *Gregg*, it is difficult to reconcile this with the decidedly vague policy appeals of the majority in *Chester*. Lady Hale may be correct in distinguishing between the two, and it will be interesting to see if the tidal wall will hold; we would point, however, to the

---

[212] Namely, that '. . . a patient's prospects of recovery are treated as non-existent whenever they exist but fall short of 50%', *ibid*, para 43.
[213] *Ibid*, para 46.   [214] *Ibid*, para 121.   [215] *Ibid*, para 192.   [216] *Ibid*, para 172.

trend that seems to be emerging elsewhere, where the courts are bowing to pressure to assist the plaintiff over the causation hurdle in medico-legal cases.[217]

INJURIES CAUSED BY MEDICAL PRODUCTS OR DEVICES

9.105　The extensive use of drugs and other medical products in modern medical practice, coupled with the wide variety of available substances and devices, inevitably leads to a high incidence of injuries for which they are held responsible.[218] It has been reported, for example, that 3–5 per cent of all admissions to hospital are due to adverse reactions to drugs, costing the NHS around £500 million a year.[219] The number of persons affected will be small in some instances due to the speedy detection of the dangers and the rapid withdrawal of the products concerned. In others, the scale of the claims may be astronomic, an example being the early series of actions brought against manufacturers of intrauterine devices.[220] For these reasons, the question of compensation becomes an intensely political issue, as it has done in relation to HIV-contaminated blood, certain tranquillisers, and more recently MMR vaccine. The regulation of medicines and medical devices is now controlled by the Medicines and Healthcare Products Regulatory Agency,[221] which was established on 1 April 2003 and replaced the Medical Devices Agency and the Medicines Control Agency. This body monitors approval mechanisms, controls licensing arrangements, and issues rapid warnings when evidence comes to light of a public danger concerning the use of a product or device. It does not, however, have any direct dealings with issues of compensation for harm occasioned as a result of such use.[222]

9.106　Compensation for injury caused by products is now largely regulated in the United Kingdom by the Consumer Protection Act 1987.[223] This derives from the EU Council

---

[217] See, for example, New South Wales (*Rufo v Hosking* [2004] NSWCA 391) and Ireland (*Philp v Ryan* [2004] 1 IESC 105).

[218] See, generally, H Teff 'Products Liability' in A Grubb (ed) *Principles of Medical Law*, 2nd edn, (2004), chapter 15.

[219] House of Commons Health Committee, *The Influence of the Pharmaceutical Industry*, Fourth Report of Session 2004–2005, HC 42-I (2005), p 8.

[220] G R Thornton 'Intrauterine Devices: Malpractice and Product Liability' (1986) 14 Law Med Hlth Care 4.

[221] www.mhra.gov.uk.

[222] It is interesting to speculate as to the Agency's own potential liability for harm caused, for example, by procedural or operational failures in drug or product approval or withdrawal. No test case has yet emerged. The Agency has, however, been criticised recently by the Parliamentary Health Select Committee for failing to scrutinise licensing data adequately and for insufficient post-marketing surveillance. The Committee has called for a fundamental review of the Agency as a result, see House of Commons Health Committee, *The Influence of the Pharmaceutical Industry*, Fourth Report of Session 2004–2005, HC 42-I (2005).

[223] This does not preclude an action in negligence, although one of the reasons for legislative reform was precisely because of the serious limitations that such an action represents for those harmed by defective products, see generally, P R Ferguson, *Drug Injuries and the Pursuit of Compensation* (1996).

Directive on product liability,[224] the aim of which was to create strict liability for most injuries which were caused by defective products; this policy had long been advocated by commentators on compensation for personal injury. Under the terms of the Act, strict liability is borne primarily by the manufacturer of a defective product, although the suppliers will also be held liable if the manufacturer cannot be identified. Products include the components and raw materials from which a product is made and, in certain circumstances, a doctor may be a supplier of a drug. Despite strong protests from the industry, pharmaceutical products are not exempted from the system of strict liability. A drug will be regarded as defective if it fails to measure up to that degree of safety which 'persons generally are entitled to expect' (s 3(1)).

9.107   In some circumstances, the manufacturer will be able to call on a development risk—or, in American terms, a 'state of the art'—defence.[225] Section 4(1)(e) of the Act provides that the manufacturer will not be liable if he can show:

that the state of scientific and technical knowledge at the relevant time was not such that a producer of products of the same description as the product in question might be expected to have discovered the defect if it had existed in his products while they were under his control.

9.108   The aim of this defence is to relieve manufacturers of liability if the existence of a defect was undiscoverable at the time.[226] Expert evidence will be important in deciding whether a manufacturer has attained this goal within the limitation that the Act does not require the highest possible standards.

9.109   Is a manufacturer entitled to market a drug which will be beneficial to many but which he knows may cause harm to a minority—in other words, is there such a thing as a socially acceptable risk? The traditional approach to this issue is by way of balancing the prospective benefit and risk. In general, sensitive users will have no claim to compensation if it is in the public interest that the drug should be available; much would then depend upon the presentation of the product and the nature of any warnings given. In this respect, s 3(2)(b) of the 1987 Act stipulates that, in assessing what constitutes defect, consideration must be given to what might reasonably be expected to be done with, or in relation to, the product. For example, it might reasonably be expected that children could gain access to drugs intended for adult use only. It is, however, unlikely that, say, suicide could be reasonably anticipated by the manufacturer. Common sense and notions of general public knowledge and understanding can also have a role to play. Thus, in *Richardson v LRC Products*[227] it was held to be common knowledge that condoms are not fail-safe and that a risk of rupture is an inherent part of their use; the happening of such an eventuality did not, therefore, make the product 'defective'.

---

[224] Council Directive 85/374/EEC.

[225] For a full exposition of the subject, see P R Ferguson, n 223 above.

[226] C Newdick 'The Development Risk Defence of the Consumer Protection Act 1987' (1988) 47 CLJ 455. See also C J Stolker 'Objections to the Development Risk Defence' (1990) 9 Med Law 783.

[227] (2000) 59 BMLR 185.

9.110   The litigation relating to transmission of HIV infection through contaminated blood products was taken in breach of a statutory duty under the National Health Service Act 1977 and in negligence.[228] Although it was for some time in doubt due to the absence of any authoritative interpretation, any argument as to whether or not strict liability applies to human blood and its derivatives is now settled—blood is a naturally occurring substance which has not been manufactured but which has been won or abstracted; it, therefore, comes within the scope of the Act.[229] Moreover, as we shall see, the production of blood for transfusion is regarded as an industrial process. In terms of the Act, the National Blood Authority would normally be the producer of the 'product' but the hospital, or even the individual doctor, responsible for its transfusion would be the supplier. The application of strict liability to blood transfusion has, inevitably, been considered at greatest length in the United States, where the principle has been applied in some courts but where, in general, transfusion has been looked upon rather as the provision of a service than of a product,[230] thereby attracting potential actions in negligence—which would, of course, still be available outside the Act in the United Kingdom.[231] Clark[232] has confirmed that the majority of the United States has legislated to the effect that the supply of human blood is a service rather than a sale; the introduction of an element of 'sale' perhaps makes the distinction more urgent there than it is in the United Kingdom.

9.111   The matter at last came to the United Kingdom courts in the shape of *A v National Blood Authority.*[233] The judgment is a High Court decision only; none the less, it is extremely thorough and it is difficult to do it justice in a book of this title.[234] For these reasons, we do no more than attempt to extract the more important points. The case was brought as a class action by a group who had been infected with hepatitis C virus (HCV) during routine blood transfusion. HCV[235] was discovered in May 1988—although its presence had been suspected since 1975; a test for the presence of the virus was not developed until September 1989 and an improved test was not approved for use in the United Kingdom until April 1991. Prior to 1988, however, the occurrence of cases of post-transfusion hepatitis of uncertain origin had prompted the introduction of so-called 'surrogate tests' in the United States in September 1986; these tests did not identify a virus but, rather, the effects of viral contamination or,

---

[228] D Brahams 'Confidential Documents in HIV/Haemophilia Litigation' (1990) 336 Lancet 805.

[229] 1987 Act, ss 1(2) and 45(1). See, in particular, A M Clark *Product Liability* (1989) ch 3.

[230] E.g. *Coffee v Cutter Biological* 809 F 2d 191 (1987).

[231] The supply of HIV-infected blood was the subject of common law-based litigation in the Australian case of *H v Royal Alexandra Hospital for Children* [1990] 1 Med LR 297.

[232] *Product Liability* p 62.   [233] [2001] 3 All ER 289, (2001) 60 BMLR 1.

[234] A very full discussion of this case—and others, including *Richardson*, n 227 above—is provided by S Williamson 'Strict Liability for Medical Products: Prospects for Success' (2002) 5 Med L Interrnat 281. The author believes *A v National Blood Authority* to be the first case to succeed against the producers of a medical product.

[235] Burton J, who tried the case, made a passionate plea for the abandonment of the abbreviation HCV; none the less, it is accepted medical terminology.

alternatively, a high-risk lifestyle on the part of the donor. Surrogate tests were not supported, nor introduced, in the United Kingdom.

9.112   The group action was brought under the Consumer Protection Act 1987 by the relatively small number of persons who were infected between the coming into force of the Act and the introduction of a screening test for blood in 1989. Claims were lodged notwithstanding the facts that HCV was not identified at the time the claims commenced nor was a screening test available. The defendants agreed that the risk was known but asserted that avoiding the risk was impossible and that it could not be right to expect the unattainable. The public was not entitled to expect 100 per cent clean blood—the most that could be expected was that every reasonable precaution had been taken or carried out. In the event, arguments for both sides were based on the Council Directive rather than the 1987 Act—largely on the grounds that the latter *had* to be interpreted so as to be consistent with the former.[236] The issues were, therefore, concentrated on Articles 6 (which defines 'defective') and 7(e) (which describes the 'development risk' defence in much the same terms as s 4(1)(e) of the 1987 Act, above) of the Directive. It is to be noted that negligence was not a feature of this particular litigation.

9.113   In essence, the court found that the blood was defective, liability being 'defect-based' rather than 'fault-based'; avoidability was not a factor which could be taken into account in so far as it is 'outwith the purpose of the Directive'; the public at large was entitled to expect that the blood would be free from infection; and it was not material to consider whether any further steps could have been taken to avoid or reduce the risk that the blood would be infected. As to Article 7(e), the development risk defence was not available on the grounds that, if there is a known risk, then the producer who continues to produce and supply the product does so at his own risk. The court concluded that it is a lack of opportunity to discover the defect in the particular product that is essential to Article 7(e). Known risks do not qualify, even if they are unavoidable, and the problem came down to whether such 'testing' as was available, but not used, would have been able to identify a risk in an individual bag of blood. The court concluded that, whereas surrogate testing on its own would not, on the balance of probabilities, have done so, the combination of surrogate testing and screening once the virus had been identified would have been effective. A defence under Article 7(e) thus failed. So, as things stand at present, it seems that strict liability means what it says—strict liability; and manufacturers or producers will find it increasingly hard to plead a 'state of the art' defence.

9.114   *A v National Blood Authority* was a case fought at an exceptionally high level of responsibility and one wonders how much it will affect the individual doctor or pharmacist.[237] Probably their major concern in respect of strict liability laws lies in the

---

[236] The European Commission had previously lodged a complaint with the European Court of Justice, later dismissed, that the United Kingdom's implementation of the 1987 Act did not comply with the Directive: *EC Commission v United Kingdom* [1997] ECR I-2649, [1997] All ER (EC) 481.

[237] It is of interest that a leading article in the BMJ stated: 'The only possible response to the judgment must be that the necessity for each transfusion is now carefully weighed up . . . and the search for alternatives

need to ensure that the manufacturer can be adequately identified in order to avoid claims being made against the individual supplier. An interesting American twist was shown in *Oskenholt v Lederle Laboratories*,[238] where a doctor, having been successfully sued for prescribing a faulty drug, himself brought an action against the manufacturers for damage to his professional reputation—a fair example of the worm turning!

9.115   The Group Litigation concerning alleged liability arising from the use of MMR (Measles, Mumps and Rubella) vaccine is currently in a procedural quagmire. The factual basis for the litigation stems from an article published in *The Lancet* in 1998 indicating that there may be a causal connection between the vaccine and autism in children.[239] Over 1,000 children allegedly affected in this way are the focus of an on-going group action which relies on the terms of the Consumer Protection Act 1987 as to the strict liability of the vaccine's manufacturers. It is important to point out in passing that for these families the provisions of the Vaccine Damage Payments Act 1979 are judged to be wholly inadequate. This Act established a strict liability scheme whereby those adversely affected by vaccines can seek compensation through the Department of Health if it can be shown that an individual has suffered at least 60 per cent disability as a result of being given the vaccine. The current payable sum is £100,000. However, this is considered to be an entirely insufficient sum for the MMR families by which to cover the potentially life-time costs of rearing mentally-handicapped children. Given that causation must be proved either way, they have sought to take their chances under the 1987 Act.[240] But the main problem for this group litigation has not been the law (thus far) but legal aid (or, rather, its absence). The Legal Services Commission withdrew funding in 2003 and the decision was upheld on appeal and survived a judicial review. While the battle continues,[241] it demonstrates all too well the considerable challenges faced by potential litigants. For, whether we are talking about the common law of negligence, statutory product liability or sui generis schemes of strict liability, the problem of causation remains. It is of course arguable that this is as it should be as a matter of principled justice; but there is also the other side of the debate that says that medical causation is of such a specific, highly complex, nature that some concessions should be made. We do, indeed, see recent examples of this in cases like *Fairchild* and *Chester*. But none of this

---

to allogeneic transfusion intensified'—P P Mortimer 'Making Blood Safer' (2002) 325 BMJ 400. Patient demand may also increase the pressure; see, for example: E S Vanderlinde, J M Heal and N Blumberg 'Autologous Transfusion' (2002) 324 BMJ 772.

[238] 656 P 2d 293 (Ore, 1982).

[239] The original paper which sparked the controversy was A Wakefield et al 'Ileal-lymphoid-nodular Hyperplasia, Non-specific Colitis, and Pervasive Development Disorder in Children' (1998) 351 The Lancet 637. Contrary evidence includes K M Madsen et al 'A Population-Based Study of Measles, Mumps and Rubella Vaccination and Autism' (2002) 347 New Eng J Med 1477.

[240] Recovery under the 1979 Act does not preclude a subsequent action in negligence, but this itself may be unattractive for reasons we have already outlined.

[241] A limited amount of public funding has been restored to a small group of claimants. For an April 2005 update on the state of this extremely complication litigation, see *Re MMR and MR Vaccine Litigation (No. 12)* [2005] EWHC 539.

matters if claimants are not even afforded their day in court: access to justice and financial support go hand-in-hand, taking us from the realm of law to that of politics. The battle must, therefore, be waged on many fronts; but in each domain the odds are staked firmly against the claimant.

CRIMINAL NEGLIGENCE

9.116   Medical negligence is predominantly a civil matter, but a spate of prosecutions in the early 1990s served to remind doctors that the loss of a patient may sometimes lead to criminal prosecution. Such prosecutions used to be rare; their increase points to heightened interest in the external regulation of medicine and to a diminution in the professional immunity which doctors may previously have enjoyed. In some respects, this process is healthy; in others, it is a matter for regret. The principle that doctors, and indeed all professionals, should be accountable for their failures is entirely acceptable; what is more dubious is that the criminal law, and particularly manslaughter prosecutions, should be the instrument chosen to perform that task. We believe that the concept of criminal liability for negligence involving a breach of duty is, at best, tenuous and that the minimum threshold for the invocation of criminal sanctions should be recklessness. We explore the implications of this below.

9.117   Criminal liability for negligence is effectively limited to prosecutions for manslaughter.[242] The requisite elements are similar to those in the civil law, namely, that there is a duty of care; there is a breach of that duty of care; and the breach amounts to gross negligence. The need for resultant harm is, of course, a given and here it is the death of the patient. The level of negligence which the doctor must have manifested is considerably above that at which civil liability may be incurred. Traditionally it has been defined as 'gross' or 'extreme' negligence and sometimes, somewhat tautologically, as 'criminal negligence'; the essential concern is that it surpasses the civil test, as was stressed in *R v Bateman*:

In order to establish criminal liability, the facts must be such that . . . the negligence of the accused went beyond a mere matter of compensation between subjects and showed such disregard for the life and safety of others as to amount to a crime against the State and conduct deserving punishment.[243]

This, of course, does not answer the question of when conduct goes beyond the compensation level but it is probably impossible to be much more specific. It is clear that what is required is conduct which gives rise to a sense of outrage—or to the conclusion that the accused deserves *punishment* for what he did. Such a conclusion,

---

[242] R E Ferner 'Medication Errors that have led to Manslaughter Charges' (2000) 321 BMJ 1212 was able to find 17 British cases between 1970 and 1999—13 of these arose in the third decade. Seven cases resulted in conviction excluding those where an appeal was successful.

[243] [1925] All ER Rep 45 at 48, 19 Cr App Rep 8 at 11, per Lord Hewart LCJ.

though, is likely to be articulated in terms of a lack of regard for the patient's welfare or safety—and therein lies the problem. If criminal negligence is defined in terms of a deliberate exposure of the patient to some form of risk, then we are in the realms of recklessness rather than negligence.[244] It is one thing to punish a person for subjective recklessness; it is quite another to punish for objective negligence. In the former case the accused has effectively said: 'I knew of the risk of harm but did not care'; in the latter, he may have been quite unaware of any risk at all—the damage caused may have been the result of incompetence or ignorance, neither of which qualities necessarily deserve criminal punishment.

9.118   The conduct involved in the relevant cases has ranged from, at one extreme, an apparent indifference with all the features of recklessness to mere incompetence at the other. In *Saha and Salim*,[245] two doctors administered an astonishing cocktail of drugs to a remand prisoner who died as a result. They were both convicted and sentenced to a term of imprisonment. By contrast, the conviction of two young and relatively inexperienced doctors for the manslaughter of a patient to whom they had incorrectly administered cytotoxic drugs was greeted with concern in medical circles and was, in due course, quashed by the Court of Appeal.[246] Somewhere in between lies the case of *R v Adomako*,[247] in which an anaesthetist failed to notice the fact that his patient was in distress when this would have been glaringly obvious to any competent practitioner. There was conflicting evidence on the question of whether the accused was out of the theatre at the time; if he had been, and if there had been a failure on his part to make adequate arrangements for the monitoring of the patient, then that would surely have amounted to a degree of recklessness which was strongly deserving of punishment. If, however, he was merely incompetent, it might be more difficult to argue for his conviction of manslaughter—although, undoubtedly, professional sanctions would still be needed. These cases were heard together on appeal,[248] when it was held that the proper test in manslaughter cases based on breach of duty was that of gross negligence rather than recklessness.[249] In contrast to that of the two young doctors, Dr Adomako's appeal failed. He did, however, carry his case to the House of Lords where his conviction was upheld.[250] The House considered that gross negligence requires 'an egregious failure' to exhibit a minimum standard of competence (judged objectively) or a gross dereliction of care: '[c]onduct so bad in all circumstances as to amount to a criminal

---

[244] A difficulty which the courts have acknowledged in those decisions where gross negligence manslaughter appears to have been replaced by reckless manslaughter: *R v Seymour* [1983] 2 AC 493, (1983) 77 Cr App R 21; *Kong Cheuk Kwan v R* (1986) 82 Cr App R 18.

[245] (1992, unreported); see D Brahams 'Death of Remand Prisoner' (1992) 340 Lancet 1462.

[246] [1991] 5 Med LR 277.

[247] *R v Prentice, R v Adomako* [1993] 4 All ER 935, (1993) 15 BMLR 13, sub nom *R v Holloway, R v Adomako, R v Prentice and Sulman* [1993] 4 Med LR 304. See C Dyer 'Manslaughter Verdict Quashed on Junior Doctors' (1993) 306 BMJ 1432.

[248] (1993) 15 BMLR 13, [1993] 4 Med LR 304.

[249] (1993) 15 BMLR 13 at 21, [1993] 4 Med LR 304 at 310, per Lord Taylor, following *Andrews v DPP* [1937] AC 576, [1937] 2 All ER 552, HL and *R v Stone, R v Dobinson* [1977] QB 354, [1977] 2 All ER 341.

[250] *R v Adomako* [1995] 1 AC 171, (1994) 19 BMLR 56, HL.

act or omission'.[251] It was further clarified that, in cases of manslaughter by criminal negligence involving a breach of duty, it was a sufficient direction to the jury to adopt the gross negligence test set out by the Court of Appeal; it was not necessary to define recklessness, although it was open to the judge to use the word 'reckless' in its ordinary meaning as part of his exposition of the law.

9.119   Thus, as the criminal law now stands, a grossly incompetent doctor is liable to conviction despite the fact that there is no element of subjective wrongdoing on his part. This might well be considered inappropriate.[252] The alternative view is that the law should protect the public and that prosecution represents one way of controlling those who cannot meet minimal professional standards. Surely, however, the law should, at the same time, recognise the difference between the reckless and the inadequate practitioner. There is, indeed, some evidence that the House of Lords was prepared to concede the inherent dangers of the gross negligence test. Thus, we have Lord MacKay commending the words of the trial judge in *R v Adomako*:

> You should only convict a doctor of causing death by negligence if you think he did something which *no reasonably skilled* doctor should have done. (Emphasis added.)[253]

which is a very severe definition.

9.120   The ruling in *Adomako* has remained controversial in the decade since it was delivered and there have been various attempts to have the House of Lords revisit their decision. Each has failed. The application for appeal was rejected in *R v Mark*, for example, because it was said that the law is perfectly clear and no decision since *Adomako* has questioned its validity.[254] It was, indeed, applied most recently to uphold the convictions of two doctors in *R v Misra; R v Srivastava*[255] in which a patient died after developing a staphylococcal infection following routine surgery. The prosecution arose not because the doctors had failed to diagnose the particular infection, but because they failed to notice that their patient was ill at all, despite his high fever, high pulse rate and low blood pressure. They did nothing to diagnose his condition until it was too late and the patient succumbed to toxic shock syndrome. The importance of the appeal lay in the questions it raised as to the compatibility of gross negligence manslaughter with the Human Rights Act 1998. Two essential arguments were made: (i) that there was no 'fair trial' (Article 6 ECHR) in such cases because they involve juries that are not required to articulate the reasoning behind their verdict, and (ii) there was a breach of Article 7 ECHR which requires a clear pre-existing criminal offence in law. The argument here was that the English law lacked clarity because of its circularity: the jury should convict if they consider the defendant's behaviour to be 'criminal'; so what is 'criminal' is what the jury considers to be such. Dismissing the appeals, however, the Court of Appeal held that the elements of the offence are very

---

[251] Per Lord Mackay [1995] 1 AC 171, at 187.

[252] For expansion of this argument, see A McCall Smith 'Criminal Negligence and the Incompetent Doctor' (1993)1 Med L Rev 336.

[253] (1994) 19 BMLR 56 at 64–65.   [254] *R v Mark (Alan James)* [2004] EWCA Crim 2490.

[255] [2004] EWCA Crim 2375, (2004) *The Times*, 13 October.

clearly defined in *Adomako* and involve no uncertainty. A doctor can easily be apprised of his obligation to his patients within the limits of the criminal law. Nor is there any valid human rights argument that can call into question the operation of the present jury system: it has, indeed, been accepted as valid by the European Court of Human Rights itself. Finally, the court, once again, refused a request for leave to appeal to the House of Lords.

9.121 But are the criminal courts the appropriate guardians of conditions in the operating theatre? The General Medical Council has been widely criticised in the past for its ineffective control of clinical standards. It now appears prepared to use its newly erupted teeth.[256] It could well be that the better route to the protection of the public from clinical error lies along the development of the investigative and restrictive powers of the GMC and the Royal Colleges, leaving only the subjective wrongdoer where he belongs—in the criminal courts.

9.122 If concern is felt in the United Kingdom over the prosecution of, often junior, doctors for causing of the deaths of patients, it was amplified in New Zealand where, under the Crimes Act 1961, criminal liability was imposed on a doctor who merely failed to show 'reasonable knowledge, skill and care' in the treatment of his patients. This extraordinarily low threshold of liability was applied in *R v Yogasakaran*[257] and confirmed on appeal.[258] In this case, an anaesthetist had not checked the label on an ampoule of a drug which he injected into a patient. The ampoule was of the appropriate shape and size and was in the right place on the trolley but, for some reason unconnected with the anaesthetist, contained the wrong drug. Presumably, the same result would have been achieved if the anaesthetist had, in fact, read the label but had read it wrongly. Such a common mistake can hardly be seen as justification for convicting a person of a crime which carries with it a very great deal of moral opprobrium—it would surely be better investigated by the Medical Practitioners' Disciplinary Committee. Concerted medical opposition to the use of the criminal law in this fashion led, in fact, to a government-sponsored amendment to the Crimes Act, which required that there should be a substantial departure from the normally expected levels of care before liability for manslaughter could be imposed.[259] This effectively raised the standard in New Zealand to the gross negligence standard applied elsewhere. Most of the New Zealand doctors or nurses who were found guilty under the old legislation would not be convicted under the new standard.[260]

---

[256] See discussion in chapter 1.   [257] [1990] 1 NZLR 399.

[258] See D B Collins 'New Zealand's Medical Manslaughter' (1992) Med Law 221. The Privy Council refused to consider what it regarded as matters of policy.

[259] Now enacted in the Crimes Act 1961, s 150A, inserted by Crimes Amendment Act 1997, s 2. On the background, see A Merry and A McCall Smith 'Medical accountability and the criminal law' (1996) Hlth Care Anal, and, by the same authors, 'Medical Manslaughter' (1997) Med J Austral 342.

[260] P D G Skegg 'Criminal Prosecutions of Negligent Health Professionals: the New Zealand Experience' (1998) 6 Med L Rev 220 describes eight such cases. Five of the prosecutions failed partly or wholly because of the difficulty of proving that the defendant's conduct was a cause of death. A recent trial in Wales, which concerned the removal of a man's only healthy kidney, was halted for the same reason: C Dyer 'Surgeons Cleared of Manslaughter after Removing Wrong Kidney' (2002) 325 BMJ 9.

10

CONSENT TO TREATMENT

10.1   The paternalist might argue that there are many examples in medical practice of situations in which treatment is justified in the teeth of the patient's objection. Arguing from such a position—that the patient may be unable to appreciate that a particular treatment is in his best interest—the decision of the doctor to impose it is seen as serving the patient's welfare in spite of what may turn out to be short-term objections. This, a paternalist would hold, cannot be wrong. Good health and physical comfort are preferable to ill health and physical discomfort: a patient will thus be happier treated than untreated.

10.2   Such arguments can, however, be sustained only in very limited conditions, such as when the patient is in an irrational state because of impaired or disturbed consciousness. Restraining a delirious patient is an instance of justifiable paternalism, as is the action of clearing the air passages of one who is about to choke to death. The intervention is justified by the conviction that this is what the patient would want, were he fully rational, or that such treatment is needed to restore him to a position in which he can make up his own mind.[1]

10.3   The case for imposed treatment can also be couched in social terms. Illness is costly to the community and it could be argued that the individual is not entitled to refuse treatment which may minimise that cost. The community may have to support the family of a person who dies as a result of refusing treatment. Non-voluntary intervention might, thereby, be justified. This argument is, however, also weak. Society may, indeed, be saved certain costs if a life is preserved, but it can be argued that the damage resulting from coercion convincingly outweighs that which it seeks to avert. A coercive society can be most cost-effective—but this does not mean it is most desirable.

10.4   A possible, although uncommon, exception to this rejection of the social cost argument exists when a person is found to be suffering from a highly infectious and dangerous illness; few would then argue that he should be allowed to refuse treatment if such treatment is the sole way to reduce the risk of spreading the disease, and we have discussed this fully in chapter 2. Here, the only caveat to the application

---

[1] See, for example, *Bolton Hospitals NHS Trust v O* [2003] 1 FLR 824, [2003] Fam Law 319 in which it was confirmed that is lawful to use reasonable force in providing treatment in a patient's best interests when that patient is incompetent.

of imposed treatment is that it should be as non-coercive as is compatible with containment of the threat.[2]

NON-CONSENSUAL TREATMENT

THE LEGAL JUSTIFICATION

10.5 The common law has long recognised the principle that every person has the right to have his bodily integrity protected against invasion by others.[3] Only in certain narrowly defined circumstances may this integrity be compromised without the individual's consent—as where, for example, physical intrusion is involved in the carrying out of lawful arrest. The legal consequences of an unauthorised invasion of bodily integrity include civil actions for damages and, in theory at least, criminal liability for assault. In practice, non-consensual medical interventions would be unlikely to result in criminal charges, although this could be so in extreme cases.[4]

10.6 The seriousness with which the law views any invasion of physical integrity is based on the strong moral conviction that everyone has the right of self-determination with regard to his body. Unless there is consent to an act of touching by another, such an act will—subject to the principle *de minimis non curat lex*—constitute a battery for which damages may be awarded. Consent can make physical invasion lawful, but the reality of such consent may be closely scrutinised by the law and is, anyway, subject to certain policy limitations. Consent will not normally render legitimate a serious physical injury; thus, it was held by Swift J in *R v Donovan*:

As a general rule to which there are well established exceptions, it is an unlawful act to beat another person with such a degree of violence that the infliction of bodily harm is a probable consequence and, when such an act is proved, consent is immaterial.[5]

10.7 This being so, it is nevertheless important to note that the degree of harm suffered goes simply to the question of damages and does not operate in constituting the tort or delict. Here it is the affront to bodily integrity which makes the conduct actionable and no actual physical harm need arise. In the same way, the motive of the aggressor is irrelevant. Thus, it matters not that the touching is designed to 'help' the person and, as a consequence, every touching of a patient by way of medical treatment is potentially a battery. The classic expression is that of Cardozo J:

---

[2] See M Brazier and J Harris 'Public Health and Private Lives' (1996) 4 Med L Rev 171.

[3] This is also a human rights issue: see *YF v Turkey* (2004) 39 EHRR 34 in which it was held that physical and psychological integrity of the person is protected by Article 8 ECHR and that compulsory medical intervention is an interference with this right irrespective of whether or not 'consent' has been obtained. It falls, therefore, to the state to justify any such interference under Article 8(2).

[4] See, for example, criminal charges for indecent assault for non-consensual touching by a doctor: *R v Healy (Timothy John)* [2003] 2 Cr App R (S) 87.

[5] [1934] 2 KB 498 at 507: endorsed in *R v Brown* [1994] 1 AC 212.

Every human being of adult years and sound mind has a right to determine what shall be done with his own body; and a surgeon who performs an operation without the patient's consent commits an assault.[6]

10.8 It is the patient's consent—either implied or expressed[7]—which makes the touching legally innocuous and there is no doubt that surgical intervention is covered by this principle.[8] The theory, then, is quite simple—the reality is somewhat different. Much jurisprudence in common law countries has focused on the consent issue and, as a result, the so-called doctrine of informed consent has assumed a significant role in the medical negligence debate. As will be seen later in the chapter, it is a doctrine which lies surprisingly uneasily in the medico-legal ambience of the United Kingdom.

IS CONSENT ALWAYS NECESSARY?

10.9 As a general rule, medical treatment, even of a minor nature, should not proceed unless the doctor has first obtained the patient's consent. This may be expressed or it may be implied, as it is when the patient presents him- or herself to the doctor for examination and acquiesces in the normal routine. This principle applies in the overwhelming majority of cases but there are limited circumstances in which a doctor may be entitled to proceed without this consent. Essentially, these can be subsumed under the heading of 'non-voluntary therapy', which has to be distinguished from involuntary treatment. The latter implies treatment against the patient's expressed wishes; the occasions on which this would be ethical are, indeed, very few, although a case can be made out when the interests of a third party or of society itself are involved.[9] Non-voluntary treatment is that which is given when the patient is not in a position to have or to express any views as to his or her management. Treatment in the absence of consent is clearly more easily justified in such circumstances. These include, first, when the patient is incapable of giving consent by reason of unconsciousness; second, when the patient is a minor; and, finally, when the patient's state of mind is such as to render an apparent consent or refusal invalid.

The unconscious patient

10.10 It is possible to see non-voluntary treatment as proceeding with consent, although that consent has not been expressed. Thus, when an unconscious patient is admitted to hospital, the casualty officer may argue that his consent could be implied or presumed on the grounds that if he were conscious he would probably consent to his life

---

[6] *Schloendorff v Society of New York Hospital* 105 NE 92 (NY, 1914).

[7] On the possibilities in the modern technological age, see P A B Galpottage and A C Norris 'Patient Consent Principles and Guidelines for E-consent: A New Zealand Perspective' (2005) 11 Health Informatics J 5.

[8] *A-G's Reference (No. 6 of 1980)* [1981] QB 715, [1981] 2 All ER 1057. The Scots equivalent, albeit indirect, lies in *Smart v HM Advocate* 1975 SLT 65.

[9] Hence involuntary treatment is often at issue in the case of psychopathic illness—for which see chapter 20.

being saved in this way. This may be true but, while the majority of patients could be expected to endorse the decision to treat in such circumstances, it is something of a fictitious approach to the problem.[10]

10.11 An alternative route is to apply the necessity principle. It is widely recognised in both criminal and civil law that there are times when acting out of necessity legitimates an otherwise wrongful act. The basis of this doctrine is that acting unlawfully is justified if the resulting good effect materially outweighs the consequences of adhering strictly to the law. In the present context, the doctor is justified, and should not have criminal or civil liability imposed upon him, if the value which he seeks to protect is of greater weight than the wrongful act he performs—that is, treating without consent—*and* there is no alternative means by which the end can be achieved.

10.12 Necessity will be a viable defence to any proceedings for non-consensual treatment where an unconscious patient is involved and there is no known objection to treatment. The treatment undertaken, however, must not be more extensive than is required by the exigencies of the situation—we do well to remember what Lord Devlin said, albeit in a rather different context: 'The Good Samaritan is a character unesteemed in English law.'[11] A doctor cannot, therefore, 'take advantage' of unconsciousness to perform procedures which are not essential for the patient's immediate survival or well-being. This was established in two well-known Canadian cases where the courts explored the distinction between procedures that are justified by necessity and those which are merely 'convenient', a distinction which is also applied by the British courts.[12]

10.13 In the first of these, *Marshall v Curry*,[13] the plaintiff sought damages for battery against the surgeon who had removed a testicle in the course of an operation for a hernia. The surgeon's case was that the removal was essential to a successful operation and that, had he not done so, the health and life of the patient would have been imperilled because the testis was, itself, diseased. Taking the view that the doctor had acted 'for the protection of the plaintiff's health and possibly his life', the court held that the removal of the testicle was necessary and that it would have been unreasonable to put the procedure off until a later date. By contrast, in *Murray v McMurchy*,[14] the plaintiff succeeded in an action for battery against a doctor who had sterilised her without her consent. In this case, the doctor had discovered during a caesarian section that the condition of the plaintiff's uterus would have made it hazardous for her to go through another pregnancy and he tied the fallopian tubes although there was no

---

[10] Although old, P D G Skegg *Law, Ethics and Medicine* (1984) remains a most valuable reference; the particular point is discussed at p 99. A rather mundane example involved a dental anaesthetist who inserted an analgesic suppository while the patient was anaesthetised in order to minimise the pain from multiple extractions. He had not discussed this particular treatment before the operation. The GMC found him guilty of serious professional misconduct: see J Mitchell 'A Fundamental Problem of Consent' (1995) 310 BMJ 43.

[11] Lord Devlin *Samples of Law Making* (1962) p 90.

[12] Per Lord Goff, *Re F* [1990] 2 AC 1, esp 74–77.   [13] [1933] 3 DLR 260.

[14] [1949] 2 DLR 442. *Devi v West Midlands Regional Health Authority* [1981] CA Transcript 491 provides an almost exact British parallel.

pressing need for the procedure to be undertaken. The court took the view that it would not have been unreasonable to postpone the sterilisation until after consent had been obtained, in spite of the convenience of doing it on the spot.[15]

10.14   The principle that emerges from these two cases is that a doctor is justified by necessity in proceeding without the patient's consent if a condition is discovered in an unconscious patient for which treatment is necessary in the sense that it would be, in the circumstances, unreasonable to postpone the operation. Postponement of treatment is, however, to be preferred if it is possible to wait until the patient is in a position to give consent. An English example arose in *Williamson v East London and City Health Authority*[16] in which the plaintiff consented to removal and replacement of a leaking breast implant. The condition was, however, found at operation to be more serious than had been anticipated and a subcutaneous mastectomy was performed. Although the evidence was conflicting, Butterfield J ruled that consent to the more serious procedure had not been given and that the plaintiff would not have agreed to it had she been given the opportunity. Damages of £20,000 were awarded despite the fact that the court agreed that the operation would have been needed at some time in the future.

10.15   The distinction between necessity and convenience is, nevertheless, often delicately balanced—particularly in the light of the sometimes vague terms of written consent forms. In an unreported Scottish case[17] the patient signed to the effect: 'I hereby give permission for myself to have a general anaesthetic and any operation the surgeon considers necessary'. The operation proposed was the comparatively simple removal of a supposed branchial cyst but, on exploration, the 'cyst' was found to be a carotid body tumour. Removal of such a mass is a far more difficult procedure and the patient, in fact, sustained paralysis of half his body. The Inner House concluded that permission was not limited by seriousness and that the patient had consented to any operation to the end of removing the swelling: 'Consent must be read as covering any operation considered by the surgeon at the time to be in the patient's interest' (per Lord Robertson). None the less, the three judges concerned could all foresee different conclusions if the operation lay outside the procedure contemplated by the patient. It is less certain that such a decision would be reached elsewhere, particularly in the United States, where it has been considered for many years that: 'the so-called authority [of such consent forms] is so ambiguous as to be almost completely worthless'.[18] Guidance on obtaining consent in the UK was provided to all health care

---

[15] Such cases seem still not infrequent and a number of pressure groups exist in the UK, including the Hysterectomy Legal Fighting Fund and Action Against Unnecessary Hysterectomies, set up with the aid of Labour MP Diana Organ in 1997.

[16] (1998) 41 BMLR 85, [1998] Lloyds's Rep Med 6. The case reads as a model moral as to the importance of filing adequate clinical notes.

[17] *Craig v Glasgow Victoria and Leverndale Hospitals Board of Management* (22 March 1974, unreported) 1st Division. One has to note that this case is thirty years old—does it, together with *Williamson*, provide an example of changing public mores?

[18] *Rogers v Lumbermen's Mutual Cas Co* 119 So 2d 649 (La, 1960).

professionals by the Department of Health in 2001.[19] Uniform model consent forms have been used in the NHS since 1990 and have recently been updated.[20]

10.16   It is possible that a member of the family, a partner or a close friend may be at hand when a patient is unconscious. In such a case, it may be wise for the doctor to obtain the agreement of that person largely in order to discover any anticipatory choice on the part of the patient or other details which might affect a clinical decision.[21] It has been, however, long established that, in the case of an adult patient, no other person, not even the next of kin, has an automatic *legal right* to consent to or refuse treatment in England and Wales.[22] Indeed, the doctor who delays unreasonably while seeking the support of family or significant others is misconceiving the law. In Scotland, a welfare attorney may have been appointed under the Adults with Incapacity (Scotland) Act 2000 with power to consent to medical treatment under Part V of that Act. If so, such a person should be consulted by medical staff prior to treating an incapable adult, provided that it is practicable to do so. None the less, in no case is the doctor's position easy and, provided that it involved no adverse effects, the fact that the spouse's, parents', partner's or friend's agreement had been obtained could be of value in that it would diminish the likelihood of the patient feeling aggrieved at the invasion of his or her bodily integrity.[23] In those common law countries which retain the parens patriae jurisdiction, the courts have the power to consent or refuse on behalf of an incapax, whether they be in that state temporarily or otherwise. This is a wide-ranging discretion which is limited only by one principle: all decisions must be taken in the best interests of the patient. We discuss this jurisdiction in more detail below together with recent statutory reforms which now allow for the appointment of donees with lasting power of attorney in England and Wales.

Proxy consent and the consent of minors

10.17   Proxy consents are truly valid only when the patient has given express authority to another person to give or withhold consent on his behalf (assuming the law supports such a regime), or when the law invests a person with such power. The commonest example of the latter would be that of parent and child. When proxy consent of this

---

[19] Department of Health *Reference Guide to Consent for Examination or Treatment* (2001).

[20] HSC 2001/023 *Good Practice in Consent* followed by a guide to implementation: see the relevant sections of the Department of Health website: www.dh.gov.uk.

[21] Note that the World Medical Association *Declaration on the Rights of the Patient* (1981, amended 1995) speaks of the need in such cases to obtain the consent of a 'legally entitled person'. This Declaration also states that the physicians 'should always try to save the life of a patient unconscious due to a suicide attempt' (Principle 4(c)).

[22] *Re T (adult: refusal of medical treatment)* [1992] 4 All ER 649 at 653, (1992) 9 BMLR 46 at 50, CA, per Lord Donaldson MR. But see now the Mental Capacity Act 2005, para 10.38 below.

[23] Many United States have enacted 'good Samaritan' legislation aimed at protecting the doctor giving emergency roadside treatment; however, these vary in terms of protection and may not provide liability protection during or after disasters. In some states, malpractice insurance policies do not cover out-of-office care, and generally a physician is not covered if there is any payment for services or an accusation of gross negligence. See also Australian legislation: Emergency Services Amendment Act 2001; Ambulance Services Act 1990, s 26 (NSW).

sort is available, the person vested with the power must use it reasonably; a third party may be justified in ignoring an unreasonable withholding of consent. In Scotland, the proxy decision-maker does not have the right to refuse—only to consent to— proposed medical treatment.[24] Specific court authority, either to consent on behalf of a minor or to declare a particular course of conduct or non-conduct in respect of an adult incapax lawful, should be sought as a matter of human rights law[25] when there is dispute between carer and health care professional.

10.18   A common occasion on which parents refuse to give consent to the medical treat- ment of their children is when they disapprove of it for religious reasons. The capacity of the 'mature minor' to consent to treatment on his or her own behalf is discussed in some detail below;[26] here, we are concerned only with the child who is evidently too young to take important decisions about his or her own medical treatment. A doctor taking steps to administer life-saving treatment such as a blood transfusion to the child against the wishes of its parents has traditionally been able to rely upon the common law as above, arguing that a decision taken in good faith and in the best interests of a child would, save in very unusual circumstances, be upheld by the courts.[27] This degree of latitude is, however, now to be doubted in light of the European Court of Human Rights decision in *Glass v the United Kingdom*.[28] Here the court held it to be a breach of the child's human right to respect for his private life—and more specifically his right to bodily integrity—for the hospital trust not to seek court authority to proceed with treatment against his parents' wishes. The gov- ernment's argument that the treatment was an 'emergency' could have been valid in justifying proceeding quickly without court intervention (under Article 8(2)), but the facts of the case did not bear this out—there was time to refer the case to the High Court and this should have been done. Procedurally, then, disputes over care should be referred to the courts in all but the most urgent of circumstances. Particular guidance appears in the guise of Practice Notes.[29]

10.19   The route to seek the assistance of the court will, to an extent, depend on administrative preference. Appeal may be made to the inherent jurisdiction of the court by way of the Children Act 1989, s 100 as, for example, in *Re O* or the applicant may seek a specific issue order. It is also technically possible for the medical advisers to

---

[24] Adults with Incapacity (Scotland) Act 2000, s 50. At best, the proxy has a 'right' to a second medical opinion and, ultimately, a right of appeal to the court: see G Laurie and K Mason 'Negative Treatment of Vulnerable Patients: Euthanasia By Any Other Name?' [2000] *Juridical Review* 159.

[25] See *Glass v United Kingdom* [2004] 1 FLR 1019, (2004) 77 BMLR 120.

[26] See para 10.27.

[27] By extrapolation from *Re F (mental patient: sterilisation)* [1990] 2 AC 1, sub nom *F v West Berkshire Health Authority* [1989] 2 All ER 545, HL.

[28] N 25 above.

[29] Practice Direction (CAFCASS: Representation of Children in Family Proceedings) [2004] 1 FLR 1190 and Practice Direction (Family Proceedings: Representation of Children) [2004] 1 WLR 1180.

initiate care proceedings.[30] The inherent jurisdiction of the court[31] and, particularly, its power to make a declaration on a 'best interests' basis[32] will probably be used in an emergency when speed may be of the essence. Whatever route is adopted, *Glass* now makes it clear that there is an obligation on the *health authority* to seek the advice of the courts in the face of serious disagreement.

10.20   Although there would be little public sympathy for parents who refuse on religious grounds to consent to blood transfusion for a perilously ill child,[33] it would be a mistake to reject their position out of hand. The refusal of blood in such circumstances may seem to many to be irrational and pointless, but there is no doubt that it is a strongly held minority position. Ignoring it involves overriding religious convictions and this is a major step in a free society—particularly one that is as diverse as the United Kingdom now is. Such action also entails a significant interference with the principle that parents should have freedom to choose the religious and social upbringing of their children. Strongest confirmation of this has come most recently from the Supreme Court of Ireland which has upheld the 'family autonomy' of parents to refuse a simple heel prick test on their new-born son for the eminently manageable condition of phenylketonuria, even although such refusal could lead to serious and irremediable brain damage.[34] While respect for parental freedom certainly suggests caution, it is more often outweighed in the UK by the counter-arguments that there has been a redefinition of the role of the parents in respect of control of their children[35] and that it is no longer possible to regard them as having an almost absolute power: 'Parental rights to control a child', said Lord Fraser, 'exist not for the benefit of the parent but for the child'.[36] The community interest in the welfare of children is demonstrated in a number of ways, some more draconian than others. Society is prepared to remove a child from its parents if it is in moral or physical danger; the

---

[30] Children Act 1989, s 31; Children (Scotland) Act 1995, s 57.

[31] *Re R (a minor) (wardship: medical treatment)* [1992] Fam 11, (1991) 7 BMLR 147. For general comment on consent and children see L Hagger 'Some Implications of the Human Rights Act 1998 for the Medical Treatment of Children' (2003) 6 Med L Internat 25.

[32] See further the discussion in respect of *Re F*, para 10.33 below.

[33] On court-ordered intervention, see *Re O (a minor) (medical treatment)* [1993] 2 FLR 149 and *Camden London Borough Council v R (a minor) (blood transfusion)* (1993) 91 LGR 623. See also *Re S (a minor) (medical treatment)* [1993] 1 FLR 377: blood transfusion was authorised by the court in the case of a four-year-old boy whose parents objected on religious grounds—notwithstanding that it was a non-emergency situation. In the American case of *In re Brown* 689 NE 2d 397 (Ill, 1997), however, the court refused to order a blood transfusion for a pregnant woman in order to save the life of her fetus. For review of current attitudes of Jehovah's Witnesses, see O Muramoto 'Bioethical Aspects of the Recent Changes in the Policy of Refusal of Blood by Jehovah's Witnesses' (2001) 322 BMJ 37.

[34] *North Western Health Board v W (H)* [2001] IESC 70. For commentary see G T Laurie 'Better to Hesitate at the Threshold of Compulsion: PKU Testing and the Concept of Family Autonomy in Eire' (2002) 28 J Med Ethics 136.

[35] See, for example, *In re J (a Minor)(Prohibited steps order: Circumcision)* [2000] 1 FLR 571, (2000) 52 BMLR 82 in which a ritual circumcision at the age of 5 was considered not to be in the child's best interests.

[36] In *Gillick v West Norfolk and Wisbech Area Health Authority* [1986] AC 112, [1985] 3 All ER 402 (see para 10.27 et seq). Following Lord Denning MR in *Hewer v Bryant* [1970] 1 QB 357 at 369: 'Parental rights start with the right of control and end with little more than advice'.

child whose life is endangered by parental refusal of consent to medical treatment may be removed from its home on precisely the same grounds as may be the battered child. Any difference in the two cases lies in motives. The parent withholding consent may be doing so for what he sees as good reasons and in the interests of the child; the parent who neglects his child is unlikely to feel the same. In spite of this difference, however, there must be few who will see the parents' good faith as justifying the imperilling of the child's life; the death of a child in such circumstances might result in prosecution of the parents for manslaughter[37]—as was said in a well-known American case: 'Parents may be free to become martyrs themselves. But it does not follow that they are free in identical circumstances to make martyrs of their children'.[38] Thus, in *Re C (a child) (HIV testing)*,[39] Wilson J held that notwithstanding the opposition of both parents who rejected contemporary medical thinking on the causes and treatment of HIV and AIDS, it was overwhelmingly in the interests of the child that her HIV status be known. Accordingly, he ordered that a blood sample should be taken from the child.[40]

10.21   The Supreme Court of Canada has ruled that to allow parents to refuse blood transfusions for their child for religious reasons 'undermines the ability of the state to exercise its legitimate parens patriae jurisdiction'.[41] Indeed, the court continued: '[a]s society becomes increasingly aware of the fact that the family is often a very dangerous place for children, the parens patriae jurisdiction assumes greater importance'.[42]

10.22   The Family Division of the English High Court in *Re C (a minor) (medical treatment)*[43] refused to respect the wishes of parents to continue treatment of their 16-month-old child, who was suffering from spinal muscular atrophy. Medical assessment of the infant's condition was to the effect that continued ventilation was futile, it only being a matter of time before she suffered a fatal collapse. The parents agreed that ventilation should be discontinued but were unwilling, on religious grounds, to stand idly by and watch a life wither away when further intervention could delay death. They insisted that the child be ventilated in the event of further collapse. We discuss this case below, and more recent developments,[44] in the general

---

[37] *R v Senior* [1899] 1 QB 283. A Rastafarian couple who had refused to allow their diabetic child to be given insulin were convicted of manslaughter in 1993—see D Brahams 'Religious Objection versus Parental Duty' (1993) 342 Lancet 1189; the author wondered why the child was not made a ward of court.

[38] *People (ex rel Wallace) v Labrenz* 104 NE 2d 769 (Ill, 1952). By the same token, the US courts are very wary to sanction state interference with personal decisions—including those based on religious faith—without an 'extraordinary degree of public concern' and where 'the public interest is very clear', see: *Eisenberg v Industrial Com'n of Illinois* 337 Ill. App. 3d 373, 381.

[39] [2000] Fam 48, [1999] 2 FLR 1004.

[40] Yet, while the principle of law may be well established, this can have little impact on the practical outcome in many circumstances. In the instant case the parents fled the country with the child before the sample could be taken.

[41] *B v Children's Aid Society of Metropolitan Toronto* [1995] 1 SCR 315 at 433.

[42] But the Supreme Court will not extend the jurisdiction to the child in utero: *Winnipeg Child and Family Services (Northwest Area) v G (DF)* [1997] 2 SCR 925.

[43] [1998] 1 FLR 384, (1997) 40 BMLR 31.

[44] See, for example, *Re Wyatt (a child) (medical treatment: parents' consent)* [2004] Fam Law 866 and *Re Winston-Jones (a child) (medical treatment: parents' consent)* [2004] All ER (D) 313.

context of withdrawal of treatment from handicapped neonates.[45] Its significance here lies in the attitude of the court in determining the point at which parental powers of consent fall away to be replaced by the court's power to exercise its inherent jurisdiction, and the extent to which parental power is subjugated to the clinical judgment of health care professionals. Importantly, whether we are concerned with the powers of the parents or the court, or with the duty of the medical profession towards the patient, the determining factor which limits interventions in each case is that of the subject's best interests. What exactly, then, was in the best interests of this child? As orthodox Jews, the parents of C firmly believed that life should always be preserved where possible and could not accept the conclusion that it was in her best interests not to be reventilated if she was subsequently unable to breathe independently. The contrary attitude of the medical profession was unequivocal. Overwhelming clinical evidence testified to the 'futile' nature of continued intervention; the carers, in their turn, were unable to contemplate such a course of action in the best interests of the child. The court, in refusing to interfere with the medical assessment of the case, assiduously followed existing precedents which had eschewed all interference with the clinical judgment of health care professionals by the courts in cases such as this.[46] There was, however, no direct mention in this case of the place for the parents' religious views. The decision was presented as involving an objective assessment of best interests and, indeed, of what counts as futility, yet as we discuss below,[47] these notions are, in reality, highly subjective. Whichever way one looks at a case such as *Re C*, one cannot avoid the conclusion that it involved a value judgment. That the values of the parents in consenting on behalf of their child were completely ignored was at best paternalistic and, at worst, culturally imperialistic.[48]

10.23   But times have changed somewhat since the decision in *Re C*. This is seen most clearly in *Re Wyatt (a child) (medical treatment: parents' consent)*[49] which again involved a dispute over neonatal care, with unanimous medical evidence on one side that continued intervention was futile, and with the parents on the other side 'hoping for a miracle'. While the court confirmed that the best interests test is the appropriate legal parameter to determine what should be done for the child, it expressly acknowledged that its determination is, in the final analysis, a subjective matter. The medical evidence therefore provides the scientific basis for determining what can or cannot be done for the patient, but the ultimate responsibility falls to the court to decide

---

[45] See chapter 16.

[46] *Re J (wardship: medical treatment)* [1991] Fam 33, [1990] 3 All ER 930; *Re J (a minor) (medical treatment)* [1993] Fam 15, [1992] 4 All ER 614; *Re R (a minor) (wardship: medical treatment)* [1992] Fam 11, (1991) 7 BMLR 147. We discuss these cases in detail in chapter 16.

[47] See chapter 16.

[48] For an account of the importance of cultural and religious tenets in withdrawal cases, see M F Morrison and S G DeMichele 'How Culture and Religion Affect Attitudes toward Medical Futility' in M B Zucker and H D Zucker *Medical Futility* (1997).

[49] N 44, above.

what—from the patient's perspective—will be in her interests.[50] In following the medical evidence that continued intervention would be useless, Hedley J none the less stated:

In reaching that view I have of course been informed by the medical evidence as to the prospects and costs to her of aggressive treatment. I hope, however, that I have looked much wider than that and seen not just a physical being but a body, mind and spirit expressed in a human personality of unique worth who is profoundly precious to her parents. It is for the personality of unique worth that I have striven to discern her best interests. It is my one regret that my search has led to a different answer than that sought be these parents.[51]

Such an approach certainly displays more sensitivity to the position of distraught parents but, at the same time, it indicates the courts' determination to adhere to what it sees as good medical practice. We seriously doubt that a court would ever require particular health care professionals to continue with treatment against their better judgment; the more probable shift that this line of precedent represents is that equivocal medical assessment might lead a court to declare that it is part of the attending doctors' duty of care to find other professionals who *are* willing to treat the patient.[52] *Wyatt* is on appeal at the time of writing.

10.24   What of human rights arguments in this field? Interestingly, the court in *Wyatt* stated that '. . . in this case at least the convention now adds nothing to domestic law'.[53] In *A NHS Trust v D*[54] it was argued that a clinical decision to withdraw and withhold life-sustaining treatment from an irreversibly brain damaged child contrary to parental wishes would be a breach of Article 2 (right to life) and Article 3 (prohibition on cruel and inhuman treatment) of the European Convention on Human Rights (ECHR). Cazalet J held, however, that there could be no such breach if the proposed action was in the best interests of the patient—and the unanimous medical opinion that it was so, arrived at in good faith, satisfied this test. Subsequent case law relating to negative treatment of both minors and incapable adults has similarly refuted any claim that this course of action is a breach of the Human Rights Act 1998.[55] The point to note is that the appropriate test remains the best interests of the patient and this has, indeed, now passed muster with the European Court of Human Rights itself.[56]

10.25   In contrast to these cases, the Court of Appeal issued an unprecedented ruling in *Re T (a minor) (wardship: medical treatment)*[57] that parents of a child suffering from biliary atresia, a life-threatening liver defect, could legally refuse a liver transplant on behalf of the infant, even although there was firmly held medical opinion that a

---

[50] See, too, *Re C (A Child) (Immunisation: Parental Rights)* [2003] 2 FLR 1095, (2003) 73 BMLR 152, [2003] Fam Law 731, which we discuss in chapter 2.

[51] *Wyatt*, n 44 above, para 39.

[52] See *R (on the application of Burke) v General Medical Council* [2004] 2 FLR 1121, (2004) 70 BMLR 126, distinguishing *Re J (a minor) (child in care: medical treatment)* [1993] Fam 15.

[53] *Wyatt*, n 44 above.   [54] [2000] 2 FLR 677, (2000) 55 BMLR 19.

[55] See chapter 16.   [56] See generally *Glass*, para 10.18 above.

[57] [1997] 1 All ER 906, (1996) 35 BMLR 63.

transplant would give the child a number of years of life beyond his current prognosis. We discuss this case in depth below.[58] Suffice it to say here that the significance of the court's ruling from the perspective of the law of consent lies in its willingness, indeed, determination, *not* to equiparate the concept of best *medical* interests with the far broader notion of *overall* best interests; and as we have seen above, this now permeates the entire application of the test.

10.26   In many respects, the decision in *Re T* was easier for the Court of Appeal to achieve than was that in *Re C* for the High Court.[59] While both involved a rejection of received medical wisdom, the parents in the latter case sought to force health care professionals to treat against their will, while in the former, the parents simply requested to be left alone. *Re C* was therefore, to all intents and purposes, founded on a 'right to health care' argument. For ethical, pragmatic and economic reasons, no such right has ever been held to exist.[60] Thus, whilst parents do not have a right to demand continuous care on behalf of their child, there is scope for argument that their right to refuse on behalf of their child has been strengthened judicially. The focus in *Re T* on the effect of forced treatment on the relationship between the child and the parents may prove to be useful in the future for parents who seek to refuse medical care for their child because of their personal beliefs. It could, for example, be legitimately argued that they, too, would come to see their child differently if treatment were imposed without their consent. They may regard their child as 'tainted' or 'soiled' by medical treatment which is administered against their conscience, leading them to reject the child or treat him or her adversely. In such cases, the argument could be put that it is in the child's *overall* best interests *not* to receive the said treatment.[61]

Mature minors

10.27   The questions of positive consent to and refusal of medical and surgical procedures by relatively mature minors in the absence of parental authority—or, indeed, knowledge—is one of the more controversial issues in this field. The status of the minor between the ages of 16 and 18 is now almost settled and we return to it briefly below; discussion is, here, confined to the child below the age of 16. The common law does not exclude such a child giving consent but the validity of that consent still falls to be considered in the light of the pivotal case of *Gillick v West Norfolk and Wisbech Area Health Authority*.[62] Although, as is well known, that case was specifically concerned with the provision of contraceptives (and is also discussed both under that heading[63] and under confidentiality)[64], many of the points made in the majority opinions can be

---

[58] See chapter 16.

[59] For discussion and comparison of these two cases, see J Loughrey 'Medical Treatment—The Status of Parental Opinion' [1998] Fam Law 146.

[60] Compare *R v Cambridge Health Authority, ex p B (a minor)* (1995) 25 BMLR 5 (first instance) with the Court of Appeal ruling at [1995] 2 All ER 129, (1995) 23 BMLR 1, discussed below in chapter 16. But see more recently, *Burke*, n 52 above, discussed at paras 16.88 et seq.

[61] A D Lederman 'Understanding Faith: When Religious Parents Decline Conventional Medical Treatment for their Children' (1995) 45 Case Western Res L Rev 891.

[62] [1986] AC 112, [1985] 3 All ER 402, HL.   [63] See chapter 4.   [64] See chapter 8 above.

taken as relating to the consent of minors to medical treatment as a whole—indeed, the term '*Gillick* competent' is now part of medico-legal lore.[65]

10.28   The dominant opinion[66] was that the parental right to determine whether or not their minor child below the age of 16 years will have medical treatment 'terminates if and when the child achieves a significant understanding and intelligence to enable him or her to understand fully what is proposed' but, until the child attains such a capacity to consent, the parental right to make the decision continues save only in exceptional circumstances.[67] Despite the general tenor of his judgment, Lord Scarman affirmed that: 'Parental rights clearly exist and do not wholly disappear until the age of majority'. It can be taken as being now accepted that a doctor treating a child should always attempt to obtain parental authority but that, provided the patient is capable of understanding what is proposed and of expressing his or her wishes, the doctor may provide treatment on the basis of the minor's consent alone. The decision to do so must be taken on clinical grounds and, clearly, must depend heavily on the severity and permanence of the proposed therapy.[68] The concurrence of Scots law on this question has scarcely been disputed and is enshrined in the Age of Legal Capacity (Scotland) Act 1991, s 2(4).

10.29   The court in *Gillick* took the view that it would be a question of fact to be decided in each case whether a child seeking advice had sufficient understanding to give a consent valid in law. An illustration of this is provided by a case in which the court agreed that a schoolgirl aged 15 should be allowed to have an abortion against the wishes of her parents. Butler-Sloss J said: 'I am satisfied she wants this abortion; she understands the implications of it'.[69] Thus, the problem of consent to treatment by minors is, to all intents, settled and is well understood. We have not, however, yet touched on refusal of treatment. This is an issue which has aroused considerable controversy. We return to it in a discussion of recent cases below.[70]

The mentally incompetent

10.30   Non-consensual treatment that can be provided for involuntary mental patients is prescribed by statute and is discussed elsewhere.[71] Such therapy is, however, specifically limited to treatment of the mental condition. Treatments of unrelated physical conditions are excluded and a therapeutic lacuna remains—how can treatment be provided legitimately to persons who are unable to consent to it? At one time, the dilemma was subsumed within the parens patriae jurisdiction under which the State,

---

[65] *Re R (a minor) (wardship: medical treatment)* [1992] Fam 11, (1992) 7 BMLR 147 at 156, CA, per Lord Donaldson. See too, *Re L (medical treatment: Gillick competence)* [1998] 2 FLR 810.

[66] [1985] 3 All ER 402 at 423, per Lord Scarman.

[67] A similar approach by Lord Denning MR in *Hewer v Bryant* [1970] 1 QB 357, [1969] 3 All ER 578 was strongly approved and the common law position in Canada, as expressed in *Johnston v Wellesley Hospital* (1970) 17 DLR (3d) 139, was also quoted.

[68] For a critical review of the *Gillick* decision with particular reference to the doctor's situation, see G Williams 'The *Gillick* Saga' (1985) 135 NLJ 1156, 1179.

[69] *Re P (a minor)* [1986] 1 FLR 272, 80 LGR 301.   [70] See para 10.44 et seq.

[71] See chapter 20.

acting through the judiciary, could consent to or refuse medical treatment on behalf of an incapax, whether that be a minor or an incapable adult.

The *parens patriae* jurisdiction and its aftermath

10.31 The parens patriae—literally, the 'parent of the country'—jurisdiction derives from the ancient powers of the English monarchy and survives in a number of countries which draw their legal systems from that of England—these include Australia, Canada, Ireland and the United States, together with Scotland by virtue of its retention of its own legal system after the Act of Union 1707. It has been used in a number of cases which we have done or will consider in this book.[72] The Australian Family Court, for example, has authorised the harvesting of bone marrow from a 12-year-old boy to help in the treatment of his aunt[73] but the power will not be used lightly. Thus, the Supreme Court of New South Wales would not use the jurisdiction to authorise the removal of sperm from an unconscious man for later fertilisation of his wife,[74] the court holding that it was not intended that this power should be invoked for the benefit of others.[75] Similarly, in *Re Eve*[76] the Supreme Court of Canada confirmed the persistence of its parens patriae role and that of the Canadian Supreme Courts, but refused to exercise the jurisdiction to authorise a non-therapeutic sterilisation of an incapax adult woman.[77]

10.32 Somewhat paradoxically, it was the passing of the Mental Health Act 1959, which was designed to preserve, so far as possible, the autonomy of the mentally disordered, that did away with the parens patriae power in England and Wales and, in doing so, ensured that, subsequently, no one, not even a court, could consent to or refuse medical treatment on behalf of an incapable adult unless it fell within the provisions of the mental health legislation.[78]

10.33 The resulting manifest prejudice to the physical well-being of the mentally ill was solved, albeit derivatively, in the very influential case of *Re F*.[79] In this sterilisation

---

[72] In Ireland, see *Re a Ward* [1996] 2 IR 79, (1996) 50 BMLR 140 and in Scotland, *Law Hospital NHS Trust v Lord Advocate* 1996 SLT 848, (1998) 39 BMLR 166.

[73] *Re GWW and CMW* (1997) 21 Fam LR 612. A similar decision was reached in *Re Y (adult patient) (transplant: bone marrow)* [1997] Fam 110, (1996) 35 BMLR 111, in which it was held to be in the best interests of a 25-year-old incapax woman to donate bone marrow to her sister.

[74] *MAW v Western Sydney Area Health Service* [2000] NSWSC 358.

[75] Cf, the outcome in *R v Human Fertilisation and Embryology Authority, ex p Blood* [1999] Fam 151 which the court arrived at on the basis of judicial review and without any need for an inherent parens patriae jurisidiction. We discuss this case in chapter 4, paras 4.13–4.16.

[76] [1986] 2 SCR 388. In a later case, *Winnipeg Child and Family Services (Northwestern) v GDF* [1997] 3 SCR 925, the court declined to extend the parens patriae jurisdiction so as to protect a fetus being carried by a glue-sniffing woman.

[77] But see the opposite result in the Australian High Court in *Secretary, Dept of Health and Community Services v JWB* (1992) 106 ALR 385.

[78] The power remained in Scotland after the passing of the Mental Health (Scotland) Act 1960 because it did not depend, in addition, on the peculiarly English order of the Sign Manual which empowered the judiciary to act on behalf of the monarch. This was revoked at the same time as the 1959 Act was passed.

[79] *Re F (mental patient: sterilisation)* [1990] 2 AC 1, sub nom *F v West Berkshire Health Authority* [1989] 2 All ER 545.

case, it was clearly stated that a doctor can provide—indeed, is professionally bound to provide—treatment for a mentally handicapped person in the absence of consent so long as that treatment is in the patient's best interests—a subsequent line of decisions has supported that view and, indeed, has extended its scope.[80] It is, however, doubtful if this professionally-orientated approach acts to the maximum advantage of the mentally handicapped. This is so for two reasons—summed up in the question: 'Who decides what constitutes best interests, and how?' Either it is the doctor acting alone—in which case there is little left of even surrogate patient consent—or, in the event that the doctor's opinion is challenged, it is the prerogative of the court which is, to an extent, hamstrung by the traditional jurisprudence which is based on the *Bolam* test.[81] We have already seen how this test operates in the context of the negligence action in chapter 9. Its importation to the context of the legitimacy of dealings with incompetent patients has raised a number of particular issues.

10.34   Essentially the operation of the *Bolam* test in the consent context states that a doctor's conduct is acceptable provided it is agreed by a responsible body of medical opinion—and this means a single body of opinion, not a consensus. We have always found this to be doubtfully acceptable, because it places the focus not on the patient's interests as such, but on the views of the medical profession as to those interests. Moreover, left in its original form, the *Bolam* test precludes the court making a choice between conflicting medical opinions;[82] as a result, the courts must pass responsibility back to the profession and the incapable patient has gained little or nothing in the process. This situation is, however, now changing rapidly due to the coincidence of two trends. First, there have been profound changes in the common law while, at the same time, the legislatures have responded to the patients' needs by way of a wave of legislation, designed at least in part to place the matter on a statutory basis, across the whole United Kingdom. While the relevant statutes have yet to show their hands in practice, it is apparent that they, together with any professional latitude remaining under the rubrics of best interests and necessity,[83] have effectively removed any need for the parens patriae jurisdiction and, for that reason, we have eschewed further discussion of the subject in this edition. The reader who is interested in what is, in the medical context, effectively legal history (at least for England and Wales) is referred to the comprehensive analysis by one of us.[84]

---

[80] Most recently, this has been clarified yet further in the context of abortion and the mentally incompetent patient in *An NHS Trust v D* [2004] 1 FLR 1110, [2004] Fam Law 415.

[81] Laid down in *Bolam v Friern Hospital Management Committee* [1957] 2 All ER 118, [1957] 1 WLR 582.

[82] *Maynard v West Midland Regional Health Authority* [1985] 1 All ER 635, [1984] 1 WLR 634.

[83] It has been held that 'necessity' here is not limited to medical and similar emergencies. See *Re G (an adult) (mental capacity: court's jurisdiction)* [2004] EWHC 2222 (Fam).

[84] G T Laurie 'Parens Patriae in the Medico-legal Context: The Vagaries of Judicial Activism' (1999) 3 Edin LR 95. See also J Seymour '*Parens Patriae* and Wardship Powers: Their Nature and Origins' (1994) 14 OJLS 159.

Recent common law developments

10.35 As already intimated, and despite what appears to be clear authority from the House of Lords on the meaning and role of best interests in respect of adults in the UK, there has been something of a groundswell of reaction among the lower courts since the last edition of this book. Thus, we have Munby J in *A v A Health Authority*[85] stating that an adult's best interests involve a welfare appraisal in the widest possible terms to include a range of ethical, social, moral, emotional, and welfare considerations. As authority, he cites Dame Butler-Sloss, President of the High Court, in *Re A (medical treatment: male sterilisation)*[86] where, indeed, she stressed that, '[i]n my judgment, best interests encompasses medical, emotional and all other welfare issues'.[87] This is repeated and expanded by the President in *Simms v Simms and Another*[88] where she is categoric that, '[i]n a case where an application is made to the court . . . it is the judge, not the doctor, who makes the decision that it is in the best interests of the patient that the operation be performed or the treatment be given'.[89] This is undoubtedly true, and a better reading of *Re F*—which emerges from concurrent developments in the law of negligence which we discuss in chapter 9—is that while it is always a doctor's duty to act with the requisite standard of care by reference to his peers, whether in relation to treatment decisions or a judgment about a patient's best interests, that standard is in no way absolute. The role and influence of the *Bolam* test have been significantly downgraded in recent years, at least in the sense that responsible medical opinion will no longer be determinative of any legal issue. Thus, in *R (on the application of N) v Doctor M and Others*,[90] where there was a responsible body of medical opinion that a particular course of treatment was *not* in the patient's best interests, the Court of Appeal held that this was '. . . relevant to the question whether it is in the patient's best interests or medically necessary, but it is no more than that'.[91] It continued, '[t]he court has to decide in light of all of the evidence in the case whether the treatment should be permitted'.[92] And, as for the role of *Bolam*, it was stated that while all treatment must satisfy the test, this is merely '. . . a necessary, but not sufficient, condition of treatment in the patient's best interests'.[93]

---

[85] [2002] 1 FCR 481, [2002] Fam 213, at para 43.   [86] [2000] 1 FCR 193.

[87] See also, *A Hospital NHS Trust v S and others* [2003] EWHC 365 (Fam), para 47: 'When considering the best interests of a patient, it is . . . the duty of the court to assess the advantages and disadvantages of the various treatments and management options, the viability of each such option and the likely effect each would have on the patient's best interests and, I would add, his enjoyment of life . . . any likely benefit of treatment has to be balanced and considered in the light of any additional suffering the treatment option would entail'.

[88] [2003] 2 WLR 1465, [2003] 1 ALL ER 669. For comment, see J Laing 'Incompetent Patients, Experimental Treatment and the "Bolam Test" ' (2003) 11 Med L Rev 237.

[89] *Ibid*, para 46. It should also be noted that the President points out that, unlike the instance cases, there was '. . . no need to investigate the meaning or the extent of the phrase "best interests" in *Re F*, *ibid*, para 45.

[90] [2003] 1 FLR 667, [2003] 1 FCR 124.   [91] *Ibid*, para 29.

[92] *Ibid*, citing with approved the European Court of Human Rights case *Herczegalvy v Austria* (1992) 15 EHRR 437, 18 BMLR 48.

[93] *Ibid*. See also *Simms*, n 88 above, para 48.

10.36   The ultimate responsibility for determining best interests, then, rests with the courts.[94] The best judicial guidance offered to date on how these interests should be assessed is that of Thorpe LJ in *Re A* which we repeat here in full for the sake of clarity:

Pending the enactment of a checklist or other statutory direction it seems to me that the first instance judge with the responsibility to make an evaluation of the best interests of a claimant lacking capacity should draw up a balance sheet. The first entry should be of any factor or factors of actual benefit. In the present case an instance would be the acquisition of foolproof contraception. Then on the other sheet the judge should write any counterbalancing dis-benefits to the applicant. An obvious instance in this case would be the apprehension of risk and the discomfort inherent in the operation. Then the judge should enter on each sheet the potential gains and losses in each instance making some estimate of the extent of the possibility that the gain or loss might accrue. At the end of that exercise the judge should be better placed to strike a balance between the sum of the certain and possible gains against the sum of the certain and possible losses. Obviously, only if the account is in relatively significant credit will the judge conclude that the application is likely to advance the best interests of the claimant.[95]

10.37   While an application to the court is not necessary when issues of capacity and best interests are self-evident, this should be made if there is doubt and/or dispute between interested parties such as family members and health care professionals.[96] Best interests can only be assessed in light of full and accurate medical (and non-medical) evidence about the patient's condition, and it is accepted that those interests will change as the patient's condition changes.[97] Moreover, it has been stated to be extremely important that the patient be given the opportunity to make representations before any final declaration on treatment is made.[98] This is true even in the context of an (emergency) interim declaration.[99] But doubt has arisen as to the correctness, indeed the legality, of procedures where the incapax person has had no opportunity to make her views known or where a declaration has been sought when incapacity has merely been raised as a possibility but not yet established. In *NHS Trust v T*, for example, Charles J sought to question the on-going validity

---

[94] For an example of this in operation see *R (on the application of PS) v G (Responsible Medical Officer)* [2003] EWHC 2335.

[95] *Re A (medical treatment: male sterilisation)* [2000] 1 FLR 549, at p 555.

[96] *An NHS Trust v D* [2004] 1 FLR 1110 (termination of pregnancy involving a severely schizophrenic woman was declared to be in her best interests). This is now also a matter of human rights law, see *Glass*, para 10.18 above.

[97] *A Hospital NHS Trust v S* (2003) 71 BMLR 188 (where the court sanctioned leaving open various medical avenues of treatment depending on how the patient progressed and would not rule out the possibility of kidney transplant on non-medical grounds such as the staff's inability to cope with the patient's behavioural problems related to alternative treatment).

[98] *NHS Trust v T (adult patient: refusal of medical treatment)* [2005] 1 All ER 387.

[99] *Ibid*; recalling none the less, that the terms of a declaration are valid only so long as the patient remains in an incapacitated state and absent any other fundamental change of circumstances.

of judicial guidance of recent years[100] as to the procedures to be followed in such circumstances.[101] In particular, he drew attention to a recent assault action involving health care professionals (HCPs) for continuing treatment against the patient's (subsequently-declared-to-be-competent) wishes;[102] this was successful even when the HCPs in question acted entirely in good faith and according to what they truly believed to be the best interests of their patient. The guidance—which states that: '. . . while the question of capacity is being resolved the patient must . . . be cared for in accordance with the judgment of the doctors as to the patient's best interests'[103]—may no longer protect HCPs from future legal action. As a result, Charles J called for reconsideration of the guidance and of the law's general approach to the problem.

Recent statutory reforms

10.38 Reforming measures have been on the horizon in England and Wales since the Law Commission's paper on Mental Incapacity in 1995.[104] Some ten years on, the Mental Capacity Act 2005[105] scraped through without adequate debate on the dissolution of Parliament after extensive consultation and vacillation over its proposals.[106] The Act reflects its Scottish counterpart—the Adults with Incapacity (Scotland) Act 2000—in its general breadth and, importantly, in providing for the appointment of substituted decision-makers (*donees* with a lasting power of attorney). The key point of departure, however, lies in the fact that, whereas the Scottish ministers shied away from the paternalistic overtones of the 'best interests test', the 2005 Act remains committed to the principle and pursues the common law concept as outlined above while seeking to clarify certain areas of doubt.

10.39 Part I of the Act lays out a checklist of issues to be considered in determining best interests, which in turn must be read against a set of guiding principles which underpin the entire instrument. The principles impose, first and foremost, a presumption of capacity and an obligation to assist individuals to make their own decisions as far as it is practicable to do so.[107] The irrational or thought-to-be-unwise decisions of

---

[100] The guidance in question includes that of the Court of Appeal in *St George's Healthcare NHS Trust v S* [1998] 3 WLR 936, discussed below at para 10.71, and that in *Re B (adult: refusal of medical treatment)* [2002] 2 All ER 449.

[101] *NHS Trust v T (adult patient: refusal of medical treatment)* [2005] 1 All ER 387, paras 72–75.

[102] *Re B (adult: refusal of medical treatment)* [2002] 2 All ER 449, discussed at para 10.63.

[103] *Re B, ibid,* para 100, point (iv).

[104] Law Commission, *Mental Incapacity,* No. 231, 1995; For comment on the Law Commission's work, see P Alldridge 'Consent to Medical and Surgical Treatment—The Law Commission's Recommendations' (1996) 4 Med L Rev 129 and P Wilson 'The Law Commission's Report on Mental Incapacity: Medically Vulnerable Adults or Politically Vulnerable Law?' (1996) 4 Med L Rev 227.

[105] The major thrust of the Act is probably aimed at those who have lost capacity through the ageing process and we return to it in chapter 12. It is clearly relevant, however, to any incompetent who needs treatment for physical disease and is, therefore, integral to the present discussion.

[106] See, for example, Lord Chancellor's Department, *Who Decides? Making Decisions on Behalf of Mentally Incapacitated Adults,* 1997, Cm 3803, and the Government's response, *Making Decisions,* 1999, Cm 4465. As a result of the speed with which the Royal Assent was obtained, there is specific warning that the Act may be due for significant reappraisal.

[107] Mental Capacity Act 2005, s 1.

competent persons must be respected, reflecting the common law position outlined below. Where incompetence has been established, decisions taken for the person must be in their best interests and in the least restrictive manner, viz, the impact on their rights, freedoms and interests. Section 4 fleshes out the meaning of best interests. This is to be an objective test—not one based in substituted judgment—and it requires that *all* factors listed in the clause be weighed in the decision-making process with none having any more importance than any other. Moreover, the incapacitated person should be an integral part of that process so far as it is possible. Consideration should also be given to the likelihood of the person recovering capacity sufficiently to be able to make the decision in the reasonably foreseeable future. The factors to be considered include: the persons' past and present wishes and feelings, their beliefs and values to the extent they might influence their decisions if they had capacity,[108] and the views of other parties interested in the incompetent's welfare (to include anyone named by the incapax, carers, any donee of a lasting power of attorney and any court-appointed deputy). The obligation, then, is to consult widely and, by implication, to gather as much relevant information as possible. Notwithstanding, 'best interests' is never defined in the Act: the task of acting within their limits thus remains one which a decision-maker must justify in each circumstance. Nor is there any explicit guidance within the Act itself on *how* balancing of factors should be done.[109] Doubtless, this will appear in due course, but in the meantime the dicta of Thorpe LJ in *Re A* (para 10.36 above) must serve as the best indication.

10.40   Subsections (8) and (9) of section 4 attempt to address the concern of Charles J about the interim grey phase where an individual's capacity may be in doubt and yet action is required to protect their interests. These provide, in essence, that it will be lawful to purport to act in a person's best interests when (a) the actor reasonably believes that the person lacks capacity and (b) he reasonably believes that what he does or decides is in the best interests of the person concerned. This, of course, does not absolve such a person of the obligation to comply with the other requirements of the section regarding the factors to be weighed in the balance when deciding what those best interests are.

10.41   Section 9 provides for the appointment of Lasting Power of Attorney which includes the authority to consent to or refuse medical treatment on behalf of the incapacitated person, subject to two important riders: (i) decisions are subordinated to valid advance directives created by the person in accordance with ss 24–26 of the Act, and (ii) the decision-making power in respect of the administration or withdrawal of life-sustaining care must be expressly provided for in the appointing

---

[108] We would comment in passing that this comes incredibly close to a substituted judgment approach, yet this approach is expressly eschewed in the Explanatory Notes to the Bill, Mental Capacity Bill, HC 15 December 2004 [HL Bill 13] para 25.

[109] At best, s 6 makes it clear that when restraint is to be used the decision must include an assessment that the action is 'necessary in order to prevent harm' and that it is a 'proportionate response' to the likelihood and seriousness of harm.

instrument.[110] Any other conditions in that instrument must also be complied with.[111] Finally, a new Court of Protection[112] will be created and would have power to declare acts, proposed acts or omissions (e.g. a failure to treat) as lawful in respect of patient's best interests; it will be assisted by the new Office of the Public Guardian.[113]

10.42   As we have already seen, reforming legislation appeared in Scotland in the guise of the Adults with Incapacity (Scotland) Act 2000, Part V of which deals with medical treatment and research and came into force on 1 July 2002. Rather than look to the patient's best interests, the Scottish Commission preferred to list a number of factors to be considered before treating an incapable adult. Nonetheless, the position of the incapable adult in Scotland remains strongly influenced by health care professionals. The 2000 Act grants a 'general authority to treat' for any practitioner primarily responsible for a patient who—in the practitioner's certified opinion—is incapable in relation to a treatment decision. This is an authority to do all that is reasonable in the circumstances 'to safeguard or promote the physical or mental health of the adult'.[114] And, while the Act makes provision for the appointment of proxy decision-makers who should be consulted prior to any action where it is practicable to do so, these persons only have a power to consent on behalf of the incapable adult—that is, to accede to medical opinion; there is no correlative power to refuse. If a dispute arises, a second medical officer must be appointed from a list held by the Mental Welfare Commission and his or her agreement with the initial medical opinion provides the legal authority to proceed. The only course then left for the proxy is to appeal to the Court of Session. The primary carer can also do so in cases where the second medical officer agrees with the proxy. Codes of practice have been issued both for proxy decision-makers[115] and for those authorised to carry out treatment or research under the Act.[116] We have commented more fully on the terms of this legislation elsewhere.[117]

[110] It should also be noted that certain 'Excluded Decisions' fall outside the authority of any decision-maker under the Act, see Mental Capacity Act, ss 27 and 28. Of relevance in the present context are: (i) any consent under the Human Fertilisation and Embryology Act 1990, and (ii) authority or consent to treat someone for mental disorder (which we discuss in chapter 20). Furthermore, specific provisions apply in the context of research and the incapacitated person by virtue of ss 30–33 of the Act, on which we say more in chapter 18.

[111] Mental Capacity Act, ss 11(7) and (8).

[112] Mental Capacity Act, Part 2, having the same powers as the High Court (s 47(1)).

[113] Mental Capacity Act, ss 57 and 58.

[114] 2000 Act, ss 47(1) and 47(2). Note, however, certain treatments such as neurosurgery, sterilisation and surgical implantation of hormones to reduce sex drive must first receive the approval of the Court of Session, while others such as electro-convulsive therapy, abortion, drugs to reduce sex drive or other procedures likely to result in sterilisation, must be cleared by the Mental Welfare Commission, see the Adults with Incapacity (Specified Medical Treatments) (Scotland) Regulations 2002, SSI 2002/275.

[115] Code of Practice for Continuing and Welfare Attorneys, March 2001, SE/2001/90 (effective 2 April 2001), and Code of Practice for Persons Authorised Under Intervention Orders and Guardians, March 2002, SE/2002/65 (effective 1 April 2002).

[116] Code of Practice for Persons Authorised to Carry Out Treatment or Research Under Part Five of the Act, April 2002, SE 2002/73, effective 1 July 2002.

[117] G T Laurie and J K Mason 'Negative Treatment of Vulnerable Patients: Euthanasia By Any Other Name? [2000] Jurid Rev 159.

10.43   It is important to note that the 2000 Act does not displace the common law in its entirety. The common law still governs the position in emergencies and negative treatment decisions, that is, those relating to the withholding or withdrawal of treatment. Moreover, the 2005 Act is not yet in force and will probably not be so for some time. For these reasons, and to assist in the general understanding of the development of the jurisprudence, we must now turn still to consider the seminal court decisions.

The cases

10.44   We noted in the sixth edition of this book that the interval between previous editions had provided a remarkable series of cases which had served to draw together, and indicate judicial attitudes to, non-voluntary treatment involving minors, mature minors and doubtfully incompetent adults. This trend has continued beyond the last edition to the present day. Several of these cases have far-reaching implications; here, we consider only those aspects which are directly related to refusal of and consent to treatment.

10.45   The first, albeit not chronologically, which is of importance in the present context is *Re J*.[118] This case concerned a 16-month-old brain damaged child whose condition was such that his medical attendants considered it inappropriate to provide invasive intensive care in the event that he suffered a life threatening event. The boy's mother sought, and obtained, an order that such treatment should be given if it served to prolong his life. This order was immediately stayed and this stay was, later, upheld on appeal. The significance of *Re J* is that, in restating[119] in the clearest terms that the medical profession could not be required to undertake treatment against its clinical judgment, it laid a base-line that, while *consent* to treatment is essential, there is no concurrent right to *demand* treatment—in short, there are 'checks and balances of consent and willingness and ability to treat'. We saw above how this ruling has been applied without question in *Re C (a minor) (medical treatment)*.[120] The dubious position whether there is ever a right to demand treatment has, however, recently been obfuscated by the decision relating to an adult in *R (on the application of Burke) v General Medical Council*[121] on which we say more below.[122] For now, we concentrate on minors.

10.46   *Re R*[123] was something of a landmark case as it constituted the first time that the concept of the mature—or *Gillick*-competent—minor had been tested in the United Kingdom courts; it also raised, but scarcely resolved, the relationship between consent to and refusal of treatment. Briefly, the case concerned a 15-year-old girl whose

---

[118] *Re J (a minor) (wardship: medical treatment)* [1992] 2 FLR 165, (1992) 9 BMLR 10.

[119] The proposition had been previously stated in *Re J (a minor) (wardship: medical treatment)* [1991] Fam 33 at 41, (1990) 6 BMLR 25 at 30 and in *Re R (a minor) (wardship: medical treatment)* [1992] Fam 11 at 22, (1992) 7 BMLR 147 at 154, both per Lord Donaldson MR. The trial judge in the present case interpreted these remarks as not binding.

[120] [1998] 1 FLR 384, (1997) 40 BMLR 31.   [121] [2004] 3 FCR 579, (2004) 79 BMLR 126.

[122] See para 16.88 et seq, but note that *Burke* has now been successfully appealed.

[123] [1992] Fam 11, (1991) 7 BMLR 147.

increasingly disturbed behaviour required sedative treatment. However, during her lucid phases—in which she appeared rational and capable of making decisions—she refused her medication and the local authority instituted wardship proceedings, the intention being to seek authority to provide anti-psychotic treatment whether or not she consented; R appealed against an order to that effect which had been obtained.

10.47 The Court of Appeal first disposed of the distinction, if any, between parental powers and those of the court in wardship and concluded that the latter were wider; the court could override both consent and refusal of treatment by the ward if that was considered to be in his or her best interests. The court then further distinguished *Gillick*, which was concerned with the developing maturity of normal children; the test elaborated in that case could not be applied to a child whose mental state fluctuated widely from day to day. But the aspect of the case having by far the most general significance lay in its definition of parental powers. Essentially, Lord Donaldson MR considered that the parental right which *Gillick* extinguished was to *determine* the treatment of a mature minor—and determination was considered to be wider in its implications than a right to consent, in so far as it included the right of veto. In explanation, Lord Donaldson introduced the concept of consent providing the key to the therapeutic door and of there being, in the case of the mature minor, two keyholders—the minor and her parents; consent by either *enabled* treatment to be given lawfully but did not, in any way, *determine* that the child should be treated. Lord Donaldson was later to regret his keyholder analogy in so far as keys can lock as well as unlock doors. It seems to us to be acceptable so long as it is modified to imply that refusal on the part of the child effectively means that the child has thrown away its key to a locked door; it is then only prudent that there should be a second key available as a fire precaution.

10.48 *Re R* raised a storm of academic protest. This was not, primarily, as to the assessment of mental incompetence, which the court considered should be based on the general condition of the patient rather than that at a given moment in time; nor was there great exception to the definition of the court's authority in wardship. Rather, the criticism was directed at the retention of the parental right to give consent in the face of the child's refusal—an interpretation of the law which Kennedy described as 'driving a coach and horses through *Gillick*'.[124] But is this, in fact, so? Lord Donaldson's distinction between a parental ability to determine a minor's treatment—which Lord Scarman considered to be overtaken by the child's developing maturity[125]—and to consent to treatment is a legitimate one and, as we have seen, a corresponding obligation to apply that treatment was firmly rejected. Moreover, the Master of the Rolls was, arguably, doing no more than interpreting the statute law of England and Wales. The Family Law Reform Act 1969, s 8(1) gives the minor aged 16–18 powers of

---

[124] I Kennedy 'Consent to Treatment: The Capable Person' in C Dyer (ed) *Doctors, Patients and the Law* (1992) ch 3. See also A Bainham 'The Judge and the Competent Minor' (1992) 108 LQR 196, which is concerned more with the Family Law Reform Act 1969, s 8(1) rather than with s 8(3).

[125] In *Gillick* [1986] AC 112 at 188, [1985] 3 All ER 402 at 423.

consent to medical and surgical treatment equivalent to those of an adult. Section 8(3), however, goes on to say:

Nothing in this section shall be construed as making ineffective any consent which would have been effective if this section had not been enacted.

10.49   It has been widely assumed that this section does no more than confirm the common law right of competent minors to decide these questions for themselves. We have always doubted this, largely because, if this is the correct interpretation, there was never any need for s 8(1)—a view which was endorsed by the absence of any such statute in Scotland prior to the Age of Legal Capacity (Scotland) Act 1991.[126] The better view, in our opinion, is that a parental right to consent on behalf of a child existed before 1969 and that s 8(3) preserves that right in the case of all those below the age of 18; this seems to have been the basis of Lord Donaldson's opinion.[127] The academic response to *Re R* demonstrates, above all, the difficulties which arise when attempting to apply general philosophical principles to particular medical cases. The opinion may have further muddied the murky waters of *Gillick* but what was the alternative? This could only have been to accede to the minor's right to refuse treatment when competent and to treat her when incompetent under the mantle of necessity. This is not only bad medicine; it also smacks of a 'cat and mouse' approach which cannot be ethically sustainable. It might have been better to confine the ratio to such narrow issues and to regard the remainder of Lord Donaldson's speech as obiter; but the Master of the Rolls, albeit with some reservations, consolidated his position in the next case—*Re W*.[128]

10.50   *Re W* takes us one step further down the road of consent in that it concerned a 16-year-old girl who, therefore, came within the provisions of s 8(1) of the Family Reform Act 1969 which states:

The consent of a minor who has attained the age of sixteen years to any . . . medical . . . treatment which, in the absence of consent, would constitute a trespass to the person, shall be as effective as it would be if he were of full age; and where a minor has by virtue of this section given effective consent to any treatment it shall not be necessary to obtain any consent for it from his parent or guardian . . .

10.51   W was suffering from anorexia nervosa and was refusing all treatment despite a rapid deterioration in her health. The Court of Appeal supported an order that she be treated in a specialist unit but, in essence, did so on the clinical grounds that the

---

[126] The Age of Legal Capacity (Scotland) Act 1991, s 2(4) gives statutory power, which is rather wider even than that envisaged in *Gillick*, to the mature minor under the age of 16 to consent to medical or dental treatment. The section is, however, *enabling* in that it provides an exception to the general rule that a person under 16 has no capacity to enter into any legal transaction. For the application of the English case law to Scotland, see L Edwards 'The Right to Consent and the Right to Refuse: More Problems with Minors and Medical Consent' [1993] JR 52.

[127] (1992) 7 BMLR 147 at 156.

[128] *Re W (a minor) (medical treatment)* [1992] 4 All ER 627, (1992) 9 BMLR 22. For a comparable Australian case, see *DoCS v Y* [1999] NSWSC 644.

disease is capable of destroying the ability to make an informed choice—the wishes of the minor thus constituted something which, of themselves, required treatment. In the course of the judgments, however, several general issues were either clarified or reinforced. First, it was reiterated that the court had extensive powers in wardship and that these existed irrespective of the provisions of the Family Law Reform Act 1969, s 8(1); moreover, Lord Donaldson held that the exercise of the court's power to make a specific issue order did not conflict with those sections of the Children Act 1989 which give a mature minor the right to refuse psychiatric or medical treatment in defined circumstances.[129] All the opinions emphasised that this attitude did not conflict with *Gillick* which was concerned with *parental* powers only. Secondly, the court disposed in clear terms of the relationship of consent to refusal of treatment with particular reference to the 1969 Act. Lord Donaldson said:

No minor of whatever age has power by refusing consent to treatment to override a consent to treatment by someone who has parental responsibility for the minor and a fortiori a consent by the court.[130]

Balcombe LJ said:

I am quite unable to see how, on any normal reading of the words of the section, it can be construed to confer [an absolute right to refuse medical treatment] . . . That the section did not operate to prevent parental consent remaining effective, as well in the case of a child over 16 as in the case of a child under that age, is apparent from the words of sub-s (3).[131]

10.52 This is, of course, a legal decision and it is true, as Balcombe LJ himself said, that, in logic, there can be no difference between an ability to consent to treatment and an ability to refuse treatment. It is undoubtedly the case that the courts will seek to respect a mature minor's autonomous wishes in respect many aspects of their life, including matters medical. Thus, for example, in *Torbay Borough Council v News Group Newspapers*[132] we find Munby J upholding the right of a young woman who was almost 17 to decide for herself whether to disclose the details of own teenage pregnancy to the press, irrespective of the wishes of her parents. But matters are not so clear cut when the decision relates to medical treatment and when a refusal may involve a serious risk of physical or mental harm, or indeed, death. In such cases, is there not a clear practical distinction to be made? It is reasonable to suppose, paternalistic though it may sound, that a qualified doctor knows more about the treatment of disease than does a child. Thus, while consent involves acceptance of an experienced

---

[129] This has been clearly restated in *South Glamorgan County Council v W and B* [1993] 1 FCR 626; [1993] Fam Law 398.

[130] [1992] 4 All ER 627 at 639, (1992) 9 BMLR 22 at 36.

[131] [1992] 4 All ER 627 at 641, (1992) 9 BMLR 22 at 37, 38. Kennedy para 10.48 above at 60–61 regarded Lord Donaldson's refusal in *Re R* to accept refusal and consent as twin aspects of the single right to self-determination as bordering on the perverse; this was because he had no stated support. The presence of such support in *Re W* serves to fill the lacuna.

[132] [2003] EWHC 2927.

view, refusal rejects that experience—and does so from a position of limited understanding. Furthermore, a refusal of medical treatment may close down the options—
and this may be regretted later in that the chance to consent has now passed. The
implications of refusal may, therefore, be more serious and, on these grounds refusal
of treatment may require greater understanding than does acceptance. A level of
comprehension sufficient to justify refusal of treatment certainly includes one to
accept treatment but the reverse does not hold; the two conditions cannot be regarded
as being on a par.[133] We accept, of course, that the same could also be true for most
adults. But we have no difficulty with the courts deeming the distinction to be necessary in the case of vulnerable persons—be they minors or incapax adults. Indeed, as
we show below,[134] just such an approach has been adopted in the case of the latter by
the courts after the decision of *Re C (adult: refusal of medical treatment).*[135]

10.53   What is clear from both *Re R* and *Re W* is that, rather like Lord Denning before
him, Lord Donaldson was concerned to protect the medical profession from the fire
of litigation—his reference to consent providing a flak-jacket for the doctor demonstrates this vividly. It is, therefore, possible to criticise the two decisions as concentrat-
ing on this aspect and taking insufficient notice of the developing autonomy of
adolescence. None the less, all the speeches in both cases are at pains to emphasise
the importance of respecting the minor's wishes—and of giving them increasing
value with increasing maturity. They emphasise that those wishes are not binding; but
their tenor is such as to retain the concept of the mature minor very firmly and to
insist that this is breached only in exceptional circumstances. It might, however, be
posited that matters have changed with the introduction of the Human Rights Act
1998, and that a failure to respect a refusal by a mature minor would now be a breach
of a considerable number of her fundamental rights, including those under Articles 2,
3, 5, and 8.[136] We doubt that this will be so, and would point to both the doctrine of
proportionality—requiring a balance of community and individual interests—and
the margin of appreciation that countries enjoy under the European Convention on
Human Rights. The English courts have made a concerted effort to demonstrate their
desire to find balance in these cases and there is little in ECtHR jurisprudence that
would lead them to upset that delicate equilibrium.

10.54   None the less, the ease with which this balance might be thought to be upset
is very clearly illustrated by *Re M (child: refusal of medical treatment)*[137] in which a
15½-year-old girl who had sustained acute heart failure was denied the right to refuse
a heart transplant operation. While the High Court emphasised the need to take
account of a mature minor's wishes as to her own medical treatment, it also endorsed
the legal view that those wishes are in no way determinative. Johnson J was keen that
his ruling be very clearly laid out for M to read for herself but, interestingly, he did

---

[133] For a contrary clinico-legal view, see J A Devereux, D P H Jones and D I Dickenson 'Can Children
Withhold Consent to Treatment?' (1993) 306 BMJ 1459.
[134] See para 10.58 et seq.   [135] [1994] 1 All ER 819, [1994] 1 WLR 290.
[136] See A Hockton, *The Law of Consent to Medical Treatment* (2002), paras 8.016–8.021.
[137] [1999] 2 FLR 1097, (2000) 52 BMLR 124.

not, himself, ascertain her views before passing judgment. Instead, these were gleaned by a local solicitor and the Official Solicitor who, together, formed the view that M was overwhelmed by her circumstances. She had said that she did not wish to die. By the same token, she had also indicated that she did not want someone else's heart, nor did she relish the thought of taking medicine for the rest of her life. In the final analysis Johnson J held that it was in M's best interests to receive a new heart and authorised her surgeons to perform the procedure. This must surely represent the outermost reaches of acceptable paternalistic practices. While it seems that she finally acquiesced, was the court really countenancing a forced transplantation if M had continued her resistance? More broadly, we question if it is ethically correct to earmark a scarce and expensive resource for someone who does not want it. Small wonder that Johnson J expressed concern at the gravity of his decision.

REFUSAL OF TREATMENT BY ADULTS

10.55   The Court of Appeal considered the adult who refuses treatment in *Re T*.[138] *Re T* appears to have been the first adult Jehovah's Witness case to have come before a British court. The case itself was fairly unexceptional. A pregnant woman was involved in a car accident and, after speaking with her mother, signed a form of refusal of blood transfusion. Following a caesarian section and the delivery of a stillborn baby, her condition deteriorated and a court order was obtained legalising blood transfusion on the grounds that it was manifestly in her best interests; the declaration was upheld by the Court of Appeal. The fundamental decision was to the effect that an adult patient who suffers from no mental incapacity has an absolute right to consent to medical treatment, to refuse it or to choose an alternative treatment[139]—'it exists notwithstanding that the reasons for making the choice are rational, irrational, unknown or even non-existent'.[140] How, then, did the court reach its decision to support the provision of apparently involuntary treatment?

10.56   First, of course, it had to transform involuntary treatment into non-voluntary. This it did by finding that T's mental state had deteriorated to such an extent that she could not make a valid choice as between death and transfusion—and if there was doubt as to how the patient was exercising her right of self-determination, that doubt should

---

[138] *Re T (adult) (refusal of medical treatment)* [1992] 4 All ER 649, (1992) 9 BMLR 46, CA. Not to be confused with quite exceptional case of *NHS Trust v T (adult patient: refusal of medical treatment)* [2005] 1 All ER 387 where transfusion was refused because the patient thought her own blood was contaminating the transfused blood.

[139] The only possible qualification mentioned by Lord Donaldson—where the choice might lead to the death of a viable fetus—is discussed below at para 10.65 et seq.

[140] [1992] 4 All ER 649 at 653, (1992) 9 BMLR 46 at 50, per Lord Donaldson.

be resolved in favour of the preservation of life.[141] But an additional factor of great importance to the doctors was added when it was stated that the effects of outside influence on a patient's refusal have to be taken into consideration; in short, the question of whether the patient means what he or she says has to be posed—and whether the decision was reached independently after counselling and persuasion or whether the patient's will was overborne is a matter to be decided by the doctors. At first glance, this looks suspiciously like opening the door to involuntary treatment— that is, until one comes to Staughton LJ, who said:

I cannot find authority that the decision of a doctor as to the existence or refusal of consent is sufficient protection, if the law subsequently decides otherwise. So the medical profession ... must bear the responsibility unless it is possible to obtain a decision from the courts.[142]

10.57   Since this will be possible only rarely in an emergency, *Re T* seems to place a well-nigh intolerable burden on the doctors, not all of whom in the middle of the night will be of consultant status. What, for example, is the young houseman to make of Lord Donaldson:

... what the doctors *cannot* do is to conclude that, if the patient still had the necessary capacity in the changed situation [he being now unable to communicate], he would have reversed his decision ... What they *can* do is to consider whether at the time the decision was made it was intended by the patient to apply in the changed situation.[143]

One of us, at least, is grateful that he is no longer likely to be faced with an uncompleted suicide attempt in a busy casualty department! Even the law is undecided on the definition of undue influence and, again, neither Lord Donaldson[144] nor Butler-Sloss LJ[145] made it any easier by including parents and religious advisers among those who might, as a result of their relationship, lend themselves more readily than others to overbearing the patient's will. The law, in fact, seems to have comparatively little difficulty in discounting religious belief. T was considered to be, at best, an uncommitted Jehovah's Witness and we have Ward J in *Re E*[146] saying of a 15-year-old '*Gillick* competent' boy who was refusing blood transfusion: 'I respect this boy's

---

[141] For an example of the difficulty given a patient of marginal mental capacity, see C W Van Staden and C Kruger 'Incapacity to Give Informed Consent owing to Mental Disorder' (2003) 29 J Med Ethics 41. See, too, M A Jones and K Keywood 'Assessing the Patient's Competence to Consent to Medical Treatment' (1996) 2 Med Law Internat 107.

[142] [1992] 4 All ER 649 at 670, (1992) 9 BMLR 46 at 68. For an excellent analysis of undue influence, see *Centre for Reproductive Medicine v U* (2002) 65 BMLR 92, [2002] Lloyd's Rep Med 93; supported on appeal: [2002] EWCA Civ 565, and applied in *Evans v Amicus Healthcare Ltd and Others* [2004] 3 WLR 681, [2004] 3 All ER 1025, [2005] Fam 1.

[143] [1992] 4 All ER 649 at 662, (1992) 9 BMLR 46 at 60.

[144] [1992] 4 All ER 649 at 664, (1992) 9 BMLR 46 at 62.

[145] [1992] 4 All ER 649 at 667–668, (1992) 9 BMLR 46 at 65–66.

[146] *Re E (a minor)* [1993] 1 FLR 386, [1994] 5 Med LR 73. Ward J did say he wished to avoid notions of undue influence. Perhaps feelings are not as strong as they once were: 'of all influences religious influence is the most dangerous and powerful'—*Allcard v Skinner* (1887) 36 Ch D 145, [1886–90] All ER Rep 90 at 99–100, per Lindley LJ, referred to by Butler-Sloss LJ in *Re T* [1992] 4 All ER 649 at 667, (1992) 9 BMLR 46 at 65. *Allcard* was recently applied in *Pesticcio v Huet* [2004] EWCA Civ 372—though not in respect of religion.

profession of faith, but I cannot discount at least the possibility that he may in later years suffer some diminution in his convictions'.

10.58   The authority of *Re T* was applied shortly afterwards in the very interesting conditions of the case of *Re C*.[147] Despite being a decision at first instance only, the case is, nevertheless, extremely important in that it was the first in which the right to refuse treatment was respected by the United Kingdom courts. The case concerned a 68-year-old patient suffering from paranoid schizophrenia who had developed gangrene in a foot while serving a term of imprisonment in Broadmoor. On removal of the patient to a general hospital, a consultant prognosed that he had only a 15 per cent chance of survival if the gangrenous limb was not amputated below the knee.[148] The patient, however, refused the operation, saying that he preferred to die with two feet than to live with one. The hospital questioned C's capacity to exercise his autonomy in this way and an application for an injunction restraining the hospital from carrying out the operation without his express written consent was lodged with the court on C's behalf.

10.59   Thorpe J held that C was entitled to refuse the treatment even if this meant his death. Quoting with approval the dicta of Lord Donaldson in *Re T*, he stated that, prima facie, every adult has the right and capacity to accept or refuse medical treatment. He acknowledged that this might be rebutted by evidence of incapacity but this onus must be discharged by those seeking to override the patient's choice. When capacity is challenged, as in this case, its sufficiency is to be determined by the answer to the question: has the capacity of the patient been so reduced (by his chronic mental illness) that he did not sufficiently understand the nature, purpose and effects of the proffered medical treatment? This depends on whether the patient has been able to comprehend and retain information, has believed it and has weighed it in the balance with other considerations when making his or her choice. As Thorpe J said:

Applying that test to my findings on the evidence, I am completely satisfied that the presumption that C has the right to self-determination has not been displaced. Although his general capacity is impaired by schizophrenia, it has not been established that he does not sufficiently understand the nature, purpose and effects of the treatment he refuses. Indeed, I am satisfied that he has understood and retained the relevant treatment information, that in his own way he believes it, and that in the same fashion he has arrived at a clear choice.[149]

10.60   Several points of interest arise from this judgment. First, it reaffirms the commitment of the law to the principle of respect for patient autonomy.[150] There is a prima

---

[147] *Re C (adult: refusal of medical treatment)* [1994] 1 All ER 819, (1993) 15 BMLR 77.

[148] This was, however, averted by intervention short of amputation: [1994] 1 All ER 819 at 821, (1993) 15 BMLR 77 at 78–79.

[149] [1994] 1 All ER 819 at 824, (1993) 15 BMLR 77 at 82. A similar situation, but one involving a self-inflicted injury, is found in *Re W (Adult: Refusal of Medical Treatment)* [2002] EWHC 901. Butler-Sloss P held that a psychopathic prisoner with mental capacity on *Re C* terms could refuse treatment even though it might lead to his death.

[150] For a critique of the decision which doubts that it pays proper respect to patient autonomy, see M Stauch 'Rationality and the Refusal of Medical Treatment: A Critique of the Recent Approach of the English Courts' (1995) 21 J Med Ethics 162.

facie presumption of its existence and value which can only be overridden in established circumstances.[151] Furthermore, the particular facts of the case show that incapacity in one or several areas of one's life does not preclude autonomous behaviour in others, nor does it remove the presumption of competence to refuse. Indeed, the injunction obtained by the plaintiff extended not only to the particular operation contemplated by the hospital but to *all* future attempts to interfere with his bodily integrity without his express written consent. The importance of this should not be underestimated. In effect, it is tantamount to judicial recognition of the validity of advance refusals of treatment.[152] If, however, incapacity can ever be established, then, as we have seen, the patient must be dealt with in a manner which furthers his or her own best interests. In passing, it is important to note that both the notion of a presumption of capacity and the validity of advance directives have been put on a statutory footing under the Mental Capacity Act 2005.[153]

10.61 The judgment in *Re C*, however, suffers from its vagueness. A patient's competence can be successfully challenged if it can be shown that he does not comprehend or absorb information to the extent that he understands it or if he is thought not to believe the information or if he cannot balance this information against other considerations when making his choice. In this way, hurdles are placed in the path of those seeking to exercise their autonomy but, at the same time, it remains uncertain how high they must jump in order to clear these hurdles. For example, the requirement that the patient must actually comprehend the information is not easy to assess—it can depend as much on the amount of information which is given to the patient and the manner in which it is provided as on the capacity of the patient to understand. Yet, the test is not '*can* the patient understand?' but, rather, '*does* the patient understand?' This imposes an obligation on medical staff to ensure that actual understanding is reached and this, in itself, is paradoxical given that treatment staff might not want the patient to understand if they disagree with the nature of his or her decision—as in *Re C*. Many of these weaknesses can also be found in the Mental Capacity Act which largely reproduces the common law test.[154]

[151] For an alternative perspective on the relationship between autonomy and best interests, see A Buchanan 'Mental Capacity, Legal Competence and Consent to Treatment' (2004) 97 J of Royal Soc Med 415.

[152] Reaffirmed in *Re AK (medical treatment: consent)* [2001] 1 FLR 129, (2001) 58 BMLR 151. In *HE v A Hospital NHS Trust* [2003] 2 FLR 408 the court held that it is not necessary for an advance directive to be in writing in order to be valid, and, by corollary, revocation of any such directive can occur other than by written means. A provision purporting to make an advance directive valid for all time coming is contrary to public policy. Doubt over the continuing validity of an advance directive must be resolved in favour of life unless clear and convincing evidence is offered to the contrary. In the instant case, the patient's change of religious faith was enough to override her prior wishes. For the professional perspective, see British Medical Association *Code of Practice: Advance Statements about Medical Treatment* (2000), for updates on which visit the BMA website www.bma.org.uk.

[153] Mental Capacity Act 2005 s 1 (2) (presumption of capacity), and ss 24–26 (advance directives).

[154] The Mental Capacity Act defines incapacity in s 2 thus: '. . . a person lacks capacity in relation to a matter if at the material time he is unable to make a decision for himself in relation to the matter because of an impairment of, or a disturbance in the functioning of, the mind or brain'. S 3 continues that: '. . . a person is unable to make a decision for himself if he is unable—(a) to understand the information relevant to the

10.62   Nor is it exactly clear *what* the patient must understand in light of the *Re C* ruling. The decision talks of the 'nature, purpose and effects' of the treatment. This is potentially very broad and can encompass elements ranging from the general aim of the procedure to the risks and the consequences of refusal and beyond. Arguably, as Grubb has pointed out, the category of 'autonomous persons' is reduced to only the most 'comprehending' individuals if excessive amounts of information are required to be disclosed and understood.[155]

10.63   The general trend of the common law was ultimately confirmed in *Re B (adult: refusal of medical treatment)*.[156] Ms B was a 43-year-old patient who was paralysed from the neck down and sustained only by means of a ventilator. Ms B refused this intervention shortly after it was introduced but she was adjudged incompetent to do so by two psychiatrists in April 2001. She was, however, declared competent by an independent clinician in August of that year and, thereafter, the hospital treated her as such. Nevertheless, her attending physicians refused to remove the ventilator, advocating instead that their patient attend a rehabilitation unit which offered a slim chance of improvement in her condition. Ms B rejected this course of action and repeated her refusal on several occasions. Ultimately, the President of the Family Division attended Ms B's bedside to hear her story. In a poignant ruling, Butler-Sloss P reiterated the fundamental principles that now govern this area, namely, that a competent patient has an absolute right to refuse treatment irrespective of the consequences of her decision, and she issued very clear guidance to health care professionals as to their responsibilities in such cases. These include keeping the patient as involved in the decision-making process as possible, moving to resolve any dispute as promptly as practicable and finding other clinicians to undertake the course of action if the primary carers feel unable to do so.[157] Perhaps most striking of all, notional damages of £100 were awarded in recognition of the technical assault that the health carers had committed by continuing to treat Ms B against her wishes.[158]

10.64   Straightforward as this may seem, these cases have to be read in conjunction with others in which the autonomy of the patient has been overridden and their right to choose for themselves has been denied.

decision, (b) to retain that information, (c) to use or weigh that information as part of the process of making the decision, or (d) to communicate his decision (whether by talking, using sign language or any other means). A broadly similar functional definition is contained in the Adults with Incapacity (Scotland) Act 2000, s 1(6).

[155] See A Grubb 'Commentary' (1994) 2 Med L Rev 92 at 95.

[156] Sub nom *B v NHS Hospital Trust* [2002] 2 All ER 449, (2002) 65 BMLR 149. We return to this case in chapter 16.

[157] Although note now the reservations of Charles J in *NHS Trust v T*, para 10.37 above.

[158] For general comment see, Special Clinical Ethics Symposium: 'The Case of Ms B' (2002) 28 J Med Ethics 232.

REFUSAL OF TREATMENT IN LATE PREGNANCY

10.65   The decision of the Court of Appeal in *Re T* was not without its caveats. Lord Donaldson said:

An adult patient who . . . suffers from no mental incapacity has an absolute right to choose whether to consent to medical treatment, to refuse it or to choose one rather than another of the treatments being offered. *The only possible qualification is a case in which the choice may lead to the death of a viable fetus.*[159]

10.66   This 'possible qualification' was tested in the soon-to-follow decision of *Re S*,[160] in which a health authority applied for a declaration to authorise the surgeons and staff of a hospital to carry out an emergency caesarian section on a 30-year-old woman who was in spontaneous labour with her third child. The woman refused to submit to a section on religious grounds. The surgeon in charge was adamant that both patient and baby would die without such intervention. After six days of Mrs S's labour, the health authority sought a judgment from the High Court. The decision of Sir Stephen Brown is approximately one page in length, one half of which is concerned with relating the facts, and there is little or no legal argument or analysis in the judgment whereby the declaration was agreed. As the President said:

I [make the declaration] in the knowledge that the fundamental question appears to have been left open by Lord Donaldson MR in *Re T* . . ., and in the knowledge that there is no English authority which is directly in point.

10.67   But it was precisely this lack of precedental authority which provoked major criticism of *Re S* in so far as the case, with all its jurisprudential limitations, bid fair to *provide* that authority. But the problems thus generated were both manifold and manifest. First, the decision was based wholly on the medical evidence. There was no discussion of how the competency of a woman to make such a choice was to be assessed. How would the choice by a woman in S's position be validated? Secondly, when Lord Donaldson spoke of a 'viable' fetus, he was speaking in relative rather than absolute terms—for viability results from a combination of gestational age and obstetric expertise.[161] At what stage, therefore, would it regarded as legally acceptable to enforce the operation? Thirdly, we have to ask what importance a court should place on the danger to the life of the woman herself? Strictly speaking, this should have no influence for, as was said in *Re T* and now confirmed in *Re B*, the right to decide whether or not to accept treatment persists even if refusal will lead to premature death. Yet we still believe that it is asking a great deal of the health care team to stand by and watch their patient die a painful death and it is probable that such

---

[159] [1992] 4 All ER 649 at 652–653, (1992) 9 BMLR 46 at 50, emphasis added.

[160] *Re S (adult: refusal of medical treatment)* [1992] 4 All ER 671, (1992) 9 BMLR 69. This case was decided only two and a half months after *Re T*.

[161] See e.g. the American case *Re AC* 573 A 2d 1235 (DC, 1990) where the enforced caesarian section of a 26-week-old fetus ended, almost predictably, with the death of the neonate within hours.

considerations were in the mind of the President when he was confronted with an emergency situation.[162] Finally, the decision depended on very doubtful logic in that it was, and is, well-established law that the fetus in utero has no rights of its own and has no distinct human personality.[163] If, then, we look upon an enforced caesarian as a means of resolving a conflict between a woman who is refusing treatment and a fetus who seeks it,[164] there is, in sporting terms, effectively 'no contest'—there can be no valid reason behind isolating this particular situation as the one occasion on which the fetus achieves legal dominance over its mother. While we have great sympathy with the President in the particular circumstances of *Re S*, it is hard to see his decision as other than logically and legally untenable.

10.68   None the less, it appeared for a time as though *Re S* had, indeed, set a precedent and, despite fierce criticism of the ruling,[165] the English courts proceeded in *Norfolk and Norwich Healthcare (NHS) Trust v W*[166] and *Tameside and Glossop Acute Services Trust v CH (a patient)*[167] to impose caesarian sections on women against their will. Indeed, in the latter case it was held that the performance of a caesarian section on a schizophrenic woman could be 'treatment' of her mental disorder within the terms of the Mental Health Act 1983.

10.69   The relationship between a pregnant woman and her fetus was, however, fully reconsidered by the Court of Appeal in *Re MB*.[168] The court was adamant in its ruling that a woman carrying a fetus is entitled to the same degree of respect for her wishes as is anyone else and reiterated the general principle that a person of full age and sound mind cannot be treated against his or her will without the door being opened to civil and criminal legal consequences. It also endorsed strongly the view that a refusal of medical treatment can be for any reason, rational or irrational, or for no reason at all. In particular, it was stressed that circumstances in which non-voluntary treatment is permissible arise only when the patient cannot give consent and when treatment is in the *patient's* best interests. The court has no jurisdiction to declare medical intervention lawful when a *competent* pregnant woman decides to refuse treatment, *even though* this might result in the death or serious handicap of the fetus

---

[162] For some judicial sympathy, see Major J dissenting in *Winnipeg Child and Family Services (Northwestern) v GDF* [1997] 2 SCR 925: 'Where the harm is so great and the temporary remedy so slight, the law is compelled to act . . . Someone must speak for those who cannot speak for themselves.'

[163] The offence of child destruction is not engaged as the Infant Life (Preservation) Act 1929 requires intention to kill the child-to-be. We know of no precedent whereby the mother could be charged with the offence.

[164] One need not, however, always approach the problem as one which necessarily involves a conflict: see J Mair 'Maternal/Foetal Conflict: Defined or Diffused?' in S A M McLean (ed) *Contemporary Issues in Law, Medicine and Ethics* (1996) ch 5.

[165] See eg A Grubb 'Commentary on *Re S*' (1993) 1 Med L Rev 92.

[166] [1996] 2 FLR 613, (1996) 34 BMLR 16. The same judge made a similar decision in *Rochdale Healthcare (NHS) Trust v C* [1997] 1 FCR 274.

[167] [1996] 1 FLR 762, (1996) 31 BMLR 93. For analysis see A Grubb 'Commentary' (1996) 4 Med L Rev 193. An interesting selection of views is to be found under the general heading 'Caesarian Section: A Treatment for Mental Disorder?' (1997) 314 BMJ 1183.

[168] *Re MB (an adult: medical treatment)* [1997] 8 Med LR 217, (1997) 38 BMLR 175, CA.

she is bearing. The question of the woman's own best interests *does not arise* in such circumstances. On the facts of the particular case, however, the pregnant woman was declared incompetent because of a fear of needles which had led her to refuse the operation—but, at the end of the day, she consented and a healthy child was delivered.

10.70   This decision clearly places the autonomy of the woman above any interests of the fetus, including an interest in being born alive.[169] Yet, it is important to bear in mind that all of this is subject to the woman being competent when she makes her refusal. If she is not, she must be treated in her best interests. In the particular circumstances of *Re MB*, the assessment that the operation was in her best interests is open to little question; both the woman and her husband wanted the child to be born—subject to her needle phobia. However, it still remains open to speculation how the patient's best interests should be assessed if there is no clear indication of how the mother feels about the birth. In the final analysis, *Re MB* does little to remove from the medical profession the discretion and power to decide on a patient's capacity to act autonomously—and ultimately, in cases of incapacity, to decide on the patient's best interests.

10.71   This discretion was not removed by the last case in this current line of authority that we intend to discuss,[170] although the Court of Appeal's ruling in *St George's Healthcare NHS Trust v S (Guidelines), R v Collins, ex p S (No. 2)*[171] does provide helpful guidance for health care professionals who must decide on the capacity of a patient to consent to or refuse treatment. The case concerned S, a 36-year-old pregnant woman with pre-eclampsia who was advised that she would require to be admitted. Fully cognisant of the risks, and wishing her baby to be born naturally, S refused. As a consequence, she was seen by a social worker and two doctors and admitted to a mental hospital for assessment. On her transfer to another hospital a declaration was sought and granted to dispense with S's consent and the baby was delivered by caesarian section. S discharged herself and appealed against the declaration.

10.72   The Court of Appeal upheld its ruling in *Re MB* to the extent that a mentally competent pregnant woman has the absolute right to refuse medical intervention. The actions of the hospital were a trespass and the former declaration was set aside accordingly. Moreover, the court castigated the use of the mental health legislation to treat an otherwise healthy woman:

> The Act cannot be deployed to achieve the detention of an individual against her will merely because her thinking process is unusual, even apparently bizarre and irrational, and contrary to the views of the overwhelming majority of the community at large.

---

[169] For consideration of whether a human rights analysis might strengthen the legal position of the fetus, see G T Laurie, 'Medical Law and Human Rights: Passing the Parcel Back to the Profession?' in A Boyle et al (eds) *Human Rights and Scots Law: Comparative Perspectives on the Incorporation of the ECHR* (2002).

[170] *St George's Healthcare NHS Trust v S, R v Collins, ex p S* [1998] 3 All ER 673, (1998) 44 BMLR 160. In a later case, *Bolton Hospitals NHS Trust v O* [2003] 1 FLR 824, [2003] Fam Law 319, Butler-Sloss followed *Re MB* in re-stating the principles but still finding a woman with post traumatic stress temporarily incompetent due to panic induced by flash-backs. The case adds nothing to the established jurisprudence.

[171] [1999] Fam 26, (1998) 44 BMLR 194.

10.73   Thus, the position of the pregnant woman of sound mind has been brought into
        line with the 'adult of sound mind' referred to in *Re T*. More significantly, the Court
        of Appeal sought to prevent a repeat of this case and, indeed, others involving the
        treatment of patients of doubtful capacity, and issued guidelines for future reference.
        These are of considerable importance and we repeat them here for the sake of
        completeness:

   (i)   The guidelines have no application where the patient is competent to accept
         or refuse treatment. In principle, a patient may remain competent notwith-
         standing detention under the Mental Health Act 1983.

   (ii) An application to the High Court for a declaration will be pointless if the
         patient is competent and refuses consent to the treatment. In this situation the
         advice given to the patient should be recorded. For their own protection,
         hospital authorities should seek unequivocal assurances from the patient (to
         be recorded in writing) that the refusal represents an informed decision: that
         is that she understands the nature of and reasons for the proposed treatment
         and the risks and likely prognosis involved in the decision to refuse or accept
         it. If the patient is unwilling to sign a written indication of this refusal, this
         too should be noted in writing. Such a written indication is merely a record
         for evidential purposes. It should not be confused with or regarded as a
         disclaimer.

   (iii) If the patient is incapable of giving or refusing consent, either in the long term
         or temporarily (eg due to unconsciousness), the patient must be cared for
         according to the authority's judgment of the patient's best interests. Where the
         patient has given an advance directive, before becoming incapable, treatment
         and care should normally be subject to the advance directive. However, if
         there is reason to doubt the reliability of the advance directive (e.g. it may
         sensibly be thought not to apply to the circumstances which have arisen), then
         an application for a declaration may be made.

   (iv) The authority should identify as soon as possible whether there is concern
         about a patient's competence to consent to or refuse treatment.

   (v)   If the capacity of the patient is seriously in doubt, it should be assessed as a
         matter of priority. In many such cases, the patient's general practitioner or
         other responsible doctor may be sufficiently qualified to make the necessary
         assessment but, in serious or complex cases involving difficult issues about the
         future health and well-being or even the life of the patient, the issue of capacity
         should be examined by an independent psychiatrist, ideally one approved
         under s 12(2) of the Mental Health Act 1983. If, following this assessment
         there remains a serious doubt about the patient's competence, and the ser-
         iousness or complexity of the issues in the particular case may require the
         involvement of the court, the psychiatrist should further consider whether the
         patient is incapable by reason of mental disorder of managing her property or

affairs. If so the patient may be unable to instruct a solicitor and will require a guardian ad litem in any court proceedings. The authority should seek legal advice as quickly as possible. If a declaration is to be sought, the patient's solicitors should be informed immediately and, if practicable, they should have a proper opportunity to take instructions and apply for legal aid where necessary. Potential witnesses for the authority should be made aware of the criteria laid down in *Re MB* and this case, together with any guidance issued by the Department of Health and the British Medical Association.

(vi) If the patient is unable to instruct solicitors, or is believed to be incapable of doing so, the authority or its legal advisers must notify the Official Solicitor and invite him to act as guardian ad litem. If the Official Solicitor agrees he will no doubt wish, if possible, to arrange for the patient to be interviewed to ascertain her wishes and to explore the reasons for any refusal of treatment.

(vii) The hearing before the judge should be inter partes. A declaration granted ex parte is of no assistance to the authority as the order made in her absence will not be binding on the patient unless she is represented either by a guardian ad litem, if incapable of giving instructions, or, if capable, by counsel or solicitor. Although the Official Solicitor will not act for a patient if she is capable of instructing a solicitor, the court may in any event call on the Official Solicitor, who has considerable expertise in these matters, to assist as an amicus curiae.

(viii) It is axiomatic that the judge must be provided with accurate and all the relevant information. This should include the reasons for the proposed treatment, the risks involved in the proposed treatment, and in not proceeding with it, whether any alternative treatment exists, and the reason, if ascertainable, why the patient is refusing the proposed treatment. The judge will need sufficient information to reach an informed conclusion about the patient's capacity and, where it arises, the issue of best interest.

(ix) The precise terms of any order should be recorded and approved by the judge before its terms are transmitted to the authority. The patient should be accurately informed of the precise terms.

(x) Applicants for emergency orders from the High Court made without first issuing and serving the relevant applications and evidence in support have a duty to comply with the procedural requirements (and pay the court fees) as soon as possible after the urgency hearing.

10.74   Detailed though these guidelines are, it is noteworthy that they concern, primarily, procedural matters—the court was clearly disinclined to interfere in clinical matters. Indeed, it emphasised that they were, at the end of the day, guidelines only and advised that rigid compliance with them was inappropriate if to do so would put the patient's health or life at risk. The ball thus remains firmly in the health carers' court—subject, of course, to its being played according to the rules. A significant feature of the case, however, lies in its challenge to the use of mental health legislation as a means of legitimising involuntary treatment. A trend in such a use had, in fact, been emerging in the lead up to this ruling, not only in relation to pregnant women, but also in the context of anorexics—whose management is discussed below.[172]

10.75 The experience of other jurisdictions in the maternal/fetal context has varied. In the United States, the issue has been affected by political pressure for the symbolic protection of the fetus—in the fiercely contested context of abortion—but this has been met by strong libertarian objections to interfering with maternal freedom during pregnancy.[173] The exemplar case is *Re AC*,[174] where a caesarian section was ordered against the wishes of a moribund woman suffering from malignant disease in an attempt to salvage a 26-week-old fetus—the mother survived only long enough to see her baby die in a matter of hours. Brahams noted that the case should sound a warning bell to all interventionists in Britain; the majority of commentators adopted a similarly cautious approach to the subject on the grounds, among others, that it is nearly impossible to balance the benefits to the fetus against the reasonableness of withheld consent, that unwanted intervention must injure the maternal doctor-patient relationship and that the standards of enforcement would be inequitable. This view was vindicated by the District of Columbia Appeal Court, where the court vacated the judgment in *Re AC* and, by a 7:1 majority, held that the right to informed consent encompassed a right to informed refusal of treatment; in this respect, a fetus cannot have rights superior to those of a person who has already been born. Even so, the door was not quite shut:

We do not quite foreclose the possibility that a conflicting State interest may be so compelling that the patient's interest must yield but we anticipate that such cases will be extremely rare and truly exceptional.[175]

10.76 The circumstances in *Re AC* were special—involving a dying woman carrying a barely viable fetus—but the political climate has changed considerably in the United States since the ruling; conservativism and sanctity of life are now very much the order of the day. The case may therefore be of more value for its representative nature of the dilemmas that can arise rather than for its weight as any kind of precedent.

10.77 In other jurisdictions with differing political trends, such as Canada, the view is very firmly taken that caesarian section is a seriously invasive technique and the consequences for pregnant women of forced interventions are too serious to

---

[172] See para 10.80.

[173] For a comparative survey, see B J Glass 'A Comparative Analysis of the Right of a Pregnant Woman to Refuse Medical Treatment for Herself or her Viable Fetus: the United States and the United Kingdom' (2001) 11 Indiana Int Comp L Rev 507.

[174] *Re AC* 533 A 2d 611 (DC, 1987). For discussion, see D Brahams 'A Baby's Life or a Mother's Liberty: A United States Case' (1988) 56 Med-leg J 156; M A Field 'Controlling the Woman to Protect the Fetus' (1989) 17 Law Med Hlth Care 114.

[175] *In re AC* 573 A 2d 1235 (DC, 1990), per Terry J. See D Brahams 'Enforced Caesarian Section: A US Appeal' (1990) 58 Med-leg J 164. For a pragmatic defence of coerced caesarians, see F A Chervenak, L B McCullough and D W Skupski 'An Ethical Justification for Emergency, Coerced Cesarean Delivery' (1993) 82 Obst Gynecol 1029.

contemplate. This perspective carried the day in the important decision of the Canadian Supreme Court in *Winnipeg Child and Family Services (Northwest Area) v GDF*,[176] the effect of which has been to dampen enthusiasm for intervening on behalf of the fetus.

OTHER VULNERABLE GROUPS

10.78   It is everywhere agreed that, to be valid, consent should be free and unfettered; unwarranted coercion may be by others or by circumstance, including environment. In this last respect, prisoners therefore constitute a further group which deserves special consideration.

10.79   The status of prisoners has been referred to briefly in chapter 1. It will be seen from this that it could be held that the incarcerated can never give a valid consent to treatment in that an element of coercion is implicit in the prison doctor-patient relationship. This proposition was considered in *Freeman*,[177] the decision in which greatly restricts this line of argument. The case turned in large measure on its own facts but the suggestion that the position of the prison psychiatrist vis-à-vis his patient voided a general consent was rejected; it was further stated that 'it was not open for it to be argued for the plaintiff that "informed consent" was a consideration which could be entertained by the courts'. While we believe that this latter opinion derived from a semantic misinterpretation of the concept which is discussed in detail below, the judgment clearly indicates that, in the absence of overt coercion, the restricted circumstances in which a prisoner's consent to treatment is given will be unlikely to affect the validity of that consent in law. An action for trespass is open to those in detention when consent to treatment has not been given[178] but mere negligence in obtaining that consent[179] will not brand the trespass as being coercive or oppressive. As an example of a valid refusal on the part of a prisoner, we have the judgment in *Secretary of State for the Home Department v Robb*,[180] a case which raised the question of whether the decision of a prisoner to go on hunger strike should be respected by the prison authorities. Somewhat unorthodoxly, the court applied a medical law approach to the case, even although the prisoner was not a patient, and upheld the individual's 'right to self-determination' to refuse food. In contrast, the attempt by the multiple murderer Ian Brady to starve himself to death was thwarted by the High Court when it refused his application for judicial review of the medical decision to force-feed him on the grounds that his personality disorder made him refuse food and therefore 'feeding' was treatment for his mental condition within the terms of the

---

[176] N 76 above. For discussion, see L Shanner 'Case Comment and Note' (1998) 36 Alberta L Rev 751.
[177] *Freeman v Home Office (No. 2)* [1984] QB 524, [1984] 1 All ER 1036.
[178] *Barbara v Home Office* (1984) 134 NLJ 888.   [179] See paras 10.94 et seq.
[180] [1995] 1 All ER 677.

Mental Health Act 1983.[181] This latter case is better considered in the context of that legislation, and we do so in chapter 20.

10.80   Another series of cases has similarly sanctioned the force-feeding of persons such as anorexics and depressives who refuse food. The rationale in each case has been that the feeding is *treatment* for the individual's *mental disorder*, this being the sole criterion under the legislation which permits health care professionals to forego consent.[182] Thus, for example, the trial judge in *Riverside Mental Health Trust v Fox*[183] held that an adult who was being treated for anorexia nervosa could be force-fed as a part of treatment for her mental condition. The Court of Appeal later overturned this decision but did so on procedural grounds and did not question the validity of the application of the 1983 Act to such a case. As if to endorse this line of reasoning, the Court of Appeal in *B v Croydon Health Authority*[184] authorised force-feeding under the 1983 Act of a woman with a borderline personality disorder, and feeding of a depressive and suicidal quinquagenarian was similarly ordered in *Re VS (adult: mental disorder).*[185] In *Re C (detention: medical treatment)*[186] an anorexic 16-year-old was detained using the High Court's inherent protective jurisdiction in order that she receive 'medical treatment' including, inter alia, force-feeding. This unusual procedure was justified as being in the child's best interests on the grounds that, because it was in her best interests to receive 'treatment' for her condition, it was also a part of those interests that she be detained—using reasonable force if necessary—so that the treatment could be carried out. It is to be noted that this order was not based on the detention provisions of the 1983 Act but, rather, on the common law powers of the High Court—which suggests that this jurisdiction is potentially very wide-ranging. Another interesting point is the use by Walls J of the three-stage test for competency laid down in *Re C (adult: refusal of medical treatment).*[187] That case concerned the competency of an adult. As we have seen, the capacity of a minor to agree to or refuse medical treatment has relied up until now on the concept of *Gillick* competence, the evaluation of which lies within the discretion of the health care professional. This equiparation of the test for competency in adults and minors is, in our view, correct, and adds judicial weight to our earlier argument that refusal of treatment by minors requires a higher standard of competency than does a decision to consent.[188]

10.81   Bearing in mind the different ambiences of an NHS and a special hospital, all of this must now be seen in light of the Court of Appeal decision in *R (on the application*

---

[181] *R v Collins, ex p Brady* (2000) 58 BMLR 173, [2000] Lloyd's Rep Med 355.

[182] In particular, Mental Health Act 1983, s 63.   [183] [1994] 1 FLR 614, (1993) 20 BMLR 1.

[184] [1995] 1 All ER 683, CA. The seminal case of *Re W (a minor) (medical treatment)* [1992] 4 All ER 627 is discussed at para 10.50 above.

[185] [1995] 3 Med L Rev 292.   [186] [1997] 2 FLR 180, [1997] Fam Law 474.

[187] Para 10.58 above.

[188] In the context of minors the Scottish courts seem not to agree with us. In *Re Houston, Applicant* (1996) 32 BMLR 93, Sheriff McGown interpreted s 2(4) of the Age of Legal Capacity (Scotland) Act 1991 in respect of a 15-year-old boy suffering from mental illness to mean that capacity to consent encompassed a capacity to refuse and, furthermore, it brings to an end the power of a parent to consent on behalf of the minor.

of Wilkinson) v RMO, Broadmoor Hospital Authority[189] which revisited these decisions in the shadow of the Human Rights Act, and emphasised procedural requirements before such treatment can be embarked upon properly. As Hale LJ said:

> Whatever the position before the Human Rights Act 1998, the decision to impose treatment without consent upon a protesting patient is a potential invasion of his rights under article 3 or article 8. Super-*Wednesbury* is not enough. The claimant is entitled to a proper hearing, on the merits, of whether the statutory grounds for imposing this treatment upon him against his will are made out: i.e. whether it is treatment for the mental disorder from which he is suffering and whether it should be given to him without his consent 'having regard to the likelihood of its alleviating or preventing a deterioration of his condition'.[190]

CONSENT TO TESTING FOR HIV INFECTION

10.82   The question of whether tests for HIV infection can be undertaken without the express consent of the patient has always been controversial.[191] There may be times when a doctor would wish to carry out such tests as part of a responsible diagnostic routine but, at the same time, be reluctant to alarm or embarrass his patient by disclosing his intention. Equally, the HIV status of a patient might be an issue after a needle-stick injury or blood contamination of medical personnel; the need to know could be urgent, yet the patient might refuse to consent to testing. Indeed, in 2002 the Royal College of Surgeons called for the right to test patients for HIV.[192] The legal problems are the same in each instance: does HIV testing exceed the bounds of any consent which the patient has already given to therapeutic or diagnostic investigation? Can such testing ever be performed *without* consent?

10.83   The GMC believes that specific consent to testing for HIV infection is required because of the serious social and financial consequences that may follow a positive diagnosis; every patient should have the opportunity to evaluate these consequences as they affect him personally. The Council has, accordingly, firmly rejected HIV testing in the absence of specific consent save in the 'most exceptional circumstances'.[193]

---

[189] [2001] EWCA Civ 1545, [2002] 1 WLR 419, (2001) 65 BMLR 15.

[190] *Ibid*, at para 83. See also, *R (on the application of Wooder) v Feggetter* [2002] EWCA Civ 554, [2002] 3 WLR 591, in which it was held that adequate written reasons to give a detained patient medication against his will must be produced by a second opinion doctor under the Mental Health Act 1983, and that these should be disclosed to the patient except in the rare circumstances where this would have an adverse effect on his physical or mental health. *Wilkinson* has most recently been applied in *R (on the application of B) v SS* [2005] EWHC 86.

[191] See K M Boyd 'HIV Infection: The Ethics of Anonymised Testing and of Testing Pregnant Women' (1990) 16 J Med Ethics 173. The position in the US, where AIDS is a notifiable disease, and elsewhere, may well be different and is not considered here. For general discussion of blood testing, see A Grubb and D S Pearl *Blood Testing, AIDS and DNA Profiling: Law and Policy* (1990).

[192] A Browne 'Surgeons Demand Right to Test Patients for HIV Infection' *The Times*, 29 July 2002, p 3.

[193] General Medical Council *Serious Communicable Diseases* (1997).

At the same time, the GMC is quite clear that non-consensual testing is permissible if it is in the patient's medical interests to do so. It is more vague on the position regarding testing in the interests of others, urging simply that a practitioner should 'reconsider the severity of risk' to himself or others. The Council does agree, however, that the best interests of a child may dictate testing even in the face of parental objection. We return to the position of the child below.

10.84   Advice from such a source carries great ethical weight but does not help as to the legality of such testing. Here, conflicting advice has been offered to doctors in the United Kingdom. Legal opinion sought by the Council of the British Medical Association was to the effect that, not only was non-consensual testing impermissible but also, to do so, might well constitute an assault;[194] by contrast, the Central Committee for Hospital Medical Services was advised that the doctor may exercise his clinical judgment unless the patient asks specifically about HIV testing;[195] finally, the Medical Defence Union obtained an opinion which eliminated the possibility of assault once permission for venepuncture had been given but, nevertheless, thought that, save in exceptional circumstances—as, for instance when the expectation of a positive result was very low—specific consent for HIV should always be obtained.[196]

10.85   It is significant that much has changed in relation to HIV and AIDS since these opinions were proffered. Where once HIV was untreatable, combination therapy now provides significant hope for many people infected with the virus. Moreover, there is less evidence of a special case being made of the disease, as is demonstrated by the GMC's Guidance which relates to serious communicable diseases generally whereas once it spoke only of HIV and AIDS.[197] Indeed, as we go to press a controversial debate is on-going on the internet pages of the British Medical Journal, sparked by an article by Edinburgh colleagues claiming that 'HIV exceptionalism' is no longer sustainable and that the practice of requiring specific and relatively lengthy counselling may actually be deterring patients from being tested.[198] The electronic 'rapid responses' to this article on the website[199] fall fairly evenly on both sides of the argument; on the one hand there are pragmatists who point to the World Health Organization's (WHO) revised policy calling for HIV testing to become a routine part of health care provision,[200] while others insist that so long as social stigma and the

---

[194] M Sharrard and I Gatt 'Human Immunodeficiency Virus (HIV) Antibody Testing' (1987) 295 BMJ 911.

[195] HMSC Advice re HIV Testing (1988) discussed by C Dyer 'Another Judgment on Testing for HIV Without Consent' (1988) 296 BMJ 1791.

[196] Medical Defence Union AIDS: Medico-Legal Advice (1988). These three opinions are discussed in detail by J Keown 'The Ashes of AIDS and the Phoenix of Informed Consent' (1989) 52 MLR 790.

[197] For support for this process, see K M De Cock and A M Johnson, 'From Exceptionalism to Normalisation: A Reappraisal of Attitudes and Practice Around HIV Testing' (1998) 316 BMJ 290.

[198] K Manavi and P D Welsby 'HIV Testing Should No Longer Be Accorded Any Special Status' (2005) 330 BMJ 492.

[199] British Medical Journal: www.bmj.com.

[200] World Health Organization 'The Right to Know: New Approaches to HIV Testing and Counselling' (2003).

possibility of discrimination remain, so should a distinct approach to HIV testing. Certainly, the WHO recognises these adverse possibilities in its recent policy statement which calls for a 'human rights approach' to HIV testing and counselling, the cornerstone of which remains informed consent.[201]

10.86   We take the view that a patient who consults a doctor gives tacit consent to the carrying out of those diagnostic tests that the doctor considers necessary—the patient's consent to each and every test to be performed on a blood sample need not be obtained and it is unreal to speak of 'informed consent' in this context. This is not a unique view—as Dyer has reported: 'some lawyers have suggested that patients with a "perplexing presentation" might be taken to have given an implied consent to any tests designed to find out what was wrong with them'.[202] The essential question is whether the HIV test is of such a nature as to remove it from the scope of those tests to which the patient may be said to consent implicitly. It is true that HIV tests carry major emotional, financial and social significance; moreover, while the disease process can be contained, the full-blown condition is probably still incurable—which distinguishes the test from one for, e.g. syphilis. The same could, however, be said for a hypothetical test which demonstrated the presence of incurable malignant disease. It would not be necessary for the doctor to obtain specific consent to undertake such a test, yet it could have consequences similar to a test for HIV infection. The similarity is, however, not absolute—the major distinction being that, irrespective of the result, the mere fact that an HIV test has been undertaken can carry serious insurance implications and has to be disclosed as a condition of many policies. We would raise, too, the potential psychological sequelae of an unexpected positive result which do not only relate to the future *health* implications of testing positive. There is no escaping the fact that our society has constructed a stigma around this disease which, even in today's more understanding climate, makes the confirmation of a positive result all the more difficult to accept. Moreover, if such a result comes 'from the blue' when no specific consent was given, the question of the patient's right *not* to know arises.[203] These factors certainly constitute grounds for treating the HIV test with special care but it is doubtful if it is a sufficiently powerful argument to exclude absolutely all testing for which no specific consent was given. None the less, the patient could argue that, had he been informed of the doctor's intention, he would not have consented to giving the sample; in such circumstances, an action for negligence might be available under the general terms of the consent doctrine.[204] The critical condition, here, is that he was informed—insurance and comparable complicating factors do not arise if the

---

[201] UNAIDS/WHO Policy Statement on HIV Testing (2004). The Statement opines: 'HIV testing without consent may be justified in the rare circumstances in which a patient is unconscious, his or her guardian is absent, and knowledge of HIV status is necessary for purposes of optimal treatment'.

[202] C Dyer 'Testing for HIV: The Medico-legal View' (1987) 295 BMJ 871. D Brahams 'Human Immunodeficiency Virus and the Law' [1987] 2 Lancet 227 shared our view so long as consent to test for HIV infection had not been specifically withheld. The issue of HIV testing is discussed extensively in R Bennett and C Erin (eds) *HIV and AIDS: Testing, Screening and Confidentiality* (1999).

[203] Discussed in the context of genetic information in chapter 7.   [204] See paras 10.94 et seq.

patient is ignorant of the facts. The professional attitude is summed up by the reported case in which a doctor was found guilty of serious professional misconduct for testing five patients for HIV without consent.[205] The GMC found that there was insufficient clinical evidence of infection in each patient, indicating, perhaps, that matters might be different were it otherwise. However, the practitioner must be prepared to justify his action, both in court and before his peers, in all cases of non-consensual testing.

10.87   We stated above that the position of the child is somewhat different. Thus, we have *Re HIV Tests (Note)*[206] from 1994—a period when there was no effective treatment for HIV infection—wherein the procedural safeguard was established that 'for the time being', and because of the 'whole range of emotional and psychological and practical problems which bear on the question', applications to determine whether HIV testing was in a child's best interests should always be considered by the High Court in the first instance. As to the nature of best interests in these cases, we then have the decision of *Re C (a child) (HIV test)*[207] in 1999, when the court held that the medical case for testing was now very strong—combination therapy having been introduced in 1996—and that the overall best interests of the child were overwhelmingly in favour of knowing her status even despite the opposition to testing of both parents. The court stated that as a matter of law there is a rebuttable presumption that the 'united appraisal' of both parents would normally be enough to correctly identify where the welfare interests of their child lay, and that the law would be reluctant to interfere in most cases; not least because such interference might itself fundamentally undermine the parent/child relationship.[208] But, in the instant case,[209] all of the evidence pointed in the opposite direction.[210] Finally, and most recently, we have yet another evolution in thinking, this time from the President of the Family Division of the High Court herself.[211] The President's Direction of 2003 reflects growing judicial experience in the course of the previous decade and it indicates that it is now no longer necessary to take a child HIV testing case to the High Court. This will only be so if the inherent jurisdiction of the court is being invoked or if a mature minor is refusing the test and parties seek to override such refusal. Moreover, if all those with parental responsibility agree to testing, and there is no opposition from the child, then no reference to court is required at all. Helpful practical guidance in respect of all minors is now provided by the Department of Health.[212]

---

[205] C Dyer 'GP reprimanded for testing patients for HIV without consent' (2000) 320 BMJ 135.

[206] [1994] 2 FLR 116, [1994] Fam Law 559.

[207] [2000] 2 WLR 270, [1999] 3 FCR 289, 50 BMLR 283.

[208] *Re T*, para 10.25 above, was quoted with approval.

[209] It should be borne in mind that an assessment of best interests must always be on a case-by-case basis—it does not follow from this case, therefore, that it will *always* be in a child's best interests to test for HIV.

[210] In it interesting to note in passing that the court refused to come 'between baby and breast' and would not order that the mother desist from breast-feeding her child. Such an order was thought to be futile and an unacceptable invasion of liberty/privacy interests.

[211] *President's Direction: HIV Testing of Children* [2003] 1 FLR 1299.

[212] Department of Health *Children in Need and Blood-Borne Viruses: HIV and Hepatitis* (2004).

10.88   All the above discussion relates to consent within the clinical setting and the patient's advantage; there can, in our opinion, be no vacillation if the advantage of testing is to another party—express consent would have to be obtained in such circumstances and action in its absence would have to be defended on the grounds of necessity or public interest.

10.89   In the earlier days of the pandemic, there were calls in some quarters for mandatory HIV testing; these were largely rejected, although a number of jurisdictions did introduce compulsory testing programmes for sections of the public. The World Health Organization has been firm in its condemnation of such measures, pointing out that there are 'no benefits either to the individual or for public health arising from testing without informed consent that cannot be achieved by less intrusive means, such as voluntary testing and counselling'.[213] In spite of this, and similar endorsements of the voluntary approach to HIV testing, there has been a creeping tendency in some countries to allow compulsory testing of particular groups—such as military recruits, job applicants or for immigration purposes.[214] In some US jurisdictions, for example, legislation has been introduced allowing testing in the health care environment (for the protection of health care staff) or in prisons (for the protection of prison officials).[215] But nor should it be thought that patients' rights are necessarily protected by the need to obtain informed consent. This, for example, is the legal position in Argentina in respect of job applicants. Consent to testing is required as a matter of law,[216] but a recent human rights report notes that lamentably there is no protection from being asked to take a test in the first place; the problem then is that a refusal to be tested will lead to adverse inferences in many cases (if you have nothing to hide then why do you not simply consent?). Moreover, the anti-discrimination law only prevents current employees from being dismissed; there is no protection of prospective employees who feel that they have been unfairly denied a position on the basis of a suspicion about their health status.[217]

10.90   Measures designed to protect health care staff from infection raise difficult issues, as do measures to protect patients from infection by staff. Would the public interest justify coercive routine testing of some or all health carers? There has been an historical tendency in this direction in the United States,[218] which has been resisted in the United Kingdom, by both the government and the medical profession. In practice, it would be an ineffective way of solving a problem which is, to all intents, insignificant. Between 1988 and 2001 there were 22 patient notification exercises in the UK

---

[213] World Health Organization Statement from the Consultation on Testing and Counselling for HIV Infections (1992), 3. This position is repeated to the same effect in the more recent 2004 Statement, n 201, above, p 3.

[214] WHO, 2004 Statement, n 201 above, p 3.

[215] See L O Gostin and D W Webber 'HIV Infection and AIDS in the Public Health and Healthcare System' (1998) 279 J Amer Med Ass 1108.

[216] National AIDS Law No. 23.798.

[217] Fundación Huésped, *Human Rights and AIDS* (2004), pp 59–61.

[218] M Morris 'American Legislation on AIDS' (1991) 303 BMJ 325.

following concerns of infection from health care workers. There was no detectable transmission of HIV from an infected worker despite around 7,000 patients having been tested.[219] It is more than doubtful if it would be morally defensible to spend millions of pounds of health service money[220] on exorcising such an ephemeral spectre. Indeed, the tendency in the UK is towards less interventionist practices. In July 2002 the Department of Health issued a consultation paper which laid out new guidance and policy on patient notification.[221] It followed advice from the Expert Advisory Group on AIDS that it is no longer necessary to notify every patient who has undergone an exposure prone procedure by an infected health care worker because of the very low levels of risk of transmission and the likelihood of wider public anxiety. Each decision should be made on a case-by-case basis and subject to clear guidelines contained in the paper. The paper itself was provoked in part by the Court of Appeal's judgment in *H v Associated Newspapers*[222] in which the very strong interests in confidentiality were stressed and weighed against the arguments in the name of freedom of expression and public safety that were mounted in support of a claim to identify an HIV-positive health care worker. The balance there was tipped most determinedly in favour of the public and private interests in maintaining confidentiality, and we discuss these in more detail in chapter 8. The general terms of the consultation paper effectively became official guidance of the Department of Health in 2003.[223]

10.91 The issue of contamination of the health carer has been raised on several occasions by the Royal Colleges of Surgeons of England and of Edinburgh.[224] Indeed, evidence indicates that the risk of transmission is greater *from* an HIV-positive patient *to* a health care worker. Data to December 2002 show that there have been 106 such cases worldwide, five of which were in the UK.[225] The principle of the need to obtain consent to testing before operation, even in an emergency, from a high-risk patient has been emphasised but the Colleges have agreed to support any surgeon who undertook non-consensual testing in the interests of seriously contaminated theatre staff— serious contamination and high-risk being, again, left to the individual surgeon's interpretation. It was said that testing before the patient had recovered from the anaesthetic could count as an assault; we confess to some difficulty in accepting this— it is hard to see where would be the element of assault provided no special invasion

[219] Department of Health, HIV Infected Health Care Workers: A Consultation Paper (2002), para 2.4.
[220] K Tolley and J Kennelly 'Cost of Compulsory HIV Testing' (1993) 306 BMJ 1202.
[221] N 219 above.
[222] *H (a healthcare worker) v Associated Newspapers Ltd; H (a healthcare worker) v N (a health authority)* [2002] EWCA Civ 195, (2002) 65 BMLR 132. For commentary, see (2003) 11 Med LR 124.
[223] Department of Health, AIDS/HIV Infected Health Care Workers: Guidance on the Management of Infected Health Care Workers and Patient Notification (2003). See also, Department of Health, Health Clearance for Serious Communicable Diseases New Health Care Workers Draft Guidance for Consultation (2003), and for Scotland, Scottish Executive/NHS Scotland, Health Clearance for Serious Communicable Diseases: New Health Care Workers Draft Guidance for Consultation (2003).
[224] A Walker 'Surgeons and HIV' (1991) 302 BMJ 136 and more recently in 2002, see n 192 above.
[225] Health Protection Agency, Occupational Transmission of HIV: Summary of Published Reports (2005). See also, Health Protection Agency, Eye of the Needle: Surveillance of Significant Occupational Exposure to Bloodborne Viruses in Healthcare Worker (2005).

were made for the express purpose of obtaining the blood sample. In the current climate, however, it would be hard to justify a failure to wait the few minutes needed for the patient's recovery in order to carry out a relatively lengthy test; the situation, however, seems to be one of more theoretical than practical importance.

10.92   Anonymised HIV testing, which may be of great epidemiological importance, is less controversial but still raises ethical issues.[226] Such tests involve either taking blood or saliva from random groups of patients who have not necessarily engaged in high-risk practices or using blood samples that have been obtained for other purposes. The morality of random testing for a specific condition depends, to a large extent and as discussed in chapter 8, on what would be done in the event of a positive result. The dilemma can be overcome by total anonymisation but this only substitutes one potential immorality by another—the knowledge obtained cannot now be used for the benefit of the individual or of his or her contacts. In general, however, the positive advantages of investigation seem to outweigh such objections provided that those tested are informed that their blood may be subjected to anonymised testing of any sort and that they will not be informed of the results. The Unlinked Anonymous Prevalence Monitoring Programme has, in fact, been in operation since 1990, providing a vital service for public health by generating data which could not be ascertained in any other way. Its work showed that, by the end of 2001, 41,000 adults were infected with HIV in the UK, over a third of whom were unaware of their infection.[227] Such figures are of major value in respect of public health and treatment planning, as well as for further research into the disease and its spread.

10.93   The question of whether it is ethically acceptable to carry out testing of this nature without the consent of the donors remains contentious. There is a strong argument for allowing it on the grounds of public interest. On this view, such testing cannot possibly harm the donor of the sample, who may well be unaware that his or her sample is being used in this way. A contrary view—which has been discussed in detail in respect of genetic testing in chapter 7—is that a wrong is done even if the donor is unaware of it, and that a person who discovers that a personal sample has been used in this way is entitled to feel that his or her privacy has been infringed, irrespective of what protections against de-anonymisation were in place. Evidence of the general tenor of the British public's attitude towards things done without their consent may be found in the results of the 2002 consultation *Human Bodies, Human Choices*,[228] which—although it related to attitudes towards tissue and not blood as such—send a general message of caution about departing from the need to obtain consent. We show in chapter 14 how this has translated to a very strong commitment to the concept of informed consent in the Human Tissue Act 2004, but it is also one which—to our mind—does not always strike an appropriate balance between private and

[226] See Boyd n 191 above.

[227] Department of Health, Prevalence of HIV and Hepatitis Infection in the United Kingdom 2001 (2002), p 1. The figure until the end of 1999 had been 33,200.

[228] Department of Health, Human Bodies, Human Choices: Summary of Responses to the Consultation Report (2003).

public interests. We have the same concerns in the present context where, basically, care and treatment in respect of HIV and other diseases simply cannot advance if we do not facilitate research. As a final point we would stress that the role of consent is as a means to respect individuals and to protect their interests. It is possible to achieve these same ends without always relying on consent.

PROCEEDING WITHOUT CONSENT—THE CONSEQUENCES

10.94   Non-consensual medical treatment entitles the patient to sue for damages for the battery which is committed. It is also possible to base a claim on the tort of negligence, the theory being that the doctor has been negligent in failing to obtain the consent of the patient. There are important differences between the two forms of action which have given rise to much legal debate.

10.95   An action for battery arises when the plaintiff has been touched in some way by the defendant and when there has been no consent, express or implied, to such touching. All that the plaintiff need establish in such an action is that the defendant wrongfully touched him. It is unnecessary to establish loss as a result and, therefore, there is no problem as to the causation of damage to be overcome. By contrast, in an action based on the tort of negligence, the plaintiff must establish that the defendant wrongfully touched him and that the negligence of the defendant in touching him without consent has led to the injury for which damages are sought. There is thus a problem of factual causation to be tackled and, for this reason, the action for battery is an easier option from the plaintiff's point of view. The measure of damages recoverable will also be different. All direct damages are recoverable in battery; only those damages which are foreseeable and which it is fair and just to compensate may be recovered in an action for negligence. Thus, an unforeseen medical complication arising from the procedure in question may give rise to something for which damages are recoverable in battery but not in negligence. Clarification of the circumstances in which each action is available was provided by the Supreme Court of Canada in *Reibl v Hughes*[229] and in the first apposite English case of *Chatterton v Gerson*.[230]

10.96   An action for battery is appropriate where there has been no consent at all to the physical contact in question. Thus, an action for battery is the suitable remedy if a patient has refused to submit to a procedure but the doctor has, nevertheless, gone ahead in the face of that refusal. Two historic Canadian cases illustrate the typical

---

[229] (1980) 114 DLR (3d) 1 at 10, per Laskin CJ. The ruling has most recently been applied without modification, inter alia, in *E (D) (Guardian ad litem of) v British Columbia* (2005) Carswell BC 523, 2005 BCCA 134 (BCCA 11 Mar 2005).

[230] [1981] QB 432, [1981] 1 All ER 257. See also *Hills v Potter* [1983] 3 All ER 716, [1984] 1 WLR 641.

circumstances. Actions were sustained in *Mulloy v Hop Sang*,[231] where the plaintiff's hand was amputated without his consent, and in *Schweizer v Central Hospital*,[232] where the surgeon performing an operation on the back of a plaintiff whose consent was related to an operation on his toe was held liable for battery. It will be seen in these cases that what the doctor actually did was quite unconnected with the procedure to which the patient had consented. There was no consent to an operation of the 'general nature' of that which was actually performed—thus, they lay within the courts' policy of restricting battery actions to acts of unambiguous hostility.

10.97   A claim based on negligence is apt when the plaintiff has given his consent to an act of the general nature of that which is performed by the defendant but there is a flaw in this consent and, as a result, there has been no consent to certain concomitant features of the act of which he was unaware. The negligence lies in a failure to apprise the patient of such features as a result of which he has sustained damage; the damage is not due to negligent performance but results from a mishap which, in this instance, was a recognised potential hazard of the procedure. The distinction between the two forms of action was sharply outlined in *Reibl v Hughes* by Laskin CJC, who remarked in his judgment:

I do not understand how it can be said that the consent was vitiated by the failure of disclosure of risks as to make the surgery or other treatment an unprivileged, unconsented to and intentional invasion of the patient's bodily integrity. I can appreciate the temptation to say that the genuineness of consent to medical treatment depends on proper disclosure of the risks which it entails, but . . . unless there has been misrepresentation or fraud to secure consent to the treatment, a failure to disclose the attendant risks, however serious, should go to negligence rather than battery.

10.98   Similarly, it was emphasised in *Chatterton v Gerson* that an action for trespass to the person is inappropriate once the patient is informed in 'broad terms' of the nature of the procedure and consent is given; an action for negligence is the proper remedy if there is a failure to disclose risks.

10.99   This, however, is not to say that an action in assault or battery is entirely irrelevant to medical law. In *Appleton v Garrett*[233] the High Court awarded both exemplary and aggravated damages against a dentist who had actively deceived patients as to their need for treatment over a number of years. Any consent offered by the patients was vitiated by the fraudulent misrepresentation of the practitioner.[234] The court held that information had been deliberately withheld and the defendant had acted throughout in bad faith, making an action in battery, rather than in negligence, appropriate. This having been said, there need not be a nefarious purpose behind the touching for an

---

[231] [1935] 1 WWR 714.   [232] (1974) 53 DLR (3d) 494.

[233] (1995) 34 BMLR 23. See also [1996] 4 Med L Rev 311, considered most recently in *Richardson v Howie* [2004] EWCA Civ 1127.

[234] Similarly, those who pose as a qualified medical practitioner and elicit consent to touching on this basis are guilty of criminal assault, see *R v Tabassum* [2000] 2 Cr App R 328; [2000] Lloyd's R Med 404.

assault to be committed, as the case of *Ms B* shows.[235] However, only notional damages are likely to be awarded in such cases in recognition of the affront to bodily integrity that the unauthorised touching represents.

THE NEGLIGENCE ACTION AND THE VAGARIES OF INFORMATION DISCLOSURE

10.100   When an undisclosed risk arises, the aggrieved patient is, in essence, claiming: 'You did not inform me of the risk which has eventuated; but for your failure, I would not have consented to the procedure; you have failed in your duty of care and, as a result, I have sustained injury'. The problem in negligence actions based on a lack of consent is, therefore, largely that of causation—the court must be satisfied that the defendant's failure to obtain the valid consent of the patient was, in fact, the cause of the patient's injury. To satisfy this requirement, the patient must prove that he would not have given his consent had he received the information of which he was allegedly deprived. We explore the whole concept of causation fully in chapter 9. Here we simply highlight the hurdles faced by a claimant in respect of inadequate information disclosure. The issues have, indeed, been addressed most recently by the House of Lords in *Chester v Afshar*,[236] wherein the majority of the House adopted a very clear policy line in favour of the patient. This stands in stark contrast, however, with the legal position in respect of the standard of care that patients can expect from their doctors in terms of disclosure of risks associated with healthcare. The line of authority as to the latter evolved some time ago and we consider it appropriate to address the question of standard of care before proceeding to causation. In this way the reader can best assess for him or herself how the law has been developing over the last twenty years.

Informed consent and standards of care

10.101   The discussion in this field centres on the issue of 'informed consent'—a concept which will always remain a classic example of the importation of a medical philosophy from across the Atlantic. Its journey has, in fact, been remarkably slow. Thus, while the first mention of 'informed consent' in the English courts seems to have been as late as 1981,[237] the seed was sown in America in 1957 in the case of *Salgo*.[238] Here, the court concluded that the doctor had a duty to disclose to the patient 'any facts which are necessary to form the basis of an intelligent consent by the patient to the proposed treatment'.[239] It is unfortunate that the phrase 'intelligent consent' was replaced in a later passage related to therapeutic privilege:[240]

---

[235] Discussed above at para 10.63. £100 in token damages was awarded.
[236] [2005] 1 AC 134, [2004] 4 All ER 587, [2004] 3 WLR 927.
[237] *Chatterton v Gerson* [1981] QB 432, [1981] 1 All ER 257.
[238] *Salgo v Leland Stanford Junior University Board of Trustees* 317 P 2d 170 (Cal, 1957).
[239] Per Bray J.   [240] See para 10.118 below.

In discussing the element of risk, a certain amount of discretion must be employed consistent with full disclosure of facts necessary to an *informed* consent (our emphasis).[241]

10.102 Informed consent was later made a requirement for all state-funded research work following a series of allegations that potentially dangerous experiments were being conducted without the consent of the experimental subjects.[242] Silverman maintained that there are, thus, two distinct forms of 'informed consent' and, certainly, this must be so as to the assessment of the quality of the information provided. Such a review *must* be prospective in the case of research whereas it can only be retrospective, for example by way of litigation, in respect of day-to-day patient management.

10.103 In either event, informed consent introduced a new element to medical treatment. It is no longer a simple matter of consent to a technical assault; consent must now be based on a knowledge of the nature, risks, consequences and alternatives associated with the proposed therapy. Bray J's definition has gone relatively unchallenged[243] across the United States but it is still no more than a broad expression of principle. It goes no way to explaining either what counts as informed consent or how we tell that the circumstances surrounding a given event satisfy the requirements.[244] In so far as it defines a doctor's duties rather than the patient's reaction, the phrase is a misnomer[245] which, we believe, has been applied in medical writing and, indeed, now almost inevitably, in official publications with inadequate exploration of its meaning.[246] Moreover, the phrase is tautologous—to be ethically and legally acceptable, 'consent' must always be 'informed'. It is interesting to note that, although the English text of the Council of Europe's *Convention on Human Rights and Biomedicine* speaks of 'informed consent' in Article 5, the French text refers merely to 'consentment' *tout simple*.[247]

10.104 The topic recalls the aphorism of Frankfurter J, albeit in a completely different context:

A phrase begins life as a literary expression; its felicity leads to its lazy repetition; and repetition soon establishes it as a legal formula indiscriminately used to express different and sometimes contradictory ideas.[248]

10.105 Thus, we suggest that, when Dunn LJ said in the fundamental United Kingdom case

[241] We are indebted to W A Silverman 'The Myth of Informed Consent: In Daily Practice and in Clinical Trials' (1989) 15 J Med Ethics 6 for many of the historical details.

[242] Surgeon General's Memorandum *Clinical Investigations Using Human Subjects* (1966). It is, of course, now an integral part of research on a global scale (see chapter 18).

[243] E.g. *Harnish v Children's Hospital Medical Center* 387 Mass 152 (1982) where the phrase 'intelligent decision' was used.

[244] G R Gillett 'Informed Consent and Moral Integrity' (1989) 15 J Med Ethics 117.

[245] T K Feng 'Failure of Medical Advice: Trespass or Negligence' (1987) 7 LS 149.

[246] For recent criticism see, O O'Neill 'Some Limits of Informed Consent' (2003) 29 J Med Ethics 4, O Corrigan 'Empty Ethics: The Problem with Informed Consent' (2003) 25 Sociology of Health and Illness 768, and A Campbell-Tiech 'The Trouble with Consent' (2003) 121 Brit J Haemat 839.

[247] Council of Europe, *Convention for the Protection of Human Rights and Dignity of the Human Being with regard to the Application of Biology and Medicine* (1997), Article 5.

[248] *Tiller v Atlantic Coast Line Railroad Co* 318 US 54 at 68 (1943).

of *Sidaway*: 'The concept of informed consent forms no part of English law',[249] he may well have been referring to consent based on a subjective patient test—for no one would deny that 'information' must nowadays be passed from doctor to patient in the United Kingdom. Yet, similar disclaimers have been repeated both in England[250] and in Scotland[251]—and have been echoed in Australia[252]—and the legal definition has become no clearer. The phrase 'informed consent' is, however, now part of the lore of medical ethics and its repetition among even the highest ranks of judiciary[253] mean that we must accept it and consider the basic nature of the information that has to be given in order to validate consent to medical treatment.

What needs to be disclosed?

10.106   Looked at from the ethical point of view, the matter is one of self-determination. A person should not be exposed to a risk of harm unless he has agreed to that risk and he cannot properly agree to—or, equally importantly, make a choice between—risks in the absence of factual information. The twin problems to be resolved are, therefore, by what general standard should the information be judged and, within that, to what extent must or should particular details be divulged?

10.107   The general standards available are conveniently described as the 'patient standard' and the 'professional standard'. The former has already been described above in the wide context of consent to battery. Precisely the same principles apply to counselling. Thus, the extreme of this school of thought would hold that, given a rational patient, the doctor must reveal all the relevant facts as to what he intends to do. It is not for him to determine what the patient should or should not hear. Obviously, there must be some medical assessment of what is or is not significant but, apart from the exclusion of irrelevant material, the patient should be as fully informed as possible so that he or she can make up his or her mind in the light of all the relevant circumstances. This approach most fully satisfies the requirements of self-determination but can be criticised on the grounds that it leaves little scope for the exercise of clinical judgment by the doctor. It is for this reason that even those most dedicated to patient

---

[249] *Sidaway v Board of Governors of the Bethlem Royal Hospital* [1984] QB 493 at 517, [1984] 1 All ER 1018 at 1030, CA.

[250] 'English law does not accept the transatlantic concept of informed consent' per Lord Donaldson in *Re T (adult) (refusal of medical treatment)* [1992] 4 All ER 649 at 663, (1992) 9 BMLR 46 at 61, CA. The use of the words 'transatlantic concept' is, itself, misleading, as probably the majority of the United States still hold to a professional standard.

[251] '[T]he law . . . has come down firmly against the view that the doctor's duty to the patient involves at all costs obtaining the informed consent of the patient to specific medical treatments': *Moyes v Lothian Health Board* [1990] 1 Med LR 463, 1990 SLT 444 at 449, per Lord Caplan.

[252] '. . . nothing is to be gained by reiterating . . . the oft-used and somewhat amorphous phrase "informed consent" ': *Rogers v Whittaker* (1992) 109 ALR 625 at 633, (1994) 16 BMLR 148 at 156 (High Court of Australia), per Mason CJ et al.

[253] See *Chester v Afshar*, para 10.100 above, per Lord Hope at para 57 and Lord Steyn at para 14 who actually states: 'Surgery performed without the informed consent of the patient is unlawful. The court is the final arbiter of what constitutes informed consent'.

autonomy will allow the doctor the 'therapeutic privilege' to withhold information which would merely serve to distress or confuse the patient.

10.108   This concession applies only to specific items selected by the doctor for specific reasons. It does not run as far as acceptance of the alternative approach to disclosure of information—that is, one based on the professional standard. Here, counselling and informing are regarded as an integral part of clinical management; the extent and detail of the information supplied is a matter for decision by the doctor who is, therein, subject to the same duty of care as when prescribing or operating. It follows that, whichever standard is adopted, litigation based on inadequate information must be taken in negligence. Any difference lies in the test to be applied. Given a patient standard, the quality of information will be judged from the viewpoint of the prudent—or the particular—patient; under the professional standard, it will be that of the prudent doctor.

10.109   The choice between a 'patient standard' and a 'professional standard' is a difficult one. There must be respect for the patient's legitimate interest in knowing to what he is subjecting himself but, at the same time, there will clearly be cases where a paternalistic approach is appropriate.[254] In addition, the practicalities of the situation must be borne in mind. Although it might be ethically desirable for patients to be as fully informed as possible, the time spent in explaining the intricacies of procedures could be considerable, particularly if a doctor is expected to deal with remote risks. Doctors—and, particularly, doctors operating in a NHS—simply do not have the time to spend on unduly lengthy explanations of all the ramifications of treatment and many would regard the practice as unnecessarily disturbing for the patient.[255] It has also been pointed out that adherence to a professional standard provides a coherent body of principles;[256] courts that are subject to this standard are, therefore, at least less likely to be inconsistent in their judgment of disputes. This clarity of approach is likely to continue in the light of detailed guidance both by the Department of Health[257] and the General Medical Council[258] as to what patients should be told in order to obtain valid consent.

10.110   A final point about the nature of the doctrine of informed consent relates to 'patient understanding'. The focus of the concept is on information given, supposedly to further the autonomy of the patient. But the consequent implication is that the

---

[254] For discussion on patient deception, see R J Sullivan, L W Menapace and R M White 'Truth-telling and Patient Diagnoses' (2001) 27 J Med Ethics 192 and M Gold 'Is Honesty Always the Best Policy? Ethical Aspects of Truth Telling' (2004) 34 Internal Medicine Journal 578.

[255] This, and other aspects, have been researched in Sheffield: D D Kerrigan, R S Thevasagayam, T O Woods et al 'Who's Afraid of Informed Consent?' (1993) 306 BMJ 298 and was found to be unmerited. The study, however, concerned the relatively innocuous repair of inguinal hernia—the authors concede that the results could be different in more serious circumstances.

[256] C Newdick 'The Doctor's Duties of Care Under *Sidaway*' (1985) 36 NILQ 243.

[257] Department of Health, Reference Guide to Consent for Examination or Treatment (2001). Numerous other documents and guidance—including that for patients—appears on the Department of Health website: www.dh.gov.uk.

[258] General Medical Council *Seeking Patients' Consent: The Ethical Considerations* (1998).

health care professional has fulfilled his duty once he has proffered the information. Such a narrow interpretation, however, ignores consideration of the patient's ability to assimilate and analyse the information.[259] If it is not also part of the doctor's duty to ensure at least a degree of understanding on the part of the patient, he can discharge his duty by offering information in a way that results in no enhancement of the patient's autonomy—the ethical basis of the doctrine is, accordingly, undermined. It is a fallacy to make consent forms longer and more detailed in an attempt to meet the requirements of the law for at least two reasons. First, this is likely to hinder rather than promote patient understanding, and, second, because a signed consent form has, in any case, no binding validity, it merely serves as *some* evidence that consent has been obtained, but this can always be rebutted if contrary evidence demonstrates that the patient was uncomprehending and did not truly provide his or her voluntary assent. This is confirmed by *Williamson v East London and the City Health Authority*,[260] which we have already looked at (see para 10.14). The surgeon maintained that she had explained that an extensive breast operation might be likely. The plaintiff did not accept that she was told this before the operation. The form which was signed related to silicon replacement, but was subsequently altered to read 'Bilateral replacement. Breast prosthesis. Right subcutaneous mastectomy'. There was no evidence that the patient had re-signed the form or initialled the amendments. The judge was satisfied that, on the balance of probabilities, the surgeon did not properly or sufficiently explain her intention to alter the operation.

The standard of care cases

10.111 Whatever standpoint one takes on information disclosure, a decision of some court can be found to endorse one's preferred approach. Within the Commonwealth, there are decisions ranging from the endorsement of the deliberate medical lie to the acceptance of the extreme patient-orientated approach which emphasises complete disclosure of risk. The United States, with its 51 independent jurisdictions, provides a useful overall view. Although a majority of the States still applies a professional standard, there is a recognisable national drift towards that of the prudent patient; it is worth recapitulating the reasons given for this in a typical case in which the onus was transferred.[261] These included:

(a) that conditions other than those that are purely medical will influence the patient's decision;

---

[259] For survey evidence suggesting that detailed descriptions do not confuse or deter, see J R T Greene 'Effects of Detailed Information about Dissection on Intentions to Bequeath Bodies for Use in Teaching and Research' (2003) 202 J of Anatomy 475.

[260] (1997) 41 BMLR 85, [1998] Lloyd's Rep Med 7.

[261] *Largey v Rothman* 540 A 2d 504 (NJ, 1988). The prudent patient standard was set in *Canterbury v Spence* 464 F 2d 772 (DC, 1972). For retention of the professional standard, see *Wooley v Henderson* 418 A 2d 1123 (Md, 1980).

(b) that following the whim of the physician is inconsistent with the patient's right to self-determination; and

(c) that the professional standard smacks of anachronistic paternalism.

10.112 In addition, the court in *Largey* specifically ruled out the criticism that the prudent patient test obliges the doctor to list every possible complication of the proposed procedure. While this appears superficially disarming, it does, in fact, serve to emphasise that the professional is bound to be unsure of his precise position; as Margaret Brazier put it: 'the doctor is left to "second-guess" the courts'.[262]

10.113 The starting point for the UK position is found in the complementary cases of *Hunter v Hanley*[263] in Scotland and *Bolam v Friern Hospital Management Committee*[264] in England, both of which define the essence of medical negligence as we have already seen in chapter 9. It will be recalled that the *Bolam* dictum runs thus: 'a doctor is not negligent if he acts in accordance with a practice accepted at the time as proper by a responsible body of medical opinion'.[265] Since it is agreed that actions based on lack of consent to medical treatment should be taken in negligence, it follows that any argument as to what needs to be disclosed in British medical practice hinges upon whether or not the *Bolam* principle applies equally to both diagnosis and treatment *and* to the giving of information.

10.114 That it does so was upheld both in *Chatterton v Gerson*[266] and in *Hills v Potter*.[267] The acid test, however, came in the seminal case of *Sidaway*[268] where the proposition was accepted in the court of first instance but was received rather less enthusiastically in the Court of Appeal; there, Sir John Donaldson MR did not regard it as self-evident that the standards applied to diagnosis and treatment should be the same as those applied to disclosure. Concern was expressed that the definition of the duty of care was a matter for the law which 'could not stand by if the profession, by an excess of paternalism, denied their patients a real choice'.[269] Although the Master of the Rolls' colleagues were unable to follow him all the way, Browne-Wilkinson LJ also believed that there was a prima facie duty on the doctor to inform the patient—the assumption of the role of adviser carried with it the duty to disclose material and unusual risks.

10.115 The House of Lords, while maintaining a professional standard of disclosure, was, similarly, prepared to modify the existing law in certain respects. Thus, Lord Bridge held:

---

[262] M Brazier 'Patient Autonomy and Consent to Treatment: The Role of the Law?' (1987) 7 LS 169.

[263] 1955 SC 200, 1955 SLT 213.   [264] [1957] 2 All ER 118, [1957] 1 WLR 582.

[265] Per McNair J [1957] 2 All ER 118 at 122.

[266] [1981] QB 432, [1981] 1 All ER 257.

[267] [1983] 3 All ER 716, [1984] 1 WLR 641.

[268] *Sidaway v Board of Governors of the Bethlem Royal Hospital* [1984] QB 493 at 517, [1984] 1 All ER 1018 at 1030, CA; affd [1985] AC 871, [1985] 1 All ER 643, HL.

[269] [1984] QB 493 at 513, [1984] 1 All ER 1018 at 1028, CA.

A judge might, in certain circumstances, come to the conclusion that the disclosure of a particular risk was so obviously necessary to an informed choice on the part of the patient that no reasonably prudent medical man would fail to make it . . .[270]

while Lord Templeman considered that:

. . . the court must decide whether the information afforded to the patient was sufficient to alert the patient to the possibility of serious harm of the kind in fact suffered.[271]

10.116   Lord Scarman, however, delivered what was, effectively, a dissenting judgment in which he indicated that: 'it was a strange conclusion if our courts should be led to conclude that our law . . . should permit doctors to determine in what circumstances . . . a duty arose to warn.' He found great merit in the American case of *Canterbury v Spence*,[272] in which it was held that, while medical evidence on this matter was not excluded, it was the court which determined the extent of, and any breach of, the doctor's duty to inform. Information includes warning. King CJ, for example, specifically instructed that the doctor's duty extends not only to disclose any real risks in the treatment but also to warn of any real risk that the treatment may prove ineffective.[273]

10.117   Two specific aspects of the information issue are confirmed as a result of *Sidaway*. The first is that material risks of a procedure must be disclosed. Following *Canterbury*, a risk can be defined as material if a reasonable person in the patient's position, if warned of the risk, would be likely to attach significance to it. Similarly, it is material if the medical practitioner is, or should reasonably be, aware that the particular patient, if warned of the risk, would be likely to attach significance to it.[274] Quite what that means in relation to chance is impossible to assess and, indeed, generalisations may be inappropriate as the test relates to the circumstances of the particular case. Moreover, significance in this field is a function not only of incidence but also of severity; as to incidence, it was agreed in *Sidaway* that a risk of 10 per cent of a stroke resulting—as was established in *Reibl v Hughes*[275]—was one which a doctor could hardly fail to appreciate as necessitating a warning; but non-disclosure was considered proper in Mrs Sidaway's case when the risk of damage to the spinal cord was of the order of 1 per cent or less. We have to admit to some concern that odds shorter than 100:1 might be regarded as immaterial in the eyes of the law.[276] A great deal will, however, hang on the *patient's* requirements as expressed by way of questioning and we return to this below.

---

[270] [1985] AC 871 at 900, [1985] 1 All ER 643 at 663, HL.

[271] [1985] AC 871 at 903, [1985] 1 All ER 643 at 665.

[272] 464 F 2d 772 (DC, 1972).

[273] *F v R* (1983) 33 SASR 189, SC. Alternative treatments should also be canvassed—particularly if there is a choice between medical and surgical procedures: *Haughian v Paine* (1987) 37 DLR (4th) 624, cited in (1987) 137 NLJ 557.

[274] Mason CJ et al in *Rogers v Whittaker* (1992) 109 ALR 625 at 634, [1993] 4 Med LR 79 at 83, Aus HC.

[275] (1980) 114 DLR (3d) 1.

[276] King JC accepted 200:1 as not being material in *F v R* (1983) 33 SASR 189, SC.

10.118   Secondly, *Sidaway* confirmed the 'therapeutic' or 'professional' privilege to withhold information that might be psychologically damaging to the patient. This, again,
follows the direction in *Bolam*, in which the judge said in his charge to the jury:

> You may well think that when a doctor is dealing with a mentally sick man and has a strong
> belief that his only hope of cure is submission to electroconvulsive therapy, the doctor
> cannot be criticised if he does not stress the dangers, which he believed to be minimal, which
> are involved in the treatment . . .[277]

This principle has since been widely adopted.[278]

10.119   It is also clear from *Sidaway* that, by way of exception to this rule, there must be
particularly good reasons, which the doctor would have to justify, for failing to answer
such questions as the patient puts and that there may, indeed, be a strict obligation to
do so.[279] Thus, Lord Bridge held, albeit obiter, that:

> When questioned specifically by a patient of apparently sound mind about risks involved in
> a particular treatment proposed, a doctor's duty must, in my opinion, be to answer both
> truthfully and as fully as the questioner requires.[280]

10.120   'The fact that the patient asked questions revealing concern about the risk would
make the doctor aware that this patient did, in fact, attach significance to the risk'[281]—
and, hence, affect its materiality; it was certainly this fact which served to turn a
1:14,000 chance of blindness into a risk which it was found negligent not to disclose in
the Australian case of *Rogers v Whittaker*.[282]

10.121   This inference was, however, disturbed in England in *Blyth v Bloomsbury Health
Authority*.[283] Here, the trial judge's decision in favour of the plaintiff was reversed on
appeal. He was found to be in error in holding that there was an obligation, when
asked, to pass on *all* the information available to the hospital; the question of what a
patient should be told in response to a general inquiry could not be detached from the
Bolam test any more than when no such enquiry was made (per Kerr LJ). Neill LJ went
further:

---

[277] [1957] 2 All ER 118 at 124, [1957] 1 WLR 582 at 590, per McNair J.

[278] It has been endorsed most recently, and once again by the House of Lords (albeit obiter), in *Chester v Afshar*, n 236 above, per Lord Steyn, para 16.

[279] For an interesting survey indicating a widespread *lack* of interest among patients in asking further questions (at least in respect of anaesthesia) see A Moores and N A Pace 'The Information Requested by Patients Prior to Giving Consent to Anaesthesia' (2003) 58 Anaesthesia 703.

[280] [1985] AC 871 at 898, [1985] 1 All ER 643 at 661, HL.

[281] Mason CJ et al in *Rogers v Whittaker* (1992) 109 ACLR 625 at 631, [1993] at 4 Med LR 79 at 82.

[282] In *Hopp v Lepp* [1980] 2 SCR 192, 112 DLR (3d) 67 the Supreme Court of Canada held that in obtaining a patient's consent a doctor must answer any specific questions put by the patient as to the risks involved, and should, even in the absence of questioning, disclose the following: the nature of the proposed intervention, its gravity, any material risks and any special or unusual risks.

[283] (1985) *The Times*, 24 May; on appeal [1993] 4 Med LR 151, CA. *Blyth* reminds us that the principles derived from surgical cases can apply equally to medication—implied consent to taking a drug cannot be assumed: *Crichton v Hastings* (1972) 29 DLR (3d) 692.

I am not convinced [from *Sidaway*] that the *Bolam* test is irrelevant even in relation to the question of what answers are properly to be given to specific enquiries or that Lords Diplock and Bridge intended to hold otherwise.[284]

10.122 However, the argument in *Blyth* centred largely on some rather obscure therapeutic notes written in the hospital and there has been no judicial enthusiasm to follow its line.

10.123 The House of Lords' approach in *Sidaway* has been subject to strong academic criticism[285] largely because of the uncertainties it left behind. A strong impression remains that the House was not at ease with *Bolam*—only Lord Diplock was prepared to carry it to its conclusion. Yet ranks continued to be closed whenever the principle was directly questioned. Thus, in *Gold*,[286] Schiemann J at first instance attempted to distinguish counselling from treatment and was firmly overruled by the Court of Appeal.[287] The House of Lords has since confirmed that the courts retain the power to establish standards of care,[288] but, as we point out elsewhere, their Lordships find it acceptable to challenge medical opinion only when the latter has no rational basis. This attitude is now becoming almost unique in face of the current universal acceptance of a patient's right to decide on his or her own treatment. The writing was already on the wall 25 years ago in Canada where, in *Reibl*, it was held:

[The] scope of the duty of disclosure ... is not a question that is to be concluded on the basis of the expert medical evidence alone ... What is under consideration here is the patient's right to know what risks are involved in undergoing or forgoing certain surgery or other treatment.[289]

and, in 1983, it was said of warning of therapeutic failure in the Supreme Court of South Australia:

The ultimate question ... is ... whether the defendant's conduct ... conforms to the standard of reasonable care demanded by the law. That is a question for the court and the duty of deciding it cannot be delegated to any profession or group in the community.[290]

10.124 The strongest attack on *Bolam* to date has, however, come from the High Court of Australia where its application to counselling was firmly rejected in *Rogers v Whittaker*. In that case, we have the majority opinion saying:

There is a fundamental difference between, on the one hand, diagnosis and treatment and, on the other hand, the provision of advice or information to the patient ... Because the choice to be made calls for a decision by the patient on information known to the medical

---

[284] [1993] 4 Med LR 151 at 157, Neil LJ concurring at 160.

[285] For full discussion see I Kennedy and A Grubb *Medical Law* (3rd edn, 2000) pp 691 et seq.

[286] *Gold v Haringey Health Authority* [1988] QB 481, [1987] 2 All ER 888, CA.

[287] The integral nature of medical attendance has been emphasised in other contexts, e.g. in the management of the mentally incompetent: *Re H (a patient)* [1993] 1 FLR 29, [1993] 4 Med LR 91.

[288] *Bolitho v City and Hackney Health Authority* [1997] 4 All ER 771, (1997) 39 BMLR 1.

[289] (1980) 114 DLR (3d) 1 at 13.

[290] *F v R* (1983) 33 SASR 189 at 194, per King CJ.

practitioner but not to the patient, it would be illogical to hold that the amount of information to be provided by the medical practitioner can be determined from the perspective of the practitioner alone or, for that matter, of the medical profession.[291]

and even more trenchantly, Gaudron J:

[E]ven in the area of diagnosis and treatment, there is, in my view, no legal basis for limiting liability in terms of the rule known as 'the *Bolam* test' . . . [It] may be a convenient statement of the approach dictated by the state of the evidence in some cases. As such, it may have some utility as a rule-of-thumb in some jury cases, but it can serve no other useful function.[292]

10.125   The ripples of *Rogers* have reached distant shores, including those of South Africa, where negligence is subsumed under a general heading of 'wrongfulness' for which the defence of *volenti non fit injuria*—i.e. voluntary assumption of risk—is available. In *Castell v De Greef*[293] the Cape Provincial Division of the Supreme Court endorsed not only the Australian High Court's patient-orientated disclosure test, but also that court's definition of material risk. It was held that, for a defence of *volenti non fit injuria* to be successful, the consenting party must have knowledge, awareness, appreciation and understanding of the nature and extent of the harm or risk involved, this being on the grounds that the patient has otherwise not voluntarily assumed the risks in question, i.e. is not *volens*. The juxtaposition of *volenti* and consent suggests that, pace *Chatteron v Gerson*,[294] an action in trespass may still be available, at least in South Africa; the fact that *Castell* was taken in negligence was dictated by the nature of the pleadings. Thus, we see how a common concept of informed consent can be recognised in legal systems with varying traditions.

10.126   In the United Kingdom, however, habits die hard and the position in Scotland has been resolved in a way that leaves little room for doubt.[295] Lord Caplan had this to say:

In my view . . . the appropriate tests to apply in medical negligence cases are to be found in *Hunter v Hanley* and *Bolam* . . . As I see it, the law in both Scotland and England has come down firmly against the view that the doctor's duty to the patient involves at all costs obtaining the informed consent of the patient to specific medical treatments . . . I can read

---

[291] (1992) 109 ALR 625 at 632, [1993] 4 Med LR 79 at 83. For a full discussion of the case, see D Chalmers and R Schwartz '*Rogers v Whittaker* and Informed Consent in Australia: A Fair Dinkum Duty of Disclosure' (1993) 1 Med L Rev 139; R C Pincus 'Has Informed Consent Finally Arrived in Australia?' (1993) 159 Med J Austral 25; and B McSherry 'Failing to Advise and Warn of Inherent Risks in Medical Treatment: When Does Negligence Occur?' (1993) 1 J Law Med 5.

[292] (1992) 109 ALR 625 at 635–636, [1993] 4 Med LR 79 at 84. This decision was reaffirmed by the High Court in *Chappel v Hart* [1998] HCA 55. However, in *Rosenberg v Percival* [2001] HCA 18, a case which was primarily concerned with information and causation, the High Court was not entirely dismissive of *Bolam*; the objection was not so much to the relevance of medical opinion as to its conclusiveness in assessing the necessary extent of disclosure.

[293] 1993(3) SA 501 and 1994 (4) SA 408.

[294] [1981] QB 432, [1981] 1 All ER 257.

[295] *Moyes v Lothian Health Board* 1990 SLT 444, [1990] 1 Med LR 463. Two further Scottish cases are known to have failed but are very poorly reported: *Comber v Greater Glasgow Health Board* 1992 SLT 22n, *Hsuing v Webster* 1992 SLT 1071n. They are reported as news items in *The Scotsman*, 24 April 1991, p 4.

nothing in the majority view in *Sidaway* which suggests that the extent and quality of warning to be given by a doctor to his patient should not in the last resort be governed by medical criteria.[296]

10.127   But, despite this, there is no doubt that a movement away from *Bolam* has developed in the last few years and there is now evidence that the British courts will not always adhere rigidly to the *Bolam* standard in disputes over information disclosure. In *Smith v Tunbridge Wells Health Authority*,[297] for example, the failure of a consultant surgeon to inform a 28-year-old man of impotence and bladder dysfunction following an operation to treat rectal prolapse was held to be negligent, despite medical support for the decision. Indeed, it was considered that disclosure of the risk was the *only* reasonable course of action. Negligence was also established in *McAllister v Lewisham and North Southwark Health Authority*,[298] when a senior consultant neurosurgeon failed to disclose the risks surrounding an operation to alleviate a weakness in the patient's leg which was linked to a neurological malformation. Among other lapses, a risk of hemiplegia was not disclosed. The trial judge held that:

I have come to the conclusion that those who say that the warnings given ... were inadequate are right and there has not been shown to me on the evidence any reputable body of responsible opinion to the contrary.

10.128   *Newell v Goldenberg*[299] was in essence a wrongful pregnancy case, involving a vasectomy which reversed and led to a fourth conception for the plaintiffs. The undisclosed risk of this happening was 1:2,300 and the plaintiffs argued that, had they been informed, Mrs Newell would also have been sterilised. Mantell J found for the plaintiffs in holding that a patient about to undergo elective or voluntary surgery is entitled to be told about its effectiveness. He opined that, although some doctors might not have disclosed the risk at the relevant time, they would not, in so doing, have been acting reasonably or responsibly: '[t]he Bolam principle provides a defence for those who lag behind the times . . . It cannot serve those who know better'.[300]

10.129   Turning to the Court of Appeal, a plaintiff's action for negligent failure to disclose the risk that a hysterectomy might not provide protection against conception was upheld in *Lybert v Warrington Health Authority*.[301] Without referring explicitly to *Bolam*, the court none the less decreed that part of the duty of care owed was to ensure that a proper and effective system existed for giving sufficient warning of failure. Ideally, that warning should be oral *and* in writing and could be given either on admission of the patient, before she agreed to the operation or before her discharge.

---

[296] 1990 SLT 444 at 449, [1990] 1 Med LR 463 at 468.

[297] [1994] 5 Med LR 334.   [298] [1994] 5 Med LR 343.   [299] [1995] 6 Med LR 371.

[300] Yet, in 1998, we have Ebsworth J in a disclosure case: '[I]t was not open to the court, while probably preferring the evidence of one expert from that of another, to choose between genuine, equally competent and logically justifiable difference of opinion as to whether decisions made about treatment, including the obtaining of consent, had been professionally justifiable': *Newbury v Bath District Health Authority* (1999) 47 BMLR 138 at 149.

[301] [1996] 7 Med LR 71.

Here the court is effectively laying down the acceptable standard of care for such cases and, in this respect, the decision represents a tentative incursion into near-virgin territory.

10.130   Most significant of all, however, is the Court of Appeal decision in *Pearce v United Bristol Healthcare NHS Trust*,[302] in which an action in negligence was brought by a couple whose child died in utero almost three weeks overdue. The mother had pleaded with the consultant two weeks after her delivery date either to induce the birth or to carry out a caesarian section, but he advised against it citing the high risks of induction and the long time for recovery from caesarian section. He did not disclose the risks of fetal death in the womb as a result of delay in delivery. In deciding whether the consultant was negligent in this regard, the court endorsed *Sidaway* as the law and accepted *Bolam* as the relevant test, but also followed Lord Bridge's caveat concerning the need to warn of 'significant risks'. Lord Woolf MR felt that Lord Templeman's views in *Sidaway* best summed up the position, whereby the patient was entitled to such information as was needed to make a balanced judgment in the circumstances. Moreover, Lord Woolf quoted with approval the passage from *Bolitho* concerning the role of the court in questioning medical opinion lacking a logical basis, which we discuss in chapter 9.[303] All of this led him to the following ratio:

> In a case where it is being alleged that a plaintiff has been deprived of the opportunity to make a proper decision as to what course of action he or she should take in relation to treatment, it seems to me to be the law . . . that if there is a significant risk which would affect the judgment of a reasonable patient, then in the normal course it is the responsibility of the doctor to inform the patient of that risk, if the information is needed so that the patient can determine for him or herself as to what course he or she would adopt.

10.131   This endorses Lord Bridge's views in *Sidaway*, and indeed, Lord Woolf cites with approval Lord Bridge's case of a 10 per cent risk of stroke as an example of a 'significant risk'. Beyond that he does not say how the significance of a risk is to be determined. However, in one, possibly significant, regard Lord Woolf shifts the emphasis of this concept. He talks of the effect of a significant risk on the judgment of a *reasonable patient*, while Lord Bridge spoke of 'disclosure . . . so obviously necessary to an informed decision on the part of the patient that no *reasonably prudent medical man* would fail to make it'. Does this represent a doctrinal shift towards a prudent patient test for Britain? It is arguable. But Lord Woolf only generated hope in half-measure, for he went on to apply his test to the facts of the case. In doing so, he concluded that there was no 'significant risk' because '[t]he doctors called on behalf of defendants did not regard that risk as significant; nor do I'. Moreover, he stated that the consultant could not be criticised when dealing with a distressed patient for not

---

[302] (1999) 48 BMLR 118.
[303] Note, however, that Lord Browne-Wilkinson in *Bolitho* made it clear that he was not dealing with an information disclosure case.

informing her of 'that very, very small additional risk'—one in the order of 0.1–0.2 per cent. In this sense, the risk was 'small' in statistical terms. However, and importantly, there is little evidence that 'significance' is determined by reference to patient-orientated criteria. While the language used by the Court of Appeal is suggestive of a movement away from the precedents of the past, and while 'the doctor, in determining what to tell a patient, has to take into account all the relevant considerations',[304] the outcome and the reasoning may simply locate the decision within the existing paradigm—namely, the *Bolam* test. A possible exception lies where there is a 'significant risk'—i.e. a self-evidently high statistical risk of serious harm occurring, which *no* reasonable person, professional or otherwise, would find it acceptable to withhold. Even so, there is little doubt that the tenor of debate surrounding these matters has been veering to the side of the patient and her right to choose for many years now. Precedents such as this can be taken either way and the future direction of the law lies as much in the attitude with which the individual courts approach such cases as in the ratio of *Pearce*.[305] Movement away from *Bolam*, as the High Court of Australia so readily accepted in *Rogers v Whittaker*, is due to recognition of the fact that the advice-giving aspect of medical practice is not entirely a matter of medical knowledge and expertise. This must be correct for, unlike diagnosis and treatment, the question of whether a patient wishes to consent to a particular procedure is bound firmly to the notion of patient autonomy—the choice of the patient is crucial and a choice can only be real and valid if it is based on adequate information. This brings us full circle and back once again to the nature of the doctrine of informed consent and its future.[306]

Causation, informed consent and the future

10.132 Much of the fate of informed consent may have been recently sealed by the House of Lords' decision in *Chester v Afshar*,[307] which we consider at para 10.136 below. Here we move from questions about the standard of care that patients can expect from their doctors to the far more technically complex area of causation where the focus shifts to the patients themselves. As we stated at the beginning of this section, information disclosure cases essentially turn on the question of causation: the patient is saying, 'if you had warned me of the risk I would not have consent to run it; I only did

---

[304] (1999) 48 BMLR 118 at 125—'which include the ability of the patient to comprehend what he has to say to him or her and the state of the patient at the particular time, both from the physical point of view and an emotional point of view . . .' These matters go to the capacity of the individual patient to absorb the information. They tell us nothing about what the patient is entitled to know as a matter of law. Moreover, they are determined by medical judgment, not by patient need.

[305] The problems involved are explicit in *O'Keefe v Harvey-Kemble* (1999) 45 BMLR 74, CA, a case involving cosmetic rather than therapeutic breast surgery. The warnings given were considered insufficient.

[306] The importance of the way in which information is given is shown in the recent case of *Thompson v Bradford* (2004) EWHC 2424, in which a child contracted poliomyelitis as a result of being operated on shortly after vaccination, both lack of care and causation were proved largely on the basis that the doctor had been unnecessarily dismissive of the parents' concerns.

[307] N 236 above.

so because I didn't know about the risk—the harm (the materialisation of the risk) has been caused by your negligent failure to disclose'. The hurdles are manifold. It may, for example, simply be a question of witness credibility. In both *Smith v Salford Health Authority*[308] and *Smith v Barking, Havering and Brentwood Health Authority*[309] the courts refused to accept that the claimants would not have proceeded with the respective medical procedures had they been informed of the risks. To be clear, these are not examples of the courts accusing witnesses of lying; rather it the courts' assessment of the 'facts' of the case that the patients would probably—on balance of probabilities—have proceeded even if they had been told.

10.133   But by what test should a patient's testimony be judged as to what he would or would not have done? There are several ways to answer this question. The first involves a purely subjective judgment—that is, what would that particular patient have considered to be adequate information? This is clearly open to the abuse of hindsight. It will be only too easy for a plaintiff, once he has suffered damage, to allege that he would not have given his consent when, in reality, he may well have been quite prepared to do so, even with full knowledge of the risks entailed—as a Californian court had it: 'Subjectively he may believe [he would have declined treatment] with the 20/20 vision of hindsight but we doubt that justice will be served by placing the physician in jeopardy of the patient's bitterness and disillusionment'.[310] The subjective standard is weighted overwhelmingly in favour of the plaintiff and only a few jurisdictions have accepted it.[311]

10.134   An alternative objective approach is to postulate a standard based on a reasonable patient. Would the reasonable patient have given his consent when confronted with full information of the risks and difficulties of the procedure in question? If the answer is 'yes', then it may be inferred that the plaintiff himself would have consented. This, like all objective tests, has the disadvantage of being potentially unfair to the plaintiff. There may be specific circumstances which are unique to the individual and it may well be that he or she genuinely would not have consented. To apply the objective standard might, then, be equally unsatisfactory: 'if it is Utopian to think one must concentrate on the particular patient, the law should surely be aiming at Utopia'.[312] The reasonable patient test has practical value in that judges are, themselves, potential patients and can, therefore, assess the evidence at first hand rather than by proxy; at the same time, this introduces the element of personal prejudice

---

[308] (1994) 23 BMLR 137.   [309] [1994] 5 Med LR 285.

[310] *Cobbs v Grant* 104 Cal Rptr 505 (1972). It is important to note, however, that this case has never been picked up as a precedent.

[311] The subjective standard was certainly used by the New Zealand Court of Appeal in *Smith v Auckland Hospital Board* [1964] NZLR 241, SC; revsd [1965] NZLR 191, NZCA, but there was no argument on the point in this very early case; a clear Antipodean preference for the subjective standard is to be found in the New South Wales Court of Appeal decision: *Ellis v Wallsend District Hospital* [1990] 2 Med LR 103. For full exposition, see D Giesen *International Medical Malpractice Law* (1988) pp 252 et seq.

[312] K McK Norrie 'Informed Consent and the Duty of Care' 1985 SLT 289. Or achieving 'the ethical optimum of patient autonomy' as put by M Brazier 'Patient Autonomy and Consent to Treatment: The Role of the Law?' (1987) 7 LS 169.

and, in *Maynard*,[313] the trial judge was considered to have been in error in preferring one body of medical opinion to another.

10.135   A third, compromise, possibility exists. The court may opt for an objective approach but qualify it by investing the hypothetical reasonable patient with the relevant special peculiarities of the individual plaintiff. In this way the edge is taken off the objective test, while the pitfalls of the purely subjective approach are avoided. The courts in Canada vacillated for some time between the alternatives of the object-ive and subjective approaches.[314] Finally, in *Reibl v Hughes*,[315] the Supreme Court came down in favour of the compromise solution. The effect of this is that one's starting point is to determine the extent to which the balance of risks was, medically speaking, in favour of the treatment in question. This allows a decision to be made as to whether a reasonable patient would have consented and, that done, the court can proceed to look at the particular patient's condition. Here the judgment in *Reibl v Hughes* emphasised the importance of taking into account the patient's questions to the doctor, as these will demonstrate his concerns and will better enable the court to assess what a reasonable patient in the plaintiff's position would have done. This is now also largely the position adopted in the United Kingdom.

10.136   But matters can be yet more complicated as *Chester v Afshar* demonstrates only too well. Here a young woman found herself in circumstances strangely similar to those of Mrs Sidaway: a surgeon treating the patient for serious back pain failed to disclose a low (1–2 per cent) but serious risk of nerve damage and paralysis inherent in the operation. This manifested itself and the patient sued in negligence claiming that had she been informed of the risk she would not have gone ahead with the operation when she did.[316] It was not established a trial, however, and indeed the plaintiff did not argue, that she would never undergo the operation (and so never run the risk). Moreover, it was accepted that the risk in question was a constant: it was an integral part of the operation in question; it was irrelevant who performed it or when. Thus a very important issue arose as to whether it could meaningfully be said as a matter of law that the surgeon *caused* the patient's harm. Lords Hoffmann and Bingham were adamant and emphatic in their rejection of the claimant's case. For Lord Bingham, she had not met the basic requirements of the 'but for' test—she had not shown that *but for* the failure to warn she would never have undergone surgery.[317] Lord Hoffmann stated, quite simply, that there was no basis on the ordinary principles of tort law for recovery, and he was not con-vinced that a special rule was needed in the instant case.[318] But it was precisely on this

---

[313] *Maynard v West Midlands Regional Health Authority* [1985] 1 All ER 635, [1984] 1 WLR 634, HL. A rather similar judicial foray into medical decision-making was rejected on appeal in *Gold v Haringey Health Authority* [1988] QB 481, [1987] 2 All ER 888, CA. *Maynard* has been widely followed but is now under scrutiny in the light of *Bolitho v City and Hackney Health Authority* [1997] 4 All ER 771, (1997) 39 BMLR 1.

[314] See e.g. *Male v Hopmans* (1967) 64 DLR (2d) 105; *Kelly v Haslett* (1976) 75 DLR (3d) 536.

[315] (1980) 114 DLR (3d) 1.

[316] The breach of the requisite standard of care requiring that the information should have been disclosed was not in doubt.

[317] *Chester v Afshar*, n 236 above, para 8.

[318] *Ibid*, para 32.

last point that the three remaining members of the bench took issue with their learned colleague.[319] While each acknowledged that, indeed, there could not be recovery on the 'standard rules', they argued, variously, that policy, justice or the particular nature of decisions relating to one's health and well-being called for a departure from those rules. And, most significantly, common to their arguments was the view that these negligence actions are essentially concerned with protecting the patient's right to choose—that is, her autonomy. They pointed out that each of their Lordships in *Sidaway* recognised this as the basic legal interest at stake; Lord Walker went as far as to emphasise the importance of the growth of autonomy-based arguments over the last twenty years as the basis for justifying an outcome in the claimant's favour in the instant case.[320]

10.137   We, too, have stressed throughout this book how fast and far autonomy-based reasoning has come to dominate medical law. As to its influence in information disclosure cases, however, we remain ambivalent. While we disapprove of the enduring role of the *Bolam* test as the measure of the standard of care because of its failure to distinguish between information disclosure and other medically-determined treatment scenarios, we find that *Chester* perhaps swings too far in the other direction, allowing obeisance to autonomy to undermine sound legal principle.[321] It is not only justice to the patient that is at stake. Moreover, even if we accept that a patient's self-determination interests have been compromised by a failure fully to inform, we agree with Lord Hoffmann that the resulting harm is more in the nature of solatium—hurt to feelings—than related to the actual physical injury itself.[322] This is important for the significant impact it would have on the measure of damages.[323] But, however one views *Chester*, it does, as we have written in another short appraisal of the case, represent 'an important shift in judicial thinking on questions of causation and has significant implications for the future. It seems, however, that *Bolam*'s place in the relevant law is likely to move regressively towards the rear of the field'.[324]

10.138   Certainly the wind of change is now blowing strongly and the question is no longer 'is the doctrine of informed consent coming to the United Kingdom?' but, rather, 'what can we do to improve on the American model?'[325]

---

[319] A lot of support was drawn from the Australian decision in *Chappel v Hart* [1999] 2 LRC 341, (1998) 72 ALJR 1344 which dealt essentially with the same issue and where there was also division of opinion among the justices.

[320] *Chester v Afshar*, n 236 above, para 92.

[321] O O'Neill 'Some Limits of Informed Consent' (2003) 29 J Med Ethics 4 is an important commentary. Its practical implications are discussed in K M Boyd 'Beyond Consent?' (2004) 34 J R Coll Physicians 290.

[322] *Ibid*, per Lord Hoffmann, para 34 (the *physical* damage being inherent in the operation and not due to negligence).

[323] We speculate tentatively whether this also reflects the motivation for creating a new measure of damages in wrongful conception cases such as *Rees v Darlington Memorial Hospital NHS Trust* [2003] 4 All ER 987. Are we moving towards the recognition of a new tort of infringement of autonomy?

[324] K Mason and D Brodie '*Bolam, Bolam*—Wherefore Art Thou *Bolam*?' (2005) 9 Edin LR 398.

[325] The various themes that can be accommodated under the umbrella of 'informed consent' are well described in a recent analysis by A R Maclean 'The doctrine of informed consent: Does it exist and has it crossed the Atlantic?' (2004) 24 LS 386.

10.139   In our view, a start might well be made by dropping the phrase 'informed consent' in favour of 'valid consent'—or, perhaps better, using the word 'understanding', for a competent adult has every right to make a decision which may appear irrational to others. Both are terms which pay due deference to patient autonomy and, at the same time, provide the doctor with a yardstick as to what is expected of him.[326] We need to ensure that any spirit of confrontation between the medical profession and the public is halted and abandoned in favour of the concept of what Teff described as a therapeutic alliance.[327]

[326] The use of other ill-defined terms such as 'effective consent' in the Human Fertilisation and Embryology Act 1990, Sch 3 or 'appropriate consent' in the Human Tissue Act 2004 do little more than compound the difficulties.

[327] H Teff 'Consent in Medical Procedures: Paternalism, Self-determination or Therapeutic Alliance?' (1985) 101 LQR 432.

11

HEALTH RESOURCES AND DILEMMAS IN TREATMENT

11.1   No resources are infinite. Even if a basic material is widely available, the costs of harvesting, treating or assembling it put some restraint on its use; moreover, the manpower required for distribution and exploitation of the finished product is also going to be limited. Applying these to medicine, it is clear that it is well-nigh impossible to provide every form of therapy for everyone—some sort of selective distribution is inevitable.

11.2   The logistics of medicine get no easier despite—or, more probably, because of—the massive technological advances of the last half century. Costs of all types are rising while even comparatively affluent countries face persistent economic difficulties. The average span of life is increasing—at least in the developed countries—and, as a result, people need treatment for longer; this treatment is not the 'easy-cure' type appropriate to infectious diseases but is rather a matter of sophisticated care for the results of degenerative change. In addition, members of the public are better informed on medical matters and are better able to assimilate the information they are given; they are subjected to a barrage of advice of varying quality on the Internet and, as a result, the choice of treatment is increasingly influenced by the patient's demands, with proportionate erosion of the doctor's discretion—in effect, while the latter may wish to treat on a productivity basis, the former views therapy in terms of feasibility.[1]

11.3   Somehow, a compromise must be achieved between demand and supply; the distribution of scarce resources poses some of the more complex ethical problems of modern medicine and permeates every aspect of its provision. They are not confined to the higher administrative echelons nor to the more esoteric departments of major hospitals. They may, indeed, arise and be answered subconsciously—every time a doctor travels to visit a patient he is distributing his resources in favour of one priority and this is possibly at the expense of others with which he could have dealt during his non-productive driving time.[2]

---

[1] It is only fair to say that these widely held views can be criticised in that the evidence for their influence is virtually untested: S Frankel, S Ebrahim and G D Smith 'The Limits to Demand for Health Care' (2000) 321 BMJ 40. None the less, we accept the fact that ever-increasing financial provision for the health service has failed to close the gap between supply and demand.

[2] This aspect was amplified in R Klein 'Dimensions of Rationing: Who Should Do What?' (1993) 307 BMJ 309.

11.4 Such an example relates to the treatment of individuals. But the ethics of health service distribution can also be considered on a global scale; the problems arising at a national level occupy an intermediate position. We propose examining these as three separate issues.

GLOBAL DISTRIBUTION OF RESOURCES

11.5 It is beyond question that the world's medical resources are distributed unevenly both in material and in human terms. The money to buy the expensive paraphernalia associated with modern hospital medicine is often not available in the developing countries; most often, the infrastructure to distribute and administer medicines and to support patients throughout their illnesses simply does not exist.[3] At the same time, there are inadequate facilities for the local training of doctors who must, therefore, travel to obtain experience. The result is a vicious circle in which doctors accustomed to the sophisticated methods of the developed nations return to their own countries only to depart again dissatisfied with what they have found; permanent emigration of doctors and, in particular, nurses adds to the problem.

11.6 All this occurs in the face of increasingly destructive pandemics of infectious disease—in particular HIV infection, tuberculosis and malaria—and the effect is amplified by a shortage of public health resources. Requests are then made of developed countries for medical assistance in the form of rapid response and the supply of cheap drugs.[4] The response, such as it is, is not necessarily entirely altruistic. Along with the development of international travel, we have created ideal conditions for the spread of such diseases and action at source may be a matter of self-preservation.[5] Supply of medicines also, of course, comes at a price; while (Western) pharmaceutical companies might be well placed to ease the plight in developing countries, they also need to protect their markets. Thus, the practice of buying up drugs cheaply in one market for importation into developing countries in an attempt to address the public health crisis has often been met by the strategic exercise of restrictive intellectual property rights by the manufacturers of the drugs. The tensions have been recognised by the World Trade Organization which issued its Doha Declaration

[3] Commission on Intellectual Property Rights *Integrating Intellectual Property Rights and Development Policy* (2002), chapter 2 (Health). See too the work of the World Health Assembly's Commission on Intellectual Property Rights, Innovation and Public Health (established 2003): www.who.int/intellectualproperty/en/.

[4] J Frenk and O Gómez-Dantés 'Globalisation and the Challenges to Health Systems' (2002) 325 BMJ 95. Note: World Health Organization *Macroeconomics and Health: Investing in Health for Economic Development* (2003).

[5] The near hysteria at the appearance of the severe acute respiratory syndrome (SARS) in the Far East in 2003 is a case in point.

in November 2001 in an attempt to reach compromise and agreement on the issues.[6] The Declaration stresses the importance of implementing international intellectual property agreements so as to promote access to medicines and to encourage the development of new ones.[7] Agreement was eventually reached in August 2003, and we have discussed this elsewhere;[8] its terms, and indeed those of almost any kind of aid provided to developing countries, are, however, heavily politically influenced and, to this extent, become a matter beyond the scope of our current discussion.[9]

THE ALLOCATION OF NATIONAL RESOURCES

11.7   We come closer to personal reality when discussing resource allocation on a national scale and, here, a mass of relevant literature has built up in recent years—much of which admits the near impossibility of a wholly just solution.

11.8   The primary problem, which is essentially political, is to establish what share of the national resources is to be allocated to health—and it is the open-endedness of claims to health care that leads to particular difficulties. The Department of Health announced 2006/07 and 2007/08 allocations totalling £135 billion in February 2005 yet, despite such largesse, claims can never be met in full. Moreover, issues of justice between claimants will inevitably arise after the broad budgetary decisions have been made. Ideally, resource allocation should provide equal access to health care for those in equal need. Attempts have been made in recent years to achieve this by systematically correlating the revenue given to the health authorities with their needs. These needs were originally based by the Resource Allocation Working Party on the standardised mortality rates which were taken as representing the underlying morbidity. This, in itself, is open to criticism, as it reflects the needs at hospital level rather than those of the provision of primary care which is particularly affected by external factors such as the degree of social deprivation. Nevertheless, RAWP, as the process continues to be known, appeared to provide an objective, albeit rough, formula which could be readily understood; inevitably, it was subject to criticism and the major discrepancies were ironed out slowly.[10] A new formula was introduced in 1991 which weights the age adjusted population of each region by the square root of its standardised

---

[6] For an account of the history and possible future of DOHA, see World Trade Organization, *The Road to DOHA and Beyond* (2002).

[7] See too the separate Declaration on public health, *Declaration on the TRIPS Agreement and Public Health*, November 2001.

[8] G Laurie 'Patenting and the Human Body' in A Grubb (ed) *Principles of Medical Law* (2nd edn, 2004).

[9] For a philosophical approach, see R Attfield 'The Global Distribution of Health Care Resources' (1990) 16 J Med Ethics 153.

[10] N Mays 'Measuring Morbidity for Resource Allocation' (1987) 295 BMJ 703; J Smith 'RAWP Revisited' (1987) 295 BMJ 1015; more recently, J Appleby 'RAWP: Weighting for A Change' (1995) 105 Hlth Serv J 34.

mortality rate for those under 75 years old;[11] this was based on empirical findings. One effect is, as pointed out by Sheldon, to open the doors to differential interpretation at sub-regional level and to political lobbying by health authorities who can gain from some of the many variables which can, legitimately, be fed into the resultant equation—moreover, by their nature, empirical data are unlikely to be fully contemporary. Some explicit measure of macroallocation of national resources is clearly needed—it was once suggested, for example, that one result of its use is that vote maximising policies become more obvious and are, thus, more difficult to carry out.[12] Even so, it may well be that it is better left at a relatively unsophisticated level and that further research is directed to how the allocations, once made, are actually used.[13]

11.9   When allocation is considered at sub-regional level, equity becomes a less significant factor and gives way to the dictates of demand. This inevitably involves a choice and this choice must be, to some extent, arbitrary. The ethical control of resources then depends, first, upon the broad base of representation on the allocation committee and, secondly, on the willingness of the constituent members not to press their own interests too hard—a process which has been described, and, to an extent, approbated, as shroud waving;[14] the lay influence on what were community health councils has been important at this point and is likely to remain so.[15]

11.10   In any event, a change in policy was laid down in the National Health Service and Community Care Act 1990 which established the district health authorities as purchasers of health services on behalf of the local population. In this role, they were required to act as good housekeepers and not only to provide what the people want but also to do this in the most cost-effective manner.[16] The choices can never be easy—is it possible to decide the relative importance between, say, strict economy, the avoidance of suffering or the prolongation of life? And how is one to identify the best route to the intended goal? If, for example, morbidity as a whole is taken as the yardstick, the alleviation of bronchitis and asthma has been found to take precedence; if, on the other hand, one considers total hospital in-patient days, mental health may be the single most important consideration. But to say that mental health and respiratory disease constitute the most serious burdens on the health service is not necessarily to say that they merit the greatest allocation of resources. There is a strong economic incentive to apply some sort of 'productivity test' in distributing the resources of

---

[11] Department of Health *Funding and Contracts for Health Services, Working Paper 2* (1989). For discussion, see T A Sheldon, G D Smith and G Bevan 'Weighting in the Dark: Resource Allocation in the New NHS' (1993) 306 BMJ 835—particularly for the mathematical analysis which is beyond the ambit of this book.

[12] See e.g. A Maynard and A Ludbrook 'Applying Resource Allocation Formulae to Constituent Parts of the UK' (1980) 1 Lancet 85.

[13] The latest formulae can be accessed at www.dh.gov.uk/assetRoot/04/02/02/72/04020272.pdf.

[14] J Rawles 'Castigating QALYs' (1989) 15 J Med Ethics 143.

[15] Community Health Councils are to be abolished (National Health Service Reform and Health Care Professions Act 2002, s 22). Community Health Partnerships are now established in Scotland: National Health Service Reform (Scotland) Act 2004. Patient and public involvement at all levels of health care is a cornerstone of current central policy on both sides of the border (see also chapter 1).

[16] See C Newdick 'Rights to NHS Resources after the 1990 Act' (1993) 1 Med L Rev 53.

society; the question is—is it ethical to do so? Analysis of the problem raises some stark and disturbing answers. Thus, it has been said that to reject opportunities to allow natural dying is costly in financial terms—in a health care service with finite resources, it is neither harsh nor unethical to accept the consequences of a financial limit.[17] And the same article expressed the grim reality of political power in the suggestion that to spend a lot on the elderly might not be supported by public opinion if it became known that younger lives were being lost because of inadequate finance.

11.11   This immediately draws attention to one major difficulty encountered in any such evaluation based on public opinion—which is that the welfare of unproductive citizens is likely to be regarded as secondary to that of the productive unless the views of voluntary representative organisations with specific interests are given consideration; the mentally handicapped and the elderly are, in fact, in double jeopardy—not only may they be seen as less deserving of resources, but they are less likely to be invited to subscribe to the opinion-making process. Geriatric patients, it is said, would not and should not expect priority over younger patients. Which is true enough—but they *would* expect equal consideration. Harris's argument,[18] which sees the saving of life as the main medical objective, is at its strongest when we are considering the use of life years as a parameter for the assessment of the disposal of scarce resources. The choice between a 20-year-old and an 80-year-old may be straightforward to the outsider. But, at the moment of decision, each patient values his or her life equally—and the problem, then, is how to decide when age alone becomes an irrelevant factor; a productivity test, for example, demands that treatment should be both beneficial *and* effective whereas an evaluation on the basis of social good may conclude that benefit alone is sufficient to justify the resultant costs to the community.[19]

11.12   It is inevitable that, so long as there is a restriction on resources, some principle of maximum societal benefit must be applied; the individual's right to equality must, to some extent, be sacrificed to the general need. The precise determination of a maximum benefit policy is difficult to make, but the decision is societal rather than medical and involves a 'cost-benefit' analysis and all that that entails as to the quality of life.[20] Essentially, there are three potential measures of a free health service— comprehensiveness, quality and availability—and the situation is that the goal of fully comprehensive, high quality medical care that is freely available to all on the basis of

[17] G S Robertson 'Dealing with the Brain-damaged Old—Dignity Before Sanctity' (1982) 8 J Med Ethics 173.

[18] J Harris 'Unprincipled QALYs' (1991) 17 J Med Ethics 185.

[19] The seriously dated paper by M A Somerville ' "Shall the Grandparents Die?": Allocation of Medical Resources with an Ageing Population' (1986) 14 Law Med Hlth Care 158 remains one of our favourites. For a more contemporary analysis, see J Hurley 'Ethics, Economics, and Public Financing of Health Care' (2001) 27 J Med Ethics 234.

[20] A particularly poignant example is to be found in the salvage of extremely premature infants. The cost of intensive care has been put at £20,000 for each baby weighing less than 1.5kg and some 50% of these may sustain brain damage sufficient to require life-long support. Would the money be better spent on research into the prevention of prematurity? Office of Health Economics *Born Too Soon* (1992). See L Hunt 'Cost "Dilemma" Posed by Premature Babies' (1993) *The Independent*, 20 January, p 6.

medical need is unattainable in the face of steadily increasing costs;[21] the temptation is to lower one standard in favour of the other two.

11.13   The difficulties are formidable because what we are discussing at this level is essentially 'horizontal resource allocation', or priority setting between different types of service, which depends not so much on professional medical assessment and advice as on public opinion and on evidence as to cost and effectiveness[22]—and the former, at least, is a fickle measuring instrument. Not only can polls be grossly distorted by the way in which questions are put but also opinion is very subject to political and other extraneous influences—particularly that of the media whose circulation depends on maintaining an aggressive and partisan attitude. Attempts that have been made in the past to sacrifice comprehensiveness in favour of 'core care' by way of translating societal attitudes into standardised decision-making[23] seem to achieve less than satisfactory results. The essential dilemma stems from the fact that the categories of choice on which a consensus may be sought are indefinable save at the margins of health care.[24] However, the new emphasis on explicitness—or transparency—in rationing strategies is an increasingly important development and may lead to surprising results; resource allocators, it has been said, should not take it for granted that their own values are shared by the general public.[25]

11.14   Given the absence of any obvious set of principles on which to act and given that the function of the NHS and primary care trusts is, on the one hand, ultimately constrained by the strategic health authority[26] and, on the other, is to provide what the public wants, it is unsurprising that the distribution of the scarcer resources is uneven and that the principles invoked in decision-making are uncertain—the factors given most weight have been found to range from the availability of other funding (e.g. the private sphere) for the service to the more obviously laudable potential for health gain in terms of length and quality of life.[27] In a survey of six districts, now a few years old, Ham found that there was a general reluctance to exclude some services entirely from their contracts. But it is from a review of a service which was *not* provided by some authorities—in this case, in-vitro fertilisation—that some of the clearest evidence of the factors likely to be considered influential is to be found. These included:

[21] A Weale 'Rationing Health Care' (1998) 316 BMJ 410.

[22] M Cochrane, C Ham, C Heginbotham and R Smith 'Rationing: At the Cutting Edge' (1991) 303 BMJ 1039.

[23] P A Lewis and M Charny 'Which of Two Individuals Do You Treat When Only Their Ages Are Different and You Can't Treat Both?' (1989) 15 J Med Ethics 28.

[24] See reply to Lewis and Charny, n 23 above: D Lamb 'Priorities in Health Care' (1989) 15 J Med Ethics 33; also B A Stoll 'Choosing Between Cancer Patients' (1990) 16 J Med Ethics 71.

[25] E Nord 'The Relevance of Health State after Treatment in Prioritising between Different Patients' (1993) 19 J Med Ethics 37. It is to be noted that the deliberations of NICE (see para 11.21 below) are now held in public.

[26] Now established by way of National Health Service Reform and Health Care Professions Act 2002.

[27] See the analysis provided by C Ham 'Priority Setting in the NHS: Reports from Six Districts' (1993) 307 BMJ 435.

(a) the presence of a prominent lobbyist for the service and the ready availability of the service;

(b) whether or not a competent public health department could be used to interpret the effectiveness of and need for the service;

(c) whether it represented a true health need;

(d) having decided that there was a need, whether the particular service offered the best way of meeting that need;

(e) notwithstanding the effectiveness of the service, whether it should be purchased at the expense of another unrelated service;

(f) whether valid reasons could be given for selective treatment when supply fell short of demand; and

(g) whether it was right to introduce a service which could not be given to everyone.[28]

11.15 Despite the obvious difficulties, we see it as self-evident that some form of cost evaluation in health care is essential at the resource purchasing level, if only to ensure impartiality—pressure groups tend to be bad advocates from the point of view of society as a whole in that success in their particular field must encourage deprivation in others. We agree with those who believe that there are no intrinsic ethical problems in applying economic considerations to health resource allocation. It should, rather, be accepted that without such control there is likely to be an unethical maldistribution of resources; as Williams put it, anyone who says no account should be paid to costs is, in reality, saying no account should be paid to the sacrifices thereby imposed on others— and there are no *ethical* grounds for ignoring the effect of an action on other people.[29] Surely, everyone would agree with this—but it still leaves open the question of in which group's favour is a marginal change in resource allocation rightly to be tilted.

11.16 We must also not lose sight of the fact that there are more reasons than cost for limiting the availability of drugs and other treatments. A health authority may, for example believe that a given therapy is useless and, accordingly, refuse to sanction its purchase. Such situations arise most commonly in those conditions for which there is, currently, no effective treatment. Sufferers from multiple sclerosis, for example, will clutch at any straw and will be unimpressed by the need for statistical evaluation of a drug before they can be given the chance to use it. So long as the adoption of a new drug remains a matter of individual advisory medical opinion, the result will be an inequality of distribution which breeds consumer dissatisfaction.[30] Alternatively, the

---

[28] S Redmayne and R Klein 'Rationing in Practice: The Case of In Vitro Fertilisation' (1993) 306 BMJ 1521.

[29] A Williams 'Cost-effectiveness Analysis: Is It Ethical?' (1992) 18 J Med Ethics 7. See also G Mooney 'QALYs: Are They Enough? A Health Economist's Perspective' (1989) 15 J Med Ethics 148.

[30] At the same time, a national policy for the provision of a service may result in *local* decisions as to collateral economies; uniformity may, as a result, be even further compromised: R Cookson, D McDaid and A Maynard 'Wrong SIGN, NICE Mess: Is National Guidance Distorting Allocation of Resources?' (2001) 323 BMJ 743.

condition itself may be questioned as to its nature—is its alleviation a truly medical matter or is it one of 'lifestyle enhancement' only? Here, we could place, for example, assisted reproduction and gender reassignment in the 'grey' area of the black to white scale where we are likely to get different answers from different authorities.[31] At the more extreme, we could consider the supply of sildenafil (Viagra) through the NHS. There are occasions when impotence—as opposed to sexual inadequacy—can be seen as a proper medical concern. But this is a far cry from supplying a drug with no intention other than to improve sexual performance. Consequently, the government foresaw an exceptional demand for sildenafil which could have had an adverse effect, both financial and healthwise, on the rest of the community; accordingly, it issued Circular no. 1998/158 which advised doctors not to prescribe sildenafil and Health Authorities not to support the provision of the drug at NHS expense other than in exceptional circumstances. The circular was, however, declared unlawful in the High Court in that its 'blanket' nature was interfering with doctors' professional judgments.[32] It is, therefore, evident that the courts will strongly uphold the right of the *individual* patient to individual consideration in the face of attempted 'rationing'—but only when it is agreed that it is the treatment of a *disease* that is in issue.

11.17   Finally, it must, of course, be conceded that societies differ and, while some form of resource rationing is, as we believe, inevitable, no single system will be universally acceptable. Britain has been described as an original sin society[33] in which tribulation in the form of ill-health is expected—a view which, incidentally, is becoming less and less acceptable as the years pass. The United States, on the other hand, are seen as a society dominated by consumerism and striving for perfectibility of man; the demand for and the use of medical resources are bound to differ. That being so, it is, perhaps, anomalous that the first experiment in public consensus health care rationing should have had its origins in the United States.[34] The State of Oregon has, as a result of research including extensive public debate, arrived at an adaptable prioritised list of treatments which will and will not be available under Medicaid and business-related private insurance arrangements. Inevitably, the plan has had its difficulties—one of which lies in the constantly changing list of priorities and the consequent inflation

[31] Even so, once the condition is classified as a disease, the authority must consider the individual's condition before refusing to fund treatment: *R v North West Lancashire Health Authority, ex p A, D and G* [2000] 1 WLR 977, (2000) 53 BMLR 148.

[32] *R v Secretary of State for Health, ex p Pfizer Ltd* [1999] Lloyd's Rep Med 289, (2000) 51 BMLR 189. Note that it would have been lawful, given the time, for the Secretary of State to 'blacklist' sildenafil under the National Health Service (General Medical Services) Regulations 1992, SI 1992/635, Schs 10 and 11.

[33] R Klein 'Rationing Health Care' (1984) 289 BMJ 143. For an updated comparative review, see R G Lee and F H Miller 'The Doctor's Changing Role in Allocating US and British Medical Services' (1990) 18 Law Med Hlth Care 69.

[34] M J Garland 'Justice, Politics and Community: Expanding Access and Rationing Health Services in Oregon' (1992) 20 Law Med Hlth Care 67; S Rosenbaum 'Mothers and Children Last: The Oregon Medicaid Experiment' (1992) 18 Am J Law Med 97; J Dixon and H G Welch 'Priority Setting: Lessons from Oregon' (1991) 337 Lancet 891. The New Zealand experience is referred to below at para 11.20.

of the basic health care package that is available.[35] Its success or failure also depends to a large extent on extraneous factors such as the strength of the state economy as a whole, which leads to fluctuation in the number of those covered. We doubt, however, if the Oregon experiment has any direct relevance to the United Kingdom. Quite apart from the disparate populations involved, the Oregon plan is directed at those who cannot, for financial and other reasons, obtain private medical insurance, whereas the NHS is open to all in the United Kingdom as of right.

11.18   The American experience of rationing within the private sector has been fraught with difficulty. The proportion of the domestic national product spent on health is substantial and people have come to expect a high level of medical attention. In an attempt to contain costs, the insurers introduced managed health care systems under which plans they undertook to provide necessary health care, the question of what is necessary being determined by the insurers themselves. These schemes have been widely criticised as limiting consumer choice and as constituting disguised rationing. The political and legal controversy surrounding them demonstrates the difficulty of imposing rationing on those whose expectations are high.[36]

11.19   There may well be lessons to be learnt from the United States but, New Zealand, being, so far as we know, the only Commonwealth country to have overtly adopted a rationing policy in a fully tax-funded health system, perhaps offers a more useful comparator. The now-called New Zealand National Advisory Committee on Health and Disability appears to have rapidly abandoned the Oregon model of a list of treatments that are and are not available and, instead, has decided to issue a series of guidelines as to how restricted, publicly funded resources are to be allocated.[37] Guidelines were developed for the treatment of specific conditions and there is little doubt that the resulting compartmentalisation of resources gives rise to some uncomfortable, albeit salutary, reading. The reasons for this discomfort are not easy to define. Probably no country in the world surpasses New Zealand in its dedication to human rights and to fair treatment for all, yet the fact that the guidelines as to eligibility for treatment of end-stage renal failure included recommendations that, in usual circumstances, persons aged over 75 should not be accepted and that other serious diseases or disabilities that are likely to affect survival or the quality of life are reasons for exclusion clearly opens the door for discrimination on the basis of value-laden judgments which may well be beyond the medical remit; we return to this problem at para 11.35.

---

[35] C Ham 'Retracing the Oregon Trail: The Experience of Rationing and the Oregon Health Plan' (1998) 316 BMJ 1965. And an interesting critique of the US system overall: E J Lamb 'Rationing of Medical Care: Rules of Rescue, Cost-effectiveness, and the Oregon Plan' (2004) 190 Amer J Obs Gynecol 1636.

[36] A C Enthoven, H H Schauffler and S McMenamin 'Consumer Choice and the Managed Care Backlash' (2001) 27 Amer J Law Med 1.

[37] The majority of our information is derived from the authoritative authorship of C M Feek, W McKean, L Henneveld et al 'Experience with Rationing Health Care in New Zealand' (1999) 318 BMJ 1346. See also C M Feek 'Rationing Healthcare in New Zealand: The Use of Clinical Guidelines' (2000) 173 Med J Austral 423.

11.20   The seminal test of the New Zealand guidelines[38] concerned a man, W, in end-stage renal failure who also suffered from diabetes and dementia.[39] A decision was taken to discontinue interim dialysis—first, on the grounds that W's moderate dementia left him outside the group of persons considered suitable for inclusion in the treatment programme but, later, on a pure clinical and 'best interests' standard. The decision was forcefully contested and the matter was ultimately heard by the New Zealand Court of Appeal. There, the Court refused to accept the case as a test of the guidelines, and, hence, as a question of rationing, and determinedly held it to be a matter of the exercise of clinical judgment within good medical practice—even to the extent of stating that the case raised no significant ethical issues; accordingly, the decision of the High Court that it was totally inappropriate for a court to attempt to direct a doctor as to what treatment should be given to a patient was upheld.[40] None the less, despite its restricted scope, *Shortland* is still relevant to the 'rationing' debate in that it shows the difficulties inherent in making subjective clinical decisions once general guidelines have been laid down for the use of resources in specific conditions. As Feek et al put it: 'Explicit rationing will work only when clinicians accept the link between clinical decision-making and resource allocation'—and one has to ask: which comes first? Moreover, whatever may be the logic that drives informed professional opinion, the public are unlikely to distinguish between the two. Feek et al quote the following press comment:

[T]he reality is that [W's] case was not a priority. First concerns have to be for patients who are not terminally ill, who do not have other complications and who have a better chance of rehabilitation.[41]

None of which provides much comfort for the elderly who are not quite as bright as they used to be.

THE NATIONAL INSTITUTE FOR HEALTH AND CLINICAL EXCELLENCE

11.21   The current United Kingdom parallel approach rests on the National Institute for Health and Clinical Excellence (NICE)[42] which resulted from an amalgamation of the National Institute for Clinical Excellence with the Health Development Agency. The latter's function was, and remains so in the new organisation, essentially within the

---

[38]   *Shortland v Northland Health Ltd* [1998] 1 NZLR 433, (1999) 50 BMLR 255.

[39]   Richardson P described this as brain damage (at BMLR 256) and his general practitioner as mild dementia. W had expressed a wish to remain alive—cf the English case of *Re D (medical treatment: consent)* [1998] 2 FLR 22, (1998) 41 BMLR 81 in which it was held that dialysis need not be imposed on a patient who could neither accept nor refuse treatment.

[40]   Salmon J at BMLR 257 relying heavily on *Re J (a minor)* [1993] Fam 15, [1992] 4 All ER 614.

[41]   From the *Nelson Mail*, 13 October 1997. The authors also refer to W's continued treatment as futile.

[42]   NICE, in the form of a National Council for Health Priorities, was forecast in an exceptionally thorough analysis of the position at the time by C Newdick 'Resource Allocation in the National Health Service' (1997) 23 Amer J Law Med 291.

public health sector and, thus, was responsible for the prevention of ill-health; the former was established as a special health authority within the NHS in 1999[43] with a remit described as being to carry out such functions in connection with the promotion of clinical excellence in the health service as the Secretary of State may direct. In essence, this wide responsibility crystallised into providing advice and guidance as to what treatments are best for patients on a national scale Such guidance for 'best practice' can be divided into three categories: clinical guidelines, recommendations as to audit and the appraisal of the clinical, and cost-effectiveness of new and existing health technologies;[44] we are, here, concerned only with the last of these functions. In this respect, the Institute was hailed as a rational response to the existing situation, already outlined above, whereby individual health authorities determined whether, or in what circumstances, a given treatment would be provided—a system which had come to be popularly known as 'post-code prescribing'. Ideally, NICE's decisions were intended to be based on pure clinical need and efficiency but, inevitably, they had to include consideration of what was best for the health service itself; as we have already seen, scientific value and social value judgments cannot be dissociated in a tax-funded service[45]—the conclusion, as a leading article in *The Times* put it, is that: 'The National Institute for Clinical Excellence is rationing made plain.'[46]

11.22   As a consequence, NICE is, to an extent, living a lie[47] and is subject to not only commercial and political pressures but also to massive influence from the media—it becomes very much easier to approve a new or expensive treatment than to refuse its use. NICE has, to date, provided guidance on the use of over 200 drugs and treatments[48] and its decisions are unashamedly moulded to a large extent by their economic effect. At its simplest, this is a matter of deciding what increase in health is likely to accrue from the increased expenditure involved in introducing a new treatment—the so-called incremental cost effectiveness ratio—and NICE's preferred measure of this is the cost per quality adjusted life year (QALY). We discuss the concept of the QALY as applied to the individual below at para 11.47. Here, it need

---

[43] National Institute for Clinical Excellence (Establishment and Constitution) Order 1999, SI 1999/220. Meetings of NICE must be open to the public (SI 1999/2219). The Scottish equivalent is the Health Technology Board for Scotland the function of which is to advise on the clinical and cost-effectiveness of new and existing treatments but a second organisation, the Scottish Intercollegiate Guidelines Network, which is based at the Royal College of Physicians of Edinburgh and is concerned mainly with the clinical appraisal of new treatments, has also been operating within the NHS since 1993. We will confine our observations to NICE.

[44] K Syrett ' "Nice Work?" Rationing, Review and the "Legitimacy Problem" in the "New NHS" ' (2002) 10 Med L Rev 1.

[45] The way in which decisions are taken is detailed by the Institute's current chairman: M D Rawlins and A J Culyer 'National Institute for Clinical Excellence and Its Value Judgments' (2004) 329 BMJ 224.

[46] Leading Article 'Not a Nice Habit' *The Times*, 12 April 2002, p 23. It is fair to say that at least one major survey suggests that NICE is more concerned with the clinical effect of a treatment than with the cost per QALY: J Raftery 'NICE: Faster Access to Modern Treatments? Analysis of Guidance on Health Technologies' (2001) 323 BMJ 1300.

[47] R Smith 'The Failings of NICE' (2000) 321 BMJ 1363. Though it is fair to say that the Institute has gained in stature in the last few years.

[48] C Shannon 'Money Must be Made Available for NICE Guidance, Minister Says' (2003) 327 BMJ 1368. T H S Dent and M Sadler 'From Guidance to Practice: Why NICE is not Enough' (2002) 324 BMJ 842.

only be said that, having established for how long a new treatment offers an enhanced quality of life, the Institute estimates what extra cost this would involve individually and, by extrapolation, what effect this would have on the overall economy of the Health Service. There is no threshold, each case being considered on its merits but, with commendable honesty, NICE says that it would be unlikely to reject a technique with a ratio of £5,000–£15,000/QALY on the grounds of cost ineffectiveness alone; on the other hand, a ratio of £25,000–£35,000/QALY would indicate the need for special reasons before it was accepted.[49]

11.23   One of the most illustrative examples of the scheme in practice related to the use of interferon beta for the treatment of multiple sclerosis. In June 2000, the Chairman of NICE confirmed that the Institute was considering a recommendation that interferon beta should not be prescribed to new patients on account of its low success rate and very high cost. Media speculation then prompted confirmation of this—but with the added rider that the Department of Health might consider ways in which the drug could be made available on a cost-effective basis. NICE issued its final guidance in February 2002 by which time the Department of Health had embarked on a risk-sharing scheme in which interferon beta would be funded only if treatment trials in individual patients showed it was effective—an attitude to research that was severely criticised by academic scientists.[50] Confusion reigns; meantime, a full review of the guidance on the treatment of multiple sclerosis is not expected until 2006.

11.24   The difficulties are not over, even when such finality is achieved—someone has to pay the bill. Money is now available from central sources by which to achieve the aim that the NHS will provide any treatment endorsed by NICE within three months of the decision. Inevitably, there have been teething problems in implementation[51] but, at least, a major criticism of the Institute has been addressed. Currently, clinical guidance is, as its name suggests, not mandatory on practitioners; the guidance is, however, binding on purchasers. While this seems a simple statement, there are difficulties in putting it into practice and NHS Trusts will inevitably interpret their instructions differently—often in respect of the way in which the budget is distributed. As a result, the distribution of selected treatments still varies across the country.[52] NICE is something of a brave attempt to rationalise, and nationalise, our health care—but it cannot eliminate all the underlying problems.

11.25   NICE guidelines raise a number of questions as to liability in the event that they are not followed—it has, for example, been suggested that the guidelines might replace

---

[49] M D Rawlins and A J Culver 'National Institute for Clinical Excellence and Its Value Judgments' (2004) 329 BMJ 224. Professor Rawlins is Chairman of NICE. Special reasons might include fairness and consideration of the features of the condition being treated and the population involved—hence, age may be a relevant factor (see para 11.44 below). NICE does not consider affordability which is a matter for the government and which may trump its decisions.

[50] S Mayor 'Health Department to Fund Interferon Beta despite Institute's Ruling' (2001) 323 BMJ 1087.

[51] Shannon, n 48 above.

[52] A very interesting break-down of how the guidance is implemented in practice is provided by T A Sheldon, N Cullum, D Dawson et al 'What's the Evidence that NICE Guidance has been Implemented?' (2004) 329 BMJ 999.

the *Bolam* test for medical negligence and, since individual clinical autonomy is not specifically suppressed, the physician or surgeon wishing to exercise his or her own judgment may be left in a quandary.[53] Our own view is that the rules should be similar to those applied to any 'guidelines'—the practitioner is not bound to follow them but, in the event of something going wrong as a result, it would be that much more difficult to justify the action taken. Margaret Brazier has recently redrawn attention to the alternative and as yet untested question—that is, what is NICE's liability in the event that its advice is faulty? Certainly, NICE's decisions are subject to judicial review but this is of small consolation to the patient who sustains injury as a result of his or her doctor following the wisdom of the Institute, possibly against his or her better judgment. This aspect of the 'legitimacy' of the Institute was addressed in depth by Syrett[54] and the test is certainly a hard one, particularly in that an essentially scientific body is being asked to make what are often moral judgments within a pluralistic society. No NICE decisions are likely to please everyone[55] and the role of the courts in enforcing 'reasonableness' becomes increasingly important. The question is, is legal intervention to be welcomed or distrusted?[56]

THE LEGAL SITUATION

11.26   Financial restraints clearly place the Secretary of State in some difficulty in discharging his statutory duty to provide, to such extent as he (or she) thinks necessary to meet all reasonable requirements, including, inter alia, hospital accommodation.[57]

11.27   In some ways it is surprising that there have not been more actions brought by patients who feel that the Secretary has failed in these duties but, on reflection, it is probable that the dearth of cases results from the extreme improbability of a successful outcome. Cases are, however, reported sporadically and the classic action is that of *Hincks*.[58] In that case, patients in an orthopaedic hospital complained that they had waited an unreasonable time for treatment because of a shortage of facilities arising, in part, from a decision not to add a new block to the hospital on the grounds of cost; accordingly, they sought a declaration that the Secretary of State and the health authorities were in breach of their duty. In dismissing the application, Wien J said it was not the court's function to direct Parliament what funds to make available to the health service nor how to allocate them. The duty to provide services 'to such extent as he considers necessary' gave the minister a discretion as to the disposition of financial

---

[53] M R Utting et al 'Total Hip Replacement and NICE' (2005) 330 BMJ 318.

[54] N 44 above.

[55] Although the World Health Organization has given its technology approval programme general approval: N Devlin, D Parkin and M Gold 'WHO Evaluates NICE' (2003) 327 BMJ 1061.

[56] An extreme view, quoted by Syrett is that: 'there is no place for the courts in rationing health care. The law is too blunt a weapon in an area of moral and ethical choices that are heavily contingent upon the circumstances prevailing in a particular case'—D Hunter 'Rationing Healthcare: The Political Perspective' (1995) 51 Brit Med Bull 876.

[57] National Health Service Act 1977, s 3.

[58] *R v Secretary of State for Social Services, ex p Hincks* (1979) 123 Sol Jo 436.

resources. The court could only interfere if the Secretary of State acted so as to frustrate the policy of the Act or as no reasonable minister could have acted; and no such breach had been shown in the particular case. Moreover, even if a breach was proved, the Act did not admit of relief by way of damages.

11.28   The case went to appeal[59] where, as might be expected, the judgment turned on the interpretation of 'reasonable requirements'. Lord Denning MR considered this to mean that a failure of duty existed only if the minister's action was thoroughly unreasonable. It was further thought that we should be faced with the economics of a bottomless pit if no limits in respect of long-term planning were to be read into public statutory duties; the further the advances of medical technology, the greater would be the financial burden placed upon the Secretary of State.

11.29   Since 1980, however, health authorities, under whatever name, have been required to balance their individual budgets.[60] Inevitably, major decisions as to the provision of health care have been moved down one hierarchical step, thus bringing the decision-makers into closer contact with those affected. Society, now in the guise of the Patient and Public Involvement Forums, has a statutory place in the process[61] and, as a corollary, is entitled to judicial review of decisions thought to have been taken improperly. Nevertheless, attempts to extend this privilege to individuals seeking improved access to treatment have foundered consistently on the rock of the reasonableness test inherent in the jurisprudence to date.

11.30   The paradigmatic case is that of *Walker*,[62] which concerned a baby whose surgery had been postponed five times because of a shortage of skilled nursing staff. The trial judge, Macpherson J, deprecated any suggestion that patients should be encouraged to think that the court had a role in cases which sought to compel the authority to carry out an operation that was not urgent; and the Court of Appeal confirmed his refusal of the application for review. Within two months, the same health authority was involved in a comparable case, the only major difference being that the child was possibly in greater immediate danger.[63] Reiterating that, to be so unreasonable as to come within the jurisdiction of the court, the Authority would have had to make a decision that no reasonable body could have reached,[64] Stephen Brown LJ said:

[59] *R v Secretary of State for Social Services, ex p Hincks* (1980) 1 BMLR 93, CA. The case was discussed by J D Finch in 'Rationing of Resources' (1985) 290 BMJ 374 and by D Brahams 'Enforcing A Duty to Care for Patients in the NHS' [1984] 2 Lancet 1224. See also C Newdick 'Rights to NHS Resources after the 1990 Act' (1993) 1 Med L Rev 53. F H Miller 'Denial of Health Care and Informed Consent in English and American Law' (1992) 18 Am J Law Med 37.

[60] National Health Service Act 1977, s 97A, inserted by Health Services Act 1980, s 6.

[61] Established under the National Health Service Reform and Health Care Professions Act 2002, s 15—Patients Forums (Functions) Regulations 2003, SI 2003/2124..

[62] *R v Central Birmingham Health Authority, ex p Walker* (1987) 3 BMLR 32, CA.

[63] *R v Central Birmingham Health Authority, ex p Collier* (6 January 1988, unreported, available on Lexis). The case was discussed by D Brahams 'Seeking Increased NHS Resources Through the Courts' (1988) 1 Lancet 133. See also Newdick n 59 above; Miller n 59 above for this case and *Walker*.

[64] *Associated Provincial Picture Houses Ltd v Wednesbury Corpn* [1948] 1 KB 223 at 229, [1947] 2 All ER 680 at 683, per Lord Greene MR, CA.

In the absence of any evidence which could begin to show that there was [such a failure] to allocate resources in this instance . . . there can be no arguable case . . . It does seem to me unfortunate that this procedure has been adopted. It is wholly misconceived in my view. The courts of this country cannot arrange the lists in the hospital . . . and should not be asked to intervene.

11.31   While expressing great sympathy with the parents, Stephen Brown LJ suggested that it might have been hoped that the publicity would bring pressure to bear on the hospital and there is no doubt that this effect could, and on occasion does, materialise —particularly in a life-saving situation. Dyer reported a typical case of a woman suffering from end-stage renal failure who was refused dialysis facilities; on her being granted legal aid to take the authority to court, an extra £250,000 was made available to the local renal units.[65] Whatever one thinks of the morality of the process, it seems to have been a very successful exercise in 'shroud waving'—and it is to be noted that the money was not 'new' but was plucked from the waiting list fund. The circumstances were such, however, as to raise a real possibility of *Wednesbury* unreasonableness. An even more spectacular 'success' concerned Laura Davies, who received, and rejected, a liver and small intestine transplant; she was then given a second transplant involving seven organs at a cost estimated as £1m, which is said to have been defrayed by a Middle Eastern potentate.[66] Perhaps the most publicised relevant incident in recent years has been that of 'Child B', in which funding for an essentially ineffective treatment was refused.[67] This case is discussed in detail below;[68] for the present, it is appropriate only to quote the Chief Executive, who was, as the mouthpiece of the health authority, taken to be responsible for the decision:

[The] case took on a symbolic importance, helping people to grasp the reality that expectation and demand had now outstripped their publicly funded systems' ability to pay without regard to the opportunity cost.[69]

11.32   It is, perhaps, worth noting that the NHS has not been singled out for judicial cheese-paring. In a case brought under the Chronically Sick and Disabled Persons Act 1970, it was held that the costs of the arrangements and the authority's resources were proper considerations in assessing whether a person had a need and whether it was necessary to make arrangements to meet it.[70] The case concerned the *removal* of social services from a disabled man; some of the difficulties involved are crystallised in the dissenting opinion of Lord Lloyd:

---

[65] C Dyer 'Going to Law to Get Treatment' (1987) 295 BMJ 1554.

[66] For a critical lay view of such disposal of both financial and organic resources, see K Muir 'Can Saving the Life of Little Laura Really Be Worth £1 million?' *The Times*, 22 September 1993, p 15.

[67] *R v Cambridge Area Health Authority, ex p B (a minor)* (1995) 25 BMLR 5; revsd (1995) 23 BMLR 1, CA.

[68] See chapter 16.

[69] S Thornton 'The Child B Case—Reflections of a Chief Executive' (1997) 314 BMJ 1838. Interestingly, reporting restrictions were lifted in order to facilitate a public appeal fund: *Re B (a minor)* (1996) 30 BMLR 101.

[70] *R v Gloucestershire County Council, ex p Barry* [1997] AC 584, (1997) 36 BMLR 69, HL.

How can resources help to measure [the man's] need? ... It cannot, however, have been Parliament's intention that local authority B should be able to say 'because we do not have enough resources, we are going to reduce your needs'. His needs remained exactly the same. They cannot be affected by the local authority's inability to meet those needs.[71]

Even so, as in the medical cases, the court was not minded to interfere with the intricacies of resource allocation.

11.33   It is to be noted, however, that resort to human rights and constitutional arguments has introduced a new element into resource allocation cases. The full impact of the Human Rights Act 1998 on the health service in the United Kingdom is still uncertain but it will, at the very least, require decisions to be made with regard to due process requirements and to claims to equality. It is very unlikely, however, that Article 2 of the European Convention on Human Rights, which protects the right to life, will provide an automatic entitlement to treatment in any particular case; it could, however, prevent the evolution of any policy which denied reasonable access to readily available resources. Such human rights arguments have been made in a number of other jurisdictions. In South Africa, for example, the Constitutional Court held that the provision in the Constitution which states that 'everyone has the right to have access to health care services . . .' did not give an absolute entitlement to any particular treatment, and that hard decisions as to the availability of expensive treatments—in this case dialysis—would have to be made by the medical authorities.[72] This very supportable approach did not prevent the South African courts later ordering the Government to provide HIV-suppressing drugs to pregnant women as a matter of constitutional entitlement.[73]

11.34   It has been suggested that more than half the British public favour unlimited funding of the NHS.[74] While this is clearly impossible, it can be argued that, once it is established that there is a reasonable requirement for a particular service, no further qualification of the Secretary of State's duty to provide it exists and that inadequate resources do not absolve him from this duty.[75] This may well be so but, in so far as one cannot make a pot of tea without tap water unless one takes the water from the coffee urn, it adds little to the solution of the inherent problems. Clearly, however, a further major ethical dilemma centres on the imposed medical limitations on treatment of the individual and it is to that aspect that we now turn.

---

[71] [1997] AC 584 at 599, (1997) 36 BMLR 69 at 96.

[72] *Soobramoney v Minister of Health KwaZulu-Natal* (1997) 12 BCLR 1696 (CC), (1999) 50 BMLR 224.

[73] *Minister of Health v Treatment Action Campaign* (2002) (5) SA 721, CC.

[74] T Groves 'Public Disagrees with Professionals over NHS Funding' (1993) 306 BMJ 673. For a recent review of public attitudes, see J Appleby and A A Rosete 'The NHS: Keeping Up with Public Expectations?' in A Park et al (eds) *British Social Attitudes: The 20th Report* (2003).

[75] G P Morris 'Enforcing a Duty to Care: The Kidney Patient and the NHS' (1983) 80 Law Soc Gaz 3156. But an extrapolation of *R v Gloucestershire County Council, ex p Barry* [1997] AC 584 suggests that this would be unlikely to be sustained.

TREATMENT OF THE INDIVIDUAL

11.35   In discussion of the medical treatment of the individual, we are faced not with the hypothetical patient who may become ill but with one who is actually at risk. Objectivity is no longer the main arbiter and is replaced by need—which, in a medical context, can be defined as existing 'when an individual has an illness or disability for which there is an effective and acceptable treatment'.[76] In practice, access to such treatments will be limited by their cost—for a limited budget will provide only a limited number of treatment units. As a result, some form of differential treatment is enforced and, in turn, the assessment of relative needs involves a value judgment.

11.36   How, then, is that judgment to be made? In practice, many decisions are made instinctively and without the need for profound analysis—thus, the single-handed doctor will unhesitatingly choose the patient in greater pain for treatment, despite the fact that this will simultaneously delay the treatment of those in lesser pain. There may well be moral arguments against such a policy—it does, for example, act to the detriment of the stoic—but the circumstances are acute and, the urgency being comparable, the doctor has selected a single criterion on which to base his judgment. Moral agonising is, in practice, reserved for the treatment of chronic, life-threatening diseases, not only because they offer the opportunity for analysis but because they attract the use of expensive resources and will consume these for a long time—at which point the dilemma extends not only to the allocation of resources but also to their withdrawal. The treatment of chronic renal diseases and of brain injury provide good examples on which to base discussion.

11.37   It is easy to say that enough dialysis machines should be made available to treat all cases of chronic renal failure but, in existing circumstances, this may merely mean that some other financially dependent resource must be curtailed. Costs can be cut by, for example, changing a policy of hospital dialysis to one of home treatment, but the fact of financial restraint is not thereby removed—only its degree is altered. At the same time, the modern patient undoubtedly regards access to high technology medicine as his individual right and such a view is readily tenable when there is an urgent or life-saving need. If the doctor is, perforce, to qualify those rights, his reason for so doing must be beyond reproach and therein lies the problem.

11.38   The case of Mr McKeown in New Zealand[77] is a classic of its type. James McKeown was a man aged 76 in end-stage renal failure. He also had coronary artery disease and prostatic cancer. Given dialysis, his expectation of life was about two years; nevertheless, he clearly failed the consensus guidelines for the treatment of renal failure and the head of the dialysis unit is quoted as saying: 'Given our resources, he had to fit into a group we said no to'. The patient's family then laid a complaint of age discrimination with the Human Rights Commission of New Zealand. As a result, the hospital

---

[76] N Bosanquet 'A "Fair Innings" for Efficiency in Health Services' (2001) 27 J Med Ethics 228.
[77] Reported by Feek et al, n 37 above.

authorities ordered a clinical review of the case, renal dialysis was started and Mr McKeown died 18 months later—presumably by way of his malignant disease. How, then, is this case to be analysed in retrospect? On one view, the treatment, at best, served no more than a doubtfully useful purpose and, at worst, may have deprived a more deserving claimant of therapy. In the alternative, one can hold that all persons who have lost their kidney function will die at the same rate; all are, therefore, equally entitled to life-saving intervention and their length of survival is immaterial.[78] Our inclination is to adopt the latter stance—but we freely admit that intuition does not solve the underlying dilemma.

11.39   Essentially, the New Zealand system involves allocating resources in terms of triage. Triage is a curiously derived expression meaning, in the present context, the separation of casualties into priority treatment groups. It is basically a military concept, the current British policy being to allocate four categories of casualty, ranging from those whose slight injuries can be managed by self-care to those who cannot be expected to survive even with extensive treatment and who are, therefore, treated on a humanitarian basis only; the policy is closely associated with that of casualty evacuation. Triage in this sense is not only good emergency surgical practice but is also ethically acceptable because it is directed to a single discernible end—that is, to win the war or the battle, and we accept that this, in itself, is a morally acceptable objective with which the medical branch of the armed services can quite properly associate itself. But can we, in ethical terms, simply transfer the concept of triage, which is an emergency procedure, to elective civilian practice? It may be possible to do so in special circumstances—it is, for example, a recognised practice following a major disaster, when the single most pressing objective is to mitigate the effects of that disaster. But we are not dealing with a single issue in normal practice. The circumstances of, and the circumstances surrounding, each patient are so disparate that triage, and its underlying principles, cannot be used as a convenient substitute, or subterfuge, for resource allocation and should be abandoned for that purpose.[79] What, then, does one put in its place?

ALTERNATIVE MODELS

11.40 There have been many attempts to find a solution[80] but none is satisfactory—all generalisations fail when applied to the particular but we will briefly outline some

---

[78] This is, roughly, the view of J Harris 'What is the Good of Health Care?' (1996) 10 Bioethics 269. The question of from whose viewpoint we are to judge the utility, or otherwise, of an eighteen-month extension of life is discussed in chapter 12.

[79] Not everyone would agree with this view: eg J Cubbon 'The Principle of QALY Maximisation as the Basis for Allocating Health Care Resources' (1991) 17 J Med Ethics 181. See also K M Boyd and B T Potter 'Priorities in the Allocation of Scarce Resources' (1986) 12 J Med Ethics 197.

[80] An exhaustive analysis of the alternatives was given in a classic paper by H J J Leenen 'The Selection of Patients in the Event of a Scarcity of Medical Facilities: An Unavoidable Dilemma' (1979) 1 Int J Med Law 161. For a more recent appraisal, see M J Langford 'Who Should Get the Kidney Machine?' (1992) 18 J Med Ethics 12.

proposals which have been made. It is, perhaps, easiest to progress from those parameters which we consider to be least appropriate at the individual patient level.

11.41   We do not believe that cost-benefit should be a major influence here. It needs no profound philosophical analysis to make one appreciate instinctively that it is right to deploy a helicopter to rescue a man on a drifting pleasure raft, despite the fact that his danger is of his own making, despite the expense and despite the fact that the helicopter is designed to carry ten persons. The immediacy of the situation has placed a very high value on life which it would be quite immoral to ignore. The value cannot, however, be infinite—otherwise, faced with the choice of saving one man on a raft or ten men in a sinking dinghy, the grounds for the 'value choice' would be equal whereas, in practice, few would doubt the correctness of choosing the larger number—always provided the operational circumstances were similar. Such choices must, however, be very rare in practice. In the chronic situation, as exemplified by dialysis, we are effectively confronted with a one-to-one choice between two individuals; at this point it might be possible to introduce a cost-benefit argument which takes the form of assessing the relative gain to society of saving one or the other. In practice, this would invoke the use of some formula such as 'earning capacity x (retiring age—actual age)'. We believe, however, that neither age nor income group should be primary criteria regulating choice per se—it might be that the aged respond less well to treatment than do others[81] but that would be a different consideration. Such an assessment would, in addition, offend 'moral' practices which have almost attained the force of common law and of which 'women and children first' is an obvious example; at least according to admittedly crude criteria based on earnings potential, women would generally come out worse if such objective cost-benefit criteria were to be applied. But this is not to say that some concern for quality or expectation of life should not be thrown into the prognostic balance as discussed below.

11.42   The corollary to this line of thought is that scarce resources should be distributed on the basis of the 'deserts' or basic merits of the recipients. One aspect of this can be seen in a United States experiment which attempted to distribute a very scarce resource—human kidneys—to those hospitals which had, themselves, provided organs; while such a system has much to commend it, any benefit accrues to the hospital rather than to the individual patient who still has to be 'chosen' by some other method. Others would look at this criterion from the opposite point of view and would exclude those who could positively endanger the treatment programme—a group that is exemplified by those carrying strains of the virus of hepatitis. But such reasoning is a purely technical matter. A more moralistic variant on this theme would hold it to be acceptable for a society which was providing the facility to exclude persons who increased the cost of care through their own choice;[82] while this is

---

[81] Hence, say, the relative acceptability of denying in vitro fertilisation to older women: *R v Sheffield Heath Authority, ex p Seale* (1994) 25 BMLR 1.

[82] H T Engelhardt 'Allocating Scarce Medical Resources and the Availability of Organ Transplantation' (1984) 311 New Engl J Med 66.

certainly arguable, it is a concept that is probably more applicable to communities in which the health of only a proportion is being supported by the taxes paid by the remainder—the beneficiaries of a national health service are more likely to see themselves as all in the same leaky boat.

11.43   More often, the assessment of 'deserts' is taken to apply to the intrinsic worth of the subject to society—and, again, we may look at this from the negative or positive aspect. First, such a method of selection inevitably discriminates against those who have some additional disability—and particularly mental disability—which limits their perceived value in a societal sense; this group, however, is, perhaps, better included among those falling to be assessed under the 'medical benefit' test discussed below. The alternative, positive, approach in the event of shortage of facilities for treatment is to select those who offer the greatest contribution to society now and in the future. In our view, allocation tests which attempt to distinguish between, for example, the philanthropic mafia millionaire and the contestant for an international prize in applied mathematics serve no useful purpose in that they are hopelessly subjective. Choices so based are clearly beyond the capacity or function of the doctor and the 'principle' can be dismissed out of hand.

11.44   The one 'deserts-related' issue which is most commonly raised is that of age. It is very widely held that the older a patient is, the less can he or she command equal opportunity in a competition for therapy. The reasons for this acquiescence differ. Some will rely on the argument 'he's had his innings'—but even this depends, to an extent, on one's position in the batting order; others, more rationally, will point to the fact that results of treatment are generally better in the young than in the old—but simply because the results of coronary surgery are commonly more satisfactory in the middle-aged patient does not mean that surgery is not worthwhile in the 75-year-old.[83] There is, moreover, a tendency to forget that not every therapy is effective for a full life-span; it matters not whether the patient treated is aged 20 or 60 if we anticipate that the treatment will result in survival for no more than five years. We suspect that the reason underlying the common assumption is that those responsible for decision-making are, by definition, below retiring age; it has been said, rightly, that there is often a wide discrepancy between the optimum solution of a problem from the perspective of society as a whole and that of the individual within that society.[84] Lewis and Charny[85] tried, by means of an opinion poll, to establish the points at which the public would be prepared to accept age-based choices and, thus, to map out decision-making boundaries which will reflect the values of society as a whole. This was a praiseworthy effort which may, indeed, be widely copied in the future as the government inspired lay participation in medical decision-making gathers momentum; for ourselves, while appreciating the value of uniformity and accepting the attractions of

[83] We discuss the problem of age—and, particularly, the recent statements from NICE—in the next chapter.
[84] Lewis and Charny, n 23 above.   [85] *Ibid.*

the development of guidelines established by way of wide societal involvement, we find it difficult to support a cold actuarial basis for making what is still a human clinical decision.

11.45   Clearly, the most widely acceptable criterion of selection would be that determined by medical benefit.[86] But, once again, this is easier to accept in theory than to put into practice. Unless one is dealing with a recoverable condition—and dialysis in the context of end-stage renal failure, which is providing the main theme for discussion, is only palliative[87]—medical benefit is a relative matter and, moreover, prognosis is unpredictable. It is also difficult to avoid the conclusion that the individual's financial and social status may influence the outcome of any therapy—despite the ultimate medical basis for any decision, access to scarce resources is, then, governed by what are, essentially, non-medical considerations.

11.46   But, even if the clinician claims absolute responsibility for allocation of his expertise, he must consider the quality of the life he is extending and it is here that he may obtain guidance from—or suffer the interference of—the health economist. Perhaps the greatest influence in this field over the last few decades has been the introduction of the concept of quality adjusted life years—or QALYs—which we have already introduced in a national context above.

Quality adjusted life years

11.47   The principle of the QALY is simple enough. A year of healthy life expectancy is scored as 1 and a year of unhealthy life as less than 1, depending upon the degree of reduction in quality; while death is taken as zero, a life considered to be worse than death can be accorded a minus score. The 'value' of treatment in terms of 'life appreciation' can then be assessed numerically. Thus far, in fact, QALY's as applied to the individual seem to be doing little more than expressing the intuitive findings of the competent clinician in a mathematical formula. And, therein lies the rub—for the 'quality scoring' will still be founded on a 'best interests' assessment made by a third party and the paternalistic element in that assessment has been scarcely modified. It is, for example, hard for a middle-class doctor not to see a middle-class life as being of higher quality than one spent 'sleeping rough'; a young physician may see a short life on the golf course as preferable to a long one tied to the television set—but this may well not be the patient's evaluation. It is thus apparent that, at this level, a QALY can only be truly evaluated with the patient's co-operation; it can then be used to decide between two possible treatments for the same condition. Here, in what has been described as 'vertical priority setting', one is on more level ground in so far as one is

---

[86] The choice made, inter alia, by Professor Gillon's remarkably prescient daughter: see R Gillon 'Justice and Allocation of Medical Resources' (1985) 291 BMJ 266. It was also the implicit choice of the court in *Re J (a minor) (wardship: medical treatment)* [1993] Fam 15, [1992] 2 FLR 165.

[87] Very different considerations might apply in the not improbable circumstances of a large number of people requiring dialysis for recoverable acute tubular renal failure, say, following an earthquake, and an inadequate number of machines was available.

comparing like with like.[88] Used in this way, QALYs may actually augment the patient's autonomy by explicitly involving him or her in the process of rational consent to therapy.[89] Even so, a note of caution may be sounded as it is not difficult to confuse the objectives. The easy phrase 'not clinically indicated' may mean either that the treatment is not considered to be of overall benefit to the patient or it may imply an inappropriate allocation of resources.[90] The distinction is conceptually important; in the latter case, the professional has a legitimate prior interest in decision making while, in the former, the views of the patient must be given proportionate consideration.

11.48   There are other more specific objections to QALYs as applied at the individualistic level. Clearly, they operate to the disadvantage of the aged; they measure only the endpoint of treatment without considering the *proportional* loss or gain in the quality of life; and there are parameters other than simple health which need to be fed into the equation. Possibly the most important moral criticism is that the QALY sets no value on life per se.[91] Harris considers that we should be saving as many lives, not life years, as possible—a proposition which simplifies the argument by removing it from the ambit of life-saving treatment which should, then, be apportioned only on a 'first come, first served' basis;[92] we also suggest that the customary use of the term 'life-saving', when what is really meant is 'death-postponing', can lead to false reasoning. What this view certainly does, however, is to emphasise that QALYs can never be used to compare the value of 'life-saving' therapies with those which are merely life-enhancing. Indeed, we may well wonder whether we have any right to pronounce on the quality of other people's lives and, hence, whether abstract formulae should ever be used to compare the management of individual persons or different disease states. We should be very careful lest we find that we have unwittingly written into the equation a constant such as that the mentally handicapped, for example, are, by definition, possessed of less QALYs than are those with no such inherent deficit.[93]

11.49   In view of these many criticisms, it is not surprising that alternatives to the QALY are being actively sought. One such system is the saved young life equivalent, in which saving the life of a young person and restoring him or her to full health is regarded as the unit of measurement—on the grounds that most people would regard that as the maximum benefit that a single individual can obtain.[94] The comparative value of treatments is then assessed in terms of how many expected outcomes of each treatment would be equivalent to one SAVE. Our specific criticism of such a system would

[88] Cochrane et al n 22 above.   [89] See para 10.106.

[90] See T Hope, D Sprigings and R Crisp ' "Not Clinically Indicated": Patients' Interests or Resource Allocation?' (1993) 306 BMJ 379.

[91] See, in particular, J Harris 'QALYfying the Value of Life' (1987) 13 J Med Ethics 117; Rawles, n 14 above.

[92] Cf the case of Mr McKeown, para 11.38 above.

[93] For something of an ethical defence of *in*equality, see J Savulescu 'Resources, Down's Syndrome and Cardiac Surgery' (2001) 322 BMJ 875.

[94] E Nord 'An Alternative to QALYs: The Saved Young Life Equivalent (SAVE)' (1992) 305 BMJ 875.

be that, even by its title, it actively promotes 'ageism'—which is little more than an incidental to the QALY concept. Moreover—and in common with all such formulae —it reduces persons to numbers and tends to dehumanise medical practice. In this respect, there is much to be said for the more recent introduction of the 'discrete choice experiment' in which the attributes of a treatment—or those features of a treatment which influence the way in which the therapeutic outcome is achieved—are fed into its evaluation; in other words, the process as well as the outcome is taken into consideration. The use of the word 'choice' indicates the importance attached to patient preference; research along these lines is, therefore, very much in line with current health care policies and it is probable that NICE will take advantage of this line of research.[95]

11.50   A final alternative is that proposed by Daniels,[96] which is reminiscent of the stand-ard legal approach to these questions in the UK. He advocates a fair, deliberative process of setting limits on difficult decisions where it is impossible to satisfy all parties; the process is typified by clear articulation of criteria for decision-making, transparency at every level, and an overall aim to reach decisions which are acceptable to (all) reasonable persons because the reasons—and values—behind them are at least understood, even if they are not agreed. This approach is clearly potentially relevant at each of the levels we have identified as giving rise to problems of resource allocation and, indeed, it could well be tested in the ongoing case of *R (on the application of Burke) v General Medical Council*.[97] Here, the court of first instance held, clearly, that a patient was entitled to demand nutrition and hydration for as long as he or she was alive as judged by a beating heart. What was left unclear was the extent to which a person who was considered, medically, to be untreatable could demand treatments of his or her own choice as of right. The implications as to the use of resources were such that the GMC was joined by the government in appealing the decision and the Secretary of State took the unusual step of explaining her reasons for so doing in a public statement.[98] As we go to press, we hear that the appeal has succeeded.

11.51   Whatever principles are invoked to establish a fair and a preferred method of distribution of resources at patient level, it is impossible to exclude the health econo-mist from decision-making even at the doctor/patient interface. It may well be salu-tary for physicians and surgeons to be forced into knowing the cost-effectiveness of any given procedure and, at base, NICE takes on the function of enforcer. Inevitably, this raises questions of professional clinical independence[99]—and, equally, to some

[95] M Ryan 'Discrete Choice Experiments in Health Care' (2004) 328 BMJ 360 quoting M Ryan and S Farrar 'Eliciting Preference for Healthcare using Conjoint Analysis' (2000) 320 BMJ 1530.

[96] The seminal work is N Daniels *Just Health Care* (1985); see too N Daniels and J E Sabin *Setting Limits Fairly: Can We Learn To Share Medical Resources?* (2002).

[97] (2004) 79 BMLR 126, QBD. See also R Gillon 'Why the GMC Is Right to Appeal over Life Prolonging Treatment' (2004) 329 BMJ 810.

[98] P Hewitt 'Appeal over Right to Medical Care' (2005) *The Times*, 24 May, letters, p 16.

[99] At the time of writing, there is opposition to NICE's proposed withdrawal of approval from several drugs used in the treatment of Alzheimer's disease: R Irving 'Anger at Drugs Removal' (2005) *The Times*, 10 March, p 53. The cost of the most expensive of these per quality of life year gained was said to be £48,000.

polarisation of views. Thus, on the one hand, it has been said that to allow clinical problems to be resolved in financial terms is to condone: 'the development by health economists of fairer methods of denying patients treatment'.[100] To which the economist would reply: 'The economic perspective is clear—to maximise health improvements from limited resources by targeting resources at those activities high in the cost-QALY league table'.[101] It is up to society to define its objectives in an area where successful compromise is hard, if not impossible, to achieve.

11.52   To some, the answer to the resource allocation dilemma is simply to increase the resources;[102] others regard this as a dangerous assumption—Klein, for example, suggested that it is only a slight exaggeration to say that the demand for health care is just what the medical profession chooses to make it.[103] We believe that the transfer of funds from, say, nuclear weapon production to health care, while being admirable in itself, does no more than move the problem one incremental stage further. The majority would agree that some form of structured distribution of facilities at microallocation level is essential even though equity and efficiency may, at times, be difficult to accommodate. Harris, for example, has made out a powerful case against the QALY[104] but one that is insufficient to convince one that the best method of resource allocation is on the basis of 'first come, first served'. McKie and his colleagues, in a continuing debate with Harris, saw QALYs, on the other hand, as a sensitive and egalitarian method of distributing scarce resources among competing individuals.[105] We doubt if they should be used in this way. To say that 'the QALY approach is egalitarian because no one's QALYs count for more than anyone else's' takes no note of the fact that, when the chips are down, the QALYs available to each player are unequally stacked. McKie et al were at their fairest when they said that they would restrict the QALY method of assessment if it was shown in a particular case to have a 'divisive and corrosive effect on the sense of community'. But to do so is to reintroduce subjective preferences into what was intended to be an objective exercise and is, to that extent, self-defeating. In the end, QALYs as they stand are no more than aids to decision-making and they are but one of a number of possible models.[106] We take leave to wonder, however, if they should be used other than as a means to choose between alternative therapies—either for general distribution, which is the function of NICE, or for the treatment of the individual patient.

11.53   We should exclude from this discussion, and treat as a special case, the patient who is using a scarce resource but who is obtaining no benefit. The most clear example of

[100] J Rawles and K Rawles 'The QALY Argument: A Physician's and A Philosopher's View' (1990) 16 J Med Ethics 93.

[101] A Maynard 'Ethics and Health Care "Underfunding"' (2001) 27 J Med Ethics 223.

[102] Rawles, n 14 above.   [103] Klein, n 2 above.

[104] J Harris 'Would Aristotle Have Played Russian Roulette?' (1996) 22 J Med Ethics 209.

[105] J McKie, H Kuhse, J Richardson and P Singer 'Double Jeopardy, the Equal Value of Lives and the Veil of Ignorance' (1996) 22 J Med Ethics 204.

[106] For a useful summing up, see R Robinson 'The Policy Context' (1993) 307 BMJ 994.

this is one who is brain damaged and is being maintained in intensive care—a situation discussed in detail in chapter 16 below. We believe that, once treatment is clearly of no avail, it is not only permissible but positively correct to discontinue heroic measures.[107] Of the many reasons for taking this view, the one which is presently apposite is that a resource, even if couched in terms of man-hours only, is thereby released for someone who is likely to benefit.

Random selection

11.54   In our search for an equitable and efficient method of providing limited treatment at the coal-face, only the option of random selection of patients—or of lottery, or 'first come, first served'—remains for discussion.

11.55   Such a policy has the advantage of apparent objectivity and, as we have seen, it could be regarded as the morally desirable choice in the context of potentially fatal disease. It is, however, a bad medical option because it takes no account of the gravity of the patient's condition and no account of 'medical benefit'—it concentrates on justice and ignores 'welfare'; moreover, the sheer length of waiting lists may prevent the most acceptable cases from the physician's point of view from ever obtaining treatment. As an option, it is also socially suspect in that it treats human beings as 'things' and pays no justice to human values and aspirations. And, finally, its acceptance may be a cloak for no more than abrogation of responsibility. Nevertheless, it may be the way of allocating scarce resources that the public prefer.[108]

11.56   It is surprising that there is no recent precedental case law on which to judge the attitudes of society in respect of allocation of resources at the micro, or individual, level.[109] The most likely reason for this is that decisions are taken in good faith and are based on principles which would be acceptable to a responsible body of medical opinion—there is, therefore, no action available in negligence; moreover, there is a tendency for well-publicised and apposite instances to be solved pragmatically. For any assistance, we suspect we must go back to the classic case of US v Holmes.[110] In this instance, a ship's officer ordered a number of passengers to be ejected from a sinking lifeboat; Holmes, who helped effect the instructions, was convicted of manslaughter. A main argument for the prosecution was that the passengers, at least, should have

---

[107] An example is that of Re G (adult incompetent: withdrawal of treatment) (2001) 65 BMLR 6. It is to be noted, however, that such cases are rarely, if ever, argued on a resource basis. We discuss this case further at para 16.119.

[108] There is, for example, no objection to 'waiting lists' for organ transplantation. Calls for more public participation and debate have been made for some time: R Smith 'Rationing Health Care: Moving the Debate Forward' (1996) 312 BMJ 1553 and, as we have seen, are an integral part of government policy.

[109] Such messages as there are conflicting. The European Court of Human Rights was reluctant to make exceptions to the member country's overall rules in the case of Sentges v Netherlands, app. 27677/02; cf. R v North West Lancashire H A, ex p A, n 31 above, in which the Court of Appeal rejected a 'blanket policy' of treatment allocation. As something of an aside, a recent case has held that Article 3 of the ECHR does not require contracting States to provide aliens indefinitely with medical treatment unavailable in their own countries: N v Secretary of State for the Home Department (2005) The Times, 5 May, HL.

[110] 26 Fed Cas 360 (1841), No 15383.

been chosen by lot. It seems fair to assume that this decision would lend support to a policy of randomisation in the event of competition for scarce medical resources; the inferred element of an 'appeal to God' adds some moral weight to the argument. A rather similar English incident is reported in relation to a ferry-boat disaster. Here, a passenger assumed a position of authority and may well have occasioned the sacrifice of one man in order to save the lives of several other passengers; the case never came to court and the coroner thought that such killing would not necessarily be criminal. The commentator, however, considered that such authority as exists is to the effect that the killing of one to save the lives of others cannot be justified or even excused.[111] But such precedents are, at best, only loosely applicable to the present discussion.

11.57　　As to the withdrawal of resources from a patient already using them, both United Kingdom and United States law is discussed in chapters 16 and 17. It is to be noted, however, that nowhere is there any authority for such action on the grounds of competing medical benefit—that is, that a further latecomer to the scene would be likely to do better. Indeed, there are strong indications that the contrary holds. In *Re J*,[112] Balcombe LJ said:

I would stress the absolute undesirability of the court making an order which may have the effect of compelling a doctor or health authority to make available scarce resources (both human and material) to a particular child, without knowing whether or not there are other patients to whom the resources might more advantageously be devoted ... [It might] require the health authority to put J on a ventilator in an intensive care unit, and thereby possibly to deny the benefit of those limited resources to a child who was much more likely than J to benefit from them.

The implication is clear—withdrawal of treatment will only be condoned when the patient can receive no further benefit.

A SOLUTION OF THE INSOLUBLE?

11.58　　We have thus reached a position where no single parameter seems entirely satisfactory. Gordon[113] in a discussion of the doctrine of necessity, speaks of it as offending 'against the feeling that no human being has a right to decide which of his fellows should survive in any situation'; but, while most would agree with this proposition in a general sense, doctors cannot opt out of such decisions. Some idea of the complexity of the dilemma was given in an early, but still interesting study of dialysis decisions.[114] In this, 40 specimen patients' records were sent to 25 renal units with the request that

111　J C Smith 'Justification and Excuse in the Criminal Law' in J C Smith and B Hogan *Criminal Law: Cases and Materials* (6th edn, 1996), p 311. The well-known case of *R v Dudley and Stephens* (1884) 14 QBD 273, [1881–5] All ER Rep 61, CCR was essentially a matter of killing and cannibalism for self-preservation and is too far removed to be appropriate to the present discussion.

112　*Re J (a minor) (wardship: medical treatment)* [1992] 2 FLR 165 at 176, (1992) 9 BMLR 10 at 20.

113　G H Gordon *The Criminal Law of Scotland* (3rd edn, 2000), vol 1, p 506.

114　V Parsons and P Lock 'Triage and the Patient with Renal Failure' (1980) 6 J Med Ethics 173. In fairness, however, it should be emphasised that this is a very dated reference.

ten patients be rejected on the grounds of inadequate treatment resources. Only 13 patients would have been accepted in all the units, but, at the same time, none was rejected by all; in the event, it was discovered that six of the ten most commonly rejected cases had already been successfully treated by the authors! Something of a lottery must have been operating despite the most earnest endeavours of physicians to improve upon the system—and it has to be remembered that far more sophisticated approaches to organ allocation have subsequently been developed.[115] We should also note that the New Zealand consensus guidelines, which we have discussed above, were introduced specifically to eliminate such anomalies—right or wrong, uniformity may be preferable to confusion.

11.59   We have not discussed a final possible criterion of selection—that is, the ability to pay for a resource. The omission probably derives from a natural repugnance to such an idea, particularly among those accustomed to a national health service. But, on reflection, we wonder if a modified concept of this type does not have its attractions as a way of alleviating scarcity while still retaining moral respectability—indeed, Dworkin has suggested that one criterion for the allocation of resources might be based on what the public *would* pay for given the need.[116] There is no shortage of dialysis machines from the manufacturing point of view; it is the shortage of money to pay for them and the associated manpower within the confines of a 'free' medical service which lies at the root of the problem. In these circumstances, it might not be unreasonable to allow patients to contribute to the purchase of 'engineering hardware' according to their means, on the principle that a machine which is bought releases another for the use of others who cannot do so.

11.60   Such a policy would be, we admit, difficult to apply with absolute equity. In particular, it could be argued that it would draw off in an unequal manner the personnel required to operate the machines and who have been trained at public expense.[117] To which one could answer that one does not expect a university graduate in law to accept only legal aid cases; one could also point out that a greater number of cases— of dialysis cases, at least—would be treated at home and that, by and large, the efficiency of domiciliary treatment and the financial status of the patient are closely related. In short, in certain circumstances, there may be a logical case for including private medicine within the public sector with possible benefit to the latter.[118] What does seem to be increasingly clear is that an ideological attachment to a monopolistic tax-funded health service is not necessarily the best approach to an ideal service. As Bosanquet[119] argued, other options for choice and competition are available and it is,

---

[115]   R W S Chang 'How Should Cadaver Kidneys Be Allocated?' (1996) 348 Lancet 453 and associated papers.

[116]   For discussion, see R Smith 'Being Creative about Rationing' (1996) 312 BMJ 391.

[117]   An effective case can be made out for an 'all or nothing' policy for health service employees: D W Light 'The Real Ethics of Rationing' (1997) 315 BMJ 112.

[118]   And, of course, this is now Government policy in respect of hospital admissions.

[119]   N 76 above. The formation of elite NHS Foundation Trusts under the Health and Social Care Act 2003, free from direct management by the Department of Health, and representing the middle ground between the public and private sectors with local governance, is a move in this direction. See R Robinson 'NHS Foundation

perhaps, a failing of modern health economics that these potentially dynamic forces for developing improved and cost-effective programmes have not been explored more fully.[120]

11.61   We appreciate that, at the end of this fairly lengthy discussion, we have come to little in the way of firm conclusions. We have approached the issues from the position of doctor and lawyer and it is, in some ways, comforting to find that philosophers may be in much the same dilemma.[121] Gillon probably summed up the debate correctly when he implied that, provided decisions are made taking into account fundamental moral values and principles of equity, impartiality and fairness, and provided the bases for decision-making are flexible in relation to the times, then the underlying system is just and is likely to yield just results. Alternatively, we can simply be stoical and acknowledge that: 'to live with circumstances that are unfortunate but not unfair is the destiny of men and women who have neither the financial nor the moral resources of gods and goddesses'.[122]

The responsibility of the individual

11.62   No discussion of this type would be complete without a passing reference to the responsibility of the individual to avoid the need for medical resources. The argument that prevention is better than cure has been widely popularised. No one would deny the importance of the theory at all levels but, equally, it is difficult to decide when friendly persuasion ceases and restriction of liberty begins. It follows that a good case can be made out for a right to choose to be unhealthy—and this not only on Kantian but also on utilitarian grounds, for every sudden death in late middle age that is prevented is potentially a long-term occupation of a bed in a psychogeriatric ward; it could well be that the quest for dementia that is inherent in many of the currently popular limitations on habit are remarkably cost-inefficient.

11.63   What does *not* follow is that there is a concomitant right to health resources when the consequences of that choice materialise. It seems that the public have little sympathy for the cavalier approach—in Williams's experience, the least unacceptable reason for discrimination in prioritisation was that the prospective patients had not cared for their own health. In making such value judgments, however, the public are not constrained by principles of professional ethics and the issue is certainly not so easily solved by health care providers. Various views were put forward in an interesting debate in the *British Medical Journal* on whether or not coronary bypass surgery

---

Trusts' (2002) 325 BMJ 506; R Klein 'The First Wave of NHS Foundation Trusts' (2004) 328 BMJ 1332—the latter suggests there is considerable lassitude as to the initiative. There are now 31 Foundation Trusts.

[120]   For alternatives adopted in Europe, see L Prudil 'Constitutional Limits to the Financing of Health Care in the Czech Republic and in Selected European Countries' (2003) 22 Med Law 659; J Rijlaarsdam 'A Reassessment of the Right to Health Care' (2004) 23 Med Law 219—the latter makes interesting reading in association with *N v S of S for the Home Department*, n 109 above.

[121]   Gillon, n 86 above.   [122]   Engelhardt, n 82 above.

should be offered to smokers.[123] The attitude of the surgeons was conditioned by the poor results obtained in smokers and the fact that they spent longer in hospital. Non-treatment could, therefore, be justified on the grounds that treatment of smokers deprived others of more efficient and effective surgery. An alternative medical view was that non-treatment of symptomatic patients is often less effective in terms of overall cost to society than is surgery, that there are many other 'self-inflicted' conditions which one would not hesitate to treat and that, at least in some cases, smoking is an addictive disease which merits sympathy. A warning was also sounded that, in regarding those who have brought medical ills upon themselves as, somehow, less deserving, the doctor is coming perilously close to prescribing punishment. We would accept the view expressed that the patient should be offered the chance when a positive therapeutic advantage—albeit a less than ideal advantage—may be attainable. The solution to the problem thus comes down to the 'best interests' of the individual; we believe, moreover, that this is the route that would be taken by the courts were such a case to be litigated—but the matter would, now, more likely be resolved on *Re S* standards[124] than by reliance on *Bolam*.

[123] 'Should Smokers Be Offered Coronary Bypass Surgery?' (1993) 306 BMJ 1047: M J Underwood and J S Bailey 'Coronary Bypass Surgery Should Not Be Offered to Smokers' at 1047; M Shiu 'Refusing to Treat Smokers Is Unethical and a Dangerous Precedent' at 1048; R Higgs 'Human Frailty Should Not Be Penalised' at 1049; J Garfield 'Let the Health Authority Take the Responsibility' at 1050.

[124] *Re S (adult patient: sterilisation)* [2001] Fam 15, [2000] 3 WLR 1288, CA—the standard being the *overall* rather than the *medical* best interests.

12

TREATMENT OF THE AGED

12.1 Old age used to present no particular medico-ethical problems—senescence carried with it an increasing susceptibility to infection and the majority of the aged died at home within the family circle, having strayed not too far from their biblical allocation of three score and ten years.

12.2 Fewer people die in middle age today than did so in the past, while the physical health of the elderly is steadily improving; thus, longevity itself and the expectation of longevity are both increasing. Thirteen per cent of the population of the United Kingdom were aged over 65 years in 1971; this proportion has now grown to 16 per cent and is expected to increase steadily so as to reach 23 per cent in 2031—persons over the age of 65 will outnumber those below age 16 before 2015 and possibly as early as 2012. The elderly population is also growing older. The greatest expected proportional rise in the population is in those over 90 years old who are likely to double in numbers between now and 2036; more significantly, because of the absolute numbers involved, the proportion of the population aged 81 or over was 1.9 per cent in 2001 and is expected to rise to 3.8 per cent by 2031.[1] Of perhaps greater importance in the present context is the projection that the number of people aged 65 or over suffering from a long-standing illness is likely to rise from some 6 million today to over 9 million in 2036. Even so, it is encouraging to note that the anticipated number of aged persons who require help with conditions of ordinary living falls according to the year in which the projection was made. For example, it was forecast in 1976 that there would be some 3 million such persons in 2036; by 1991, the figure was revised to 800,000. Thus, the functional health of old people is improving as their numbers increase[2]—the relationship of their total number and the consequent drain on the social services is, therefore, not that of simple parallelism. Improved physical status, however, is not necessarily accompanied by improved mental capacity; indeed, a longer life provides more time during which the inevitable wastage of a limited supply of brain cells can occur. The stage is then set for a swelling proportion of the population that is suffering from various degrees of dementia; this may, itself, be of primary degenerative type or be secondary to disease of the cerebral vasculature. Long-stay is likely when such patients are admitted to hospital and the dilemma in respect of

---

[1] These figures are based on Office for National Statistics *National Population Projections; 2001 based* (2003).

[2] M R Bone, A C Bebbington, C Jagger et al *Health Expectancy and its Uses* (1995).

resource allocation scarcely needs emphasis[3]—in 1997–98, two-thirds of acute hospital beds were occupied by people over 65 who comprised 16 per cent of the general population[4] and this is one of the health imbalances associated with age that the current government initiatives on behalf of the elderly are hoping to alter.[5] Population projections are now sufficiently sophisticated to indicate the problems likely to be met in deciding on the means by which to cope with conditions in the future—those means cannot be determined on the basis of administrative convenience alone but must also involve both ethical and legal considerations.

AUTONOMY AND PATERNALISM IN THE TREATMENT OF THE AGED

12.3   The conflict between autonomy—or the exercise of choice—and paternalism—or the efforts of others to protect those who they consider to be in need of protection— lies at the heart of modern-day medical jurisprudence and is far more complex in the context of geriatric medicine than it is, say, in the relatively straightforward field of consent to surgical treatment by a competent adult. The elderly person is constrained in his—or, more likely, her[6]—choice of action by many factors, some of which are endogenous—such as the effects of early dementia—but others of which are extraneous—for example, poverty. The impetus to paternalistic protection of the aged, no matter how it is ultimately applied, is likely to come from that person's family and, although the factor may be minimised in individual cases, it is undeniable that, in general, it is easier to live without the burden of caring for one's ageing parents; children take on the mantle of paternalism when they seek institutional care for their parents and there is no way in which subjectivity can be wholly eliminated from such action. It is arguable that children have neither a legal nor a moral obligation to support their parents[7] and, regrettable as it may seem, no such obligation has ever existed in English law; moreover, the common law duty which existed previously in Scotland has been removed by statute.[8] The public is probably insufficiently aware of

[3] See K Andrews 'Demographic Changes and Resources for the Elderly' (1985) 290 BMJ 1023 for an early analysis.

[4] Undated and anonymous King's Fund briefing note: *Age Discrimination in Health and Social Care*: www.kingsfund.org.uk/pdf/AgeDisc/pdf.

[5] Department of Health *National Service Framework for Older People* (2001). Numerous progress reports are available on the DoH website.

[6] The life expectancy for males in 1901 was 45 and, for females, 49 years. The current figures are 76.2 and 80.6 years and they are expected to be 81 and 84.9 years respectively in 2031: Office of National Statistics, n 1 above.

[7] N Daniels 'Family Responsibility Initiatives and Justice Between Age Groups' (1985) 13 Law Med Hlth Care 153. Also by the same author *Am I My Parents' Keeper?* (1988).

[8] Family Law (Scotland) Act 1985, s 1(1)—by non-inclusion of a child/parent obligation to aliment. But this is not universal. A duty to care for one's indigent parents exists, say, in South Africa: P Q R Boberg *The Law of Persons and the Family* (1991) quoting *Re Knoop* (1893) 10 SC 198.

the extent of intra-familial abuse of the elderly; the degree of ignorance—or, in this case possibly, of indifference—is comparable to that which applied to child abuse 50 years ago. There is little doubt that abuse is extensive and that it occurs in various forms including verbal, physical and by way of neglect or deprivation; figures of between 5 per cent and 65 per cent of elderly persons being at risk are quoted, the incidence depending on the criteria used by the reporting agencies.[9] In one prospective study in England, 45 per cent of carers admitted to some form of 'elder abuse'[10]—and the situation does not seem to have altered greatly over the last few decades.[11] It follows that any attempt to enforce a filial duty of care for the aged would be likely to exacerbate domestic violence or neglect and, thus, provoke further deterioration in the geriatrics' conditions. Much of the care of the elderly must, therefore, devolve on the medical and social services and both of these must be supported by the law.[12]

INSTITUTIONAL TREATMENT

12.4   Medical treatment of the aged in the United Kingdom has, as in all advanced societies, moved a long way since the chronically sick, including those who were simply homeless, were almost arbitrarily assigned to hospital wards which have been described as little more than 'human warehouses'.[13] Attention is now concentrated on maintaining the old person's preferred environment as far as is possible. Such a policy must include as a starting point a system of pre-admission home visits by specialists in geriatric medicine; the fact that an inability to appreciate one's disablement is a concomitant of dementia has also dictated positive case-finding.[14] Both these activities may raise problems of etiquette, if not of ethics, between specialists and general practitioners; moreover, there is a strong possibility that case-finding imposes an excessively heavy load on general practitioners. Antipathy to institutionalising the psycho-geriatric patient, however, inevitably calls for concomitant improvements in home help. Given a good relationship, much of this can be provided by the family— particularly if they are given assistance. The local authority has a duty to assess the needs of anyone who appears to be in need of community care[15] and, once the

[9] B Pitt 'Abusing Old People' (1993) 305 BMJ 968.

[10] A C Homer and C Gilleard 'Abuse of Elderly People by their Carers' (1990) 301 BMJ 1359. It is fair, however, to say that such figures do not always obtain: J Ogg and G Bennett 'Elder Abuse in Britain' (1992) 305 BMJ 998.

[11] A Tonks and G Bennett 'Elder Abuse' (1999) 318 BMJ 278.

[12] See A Griffiths and G Roberts The Law and Elderly People (2nd edn, 1995).

[13] T Howell 'The Birth of British Geriatrics' (1983) 13 Geriat Med 791.

[14] M Arcand and J Williamson 'An Evaluation of Home Visiting of Patients by Physicians in Geriatric Medicine' (1982) 283 BMJ 718.

[15] Disabled Persons (Services, Consultation and Representation) Act 1986. The quality of such assessment and the consequent disposal of the subjects is open to criticism: E Dickinson 'Long Term Care of Older People' (1996) 312 BMJ 862. See also National Health Service and Community Care Act 1990, s 47.

authority is satisfied of that person's needs, it has a duty to make suitable arrangements.[16] These are available by way of rather complex legislation. In essence, a disability living allowance, divided into care and mobility components, is payable to a person who, inter alia, is so physically or mentally disabled as to require the constant attention of another person by day (or prolonged or repeated attention at night) to assist with his or her bodily functions or for his or her protection from danger. Disability living allowance is payable only if the disability arose before the age of 65; it is replaced by attendance allowance if it arose later—and there is no age limit applied to this benefit.[17] Elective and temporary admission to hospital, thus allowing the carers time for relaxation, can be a most useful adjunct. By and large, however, home assistance must be a function of the social services and the local authority is under an obligation to provide such aid in a 'preventive' mode. This includes help with the design of the house and the provision of meals, facilities for recreation and home helps.[18]

12.5   It may be, however, that such treatment is cost ineffective and is difficult to apply. In a case brought under the Chronically Sick and Disabled Persons Act 1970, which we have already noted at para 11.32 above,[19] it was held that a chronically sick and disabled person's need for services could not sensibly be assessed without some regard to the cost of providing them. There is a suspicion that the House was not entirely happy with its decision which depended to an extent on a fairly subtle distinction between statutory duties and powers; it is not surprising that such cases become complex and depend to a large extent on the precise legislation involved. Thus, in a later case taken under the National Assistance Act 1948, the Court of Appeal held that the local authority could not manipulate the regulations so as to tie an applicant's point of entitlement to assistance to the level of its resource[20]—and there are numberless similar cases, both reported and unreported, in point.

12.6   Even so, as we have seen in the previous chapter in relation to the National Health Service, the courts are generally loath to interfere with the distribution of public funds—and much the same applies to the social services provided by the local

---

[16] Chronically Sick and Disabled Persons Act 1970, s 2.

[17] Social Security Contributions and Benefits Act 1992, ss 71, 75 and 64. These benefits are to be distinguished from invalid care allowance which is paid to the carer (s 70). The rights of married daughters to invalid care allowance have been upheld by the European Court of Justice: *Drake v Chief Adjudication Officer* [1986] 3 All ER 65, [1986] ECR 1995.

[18] For a useful, simple review, see P Wanklyn 'Homes and Housing for Elderly People' (1996) 313 BMJ 218. Boarding accommodation, which is something less than residential care, can also be provided under the Health and Social Services and Social Security Adjudications Act 1983, Sch 9, Pt II; Social Work (Scotland) Act 1968, s 14. A general duty to care for the welfare of the elderly also rests on the local social service authority (Health Services and Public Health Act 1968, s 45).

[19] *R v Gloucestershire County Council, ex p Barry* [1997] AC 584, [1997] 2 All ER 1, HL. For commentary, see Lord Browne-Wilkinson in *R v East Sussex County Council, ex p Tandy* [1998] AC 714, (1998) 42 BMLR 173 at 180.

[20] *R v Sefton MBC, ex p Help the Aged* [1997] 4 All ER 532, (1997) 38 BMLR 135, CA. There are, also, times when the local authority *must* give support irrespective of resources: *R v Birmingham City Council, ex p Mohammed* [1998] 3 All ER 788, [1999] 1 WLR 33 (payment of disabled facilities grant under Housing Grants, Construction and Regeneration Act 1996, s 23).

authority. The House of Lords was not minded to dictate the tactical allocation of resources in Mr Barry's case and it has been said at first instance that:

The council is entitled to a substantial degree of deference relating to the way in which it allocates resources and provides services.[21]

12.7 The economic return from this type of management depends, to an extent, on the degree of dependency—the expense of domicillary care increases with increased dependency and, at some point, it will become inequitable for a disabled person to expect cost-ineffective support at the expense of others who are, thereby, deprived of care;[22] clearly, however, the wishes—or autonomy—of the subject must be fed into the balance, and this demands the provision of adequate information.[23] The current proliferation of privately-run nursing homes makes it very difficult to generalise as to the comparative prognosis of those cared for at home and those who are institutionalised. Inevitably, much depends upon the degree and efficiency of supervision of residential and nursing homes and we return to the subject below.

12.8 Nevertheless, some old people, who are fit other than in the mind, must be institutionalised to an extent which will depend upon the severity of dementia. The simplest form of such care is by way of sheltered housing—which may be provided by the local authority, housing associations or as a private venture—but the degree of available supervision is generally so low as to eliminate it as a resort for persons who are anything greatly less than fully independent; sheltered housing might, however, be the ideal refuge for the elderly person who is subject to domestic abuse and, thereby, among those eligible for priority accommodation.[24] Beyond this, it may be possible to arrange for residential care in accommodation which the local authority has a duty to provide by virtue of the National Assistance Act 1948, s 21. Practice, however, falls short of the theoretical ideal. The local authority has no obligation to provide specialist or hospital-type medical facilities in such institutions,[25] which are already accepting patients whose requirements exceed those for which this method of disposal was designed; so-called 'Part III accommodation'—i.e. provided under the National Assistance Act 1948, ss 21 to 26—tends to revert to the conditions which are less than ideal.

12.9 The result has been a growth of private homes, which has been encouraged by government policy that the local authorities should utilise the private sector.[26] Homes which must be registered under the Care Standards Act 2000 are known as care homes

---

[21] *R (Haggerty and others) v St Helens Borough Council* [2003] EWHC 803, (2003) 74 BMLR 33 per Silber J at [61]. *Haggerty* is an interesting case in that a claim under Article 8 of the Human Rights Act 1998, Sch 2 was rejected on the grounds that 'the financial resources of the council were an important element to be considered in the balancing exercise required in the application of article 8(2)'.

[22] J G Evans 'Institutional Care and Elderly People' (1993) 306 BMJ 806.

[23] This aspect of duty to the aged is emphasised by K Lothian and I Philp 'Maintaining the Dignity and Autonomy of Older People in the Healthcare Setting' (2001) 322 BMJ 668.

[24] Housing Act 1996, s 167. Vulnerability can only be defined following wide-ranging inquiry: *R v Lambeth Borough Council, ex p Carroll* (1988) 20 HLR 142.

[25] Health and Social Care Act 2001, s 49.

[26] Community Care (Residential Accommodation) Act 1992, amending National Assistance Act 1948, s 26.

and include those which provide either board and personal care to those in need of it[27] (residential care homes) and those which, in addition, provide nursing care (nursing homes). The 2000 Act makes no nominal distinction between the two but the nature of the building, the staff requirements and the like will be reflected in the grant of registration.[28] The extension of private nursing homes, with governmental assistance as to charge, has provided some sort of solution to the problem of the scarcity of residential accommodation although the situation is not as good as it once was due to the continuing closure of private homes on economic and commercial grounds.[29] The cumulative result is that hospital beds are blocked by older patients who cannot be moved—not only are the elderly thus retained in conditions that were not designed for such use but those who would benefit most are deprived of hospital accommodation.[30]

12.10   The government's response has been surprising, albeit, perhaps, predictable in that it places responsibility for improvement on the local authorities and the National Health Service. Under the Community Care (Delayed Discharge etc.) Act 2003, the local authority must pay a fine of £100 for every day, beyond two, that a patient has to remain unnecessarily in an acute hospital bed because a suitable package of care— whether domiciliary or in alternative accommodation—has not been arranged. Admittedly, the Government has allocated £100m annually to defray the inevitable costs to the local authorities but the probable clash of interests between the two forms of authority—to the disadvantage of patients—is almost self-evident.[31]

12.11   One of the government's newer initiatives in this respect involves the creation of some 5000 intermediate care beds together with supported intermediate care places which will be used to expedite discharge from hospital, to prevent unnecessary admissions and, also, to avoid premature admission to long-term residential care.[32] Inevitably, this is regarded in some quarters as being less than satisfactory and even contrary

---

[27] Personal care essentially means bodily care for those who cannot manage for themselves. The fact that a person is not receiving assistance with bodily functions does not, however, mean that he or she cannot be in need of personal care: *Harrison v Cornwall County Council* (1990) 11 BMLR 21.

[28] The functions of the National Care Standards Commission, which was responsible for registration, passed to the Commission for Health Care Audit and Inspection in respect of independent hospitals and clinics and to the Commission for Social Care Inspection in respect of care homes and the like: Health and Social Care (Community Health and Standards) Act 2003, Sch 9, Pt 2, para 17. Note that the government is committed to combining the CSCI and the Health Care Commission in 2008.

[29] 13,400 care home places were closed between January 2002 and April 2003: Laing and Buisson *Care of Elderly People: UK Market Survey 2003* www.laingbuisson.co.uk/Longtermcare.htm.

[30] The Health and Social Care Change Agent Team was established in 2002 to advise on the problem.

[31] The figures come from a scathing article by D R Rowland and A M Pollock 'Choice and Responsiveness for Older People in the "Patient Centred" NHS' (2004) 328 BMJ 4. The authors particularly note the curtailment of choice for those with long-term illness.

[32] National Health Service *The NHS Plan: A Plan for Investment, A Plan for Reform* (2000) (Cm 4818–1) para 15.14. Some 10% of all patients over the age of 65 discharged from hospital are discharged to intermediate care which is far less than, say, in the United States. Nearly 3% are discharged to residential homes or hospices: 'Dr Foster's Case Notes' (2004) 328 BMJ 605.

to accepted geriatric practice[33]—but there is little doubt that the health care of old people has assumed a new political significance in the early twenty-first century.[34]

12.12 The resulting pressures at all levels lead to what many would regard as manifest inequity. So long as the old person remains in hospital, his or her needs are met free through the medium of the NHS. The use of a local authority's residential or nursing home is, however, subject to a means test.[35] Effectively, a person who has a capital of £20,500[36] or more, which includes the value of his or her own home, has to pay his or her charges in full; the local authority will pay the difference between their basic and the actual costs until the person's savings have been reduced to £12,500; the authority will then pay the full fee.[37]

12.13 Something of a conflict may, therefore, develop between the local health authorities, who are anxious to clear their bed-space, and the elderly, backed by their families, many of whom would, quite reasonably, wonder why they have been singled out as a group to whom the facilities of a comprehensive health service are denied when most needed—it is estimated that some 40,000 houses are sold each year in order to finance long-term nursing care.[38] Health authorities may, and do, claim that their duty of care is limited by the resources available and, as a result, policies on the limitation of long-term care are variable—in fact, very few Health Authorities provide nursing home care; at the same time, the social services cannot find places for an indefinite number of persons discharged from hospital. Thus, not only may the older patient be discharged from hospital prematurely, but he or she may be moved from NHS to local authority accommodation with corresponding financial penalty.[39]

12.14 An interesting example arose in the case brought by Mrs Coughlan in 1999.[40] Here, a paraplegic woman had been assured of a 'home for life' in a nursing home controlled by the NHS; she applied for judicial review of the Health Authority's decision to close the home and transfer the residents to local authority care where 'nursing

---

[33] J G Evans and R C Tallis 'A New Beginning for Care for Elderly People?' (2002) 322 BMJ 807.

[34] For which, see I Heath 'Long Term Care for Older People' (2002) 324 BMJ 1534.

[35] The assessment of whether or not a person is 'in need' is not resource dependant. It is only after the need has been established that means affect charging for the services provided—at least in Scotland: *Robertson (AP) v Fife Council* 2003 SCLR 39, (2002) 68 BMLR 229, HL.

[36] National Assistance (Sums for Personal Requirements and Assessment of Resources) (Amendment) (England) Regulations 2005, SI 2005/708, r 3.

[37] Health and Social Services and Social Security Adjudications Act 1983, s 17; J Warden 'The Lottery of Long Term Care' (1994) 308 BMJ 742.

[38] Leading Article 'The Age of Health' *The Times*, 24 July 2000; M Dean 'UK's Long-term Nightmare on Nursing-care Costs' (1996) 347 Lancet 681. Predictably, the NHS has denied that it is neglecting the long-term health care of the elderly: Community Care Unit, NHS Executive *NHS Responsibilities for Meeting Longterm Health Care Needs* (1994).

[39] The near absurdity of the schizoid approach to management is exemplified by the proposal that elderly persons discharged from hospital will receive direct cash payments to provide services that the local authorities' budgets cannot meet: A Vass 'Elderly Patients to Receive Cash to Speed up Hospital Discharge' (2002) 325 BMJ 179.

[40] *R v North and East Devon Health Authority, ex p Coughlan* [2001] QB 213, [2000] 3 All ER 850. For brief discussion, see A Loux, S Kerrison and A M Pollock 'Long Term Nursing: Social Care or Health Care?' (2000) 320 BMJ 5.

care' would be paid for according to the patients' means. The Court of Appeal carefully considered the concept of 'nursing care' and, while admitting the difficulties involved in the marginal case, distinguished between that which might be expected from an authority providing 'social care' and that which was required by way of a primary health need—in essence, the test was both quantitative and qualitative. The Court considered that the Health Authority was at fault in imposing eligibility criteria for admission to its nursing home which were so severe as to force the local authority to accept responsibilities for which it was unsuited under the terms of the National Assistance Act 1948, s 21.[41] *Coughlan* can, thus, be said to have clarified, but not resolved, the inequities of the current situation—as it has been said: 'the demarcation between nursing (health) and personal (social) care . . . is "unworkable, unfair and unjust" '.[42]

12.15   It is, however, fair to say that the government has, at last, recognised these anomalies and, largely as a result of the recommendations of the Sutherland Commission,[43] a number of initiatives have either been, or are about to be, launched at the time of writing.[44] Amongst these, arguably the most important is that nursing care is now provided free in nursing homes controlled by the local authority; personal care is, however, still means tested.[45] A second major concession is that the value of a person's house is not now counted against his or her capital assets for the first 12 weeks of residential care, thus allowing the old person time for reflection and adjustment.[46] Finally, though not exclusively, and although one views the establishment of yet more quangos with some scepticism, Commissions to oversee the provision of care have been authorised on both sides of the Border—and their remit will certainly include regulation of the care of the aged.[47] It is also to be noted that the difficulties associated

[41] As amended by National Health Service and Community Care Act 1990, ss 42 and 66.

[42] See Heath, n 34 above, at 1535. It is also a cause for confusion and has been a subject for investigation by the health service ombudsman: A Gulland 'Health Authorities Face Big Payouts after Ombudsman's Ruling' (2003) 326 BMJ 466. A critical report was commissioned by the DoH: M Henwood *Continuing Health Care: Review, Revision and Restitution* (2004).

[43] Royal Commission on the Funding of Long Term Care (Sir S Sutherland, chairman) *With Respect to Old Age: Long Term Care—Rights and Responsibilities* (1999) (Cmnd 4192–1).

[44] See, in particular, National Health Service *The NHS Plan: The Government's Response to the Royal Commission on Long Term Care* (2000); Department of Health National Service *Framework for Older People* (2001).

[45] A situation that has been described as 'futile and destructive': I Heath 'Long Term Care for Older People' (2002) 324 BMJ 1534. Personal care is, however, free in Scotland: Community Care and Health (Scotland) Act 2002, s 1—defined as concerned with day-to-day physical [and mental] tasks and needs: Regulation of Care (Scotland) Act 2001, s 2(28). There are, in fact, serious doubts as to whether the Scottish system is sustainable: Anonymous 'Free Personal Care for Elderly Scots Cost £60m a Year More than Forecast' (2005) *The Times*, 22 March, p 28. Against this, powerful voices call for the rest of the United Kingdom to follow the Scottish lead: K Burke 'Long Term Care Will "Implode" unless Personal Care Comes Free' (2003) 327 BMJ 770. For a comparative review of alternative systems, including compulsory insurance, see (2002) BMJ pp 1542–1543.

[46] National Assistance (Assessment of Resources) 1992, SI 1992/2977, Sch 4, para 1A inserted by National Assistance (Assessment of Resources) (Amendment) (No. 2) (England) Regulations, SI 2001/1066, r 5.

[47] Health and Social Care (Community Health and Standards) Act 2003, ss 41 and 42; Regulation of Care (Scotland) Act 2001, s 1.

with the placement of elderly people under the care of either the health or local authorities was eased by the introduction of a single assessment process that is governed by relatively strict guidelines.[48]

12.16   No-one expects that good intentions will always be crowned with success. The care of the disabled elderly is a relatively thankless task and, at the end of the day, the management and conditions within residential and nursing homes depend on a dedicated 'coal-face' staff which is unlikely to be available in the numbers needed. Some years ago, institutional care was found to be of less than ideal quality[49]—but this was probably so on a global scale. Methods of placement have become more sophisticated and more money is being made available for the general care of the aged. When we add to these the anti-discriminatory measures which are being introduced for the protection of the aged (see para 12.42 below), we can hope—and perhaps anticipate—that a new deal for this vulnerable group is on the way.

THE INDIVIDUAL PATIENT

12.17   So far, we have considered the problems of the aged in general terms only; they become even more acute when applied to the individual patient. Thus, in the conditions of housing supplied by the local authority under Part III of the 1948 Act, injuries due to falls and other mishaps are likely to arise in an unsupervised situation; deaths which occur later, and which are no more than temporarily associated, are likely to be the subject of inquiry by either the Coroner or the Procurator Fiscal.[50] Many such incidents may be beyond the control of insufficient and inexperienced staff, notwithstanding their dedication; yet the fear of culpability can rebound to the overall detriment of the patient—'defensive' action by the nurses may result in unnecessary restraint of their charges.[51] Of greater immediate importance are the ethical problems surrounding those old persons who clearly need care and attention but want to retain their independence and resist removal to an institution. The danger, then, is that the 'cussedness' of old age may be designated as mental illness and the aged person is compulsorily restricted under statute—and the definition of mental disorder, as we will see in chapter 20, is so wide that it may well be possible for the doctor to take such action and yet retain his or her ethical integrity.

12.18   Given, however, that the person has no recognisable mental disorder yet his or her behaviour is so deviant as to give rise to both medical and social concern, it is still possible to remove him or her to a place of safety by way of the National Assistance

---

[48] Department of Health *Single Assessment Process* (2002), HSC 2002/001, LAC (2002) 1.

[49] See, for example, E Dickinson 'Long Term Care of Older People' (1996) 312 BMJ 862.

[50] For a useful review of accidents in the home, see S M Cordner and J Ozanne-Smith 'Accidental Death and Injury in the Home' in J K Mason and B Purdue (eds) *The Pathology of Trauma* (3rd edn, 2000).

[51] A very full discussion is to be found in S H Johnson 'The Fear of Liability and the Use of Restraints in Nursing Homes' (1990) 18 Law Med Hlth Care 263.

Act 1948, s 47 and the National Assistance (Amendment) Act 1951, s 1 which have not been repealed—largely because the modern legislation still leaves a gap in the protection of those who retain capacity but are, still, socially inadequate. The 1948 Act allows the compulsory removal from their homes of persons who are not mentally ill but who are suffering from grave chronic disease or, being aged, infirm or physically incapacitated, are living in insanitary conditions and are unable to devote to themselves, and are not receiving from other persons, proper care and attention. Removal may be effected in the person's own interest or in order to prevent injury to the health of, or serious nuisance to, other persons. The medical officer of health can apply for a magistrate's order giving seven days' notice of removal. The order allows for detention in a 'suitable hospital or other place' for up to three months; emergency removal for a period of three weeks, thus avoiding the seven day notification period, can be achieved on the recommendation of the community physician if this is backed by another practitioner—who is normally the person's general practitioner—and the removal is in the interests of the person concerned.[52] The fact that this accelerated procedure is used in the majority of cases is a cause of anxiety as to the operation of the legislation.

12.19   It has been estimated that the powers under s 47 and its amendment are invoked annually less than some two hundred times in England[53] and 15 times in Scotland. The Act merely stipulates that the subject may be removed to 'a suitable hospital or other place'—and the seven day notification requirement applies to the manager of the premises unless he or she has agreed to receive the 'patient'. As to the place of removal, the order does not provide for compulsory treatment—a fact which must lead to some antipathy on the part of hospital managers.[54] If the subject is sent to hospital, it is likely to be to a geriatric hospital rather than to a specialised geriatric unit; admission to a general hospital is likely to be looked on as a contradiction in terms unless the admission is on the grounds of grave chronic disease. The moral issues were elegantly argued some time ago by Gray[55] who, first, questioned the justification for removing an elderly person from his or her home for the benefit of 'other persons'—as he pointed out, powers of compulsory home cleaning and the like are already available under the relevant public health legislation. Secondly, the arguments balancing paternalism against personal liberty are raised in a particularly acute form. Thirdly, the use of statutory powers may be little more than a cloak for inadequate social services or family care—which, taken together, are to be preferred to institutionalisation. And finally, and perhaps of greatest importance, there is a strong

---

[52] National Assistance (Amendment) Act 1951, s 1(1).

[53] P Nair and J F Mayberry 'The Compulsory Removal of Elderly People in England and Wales under Section 47 of the National Assistance Act and its 1951 Amendment: A Survey of its Implementation in England and Wales in 1988 and 1989' (1995) 24 Age and Ageing 180. This analysis is rather old but, since there is no requirement to report such removals, data are very hard to come by.

[54] Refusal of treatment was given as the reason for removal in 19% of cases in the above study.

[55] J A M Gray 'Section 47' (1981) 7 J Med Ethics 146.

implication that the powers may be based on disapproval of unusual, rather than of dangerous, behaviour.[56]

12.20   The contrary view was put by Greaves[57] who concluded that reference to the standard philosophical alternatives do not do justice to the moral issues at stake; he saw the answer to the problem as lying somewhere between the application of rational principles and personal prejudices. Greaves gave no firm answer as to how this level is to be achieved, but accepted that, in certain circumstances, a decision must be taken by proxy on behalf of the old person—and that this is best done by a doctor whose personal ethical sensitivity is unlikely to be suppressed by the blanket application of a principle. Gray,[58] in fact, pointed out that s 47 and its forerunners was originally seen as a mechanism for protecting the elderly against the whims of officialdom and the Medical Officer of Health was thought to be the best person to do this. While criticising the Draconian powers available under s 47, he did not believe that it should be repealed—but this was largely because other coercive or frankly immoral practices would evolve in order to persuade old people to resign their homes; there is an ingrained way of public thought that, given the same abnormality, old people 'must' be protected while others merely 'ought' to be persuaded. There is, in fact, no easy solution. In a more recent attack on the current legislation, it was admitted that there are underlying problems involving individuals in need of care which cannot, at present, be answered in any way other than by the use of s 47 and it was asked whether it is right to deny what may be the best, albeit imperfect, option to one person in the hopes of improving the law for others. None the less, the author concluded that all suggested justifications for the use of s 47 fail.[59] For our part, perhaps the most damning aspect of the legislation is that there was no record of the outcome of 24 per cent the compulsory removals recorded by Nair and Mayberry.

12.21   It is for this and for allied reasons that more modern legislation designed to achieve the same objective is at pains to respect the interests of the 'patient'. Foremost among this, even if on no more than a temporal basis, are the emergency statutory provisions within the Mental Health Act 1983 and the Scottish equivalent of the Mental Health (Care and Treatment) (Scotland) Act 2003. There are, first, the extensive powers available under s 135 (s 292 in Scotland) whereby a justice, acting on information from an approved social worker, can authorise the police to enter and remove to a place of safety a mentally disordered person who is at risk and living alone (this can only be done in Scotland after a mental health officer or a medical commissioner has been refused entry). The subject can then be detained for only 72 hours and,

---

[56] For further criticism, see J D Fear, P Hatton and E B Renvoize 'Section 47 of National Assistance Act: A Time for Change?' (1988) 296 BMJ 860.

[57] D A Greaves 'Can Compulsory Removal Ever Be Justified for Adults Who Are Mentally Competent?' (1991) 17 J Med Ethics 189.

[58] J A M Gray 'Section 47—Assault On or Protection Of the Freedom of the Individual?' (1991) 17 J Med Ethics 195.

[59] S J Hobson 'The Ethics of Compulsory Removal under Section 47 of the 1948 National Assistance Act' (1998) 24 J Med Ethics 38.

unsurprisingly, the section is used very rarely.[60] Very much more important are the powers relating to compulsory admission to hospital for assessment (s 2 (s 44(S)) or for emergency assessment (s 4 (s 36(S)) of the person's mental status. These are discussed in greater detail in chapter 20; for the present it is necessary only to note that it might not be difficult to invoke them in cases where s 47 is appropriate—indeed, the Mental Health Act has, in the past, been seen as the preferred route in an emergency.[61] We take the view, however, that committal under the 1983 and 2003 Acts inevitably classifies the elderly and confused as being mentally abnormal—and, to many, such classification represents a stigma; despite the simultaneous provision of a recognised system of appeal, the use of what is, effectively, a ruse as a matter of administrative convenience seems to us to be more morally reprehensible than is the use of the more straightforward s 47. Moreover, the effective use of the Acts depends upon proof of incompetence. As has been emphasised in the Court of Appeal:

The Act[s] cannot be deployed to achieve the detention of an individual against her will merely because her thinking process is unusual, even apparently bizarre and irrational, and contrary to the views of the overwhelming majority of the community at large.[62]

Although stated in a different context, the principle cannot be altered simply on the grounds that the patient is elderly.

12.22   The final possibility by which to effect emergency removal of a social incompetent lies in an application for guardianship[63]—the purpose being to empower the guardian, who may be the local authority, to dictate the place of residence of the disordered person. Once again, the practice is seldom adopted due, largely, to the fact that the essential function of a guardian is to maintain the incompetent in the community; to order removal to residential care is, in its way, to defeat the object of the exercise. Moreover, the guardian has no power to order treatment and the guardianship is open to challenge. Thus, until recently, no current way of achieving compulsory residential care of the elderly can be said to have been wholly satisfactory. The result was that, in the majority of cases, the legal process was avoided and the elderly person was 'talked into' abrogating his or her independent status.

12.23   The removal of an elderly person to a home or hospital does not, of course, solve all treatment dilemmas. He or she may, like any other, refuse to accept treatment. Compulsion from the legal point of view is out of the question so long as the subject is competent, although, in practice, relatives and others may resort to pressure of various sorts to ensure compliance. The position of one who is dementing, or whose capacity is otherwise diminished, will, however, be different. Almost by definition, such a

---

[60] Section 136, which refers to persons in public places, is used more commonly as the proportion of patients in community care increases.

[61] E Murphy 'What to do with a Sick Elderly Woman Who Refuses to go to Hospital' (1984) 289 BMJ 1435.

[62] *St George's Healthcare NHS Trust v S* [1998] 3 All ER 673 at 692, (1998) 44 BMLR 160 at 180, per Judge LJ. See more recently *NHS Trust v T (Adult Patient: Refusal of Treatment)* [2005] 1 All ER 387, (2004) 80 BMLR 184.

[63] Mental Health Act 1983, s 7, Adults with Incapacity (Scotland) Act 2000, s 57.

patient is unlikely to understand fully the nature of his or her condition and the treatment available. It might be argued that an analogy with the unconscious patient is applicable and, in that case, a doctor may justify the non-consensual treatment of his patient on the grounds of necessity. Dementing patients, however, are not unconscious. Moreover, the nature of the condition is such that they will rarely be wholly competent or wholly incompetent. Their comprehension may be affected but, equally, they may still be capable of holding and articulating views.[64] It follows that a generalised label of 'incompetence' is likely to be justifiable only in the later stages of the condition and a person's competency should be judged in respect of each decision made.[65] Put another way, it might be better to consider such treatment as an acceptable instance of paternalistic intervention of the sort under which children who are incapable of full understanding are treated. A 'best interests' argument could be advanced should specifically legal justification be called for.[66] In short, it is the doctrine of necessity rather than court sanction that underpins the general medical and surgical treatment of the mentally disordered.[67]

Recent legal protection of the incapax

12.24 Until comparatively recently, the legal protection of persons who are vulnerable by reason of being unable to manage their own welfare has founded upon an uneasy amalgam of mental health and social security law which is not easy to assimilate within the classic statutory framework. Moreover, the Mental Health Acts relate to a very particular group of patients and their terms leave therapeutic lacunae that are often difficult to fill. As result, legislation has now been passed in both England and Scotland that is specifically aimed at protecting those who have lost, or are losing, their mental capacity but who need a more flexible form of management than is provided by the mental health legislation. It is, perhaps, worth stressing at this point that loss of mental capacity is not necessarily confined to the aged and, for that reason, we have already considered some of the important developments in chapter 10. Nevertheless, it is clear that the majority of incapaces will be elderly and we revisit the legislation here with that in mind.

12.25 As has already been stated, the Scottish Executive led the way with the Adults with Incapacity (Scotland) Act 2000.[68] The Westminster Parliament has now followed suit with the Mental Capacity Act 2005. Naturally, both Acts follow much the same

---

[64] For a seminal study, see M J Gunn 'Treatment and Mental Handicap' (1987) 16 Anglo-Am L Rev 242.

[65] See, in general, *Re C (adult: refusal of treatment)* [1994] 1 All ER 819, (1993) 15 BMLR 77.

[66] Note that the incompetent patient who is admitted to hospital under the Mental Health Acts may be treated compulsorily only for the mental disorder which forms the basis of his admission or detention.

[67] *Re F (mental patient: sterilisation)* [1990] 2 AC 1, sub nom *F v West Berkshire Health Authority* [1989] 2 All ER 545 at 551 per Lord Brandon at AC 55, HL. It will be seen throughout this book that this case has been cited as the basis for treatment of the incompetent in a number of ways. The European Court of Human Rights has, however, recently held that the 'informal patient' regime instituted on the basis of necessity is unlawful: *HL v United Kingdom* (2005) 40 EHRR 32, (2005) 81 BMLR 131.

[68] Now backed by the Mental Health (Care and Treatment) (Scotland) Act 2003. The interaction of the two statutes will have to evolve. The comparable draft English Bill was lost but is likely to be reintroduced.

pattern but there are a number of relatively subtle differences; we illustrate the general principles mainly by reference to these.

12.26 Both Acts begin by outlining the principles underlying the justification of intervention on behalf of an incapax. As might be expected, the 2005 Act centres on whether the person's 'best interests' are to be served by intervention. In assessing these interests, the assessor must, inter alia, consider the person's past and present wishes and feelings together with 'any other factors he would be likely to consider if he were able to do so' (s 4(5)). The Scottish Act is content to specify that any action taken must be to the benefit of the adult—adding the rider that the benefit cannot reasonably be achieved without that intervention.[69] While deliberately avoiding the concept of best interests, the 2000 Act also appeals to the past feelings of the adult (s 1(4)); the marked similarity between the two Acts in this connection draws attention, once again, to the increasing conflation of the principles of 'best interests' and 'substituted judgment' in United Kingdom law.[70]

12.27 Both Acts define incapacity in terms of an inability to make decisions and both, in effect, rely heavily on the interpretation provided in the well-known case of *Re C*[71] (for which see para 10.58). This relates the inability to make decisions to defective understanding or retention or assessment of information. Additionally, a person may be incapacitated by virtue of being unable to communicate, with or without aids. The underlying cause of incapacity lies, in English terms, in an impairment of, or disturbance in the functioning of, the mind or brain, whether permanent or temporary (s 2); in Scotland it results from mental disorder or inability to communicate because of physical disability (s 1(6)), which suggests that the Scottish mental requirement is more specific than that in England.[72] In either case, the close similarity to the language used in the Mental Health Act 1983 and the Mental Health (Care and Treatment) (Scotland) Act 2003 leads, from the start, to some confusion as to the practical application of the mental health and the mental capacity legislation in both jurisdictions.[73] Nevertheless, it is clear that Parliament's intention is to keep the two distinct to the extent that nothing in the 2005 Act authorises anyone to give treatment or to consent to treatment for a mental disorder if, at the time, his treatment is regulated by the Mental Health Act 1983, Part IV—that is, treatment for which the 1983 Act requires either special consent or no consent.[74] (2005 Act s 28). The types of treatment which cannot be given in Scotland are subsumed under s 48(2) of the 2000 Act which gives

---

[69] The distinction is probably one without a difference though it could be argued that someone, say in the permanent vegetative state, could have no interests.

[70] In addition, the views of near relatives, carers, proxy-decision makers and, in Scotland, 'any other person appearing to have authority to intervene' must be considered—which leads to the fear that, in the absence of prioritisation, conflicting views might result in inaction. But all this is, of course, at an early stage of interventionist activity.

[71] *Re C (adult: refusal of treatment)* [1994] 1 All ER 819, (1993) 15 BMLR 77.

[72] See Mental Health (Care and Treatment) (Scotland) Act 2003, s 328.

[73] It is noted, however, that mental incapacity is defined as resulting from 'mental disorder (within the meaning of the Mental Health Act)' in Sch 4, c 23 of the 2005 Act.

[74] For which see chapter 20, para 20.59.

the Scottish Ministers a broad brush approach to such limitations. Paradoxically, it is this very limitation, taken in conjunction with the very similar semantics of the 1983 and 2005 Acts in England and Wales, which paves the way to the treatment of physical disease in those who cannot decide for themselves. Non-consensual treatment of such disease is effectively barred by the terms of the Mental Health Act 1983, s 63 and, as we have seen, could, until recently, be provided only under common law. The 'best interests' terms of the 2005 Act now, however, provide a statutory basis for essential treatment of anyone who is incapacitated by reason of impaired functioning of the mind—and this clearly includes not only the aged dement but also both voluntary and involuntary mental patients. The situation in England and Wales is, thus, now on a par with that in Scotland.

12.28   This, however, obscures what seems to us to be a real difficulty—that is, deciding under which instrument—mental health or mental capacity—the carer should invoke interventionist powers; each case has its own particular circumstances and the assessment of these is a matter for the specialist in mental illness. Two aspects do, however, strike us as being of special significance. First, there is little doubt, unfortunate though it may be, that 'sectioning' under the Mental Health Acts does carry with it an element of stigma; we fancy that most practitioners would hope to circumvent this if it were possible. Second, and allied to this, the mental capacity Acts across Great Britain[75] allow a considerable power to the primary health carer. It is certainly true that the person who determines the provision of treatment to an incapax is constrained by the conditions of the 2005 Act, ss 4, 5 and 6 but, when summarised, these effectively do no more than impose good medical practice on the practitioner. Similarly, in Scotland, once the medical practitioner primarily responsible for the treatment of an adult has certified that his patient is incapable of making decisions related to his treatment, the practitioner has a relatively free therapeutic hand for up to a year.[76] On all counts, then, it seems that one effect of the 2003 and 2005 Acts will be to cut down considerably the use of the mental health legislation in respect of the mentally disordered aged.

12.29   Treatment of the incapax is not, however, simply a matter of the doctor's opinion. The Scottish Act of 2000 allows for the appointment of a guardian or a welfare attorney who can act on behalf of an adult who is deemed by the Sheriff to be incapable. The former has powers in relation to decisions about the patient's property and financial affairs; the latter as to his or her personal welfare.[77] The interests of the incapax are carefully protected throughout the Act and the activities of any guardian are subject to the supervision of the Public Guardian. The duties and limitations of the welfare attorney are discussed in greater detail in chapter 10. The English Act

---

[75] The 2005 Act does not run to Northern Ireland.

[76] He cannot, however, subvert the Mental Health (Care and Treatment) (Scotland) Act 2003 by using this power to place an adult in a hospital for the treatment of mental disorder (2000 Act, s 47(7)).

[77] Section 80 of the 2000 Act abolishes the appointment of a curator bonis, tutor-dative or tutor-at-law in respect of persons over the age of 16 years.

follows this format closely save that the person responsible for the incapax's affairs and welfare are combined in the *donee*—that is, the person who has been given a lasting power of attorney.[78] The limitations and restrictions placed on the donee are spelled out in detail and are, effectively the same as those constraining a health care provider since the latter cannot act in a way that conflicts with the decisions of the former (s 6(6)).

12.30   Thus, the provision of health care for the incapacitated is treated relatively informally, albeit a trifle didactically, under the English statute. The Adults with Incapacity (Scotland) Act, by contrast, sets out a more precise protocol to be followed in the event that a welfare attorney has been appointed. Treatment can go ahead if there is agreement.[79] In the event of disagreement, the doctor responsible for treatment must ask the Mental Welfare Commission to nominate a medical practitioner from their list of such referees to give an opinion as to the proposed treatment—which, in the event of approval, can go ahead irrespective of opposition from the welfare attorney. If the nominated practitioner disagrees with the doctor in charge, the latter—together with any other interested person—can appeal to the Court of Session for a ruling. The impression gained, therefore, is that, where there is difficulty in relation to treatment of the incapax, the Scottish Act gives priority to professional opinion; the 2005 Act, rather, tends to assume that the donee is, in fact, the voice of the patient; accordingly, he can both give and refuse consent to treatment (s 11(7)(c)).[80]

12.31   Finally,[81] in respect of the individual patient, both jurisdictions allow for 'patient advocacy' on behalf of the incapacitated in the event of disputes or uncertainties arising in his or her management. The complex interplay between the mental incapacity and health legislations is, again, demonstrated by the fact that this appears in the mental health legislation in Scotland (2003 Act, Chapter 2) but in the Mental Capacity Act, s 35 in England;[82] however, in the latter situation, the advocate can only intervene when 'serious medical treatment' as yet undefined, is being considered outwith the conditions of the Mental Health Act 1983, Part 4.

12.32   It will be seen, then, that the new Acts, virtually for the first time, lay out in detail provisions for the welfare of the incapax by way of medical and allied treatment and that the underlying principle has been to balance the paternalism that is inevitable in

---

[78] There may be more than one donee who can act either together or separately in respect of all or different functions (s 10(4)).

[79] Although, throughout the legislation, there is a disturbingly open-ended rider to the effect that '*any person* having an interest in the personal welfare of the adult' may appeal a decision to the Court of Session (our emphasis).

[80] Although the power to refuse is limited in the case of life-saving treatment (s 11(8)). In the event of disagreement, the doctor could provide life saving treatment pending a decision by the Court of Protection (s 6(7)). In other cases of disagreement, the donee would have unrestricted access to the court (s 50(1)); it seems that the doctor would have to apply for access which would surely be allowed (s 50(3)).

[81] The regulation of research on incapacitated persons is discussed in chapter 18.

[82] We suspect that the difference may well be due to the difficulty in introducing new mental health legislation that has been experienced in England and Wales. There is a similar dichotomy in respect of the significance of advance directives (for which, see para 17.81).

such a relationship against the preservation of the patient's surviving autonomy and dignity. In this respect, the status of any advance statement or directive made prior to incapacity merits special consideration.

12.33   This has already been mentioned in chapter 10. Here, it can be said that the 2005 Act reflects the almost total obeisance to patient autonomy that is now such a feature of Westminster-driven medical jurisprudence. The terms of a valid[83] advance decision *must* be followed in respect of any specified treatment (s 26(1)) and such a decision takes precedence over that of a person with lasting powers of attorney (s 25(7)). The comparable Scottish Act of 2000 is silent on the point which is addressed, in regard to the treatment for mental disorder only, in the Mental Health Act of 2003. It is noteworthy that, in Scotland, the requirement is that the Mental Health Tribunal and the principal carer need do no more than 'have regard' to the contents of the directive— although the reasons for taking any contrary steps must be recorded (s 276). It seems, therefore, that the authority of advance directives as to treatment for conditions other than mental disorder is currently uncertain in Scotland; it is probably expressed in s 1(4) of the 2000 Act which says that *account shall be taken* of the present and past wishes of the adult when any interventionist activity is being taken. We doubt if there is any major practical distinction between the two jurisdictions as related to medical treatment because the conditions laid down in such directives are, by their nature, generally in accord with accepted medical practices; the doctor is unlikely to wish to gainsay them unless he or she is swayed by conscience—in which case, the correct legal procedure would be to demit the care of the patient to a colleague who was not so constrained.

Legal protection of the incapacitated in general

12.34   At the same time as considering their medical interests, the Acts collect and codify the regulatory protection of incapacitated persons' material well-being. This is largely beyond the remit of medical ethics but we note the following points. Both the 2005 and the 2000 Acts provide for the establishment of the Public Guardian[84] whose function is, in essence, to supervise and administer any donees of lasting powers of attorney or guardians appointed to administer the property or financial affairs of the incapacitated adult.[85] In England, therefore, the Office of the Public Guardian, is by way of being the administrative arm of the Court of Protection which is re-established as a superior court of record under Part 2 of the 2005 Act.[86] It is beyond the scope of

---

[83] The decision is valid if the person making it has capacity and it is in writing and is countersigned by a witness. An advance decision is, however, only applicable to life-sustaining treatment if it is verified that it is to apply even if, as a result, life is at risk (s 25(5) and (6)).

[84] Mental Capacity Act 2005, s 57; Adults with Incapacity (Scotland) Act 2000, s 6.

[85] The English donee also has powers related to the incapax' welfare. The Public Guardian, accordingly, has unfettered access to health records in carrying out his functions (2005 Act, s 58(5)).

[86] The previous Court of Protection which was an office of the Supreme Court now ceases to exist and the new court is no longer tied to the Mental Health Act.

this book to discuss the function of the Court of Protection.[87] Suffice it to say that the Court has, or will have, extensive powers devoted to the well-being, in all senses of the word, of the incapacitated. In considering questions relating to a person, it can institute reports relevant to that person from its agents—the Public Guardian or a Court of Protection Visitor—or it can call for reports from other public bodies, and the health records of the person concerned must be made available (s 49). Applications to the Court can be made without previous permission by the incapax or his or her representatives—including the parent of a person under 18 years of age.

12.35 Outwith the context of these formal legal institutions, the law also takes account of particular situations involving the elderly person. Contractual capacity may be denied in England and Wales to one who cannot understand the implications of a contract and contracts which are entered into by persons whose mind is affected by dementia may, of course, be set aside. Similarly, testamentary capacity is restricted to those who can comprehend the nature and extent of their estate and the claims which people may have upon them. In assessing such capacity, however, the law is not so much concerned to place a psychiatric label on a testator as to determine the impact which an apparent specific delusion may have on the contents of the will.[88] The rules of testamentary capacity were, in fact, developed with the interests of others in mind.

ETHICAL CONSIDERATIONS

12.36 There remain for consideration the practical and ethical aspects of the treatment of geriatric patients. These are often discussed in the context of euthanasia which we deal with later in chapter 17. But, while it is true that many old persons may be suffering from terminal or incapacitating physical disease, an equal or greater number may be the victims of no more than intellectual deterioration; the greater part of geriatric medicine relates, in fact, to the management of incurable, rather than of life-threatening, disease.[89] If the patient's best interests or benefit represent the therapeutic yardstick—as they must—the inner world of the geriatric must be assessed subjectively and not related to the observer's own youthful or middle-aged experience. The demented but otherwise physically capable old person is not in pain and, for all we know, is passing a reasonably contented life. The parallel in controversial treatment issues is to be found in the uncomplicated Down's syndrome infant who, as we have already argued, is as entitled to medical treatment as is his mentally normal counterpart. Glib phrases such as 'pneumonia is the old man's friend' come easily to the lips in this discussion and can be dangerously emollient unless they are qualified;

---

[87] For powers of the previous Court of Protection, see *Re W (EEM)* [1971] Ch 123 at 143, per Ungoed-Thomas J. It is, of course, too early for publication of an authoritative analysis of the new Court.

[88] *Banks v Goodfellow* (1870) LR 5 QB 549.

[89] In this connection, we have noted a rather disturbing report from the Netherlands that a case of Alzheimer's disease has been held to satisfy the requirements for lawful euthanasia in that country: T Sheldon 'Dutch Approve Euthanasia for a Patient with Alzheimer's Disease' (2005) 330 BMJ 1041.

death may certainly be a blessed relief to the patient in severe pain but problems raised in the treatment, say, of intercurrent infection in the contented dement are of the same order as are those faced by the mentally competent—one wonders if the more honest aphorism is not that 'pneumonia in an old man is his associates' best friend'.

12.37   We would, therefore, disagree to an extent with those who, effectively, call for a policy which is generally biased towards non-treatment of the elderly demented patient on grounds of the 'quality of cognitive life'.[90] At one time, this was frequently expressed by including in the hospital notes the instruction 'do not resuscitate', the morality and practicality of which is discussed below.[91] Similar instructions to withhold resuscitative measures in the event of cardiorespiratory arrest are known as 'No-code orders' in the United States where their validity has been upheld.[92] The judicial reliance on good medical practice that is evident on both sides of the Atlantic emphasises the importance of considering each patient as an individual problem. Following our analogy with the newborn, there is a case to be made out for selective non-treatment of the aged—but selection must be based on the individual patient's circumstances. Guidelines for treatments are just that—they do no more than provide a useful setting in which to formulate a decision; they should not be seen as instructions which transcend the realities of the particular patient's condition.[93]

12.38   The issues crystalise in the place of the elderly in the allocation of resources which, as we have seen, is inevitable in an expanding medical technological ambience—and the arguments are finely balanced. The views of the authoritative commentator Callahan, although somewhat dated, are particularly interesting in this context.[94] In brief, Callahan saw the need for objective planning if the otherwise certain breakdown in resources is to be avoided. The aged, it was said, have some claim to public funds but these are not unlimited—the goal is a balanced, affordable system of care for the elderly which admits of a good balance between length and quality of life. Effectively, we should see ageing as an inevitable part of life and accept that society discharges its principal duty to the elderly by avoiding premature death. Callahan admitted that any serious form of setting limits to treatment will be unpleasant but, since the possibilities of spending money in an attempt to turn old age into permanent middle age

[90] G S Robertson 'Ethical Dilemmas of Brain Failure in the Elderly' (1983) 287 BMJ 1775 remains a most useful reference.

[91] See para 17.93. For an excellent legal appraisal, see J Hendrick and C Brennan 'Do Not Resuscitate Orders: Guidelines in Practice' (1997) 6 Nottingham LJ 24.

[92] *Re Dinnerstein* 380 NE 2d 134 (Mass, 1978). On the other side of the coin, it was later said that the law begins with a presumption that the incompetent patient would consent to life saving treatment—hence, *consent* to such treatment can be given by surrogates: *Re Spring* 399 NE 2d 493 (Mass, 1979). For attempts in the US to codify the DNR process, see T E Miller 'Do-Not-Resuscitate Orders: Public Policy and Patient Autonomy' (1989) 17 Law Med Hlth Care 245.

[93] See General Medical Council *Withholding and Withdrawing Life-prolonging Treatments* (2002); British Medical Association *Withholding and Withdrawing Life Prolonging Medical Treatment* (2001), upgraded in 2004.

[94] D Callahan *Setting Limits* (1987). This sort of view was well criticised by H R Moody 'Should We Ration Health Care on Grounds of Age?' in *Ethics in an Ageing Society* (1992) ch 9.

are infinite, we should impose an age limit upon ourselves. These views, needless to say, have attracted opposition particularly from those who see the welfare of the individual as transcending a policy of general societal benefit[95]—the argument that we should *always* prefer a younger patient before an older one on the grounds that society's net life gain is, thereby, more evenly distributed is attractive but too dispassionate for comfort. While we would agree that difficult decisions may have to be taken, we prefer the egalitarian philosophy which will avoid positive discrimination against the elderly—expressed as the age-indifference principle which asserts that each person is entitled to the same concern, respect and protection of society as is accorded to any other person in the community.[96] Therapeutic decisions are intensely individual matters which cannot be covered by way of restrictive formulae; age, and the effect of age, may be one factor in the decision to treat but it cannot be the *only* factor.[97] To quote Harris:

All of us who wish to go on living have something that each of us values equally although for each it is different in character . . . This thing is of course 'the rest of our lives'. So long as we do not know the date of our deaths then for each of us the 'rest of our lives' is of indefinite duration. Whether we are 17 or 70 . . . so long as we each wish to live out the rest of our lives . . . we each suffer the same injustice if our wishes are deliberately frustrated and we are cut off prematurely.[98]

12.39   In short, the commonly-voiced argument that the old person has 'had a good innings' and must make way for the young is incomplete; the retiring batsman is fully entitled to a respected rest in the pavilion. The argument is, in practice, sterile—we must surely agree that 'explicit age-based rationing . . . is highly unlikely to be politic-ally acceptable in the UK'.[99] Such problems may, however, confront the surgeon with particular force; the application of the productive/non-productive test[100] must always affect his decision whether or not to operate on the elderly. A negative response to advanced malignant disease may be a simple matter but the improvement in operative techniques is such that the results of elective general surgery in the aged, even of an advanced technological nature such as coronary artery replacement, may be both

[95] See e.g. R W Hunt 'A Critique of Using Age to Ration Health Care' (1993) 19 J Med Ethics 19. The obvious difficulties of involving the law in this area are summarised by M Rivlin 'Should Age Based Rationing of Health Care Be Illegal?' (1999) 319 BMJ 1379.

[96] J Harris 'The Principle of Age Indifference' in Age Concern Millennium Paper *Values and Attitudes in an Ageing Society* (1998).

[97] Much the same view has been expressed by the authoritative National Institute for Health and Clinical Excellence *Social Value Judgements: Draft for Consultation* (April, 2005) www.nice.org.uk/pdf/CC SVJ 0405.pdf—the consultation has since closed.

[98] J Harris *The Value of Life* (1985) p 89.

[99] Taken from a very useful, but undated and anonymous, briefing note from the King's Fund *Age Discrimination in Health and Social Care*: www.kingsfund.org.uk/pdf/AgeDisc.pdf.

[100] See para 17.73. Decisions to operate may be heavily influenced by the 'biological age'—of the patient; operation is more likely in those capable of living independently: S M Farquharson, R Gupta, R J Heald and B J Moran 'Surgical Decisions in the Elderly: The Importance of Biological Age' (2001) 94 J Roy Soc Med 232.

satisfactory and rewarding—the fact that results may be generally better in the young does not mean that the same procedure in the old is necessarily not worthwhile.[101] It has, in addition, been suggested that relatively risky surgery, offering either good health or a quick death, may be particularly attractive to the old who should not be denied the choice.[102] In any event, it is relatively unlikely that considerations of productivity can be applied to an acute surgical emergency occurring in an elderly patient with no other mortal disease. The only acceptable test is then one of feasibility—there can seldom be an ethical alternative to treatment if it can be given but, inevitably, high morbidity and mortality rates must be accepted.

12.40   The dilemma remains as to what to do in the event that a geriatric patient refuses treatment. There can be no doubt as to the rights of the competent adult to refuse treatment and these rights would certainly include opposition to enforced feeding— but the problem is different from forced feeding in, say, the prison context.[103] The difficulty here, as we know, is that the borderline between competence and incompetence is often indistinct in old age.[104] Court judgments or decisions on the part of those responsible may well be sought in dramatic situations such as the removal of life-support but are unlikely to be invoked for apparently trivial matters such as the manner of oral feeding; it is probable that many old people, no matter what their situation, are fed with a varying degree of force but the action is taken on the assumption that refusal to eat is non-volitional. The process is degrading both to the patient and to the staff and, moreover, carries considerable medical hazard. It is, however, difficult to see the alternative to compassionate and moderate coercion in such cases.

12.41   Positive refusal of treatment by the competent old person is a different matter and one which has attracted considerable attention in the courts of the United States. There, the right to be let alone has been described as 'the most comprehensive of rights and the right most valued by civilised men'[105] and the courts have, in general, upheld such rights—perhaps the most apposite example still being that concerning an 85-year-old, yet alert, man who frankly chose suicide by self-starvation in preference to medical care.[106] The problem of the management of the partially competent

---

[101] From 2000 to 2002, coronary artery bypass surgery increased by 32% in those aged 75 or over: Department of Health *Standard One—Rooting out Age Discrimination* (2004). The 'jury is still out' as to the end results of cancer treatment as related to age: N J Turner, R A Haward, G P Mulley and PJ Selby 'Cancer in Old Age—Is It Inadequately Investigated and Treated?' (1999) 319 BMJ 309.

[102] T Hope, D Sprigings and R Crisp ' "Not Clinically Indicated": Patients' Interests or Resource Allocation?' (1993) 306 BMJ 379.

[103] Discussed at para 10.79.

[104] In an interesting unpublished paper: C Heginbotham 'Mental Disorder and Decision Making: Respecting Autonomy in Substitute Judgments' (1992), Paper presented to the UK Forum on Health Care Ethics and the Law, London, the author drew attention to the distinction between capacity, which hinges on cognitive and volitional attributes of the individual, and competence. Capacity, being a necessary, though insufficient, condition for competence is, thus, the more important.

[105] *Griswold v Connecticut* 381 US 479 (1965).

[106] *Re Plaza Health and Rehabilitation Center of Syracuse* S Ct, Onandaga Cty, NY, 4 Feb 1984.

geriatric who depends upon artificial feeding can be more difficult; this was well exemplified in the various stages of the now historic case of *Conroy*,[107] where, although the Court of Appeal and the Supreme Court of New Jersey disagreed on the definition of medical treatment, both had misgivings as to the possible impact that the decision to abandon nasogastric feeding might have on the general treatment of the elderly incompetent. Indeed, in attempting to resolve the ethical issues in this area, it has been rightly, and prophetically, said that: 'Society should be wary of moving from a recognition of an individual's right to die to a climate of enforcing a duty to die.'[108]

CARE OF THE ELDERLY IN THE FUTURE

12.42   It may well be true that loss of dignity in the elderly derives from the way that we care for our sufferers from dementia, not from the illness itself.[109] The condition is a challenge to society's attitudes to the aged and is to be met by the provision of appropriate facilities. In our previous editions, we have been sceptical as to the likelihood of any political initiative designed to improve the lot of our oldest citizens and there is some evidence to suggest that that scepticism was not misplaced.[110] The *National Service Framework for Older People*[111] was launched in 2001 and, since then, there have been a number of follow-up governmental publications; the majority of these, however, are still at the consultation phase.[112] The Scottish initiative and the passing of the Mental Capacity Act 2005 are great strides forward but their impact is, in essence, confined to those who are clinically mentally disordered. There is little practical evidence of a dramatic change in the care of those who are 'different' in that they are old, lonely and poor. Perhaps this is something beyond the control of politicians and is a matter for society as a whole. Nevertheless, the current plethora of government publications does indicate a sincere dedication to improving the lot of

[107] *Re Claire C Conroy* 464 A 2d 303 (NJ, 1983), CA, 486 A 2d 1209 (NJ, 1985), SC.

[108] This very old quotation merits as much—if not more—attention today as it did when it was written: M Siegler and A J Wiesbard 'Against the Emerging Stream' (1985) 145 Arch Int Med 129.

[109] This memorable comment is taken from E Murphy 'Ethical Dilemmas of Brain Failure in the Elderly' (1984) 288 BMJ 61.

[110] E Roberts, J Robinson and L Seymour *Old Habits Die Hard: Tackling Age Discrimination in Health and Social Care* (2002).

[111] N 5 above.

[112] We draw attention to two which are well worth consulting: Department of Health *Better Health in Old Age: Report from Professor Ian Philp* (2004) www.dh.gov.uk/PublicationsAndStatistics/PublicationsPolicy AndGuidance/PublicationsPolicyAndGuidanceArticle/fs/en?CONTENT; *Independence, Well-being and Choice* (2005), Cm 6499. Among other interesting 'visions' in the latter is that direct payments, which allow the beneficiaries to choose their own brands of social services, should be encouraged. (See now Health and Social Care Act 2001, s 57.)

the elderly—even if some of them carry an aura of propaganda. Ideas, or 'vision', cannot be translated into practice overnight and we have to remember that the *Framework for Older People* is in the nature of a 10-year plan. As we anticipated in our last edition, it is still possible to see the management of the aged in a rosier light than that of a few years back.

13

THE DIAGNOSIS OF DEATH

13.1   Death is defined in *Chambers Twentieth Century Dictionary* as 'the state of being dead; extinction or cessation of life'. *Steadman's Medical Dictionary* adds to this 'in multicellular organisms, death is a gradual process at the cellular level with tissues varying in their ability to withstand deprivation of oxygen'. There is, therefore, a conceptual conflict between layman and doctor. To the former, a person is either alive or dead, and this is generally based on the appearances in a *fait accompli*; the doctor, however, is involved in death as a process; he must, therefore, seek a definable end-point. Prior to the mid-twentieth century, death could be seen without qualm as being 'a permanent state of tissue anoxia'. Indeed, this remains the *ultimate* definition; we will see that the great majority of modern discussion is concerned solely with whether or not, and to what extent, we can pre-empt that truism and declare a *person* to be dead. Tissue anoxia arises naturally in two ways—either respiration ceases, in which case there is a failure to harvest oxygen, or the heart fails, when oxygen is no longer distributed to the tissues. In either case, the diagnostic problem lies in the definition of permanence.

13.2   In practice, it is astonishing how often the moment of 'death of the person' is perfectly clear. One can generally tell immediately when a loved one or a carefully observed patient 'dies' in cardiorespiratory terms.[1] The patient has 'breathed his or her last' and the heart stops beating; this is 'somatic' death. But the individual cells of the body are not dead; they will continue to function until their residual oxygen is exhausted. How long this takes depends upon their oxygen consumption which, in turn, is correlated with their specialised activity. Theoretically, therefore, there should be evidence of cellular death before the state of permanence is accepted but, in practice, the doctor can rely on his senses and on his stethoscope because death is to be expected and is accepted on the vast majority of occasions when it visits.[2] Even so, one is left with the disquieting realisation that brain cells will withstand anoxia for a time, albeit for only a few minutes. If we are to accept the concept of 'brain death', as argued below, we should treat the patient in irreversible cardiorespiratory failure as

---

[1] The words 'carefully observed' deserve emphasis. The distinction between death and 'suspended animation' may be difficult to make *post facto* in some circumstances—e.g. in cases of drug overdose or hypothermia.

[2] Even so, some jurisdictions demand visible evidence of pooling, or non-circulation, of the blood—so-called hypostasis—before death is finally certified.

dying rather than dead—for the true agonal period in natural death is that which lies between cardiac and cerebral failure.

13.3   But what if death is unheralded and unexpected? It is common knowledge that an apparently permanent cessation of the respiration or blood flow can, in many instances, be challenged by physical or mechanical intervention. Thus, sudden heart failure may, in suitable cases, be reversed by electrical stimulation (cardioversion) or by cardiac massage coupled, perhaps, with artificial respiration or ventilation. But, while the patient has been 'saved from the dead', the process of cellular death has been initiated by the temporary failure of oxygen distribution. The majority of organs will recover from such an insult but the cells of the brain are outstandingly the most sensitive in the body to oxygen deprivation and, moreover, they are irreplaceable. Thus, a situation may arise whereby the body as a whole is brought back to life but where it is now controlled by a brain which is damaged to an uncertain degree. The decision to restore an interrupted cardiac function is not, therefore, a simple choice between the good (life) and the bad (death). It poses serious and urgent ethical problems which provide a base from which to discuss the more measured, and in some ways more complicated, issues arising from ventilator deaths.

13.4   When death strikes unexpectedly on its second front—by way of acute respiratory failure—it may be countered by the use of artificial ventilation. This may be accomplished by a mechanical respirator which simulates the movements of the chest wall or, more commonly in the context of the present discussion, by a ventilator which forces air in and out of the lungs.

BRAIN FUNCTION AS A MEASURE OF DEATH

13.5   The mechanisms underlying acute heart failure and respiratory failure need to be distinguished. Given an adequate oxygen supply, the heart will continue to beat independently of higher control—it did, for instance, often beat for some 20 minutes following the broken neck of judicial hanging; the cause of acute cardiac failure, therefore, lies within the heart itself. Respiration, on the other hand, is controlled by the respiratory centre—a nervous 'battery' situated in the brain stem—and, in practice, acute respiratory failure of the type which is important in the present context is almost invariably the result of central damage—that is, damage to the brain stem.[3] Oxygenation of the tissues, or cellular life, is, thus, based on a servo-type mechanism: the heart depends for its own tissue oxygen on the lungs which, in turn, are useless without the heart; together they supply oxygen to the brain which, therefore, cannot function in the absence of competent heart and lungs; yet the lungs are, themselves, dependent upon a functioning brain stem. We have, however, seen that the only

---

[3] Now that acute anterior poliomyelitis ('infantile paralysis') has been virtually eradicated, there are very few extra-cerebral causes of acute respiratory failure that cannot be corrected by the ventilator.

segment of this triad which cannot be substituted is the brain. There are, therefore, strong logical arguments for defining death in terms of brain death rather than in the generally accepted terms of cardiorespiratory failure; indeed, Pallis taught that all death is, and always has been, brain stem death and that circulatory arrest just happens to be the commonest way to bring such death about,[4] a point to which we have already alluded. We prefer, however, to visualise the brain, the heart and the lungs as forming a 'cycle of life' which can be broken at any point; looked at in this way, there is no need to speak of two *concepts* of death—that is, cardiorespiratory death or brain death; it is simply that different criteria, and different tests, can be used for identifying that the cycle has been broken.[5] Be that as it may, it is also clear that we *must* turn to the brain when the natural functional condition of the lungs—or, occasionally, of the heart—is obscured by the intervention of a machine.

13.6   The brain itself is not uniformly sensitive to hypoxia.[6] Simplistically, it can be divided into three main areas: the cortex, which is responsible for our human intellectual existence and is the least able to withstand oxygen deficiency; the thalamus, which roughly regulates our animal existence; and the brain stem, which controls our purely vegetative functions including breathing. The brain stem is least affected by hypoxia; if it is so damaged, it can be assumed, as near certainly as is possible, that the rest of the brain is damaged to a similar or greater extent.[7] Generalised hypoxia will affect all tissues of the body but to a varying degree—the brain being pre-eminently at risk. Conditions producing such hypoxia may be natural—e.g. heart failure or severe internal haemorrhage—or unnatural, of which drug overdose or a reduced oxygen intake, due, for instance, to a poorly given anaesthetic, are probably the most important in the present context. Violence may be such as to reduce the chest movement—as in conditions of overcrowding—or, more likely, will cause 'surgical shock', in which a lowered blood pressure results in inadequate oxygen perfusion of the tissues. Other causative lesions—which can be natural or associated with injury—may be localised within the skull and injure the brain in secondary fashion by occupying the confined space and, effectively, squeezing the vessels carrying the blood. Whatever the cause, hypoxic *anatomic damage* to the brain is irreversible, but further damage is prevented once an efficient oxygen supply is restored. In such a situation, therefore, one can speak of *degrees* of brain damage and resultant coma but not of *stages* of coma because, once the oxygen supply is restored, the condition is no longer progressive.

13.7   The clinical condition of a person who is brain damaged but treated will vary with the degree of hypoxic insult sustained. Four degrees of coma were recognised by the

---

[4] C Pallis 'Return to Elsinore' (1990) 16 J Med Ethics 10.

[5] This was much the view taken by the original United States President's Commission for the Study of Ethical Problems in Medicine *Defining Death: Medical, Legal and Ethical Issues in the Definition of Death* (1981).

[6] The relative term 'hypoxia' is used advisedly to emphasise that oxygen lack need not be absolute—'anoxia'—in order to cause brain damage.

[7] Lesions which affect the lower brain and leave the cortex intact are the result of local vascular damage—not of generalised hypoxia.

early French writers:[8] *coma vigile*, which represents no more than a blurring of consciousness and intellect; *coma type* and *coma carus*, which are characterised by increasing loss of relative functions followed by vegetative functions; and, finally, *coma depassé*—something beyond coma in which all functions are lost and the patient can only be maintained by artificial means.

13.8   Thus, while all appropriate cases may properly be given intensive care for the purposes of diagnosis and assessment, it would be well-nigh impossible to justify the initiation of long-term treatment for a patient who was likely to retain no cortical and only minimal thalamic function. The identification of such a case presents a formidable technical dilemma because some *functional* or *physiological* damage may be recoverable while some 'dormant' brain cells may have survived to become activated later. This potential for evidence of clinical recovery underlies the distinction between a persistent and a permanent stage of cerebral dysfunction; it also accounts, at least in part, for the fact that recovery of brain function is more likely when it has been lost as a result of direct head injury than when a comparable loss is due to pure hypoxic damage.[9]

13.9   The wholly decorticated patient falls into the category originally defined by Jennett[10] as the persistent vegetative state. Such a person will have periods of wakefulness but is, nevertheless, permanently unconscious; the state has been described as eyes-open unconsciousness.[11] The definition and management of such persons is discussed in detail in chapter 16. For the present, it will be clear that a human who has lost cortical function has, simultaneously, lost his human personality but, in so far as he is capable of oxygenating his tissues naturally and without mechanical support—i.e. his cardiorespiratory system is intact—he is equally certainly not dead. There have been serious suggestions that the decorticated patient should be regarded as dead—may not *homo sapiens* be weakened in its own fight for survival if it devotes strength and resources to maintaining *homo* when he is no longer *sapiens*?[12]—and the equation of permanent loss of personality with no longer being alive is a philosophy that is gaining relatively wide acceptance.[13] Such an attitude may be tenable in a general discussion on euthanasia but, when related to the definition of death, it can only confuse the issue and enhance the already strong public apprehension of premature disposal of the body; a particularly powerful article, for example, concluded that, while neocortical death may be compatible with our current concepts of death, it ought not to be introduced as public policy simply because the general public would

---

[8] P Mollard and M Goulon 'Le Coma Depassé' (1959) 101 Rev Neurol 3.

[9] R S Howard and D H Miller 'The Persistent Vegetative State' (1995) 310 BMJ 341.

[10] B Jennett and F Plum 'Persistent Vegetative State after Brain Damage' (1972) 1 Lancet 734.

[11] R E Cranford and D R Smith 'Consciousness: The Most Critical Moral (Constitutional) Standard for Human Personhood' (1987) 13 Am J Law Med 233.

[12] Lord Scarman 'Legal Liability in Medicine' (1981) 74 J Roy Soc Med 11.

[13] For a comparatively early exposition, see D R Smith 'Legal Recognition of Neocortical Death' (1986) 71 Cornell L Rev 850. For continuation, see R M Veatch 'The Impending Collapse of the Whole-Brain Definition of Death' (1993) Hastings Center Report 23, no. 4, 18. And see M Angell 'After *Quinlan*: The Dilemma of the Persistent Vegetative State' (1994) 330 New Engl J Med 1524.

not understand the issues and it would be needlessly divisive for society.[14] Put another way, could a non-cognitive, decorticated person with continuing cardiopulmonary function be buried?[15] Death must remain an absolute; there is no place in medical jurisprudence for conditional phrases such as 'at death's door' or 'as good as dead'. The definition of death has not—or should not have—changed; and, if we are to alter our diagnostic methods, the diagnosis of death must be as sure as it was when we were using the heart and lungs as its sole parameters.[16]

13.10   It follows that, if we are to adjudge death by way of cerebral non-function, we must be certain that there is *permanent* physical destructive damage to the *whole* brain[17]— and, as we will see later, this must include the brain stem. This principle has been unintentionally confused semantically by the Harvard group, who introduced the term 'irreversible coma'.[18] One's first reaction would be to equate such a condition with the persistent vegetative state—or decorticated patient—or an even lesser degree of cerebral incompetence.[19] It is, however, clear that the committee was describing what other Americans and, later, the British Royal Colleges dubbed 'brain death'.[20] Even this term is capable of misinterpretation—in particular, it can be taken as including 'partial brain death'. The alternative is to speak only in terms of 'brain stem death', a term which derives from the logical assumption that somatic life is impossible in the absence of a functioning brain stem.[21] Conceptual difficulties still remain which are concerned, for the most part, with such differences as there may be between 'brain stem death' and 'whole brain death'.[22] We are very doubtful whether the distinction needs to be emphasised. Natural diseases in the form of destructive primary lesions of

---

[14] R J Devettere 'Neocortical Death and Human Death' (1990) 18 Law Med Hlth Care 96. This paper summarises the views of others in the field. More recently, J Fisher 'Re-examining Death: Against a Higher Brain Criterion' (1999) 25 J Med Ethics 473.

[15] D J Powner, B M Ackerman and A Grenvik 'Medical Diagnosis of Death in Adults: Historical Contributions to Current Controversies' (1996) 348 Lancet 1219.

[16] J M Stanley 'More Fiddling with the Definition of Death?' (1987) 13 J Med Ethics 21. It is disturbing to read in the modern literature '[This] reflects the medical community's use of the terms "brain dead" or "clinically dead" for persons who are unconscious, comatose, and terminally ill without any reasonable prognosis of recovery': G J Banks 'Legal and Ethical Safeguards: Protection of Society's Most Vulnerable Participants in a Commercialized Organ Transplantation System' (1995) 21 Am J Law Med 45.

[17] We use the term in a gross anatomical sense. It does not imply, as many US writers have suggested, that a search must be made for residual pockets of cellular survival before death can be certified. See, as an example, R Hoffenberg 'Christiaan Barnard; His First Transplants and their Impact on Concepts of Death' (2001) 323 BMJ 1478.

[18] H K Beecher (chairman) 'A Definition of Irreversible Coma', Report of the ad hoc Committee of the Harvard Medical School to examine the definition of brain death (1968) 205 J Amer Med Ass 337. It is still suggested that this may cause confusion: R Cohen-Almagor 'Language and Reality at the End of Life' (2000) 28 J Law Med Ethics 267.

[19] An authoritative report in the UK emphasises the distinction to be made between coma and the permanent vegetative state: Working Group of the Royal College of Physicians 'The Permanent Vegetative State' (1996) 30 J R Coll Physicians Lond 119. Coma classically presents as eyes-closed unconsciousness.

[20] Conference of Medical Royal Colleges and their Faculties in the UK 'Diagnosis of Brain Death' [1976] 2 BMJ 1187.

[21] The concept originally introduced by A Mohandas and S N Chou (1971) 35 J Neurosurg 211.

[22] C Pallis *ABC of Brain Stem Death* (1983).

the brain stem—generally in the form of haemorrhage—which do not simultaneously affect the rest of the brain are rare and are either partial in type or, more commonly, rapidly fatal; in the event of survival, the resulting 'locked in' syndrome, characterised by quadriplegia and inability to speak but with preservation of consciousness and some eye movements, is a terrifying example but its existence is well appreciated by neurologists.[23] The only unnatural ways in which death or destruction of the brain stem can reasonably be expected in the presence of a normal cerebrum are following accident involving the cervical spine, judicial hanging or beheading—none of which are germane to the present discussion. For the rest, it is difficult in the extreme to conceive of a generalised, fundamentally hypoxic condition destroying the brain stem while sparing the highly specialised tissue of the cerebral cortex; and, even were this possible, continued attempts to maintain such a body artificially would be hopelessly non-productive and positively unethical. We believe that the common terms used to define the irreversible cessation of all brain function—'brain stem death' and 'whole brain death'—can be regarded as synonymous in both practice and theory.[24] But, since the tests devised for diagnosis are, essentially, tests of brain stem function, we prefer the former term which is, in addition, in general use in the United Kingdom.

13.11   We do, however, accept that many misconceptions are founded on misunderstanding of the British standards for the diagnosis of brain stem death. These include three equally important phases. First, there is the exclusion of coma being due to reversible causes including drug overdose, hypothermia and metabolic disorders while, at the same time, making a positive diagnosis of the disorder which has caused the brain damage and ensuring that this, in turn, is irremediable. Secondly, there is the carrying out of a number of tests specifically designed to demonstrate destruction of the several components of the brain stem—which include the respiratory centre and, hence, the ability to breathe naturally. Thirdly, there is a carefully controlled system whereby a patient's inability to breath spontaneously is proved. These tests should be repeated although the recommendations are, of necessity, somewhat open on this point and depend, mainly, on the nature of the precipitating condition.

13.12   These criteria have been criticised on the grounds that the patient is 'being asked to prove he is alive' rather than that the physician is proving death. Positive tests, such as an electroencephalogram (EEG) or an angiogram—by which cessation of the blood flow in the brain can be visualised—are, therefore, often sought and one or other is, indeed, mandatory in some countries of the European Union.[25] It is hard to believe

[23] See C M C Allen 'Conscious but Paralysed: Releasing the Locked-in' (1993) 342 Lancet 130 and, for a thorough, up-to-date review: E Smith and M Delargy 'Locked-in Syndrome' (2005) 330 BMJ 406.

[24] Even so, the open-ended definition can lead to concern: J L Bernat 'How Much of the Brain Must Die in Brain Death?' (1992) 3 J Clin Ethics 21.

[25] Pallis, n 22 above, quoted France, Greece and Italy as so requiring. The UK, Eire, Belgium, Germany and the Netherlands are said to accept medical criteria alone as being diagnostic of brain stem death. Among countries in which there is specific legal recognition of the brain as an indicator of death are at least 33 of the United States, Canada and the States of Australia although this relates only to transplantation procedures in Queensland and Western Australia.

that an EEG, which measures the surface electrical activity of the cerebral cortex, would be positive in the presence of properly performed confirmatory tests for brain stem death but there is no reason why such a test should not be added if it would serve to allay any fears among the next of kin as to the certainty of death.

13.13   There is little doubt that any residual public misgiving would be lessened if the purposes of defining brain stem death were more fully understood. Certainly, it is a valuable tool in the provision of high quality organs for transplantation (see chapter 14) but this is only part of the story. The major purpose of the procedure is to establish a consensus by which patients who can no longer benefit can be removed from ventilator support. This is essential if the patient is to die with dignity, if the relatives are to be spared wholly unnecessary suffering and if resources, both mechanical and human, are to be properly apportioned. Accepting brain stem death is not a way of 'hurrying death along'; rather, the ventilator allows the pace of investigation, assessment and prognosis to be slackened; when it comes to the point, the diagnosis of brain stem death is, in the great majority of cases, only confirming what is clear from clinical observation—that the patient is dead.

13.14   Nonetheless, there are still those who believe that the word 'death' should be reserved for those whose heart has stopped beating, the underlying philosophy being, in effect, that loss of brain function should be regarded as the irreversible onset and loss of cardiac function as the termination of the process of death.[26] Clearly, such a formula can apply only when the patient is maintained on a ventilator and, even within that limited parameter, it positively excludes cardiac transplantation as an ethically acceptable procedure. More worryingly, it lends support to suspicions that different concepts of death are being used by the profession and the public and that special criteria apply in association with transplantation.[27] Understanding, or its lack, lies at the root of the problem. Evans, who has been a major opponent of the brain stem death concept, has suggested that our moral convictions stand independent of rational account or explanation[28]—and has been criticised for, thereby, rendering philosophical inquiry superfluous.[29] Yet, in simply calling for better 'education' of the public, it is easy to minimise the importance of religious and cultural traditions. Transplant operations involving brain dead donors have been legalised only within the last decade in Japan and a major reason for this must lie in the unique attitude to death that is widely held in that country. The Western critic should be wary before

[26] Such a view was put forward by the influential Danish Council for Medical Ethics. See B A Rix 'Danish Ethics Council Rejects Brain Death as the Criterion of Death' (1990) 16 J Med Ethics 5. For commentary on the Danish recommendations, see R Gillon 'Death' (1990) 16 J Med Ethics 3 and D Lamb 'Wanting It Both Ways' (1990) 16 J Med Ethics 8.

[27] The issue has been reopened recently by C Machado 'A Definition of Human Death should not be Related to Organ Transplants' (2003) 29 J Med Ethics 201 replying to I H Kerridge, P Saul, M Lowe et al 'Death, Dying and Donation: Organ Transplantation and the Diagnosis of Death' (2002) 28 J Med Ethics 89. These authors suggest that those who are brain dead are not 'dead' but should be legally available as organ donors—a distinction that, in our view, only compounds the confusion.

[28] M Evans 'A Plea for the Heart' (1990) 3 Bioethics 227; 'Death in Denmark' (1990) 16 J Med Ethics 191.

[29] D Lamb 'Death in Denmark: A Reply' (1991) 17 J Med Ethics 100.

suggesting that centuries of cultural tradition should be swept aside in the name of modern medical technology.[30]

13.15 Perhaps we *are* 'fiddling with definitions' and should, rather, concentrate on what it is or is not ethical to do with a dying or a dead body. Gillett[31] has suggested that we do not and cannot require to prolong a life that will never again be engaged with the world; that we require a decent end to that life; and that we require that human remains should be treated with respect—and there is much to commend this rational-isation. Within such a framework, the problems of removal from the ventilator become technical rather than ethical. In this respect, it has been advised that the diagnosis of brain stem death should be made by two doctors, one of whom should be the consultant in charge of the case and the other suitably experienced and clinically independent of the first;[32] but, while the vast majority of practitioners would abide by authoritative guidelines, there is no United Kingdom law on the point.

THE LEGAL EFFECT OF APPLYING BRAIN STEM DEATH CRITERIA

13.16 The application of brain stem death criteria has obvious implications as to caus-ation in cases of unlawful killing—who has killed the victim if he or she is removed from intensive care? Any difficulties disperse once it is conceded that brain stem death means death of the person.[33] It is then clear that the effect of treatment has been no more than to delay the inevitable result of the initial insult to the brain and there is no break in the chain of causation. This was, first, accepted many years ago in America in *People v Lyons*[34] where it was found that the victim of a shooting incident was legally dead before being used as a transplant donor. The British position was summed up in two leading cases to which we return in chapter 17. Thus, in Scotland, it was held:

Once the initial reckless act causing injury has been committed, the natural consequence which the perpetrator must accept is that the victim's future depended on a number of

---

[30] For discussion, see K Hoshino 'Legal Status of Brain Death in Japan: Why Many Japanese Do Not Accept "Brain Death" as a Definition of Death' (1993) 7 Bioethics 234; J Wise 'Japan to Allow Organ Transplants' (1997) 314 BMJ 1298. The Muslim Law Council also accepts brain stem death as a proper definition of death: V Choo 'UK Shariah Council Approves Organ Transplants' (1995) 346 Lancet 303.

[31] G Gillett 'Fiddling and Clarity' (1987) 13 J Med Ethics 23. For a rather similar US view, see D Wickler and A J Weisbard 'Appropriate Confusion over "Brain Death" ' (1989) 261 J Amer Med Ass 2246.

[32] Lord Smith (chairman of Working Party) *The Removal of Cadaveric Organs for Transplantation: A Code of Practice* (1979). There is such legislation, for example, in the Australian States and in South Africa (e.g. Trans-plantation and Anatomy Act 1983 (South Australia), s 24). A very useful protocol for the diagnosis of brain stem death was published by M D O'Brien 'Criteria for Diagnosing Brain Stem Death' (1990) 301 BMJ 108.

[33] Conference of Royal Medical Colleges and their Faculties in the United Kingdom 'Diagnosis of Death' [1979] 1 BMJ 332.

[34] Sup Ct No 56072, Alameda Co (Cal, 1974).

circumstances, including whether any particular treatment was available and, if it was available, whether it was medically reasonable and justifiable to attempt it and to continue it.[35]

The later English decision was fully confirmatory:

Where a medical practitioner, using generally acceptable methods, came to the conclusion that the patient was for all practical purposes dead and that such vital functions as remained were being maintained solely by mechanical means, and accordingly discontinued treatment, that did not break the chain of causation between the initial injury and the death.[36]

It is therefore clear that the law has never regarded doctors who remove a brain stem dead patient from the ventilator as being, thereby, responsible for his death

13.17   Although it is doubtful if it is needed, there is case law which confirms the medical view that persons whose brain stems are dead are, themselves, dead. In the unusual case of Re A[37]—in which the parents of a child sought to have him retained on a ventilator for medico-legal reasons—the judge made a declaration that A, who had been certified as brain stem dead, was dead for all legal as well as all medical purposes and that a doctor who disconnected the apparatus was not acting unlawfully; the fact of death was emphasised when the judge held that he had no inherent jurisdiction over a dead child who could not be made a ward of court for the same reason.

13.18   The major legal problem still outstanding relates to the precise time that death occurs in such circumstances; there are several issues which depend upon that determination, and it is surprising that none appears to have been brought to the courts.

13.19   Lawyers are inclined to dismiss the problem of when death occurs on the assumption that the time of death can be equated to the time the diagnosis is made or to the time the ventilator support is removed. But a moment's reflection makes it clear that the diagnosis of brain stem death, and the consequent ending of treatment, must be retrospective—death has already occurred and the precise time at which it occurred is unknown and unknowable. Moreover, the choice of the time at which the necessary tests are undertaken is as likely to be based on convenience as on anything else. It is difficult to see how the doctor can conscientiously certify the 'date and time of death'—which is not the same as the 'date and time of death certification'—but it is easy to think of occasions on which he might be called upon to do so urgently.

13.20   One very real difficulty lay in the 'year and a day' rule, under which death could not be attributed to murder, manslaughter, infanticide or suicide if it occurred more than a year and a day after the precipitating cause. This rule was repealed by the Law Reform (Year and a Day Rule) Act 1996—a statute which was introduced for the specific reason that ventilator support can often be continued indefinitely; as a result, the time when 'death on the ventilator' occurs is largely in the hands of the intensive

---

[35] Finlayson v HM Advocate 1978 SLT 60 at 61, per Lord Emslie LJ-G.

[36] R v Malcherek; R v Steel [1981] 2 All ER 422 at 428–429, CA, per Lord Lane LCJ.

[37] [1992] 3 Med LR 303. Re A is sometimes taken as establishing that brain stem death constitutes the legal definition of death in England. In our view, it does no more than confirm that a person who is brain stem dead is legally dead.

care team. Time-related factors in the payment, or withholding, of life or personal accident insurance policies remain as being possibly important; one example could concern the application of a suicide clause which would be lifted on a given day. Problems as to the payment of estate duty might also arise.

13.21 But the most intractable issue seems to be that related to succession and the possibility of disputed survival. What is to be said as to the deaths of a husband and wife who are injured in the same accident, who are both ventilated and who are both declared brain stem dead? One thing is certain—survivorship cannot be judged on the basis of the technical diagnosis because the order in which death is determined could well be purely arbitrary. To remove ventilator support from both simultaneously and measure the time for the individual heart to stop beating would be confusing and would raise considerable difficulties in those jurisdictions which allow for *alternative* means of diagnosing death (see below); it is essential to hold on to the premise that 'brain-stem dead' patients are certified as being *already* dead. It would be wholly illogical to vary one's criteria to accommodate a specific situation—alternative methods in diagnosis are acceptable but double standards of death are not.[38] The rules of succession are bound by statute and, accordingly, this is one aspect of brain stem death which could be subject to legislative action. It seems to us that a positive solution to 'ventilated commorientes' is currently impossible; but a negative direction on the lines that evidence as to the time of removal of ventilator support cannot, by itself, be regarded as sufficient to rebut the statutory presumptions might, at least, be equitable and, at the same time, relieve the doctor of one more moral problem.

THE ETHICAL POSITION OF THE DOCTOR

13.22 Thus, while we have said that the act of terminating treatment once brain stem death is diagnosed is a technical problem which raises no ethical issues, the time at which this is done unfortunately may do so. It is facile merely to remark that the doctor's decisions should be uninfluenced by extraneous factors because, in practice, he can scarcely avoid being aware of them—and influence is inseparable from awareness. The problems posed, say, by insistent pressure from relatives who are concerned for the terms of an insurance policy could be intolerable.

13.23 Other dilemmas of a purely moral nature may also arise. Thus, some religious faiths—in particular, orthodox Judaism—still find the concept of brain stem death unacceptable. Is it, then, right to continue ventilation of a dead body in order to respect the cultural traditions of the deceased's family? Some would say—yes, and this largely on the grounds that the heart will, in any case, probably stop beating within a few days of death of the brain stem irrespective of continued support.[39] For our part,

---

[38] See P D G Skegg *Law, Ethics, and Medicine* (1984) ch 9; Lamb, n 29 above.

[39] This is based on very early teaching: B Jennett and C Hessett 'Brain Death in Britain as Reflected in Renal Donors' (1981) 283 BMJ 359. Doubts have, however, arisen on this score (see para 13.26 below). For long-term support, see D A Shewmon 'Chronic Brain Death: Meta-analysis and Conceptual Consequences' (1998) 51 Neurology 1538.

we must prefer the view that it is more respectful of the dead, kinder to the staff and, in the end, probably kinder to the relatives and certainly less sophistic to support good medical practice—albeit with the maximum compassion.[40]

13.24   In recent years, however, doctors and the public have been confronted by the picture of brain dead women being retained on support for the sole purpose of bringing a fetus to viability.[41] A plethora of moral problems then arise, the answers to which, if there are any, depend, first, on the gestational age of the fetus and, second, on whether the individual woman has or has not expressed her wishes or intentions while alive.[42] The classic situation is illustrated by an instance from Germany which concerned an unmarried, brain stem dead 18-year-old who was only 15 weeks' pregnant; the hospital ethics committee (see chapter 18) recommended continuation of the pregnancy—a decision which was, in our view surprisingly, widely supported by all other than women's groups.[43] The fetus was still born after six weeks of intensive effort. The President of the Federal Chamber of Physicians is reported as commenting: 'Due to scientific advances, medicine will, again and again, have to infringe ethical borders';[44] the alternative view, which we share, sees such actions as incremental nudges which may, ultimately, push this branch of medicine into areas of doubtful morality. Even so, we wonder if we would have been so sceptical had the fetus been of, say, 24 weeks' gestation? In the absence of any indication as to the woman's wishes— which is the probable scenario—the temptation is to say that to maintain her as an oxygenated cadaver would be an unacceptable invasion of a dying person's dignity and privacy. On the other hand, it would certainly not be unreasonable to hold that the fetus now constituted the living patient who should be treated in his or her best interests. Arguments based on a potential fetal/maternal conflict, such as have been raised under the heading of 'Abortion', would be invalidated once the mother was declared dead—yet, in the alternative, could the doctor be seen as acting unethically in failing to treat an organism that has no legal personality? Death does not, for example, extinguish all interests that a person has; even the brain stem dead can retain interests in how the corpse is treated and respected.

[40] See D Inwald, I Jacobovits and A Petros 'Brain Stem Death: Managing Care when Accepted Medical Guidelines and Religious Beliefs are in Conflict' (2000) 320 BMJ 1266 and accompanying comment by M Fisher and R F Raper. See also the closely allied case *Re C (a minor) (medical treatment)* [1998] 1 FLR 384, (1998) 40 BMLR 31.

[41] For thorough discussions, see N S Peart, A V Campbell, A R Manara et al 'Maintaining a Pregnancy Following Loss of Capacity' (2000) 8 Med L Rev 275 and D Sperling 'Maternal Brain Death' (2004) Amer J Law & Med 453. The problem is not, however, as recent as might be supposed; see, for example a thoughtful article by D R Field, E A Gates, R K Creasy et al 'Maternal Brain Death during Pregnancy: Medical and Legal Issues' (1988) 260 J Amer Med Ass 816.

[42] Peart et al, n 41 para above, also discuss the situation in which the woman is unconscious and we return to that problem briefly in chapter 14.

[43] For full discussion, see C Anstötz 'Should a Brain-dead Pregnant Woman Carry her Child to Full Term? The Case of the "Erlangen Baby" ' (1993) 7 Bioethics 340.

[44] A Tuffs 'Keeping a Brain-dead Pregnant Woman "Alive" ' (1992) 340 Lancet 1029.

13.25   The situation is not greatly eased if the woman has expressed her intentions. Suppose she wishes to be ventilated for the sake of her fetus—which might be regarded as an autonomous choice of a competent adult? Does the doctor *have* to follow such a choice? Or what if the woman has expressed a wish not to be maintained after death and the fetus is viable? Is it impossible that the doctor who causes its death by following its mother's dictates could be charged under the Infant Life (Preservation) Act 1929?[45] It is inviting to try to fit such a case within the legislation surrounding the use of human tissues after death but we can see no way by which post-mortem pregnancy can be accommodated within the scheduled purposes governed by the Human Tissue Act 2004.[46]

13.26   Fortunately, the conditions envisaged must arise extremely rarely and we suggest that, should the issue be raised, it would be a matter to be decided by discussion between the doctor responsible for intensive care and, perhaps ideally, the person likely to be responsible for the welfare of the living child—although the Act might well be invoked so as to involve the woman's 'nominated representative' in the discussion, or to identify the appropriate person within a 'qualifying relationship'[47] who might be called on. In the event of disagreement, we imagine that the courts would decide any issue on the common sense aspects of the individual case while bearing in mind the best interests of the proposed neonate. What is more important in the context of the diagnosis of death is how such cases can occur—bearing in mind Jennett's advice which we have already mentioned.[48] Many of these cases are said to have been ventilated for more than 50 days—which must suggest the possibility of diagnostic inconsistency.[49] This being so, attempts to incubate a fetus to viability in a woman who has been declared dead may not only be unethical but may also contribute to the confusion and distrust which, even today, colour the concept of brain stem death.

THE CASE FOR LEGISLATION

13.27   It is because of this latent unease that the case for a modern statutory definition of death has been widely canvassed and is applied in many jurisdictions.

13.28   The main difficulty in framing legislation is to allow for all modes of death—from

---

[45] Peart et al cite *R v Woollin* [1999] 1 AC 82, [1998] 4 All ER 103 in support of this but we are doubtful if the law of murder can be easily extrapolated to that of child destruction.

[46] See chapter 15.

[47] Human Tissue Act 2004, ss 4 and 54(9).

[48] N 39 above. Further early disagreement is to be found in: J F Parish, R C Kim, G H Collings et al 'Brain Death with Prolonged Somatic Survival' (1982) 306 New Engl J Med 14.

[49] Yet there was, apparently, no doubt in the case of Ms Marshall who was maintained for 105 days before being delivered of an approximately 32 weeks' fetus which survived—quoted by Fisher, n 14 above. Sperling, n 41 above, gives a comprehensive list of such reports—including four in which the woman is said to have survived for 60 days or more.

the elementarily obvious to the complex ventilator case; it would be absurd to demand that criteria designed for the latter be applied to the former. As a result, most statutes, either existing or proposed, have applied some form of dual criteria of proof of death.[50] A typical expression is to be found in the United States Uniform Determination of Death Act 1980,[51] which reads:

1. An individual who has sustained either: (a) irreversible cessation of circulatory and respiratory functions; or (b) irreversible cessation of all functions of the entire brain, including the brain stem; is dead.

2. A determination of death must be made in accordance with accepted medical standards.

And, as an example of Commonwealth legislation, we quote the Human Tissue Act 1982 (Victoria), s 41:

A person has died when there has occurred:

(a) Irreversible cessation of the circulation of the blood in the body of the person, or

(b) Irreversible cessation of all functions of the brain of the person.

There are similar provisions in the Human Tissue Act 1983 (NSW), s 33.

13.29   But, in essence, all these measures do is to spell out good medical practice within a legal framework—and many would feel this to be unnecessary. They lay down no specific methods; these being relegated to codes of practice—and this, we believe, is rightly so. We would certainly agree with the great majority of commentators that any statutory definition of death must be limited to an enabling concept. Medical facilities and expertise alter and do so faster than can the law; it is, therefore, essential that the evaluation of diagnostic techniques remains in the hands of the medical profession. In fact, the ethical, philosophical and social problems inherent in the definition of death seem to have been largely solved in recent years;[52] definitive legislation might do little more than reanimate concerns which have, at least to a large extent, been put to rest and might, as a result, be self-defeating. The stethoscope and the CT scanner have it in common that both depend upon the expertise of their user—no Act of Parliament can alter that basic fact.

---

[50] State statutes in the USA can be divided into three categories: those which provide for brain death as an express alternative to heart-lung orientated death, those which admit the use of brain-based criteria when a cardiorespiratory diagnosis is obviated by artificial maintenance; and those which recognise brain death simply as a means of determining or defining death. All states have now adopted the concept of brain death either by statute or by court recognition. See A M Capron 'Brain Death—Well Settled yet still Unsettled' (2001) 344 New Engl J Med 1244.

[51] 12 Uniform Laws Annotated (ULA) 589 (West 1993 and West Supp. 1997).

[52] Pallis, n 22 above.

14

THE DONATION OF ORGANS AND TRANSPLANTATION

14.1 The juxtaposition of chapters on the diagnosis of death and on transplantation of organs should not be taken to indicate that they are *necessarily* associated. It is again emphasised that the concept of brain stem death is equally important to neurosurgeons, who can, as a result, allow their hopeless patients to die in peace, and to the relatives, who can now accept the fact of death in a ventilated body with good conscience. Nevertheless, and despite the introduction of new techniques to which we refer later, optimum transplantation—and, with it, maximum saving of lives—depends upon the acceptance of brain stem death; furthermore, the two conditions are closely linked in the public mind. This is, therefore, a not inappropriate point at which to discuss the ethics and legality of a procedure which, although now firmly established as accepted medical treatment, nevertheless still provokes some public disquiet.[1]

TECHNICAL ASPECTS OF TRANSPLANTATION

14.2 Aside from the technical expertise required, there are three major biological hurdles to be overcome in successful transplantation therapy: (i) ensuring that the donated organs are healthy; (ii) preserving the viability of those organs in the period between their becoming available and their reception; and (iii) neutralising the 'tissue immunity' reaction.

ACCEPTABILITY OF THE TISSUES

14.3 It is axiomatic that an organ intended as a replacement for a diseased tissue must, itself, be normal. The practical result is that donors must either be living or have died from accident or from localised natural disease which has no effect on the donated tissue. Arbitrary age limits for donation have been adopted in the past; present policy,

---

[1] For a recent short overview and discussion, see C Machado 'A Definition of Human Death should not be Related to Organ Transplants' (2003) 29 J Med Ethics 201.

however, is to assess the health of the potential donor and to use or reject the available tissues on that basis alone.

14.4   Viability, or continued functional competence, of the donated organ is the essential element for success and it is the assurance of viability which combines most clearly the technical and ethical problems of transplantation surgery. As has been discussed in chapter 13, the cells of the body will deteriorate when deprived of oxygen; the process of deterioration can be slowed markedly by chilling the organ, the viability of which then depends on the 'warm anoxic time'—that is, the interval between cessation of the circulation and chilling of the specimen. In terms of practical transplantation, it becomes increasingly pointless to transplant a kidney after more than one hour's warm anoxia. Even so, the acceptable cold anoxic time is also finite and varies with the tissue involved—not only as regards its metabolic activity but also as to the urgency with which it must assume full function after transplantation; in general terms, the heart and lungs can be used up to four hours after harvesting, the liver up to 8–12 hours and the kidneys can be maintained in vitro for more than 24 hours. Imposed delays must, therefore, jeopardise the validity of the operation.[2]

14.5   A tissue immunity reaction results from the recognition by the body of antigenically foreign material which it will then reject with a degree of determination that depends, to a large extent, on *how* different is the donated tissue from that of the recipient. From this point of view, we can distinguish three main forms of transplantation therapy:

   (a) Autotransplantation, or the resiting of portions of the same body. This is effectively limited to skin or bone grafting and poses only the difficulties of highly complex surgery. It is of no concern in the present context.

   (b) Homotransplantation or allografting, which involves the transfer of viable tissue from one human being to another.

   (c) Heterotransplantation or xenotransplantation—that is, the successful transplantation of organs from one species to another. This last format is highly experimental and is of minimal practical significance at the present time. It will, therefore, be convenient to deal with it first as something of a separate subject.

XENOTRANSPLANTATION

14.6   Clearly, xenotransplantation is that form of organ grafting which will stimulate the maximum immune reaction. The reaction will be quantifiably different when involving so-called concordant species—for example, within the primates—and discordant

---

[2] Cold perfusion of the whole body or of individual organs in situ is now used to reduce these difficulties. The non-heart-beating donor may be returning and improving the supply of organs. G Kootstra, R Wijnen, J P van Hooff and C J van der Linden 'Twenty Percent More Kidneys through a Non-heart Beating Program' (1991) 23 Transplant Proc 910. For a review of the current position, see V Papalois, K Vlachos, A Barlas et al 'Ethical Issues in Non-heart-beating Donation' (2004) Bull Med Ethics, No. 202, 13.

species—when the species are widely separated, as in pig to man transplants; the reaction is then of a quite different order from that seen with the customary allograft and is known as hyperacute rejection of the donated organ.

14.7   Even so, there is no doubt that, although it is not, as yet, a practical possibility, xenotransplantation has moved relatively rapidly towards realisation in the last ten years.[3] The increasing sophistication of immunosuppressant drugs and of immuno-suppressant techniques—in particular those involving genetic replacement whereby transgenic animals, modified so as to contain human genetic material, are produced and, thus, take xenografting[4] closer to allografting[5]—are, however, changing the scene to the extent that a man has survived for 70 days following the transplantation of a baboon's liver.[6] These rapid advances have precipitated precautionary governmental action which has, thus far, culminated in the establishment of a Xenotransplantation Interim Regulatory Authority (UKXIRA); the Authority oversees the development of xenotransplantation and its co-ordination pending the introduction of primary legis-lation. The government's approach to this potential therapy is, therefore, very similar to that it adopted in respect of assisted reproduction (see chapter 4). One of the first actions of the UKXIRA was to declare a moratorium on clinical trials of xenografting pending further research. Thus, consideration of the subject can still be pitched at a relatively superficial level in a book of this type. This, however, should not cloud the fact that xenotransplantation stimulates a host of ethical problems in addition to those which are severely practical.[7]

14.8   As to the latter, in addition to the establishment of an immune response in the individual case, the community-based possibility of transmitting animal micro-organisms—in particular, viruses—to humans, and of their becoming adapted to the new environment and of consequent human to human spread, is very real and consti-tutes one of the main reasons why xenotransplantation is suspect.[8] A corollary to this, which crosses the ethical/practical boundary, is that animals destined to be donors

---

[3] For a state of the art report on the technology from the Council of Europe as of 2003 see: www.coe.int/T/ E/Social_Cohesion/Health/Activities/Organ_transplantation/.

[4] Xenotransplantation and xenografting can be regarded as interchangeable terms.

[5] A James 'Transplants with Transgenic Pig Organs?' (1993) 342 Lancet 45.

[6] T E Starzl, J Fung, A Tzakis et al 'Baboon-to-human Liver Transplantation' (1993) 341 Lancet 65. Even so, we remain unconvinced that such a result should be classified as a success. For analysis from the US, see J K Fredrickson 'He's All Heart . . . and a Little Pig Too: A Look at the FDA Draft Xenotransplant Guidelines' (1997) 52 Food Drug LJ 429; J M Kress 'Xenotransplantation: Ethics and Economics' (1998) 53 Food Drug LJ 353.

[7] For a recent inquiring review, see S A M McLean and L Williamson 'Xenotransplantation: A Pig in a Poke?' (2004) 57 CLP 443.

[8] See Nuffield Council on Bioethics *Animal-to-Animal Transplants* (1996) ch 6 and its follow up: D A Muir and G E Griffin *Infection Risks in Xenotransplantation* (Prepared for the Department of Health, 2001). Also M Fox and J McHale 'Regulating Xenotransplantation' (1997) 147 NLJ 139 and F H Bach, A J Ivinson and C Weeramantry 'Ethical and Legal Issues in Technology: Xenotransplantation' (2001) 27 Amer J L Med 283 where the global nature of the risks are emphasised. It is fair, however, to direct attention to the fact that no evidence of a severe threat to public health can be derived from a study of those who have already been treated with porcine tissues: J H Tanne 'Study Gives Reassurance on Safety of Xenotransplantation' (1999) 319 BMJ 533.

would have to be reared in 'pathogen-free' environments which are hard, if not impossible, to define and maintain but which would also involve much animal suffering—and the morality of xenotransplantation depends on there being a positive balance in favour of human advantage over animal disadvantage.[9] Given that it is acceptable to use animals in this way, one has to ask—what sort of animals? Clearly, tissue rejection would be minimised if non-human primates were used. It is, however, widely accepted that primates have special characteristics and constitute such a natural resource as to exclude them as organ donors.[10] Current interest, therefore, centres on the pig—an animal which has no antigenic but remarkable physiological affinities with man. Modern molecular biological techniques have already produced transgenic pigs in which at least one of the mechanisms leading to graft rejection appears to have been eliminated; there is little doubt that clinical trials using such organs are on the horizon, albeit not just around the corner.

14.9   All of which may be good scientific medicine but, like so many such 'advances', it raises both intuitive and philosophical doubts. Undoubtedly, there is a 'gut' distaste for being maintained by a porcine heart. More importantly, one must wonder at the morality of maintaining and, worse, breeding animals for the express purpose of substituting human body parts. The simple response that this is no different from eating pork in order to avoid starvation seems unsatisfactory—Downie,[11] for example, saw a moral difference between 'natural' feeding and 'unnatural' organ substitution. We feel, however, that the subject—which should include an analysis of the philosophy of speciesism—is too wide to be tackled here.[12] In fact, while very much appreciating the potential human advantages of xenotransplantation, we are equally concerned as to the possible ill effects on our human society. It is not wholly unreal to foresee human organs being replaced by those of animals as they fail in sequence; we are then left with the unedifying picture of replacement therapy being continued until the irreplaceable and paradigmatic human organ, the brain, wears out. Moreover, since no health service could contain the costs of such a programme, longevity would become the prerogative of the rich; the structure of human society could be altered dramatically.

14.10   In addition to these relatively practical concerns, we have to ask if xenotransplantation can be accommodated within our existing medical jurisprudence. Writing from within the strongly consent-orientated Canadian jurisdiction, Caulfield and

---

[9] That such a balance exists was accepted by both the government appointed Advisory Group on the Ethics of Transplantation *Animal Tissue into Humans* (1996) and the Nuffield Council. Individuals are less convinced: see R Downie 'Xenotransplantation' (1997) 23 J Med Ethics 205.

[10] While stating this firmly, the Advisory Group, considered that primates could, in strictly circumscribed conditions, be used for research into xenotransplantation. They would, of course, be protected by the Animals (Scientific Procedures) Act 1986.

[11] Others are less convinced: e.g. J Hughes 'Xenografting: Ethical Issues' (1998) 24 J Med Ethics 18. For a comprehensive analysis, see M Fox and J McHale 'Xenotransplantation: The Ethical and Legal Ramifications' (1998) 6 Med L Rev 42. We also wonder at what stage of modification does a transgenic pig become human?

[12] This aspect is well considered by W Cartwright 'The Pig, the Transplant Surgeon, and the Nuffield Council' (1996) 4 Med L Rev 250.

Robertson[13] have pointed out that the needs for continued surveillance and for man-datory autopsy following xenografting must lead to concepts of 'contracts to undergo treatment' rather than consent to do so. Moreover, is the public not entitled to con-sent or dissent to a programme which undoubtedly threatens its well-being? The appointment of a supervisory authority is, of course, a step in the right direction but a strong case can be made out for insisting on a wide-based popular expression of agreement before all moratoria are lifted.[14] In practical terms, no xenografts have, as yet, been performed in the United Kingdom; it is to be noted, however, that current government policy on the subject is very cautious but is by no means exclusive.[15]

14.11   Even so, the great majority of commentators would prefer to see improvements in the existing homotransplantation programme rather than the development of xeno-grafting and the remainder of this chapter is devoted to organ replacement as it is generally understood.

HOMOTRANSPLANTATION

14.12   Here, despite the fact that we are dealing with tissues from the same species, an immunity problem persists because, for practical purposes, no two persons other than monovular twins are genetically identical; the body can still recognise, and will reject, tissues of the same species which are 'non-self'.[16] This intra-species immune reaction can be increasingly well suppressed by the use, inter alia, of the ciclosporine group of drugs and monoclonal antibodies. The general principle remains, however, that such suppression will be effective—and will have less adverse side effects—in proportion to the genetic similarity of donor and recipient. Thus, sibling donation will be especially satisfactory and intra-familial exchanges in general are likely to show less antigenic discrepancies than are those between random strangers. Other variables, however, intrude and complicate the picture. Immunosuppression is non-specific; there-fore, while the graft rejection process is being controlled, other desirable immune reactions—such as the body's defence against microbiological invasion—are also affected. Thus, micro-organisms that are normally resisted with ease will be increas-ingly able to establish themselves in the vulnerable body—the most specifically

---

13 T A Caulfield and G B Robertson 'Xenotransplantation: Consent, Public Health and Charter Issues' (2001) 5 Med L Internat 81.

14 This line of argument is well expressed by M A Clark 'This Little Piggy Went to Market: The Xenotrans-plantation and Xenozoonose Debate' (1999) 27 J Law Med Ethics 137. The paper should, however, be read in conjunction with its sibling written by a member of the FDA's Subcommittee on Xenotransplantation: H Y Vanderpool 'Commentary: A Critique of Clark's Frightening Xenotransplantation Scenario' (1999) 27 J Law Med Ethics 153.

15 Official Reports HC, 15 February 1993, vol 219, col 80. See also *Government Response to 'Animal Tissue into Humans'* (1997). Extensive recommendations and guidelines from the Council of Europe Committee of Ministers are posted on www.coe.int/T/E/Social-Cohesion/Health/Recommendations/Rec(2003)10.asp which do not preclude actual treatment.

16 The alternative—where the transplanted material attacks the host—is a difficulty of bone marrow transplantation. See the still very useful article: A M Denman 'Graft versus Host Disease: New Versions of Old Problems?' (1985) 290 BMJ 658.

significant of these are viruses which are responsible for certain forms of malignant disease of the lymphoid system. Thus, although the newer agents allow for increased selectivity and for 'tailoring' to the needs of the individual patient,[17] the rising success of transplantation therapy is not simply a matter of discovering more powerful immunosuppressants.

14.13   As to the source of homotransplants, it will be evident that suitable organs can be provided by the living or by the dead. Living donation offers many technical advantages—tissue compatibility can be measured at leisure, the operation can be elective and the warm anoxic time can approach zero.[18] In theory, potential cadaver donors are widely available. In practice, however, their recovery is often capricious and both donor and recipient operations must then take on the character of emergency surgery. The recognition of brain stem death, however, offers the possibility of a variation on cadaver donation—the 'beating heart donor'—which bridges the gap between the living and the conventionally dead and carries with it many of the advantages of both types of donor. The legal and ethical limitations of all three methods must be considered.

THE LIVING DONOR

14.14   The donation of tissues which can be replaced rapidly—such as blood and bone marrow—presents, in practice, few technical or ethical problems other than that of commercialism to which we refer below.[19] We are concerned here only with non-regenerative tissues.

14.15   The legal regulation of living donations in the United Kingdom lies in both common and statute law. As to the former, the starting-point must be the principle that no person is to be deemed capable of consenting to his being killed or seriously injured. The living donation of a heart is, thereby, precluded. This, of course, is the extreme case and, beyond it, legality would depend upon the presumed risk-benefit ratio involved in the procedure—and assessment of this is difficult because the technological boundaries of medicine are always expanding. A few years ago, one would have said the same about the liver as about the heart; today, the use of segments of adult liver in paediatric transplantation therapy is recognised as part of the norm while partial liver transplantation between adults is also widely practiced[20]—in fact, since

---

[17] P A Andrews 'Recent Developments: Renal Transplantation' (2002) 324 BMJ 530.

[18] The 1-year survival rate following live transplantation is 95% as compared with some 88% in the case of cadaver donations: P A Andrews 'Renal Transplantation' (2002) 324 BMJ 530. The Royal College of Surgeons has called for a doubling of the number of live transplants in the UK: *Report of the Working Party to Review Organ Transplantation* (P Morris, chairman) (1999) www.rcseng.ac.uk/services/publications/publications/pdf/rep_orgt.

[19] Though bone marrow donation is certainly a procedure which cannot be undertaken light-heartedly.

[20] A Marcos, R A Fisher, J M Ham et al 'Right Lobe Living Donor Liver Transplantation' (1999) 68 Transplantation 798.

the liver regenerates both anatomically and functionally,[21] it may be that live liver donation is more akin to bone marrow donation than to organ transplantation.[22] Much the same is now true of donation of lobes of the lung—a matter of great importance in the treatment of the relatively common, life-threatening genetic condition of cystic fibrosis.[23] Given that the relative risks and benefits of a given procedure are both assessable and acceptable, the common law legality and the morality of live organ donation is now settled; consent to a surgical operation which is, in itself, non-therapeutic will be valid so long as the consequent infliction of injury can be shown not to be against the public interest.[24]

14.16   The statutory regulation of live donation is to be found in the Human Tissue Act 2004, s 33 for England, Wales and Northern Ireland and the Human Organ Transplants Act 1989 for Scotland.[25] Both create an offence if a live organ transplant is performed other than in accordance with the regulations. No regulations under the 2004 Act have been promulgated at the time of writing and we propose, here, to assume that the conditions governing living donation laid down in the 1989 Act will remain in force throughout the United Kingdom for some time. The essential feature of the 1989 Act and its associated regulations was to prohibit a transplant operation between living persons who are not genetically related unless it was undertaken with the agreement of the Unrelated Live Transplant Regulatory Authority (s 2).[26] Genetically related transplantation is not subject to statutory control. Section 2(2) of the 1989 Act defines a genetic relationship. This can be so wide—it includes, for example, uncles and aunts by half blood—as to raise the suspicion that Parliament was concerned more with family loyalties than genetic niceties;[27] even so, it is surprising

---

[21] S Kawasaki, M Makuuchi, S Ishizone et al 'Liver Regeneration in Recipients and Donors after Transplantation' (1992) 339 Lancet 580.

[22] The Human Organ Transplants Act 1989, s 7, which remains in force in Scotland, defines an organ as any part of the human body consisting of a structured arrangement of tissues which, *if wholly removed*, cannot be replicated by the body (our emphasis). This would include a liver but not necessarily a segment of liver. Transplantable material in terms of the Human Tissue Act 2004 has yet to be defined (s 33(7)).

[23] The mortality associated with lung lobe donation is said to be approaching that of live kidney donation. However, two donors are needed to treat a single child. M E Hodson 'Transplantation using Lung Lobes from Living Donors' (2000) 26 J Med Ethics 419.

[24] *R v Coney* (1882) 8 QBD 534. The obiter remarks of Denning LJ in *Bravery v Bravery* [1954] 1 WLR 1169 at 1180 have been endorsed: *A-G's Reference (No. 6 of 1980)* [1981] QB 715, [1981] 2 All ER 1057.

[25] The 1989 Act is repealed by the 2004 Act outwith Scotland. The 1989 Act and the Human Tissue Act 1961 are unlikely to be replaced in Scotland in the near future.

[26] See also particularly Human Organ Transplants (Establishment of Relationship) Regulations 1989, SI 1989/2107 and Human Organ Transplants (Unrelated Persons) Regulations 1989, SI 1989/2480. It seems that the functions of the Authority will be subsumed within the remit of the new Human Tissue Authority.

[27] Human Fertilisation and Embryology Act 1990, ss 27–29 do not apply for the purposes of the section. It is, however, fair to say that, consequent upon the major improvements in immunosuppression, not everyone is uncritical of the current restrictions which are not applied in some other European jurisdictions—e.g. Germany. It is probable that the only genetic match that is *essential* to, say, kidney donation is the ABO grouping—transplants between spouses and partners are, therefore, not only emotionally indicated but are also as technically satisfactory as are those between genetic relations. For doubts as to the usefulness of the Authority, see S Choudhry, A S Daar, J Radcliffe Richards et al 'Unrelated Living Organ Donation: ULTRA Needs to Go' (2003) 29 J Med Ethics 169.

that inter-spousal donations, and donation by 'in-laws' or God-parents, are still subject to restriction. Authority for an unrelated donation is, however, subject to very strict rules as to the absence of commercial involvement (which we discuss in greater detail in paras 14.27 et seq below) and as to the consent of the donor and counselling of both parties—additionally, the Authority must be informed of any difficulties in communication between the counsellor and the donor and/or recipient.[28] An interesting variation on the normal conditions for consent (for which see chapter 10) is that the donor *must* understand the processes involved—there is no scope here for 'professional privilege' in providing information; live organ donations involving unrelated incompetents are, therefore, very nearly legally impossible—the position as regards minors is discussed below. These rules, other than those associated with non-payment, are waived in the event that the donation is part of the treatment of the donor[29]—a circumstance which arises most commonly in what is known as the 'domino transplant'. Thus, in the treatment of cystic fibrosis by cadaver donation, for example, it is clinically more satisfactory to use a heart/lung preparation obtained from the dead donor than to implant a lung alone; this leaves the live recipient's heart available for donation in what will almost certainly be a non-related context. A large proportion of unrelated donations are, in fact, of this type.[30]

14.17   The proportion of renal transplants from living donors has been rising in the United Kingdom since 1992. In 1994, it was 7 per cent; the comparable figure in 2003–4 was 24 per cent.[31] Similar trends have been noted worldwide. The proportion in Australia, where the overall donation rate is very low, is 34 per cent while the number of live donations has actually exceeded those from deceased persons in the United States since 2001.[32] Despite the fact that there is no statutory protection in the United Kingdom for the *related* donor, there can be no doubt as to the legality of the removal of a kidney from a live adult for the purpose of saving the life of a seriously ill patient—subject, of course, to free and rational consent to the operation.[33] Living donation by children, however, raises a number of thorny issues.

---

[28] Human Organ Transplants (Unrelated Persons) Regulations 1989, SI 1989/2480, reg 3(2)(e).

[29] SI 1989/2480, 3(1)(c).

[30] B New, M Solomon, R Dingwall and J McHale *A Question of Give and Take: Supply of Organs for Transplantation* (1994), p 35. Three out of 10 living liver transplants performed in 2003–4 were also of 'domino' type.

[31] UK Transplant Activity Report 2003–2004. The annual total of renal transplants has remained remarkably steady over the decade but the waiting list in 2004 stood at an all time high of 7,236.

[32] OPTN/SRTR Annual Review 2003. For a general overview, see N Biller-Andorno and H Schauenburg 'It's Only Love? Some Pitfalls in Emotionally Related Organ Donation' (2001) 27 J Med Ethics 162. The very high proportion of live transplants in the Scandinavian countries is remarkable (50% in Norway). It should be noted that live donation is the preferred method in some societies. In Japan, for example, the concept of brain stem death has only recently become acceptable, some 70% of donations were of live type. Virtually all transplants in India are 'live' but this is probably an administrative rather than cultural consequence (see para 14.33 below).

[33] This is now confirmed in the European dimension in the second Additional Protocol to the Convention on Human Rights and Biomedicine (1997), Chapter III.

THE MINOR AS A DONOR

14.18 The donation of organs by children is required surprisingly often; clearly, the advantages of live donation will apply here as much as they will in the adult situation. The legality of such operations on children below the age of 16 has not been decided by British courts and the issue must thus be considered in the light of the general legal principles applied to the medical treatment of minors. As discussed in chapter 10, consent to an operation on a minor below the age of 16 years should normally be obtained from the parents, subject only to the possible common law rights of the child.[34] Valid parental consent, however, refers to treatment for the advantage of the child; troublesome questions arise in relation to procedures which are not calculated to be to his or her benefit—does parental consent in such circumstances constitute an abuse of parental power?

14.19 It has been argued that the principle that a minor—or an incompetent adult—cannot legally be subjected to any procedure which is not to his or her advantage is not an absolute one. It is also possible that a court might consider that the donation of an organ is not only in the public interest but that it is also in the interest of the minor donor, who will, almost certainly, be a sibling of the recipient. In such circumstances it might be supposed that it is in the interests of the minor that a member of his family should be saved rather than die. This line of argument was successfully pursued in the index American decision in *Strunk v Strunk*.[35] In this case, the donor, who, although adult, had a mental age of six, was chosen to donate a kidney to his brother, who was critically ill. The court came to the conclusion it would be in the donor's best interests for his brother's life to be saved after hearing evidence of the close relationship which existed between them. Consequently, the operation was allowed although the donor was not in a position to give consent. *Strunk* has not, however, had an easy ride.[36] There is no assurance that it represents the general rule in the United States; indeed, it has been rejected in a more recent case involving a bone marrow transplant between three-year-old twins.[37] Again, this decision can be compared with that in the English case *Re Y*. Here, a bone marrow transplant was authorised between siblings largely on the grounds that, absent treatment for the lymphomatous child, the mother would have less time to devote to the incapax; the procedure was, accordingly in the best

---

[34] P D G Skegg 'English Law relating to Experimentation on Children' (1977) 2 Lancet 754 took the view that the Family Law Reform Act 1969, s 8 has no application to non-therapeutic procedures and that the rules of non-statutory law do not vary with different categories of persons. See Lord Donaldson in *Re W (a minor) (medical treatment)* [1992] 4 All ER 627, (1992) 9 BMLR 22, discussed para 14.21 below. The position in Scotland under the Age of Legal Capacity (Scotland) Act 1991, s 2(4) is uncertain.

[35] 445 SW 2d 145 (Ky, 1969).

[36] It was followed in *Hart v Brown* 289 A 2d 386 (Conn, 1972) (identical twins) and in *Little v Little* 576 SW 2d 493 (Tex, 1979) (14-year-old incompetent) but rejected in *In re Richardson* 284 So 2d 185 (La, 1973) (17-year-old incompetent) and in *In re Guardianship of Pescinski* 226 NW 2d 180 (Wis, 1975) (adult incompetent). It is interesting that, despite attempts to apply a substituted judgment test, all the relevant cases have been decided on the basis of the donor's best interests.

[37] *Curran v Bosze* 566 NE 2d 1319 (Ill, 1990). It seems that there have been no transplants involving minors in the United Sates in recent years—OPTN/SRTR Annual Review for 2003.

interests of the donor. It is clear that no rule can be anticipated. Each case will stand on its own merits and, in view of the existing jurisprudence, it is significant that the Council of Europe's protocol on transplantation envisages donation involving a live incompetent as being permissible only between siblings.[38]

14.20   In practice, while donation of regenerative tissue is permissible given stringent conditions, most jurisdictions are reluctant to allow the taking of non-regenerative tissues from minors and a blanket ban on the use of minors as organ donors has been advocated by the World Health Organization.[39] While the complete exclusion of minor donors might seem to many to be too extreme, there are powerful reasons why some limits should be placed on the use of children as donors of non-regenerative tissue and very great caution should be exercised in the case of young children in whom there is unlikely to be any significant understanding of what the donation entails. Even if a minor shows a reasonable degree of understanding of the donation and of the risks involved, a sharp distinction is to be made between instances when the recipient is a member of the immediate family and when he or she is not. As we have already intimated, it might be regarded as ethically acceptable for a minor to be used as a donor in the former case; generosity towards a brother or sister is to be encouraged and may even be regarded as a social duty.[40] The situation is less clear with relatives other than siblings. Should one apply the same rule to a situation where the prospective recipient is a cousin in the first degree? It is possible that the minor donor may be as fond of such a cousin as he is of a brother or sister and the illness of the cousin may be as distressing to him as would be the illness of a sibling. Nevertheless, a policy of limiting approved donation by minors to the immediate family has the attraction of certainty. In summary, the general approach seems to be that, while blood and bone marrow donation by children is acceptable given fairly rigid conditions as to authorisation, the therapeutic use of living minors' non-regenerative organs will not be countenanced.[41] The caution shown by countries that are subject to both common and civil law jurisdictions is noteworthy[42] given the somewhat *laissez-faire* attitude adopted in the United Kingdom where statute is either ambivalent or

---

[38] N 33 above. It is to be noted that the Convention on Human Rights and Biomedicine has not been ratified by the United Kingdom at the time of writing.

[39] World Health Organization *Guiding Principles on Human Organ Transplantation* (1994) principle 4, discussed by M N Morelli 'Organ Trafficking: Legislative Proposals to Protect Minors' (1995) 10 Am U J Int Law Pol 917.

[40] L F Ross 'Moral Grounding for the Participation of Children as Organ Donors' (1993) 21 J Law Med & Ethics 251 introduces the interesting concept of the family as an autonomous unit which can aspire to a collective purpose. Intrafamilial donation by a child advances the family's interests, which is a means of promoting the child's own interests. None the less, the author was extremely chary of exposing minors to risks they do not understand.

[41] See, for example, France: Law no. 2004–800 of 6 August 2004 maintaining Articles L.1231–1 (adults) and L.1231–2 and L.1241–3 (minors) of the Public Health Code.

[42] Scandanavia seems to provide exceptions to the rule in Europe: donation of organs by minors is permissible, subject to varying regulation, in Denmark (Law no. 402 of 13 June 1990), Norway (Law no. 6 of 9 February 1973) and Sweden (Transplantation Law no. 190 of 15 May 1975). Interestingly, none of the Australian States allows live organ donation by a minor.

silent on the matter. Partial clarification of the current legal position here has, however, come from the Court of Appeal.

14.21   The case of Re W[43] dealt with consent to treatment by a 16-year-old and was concerned, in the main, with the application of the Family Law Reform Act 1969, s 8(1).[44] The problem of organ transplantation was not in issue but was touched upon by the then Master of the Rolls; his views must, we feel, be regarded as obiter but are, nevertheless, persuasive. Lord Donaldson first disposed of the statute on the grounds that the section related to treatment and diagnosis; it could not, therefore, extend to the donation of organs as this did not satisfy either condition in respect of the donor. He went on:

Organ donations are quite different and, as a matter of law, doctors would have to secure the consent of someone with the right to consent on behalf of a donor under the age of 18 or, if they relied on the consent of the minor himself or herself, be satisfied that the minor was 'Gillick competent' in the context of so serious a procedure which would not benefit the minor.[45]

14.22   As to the latter, he added, somewhat equivocally: 'This would be a highly improbable conclusion.' The whole passage is, in fact, a trifle confusing as, logically, 'Gillick-competence' applies only to the under 16-year-old, whereas s 8(1) of the Act relates to the 16–18-year-old. However, Lord Donaldson continued:

It is inconceivable that [the doctor] should proceed in reliance solely upon the consent of an under-age patient, however 'Gillick-competent', in the absence of supporting parental consent and equally inconceivable that he should proceed in the absence of the patient's consent. In any event he will need to seek the opinions of other doctors and may be well advised to apply to the court for guidance . . .[46]

which seems clear enough until we look at the summary provided by the Master of the Rolls:

A minor of any age who is Gillick-competent in the context of a particular treatment has a right to consent to that treatment which again cannot be overridden by those with parental responsibility, but can be overridden by the court. Unlike the statutory right this common law right extends to the donation of blood or organs.[47]

14.23   We can only suggest that, however this is interpreted, it would be a brave surgeon who ignored Lord Donaldson's advice-in-chief. The minor's right to refuse is, however, clearly preserved.

14.24   That is, the minor's right to refuse to donate. But what of the minor's rights to refuse to receive a transplant? We discuss the case of Re M (child: refusal of medical

43 Re W (a minor) (medical treatment) [1992] 4 All ER 627, (1992) 9 BMLR 22.
44 Already discussed in greater detail at para 10.50 above.
45 [1992] 4 All ER 627 at 635, (1992) 9 BMLR 22 at 31.
46 [1992] 4 All ER 627 at 635, (1992) 9 BMLR 22 at 31.
47 [1992] 4 All ER 627 at 639, (1992) 9 BMLR 22 at 35.

treatment)[48] in chapter 10. Here, it need only be said that to authorise a non-consensual heart transplant on a determinedly reluctant 15½-year-old girl seems to be a remarkable example of the power of the 'best interests test'.

14.25   It appears, in fact, that transplant surgeons in general have developed their own code of practice in respect of live donation by minors. Our inquiries indicate that no currently practising British transplant surgeon would accept a live child as an organ donor; only one such instance, involving an identical twin aged 17 years, has arisen in the United Kingdom in the last 20 years. Discussion of the matter thus lies at the academic rather than the practical level.

PATIENTS IN THE PERMANENT VEGETATIVE STATE

14.26   The current pressure to accept cognitive death as equivalent to somatic death[49] is such as to dictate a brief word on the permanent vegetative state. It is, perhaps, necessary to do no more than recapitulate our view that, tragic as their state may be, persons in the persistent vegetative state are existing by means of their own cardiovascular system and are not dead. There can surely be no question of using them as non-voluntary donors whether or not to do so would limit their existence.[50] Predictably, this view is shared by the British Medical Association.[51] Very little is, however, certain in the medico-ethical field and an authoritative paper published on behalf of an International Forum for Transplant Ethics inferred that to exempt PVS patients from the normal legal prohibitions against 'killing' would be humanitarian in that it would obviate the futile use of resources and would release organs that were suitable for transplantation.[52] We have already implied our strong antipathy to such a policy. To confuse the concept of brain stem death and to associate the permanent vegetative state with transplantation could only fan any embers of public distrust for 'premature grave robbing' which still remain. Burke and Hare attracted much sympathy in their role of exhumers; it was when they became pre-emptive that they fell from grace!

THE DONOR AS VENDOR

14.27   The commercialisation of transplant surgery remains one of the most urgent issues in the context of living organ donation. Its acceptability or rejection involves a complex amalgam of public policy and the validation of individual consent in exceptional circumstances. On the latter score alone, it is to be distinguished from payment for

---

[48] [1999] 2 FLR 1097, (2000) 52 BMLR 124. Johnson J fully expressed the difficulty and the gravity of his decision.

[49] See para 13.9 above.

[50] Discussed by J Downie 'The Biology of the Persistent Vegetative State: Legal, Ethical, and Philosophical Implications for Transplantation' (1990) 22 Transplant Proc 995.

[51] BMA 'Guidelines Relating to the Persistent Vegetative State' reproduced in (1993) 3 Bull Med Ethics 8, para 9.

[52] R Hoffenberg, M Lock, N Tilney et al 'Should Organs from Patients in Permanent Vegetative State Be Used for Transplantation?' (1997) 350 Lancet 1320.

cadaver organs—a matter which is better considered as an aspect of the availability of organs rather than of ethical principle.

14.28   Inevitably, a British view on donation for recompense must be coloured by one's experience of a national health service. Within that framework—and given that live donation, at least, of kidneys is an accepted form of medical practice—it is difficult to visualise the sale of organs as other than a way for the rich to obtain priority essential care. But it is only fair to remark that those working in a health care system that is governed by a market economy could see the situation as one in which an anxious buyer meets a willing seller. It is not easy to occupy an objective middle ground.

14.29   The problem may have existed in England before 1989 but it was then that it presented acutely. It transpired that impoverished Turkish donors were being recruited and paid to donate their kidneys to genetically and ethnically unrelated recipients; there were wide-ranging repercussions at both legislative and professional levels and these, of themselves, provoked further ethical debate. The response of the legislature was to rush through the Human Organ Transplants Act 1989, which pro-hibited the exchange of money, other than legitimate expenses, for the purpose of organ donation by the living (s 1(1));[53] it also made it an offence to advertise for the purpose (s 1(2)). Clearly, the legislative intention was to distinguish altruism from commercialism and to approve the former while condemning the latter. This ethos is perpetuated in the Human Tissue Act 2004, ss 32 and 33.[54] Section 32 criminalises the giving or receiving of reward for the supply of, or offer to supply, any controlled material or of advertising to that effect. For the purposes of the section, controlled material is defined as any material which consists of or includes human cells, is removed, or intended to be removed, from a human body and is intended to be used for the purpose of transplantation; it excludes gametes, embryos and 'material which is the subject of property because of an application of human skill'.[55] Section 32(1)(c) makes it an offence for a person to offer to supply any controlled material for reward and this, presumably, includes the potential donor. Certainly, this is the position under the 1989 Act. Section 33 makes it an offence either to remove and/or to implant any transplantable material from a living person unless the regulations provide otherwise.[56] Again, no new regulations have been published at the time of writing so that those made under the 1989 Act still apply until the 2004 Act comes into force.[57]

14.30   The total ban on reward for the provision of transplantable material from living donors is generally accepted on a global scale and is dictated by the consent doctrine in that it is assumed that a free, uncoerced consent is impossible in the face of

---

[53] And also from the dead—see para 14.60. Interstate commerce in organs is illegal in the United States—National Transplantation Act 1984, Public Law 98–507—and this has been followed within many States: Joralemon, n 126 below.

[54] As already noted, the 1989 Act currently persists in Scotland.

[55] For discussion of which last, see chapter 15. Gametes and embryos are covered by the Human Fertilisa-tion and Embryology Act 1990.

[56] Transplantable material remains to be defined by regulation (s 33(7)).

[57] See n 25 above.

financial inducement. To which one might add the widely held moral objection to *any* commercialisation of the human body (see chapter 15).[58] Yet, it is undeniable that, in accepting these restrictions on the individual's power over his or her own body, one is, simultaneously accepting a degree of paternalism which could be regarded as unjustifiable.[59] Is it impossible that a commercial donor could make his or her decision in a reasoned manner and on his own altruistic grounds?[60] And who, in quest of unfettered consent, is to distinguish between external financial pressure and moral pressure exerted within the family?[61] It is at least arguable that, in closing the door on the use of an inessential part of one's body for gain, Parliament is striking at the individual publican's autonomy in favour of the corporate pharisee's inner virtue.

14.31   As a result, a significant underswell of opposition to the 'no reward' imperative has developed[62]—and it has to be admitted that the philosophical discourse has been fuelled by pragmatic concern over the general shortage of organs for therapeutic use.[63] The considerable force of the counter-argument cannot be denied and can be précied in the words of the International Forum:

> [F]eelings of outrage and disgust that led to an outright ban on kidney sales . . . typically have a force that seems to their possessors to need no further justification. Nevertheless, if we are to deny treatment to the suffering and dying we need better reasons than our own feelings of disgust.[64].

14.32   Against this, it will be said that to allow payment would be to open up a traffic in organs and there is little doubt that this threat is both real and actual. There are wide differences in culture and transplantation practice between Western and Eastern civilisations which are certainly conducive to a two-way traffic in organ procurement on a commercial scale while the economic discrepancies between European countries, including those within the free-movement European Union, have led to a recognised

---

[58] We are unconvinced by the philosophical argument that the wrong lies in the invasion of bodily integrity—a wrong which is offset by the good of altruism but which finds no such exculpation in the commercial situation: S Wilkinson and E Garrard 'Bodily Integrity and the Sale of Human Organs' (1996) 22 J Med Ethics 334. The money that accrues can be put to good use.

[59] The point is made succinctly by J Savulescu 'Is the Sale of Body Parts Wrong?' (2003) 29 J Med Ethics 138.

[60] It is reported that one of the Turkish donors intended to devote the proceeds to the medical treatment of his daughter. See a sympathetic contribution by J Harvey 'Paying Organ Donors' (1990) 16 J Med Ethics 117.

[61] For an interesting review of the subtle intra-familial pressures that can be exerted, see Biller-Andorno and Schauenburg, n 32 above.

[62] See the powerful argument mounted by A S Daar 'Paid Organ Donation—the Grey Basket Concept' (1998) 24 J Med Ethics 365—among other writings by the same author.

[63] This two-pronged argument as been well expressed by L D de Castro 'Commodification and Exploitation: Arguments in Favour of Compensated Organ Donation' (2003) 29 J Med Ethics 142. In the same issue J Radcliffe Richards 'Commentary: An Ethical Market in Human Organs' (2003) 29 J Med Ethics 139 points out that, so long as it is accepted that the sale of organs would improve their availability, it is difficult to justify *any* restriction. It is, however, unlikely that public or political opinion could be altered to that extent.

[64] J Radcliffe-Richards, A S Daar, R D Guttmann et al 'The Case for Allowing Kidney Sales' (1998) 351 Lancet 1950. It is to be noted that the possibility of payment for organs is still alive in the United States: D Josefson 'AMA Considers whether to Pay for Donation of Organs' (2002) 324 BMJ 1541.

market in organs far closer to home.[65] The danger is there, yet it is difficult to see why it could not be obviated by legalising paid donations only by way, say, of the Unrelated Live Transplant Regulatory Authority;[66] this would, at the same time, exclude what is probably the main cause of distaste for rewarded donation—that is, the involvement of the commercial middle-man. There is some empirical evidence that public opposition to payment is not as strong as might be supposed—between 40 per cent and 50 per cent may find the practice permissible[67] and it has been noted that: 'As long as there are adequate safeguards, any ethical or legal fastidiousness demanding that donation be only gratuitous could condemn the sick'.[68]

14.33   The overriding practical difficulty lies in the fact that it is now almost impossible to confine a market in organs within one jurisdiction. Networks for their commercial provision already exist; clearly any restrictions on the practice must be international if they are to be effective and, in this respect, the fact that the recorded antipathy reflects a specifically Western view merits repetition. It is at least arguable that, in a country such as India, where there is no cadaver transplant programme and where long-term dialysis is impracticable, paid organ donation may be not only ethical but also desirable.[69] As has been said,[70] the ethical distinction between allowing one poor and needy citizen to run the risk of brain damage in the boxing ring and denying another the right to sell a kidney may be hard to define—and the point being made is equally easy to accept. That is, until one reads of the reality of the situation in the investigative news media;[71] it is then that one begins to appreciate the extent of the evil that is inherent in commercial trafficking in live human body parts.

CADAVER DONATIONS

14.34   A person has very limited rights as to the future disposal of his dead body in common law and the wishes of the executors would normally be supported rather than those of the dead person in the event of conflict. Statute law has, however, largely

[65] R Watson 'European Parliament Tries to Stamp Out Trafficking in Human Organs' (2003) 327 BMJ 1009. See the Council of Europe Report *Trafficking in Organs in Europe:* http://assembly.coe.int/documents/workingdocs/doc03/edoc9822.htm.

[66] The Manchester School has consistently supported a similar initiative: J Harris and C Erin 'An Ethically Defensible Market in Organs' (2002) 325 BMJ 114; C A Erin and J Harris 'An Ethical Market in Human Organs' (2003) 29 J Med Ethics 137.

[67] A Guttmann and R D Guttmann 'Attitudes of Health Care Professionals and the Public towards the Sale of Kidneys for Transplantation' (1993) 19 J Med Ethics 148.

[68] I Davies 'Live Donation of Human Body Parts: A Case for Negotiability?' (1991) 59 Med-Leg J 100.

[69] The Indian Government has, in fact, outlawed payment for organs but the ban is not water-tight and the demand is relentless. See: A K Singh, P A Srivastava and A Kumar 'Current Status of Transplant Coordination and Organ Donation' (1998) 30 Transplant Proc 3627; G Mudur 'Kidney Trade Arrest Exposes Loopholes in India's Transplant Laws (2004) 328 BMJ 246.

[70] J Bignall 'Kidneys: Buy or Die' (1993) 342 Lancet 45.

[71] There are, of course, a vast number of such articles. We were particularly impressed by L Rohter 'Tracing a Kidney's Path of Poverty and Hope' (2004) New York Times, 27 May, p 1.

replaced common law and the collection and use of cadaver organs and tissues has been regulated in Great Britain since 1961 by the Human Tissue Act. Revision of the Act was hurried forward in England and Wales as a result of the exposure at the turn of the century of what had been, undoubtedly, widespread breaches of the law—and which are discussed in greater detail in chapter 15; this resulted in the Human Tissue Act 2004. No similar legislation has yet been promulgated in Scotland where the Human Tissue Act 1961, the Anatomy Act 1984,[72] the Corneal Tissue Act 1986 and, as we have seen, the Human Organ Transplants Act 1989, have not been repealed as they have in England. Moreover, there is no certainty that any subsequent Scottish legislation will duplicate the 2004 Act. We are, therefore, in another editorial difficulty which is compounded by limitations as to space. We intend to do not more than outline the two-page 1961 Act as it still applies to Scotland and to draw attention to some of its defects which, amazingly, have been allowed to persist for nearly half a century. Thereafter, we will concentrate of the 2004 Act which, by contrast, extends to 61 sections and 7 schedules.

14.35   The 1961 Act provides, in s 1(1), that removal of an organ is authorised if there has been a specific prior indication to this effect by the deceased; the removal may be for therapeutic, educational or research purposes. In the absence of such authority, s 1(2) provides for the authorisation of organ removal if the person 'lawfully in possession of the body' has, after making such 'reasonable enquiry as may be practicable', no reason to believe that the deceased had expressed any objection to organ removal or that the surviving spouse or 'any surviving relative' of the deceased objects to the body being so dealt with. It is to be noted that, under the 1961 Act, the power of the surviving relatives is confined to objection to the use of the body in the absence of any advance directive on the part of the deceased.

14.36   The rather loose wording of the Act has given rise to some difficulties. This was particularly so as to the definition of the person in lawful possession. For some time it was considered that the term implied one with a right to possession, that is, the executors. The alternative view was that it refers to the person who has physical possession of the body who is, in practical terms, the hospital administrative officer. This latter interpretation is supported by the wording of other sections of the Act and is now widely accepted but the point has not been tested in the courts.[73] Clarity on the point is important in that, were the executors to be in lawful possession, they could overrule any specific request made by the deceased. Even allowing for the fact that the relatives have no locus standi to object to the removal of organs under s 1(1), which

---

[72] The Anatomy Act 1984 was specifically limited to dissection of a body for the purposes of studying morphology—i.e. examination in an anatomy school. Post-mortem examinations for medico-legal or clinical purposes were excluded (s 1(4)). The Human Tissue Act 1961 will still take precedence in Scotland when authority for study derives from both Acts (s 1(5)). There is extensive and distinct legislation in the 2004 Act replacing the substance of the 1984 Act. However, although donation of the body for anatomical dissection is not uncommon, it raises few distinct ethico-legal problems and the remnants of the 1984 Act are not considered further in this chapter. Similarly, we are ignoring the very specific Corneal Tissue Act.

[73] In fact, the Transplant of Human Organs Bill 2001 proposed substituting the words 'health authority or NHS Trust' for 'person lawfully' but the Bill lapsed.

clearly expresses the law, the doctor is in a difficult position in the event of their objections being voiced. On the one hand, he has legal justification to proceed and he may, rightly, be thinking of the potential recipients. On the other, it would be extremely hard to justify in ethical terms a decision to add further suffering to the bereaved. It is fortunate that such conflicts are rare in practice but we return to the point when considering the shortfall in organs available for treatment. It should be noted, in passing, that the procurator fiscal may veto any authorisation if the death comes within his or her jurisdictions and it is concluded that organ retrieval might jeopardise his or her inquiries (s 1(9)).

14.37   The concept of 'such reasonable enquiry as may be practicable' is also vague, reasonableness being a matter of highly subjective judgment. The partial solution is to consider what is *un*reasonable—and it would clearly be unreasonable to prolong one's enquiries until the intended donor organ was non-viable. Such a pragmatic approach is, however, less tenable in the context of the beating heart donor, which is discussed below. Finally, the wording 'any surviving relative' is confusingly open-ended and must again be interpreted in a practical sense—the phrase must be taken to mean 'any relative who can reasonably be contacted within the limited time available', which effectively limits one to the immediate next of kin.

14.38   The Human Tissue Act 1961 is unusual in that it prescribes no sanctions in the event of its non-observance. This has been addressed in the 2004 Act from the criminal aspect. To the best of our knowledge, civil liability was never tested in the courts although there seems no reason in principle why an action in tort for nervous shock should not have been available to a close relative who thought that the conditions of reasonable inquiry had not been met and who was confronted with what he or she regarded as a mutilated corpse. Success in such actions is notoriously difficult to achieve but there are good reasons to suppose that an action for 'affront to feelings'— *actio iniuriarum*—might still succeed in Scotland.[74]

14.39   In our view, the 2004 Act was born under the wrong star. As will be discussed in the next chapter, it was forced into service as a result of the widespread unauthorised retention of tissues following post-mortem examination. Although the 1961 Act covered post-mortem examinations (at s 2),[75] it did so only as a small part of the Act, the main purpose of which was to regulate transplantation therapy. To revise the 1961 Act on the basis of offences related to the autopsy room was, therefore, some-thing in the nature of the tail wagging the dog and, indeed, other than in respect of trafficking, the therapeutic use of cadaver organs is scarcely mentioned in the Act— transplantation is no more than one of twelve 'scheduled purposes' for the use

---

[74] N R Whitty 'Rights of Personality, Property Rights and the Human Body in Scots Law' (2005) 9 Edin LR 194 relying in part on the old cases of *Pollok v Workman* (1900) 1900 2 F 354, *Conway v Dalziel* (1901) 3 F 918 and *Hughes v Robertson* 1913 SC 349.

[75] And, accordingly, retention of tissues was, prima facie, an offence—albeit one with no attached penalty. However, it could have been argued, possibly successfully, that the actions were governed by the Coroners Act 1988.

of human tissues with which the Act is concerned.[76] As a result, the regulation of transplantation is now dominated by the concept of consent.[77]

14.40   In essence, the Act now states that the use of a body or the removed organs of a deceased person for transplantation is lawful if done with 'appropriate consent' (s 1(1)(b & c)). Appropriate consent to donation, in the case of an adult, means his or her consent.[78] In the absence of a directive, consent may be given or withheld by a person or persons who can be nominated under s 4 by a living adult to act in his or her interests after death.[79] Authority is vested in a person who stood in a qualifying relationship to the deceased if neither of these options is available.[80] The consent of a child to organ donation after death is valid; in its absence, authority to consent passes to the person who has parental responsibility or, failing that, to a person who stood in a qualifying relationship to him or her.[81]

14.41   Almost inevitably in the current climate, transplantation will come under the aegis of an overriding Authority—in this case, the Human Tissue Authority. Transplant surgeons are excluded from the need to have a licence to operate (s 16(2)(c)) though it seems that the Authority must ensure that a relevant Code of Practice (s 26(2)(h) is in place and that this Code must pay particular attention to consent.[82]

14.42   One's immediate reaction to the 2004 Act was that, insofar as the therapeutic use of tissues is so far separated in the public mind from activities such as research and education, it was a matter for regret that the opportunity was not taken to legislate for the first on a distinct conceptual plane. Nonetheless, it seems that the practice of transplantation therapy is relatively undisturbed by the new Act while, at the same time, many of the legal issues raised by the 1961 Act have been resolved—and, in ethical terms, often for the better. It remains to be seen what will be the practical effect on the procurement of organs (see paras 14.46 et seq below).[83] In this connection it is

---

[76] Schedule 1, Parts 1 and 2.

[77] Advice in Scotland is to the effect that relatives should be entitled to authorise rather than consent to cadaver donation but the point is of academic rather than practical significance. See S A M McLean (chair) *Independent Review Group on Retention of Organs at Post-mortem* Final Report (2001), section 1, para 17. For comment see M Brazier 'Retained Organs, Ethics and Humanity' (2002) 22 LS 551.

[78] S 3(6)(a) does not stipulate consent in writing.

[79] An appointment, if made orally, is valid only if it is made before two witnesses together (s 4(4)). A written appointment must be attested by at least one witness or may be part of a will (s 4(5)).

[80] The ranking of qualifying relationships is set out in s 27(4).

[81] The overriding powers of the Coroner in respect of bodies subject to his or her authority are preserved in s 11.

[82] The relationship between the Human Tissue Authority and UK Transplant—a Special Health Authority that provides central support for transplantation—has yet to be decided (2004 Act, s 35). A UK Code of Practice for Therapeutic Tissue Banking was published in 2001. The HTA may be short-lived as there are plans to merge it with the Human Fertilisation and Embryology Authority to form the Regulatory Authority for Fertility and Tissue (RAFT). Similarly, UK Transplant is to be merged with the National Blood Authority in England to become NHS Blood and Transplant.

[83] An interesting Australian study, admittedly undertaken in the 1980's, found that, whereas some 65% of people said they would definitely or probably donate organs after death, only 38% would do so on behalf of the next of kin: P Dye 'Donation in Australia: An Historical Overview, Current Directions and Future Principles' (1995) 23 Anaesthesia Int Care 65.

to be noted that the power of the 'person lawfully in possession of the body' is retained to a limited extent in that, given that parts of a body lying within the hospital or similar institution may be suitable for transplantation, the hospital management may take minimally invasive steps to preserve the parts and to retain the body for the purposes of transplantation until it is established that consent has not been, and will not be, given (s 43).[84]

BEATING HEART DONORS

14.43   It is apparent that several of the major practical criticisms levelled at the Human Tissue Act 1961 derive from the prolongation of the warm anoxic time entailed in strict adherence to its terms. But such objections arise only when death is measured by the irrevocable failure of the cardiovascular system. In practice, the largest proportion of cadaver-donated material will come from patients who have been maintained on ventilator support and in whom it will be appropriate to reach a diagnosis of death by means of brain stem criteria.[85] There is no logical reason why ventilation should not be continued after death and the heart beat be maintained during an operation for organ donation. Despite the considerable expertise required, the ideal characteristics of the living donor are, in this way, achieved in a cadaver.

14.44   The technical advantages of a beating heart donation are not in dispute and the process is essential to the success of some transplantations.[86] Why, then, is there any residual antipathy to the procedure? Much must stem from an inherent revulsion at performing what is a lethal operation amid the conditions pertaining to a living patient, but this is irrational once the concept of brain stem death has been accepted—any emotional bias should be directed towards the recipients. Perhaps the major problem lies in the fact that there are still those who, in all good conscience, cannot accept the technical criteria advocated for the diagnosis of brain stem death— doubts which affect both doctors and relatives;[87] some surgeons, while accepting a ventilated donor, will not operate until the patient is disconnected from the machine and shows a flat electrocardiogram. While fully accepting that every doctor is entitled to his own clinical judgment, we do suggest that the subject would be, so to speak, defused were it to be made compulsory for a death certificate to be issued, and the notification handed to the next of kin, before any donation could be effected. This would serve, first, to ease matters for the professionals involved—it is not entirely satisfactory for the surgeon undertaking a beating heart donation to have to 'satisfy

---

[84] See para 14.56 below for the relevance of this in the context of the non-heart beating donor.

[85] 68% of kidney donations in 2003–4: UK Transplant Activity Report 2003–2004. Less than 1% of all deaths are of this type.

[86] E.g. heart transplants.

[87] For review, see J M A Swinburn et al and associated papers 'Discontinuation of Ventilation after Brain Stem Death' (1999) 318 BMJ 1753. For theoretical scepticism, see H Jonas 'Against the Stream: Comments on the Definition and Redefinition of Death' in T L Beauchamp and R M Veatch (eds) *Ethical Issues in Death and Dying* (2nd edn, 1996).

himself by personal examination of the body that life is extinct' (Human Tissue Act 1961, s 1(4)) from a mere perusal of the hospital notes; secondly, we feel the process might set the minds of at least some relatives at rest.

14.45   In any event, relatives must be confused and distraught unless given sympathetic counselling and, in practice, this should always be possible in modern circumstances when, as a result of ventilator support, relatives will have been aware of the impending death for some time and will, no doubt, have been attending at the hospital— transplant co-ordinators are now widely established and can assist in the task to great advantage.[88] Relatives should be given every available assistance. Thus, while we accept the view that an electroencephalogram is not necessary to establish the fact of death, we also believe that the relatives should have the right to such evidence should they ask for it. It is only by such pragmatic adaptations of the statutory law that beating heart donation will become universally accepted and that, as a consequence, the maximum proportion of high quality organs will be obtained.[89]

THE PROCUREMENT OF SUITABLE ORGANS

14.46   It is now trite to say that the procurement of organs is in an unsatisfactory state in the United Kingdom. We use the word 'procurement' here advisedly. To deprecate the shortage of organs in terms of 'availability'—as is so often done—is to obscure the fact that some 50 per cent of cadaver organs derive from fit young adults who die as a result of trauma; to that extent, it is arguable that we should, rather, be concerned that *any* of their organs are 'available' for donation—and it may be that the small, but significant, annual decline in the number of cadaver donors[90] is due, in part, to a simultaneous reduction in road traffic deaths. That having been said, it is clear that accidents will always happen and the problem is, then, to recoup the maximum benefit from a bad situation. It follows that the cause for concern lies in the relatively poor procurement of organs from the available pool.

14.47   Some 7,236 patients were awaiting transplants in 2003–4[91]—an all-time high which must, inevitably, increase in the absence of some radical action. This is not because there is a shortage of potential donors but, rather, it is because nearly half

[88] For the modern function of the transplant co-ordinator, see Department of Health Draft Consultation Document for Comment *Organ and Tissue Transplantation: A Plan for the Future* (2001), para 13.

[89] In respect of corporate antagonism, the Japanese Parliament has officially recognised the concept of brain stem death so long as transplantation is involved; this has resulted in a dual definition of death: J R McConnell 'The Ambiguity about Death in Japan: An Ethical Implication for Organ Procurement' (1999) 25 J Med Ethics 322. It is also to be noted that Muslim law now allows donation and receipt of organs using a brain stem death approach: V Choo 'UK Shariah Council Approves Organ Transplants' (1995) 346 Lancet 303.

[90] There were 878 cadaveric donors in 1994–5 and 772 in 2003–4: Most of the figures quoted here come from the UK Transplant Activity Report 2003–2004: www.uktransplant.org.uk/ukt/statistics/transplant_activity/transplant_activity.jsp.

[91] N 31 above. The cost of hospital dialysis averages £25,000 per year and of home dialysis £15,000; following an initial operative cost of between £10,000 and £15,000, the follow-up treatment of the transplant recipient costs around £3,000 per year.

the potential donors fail to become actual donors and it is this deficit in procurement which needs to be corrected. The Government has clearly been concerned at what is, at best, a stalemate but initiatives such as its *Plan for the Future*[92] can be seen as only scratching the surface; what is needed is an in-depth appraisal of the underlying philosophy. In the meantime, the International Forum have stated: '[I]t is morally unjustified to perpetuate a system that falls short of increasing the availability of organs to people who might benefit from transplantation'.[93]

14.48   There are essentially two avenues to explore: to reform the law and to change professional and public attitudes. As to the former, it is clear that a main source of cadaver organs under the Human Tissue Acts results from a system of 'contracting in' to the transplant service, something which dictates a conscious effort that many healthy persons—and particularly young persons—find difficult to make.[94] It is widely suggested that the Act could profitably be altered so as to adopt a 'contracting out' position—that is, one in which consent to donation is presumed unless it is specific-ally withheld.[95] Such a system operates in several European countries, although with varying rigidity. Thus, a right of veto is still vested in the next of kin in Italy and Spain, while the sensitivities of the relatives are deeply respected in Belgium—very few trans-plant centres would apply the law in that country in the face of their opposition. The views of the next of kin are held at a minimum in Austria where, interestingly, the cadaver kidney donor rate is the highest among the leading 'transplant countries'.[96] Thus, a good case for 'presumed consent' can be made out—and contracting out on the Belgian model is clearly the preferred choice of the International Forum;[97] nevertheless, it carries with it a hint of coercion and it is hard to foresee a British government making such a major policy change. The consultation document *A Plan for the Future* states that, as part of the screening process for donation, relatives and friends are asked about the donor's recent medical history and unequivocally:

If they object to donation, organs will not be retrieved whatever the legal framework.[98]

14.49   One would suppose, then, that there is little purpose in speculating whether objections from the next of kin would remain at the same level given a change of

[92] N 88 above.

[93] I Kennedy, R A Sells, A S Daar et al 'The Case for "Presumed Consent" in Organ Donation' (1998) 351 Lancet 1650.

[94] Even so, it does not seem to deter them in Holland where what is possibly the most advanced and comprehensive legislation is to be found. Under the Organ Donation (Wet op de Orgaandonatie) Act 1998, everyone over the age of 18 is invited to register with a central registry. The individual can register one of four options as to post-mortem donation—a consent to donate any or specified organs, a refusal to donate, delegation of consent to the next of kin or delegation to a nominated person. The choice may be altered at any time. Access to the Central Register is available 24 hours a day. Living donation of organs and bone marrow is also covered by the Act. The Act is also fully acceptable on ethical grounds in so far as a coercive element is avoided by providing an equal opportunity to consent or refuse.

[95] C A Erin and J Harris 'Presumed Consent or Contracting Out' (1999) 25 J Med Ethics 365 maintain, correctly, that there is a distinction to be made between the two. Rather than speak in terms of consent, they prefer to look upon both approaches as being morally right.

[96] New et al, n 30 above, fig 11.   [97] See n 93 above.   [98] At para 28.

policy—yet the 2004 Act leaves the door at least ajar. Section 3(6)(a) defines 'appropriate consent' to the use of the body for a purpose specified in Schedule 1 in the case of an adult as the deceased's consent if a decision of his or hers was in force immediately before he or she died; but, in the absence of such a decision, consent by his or her appointed person or a qualified relative becomes 'appropriate'. It is quite clear that signing a donor card is a legally effective written expression in life of a request that one's body should be used for therapeutic purposes, yet it is recognised that the great majority of transplant surgeons will be reluctant to press the matter if the relatives express an objection. While this may be laudably sympathetic medicine, it is, paradoxically, doubtful medical ethics—effectively, the last autonomous wish of the individual is being thwarted simply because he or she is in no position to object. Whether or not a firmer attitude would result in significantly more donations is uncertain, but it appears that the new Act still allows for such an approach.[99]

14.50 Antipathy to or apathy in seeking the co-operation of relatives may be a further important factor; this has led to a movement in favour of 'required request' for organ donation—a format which imposes a legal obligation on doctors to seek permission from the relatives for the removal of tissues from suitable dead persons. This is now the subject of federal law in the United States.[100] There has been, in fact, considerable debate in the United Kingdom as to the efficacy of this type of legislation[101] and 'required request' undoubtedly compromises the clinical autonomy of the medical staff concerned. The Government seems to be appreciating some of these difficulties and is clearly moving towards the wider establishment of dedicated transplant co-ordinators who will relieve the clinical staff of many of these tasks and, particularly, interview the relatives of any potential donor—which appears in some ways rather like required request in a different guise.

14.51 The Parliament and the Government will have the final word but the indications are that this is still some way off. As the Expert Committee of the Council of Europe has said:

> It is strongly advisable to ascertain the public's and health professionals' opinion about presumed or informed consent for organ donation before promoting legal changes that might be potentially detrimental.[102]

14.52 Which leaves us still with the opportunity to consider the virtually revolutionary view that the interests of the main protagonists in the debate—the donor and the recipient—are so disproportionate as to render 'consent' an invalid determinant of the outcome. As to the former, the maximum at stake is a potential emotional

---

[99] We have already noted that the Act is mainly concerned with disposal of body parts other than by transplantation and it may well be that such matters will be dealt with in a Code of Practice.

[100] US Public Law 99–509 9318.

[101] G D Chisholm 'Time to End Softly Softly Approach on Harvesting Organs for Transplantation' (1988) 296 BMJ 1419 regarded it as 'positive'; R M R Taylor and J H Salaman 'The Obligation to Ask for Organs' (1988) 1 Lancet 985 saw it as the only answer to a dialysis 'crisis'; A Bodenham, J C Berridge and G R Park 'Brain Stem Death and Organ Donation' (1989) 299 BMJ 1009 were doubtful.

[102] *A Plan for the Future*, n 88 above, para 27.

disturbance for his or her relatives; for the latter, the issue is one of restoration of life. As a result, it is morally impermissible to pit the one against the other.[103] The difficulty about such an argument is that it dictates a completely novel approach to possessory rights in the cadaver—essentially that, in some way, the dead body falls to the custody of to the State. Innovatively, Emson justifies this by seeing the human body—as opposed to the human spirit—as being 'on extended loan from the biomass to the individual of which it forms a part'.[104] Harris, who is, perhaps, the protagonist of such an approach, needs no such ecological support but, rather, sees organ donation as no more than an example of a 'small but significant class of public goods, participation in which [should be] mandatory'.[105]

14.53   Harris believes that people would soon get used to the idea. But, so contrary is it to the current extensive and expansive doctrine of autonomy, that we doubt it would be so. Given our reservations as to the ethics of the transplant programme as a whole, we are unable to accept Harris's assessment of its place in the hierarchy of therapeutic imperatives. None the less, a strong case can be made for regarding cadaver organs as a community asset that it is immoral to allow to go to waste.[106] One is reminded of the words of O'Donovan and Gilbar:

> Calling on individualistic autonomy as the primary value in medical ethics, or on self-determination as central to medical law, whilst simultaneously overlooking the patient's identity in relationships with others is too narrow an approach to the complexities of human lives.[107]

The difficulty in finding the right balance is particularly evident in the field of transplantation therapy.

Non-heart beating donation

14.54   An alternative—or, perhaps, complementary—approach to reducing the 'wastage' of organs would be to acknowledge the layman's possible distrust of brain stem death and revert to a cardio-respiratory definition of death. To do so, or to use the definitions of death in parallel,[108] takes us into the realm of what is now known as non-heart beating donation. Such donors can become available in two main ways. In the first, mechanical support is removed from a 'brain dead' ventilated patient whose

---

[103] H E Emson 'It Is Immoral to Require Consent for Cadaver Organ Donation' (2003) 29 J Med Ethics 125.

[104] *Ibid* at 125–126.

[105] J Harris 'Organ Procurement: Dead Interests, Living Needs' (2003) 29 J Med Ethics 130. See also the same author's larger contribution: 'Law and Regulation of Retained Organs: The Ethical Issues' (2002) 22 LS 527.

[106] The other side of the debate is provided in the same issue by C L Hamer and M M Rivlin 'A Stronger Policy of Organ Retrieval from Cadaveric Donors: Some Ethical Considerations' (2003) 29 J Med Ethics 196. Harris's counter-argument is, however, very telling.

[107] K O'Donovan and R Gilbar 'The Loved Ones: Families, Intimates and Patient Autonomy' (2003) 23 LS 332.

[108] This approach is adopted in the United States' Uniform Determination of Death Act—see chapter 13 above for discussion.

heart will then cease to function as a result of respiratory failure. This is little more than a matter of raising public confidence and we have already seen that many surgeons adopt this procedure as a routine. Alternatively, suitable patients who have died suddenly and who have not been ventilated can be used as donors[109] and this raises a number of both legal and ethical questions.

14.55   First, the questions arise as to whether the use of a 'second-best' organ is better than no transplant and, collaterally, whether it is an either ethically or legally appropriate procedure. As to the first part, there is little doubt that transplantation is almost always the preferred treatment of end stage renal failure so long as the organ has a reasonable chance of survival; nevertheless, a discussion of any likely shortcomings in the procedure would be an essential part of informed consent to the operation. As to the latter, the current attitude of transplant surgeons would be essential to the resolution of any dispute as to negligence; the *Bolam* principle, which is discussed in chapter 9, would undoubtedly apply both as to disclosure of information and the operative technique. It must be said, however, that the extent of the problem is uncertain; some hold that the differences in outcome between non-heart beating and beating heart donations are of a subtle nature only[110] while others report considerable variations on the ideal depending, to an extent, on the precise source of the donor.[111]

14.56   More importantly, however, in returning to the original use of unventilated, non-heart beating donors, we have come full circle and we are, at the same time, restarting the 'race against time to save a life'. Moreover, the pressures to reduce the warm anoxic time are even greater than they were now that we are fully aware of, at least, the theoretical advantages of the beating heart donation. Several techniques—of which, cold perfusion of the organs in situ is the most commonly used—are available to reduce the effects of anoxia[112] but conditions often dictate that these are put to use without the consent of the appropriate person. Section 43 of the 2004 Act, which allows the institutional authorities to take steps to preserve parts of the body for use for transplantation, renders this lawful. Section 43(2) limits non-consensual interference to the minimal and least invasive steps *necessary for the purpose*; subject to the 'good medical practice' test. This clearly allows for procedures which are, even so, undeniably invasive.

14.57   Rapid response lies at the heart of non-heart beating donation. This being so, major significance attaches to what can be regarded as the true 'agonal period'—that is, the

---

[109] G Kootstra, R Wijnen, J P van Hooff and C J van der Linden 'Twenty Percent More Kidneys through a Non-heart Beating Program' (1991) 23 Transplant Proc 910.

[110] R M H Wijnen, M H Booster, B M Stubenitsky et al 'Outcome of Transplantation of Non-heart-beating Donor Kidneys' (1995) 345 Lancet 1067.

[111] S Balupuri, P Buckley, C Snowdon et al 'The Trouble with Kidneys derived from the Non-heart-beating Donor: A Single Centre 10 Year Experience' (2000) 69 Transplantation 842. The likely sources are patients who are dead on arrival at hospital, those who have been unsuccessfully resuscitated and those from whom care is withdrawn.

[112] Cold perfusion of the whole body or of individual organs in situ is used to reduce these difficulties: Y W Cho, P I Terasaki, J M Cecka et al 'Transplantation of Kidneys from Donors whose Hearts have Stopped Beating' (1998) 338 New Engl J Med 221.

so-far undefined period between the beginning and the end of the somatic death process. In our view, this is classically limited by, on the former hand, irrevocable cardiorespiratory failure and, on the latter, by irrevocable failure of cerebral cortical function. We do not know how long this period lasts—indeed, it almost certainly varies with the individual—but it may be the most profound period of a person's existence and is deserving of the greatest respect. It is, therefore, surprising to find that, at least in the United States, there is no standard imposed delay between cessation of cardio-respiratory function and the harvesting of organs—the Institute of Medicine suggests five minutes[113] but it seems it can be anything from ten minutes[114] to being discounted altogether.[115] It is at least possible that such discrepancies are founded on misconceptions. Those who support the shorter times do so on the assumption that death may be defined as the irreversible failure of the cardiorespiratory system only when the heart beat has stopped for such a period as precludes the possibility of cardiac autoresuscitation—and this could well be five minutes. But the fact that the body is irreversibly dead does not mean that the persona, as represented by cerebral function, is also dead; hypoxic death of the brain cells—and, with it, a total loss of mind—cannot be assumed for a longer period.[116] In our view, death should not be regarded as complete until some fifteen minutes have elapsed since cessation of cardiac and pulmonary function—and, in parentheses, we believe that this should be a matter of hospital routine independent of the transplant programme. We are certainly not alone in our concern over both the ethics and practicalities of non heart beating donation as currently practiced.[117] Nonetheless, the Government intends to support non-heart-beating donation and hopes to achieve an annual rate of such donations of 10 per million population—this, it is anticipated, will result in 500 extra operations per year.[118] It will be interesting to see how an associated Code of Practice will address the several difficulties.

14.58   Ethical consideration of this 'agonal period' assumes equal practical importance in the suggested extension of non-heart-beating donation—that is, the even more

[113] As reported in an extremely critical article by J Menikoff 'Doubts about Death: The Silence of the Institute of Medicine' (1998) 26 J Law Med Ethics 157. The author implies that the better limit would be 15 minutes. Members of the Institute of Medicine's Committee on Non-Heart-Beating Organ Transplantation refute his criticisms in a follow-up article at p 166.

[114] Derived from the so-called Maastricht Workshop: G Koostra 'The Asystolic or Non-Heart-Beating Donor' (1997) 63 Transplantation 917.

[115] J M DuBois 'Non-Heart-Beating Organ Donation: A Defense of the Required Determination of Death' (1999) 27 J Law Med Ethics 126.

[116] We are, thus, side-stepping a metaphysical argument as to 'what is death'. We would, however, support the expressed view that to allow for both cardio-respiratory and cerebral definitions of death is, essentially, measuring different manifestations of the same phenomenon: A M Capron and L R Kass 'A Statutory Definition of the Standards for Determining Human Death: An Appraisal and a Proposal' (1972) 121 Univ Penn L Rev.

[117] For a very full consideration, see M D D Bell 'Non-heart-beating Organ Donation: Old Procurement Strategy—New Ethical Problems' (2003) 29 J Med Ethics 176. The accompanying article: N Zamperetti, R Bellomo and C Ronco 'Defining Death in Non-heart-beating Organ Donors' (2003) 29 J Med Ethics 182 is, perhaps, even more disturbing in its implications.

[118] A Plan for the Future, n 88 above, para 48.

controversial practice of 'elective ventilation'. Essentially, the concept involves extending the sources of donors so as to include the medical wards. Deeply comatose patients dying from strokes or other cerebral medical conditions are transferred to the intensive care unit and are there supported until brain stem death supervenes and organ retrieval can be arranged. The procedure was pioneered in Exeter,[119] where a rigid protocol was drawn up before the work began. However, while accepting the caution that was expressed by the authors, we still believe that the procedure raises a number of legal and ethical difficulties.[120] As to the former, the 2004 Act remains to be tested. In so far as s 4(1) allows for the appointment of a nominated representative to act *after* the appointer's death and s 3(6) provides authority for qualified relatives to act only on behalf of a *dead* person, we doubt if the Act adds anything to their existing powers. Removing a patient from the calm of a medical ward to the activity of the intensive care unit can hardly be seen as being in his or her best interests and it seems unlikely that the patient's relatives have any common law power to consent to the procedure. Even were this to be seen as no more than a legal quibble, the ethical question remains as to whether it is right to alter radically the mode of death, and, perhaps, to prolong the dying process, purely for the benefit of others.[121] The concurrent problem of whether intensive care beds should be utilised in this way is, in our view, a purely practical matter to be resolved by the doctors in charge. In the event, it has been agreed that the procedure is unlawful given the current regulations and the abuse of the 'best interests' test[122] and elective ventilation has now been discontinued, at least for the time being. Despite the obvious advantages to the organ harvest, we believe this to be correct—one cannot exorcise a feeling that death is being pre-empted and it is certain that this form of organ husbandry must be very carefully controlled if a backlash of public reaction—and a return to a public fear of 'pre-empted death'—is to be avoided.[123]

14.59   This is of immense overall importance as it is probable that British policy in the

[119] T G Feest, H N Riad, C H Collins et al 'Protocol for Increasing Organ Donation after Cerebrovascular Deaths in a District General Hospital' (1990) 335 Lancet 1133. The protocol was also used elsewhere: M A M Salih, I Harvey, S Frankel et al 'Potential Availability of Cadaver Organs for Transplantation' (1991) 302 BMJ 1053. These authors suggested that, realistically, including potential medical donors aged 50–69 would have provided a harvest of 36 kidneys per million population per year, which is coming somewhere near the estimated need for 48 kidneys per million population per year.

[120] For similar misgivings, see J V McHale 'Elective Ventilation—Pragmatic Solution or Ethical Minefield?' (1995) 11 Prof Neg 23; S A M McLean 'Transplantation and the "Nearly Dead": The Case of Elective Ventilation' in S A M McLean (ed) *Contemporary Issues in Law, Medicine and Ethics* (1996).

[121] This was denied on the grounds that it is a corpse that is being ventilated: A Nicholls and H Riad 'Organ Donation' (1993) 306 BMJ 517. But are the patients dead when the ventilation is instituted? The Exeter group put up a strong defence of their procedure, only to be contradicted: see H Riad and A Nicholls 'Elective Ventilation of Potential Organ Donors' (1995) 310 BMJ 714 and associated debate.

[122] NHS Executive *Identification of Potential Donors of Organs for Transplantation* HSG (94) 41. For support for changing the law to accommodate elective ventilation, see A B Shaw 'Non-therapeutic (Elective) Ventilation of Potential Organ Donors: The Ethical Basis for Changing the Law' (1996) 22 J Med Ethics 72.

[123] G Routh 'Elective Ventilation for Organ Donation—The Case Against' (1992) 8 Care Crit Ill 60. For the opposite view, see C H Collins 'Elective Ventilation for Organ Donation—The Case in Favour' (1992) 8 Care Crit Ill 57.

quest for more donated organs will depend upon continuing public education for the foreseeable future. One still has to wonder, most particularly, at the basic reasons underlying the obdurate refusal of a significant proportion of relatives to consent to the harvesting of organs even when the deceased is carrying a donor card. We suggest that misunderstanding of the modern concepts of death is probably the main factor and it is probable that the increasing availability of dedicated transplant co-ordinators, each armed with a specific remit, may provide the most effective corrective measure. This will, at the same time, spare those who have been responsible for the treatment of the deceased; the distressing, and somewhat anomalous, change of therapeutic role that is involved in seeking consent to donation; the intervention of a neutral party will, at least, ensure that more qualifying relatives are *asked* to consent. We also believe that the best strategy for counsellors lies in maximising the concept of the multiple organ donor. It is not easy to enthuse about a treatment whereby one family's joy at the availability of a donor must be balanced against another's tragedy; the public's imagination might well be fired were it generally appreciated that one regrettable death could be compensated by the salvage of four or, increasingly, more lives. The suggestion in *A Plan for the Future* that co-ordinators should be encouraged to keep the donor family informed as to the outcome would do much to improve the sense of community involvement in what is, essentially, a community project.

Payment for tissues

14.60   Any discussion on the availability of organs must take into account the possibility of their provision on a commercial basis. We have discussed the ethics of donation for reward by the living and have concluded that this is, at least in part, a matter for decision by the potential donor. But the selling of cadaver organs is, at root, directed to the enticement of the next of kin. Put this way, the proposition can be seen as appealing to the less than humanistic instincts of vulnerable persons and as something with which the medical profession should have no truck—typically put:

A shift into any form of commercialism or its currently more fashionable cousin 'rewarded gifting' holds the potential of threatening the entire spiritual structure upon which organ transplantation is based at present.[124]

14.61   The possibility is, however, by no means excluded and seems to be gaining ground in the United States.[125] Manoeuvres to avoid ethical restrictions such as wholesale to kidney banks rather than to individuals have been mooted; standardised cash awards in various forms—such as payment of donors' funeral expenses[126]—have been suggested; and an 'insurance policy' in the form of preferred status was, perhaps surprisingly, found to be the top-ranked option in the United States, where over half

---

[124] F T Rapaport 'Progress in Organ Procurement: The Non-Heart-beating Cadaver Donor and Other Issues in Transplantation' (1991) 23 Transplant Proc 2699.

[125] D Josefson 'AMA Considers whether to Pay for Donation of Organs' (2002) 324 BMJ 1541.

[126] The so-called 'Pennsylvania Plan': for discussion, see D Joralemon 'Shifting Ethics: Debating the Incentive Question in Organ Transplantation' (2001) 27 J Med Ethics 30.

those responding to a survey approved the introduction of incentives to improve the supply of organs.[127] Commenting on this, Peters, who supported payment of a fixed death benefit to donors through an organ procurement organisation, suggested that those in the transplant field have wrongly adhered to certain moral values of their own—values which are not necessarily accepted by those at the giving and receiving end of the process;[128] Sells has also pointed out that antagonism to incentive represents an essentially Western view of ethics as we think they ought to be practised:

Western societies have prescribed for the rest of the globe without giving much thought, evidently, to the differing ethical and medical circumstances in which our less-affluent colleagues have to operate.[129]

14.62   This is not to say that we approve of a traffic in human organs—in fact, we find payment for the organs of the dead far less easy to justify than payment to the living donor.[130] Given, however, that the process was strictly controlled—say, through a successor to the Unrelated Live Transplant Regulatory Authority—and supposing that it *succeeded* in providing life-saving treatment for those dying on the waiting list, reward for donation of cadaver organs appears in a less scandalous light than it did at first sight. The following observation from America is, perhaps, indicative of the trend in that country:

It is only a matter of time before this country will be forced to decide on *the type of commercial system* which should be adopted in order to meet the demand of transplantable human organs. (Emphasis added.)[131]

14.63   In fact, we suggest the far simpler option of displaying a permanent 'roll of donors' in hospital entrance halls. Not only is this virtually free from ethical criticism but it is a form of recognition which, we believe, large numbers of bereaved relatives would positively endorse.

Conditional donation

14.64   It is possible that the impersonality of donation as currently practised may exert a

---

[127] D S Kittur, M M Hogan, V K Thukral et al 'Incentives for Organ Donation?' (1991) 338 Lancet 1441. The 'carrot' of preferred treatment for registered donors was discussed and approved by R Jarvis 'Join the Club: A Modest Proposal to Increase Availability of Donor Organs' (1995) 21 J Med Ethics 199, but was rejected in the same issue by R Gillon 'On Giving Preference to Prior Volunteers when Allocating Organs for Transplantation' (1995) 21 J Med Ethics 195.

[128] T G Peters 'Life or Death: The Issue of Payment for Cadaveric Organ Donation' (1991) 265 J Amer Med Ass 1302. For criticism of his arguments, see E D Pellegrino 'Families' Self-interest and the Cadaver's Organs: What Price Consent?' (1991) 265 J Amer Med Ass 1305. Opposition also comes from R W Evans 'Incentives for Organ Donation' (1992) 339 Lancet 185; 'Organ Procurement Expenditures and the Role of Financial Incentives' (1993) 269 J Amer Med Ass 3113. For support from an unlikely source of payment for cadaveric organs, see G P Smith 'Market and Non-market Mechanisms for Procuring Human and Cadaveric Organs: When the Price is Right' (1993) 1 Med Law Internat 17.

[129] R A Sells 'Commerce in Human Organs: A Global Review' (1990) 19 Dialysis Transplant 10.

[130] A very suspicious attitude was adopted by Joralemon, n 126 above.

[131] G J Banks 'Legal and Ethical Safeguards: Protection of Society's Most Vulnerable Participants in a Commercialized Organ Transplantation System' (1995) 21 Am J Law Med 45.

negative influence on a deceased's relatives—more organs might be donated if they were aware of their intended use. Thus, the possibility exists that a form of conditional donation might succeed where failure is, consciously or subconsciously, due to the present requirement for open-ended consent.

14.65   Discussion of this possibility was stifled by the fact that the first publicised offer was based on ethnic conditions—and racial discrimination is almost universally considered unacceptable in a modern democratic society. The panel set up by the Government to report on the case rejected decision-making on the particularities of individual cases and, rather, condemned all conditional donation as being contrary to the principles of altruism that govern the transplantation programme;[132] this is now established policy—a policy which, once again, has the aura of a knee-jerk reaction.

14.66   Just as there are many faces of discrimination, there are also many measures of altruism. It is altruistic to donate to the Salvation Army; the fact that the money does not go to the fighting forces does not detract from its intrinsic value. Closer to home, and without intending to reopen any racist canard, it is notable that the Government's plan for the future emphasises the Asian community's shortage of donations; would it be wrong to insist on one's organs being used for that community alone on the grounds that it was in greatest *need*? Conditional donation may have its difficulties and contraindication, but the availability of organs should not be compromised on the altar of a doubtful ethical imperative. As others have indicated, there is a major divide between an offer and its acceptance.[133] A blanket rejection of any motivation other than indifference as to the outcome might well be perverse; selective acceptance of directive donation might, at least, be worth considering in the greater interest.

THE FETUS OR NEONATE AS A TRANSPLANT DONOR

14.67   Transplantation therapy in infancy is now a standard part of paediatric surgery. Suitable organs, such as the liver, may become available from other neonates suffering from fatal conditions; such opportunities are rare but no new issues are then involved because the infant is subject to the conditions of the relevant Human Tissue Acts in just the same way as is the adult or the minor. This, however, is not always so in the case of the fetus who may be involved as an organ donor at maturity or as a cell donor at an early stage of development.

14.68   In the former circumstance, the fetal organs must be both mature and viable if they are to be used to good purpose. One potential source of mature organs is the stillbirth which, by definition, must be of more than 24 weeks' gestation.[134] Equally by definition, however, the stillbirth must neither have breathed nor shown any other

---

[132] Department of Health *An Investigation into Conditional Organ Donation* (2000).

[133] T M Wilkinson 'What's Not Wrong with Conditional Organ Donation?' (2003) 29 J Med Ethics 163.

[134] Still-Birth (Definition) Act 1992.

sign of life once separated from its mother. It follows that its organs must have been anoxic for an uncertain, but almost certainly significant, time; the chances of their being viable in the sense of being transplantable are, therefore, very slight and, save in exceptional circumstances, the stillbirth can be ignored as a possible source of *organs*. It follows that the 'fetal' donor must be alive when born and we are, in fact, considering the neonate as a donor. None the less, it is convenient to retain the term 'fetal donor' in order to distinguish him or her from the neonate that has been under treatment for a significant time.

14.69   The 'live fetal' donor might derive from a therapeutic abortion—a possibility which is rendered more real by the 1990 amendments to the Abortion Act 1967 which, inter alia, permit an abortion on the grounds of fetal abnormality without limit of gestational age (s 1(1)(a)) and absolve the doctor from liability under the Infant Life (Preservation) Act 1929 when terminating a pregnancy within the provisions of the 1967 Act (s 5(1)). The use of a living abortus as a transplant donor would be constrained by the terms of the Polkinghorne Report and is best regarded as an aspect of fetal research.[135] Ultimately, therefore, discussion of the fetal organ donor is limited in practice to that of the anencephalic fetus; new ethical ground is, thereby, broken.

14.70   The status of the anencephalic neonate is considered further in chapter 16. Here, it need only be said that maintenance treatment of the infant who exists only by virtue of a residual brain stem is, perhaps, the quintessential example of medical futility.[136] On the other hand, the anencephalic is, by existing standards, legally a 'creature in being' to whom the existing rules of homicide apply. Thus, the anencephalic neonate must be allowed a natural death which, save in exceptional circumstances, will occur within about one week.[137] Two major difficulties arise from this—first, as to the diagnosis of death in such circumstances and, secondly, as to the unpalatable corollary that the *dead* neonate or abortus must be reanimated if it is to provide undamaged organs. As to the former, the Royal Colleges and their Faculties in the United Kingdom concluded that: 'organs for transplantation can be removed from anencephalic infants when two doctors who are not members of the transplant team agree that spontaneous respiration has ceased'.[138] On the face of things, this seems to be doing no more than restating a diagnostic test for death which has been, and still is, the norm— moreover, the test is equally applicable to fetuses who have been fatally brain damaged during delivery and who might, exceptionally, be considered as donors. More importantly, perhaps, it pre-empts suggestions that anencephaly per se should carry a presumption of death—for the surviving anencephalic neonate is in the same position as

---

[135] For which see para 19.29 below.

[136] See para 16.60 below for the illustrative US case *In the matter of Baby K* 16 F 3d 590 (4th Cir, 1994). The findings at first instance were recapitulated in T L Beauchamp and R M Veatch *Ethical Issues in Death and Dying* (2nd edn, 1996), chapter 8, p 376.

[137] Paradoxically, an exception arose in the high profile case of Baby K, above, who survived for over two years.

[138] *Report of the Working Party of the Conference of Medical Royal Colleges and their Faculties in the United Kingdom on Organ Transplantation in Neonates* (1988).

is the adult in the permanent vegetative state.[139] It is, therefore, both unnecessary and impracticable to attempt to introduce a brain death standard. There is, however, a further practical difficulty in that fetal tissues—and particularly the heart—are extremely sensitive to 'warm anoxia'—the best results from the small number of cases reported are said to have come from those infants who were placed on life support and the organs used as soon as possible without regard to the existence of brain stem activity.[140] The time required to satisfy the Royal Colleges' criterion of cessation of respiration may, therefore, dictate an unacceptable deterioration in the quality of the donor organs which, in general, must be recovered from a 'beating heart' donor. But this practice depends, as we have seen, on the acceptance of 'brain stem death' and the transplant surgeon is left with a well-nigh insoluble dilemma—so much so that at least one authoritative commentator has questioned whether it is possible to establish death legally in an anencephalic and, at the same time, preserve the best interests of the recipient of its organs.[141] Attempts to redefine death in the anencephalic as a state of 'brain absence' or to regard such a neonate as 'not being a reasonable creature in being' seem to us to be examples of semantic juggling which should be resisted; the same applies to the more extreme suggestion that the definition of death should be extended so as to include anencephalics as a group[142]—as McCullagh has observed:

Classification as 'dead' will not cause an anencephalic who is breathing to cease doing so . . . One would require also to accept the burial of a spontaneously breathing patient.[143]

14.71   The more honest approach is to accept that, at the least, the legality and morality of anencephalic donations are matters for concern and that it is probable that their eventual solution will be founded on strongly utilitarian rather than strict deontological principles.

14.72   The implicit result of using the Royal Colleges' criteria is that anencephalic dona-tion must involve some form of 'reanimation ventilation'. This inevitably introduces moral qualms—not the least being that the period of 'deanimation' will be unaccept-ably short—and, eventually, one has to ask whether the manifest invasion of normal ethical standards is justified by results. No exercise in semantics will obscure the fact that 'reanimation' is defensible only by the use of unqualified utilitarian ethics.

14.73   It has been estimated that the use of anencephalic neonates would result in the availability of not more than 20 suitable donors each year in the United Kingdom;[144]

---

[139] See chapter 16.

[140] The Medical Task Force on Anencephaly 'The Infant with Anencephaly' (1990) 322 New Engl J Med 669.

[141] S McLean 'Facing the Dilemma of a Life and Death Issue' (1991) *The Scotsman*, 26 August, p 9. For a similar US view, see J L Peabody, J R Emery and S Ashwal 'Experience with Anencephalic Infants as Prospective Organ Donors' (1989) 321 New Engl J Med 344.

[142] For review, see W F May 'Brain Death: Anencephalics and Aborted Fetuses' (1990) 22 Transplant Proc 885.

[143] P McCullagh *Brain Dead, Brain Absent, Brain Donors* (1993) p 168.

[144] See J R Salaman 'Anencephalic Organ Donors' (1989) 298 BMJ 622.

the surprisingly low yield of organs which would accrue in the United States has been emphasised[145] as has their poor quality and associated distressingly bad therapeutic success rate.[146] All these factors were considered in what appears to be the only extant judicial consideration of the status of the anencephalic—at least in the anglophone jurisdictions.[147] The circumstances of T's birth were widely publicised. She was born anencephalic and, during her life of nine days, her parents sought to have her declared dead so that her organs could be used to save other lives. The circuit court judge held that she was not brain dead but, nevertheless, gave permission for a single kidney to be removed on the grounds that this was not harming her. This ruling was upheld in the District Court of Appeal but, despite the fact that the baby was now dead, the Supreme Court of Florida then agreed to accept the case as one which 'raised a question of great public importance requiring immediate resolution'. Much of the court's deliberation concerned the common and statute law of Florida but questions of principle were also addressed. Having established that T was legally alive at the relevant time, the parents' request that an additional common law standard of death applicable to anencephalics was considered in the light of current technology. It was held:

> Our review of the medical, ethical, and legal literature on anencephaly discloses absolutely no consensus that public necessity or fundamental rights will be better served by granting this request.[148]

and, later:

> We acknowledge the possibility that some infants' lives might be saved by using organs from anencephalics who do not meet the traditional definition of 'death' we affirm to-day. But weighed against this is the utter lack of consensus, and the questions about the overall utility of such organ donations. The scales clearly tip in favor of not extending the common law in this instance.[149]

14.74   Thus, the essential ethical problem is to decide whether the utilitarian advantages stemming from anencephalic organ donation are sufficient to offset the inherent deontological doubts raised by the procedure.[150] A 'cost-benefit' analysis inclines us to the view that the price is too high. The balance is, however, finely adjusted;[151] there might well be a case for further consideration should transplantation techniques improve to the extent that it can be shown clearly that, once obtained, organs from anencephalics offer a genuine prospect of life to those who are otherwise condemned to death.

---

[145] See May, n 142 above, reporting the findings, in particular, of Shewmon.

[146] D A Shewmon, A M Capron, W J Peacock and B L Schulman 'The Use of Anencephalic Infants as Organ Sources' (1989) 261 J Amer Med Ass 1773.

[147] *Re T A C P* 609 So 2d 588 (Fla, 1992).   [148] *Ibid* at 594.   [149] *Ibid* at 595.

[150] M Harrison 'Organ Procurement for Children: The Anencephalic Fetus as Donor' (1986) 2 Lancet 1383. For criticism of the utilitarian view, see A Davies 'The Status of Anencephalic Babies: Should Their Bodies Be Used as Donor Banks?' (1988) 14 J Med Ethics 150.

[151] For an international assessment, see L S Rothenberg 'The Anencephalic Neonate and Brain Death: An International Review of Medical, Ethical and Legal Issues' (1990) 22 Transplant Proc 1037.

14.75   The question would then remain whether a woman can properly choose to carry an affected baby close to term purely to provide transplantable organs. Such a programme appears, at first sight, to be unethical on the grounds that a human being is being used as a means. Yet, to prevent it could be seen as unreasonable paternalism. A veto not only *might* deprive potential recipients of life but it would also strike a direct blow at a woman's right to control her body. We would not support a total ban on what may be a truly altruistic endeavour—but it is an aspect of transplantation therapy which must merit very careful scrutiny.

FETAL BRAIN IMPLANTS

14.76   Normal adult nerve cells cannot replicate, whereas fetal cells are actively growing and multiplying; theoretically, therefore, an implanted fetal nerve cell will grow and provide a source of important cellular metabolites that are often deficient in the aged. The use of fetal neural tissue for the treatment of Parkinsonism[152] in the elderly—and its extension to the treatment of other degenerative diseases of the ageing brain—was, at one time, a burning issue. Much of the urgency has now been dispelled as a moratorium has been agreed as to further clinical trials. Moreover, enthusiasm for the procedure has been, to a large extent, diverted to the quest for stem-cell therapy (for which, see chapter 19). As a consequence, there is little, if anything, new to say on the subject. None the less, the procedure raises a number of legal and ethical problems which should be kept in mind—and we see four of these as being of major importance.

14.77   In contrast to fetal organs, fetal brain cells must be immature and are ideally harvested at 10–14 weeks' gestation. Thus, the first problem is that, excluding the rare opportunities derived from natural spontaneous miscarriage, from which a clear moral distinction to be made, the process is inextricably linked to abortion. The legal consequence is that fetal brain therapy is largely governed by the Abortion Act 1967; morally speaking, those who are opposed to abortion can accept fetal brain implantation only on the basis that it is desirable to extract some good from an intrinsically bad action if it is possible to do so[153]—and by no means all moralists would agree to such a proposition.[154] Certainly, virtually everyone would agree that a termination of

---

[152] Note that there is a clinical distinction to be made between idiopathic Parkinson's disease and the signs of Parkinsonism which occur in several other conditions: Editorial Comment 'Parkinson's Disease: One Illness or Many Syndromes?' (1992) 339 Lancet 1263.

[153] J A Robertson 'The Ethical Acceptability of Fetal Tissue Transplants' (1990) 22 Transplant Proc 1025 argues, persuasively, that the physician using the material has no complicity in obtaining it. The discussion is continued by K Nolan 'The Use of Embryo or Fetus in Transplantation: What There Is to Lose' (1990) 22 Transplant Proc 1029, who concludes that the use of fetal tissues obtained after elective abortion is justified only as a last resort.

[154] For extended analysis, see D G Jones 'Fetal Neural Transplantation: Placing the Ethical Debate Within the Context of Society's Use of Human Material' (1991) 5 Bioethics 23.

pregnancy and any subsequent transplantation must be dissociated; the prospect of a woman becoming pregnant in order to provide therapeutic material for an aged relative is scarcely acceptable—as Nolan has put it, it involves seeing fetuses as valuable primarily for their medicinal properties rather than for their stunning developmental potential. Secondly, it is obvious that the individual brain cells must be viable in themselves; can it then be said that the fetus is dead when subjected to surgery? Here, we must rely to an extent on semantic and pragmatic arguments. A 10–14-week-old fetus is not viable—it has no organised heart beat, its lungs cannot conceivably function as oxygenators and, once delivered, it is so clearly not born alive that its existence will go unrecorded save in respect of the abortion regulations; it follows that it is born dead. Moreover, in practice, the technique of abortion will have been so traumatic to the fetus as to preclude any form of life as it is generally accepted. But, be that as it may, it is still very difficult to answer the question: 'Is it brain dead?' in the affirmative.

14.78   Thirdly, we cannot overlook the revulsion with which most people view any form of tampering with the brain and, particularly, the idea of 'brain transplants'. As a consequence, the BMA's recommendation that nervous tissue should only be used for transplantation in the form of isolated neurones or tissue fragments[155] should be fully endorsed.[156] Finally, there is some moral repugnance to the use of tissues from the very young to sustain the aged. This is unfair in the present context for the aged are just as entitled to available treatment as is any other population group. But we must ensure that it is true treatment designed to ameliorate specific disease processes. Dr Faustus, in his quest for eternal youth, is scarcely admirable but there are few who have passed middle age who could honestly deny at least a touch of sympathy for his objectives; it is important that we do not seek to force the role of Mephistopheles upon the neurosurgeon.[157]

[155] Medical Ethics 'Transplantation of Fetal Material' (1988) 296 BMJ 1410.

[156] The question of the persona and brain tissue transplants is discussed in G Northoff 'Do Brain Tissue Transplants Alter Personal Identity? Inadequacies of some "Standard" Arguments' (1996) 22 J Med Ethics 174. See the associated editorial comment R Gillon 'Brain Transplantation, Personal Identity and Medical Ethics' (1996) 22 J Med Ethics 131.

[157] For an excellent review of the agonies of a Research Review Committee, see A S MacDonald 'Foetal Neuroendocrine Tissue Transplantation for Parkinson's Disease: An Institutional Review Board Faces the Ethical Dilemma' (1990) 22 Transplant Proc 1030.

15

THE BODY AS PROPERTY

15.1   We have encountered examples of moral, ethical and legal recognition of the relationship between the concept of 'self' and the physical entity known as 'the human
body' at many junctures in the discussion thus far. In particular, the central position
in medical law of the principle of respect for the patient's autonomy determines that
the individual patient has the ultimate right to control his or her body and what is
done with or to it. Primarily, that control is exercised through the concept of consent
to, and its correlate, refusal of, treatment. Thus, we have seen in chapter 10 that
disrespect of a refusal to an invasive procedure can result in actions in negligence or
for assault, and the use and storage of gametes is strictly controlled according to the
written consent of the donor under the Human Fertilisation and Embryology Act
1990 (see chapter 4). That said, it is by no means the case that we have an absolute
right, either ethically or legally, to do whatever we want with our bodies—we have
noted how the Human Tissue Act 2004 will prohibit 'trafficking' in human material[1]
(while its predecessor, the Human Organ Transplants Act 1989, has been concerned
with a 'trade in organs'),[2] and the House of Lords was categoric in *R v Brown*[3] that
ritual physical abuse of the body for sexual pleasure remains criminal even when
undertaken within the envelope of full and informed consent by the parties involved.
The question, therefore, arises as to what limits are set to the right to control our
bodies. In recent years, this debate has centred around the very important issue of the
status of the body as property. This chapter will consider three aspects of that debate:
property in material taken from living persons; property in material taken from
cadavers; and the granting of intellectual property rights in human material.[4]

---

[1] Human Tissue Act 2004, s 32. It is thought that the majority of the Act will come into force in the course
of 2006.

[2] It should be noted that the Human Organ Transplants Act 1989 is not repealed in so far as it extends to
Scotland; nor, for that matter are the provisions of the Human Tissue Act 1961.

[3] *R v Brown* [1994] 1 AC 212, [1993] 2 All ER 75.

[4] Consider the on-going work of the PropEur project which is examining new approaches to law and
ethics in property concerning, inter alia, the human genome and human tissue: www.propeur.bham.ac.uk.

PROPERTY IN LIVING HUMAN MATERIAL

15.2   Intuitively, it is perfectly natural for one to talk of 'my body' and to infer that, because it is 'my' body, I can determine precisely what is done to it or its parts. Moreover, for most people, this feeling is inherently bound up with the proprietary notion that, because my body is my own, I 'own' my body. However, it is far from clear that there is support for this in either legal or ethical terms. No single ethical principle or imperative exists on which one can ground a property right in oneself.[5] And, as Harris has pointed out, it is a 'spectacular non sequitur' to deduce that, because no one can make a slave of me and own my body, I necessarily own my body myself.[6] Indeed, the idea of property is primarily a legal one. It is a construct which allows us to order our society according to a chosen value system which, in turn, greatly facilitates the achievement of certain of our social goals—in our case, those of most Western states which encourage commerce and sanction commodification. The role of ethics lies not so much in grounding a property right but in determining whether it is appropriate to commodify something such as the human body which, for reasons we have already discussed in chapter 1, has a particular moral status deserving of respect. Thus, for many, the idea that one can buy or sell body parts is repugnant in that it shows disrespect for the status of 'the human body'.[7] A British doctor was struck off the medical register in 2002 for offering to broker a sale of a kidney with a journalist who posed as the son of a terminally ill man.[8] Trade in body parts gives rise to the spectre of exploitation, which is ethically questionable because it has the potential to harm those who are exploited.[9] The counter to this, of course, is that, while no one would sanction forced participation in the trade of body parts, it is unduly paternalistic to eschew the consent of individuals who would willingly sell their tissues.[10] It is on just such a basis, amongst others, that the Human Organ Transplants Act 1989 has been criticised as being an unsophisticated knee-jerk reaction to a serious problem open to a workable solution.[11] None the less, as we have indicated, its prohibitory terms are largely reproduced in the Human Tissue Act 2004 and indeed these are potentially considerably extended since the 1989 Act was concerned with

---

[5] However, for argument to this effect, see D Beyleveld and R Brownsword *Human Dignity in Bioethics and Biolaw* (2001), ch 8.

[6] J W Harris 'Who Owns My Body?' (1996) 16 OJLS 55 at 71.

[7] L Skene 'Arguments Against People Legally "Owning" Their Own Bodies, Body Parts and Tissue' (2002) 2 MacQuarie LJ 165. Also cf, S R Munzer 'An Uneasy Case Against Property Rights in Body Parts' (1994) 11 Soc Philosoph Pol 259, and A Ryan 'Self-Ownership, Autonomy and Property Rights' (1994) 11 Soc Philosoph Pol 241.

[8] C Dyer 'GP Struck Off for Offering the "Fix" Kidney Sale' (2002) 325 BMJ 510.

[9] For an argument in favour of a defensible system, see C A Erin and J Harris 'An Ethical Market in Human Organs' (2003) 29 J Med Ethics 137.

[10] J Savulescu 'Is the Sale of Body Parts Wrong?' (2003) 29 J Med Ethics 138 and M M Friedlaender 'The Right to Sell or Buy a Kidney: Are We Failing Our Patients?' (2002) 359 Lancet 971.

[11] J Radcliffe-Richards et al 'The Case of Allowing Kidney Sales' (1998) 351 Lancet 1950.

'organs' while its successor extends to 'controlled material'. 'Organ' is defined by the 1989 Act as: 'any part of the human body consisting of a structured arrangement of tissues which, if wholly removed, cannot be replicated by the body'.[12] The 2004 Act defines 'controlled material' as: 'any material which (a) consists of or includes human cells, (b) is, or is intended to be removed, from the human body . . ., excepting (a) gametes, (b) embryos, or (c) material which is the subject of a property right because of the application of human skill'.[13] Thus the new definition is considerably wider— extending the application of the no-trade rule—although, somewhat ironically, it simultaneously recognises not only that property rights *can* accrue in human material but that these will be allowed to endure. We return to the means of acquisition of such rights in due course. For present purposes, we question the mixed messages that continue to be sent out. The 2004 Act is the first piece of legislation to recognise expressly the potential existence of property rights in human material although it does so merely by repeating unquestioningly the pre-existing common law position which, as we see below, has been unclear and unsatisfactory.[14] It is to be regretted that the government did not take the opportunity to clarify the law after the extensive public consultation exercise that preceded the Act. This is yet a further example of the reluctance of the legislature to address property issues directly. The Human Organ Transplants Act 1989 says nothing about property in organs as such and merely criminalises those who would attempt to trade in the material, while the Human Fertilisation and Embryology Act 1990 relies on the expressed written wishes of donors in controlling the use and storage of gametes—all of which falls far short of acknowledging a property right in any sample.[15]

15.3   The opaqueness of the common law as to the actual status of body parts in property terms has endured for many years. Thus, while there is evidence in the case law which suggests that regenerative body material such as hair,[16] blood[17] and urine[18] can be the subject of property,[19] a 'no property in a corpse' rule remains the foundation of the law in respect of the deceased;[20] this too, however, admits exceptions whereby sufficient work or skill can been exercised on the material to convert it into an ownable 'thing'. Some foreign jurisdictions do grant direct recognition of property rights in human material. For example, the German Bundesgerichtshof has ruled that excised

---

[12] Human Organ Transplants Act 1989, s 7(2).

[13] Human Tissue Act 2004, s 32(8) and (9).   [14] *Ibid*, s 32(9).

[15] For recent discussion see J W Berg 'You Say Person, I Say Property: Does it Really Matter what We Call an Embryo?' (2004) 4 Amer J Bioethics 18.

[16] *R v Herbert* (1961) 25 JCL 163.

[17] *R v Rothery* [1976] RTR 550, (1976) 63 Cr App R 231.   [18] *R v Welsh* [1974] RTR 478.

[19] In each of these criminal cases, the accused was convicted of theft for removing the 'property' of another without permission. E.g. in *Rothery* the accused gave a sample of blood to be tested for alcohol levels and then 'stole' it by removing it from the police station.

[20] For an in-depth discussion of the position in Scots law see N Whitty 'Rights of Personality, Property Rights and the Human Body in Scots Law' (2005) 9 Edin LR 194.

body parts that are not intended for another (such as transplant organs) or for return to the individual (such as stored sperm), are subject to the normal rules of personal property.[21] Often, however, the courts use an appeal to property rights as a means to other legal ends. An illustration of this is the decision by the Supreme Court of Western Australia in *Roche v Douglas*[22] where it was held that human tissue taken from a deceased person was 'property' for the purposes of the court rules; this allowed the court then to claim dominion over the sample in order to authorise testing to settle a familial paternity dispute. A similar technique was employed by the Californian Court of Appeal in *Hecht v Kane*,[23] in which the court held that a deceased man who had previously deposited sperm for the use of his partner had an interest 'in the nature of ownership' of the samples such as to render them 'property' within the meaning of the Probate Code and, accordingly, disposable property on his death.[24] And, the Tennessee Supreme Court held in *Davis v Davis*[25] that the embryo occupied an 'interim category' as neither 'person' nor 'property', yet which entitled it to a special respect. While the parties were denied 'a true property interest' they retained an interest, 'in the nature of ownership' in relation to the use and disposal of their pre-embryos. Reflections of this are also to be found in the British Isles where, in *In the Matter of X*,[26] the Jersey Royal Court relied on the 'interest in the nature of ownership' of a minor in respect of her aborted fetus as the reason to respect her refusal to release fetal tissue to the police.[27]

15.4   In each of these cases the central issue is one of control.[28] Property is a powerful control device for the bundle of rights that it confers. It also carries a particular message—one of the potential for commerce and trade; of market advantage and disadvantage. To recognise a 'quasi-property' claim to material is to support a normatively strong connection to that material and, accordingly, to establish a strong, justiciable

---

[21] Bundesgerichtshof, 9 November 1993, BGHZ, 124, 52.

[22] [2000] WAR 331. For a full discussion from the Australian perspective with elements of universal interest, see Australian Law Reform Commission (ALRC), *Protection of Human Genetic Information: Discussion Paper 66* (2002); the final report appears as ALRC, *Essentially Yours: The Protection of Human Genetic Information in Australia* (2003).

[23] 16 Cal App 4th 836 (1993).

[24] On the issues from an ethical perspective, see L Cannold 'Who Owns a Dead Man's Sperm?' (2004) 30 J Med Ethics 386.

[25] 842 SW 2d 588 (1992).   [26] [2002] JRC 202.

[27] This was sought in the pursuit of a prosecution against the child's sexual partner for under-age intercourse. In the final analysis the Jersey Court of Appeal overrode the child's refusal in the interests of justice: [2003] JCA 050. For commentary see, A Grubb 'Access to Fetal Material: Property Rights and PACE' (2003) 11 Med L Rev 142.

[28] These decisions should be contrasted with the French case of *Parpalaix v CECOS* JCP 1984.II.20321 in which the court ordered the return of frozen sperm to the wife of the depositor on the basis of an agreement which had been made between him and the sperm bank and his original intent. It refused, however, to go so far as to recognise any property interest in the sperm. In subsequent cases the French court struggled to find a valid basis in law for dealing with embryos and sperm, vacillating between the law of obligations on the one hand and the principle of 'the established family' on the other: see (1996) *La Semaine Juridique* Ed G, No. 27, 22666.

legal interest; by the same token, these examples indicate that 'full' property rights will only be recognised where there is little or no prospect of exploitation or other harm, which can include the 'harm' of disrespect for the dignity of the human organism. We see, then, a wide-spread ambivalence about property in human material. Other devices, such as consent or contract, are often used instead of property to establish rights and resolve conflicts. Moreover, there is arguably nothing inherently valuable in an appeal to property itself save when such an appeal can furnish rights or solutions to disputes which escape other legal concepts. It is with just such a critical eye that we should consider the entire gamut of legal mechanisms that are employed in the medico-legal sphere, from which, we contend, *property* should not be excluded without careful consideration of its own utility and limits.

THE EMBRYO IN VITRO

15.5   The Human Fertilisation and Embryology Authority faces the dilemma of the disposal of embryos which are created for assisted reproduction but which are not used for the purpose. As we have stated, the 1990 Act avoids any recognition of property rights and control over the use and disposal of frozen embryos falls to be determined by the will of the parties contributing to their formation. However, unlike gametes, two parties provide the genetic material contained in embryos. Who, then, has the power to dispose of them?

15.6   In this respect, Sch 3 to the 1990 Act provides that effective written consent must be given by each person whose gametes have contributed to the embryo.[29] In practice, this gives either contributor a veto over its use but it provides neither with rights of disposal—the embryos must be allowed to perish if the gamete providers cannot agree and the storage time for the embryo has exceeded the statutory limit.[30]

15.7   The regulations which govern storage of gametes and embryos provide that the initial storage period of five years may be extended up to ten years, and in some cases longer, so long as the gamete providers do not lodge an objection when asked to reaffirm their consent to storage. It is important to note here that actual written reconfirmation of such consent is required. This can be problematic at a number of levels, particularly if a couple who have provided gametes has separated or if gametes have been supplied by a donor who is no longer traceable or who has died.[31] In each case, the embryos will be allowed to perish if no reconfirmation is obtained.[32] Such a system is effectively designed for stalemate, and just such an eventuality materialised

---

[29] Schedule 3, para 6(3).

[30] Human Fertilisation and Embryology (Statutory Storage Period for Embryos) Regulations 1996, SI 1996/375, r 14(1)(c).

[31] In this latter respect and for a challenge to prevalence of the consent model, see M Parker 'Response to Orr and Seigler—Collective Intentionality and Procreative Desires: The Permissible View on Consent to Posthumous Conception' (2004) 30 J Med Ethics 389.

[32] Schedule 3, para 6(3).

in the case of *Evans v Amicus Healthcare Ltd and Others* [33] which we discuss in chapter 4. The reader will recall that the Court of Appeal stuck rigidly to the letter of the law in this case, holding that the refusal to cooperate by the estranged partners of two women who sought possession of their frozen embryos meant that there was no other legal option but to deny access to the embryos, effectively condemning the organisms to destruction.

15.8   We view this system of consents with a degree of concern. [34] In the absence of any property right in embryos, the aim for which they have been created can be thwarted easily by the absence or withholding of consent by a potentially disinterested, bitter or uncontactable contributor. Thus, the person for whom they were intended, that is the woman who was to carry one or more of them, is denied the opportunity to benefit from the original treatment proposed. While we do not suggest that a property system would be problem-free, we believe that to recognise a property right in embryos which vests, in the first instance, in the woman who is to receive treatment would go a long way to resolving the current controversies surrounding these issues. It should not be forgotten that a considerable number of embryos had to be destroyed at the end of the first five-year period of storage precisely because of the difficulties outlined above [35] and the mere creation of a facility to extend the storage period will not make the problems go away. By the same token, it could not be the case that a male partner could be forced to be the legal father of any progeny against his wishes. This, of course, could be addressed from within the existing law where any presumption of fatherhood can be rebutted on relevant evidence. [36] It would not, however, tackle the social consequences of the child who seeks contact with her biological father at a future date. Such eventualities would require to be fully disclosed to parties at the beginning of any reproductive therapy and those with the slightest doubts should be encouraged to reconsider seriously their position.

THE FETUS IN VIVO AND FETAL MATERIALS

15.9   Whatever may be said about the embryo in vitro, there should be no support for extending a woman's property right to an implanted fetus. A clear moral distinction is to be made between the in vitro and the in vivo human organism, not least because of the immediate potentiality of the latter to become a complete human being. [37] It is to be noted that the Polkinghorne Committee [38] suggested that provision be made in any consent to fetal research procedures for the relinquishment of property rights 'if,

---

[33] [2004] 3 WLR 681, [2004] 3 All ER 1025. Leave to appeal to the House of Lords has since been denied and we understand that the claimants are to take their case to the European Court of Human Rights.

[34] J K Mason 'Discord and Disposal of Embryos' (2004) 8 Edin LR 84.

[35] K D Hopkins 'First Batch of Human Embryos Destroyed in UK' (1996) 348 Lancet 399.

[36] See further chapter 4.

[37] Although the fetus is not a legal person, the concept of it being 'property' is too close to that of slavery for comfort.

[38] *Review of the Guidance on the Research use of Fetuses and Fetal Material* (Cm 762, 1989).

indeed, there be any' (para 8.4). This clearly refers to maternal rights in respect of the fetus. Times have, however, changed since 1989. While the Polkinghorne Committee regarded the dissociation of the use of fetal tissues and abortion as the overriding consideration, others might now see it as anomalous if a 'profit sharing' agreement were enforceable between a biotechnological institute and the donor when the tissues of a living person were used but the institute could escape any duty of financial recompense by using tissues from a fetus.

15.10   But what of a non-viable or stillborn fetus and/or fetal material that is discharged from the mother as the result of either a medical termination or a spontaneous miscarriage? The potentiality for viable human life has clearly ended in such a case[39] and we must consider the possibility of property rights afresh. The Polkinghorne Committee refused to address this issue and preferred, instead, to recommend that the full and informed consent of the woman be obtained concerning the use and/or disposal of the material. While we acknowledge that, in moral terms, a dead fetus might command greater respect than fetal material *in se*, we do not consider that the recognition of a property interest in either necessarily involves such a degree of disrespect as would lead us to refuse to recognise any such interest. The potential value of any tissue is,[40] nowadays, uncertain but is surely increasing and we suggest that the mother of the dead fetus should retain any available property claim not only in respect of the fetus itself but also of its associated materials. Of course, the matters of ownership and disposal should be approached cautiously and with sensitivity at such an emotional time. We have already mentioned the decision *In re the Matter of X*[41] in which the court of first instance expressly relied on the analogy of a property-type interest of the mother in her dead fetus to strengthen her claim to respect for her choices about what was done with the fetal material. While her refusal was ultimately overridden by the Jersey Court of Appeal in furtherance of the public interest in the investigation and prosecution of crime, this does not detract from the significance of the appeal to property as a *complement* to an autonomy-based interest. Here, the autonomy claim was weaker because of the mother's status as a minor. Moreover, the fact that property or quasi-property rights might be trumped by stronger competing public interests should come as no surprise for the former are never absolute in any context.

THE NUFFIELD REPORT

15.11   The report of the Nuffield Council on Bioethics on Human Tissue[42] has recently enjoyed its 10th birthday, but it remains a valuable resource for its comprehensive discussion of the issues surrounding the question of property in body parts—including gametes, embryos and fetal material. After reviewing the legal and ethical

---

[39] The possible exception to this is the living abortus which we discuss in chapter 5.
[40] See para 15.15 et seq below.   [41] Para 15.3 above.
[42] Nuffield Council on Bioethics *Human Tissue: Ethical and Legal Issues* (1995).

position on human tissue, the Council made its recommendations in light of the provisions of the Human Tissue Act 1961, the Human Organ Transplants Act 1989 and the Anatomy Act 1984—all of which are now to be repealed in England and Wales by the Human Tissue Act 2004, although they will remain in force in Scotland for the time being.[43] The conclusions of the Council none the less remain as valid today as they were in 1995—the medical institutional expectation is that any tissue given or taken from individuals is received free of all claims and, second, the common law position is unsettled. The Council recommended that any disputed claim over material should be determined with regard to the nature of the consent given to the initial procedure for removal. Moreover, it was the Council's view that it should be implied in any consent to medical treatment which involves the removal of tissue that the tissue has been abandoned by the person from whom it was removed.[44] It was recommended that tissue removed from an individual who is unable to give valid consent should not be the subject of any claim, either by the incapax or by his or her representatives.[45]

15.12   The Council's recommendations are certainly in keeping with the trend which has emerged in the United Kingdom to date.[46] Yet, we cannot help but feel that the Council, like the courts and legislature before it, was reluctant to face the real issues concerning body ownership head-on.[47] The Council acknowledged that trading in bodily materials, products or by-products inside and outside the NHS is an essential part of the Service, although it also pointed to legal provisions that restrict financial return to necessary expenses.[48] The Council recommended that organisations responsible for the procurement and handling of human tissue should operate on a non-commercial basis, and the Department of Health followed the Council in large part by producing a Code of Practice on tissue banks in the public sector in 2001;[49] this, however, explicitly excludes coverage of commercially manufactured therapeutic products that utilise human tissues. In fact, commercial tissue banks have proliferated in the years since the Nuffield Report, with recent examples including the

---

[43] For recommendations as to reform in Scotland, see the work of the Independent Review Group on Retention of Organs at Post-Mortem: www.scotland.gov.uk. See, too, Whitty, n 20 above, for a full account of the Scots law historical position.

[44] N 42 above, ch 9, in particular para 9.14.   [45] N 42 above, paras 9.15–9.17.

[46] E.g., the Medical Research Council has stated that: 'The human body and its parts shall not, as such give rise to financial gain. Researchers may not sell for a profit samples of human biological material that they have collected as part of MRC funded research, and research participants should never be offered any financial inducement to donate samples', see MRC *Human Tissue and Biological Samples for Use in Research: Operational and Ethical Guidelines* (2001), Part 2. This reflects the terms of Article 21 of the Council of Europe Convention on Human Rights and Biomedicine, although it is important to note that both the Convention and the MRC draw a distinction between no property in the body and its parts *as such* and 'inventions' using human material which may be subject to intellectual property rights. We discuss this further below.

[47] For a full discussion, see P Matthews 'The Man of Property' (1995) 3 Med L Rev 251.

[48] Nuffield Council, n 42, above, paras 10.8—10.10.

[49] Department of Health *A Code of Practice for Tissue Banks Providing Tissues of Human Origin for Therapeutic Purposes* (2001).

establishment of stem cell banks.[50] Indeed, the European Parliament and Council have adopted a Directive on standards and processing human tissues and cells to harmonise regulation throughout the Union.[51] The European Group on Ethics has been asked to comment on this Directive and, in contemplation of commercialisation practices, it has said, inter alia, that '[w]hen the donated cells may become part of a patent application, donors should be informed of the possibility of patenting and they are entitled to refuse such use'.[52] By the same token, the Group reiterates that '. . . Apart from justified compensation, donors ought not to get a reward which could infringe the principle of non-commercialisation of the human body.'[53] In the UK, the Human Tissue Act 2004 now affords a power to the new Human Tissue Authority to authorise financial returns beyond mere expenses for the handling of, or trade in, human tissues. For example, s 32(6) of the Act allows licence terms for the transporting, removing, preparing, preserving and storing of controlled material to include payments on a commercial basis. The point, then, is that a market in materials exists and that property rights are generated. The Nuffield Council's recommendations of a decade ago must now be read in light of these developments.

15.13   Perhaps of most interest is the trend that shows that, in many cases, property rights flow to parties other than the persons from whom the material has been taken. Why should this be so? Stark et al studied the attitudes of a small sample of in-patients but this sheds little light on the major current ethical debate over body parts and does not help us as to the actual or potential legal position.[54] It is telling, none the less, that few of those surveyed had been told about the possible uses of the material.[55] Indeed, more recent evidence suggests a shift in cultural attitude towards self-ownership among certain sectors of the community. The Medical Research Council's survey on the perceptions of the public on the collection and use of human biological samples found that of those surveyed, younger people tended to view payment for such samples as a matter of right—or they were, at least, open to the prospect.[56] This was especially so when research was likely to generate income for commercial organisations.[57] In contrast, members of the older generation tended to adhere to the classic

---

[50] For the UK Stem Cell Bank which was established in 2003 see: www.ukstemcellbank.org.uk. See too, European Group on Ethics *Opinion No.19: Ethical Aspects of Umbilical Cord Blood Banking* (2004).

[51] Directive 2004/23/EC on setting standards of quality and safety for the Donation, Procurement, Testing, Processing, Preservation, Storage and Distribution of Human Tissue and Cells (OJ L102 7.4.2004 p 48–58).

[52] European Group on Ethics *Report of the European Group on Ethics on the Ethical Aspects of Human Tissue Engineered Products* (2004), p 3.

[53] *Ibid*, p 5.

[54] The survey showed that only 10% of hospital patients believed that they retained ownership of tissue removed after surgery, while 47% thought that the material belonged either to the hospital (27%) or to the laboratory (20%). Only 27% of those surveyed were of the opinion that no one owned the material: R D Start et al 'Ownership and Uses of Human Tissue: Does the Nuffield Bioethics Report Accord with Opinion of Surgical Inpatients?' (1996) 313 BMJ 1366.

[55] This is expressly disapproved of by the EGE in its recent opinion on the Tissue Directive, n 52 above, p 2

[56] Medical Research Council *Public Perceptions of the Collection of Human Biological Samples* (2000).

[57] Compare A L Jack and C Womack, 'Why Surgical Patients Do Not Donate Tissue for Commercial Research: Review of Records' (2003) BMJ 262.

gift paradigm, expecting nothing in return for altruistic and public spirited dona-tions.[58] However, support for allowing volunteers to retain a degree of ownership in donated samples was also found among GPs and nurses who took part in the survey.[59] Numerous public engagement studies indicate that public confidence is shaken by the prospect of private profit from public involvement in biotechnological research, and most especially by the prospect of patents over the products of that research.[60]

15.14   The Nuffield Council's report was based, in the main, on the premise that people see no value in their excised body parts; this premise has long dominated this area of debate, yet it is one which has always been questionable and is easily challenged today. 'Value' exists in a variety of forms. Consider the value which we attach to fetal tissue and the controversy which has surrounded proposed research and therapies using such tissue (see chapter 19). Consider, too, the fact that we find it meaningful to continue to talk about '*my* appendix' and '*my* gall stones' even when these materials have been removed from our bodies. Perhaps most significantly of all, the advent of the biotechnological age has meant that there can be considerable economic value which accrues to biotechnological products produced using human material. Thus, to assert, as the Council does, that patients should be deemed to abandon their tissues, is to ignore the potential values which those very persons may well hold in retaining control over such material. A system of consents does not permit that control to be exercised as fully as might be desirable.[61]

COMMERCIALISM AND HUMAN MATERIAL

15.15   Gold has noted, for example, that, because the courts tend to ignore sociological, psychological and anthropological attitudes towards the body and, instead, reduce everything to economics, they ignore the signs of people's ambiguity about techno-logical advancement.[62] It is widely assumed that the interposition of commercial interests between the source of valuable material and its user is unacceptable because it leads necessarily to exploitation. At the same time, it is accepted that the encouragement of commercial profit-making by users, primarily by the biotechnol-ogy industry, can only bring benefits to the community in the guise of more therapies and cures. But, as Gold correctly observes, giving property rights to biotechnology researchers focuses the medical industry primarily on cure and shifts attention away

---

[58] At para 6.12.   [59] At para 17.

[60] See, for example, Cragg Ross Dawson, *Public Perceptions of the Collection of Human Biological Samples*, (2000): www.wellcome.ac.uk and R Hapgood, C McCabe and D Shickle 'Public preferences for participation in a large DNA cohort study: a discrete choice experiment' (2004): www.shef.ac.uk/~sheg/discussion/04_5FT.pdf.

[61] Something of an outcry arose in 2001 when it transpired that thymus glands taken from paediatric cardiac surgery cases were being sold for nominal amounts to drug companies. This, despite the fact that wastage of the glands was a necessary part of the operation and the parents consented to 'retention of tissues for research purposes': BBC News 'Milburn Condemns "Body Part Trade" '(2001) 26 January.

[62] E R Gold *Body Parts: Ownership of Human Biological Material* (1996).

from the equally, or more, important pursuit of determining—and eradicating—the underlying causes of illness and disease.[63] Similarly, as we discuss in the context of surrogacy (see chapter 4), it is not necessarily exploitative *in se* to offer financial incentives or rewards to individuals to use their bodies in certain ways. As Andrews has said in the context of that debate, it may be more devaluing to persons not to recognise their worth in monetary terms for the contributions they can make to society from the use of their bodies than it is to protect them from potential predators—provided, always, that the value that they represent is not entirely reducible to those terms.[64] That something is potentially exploitative does not mean that it must always be so, and it certainly does not justify the courts' refusing to deal directly with the real interests and issues.

15.16   The case which most clearly betrays the skewed attitude of the judiciary towards these matters is *Moore v Regents of the University of California*.[65] John Moore suffered from hairy cell leukaemia and his spleen was removed at the Medical School of the University of California at Los Angeles. His doctor, Dr Golde, discovered that cells from the spleen had unusual and potentially beneficial properties and developed an immortal cell-line from them without his patient's knowledge or consent. Moreover, Dr Golde sought, and obtained, a patent over the cell-line which he subsequently sold to a drug company for $15m—and it has been reported that the drugs and therapies which were developed from the patented product are now worth in excess of $3b.[66] Moore brought an action against the researchers, the university and the drug company when he discovered the truth about his cells. He filed 13 causes of action in total but those concerning the questions of property and consent are of most direct interest. In particular, he alleged *conversion*—that, as the 'owner' of the cells, his property right had been compromised by the work carried out on the cells by the defendants. He also alleged breach of fiduciary duty and lack of informed consent because he had never been told of the potential use of his cells and, correspondingly, he had never given his full and informed agreement to the initial operation. The Californian Supreme Court upheld these two last claims but rejected the argument in conversion. The court opined that it was inappropriate to recognise property in the body, first, because no precedent could be found on which to ground such a claim and, secondly, because to recognise individual property rights in body parts would be to hinder medical research 'by restricting access to the necessary raw materials'—a pure utilitarian consideration. Moreover, the court was concerned that a contrary decision would '[threaten] to destroy the economic incentive to conduct important medical research' because '[i]f the use of cells in research is a conversion, then with every cell sample a

[63] *Ibid*, p 37.
[64] L B Andrews 'Beyond Doctrinal Boundaries: A Legal Framework for Surrogate Motherhood' (1995) 81 Virginia Law Rev 2343.
[65] 793 P 2d 479 (Cal, 1990). See also, *Brotherton v Cleveland* 923 F 2d 661 (6th Cir, 1991).
[66] B Merz, 'Biotechnology: Spleen-Rights' *The Economist*, 11 August 1990, p 30.

researcher purchases a ticket in a litigation lottery'.[67] The irony of this decision is
pointed out in the dissent of Broussard J:

> . . . the majority's analysis cannot rest on the broad proposition that a removed part is not
> property, but . . . on the proposition that a *patient* retains no ownership interest in a body
> part once the body part has been removed. (Emphasis added.)

15.17   Thus, while each of us is denied recognition of a property interest in excised parts
of our bodies, third parties may not only gain such an interest but can go on to protect
it using forms of property law such as the law of patents.

15.18   But does not such an example demonstrate precisely the kind of value which
individuals could retain in their excised parts? The properties of the patient's cells are
a *sine qua non* of the ultimate invention. And, while no one would deny that much
time and money would need to be expended in turning the natural material into a
patentable product, is the view of the Supreme Court in *Moore* not something of an
over-reaction to the *possible* consequences of applying property law to the human
body? It is entirely reasonable to hold that some financial reward should also be given
to the source of the valuable sample while, at the same time, accepting that the
majority of the spoils should return to those who have done the work in creating a
patentable invention. It is *not* reasonable to exclude completely from the equation
the one person who can make everything possible. Furthermore, policy is not always
on the side of the researchers, as another American dispute demonstrated well.[68] In
Greenberg et al v Miami Children's Hospital Research Institute Inc,[69] a law suit was
brought by parents of children affected by a rare, fatal and incurable genetic disorder
called Canavan disease against researchers who developed and patented a test for the
disease using samples donated by the families. The defendants had worked closely
with afflicted families, receiving samples and gaining access to registers containing
details of other affected groups around the world. However, when the Canavan gene
was eventually identified, the researchers sought a patent over it and a related test and
proceeded to restrict access to the latter save through tightly controlled exclusive
licences. The plaintiffs objected strongly and, in much the same way as happened in
Moore, mounted an action on a number of grounds, including lack of informed
consent, unjust enrichment, breach of fiduciary duty and conversion. In this last
respect, the plaintiffs claimed a property interest in their samples, the genetic information therein and information contained in the Canavan Register. Paradoxically,
however, the case stood in stark contrast to *Moore* for, here, policy favoured the

---

[67] For comment on *Moore*, see B Hoffmaster 'Between the Sacred and the Profane: Bodies, Property, and
Patents in the *Moore* Case' (1992) 7 Intellect Prop J 115 and E B Seeney 'Moore 10 Years Later—Still Trying to
Fill the Gap: Creating a Personal Property Right in Genetic Material' (1998) 32 New Engl L Rev 1131.

[68] For an account of the American regulatory position, see R Hakimian and D Korn 'Ownership and Use
of Tissue Specimens for Research' (2004) 292 J Amer Med Ass 2500.

[69] *Greenberg et al v Miami Children's Hospital Research Institute Inc. et al* 264 F Supp 2d 1064 (SD Fla,
2003), settled action; for comment see M R Anderlik and M A Rothstein 'Canavan Decision Favors
Researchers Over Families' (2003) 313 *Journal of Law, Medicine and Ethics* 450.

plaintiffs—the families wanted information about the disease and the test to be freely available, while it was the patent holders who wished to restrict access and so potentially hinder research. The case was eventually abandoned after a preliminary hearing in which the judge rejected the property claim but suggested that the argument in unjust enrichment might succeed. While the precise basis for this remains unclear, the outcome, nevertheless, reveals the continuing antipathy to property model approaches to individual rights.[70]

15.19   We have argued elsewhere that the time has now come to recognise a modified form of property rights for individuals in their own (excised) body parts.[71] We should not be distracted from the property debate by the illusion that consent is the sole, or optimal, ethico-legal solution to the dilemmas thrown up by modern medicine, as many official bodies would have us believe.[72] A consent model disempowers individuals to the extent that the single 'right' that it gives is a right to refuse. How does this help the person who is willing to participate in medical research but has qualms about the subsequent use of his samples towards undesirable ends? It does not, for his only option is not to participate.[73] A property right would, at least, allow an element of continuing control over such samples after surrender and would allow for a legally recognised voice in how they are used. The same is not true once an initial consent has been obtained, for so long as the requisite information is disclosed at the time the sample is provided the sample source's 'rights' have, thereby, been exhausted.[74] It is uncertain how far these views would be accepted in the courts in the United Kingdom.

15.20   This does not, however, take us very far with the question of disposal of the commercially valueless specimen. We suggest that a consent-based action in negligence would be available if, for example, a patient's susceptibilities were outraged by his tissues being used for demonstration purposes but this is by no means certain. Fortunately, the question is of no more than academic interest in the overwhelming majority of cases.[75]

---

[70] For discussion see J A Bovenberg 'Inalienably Yours? The New Case for an Inalienable Property Right in Human Biological Material: Empowerment of Sample Donors or a Recipe for a Tragic Anti-commons?' (2004) 1:4 SCRIPT-ed 591, available at: www.script-ed.org.

[71] K Mason and G Laurie 'Consent or Property? Dealing with the Body and its Parts in the Shadow of Bristol and Alder Hey' (2001) 64 MLR 711. Cf L Skene 'Proprietary Rights in Human Bodies, Body Parts and Tissue: Regulatory Context and Proposals for New Laws' (2002) 22 LS 102 and C H Harrison 'Neither Moore nor the Market: Alternative Models for Compensating Contributors of Human Tissue' (2002) 28 Am J L and Med 77.

[72] See, e.g., Nuffield Council, n 42 above, and Human Genetics Commission Inside Information: Balancing interests in the Use of Personal Genetic Data (2002), para 5.25: '. . . best practice requires that the question of commercial involvement in research or access to genetic databases should be fully explained at the time of obtaining participants' consent.'

[73] Nor could he seek to impose conditions on his donation as there is no obvious legal right to have those conditions respected, absent a contractual relationship—rare in this context.

[74] For further comments on the limits of consent in the commercialisation context see G Laurie 'Patents, Patients and Consent: Exploring the Interface between Regulation and Innovation Regimes' in J Somsen (ed), Regulating Biotechnology (2005).

[75] Support for this might now have arrived in the guise of AB v Leeds Teaching Hospital NHS Trust, discussed below, para 15.28. The criminal law is just as uncertain—a man who 'stole' a brain from a Scottish hospital mortuary was convicted of breach of the peace (2001) The Times, 12 October, p 18.

TISSUES AT MOLECULAR LEVEL

15.21   As a final point, we note the United States model federal Genetic Privacy Act 1995, which we also discuss in the context of control over genetic information in chapter 7. In an unprecedented move, this legislative framework vests a right of property in a DNA sample in the source of that sample. Thus, in addition to requiring clear written consent from the donor in respect of the gathering and use of any DNA material, the Act puts him in a stronger bargaining position in respect of any potentially profitable research work which might be carried out on his sample. Lin has argued that this approach promotes, rather than hinders, research because those previously hesitant to provide samples now have an incentive to do so.[76] We would agree, and add that it also clarifies the legal position and makes for a more principled approach to the question of ownership of body parts. The terms of such an Act could be but the first step on the road to proper recognition of ownership of one's own body and its parts. However, the experience in Oregon does not augur well. There, a property right in genetic samples was granted to citizens in 1995, but after several years of intensive lobbying by the pharmaceutical industry and research institutes, a reforming Bill was passed in June 2001 that removed this right and replaced it with more stringent privacy protection.[77] The claim was that Oregon would then have the most far-reaching privacy legislation of its kind in the United States to protect citizens' interests, but we remain convinced that the Oregon experiment was not given sufficient time for the promise and the pitfalls of a property paradigm to be addressed and explored. Similar antipathy to property rights is found elsewhere. The Australian Law Reform Commission (ALRC) recently undertook a consultation on use of human genetic material part of which contemplated whether individuals should have a form of property right in their own genetic material. The ALRC pointed out in the Issues Paper that: '[t]he recognition or creation of donor property rights might allow donors to negotiate with researchers for the use of their genetic samples and contract to share in any resulting commercial benefits'.[78] This consultation was partly prompted by the Genetic Privacy and Anti-discrimination Bill 1998 which was based on the 1995 American Act and which appeared before the Australian Parliament but was defeated. Although the Australian Bill did not go as far as to recognise a property right in samples, it did require individuals' authorisation either to waive or to receive economic benefits deriving from their samples.[79] In the final analysis, however, and having weighed the pros and cons of property and privacy approaches, the ALRC recommended that the protection of genetic samples could be achieved most effectively by changes to the

---

[76] M M J Lin 'Conferring a Federal Property Right in Genetic Material: Stepping into the Future with the Genetic Privacy Act' (1996) 22 Amer J Law Med 109.

[77] Senate Bill 114 was before the 71st Oregon Legislative Assembly (8 January–7 July 2001).

[78] ALRC *Protection of Human Genetic Information* (Issues Paper 26, 2001) para 7.47.

[79] See Senate Legal and Constitutional Legislation Committee *Provisions of the Genetic Privacy and Non-discrimination Bill 1998* (1999). There was also a right that records and samples be returned or destroyed.

Australian Privacy Act.[80] It acknowledge that '... property rights have some clear benefit: they clarify the legal rights of donor and recipient; they facilitate on-going control by the donor until such time as the property is alienated; they enable the donor or other property owner to seek legal remedies for unlawful interference with proprietary rights; and they enable a donor to share in the financial benefits that may accrue from use of the tissue'.[81] Nevertheless, the Commission ultimately felt that the disadvantages of the approach, and some potentially unlooked-for consequences, meant that 'property law may be a rather "blunt instrument" for protecting a person's interest in his or her genetic sample'.[82]

15.22   In the UK, the Human Genetics Commission did not address the prospect of a property model directly, preferring instead to fall back, once again, on the familiar consent approach.[83] In contrast, one of its more Draconian recommendations—that is, to protect genetic material by creating a criminal offence of deceitfully obtaining and analysing a person's genetic information[84]—has found its way into law. Section 45 of the Human Tissue Act 2004 creates an offence of non-consensual analysis of DNA.[85] A person commits an offence if he has bodily material *intending* that it be analysed without consent and that the results will be used other than for an 'excepted purpose'. Such purposes include medical diagnosis or treatment, discharging the functions of a coroner or procurator fiscal, prevention or detection of crime, the conduct of prosecution, national security and the implementing of court orders.[86] Research purposes can amount to 'excepted purposes' on an order of the Secretary of State. Existing holdings of material can be used lawfully for a range of health-related purposes, including clinical audit, public health monitoring and research. It should be noted that the offence is one of having possession of material *with the requisite nefarious intent*; actual analysis need not therefore take place. To this extent the offence is wider than that initially recommended by the HGC. The penalty extends to up to 3 years in prison, a fine, or both.[87]

PROPERTY IN CADAVERS AND CADAVER TISSUES

15.23   The concept that third parties can own body parts while the person from whom those parts are taken cannot do so, is also to be found in the law relating to cadavers.[88] For a long time the 'no property in a corpse' rule was thought to exclude all possibility

---

[80] Australian Law Reform Commission *Essentially Yours: The Protection of Human Genetic Information in Australia* (2003), para 20.37.

[81] *Ibid*, para 20.33.   [82] *Ibid*, para 20.34.

[83] Human Genetics Commission, n 72 above.   [84] *Ibid*, para 3.60.

[85] This is the only provision of the legislation that also extends to Scotland.

[86] S 45 and Schedule 4 of the Human Tissue Act 2004.

[87] For comment see L Skene 'Theft of DNA: Do We Need A New Criminal Offence?', available at www.ccels.cardiff.ac.uk.

[88] See, Mason and Laurie, n 71 above.

of property in a dead body or its parts in England and Wales[89]—although there is some authority in Scotland that property can exist in a corpse, at least until it is buried or otherwise disposed of.[90] The case of *R v Kelly*[91] established, however, that there are serious limitations to any such rule which may have important consequences for the users of human tissue removed from cadavers. In *Kelly* the Court of Appeal was faced with the question of whether it was theft for a junior technician of the Royal College of Surgeons to remove body parts for use, and ultimate disposal, by an artist who was interested in employing them as moulds for his sculptures. The defendants relied on the 'no property' rule as their defence. The court held that the rule refers only to a corpse or its parts which remain in their natural state, but that:

> ... parts of a corpse are capable of being property ... if they have acquired different attributes by virtue of the application of skill, such as dissection or preservation techniques, for exhibition or teaching purposes.[92]

15.24   So it was in the *Kelly* case. Work had been done on the body parts in question, such that they became specimens owned by the Royal College. To remove them without authority was, therefore, theft. The court opined, however, that the 'no property' rule is so deeply entrenched in English jurisprudence that legislative action would now be required for it to be changed *in se*. That having been said, the court went on to speculate that the common law might recognise property in human body parts even when those parts had not acquired different attributes, but if they had attracted a 'use or significance beyond their mere existence'.[93] What we are not told is who would be the holder of any such right. An answer is found, however, in an earlier ruling by the Court of Appeal, which was approved in *Kelly*.

15.25   In *Dobson v North Tyneside Health Authority*[94] the relatives of a woman who had died from brain tumours brought an action in negligence against the health authority for failure to diagnose the nature of the deceased's condition properly and in time. In order to succeed, however, it was important to establish whether the tumours were malignant or benign and this could only be done by examining samples from the deceased's brain. The brain had been removed by the hospital at an autopsy directed by the coroner; it was preserved in paraffin[95] but it had been disposed of later. The relatives therefore brought a further action against the hospital alleging that it had converted 'property' to which the relatives were entitled and that, at best, it acted as a bailee having no right of unauthorised disposal. In rejecting these claims, the Court of Appeal held that no right of possession or ownership of the brain, or indeed of the

---

[89] Nuffield Report, n 42 above, para 10.2. The Australian case *Doodeward v Spence* (1908) 6 CLR 406 is frequently cited in this regard.

[90] *Dewar v HM Advocate* 1945 JC 5 at 14. See also Whitty, n 20 above.

[91] [1998] 3 All ER 741.   [92] At 749–750.   [93] At 750.

[94] [1996] 4 All ER 474, (1996) 33 BMLR 146.

[95] One of us finds this hard to understand. Normal procedure would be to preserve the brain in formalde-hyde and to remove small pieces which would be processed into small 'paraffin blocks' for examination. The latter would present a negligible storage problem.

corpse, vested in the relatives. At best, a limited possessory right to a corpse is enjoyed by the executor or administrator of a deceased person but this right is only to possess the corpse with a view to its burial or disposal.[96] More importantly, the court held that the next of kin have no such legal right unless they assume the role of executor or administrator. Secondly, the court held that property rights could arise in respect of body parts where some work or skill differentiates the body or its parts from a corpse in its natural state. It quoted, with halting approval, the following passage from the Australian decision *Doodeward v Spence*,[97] which involved a dispute over the 'ownership' of a two-headed fetus:

... when a person has by lawful exercise of work or skill so dealt with a human body or part of a human body in his lawful possession that it has acquired some attributes differentiating it from a mere corpse awaiting burial, he acquires a right to retain possession of it, at least as against any person not entitled to have it delivered to him for the purposes of burial.

15.26   Two elements from this passage are worth noting. First, any such property right which accrues, does so to the person who does the work. Second, the property right which springs into existence is subject to the right of those with the right to possession for burial. We have already seen that no possessory right for burial purposes existed in *Dobson*. But had the brain become property? Gibson LJ did not seem to think so. The brain had not been preserved for the purposes of teaching or exhibition, nor was the case analogous to a stuffing or an embalming, which displays an intention to retain the part as a specimen. The brain had been removed and preserved only under the obligation to remove material bearing on the cause of death imposed by the Coroners Rules 1984.[98] The hospital intended to abide by these rules and was at liberty to destroy the brain once the material was no longer required by the coroner.

15.27   *Dobson* is as interesting for the questions that it does not answer as it is for those that it does. For example, as to the possessory right of executors, must the body and *all* of its parts be returned? Similarly, what is the role of intention in creating property rights? Reading *Dobson* and *Kelly* in conjunction, it seems that property rights can arise if work is done on a tissue *with the intention* of retaining the sample as a specimen or for some other purpose. But just how much, or little, work needs to be done? In *Kelly* the court indicates that dissection or preservation techniques are enough to make a sample 'property'.[99] If so, then merely to carry out an autopsy or to place a sample in formaldehyde is enough to create 'property'.[100] And, as we have seen

---

[96] No executor or administrator had been appointed in the present case until after the body had been disposed of.

[97] (1908) 6 CLR 406 at 414, per Griffith CJ.   [98] Coroners Rules 1984, SI 1984/552, r 9.

[99] [1998] 3 All ER 741 at 749–750.

[100] The Nuffield Council is of the view that 'a hospital which has tissue in its possession, for example for transplant, has such property rights over the tissue as to exclude any claim of another to it, as does a coroner or pathologist who has carried out a post-mortem and retains body parts for examination': Report at para 10.6. Without wishing to labour the point, there is a world of difference between placing a brain in preservative and preparing blocks for microscopic examination; the precise conditions obtaining in *Dobson* are, therefore, of some significance.

from *Dobson*, that property belongs to he who would 'use' the goods and certainly not to the source or his/her significant others. Thus, if the Court of Appeal in *Kelly* is correct and the common law does one day move to the position that property rights may arise because of the 'inherent' valuable attributes in tissue samples, it is undoubtedly the case that such rights will vest in the 'discoverer' of those properties. As we have seen, the long-overdue reforms of the law relating to cadavers as embodied in the Human Tissue Act 2004 leave open the position on accrual of property rights, but also leave the common law 'no property' rule untouched—including the attribution of property because of 'an application of human skill'. At the same time, the reforms extend the consent model by allowing third parties, such as next-of-kin, parents or partners, to authorise, or veto, dealings with the remains of a loved one.[101] We simply point out that consent and property are not mutually exclusive concepts; indeed, to the extent that they are both a means of furnishing respect, they should perhaps be made to work together towards a common end.[102]

15.28   Finally, a recent ruling from Gage J confirms much of the discussion above about the nature and existence of property rights in cadaver material at common law. *AB v Leeds Teaching Hospital NHS Trust*[103] concerned actions brought by aggrieved parents in respect of post-mortems performed on their dead children. Inter alia, claims were made in negligence for psychiatric injury and for wrongful interference with the body—a tort not previously recognised in English law.[104] The premise was that inadequate care and attention was exercised when obtaining parental consent to the post-mortems and that body parts of the children should not have been retained without express authority. Gage J confirmed the 'no property in a corpse' rule but that, following *Kelly*, parts of a body may acquire the character of property provided sufficient work and skill has been expended. In the particular case of the pathologist, it was stated: '. . . to dissect and fix an organ from a child's body requires work and a great deal of skill . . . The subsequent production of blocks and slides is also a skilful operation requiring work and expertise of trained scientists'.[105] Moreover, in each case the court held that the post-mortem examinations were lawfully executed and therefore capable of giving rise to possessory rights on the part of the pathologists to retained samples.[106] Any right of possession of the parents for the purposes of burial could not, from a pragmatic stance, be a right to return of every part of the body after post-mortem.[107] But what if parents make it an express stipulation of their consent to post-mortem that all body samples be returned? Here Gage J refused to create common law torts where none currently exists, namely, a tort of wrongful interference with the body or of conversion in the body. Rather, he held that such matters fall to be

---

[101] Ss 27(4) and 54(9) of the Human Tissue Act 2004.
[102] Mason and Laurie, n 71 above.   [103] [2004] 2 FLR 365, [2004] 3 FCR 324.
[104] But probably recognised in Scotland, see *Pollok v Workman* [1900] 2 F 354 and *Hughes v Robertson* [1930] SC 394, fully discussed in Whitty, n 20 above.
[105] *AB v Leeds Teaching Hospital NHS Trust*, para 148.
[106] *Ibid*, para 160.   [107] *Ibid*, para 158.

considered as a matter of negligence: the doctor who receives such instructions from parents has a duty of care to pass these on to the pathologist; he in turn is obliged to heed such a condition lest he be found to be in breach of his own duty of care.[108] We see, then, and once again, that other devices are to be employed to protect the interests at stake. It is helpful, however, to contemplate the differences here. While recognition of a property-type claim would entitle the right-holder to control (and return) of the thing itself[109]—which is what the parents sought in this case—a negligence action is for monetary compensation and requires proof of causation of a recognised form of harm, such as psychiatric injury, which can be a difficult hurdle to overcome. Property reveals different aspects to the rights currently enjoyed by patients and their families in respect of their bodies. The interests that it protects cannot wholly be subsumed within other concepts or under other rights of action.[110]

INTELLECTUAL PROPERTY LAW AND THE HUMAN BODY

15.29   We end this chapter with a consideration of intellectual property rights in the human body. We have already seen in *Moore* how a patent was granted over the 'Mo' cell-line produced using Mr Moore's cells. Certainly, patent law has had to adapt rapidly in the last few decades to meet the demands of the biotechnology industry. Astronomical sums are invested in research and development by drug companies and the industry has fought long and hard to ensure that its products receive patent protection. This, it is thought, assures a degree of return on the investment. The earning potential of the industry is tremendous. It is estimated that the world revenue for biotechnology products exceeded £70 billion in 2000, £9 billion of which was concentrated on the UK market.[111]

15.30   A patent offers an absolute monopoly for up to 20 years over an invention to the extent that all others can be excluded from competing in the marketplace with the

---

[108] *Ibid*, para 161. The court also recognised the relevance of human rights arguments to the circumstances where body parts are retained for research purposes, viz, unauthorised retention with a view to research ends is capable of engaging the right to respect for private and family life under Article 8(1) ECHR and that the circumstances in which this could be justified by the public authority under Article 8(2) '. . . will probably be rare', paras 287–300.

[109] Absent its destruction or the operation of other supervening property rights such as commixtion, confusion or specification (to use the Scottish terminology).

[110] The circumstances of this case arose from the concerns generated by the practices at Alder Hey and Bristol which became the subject of two public inquiries (see further chapter 14). This also saw the establishment of the Retained Organs Commission which issued *Recommendations on the Legal Status of Tissue Blocks and Slides* (2003; ROC17/6) in which it supported the suggestion that 'straightforward legal ownership was not a preferred option . . . tissue blocks and slides should be subject to some form of custody or stewardship . . .', *ibid*, p 1.

[111] Department of Trade and Industry *Biotechnology Clusters* (1999), para 2.1.

same, or a similar, product.[112] Strict criteria must be met to obtain protection but, once secured, a patent can protect a commercial enterprise against all comers. Yet patenting is not a morally neutral exercise and the biotechnology industry has faced considerable problems in obtaining protection for itself.[113] These problems have been particularly acute in Europe and arise because the work of the industry involves the manipulation of living organisms.[114] Thus, for many, to patent a biotechnological invention is to patent 'life' itself.[115]

15.31   Standard criteria for patentability are accepted in most countries of the world.[116] To be patentable, an invention must be new, it must involve an 'inventive step'—in the sense that the development should not be obvious to a person skilled in the particular field—and it must have utility or be made or used in any kind of industry. In the United States, there is no provision in the law to refuse registration of a patent on the grounds of morality. Thus, while it was argued in *Diamond v Chakrabarty*[117] that a patent for a genetically hybridised oil-eating bacterium should be revoked on the grounds that no patent should be given over 'life', this was rejected by the Supreme Court which held that 'Congress intended statutory subject matter to include anything under the sun that is made by man'. Similarly, when, in 1988, Harvard University sought a patent for its *ONCOmouse*—a mouse genetically engineered with a human cancer gene in such a way that it develops cancer as a matter of course—the US Patent and Trademark Office granted the patent without question.

15.32   Harvard faired significantly less well in Europe. Although an application for a patent over *ONCOmouse* was filed in 1985, this was not granted until 1991,[118] and even then its validity has been in constant doubt with further restrictions on the scope of its monopoly being imposed in 2001[119] and 2004;[120] thus, while the monopoly was

[112] See, generally, G Laurie 'Patenting and the Human Body' in A Grubb (ed) *Principles of Medical Law* (2nd edn, 2004), pp 1079–1101.

[113] For a useful historical account, see: Nuffield Council on Bioethics *The Ethics of Patenting DNA* (2002), Appendix 2. For a discussion of the practicalities in the UK healthcare context, see W R Cornish, M Llewelyn and M Adcock *Intellectual Property Rights and Genetics: A Study into the Impact and Management of Intellectual Property Rights within the Healthcare Sector* (2003) and for an interesting comparative analysis, see Australian Law Reform Commission *Genes and Ingenuity: Patenting and Human Health* (2004).

[114] S J R Bostyn 'The Prodigal Son: The Relationship Between Patent Law and Health Care' (2003) 11 Med L Rev 67.

[115] Compare A J Wells 'Patenting New Life Forms: An Ecological Perspective' (1994) 3 Euro Intellect Prop Rev 111 and S Crespi 'Biotechnology Patents: The Wicked Animal Must Defend Itself' (1995) 9 Euro Intellect Prop Rev 431.

[116] In the US the law is contained in 35 USC paras 101, 102 and 103. The UK equivalent is found in the Patents Act 1977, s 1(1). This embodies the terms of the European Patent Convention (1973) which now has 30 signatory states (as of 1 January 2005). A degree of harmonisation of patent criteria was achieved with the establishment of the TRIPS Agreement (Trade Related Aspects of Intellectual Property Rights) at the Uruguay Round of GATT in 1994. The Agreement is administered by the World Trade Organization which had 148 member countries as of 16 February 2005.

[117] 447 US 303, 66 L Ed 2d 144 (1980).   [118] [1991] EPOR 525.

[119] A Abbott 'Harvard Squeaks Through Oncomouse Patent Appeal' (2001) 414 Nature 241. This reduced the scope of claim from 'transgenic mammals' to 'transgenic rodents'.

[120] T315/03 Oncomouse/Harvard, EPO, July 2004, summary available at: www.european-patent-office.org.

originally granted to cover 'transgenic mammals', it is now restricted only to 'transgenic mice'. In essence, the problem of patent protection faced by the biotechnology industry in Europe stems from the 'morality provisions' of the European Patent Convention 1973 (EPC), which embodies the patent law of 30 European countries as of 1 January 2005. Article 53 of the EPC states:

European patents shall not be granted in respect of:

(a) inventions the publication or exploitation of which would be contrary to *ordre public* or morality, provided that the exploitation shall not be deemed to be so contrary merely because it is prohibited by law or regulation in some or all of the Contracting States;

(b) plant or animal varieties or essentially biological processes for the production of plants or animals; this provision does not apply to microbiological processes or the products thereof.

15.33   The Harvard patent was challenged both on the grounds that it was inherently immoral to patent 'life' under Article 53(a) and because it was an attempt to patent an 'animal variety' under Article 53(b).[121] Yet, in *HARVARD/ONCOmouse*,[122] the Examining Division of the European Patent Office allowed the patent in respect of (a) because it held that the morality question is to be tested by balancing, on the one hand suffering of the animal, with, on the other, the potential benefits to humanity. The 'carrot' of a potential cure for cancer tipped the scales in favour of patentability. In respect of (b) it was held that the 'invention' being claimed was a 'non-human mammal' and this was much broader than a mere 'animal variety'; therefore, no problem arose under Article 53(b).[123] Neither of these interpretations has been disturbed by the latest edicts from the Opposition Division. Such linguistic gymnastics are clearly driven by policy concerns as to the attractiveness of Europe to the investor in biotechnology. Laws which are too strict act as a disincentive and encourage more investment in the United States where morality in this field is, seemingly, not a problem. But when we enter the domain of human material we find that a broader range of policy considerations enters the fray, setting off a whole new set of interpretative cartwheels on the part of the European Patent Office.

15.34   Patents over human material have been granted for a number of years. For example, over 1,175 human DNA patents were granted in the period 1981–95, mainly in the United States. Yet, as with ONCOmouse, the European Patent Office (EPO) has had to deal with moral objections to such patents. The invention in dispute in *HOWARD FLOREY/Relaxin*[124] concerned H2 Relaxin, a protein produced naturally by women at the time of childbirth which softens the pelvis and so eases the passage of the child.

---

[121] *HARVARD/ONCOmouse* [1990] EPOR 4.   [122] [1991] EPOR 525.
[123] Opposition proceedings were immediately started by 16 groups after this decision.
[124] [1995] EPOR 541.

Howard Florey genetically engineered this protein and sought a patent for the artificial chemical. It was argued before the Opposition Division of the EPO, first, that it would be tantamount to slavery to grant a patent for such a product, in that it involved the sale of human tissue; secondly, that this too was exploitative and an offence to human dignity; and, finally, that any patent over DNA is inherently immoral because DNA is 'life'. Each of these arguments was rejected out of hand by the Division. It held that there can be no question of slavery because no woman is forced to surrender material—all the subjects consented. Similarly, it was not necessarily exploitative to use human material because free and informed consent was given; the Division pointed out that human material is used in a variety of contexts without the question of exploitation arising. Finally, it was held that DNA is not 'life' but a chemical substance which carries genetic information: 'no woman is affected in any way by the present patent.'[125] The general policy of the EPO has been to interpret the exceptions to patentability narrowly and to presume that the protection criteria are satisfied unless a strong contrary case can be shown.[126]

15.35   The controversy surrounding the morality of patenting DNA and genetically engineered products has also been addressed by European law, primarily in the name of protecting the EU's Single Market. After a very difficult passage lasting 10 years, a European Directive was eventually adopted in July 1998 in an attempt to clarify the legal position in respect of biotechnological patents.[127] Guidance is given on the kinds of invention which will never receive patent protection,[128] and the morality provision as defined in *ONCOmouse* is incorporated in a modified, although still relatively imprecise, form.[129] Indeed, a number of member states have yet to implement the Directive because of general uncertainty about its terms,[130] while others have unsuccessfully challenged its validity alleging, inter alia, that it entails a breach of the principle of legal certainty and a breach of the fundamental right to respect for human dignity.

15.36   Once again, however, the interpretative authority in charge—this time the European Court of Justice—took a narrow view of the circumstances, and upheld the

---

[125] At 550–551.

[126] See, e.g., *PLANT GENETIC SYSTEMS/Glutamine Synthetase Inhibitors* [1995] EPOR 357 and *LELAND STANFORD/Modified Animal* [2002] EPOR 2 (immuno-compromised chimera mouse was patentable—controversial technology not in itself a bar to patenting).

[127] Directive of the European Parliament and of the Council on the Legal Protection of Biotechnological Inventions, No 98/44/EC of 6 July 1998.

[128] Under Article 6 the following are unpatentable: (a) processes for cloning human beings; (b) processes for modifying the germ line genetic identity of human beings; (c) uses of human embryos for industrial or commercial purposes; (d) processes for modifying the genetic identity of animals which are likely to cause them suffering without any substantial medical benefit to man or animal, and also animals resulting from such processes.

[129] Article 6 requires that a *substantial medical* benefit accrue to humanity or animals before the morality test will be satisfied.

[130] Eight members were referred to the European Court of Justice in July 2003 when further negotiations with the Commission came to nothing (IP/03/911, 10 July 2003).

Directive both as to its legitimacy as an instrument of European law and as to its substantive content re: European patent law.[131]

15.37 This narrowness of approach in respect of interpreting patent law has, however, most recently been challenged by the advent of human embryonic stem cell patents.[132] While it has been possible to derive stem cells from adults for over 40 years, and from animals, including animal embryos, for almost a quarter of a century, human embryonic stem cells were only first isolated in 1998. This date is significant, being also the year when the EC Directive on the legal protection of biotechnological inventions was adopted. Accordingly, there are no specific provisions on human embryonic stem cells contained within that document. None the less, certain key provisions of the Directive can be seen to have direct application. These are:

Article 5(1): The human body, at the various stages of its formation and development, and the simple discovery of one of its elements, including the sequence or partial sequence of a gene, cannot constitute patentable inventions.

Article 6(1) Inventions shall be considered unpatentable where their commercial exploitation would be contrary to *ordre public* or morality; . . . (2) the following, in particular, shall be considered unpatentable: (a) processes for cloning human beings; . . . (c) uses of human embryos for industrial or commercial purposes . . .;

15.38 From the ethical perspective, research using the human embryo is problematic for a number of reasons, all of which centre around the moral status of this organism. The concern surrounding embryonic stem cell technologies is that—*at the present time*—we must both use and destroy a human embryo to produce valuable embryonic stem cell cultures.[133]

15.39 The European Group on Ethics reported on stem cell patents in 2002,[134] noting that by that time over 2000 applications had been lodged worldwide in respect of stem cell technologies, 500 of which related to Embryonic Stem Cells (ES cells). Of these ES cells applications, around 25 per cent had been granted, that is, there had been around 125 patent grants. But because of the ethical concerns surrounding embryonic stem cell technologies and the prospect of commercialisation through patenting, the EGE opined that certain *early stage interventions* should be excluded from protection. These can best be understood through the use of the diagram below.

But the EGE Opinion was dealt a fatal blow by the Opposition Division (OD) of the European Patent Office (EPO) in a decision that followed only a few months after the Opinion's release. In July 2002, the OD considered the opposition arguments to the

---

[131] *Netherlands v European Parliament (C377/98)* [2002] All ER (EC) 97. Note, the Directive only harmonised the law in the 15 member states of the European Union (now 25), but the implementing regulations of the European Patent Convention have been amended to reflect the terms of the morality provisions of the Directive to ensure consistency of approach across the 30 signatory countries to the EPC.

[132] For a discussion, see G Laurie 'Patenting Stem Cells of Human Origin' [2004] European Int Prop Rev 59.

[133] For a recent moral evaluation, see J C Polkinghorne 'The Person, The Soul, and Genetic Engineering' (2004) 30 J Med Ethics 593.

[134] European Group on Ethics in Science and New Technologies *Ethical Aspects of Patenting Inventions Involving Human Stem Cells*, Opinion No. 16, 17 May 2002.

Time	EUROPEAN GROUP ON ETHICS
	• Processes for *creation* of embryo by cloning for stem cells [unpatentable]
	DAY '0'—CREATION OF EMBRYOS
	• Isolated stem cells [unpatentable] • Unmodified stem cell lines [unpatentable] • Inventions allowing the transformation of unmodified stem cells into modified stem cell lines [patentable] • All processes involving stem cells of whatever source [patentable]

so-called 'Edinburgh patent', held by the University of Edinburgh, and relating to *animal* transgenic stem cells. This had raised concerns when it was suggested that it might extend to human cloning because, in scientific terms, the taxonomy of 'animal' includes 'human'. Accordingly, the patent was amended so as to exclude mention of human or animal embryonic stem cells, although it still covers other *modified* human and animal stem cells.

15.40   The OD was called upon to interpret Article 53(a) of the European Patent Convention (EPC) and Rule 23d(c) EPC, following which European patents shall not be granted for *uses of human embryos for industrial or commercial purposes*. The OD noted that the provision could be interpreted in two ways: *narrowly*, to mean that only commercial uses of human embryos *as such* are excluded from patentability, or *broadly*, to mean that human embryonic stem cells—which as we have noted can only be obtained by destroying an embryo—are also not patentable. The OD preferred the latter approach, arguing that since embryos *as such* are already protected by Rule 23(e) (equivalent of Article 5(1) of the EC Directive), a similar interpretation of Rule 23(d)(c) (equivalent of Article 6(2)(c) of the EC Directive) would be redundancy and this could not have been the intention of the legislator.

15.41   Although the EGE Opinion was considered for guidance by the OD in reaching its decision, it was rejected *in toto* because 'classic concepts of patent law are misinterpreted and confused'. While this is not the place to engage with the relative merits of the Opinion or the views of the OD, it is pertinent to point out that the OD felt confident in rejecting entirely the considered views of a group of ethical experts on the essential questions and the approach to be adopted. This is in stark contrast with the earlier cautious approach of the OD and Examining Divisions (ED) of the EPO which demonstrated extreme reluctance to engage with ethical issues—indeed one ED professed no authority in this domain.[135]

15.42   Such an approach has, none the less, recently been reinforced and even extended by a ruling of the Examining Division in July 2004. The Wisconsin Alumni Research Foundation (WARF) was responsible for developing the first techniques to isolate

---

[135] *Harvard/Oncomouse* [1990] EPOR 4.

human embryonic stem cells in 1998,[136] and holds a patent over the technology in a number of jurisdictions. This ruling concerned an application for 'European' patents from the EPO in respect of 'primate embryonic stem cells'. The application was for embryonic stem cell cultures themselves—i.e. stem cell *products*—but the application also disclosed the means to make such products, as one would expect. Thus the application disclosed a method for preparing ES cells from primate blastocysts. It was accepted, but not demonstrated in the application, that this method was also enabling of the production of human ES cells. Moreover, the sole method of production of the stem cell cultures that was described involved the use, and destruction, of embryos.

15.43　　The Examining Division held that all of the claims which could be extended to human embryonic stem cells were invalid on grounds of immorality. It did so on the basis of an extremely literal and broad interpretation of Rule 23(d)(c): 'European patents are not to be granted in respect of . . . inventions which concern . . . uses of human embryos for industrial or commercial purposes.' In sum, the Division held that: 'The use of an embryo as starting material for the generation of a product of industrial application is considered equal to industrial use of this embryo'. The rationale here is that the claimed cultures are inseparable from the means to make them. It is, therefore, in a literal sense, necessary to 'use' embryos to create the claimed invention. The message from this ruling is that the moral concern goes far beyond patenting itself and extends to general instrumentalisation. It implies that mere involvement—use—of embryos in the research and development of an invention is sufficient to bar the patentability of that invention.

15.44　　We consider that, well-intended as it is, the morality provision in European patent law is ill-placed. Primarily, this is because it can never attain that which it was designed to achieve. The crucial point is that the refusal of a grant of a patent does nothing directly to prevent the creative process from continuing. Thus, Harvard could continue to produce the mouse for sale on the open market even if ONCOmouse had never been given a patent—all that would be lost would be a chance to monopolise that market. If one is concerned by the act of creation itself, and this must be the main concern in these cases, then attention should be turned not to the point at which protection is offered, but to the point at which the creation takes place.[137] This cannot be done through the law of patents but, rather, through other mechanisms such as the introduction of regulatory schemes or the creation of authorities which can monitor the industry. Making morality part of patent law does nothing to regulate the biotechnology industry. Moreover, allowing patent law to drive the regulatory and innovation systems is a dangerous formula.

15.45　　Some insight into the problems of failing to maintain some sort of boundary

---

[136] J A Thomson et al 'Embryonic Stem Cell Lines Derived from Human Blastocysts' (1998) 282 Science 1145.

[137] This is argued more fully in G T Laurie 'Biotechnology: Facing the Problems of Patent Law' in H L MacQueen and B G M Bain (eds) *Innovation, Incentive and Reward: Intellectual Property Law and Policy* (1997) Hume Papers on Public Policy 46.

between patent law and regulatory regimes can be gained by considering the possible effect of the current stem cell patent rulings on countries where stem cell research is both legal and encouraged. The United Kingdom is one such country. The UK has a robust regulatory framework for embryo research administered by the Human Fertilisation and Embryology Authority (HFEA). As we saw in chapter 4, the HFEA operates a licensing system whereby research is only authorised under licence and it is a criminal offence to conduct it otherwise. At present, the HFEA has granted licences in respect of 28 research projects, 10 of which relate to embryonic stem cells and 2 on parthenogenesis.[138] The HFEA has also recently granted the first licence in Europe to allow therapeutic cloning to produce embryonic stem cells.[139] The British government provides millions of pounds a year to encourage research in this field. The ethics of embryo research and stem cell research have been considered by a number of respected national bodies before legal authority was given for the work to be done.[140] But now, in light of the rulings from the EPO in terms of patent incentives, what will be the impact on the future of the UK's research programme? While the possibility remains for national patents only, the influence of the European framework cannot be ignored in practice nor should it be overlooked in principle.

15.46   Other features of patent law are problematic for the health care sector, especially in the realm of pharmaceuticals.[141] The monopolistic right that a patent gives to an inventor potentially prevents many individuals from gaining access to vital medicines, as the recent South African AIDS drugs debacle demonstrated only too well.[142] The European Parliament issued a Resolution in October 2001 calling on the EPO to reconsider the grant of patents to Myriad Genetics over the genes for breast cancer, BRCA1 and BRCA2,[143] and the patents were the subject of opposition proceedings before the EPO instigated by the Institut Curie, the Assistance Publique-Hôpitaux de Paris and the Institut Gustave-Roussy. The concern is summed up by the Nuffield Council on Bioethics in its discussion paper on the ethics of patenting DNA:

The opposition is aimed at curtailing any possible deleterious consequences which might stem from sanctioning the monopoly conferred on Myriad Genetics, including the possible threat to the development of research and the identification of new tests and diagnostic methods. It has also been argued that the patent will have a serious impact on equitable

---

[138] Human Fertilisation and Embryology Authority homepage: www.hfea.gov.uk/Home.

[139] 'Scientists given cloning go-ahead', BBC News, 11 August 2004: http://news.bbc.co.uk/1/hi/health/3554474.stm.

[140] The entire field was the subject of the influential Warnock Report, *Report of the Committee of Inquiry into Human Fertilisation and Embryology* (Cmnd 9314, 1984), which paved the way for the legislation. More recently, the advent of stem cells has been considered by the Nuffield Council on Bioethics, *Stem Cell Therapy: The Ethical Issues*, 2000.

[141] B Domeij 'Patent Claim Scope: Initial and Follow-on Pharmaceutical Inventions' [2001] EIPR 326.

[142] In which the companies sought, quite legally, to forestall the production of cheaper generic drugs 'Drug Giants Bow to AIDS Campaign' *The Times*, 20 April 2001, p 23. See further, Laurie n 112 above.

[143] European Parliament *Resolution on the Patenting of BRCA1 and BRCA2 ('Breast Cancer') Genes* (4 October 2001, B5–0633, 0641, 0651, and 0663/2001).

access to testing. It is suggested that the monopoly is antithetical to an approach to public health that is based on a commitment to the comprehensive care of patients at high-risk.[144]

15.47 Moreover, and as the Council goes on to point out, there are currently no other methods of diagnosing the presence of the breast cancer susceptibility gene BRCA1 that can be used without infringing the patents because of the way in which Myriad Genetics has used its patent monopolies worldwide.[145] The patents were eventually revoked in 2004[146] but for technical reasons of patentability rather than on a principled approach as to whether and to whom patent monopolies should be granted.

15.48   There are numerous responses that we might have to these principled arguments. One could be to deny patent protection altogether, but this is an unrealistic prospect and may be counter-productive if the venture capitalists are to be believed—they would simply cease funding the research necessary to produce the products in the first place.[147] More realistically, there is much that can be done to work within and to improve the current patent system. For example, standards of drafting patent applications should be strengthened to ensure (i) that inventions are properly described and (ii) that unsustainable claims to protection are not made. This, in turn, would facilitate a more rigorous examination process that should ensure that protection is granted only to innovations that are truly inventive and which have never been made available to the public. Indeed, the Nuffield Council has argued that patents over gene sequences themselves would become the exception, not the norm, if the criteria for patentability were more properly applied.[148] Ultimately, patent offices and courts must work together more closely so as to limit the effects of overly broad patents, by restricting protection to the precise contribution that an invention makes to human knowledge and no further.[149] A recent novel approach—and unique as far as we know—is illustrated by the case of PXE International which is a patient and family support group for those affected by the genetic disorder pseudoxanthoma elasticum. The group announced in 2004 that one of its leading members had been named as a co-inventor of the gene associated with the condition together with the scientists responsible for its isolation. All rights have been assigned to PXE International which considers itself the 'steward of the gene'. The Group has now entered various

---

[144] Nuffield Council, n 113 above, para 4.6. This specific problem is discussed in G Matthijs 'Patenting Genes' (2004) 329 BMJ 1358.

[145] At para 5.4.

[146] See the European Patent Office website: www.european-patent-office.

[147] This consideration influenced the European Group on Ethics in Science and New Technologies (EGE) in its report on patenting human stem cells wherein it concluded that it would not be in the public interest to exclude patent protection altogether. Instead the Group recommended more rigorous ethical evaluation of controversial patent applications, see EGE Opinion No. 16, n 134 above, paras 2.1 and 2.10.

[148] A similar view is expressed by the British Medical Association *Gene Patenting: A BMA Discussion Paper* (2001). A key feature of the argument is the assertion that much of the work of the biotechnology industry to produce gene sequences is 'obvious' i.e. lacks 'inventive step' and so would not attract patent protection.

[149] Another option is to make more use of compulsory licences, but there is a significant industry cultural resistance to this in many quarters, especially in the United States.

agreements to pursue further research and develop a diagnostic kit.[150] This is an example of interest groups working together within the patent system to pursue mutually beneficial ends. The only negative comment that could be made about the arrangement is that it is, at present, a very rare beast indeed.

15.49   Most radically, however, the grant of a patent could be made conditional on the assumption of certain attendant responsibilities to the community. For example, the Human Genome Organisation's Ethics Committee (HUGO) recommended in April 2000 that: 'profit-making entities dedicate a percentage (e.g. 1–3 per cent) of their annual net profit to healthcare infrastructure and/or to humanitarian efforts'.[151] There is no reason why this quid pro quo should not become part of patent law, provided that there is sufficient political will to make it so. It is a form of benefit-sharing that could go a long way to restoring public trust in privately-funded research,[152] and it might give a more acceptable face to the prospect of patenting the human genome.[153]

CONCLUSION

15.50   It seems that whether we are dealing with living or dead human tissue, whether we are looking at humanity at the structured or the molecular level, or whether we are considering domestic or international regulation, we are faced with a schizoid approach to property rights in human material. On the one hand, there is an innate antipathy to the concept; on the other, we accept the inexorable march of 'science' knowing that, if something is there to be discovered, someone will discover it—and with little concern for the consequences. Governments may set up regulatory authorities as the significance of each scientific advance becomes apparent but they are relatively powerless in the face of global international pressures. What does seem clear is that, so far as the domestic scene is concerned, our courts must appreciate that this is a field in which technology and societal attitudes are advancing and being fashioned rapidly—and the common law must keep pace and accelerate as is necessary. Put in a nutshell, the legal issues involving the DNA double helix can no longer be resolved by way of authority derived from the exhibition of an anatomical aberration in a nineteenth-century fairground.

---

[150] See the PXE website: www.pxe.org.

[151] HUGO Ethics Committee, *Statement on Benefit-Sharing* (2000).

[152] We discuss this further in G Laurie and K G Hunter 'Benefit Sharing and Public Trust in Genetic Research' in G Arnason, S Nordal and V Arnason (eds) *Blood and Data: Ethical, Legal and Social Aspects of Human Genetic Databases*, University of Iceland Press, 2004, pp 323–331.

[153] At least one governmental advisory body has recommended the adoption of such a scheme, see Canadian Biotechnology Advisory Committee *Patenting of Higher Life Forms and Related Issues: Report to the Government of Canada Biotechnology Ministerial Coordinating Committee* (2002), p 18.

16

MEDICAL FUTILITY

PART I: THE BEGINNING OF LIFE

16.1   It is probably fair to say that the health care professional will, intuitively, seek to prolong life so long as it is possible to do so. The massive technological advances of the last half century have increased our capabilities in this respect and, perhaps because of this, we have become more and more aware that, occasionally, the preservation of life can be a negative blessing. Such an assessment may come from the patient him- or herself—in which case we are in the field of euthanasia, which we discuss in chapter 17. Alternatively, the health carers may, themselves, raise the question, not as to whether it is in the patient's interest that he or she should live or die but, rather, whether his or her death should be prolonged by medical care. In other words, there are times when we must ask ourselves if treatment should be considered futile and should be abandoned—and such moments will arise with patients of any age. Even so, there are two situations in which life and death decisions become fundamental and unavoidable—when we are born and when we are dying. It is for this reason that we have divided the discussion into two sections dealing, respectively, with the beginning and the end of life; it must, at the same time, be recognised that the principles derived can be applied at any intervening time.

16.2   When the first edition of this book was written, selective non-treatment of the newborn and, most particularly, withholding the means of survival from mentally handicapped infants were burning issues; it is fair to say that the legal and ethical standards in this area are, now, relatively stable. In the interim, however, a comparable flurry of interest developed around the management of the incompetent adult, with greatest importance attaching, in this instance, to the patient in the persistent or permanent vegetative state. Categories have become blurred in the process. Much as we predicted originally, selective non-treatment of the newborn has progressed to selective non-treatment of the defective child, while the infant whose brain has been destroyed by meningitis can be used as a model for the adolescent who is similarly affected. It is somewhat ironic that the long and careful deliberations of the House of Lords in *Bland*[1] can trace their origins to the thoroughly unsatisfactory case of *Arthur*.[2]

---

[1] *Airedale NHS Trust v Bland* [1993] 1 All ER 821, (1993) 12 BMLR 64, Fam D, CA, HL.
[2] *R v Arthur* (1981) 12 BMLR 1.

16.3   All such situations, which form a continuum from neonatal deformity, through the permanent vegetative state, to the catastrophically afflicted adult, have it in common that treatment may be contraindicated on the grounds either that it is achieving no medical effect or that continued treatment can be seen as being against the patient's best interests. These can be subsumed together under the general heading of futility. Simple as this analysis appears to be, attempts to reach a universally satisfactory definition of 'futility' do little more that open a Pandora's box of conflicting moral values—for it cannot be denied that it raises the curtain on what is no less than the first act in the wider drama of euthanasia. Thus, while we find the concept useful, albeit in a restricted way, we cannot introduce it without some consideration of its limitations.

THE CONCEPT OF MEDICAL FUTILITY

16.4   Before starting the discussion, however, it is well to clear up what may become a source of trans-Atlantic misconception. The term in the United States has been seen generally as a shorthand way to describe the situation in which a patient demands and a physician objects to the provision of a particular medical treatment on the ground that the treatment will provide no medical benefit to the patient.[3] This definition, in introducing an element of conflict, is restrictive and, we believe, self-defeating. Conflict there may be, but an essential aspect of the regime is that it should be carried out, so far as is possible, in an atmosphere of mutual understanding and agreement—and it is with this aim in mind that we address the subject.

16.5   The basis for the concept of futility is certainly not new. More than three decades ago, it was said:

> The whole resources of an advanced medical service are currently deployed in the pursuit of the preservation of life. It is becoming obvious that the costs of this policy are becoming insupportable . . . We must face an inescapable duty to let some patients die.[4]

16.6   The philosophy behind this approach was widely accepted during the 1980s but has since been challenged on several grounds. First, it confuses futility or non-productivity of treatment with rationing of resources; secondly, it suggests that doctors can and should select their patients for treatment by way of their own judgments as to their relative worth; thirdly, the statement, as it stands, conflicts head-on with the rapidly evolving respect for the principle of patient autonomy; and, finally, it speaks in the language of duty while, at the same time, failing to identify the beneficiary of that duty. All of which lead us directly to the question—what do we mean by futility?

---

[3] J F Daar 'Medical Futility and Implications for Physician Autonomy' (1995) 21 Am J Law Med 221.
[4] E Slater 'Severely Malformed Children: Wanted—A New Approach' (1973) I BMJ 285.

16.7   Even then, this question can be formulated in a number of ways. Who is to make the definition—the patient, his surrogate or the doctor? And, if it is the last, what is his objective standard—for one man's futility is another's courageous effort.[5] Equally, reliance on, say, the surrogate is bound to end in conflict because, as we will see later—and despite some moral doubts on the part of respected American bio-ethicists[6]—no doctor in the United Kingdom can be compelled to provide a particular treatment against his better judgment.[7]

16.8   Can we refine this choice more closely by considering the quality of the decision to be made? We could, for example, define futile treatment as care that does not accomplish its intended purpose—in which case, a respirator that kept a person breathing could never be classed as providing futile treatment irrespective of the status of the patient. Despite later legal intervention,[8] this is clearly not how the medical profession intended the term to be used; Jecker and Pearlman[9] reviewed the literature and identified four major alternative definitions of futility:

(a) treatment which was either useless or ineffective;

(b) that which fails to offer a minimum quality of life or a modicum of medical benefit;

(c) treatment that cannot possibly achieve the patient's goals; or

(d) treatment which does not offer a reasonable chance of survival.

16.9   This mix demonstrates very well the fundamental distinction which must be made between, on the one hand, the *effect* of a treatment—which is no more than an alteration in some bodily function—and, on the other, the *benefit* of a treatment—which is something that can be appreciated by the patient.[10] Put another way, the need is to distinguish between physiological and normative futility[11]—in which case, it is arguable that the former is to be decided on purely medical grounds while the latter involves a quality or value judgment which is the prerogative of the patient or his surrogates.[12] Against which, it has been said that medical judgments are never value-free[13] and that to abandon such judgments at the behest of the patient is to subvert the

[5] R Lofmark and T Nilstun 'Conditions and Consequences of Medical Futility—From a Literature Review to a Clinical Model' (2002) 28 J Med Ethics 115.

[6] E.g. R M Veatch and C M Spicer 'Futile Care: Physicians Should Not Be Allowed to Refuse to Treat' in T L Beauchamp and R M Veatch *Ethical Issues in Death and Dying* (1996) p 392.

[7] At best, a doctor who refuses to pursue a particular course of action will have a duty of care to find a colleague is prepared to do so, see *R (on the application of Burke) v General Medical Council* [2004] 3 FCR 579, discussed further below at paras 16.88 et seq.

[8] See para 16.21 et seq below.

[9] N S Jecker and R A Pearlman 'Medical Futility: Who Decides?' (1992) 152 Arch Intern Med 1140.

[10] L J Schneiderman and N S Jecker 'Futility in Practice' (1993) 153 Arch Intern Med 437.

[11] Veatch and Spicer, n 6 above.

[12] The major part of an issue (1992) 20 Med Law Hlth Care was given over to the problem. See, in particular, R Cranford and L Gostin 'Futility: A Concept in Search of a Definition' at 307.

[13] For recognition and engagement with this reality, see S Bailey, 'The Concept of Futility in Health Care Decision Making' (2004) 11 Nursing Ethics 77.

core of medical professionalism.[14] The doctor's dilemma can, perhaps, best be appreciated in terms of objective. When the primary aim of the health carer is to preserve life, futility only has a role to play when life can no longer be preserved—a relatively simple concept. However, matters become altogether more complicated when the doctor assumes the role of quality of life provider—futility then assumes a role which is far less clear cut and this is particularly so when decisions are made as to life or death. In such cases, medical intervention *may* keep the patient alive but, none the less, futility is advanced as a justification for allowing him or her to die. Futility then becomes not futility in the face of death but, rather, futility in the face of an unacceptable quality of life, which is a far more subjective construct, and one on which the competent patient himself will doubtless have views.[15]

16.10   Thus, the whole topic of medical futility—when seen as a concept rather than as a series of problem-solving exercises—is fraught with difficulties and contradictions.[16] It has been said that futility is not only a word which is foreign to the families of handicapped neonates but it is also one which is unacceptable because of its hopelessness; its use militates against achieving the proper societal response.[17] Gillon believed that 'when judgments are to be used as a basis for withholding or withdrawing potentially life prolonging treatment, they had better be made rather precisely and preferably expressed in terms that are less ambiguous, complicated and distressing'.[18] While it is clear that we accept the *medical* principles behind selective non-treatment of the newborn,[19] of 'do-not-resuscitate' orders and of withdrawal of treatment from persons in the permanent vegetative state, we have great sympathy with those who object to futility on *semantic* and *philosophical* grounds. We much prefer to speak of non-productive treatment, which places the problem firmly in the medical field and, as a result, carries the added advantage of clarity of intention.[20] Meantime, it is suggested that non-productivity and futility can be reconciled if the latter concept is confined to Schneiderman and Jecker's summary definition:

A treatment which cannot provide a minimum likelihood or quality of benefit should be regarded as futile and is not owed to the patient as a matter of moral duty.[21]

[14] J F Drane and J L Coulehan 'The Concept of Futility: Patients Do Not Have a Right to Demand Medically Useless Treatment' (1993) 74 Hlth Prog 28; H Brody 'Medical Futility: A Useful Concept?' in M B Zucker and H D Zucker (eds) *Medical Futility* (1997), ch 1. This is an outstanding book on the subject.

[15] See A Lelie and M Verweij 'Futility Without Dichotomy: Towards an Ideal Physician-Patient Relationship' (2003) 17 Bioethics 21.

[16] See D L Kasman 'When is Medical Treatment Futile?' (2004) 19 J Gen Intern Med 1053.

[17] B Anderson and B Hall 'Parents' Perceptions of Decision Making for Children' (1995) 23 J Law Med & Ethics 15; C Weijer and C Elliott 'Pulling the Plug on Futility' (1995) 310 BMJ 683.

[18] R Gillon ' "Futility"—Too Ambiguous and Pejorative A Term?' (1997) 23 J Med Ethics 339.

[19] We have retained this expression because it is well established. Paediatricians will, however, point out that it covers a period of care which demands particular clinical and nursing skills. Everyone should read I Laing 'Withdrawing from Invasive Neonatal Intensive Care' in J K Mason (ed) *Paediatric Forensic Medicine and Pathology* (1989).

[20] We discuss this concept in greater detail at para 16.15 et seq.

[21] See n 10 above.

16.11 Schneiderman and Jecker have also reminded us that there are *positive* dangers of abuse if the term 'futile treatment' is adopted uncritically within the medical vocabulary. These include the resurgence of inappropriate paternalism, the erosion of patient autonomy, the unjustified avoidance of the duty to treat—or, we might add, the creation of an ephemeral duty *not* to treat—and the introduction of disguised and arbitrary rationing of resources.[22] Many of these pitfalls are revealed in the cases which follow.

SELECTIVE NON-TREATMENT OF THE NEWBORN

16.12 It is apparent that we regard the problem of non-productive treatment as one that is common to all ages; nevertheless, selective non-treatment of the newborn retains some unique features. First, it is intimately bound up with the subject of abortion—in so far as a large proportion of conditions which call for 'futile' neonatal treatments were present and were diagnosable in utero and, as such, constituted grounds for legal termination of pregnancy by way of the Abortion Act 1967, s 1(1)(d). What, then, of those affected fetuses which come to full term undiagnosed? Where do public opinion and the law stand between the opposite extremes, on the one hand, of upholding a right to life and, on the other, of supporting medical assessments that intervention to sustain life is a pointless exercise? There has to be a middle road but, in the case of the neonate, we have had to find it without the aid of statute.

16.13 Second, treatment decisions taken immediately after birth concern human beings who are at the most vulnerable period of their lives—human beings, moreover, who cannot express their feelings for the present or the future and who clearly cannot have indicated their preferences to their surrogates. Parents faced with decision-making at this point are likely to agree with their medical advisers simply because they have no evidence on which to *disagree*. It is only when the bonds of adversity have been cemented between the parents and the disabled infant that the former are likely to have developed strong independent opinions as to which treatments are appropriate. As a result, the majority of cases in which the court is called upon to adjudicate concern disabled infants rather than neonates. But in both cases the nascent personality of the child often acts like a blank page on which the court will write its own version of the child's interests in his life; in contrast, the seriously-compromised adult has at least experienced enough to create his own biographical life, and this can lead the courts to differing interpretations of 'best interests' in the cases of adults compared to the newborn, as we shall see.

16.14 Whatever the age or condition of the patient, however, the 'futility' debate is, as discussed above, likely to be conducted at the 'quality of life' level. We have, however, not yet considered whether this is, of itself, a morally tenable level. Have we the right to place relative values on lives or is all life sacrosanct? This question represents the foundation stone of the futility argument and, while it is applied throughout the

---

[22] M Wreen 'Medical Futility and Physician Discretion' (2004) 30 J Med Ethics 275.

spectrum of selective treatment, it is convenient to discuss it in the context of the early stages of human development.

Sanctity or quality of life?

16.15   The doctor's dilemma is self-evident—is he or she practising truly 'good' medicine in keeping alive a neonate who will be unable to take a place in society or who will be subject to pain and suffering throughout life? In short, is one to displace a concept of the sanctity of life based on a Hippocratic and theological foundation by a standard related to the quality of life which is, essentially, justified by a utilitarian ethos?[23] The situation gives rise to a catalogue of questions—of which the first might well be to ask if there is, in fact, any solid basis for what has become known as the 'sanctity of life doctrine'. This seems to us to be, at least, doubtful, particularly if the doctrine is to be interpreted in terms of vitalism—or 'the sanctity of life at any price'. The Hippocratic Oath proscribes euthanasia but neither it, nor the more contemporary Declaration of Geneva impose an obligation to provide treatment at all times; rather, the emphasis is on doing no harm—an approach which clearly allows for pragmatic interpretation. A persuasive case can also be made out for there being no theological imperative to regard human life as sacrosanct.[24]

16.16   Even so, while vitalism has been largely rejected, a modified concept of the sanctity of life is widely endorsed; the debate continues as to the acceptable extent of that modification and, in its turn, raises a number of derived questions, many of which are unanswerable in the abstract. Who is to determine the minimum quality of life? Whose life are we considering—the infant's? or are we also taking into account that of the parents or, indeed, the well-being of society? Do we, in fact, *want* a society in which the right to life depends upon achieving a norm which is largely measured in material terms? Should the disabled infant whose dying is needlessly prolonged be helped on its way?—and, if so, is this help to be a matter of omission or should positive steps be taken to end life? And, behind all these, now lies the Human Rights Act 1998 with its implications under Article 2 (the right to life), Article 3 (the right not to be subjected to inhuman or degrading treatment) and Article 8 (the right to respect for private and family life) of the European Convention.

16.17   In the discussion of euthanasia which follows in chapter 17, stress is laid on the relationship between the quality of life and the proportionate or disproportionate treatment which is needed to maintain that quality. But the quality of the therapeutic environment at the beginning of life is very hard to assess. Not only can the patient express no opinion but, were it possible, he or she has no yardstick by which to judge; as put by McKenzie J in Canada:

---

[23] A classic review is to be found in L Gostin 'A Moment in Human Development: Legal Protection, Ethical Standards and Social Policy in the Selective Non-treatment of Handicapped Neonates' (1985) 11 Am J Law Med 31.

[24] K Boyd 'Euthanasia: Back to the Future' in J Keown (ed) *Euthanasia Examined* (1995) ch 7.

... he would not compare his life with that of a person enjoying normal advantages. He would know nothing of a normal person's life having never experienced it.[25]

16.18   As an inevitable result, parents must be invited to make 'life or death' decisions on behalf of their physically or mentally challenged offspring—and they will be guided by the doctor whose advice is likely to be on the lines that consideration for the preservation of life is secondary to that of preventing suffering. But the early cases fail to address the solution of conflict between the medical carers and the parents. As we have seen, this underlies the concept of medical futility which, as a result, can be seen as developing in the United Kingdom only since the 1980s. Thus, we have the evidence of Dr Dunn at the trial of Dr Arthur: 'no paediatrician takes life but we do accept that allowing babies to die is in the baby's interest at times'[26]—and the wealth of distinguished supporting evidence showed that this paediatric practice was clearly acceptable at the time. It does, however, involve a number of assumptions:

(a)   that there is an essential difference between activity and passivity when the same end—death—is realised by either and, arising from this, that passivity does not conflict with the doctor's duty to 'maintain life from the time of conception';[27] moreover, it presupposes that passivity is clinically preferable from the patient's viewpoint;

(b)   that there is a point at which death is preferable to life; and

(c)   that some, as yet unidentified, person can decide that point in surrogate fashion and that it is right and proper for others to follow that judgment through.

16.19   Yet this seems to come perilously close to breaking the law. To kill a living human being deliberately is murder and, except as to the specific crime of infanticide,[28] the age of the victim has no relevance. Killing a child by omission could be prosecuted under the Children and Young Persons Act 1933, s 1;[29] it is more likely to be charged as manslaughter although it could be murder[30]—the paramount considerations being whether or not there is a duty of care and, if there is, what is the extent of that duty.[31] It is difficult to see how the consultant in charge of the paediatric ward could be seen as not having a duty of care to his patients. Yet, it has been suggested that anything up to 30 per cent of deaths in a neonatal intensive care unit follow the deliberate

---

[25] *Re Superintendent of Family and Child Services and Dawson* (1983) 145 DLR (3d) 610 at 621.

[26] *R v Arthur* (1981) 12 BMLR 1 at 18. Dr Dunn subsequently stated that he would limit withholding life-saving treatment only to three groups of neonate: those with severe malformations, those with severe hypoxic/traumatic brain damage; and those of extreme prematurity with major problems such as brain haemorrhage: P M Dunn 'Appropriate Care of the Newborn: Ethical Dilemmas' (1993) 19 J Med Ethics 82.

[27] Declaration of Geneva (see Appendix B).

[28] Infanticide Act 1938.

[29] The section probably applies only to parental obligations. If this be so, it would not constitute a potential sanction against the health care team. See I Kennedy and A Grubb *Medical Law* (3rd edn, 2000), p 2165.

[30] *R v Gibbins and Proctor* (1918) 13 Cr App R 134, CCA.

[31] *R v Stone; R v Dobinson* [1977] QB 354, [1977] 2 All ER 341, CA.

withdrawal of life support[32] and we have Farquharson J charging the jury in the leading apposite criminal case:

I imagine that you will think long and hard before concluding that doctors, of the eminence we have heard . . . have evolved standards that amount to committing a crime.[33]

16.20   Moreover, we have not yet fed the rights of the neonate into the equation. The newly born baby has the same rights to respect as has every human being, certainly as a matter of law. From the ethical and philosophical perspective, however, this proposition is increasingly under attack as the definition of personhood in terms of intellect is developed. We have already observed that, if it is valid to treat the fetus as a non-person, it is also valid to use the same parameters by which to deny personhood to the neonate; there are, indeed, those who are prepared to equate the status of 'infanticide' with that of 'feticide'[34]—or even of contraception. It is against this conflicting legal and ethical background that we can trace the absorption of the concept of medical futility into the medical jurisprudence of the United Kingdom as, first, related to the neonate and infant.[35]

Futility or a duty not to treat?

16.21   Although *R v Arthur*[36] was, chronologically speaking, not the first instance of selective non-treatment of the newborn to come before the English courts, it was undoubtedly that which brought the whole subject before the public conscience. In so far as it was taken through the criminal courts, it is an unsatisfactory prototype; nevertheless, it has been said that there are surprisingly few substantive issues in medical ethics that Dr Arthur's case does not raise[37] and it remains an important landmark.

16.22   Put briefly, the salient features of the case are that a baby was born with apparently uncomplicated Down's syndrome and was rejected by his parents; Dr Arthur, a paediatrician of high repute and impeccable professional integrity, wrote in the notes 'Parents do not wish it to survive. Nursing care only'; the baby died 69 hours later. Dr Arthur was charged with murder but, during the course of the trial, medical evidence was adduced to the effect that the child had not been physically healthy; accordingly, the charge was reduced to one of attempted murder and Dr Arthur was acquitted.

16.23   The central question raised by the trial is why, in the light of the acknowledged

---

[32] A Whitelaw 'Death as an Option in Neonatal Intensive Care' [1986] 2 Lancet 328; C H M Walker '. . . Officiously to Keep Alive' (1988) 63 Arch Dis Child 560. A very surprising recent report from Belgium indicates that some 13% early neonatal deaths were assosiared with the administration of lethal drugs: V Provvoost, F Cools, F Mortier et al 'Medical End-of-life Decisions in Neonates and Infants in Flanders' (2005) 365 Lancet 1315. See chapter 17 for the attitude to euthanasia in the Low Countries.

[33] *R v Arthur* (1981) 12 BMLR 1 at 22.

[34] See in particular H Kuhse and P Singer *Should the Baby Live?* (1985) ch 6.

[35] See further, R J Boyle, R Salter and M W Arnander 'Ethics of Refusing Parental Requests to Withhold or Withdraw Treatment from their Premature Baby' (2004) 30 J Med Ethics 402 and H McHaffie 'A Scottish Researcher's Response' (2004) 30 J Med Ethics 406.

[36] (1981) 12 BMLR 1.

[37] R Gillon 'An Introduction to Philosophical Medical Ethics: The Arthur Case' (1985) 290 BMJ 1117.

developments in neonatal intensive care, was Dr Arthur singled out for prosecution?[38] In our view, the most logical answer lies in the application of a 'treatability' test. Dr Arthur's patient was in no physical pain and, so far as was known prior to autopsy, he required no treatment. Death in such circumstances depends on the withholding of nourishment and to take away such a life is to make a social rather than a medical decision—the fact that it was taken by a doctor rather than a member of the public should be irrelevant. The prosecution of Dr Arthur led to a storm of resentment on the part of the leaders of the medical profession but this was almost entirely due to a failure to appreciate that there is a world of difference between withholding treatment from a dying patient and refusing sustenance to one who shows firm evidence of a will to live.[39] Any confusion as to the doctor's role is dispersed once it is appreciated that there is a fundamental distinction to be drawn between physical defect—for which invasive treatment remains an option—and mental defect for which no curative treatment is available. The failure of the medical establishment in this respect is exemplified in the statement of the President of the Royal College of Physicians:

Where there is an uncomplicated Down's case and the parents do not want the child to live . . . I think there are circumstances where it would be ethical to put it upon a course of management that would end in its death. . . I say that with a child suffering from Down's and with a parental wish that it should not survive, it is ethical to terminate life.[40]

16.24 By any standards, this is a remarkable interpretation of both medical and parental responsibilities and powers. In the light of later judicial decisions, which are discussed below, it is unlikely that Dr Arthur's regime would be acceptable today and the case has lost any credibility as a precedent. In our view, the management pattern disclosed in *R v Arthur* is best seen as an example of the dangers of extrapolating the concept of 'futility' to one of an obligation not to treat in the face of parental pressure.

Case law other than *Arthur*

16.25 With, perhaps, one major exception,[41] the law in this area has shown a remarkably steady development in the last 25 years.[42] None the less, the template was undoubtedly established in the prototype case of *Re B (a minor)*,[43] the judgment in which has been

---

[38] Only a few weeks previously, the Director of Public Prosecutions had decided that no action would be taken against a doctor who had allegedly refused to sustain a baby, Stephen Quinn, who was suffering from spina bifida: *The Times*, 6 October 1981, p 1.

[39] E.g. Editorial Comment 'Paediatricians and the Law' (1981) 283 BMJ 1280.

[40] (1981) 12 BMLR 1 at 21–22. See also the leading article at the time, 'After the Trial at Leicester' (1981) 2 Lancet 1085. It is possible that a similar attitude persists: Z Kmietowick 'Down's Children Received "Less Favourable" Hospital Treatment' (2001) 322 BMJ 815 commenting on R Evans (chairwoman) *The Report of the Independent Inquiries into Paediatric Cardiac Services* (2001).

[41] *Re T (a minor) (wardship: medical treatment)* [1997] 1 All ER 906, discussed in greater detail at para 16.76 et seq below.

[42] These cases are collected and reviewed very succinctly in J Read and L Clements 'Demonstrably Awful: The Right to Life and the Selective Non-treatment of Disabled Babies and Young Children' (2004) 31 J Law & Soc 482.

[43] (1981) [1990] 3 All ER 927, [1981] 1 WLR 1421, CA.

said still to represent the law in this particular field.[44] Thus, despite its antiquity, *Re B* still merits close consideration.

16.26　In essence, B was an infant suffering from Down's syndrome complicated by intestinal obstruction of a type which would be fatal per se but which was readily amenable to surgical treatment. The parents took the view that the kindest thing in the interests of the child would be for her not to have the operation and for her to die—in passing, a decision which was later described by Dunn LJ as 'an entirely responsible one'. The infant was made a ward of court and, in the face of both judicial indecision and medical disagreement, the question 'to treat or not to treat?' came before the Court of Appeal.

16.27　The summary answer to the basic question was provided by Dunn LJ in saying: 'She should be put in the position of any other mongol child and given the opportunity to live an existence.'[45] For the major analysis, however, we must look to Templeman LJ who, adhering to the general principles relating to the affairs of minors,[46] concluded that the judge of first instance, in refusing to authorise the operation, had been too much concerned with the wishes of the parents; the duty of the court was to decide the matter in the interests of the child. In coming to the conclusion that these interests were best served by treatment, he said:

> . . . it devolves on this court . . . to decide whether the life of this child is demonstrably going to be so awful that in effect the child must be condemned to die or whether the life of this child is still so imponderable that it would be wrong for her to be condemned to die . . . Faced with [the] choice, I have no doubt that it is the duty of this court to decide that the child must live,[47]

and it was this that led Lord Donaldson to look upon *Re B* as close to a binding authority for the proposition that there is a balancing exercise to be performed in assessing the course to be adopted in the best interests of such children.

16.28　Templeman LJ did, however, clearly leave the door open for an alternative decision in saying:

> There may be cases . . . of severe proved damage where the future is so certain and where the life of the child is so bound to be full of pain and suffering that the court might be driven to a different conclusion.[48]

16.29　Thus, the court clearly accepted that there is an essential prognostic difference between mental and physical handicap and, as to the latter, laid the foundations for a quality of life therapeutic standard rather than one based on a rigid adherence to the principle of the sanctity of human life. Even so, the medical profession was now left in

---

[44] *Re J (a minor) (wardship: medical treatment)* [1990] 3 All ER 930, (1990) 6 BMLR 25, CA paraphrasing Lord Donaldson MR [1990] 3 All ER 930 at 938, (1990) 6 BMLR 25 at 34.

[45] [1990] 3 All ER 930 at 931, [1981] 1 WLR 1421 at 1425.

[46] Guardianship of Minors Act 1971, s 1. See, now, Children Act 1989, s 1.

[47] [1990] 3 All ER 930 at 931, [1981] 1 WLR 1421 at 1424.

[48] [1990] 3 All ER 930 at 931, [1981] 1 WLR 1421 at 1424.

a cleft stick. Allowing for the fact that they relate to different jurisdictions, *Re B* and *Arthur* are virtually impossible to reconcile. Legally speaking, it is difficult to see why the parents' wishes as to the death of their offspring should be overruled when major surgery is involved, yet be regarded as ultimately decisive when it is not and, in a clarification which seems only to add to the confusion, the Attorney-General said shortly after Dr Arthur's trial:

I am satisfied that the law relating to murder and to attempted murder is the same now as it was before the trial; that it is the same irrespective of the age of the victim; and that it is the same irrespective of the wishes of the parents or of any other person having a duty of care to the victim. I am also satisfied that a person who has a duty of care may be guilty of murder or attempted murder by omitting to fulfil that duty, as much as by committing any positive act.[49]

16.30   This unsatisfactory situation persisted for almost a decade but was then greatly clarified in a series of cases overseen by Lord Donaldson MR.[50] The decisions in these cases relate to treatment of infants rather than of the newborn. They can, therefore, be taken as early examples of the application of medical futility across the whole span of life.

SELECTIVE NON-TREATMENT IN INFANCY

16.31   *Re C*[51] concerned a moribund child and the essence of the decision was that the hospital were given authority to treat her so as to allow her life to come to an end peacefully and with dignity; such treatment as would relieve her from pain, suffering and distress would be given but it was specifically said to be unnecessary to use antibiotics or to set up intravenous infusions or nasogastric feeding regimes. It was emphasised that the decision was based on the paramountcy of her welfare, well-being and interests. *Re C* thus represents the antithesis of *Re B* in respect of physical disability and, in retrospect, neither case was difficult to decide.

16.32   Baby J[52] was, however, not dying and the case illustrates more clearly the real dilemma presented by these cases. The situation was that the brain-damaged child suffered from repetitive fits and periods of cessation of breathing for which he required ventilation. There was no doubt that he could be rescued in the probable event that he sustained further episodes of respiratory failure but it was equally certain that he would die if the necessary treatment was withheld. Non-treatment in these circumstances cannot be dressed in such euphemisms as 'allowing a peaceful and dignified death' and the question before the court was what was to be done if he

---

[49]   19 HC Official Reports (6th series) written answers, col 349, 8 March 1982.

[50]   For review of these cases, see J K Mason 'Master of the Balancers: Non-voluntary Therapy under the Mantle of Lord Donaldson' [1993] JR 115.

[51]   *Re C (a minor) (wardship: medical treatment)* [1989] 2 All ER 782, [1990] Fam 26.

[52]   *Re J (a minor) (wardship: medical treatment)* [1990] 3 All ER 930, (1992) 6 BMLR 25.

sustained a further collapse. The Court of Appeal had little difficulty in agreeing with the judge of first instance that:

it would not be in J's best interest to reventilate him [by machine] in the event of his stopping breathing unless to do so seems appropriate to the doctors caring for him given the prevailing clinical situation.[53]

16.33 In the course of his judgment, the Master of the Rolls made several observations which we see as being of particular importance. In the first place, he stressed that, while there was a strong presumption in favour of a course of action that will prolong life, nevertheless, the person who makes the decision must look at it from the assumed view of the patient.[54] Following on from this, consideration must be given to the prognosis in terms of pain and suffering—including the distress caused by any treatment of itself; in J's case, the quality of life, even without the added effect of further hypoxic episodes, was extremely low. Thirdly, the court held that decision making was a co-operative effort between the doctors and the parents—or, in the case of wardship, between the doctors and the court with the views of the parents being taken into consideration;[55] any choice must be made solely on behalf of the child in what was believed to be his best interests. Finally—and this we see as especially significant—it was emphasised that any decision taken was one which would affect death by way of a side-effect; the debate was not about terminating life but solely about whether to withhold treatment designed to prevent death from natural causes:

The court never sanctions steps to terminate life. That would be unlawful. There is no question of approving, even in a case of the most horrendous disability, a course aimed at terminating life or accelerating death. The court is concerned only with the circumstances in which steps should not be taken to prolong life.[56]

16.34 Re C and Re J must, however, be looked at in conjunction with a third case which was unfortunately also named Re J[57]—and called here Re J(2). In this instance, a mother attempted to enforce the intensive care of her child who had sustained severe brain damage as a result of a fall. The Court of Appeal, however, refused to entertain the

---

[53] [1990] 3 All ER 930 at 933, (1992) 6 BMLR 25 at 29.

[54] Lord Donaldson demonstrated a sympathy with the 'substituted judgment' test throughout this series of cases (see para 16.36–16.37 below).

[55] The nurses were singled out for praise in the Court of Appeal in Re C, where there were clear indications that their views should also be considered.

[56] [1990] 3 All ER 930 at 943, (1990) 6 BMLR 25 at 40, per Taylor LJ. In Re C, the Court of Appeal would not even tolerate the expression 'treat to die'.

[57] Re J (a minor) (medical treatment) [1993] Fam 15, [1992] 4 All ER 614. Two supportive decisions were also reached in Scotland. The determination in the fatal accident inquiry concerning the death of Rebecca Cassidy supported a decision not to treat an extremely low birth-weight premature infant: see S English 'Doctor was Right not to Resuscitate "Unviable" Baby' The Times, 27 June 1997, p 11. The decision not to provide a liver transplant for a teenage girl was accepted as good medical practice in the inquiry into the death of Michelle Paul: see G Bowditch 'Surgeon Right to Refuse Teenager a Liver Transplant' The Times, 23 July 1997, p 7.

suggestion that it should direct clinicians to provide treatment against their best clinical judgment:

I agree with Lord Donaldson that I can conceive of no situation where it would be proper . . . to order a doctor, whether directly or indirectly, to treat a child in the manner contrary to his or her clinical judgment. I would go further. I find it difficult to conceive of a situation where it would be a proper exercise of the jurisdiction to make an order positively requiring a doctor to adopt a particular course of treatment in relation to a child.[58]

Thus, this series of cases indicates a strong judicial belief in the doctor's clinical autonomy. It also shows a very determined stance in favour of a quality of life standard which is founded on the principle of the patient's 'best interests'.

16.35   The use of this standard is best considered under the management of the permanent vegetative state.[59] For present purposes, we consider only the relationship between 'best interests' and 'no interests' in which we are, in fact, reverting to the problem of distinguishing mental from physical disability. It may well be permissible to see death as a blessed relief from severe pain or unacceptable bodily invasion and, therefore, an outcome of a treatment that is in the patient's 'best interests'. By contrast, the patient who has sustained brain damage of such degree as to permanently deprive him or her of sensation and cognition has no immediate interests as between death or survival.[60]

16.36   We believe that some other test is called for in the latter circumstance and that it is there, in particular, that we can legitimately call on the concept of medical futility to guide our therapeutic programming. However, as we have seen, this can conflict with the respect due to *patient* autonomy and, to avoid this, it may be preferable to rely on the principle of substituted judgment—or, in other words, to follow the regime that one assumes the patient him- or herself would have opted for if given the chance.[61] The objections to such a test are discussed in greater detail below.[62] For the present, we will only observe that its acceptance relieves one of an element of hypocrisy that is inherent in the 'best interests' test. We are constantly assured that judicial treatment/non-treatment decisions are founded on the best interests of the patient alone and that the interests of the relatives, carers and, indeed, the state are entirely secondary, if not irrelevant—yet, in all honesty, it is hard, if not impossible, to separate these extraneous interests. Substituted judgment allows us to take the latter into consideration with a relatively clear conscience. A competent patient may opt for non-treatment rather than treatment and the effects of the decision on his or her family

---

[58] [1993] Fam 15 at 29, [1992] 4 All ER 614 at 625, per Balcombe LJ.

[59] See para 16.95 et seq below.

[60] Although Dworkin, for one, speaks in terms of critical interests which persist despite the loss of appreciative capacity: R Dworkin *Life's Dominion* (1993), discussed extensively by A Grubb 'Commentary on *Law Hospital NHS Trust v The Lord Advocate*' (1996) 4 Med L Rev 301.

[61] 'Donning the mental mantle of the incompetent patient': see *Superintendent of Belchertown State School v Saikewicz* 370 NE 2d 64 (Mass, 1977).

[62] See para 16.130 et seq.

can legitimately form part of its foundation; there is no reason why this should not be incorporated in the substituted judgment.

16.37   In fact, the English courts, in their anxiety to maintain the welfare principle, have tended to confuse the two tests.[63] Thus, we have, again, Lord Donaldson[64] quoting McKenzie J:[65]

It is not appropriate for an external decision maker to apply his standards of what constitutes a liveable life . . . The decision can only be made in the context of the disabled person viewing the worthwhileness or otherwise of his life in its own context as a disabled person.[66]

And although it was taken as expressing the best interests of J, this is as clear a description of the principle of substituted judgment as one is likely to find. It also re-emphasises the mental/physical divide—a divide which has become even more apparent in some relevant cases which have been reported since the era of Lord Donaldson.

Important cases post-*Donaldson*

16.38   *Re C (a baby)*[67] concerned a premature infant who developed meningitis resulting in her being blind and deaf and suffering from repeated convulsions. She could survive only by virtue of artificial ventilation but, given that support, it was thought that she could live for months or even up to two years. Meantime, her pain and distress were expected to increase. She was described as not being in coma but as having 'a very low awareness of anything, if at all'; Sir Stephen Brown P summed up her condition as 'almost a living death'. Medical opinion was that she had no independent existence and that it was in her interests that ventilation should be discontinued—in which case she would die within hours. The President had no doubt that he should grant leave to the medical staff to adopt this recommended regime. Sir Stephen was invited to make observations as to when it would be appropriate for doctors placed in this position to seek the leave of the court; he thought, however, that it would not be right to make any general observation about that matter—medical and legal opinion concurred in believing that each case should be considered on its particular facts.

16.39   The parents in *Re C (a baby)* agreed with the recommendations of their medical advisers. In the second important case, *Re C (a minor) (medical treatment)*,[68] however, the parents were orthodox Jews, who firmly believed that life should always be preserved. Their child, aged 16 months, suffered from spinal muscular atrophy—a progressive condition for which it was agreed there was no curative treatment. Nevertheless, she was conscious, able to recognise her parents and was able to smile. The recommended plan was to undertake a form of therapeutic test by removing her from

---

[63] We would point out that this confusion persists in the Mental Capacity Act 2005, which we discuss in chapters 10 and 12.

   [64] In *Re J* [1990] 3 All ER 930, (1990) 6 BMLR 25.

   [65] In *Re Superintendent of Family and Child Services and Dawson* (1983) 145 DLR (3d) 610.

   [66] [1990] 3 All ER 930 at 936, (1990) 6 BMLR 25 at 32.

   [67] *Re C (a baby)* [1996] 2 FLR 43, (1996) 32 BMLR 44.   [68] *Re C (a minor)* (1997) 40 BMLR 31.

supportive ventilation; if, as was probable, she suffered a further respiratory relapse, she would not be reventilated but would be allowed to die. The parents accepted the first part of the plan but were unable to consent to the second.

16.40   In the event, the President relied heavily on Lord Donaldson's leading cases[69] in defining the legal limits of the doctor's duties. In particular:

[To follow the wishes of the parents] would be tantamount to requiring the doctors to undertake a course of treatment which they are unwilling to do. The court could not consider making an order which would require them so to do.[70]

16.41   The situation was one in which the hospital trust sought the court's consent in the absence of consent by the parents. The medical evidence was not in dispute and was backed by the general recommendations issued by the Royal College of Paediatrics and Child Health[71]—under which, spinal muscular atrophy would be regarded as a 'no-chance situation' in which medical treatment may be deemed inappropriate. Leave was granted to the hospital to withdraw treatment and to exclude resuscitation in the event of respiratory arrest—such a regime being justified as being in C's best interests.

16.42   Much the same situation underlay *A National Health Service Trust v D*[72] which is probably the first case in this line which considered the issues from a human rights perspective. It concerned a child who had been born with irreversible lung disease and multi-organ failure. Any therapeutic 'progress' could be measured no more than in terms of an occasional voluntary movement of a digit or hand. The Trust applied for a declaration that, in the event of a further cardio-respiratory arrest, it would be lawful not to resuscitate him but to initiate treatment designed to let him end his life peacefully and with dignity. Medical opinion was unanimously in favour of this approach which was strongly opposed by the parents on the grounds that it was premature. Cazalet J, relying heavily on the previous Donaldson judgments, granted the declaration on the grounds that it was in the child's best interests that he be so managed; in so doing, the judge stated the law in clear terms:

[T]he court's prime and paramount consideration must be the best interests of the child. This of course involves . . . consideration of the views of the parents concerned . . . However, . . . those views cannot themselves override the court's view of the ward's best interests.[73]

16.43   Cazalet J also considered the implications of compliance with the European Convention on Human Rights and concluded that there could be no infringement of Article 2 insofar as the order was made in the best interests of D. At the same time, he

---

[69] *Re J (a minor)* [1990] 3 All ER 930, (1992) 6 BMLR 25; *Re J (a minor)* [1993] Fam 15, [1992] 4 All ER 614; *Re R (a minor) (wardship: medical treatment)* [1992] Fam 11, (1991) 7 BMLR 147.

[70] (1997) 40 BMLR 31 at 37.

[71] Royal College of Paediatrics and Child Health (RCPCH) *Withholding or Withdrawing Life Saving Treatment in Children: A Framework for Practice* (1998), confirmed in RCPCH *Good Medical Practice in Paediatrics and Child Health: Duties and Responsibilities of Paediatricians* (2002).

[72] [2000] 2 FLR 677, (2000) 55 BMLR 19.

[73] [1992] 2 FLR 667 at 686, (2000) 55 BMLR 19 at 28.

confirmed that Article 3 encompassed the right to die with dignity[74]—an increasingly commonly used phrase which seems to us to be becoming equivalent to 'without the encumbrance of invasive forms of treatment'.

16.44   The two latest cases in this chain of authority have received much public attention; in legal terms, however, they largely confirm the already well-established precedents outlined above.[75] *Portsmouth NHS Trust v Wyatt*[76] and *Re Winston-Jones (a child) (medical treatment: parent's consent)*[77] can, therefore, be taken together. Baby Wyatt was 11 months old. She had been born very prematurely and suffered all her life from severe respiratory failure and was going into heart and renal failure. She was blind, deaf and could make no voluntary movements. Medical opinion was unanimous that she would have minimal cognitive function but would be able to experience pain of any future treatment. Prognosis for 12 months' survival lay between 25 per cent and 5 per cent. Baby Winston-Jones was 9 months old and suffered from an incurable genetic condition resulting in severe cardio-respiratory dysfunction. In both cases, the hospitals sought a declaration that it would not be unlawful to withhold ventilation should it be needed. Both sets of parents strongly opposed the request. In granting the relief sought in the case of Baby Wyatt, the Judge applied *Re J* and, while accepting that further invasive intervention would be intolerable, he preferred to base his decision on what was the best that could be done for her. In the case of Baby Winston-Jones, Dame Butler-Sloss decided that it was not in his best interests to be mechanically ventilated. Each court confirmed the centrality of the best interests test to such decisions, and Hedley J even expressly acknowledged that this is essentially a subjective analysis. Moreover, and in keeping with trends elsewhere in medical law, the courts stressed that the role of medical assessments in these determinations are but one factor to be considered; the ultimate responsibility for deciding the child's overall best interests falls to the court. Thus we have Hedley J in *Wyatt*:

. . . I have of course been informed by the medical evidence as to the prospects and costs to her of aggressive treatment. I hope, however, that I have looked much wider than that and seen not just a physical being but a body, mind and spirit expressed in a human personality of unique worth who is profoundly precious to her parents. It is for the personality of unique worth that I have striven to discern her best interests. It is my one regret that my search has led to a different answer than that sought by these parents.[78]

---

[74] Quoting *D v United Kingdom* (1997) 24 EHRR 423. Cazalet J did not enlarge on his interpretation of either article.

[75] For comment see, D W Meyers, '*Wyatt* and *Winston-Jones*: Seriously Ill Babies and Who Decides to Treat or Let Die?' (2005) 9 Edin LR 307. See also M Brazier 'Letting Charlotte die' (2004) 30 J Med Ethics 519.

[76] [2005] 1 FLR 21, [2004] Fam Law 866.   [77] [2004] All ER (D) 313.

[78] *Wyatt*, n 76 above, para 39. At the time of going to press, Baby Wyatt is still alive and the parents, having once been unsuccessful (*Portsmouth NHS Trust v Wyatt* [2005] EWHC 117), are making further efforts to have the order lifted: S-K Templeton 'Life or Death Day for Baby Charlotte' (2005) *Sunday Times*, 17 April, p 1.9.

16.45 The fundamental tension that this reveals, however, is what will a court do if it prefers the parents' assessment of the child's interests? We have no authority which indicates that a court will *require* doctors to treat against their better judgment; indeed, as we have seen, this was expressly rejected by Lord Donaldson in *Re J* above. At most, it is likely that a court will declare it to be part of the attending doctor's continuing duty of care to his patient to refer him or her to a colleague who is prepared to follow the parents' wishes. As a final point, and as we have indicated elsewhere,[79] human rights law now requires that all disputes over the care of a child should be referred to the court as ultimate arbiter. Thus in *Glass v UK*,[80] a case in which there was violent dissension between the parents and the doctors as to the treatment of their brain damaged son, the European Court of Human Rights considered that treating a child against the wishes of his mother constituted an interference with his bodily integrity and, hence, a breach of Article 8; however, the primary reason why Article 8(2) was not engaged lay in the fact that the case was not taken to the court when the dispute developed. Accordingly, non-pecuniary damages of 10,000 euros were awarded.

16.46 While all the cases cited could be subsumed under the rubric of medical futility, we see them as illustrating a relatively steady—and significant—extension of the conditions which render non-treatment lawful. Two common threads are to be seen. On the one hand, the courts will not, and are unlikely ever to, order doctors to provide treatment against their better judgment—especially for those who are severely brain damaged. As a corollary, it is clear that, no matter what may be the practical clinical situation, parents and other guardians have no *legal* right to insist on treatment which the doctors can justifiably regard as being inappropriate. This, however, depends upon the weight of the medical opinion expressed and is subject to the vagaries of medico-legal trends whereby emphasis shifts between the fundamental values that inform our laws. We discuss such shifting trends further below.[81] It is to be noted that the medical evidence has never been seriously challenged by the amicus curiae in the reported cases and one wonders what would be the outcome were it to be otherwise. The general tenor of the decisions since *Re B* through the two *Re Js* suggests that the courts would opt for the salvaging of life—as Lord Donaldson put it: 'There is without doubt a very strong presumption in favour of a course of action which will prolong life' albeit adding the rider 'but . . . it is not irrebuttable'.[82] At the same time, the more recent *Re C* cases raise the possibility of a subtle change of emphasis leading to supremacy of the 'quality of life' as the basis of assessment. It is true that all life and death decisions—and the applications themselves—have been based on a 'best interests' test, but the facts of each successive case point to an incremental erosion of the pure concept—is it not, in fact, possible to discern the glimmers of a legal recognition of the 'personhood' construct? The *C* cases can also be distinguished from the *J* cases,

---

[79] Chapters 1 and 10.
[80] *Glass v United Kingdom* [2004] 1 FLR 1019, (2004) 77 BMLR 120.   [81] See paras 16.67 et seq.
[82] *Re J (a minor) (wardship: medical treatment)* [1990] 3 All ER 930 at 938, (1990) 6 BMLR 25 at 34.

D, Wyatt and *Winston-Jones* in that, while the latter are concerned with the non-provision of treatment that interferes with the natural process, the former relate to the withdrawal of treatment that is already in place; it is difficult in the extreme to deny that the *C* cases sanction a regime which will inevitably bring about a death which would not otherwise have occurred—barely distinguishable from that which Taylor LJ excluded in *Re J*[83] and which was foreseen by Balcombe LJ in *Re J(2)*.[84] Can this be looked on as a tentative step towards legalised euthanasia? We can understand how such a view might be taken.

16.47   Finally, the more recent cases illustrate vividly the difficulties surrounding the whole concept of futility. Continued treatment was futile from the perspective of the doctors in *Re C (a baby)*[85] and *Re C (a minor)*[86] and this constitutes the justification of its withdrawal; it is, surely, carrying sophistry too far to plead 'best interests'—we discuss the matter again at para 16.66 et seq below but, meantime, we suggest that it is better to be honest. But, if a procedure is to be regarded as futile, it must be devoid of utility and, certainly, the 'futile' treatment of C in *Re C (a minor)* and the potential treatment of the children in *National Health Trust v D, Wyatt* and *Winston-Jones* was of major utility to their parents. In other words, there is a practical as well as a theoretical distinction to be made between futile treatment and *medically* futile treatment. The doctor is entitled to assess the latter and to argue in favour of its non-provision or withdrawal. But, in the end, to do so is no more than a powerful contribution to the overall assessment of the former—which goes some way to supporting Sir Stephen Brown P in his resistance to generalising in this field.[87]

Conjoined twins

16.48   Many of the cases of 'futile' medical treatment that have been considered by the courts relate to the withholding or withdrawal of mechanical means to oxygenate the tissues. Perhaps the most controversial case that has arisen in recent years concerned the management of conjoined twins.[88] One of the twins, Mary, was so disabled as to be incapable of an independent existence. Thus, it was possible to regard separation from her sister, Jodie, as akin to disconnecting her source of oxygen—or life support machine—when its continued use was medically futile.[89] We can pre-empt discussion of the case by quoting Walker LJ:

---

[83] [1990] 3 All ER 930 at 943, (1990) 6 BMLR 25 at 40.

[84] [1993] Fam 15 at 30, (1992) 9 BMLR 10 at 20, CA.

[85] (1996) 32 BMLR 44.   [86] (1997) 40 BMLR 31.

[87] *Re C (a baby)* (1996) 32 BMLR 44. See also Waite LJ: 'All these cases depend on their own facts and render generalisations . . . wholly out of place' in *Re T (a minor) (wardship: medical treatment)* [1997] 1 All ER 906 at 917, (1996) 35 BMLR 63 at 75. The Ethics Committee of the BMA has published comprehensive guidelines covering all age groups: *Withholding and Withdrawing Life Prolonging Medical Treatment* (2001). These were updated in October 2004 to take account of recent domestic and European Court of Human Rights rulings: see www.bma.org.uk.

[88] *Re A (children) (conjoined twins: surgical separation)* [2001] Fam 147, (2001) BMLR 1, CA.

[89] This reconstruction was not, however, accepted by the majority of the court.

If Mary had been born separated from Jodie but with the defective brain and heart and lungs which she has, and if her life were being supported, not by Jodie but by mechanical means, it would be right to withdraw that artificial life-support system and allow Mary to die.[90]

It is for this reason that we have chosen to discuss the case, which has multiple facets,[91] at this particular point.

16.49   In brief, *Re A (children) (conjoined twins: surgical separation)* concerned conjoined twins, one of whom, Jodie, had a normal heart and lungs. Mary, by contrast, had no functioning heart and her lungs were unusable; her tissues were oxygenated only because she shared a common aorta and venous return with her sister. Mary would die immediately were the twins to be separated whereas, in such circumstances, Jodie would be expected to live a near normal life; both would die in a matter of months if no action was taken. Since it was never disputed that the twins constituted two living individuals,[92] the medical alternatives were stark. Either the hospital could do nothing and accept 'the will of God' that both would die—which was the parents' strong preference and which would have been legally 'acceptable' practice[93]—or they could be separated, in which case, Mary's life of a few months would be sacrificed so as to ensure Jodie's survival.

16.50   It would be convenient to be able to see this as a purely moral problem. In practice, however, the undoubtedly far from satisfactory ruling of the Court of Appeal[94] was, throughout, overshadowed by considerations of the criminal law—before any decision involving the death of Mary could be accepted, it had to be cleansed of a suspicion of murder. A number of strategies were deployed to this end. These included self-defence or its support on behalf of Jodie, the necessity of avoiding an inevitable wrong[95] and absence of intention to kill. At least one of these factors was sufficient to convince all three judges of the lawfulness of the operation and it is beyond the scope of this book to argue these uncertain areas of the criminal law.

16.51   But, even when the problem of criminality is settled,[96] the case raises ethical questions of equivalent complexity. Fundamental to these is the problem of what constitutes 'best interests' in this and comparable cases. Here, Johnson J, at first instance,

---

[90] (2001) 57 BMLR 1 at 109.

[91] An entire issue of the Medical Law Review (2001) 9, no 3 was devoted to the case on which there is now a massive bibliography.

[92] Though it is possible to see them as an integrated 'item' sharing common assets: B Hewson 'Killing Off Mary: Was the Court of Appeal Right?' (2001) 9 Med L Rev 281.

[93] Per Ward LJ at BMLR 36. This was also the preferred option of R Gillon 'Imposed Separation of Conjoined Twins—Moral Hubris by the English Courts?' (2001) 27 J Med Ethics 3 and H Watt 'Conjoined Twins: Separation as Mutilation' (2001) 9 Med L Rev 237.

[94] For a powerful step by step criticism, see J McEwan 'Murder by Design: The "Feel-Good Factor" and the Criminal Law' (2001) 9 Med L Rev 246.

[95] The reasoning, which precluded a defence of necessity in *R v Dudley and Stephens* (1884) 14 QBD 273, was specifically rejected in *Re A*.

[96] And a case can be made out that it was not: S Uniacke 'Was Mary's Death Murder?' (2001) 9 Med L Rev 208.

and Walker LJ on appeal were happy in the notion that it was not in Mary's best interests to be maintained alive—this being based on the quality of life she could anticipate. Other members of the Court of Appeal, however, could not accept this—Ward LJ holding that separation would bring her life to a close before it had run its natural span without providing any countervailing advantage. Thus, the difference of opinion clearly highlighted the distinction to be drawn between the concepts of the sanctity and the quality of life to which we have already drawn attention. The further distinction between commission and omission, or between activity and passivity, in end of life decision making is closely bound to this fundamental issue. We discuss the question of whether there is an *ethical* distinction to be made elsewhere (see para 17.23 et seq); whatever the answer may be, there certainly is an important *legal* difference which we address more fully in chapter 17. Suffice it to say, here, that, having accepted that Mary was receiving no treatment which could be withdrawn in passive fashion, the Court of Appeal in *Re A* concluded that the operation to separate the twins constituted an assault on Mary. Thus, it was a positive action that would end her life and, as such, was dangerously close to, if not actually, crossing the Rubicon of euthanasia—a journey that the court was unwilling to make.[97] Thirdly, *Re A* reopens the controversy surrounding the moral doctrine of double effect and its associated concept of intent (for which, see chapter 17). The case particularly asks whether the 'good' effect—in this instance, Jodie's long term survival—can be justified if the 'bad' accompaniment is at the expense of *another* non-consensual party as represented here by Mary's premature death. In the event, only Walker LJ was prepared to hold that Mary's death could be seen as an unintentional result of Jodie's survival. Given the proportionality provided by Mary's negligible advantage, if any, in remaining alive, it is difficult to see why the majority of the court rejected a not unreasonable escape route from a hideous moral dilemma.[98]

16.52   We have previously suggested that many of these difficulties could have been avoided by accepting Mary as a still-birth which, it seems, would have been possible given that she never had any lung function.[99] To do so would also have limited the effect of the ruling in *Re A* to separation of a still-birth which would be completely lawful; as things stand, many are concerned at the potential effect of the decision on the law of murder. None the less, the court rejected this solution unanimously and we suspect that this may have been because of the somewhat conflicting way in which much of the relevant medical evidence was presented. Walker LJ, for example, quoted

---

[97] Johnson J in the High Court was prepared to equate cutting off Mary's oxygen supply with withdrawing food from those in coma—see discussion of Bland at para 16.95 et seq below—which can be regarded as an omission; the Court of Appeal rejected this unanimously.

[98] See, for example, Uniacke, n 96 above. Though, as the other members of the court noted, it is not certain that double effect will always survive following *R v Woollin* [1999] 1 AC 82, [1998] 4 All ER 103. Effectively, this says that a 'bad' result cannot be seen as unintentional if it was inevitable. For a discussion in the medical context see, *R v D* [2004] EWCA Crim 1391.

[99] J K Mason 'Conjoined Twins: A Diagnostic Conundrum' (2001) 5 Edin LR 226. For the diagnosis of still-birth, see para 5.92 above.

the leading surgeon as saying; 'Mary was not still-born but she could not be resuscitated and was not viable'[100] which, by *Rance* standards, seems to be something of a contradiction in terms. Ward LJ was content to quote the then Brooke J's definition of live birth in *Rance* and to comment: 'I think I can guarantee that when my Lord said that, he did not relate his observations to Siamese twins'—which is scarcely a robust rejection of our hypothesis.

16.53   The Court of Appeal was, then, left to solve the almost insoluble and, in the end, very nearly acknowledged that. Faced with alternatives that could never satisfy everyone, it relied on a balancing act—which decision, it asked, contained the less wrong? The Court decided unanimously in favour of separation—with the proviso that the authority of the case was confined by its very unique circumstances—and, in strict utilitarian terms, this has to be seen as correct; one cannot be so certain when speaking deontologically.

16.54   A final comment on the ethical components of *Re A* relates, once again, to the question of parental rights and responsibilities in such cases. The Court of Appeal took full cognisance of the parents' wishes yet barely questioned its own right to have the final say. Looked at dispassionately, the reasons given by the parents for their opposition to the operation—including deeply held religious convictions and the anticipated difficulties in maintaining a family unity that would be imposed by a disabled child—are, essentially, based on parental interests. Whether or not one agrees with the logic of the decision, it was based on wide-ranging analysis and careful thought rather than on custom, and this must have been to the 'better' interests of the children; as Freeman put it: 'there are more important rights to confer upon children than the right to autonomous parents.'[101] Against this, one must also quote Harris: 'This is a finely balanced judgment, but perhaps just because it is, the justification for overturning the choice of the parents is absent.'[102] It is perhaps a sobering thought that a case which provoked so much controversy and which could have a profound influence on the law might never have been heard had the twins not been in the care of an authority that was anxious to proceed in circumstances where many might not have done so.

COMPARATIVE EXPERIENCE IN THE UNITED STATES

16.55   The American experience in this field of neonatal and paediatric medicine demonstrates a somewhat turbulent history. Thirty or so years ago, there was a strong legal bias in favour of a sanctity of life approach. Opinions were handed down such as: 'If there is any life-saving treatment available, it must be given regardless of the quality of

---

[100] (2001) 57 BMLR 1 at 105.
[101] M Freeman 'Whose Life Is It Anyway?' (2001) 9 Med L Rev 259.
[102] J Harris 'Human Beings, Persons and Conjoined Twins: An Ethical Analysis of the Judgment in Re A' (2001) 9 Med L Rev 221.

life that will result'[103] or 'Children are not property whose disposition is left to parental decision without hindrance'[104] and, in general, extensive surgery was ordered so long as it was feasible.

16.56　　However, a change appeared in the next decade. In *Weber v Stony Brook Hospital*,[105] the Court of Appeal in New York would not overturn a judgment to the effect that, in refusing permission for surgery, the parents had 'elected a treatment which was within accepted medical standards'; 'to allow [a guardian]' it was said 'to bypass the statutory requirements would catapult him into the very heart of a family circle to challenge the parents' responsibility to care for their children'. The decision in *Re Infant Doe*[106] was that the value of parental autonomy outweighed the infant's right to live when 'a minimally adequate quality of life was non-existent'—this despite the fact that the anatomic abnormality present in association with Down's syndrome was amenable to relatively routine surgery; moreover, the case arose in Indiana, which was, at the time, the only state in which the life of the newborn was protected by statute. It has been described as a case: 'in which a baby whose life could almost certainly have been saved was starved to death under color of law'.[107]

16.57　　The position then became even more turbulent. *Infant Doe* provoked presidential reaction on the grounds that selective non-treatment contravened federal laws protecting the handicapped; hospitals receiving federal aid were reminded that they were prohibited from withholding life-saving medical or surgical treatment from handicapped infants. Particular attention was paid to the provision of nourishment, fluids and routine nursing care—items which were not considered options for medical judgment: 'no health care provider should take it upon itself to cause death by starvation or dehydration'. Nevertheless, the United States District Court for the District of Columbia rapidly invalidated these rules by declaring, inter alia, that the Rehabilitation Act 1973, s 504, which protects the rights of the handicapped, 'could never be applied blindly and without any consideration of the burdens and intrusions which might result'.[108] The Federal regulations were, therefore, revised but were again struck down.[109]

16.58　　The call for legislation was strong in the United States and was ultimately met by the Child Abuse Amendments of 1984 which amend the Federal Child Abuse Prevention and Treatment Act 1974.[110] The essential thrust is that, having defined medical neglect, the amendments lay down the circumstances in which withholding medically indicated treatment would not be so described. These include the presence

---

[103]　*Re McNulty* No. 1960 Probate Court (Mass, 1980) following *Maine Medical Center v Houle* No. 74–145, Sup Ct (Me, 1974).

[104]　*Re Cicero* 421 NYS 2d 965 (1979).　　[105]　456 NE 2d 1186 (NY, 1983).

[106]　(1982) GU 8204–004 A (Monroe County Cir, 12 April), cert denied 52 USLW 3369 (US, 1983).

[107]　N Lund 'Infanticide, Physicians and the Law' (1985) 11 Am J Law Med 1.

[108]　*American Academy of Paediatrics v Heckler* 561 F Supp 395 (DDC, 1983).

[109]　*American Hospital Association v Heckler* 105 S Ct 3475. The death knell was sounded in *Bowen v American Hospital Association* 106 S Ct 2101 (1986).

[110]　The onus of monitoring and enforcing the Act remains with the individual states.

of irreversible coma, when treatment would merely prolong dying and when treatment would be futile or inhumane—but correction of a simple complication of Down's syndrome is not included as an exception.

16.59   There have been two notable developments in more recent years. First, the United States appears to be the only country in which xenotransplantation has been actually attempted as a treatment of last resort. Given the current state of the art, we would regard the procedure as an outstanding example of medical futility; the subject in general and the case of Baby Fae in particular are, however, discussed in chapter 18.[111] Second, and very much to the point in the present discussion, we have had the case of *Baby K*.[112]

16.60   Baby K was born an anencephalic and, accordingly had no cognitive abilities or awareness; she was, however, placed on a ventilator because of respiratory distress. Given a prognosis of death within a few days, the hospital doctors recommended supportive care only; in so far as there is no cure for anencephaly and, hence, there was no remedy for the child's mental state, treatment was considered futile and both medically and ethically inappropriate. However, her mother, who had already refused a recommended termination of pregnancy, had a firm belief in God's unique responsibility for human life;[113] accordingly, she insisted on mechanical ventilation when required—and this was, in fact, provided on at least three occasions. The hospital then sought a declaration that it was not required to provide respiratory support and this application was refused by the district court. It is, for present purposes, unfortunate that the Appeals Court was constitutionally unable 'to address the moral or ethical propriety of providing emergency stabilizing medical treatment to anencephalic infants' and the issue became one of the interpretation of statute— EMTALA[114]—which, effectively, requires hospitals to provide 'stabilising' treatment in an emergency situation to any person who comes to hospital and requests treatment.

16.61   In the event, the case was decided in favour of the mother on the narrow ground that the statute applied—but this was because the treatment requested was for respiratory distress rather than for anencephaly. But, in so concluding, a number of other problems were addressed. First, it was held that the parents have a constitutional right to make medical decisions on behalf of their children[115] and that no such right is

---

[111] See para 18.72 below.

[112] *Re Baby K* 832 F Supp 1022 (ED Va, 1993); affd 16 F 3d 590 (4th Cir, 1994); cert denied 1994 US App Lexis 5461. The greater part of the information on this case is taken from E J Flannery 'One Advocate's Viewpoint: Conflicts and Tensions in the Baby K Case' (1995) 23 Law Med & Ethics 7 and E W Clayton 'Commentary: What is Really at Stake in Baby K?' (1995) 23 Law Med & Ethics 13. For further commentary, see 'Anti-dumping Law: Application to Anencephalic Infants' (1993) 19 Amer J Law Med 548.

[113] One wonders, then, whether the only acceptable treatment should not have been inactivity.

[114] Emergency Medical Treatment and Active Labor Act 1992. Other statutes were cited including the Rehabilitation Act 1973, which prohibits health providers from discriminating on the basis of handicap or disability in the provision of medical care.

[115] This cannot, however, be absolute, as argued by Clayton, n 112 above. It is to be noted that exceptions such as those associated with the management of children of Jehovah's Witnesses (see para 10.18 et seq above) can be explained in that these may cause harm to the child who is, then, covered by the child abuse laws.

accorded to physicians in their choice of treatments. At first glance, this seems entirely contrary to the British position as expressed in *ex p B*;[116] it has to be remembered, however, that the court in *Baby K* was concerned only with statute and not the 'best interests' of K. Second, the courts in *Baby K* rejected the hospital's submission on the grounds that its proposals for non-treatment were based on the child's disability rather than on its respiratory condition. Although the reasoning was different, this is, to an extent, a reflection of the seminal English case of *Re B*; there is, however, a world of difference between Down's syndrome and anencephaly—there is little doubt that, were a *Baby K* case to come to the English courts, it would be treated as one of Templeman LJ's exceptions destined to a demonstrably awful life.[117] Finally, *Baby K*, again, leads us to the definition of futility. It is arguable that intensive care was 'useful' to K in that it restored her respirations. Equally, however, it can be seen as 'futile' in that to do so was not a worthwhile achievement from the patient's point of view. We are then faced with the recurring problem—ought we, and can we, isolate the patient's interests from those of other involved parties, including those of the state? And if we cannot, ought treatment decisions to be left solely in the hands of the physician? In the end, the *Baby K* decision was policy-based—the courts were unwilling to undermine a general statute in order to solve a particular dilemma; the outcome might have been very different had the courts been able to consider the patient's 'best interests' but there seem to have been no further developments.[118]

A NEED FOR LEGISLATION IN THE UNITED KINGDOM?

16.62   Despite the reluctance of the courts to interfere with clinical judgments, it might still be thought that the medical practitioner needs more official guidance and legal protection when undertaking selective non-treatment decisions. The current vogue in the United Kingdom when the common or statute law is unclear as to detail is for the creation of 'guidelines' by an authoritative body. These generally do not have the force of law but their non-observance will reflect adversely on the person who fails to follow them. Numerous documents relating to paediatric practice are now available.[119] That from the Royal College of Paediatrics and Child Health is the most detailed, practical

---

[116] For discussion, see F H Miller 'Infant Resuscitation: A US/UK Divide' (1994) 343 Lancet 1584. Baby K is a very interesting case in the present context but is probably not a particularly influential US case in relation to parental rights—for which see *Weber v Stony Brook Hospital* 456 NE 2d 1186 (NY, 1983); *Bowen v American Hospital Association* 476 US 620, 106 S Ct 2101 (1986).

[117] *Re B (a minor)* (1981) [1990] 1 All ER 927 at 929, [1981] 1 WLR 1421 at 1424.

[118] For a wide-ranging review of the European situation, see H E McHaffie, M Cuttini, G Brölz-Voit et al 'Withholding/Withdrawing Treatment from Neonates: Legislation and Official Guidelines across Europe' (1999) 25 J Med Ethics 440.

[119] See Royal College of Paediatrics and Child Health *Withholding or Withdrawing Life Saving Treatment in Children: A Framework for Practice* (1998), BMA *Withholding and Withdrawing Life-prolonging Medical Treatment* (2001) and GMC *Withholding and Withdrawing Life-prolonging Treatments: Good Practice in Decision-making* (2002), paras 67–77. See also BMA *Parental Responsibility* (2004).

and definitive. In summary, it outlines five situations where the withholding or withdrawal of curative medical treatment might be considered:

(a) *The brain dead child.* Once the diagnosis of brain death has been made, it is agreed within the profession that treatment in such circumstances is futile and withdrawal is appropriate.[120]

(b) *The permanent vegetative state.* We discuss this state below.[121]

(c) *The 'no chance' situation.* The child has such severe disease that life sustaining treatment simply delays death without alleviation of suffering. Medical treatment may, thus, be deemed inappropriate.

(d) *The 'no purpose' situation.* Although the patient may be able to survive with treatment, the degree of physical or mental impairment will be so great that it is unreasonable to expect them to bear it. The child in this situation will never be capable of taking part in decisions regarding treatment or its withdrawal.

(e) *The 'unbearable' situation.* The child and/or family feel that, in the face of progressive and irreversible illness, *further* treatment is more than can be borne. These wishes are irrespective of the medical opinion on its potential benefit.

In situations that do not fit these five categories, or where there is dissent or uncertainty about the degree of future impairment, the child's life should be safeguarded in the best possible way.

16.63   The guidelines from the British Medical Association in 2001 are more general and, effectively, set the ethical framework within which to work. The basic presumption is that life-prolonging treatment should be initiated where there is reasonable uncertainty as to its benefit. On the other hand, best interests are not necessarily synonymous with prolongation of life and there are circumstances in which active intervention would be inappropriate. These are:

— that the child has no potential to develop awareness;

— he or she will be unable to interact or to achieve the capacity for self-directed action; and that

— the child will suffer severe unavoidable pain and distress.

16.64   If the child's condition is incompatible with survival or where there is broad consensus that the condition is so severe that treatment would not provide a benefit in terms of being able to restore or maintain the patient's health, intervention may be unjustified. Similarly, where treatments would involve suffering or distress to the child, these and other burdens must be weighed against the anticipated benefit, even if life cannot be prolonged without treatment.

---

[120] It will be seen from chapter 13 that we regard this as something of a contradiction; the child is dead and you cannot treat a corpse. There is specific case law to the effect that the health carers cannot be compelled to do so: *Re A* [1992] 3 Med LR 303.

[121] See para 16.95 et seq.

16.65   The BMA firmly believes that parents are generally the best judges of their young
children's, and the family's, interests; doctors take the lead in judging the clinical
factors and parents the lead in determining best interests more generally. When a
decision is reached to withhold or withdraw a particular treatment, it is the value of
the treatment which is being assessed, not the value of the child—the overall objective
of providing benefit does not change. While those with parental responsibility have
the legal power to give or withhold consent to treatment for a child, this is provided
they are not acting against his or her best interests; parental power to withhold
consent for a child's treatment is likely to be curtailed where the treatment refused
would provide a clear benefit to the child, where the statistical chances of recovery are
good or where the severity and burdens of the condition are not sufficient to justify
withholding or withdrawing life-prolonging treatment. Perhaps the only controversial
statement from the BMA lies in para 15.1 where it is said: 'Where there is genuine
uncertainty about which treatment option would be of most clinical benefit, parents
are usually best placed and equipped to weigh the evidence and apply it to their child's
own circumstances.' Clearly, this depends, and is so conceded, upon full discussion
between doctors and parents, but the paragraph is, in our view confusing when it
adds: 'the actual treatment decision will depend upon the medical assessment of
benefit'.[122]

16.66   There is ample authority supporting the premise that there are some infants who
ought not to be assisted to live by invasive methods. The incapacitated child has as
much right to die in peace as has his grandfather and there are times when it is
obvious that that right should be respected. Moreover, it is now evident that a responsible clinician who believes that to be the right course cannot be compelled to provide
treatment with which he disagrees.[123] Almost two decades ago one of us suggested
that the problem of selective non-treatment of the newborn would best be settled by
well-drafted legislation.[124] The cases of *Wyatt* and *Winston-Jones* appear, however, to
have so set the seal on established jurisprudence that this may now seem unnecessary.
The common law is really quite clear; the courts are rightly established as the final
arbiters when there is disagreement between those with parental responsibility, or
concerned relatives, and the health carers; the unassailable legal parameter for
decision-making is the patient's own best interests. As recently as 2002, however, the

---

[122] For a full empirical study of how decisions are made in practice, see H E McHaffie, I A Laing, M Parker
and J McMillan 'Deciding for Imperilled Newborns: Medical Authority or Parental Autonomy?' (2001) 27 J
Med Ethics 104.

[123] *Re J (a minor) (medical treatment)* [1993] Fam 15, (1992) 9 BMLR 10. Interestingly, one of the reasons
given was that to do so might require the health authority to use intensive care resources and, thereby, to deny
them to someone who might derive greater benefit ([1993] Fam 15 at 29, (1992) 9 BMLR 10 at 20, per
Balcombe LJ). The implication is that the courts see a difference between not starting a life-saving treatment
and withdrawing it. But see our commentary, J K Mason and G T Laurie 'Personal Autonomy and the
Right to Treatment: A Note on *R C (on the application of Burke) v General Medical Council*' (2005) Edin
LR 123

[124] J K Mason and D W Meyers, 'Parental Choice and Selective Non-Treatment of Deformed Newborns: A
View from Mid-Atlantic' (1986) 12 J Med Ethics 67.

GMC reasonably pled that 'the profession and patients [and parents] want more guidance on what is considered ethically and legally permissible in this area'.[125] Its guidelines, ironically, have since been subject to legal attack, albeit in the context of the rights and interests of adults. We discuss that on-going process below. And statutory reform is, of course, now forthcoming for the position of adults in the guise of the Mental Capacity Act, which we explore in chapter 12. This aims to put flesh on the bones of the common law concept of best interests, and will complement rather than supplant the jurisprudence that has been established to date. But this, in turn, raises questions about the relationship between the areas of law concerning, respectively, children and adults. Court jurisdictions and powers apart, is the concept of 'best interests of the patient' amenable to division? Put another way, can a case continue to be made that infants should be treated differently from adults when it comes to their medical care?

IS THE TREATMENT OF INFANTS A SEPARATE ISSUE?

16.67 There are at least two good reasons for isolating the issues in early life from those in adulthood or those which are essentially perimortal. In the first place, decisions in the first situation rest almost entirely on prognosis, which is another way of expressing an informed guess as to the future. This may, in any event, be difficult and, while we know that we are dealing with only short-term survival at the end of life, this is not the case at birth—we may be confident of what will be the state of affairs next week but we cannot say the same about the next decade. Moreover, the neonate is not passing from a settled norm into a progressively less satisfactory condition; he is developing in a sub-optimal milieu which is his norm—can one say with any certainty that the Down's syndrome child, who has never known anything different, is dissatisfied with his existence within himself? Thus, we would take issue with the reasoning of Professor Williams, who wrote: 'If a wicked fairy told me she was about to transform me into a Down's baby and would I prefer to die I should certainly answer yes',[126] because this is not the question being asked of the infant. The better view is that of Lord Donaldson—that the starting point in analysing the defective's condition is not what might have been but what is.[127]

16.68 The second major distinction between life and death decisions at the extremes of life is that, while the adult sufferer is likely to be able to express an opinion or, save in a few cases, to have previously intimated his wishes, there is no way in which the neonate can consent to treatment, suffering or death. Consent must be parental and one then asks where, in fact, do lie the parents' rights that it is feared will be usurped

[125] General Medical Council *Withholding and Withdrawing Life-prolonging Treatments: Good Practice in Decision-making* (2002), para 5.

[126] G Williams 'Down's Syndrome and the Duty to Preserve Life' (1981) 131 NLJ 1020.

[127] In *Re J (a minor) (wardship: medical treatment)* [1990] 3 All ER 930 at 936, (1990) 6 BMLR 25 at 32, paraphrasing McKenzie J.

by the courts? Have they any more right to reject a child than to abandon it? If it can be criminal to disbar an older child from treatment,[128] why is it less culpable to fail, or to connive at failure, to provide the minimum of neonatal treatment—infant feeding? How do these rights differ when exercised in the light of medical advice rather than by way of simple intuition in the privacy of the home? Is it likely that a blind eye would be turned on parents who, on their own initiative, decided to abandon their disabled child? And can the parents who are, in addition to their emotional involvement, economically and socially concerned, make a truly objective decision on behalf of the child?[129]

16.69   These questions have, in the main, an ethical or social dimension. *Re C* and the *Re J* cases have, we suggest, clarified the criminal aspects of neonaticide and there is little doubt that non-treatment decisions are now taken on a daily basis in the United Kingdom.[130] Campbell,[131] writing on severely brain damaged children, believed that anything, including feeding, that prolongs such non-human or artificial life is 'wrong for the child, wrong for the family and wrong for society'. This, however, clearly depends on a value evaluation of the quality of life and, consequently, on a largely undefined discretion.[132] While it may well be an expression of the current state of the law, we suggest that decision-makers in the field should be wary of extending the bounds of *Re J* with impunity—life clearly carried great weight in Lord Donaldson's balance pan and does so in those of his successors.

16.70   What we *have* seen, is that the English courts are resolute in distinguishing between non-treatment and euthanasia and, in this respect, the fundamental distinction to be made is between, on the one hand, infants with pure mental defects and, at the other extreme, those with severe physical incapacity resulting, for example, from neural tube defects. Treatment of the latter is a matter of careful medical management which must incorporate an element of selection.[133] Many such handicapped children will inevitably die and many should be allowed to do so; the principle of 'allowing nature to take its course' on the basis of a shared decision between doctor and parents is acceptable in both a moral and a legal sense provided that the decision is taken in the

---

[128] *R v Senior* [1899] 1 QB 283, CCR.

[129] A useful overview is to be found in S Moor 'Euthanasia in Relation to Newborn Babies—A Comparative Study of the Legal and Ethical Issues' (1996) 15 Med Law 295 and 537. The problem of responsibility surfaced dramatically in England in 2002 when the parents of a baby suffering from the severely disfiguring Goldenhar's Syndrome refused a tracheostomy to alleviate the child's breathing difficulties. Their reason was not related to futility but, rather, to fears for the baby's safety. The operation was agreed after some seven hours' discussion in the Family Court: C Dyer 'Parents Agree to Surgery for Disfigured Baby' (2002) 324 BMJ 632.

[130] See A G M Campbell and H E McHaffie 'Prolonging Life and Allowing Death: Infants' (1995) 21 J Med Ethics 339.

[131] A G M Campbell 'Children in a Persistent Vegetative State' (1984) 289 BMJ 1022.

[132] See, in particular, C Wells ' "Otherwise Kill Me": Marginal Children at the Edges of Existence' in R Lee and D Morgan (eds) *Birthrights* (1989) ch 11.

[133] For a philosophical assessment, see J Harris 'Ethical Problems in the Management of Some Severely Handicapped Children' (1981) 7 J Med Ethics 117. Results from the coalface are reported by I M Balfour-Lynn and R C Tasker 'Futility and Death in Paediatric Medical Intensive Care' (1996) 22 J Med Ethics 279.

best interests of the child.[134] By contrast, if the mentally handicapped child is not to live, it must be encouraged and guided towards death. There is no non-treatment for the anatomically normal Down's baby because it needs no treatment and failure to feed in the latter instance can only be categorised as neonaticide—ie *killing* of the neonate, which brings us back to the question of whether there is, in fact, any true difference between non-treatment and euthanasia. Kuhse,[135] in the early stages of the debate, argued most persuasively that there is no moral or legal distinction to be drawn between activity and passivity in this area of medical practice. Gillon[136] put it:

While there may be some social benefit in distinguishing between actively 'allowing to die' and painlessly killing such infants, there is, I believe, no other moral difference and doctors who accept such 'allowing to die' of severely handicapped newborn infants should not deceive themselves into believing that there is such a difference.

16.71 Elsewhere, the same author emphasised that, while there is no *necessary* moral difference between killing and letting die, it does not follow that there is a moral equivalence.[137] Were this so, we would have to approve the spectre of the paediatrician armed with a lethal syringe—and the concept is quite unacceptable. As we discuss below in relation to the permanent vegetative state, it is hard to assail the logic which says that a quick death is preferable to one which depends upon the vagaries of nature; nevertheless, we believe that natural death is the only acceptable concomitant of a decision not to treat a severely physically defective infant—and we also believe that food and water should be provided for any child which is capable of taking nourishment by mouth. In so saying, we admit to being guided, to a very considerable extent, by moral intuition alone—as a well-respected medical philosopher once put it: 'We are, here, noting a deep human inhibition which it might be unwise to tamper with in the name of logic'.[138] Clinicians are similarly beset by the illogic of intuition:

There is a powerful psychological distinction [between 'killing' and 'allowing to die'] which is important to the staff of intensive care units. To them, there is a big difference between not using a respirator to keep an infant of 600g alive and giving a lethal injection, although the end result is the same.[139]

16.72 Advances in modern medicine have, at the same time, brought their own problems

---

[134] D D Raphael 'Handicapped Infants: Medical Ethics and the Law' (1988) 14 J Med Ethics 5 was one of the first to point to the conceptual difficulty in attributing any interest in death—'the most you can say is that someone would prefer to die'.

[135] H Kuhse 'A Modern Myth. That Letting Die is not the Intentional Causation of Death: Some Reflections on the Trial and Acquittal of Dr Leonard Arthur' (1984) 1 J Appl Philos 21. The same point is made by Harris n 133 above.

[136] R Gillon 'Conclusion. The Arthur Case Revisited' (1986) 292 BMJ 543.

[137] R Gillon 'Euthanasia. Withholding Life-Prolonging Treatment and Moral Differences between Killing and Letting Die' (1988) 14 J Med Ethics 115.

[138] R S Downie 'Modern Paediatric Practice: An Ethical Overview' (1989) in Mason, p 366, n 19 above, ch 31.

[139] A G M Campbell 'Ethical Issues in Child Health and Disease' in J O Forfar (ed) *Child Health in a Changing Society* (1988).

to the neonatal period. It is increasingly possible to maintain and rear premature infants of low birth weight and evidence is accumulating that a number of such children are disadvantaged to an extent which is inversely proportionate to their birthweight.[140] The discussion of selective non-treatment is, accordingly, being extended to include attitudes to intensive care of the premature infant. It is trite medicine to say that premature births should be prevented by improved ante-natal care. The fact remains that they will continue and their numbers will be augmented not so much due to poor maternal care as by the improved medical management of high-risk pregnancies. In these circumstances, we can see little alternative but to agree with those who believe that, since an accurate prognosis is generally impossible, such infants should always be offered treatment until such time as it is clearly ineffective— the test for treatment is, on these terms, one of feasibility—not of futility.[141] The difficulty of such a rule is that, while resuscitation may be successful, the end result may be a severely handicapped survivor; quite apart from the individual clinical result, there may also be a serious problem of resource distribution:

The ability to preserve the lives of these infants must be weighed against the resultant increase in the numbers of impaired children, the distress and suffering caused by lengthy treatment and hospitalisation, their eventual expected quality of life, and the socio-economic consequences for society as a whole.[142]

16.73   There is a paucity of judicial commentary in the United Kingdom. We have discovered only one relevant case—and this from a Scottish fatal accident inquiry which was poorly reported. The case involved the death of a 23-week-old neonate which was not taken into intensive care. The sheriff ruled that 'the doctor's decision not to resuscitate was made in the best interests of the child and was a reasonable clinical decision in the circumstances . . . The doctor's clinical judgment had to take precedence over the wishes of the parents'. Since this is one of the clearest judicial statements on the relative rights of the parents to come from Scotland, it is something of a pity that the case went no further.[143]

---

[140] L W Doyle, L J Murton and W H Kitchen 'Increasing the Survival of Extremely-immature (24–28 weeks' gestation) Infants—At what Cost?' (1989) 150 Med J Austral 558 and, more recently, R J Boyle, R Salter and M W Arnander 'Ethics of Refusing Parental Requests to Withhold or Withdraw Treatment from their Premature Baby' (2004) 30 J Med Ethics 402 and H McHaffie 'A Scottish Researcher's Response' (2004) 30 J Med Ethics 406.

[141] The Texas case of *Miller v Hospital Corporation of America* 118 SW 3d 758 (Tx, 2003) is interesting in that the parents of a 23-week gestation baby who was resuscitated against their wishes were awarded $59.9m at first instance. This was reversed, however, on appeal and in the Supreme Court of Texas on the grounds that parents have no right to refuse treatment with non-terminal impairments regardless of its severity. For review, see J M Lorenz 'Ethical Dilemmas in the Care of the Most Premature Infants: The Waters are Murkier than Ever' (2005) 17 Current Op Pediat 186.

[142] J Griffin, quoted by L Hunt 'Cost "Dilemma" Posed by Premature Babies' (1993) *The Independent*, 20 January, p 6 in discussion of Office of Health Economics *Born Too Soon* (1993). The precise gestation period is critical. In a recent study, 30% of surviving infants of 24 weeks' gestation or less suffered from cerebral palsy: S Shankaran et al 'Outcome of Extremely-low-birth-weight Infants at Highest Risk' (2004) 191 Amer J Obs Gynec 1084.

[143] S English 'Doctor Was Right not to Resuscitate "Unviable" Baby' *The Times*, 27 June 1997, p 11.

THE INTERESTS OF OTHERS

16.74 No practical solutions to the ending of life can be applied without giving thought to those who must participate in any process and, in particular to those who have a conscientious objection to the procedures. Were there to be any legislation which legalises the withholding or withdrawal of treatment in specified circumstances, it must, in our view, include a discretionary clause similar to that in the Abortion Act 1967, s 4. We emphasise the role of the nursing staff and the importance of safeguarding their position both now and in the event of legislation. It is the nurses, not the doctors, who will bear the brunt of selective non-treatment; not only must they be spared responsibility for carrying out instructions but, also, their sensitivities must be fully respected. We strongly commend the increasingly accepted principle of a team approach to neonatal intensive care.[144]

16.75 We believe that current court decisions have done much to define parental powers in this area. No one would deny that the parents' views should be ascertained, nor that they should carry great weight—but they cannot be fully determinative. Common attitudes to the management of disabled infants are based on the assumption of marital harmony, in that they relate so firmly to the wishes of 'the parents'—what if there is disagreement? Fortunately, the situation must arise only rarely. There can, however, be little doubt that, while the birth of a handicapped child may uncover qualities of goodness in the parents that are beyond expectation, an opposite reaction can be provoked.[145] Certainly, there are always the courts—but who is to say that judges qua judges are uniquely fitted to decide controversial questions of the value of infant life?[146] It is essential that the medical and legal professions—as well as society at large—should make sure of the lines they intend to draw in the face of potential conflict, whether this be inter-professional, inter-parental or between the parents and the professionals carers themselves.

16.76 *Re T (a minor) (wardship: medical treatment)*,[147] is of considerable interest not only as an example of parental views winning out against overwhelming medical opinion, but also for the fact that the parents supported non-intervention in this case when there was much that could be done to save their child's life. Here, the child, curiously designated as C, was born with biliary atresia—a condition likely to be fatal within 2½ years in the absence of transplantation therapy. Remedial surgery at the age of 3½

---

[144] The point was well taken in the judgment in *Re C (a minor) (wardship: medical treatment)* [1990] Fam 26, [1989] 2 All ER 782.

[145] See B Shepperdson 'Abortion and Euthanasia of Down's Syndrome Children—The Parents' View' (1983) 9 J Med Ethics 152. And, for an interesting debate: 'Informed Dissent': M Simms 'The Views of Some Mothers of Severely Mentally Handicapped Young Adults'; A Davis 'The View of a Disabled Woman' (1986) 12 J Med Ethics 72, 75.

[146] See Walker LJ in *Re A (children) (conjoined twins: surgical separation)* (2000) 57 BMLR 1 at 16, quoting Scalia J in *Cruzan v Director*, Missouri Department of Health (1990) 497 US 261 at 294.

[147] [1997] 1 All ER 906, (1996) 35 BMLR 63. For discussion, see M Fox and J McHale 'In Whose Best Interests?' (1997) 60 MLR 700; A Bainham 'Do Babies Have Rights?' (1997) 56 CLR 48; A Grubb 'Commentary' (1997) 4 Med L Rev 315.

weeks produced no improvement but medical opinion was unanimous in believing that the chances of a successful transplant were good and that the operation was in C's best interests. This included the opinion of a consultant engaged on behalf of the mother who opposed a further operation on the grounds of the pain and suffering C had sustained following the first procedure and who even took her child abroad where there were no facilities for a liver transplant. The child's local authority then raised the matter as a special issue under the terms of the Children Act 1989, s 100(3). As a result, the trial judge found that the mother's conduct was not that of a reasonable parent and directed that C be admitted to a hospital that was prepared to undertake a transplant operation.

16.77   The Court of Appeal, however, unanimously reversed this decision, largely on the grounds that the judge had failed to give adequate weight in the necessary balancing exercise to the objections of the parents—which, it was said, were supported by qualities of devotion, commitment, love and reason. These included an assessment of the pain and suffering likely to be imposed by a second major operation and of the chances and consequences of failure. In addition, the court agreed with one expert opinion that passing back responsibility for parental care to the mother and expecting her to provide the essential commitment to the child after the operation in the face of her opposition was, in itself, fraught with danger for the child. 'How would the mother cope with having to remain in England?' asked Butler-Sloss LJ. The mother and the child were one for the purposes of the case and the decision of the court to assent to the operation jointly affected the mother and son and also the father. Waite LJ went so far as to hold that the child's subsequent development could be injuriously affected if his day-to-day care depended upon the commitment of a mother who had suffered the turmoil of her child being compelled against her will to undergo a major operation 'against which her own medical and maternal judgment wholeheartedly rebelled'.[148] The appeal was upheld and the orders of the trial judge, to the effect that surgery should be performed notwithstanding the refusal of the mother to consent, were set aside.

16.78   *Re T* raises a number of questions—both general and particular. It is, first, reasonable to question whether it is right to place discussion of the case within a section devoted to medical futility. Our view is that it represents one side of the wide concept—albeit the rather unusual reverse in which the parents, on behalf of their child, are claiming treatment to be futile in so far as it is, on balance and in their view, offering minimal benefit. It will be seen below that we reject this prognostic assessment and it may be that the importance of the case lies in providing a measure of how far the concept of futility can be stretched without incursion into areas such as euthanasia—it is possible, but it is certainly not easy, to accommodate phrases such as: '. . . the prospect of forcing the devoted mother of this young baby to the consequences of this major invasive surgery . . .'[149] within the envelope of the child's unaffected best interests. Equally to the point, one has to ask if the decision in *Re T* does, in fact,

---

[148] [1997] 1 All ER 906 at 917, (1996) 35 BMLR 63 at 75.
[149] *Re T* [1997] 1 All ER 906 at 916, (1996) 35 BMLR 63 at 74, per Butler-Sloss LJ.

represent a watershed in the medico-legal symbiosis that has developed in this area. C's parents were described as health professionals; their status is unstated but the Court of Appeal was clearly impressed by their understanding of the situation—so much so that, at times, the mother's views appear to take on the significance of another expert medical opinion. Moreover, previous court decisions represent not so much a judicial submission to the medical will as, rather, a reluctance to impose a duty to treat on unwilling doctors. *Re T* was an antithetical proposition, the end result of which was to place an embargo on treatment which at least some experts were willing to provide. It may not, therefore, be a decision taken against the stream.

16.79   Whether it was a 'good' decision in medical jurisprudential terms is, again, questionable. Despite the protestations of all three judges, and despite the court's repeated assurance as to the responsibility and devotion of the parents, an unavoidable impression remains that their interests weighed heavily in the balance at the expense of the paramountcy of those of the child. Certainly, there is great good sense in the opinion of the trial judge. There are few fields of modern medicine in which progress is as fast as it is in transplantation therapy. It is at least possible that additional technology would become available during the several years of good quality life available within the current state of the art; not only might these then be extended beyond current expectation but, in the interim, the mother's attitude might well change. It is hard to dismiss such gains as *medically* futile objectives.

FUTILITY OR SCARCITY OF RESOURCES?

16.80   We have suggested already that the concept of futility carries with it the real danger that it can be used as a means to the disguised and arbitrary rationing of resources. This may well be so but, before accepting this as wholly pejorative, it is well to note the underlying practicalities.

16.81   In the first place, the one necessarily follows the other. Thus, if one patient is removed from futile treatment, that resource automatically becomes available to another for whom it will be useful—but the motive behind the exchange remains subject to interpretation. Secondly, given that resources are not infinite, therapeutic merit is a good candidate for the most acceptable basis for their distribution; as we discuss in chapter 11, the 'first come, first served' regime fails in principle because it dictates the provision of treatment in medically futile circumstances. Thirdly, the law clearly accepts that resource allocation forms a proper part of medical decision making. Thus, we have Balcombe LJ:

[M]aking an order which may have the effect of compelling a doctor or health authority to make available scarce resources . . . to a particular child . . . might require the health authority to put J on a ventilator in an intensive care unit, and thereby possibly to deny the benefit of those limited resources to a child who was much more likely than J to benefit from them.[150]

---

[150] *Re J (a minor) (wardship: medical treatment)* [1993] Fam 15 at 30, (1992) 9 BMLR 10 at 20.

16.82   None the less, the seeds of conflict are there to be sown and are well illustrated in
         R v Cambridge Health Authority, ex p B,[151] which concerned a 10-year-old child who
         had been suffering from lymphoma since the age of five. By the time of the action, she
         had received two courses of chemotherapy and had undergone whole body irradi-
         ation and received a bone marrow transplant before she suffered a further relapse. At
         this point, her doctors determined that no further treatment could usefully be given
         and estimated her life expectancy as between six and eight weeks. Her father had,
         meantime, obtained a second opinion from the United States which, effectively, sug-
         gested that further treatment carried an 18 per cent chance of a full cure. Doctors who
         were prepared to continue treatment in the United Kingdom regarded this as unduly
         optimistic and set the chance of success at anything between 10 per cent and 2.25 per
         cent—which was, of course, to be set against the risk to the patient's life and the
         distress associated with the proposed treatment; due to a shortage of beds, this would
         have to be carried out in the private sector and the cost was estimated to be in the
         region of £75,000. Taking into account the judgment of their own clinicians, the
         nature of the treatment and its chances of success, the health authority declined to
         provide the funding, giving as its reasons, first, that the treatment would not be in B's
         best interests and, second, that the expenditure of so much money with so little
         prospect of success was an ineffective use of their limited resources bearing in mind
         the present and future needs of other patients. The father sought judicial review of
         this decision.

16.83   In the High Court hearing, Laws J began his determination with the words: 'Of all
         human rights, most people would accord the most precious place to the right to life
         itself.' Even if this is true, which it probably is, we doubt if it follows that there is a
         rights-based entitlement to any particular treatment; the 'right to life' in this context
         means no more than the right not to have one's life taken away and this right is in no
         sense infringed if it is agreed that the available treatment is either futile or against the
         patient's best interests. In confronting such criticism, Laws J opined that, in contrast
         to the position in criminal law, public law allowed no difference of principle between
         act and omission and, accordingly, the decision of the health authority assaulted the
         child's right to life. He then considered the justification for such an assault and
         concluded that, while the doctors could rightly assess the chances of success of the
         proposed treatment and its objective disadvantages in terms of risk and suffering, the
         assessment of the patient's best interests was not, in the end, a medical question at all.
         Rather, it was a matter to be decided by the child's father acting as a surrogate
         responsible for her overall care. Thus, in the end, the issue turned on the provision of
         funds—and the learned judge considered that, when the question was whether the life
         of a 10-year-old might be saved, by however slim a chance, the authority should do
         more than 'toll the bell of tight resources'. In conclusion, while admitting that there
         might still be cogent reasons for withholding funding which had not been explored,

---

[151] (1995) 25 BMLR 5, QBD; revsd [1995] 2 All ER 129, (1995) 23 BMLR 1, CA.

Laws J ordered that the authority's decision be reconsidered in the light of his judgment.

16.84 Almost predictably in the light of previous decisions in which the allocation of resources formed a part,[152] the Court of Appeal reversed this order emphasising, in general, that its function was to rule upon the lawfulness of decisions—not to express opinions as to the merits of medical judgment. In particular, the court rejected the suggestion that the wishes of the parents had been inadequately considered; in fact, the authority was under great pressure from the parents and had taken its decision in response to that pressure. Secondly, Sir Thomas Bingham MR considered that, by any showing, the treatment was at the frontier of medical science. Thirdly, he held:

I have no doubt that in a perfect world any treatment which a patient . . . sought would be provided if doctors were willing to give it, no matter how much it cost . . . It would, however, be shutting one's eyes to the real world if the court were to proceed on the basis that we do live in such a world.[153]

And, further, the court cannot make a judgment as to how a limited budget is to be best allocated. In the end, it was open to the health authority to reach the decision they had already reached. We should, as a coda, note that B's treatment was ultimately funded from both private and public sources; she died 14 months after the hearing. All the doctors involved agreed that B's life under treatment was likely to be oppressive; can one say that the gain of a year of such life negates the imprint of medical futility?—it is an arguable point but we have our doubts.

16.85 The case of Child B provided the perfect setting for 'shroud-waving' in the popular press; an in-depth analysis of the media coverage shows the extent of the pressures exerted.[154] It was, of course, unfortunate that clinical and economic considerations became entwined and, inevitably, the press saw the issue almost exclusively in financial terms; the situation was, however, bound to arise as the funding for what are known as 'extra-contractual referrals'—or the purchase of medical services outside the particular health authority—is subject to special regulation. But was *ex p B* an attempt to impose resource rationing under the cloak of medical futility? We think not. An authority must abide by the decisions of its expert advisers who were unanimous that the suggested treatment was contraindicated. In the circumstances, the authority might well have been regarded as behaving unreasonably if it *had* persisted with treatment. At the most, its attitude could be seen as part of the now familiar balancing exercise; we will never know what would have been the decision had the proposed regime not been quite so extravagant of public money—or, on the other side of the coin, had not involved quite such risk and discomfort to the patient.

16.86 *Re T* and *ex p B* may seem to be at odds, in that the Court of Appeal recognised the interests of the parents as having a high priority in the former and rejected them in

---

[152] See para 16.80 et seq above. [153] (1995) 23 BMLR 1 at 8–9.

[154] V A Entwistle, I S Watt, R Bradbury and L J Pehl 'Media Coverage of the Child B Case' (1996) 312 BMJ 1587.

the latter. The cynic might say that this is simply a matter of health care economics—that parental interests will be supported when they pose no threat to the pocket of the NHS. The alternative and, in our view, better approach is to see the two decisions as consistent. We do not disguise our suspicions as to the correctness of that taken in *Re T*. The fact remains that the court conducted a balancing act in both cases and, rightly or wrongly, concluded that the risks and suffering involved in treatment outweighed the chances of success. Certainly, the decisive evidence came from opposing corners but, at the end of the day, the lesson is that the courts will not impose what they, having heard the medical evidence, regard as medically futile—or, better, non-productive—treatment of children whose management is in dispute. Although they were stated in a rather different context, the words of Sir Thomas Bingham MR provide the foundation for our current jurisprudence:

[T]he decision of a devoted and responsible parent should be treated with respect . . . But the role of the court is to exercise an independent and objective judgment. If that judgment is in accord with that of the devoted and responsible parent, well and good. If it is not, then it is the duty of the court, after giving due weight to the view of the devoted and responsible parent, to give effect to its own judgment. That is what it is there for.[155]

16.87   But what is to guide the court it its decisions? Concepts such as 'futility' and 'best interests' have strong normative appeal but, as we have hopefully shown, the search for objectivity in their application may itself be a futile exercise. The reality is that decision-makers are involved in a value-laden process, and this is no less true when the decision is taken in a court rather than at the patient's bedside. Often the values to which we appeal are merely implicit in our decisions, and courts often take refuge in legal constructs which may reveal little about the underlying reasons for a particular outcome. But a trend has emerged in recent years whereby the courts have been more willing to state clearly which values inform their decisions. Nowhere is this illustrated more clearly than in *R (on the application of Burke) v General Medical Council*[156] and consideration of this case provides us with the perfect bridge between our discussions of futility at the beginning and at the end of life.

PART 2: THE END OF LIFE

16.88   Mr Burke suffered from the degenerative disease cerebellar ataxia which would, eventually leave him unable to communicate while still retaining his mind. Essentially, he challenged the Guidance issued by the GMC[157] that it would be within the bounds of good medical practice to withhold or withdraw artificial nutrition and hydration (ANH) when the conditions were considered to be so severe and the prognosis so

---

[155] In *Re Z (a minor) (freedom of publication)* [1997] Fam 1 at 32, [1995] 4 All ER 961 at 986.
[156] [2004] EWHC 1879, [2004] 3 FCR 579.   [157] N 119 above.

poor that providing ANH would be too burdensome for the patient in relation to the possible benefits. Mr Burke did not want ANH to be removed under any circumstances, no matter his state of health. For him, ANH would never be futile and it would be in his own best interests to continue to receive such care even when nothing else could be done for him medically and when the sole function of that care would be to keep his body alive. In an controversial ruling, the court held that (a) the Guidelines concentrated too much on the right of the competent patient to refuse treatment rather than to require treatment; (b) they did not stipulate that a doctor who did not wish to follow the patient's wishes must continue to treat until a doctor who was willing to do so was found; (c) they failed to acknowledge a very strong presumption in favour of prolonging life, and (d) that the standard of best interests was intolerability from the patient's own perspective. Article 8 ECHR implied that it was for the competent patient, not the doctor, to decide what treatment should be given to achieve what the patient thought was conducive to his or her dignity. However, there would be no breach of Articles 2, 3 or 8 if ANH was withdrawn when it was serving absolutely no purpose and was, indeed, futile, but this would not be the case in Mr Burke's circumstances.

16.89   Munby J's analysis is founded on ethical principles for which he finds support in human rights law. Thus, prominence is given to *sanctity of life* (protected by Article 2, ECHR), *dignity* (which underpins the entire human rights Convention but is most clearly seen in Article 3, ECHR), and *autonomy* or *self-determination* (which the Strasbourg Court and its domestic counterparts are in the process of 'interpreting out' of Article 8, ECHR). Munby J rates dignity highly[158] as a fundamental recognition of our humanity and a recognition, in particular, of a person's interest in the manner of his or her death.

16.90   Dignity can, of course, be seen from a subjective or objective perspective, and both feature in Munby J's analysis. They divide along the categories of competency. Thus, it is for the competent patient to *determine*—and we should note with care the use of this expression—'. . . what treatment *should* or should not be given in order to achieve what the patient believes conduces to his dignity and in order to avoid what the patient would find stressing'.[159] Where the patient is incompetent, best interests applies, and the dignity test is what 'right-thinking persons' would consider undignified in such circumstances. Munby J is clearly suspicious of the several cases he quotes which seek, progressively, to modify the concept of the sanctity of life in favour of one which admits of a value judgment; his starting point, as he says, lies in the very strong presumption in favour of taking all steps which will prolong life—'Save in exceptional circumstances, or where the patient is dying, the best interests of the patient will normally require such steps to be taken'. The benchmark at which the sanctity of life gives way to the principle of best interests is the 'intolerability of life' and, where the

---

[158] Quoting his judgment in *R (on the application of A, B, X and Y) v East Sussex CC* and the *Disability Rights Commission (No. 2)* [2003] EWHC 167 (Admin) at [86].

[159] *Burke*, n 156 above, para 130.

patient is competent, this is to be judged by reference to the patient's own assessment of his condition. Where the patient is incompetent, intolerability is to be objectively assessed. But whether the life of an insensate patient is couched in terms of 'quality' or 'tolerability', the assessment is still a matter of clinical judgment.[160] The most troubling aspect of the judgment, however, arises from the court's view of patient autonomy, to which even the sanctity of life principle is subordinated for the patient's decision 'as to what life-prolonging treatment he should or should not have is in principle *determinative*'.[161] Here Munby J is contemplating ANH, and few could argue that the removal of such basic care would be a fundamental indignity and self-evidently objectionable. But the danger in this ruling is that there is insufficient emphasis placed on the reasons why and how it is possible to distinguish between ANH and other forms of treatment. The risk is that subsequent courts will be unsuccessful in doing so. We see below in the case of persistent vegetative state (PVS) how the courts have struggled to hold the line on a precedent. The consequences of *Burke* could be profound and far-reaching. We have argued elsewhere[162] that this decision contains elements which suggest entitlement to care in general, implying a *right* to that care. These elements centre on the language of the case—first, the notion that the patient's views are *determinative* of his interests, even when those interests are *in favour of* care and, second, the linking of autonomy-based arguments under Article 8 ECHR with dignity-based arguments under Article 3 ECHR, which reinforces a subjective approach to dignity in law. If this is indeed the case, why should the nature of the care in question matter at all? Even if it is possible to contain this precedent within the parameters of ANH, it cannot be divorced from its fiscal consequences. And this, ultimately, reveals one of the great fallacies of the 'best interests' test—while the patient and his interests may be our primary focus of attention, all decisions taken in respect of care necessarily engage a far broader range of interests with implications that can reach far beyond the instant case. The test itself, however, barely admits consideration of this reality.

16.91   We have suggested already that the concept of medical futility can be applied as a continuum from the neonate to the terminally ill. The full picture is, however, not quite so simple, as the underlying reasons for, and the management of, non-treatment will vary according to age. Thus, non-treatment in infancy has been, at least in part, a matter of the management of physical disability. But this has been morally permissible only because treatment of itself would result in an intolerable life which it would be inhumane to enforce on the child who would, at the same time, die naturally if he or

---

[160] Cf, A G Lawthers, G S Pransky, L E Peterson and J H Himmelstein 'Rethinking Quality in the Context of Persons with Disability' (2003) 15 Intl J Quality in Health Care 287 who call for a multi-disciplinary approach to quality assessment.

[161] *Burke*, n 156 above, para 116(11) emphasis added.

[162] J K Mason and G T Laurie 'Personal Autonomy and the Right to Treatment: A Note on *R (on the application of Burke) v General Medical Council'* (2005) 9 Edin LR 123. As we go to typesetting, it is reported that the GMC has successfully appealed the decision in *Burke* on much the same grounds as we have remarked: A Frean 'Doctors get final say on treating the dying' (2005) *The Times*, 29 July, p 17.

she were untreated. Such conditions are uncommon in adult life and, when they do occur—as, for example, in accidental quadriplegia—their management is more allied to euthanasia[163] than to selective non-treatment.

16.92　　Disability due to brain damage is, however, common to both infancy and adulthood and we have seen that, while the courts will not tolerate the deliberate shortening of life, they are fully prepared to accede to non-treatment of associated lethal disease in the severely brain-damaged child—and to base this on an undeniably 'quality of life' standard as measured by a 'best interests' test. It is of some interest to speculate on why it is that this has been accepted relatively easily in the case of children while the legal attitude to the management of the brain damaged adult has taken so long to mature and has done so amid so much controversy. Is it that we give greater weight to life that has 'been lived' than to life which has no past? Do we see a sustainable distinction between starting on a life with handicap and continuing life in a disabled state? Are we less concerned with any residual cognitive ability in the infant than we are with comparable but expressible brain activity in the adult? And are we frightened of an ever-widening definition of what is perceived as intolerable in the adult? Possibly the most important delineator lies in the purely pragmatic reason that fatal intercurrent disease is simply less common in the brain damaged adult in whom, accordingly, non-treatment moves ever closer to euthanasia and, as a result, becomes less acceptable.

16.93　　Yet we are constantly assured that we are *not* practising euthanasia in allowing such persons to die. Thus, we have Hoffmann LJ saying:

This is not a case about euthanasia because it does not involve any external agency of death. It is about whether, and how, the patient should be allowed to die.[164]

16.94　　It is for this reason that we have detached the management of the brain damaged adult—and, particularly, the adult in the permanent vegetative state—from our discussion of euthanasia. Legally—if less certainly logically—it sits easier under the heading of 'futile treatment'; as Lord Goff put it in the House of Lords in *Bland*, 'it is the futility of the treatment [of Anthony Bland] which justifies its termination'.[165]

THE PATIENT IN THE PERMANENT VEGETATIVE STATE

16.95　　We have already discussed the effect of hypoxia on the various sectors of the brain. In clinical terms, this means that depriving the brain of oxygen can result in anything from mild intellectual deterioration to death—the outcome being determined almost

---

163　See chapter 17.
164　In *Airedale NHS Trust v Bland* [1993] 1 All ER 821 at 856, (1993) 12 BMLR 64 at 101, CA.
165　[1993] 1 All ER 821 at 870, (1993) 12 BMLR 64 at 116.

exclusively by how rapidly normal oxygenation can be established. How much consciousness or cognitive ability is retained then depends on the degree of permanent cortical damage and this can be of very considerable moral and medico-legal significance. In any event, the brain stem—which controls our vegetative functions—will survive an hypoxic insult better than will the cortex, and the truly critical situation arises when the cortex is wholly destroyed but the brain stem continues to function. This is the condition which was originally described as the 'persistent vegetative state' by Jennett and Plum.[166] The patient then has no consciousness and the awesome nature of the condition is summed up in the phrase: 'Consciousness is the most critical moral, legal, and constitutional standard, not for human life itself, but for human personhood'[167]—the unconscious or comatose patient is incapable of fulfilling his human function in a way which transcends the loss of any other capacity; it follows that the whole status of the person in a position of persistent unconsciousness is in doubt.

16.96   It is notoriously difficult to identify a satisfactory definition of the persistent vegetative state. The distinguishing features include an irregular but cyclic state of circadian sleeping and waking unaccompanied by any behaviourally detectable expression of self-awareness, specific recognition of external stimuli, or consistent evidence of attention or inattention or learned responses.[168] It is important to note that patients in this state, while generally being in a spastic condition, are not immobile and, to a varying extent, retain both cranial-nerve and spinal reflexes, including those related to visual and auditory stimuli. Again, this reflects the degree of brain damage; we can, therefore, speak in terms of degrees of vegetativeness, although it requires skilled neurological expertise to distinguish retained—or recovered—cortical function from sub-cortical reflex activity. In addition, the concept has its built-in semantic difficulties, the most urgent of which lies in the word 'persistent'. A persistent state is one which persists until it is relieved—from which it follows that the diagnosis of the persistent vegetative state envisages a potential for recovery; this was the understanding of those who coined the term.[169] It is, in our opinion, essential that discussion—and any legislation based upon it—should be devoted to the management of the *permanent* vegetative state (PVS).[170] Even then, the difficulties are not all eliminated. Permanence is a presumption rather than a certainty; whether or not that presumption is acceptable depends on empirical evidence which must, also, bow to practicality. Thus, the Multi-society Task Force in America defined the persistent

---

[166] B Jennett and F Plum 'Persistent Vegetative State after Brain Damage' (1972) 1 Lancet 734 and more recently B Jennett *The Vegetative State: Medical Facts, Ethical and Legal Dilemmas* (2002).

[167] R E Cranford and D R Smith 'Consciousness: The Most Critical Moral (Constitutional) Standard for Human Personhood' (1987) 13 Am J Law Med 233.

[168] Multi-society Task Force on PVS 'Medical Aspects of the Persistent Vegetative State' (1994) 330 New Engl J Med 1499 (Pt 1), 1572 (Pt 2).

[169] See S Laureys, M-E Faymonville and J Berre 'Permanent Vegetative State and Persistent Vegetative State are not Interchangeable Terms' (2000) 321 BMJ letters, 17 October.

[170] See, especially, Royal College of Physicians *The Vegetative State: Guidance on Diagnosis and Management* (2003).

vegetative state as a vegetative state present one month after acute traumatic or non-traumatic brain injury; it concluded that a permanent state can be assumed if the patient has been vegetative for one year.[171] But to say that a state is permanent if it has been present for a year[172] involves a balancing act between reasonableness and certainty. The compromise, no matter how high is the degree of clinical certainty, is unlikely to satisfy everyone and the possibility of exceptions to the rule cannot be denied; nevertheless, the advantages of establishing a cut-off point outweigh the disadvantages of prolonging the decision indefinitely. Of equal importance is the fact that, as we have already noted, the word 'vegetative' fails to define the degree of brain damage involved. Therapeutic decisions in PVS thus depend not only on its permanence but also on the definition of vegetative which must, to an extent, involve a value judgment.

16.97　　Having reached a diagnosis, however, we are left with what may well be regarded as the ultimate tragedy in human life—a human being who is alive in the cardiovascular sense in that he or she can breathe and maintain a heart beat, and who is, equally, not brain stem dead, but who, at the same time, has no contact with the outside world and will never have such contact again. We have discussed the concept of neocortical death above.[173] At this point we need only reiterate that it has no place in the law of the United Kingdom. The law as to killing is unaffected by the mental state of the victim—dements and aments are still protected in so far as the term 'reasonable being' implies no more than 'human being'—and persons in the permanent vegetative state still represent 'persons in being'. They present an extra jurisprudential difficulty in that, being unconscious, they are free from pain—or, at least, pain cannot be expressed in a manner which makes it treatable; the doctrine of 'double effect' cannot, therefore, be applied within their management—and, in this respect, it is to be noted that, absent an intercurrent infection or similar complication, well-managed PVS patients have a life expectancy that is to be measured in years. Lord Scarman,[174] while appreciating—

that there are great social problems not only in the life support of the human vegetable but also in the survival of barely sentient people who cannot look after themselves,

also added:

there are implications in the right to terminate another's existence of which it is well to be fearful in the absence of a more prolonged analysis of the problem than that which it has received.

---

[171] See n 168 above.

[172] Agreed by the BMA: BMA *Guidelines on Treatment Decisions for Patients in Persistent Vegetative State* (1996) and by the Working Party of the Royal College of Physicians 'The Permanent Vegetative State—Review by a Working Group Convened by the Royal College of Physicians and Endorsed by the Conference of Medical Royal Colleges and their Faculties of the United Kingdom' (1996) 30 J R Coll Physicians Lond 119 (revised 2003, see n 170 above).

[173] See chapter 13.

[174] Lord Scarman 'Legal Liability and Medicine' (1981) 74 Proc Roy Soc Med 11.

16.98   These extra-judicial remarks were made some time ago; since then, the topic has
          been subject to intense moral scrutiny and to extensive legal analysis. We have spent
          some time on the definitional difficulties of the condition because, without an under-
          standing of them, it is impossible to appreciate the distinctions which have been made
          in the various cases that have come before the courts in recent years and the reasons
          underlying them. All those that we discuss have it in common that the courts were
          being invited to pronounce on the lawfulness of withdrawing physiological support
          from severely brain-damaged patients.

THE ENGLISH CASES

16.99   The first, and most important case in which the matter was addressed in the United
          Kingdom was *Airedale NHS Trust v Bland*.[175] Anthony Bland was crushed in a football
          stadium in April 1989 and sustained severe anoxic brain damage; as a result, he
          relapsed into the persistent vegetative state. There was no improvement in his condi-
          tion by September 1992 and, at that time, the hospital sought a declaration[176] to the
          effect that they might lawfully discontinue all life-sustaining treatment and medical
          support measures, including ventilation, nutrition and hydration by artificial means;
          that any subsequent treatment given should be for the sole purpose of enabling him to
          end his life in dignity and free from pain and suffering; that, if death should then
          occur, its cause should be attributed to the natural and other causes of his present
          state; and that none of those concerned should, as a result, be subject to any civil or
          criminal liability. This declaration—save for the final clause, which was considered
          inappropriate[177]—was granted in the Family Division essentially on the grounds that
          it was in AB's best interests to do so; the court considered there was overwhelming
          evidence that the provision of artificial feeding by means of a nasogastric tube was
          'medical treatment' and that its discontinuance was in accord with good medical
          practice. An appeal was unanimously dismissed in the Court of Appeal. From three
          exceptionally well-considered opinions, we extract only that of Hoffmann LJ:

          This is not an area in which any difference can be allowed to exist between what is legal and
          what is morally right. The decision of the court should be able to carry conviction with the
          ordinary person as being based not merely on legal precedent but also upon acceptable
          ethical values.[178]

---

[175] [1993] 1 All ER 821, (1993) 12 BMLR 64, Fam D, CA, HL.

[176] The English courts have been in something of a dilemma in such cases since their authority under the
parens patriae jurisdiction was removed by way of the Mental Health Act 1959 and revocation of the last
warrant under the Sign Manual. The court cannot now give effective consent to medical treatment on behalf
of a mentally incompetent adult unless that treatment is directed to the cause of the incompetence. The court
can, however, make an anticipatory declaration as to the lawfulness or otherwise of a proposed action: see
discussion of *Re F* at para 10.33 et seq above.

[177] This problem was considered in greater detail in the comparable Scottish case *Law Hospital NHS Trust
v Lord Advocate* 1996 SLT 848, (1996) 39 BMLR 166, for which see para 16.123 et seq below.

[178] [1993] 1 All ER 821 at 850, (1993) 12 BMLR 64 at 95.

and, later:

In my view the choice the law makes must reassure people that the courts do have full respect for life, but that they do not pursue the principle to the point at which it has become almost empty of any real content and when it involves the sacrifice of other important values such as human dignity and freedom of choice. I think that such reassurance can be provided by a decision, properly explained, to allow Anthony Bland to die.[179]

16.100 The inherent difficulty of the declarator procedure is that it is concerned only with the *lawfulness* of an action[180] and, when the *Bland* case came to the House of Lords, Lord Browne-Wilkinson and Lord Mustill were at particular pains to emphasise that the ethical issues should be considered and legislated for by Parliament:

[I]s this a matter which lies outside the legitimate development of the law by judges and requires society, through the democratic expression of its views in Parliament, to reach its decisions on the underlying moral and practical problems and then reflect those decisions in legislation? I have no doubt that it is for Parliament, not the courts, to decide the broader issues which this case raises.[181]

16.101 It was, therefore, not surprising that, although the House could not entirely avoid addressing the ethical and moral problems involved, it did so to a lesser extent than did the Court of Appeal. In this respect, the fundamental conflict lies in the inevitable distortion of the principle of the sanctity of life which would result from a decision to terminate the care on which life depended.[182] The majority of the House was able to dispose of this on the grounds that the principle was certainly not absolute. Moreover, since the right to refuse treatment—including life-sustaining treatment—is now firmly part of common law and medical ethics, the principle of the sanctity of life must yield to that of the right to self-determination and, of the many lines of argument considered, it is this which seems to us to bind all five Law Lords most closely together. As Lord Goff put it,[183] the right to self-determination should not be eclipsed by the fact of incompetence—it must always be present. This also forms the basis of Lord Mustill's reasoning, which is summarised below and which, essentially, justifies the withdrawal or withholding of treatment. We are less happy with the alternative view taken, in particular, by Lord Lowry and Lord Browne-Wilkinson. In essence, this also started from the premise that non-voluntary treatment was lawful only so long as it was justified by necessity; but, once necessity could no longer be claimed—by reason of the futility of treatment—further invasion of the patient's body constituted either the crime of battery or the tort of trespass. On this view, any potential medical offence lies not in *withholding* treatment but in *continuing* it to no purpose. This argument seems to us to be dangerously open-ended in relation to conditions less

---

[179] [1993] 1 All ER 821 at 855, (1993) 12 BMLR 64 at 100.

[180] See J Bridgeman ' "Declared Innocent?" '(1995) 3 Med L Rev 117.

[181] [1993] 1 All ER 821 at 878, (1993) 12 BMLR 64 at 124, per Lord Browne-Wilkinson.

[182] For major discussion, see J Keown 'Restoring Moral and Intellectual Shape to the Law after *Bland*' (1997) 113 LQR 481.

[183] [1993] 1 All ER 821 at 866, (1993) 12 BMLR 64 at 112.

clear-cut than the persistent vegetative state—a situation which Lord Mustill was clearly anxious to avoid. None the less, this concern has been borne out more recently in guidance from the British Medical Association which proposes extending the PVS ruling to other incapacitated patients.[184] We discuss this further below.[185]

16.102   The greater part of the opinions in *Bland* was concerned for the doctors' position vis-à-vis the criminal law. First, it was essential to elide the possibility of murder by classifying removal of support as an omission rather than as a positive act.[186] There was wide agreement that, while there was no moral or logical difference, a distinction was certainly to be made in law. The House came to a unanimous conclusion that discontinuance of nasogastric feeding was an omission; their Lordships achieved this in various ways but, in general, it was considered impossible to distinguish between withdrawal of and not starting tube feeding—and the latter was clearly an omission. Next, the problem of the duty of care had to be addressed. Lord Mustill's argument can be summarised:

(a) Treatment of the incompetent is governed by necessity and necessity is, in turn, defined in terms of the patient's best interests.

(b) Once there is no hope of recovery, any interest in being kept alive disappears and, with it, the justification for invasive therapy also disappears.

(c) In the absence of necessity, there can be no duty to act and, in the absence of a duty, there can be no criminality in an omission.

16.103   This, however, leads to what was, perhaps, the major hurdle—can feeding be regarded as medical treatment and, therefore, a fit subject for medical decision-making, or is it always such a fundamental duty that it can never be wilfully withheld? The Lords in *Bland* had rather more trouble with this than have had their counterparts in the United States.[187] Eventually, however, a consensus was reached that nasogastric feeding at least formed part of the general medical management. While it is certainly more difficult to see nasogastric feeding as medical treatment than it is to accept gastrostomy feeding as such, we do not share some of the academic distrust of the concept that has been expressed.[188]

16.104   At the end of the day, the House of Lords was able to justify its unanimous decision on the basis of the patient's best interests. All the opinions stressed that it was not a matter of it being in the best interests of the patient to die but, rather, that it was not in his best interests to treat him so as to prolong his life in circumstances where 'no affirmative benefit' could be derived from the treatment.[189] We confess to some difficulty in accepting a 'best interests' test in these circumstances and we return to the

---

[184] British Medical Association *Withholding and Withdrawing Life-Prolonging Medical Treatment: Guidance for Decision Makers* (2nd edn, 2001).

[185] See para 16.120.   [186] For further discussion of which, see chapter 17 below.

[187] See para 16.137 et seq.

[188] See, e.g., J M Finnis 'Bland: Crossing the Rubicon?' (1993) 109 LQR 329.

[189] [1993] 1 All ER 821 at 883, (1993) 12 BMLR 64 at 130, per Lord Browne-Wilkinson. See also [1993] 1 All ER 821 at 865, (1993) 12 BMLR 64 at 115.

matter below.[190] For the present, we point out that its application dictates the concurrent acceptance of 'good medical practice' as the yardstick of assessment. This led the House of Lords to conclude that the *Bolam* test [191]—that the doctor's decision should be judged against one which would be taken by a responsible and competent body of relevant professional opinion—applied in the management of PVS. This gives considerable discretion to the medical profession to decide what amounts to the patient's best interests by reference to its own standards[192] and, in deciding that artificial feeding was, at least, an integral part of medical treatment, the House of Lords opened the door to the health carers to withdraw alimentation. Nevertheless, the requirement to seek court approval in every case was maintained[193]—subject to the hope that the restriction might be rescinded in the future—and there was, in fact, a strong undercurrent to the effect that the decision was specific to *Bland* rather than a general statement on the removal of alimentation from brain damaged persons.

English cases post-*Bland*

16.105   Consideration of the later cases suggests that a note of caution may not have been misplaced. Almost exactly a year later, we had the case of *Frenchay Healthcare NHS Trust v S*.[194] This concerned a young man who had been in apparent PVS for two and a half years as a result of a drug overdose. When it was discovered that his gastrostomy tube had become detached, a declaration was sought that the hospital could lawfully refrain from renewing or continuing alimentary and other life-sustaining measures and could restrict any medical treatment to that which would allow him to die peacefully and with the greatest dignity. The declaration was granted and the decision was upheld on appeal.

16.106   *Frenchay v S* differs from *Bland* in a fundamental respect—that, although the prospect had been mooted, the actual decision to discontinue treatment was not a considered one but was one forced by events. As a corollary, the judicial inquiry was certainly hurried and this was the factor which most concerned Waite LJ in the Court of Appeal. The decision has also been subject to academic criticism on these grounds.[195] More importantly, Sir Thomas Bingham MR considered it plain that the evidence in *Frenchay* was neither as emphatic nor as unanimous as that in *Bland*'s case.[196] We must also consider the potential results of failing to make or countermanding the

---

[190] See para 16.130 et seq.

[191] *Bolam v Friern Hospital Management Committee* [1957] 1 WLR 582, (1957) 1 BMLR 1.

[192] See [1993] 1 All ER 821 at 883, (1993) 12 BMLR 64 at 130, per Lord Browne-Wilkinson: '... on an application to the court for a declaration that the discontinuance of medical care will be lawful, the courts only concern will be to be satisfied that the doctor's decision to discontinue is in accordance with a respectable body of medical opinion and that it is reasonable ...' (emphasis added).

[193] *Practice Note* [1996] 4 All ER 766, (1996) 34 BMLR 20, and see now *Practice Note (Official Solicitor: Declaratory Proceedings: Medical and Welfare Decisions for Adults Who Lack Capacity)* [2001] 2 FCR 569 and *Practice Direction* [2002] 1 WLR 325.

[194] [1994] 2 All ER 403, (1994) 17 BMLR 156, CA.

[195] See e.g. A Grubb 'Commentary' (1994) 2 Med L Rev 206.

[196] [1994] 2 All ER 403 at 411, (1994) 17 BMLR 156 at 163.

declaration sought—either the doctors would have been forced into an operation which was, in the opinion of the consultant in charge, of no benefit to the patient and which possibly verged on criminal intervention or they would have had to do nothing and take their chance with the law.

16.107   Sir Thomas accepted such medical opinion as was provided but was, himself, conscious of a qualitative difference between the two cases. The question thus arises as to whether *Frenchay* represents a 'slippery slope' on which we could descend from PVS to little more than physical or mental disability when assuming that the patient's 'best interests' lie in non-treatment; alternatively, is it a judicial effort to homogenise non-treatment decisions—during which process, PVS becomes merely the end-point for decision-making rather than a condition to be considered on its own? We discuss below[197] the difficulties in harmonising the 'specific-case' stance adopted in *Bland* with the relatively open-ended direction as to withholding 'futile' treatment that was provided in *Re J*.[198] Meantime, perhaps the main inference to be drawn is that each case is special and must be judged on its own facts.[199]

16.108   Later English cases have been reported only spasmodically. We comment briefly on some of these mainly to indicate the quality of the evidence.

16.109   *Re C*[200] concerned a 27-year-old man who had been in PVS for four years following an anaesthetic disaster. Clinically, the case was of great severity and the judge appears to have accepted without demur the evidence provided by the relatives as to the likely wishes of the patient.

16.110   *Re G*[201] related to a young man whose brain damage, sustained in a motorcycle accident, was intensified by a later anoxic episode. The case was of particular interest in that there was some dispute amongst the relatives as to the course to be adopted. Sir Stephen Brown P concluded that the dissenting views of the patient's mother should not be allowed to operate as a veto when his best interests—as defined by the surgeon in charge—favoured removal of nutrition. It seems likely, therefore, that the comments of Lord Goff in *Bland*[202] to the effect that the attitudes of relatives, while due great respect, should not be determinative will be followed in the event of conflict.

16.111   *Swindon and Marlborough NHS Trust v S*[203] was unique among reported cases in being concerned with a patient who was being nursed at home. Rather as in *Frenchay*,

---

[197] See para 16.139.

[198] *Re J (a minor) (wardship: medical treatment)* [1990] 3 All ER 930, (1990) 6 BMLR 25.

[199] A point which was emphasised in *Bland* and also in the even more doubtful Irish case of *In the matter of a Ward* (1995) 2 ILRM 401. Precisely the same result was achieved in this case although the reasoning was complicated by considerations of Irish constitutional law. For discussion, see J K Mason and G T Laurie 'The Management of the Persistent Vegetative State in the British Isles' [1996] JR 263; J Keown 'Life and Death in Dublin' [1996] CLJ 6.

[200] R Ford 'Patient in coma may die in dignity' *The Times*, 18 November 1995, p 1. The importance of continued post-mortem anonymity was considered in *Re C (adult patient: restriction of publicity after death)* [1996] 2 FLR 251 and see, more recently, *Practice Direction* [2002] 1 WLR 325. For professional guidance to this effect, see General Medical Council, *Confidentiality: Protecting and Providing Information* (2004), para 30.

[201] [1995] 3 Med L Rev 80. In passing, it was held that the public interest in these cases determined that they should be heard in open court: *Re G (adult patient: publicity)* [1995] 2 FLR 528.

[202] [1993] 1 All ER 821 at 872, (1993) 12 BMLR 64 at 118.   [203] [1995] 3 Med LR 84.

however, the issue was forced by blockage of the gastrostomy tube; further treatment would, therefore, have involved hospitalisation. Ward J held that, given the certain diagnosis of PVS, to discontinue life-sustaining measures would be in accordance with good medical practice as recognised and approved within the medical profession. Once again, as in *Re G*, the court firmly adopted *Bolam* as the benchmark—there is a strong suggestion that good medical practice is being seen as a test of lawfulness.

16.112　　There was no doubt as to the diagnosis in any of these three cases. *Re D*,[204] however, concerned a 28-year-old woman who had sustained very severe brain damage following a head injury some six years before. Again, an emergency arose when her gastrostomy tube became displaced. All medical opinion was to the effect that D was totally unaware of anything or anyone but she did not fully satisfy the conditions laid down by the Royal College of Physicians for the diagnosis of the permanent vegetative state.[205] The President of the Family Division regarded her as suffering 'a living death' and was unable to accept that, because she did not fulfil one of the diagnostic criteria, she was not in a permanent vegetative state. He, therefore, did not believe he was extending the range of cases in which a declaration as to the removal of feeding and hydration might properly be considered. It was appropriate and in her best interests to make such a declaration.

16.113　　*Re H*,[206] involved a 43-year-old woman who had existed for three years in a severely brain damaged state following a vehicular accident. She, too, was agreed to be wholly and unalterably unaware of herself or her environment but, equally, it was agreed that she did not fit squarely within one of the College of Physicians' diagnostic criteria. Sir Stephen Brown P thought that, in this instance 'it may be that a precise label is not of significant importance'. Indeed, the whole area is prey to semantic juggling—one expert, while agreeing that the case did not fit the criteria for the permanent vegetative state, nevertheless thought that H was in a vegetative state which was permanent. The court reiterated that, while it was aware of the consequences that would follow the suspension of treatment, it did not in any sense sanction anything which is *aimed* at terminating life:

The sanctity of life is of vital importance. It is not, however, paramount and ... I am satisfied that it is in the best interests of this patient that the life sustaining treatment ... should be brought to a conclusion.[207]

16.114　　Thus, while all these cases show distinctive variations, they also have common features which serve as pointers to the future. The first is that, the precedents having been set, the baseline lies in the confirmed diagnosis of PVS. Once that is made, the conclusion follows automatically that the patient's best interests dictate the termination of assisted feeding and, indeed, there may well be an obligation on the doctor to discontinue treatment.[208] Second, and following from this, the Official Solicitor has

---

[204] (1997) 38 BMLR 1.　　[205] See n 170 above.
[206] *Re H (adult: incompetent)* (1997) 38 BMLR 11.　　[207] (1997) 38 BMLR 11 at 16.
[208] Following the argument put forward by Grubb in 'Commentary' [1995] 3 Med L Rev 83, 85.

been loath to oppose any applications for withdrawal of support once the diagnosis is confirmed. Complete medicalisation of treatment decisions in the condition may, then, be only a short step away. This having been said, a Practice Direction makes it clear that High Court approval should be sought in almost all cases where removal of feeding and hydration is contemplated.[209] The court is charged with weighing the advantages and disadvantages for the patient of removal in light of the available medical evidence, although it is difficult to see how any conclusion other than withdrawal could be reached when faced with a good faith assessment of medical futility by the care team. We say this in light of recent developments which—contrary to the expectations of some—demonstrate that the provisions of the Human Rights Act 1998 make virtually no difference to the position of patients in PVS.

16.115   In *NHS Trust A v Mrs M, NHS Trust B v Mrs H*[210] declarators of legality were sought on the proposed withdrawal of feeding and hydration from two patients in PVS. In authorising this the High Court not only endorsed the pre-existing position under *Bland*, but went further in testing this precedent against possible human rights objections under the 1998 Act, namely Article 2 (right to life), Article 3 (prohibition of cruel and inhuman treatment), and Article 8 (right to respect for private life). Rather than considering the particularised reasoning of Butler-Sloss P in respect of each of these provisions,[211] a few points of principle and policy should be noted.

16.116   The court clearly adopted a *good faith* approach to the issue, focusing on the fact that, because a 'responsible body of medical opinion' has reached a conclusion as to futility, there is little more to be said on the matter. This, however, makes professionalism rather than principle the measure of patient protection. We have already shown that medical professionals are qualified only to comment on the medical futility of any proposed course of action and that that the court retains for itself the ultimate role as arbiter of best interests,[212] but, as the Official Solicitor's Practice Note of 2001 also makes clear,[213] an application to the High Court is little more than a confirmatory exercise in respect of the diagnosis of PVS from which a declarator of legality of withdrawal should follow.[214]

16.117   Second, in examining the content of the human rights laid before it, the court fixed on the principle of respect for personal autonomy and concluded that, because the PVS patient could not consent to continued intervention, to continue to intervene against his or her best interests—as determined by (medically qualified) others— would *violate* protection under Article 8. This, however, turns self-determination on

---

[209] *Practice Direction (Declaratory Proceedings: Incapacitated Adults)* [2002] 1 WLR 325, 65 BMLR 72. See also *Practice Note (Official Solicitor: Declaratory Proceedings: Medical and Welfare Decisions for Adults Who Lack Capacity)* [2001] 2 FCR 569.

[210] [2001] 2 WLR 942, (2001) 58 BMLR 87.

[211] For such an analysis, see A R MacLean 'Crossing the Rubicon on the Human Rights Ferry' (2001) 64 MLR 775.

[212] As we discuss further in chapters 9 and 10.

[213] *Practice Note (Official Solicitor: Declaratory Proceedings: Medical and Welfare Decisions for Adults Who Lack Capacity)* [2001] 2 FLR 158.

[214] *Ibid*, Appendix 2.

its head. Indeed, why is this a relevant consideration in the context of someone who cannot meaningfully experience or exercise this state? It is precisely because the patient cannot do so that 'best interests' enters the equation. The error lies in the failure to appreciate that it is *respect* for the human being that is required, not only (or necessarily) respect for her 'right to choose'.

16.118   The court also relied upon the incapacity of these patients to restrict their rights in another respect. It held that, because PVS patients are insensate and cannot appreciate their state of being, it is not cruel and degrading to subject them to the vagaries of withdrawal of feeding and hydration—thus adopting the excessively narrow interpretation of Article 3 that a victim must be able to experience the inhuman treatment before a violation will occur.[215] This, however, is a distorted view of European jurisprudence which has held only that a victim's own subjective reactions to treatment can impact on the question of whether violation has occurred.[216] In no way does it follow, however, that subjectivity is a pre-requisite to violation.

16.119   We see Lord Mustill's fears as to extending the precedent in *Bland* to other, non-PVS, cases being realised in the next English case to be considered. In *Re G (adult incompetent: withdrawal of treatment)*[217] the patient was a 45-year-old woman who had suffered serious anoxic brain damage after inhaling her own vomitus following surgery. She had been kept alive for nine months by means of artificial nutrition and hydration when the NHS trust responsible for her care brought the matter to court for a declaration of legality as to the withdrawal of her means of artificial sustenance. G's family supported the application, stating that she would not have wished to remain in such a state. One expert witness was enough to convince the court that there was no reasonable prospect of her ever recovering and that she should be allowed to 'die with dignity'. Moreover, it was held not to be inconsistent with her human right to life that a decision be made to discontinue treatment, despite her inability to give a valid consent to its withdrawal. A declaration to this effect was granted.

16.120   We view this decision with a degree of concern. It comes very close to the controversial guidance of the British Medical Association, already mentioned, which suggests that an assessment of futility leading to the withdrawal of feeding and hydration may be appropriate for patients with dementia or for those who have suffered serious stroke.[218] This is highly problematic as we have argued elsewhere,[219] not least because the heavy and continuing emphasis placed on medical assessment rather than on a robust and principled approach to individualised human and patients' rights may mean that an expansionist development of clinical discretion is inevitable.

---

[215] Article 3 states: 'No one shall be subjected to torture or to inhuman or degrading treatment or punishment.'

[216] *Campbell and Cosans v UK* (1983) 7 EHRR 165, para 28.

[217] (2001) 65 BMLR 6.

[218] BMA *Withholding and Withdrawing Life-prolonging Medical Treatment*, n 184 above. See also GMC *Withholding and Withdrawing Life-prolonging Treatments: Good Practice in Decision-making* (2002) paras 22–24.

[219] See G T Laurie and J K Mason 'Negative Treatment of Vulnerable Patients: Euthanasia by Any Other Name?' [2000] JR 159.

16.121   The latest ruling from the Court of Appeal reflects our views and concerns, but at the same time it reveals the tragedy of so many of these cases which often feel like lose-lose scenarios. *W Healthcare NHS Trust v H and Another*[220] concerned KH who had suffered from multiple sclerosis for 30 years. She had required artificial feeding for 5 years and needed 24 hour nursing care to survive. She could scarcely speak and recognised nobody; she was however conscious and sentient. Her feeding tube had fallen out and her health carers wished to replace it. The family was opposed to this and appealed the trial judge's opinion in favour of continued treatment. The Court of Appeal upheld the trial judge's ruling that KH should continue to be fed while expressing the deepest of sympathy for her and her family. The court stated that three tests have to be applied in cases such as this. First, is the patient capable of taking an informed decision herself? There was no doubt as to the negative response in the instant case. Second, is there a valid advance statement or directive which covers the present circumstances? We discuss this matter more fully in chapter 10; in KH's case there was insufficient evidence of what she would have wanted to justify relying on an advanced refusal. Finally, if neither test applies, what is in the patient's best interests? It is important to note, as the court itself does, that the legal test in the UK is not substituted judgment, which we explore below at para 16.130 et seq. Thus, the court could not rely on the strong evidence from the family that KH would not have wanted to continuing living in this undignified state to refuse on her behalf. The onerous task for the court was to ask: what is in the patient's best interests given that the decision not to feed would effectively mean that the patient would starve to death? Unlike the PVS cases, KH would have some level of awareness of the process. Brooke LJ emphasised the high value that English law places on life and stated:

> The Court cannot in effect sanction the death by starvation of a patient who is not in a PVS state other than with their clear and informed consent or where their condition is so intolerable as to be beyond doubt . . . I cannot say that life-prolonging treatment . . . would provide no benefit . . . death by this route would . . . be even less dignified than the death which she will more probably face at some time in the more distant future.[221]

16.122   Intolerability, therefore, becomes the touchstone in cases outside the realm of PVS. As to the process of establishing overall best interests, the Court of Appeal approved Thorpe LJ's suggested 'balance sheet' of pros and cons which we discuss in chapter 10.

The position in Scotland

16.123   The outcome of a case similar to *Bland* was awaited with some interest in Scotland, accentuated in part by some very real jurisdictional variations between the two countries. The difficulty of deciding what were, essentially, criminal matters in a civil court was common to both jurisdictions. The House of Lords, while being unanimously

---

[220] [2004] EWCA Civ 1324, [2005] 1 WLR 834.   [221] *Ibid*, para 22.

wary on the point,[222] was quite prepared to accept a fait accompli: 'This appeal', said Lord Mustill, 'has reached this House, and your Lordships must decide it'. There was, however, no certainty that such pragmatism would be available to the Scottish courts. On the other hand, the English court in *Bland* was undoubtedly hampered by the absence of any residual powers of *parens patriae* and, again, the issue was in some doubt in Scotland. This, then, was the uncertain position when Scotland's first PVS case to come to the Inner House of the Court of Session by way of *Law Hospital NHS Trust v Lord Advocate*,[223] in which authority was sought by relatives of a middle-aged woman in PVS (Mrs Johnstone), and by the hospital treating her, to discontinue feeding.

16.124   In the event, the Inner House confirmed that it was not competent to issue a declarator to the effect that a proposed course of action was or was not criminal—it could, however, authorise a declaration in the knowledge that it would not bar proceedings in the High Court but in the hope that it would, in practice, ensure that no prosecution was undertaken there.[224] The court did, however, find that, in contrast to the position in England, the *parens patriae* jurisdiction survived in Scotland and that any authority thus given would have the same effect in law as if consent had been given by the patient. The court, in deciding as to the withdrawal of treatment, could act on its own initiative and would do so in the future.

16.125   The Inner House considered the numerous rulings that had been reached in several common law jurisdictions as to the correct test for exercising the power of consent or refusal of treatment on behalf of incompetents and concluded that the common denominator is that the decision should be taken in the patient's best interests. It followed that if, as in Mrs Johnstone's case, treatment could be of no benefit, then there were no longer any best interests to be served by continuing it.[225] Accordingly, the Lord Ordinary was authorised to provide a declarator to the effect that removal of life-sustaining treatment from Mrs Johnstone would not be unlawful in respect of its civil law consequences.[226]

16.126   The Lord President also remarked that nothing in his opinion was intended to suggest that an application must be made in every case where it is intended to withdraw treatment:

The decision as to whether an application is necessary must rest in each case with those who will be responsible for carrying that intention into effect, having regard in particular . . . to

---

[222] See [1993] 1 All ER 821 at 864–865, 876, 880, 886–887, (1993) 12 BMLR 64 at 110, 122, 127, 133–134, per Lord Goff, Lord Lowry, Lord Browne-Wilkinson and Lord Mustill respectively.

[223] *Law Hospital NHS Trust v Lord Advocate* 1996 SLT 848, (1996) 39 BMLR 166. The case was reported by Lord Cameron from the Outer House to the Inner House without any preliminary judgment.

[224] 1996 SLT 848 at 855, (1996) 39 BMLR 166 at 176, per Lord President Hope.

[225] 1996 SLT 848 at 859, (1996) 39 BMLR 166 at 182–184, per Lord Hope.

[226] It is clear that such a complex manoeuvre will be unnecessary in the future when the Inner House will use its *parens patriae* powers but it was convenient to use it in the instant case. See *Law Hospital NHS Trust v Lord Advocate (No. 2)* 1996 SLT 869, (1996) 39 BMLR 166 at 197.

any statements of policy which may, in the light of this case, be issued by the Lord Advocate.[227]

16.127   And it is here that we run into some difficulties following a statement by the Lord Advocate[228] to the effect that the policy of the Crown Office will be that no criminal prosecution will follow a decision to withdraw feeding but that this is subject to authority to do so having first been obtained by way of the civil law. This appears to pre-empt the direction by the Inner House. However, the Lord Advocate did not say he *would* prosecute in any case that was not so authorised and he went on to say, admittedly in an unofficial ambience:

In Scotland, a decision to withdraw treatment in any case cannot be *guaranteed* immunity from [prosecution] unless the withdrawal has first been authorised by the Court of Session.[229] (Emphasis added.)

Thus, both the Lord President and the Lord Advocate of the time agreed that decisions could be made on medical grounds and independently of the courts—but neither gave any guidance as to when it would be either necessary or unnecessary to seek judicial approval. The latter concluded in his paper: '... it is for doctors and relatives involved in such tragic situations to decide which course of action they wish to adopt'.

16.128   We would hope, and expect, that good common sense would prevail but, meanwhile, we suggest that not many doctors will be prepared to trust to chance that they have 'got it right'. It is reasonable to expect the criminal law to set out the boundaries of impermissible conduct in advance. Vagueness in criminal law offends the widely recognised principle of legal certainty, which requires that crimes should be clearly defined. The situation has now arisen where the doctor may be required to second guess the criminal law—a position that is hardly defensible.

16.129   This common law position remains unchanged after the passing of the Adults with Incapacity (Scotland) Act 2000. The Act allows for the appointment of a welfare guardian to act on behalf of the incompetent patient[230] but it is determinedly not concerned with any form of 'negative treatment', i.e. treatment which results in the death of the patient. Indeed, the Scottish Executive made it very clear that withdrawal or withholding decisions are outside the remit of the legislation.[231] However, we have argued elsewhere[232] that it will be impossible to maintain a clear distinction between positive and negative treatment decisions involving incapable adults, not least because the courts will invariably become involved in settling disputes as to the best thing to do under the Act: to treat or not to treat? Thus, although the powers of a proxy

---

[227]   1996 SLT 848 at 860, (1996) 39 BMLR 166 at 184.

[228]   J Robertson 'Policy on right to die welcomed' *The Scotsman*, 12 April 1996, p 1.

[229]   Lord Mackay of Drumadoon 'Decision on the Persistent Vegetative State: Law Hospital' (1996), paper presented at the Symposium on Medical Ethics and Legal Medicine, Royal College of Physicians and Surgeons of Glasgow, 26 April 1996.

[230]   And replaces the office of tutor dative which is abolished by s 80.

[231]   Scottish Executive Policy Memorandum, 8 October 1999.   [232]   Laurie and Mason, n 219 above.

decision-maker under s 50 do not include a 'right' to refuse as such,[233] his 'right' to a second opinion challenging a medical decision to continue intervention, and ultimately the 'right' to appeal to the court, will necessarily mean that a jurisprudence relating to negative treatment will develop around this recent legislation. There have, however, been, no recent cases on which to test this hypothesis.

THE BEST INTERESTS TEST

16.130   The best interests test has been widely accepted as the measure of good practice in surrogate medico-legal decision-making not only as to PVS but also as to allied problems confronting those caring for incompetent adults.[234] We have, however, to express our doubts as to its validity in respect of the removal of feeding and hydration from (PVS) patients. This is so for three main reasons.

16.131   First, it lends itself to interpretation. Certainly, Lord Goff in *Bland* was of the opinion that the correct framing of the question in these cases was of crucial importance. He said:

> The question is not whether the doctor should take a course which will kill his patient, or even take a course which has the effect of accelerating death. The question is whether the doctor should or should not continue to provide his patient with medical treatment or care which, if continued, will prolong his patient's life . . . [T]he question is not whether it is in the best interests of the patient that he should die. The question is whether it is in the best interests of the patient that his life should be prolonged by the continuance of this form of medical treatment or care.[235]

16.132   Then, we have Lord Hope in *Law Hospital*[236] using the negative approach—'there are no longer any best interests to be served by continuing treatment'—which can be compared with Lord Browne-Wilkinson's medical orientation in *Bland*:[237] 'unless the doctor has reached the affirmative conclusion that it is in the patient's best interest to continue the invasive care, such care must cease.' Our sympathies lie with Lord Clyde:[238]

> [W]hile in the context of some medical situations expressions [such as for the welfare of or

---

[233] See further chapter 10, paras 10.42.

[234] E.g. in sterilisation of the mentally incompetent: *Re F (mental patient: sterilisation)* [1990] 2 AC 1; *L, petitioner* 1996 SCLR 538.

[235] [1993] 1 All ER 821 at 869, (1993) 12 BMLR 64 at 115.

[236] 1996 SLT 848 at 859, (1996) 39 BMLR 166 at 183.

[237] [1993] 1 All ER 821 at 883, (1993) 12 BMLR 64 at 129.

[238] In *Law Hospital* 1996 SLT 848 at 863, (1996) 39 BMLR 166 at 196. The case against reliance on 'best interests' in the context of PVS is argued by A J Fenwick 'Applying Best Interests to Persistent Vegetative State—A Principled Distortion?' (1998) 24 J Med Ethics 86. An alternative view is given in the same issue: R Gillon 'Persistent Vegetative State, Withdrawal of Artificial Nutrition and Hydration, and the Patient's "Best Interests" ' (1998) 24 J Med Ethics 75.

in the best interests of] may be of value, I find less assistance in such language when the choice is between life of a sort and death.

16.133   Secondly, it is difficult to accept Lord Goff's argument in *Bland* as to the nature of the question to be asked: 'we are not saying that it is your best interests to die, just that it is in your best interests not to receive essential physiological support.' How can these two be separated?[239] How can one avoid the conclusion that to argue that it is in one's best interests to be starved is to say anything other than that it is in one's best interests to die? To ask the truly honest question fatally undermines the best interests test. How, then, can one depend upon such a test?

16.134   Thirdly, we believe that the concept of consent is of major importance to the jurisprudence of the vegetative state and it is difficult to fit 'consent' into the inherently paternalistic concept of 'best interests'. It is possible to hold that the best interests of the patient are best served by respecting his autonomy but the argument has something of a hollow ring, as we argue above in respect of *NHS Trust A v Mrs M, NHS Trust B v Mrs H*. We believe that an alternative basis on which to decide what an incompetent person would have consented to or refused must be found and, here, we suggest that the use of the 'substituted judgment' test might be a preferred alternative in the circumstances under consideration.

16.135   The English courts, at least, have consistently rejected this approach in favour of a best interests test but, like it or not, an element of substituted judgment pervades many of the relevant cases,[240] and now, as we suggest in chapter 12, also the terms of the Mental Capacity Act.[241] Our reasons for seeking what is, in effect, compliance with the patient's supposed wishes are several. In so far as substituted judgment acknowledges the autonomy of the patient, it is ethically preferable to a best interests test which is, at base, paternalistic. The absolute right of a competent adult to consent to or refuse treatment is now established in all common law jurisdictions; it is wrong to deprive a person of his or her rights to autonomy on the grounds that he or she is incompetent to express that freedom of choice.[242] Moreover, it eliminates many of the more obvious objections to the latter formulation—'how can it be in the best interests of anyone to die?'; 'how can a person with no interests have any best interests?', and the like. The Court of Appeal recently seemed to lament the non-availability of the substituted judgment test in English law in *W Healthcare NHS Trust v H and Another*, discussed above, and expressly acknowledged that its application in the instant case might have produced a different result (allowing the patient to die)

---

[239] Lord Lowry in *Bland* had similar reservations: [1993] 1 All ER 821 at 887, (1993) 12 BMLR 64 at 123.

[240] See e.g. the reasoning of the Master of the Rolls in *Re J (a minor) (wardship: medical treatment)* [1990] 3 All ER 930 at 936, (1990) 6 BMLR 25 at 32, quoting McKenzie J in *Superintendent of Family and Child Services and Dawson* (1983) 145 DLR (3d) 610. Substituted judgment was quite clearly used in *Re D* (1997) 38 BMLR 1 on the evidence of her mother and in *Re G* (2001) 65 BMLR 6 on the evidence of the family.

[241] See para 12.25.

[242] See Lord Goff in *Bland* [1993] 1 All ER 821 at 866, (1993) 12 BMLR 64 at 112, quoting the Supreme Judicial Court of Massachusetts in *Superintendent of Belchertown State School v Saikewicz* 373 Mass 728 (1977).

rather than the outcome supported by the best interests test (which favoured continued treatment).[243]

16.136   The main ground for objection to the concept of substituted judgment lies in its inapplicability to those who have never been competent to take such decisions.[244] But to limit its application to a subjective evaluation of the patient's previously expressed wishes—an interpretation that is very much a part of the doctrine as used in the United States—is, we believe, to take too narrow a view of the test. Judgments on which treatment decisions are made do not have to be substituted for written or clearly expressed preferences on the part of the patient; nor must they be rejected simply because no such declarations of intent are available. In the absence of indications of any sort, there seems no reason why an objective assessment cannot be made—what would a reasonable person of similar type and character have decided in the prevailing circumstances? It could be said that this is no more than semantic pedantry as, given no previous indications, it is almost impossible to conceive of a situation where the 'substituted judgment' and the 'best interest' tests would not coincide.[245] There is also the view that the best interests test—sensitively applied—may take the claims of autonomy into account. It is surely not in a person's best interests to have his explicit or implicit preferences ignored.[246] Even so, on balance, substituted judgment fits the concept of consent more closely and this is particularly so when considering how consent by proxy can be applied.

16.137   But no conceptual construct can avoid all conflict. The tragic case of Terri Schiavo was recently played out in the US courts and legislatures and merits mention if only as an indication of how other jurisdictions approach these sensitive issues. Previous editions of this book have included a discussion of the legal position in the United States in respect of the PVS patient, but increasingly this is not of major concern to the British reader, as this is one of numerous areas in which the United Kingdom courts are forging a particularly independent path. Mrs Schiavo's case reveals how varied the paths can be. The fundamental distinction between the US and UK jurisdictions lies in the test by which to justify termination of treatment which, we have seen, is firmly held to be that of the best interests of the patient in the United Kingdom. By contrast, the substituted judgment test—in which the surrogate makes his or her best approximation of what management schedule the patient would have wanted—is a prominent standard in the United States[247] but this is adopted only if the subjective test, which is based on what wishes the patient actually expressed, is not

[243] N 220 above, para 23.

[244] But the test has academic support otherwise. See I Kennedy and A Grubb 'Commentary on Airedale NHS Trust v Bland' (1993) 1 Med L Rev 359 at 362; D Tomkin and P Hanafin 'Medical Treatment at Life's End: the Need for Legislation' (1995) 1 Med-Leg J Ireland 3.

[245] An exception could lie in the management of the mentally disabled neonate. See discussion of *R v Arthur* (1981) 12 BMLR 1, n 2 above.

[246] This is precisely what the formulation of best interests in s 4 of the Mental Capacity Act 2005, attempts to do, discussed in chapter 10.

[247] A Meisel 'A Retrospective on *Cruzan*' (1992) 20 Law Med Hlth Care.

available. In Terri Schiavo's case, her husband was appointed as guardian and, so, surrogate decision-maker in respect of his wife's care. Mrs Schiavo had been in PVS since 1990 and her husband sought to discontinue her feeding and hydration some 10 years after her accident. An Order was made to this effect in 2003 by the Florida Circuit Court after an appeal court had rejected Mrs Schiavo's parents' objection to the withdrawal.[248] The on-going dispute eventually embroiled both the state legislature and the Governor himself, who issued an Executive Order that the patient's feeding tube should be reinstated. That Order was subsequently declared to be unconstitutional by the Florida Supreme Court,[249] and ultimately, the matter went to the US Senate, a request for appeal having been denied by the Supreme Court.[250] In a highly unusual move, Senate passed legislation—tailored directly to Mrs Schiavo's circumstances—giving authority to re-hear the case to the federal courts. Notwithstanding, the authority to remove her ANH was upheld[251] and Mrs Schiavo died on 31 March 2005.

16.138   Such political and legislative machinations simply do not form part of the British system—moreover they are doubtless motivated in large part by the wider pro-life movement that is active in the United States. To this extent, there is little that we can learn from Mrs Schiavo's case save, perhaps, that, no matter what test is to be applied in deciding what is 'best' done for the patient, every effort should be made from the earliest stages to reach consensus.

ARE WE BEING HONEST?

16.139   An alternative, and perhaps radical, approach to the whole problem of the management of PVS is to look the truth in the eye and admit that the deliberate removal of sustenance from a vegetative patient is indistinguishable from euthanasia. While this would remove a great deal of what must be regarded as paralogical argument, it would, of course, also involve a complete change of direction in the current jurisprudence—a change on which the courts would be reluctant to embark without the support of the legislature. None the less, we should not shrink from considering the proposition.

16.140   The fears of the judiciary and of many ethicists are summed up by Lord Goff in *Bland*, who declined to allow active steps to bring about death in PVS patients because this would be to authorise euthanasia and: 'once euthanasia is recognised as lawful in these circumstances, it is difficult to see any logical basis for excluding it in others'.[252]

---

[248] *Schindler v Schiavo* 851 So 2d 182 (Fla 2d DCA, 2003).

[249] *Bush v Schiavo*, Supreme Court of Florida, 23 September 2004, No. SC04–925.

[250] *Schlinder v Schiavo* 17 March 2005 (Order list 544 US).

[251] *Schindler Schiavo* et al *v Schiavo* et al, US Court of Appeals for the 11th Circuit, No. 05–11628, 25 March 2005.

[252] [1993] 1 All ER 821 at 867, (1993) 12 BMLR 64 AT 113.

We question this view, first, on the grounds that, once the concept of substituted judgment is accepted, removal of sustenance from PVS patients equates, at most, to passive, voluntary euthanasia which is already practised widely under one name or another. PVS cases occupy a unique niche in the spectrum of euthanasia. All higher brain function has been permanently lost, there is no awareness and no sensation. There is no alternative of palliative care because there are no senses to palliate—as Lord Goff put it: 'there is no weighing operation to be performed.' Only the vestiges of the person remain as the breathing body. Put another way, the patient is truly 'dead to the world' and, once his or her close relatives have come to terms with the situation, it is futile to maintain that respiration.

16.141   All this, however, depends upon the certainty of definition and diagnosis. Anthony Bland's and Mrs Johnstone's conditions were unequivocal but one cannot avoid the impression that the precedents laid down in their cases are being extended to include less well defined conditions than was intended at the time. The House of Lords distinguished *Bland* from other 'quality of life' cases such as *Re J*.[253] The two cases have very different ratios. In the former, a wholly insensate patient was deemed to have no interest in continued treatment which could, therefore, be discontinued as being futile. In the latter, it was accepted that some benefit could be derived from treatment of a patient who was not insensate but it was held that non-treatment was to be preferred when any supposed benefit was weighed against other considerations such as pain and suffering. *S*,[254] *Re D*,[255] *Re H*,[256] and now *Re G*[257] in particular, demonstrate a shift in thinking from that adopted in *Bland* towards that involved in *Re J* and one wonders if this is not something of a move towards acceptance of active euthanasia; the cases provide the most impressive example to date of the willingness of the British courts to take 'quality of life' decisions and, in our view, represent a significant step in this area of law. It should always be borne in mind, however, that these cases involved wholly or nearly wholly insensate patients. They are to be contrasted with *W Healthcare NHS Trust* where the Court of Appeal placed considerable weight on the impact of the dying process on the sentient patient: only intolerability of living would justify a course of action that would hasten death. At the end of the day, all the cases discussed, from *Bland* to *Re H* and beyond, represent variations on what is meant by 'best interests'; the fundamental question is, then, whether the jump from 'no interests' to 'a balance of interests' is acceptable in the management of the vegetative state or other chronically incapacitated states whether it represents a quantum leap onto the slippery slope of ending 'valueless lives'.

16.142   It has to be remembered that all the post-*Bland* cases have been scrupulously examined and all were supported not only by respected medical opinion but also by the Official Solicitor. All the patients were, by any standards, existing in appalling conditions and we have the gravest doubts as to whether the failure of a single

---

[253] [1990] 3 All ER 930, (1990) 6 BMLR 25, discussed above at paras 16.32 et seq.
[254] *Swindon and Marlborough NHS Trust v S* [1995] 3 Med LR 84.
[255] (1997) 38 BMLR 1.   [256] (1997) 38 BMLR 11.   [257] (2001) 65 BMLR 6.

arbitrary clinical test should be allowed to distinguish them in any significant way—and it is at least arguable that the near-vegetative state is a more horrifying condition than is PVS itself.[258] We have long submitted that the approach adopted by the courts in *Re J* could properly be applied to the withdrawal of feeding (or other vital treatment) from severely damaged adult patients. *Re J* and its allied cases went a long way to medicalising the whole approach to termination of treatment decisions and, provided medical authority is tempered by the sensitive handling of close relatives, there seems to be no fundamental reason why it should not be applied irrespective of age—the courts would then be involved only in those cases in which there is serious dispute between or within the health caring and family groups. Public acceptance of this policy would be greatly eased by an open acceptance by the medical profession of the futility of treatment of patients.[259] This is already the position advocated by the BMA in respect of patients with severe dementia or who have suffered catastrophic stroke.[260] The latest ruling from the Court of Appeal in *W Healthcare NHS Trust* may have moved us someway along this path: *Re J* was approved and the court accepted a quality of life threshold beyond which withdrawal or withholding decisions will be condoned: that threshold is high, however, and is set at the intolerability of life itself.

16.143   Inevitably, one is reminded of the calls in the House of Lords and the Court of Session for Parliamentary intervention—and, while this has its attractions, the proposal is not of unquestionable merit. To legislate for PVS alone would be to concentrate on its particular clinical status and to segregate it from the general euthanasia debate—which is as it should be.[261] Other advantages of legislation could be that the limits of PVS were statutorily determined[262] and that a clear framework could be devised within which doctors withdrawing treatment could be seen to be acting lawfully without the need for routine approval by a court. A line could thus be drawn between unequivocal and doubtful cases and a barrier placed at the edge of any developing slippery slope. On the other hand, legislation of this type could be seen as disadvantageous in that it would be restrictive—while withdrawal of support from the *Bland*-type patient would be permissible, non-treatment options might be barred in many cases of brain damage in which only minimal cognitive function remained such as in *S, D, H* and *G*. To many, this would represent the primary function of the legislation; to others, it might seem an unacceptable price to pay for the loss of individual judgment—as we have already suggested, generalisations are difficult to apply in a medical context. It might, therefore, be thought preferable to introduce purely enabling legislation.

16.144   The argument is one of long-standing and is likely to continue for even longer. Meantime, we suggest that there is one step on the path to honesty that we could take

[258] R Cranford 'Misdiagnosing the Persistent Vegetative State' (1996) 313 BMJ 5.

[259] See K R Mitchell, I H Kerridge and T J Lovat 'Medical Futility, Treatment Withdrawal and the Persistent Vegetative State' (1993) 19 J Med Ethics 71.

[260] BMA, *Withdrawing and Withholding Treatment*, n 184 above.

[261] J K Mason and D Mulligan 'Euthanasia by Stages' (1996) 347 Lancet 810.

[262] Perhaps based on the guidelines of the Royal College of Physicians, n 170 above.

without giving offence. In their anxiety to avoid conflating the final management of the permanent vegetative state with euthanasia, the courts in England, Scotland and the Republic of Ireland have been at pains to emphasise that the cause of death in PVS cases is the original injury. But, while it is true to say that this was the ultimate cause of death, the proximate cause, given that the patient has survived for a minimum of a year, must be the results of starvation—otherwise, there would be no death and, hence, no cause of death. There would be no difficulty in certifying death as being due to:

(a) inanition due to lawful removal of life support due to

(b) severe brain damage due to

(c) cerebral hypoxia.

This concession to transparency would, we feel, actually help to defuse the emotionalism that surrounds the ultimate management of PVS. A further purely practical advantage would be that the mortality statistics would be maintained correctly—and it would be possible to discover how often such decisions are made.

'DO NOT RESUSCITATE' ORDERS

16.145   The last aspect of medical futility that falls to be discussed is the so-called 'do not resuscitate' (DNR) order. There can be no doubt that it is often undesirable, effectively, to prolong the process of dying—irrespective of the competence of the patient at the time.[263] Nevertheless, in extending the concept of non-treatment to the incapacitated rather than the incompetent, it is possible that our attitudes are being moulded overly in favour of death, rather than treatment, as a management option. Moreover, we have to ask ourselves whether the DNR option is a valid example of an exercise of the principle of futility—there is a physical and moral divide between the PVS patient and the patient who is reaching the end of life in a natural fashion, albeit often in a state of diminished competence. Where one places the DNR order is a matter of ethical importance.[264] After much consideration, we doubt if it is correctly sited under 'futility' and will discuss the matter under the heading of euthanasia.[265]

[263] A particularly effective series of commentaries is to be found related to E L Schucking 'Death at a New York Hospital' (1985) 13 Law Med Hlth Care 261. See also the papers associated with R F Weir 'Betty's Case: An Introduction' (1989) 17 Law Med Hlth Care 211.

[264] See E P Cherniack 'Increasing Use of DNR Orders in the Elderly Worldwide: Whose Choice Is It?' (2002) 28 J Med Ethics 303 and P Biegler 'Should Patient Consent Be Required to Write a Do Not Resuscitate Order?' (2003) 29 J Med Ethics 359.

[265] See chapter 17.

17

EUTHANASIA

17.1 Thus far, we have looked at the ending of life in the general context of withdrawal of treatment that was regarded as inappropriate. The legal insistence that this did not constitute euthanasia has been a feature of all the cases discussed—and, indeed, it is this which underwrites their legality. In this chapter, we consider the occasions when the premature termination of life is the intended aim—and this is, at least, one definition of euthanasia. Euthanasia can, however, also be seen as providing a 'good' death or 'easing the passing' and we will, where necessary, include this in our discussion. We have already considered the infant or young child as a separate issue and have explained our reasons for isolating such cases; here it is proposed to discuss the subject only in relation to the adult patient.

17.2 Conditions at each end of life differ significantly from both the legal and ethical viewpoints. Unlike the infant, the adult patient may well be able to express his wishes as to the quality of his own life. In default of this, those responsible for the patient's management have a background of previous abilities and aspirations from which to measure the likely shortfall; clinical decisions can be based on history rather than on clairvoyance. On the other hand, the aged present a bewildering array of mental and physical variations which virtually preclude generalisations as to management—and attitudes to the elderly are inevitably coloured by the fact that their potential for meaningful relationships is waning rather than developing.

17.3 The prohibition on the taking of human life is based on fundamental and deeply held convictions. These may have different roots, and may be expressed in a wide variety of ways, but whatever their basis, they form a fundamental part of our moral lives. Historically, the prohibition against killing has most frequently been expressed in religious terms, human life being seen as a gift over which we may have stewardship but no final control. That position is still widely supported in some societies but, even in societies where religious morality has been dethroned, the right to life is still accorded particular weight. This is reflected in the modern human rights debate, where the right to life is treated as being at the heart of the liberal position. The European Convention on Human Rights, for example, provides in Article 2 that 'everyone's right to life shall be protected by law', a proposition which is similarly entrenched in many other statements of human rights and numerous nation-state constitutions. Nevertheless, few of those who recognise its value will deny that life may be taken in at least some circumstances. Article 2 of the ECHR admits various exceptions, and the principle of self-defence—either in the private context or in the course of a just war—is widely accepted as a justification for the killing of others. Similarly, some, at least, of those who would normally condemn murder might, none the less, see legal execution as an appropriate part of the process of criminal justice. In medicine, too, stout opponents of euthanasia may accept the legitimacy of abortion— a process which, by any standards, involves the taking of *some* form of life. Many people now admit the right of a person to commit suicide and do this on the grounds that, in general, the right to self-determination is among the most fundamental of all human rights. The door is thereby opened to a debate on whether euthanasia in some forms might be a morally acceptable practice.[1]

A CLASSIFICATION OF ASSISTED DYING

17.4   We use the term assisted dying advisedly insofar as we hope to demonstrate that euthanasia is a far narrower concept than is often implied by the use of the term. This is exemplified by the difficulty encountered when attempting to define the boundaries of 'euthanasia'. On the one hand, we can look at it from the point of view of the patient and divide it into voluntary, non-voluntary and involuntary categories depending on whether the patient seeks death, is unable to express an opinion on the matter, or is ignored in the decision-making process altogether. On the other hand, we can consider the actor who helps to bring about death: is his or her role in the process one of passivity or activity?—or, put another way, is death achieved by way of omission or of commission? Terms like 'active voluntary euthanasia' are, therefore, descriptive of a relationship that is an essential requirement of assisted dying. Such phrases describe, simultaneously, the respective positions of the parties involved in bringing death about; in this particular example, the doctor is 'active' in the process and the patient is 'voluntary'—that is, compliant in the act. In this simplistic fashion, we can identify six classic different forms in which euthanasia might be practiced. Even so, we still have to feed in the ambience of that practice. It is already apparent from the above that the patient may be conscious or unconscious; in addition, he or she may be incurably or terminally ill. Moreover, the role of the actor is not as simple as has been suggested above—activity can be engaged at any point on the spectrum that runs from counselling to perpetration. We have attempted to illustrate this mosaic in Fig. 17.1 which shows, incidentally, that we believe there are alternative and

---

[1] The literature on the moral status of euthanasia and of its legal implications is vast. A useful starting point is R Dworkin *Life's Dominion: An Argument About Abortion and Euthanasia* (1993). The fundamental issue of the moral status of human life is considered by M A Warren *Moral Status* (1997) and by J Finnis 'A Philosophical Case Against Euthanasia' in J Keown (ed) *Euthanasia Examined* (1995) pp 23–35. See also, J McMahon *The Ethics of Killing: Killing at the Margins of Life* (2002). Works concerned with specifically legal issues include: M Otlowski *Voluntary Euthanasia and the Common Law* (2001) and H Biggs *Euthanasia, Death with Dignity and the Law* (2001). John Keown is a consistent critic of the legalisation of euthanasia: see his *Euthanasia, Ethics and Public Policy: An Argument against Legalisation* (2002).

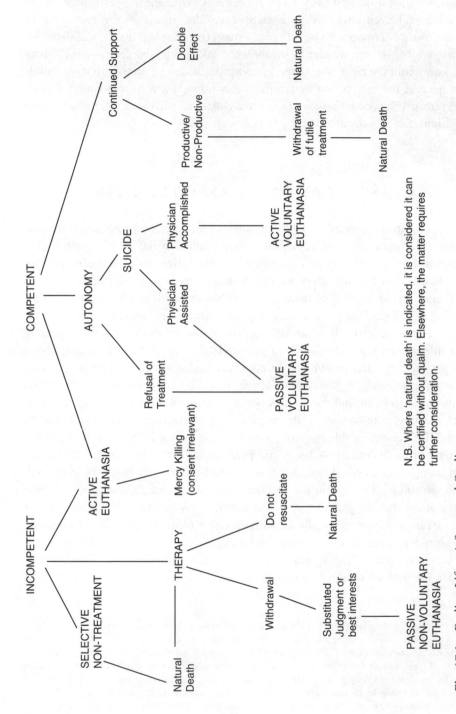

Fig. 17.1   Ending Life—A Suggested Outline

N.B. Where 'natural death' is indicated, it is considered it can be certified without qualm. Elsewhere, the matter requires further consideration.

better interpretations of the categories outlined above. Nevertheless, for descriptive ease, we intend to follow the standard classification in what follows.

VOLUNTARINESS IN EUTHANASIA

INVOLUNTARY EUTHANASIA

17.5   The major thrust of those concerned to legalise the termination of life on medical grounds has always been concentrated on what is generally known as voluntary euthanasia. This form of words implies that the patient specifically requests that his life be ended. He can, therefore, be seen as expressing his autonomy—a seminal proposition to which we will return later. Involuntary euthanasia is a quite different concept and is one from which most groups pressing for reform of the law have been careful to distance themselves. An act of involuntary euthanasia involves ending the patient's life in the absence of either a personal or proxy invitation to do so. Clearly, any person in contact with the subject can be the actor in such circumstances and perhaps the most common examples are of 'mercy killing' by relatives or carers. This book, however, is concerned with *medical* law and ethics and, for the greater part of the discussion, we confine ourselves to assisted death in the context of the doctor/ patient relationship. The fact that we are making this distinction leads us, at this early point, to the problem of the 'slippery slope'—an aspect of moral reasoning which has attracted much comment,[2] even though its mere existence is a matter of fierce debate.[3] We also return to this concept later in the context of voluntary euthanasia. For the present, we do no more than remark that it is not difficult to see an incremental continuum, on the one hand, between the doctor and the carer and, as to the former, between Dr Moor, who treated his dying patient by way of an easeful death, Dr Adams, who assisted a number of elderly patients in similar fashion, and Dr Shipman, who embellished the plot to include, perhaps, hundreds of such patients. It is this potential movement from the best to the worst of intentions which pervades the whole topic of euthanasia and, while terminating life in an involuntary context represents only a small part of the subject, it is, nonetheless, the extreme position which can tends to dominate the debate. For this reason, we think it will be useful to discuss it—and dispose of it—at the outset.

17.6   Criminal cases are rarely reported unless they demonstrate some specific point of law. Even so, it is surprising how few relevant trials there have been—and this despite

---

[2] See, for example, D Enoch 'Once You Start Using Slippery Slope Arguments, You're on a Very Slippery Slope' (2001) 211 OJLS 629; S Smith 'Evidence for the Practical Slippery Slope in the Debate on Physician-Assisted Suicide and Euthanasia' (2005) 13 Med L Rev 17 and, in particular, Keown (2002), n 1 above.

[3] R S Downie and K C Calman *Healthy Respect: Ethics in Health Care* (2nd edn, 2001).

the number of doctors who claim to have taken part in some form of euthanasia.[4] The great majority of the few who have come to trial in these circumstances on charges of murder, manslaughter or culpable homicide have been accused of no more than using therapeutic drugs in overdose and all the relevant verdicts have indicated the reluctance of British juries to convict a medical practitioner of serious crime when the charge arises from what they see as his considered medical judgment. In *R v Carr*[5] a doctor was accused of attempted murder by injecting a massive dose of pheno-barbitone into a patient whose lung cancer had been declared inoperable some seven months previously. He was acquitted of the charge but, in the course of the summing-up, Mars-Jones J had this to say:

However gravely ill a man may be . . . he is entitled in our law to every hour . . . that God has granted him. That hour or hours may be the most precious and most important hours of a man's life. There may be business to transact, gifts to be given, forgivenesses to be made, 101 bits of unfinished business which have to be concluded,

which is as good a comment on misplaced paternalism as is likely to be found.

17.7   Nevertheless, the sympathetic attitude of the courts is deeply entrenched and was confirmed in the case of Dr Moor. This GP, who admitted in the course of a public debate to having used painkillers to bring about the easy deaths of patients, was charged with the murder of a terminally ill patient into whom he was alleged to have injected a lethal dose of diamorphine. The judge left the jury in no doubt as to his own view of the matter, saying:

You have heard that this defendant is a man of excellent character, not just in the sense that he has no previous convictions but how witnesses have spoken of his many admirable qualities. You may consider it a great irony that a doctor who goes out of his way to care for [the deceased] ends up facing the charge that he does.[6]

The jury responded by acquitting Dr Moor within an hour.

17.8   Dr Adams' case, *R v Adams*,[7] was different because the index patient of whose murder he was charged was one amongst several who were incurably but not termin-ally ill; it is thought that he treated her with increasing doses of opiates, and, following her death, he was tried for murder. He was nonetheless acquitted. In the course of his summing up, Devlin J said: 'The doctor is entitled to relieve pain and suffering even if the measures he takes may incidentally shorten life', which is a clear direction leaving little in the way of doubt for the jury. The key term here, however, is 'incidental',

---

[4] And not only in the United Kingdom. See, e.g., C Zinn, who reported that 'A Third of Surgeons in New South Wales Admit to Euthanasia' (2001) 323 BMJ 1268. Other views are discussed further below.

[5] *R v Carr* (unreported, but see *The Sunday Times*, 30 November 1986, p 1). In Scotland, a doctor who injected an elderly patient with ten times the normal dose of diamorphine was acquitted of culpable homicide—the defence was, however, one of accidental error: *HM Advocate v Watson* (1991) *The Scotsman*, 11 June, p 8, 14 June, p 3.

[6] C Dyer 'British GP Cleared of Murder Charge' (1999) 318 BMJ 1306. For discussion, see R Gillon and L Doyal 'When Doctors Might Kill their Patients' (1999) 318 BMJ 1431.

[7] H Palmer 'Dr Adams' Trial for Murder' [1957] Crim LR 365.

meaning most obviously 'non-intentional'. This may, also, be an invocation of the ethical doctrine of double effect, which we discuss below at para 17.90.

17.9 Finally, and at the extreme end of our spectrum, it is trite to confirm that intentional involuntary euthanasia performed by the doctor leaves him as guilty of murder as anyone else who deliberately takes human life. Dr Shipman is the most infamous contemporary example that proves this point. Harold Shipman was convicted in 2000 of the murder of 15 patients—an example of serial killing which has cast a long shadow over the medical profession in the United Kingdom and which bears indirectly on the euthanasia argument.[8] Dr Shipman, of course, was quite different from other doctors who may have risked prosecution to end what they saw as the unbearable suffering of terminally ill patients; he killed patients for reasons which are not altogether apparent but which may have been connected with a pathological desire to exercise control over life and death. The case seriously dented trust in the medical profession and could be used as an argument against lifting the current strict prohibitions on the taking of life. Dr Shipman's imitators—if there are any—might find welcome opportunities in a system of legalised euthanasia in which they would play the role of dispatchers.[9]

17.10 The critical distinction to be derived from this series of cases lies in the 'medicalisation' of the deaths. At one end, we have dying patients undergoing treatment for serious pain; as we will see later, it is then possible to see death as a concomitant of necessary pain relief and the courts have been consistently prepared to apply the doctrine of necessity in such circumstances. Dr Adams' patient was not dying though she was in some pain; one wonders if the same approach would be adopted today.[10] Dr Shipman's patients were in no more discomfort than merited a visit to the doctor's surgery; medicalisation of their deaths by way of an overdose of opiates was impossible and the court had no difficulty in regarding the case as one of multiple murder. The importance of the distinction will be re-examined in later sections of the chapter.

VOLUNTARY EUTHANASIA

17.11 An expression of the will of the individual whose life was brought to an end was absent in all these cases. We know well by now that the will of the person deserves, and receives, the utmost respect of the law in the United Kingdom, but we have also seen

---

[8] *The Shipman Inquiry* has produced a series of reports on the affair, culminating in the *Final Report* (2005), all available at: www.the-shipman-inquiry.org.uk. The final number of patients killed by Dr Shipman will probably never be known. The Inquiry, however, has at least addressed operational matters that may have contributed to the tragedy, including questions over death and cremation certification, the use and monitoring of controlled drugs, single-practitioner practices, and professional monitoring and disciplinary systems.

[9] H G Kinnell 'Serial Homicide by Doctors: Shipman in Perspective' (2000) 321 BMJ 1594.

[10] See the review of the case: P Devlin *Easing the Passing: The Trial of Dr Bodkin Adams* (1986).

that it is not always determinative of any given issue, and this is especially so when the criminal law enters the fray. The paradigm example of this is voluntary euthanasia as demonstrated by the case of Dr Cox—a consultant rheumatologist who was convicted of attempted murder after succumbing to the repeated requests of his patient to relieve her of the excruciating pain of her rheumatoid arthritis.[11] Dr Cox's case contained all of the necessary elements of the classic murder case: intention to bring about death, direct action precipitating that death, and the absence of any reasonable defence or excuse of medicalisation in that the toxic substance administered had no palliative or curative properties—it was designed for death. Moreover, and in keeping with general criminal dogma, the patient's consent was irrelevant. Medical law must bow to criminal law is such cases. Notwithstanding, Dr Cox was not treated like an 'ordinary criminal' as we see below when we discuss his case further. Yet, while the 'voluntary' nature of the euthanasia is this case made no difference to the outcome, its 'active' nature very much did, and it is to a consideration of the distinctions between active and passive practices that we now turn.

ACTIVE AND PASSIVE EUTHANASIA

17.12   A patient's life may be terminated, or death accelerated, either actively or passively. This distinction—or whether there is, indeed, any true distinction—is one of the most hotly argued issues in the euthanasia debate and one which can be addressed on either the legal or the moral plane.

17.13   Despite the rarity of cases involving the medical profession, there is no ambiguity in the attitude of the law in the United Kingdom towards a positive act of euthanasia. It is summed up in the words of Devlin J:

> If the acts done are intended to kill and do, in fact, kill, it does not matter if a life is cut short by weeks or months, it is just as much murder as if it were cut short by years.[12]

17.14   While motive is irrelevant, intention is all-important. If a doctor intends to kill, he is as liable to prosecution as is the layman, as Drs Shipman and Cox demonstrate. There have, however, been recommendations for the introduction of a specific offence of 'mercy-killing'[13] and, although these have not been translated into legislation, there is an innate reluctance on the part of the courts to convict the genuine 'mercy-killer' of an offence which carries a mandatory sentence of life imprisonment. This is particularly so when relatives have been caring for the sick with great devotion. In such circumstances, the prosecutor may well exercise his discretion and accept a plea

---

[11] *R v Cox* (1992) 12 BMLR 38.
[12] Palmer, n 7 above.
[13] See R Leng 'Mercy Killing and the CLRC' (1982) 132 NLJ 76.

of manslaughter;[14] alternatively, the court may accept a plea of diminished responsibility on the grounds of mental abnormality[15]—psychiatrists are just as ready to diagnose or to infer a reactive depression in the accused.[16]

17.15 It is perfectly possible to see the caring doctor in the same light and, until quite recently, one would have supposed that the public was content with such a practical solution and had little or no wish to see it extended. One might also have supposed that developments in palliative care, and greater interest in the hospice movement, might have led to a decreased demand for medical assistance in dying. Such assumptions have been shown to be wrong: the euthanasia debate has continued, and, if anything, has sharpened with each lowering of legal barriers to the practice. Lawful active euthanasia has now arrived in more than one jurisdiction.

ACTIVE VOLUNTARY EUTHANASIA

THE DUTCH EXPERIENCE

17.16 One of the focal points of the debate has been the Netherlands, where medically-practised euthanasia became lawful in November 2000. This ended the previous halfway house arrangement in Dutch law under which euthanasia remained illegal but, at the same time, doctors who carried out acts of euthanasia on their patients would not be prosecuted, provided they complied with certain requirements. The novelty of the current Dutch legislation warrants its examination in some detail.

17.17 The Termination of Life on Request and Assisted Suicide (Review Procedures) Act, Article 293 amends the Penal Code of the Netherlands to read as follows:

(1) A person who terminates the life of another person at that other person's express and earnest request is liable to a term of imprisonment of not more than twelve years or a fine of the fifth category.

---

[14] E.g. *R v Johnson* (1961) 1 Med Sci Law 192. A typical Scottish case, *HM Advocate v Brady* (1996 unreported), involved a man who smothered his brother who was suffering from Huntington's disease; he was found guilty of culpable homicide and was admonished: B Christie 'Man Walks Free in Scottish Euthanasia Case' (1996) 313 BMJ 961. However, there are limits, and relatives who assume that the prosecution authorities and the courts will be sympathetic are running a major risk. An example of this is *R v Latimer* [2001] 1 SCR 3, in which the Supreme Court of Canada upheld the murder conviction of a father who had killed his 12-year-old daughter who suffered from a severe form of cerebral palsy. The father invoked a defence of necessity, arguing that the killing was the lesser of two evils. This was roundly rejected by the court, which pointed out: 'Killing a person—in order to relieve the suffering produced by a medically manageable physical or mental condition—is not a proportionate response to the harm represented by the non-life-threatening suffering resulting from that condition'.

[15] See Homicide Act 1957 s 2(1).

[16] S Dell *Murder into Manslaughter* (1984) p 35 et seq. In *R v Taylor* [1979] CLY 570, a man who battered his autistic child to death was placed on probation for 12 months. Perhaps the most remarkable example comes from the USA, where no charges were pressed against a man who held the staff at gun-point while disconnecting his son from the ventilator: see e.g. J D Lantos, S H Miles and C K Cassel 'The Linares Affair' (1989) 17 Law Med Hlth Care 308.

(2) The offence referred to in the first paragraph shall not be punishable if it has been committed by a physician who has met the requirements of due care [referred to in Article 2 of this law] . . . and who informs the municipal autopsist of this . . .

17.18   The concept of due care is defined in the legislation as requiring the doctor to believe that the patient's request was 'voluntary and well-considered' and that the patient's suffering was 'lasting and unbearable'. For his part the patient, having been informed about his situation, must believe that there is no other reasonable solution. The doctor must also have consulted an independent physician who has seen the patient and has given a written opinion on compliance with the due conditions.[17] In addition to setting out these criteria for the administration of euthanasia, the Act provides for the reporting of instances of euthanasia to regional review committees, which have power to refer non-compliance cases to the public prosecutor.[18]

17.19   The Dutch legislation allows for advance consent, thus recognising the validity of a living will. A written declaration of this nature has the effect of a concrete request for euthanasia which may be exercised when the patient is no longer capable of expressing his will. One consequence of this is that a patient who does not have the capacity to object, but who may, in fact, not now want to die, could be killed by a doctor who, possessing an earlier written authorisation, decides that it would be better for the patient to do so—or even to bring a slow and prolonged process of dying to a 'tidy end'.

17.20   The scale of the practice of euthanasia in the Netherlands, under both the earlier transitional provisions and now under the fully-legalised system, is a matter of dispute, although most studies suggest that it is extensive. In 1991, it was said that nearly 2 per cent of deaths in the Netherlands resulted from euthanasia; these involved approximately 2,300 cases of euthanasia and 400 of assisted suicide each year.[19] In 1995, it was estimated that requested deaths accounted for 2.7 per cent of all deaths.[20] This high incidence might, in itself, give rise to concern: the House of Lords has recently estimated,[21] for example, that if the Dutch model were to be implemented in Britain it could lead to 13,000 deaths a year. This is to be compared to 650 deaths per year if the Oregon model were adopted (for which see below).[22] Beyond even this, however, the evidence that has emerged of widespread disregard among doctors in the

---

[17] Article 2.

[18] Controversially, the Netherlands Act provides for the carrying out of euthanasia on minors (Article 2(3) and (4)). Children between 12 and 16 who are deemed to have a 'reasonable understanding' (the statute's language) of their interests may give consent to euthanasia, provided that their decision is agreed to by parents. Children aged 16 and 17 may opt for euthanasia, but this may only be carried out if the parents (or those exercising parental authority) have been involved in the decision process.

[19] H Hellema 'Euthanasia—2% of Dutch Deaths' (1991) 303 BMJ 877.

[20] See the *Welcome to the Netherlands* website, 'Euthanasia Policy': www.minbuza.nl.

[21] House of Lords Select Committee on the Assisted Dying for the Terminally Ill Bill, *Assisted Dying for the Terminally Ill Bill—First Report* (2005), para 243.

[22] It does, of course, depend on how one reads these figures. If these are seen as a measure of 'assistance' to those in need then the Dutch model is far more 'helpful'. If, however, they are taken as instances of 'dubious deaths' then the Dutch experience emerges as distinctly far more 'dubious'.

Netherlands of the formal requirements laid down in the transitional regime is even more disquieting.[23] Such failures suggest that administrative or internal medical control of the practice is unlikely to prevent abuses, a conclusion which robs the argument based on voluntariness of much of its force. It appears, in fact, that euthanasia has been practised in many cases without the consent of the patient.[24] This might provide grounds for asserting that it becomes far more difficult to control the practice once an absolute prohibition against killing is removed—and this leads us back to the famous slippery slope. If there is a slippery slope in the Netherlands, then there are certainly several prominent milestones on it, including the call by the Dutch Commission for the Acceptability of Life Terminating Action for public debate on whether the life of a patient suffering from severe dementia without serious physical symptoms might be terminated with or without he or she having executed an advance directive on the point.[25]

17.21   Opponents of the Netherlands approach of euthanasia have expressed concern that the grounds for its exercise will inevitably become more trivial until what matters is not the grounds for wanting to die, but the want itself.[26] This could rapidly lead to an acceptance of euthanasia in the face of relatively minor discomfort or of conditions which, although distressing, are not necessarily either permanent or terminal. Such concerns do not appear ill-founded when one reads that a Dutch psychiatrist has been found to be medically justified in assisting the suicide of a physically healthy woman who was depressed[27]—precisely the situation foreseen by those who oppose legalising the termination of life. The Dutch experience could, in fact, be taken as an object lesson rather than as a paradigm.[28]

17.22   The pioneering legislation in the Netherlands has not led to a large number of other jurisdictions following suit; it would, however, be surprising if this situation were to persist, given that the acceptance of a practice in one jurisdiction often influences the decision to allow a practice elsewhere. Indeed, a similar measure has

[23] H Hendin 'Euthanasia Consultants or Facilitators' (1999) 170 Med J Austral 351; P J van der Maas, G van der Wal, I Haverkate et al 'Euthanasia, Physician-Assisted Suicide, and other Medical Practices Involving the End of Life in the Netherlands, 1990–1995' (1996) 335 New Engl J Med 1699.

[24] Indeed, specific studies have been made on the point: L Pijnenborg, P J van der Maas, J J M van Delden and C W M Looman 'Life-terminating Acts without Explicit Request of Patient' (1993) 341 Lancet 1196.

[25] H Hellema 'Dutch Doctors Support Life Termination in Dementia' (1993) 306 BMJ 1364.

[26] A concern that becomes even more real when one reads a heading: 'Dutch euthanasia law should apply to patients "suffering through living" report says'—T Sheldon (2005) 330 BMJ 61.

[27] 'Mercy-killing Doctor Freed' (1993) The Scotsman, 22 April, p 8. See also T Sheldon 'Dutch Approve Euthanasia for a Patient with Alzheimer's Disease' (2005) 330 BMJ 1041.

[28] For a major advocate of the Dutch system, see P Admiraal 'Voluntary Euthanasia' in S A M McLean (ed) Death, Dying and the Law (1996) ch 7. A forceful opposition view is to be found in J Keown 'Some Reflections on Euthanasia in the Netherlands', 'Further Reflections on Euthanasia in the Netherlands in the Light of the Remmelink Report and the Van der Maas Survey' in L Gormally (ed) Euthanasia, Clinical Practice and the Law (1994) chs 4 and 5. For a good factual review, see J Griffiths 'The Regulation of Euthanasia and Related Medical Procedures that Shorten Life in the Netherlands' (1994) 1 Med Law Internat 137. An interesting critique of the Dutch experience, which reveals how the availability of euthanasia can obscure other options, is H Henden Seduced by Death: Doctors, Patients and Assisted Suicide (1998).

now been introduced in Belgium,[29] where, in 1997, the Council for Bioethics recommended that euthanasia be legalised, a recommendation which probably reflects what was, anyway, happening in practice.[30]

17.23   A major difficulty in assessing the Dutch experience lies in definition and this probably derives from their use of the term 'medical decisions concerning the end of life' (MDEL).[31] MDEL includes a wide spectrum of activity ranging from manifest euthanasia, through the concept of 'double effect',[32] to the most controversial, and hard to unravel, group involving termination of life without an explicit request. Griffiths extrapolated the available data to suggest that, on these grounds, an MDEL is the immediate cause of death in more than half all the deaths in the Netherlands due to chronic disease. Nevertheless, only some 5 per cent of MDELs are instances of true euthanasia and euthanasia in the Netherlands clearly includes both the active killing of the patient and assisting the patient to precipitate his or her own death—a procedure which is now widely known as physician-assisted suicide (PAS). Is there, in fact, a distinction to be made? We return to consider this at para 17.34 et seq.

THE POSITION IN THE UNITED KINGDOM

17.24   By contrast with the foregoing, and as we have already pointed out, there can be no doubt that active, even voluntary, euthanasia is unlawful in the United Kingdom. This was unequivocally restated in the landmark case of *Bland*, where we have Lord Mustill:

[T]hat 'mercy killing' by active means is murder . . . has never so far as I know been doubted. The fact that the doctor's motives are kindly will for some, although not for all, transform the moral quality of his act, but this makes no difference in law. It is intent to kill or cause grievous bodily harm which constitutes the mens rea of murder, and the reason why the intent was formed makes no difference at all.[33]

This, then, was the position when Dr Cox was charged with the attempted murder of Mrs Boyes, his patient of 13 years' standing (see para 17.11 above).[34] Mrs Boyes' rheumatoid arthritis was not, of itself, a fatal condition, but it caused intense pain and distress leading her to express a wish to die; she was, indeed, already categorised as 'not for resuscitation'.[35] At trial, it was admitted that Dr Cox injected her with

[29] Act on Euthanasia of 28 May 2002.

[30] In 2000, it was revealed that the incidence of euthanasia in the Flemish-speaking part of the country was similar to that revealed in the earlier Netherlands studies: L Deliens, F Mortier, J Bilsen et al 'End of Life Decisions in Medical Practice in Flanders, Belgium: a Nationwide Survey' (2000) 356 Lancet 1806.

[31] Griffiths, n 28 above, supports the suggestion that this would be better expressed as 'medical procedures that shorten life'.

[32] See para 17.90 below.

[33] *Airedale NHS Trust v Bland* [1993] 1 All ER 821 at 890, (1993) 12 BMLR 64 at 137.

[34] *R v Cox* (1992) 12 BMLR 38. Dr Cox was charged with attempted murder presumably because Mrs Boyes had been cremated before her death was regarded as suspicious. Any arguments as to the cause of death would, therefore, have been speculative.

[35] For which see para 17.93 below.

two ampoules of potassium chloride, which is known to be potently cardiotoxic but, at the same time, is a substance which the majority of practitioners would regard as having no analgesic value—and it is this which distinguished Dr Cox's case.[36] The only issue at trial was, therefore, that of intent—as Ognall J put it at the outset of his summing up:

If he injected her with potassium chloride with the primary purpose of killing her, of hastening her death, he is guilty of the offence charged[37]

and later:

If a doctor genuinely believes that a certain course is beneficial to his patient, either therapeutically or analgesically, then even though he recognises that that course carries with it a risk to life, he is fully entitled, nonetheless, to pursue it. If in those circumstances the patient dies, nobody could possibly suggest that in that situation the doctor was guilty of murder or attempted murder.[38]

17.25   Essentially, therefore, the problem for the jury was one of intention—did Dr Cox *intend* to kill his patient[39] or did he hope to grant her a short pain-free period during the process of dying? In the event, Dr Cox was found guilty of attempted murder.

17.26   So, what distinguished Dr Cox from Dr Carr or Dr Moor whose cases we have discussed above? Obviously, we can never know the precise reason for a jury verdict but we can extract some factors which they may have found important—even if only subliminally. First, Mrs Boyes was incurably but not terminally ill. It is interesting that none of the sporadic attempts to legalise 'euthanasia'—at least in the United Kingdom —has attempted to go beyond the confines of terminal disease. There may well be an intuitive distinction to be made which we suggest would be rightly founded on the difficulty of limiting the definition of incurable or intolerable disease. Secondly, Dr Cox injected a non-therapeutic substance and it is reasonable to assume that, while public opinion in the United Kingdom will give great latitude to the medical profession in its fight against suffering, it is not yet prepared to accept the use of a substance which has no analgesic effect and is known to be lethal when injected in concentrated form. Thirdly, and as a direct result of this, he was unable to plead 'double effect' or necessity—moral and legal concepts which we introduce below at para 17.90.

17.27   Even so, sympathy for Dr Cox was widespread.[40] No immediate custodial sentence was imposed; the Vice-President of the Voluntary Euthanasia Society castigated what

---

[36] Another trial concerned with voluntary euthanasia by way of injection of potassium chloride and lignocaine was aborted when the prosecution offered no evidence: *R v Lodwig* (1990) *The Times*, 16 March.

[37] *R v Cox* (1992) 12 BMLR 38 at 39.

[38] (1992) 12 BMLR 38 at 41.

[39] Whether or not it was 'an act of mercy' was a matter only for the judge in sentencing, motive being irrelevant to the jury.

[40] It is reported that 11% of doctors in the USA who are closely associated with relevant cases had received requests for a lethal injection and 4.7% had complied with the request at least once: D E Meier, C-A Emmons, S Wallenstein et al 'A National Survey of Physician-Assisted Suicide and Euthanasia in the United States' (1998) 338 New Engl J Med 1193.

he saw as a supine jury; the General Medical Council was content to admonish him on the grounds that, although his actions had fallen short of the high standards which the medical profession must uphold, he clearly acted in good faith; and the responsible regional health authority offered continued employment subject to certain restrictions.[41]

17.28   We believe that the jury decision was certainly right in law but that public dissatisfaction ultimately stems from the law's determination to dissociate motive from intent when faced with unlawful killing[42]—as in the case of Dr Arthur, whose case has been discussed in chapter 16. Dr Cox was certainly not a murderer as the word is commonly interpreted.

17.29   Jackson has summarised some of the resultant anomalies in a particularly powerful article.[43] She points out that the absolute prohibition of physician accomplished active euthanasia is in direct contradiction to the current movement towards the interests of the individual patient as the driving force in medicine; she concludes that the only logical reason for prohibiting doctors from complying with their patients' requests for euthanasia lies in the protection of an abstract idea as to the proper role of the medical profession[44]—and this she sees as being deeply anachronistic. None the less, for reasons which appear elsewhere in this chapter, we cannot accept that individual doctors should be given free rein in this field absent specific legislation.[45] Moreover, any such legislation must, itself, be suspect. It has been said that current attitudes to euthanasia are comparable to the attitudes to abortion in the early 1960s;[46] it is precisely the fear that current attitudes to abortion may become those to euthanasia in the twenty-first century that tempers our intuitive sympathy for both Dr Cox and his patient.

PASSIVE VOLUNTARY EUTHANASIA

17.30   In so far as suicide is a form of premature and intentional termination of life, it is impossible to exclude it from the spectrum of euthanasia. Even so, few would instinctively regard it as such and, more importantly, suicide simpliciter does not include the

---

[41]   C Dyer 'GMC Tempers Justice with Mercy in Cox Case' (1992) 305 BMJ 1311.

[42]   This view is central to the persuasive argument in K Boyd 'Euthanasia: Back to the Future' in J Keown (ed) *Euthanasia Examined* (1995) ch 7.

[43]   E Jackson 'Whose Death is it Anyway? Euthanasia and the Medical Profession' (2004) 57 CLP 415.

[44]   A case can be made for hiving off a 'duty' to provide euthanasia to specialists in the care of the terminally ill—innovatively referred to as 'telostricians': R Crisp 'A Good Death: Who Best to Bring It?' (1987) 1 Bioethics 74. One of us has previously flirted with much the same idea: J K Mason 'Death and Dying: One Step at a Time?' in S A M McLean (ed) *Death, Dying and the Law* (1996).

[45]   For an interpretation of the relationship between the law and the medical profession see Hoffmann LJ in *Airedale NHS Trust v Bland* [1993] 1 All ER 821 at 858, (1992) 12 BMLR 64 at 103: 'The court [has been invited] to decide whether, on medical facts which are not in dispute, [the action] would be justified as being in the best interests of the patient. This is a purely legal (or moral) decision which does not require any medical expertise and is therefore appropriately made by the court'.

[46]   R Smith 'Euthanasia: Time for a Royal Commission' (1992) 305 BMJ 728.

relationship that we regard as so essential to the concept of euthanasia. In addition, suicide and attempted suicide are no longer criminal offences.[47] Whether or not this implies a legal right to end one's life is debatable but we are not, here, concerned with the morality of suicide per se. Our interest for present purposes lies in the residual offence of counselling, procuring, aiding and abetting suicide which remains an offence in England and Wales by virtue of the Suicide Act 1961, s 2(1). In passing, it may be mentioned that there is some doubt as to whether an offence of abetting suicide exists in Scotland, where the Suicide Act never applied—it is difficult to imagine a common law offence of aiding an act which is not, itself, a crime.[48] Concerning ourselves only with England, then, we must consider the relationship of outside agencies to the would-be suicide and, particularly, the standing of the doctor in that context.

17.31   As to the general outsider, it is now clear that, while counselling or assisting a suicide remains an offence, this can only be illegal if conducted on a basis of immediacy and intent—the impersonal distribution of advice or information is unlikely to attract legal sanction.[49] As we have seen in chapter 3, however, there is now free movement in the search for medical interventions throughout the European Union and there is, of course, no reason why a person should not make such private arrangements in any part of the Union, or indeed the rest of the world. Such arrangements must include seeking assistance with suicide which is now legally available in a number of jurisdictions (see para 17.16 et seq above). As a result, a new problem has arisen in the shape of assistance in travel arrangements and the like.

17.32   This has recently been tested in *A Local Authority v Z*,[50] in which a local authority sought to continue an interim injunction preventing a husband from taking his wife to Switzerland so that she might avail herself of the assisted suicide procedures available in that country. Mrs Z was suffering from cerebella ataxia, an incurable and irreversible condition that left her physically incapable of fending for herself. The local authority had initially sought the injunction both to protect Mrs Z as someone it saw as vulnerable and because, in its opinion, Mr Z was committing a criminal offence. At the substantive hearing Hedley, J refused the request. He held that the powers and responsibilities of an authority in such cases were to investigate and to protect incompetent individuals and/or those subject to undue influence. Any suspicion of criminality should be reported to the appropriate authorities. But given that the criminal prosecution service had been informed, and Mrs Z found to be competent, the authority's duties did not extend any further. The criminal authorities have all the necessary powers to act should they exercise their discretion to do so. Interference through civil action was inappropriate. It was explicitly stated that the case 'afforded

---

[47] Suicide Act 1961.

[48] By contrast, it could be that assisting a person to commit suicide would be considered to be culpable homicide: see R A McCall Smith and D Sheldon *Scots Criminal Law* (2nd edn, 1997) p 171. The topic has been re-assessed by: P R Ferguson 'Killing "Without Getting into Trouble?": Assisted Suicide and Scots Criminal Law' (1998) 2 Edin LR 288.

[49] *A-G v Able* [1984] QB 795, [1984] 1 All ER 277.   [50] [2005] 1 FLR 740.

no basis for trying to ascertain the court's views about the rights or wrongs of suicide, assisted or otherwise'. The legal point was simply that competent persons are entitled to make their own decisions and that they—and those who assist them—bear the responsibility for any decisions so taken. A civil court should be slow to attempt to restrain behaviour consistent with the rights of others 'simply because it is unlawful' especially when the criminal authorities have all the necessary powers to intervene.[51]

17.33   As we have said, however, our main concern is at the doctor/patient interface and this leads to the major medico-ethical problem of physician assisted suicide.

PHYSICIAN-ASSISTED SUICIDE

17.34   The classic case of Physician Assisted Suicide (PAS) involves the doctor in no more than providing the means of ending life—most commonly by the provision or pre-scription of the necessary drugs. The patient him or herself will complete the act which can, then, be properly described as an act of suicide, albeit assisted. Given this scenario, the doctor is the passive agent in the assisted dying relationship which can then be subsumed within the category of passive voluntary euthanasia. This concept is important in that it serves to contrast vividly with the situation in which the patient physically cannot or prefers not to perform this final task and in which the doctor, in person and on request, administers the *coup de grâce*; we are, then, in the realm of active voluntary euthanasia as has been discussed above – and arguably, as a result, in a different legal ambience. The complicating factor is that such distinctions will not always be so simple. Take, for example, the doctor who responds to a request to disconnect the ventilator in a case of progressive neurological disease—is this to be classed as refusal of treatment by the patient or as assisted suicide? And what of the paralysed patient who wishes to die but is receiving no treatment that can be refused—is the ending of that life a matter of assisting suicide or of active euthanasia? Or, what is the position of the doctor who performs the venepuncture and then holds the syringe while the patient presses the plunger?[52] Clearly, then, hard as one may try to represent one, there is no bright dividing line between refusal of treatment, suicide, assisted suicide and euthanasia. For many, then, it may seem curious that Belgium legislated in 2002 to legalise active euthanasia yet made no mention whatsoever of PAS, leaving the practice in legal limbo-land.[53]

17.35   Others, however, perhaps intuitively, may perceive a distinction. Sometimes this may be subtle—as between the first two, for example, we have Lord Donaldson saying:

---

[51] It has been reported that 22 UK nationals may have been assisted to die between 2002 and 2004, see D Martin and V Dodd 'Euthanasia Group May Have Helped 22 Britons to Die', *The Guardian*, 3 Sept 2004, p 2.

[52] These examples are taken from D W Meyers and J K Mason 'Physician Assisted Suicide: A Second View from Mid-Atlantic' (1999) 28 Anglo-Am L Rev 265 in which the comparative Anglo-American scene is discussed in detail.

[53] H Nys, 'Physician Assisted Suicide in Belgian Law' (2005) 12 Euro J Health L 39.

This appeal is not in truth about 'the right to die'. There is no suggestion that Miss T wants to die . . . This appeal is about the 'right to choose how to live'. This is quite different, even if the choice, when made, may make an early death more likely,[54]

which, taken in the context of refusal of a life-saving blood transfusion, attracts something of an aura of legal expediency. Again, we have the Court in the American case of *Vacco v Quill*:[55]

[The] distinction between assisting suicide and withdrawing life-sustaining treatment in hopeless cases is logical, widely recognized and endorsed by the medical profession and by legal tradition,

and we only wish it *were* always so. On other occasions, however, the difference may be obvious. In respect of assisted suicide and euthanasia, for example, it is not difficult to see a practical difference between the classic ploy of 'leaving the pills' and undertaking a lethal injection—and it is this sort of comparison that most people have in mind when addressing the subject.[56]

17.36   There is also legislative precedent for distinguishing physician-assisted suicide as a separate entity. Having seen initiatives designed to decriminalise active voluntary euthanasia fail in both California[57] and the state of Washington by narrow majorities,[58] Oregon introduced its Death with Dignity Act of 1994, which concerned assisted suicide only.[59] This was passed by an even more slender majority but, after a series of stays on constitutional grounds, the measure was re-enacted by a majority of 60:40.[60] Under the Oregon Act, it is lawful for a doctor to prescribe a lethal dosage of a drug for a patient who wishes to end his or her life—but not to involve him- or herself in the suicidal act. Certain conditions must be satisfied, including those of competence on the patient's part to make the decision. The patient must make the request voluntarily and must be suffering from a terminal illness. Critics of the law have pointed out that it empowers the physician to determine matters such as competence and voluntariness, and it has been suggested that it naively accepts

---

[54] *Re T (adult: refusal of medical treatment)* [1992] 4 All ER 649 at 652, (1992) 9 BMLR 46 at 49.

[55] 117 S Ct 2293 (1997).

[56] For commentary, see L R Churchill and N M P King 'Physician Assisted Suicide, Euthanasia, or Withdrawal of Treatment' (1997) 315 BMJ 137.

[57] A further Bill is proceeding through the Californian legislature as we go to press; details of the *Compassionate Choices Bill 2005* can be found here: www.aroundthecapitol.com/billtrack/billview.html?bill=AB_654.

[58] Only one jurisdiction has passed such legislation: Rights of the Terminally Ill Amendment Act 1996 (NT, Australia). Four persons died under its provisions before the Australian Senate declared the measure to be unconstitutional and nullified by the national Euthanasia Laws Act 1997.

[59] For an up-to-date account see Department of Human Services, *Seventh Annual Report on Oregon's Death with Dignity Act* (2005), available at:http://oregon.gov/DHS/ph/pas/ar-index.shtml.

[60] The United States Supreme Court has decreed that statutes which *prohibit* assisted suicide—and which are in force in the majority of states—are not unconstitutional; the arguments are, however, essentially based on US constitutional law and have very little relevance outside the US: *Vacco v Quill* 117 S Ct 2293 (1997), (1997) 521 US 793; *Washington v Glucksberg* 117 S Ct 2258 (1997). For discussion, see V J Samar 'Is the Right to Die Dead?' (2000) 50 DePaul Law Rev 221.

medical reassurances of compliance with the requirements.[61] The fact that Oregon's Medicaid Plan, which provides medical cover for indigent patients, will pay for physician-assisted suicide while it will not do so for certain other treatments is of particular interest. Those who believe that financial pressure has the potential to encourage dispirited and vulnerable people to take a convenient way out, might take particular note of this.[62] The Act's passage into law was, however, not the end of the issue. A number of challenges have been mounted, including the introduction into Congress of the proposed Pain Relief Promotion Act of 1999, which would have directly banned the use of controlled drugs to end life, even where it was legal under assisted suicide legislation.[63] The failure of this Bill has not deterred the United States Government from further attempts to prevent assisted suicide through the use of drug administration regulations[64]—attempts which are largely motivated by a desire to avoid the use of Federal funds for the purpose. Indeed, the US Supreme Court will hear the case of *Gonzales v Oregon* on precisely this point in its October 2005 term.[65]

17.37   As something of an envoi to the Oregon position, it is worth noting how often and with what success the Act has been used in recent years. Thirty-seven Oregonians died as a result of PAS in 2004 and the seven-year total since it was introduced is 208. Interestingly, 25 out of 60 persons who were prescribed a lethal dose in 2004 did not take the drug. All the patients who did became unconscious within 30 minutes and all died within 31 hours, half of them within 25 minutes. So far as is known, there has been only one Oregonian failure in a man who woke up three days after taking his drug.[66] Readers are left to judge the significance of these figures for themselves.[67]

17.38   Assisted suicide was decriminalised in Switzerland in 1942 (Article 115 of the Swiss Penal Code).[68] The essential element of the law is the motive of the assisting person for, provided that the assistance is a selfless act—that is, without personal motive—it

---

[61] S R Martyn and H J Bourguignon 'Now is the Moment to Reflect: Two Years of Experience with Orgeon's Physician-Assisted Suicide Law' (2000) 8 Elder LJ 1. For early reports on the working of the law, see A Chin et al 'Legalized Physician-Assisted Suicide in Oregon—the First Year's Experience' (1999) 340 New Engl J Med 577; A D Sullivan et al 'Legalized Physician-Assisted Suicide in Oregon—the Second Year' (2000) 342 New Engl J Med 598.

[62] The economic implications are discussed by S Graboyes-Russo 'Too Costly to Live; the Moral Hazards of a Decision in *Washington v Glucksberg* and *Vacco v Quill*' (1997) 51 U Miami L Rev 907.

[63] D Orentlicher 'The Pain Relief Promotion Act of 1999' (2000) 283 JAMA 255.

[64] F Charatan, 'US Government Moves against Doctor Assisted Suicide' (2001) 323 BMJ 1149.

[65] The case was formerly known as *Oregon v Ashcroft* (2004) 368 F 3d 1118; the 9th Circuit Court of Appeals delivered its opinion in 2004 upholding the validity of the Oregon law. The appeal is at the behest of Attorney General Gonzales and is largely a matter of US constitutional law.

[66] D Colburn 'Fewer Turn to Assisted Suicide' (2005) *The Oregonian*, 11 March. But the dangers associated with 'undercover' PAS (in Australia) are stressed in R S Magnusson 'Euthanasia: Above Ground, Below Ground' (2004) 30 J Med Ethics 441. The author argues that legalising PAS may be a safer option than prohibition.

[67] A recent analysis suggests that there is, at least, no evidence of a 'slippery slope' effect which must be so. But the author similarly concludes that the same applies to the Dutch jurisdiction—and this, we feel, is a far less convincing proposition. See S W Smith 'Evidence for the Practical Slippery Slope in the Debate on Physician-assisted Suicide and Euthanasia' (2005) 13 Med L Rev 17.

[68] O Guillod and A Schmidt 'Assisted Suicide Under Swiss Law' (2005) 12 Euro J Health L 23.

is not criminal to assist another in their own suicide.[69] Perhaps surprisingly, this provision is not directed only to the medical profession. The position for mercy killing is, however, different because direct assistance to die in these circumstances remains liable to prosecution in the absence of a 'suicide'. Most recently, the Swiss National Advisory Committee on Biomedical Ethics has supported the *status quo*—that is, that assisted suicide should remain legal—but it has added the important proviso that regulation be introduced in respect of institutions who undertake the practice. More particularly, there is no suggestion of introducing residency requirements, meaning that the current trickle of terminally ill patients into Switzerland from more conservative countries in search of an 'easy death' may grow substantially in future years if other jurisdictions maintain their *stati quo*.[70]

17.39   The chances of legislation which legalises active euthanasia being accepted in the United Kingdom are slim;[71] but opposition might be very much less were it possible to legislate for PAS alone[72]—an electorate that, rightly, could not accept the doctor as an executioner might be less hostile to a doctor who could be regarded as a friend when one was in need.[73] Whatever their reasons, there is some evidence that both doctors and the public will accept the distinction. In a major survey undertaken in Scotland, McLean and Britton[74] found that, given a change in the law, 43 per cent of doctors across the United Kingdom would opt for the legalisation of PAS—defined as the person's action leading to their own death—and 19 per cent for active euthanasia in which the actions of other persons leads to death; the high proportion of undecided respondents (38 per cent) should be noted. As opposed to this, 42 per cent of Scottish people would prefer voluntary euthanasia while 28 per cent would choose PAS. It is difficult to avoid the conclusion that, in this very sensitive situation, most people would wish to pass the ultimate responsibility to others.

17.40   The diversity of results from opinion polls makes it hard to define the public attitude to either euthanasia or PAS—indeed, the public itself can appear confused.[75]

---

[69] This even extends, theoretically, to assistance borne out of indifference, that is, when the party assisting the suicide has neither a selfish nor a selfless motive.

[70] For a comparison with the German position, see K Becker-Schwarze 'Legal Restrictions of Physician Assisted Suicide' (2005) 12 Euro J Health L 9.

[71] House of Lords *Report of the Select Committee on Medical Ethics* (HL Paper 21–1, 1994)—which, admittedly, would have no truck with physician-assisted suicide either. The Government supported this aspect of the report: 'The Government can see no basis for permitting assisted suicide. Such a change would be open to abuse and put the lives of the weak and vulnerable at risk' (May 1994, Cmnd 2553). The Assisted Dying for the Terminally Ill Bill 2004 may or may not be revived in the new Parliament. A draft proposal for a Bill in the Scottish Parliament *Dying with Dignity* has been prepared by Jeremy Purvis MSP but it is no more than that.

[72] We discuss the terms of the Assisted Dying for the Terminally Ill Bill 2004 below at para 17.121.

[73] See para 17.120 below for further discussion.

[74] S A M McLean and A Britton *Sometimes a Small Victory* (1996).

[75] For a very recent overview including an assessment of various public surveys, see House of Lords Select Committee on the Assisted Dying for the Terminally Ill Bill, *Assisted Dying for the Terminally Ill Bill—First Report* (2005), chapter 6 (Public Opinion).

Thus, in McLean and Britton's survey, 67 per cent thought that human beings should have the right to choose when to die (with 20 per cent opposed) but only 55 per cent (with 30 per cent opposed) agreed that PAS should be made legal in Great Britain.[76] One powerful piece of evidence as to opinion in Great Britain is to be found in the survey carried out by Social and Community Planning Research in 1996,[77] where 82 per cent of the survey population thought that doctors should be allowed to end a person's life when requested. The opinion was, however, selective. Thus, while 86 per cent supported the procedure in comatose, incurably ill patients who were on ventilator support, the proportion dropped to 42 per cent when the patient had an incurable, painful but not fatal illness—the situation faced by Dr Cox.[78] It does seem that there is a groundswell in favour of a change in the law,[79] although it would be useful, were it possible, to survey the opinions of those who are close to death—even so, generalisations can never provide a satisfactory template in such intensely individualised conditions.[80]

17.41   There are also uncertainties as to the attitudes of the medical professions. McLean's survey disclosed only 30 per cent of doctors opposed to a change in the law to allow physician-assisted suicide; by contrast, this rose to 57 per cent in a study carried out at much the same time by the BMA.[81] Similarly, 55 per cent of the BMA sample would not take part in PAS if asked while only 37 per cent of McLean's study group would never do so. A more recent telephone survey in France found that support for euthanasia was relatively high among neurologists (46.5 per cent), slightly less among general practitioners (44.8 per cent), but, most interestingly, was lowest (35.5 per cent) among oncologists who had the most experience of end of life care of all those surveyed.[82] Whatever one is to make of these figures, it is interesting to note that the

---

[76] It was stated in *Compassion in Dying v State of Washington* 79 Fed 3d 790 (1996) that US opinion polls show majorities of between 64% and 73% in favour of physician-assisted suicide. In a study involving oncologists and oncology patients, the latter were consistently more in favour of PAS than were their physicians: E J Emanuel, D L Fairclough, E R Daniels and B R Clarridge 'Euthanasia and Physician-Assisted Suicide: Attitudes and Experiences of Oncology Patients, Oncologists, and the Public' (1996) 347 Lancet 1805.

[77] See J Wise 'Public Supports Euthanasia for Most Desperate Cases' (1996) 313 BMJ 1423.

[78] See para 17.26 above.

[79] See, for example, Voluntary Euthanasia Society *National Opinion Poll on Euthanasia* (2003): www.ves.org.uk/pdf/PublicOpinion_Apr03.pdf, BBC News, 'Half Would Help Loved Ones Die', 9 September 2004, http://ves.c.topica.com/maacDiZaa9QNpb23Jjvb/, and Guardian Unlimited 'Many Britons Would Assist Suicide', 9 September 2004, www.guardian.co.uk/uklatest/story/0,1271,-4483405,00.html.

[80] Although, in fact, a group of American oncology patients (i.e. with malignant disease) did not differ in any significant way from the general public: see Emanuel et al, n 76 above.

[81] J Coulson 'Doctors Oppose Legal Mercy Killing for Dying' (1995) BMA News Review (March) p 15. The BMA sample was, however, small and, one suspects, relatively selected. However, in a poll taken by the BMA eighteen months later, the gap between the two series narrowed—e.g. 46% of doctors opted for a change in the law to allow active medical intervention to terminate life if asked as opposed to 44% who were against. The proportion who would not intervene if so requested fell to 48%: J Coulson 'Till Death Us Do Part?' (1996) BMA News Review (Sept) p 23.

[82] P Peretti-Watel et al 'Doctors' Opinions on Euthanasia, End of Life Care, and Doctor-Patient Communication: Telephone Survey in France' (2003) 327 BMJ 595, cf EJ Emanuel et al 'Attitudes and Practices of US Oncologists regarding Euthanasia and Physician-Assisted Suicide' (2000) 133 Ann Intern Med 527.

majority of Western anglophone medical 'establishments'—as represented by their national Associations—want nothing to do with either PAS or euthanasia.[83] Nor, one might perhaps reflect, are moral questions to be determined on the basis of straw polls.[84] The fact that a majority believes that something is right does not *make it* morally right. There is ample evidence of considerable public enthusiasm in the United States for the death penalty; those who argue that public (or indeed professional) acceptance of physician-assisted suicide contributes weightily to its legalisation might consider whether consistency requires them to accept the morality of the death penalty in communities in which it is widely endorsed.

17.42   We are on equally difficult ground when we move from opinion to theory. There is a widely-held belief that assisting another to take his or her life is morally different from taking that life oneself. But where do the grounds of this difference lie? To assist in bringing about a result involves moral responsibility for that result on causal grounds, as is recognised in the criminal law doctrine of complicity. To argue that simply because one sets in motion, but does not complete a sequence of events, one is relieved of responsibility for the outcome is unconvincing. A rather more fruitful approach for the proponents of physician-assisted suicide is to defend the right to commit suicide and to characterise the provision of assistance as being legitimate in view of that right.[85] This then shifts the debate to an examination of the moral significance of the act of suicide and to the issue of whether, if this right is acknowledged, there are counterbalancing conflicting interests. This raises questions of greater moral complexity than many proponents of physician-assisted suicide imagine to be necessary. There are, for example, real moral doubts about suicide itself, which in one view can be seen as a conscious rejection of the value of human personhood.[86] And, at the end of the day, there may be strong pragmatic reasons for the view that the medical profession simply should not involve itself in actions which confuse its role. In this respect, the classic words of Capron still merit consideration:[87]

[83] American Medical Association, 'Decisions near the End of Life' (1992) 267 JAMA 2229; updated 1996, see C-G McDaniel 'US Doctors Reaffirm Opposition to Euthanasia' (1996) 313 BMJ 11. A Working Party of the British Medical Association concluded, in 1988, that the deliberate taking of a human life should remain a crime and that the doctor who feels compelled by conscience to end a patient's life must take his chance with the scrutiny of the law. The organisation repeated this view in its statement 'End of Life Decisions' in 2000, available at www.bma.org.uk and apparently remains unmoved by recent pressures: K Godfrey 'BMA Continues to Oppose Assisted Suicide and Euthanasia' (2004) 329 BMJ 997.

[84] This is largely the view of the House of Commons Select Committee on the 2004 Bill, para 17.121 below.

[85] A major review is to be found in M Blake 'Physician-assisted Suicide: A Criminal Offence or a Patient's Right?' (1997) 5 Med L Rev 294.

[86] For a useful survey of the moral arguments surrounding suicide, see M P Battin, *Ethical Issues in Suicide* (1994). For an example of the rejection of a right to commit suicide, see D J Velleman 'A Right of Self-Termination?' (1999) 109 Ethics 606.

[87] A M Capron 'Legal and Ethical Problems in Decisions for Death' (1986) 14 Law Med Hlth Care 141. See also the view of a hospice practitioner R C Twycross 'Assisted Death: A Reply' (1990) 336 Lancet 796. Practical implications (including statistical estimates of demand) are also considered by E J Emanuel 'What is the Great Benefit of Legalizing Euthanasia or Physician-Assisted Suicide?' (1999) 109 Ethics 629.

I never want to have to wonder whether the physician coming into my hospital room is wearing the white coat (or the green scrubs) of a healer, concerned only to relieve my pain and restore me to health, or the black hood of the executioner. Trust between patient and physician is simply too important and too fragile to be subjected to this unnecessary strain.

17.43   This concern over trust has been the subject of close scrutiny. Emanuel and his colleagues found, in their survey of cancer patients and members of the public in general, that 19 per cent of the former and 26.5 per cent of the latter would change doctors if their doctor spoke to them about euthanasia or physician-assisted suicide.[88] We suggested above that statistics as to what people think should not drive the debate—but these figures are not about moral attitudes, they are about the fears of, in some cases, very vulnerable people.[89]

17.44   Trust is only one of many considerations which have to be borne in mind. In addition, there are the familiar issues of coercion and abuse, both of which may serve to render decisions to end life less than fully voluntary, as, indeed, may confusion. The idea of the entirely rational person deciding to take his or her life after due reflection, and with no pressure from others or idea as to the expectations of others, may well not fit the reality.[90] If, however, there are such unequivocal cases, they are likely to involve, pre-eminently, cases of progressive neurological disease in which the patient may wish to commit suicide but is physically unable to do so without assistance. These cases constitute a very specific group which has its own special ethical problems.

PROGRESSIVE NEUROLOGICAL DISEASE

17.45   In so far as the right of the competent adult to refuse life-saving treatment is now universally established,[91] and that the legal right to control one's body has found expression in the decriminalising of suicide, it is but a short step to holding that to refuse assistance in dying to a person who is incapable of ending his or her own life is an affront to that person's rights of autonomy. It is important, though, to isolate two separate issues. One is the right to reject treatment, even if one is incapable of physically

---

[88] Emanuel et al, n 76 above.

[89] See R S Magnusson 'Euthanasia: Above Ground, Below Ground' (2004) 30 J Med Ethics 441 for a discussion of likely current rates of euthanistic practices (suggesting up to 10% of professionals have been involved at some time) and an argument in favour of legalisation to better protect vulnerable patients.

[90] But for a contrary, well-argued view from America, see S I Fraser and J W Walters 'Death—whose Decision? Euthanasia and the Terminally Ill' (2000) 26 J Med Ethics 121.

[91] For the UK, see *Re T (adult: refusal of medical treatment)* [1992] 4 All ER 649, (1992) 9 BMLR 46; *Re MB (an adult: medical treatment)* [1997] 2 FLR 426, (1997) 38 BMLR 175; *Ms B v An NHS Hospital Trust* [2002] EWHC 429. For a Canadian decision, see *Ciarlariello v Schacter* [1993] 2 SCR 119. Examples of leading cases from the US include: *Re Kathleen Farrell* 529 A 2d 404 (NJ, 1987); *Bouvia v Superior Court of Los Angeles County* 179 Cal App 3d 1127 (1986).

resisting the imposition of treatment. The second is more controversial and involves an attempt to assert a legal right to assistance in suicide.[92]

The right to refuse treatment

17.46   The *general* right to refuse treatment is discussed in detail at para 17.75 below. Here, we are concerned only with that right as it applies to the extreme example of progressive neurological disease. The application of the right in these circumstances was first upheld in the very significant Canadian decision of *Nancy B v Hôtel-Dieu de Québec.*[93] Ms B, who suffered from the Guillain-Barré syndrome, was existing by virtue of ventilation; she sought to have her ventilator disconnected and was supported in this by her family and the hospital. In making the required order, Dufour J called upon the Civil Code of Lower Canada, which held:

19.1 No person may be made to undergo care of any nature whether for examination, specimen taking, removal of tissue treatment or any other act, except with his consent,

and concluded that this encompassed ventilation. He proceeded:

What Nancy B is seeking . . . is . . . that nature may take its course; that she be freed from the slavery of a machine as her life depends on it. In order to do this, as she is unable to do it herself, she needs the help of a third person. Then, it is the disease which will take its natural course.

17.47   As a result, the person responsible for the actual cessation of treatment would not violate the criminal law in so doing. At the same time, however, the judge ruled that, not only would it not be homicide, it would also be neither suicide nor assisted suicide.

17.48   *Nancy B* has been followed in England by the equally important, although rather confusingly named, case of *Ms B v An NHS Hospital Trust.*[94] The facts of the two were very similar in that the 'English' Ms B was suffering from progressive paralysis due to a haemorrhage into her spinal cord and was, at the time of the hearing, maintained by the use of a ventilator. She had already effected an advance directive (see para 17.81) and repeatedly asked that she be disconnected from her machine but the clinicians refused to do so, preferring an attempt to wean her from life support. Ms B then sought a declaration that the treatment she was being given was an unlawful trespass. Butler-Sloss LJ, who heard the case herself at first instance, made it clear that, in the circumstances, it was not concerned with the patient's best interests but solely with

---

[92] For a very comprehensive review of such cases, see J H Veldink, J H J Wokke, G van der Wal et al 'Euthanasia and Physician-assisted Suicide among Patients with Amyotrophic Lateral Sclerosis in the Netherlands' (2002) 346 New Engl J Med 1638.

[93] (1992) 86 DLR (4th) 385, (1992) 15 BMLR 95.

[94] Para 10.63 above. A very similar case had been heard before but had received little attention: *Re AK (adult patient) (medical treatment: consent)* [2001] 1 FLR 129, (2001) 58 BMLR 151.

her legal capacity to accept or refuse treatment.[95] Ms B's case can, therefore, be dealt with in précis at the moment. Suffice it to say that she was found to have full capacity; she was moved to another hospital that was willing to disconnect her and she died some four weeks later. Butler-Sloss LJ emphasised the importance of a competent patient's free choice by imposing nominal damages of £100 against the hospital for their unlawful trespass.

17.49   In one respect, the effect of *Ms B* is merely to rehearse the well-established proposition that the competent adult may reject treatment, even if this will result in death. But the case also demonstrates the limitation of the *doctors'* autonomy that is inherent in the doctrine and we return to this below at para 17.105.

17.50   We should also remind readers that there is abundant evidence that removal of life support mechanisms at the request of the patient is not only acceptable but may be obligatory in the United States. Thus, in *Farrell*,[96] a motor neurone disease case, not only was a request for disconnection from the ventilator agreed, but the right to professional assistance during the agonal phase was upheld. An equally emphatic case arose in California, where the health care team was instructed to provide full facilities in order to ease the patient's dying.[97] It is thus clear that the United States' jurisdictions recognise a practical as well as a theoretical distinction between refusal of treatment and assisted suicide.[98]

Assistance with suicide

17.51   The second issue—that of whether there is a legal right to assistance with suicide in the case of a person who cannot exercise his or her own discretion—was considered by the Supreme Court of Canada in *Rodriguez v A-G of British Columbia*.[99] The arguments in Ms Rodriguez's case, which concerned the setting up of a mechanism she could use to end her life should she become paralysed as a result of her motor neurone disease, were, in the main, based on Canadian constitutional law and, in particular, related to possible conflicts between the Canadian Charter of Rights and Freedoms and the Criminal Code; these are issues specific to Canadian law, but their relevance in the United Kingdom has greatly increased with the passage of the Human Rights Act 1998. It was held by a majority of 5:4 that, while the patient's autonomy was at stake in such cases, the deprivation of rights consequent on the refusal of such a request was not contrary to the principles of fundamental justice, which required a fair balance to be struck between the interests of the state and those of the individual; neither were the liberty and security of the person compromised—one reason being

---

[95] The matter is discussed in detail in chapter 10. Effectively a medical assessment of 'best interests' is applicable only when the patient is incompetent. Guidelines were given in *Ms B* but originated in *St George's Healthcare NHS Trust v S* [1999] Fam 26.

[96] *Re Kathleen Farrell* 529 A 2d 404 (NJ, 1987).

[97] *Bouvia v Superior Court of Los Angeles County* 179 Cal App 3d 1127 (1986).

[98] See *Vacco v Quill* (1997) 117 S Ct 2293, (1997) 521 US 793. For discussion of the position in the United States, see N L Cantor and G C Thomas 'The Legal Bounds of Physician Conduct hastening Death' (2000) 48 Buffalo L Rev 83.

[99] *Rodriguez v A-G of British Columbia* (1993) 107 DLR (4th) 342, (1993) 50 BMLR 1.

that the provisions in the Criminal Code, s 241[100] prohibiting assisted suicide were there as a *protection* for the terminally ill who were particularly vulnerable as to their life and will to live:

[T]his protection is grounded on a substantial consensus among Western countries . . . that, in order to effectively protect life and those who are vulnerable in society, a prohibition without exception on the giving of assistance to commit suicide is the best approach . . . The formulation of safeguards to prevent excesses has been unsatisfactory and has failed to allay fears that a relaxation of the clear standard set by the law will undermine the protection of life and will lead to abuses of the exception.[101]

17.52 Despite the rather narrow basis for the judgment, some of the dissenting opinions expressed important general principles. In particular, the 'floodgates' argument was dismissed, not because it might not occur, but because a person should not be denied a choice which others have open to them simply on the grounds that, as a consequence, others may then abuse such powers as they have over the weak and ill[102]— effectively, each individual person must be treated fairly by the law and not made a scapegoat for the fallibility of others (per McLachlin J). Finally, the opinion of Cory J merits repetition:

[D]ying is an integral part of living . . . It follows that the right to die with dignity should be as well protected as is any other aspect of the right to life. State prohibitions that would force a dreadful, painful death on a rational but incapacitated terminally ill patient are an affront to human dignity.[103]

17.53 Thus, the arguments for and against assisted suicide of this type are finely balanced but all the dissenting opinions in *Rodriguez* stressed that it was for Parliament, not the courts, to make such fundamental decisions.

17.54 The issue first came to the attention of the United Kingdom courts in the *Linsell* case,[104] in which a patient in the terminal stages of motor neurone disease sought a declaration that her doctor would not be prosecuted if he administered potentially lethal doses of analgesics when her condition deteriorated. The patient withdrew her application when she heard that a substantial body of medical opinion had endorsed her doctor's planned palliative management regime, which meant that no ruling was required. A similar plight was brought before the courts some four years later by Mrs Pretty,[105] whose application was, ultimately, heard in the European Court of Human Rights. In this case the patient, who was just able to communicate, sought the

---

[100] Criminal Code of Canada, RSC (1985), C-46, s 241.

[101] (1993) 107 DLR (4th) 342 at 410, per Sopinka J.

[102] We do not intend, here, to discuss the bizarre case of Dr Kevorkian in America who is said to have invented and promoted a 'suicide machine'—he faced a Grand Jury and was acquitted of all charges. He then filmed his operation and, as a result, was tried and convicted of second degree murder. In 2002, the Michigan Supreme Court refused to review the rejection of his appeal by the State Court of Appeal.

[103] (1993) 107 DLR (4th) 342 at 413.

[104] E Wilkins 'Dying Woman Granted Wish for Dignified End' *The Times*, 29 October 1997, p 3.

[105] *R (on the application of Pretty) v DPP* [2001] UKHL 61, [2002] 1 All ER 1, (2002) 63 BMLR 1, HL.

assurance of the Director of Public Prosecutions (DPP) that he would not bring charges against her husband under the Suicide Act, s 2(1) if the latter took steps to end her life at her own request but by unspecified method.[106] The DPP declined to give this assurance, saying that it was improper for him to decline in advance to prosecute a breach of the criminal law.[107] This refusal was challenged by Mrs Pretty, by means of judicial review, on the grounds that the decision infringed rights which were protected under the Human Rights Act 1998.

17.55   Mrs Pretty based her claim on five Articles in the European Convention on Human Rights: Article 2 (the right to life); Article 3 (the prohibition of torture and cruel and degrading treatment); Article 8 (the right to respect for private life); Article 9 (the right to freedom of thought, conscience and religion) and Article 14 (the prohibition of discrimination). Although the court was clearly sympathetic to her plight, none of these Articles was deemed to be grounds on which to base a right to assistance with suicide. The court rejected the argument that Article 2 created a right of self-determination in relation to life and death, holding that the right was clearly concerned with preventing the unjustified taking of life. The appellant's argument in respect of Article 3 was that there was an obligation on the part of the state to provide assistance in the prevention of suffering—a positive rather than a negative duty. This was rejected by the court, which held that the state in this case was not in breach of its duty to prevent the infliction of suffering—and Mrs Pretty's suffering resulted from a disease rather than from the act of any person.

17.56   In dealing with the right to respect for private life (Article 8), the House of Lords did not consider a prohibition of assistance in suicide to amount to an infringement of autonomy for the purposes of the Article in question. The right of autonomy protected by the Article was the right to exercise autonomy while living one's life, and, as pointed out by Lord Bingham, there was nothing in the Article to suggest that it has any bearing on the choice to live no longer.[108] This narrow interpretation is open to criticism in that the concept of autonomy, as it is generally understood, includes decisions about dying.[109] Dying is a part of life, even if death is not, and it is difficult to imagine how at least some decisions about the nature of one's death could be seen to have nothing to do with the exercise of self-determination.[110] The European Court

---

[106] It will be seen from the discussion at para 17.34 above that, by our definition, assisted suicide was not a real possibility in that Mrs Pretty would have been unable to complete the act herself. This issue does not seem to have been considered in any of the judgments.

[107] It was also constitutionally impossible—Lord Bingham in the House of Lords drew attention to the Bill of Rights 1688 which denies the Crown and its servants any power to alter laws without the consent of Parliament ((2002) 63 BMLR 1 at 44).

[108] (2002) 63 BMLR 1 at 39.

[109] This aspect of the case has been emphasised by many writers. See, for example, H Biggs 'A Pretty Fine Line: Death Autonomy and Letting It B' (2003) 11 Feminist LS 291 who maintains that *Pretty* and *Ms B* are on a par. Lady Hale has, herself, discussed the problems in a non-judicial capacity: B Hale 'A Pretty Pass: When Is There a Right to Die?' (2003) 32 CLWR 1.

[110] Mrs Pretty's case is well argued by R English 'No Rights to Last Rites' (2001) 151 NLJ 1844. See also K M Boyd 'Mrs Pretty and Ms B' (2002) 28 J Med Ethics 211; A Pedain 'The Human Rights Dimension of the Diane Pretty Case' (2003) 62 CLJ 181.

did, in fact, appreciate the force of this argument but preferred to consider whether interference on the part of the state was justified under Article 8(2) which lists a number of exceptions that could be regarded as 'necessary in a democratic society'. In the event, the ECtHR agreed with the House of Lords in finding that the 'blanket' application of the Suicide Act 1961, s 2(1) infringed none of the five Articles considered. In particular, Article 2 imposed a duty on the state to protect life and there was no implication that this created a right to die; the prohibition of assisted suicide was not disproportionate to the need to protect the state's vulnerable citizens (Article 8); and that to distinguish between those who could and those who physically could not commit suicide—and, thus, to avoid any supposed discrimination against the latter contrary to Article 14—would be to undermine the protection of life that the 1961 Act was designed to safeguard.

17.57   Both the House of Lords and the ECtHR appreciated, and were much influenced by, the fear that permitting assisted suicide would open the door to abuse of the sick and the elderly, an attitude that was summed up well by Lord Bingham when quoting with approval the conclusions of the House of Lords Select Committee on Medical Ethics:

> The message which society sends to vulnerable and disadvantaged people should not, however obliquely, encourage them to seek death, but should assure them of our care and support in life.[111]

17.58   Be that as it may, it forms the basis for one of the main criticisms of the *Pretty* decision in that it could be held that the interests of the individual are being sacrificed in order to establish an important social policy—in short that we are coming dangerously close to the suggestion that 'it is expedient that one man should die for the people';[112] it is, at least, arguable that it is morally unacceptable to do so and, more tangibly, that such a policy is a clear infringement of the subject's basic human rights. Trenchant legal criticism can also be leveled at the Suicide Act itself and, somewhat innovatively,[113] particularly at s 2(4)—'no proceedings shall be instituted for an offence under this section except by or with the consent of the Director of Public Prosecutions'. Tur discusses the meaning of this and points out that it can either be definitional—i.e. there is no crime in the absence of the DPP's consent—or it is dispensing—i.e. it is always a crime but the DPP can dispense with prosecution in suitable cases. The judges in Mrs Pretty's case assumed the latter—as, we fancy, would most people—but, since the circumstances can only be assessed *after* the event, a dispensation is likely to lead to inconsistency and will surely lead to uncertainty— which is something the law should avoid. Section 2(4) needs amendment and the ideal is that it should spell out the conditions under which there *would be no* prosecution.

17.59   It would be undesirable, indeed unacceptable, to give carte blanche to the

---

[111] Report, para 239, p 49. Per Lord Bingham (2002) 63 BMLR 1 at 42.   [112] John 11:50.
[113] R H S Tur 'Legislative Technique and Human Rights: The Sad Case of Assisted Suicide' [2003] Crim LR 3.

self-appointed 'mercy killer' and it has been pointed out that any proposal for relaxing s 2(1) would have to accept that only help provided by medically qualified persons could be lawful.[114] This suggests that legitimising physician assisted suicide might be an acceptable half-way house.

THE INACTIVE PHYSICIAN

17.60   The procedures we have discussed thus far have focused on *some* positive action on the part of the attending physician and we must now move to the conditions in which the shortening of life is achieved by way of an omission to act. Logically, it should follow as a sub-section of passive voluntary euthanasia. It must, however, also include situations in which the patient is unable to contribute to end of life decision-making (as opposed to the final act)—that is, we are now entering the realms of non-voluntary euthanasia. Accordingly, we have treated it as a separate subject.

17.61   A comprehensive definition of passive euthanasia presents a number of problems in so far as death resulting from inaction of one sort or another is spread across a wide spectrum and includes, inter alia, non-treatment of a treatable condition, withdrawal of treatment and refusal of treatment—and we have already discussed this last variant in chapter 10. Sub-categories exist even within this framework. Thus, treatment can be withdrawn either because it is non-productive or because, based on an anticipated quality of life, it is in the patient's best interests to do so; alternatively, treatment can be refused because the competent patient wishes to die or, simply, because he or she has an aversion to a particular form of treatment.[115]

17.62   What one regards as passive euthanasia, then, depends not only on whether one is speaking in legal, moral or medical terms but also on personal preference or prejudice. As to the latter, we have tended to use the death certificate as our benchmark—would the patient have died if the physician had not retreated into his passive mode or, put another way, could we certify death as being due to natural causes with a clear conscience? On this definition, passive euthanasia is confined to withdrawal of life-sustaining treatment in the incompetent and refusal of further treatment by the competent patient where death is the intended outcome—with the 'do not resuscitate order' providing a virtually distinct category. The concept of 'double effect' (see para 17.90) is also so bound to the subject of passive euthanasia that it cannot be ignored in this context. Such a classification will seem unsatisfactory to some; nevertheless, it forms the basis for the discussion that follows.[116]

[114] D Morris 'Assisted Suicide under the European Convention on Human Rights: A critique' (2003) 1 EHRLR 65.

[115] For a discussion of the relationship between suicide and the refusal of treatment, see J Fletcher 'The Courts and Euthanasia' (1987/88) 15 Law Med Hlth Care 223. D Lanham 'The Right to Choose to Die with Dignity' (1990) 14 Crim LJ 401, considers the subject in detail.

[116] The problems of classification of assisted death have recently been critically examined by S A M McLean and S J Elliston 'Death, Decision Making and the Law' [2004] JR 265.

17.63   The question of whether allowing an event to happen through inaction is morally different from taking positive steps to bring it about has been extensively debated in moral philosophy. Criticism of the act/omission distinction has been intense and sustained over recent decades. Thus, the position advanced by Philippa Foot in her classic paper 'The Problem of Abortion and the Doctrine of Double Effect'—that our duty not to harm others is stronger than our duty to assist[117]—finds fewer supporters today than it did when it was first published in 1976. This change has even had its effect on the legal world, within which commentators—and occasionally judges— have expressed disquiet over the drawing of a sharp distinction between act and omission for the purposes of attributing liability for the consequences. In spite of this, there remain grounds for making this distinction in relation to euthanasia, even if its validity has been called into question elsewhere. One reason for arguing against the distinction is that it tolerates inconsistency and may merge into moral cowardice. On this view, a doctor who knows that his failure to treat will result in death should accept the same responsibility for that death as if he had brought it about through a positive act.[118]

17.64   How, then, is this objection to be answered? One response is to say that the distinction reflects a widely held moral intuition which, even if it involves inconsistency, allows for the practical conduct of day to day moral life. Morality, like the law, needs to be rooted in daily experience. Doctors who engage in the classic forms of passive euthanasia need—and maybe are entitled to—the comfort of thinking they are not actually killing their patients. A sophisticated morality will recognise such ordinary human needs. A second response would be consequentialist in nature. The act/ omission distinction plays an important role in the preservation of a near-absolute prohibition of killing. The weakening of this prohibition could have the effect of blunting the respect which we accord to human life. The combination of these two approaches is sufficient to tip the scales in favour of retaining the distinction.[119]

17.65   Selective non-treatment is practised fairly widely while only a very small number of physicians would work actively to end the life of a patient.[120] The medical profession as a whole accepts the distinction as argued above. As one commentator put it: 'Our gut intuition tells us that there is a difference between active and passive euthanasia and we are not going to be browbeaten into changing our minds by mere logic'[121]— and it is not beyond the capacity of moral philosophy to support this: 'We cannot

---

[117] P Foot in S Gorovitz et al (eds) *Moral Problems in Medicine* (2nd edn, 2003).

[118] Strongly argued by Jackson, n 43 above.

[119] The contrary argument, which, clearly, we find difficult to accommodate, has been put in an editorial article by L Doyal and L Doyal 'Why Active Euthanasia and Physician Assisted Suicide should be Legalised' (2001) 323 BMJ 1079.

[120] In one of many such studies, this one undertaken by the BMA, 22 out of 750 doctors admitted to having actively ended the life of a patient on request although a surprising 46% believed that they should be legally permitted to do so. 90% supported passive euthanasia and 75% recognised a moral distinction between active and passive euthanasia: J Coulson 'Till Death Us Do Part?' (1996) BMA News Rev, Sept, p 23.

[121] T B Brewin 'Voluntary Euthanasia' (1986) 1 Lancet 1085. See also D P Sulmany 'Killing and Allowing to Die: Another Look' (1998) 26 J Law Med & Ethics 55.

capture our moral judgments by appeal to argument alone . . . in the area of dying; intuitions and conceptions formed by actual experience must be given weight'.[122]

17.66 The legal position is, in one sense, clear. We can return to *Bland*, per Lord Mustill:[123]

The English criminal law . . . draws a sharp distinction between acts and omissions. If an act resulting in death is done without lawful excuse and with intent to kill it is murder. But an omission to act with the same result and with the same intent is in general no offence at all.

So far, so good, but Lord Mustill went on to say:[124]

There is one important general exception at common law, namely that a person may be criminally liable for the consequences of an omission if he stands in such a relation to the victim that he is under a duty to act.

And there is Lord Keith:[125]

In general it would not be lawful for a medical practitioner who assumed responsibility for the care of an unconscious patient simply to give up treatment in circumstances where continuance of it would confer some benefit on the patient. On the other hand, a medical practitioner is under no duty to treat such a patient where a large body of informed and responsible medical opinion is to the effect that no benefit at all would be conferred by continuance.

17.67 Lord Keith was, of course, speaking of the permanent vegetative state. There is, however, no doubt that, despite his obvious duty of care—and despite his potential liability—the doctor who discontinues treatment of an incompetent patient in the circumstances envisaged will not be prosecuted provided his inaction is covered by the doctrine of good medical practice.

17.68 An illustrative example of this comes from New Zealand.[126] The circumstances surrounding the case were very similar to those in *Nancy B*,[127] save that the patient, L—also suffering from the Guillain-Barré syndrome—was incapable of expressing his wishes. His existence depended on artificial ventilation and the question put to the High Court was in the rather stark terms: would the doctors' action in withdrawing ventilator support make them guilty of homicide?[128]

17.69 Thomas J approached this issue by asking whether a doctor is obliged to continue treatment which has no therapeutic or medical benefit notwithstanding that the withdrawal of the treatment may result in the clinical death of the patient. He commented that all natural life has ceased in such a case; it was the *manifestations* of life which were maintained artificially and which were brought to an end by the doctor's

---

[122] G Gillett 'Euthanasia, Letting Die and the Pause' (1988) 14 J Med Ethics 61. This attitude was challenged by M Parker 'Moral Intuition, Good Deaths and Ordinary Medical Practitioners' (1990) 16 J Med Ethics 28.

[123] [1993] 1 All ER 821 at 890, (1992) 12 BMLR 64 at 137.

[124] [1993] 1 All ER 821 at 890, (1992) 12 BMLR 64 at 137.

[125] [1993] 1 All ER 821 at 861, (1992) 12 BMLR 64 at 106–107.

[126] *Auckland Area Health Board v A-G* [1993] 1 NZLR 235, [1993] 4 Med LR 239.

[127] See para 17.46.

[128] Crimes Act 1961, ss 151(1) and 164, NZ. A Death with Dignity Bill was narrowly defeated in 2003.

intervention. He proceeded on the twin principles of humanity and common sense. On this basis, he concluded that life support provided *only* for the purpose of deferring certain death could not be regarded as a necessity of life; moreover, doctors have a lawful excuse to discontinue treatment when there is no medical justification for continuing that medical assistance. Withdrawal of treatment would not be unlawful if it was carried out within the accepted confines of 'good medical practice'—or adhering to a procedure which provided safeguards against the possibility of individual error. Within this scenario, withdrawal of life support would not be the cause of death *as a matter of law*—and this would coincide with the common-sense perception.

17.70　　Thomas J's admirable analysis attracted particularly favourable comment in the House of Lords in *Bland*. Jurisprudentially, it owes much to the reasoning in PVS cases and this is inevitable in that L's disease state was more advanced than was that of Ms Rodriguez or Nancy B. The judge was able, however, to medicalise the dilemma fully and thus avoid what is, in our view, the sophistry of the 'best interests' test.

17.71　　It is to be noted that all these cases of 'assistance in dying' have it in common that the courts have been anxious to ensure that the cause of death was attributed to natural disease. We suggest, and have argued already in respect of PVS,[129] that the cause of death following withdrawal of any form of life support should depend on whether the support was removed before or after brain stem death has occurred. If the person is dead at that time, the cause of death is clearly the original anoxic or other insult sustained by the brain. When, however, a treatment is discontinued solely by reason of its futility, there is nothing to be lost—and much to be gained by way of intellectual honesty—in attributing death, correctly, to 'Lawful withdrawal of life support systems which were necessitated by [the disease]'.

ALLOWING THE PATIENT TO DIE

17.72　　While selective non-treatment has gained general acceptance as being a part of good medical practice, it is clear that it will not find moral endorsement in all its forms— much will depend on the nature of the treatment that is being withheld. The issue thus focuses on the distinction between what have become known as ordinary and extraordinary treatments. There is a general consensus, now established in both legal and medical opinion, that the doctor need not resort to heroic methods to prolong the life—or, perhaps better, to prolong the dying—of his patient; considerations of cost and of the distribution of other resources are important here, although they must be secondary to the well-being and the dignity of the patient.[130] These principles are embodied in the classic expression of the ordinary/extraordinary treatment test which is to be found in the directive issued by Pope Pius XII in 1957:[131]

---

[129]　See chapter 16.

[130]　It is clear from at least two speeches in *Bland* ([1993] 1 All ER 821 at 879, 893, (1992) 12 BMLR 64 at 125, 140, per Lord Browne-Wilkinson and Lord Mustill), that resources might be a legitimate concern of the clinician.

[131]　(1957) 49 Acta Apostolicae Sedis 1027.

Man has a right and a duty in case of severe illness to take the necessary steps to preserve life and health. That duty ... devolves from charity as ordained by the Creator, from social justice and even from strict law. But he is obliged at all times to employ only ordinary means ... that is to say those means which do not impose an extraordinary burden on himself or others.

17.73 This statement represents the core of Roman Catholic teaching on the matter and a similar approach has found widespread support in non-religious discussions of the issue, where the denial of the need to resort to extraordinary measures may be based on quite different grounds. Clearly, however, the difficulty about such a test lies in making the fundamental distinction between ordinary and extraordinary treatments and the Pope, himself, qualified 'ordinary' as 'according to personal circumstances, the law, the times and the culture'. Thus, the ordinary/extraordinary test should not and cannot be applied as a general, all embracing rule.[132] Some have, accordingly, suggested that the comparison should be between proportionate and disproportionate therapy; we would take this concept one stage further in preferring the contrast of medically productive and non-productive means—the test being whether or not a particular treatment is doing the condition any good. Factors such as the physical and psychological pain involved in the treatment, its claim on scarce resources and the general prospects for the patient and his family may all be taken into account in deciding whether or not a treatment is productive.

17.74 Clearly, non-productivity and medical futility have much in common as a treatment standard and, as we have already discussed, the arguments for and against their adoption are very similar. The scope for ethical and legal disagreement is wide and, in the long term, social consensus must be sought on ways to resolve the conflicts engendered by the notion of futility[133]—which we are convinced must come to be accepted in some way. Meantime, imperfect and value-laden as the concepts of futility and non-productivity may be, their practical value should not be discarded for fear of offending what Miles has described as an elitist view of 'autonomy'.[134]

---

[132] We have expressed reservations elsewhere about the abilities of the courts to maintain a distinction between an entitlement to artificial nutrition and hydration as a form of 'basic care' (to which a patient is entitled based on his own assessment of his best interests), and other forms of care, see J K Mason and G T Laurie 'Personal Autonomy and the Right to Treatment: A Note on *R (on the application of Burke) v General Medical Council* (2005) 9 Edin LR 123.

[133] For a UK approach, see K R Mitchell, I H Kerridge and T J Lovat 'Medical Futility, Treatment Withdrawal and the Persistent Vegetative State' (1993) 19 J Med Ethics 71. Guidelines have been drawn up in New South Wales to cover cases in which life support treatment is deemed futile. Life supporting therapy is widely defined and includes chemotherapy, radiotherapy and renal dialysis: NSW Department of Health *End of Life Care and Decision-Making—Guidelines* (2005). In the United States the American Medical Association has issued guidance on the notion of futility. The Association accepted that it would be difficult to establish a consensus on this issue, and therefore recommended a process-based approach: Council on Ethical and Judicial Affairs, 'Medical Futility in End-of-Life Care: Report of the Council on Ethical and Judicial Affairs' (1999) 281 JAMA 937. For a wide-ranging overview, see M B Zucker and H D Zucker *Medical Futility* (1997).

[134] S H Miles 'Medical Futility' (1992) 20 Law Med Hlth Care 310.

WHOSE BODY IS IT?

17.75 The individual's right of self-determination, which we have discussed above within the confines of progressive neurological disease, is now established as the determining factor in *any* situation of therapeutic conflict—whether it is a problem of abortion, consent to treatment or euthanasia. Yet the question can still be properly asked—are there circumstances in which the wishes of the individual should be looked upon as being qualified by other considerations?

17.76 The theologian might well answer Yes; the Roman Catholic church, for example, allows no right to suicide and declining treatment might be regarded as suicide in certain circumstances. Others might hold that to diminish the seriousness and awe with which we view life is but a step towards the rejection of values which are of crucial importance to society. We would do well to reflect on the moral steps which are being taken when we pay homage to the cult of self-determination.[135] None the less, the principle of respect for autonomy is now firmly established and is reflected legally in the offence of battery—the concept of (informed) refusal has achieved the same standing in medical jurisprudence as that of (informed) consent.[136]

17.77 The common law basis for these decisions lies in the assumption that the rights of the competent individual to self-determination will normally outweigh the interests of the state in the preservation of life.[137] In addition, there are human rights principles which underpin the proposition that treatment may not be imposed on the competent adult. This would almost certainly amount to an infringement of rights protected by the Human Rights Act 1998 should it ever be necessary to invoke that statute; Article 3 of the European Convention on Human Rights[138] prohibits the infliction of inhuman measures, into which category non-consensual treatment would be likely to fall.[139] To the same effect, the Council of Europe's Convention on Human Rights and Biomedicine provides in Article 5 that any intervention in the health field may only be carried out if the patient gives a free and informed consent. In some jurisdictions, the right to reject medical treatment has been specifically recognised in legislation. Pioneering statutory action in this field is to be found in the Medical Treatment Act 1988 of Victoria which, among other things, introduced the offence of medical trespass which is committed by a medical practitioner who knowingly treats contrary to the certified wishes of the patient; thus, the practitioner cannot plead his own ethos and there is no 'conscience clause'. Simultaneously,

---

[135] For a searching analysis, see O O'Neill *Autonomy and Trust in Bioethics* (2002). See also the Israeli Patients' Rights Act 1996 which, inter alia, permits a right to informed consent but, on communitarian grounds, refers refusals to a committee.

[136] *St George's Healthcare NHS Trust v S R v Collins, ex p S* [1998] 3 WLR 936, [1998] 3 All ER 673 is probably the strongest authority in the United Kingdom.

[137] This is argued in a wide-ranging article by E Wicks 'The Right to Refuse Medical Treatment under the European Convention on Human Rights' (2001) 9 Med L Rev 17.

[138] Now Sch 1 to the 1998 Act.

[139] On the other side of the coin, a *failure* to provide treatment in the patient's best interests does not contravene the Convention: *A NHS Trust v D* [2000] 2 FLR 677, (2000) 55 BMLR 19; *NHS Trust A v M, NHS Trust B v H* [2001] Fam 348, (2001) 58 BMLR 87; cf *Burke*, n 148 below.

however, the Act exonerates the doctor who fails to treat in accordance with a certificate of refusal from professional, criminal and civil liability (s 9).[140]

17.78 The Victorian legislation is far-reaching. In particular, no distinction is made between terminal and other illness. Moreover, the right to refuse treatment is unqualified; it is subject neither to the interests of the state nor to those of third parties—non-consensual caesarian section on behalf of the fetus, for example, now has no place in Victorian medical practice.[141] The Act specifically excludes palliative treatment—or the provision of reasonable medical procedures for the relief of pain, suffering and discomfort (s 3)—from that which can be refused but, at the same time, preserves the patient's rights at common law in this respect. On the face of things, therefore, the Medical Treatment Act 1988 is a particularly firm expression of the doctrine of patient autonomy; it is also a remarkable example of the denial of a physician's autonomy—and, pace those who are untroubled by the distinction,[142] it is difficult to see it as other than legislative approval of passive euthanasia of either voluntary or non-voluntary type.

17.79 The interpretation of the Act was recently tested by the Supreme Court of Victoria in *Gardner; re BWV*[143] which concerned the legality of removing artificial feeding and hydration (ANH) from a woman in PVS. Relatives of the patient attested to her prior expressed wishes not to be maintained in such a debilitated state but the central legal question was whether the intervention (ANH) was 'medical treatment' (which can be refused under the Act) or 'palliative care' (which cannot be rejected). In holding that ANH is medical care, the Supreme Court sought to make treatment decisions involving ANH a matter of clinical judgment in each case wherein the opinions of relatives and proxy decision-makers can also feature. It has been hailed as a vindication of the rights of incompetent patients.[144]

17.80 It is to be noted that informed lay and medical opinion[145] has rejected the need for a similar statute in the United Kingdom where the common law and the advance directive/decision offer alternative solutions. As we have seen, there is ample evidence that the right of the competent individual to refuse treatment is ingrained in both the common law and human rights law—and this right persists even though it may result

---

[140] The power to appoint an agent in the event of supervening incompetence is granted by s 5A of the 1988 Act, as amended by the Medical Treatment (Enduring Power of Attorney) Act 1990. For description of the 1988 Act, see D Lanham 'The Right to Choose to Die with Dignity' (1990) 14 Crim LJ 401.

[141] Neither has it in England: *St George's Healthcare NHS Trust v S, R v Collins, ex p S* [1998] 3 WLR 936.

[142] For example, Rehnquist CJ in *Vacco v Quill* (1997) 117 S Ct 2293 at 2298. For an interesting tour of the semantics of euthanasia, see D P T Price 'Assisted Suicide and Refusing Medical Treatment: Linguistics, Morals and Legal Contortions' (1996) 4 Med L Rev 270.

[143] [2003] VSC 173.

[144] M A Ashby and D Mendelson '*Gardner; re BWV*: Victorian Supreme Court Makes Landmark Australian Ruling on Tube Feeding' (2004) 181 Med J Aus 442.

[145] House of Lords Report of the Select Committee on Medical Ethics HL Paper 21–1 (1994).

in the patient's death;[146] moreover, a refusal can take the form of a declaration of intention never to consent in the future.[147]

17.81   In theory, the principle of the advance directive/decision is simple—the individual executes a document expressing his or her wishes as to treatment in the event of being disabled from doing so verbally in the future and the physician acts upon it when the occasion arises. It is important to remember that, while the advance directive/decision commonly expresses a refusal of treatment, it may, equally, authorise that life-prolonging measures be maintained—though it cannot, of course, *require* that such treatment be given;[148] looked at in this way, the advance directive becomes an aspect of the right to choose rather than the right to die.[149]

17.82   The difficulty is, however, that, while the theory may be simple, practice has its complications. Perhaps the main concern lies in the fact that it is extremely difficult to devise an intelligible document which will be unambiguous in all circumstances—in particular, who is to define words such as 'severe', 'advanced' or 'comparable gravity'. Secondly, there is the persistent concern that the patient has, during the critical phase, changed his or her mind; Dworkin, in his classic *Life's Dominion*,[150] points out that the person who drafts a 'living will' and the incompetent who benefits from it are, effectively, different persons and the one need not necessarily be empowered to speak for the other. Given these imponderables, the doctor's dilemma is summed up in the words of Lord Donaldson:

> ... what the doctors *cannot* do is to conclude that, if the patient still had the necessary capacity in the changed situation [he being now unable to communicate], he would have reversed his decision . . . what they *can* do is to consider whether at the time the decision was made it was intended by the patient to apply in the changed situation,[151]

from which it is clear that the doctor should, and probably must, apply his own interpretation to an advance directive.

17.83   In *W Healthcare NHS Trust v H*[152] the Court of Appeal upheld the correctness of the judge's conclusion that the patient was incompetent in respect of the relevant

---

[146] The question of the capacity to refuse has been dealt with in chapter 10. A 2002 poll of 300 UK doctors revealed that 96% accepted the right of the competent patient to refuse treatment. However, only 61% were prepared to end a patient's treatment knowing that it would kill them. Perhaps predictably, only 49% thought that the courts should decide on competence—the preferred alternative being a mixed tribunal: G Clews 'Doctors Back Patients' Right to Refuse Treatment' (2002) BMA News, 30 March, p 12.

[147] *Re C (adult: refusal of medical treatment)* [1994] 1 All ER 819, sub nom *Re C (mental patient: medical treatment)* (1993) 15 BMLR 77 at 82. But, more recently, Munby J has held that any condition purporting to make an advance directive irrevocable is contrary to public policy and void: *HE v A Hospital NHS Trust* [2003] 2 FLR 408, [2003] Fam Law 733.

[148] Cf, *R (on the application of Burke) v General Medical Council* [2004] 3 FCR 579, (2004) 79 BMLR 126, and related commentary, Mason and Laurie n 132 above.

[149] An elegantly neutral consideration of advance directives is to be found in A Sommerville 'Are Advance Directives Really the Answer? And What Was the Question?' in S A M McLean (ed) *Death, Dying and the Law* (1996).

[150] R Dworkin *Life's Dominion* (1993).

[151] In *Re T (adult: refusal of medical treatment)* [1993] Fam 95 at 115, (1992) 9 BMLR 46 at 60.

[152] [2005] 1 WLR 834.

decision and that none of her earlier statements amounted to an advance decision that she would prefer to starve to death than be kept alive. The best interests test then fell to be applied and this supported the reinsertion of her feeding tube.

17.84   Although the court in *AK (adult patient) (medical treatment: consent)*,[153] stated quite clearly that an advance declaration by a patient should be observed by those treating him, the precise authority of advance decisions has, until recently, been equivocal.[154] The most official statement was to be found in a Practice Note of 1994: 'In summary, the patient's [previously] expressed views, if any, will always be a very important component in the decisions of the doctors and the court'.[155] However, sections 24–26 of the Mental Capacity Act 2005 now place them on a statutory footing. Even so, while this puts their legal validity beyond doubt, it still leaves room for debate as to their scope. Briefly, written, signed and witnessed (one person) advance statements from competent adults about the withdrawal or withholding of future treatments must be respected; if this relates to life-sustaining treatment there must be clear and specific statement from the person to this effect. The decision can be altered or withdrawn at any time without the need for a written statement (save in the case of withholding life-sustaining treatment); it need not be followed if there is evidence of the individual acting in a manner inconsistent with his prior-expressed wishes or if it is 'reasonable' to believe that he did not envisage the circumstances in which he finds himself. At the end of the day, then, we may not be much further forward. If one revisits the concerns and objections discussed above it is possible to see that they apply wholesale to the new legislative measures.

A limited concept?

17.85   We have already remarked on how blurred are the boundaries of 'passive euthanasia' and on the subjective nature of its definition. Thus, treatment of the patient in the permanent vegetative state is, in our opinion, best regarded as an example of medical futility and has been discussed under that heading.[156] At the other end of the scale, we find the voluntary removal of life support from the competent patient indistinguishable from physician-assisted suicide and continued treatment in the face of refusal has now been seen to constitute an assault.[157] Effectively, therefore, 'pure' passive euthanasia is limited to those relatively rare management decisions involving non-voluntary patients who have retained some cortical activity but are unable to make competent decisions and who, at the same time, are not known to have previously expressed an unequivocal preference as to treatment in the prevailing conditions.

17.86   Examples of such patients who have had their circumstances considered by a court are extremely rare in the United Kingdom; indeed, we contend that the only apposite

---

[153] N 94 above. The case concerned a 19-year-old man with motor neurone disease who wished nutrition and hydration to be discontinued two weeks after he lost all capacity to communicate.

[154] They still remain so in Scotland where there is no clarification in the Adults with Incapacity (Scotland) Act 2000. See chapter 20 below for further discussion.

[155] *Practice Note* [1994] 2 All ER 413.   [156] See chapter 16 above.

[157] *Ms B v An NHS Trust*, para 17.48 above.

example is the recent decision in *W Healthcare NHS Trust v H* which we discuss above at para 17.83. The more frequent recourse to the law courts in the United States—particularly as represented by a flurry of activity in the 1980s—has, however, served to demonstrate certain principles and, at the same time, the difficulties which may be encountered.

17.87   Taking into account our 'limited concept' of passive euthanasia, the most instructive case remains that of Ms Conroy;[158] *Conroy* was, admittedly concerned primarily with assisted feeding but we have established that feeding is, for current purposes, an aspect of treatment—and is certainly so regarded in the United States.[159] Ms Conroy was an elderly incompetent diabetic, severely malformed and with an intellectual capacity above that of a person in the persistent vegetative state—even if only marginally so. Permission to remove her nasogastric tube was sought and granted by the trial court on the grounds that no valid purpose was served by needlessly prolonging such a life. Although the subject had, meantime, died, the finding was appealed and was reversed—the Court of Appeal considering that death following removal of the feeding tube would have been due to dehydration and starvation; this implied active killing and they were not prepared to condone active euthanasia. Great concern was also expressed as to the knock-on effect which might seriously compromise the standards of treatment of the mentally retarded and of the senile demented. Even so, the Supreme Court of New Jersey reversed the appellate decision, holding that:

artificial feeding by means of a nasogastric tube . . . can be seen as equivalent to artificial breathing by means of a respirator. Both prolong life through mechanical means when the body is no longer able to perform a vital bodily function on its own,[160]

the extrapolation being that the patient has the right to refuse both. While the Supreme Court commended the appointment of a guardian to act as proxy for the incompetent, it still laid down very strict criteria—including investigation by an ombudsman—before such decisions could be taken by the medical staff and the guardian or relatives. In the absence of *any* indications of the patient's wishes—under what the court referred to as the 'pure objective test':[161]

the net burdens of the patient's life with treatment should clearly and markedly outweigh the benefits that the patient derives from life. Further, the recurring, unavoidable and severe pain of the patient's life with the treatment should be such that the effects of administering life-sustaining treatment would be inhumane.

17.88   The court expressly declined to authorise decision-making based on the personal worth or social utility of another's life, or the value of that life to others:

---

[158] *Re Claire C Conroy* 464 A 2d 303 (NJ, 1983); on appeal 486 A 2d 1209 (NJ, 1985).

[159] E.g. *Re Severns* 425 A 2d 156 (Del, 1980); *Re Mary Hier* 464 NE 2d 959 (Mass, 1984); *Brophy v New England Sinai Hospital* 497 NE 2d 626 (Mass, 1986); *Corbett v D'Alessandro* 487 So 2d 368 (Fla, 1986). In *Re Brown* 517 A 2d 893 (NJ, 1986), a hospital was ordered to retain a patient who refused to consent to artificial feeding and to honour her decision.

[160] 486 A 2d 1209 at 1236.

[161] It should be noted that the Supreme Court regarded this as a 'best interests' test rather than one of substituted judgment.

We do not believe that it would be appropriate for a court to designate a person with the authority to determine that someone else's life is not worth living simply because, to that person, the patient's 'quality of life' or value to society seems negligible.

17.89   The most recent chapter in the US debate involved the circumstances of Terri Schiavo which we discuss in chapter 16. The case concerned a decision to withdraw feeding and hydration from the patient to release her from a 15-year-long period in PVS. For present purposes the most relevant features of the case are two-fold: first, despite the clear legal authority of the patient's ex-husband to act as her guardian and proxy decision-maker, the parental challenge to his refusal was entertained by both state and federal courts alike and even resulted in the passing of a special Act of Congress addressed solely to the patient's circumstances; second, and relatedly, the highly public and political nature of the case cannot but lead to the conclusion that these deeply personal and private decisions are becoming the fodder of bodies interested in far wider agenda designed to control and manipulate the values (and rights) of the American people. The sanctity of life argument here plays a crucial central role as never before and it seems that the tension between 'private' decisions and 'public/ state' values is set to heighten.

'DOUBLE EFFECT'

17.90   We have seen that the law condemns active euthanasia on the grounds of intent. The terminally ill are beyond curative therapy by definition, and their management becomes a matter of the relief of suffering. Achieving this may, inevitably, involve some risk to life—but it is the patient's comfort, not his or her premature death, which is the intended outcome. The terminally ill patient thus most clearly sets the scene for the application of the philosophical concept of 'double effect'.[162]

17.91   The principle of double effect, as invoked in this context, is that an action which has a good objective may be performed despite the fact that the objective can only be achieved at the expense of a coincident harmful effect. This analysis has, however, to be qualified—the action itself must be either good or morally indifferent, the good effect must not be produced by means of the ill-effect and there must be a proportionate reason for allowing the expected ill to occur.[163] It is implicit in this doctrine that the good effect must outweigh the bad and this may involve a value judgment. Thus, it might well be ethically right to administer pain-killing drugs in such dosage as simultaneously shortens the life of a terminally ill patient; it would not be justifiable to give the same dose to a young man with identical pain who stood a reasonable chance of recovery. The seminal case in the United Kingdom is that of *R v Adams*,

---

[162] For a wide-ranging analysis of double effect, see D Price 'Euthanasia, Pain Relief and Double Effect' (1997) 17 LS 323. See also, D Mapel 'Revising the Doctrine of Double Effect' (2001) 18 J Appl Philosoph 257; G Williams 'The Principle of Double Effect and Terminal Sedation' (2001) 9 Med L Rev 41.

[163] It will be seen that Dr Cox (see para 17.24 above) would have failed on at least two counts to establish a 'double effect' justification for his action.

which we have already briefly mentioned,[164] but it is nonetheless worth reiterating the dictum of Devlin J, who said: 'The doctor is entitled to relieve pain and suffering even if the measures he takes may incidentally shorten life'. Twenty years after the *Adams* verdict, Lord Edmund Davies commented: 'Killing both pain and patient may be good morals but it is far from certain that it is good law'.[165] Williams,[166] by contrast, found the proposition easily justified by necessity. Any conflict has now been resolved. Devlin J's classic direction was followed in *R v Cox*[167] and the charge to the jury in the latter case was cited with approval by the House of Lords in *Bland*, where we have Lord Goff:

[It is] the established rule that a doctor may, when caring for a patient who is, for example, dying of cancer, lawfully administer painkilling drugs despite the fact that he knows that an incidental effect of that application will be to abbreviate the patient's life . . . Such a decision may properly be made as part of the care of the living patient, in his best interests; and, on this basis, the treatment will be lawful.[168]

17.92 And this is so whether the management regime is justified under the essentially moral doctrine of double effect or under the legal principle of necessity. However, since the judgment in *Bland*, the House of Lords has pronounced on intention in the case of *R v Woolin*,[169] in which a consequence was said to be intentional if the actor was 'virtually certain' that it would occur. In the Court of Appeal decision in *Re A (children) (conjoined twins: surgical separation)*,[170] Ward LJ said that it could be difficult to reconcile the doctrine of double effect with *Woolin* but, nonetheless, he could 'readily see' how the doctrine would work in cases where pain-killers are administered to deal with acute pain.

THE 'DO NOT RESUSCITATE' ORDER

17.93 There can be no doubt that it is often undesirable, effectively, to prolong the process of dying[171]—the problem, however, is to establish an acceptable general policy in an area that is so susceptible to subjective judgments. In a very influential document on the subject, the British Medical Association and the Royal College of Nursing have issued a set of guidelines which they stressed can only be viewed as a framework on which

---

164 H Palmer 'Dr Adams' Trial for Murder' [1957] Crim LR 365.
165 'On Dying and Dying Well—Legal Aspects' (1977) 70 Proc Roy Soc Med 73.
166 G Williams *Textbook of Criminal Law* (2nd edn, 1983), p 416.
167 (1992) 12 BMLR 38.
168 [1993] 1 All ER 821 at 868, (1993) 12 BMLR 64 at 114.
169 [1999] 1 AC 82, [1998] 4 All ER 103.
170 [2001] Fam 147, [2000] 4 All ER 961.
171 For a classic example, see the papers associated with R F Weir 'Betty's Case: An Introduction' (1989) 17 Law Med Hlth Care 211. For an American review assessing the moral grounds for providing or withholding treatment, see M Hilberman, J Kutner, D Parsons and D J Murphy 'Marginally Effective Medical Care: Ethical Analysis of Issues in Cardiopulmonary Resuscitation (CPR)' (1997) 23 J Med Ethics 361.

policy can be based.[172] In essence, the guidelines emphasise that an informed, non-coerced, advance directive must be respected and that, in the absence of such information, the presumption should be in favour of attempting resuscitation. An advance decision that cardiopulmonary resuscitation (CPR) will not be attempted (providing a 'do not resuscitate (DNR) order')[173] can only be made in the light of the likely outcome, the patient's ascertainable wishes and his or her human rights; adequate communication in respect of a decision is all important, but information should not be forced on patients who are unwilling to receive it. The key question is whether CPR will provide any benefit to the patient but the wishes of one who wants to be resuscitated irrespective of the prognosis should be respected.[174] The views of the relatives of incompetent adults must be taken into account but it should be made clear that their role is not to take decisions on behalf of the patient.[175] The guidelines recommend recourse to the courts if there is disagreement in respect of the management of a child. It is appropriate to consider making a DNR order when attempted CPR will almost certainly not restart the patient's heart, when there is no benefit in so doing or when the expected benefits are outweighed by the burdens. Decisions must always be made on an individual basis—blanket policies are regarded as being unethical and probably unlawful under the Human Rights Act 1998. The guidelines also stress the importance of adequate documentation of the decisions and of how they were reached.[176]

17.94   Well meaning though such guidelines may be, it is clear that they conceal a hornet's nest of moral dilemmas. Exclusion from resuscitation in British hospitals is said to be more likely in patients with a current diagnosis of malignancy, dementia or pneumonia or with a past or present history of stroke.[177] But at what stage of the disease is the patient with cancer to be regarded as not to be salvaged? How are we to assess what is the patient's idea of an acceptable quality of life? To what extent is dementia a contraindication imposed for the benefit of the carers?[178] Perhaps most importantly—who is to make the decisions and how deeply involved should the patient be in the process? Despite the Council's and the GMC's guidance that the patient's consent is highly desirable, one would have thought that obtaining such consent would raise

---

[172] Resuscitation Council (UK) *Decisions Relating to Cardiopulmonary Resuscitation—A Joint Statement from the BMA, Resuscitation Council and RCN* (2002): www.bma.org.uk/ap.nsf/Content/cardioresus/$file/cardio.pdf.

[173] A 'do not *attempt* resuscitation (DNAR) order' would be more logical but DNR is part of popular usage.

[174] Subject to the proviso that the doctor cannot be required to provide treatment against his clinical judgment: *Re J (a minor) (medical treatment)* [1993] Fam 15.

[175] The 'proxy' terms of the Adults with Incapacity (Scotland) Act 2000 and the Mental Capacity Act 2005 must be honoured.

[176] The latest advice from the GMC is to be found in *Withholding and Withdrawing Life-prolonging Treatments: Good Practice in Decision-making* (2002), paras 84–94. The GMC positively recommends the Resuscitation Council's guidelines at para 26.

[177] R M Keating 'Exclusion from Resuscitation' (1989) 82 J Roy Soc Med 402.

[178] See *Re D (medical treatment)* (1998) 41 BMLR 81, [1998] 2 FCR 178, in which treatment was lawfully suspended in a man whose long-standing mental disability made it impossible for him to commit himself to co-operate in his haemodialysis.

intractable practical difficulties. Surprisingly, however, it is said that the majority of patients actually welcome appropriate consultation.[179]

17.95   Finally, we might revert to the question of age. There is little doubt that DNR orders are issued more often and more freely in older patients; irrespective of the diagnosis and prognosis—DNR orders were written in five major American medical centres for 22 per cent of patients under 54 years old, rising to 56 per cent for those aged more than 85.[180] In our opinion, it is particularly important to ensure that junior doctors in the prime of life are trained to understand the needs of the elderly disabled. The somewhat chilling observation of Rhoads, albeit from across the Atlantic and made some time ago, bears preservation: 'How large a factor is age in deciding to relax therapeutic efforts seems to depend somewhat on the age of the physicians making the decisions'.[181]

17.96   Cases involving DNR orders come to the attention of the courts only rarely. An exception lies in the significant case of *Re R*,[182] which concerned a 23-year-old man who could not sit up, chew food or communicate in any formal way. He was probably blind and deaf and other physiological disabilities indicated that his condition was appalling. Nevertheless, he could not be regarded as being in the permanent vegetative state. A DNR order in the event of cardiac arrest was signed by the consultant psychiatrist and agreed by the patient's mother. However, a member of the staff at the day centre at which he was treated arranged for an application for judicial review of the order. The health authority then sought a declaration that it would be lawful to withhold life-sustaining treatment—which included resuscitation and ventilation, nutrition and hydration by artificial means and the administration of antibiotics— and to treat the patient so that he suffered minimum distress until his death. The application was later amended so as to exclude withholding of nutrition and hydration —and, in fact, it was proposed to perform a non-consensual gastrostomy.

17.97   At the hearing, all the medical witnesses expressed the view that cardiopulmonary resuscitation (CPR) would not be appropriate in R's case, this being largely on the grounds that it was unlikely to be successful. Withholding antibiotics was, however, considered as a separate issue and was recommended subject to the approval of the patient's general practitioner and to the consent of one or both parents—and this distinction was recognised by the court in its determination.

17.98   In granting the declaration as sought, the President, Sir Stephen Brown, repeated that there was no question of the court being asked to approve a course aimed at terminating life or accelerating death. In tying *Re R* to *Re J*,[183] however, the President

---

[179] M E Hill, G MacQuillan, M Forsyth and D A Heath 'Cardiopulmonary Resuscitation: Who Makes the Decision?' (1994) 308 BMJ 1677.

[180] R B Hakim, J M Teno, F E Harrell et al 'Factors Associated with Do-Not-Resuscitate Orders: Patients' Preferences, Prognoses, and Physicians' Judgments' (1996) 125 Ann Int Med 284.

[181] J E Rhoads 'The Right to Die and the Chance to Live' (1980) 6 J Med Ethics 53. A brief but informative review of patient and physician attitudes is to be found in R Morgan, D King, C Prajapati and J Rowe 'Views of Elderly Patients and their Relatives on Cardiopulmonary Resuscitation' (1994) 308 BMJ 1677.

[182] *Re R (adult: medical treatment)* (1996) 31 BMLR 127, [1996] 2 FLR 99.

[183] *Re J (a minor) (wardship: medical treatment)* [1991] Fam 33, (1990) 6 BMLR 25.

clearly admitted a 'quality of life' standard for decisions involving adults—approving Taylor LJ in *Re J*:

[T]he correct approach is for the court to judge the quality of life [the patient] would have to endure if given the treatment and decide whether in all the circumstances such a life would be so afflicted as to be intolerable . . .[184]

17.99   Approved management regimes thus seem to be following the course we antici-pated in chapter 16. The case also strongly indicates that non-treatment decisions in the case of the incapacitated should normally be taken by health professionals in concert with people close to the patient; it is only in the event of serious challenge to the clinical opinion that court intervention will be required. At the same time, *Re R* raises, once again, the question as to whether feeding and hydration are to be seen as different in quality from other medical treatments.[185] Our own tentative view is that any apparent divergence from the House of Lords decision in *Bland* derives from the rather specialised wording of the application in *Re R* and has no significant general application.

THE INCURABLE PATIENT

17.100   The relative simplicity of the euthanasia debate has, thus far, depended upon the use of the adjective 'terminal', which defines a patient status which can only deteriorate—and, as we have already noted, attempts to legalise euthanasia in the English-speaking world have never extended beyond the concept of the management of the dying patient. The problems for the doctor, and for the ethicist, become more complex when discussion is extended to the incurably ill whose condition may certainly get worse but which is also likely to remain static, often for long times. Many variations on such a state can be envisaged and different therapeutic solutions adduced. There are, how-ever, two overriding considerations likely to influence one's thinking—first, whether the patient is sentient or non-sentient and, secondly, whether or not the distinction between incurable illness and death depends upon the use of artificial means.

THE INCAPACITATED PATIENT

17.101   Thus, at one extreme, we have the fully conscious, incapacitated patient able to breathe naturally, as exemplified by the paraplegic or tetraplegic whose condition results from an accident or localised brain-stem haemorrhage. The clinical and moral solutions here are based on the same principles as relate to the terminally ill but conscious patient—any differences are those of emphasis. Once again, we are at the grey interface of passive euthanasia, assisted suicide and refusal of treatment and, as a

---

[184] (1990) 6 BMLR 25 at 42.   [185] For the BMA's position, see para 16.120 above.

result, major weight must be given to patient autonomy. Much of the discussion in this area has been approached from the theoretical angle and concentrates on the right to die.[186] By contrast, most of those who have been involved in the hands-on care of disabled persons have been impressed by their tenacity to life and their ability to adapt.[187] This was demonstrated vividly in an old, but emotionally influential, study of tetraplegia—a condition which must be as near to wholly intolerable as can be imagined; 18 out of 21 sufferers said that they wished to be resuscitated in the event of their degenerating into coma.[188]

17.102   Subject to the consent of a sentient patient, both the double effect doctrine and the productive/non-productive treatment test are available in the management of those who are incapacitated; their rationale needs to be just that much more firmly based than is so in the case of the terminally ill.

THE CONSCIOUS PATIENT MAINTAINED ARTIFICIALLY

17.103   The medico-legal response to a positive request for the doctor to disconnect the mentally competent patient from the mechanical respirator on which he or she depends has already been discussed in some detail. The international case law indicating that not to do so would constitute non-consensual treatment and, as a result, battery is now overwhelming—but the underlying implications of compliance are disturbing. It is almost trite to say that the ethical difficulties concerning the removal of mechanical respiratory support from those who can no longer benefit originate from the *provision* of that support—the primary decision is more important than those which follow as a consequence of that action.[189] But the doctor presented with an accident or an acute neurological emergency has virtually no choice of initiative action. He is dealing with a conscious but suddenly paralysed patient and he must provide support because he cannot know whether an individual patient is going to respond either physically or emotionally to heroic treatment—and, if the doctor does not know, the patient cannot give or withhold his informed consent to setting the therapeutic train in motion. Can the doctor, then, accede to a later request to remove support?

17.104   It has been suggested that switching off a mechanical support is an omission and is, therefore, both morally and legally acceptable. This is, in our opinion, untenable in practical terms. It would be an omission not to switch *on* the emergency supply in the event of a central power failure; that is easily distinguished from a deliberate, premeditated decision to remove the power—one has to *act* to turn off the television and the

---

[186] M Ford 'The Personhood Paradox and the Right to Die' (2005) 13 Med L Rev 80.

[187] The contrary impression given by the litigation involving Ms B and Mrs Pretty may well be due to the media exposure given to 'high profile' cases.

[188] B P Gardner et al 'Ventilation or Dignified Death for Patients with High Tetraplegia' (1985) 291 BMJ 1620. See also M Siegler and A J Weisbard 'Against the Emerging Stream' (1985) 145 Arch Int Med 129 which remains an instructive read.

[189] I M Kennedy 'Switching Off Life Support Machines: The Legal Implications' [1977] Crim LR 443.

same will apply to the respirator.[190] Kennedy[191] has pointed out that a well-wisher disconnecting a conscious patient from his respirator would be guilty of homicide or perhaps of abetting suicide—and, in the United States, Mr Linares was, at least, brought before a grand jury.[192] The difference adduced by Lord Goff in *Bland*[193] was that, whereas the doctor was allowing the patient to die from his pre-existing condition, the interloper was actively intervening to stop the doctor from prolonging the patient's life. *Bland*, in fact, very nearly solves the problem—albeit indirectly. Thus, if, as was decided, the withdrawal of nasogastric feeding is an omission, it is but a short step to conclude that withdrawal of respiratory support is, likewise, an omission—and Lord Browne-Wilkinson, for one, was happy to see them as similar. The analogy admittedly involves some elasticity of conscience. So, while Lord Browne-Wilkinson further concluded that a nasogastric tube did nothing, of itself, to sustain life and that its removal could not be said to cause death, it is difficult to say the same of the ventilator of which the air-bag is an integral part. The main practical difference between the two must lie in the immediacy and the certainty of death when the respirator is turned off; the care team is, effectively, being asked to suffocate their patient.[194]

17.105   The modern doctor's dilemma was vividly exposed in the English case of *Ms B v an NHS Hospital Trust*[195] which we have discussed in some detail above. The clinicians in charge of Ms B may have been badly advised but, whether or not they misinterpreted their legal position, they clearly thought that medical options other than death of their patient were available. The frank admission by the responsible doctors that they could not bring themselves to take the step of withdrawing ventilation from a viable patient is a striking and significant aspect of the case. In the event, another hospital was found that was willing to do so—and the use of the phrase 'to do so' surely pulls the carpet from under those who would identify 'switching off' as an omission. The doctors' evidence, set out in some detail in the judgment, serves as a reminder of the difficulties which medical staff may experience if they are expected to act contrary to their impulses to preserve life rather than to extinguish it.[196]

THE UNCONSCIOUS PATIENT AND THE PATIENT IN INTENSIVE CARE

17.106   The management of the unconscious, breathing patient has been fully discussed in chapter 16. There remain for consideration those comatose patients who are unable to sustain their cardiorespiratory functions without the aid of mechanical ventilation.

---

[190] For an authoritative alternative view see Williams para n 166 above, p 282.

[191] [1977] Crim LR 443.   [192] Lantos et al, n 16 above.

[193] [1993] 1 All ER 821 at 867–868, (1992) 12 BMLR 64 at 113–114.

[194] It is very difficult to avoid the corollary—that Bland's carers were being asked to starve him to death.

[195] Para 17.48 above.

[196] The medical correspondent of *The Times* (T Stuttaford, 23 March 2002, p 5) indicated that 'Standard medical teaching remains that we should never willingly and deliberately shorten life'. Since removal from ventilation is clearly done deliberately and, equally clearly, shortens life, the determining issue is simply one of willingness—or, put another way, of autonomy.

17.107   The vast majority, perhaps all, of living patients with severe brain damage must be offered such care when they present at hospital. Recourse is automatic for the purposes of facilitating diagnosis and assessment; there is, then, no legal or ethical objection to regarding the ventilator as merely a part of the diagnostic machinery nor to dispensing with it once a diagnosis of irretrievable functional brain loss has been made. But a decision to treat, which, in this case, is within the doctor's clinical choice, is a different matter carrying with it the inescapable consequence that, at some time and for some reason, the treatment must be withdrawn. The critical point for applying the productive/non-productive ethical test is, as we have already indicated, at the beginning. With one exception, any later decisions are based on clinical or technical considerations alone.

17.108   This exceptional ethical decision relates to the allocation of scarce resources which include machines, beds, doctors and nursing staff, together with the necessary technical back-up. It may be necessary for a resource-based value judgment to be made at some point. Making a choice between patients may be among the doctor's most agonising moments and the weight to be given to economic and policy considerations can only be judged by the individual physician or surgeon on such factors as are outlined in chapter 11. There are now sufficient obiter statements from a variety of English cases to allow one to say with confidence that the courts will be sympathetic to resource-based management arguments. We do, however, suggest that this relates only to a competition for an *available* facility. There is nothing to support the suggestion that it would be acceptable to *remove* a patient from essential intensive care for no reason other than that a medically more rewarding case required the bed.[197]

17.109   Resources aside, the removal of a patient from intensive care depends, primarily, on a simple alternative—either he is dead or he is not dead. It can be taken that the whole brain is dead once the criteria for brain stem death have been met and we have the authority of the Conference of the Royal Medical Colleges and their Faculties[198] that the individual is dead when the whole brain is dead. In such circumstances, continued treatment is no more than treatment of a corpse—far from being unethical to withhold support, it would be positively immoral to continue other than to serve the purpose of beating heart organ donation or, conceivably, of post-mortem parturition (for which, see para 13.24). Withdrawal of treatment would also be legally indicated.[199]

17.110   However, it may still be proper to discontinue artificial ventilation even if death is not diagnosed. The closely allied considerations of productive/non-productive treatment and of 'death with dignity', untrammelled by tubes and wires, may be regarded by some as being related to the moral sphere and by others as being clinical in nature. Even so, the purely clinical consideration—that the treatment is doing, and will do, no

---

[197] See Balcombe LJ in *Re J (a minor) (wardship: medical treatment)* [1993] Fam 15 at 30, (1992) 9 BMLR 10 at 20, discussed previously at para 16.81 above.

[198] 'Diagnosis of Death' [1979] 1 BMJ 332. Legislation to this effect is generalised in the English-speaking world.

[199] *Re A* [1992] 3 Med LR 303.

good—will justify removal of support. One of two things may then happen—the patient will either continue to breathe of his own accord or he will die. In the former case, the patient has reverted to a state of irreversible coma, the management of which has already been discussed. No moral or legal problem arises in the latter situation; the outcome will have resulted from a clinical decision taken in good faith and after due deliberation based on a productive/non-productive treatment test. As we have already discussed, consent of the next of kin would be desirable but not essential to the question of lawfulness, absent a proxy decision-maker.

ARTIFICIAL NUTRITION AND HYDRATION: FEEDING AS A PART OF TREATMENT

17.111   We have already referred to feeding as a part of treatment in relation to *Bland* in chapter 16. The definition of artificial feeding—or more properly Artificial Nutrition and Hydration (ANH)—was not, however, addressed in either *Bland* or *Re R (adult: medical treatment)*[200]—or in any of the other relevant British cases.[201] As Strong[202] pointed out many years ago, when we speak of providing nourishment, we are referring to a continuum which runs from natural breast feeding through feeding by mouth to seriously invasive procedures which may even entail surgical operation. Once discomfort and danger are introduced, so too is balancing the advantages and disadvantages—or, in practice, applying a productive/non-productive treatment test.[203] The fundamental question is, therefore, at what *stage* does the act of feeding become medical treatment?

17.112   Increasing invasiveness carries increasing risk—it, therefore, seems logical to classify anything which involves invasion as medical treatment. At the other end of the scale, it is difficult to conceive of purely natural feeding as treatment and, so far as we are aware, no court in either the Commonwealth or America has ever suggested that normal feeding could properly be withheld on clinical grounds from someone able to accept it. None the less, even this distinction is over-simplistic. At one extreme, spoon feeding of a reluctant ament can be regarded as invasive and, accordingly, as medical treatment; at the other, the instillation of fluid through a tube can be seen as simple care involving no risk—but it can be done only as a *result* of invasion. The difficulties

---

[200] [1996] 2 FLR 99, (1996) 7 Med L Rev 401.

[201] The Supreme Court of Victoria held in *Gardner; re BWV* [2003] VSC 173 that artificial nutrition and hydration by means of a percutaneous endoscopic gastrostomy (PEG) was a 'medical procedure' because it depends on 'protocols, skills and care which draw from, and depend upon, medical knowledge'; the practice itself, then, was deemed 'medical treatment' for the purposes of the Medical Treatment Act 1988 (see para 17.77 above).

[202] C Strong 'Can Fluids and Electrolytes be "Extraordinary Treatment"?' (1981) 7 J Med Ethics 83.

[203] K C Micetich et al 'Are Intravenous Fluids Morally Required for a Dying Patient?' (1983) 143 Arch Int Med 975. The complication rate of intravenous hyperalimentation may approach 50%.

are exemplified in the drafting of the Victorian legislation which includes 'the reasonable provision of food and water' under the heading of palliative treatment—and, therefore, outwith the statutory control of the patient[204]—and, then, fails to define 'reasonable provision'. An all-embracing definitional solution seems impossible. We can only look to a minimum standard and suggest that any form of feeding which requires some *medical* training and expertise can be considered medical treatment and, accordingly, may properly be subject to selective provision. The insertion of a nasogastric tube involves a surprising degree of skill and, on this basis, nasogastric feeding would qualify as medical treatment; thus, the decision in *Bland* is, to us, unexceptional. By contrast, the provision of food and water by normal means—that is, by mouth and dependent on the patient's swallowing reflexes—is a matter of skilled nursing care. It may also be seen as the quintessential example of kindness and humanity.[205]

17.113   The first instance case of *R (on the application of Burke) v General Medical Council*[206] has added a latest twist to the tale of ANH. Here the issue was, in essence, the opposite to our present discussion—the patient did *not* want to die and did *not* want his ANH removed when he eventually succumbed to the incapacitating brain condition that would leave him unable to communicate for himself. The court held that he had this right, largely on the basis of his human rights to respect for dignity and private life, but also, apparently, on the nature of ANH as fundamental and basic care. We suspect that, by the time *Burke* has run its course, it will add little to the existing jurisprudence. Effectively, one can answer the yes or no question of whether ANH is or is not medical treatment either way with equal moral support. The current climate is such, however, that we doubt if anyone would seek to *deny* ANH to anyone who wanted it. *Burke*, in our view was appealed primarily to establish how far, if at all, that principle can be extended to more sophisticated medical expertise.

CRIMINAL LIABILITY FOR WITHHOLDING TREATMENT

17.114   The historic case of *Quinlan*[207] settled the problem of criminal liability for withdrawal of ventilation in the United States and there have been many later confirmations of this.[208] The position in the United Kingdom was resolved, first through the Scottish case of *Finlayson*[209] and, later, in the English case of *Malcherek*,[210] both of which have been discussed in relation to causation in chapter 13. Although *Finlayson* was not

---

[204] Medical Treatment Act 1988 (Vict), s 3.

[205] *Airedale NHS Trust v Bland* [1993] 1 All ER 821 at 856, (1992) 12 BMLR 64 at 101, per Hoffmann LJ.

[206] N 148 above.   [207] *Re Quinlan* 355 A 2d 664 (NJ, 1976).

[208] E.g. *Re Bertha Colyer* 660 P 2d 738 (Wash, 1983); *Re Nancy Ellen Jobes* 529 A 2d 434 (NJ, 1987); *Barber v Superior Court* 147 Cal App 3d 1006 (1983).

[209] *Finlayson v HM Advocate* 1978 SLT (Notes) 60.

[210] *R v Malcherek* [1981] 2 All ER 422, [1981] 1 WLR 690, CA (*R v Steel* being heard simultaneously on appeal).

cited in *Malcherek*, the two decisions have remarkable similarities in that, in excluding criminality, the judges, first, relied on the concept of good medical practice and, second, declined to define death in both cases. This latter omission might, at first glance, be interpreted as vacillation on the part of the law; in fact, it reinforces the former principle in leaving the clinical decision firmly in the hands of the clinician.[211]

17.115   There is no reason to suppose that these decisions would not be applied in the civil courts and it would now be necessary to prove negligence—with all that entails— before a doctor could be considered culpable of a ventilator death; that is, of course, in the absence of conduct meeting the requirements for criminal negligence (for which see chapter 9). There are no United Kingdom authorities but a similar policy line has been adopted in the United States.[212] We doubt very much if the passing of the Human Rights Act 1998 has affected this view. Since death is an evitability, there can be no right to life per se—the 'right' lies in not having one's life taken away in 'super-*Wednesbury*'[213] terms of reasonableness which will be satisfied by 'good medical practice'.[214]

TERMINAL SEDATION

17.116   The relatively recent concept of terminal sedation lies dormant beneath virtually all the management scenarios we have discussed thus far in this chapter. We have left it until last for this reason but the fact that we have allocated a separate section for the topic should not be interpreted as giving it a special significance—however else it is regarded, it is certainly seen as a last resort option for the management of intractable pain.[215]

17.117   The concept is unusual and is defined by Williams as: 'the administration of a sedating drug for the purpose of relieving suffering by diminishing consciousness at the end of life' which is a reasonably innocuous goal. McStay, however, speaks of the 'induction of an unconscious state' and adds 'which is frequently accompanied by the withdrawal of any life-sustaining intervention, such as hydration and nutrition'—and this, in our view implies a far less easily acceptable motivation and is one, moreover,

---

[211] Some concern was shown in Scotland when the Solicitor General stated that the prosecuting authorities were not in a position to give an assurance that withdrawing life support would not lead to prosecution: G Duncan 'Doctors Warned about Decision to Withdraw Life Support' *The Scotsman*, 1 April 1993, p 3. We believe, however, that this was no more than a reminder as to procedure, not as to principle.

[212] E.g. *Lovato v District Court* 601 P 2d 1072 (Colo, 1979).

[213] *R v Ministry of Defence, ex p Smith* [1996] QB 517, [1996] 1 All ER 257.

[214] For a human rights discussion see *Burke*, n 148 above.

[215] For an excellent review, see G Williams 'The Principle of Double Effect and Terminal Sedation' (2001) 9 Med L Rev 41. The American scene is described by R McStay 'Terminal Sedation: Palliative Care for Intractable Pain, post *Glucksberg* and *Quill*' (2003) 29 Amer J Law Med 45 which draws heavily on T Quill et al 'Palliative Options of Last Resort' (1997) 278 J Amer Med Ass 2099.

that is admitted by Williams. Confusion is compounded when the potential uses of terminal sedation are considered. These include:

(a) to produce unconsciousness before the removal of artificial life support;

(b) to relieve physical pain where other options have failed; and

(c) to relieve non-physical suffering.

17.118 Thus, it seems that, while terminal sedation could be used in the normal process of good medical practice, it is far more likely to represent a part of active euthanasia or physician-accomplished suicide hiding under emollient terminology.[216]

17.119 Clearly, then, the subject is open to extensive argument and diversity of opinion, these being both on medical grounds—is, for example, the use of barbiturates in terminal sedation distinguishable from their use in deliberate active euthanasia?—and on the legal significance of intention—i.e. is the intention to sedate or to kill? We feel that problems of space prevent a deeper analysis at this point—but would still record out distrust of anything that appears to be a semantic smoke-screen.[217]

A NEED FOR LEGISLATION?

17.120 It will be appreciated that, throughout this discussion, we have tended to the view that there is little need for legislation in respect of the incurably or terminally ill adult patient; the great majority of life or death decisions can be based on good medical practice which is contained by relatively clear legal and moral guidelines—when put to the test, the euthanasia calculus needs to be enlisted only in the cases of 'mercy killing' and physician assisted or physician accomplished suicide. The movement in favour of formally legalising voluntary euthanasia and PAS is, however, maintaining its momentum, and the autonomy-based arguments advanced by its supporters merit a response. As will be apparent from our discussion above, we believe that there are persuasive reasons for rejecting the legalisation of voluntary euthanasia, not the least of these being the extent to which the policy of euthanasia in the Netherlands has been inadequately policed and progressively more widely interpreted. The uncertainty of the common law has been used in the past as a justification for change in the law, but the law is now much clearer in the light of recent decisions. The rulings in *Pretty*

---

[216] Nevertheless, the US Supreme Court has been interpreted as approving the practice in *Washington v Glucksberg* 521 US 702 (1997), *Vacco v Quill* 521 US 793 (1997).

[217] Almost inevitably, terminal sedation and the withdrawal of artificial nutrition and hydration are distinguished from euthanasia in the Netherlands on the grounds that the former are normal medical treatment: T Sheldon ' "Terminal Sedation" different from Euthanasia, Dutch Ministers Agree' (2003) 327 BMJ 465.

and in *Ms B*,[218] and more recently *A Local Authority v Z*,[219] clarify the boundaries of intervention in the case of a competent adult patient, and the legality and persuasiveness of advance declarations are, also, now well established. These decisions, together with the body of cases concerning treatment decisions in the case of children and adults without capacity, create a medico-legal landscape which is much more certain today than it was a decade ago. The law on euthanasia is now very clear: acts committed with the principal intention of bringing an end to life are legally impermissible, except where the patient himself or herself performs them. Treatment must be withdrawn after a request from a competent adult and this will not amount to homicide if death results. Equally, treatment can be legitimately withdrawn if it can be shown to be medically futile. The legal prohibition of assisted suicide remains in place. All of this involves a restriction on the autonomy of the individual and, for some, that will be unacceptable. The restrictions are not, however, arbitrary—as the Canadian Supreme Court made clear in *Rodriguez*[220] and the House of Lords, and the European Court of Human Rights, reiterated in *Pretty*.

17.121   Notwithstanding this, legislative moves have been afoot in the UK since the last edition of this book. Lord Joffe introduced two Bills to the House of Lords in 2003 and 2004 respectively, the second of which—the Assisted Dying for the Terminally Ill Bill—became the subject of a House of Lords Select Committee report. In essence, the Bill was designed to provide legal authority for a terminally ill and mentally competent adult to request either PAS or active euthanasia. The qualifying criteria included the need for there to be 'unbearable suffering' (defined as 'suffering whether by reason of pain or otherwise which the patient finds so severe as to be unacceptable and results from the patient's terminal illness'); the provision of adequate information and counselling (including the offer of palliative care, where appropriate); repeated informed requests to die from the patient; a written declaration to this effect from the patient in front of two witnesses; a 14-day waiting period, and a final verification of consent. A conscience clause for professional staff was also included with an attendant obligation to refer the patient to another colleague in the event of its being invoked. While the primary aim of the Bill was to legalise PAS, it also sought to provide for active euthanasia in cases where someone—such as an individual in the circumstances of Dianne Pretty—is not physically able to take their own life.

17.122   The Bill fell with the dissolution of Parliament for the May 2005 elections, and this fact was given due consideration by the Select Committee in its report.[221] Thus, among its recommendations was the suggestion that an early opportunity should be taken to debate the report in the House of Lords in the new parliamentary session.

---

[218] *R (on the application of Pretty) v DPP* [2001] UKHL 61, [2002] 1 All ER 1, (2002) 63 BMLR 1; *Re B (adult: refusal of medical treatment)* sub nom *Ms v An NHS Hospital Trust* [2002] EWHC 429 (Fam), [2002] 2 All ER 449, (2002) 65 BMLR 149.

[219] [2005] 1 FLR 740.

[220] *Rodriguez v A–G of British Columbia* (1993) 107 DLR (4th) 342, (1993) 50 BMLR 1.

[221] Select Committee on the Assisted Dying for the Terminally Ill Bill, *Assisted Dying for the Terminally Ill Bill—First Report* (2005).

Beyond this, the Committee recommended that any future bill should consider a number of matters, including: (a) a clear distinction between assisted suicide and active euthanasia, (b) a better articulation of a doctor's powers and responsibility under the legislation, (c) the need for concepts such as 'terminal illness' and 'competence' to reflect current clinical practice, (d) consideration of replacement of the criterion of 'unbearable suffering' with notions of 'unrelievable' or 'intractable' suffering, and (e) the abandonment of an obligation on the conscientious objector to refer a patient to a willing colleague. Evidence of public views on euthanasia were largely dismissed as inconclusive and unrepresentative, but the important point to note is the discernible, albeit subtle, shift in attitude of the House—being more open to the arguments—since the last time it considered such issues.[222]

17.123   We have long supported a more straightforward approach. The opportunity exists in England to insert a subsection in the Suicide Act 1961 amending s 2(1)—which criminalises aiding or abetting suicide. Suitable wording might be:

The provisions of s 2(1) shall not apply to a registered medical practitioner who, given the existence of a competent directive, is providing assistance to a patient who is suffering from a progressive and irremediable condition and who is prevented, or will be prevented, by physical disability from ending his or her own life without assistance.[223]

17.124   Having said which, we concede that many would regard this as allowing too much discretion to the medical profession and that they would prefer a positive, and possibly restrictive, approach.[224] Either route would achieve the desired result of legislating for a specific, relatively uncontroversial aspect of assistance in dying and, for our part, we would go no further.

---

[222]   House of Lords Report of the Select Committee on Medical Ethics HL Paper 21–1 (1994).

[223]   See J K Mason and D Mulligan 'Euthanasia by Stages' (1996) 347 Lancet 810.

[224]   For an example, see Professor McLean's draft Bill, n 74 above. Positive legislation would certainly be needed in the United States and, with this in mind, we have produced our own suggested Bill: see Meyers and Mason, n 52 above.

18

BIOMEDICAL HUMAN RESEARCH AND EXPERIMENTATION

18.1   At one time, biomedical research using human subjects proceeded almost as a routine. The researchers justified their activities as benefiting mankind; the subjects were generally happy to 'oblige' or to be reasonably recompensed; and research was of manageable quantity. Attitudes and conditions have, however, changed. The reaction against paternalistic medicine has gained momentum pari passu with an increasing concern for the rights of the individual; the potential investigations and the instrumental and other means for conducting them have greatly increased; and there has been something of an explosion not only in the production of new therapeutic agents but also in control of their distribution. But the greatest single impulse to regulate experiments on human beings sprang from a realisation of the appalling depths which were plumbed in the genocidal era of the Second World War when, undoubtedly, much valuable information was gathered but only at the cost of immense suffering. The awareness of what had happened in the medical laboratories of Nazi Germany and Japan led to a determination that medical research should never again be tainted by such callous disregard for the rights of the individual and it is this determination which led to the promulgation of international codes on the ethics of research. Such endeavours were not supported everywhere, however, and the end of the Soviet era in Eastern Europe resulted in a frank acknowledgment in a number of countries that medical science in the Soviet Union and its satellite countries had been far from meeting the ethical standards expected it the West.[1] This was translated into action in Poland, for example, by the introduction of a code of medical ethics which, in a remarkable judgment of the Polish Constitutional Court in 1992, was held to outrank contradictory provisions of the law.[2] Many of the former Soviet Union eastern European countries joined the European Union in May 2004 obliging them to

---

[1] Z Szawarski 'Research Ethics in Eastern Europe' (1992) 82 Bull Med Ethics 13.
[2] The English text of this code was published in (1992) 82 Bull Med Ethics 13; the decision of the Constitutional Court is discussed by E Zielinska at p 25 of the same issue.

meet the legal and ethical standards prevailing, or yet to be adopted, with the Union. This remains a big challenge for many.[3]

ETHICAL CODES AND LEGAL INSTRUMENTS IN HUMAN BIOMEDICAL RESEARCH

18.2 The first internationally accepted set of ethical guidelines in this context was known as the Nuremberg Code and was a direct consequence of the war-crimes trials.[4] It was, however, apparent that the medical profession itself should publicly endorse the principles expressed in the ten clauses of the Nuremberg Code; this movement culminated in the Declaration of Helsinki—drawn up by the World Medical Association in 1964 and revised several times between 1975 and 2000[5]—which is reproduced as Appendix D.[6] Many national authorities have attempted to explain or expand upon the basic principles established at Nuremberg and, for the British reader, important examples include the comprehensive set of guidelines issued by the Medical Research Council[7] and the Wellcome Trust.[8] In the European context, an Additional Protocol to the Council of Europe's Convention on Human Rights and Biomedicine (1997)[9] specifically relating to biomedical research was opened for signature in January 2005.[10] This sets out the broad principles which govern research on human subjects—under which such research is justified only if there is no comparable effectiveness (Article 5). Of greater immediate importance—at least in terms of domestic UK law—is the fact that

---

[3] See, generally, the European Union's *Science and Society in Europe* website: http://europa.eu.int/comm/research/science-society/index_en.html.

[4] There is a wide discussion of the problem of the significance of Nuremberg in G J Annas and M A Grodin (eds) *The Nazi Doctors and the Nuremberg Code: Human Rights in Human Experimentation* (1992).

[5] Notes of clarification were added in 2002 and 2004 relating respectively to paragraphs 29 (circumstances in which a placebo-controlled trial is ethically acceptable) and 30 (design of research protocols to include access provisions for participants regarding best treatment methods identified by trial).

[6] Other international codes include the International Ethical Guidelines for Biomedical Research involving Human Subjects published in Z Bankowski and R J Levine *Ethics and Research on Human Subjects: International Guidelines* (1992). For discussion of the various guidelines, see K M King 'A Proposal for the Effective International Regulation of Biomedical Research Involving Human Subjects' (1998) 34 Stanford J Int Law 163.

[7] The Medical Research Council (MRC) actually produced guidelines before the Helsinki Declaration: Annual Report of the MRC *Responsibility in Investigations on Human Subjects* (1962–63) Cmnd 2382. Since then, a stream of guidance has flowed from the Council, including most importantly, *Good Research Practice* (2000), *Human Tissue and Biological Samples for Use in Research—Operational and Ethical Guidelines* (2001/2005) and *Position Statement on Research Regulation and Ethics* (2005). All can be found at: www.mrc.ac.uk.

[8] See, *Guidelines on Good Research Practice* (2002) and *Statement on the Handling of Allegations of Research Misconduct* (2002). Both available at: www.wellcome.ac.uk.

[9] Council of Europe Convention for the Protection of Human Rights and Dignity of the Human Being with Regard to the Application of Biology and Medicine (1997). This has not been ratified by the United Kingdom.

[10] Additional Protocol to the Convention on Human Rights and Biomedicine Concerning Biomedical Research (2005), available at: http://conventions.coe.int/.

the deadline has now passed for implementing the European Union Directive on the conditions under which research in the development of medicinal products is to be conducted.[11] The emphasis here is on good clinical practice which is defined in Article 1(2) as:

[A] set of internationally recognised ethical and scientific quality requirements which must be observed for designing, conducting, recording and reporting clinical trials that involve the participation of human subjects. Compliance with this good practice provides assurance that the rights, safety and well-being of trial subjects are protected, and that the results of the clinical trial are credible.

18.3   The Directive does not apply to non-interventional trials which are, essentially, trials in which the recipient of the medicinal product is being treated in the normal way without assignment to treatment by way of an advance protocol. Moreover, it relates only to the conduct of clinical trials; other forms of research are unaffected.[12] Thus, the obligation on member states to change their laws in conformity with the Directive relates only to CTIMPs (Clinical Trials of an Investigational Medicinal Product). That having been said, the Directive's harmonising effect invoking fundamental principles and its requirements for structural and regulatory changes to systems of research governance led the British government to overhaul its system of research regulation in light of its obligation to implement the Directive. It did not take the opportunity, however, to ensure that CTIMPs and other types of research are necessarily subject to the same provisions. We return to the details of the new regimes below.

18.4   All modern ethical codes have it in common that they appreciate the need for human research and, at the same time, accept that this can often only be accomplished at the expense of some of the subjects' rights to self-determination. It is, however, universally accepted that the morality of this sacrifice depends upon the grant of 'informed' consent—which we have discussed in detail in chapter 10. All codes contain specific instructions as to the inclusion of minors and mentally incompetent research subjects. In addition, the doctor's classic ethical position must be flexible. The Hippocratic Oath states: 'I will follow that regimen which . . . I consider for the benefit of my patients and abstain from whatever is deleterious and mischievous'; the absolutist could say that this precludes all experimentation on patients, yet it is clear that progress in medicine depends upon some form of trial in which the trialist him or herself is uncertain of the result—the so-called position of equipoise; in allowing his patients to be involved, the primary clinical carer commits himself to accepting a

---

[11] European Parliament and the Council of Europe Directive 2001/20/EC of 4 April 2001 relating to the implementation of good clinical practice in the conduct of clinical trials on medicinal products for human use. The Directive was implemented in the United Kingdom by the Medicines for Human Use (Clinical Trials) Regulations 2004, SI 2004/1031.

[12] It has been joined most recently by Commission Directive 2005/28/EC of 8 April 2005 laying down principles and detailed guidelines for good clinical practice as regards investigational medicinal products for human use, as well as the requirements for authorisation of the manufacturing or importation of such products.

similar, more dubious, role. The commonest strategy adopted is that of the random-ised control trial which, in turn, provides the paradigm representation of the ethical problems in research. A balance determined by the interests of all the parties involved must be sought if the programme is to be regarded as acceptable.[13]

WHAT IS RESEARCH?

18.5   Research and experimentation are commonly used as interchangeable terms—we, however, believe that there is a distinction to be made. Research implies a predeter-mined protocol with a clearly defined end-point. Experimentation, by contrast, involves a more speculative, ad hoc, approach to an individual subject. The distinction is significant in that an experiment may be modified to take into account the individual's response; a research programme, however, ties the researcher to a particu-lar course of action until such time as its general ineffectiveness is satisfactorily demonstrated.[14] Moreover, while the aim of experimentation is usually linked to the interests of the subject upon whom the experiment is being conducted—for example, the deployment of a last-change experimental technique to improve the patient's diminishing health—the overall objective of research is to acquire generalisable knowledge which, by and large, has nothing directly to do with the health state or interests of the research subjects.[15]

18.6   The Department of Health spent approximately £540m on research in 2002–2003. Research activities can be broadly categorised as *therapeutic* research, which is aimed at improved treatment for the class of patients from which subjects have been drawn, and as *non-therapeutic*—in which the essential object is the furtherance of purely scientific knowledge which may, eventually, have a wider application than patient care.[16] This distinction makes little conceptual difference to the general requirements for ethical research. The mere fact that the research subject, being a patient at the time, may receive benefit does not mean that the programme can be undertaken unregulated by research codes—indeed, the fact that a relatively vulnerable group is

---

[13] For a simplified overview, see S J L Edwards, R J Lilford and J Hewison 'The Ethics of Randomised Control Trials from the Perspectives of Patients, the Public, and Healthcare Professionals' (1998) 317 BMJ 1209.

[14] For an excellent, albeit dated, discussion, see B M Dickens 'What is a Medical Experiment?' (1975) 113 Can Med Assoc J 635.

[15] The latest version of the Department of Health research governance framework defines research as: '. . . the attempt to derive generalisable new knowledge by addressing clearly defined questions with system-atic and rigorous methods', see Department of Health *Research Governance Framework for Health and Social Care* (2005), p 3.

[16] The eminent researcher, Doll, rightly points out that there are other forms of research available that do not involve actual human subjects—e.g. research by questionnaire, study of records etc: R Doll 'Research Will Be Impeded' (2001) 323 BMJ 1421.

involved emphasises the care with which the project should be monitored.[17] Only the degree of risk to be permitted in proportion to the expected outcome is affected by the nature of the research.

18.7   It follows from this classification that research subjects may be of four types: individual patients; a group of patients who are suffering from one particular condition; patients who have no association with the disease or process under review but who are readily available; and, finally, healthy volunteers—a heterogeneous group which is of importance because it may involve other 'captive' populations, including the researchers themselves.

18.8   The logical implication of this division of subjects is that researchers should also be categorised. Thus, the individual patient is under the care of a doctor. Any experimental procedure or treatment is, therefore, performed on a care-associated basis and, while there may be difficulties in a hospital setting where 'care' is very much a team concept, the essential doctor-patient relationship is, and should be, maintained. But it cannot be said with reference to any of the other types of research subject that 'the health of my patient [and the singular noun is to be noted] is my first consideration'; consequently, the researchers should not normally include the patients' physicians. Even so, doctors must be involved whenever human subjects are subject to medical research; the danger of non-medical researchers being, not so much callous, as uncomprehending of their subjects' reactions, is such that a situation excluding doctors would only be acceptable in the event that the researchers were their own experimental subjects.

THE RISKS INVOLVED

18.9   All research involves some risk and it is the art of the good investigator to minimise that risk. But there are certain guidelines to be followed which are spelled out in the Declaration of Helsinki,[18] the Additional Protocol[19] and the EU Directive.[20] A risk/benefit analysis must be undertaken in each case and patients may be involved only when the benefit to them clearly outweighs the inconvenience, discomfort or possible harm which the protocol may impose. The Royal College of Physicians in their own report[21] distinguished between research involving 'less than minimal risk' and that involving 'minimal risk'. The former is the risk of the sort involved in giving a sample of urine or a single venous sample in an adult; the latter arises where there is a reasonable chance of a mild reaction—such as a headache or a feeling of lethargy—or where there is a remote chance of serious injury or death. The College took the view that, if the level rises above that of minimal risk, patients should be involved only if:

---

[17] Edwards et al (n 13 above) emphasise the interesting observation that a high proportion of participants in a research programme enter because the think they have something to gain—and this is tied to the question of how much they actually understand when consenting.

[18] Paras 16–18.   [19] Articles 6, 13, 15, 16, 17 and 21.   [20] Especially, Articles 3(2), 4 and 5.

[21] Royal College of Physicians *Research Involving Patients* (1990).

(a) the risk is still small in comparison with that already incurred by the patient as a consequence of the disease itself;

(b) the disease is a serious one;

(c) the knowledge gained from the research is likely to be of great practical benefit;

(d) there is no other means of obtaining that knowledge; and

(e) the patient gives a fully informed consent

and these still represent the views expressed in the very large number of comparable documents that have been produced since this report was published.

18.10　　The question of whether healthy volunteers may ever be exposed to serious risks in the course of medical research is problematic. The Declaration of Helsinki states:

Medical research involving human subjects should only be conducted if the importance outweighs the inherent risks and burdens to the subject. This is especially important when the human subjects are healthy volunteers. (para 18)

18.11　　Thus, a project would have to be of exceptional importance before a substantial risk to the healthy volunteer would be acceptable. On the face of things, the Additional Protocol to the Council of Europe Convention on Human Rights and Biomedicine allows more discretion in stating that research that does not have the potential to produce results of direct benefit to the health of the research participant may only be authorised if it 'entails no more than acceptable risk and acceptable burden for the research participant'. (Article 6); here, the accent appears to be more on risk taking than on assessment of risk. Both are, however, subjective exercises. What, for example, is one to say of the use of volunteers in, say, potentially harmful research into the development of vaccines against diseases that may affect the community? Indeed, one can interpolate a further question—at what stage does a prophylactic exercise directed against an unknown hazard become, or cease to be, a research project?[22] The ethics depend on an uncertain amalgam of necessity, altruism and courage, the contribution of each being difficult to quantify.

18.12　　There will clearly be differing views as to which risks are justifiable; it is equally clear that there will be those who would accept risks of a very high order on communitarian grounds and it is questionable whether they should be prevented from so doing. There are legal limits to the extent to which consent decriminalises the infliction of harm[23] and it is interesting to speculate how far the consent of a volunteer

[22] For an interesting discussion of the development and use of a vaccine designed to protect against biological warfare, see T M Gibson 'A Shot in the Arm for the Military: Consent to Immunisation against Biological Warfare Agents' (2002) 5 Med L Internat 161.

[23] A-G's Reference (No. 6 of 1980) [1981] QB 715, [1981] 2 All ER 1057, CA; Smart v HM Advocate 1975 SLT 65; R v Brown [1994] 1 AC 212, [1993] 2 All ER 75. See also The Law Commission Consent in the Criminal Law (Law Com No. 131, 1995).

to a dangerous medical experiment would serve as a defence to a charge of assault or homicide.[24]

18.13   The AIDS pandemic brought the issue of participation in risky research into focus at a time when infection with HIV was effectively a 'death sentence'. On one view, the threat which HIV posed at that time justified the suspension of normal controls on research. This would mean that the normal procedures for investigating the safety of promising drugs might be circumvented and volunteers would be allowed to run risks which would, in normal circumstances, be considered excessive. While it was agreed that it would be unwise, and scientifically inappropriate, to suspend all regulation of AIDS-related research, it was argued that the necessity of the situation justified such measures as 'fast-track approval' of therapeutic drugs[25]—and the same may well apply in other similar situations. Volunteers who accept high risks are likely to be regarded as scientific heroes if they are also researchers. In the case of patients, willingness to explore any avenue of hazardous treatment might be regarded as lying within the range of acceptable personal risk-taking. Why, then, should we refuse the help of the consenting research subject?[26] It may be, of course, that the interests of others are necessarily also in play. As we discuss in chapter 14, the unknown risks of retroviruses spreading to the human population through xenotransplants would be reason enough to refuse all volunteers willing to make a personal sacrifice. When the threat of harm is only at the individual level, however, the choice to volunteer may be cast as one of the ultimate expressions of personal autonomy, namely, pure altruism, and the rejection of such wholly selfless acts becomes far more difficult to justify (certainly on a felicific calculus).[27]

RESEARCH GOVERNANCE

18.14   Risk—voluntarily assumed or otherwise—is but one factor to consider in terms of the overall regulation of ethical research. Yet, the United Kingdom's approach to research governance has been a haphazard affair, there being, for example, no piece of legislation directed towards the regulation of human research conduct prior to the passing of the Clinical Trials Regulations in 2004 (implementing the 2001 Directive).[28] Systematic ethical review of research protocols is also a relatively recent phenomenon, with the first formal guidance being issued by the Department of Health only in

---

[24] It is to be noted, however, that no such charges were brought in something of a *cause-célèbre* at a noted US hospital: J Savulescu and M Spriggs 'The Hexamethonium Asthma Study and the Death of a Normal Volunteer in Research' (2002) 28 J Med Ethics 3.

[25] L C Fentiman 'Aids as a Chronic Illness: A Cautionary Tale for the End of the Twentieth Century' (1998) 61 Albany LR 989.

[26] The issue was discussed by C Levine 'Has AIDS Changed the Ethics of Human Subjects Research?' (1988) 16 Law Med Hlth Care 167.

[27] For discussion see T Hope and J McMillan 'Challenge Studies of Human Volunteers: Ethical Issues' (2004) 30 J Med Ethics 110.

[28] See n 11 above. Earlier provisions tangentially impacting on the work of RECs included the Health Service (Control of Patient Information) Regulations 2002, SI 2002/1438.

1991.[29] While NHS-based Local Research Ethics Committees have been around in one form or another since 1975, they have not enjoyed statutory authority, and oversight of their working practices has been, at best, patchy. Responsibility for governance has been split up between each of the areas of England, Scotland, Northern Ireland and Wales, with responsibility for the English system falling to COREC (Central Office for Research Ethics Committees).[30] The work of COREC has most recently been subsumed into that of the National Patient Safety Agency (as of 1 April 2005),[31] and we have also witnessed the creation of the United Kingdom Ethics Committee Authority (UKECA) which has the task of establishing, recognising and monitoring ethics committees to ensure compliance with the 2004 Regulations.[32] And, while the Regulations relate only to CTIMPs, it is the policy intention of the Department of Health that their terms will be treated as covering all types of work carried out by research ethics committees. This can, of course, only be by convention, leaving us with the rather odd legal position whereby the work of some ethics committees is clearly covered by legal provisions (and the rules of liability) and that of others is governed by the stated will of a government department.

18.15   The Department of Health issued the second edition of its Research Governance for Health and Social Care in April 2005.[33] This sets outs principles for good research governance applying to all research conducted within the remit of the Secretary of State for Health. It lays out principles, requirements and standards for acceptable research, mechanisms to meet these criteria, methods for monitoring compliance and issues concerning the proper protection of research participants and the wider public. The document points out that good health and social care research is a multidisciplinary affair, covering areas as diverse as ethics, science, information, health, safety and employment and finance and intellectual property. Here, we concentrate on the ethical dimension.

18.16   Given the crucially important nature of the ethical and personal issues at stake, the Department of Health makes it clear that it requires that research involving patients, their organs, tissues or data must undergo prior independent scrutiny to ensure that ethical standards are met. Indeed, it is now a criminal offence under the 2004 Regulations to commence a CTIMP without such prior approval.[34] Before these regulations there was no legal compunction to seek ethical review for any type of research involving human subjects.

18.17   The Research Governance Framework makes it clear that consent is the lynchpin to ethically acceptable research and it goes on to point out that additional legal

---

[29] See, Department of Health *Local Research Ethics Committees* HSG (91)5. Department of Health policy prior to this, since 1975, required all district health authorities to establish local ethics committees, see M Brazier, *Medicine, Patients and the Law*, 3rd edn, 2003, pp 398–99. Prior to this examples of RECs can be found dating back to the 1960s but their constitution and use was sporadic and lacking centralised control.

[30] www.corec.org.uk. The responsibility in the other countries falls to the relevant Ministers.

[31] www.npsa.nhs.uk.   [32] See Part II of the 2004 Regulations, n 11 above.

[33] Department of Health *Research Governance Framework for Health and Social Care* (2005) available at www.dh.gov.uk.

[34] 2004 Regulations, n 11 above, reg 49.

requirements may come into consideration in particular circumstances depending on the type of research to be carried out or the state of the research subject. Thus, research on those of reduced capacity may invoke the provisions of the Mental Capacity Act 2005 or investigations seeking to use human material may engage the Human Tissue Act 2004. The reader is referred to the relevant chapters where these instruments are examined in more detail. We discuss the particular elements of consent to research in due course below.

18.18   Responsibility and accountability have become the watchwords of the modern research governance culture. The 2001 Directive requires that a 'sponsor' now be named in each ethical review application, being the body/person(s) with overall legal responsibility for the various elements of the conduct and management of the research. The Department of Health has rolled this out for all research undertaken in the context of the NHS or social care services in England. The Framework also spends considerable time outlining the respective duties of others involved in the research process, such as researchers themselves, funders, care professionals and research participants. Finally, the Framework points to the current unmet need for adequate monitoring systems to ensure compliance with the framework. This is a legal obligation under the 2001 Directive in respect of CTIMPs but, once again, the Department of Health's policy is that appropriate systems of surveillance and reporting will be developed in respect of all NHS research.

RESEARCH ETHICS COMMITTEES

18.19   It should be obvious that ethics committees are central to any research governance framework but it is important to distinguish two major types of committee. Institutional ethics committees[35] are common and wield considerable power in the United States, where their function generally includes therapeutic and prognostic decision-making; there is little doubt that they are being increasingly introduced elsewhere as an aid to ethical decision making in a clinical setting. A number of such committees or variations on the theme have been established in the United Kingdom following a pioneer effort in 1993,[36] and it was reported in 2001 that some 18 per cent of NHS hospital trusts had some form of decision-making ethical back-up; only 17 per cent of these, however, included established committees.[37] Beyond this clinical setting, many private and public institutions establish ethics committees to vet research being carried out under their name; examples include private research establishments, universities, and the Medical Research Council.

---

[35] These are known as Institutional Review Boards (IRBs).

[36] 'UK's First Hospital Ethics Committee' (1993) 90 Bull Med Ethics 5, reporting the setting up of an ethics committee within an NHS trust hospital in Northwest London.

[37] A Slowther, C Bunch, B Woolnough and T Hope 'Clinical Ethics Support Services in the UK: An Investigation of the Current Provision of Ethics Support to Health Professionals in the UK' (2001) 27 J Med Ethics, Supp I, 112. This paper forms part of a larger symposium—see, in particular, J Hendrick 'Legal Aspects of Clinical Ethics Committees' at p 150, which considers the uncertainties as to liability.

18.20   Research Ethics Committees, such as are set up within the NHS under the auspices of the Department of Health, are, however of a different genre. Official local research ethical committees (LRECs) are set up by Health Authorities to scrutinise research projects involving patients from within the specific Authority. Where research involves patients/persons from a number of Authorities (or, indeed, from abroad), then ethical clearance is required from a Multi-Centre Research Ethics Committees (MRECs); these were established for the first time in 1997. The composition of ethics committees in the UK, along with matters of procedure, are regulated by guidelines issued by the Department of Health,[38] as well as through nationwide Standard Operating Procedures (SOPs) which were updated most recently in October 2004.[39] Further reforming measures are afoot. An independent advisory group was established in late 2004 to initiate a review of the systems which support NHS Research Ethics Committees in England,[40] while the launch of a new UK Panel for Health and Biomedical Research Integrity was announced in early 2005 to promote the best practice in biomedical research throughout the country.[41]

18.21   In summary, each local committee should include both sexes and cover a range of ages; hospital staff and general practitioners should be represented and the committee must include a sufficiently broad range of expertise so that the scientific and methodological aspects of proposals can be reconciled with the ethical implications. A quorum consists of at least seven members of the committee which must not, itself, exceed 18 members. The Committee can, when indicated, seek the advice of specialist referees. At least one-third of the membership must be lay members and at least half of these must be people who have never been associated with the health or social services and have never undertaken research. The inclusion of 'average citizens' can be seen as no more than a necessary political gesture; on the other hand, lay members may be better placed than professionals to appreciate the effects of different treatments on the day-to-day lives of the patients and their inclusion may, therefore, have definite practical advantages. One such member must be present in a quorum as must one expert member in order to facilitate understanding of the clinical and/or methodological components of the project under review.[42] It is to be noted that Health Authorities can set up as many LRECs within their boundaries as is

[38] Obligatory guidelines are embodied in Department of Health *Governance Arrangements for NHS Research Ethics Committees* (2001). The Arrangements are due for revision in light of consultation to be undertaken in the course of 2005. Similar guidelines are available for Scotland (2001): www.show.scot.nhs.uk/cso and are currently also under review. For notes on the relationship between LRECs and MRECs, see 'Research Ethics Committee Update' (1998) 138 Bull Med Ethics 13.

[39] COREC *Standard Operating Procedures for Ethics Committees in the United Kingdom* (2004), available at www.corec.org.uk.

[40] Reported on the COREC website, *ibid*, November 2004.

[41] C White 'UK Agency to Combat Research Misconduct' (2005) 330 BMJ 616. It is to be noted that standards are not necessarily identical throughout the European community: H Hearnshaw 'Comparison of Requirements of Research Ethics Committees in 11 European Countries for a Non-invasive Interventional Study' (2004) 328 BMJ 140.

[42] The government sees the need for, and will provide facilities for, education and training of REC members and administrators (see Governance Arrangements, n 38 above).

commensurate with the work-load.[43] In every circumstance, an ethics committee is empowered to require the researchers to resubmit their request after further review if it is not satisfied with the existing standards.[44]

18.22   The SOPs outline the kinds of factors to be considered by ethics committees.[45] Annex B concerns the standard conditions for approval of research relating to CTIMPs; Annex C contains the conditions for approving all other research. In the main these are very similar, although notable difference include, (a) that approval for CTIMPs must also be given from the Medicines and Healthcare Products Regulatory Agency (MHRA), (b) sites to be used to conduct the trials must be subject to inspection and approval, and (c) an obligation of *pharmacovigilence* is imposed throughout the trial, such that any Suspected Unexpected Serious Adverse Reactions (SUSARs)[46] must be notified to the ethics committee in accordance with European Commission guidance.[47] More extensive and effective monitoring procedures are now in place for all kinds of research. For example, Annex C talks of the need to notify Serious Adverse Events (SAEs), that is, an untoward occurrence that: (i) results in death; (ii) is life-threatening; (iii) requires hospitalisation or prolongation of existing hospitalisation; (iv) results in persistent or significant disability or incapacity; (v) consists of a congenital anomaly or birth defect; or (vi) is otherwise considered medically

---

[43] Special guidelines for multi-centre research ethics committees are detailed in Chapter 8 of the governance arrangements. Applications for research involving gene therapy, xenotransplantation and human fertilisation must be made to the appropriate regulatory authorities.

[44] Department of Health *Governance Arrangements for NHS Research Ethics Committees* (2001), paras 9.9, 9.10.

[45] See, too, reg 15(5) of the 2004 Regulations, n 11 above: 'In preparing its opinion, the committee shall consider, in particular, the following matters—(a) the relevance of the clinical trial and its design; (b) whether the evaluation of the anticipated benefits and risks as required under paragraph 2 of Part 2 of Schedule 1 is satisfactory and whether the conclusions are justified; (c) the protocol; (d) the suitability of the investigator and supporting staff; (e) the investigator's brochure; (f) the quality of the facilities for the trial; (g) the adequacy and completeness of the written information to be given, and the procedure to be followed, for the purpose of obtaining informed consent to the subjects' participation in the trial; (h) if the subjects are to include persons incapable of giving informed consent, whether the research is justified having regard to the conditions and principles specified in Part 5 of Schedule 1; (i) provision for indemnity or compensation in the event of injury or death attributable to the clinical trial; (j) any insurance or indemnity to cover the liability of the investigator or sponsor; (k) the amounts, and, where appropriate, the arrangements, for rewarding or compensating investigators and subjects; (l) the terms of any agreement between the sponsor and the owner or occupier of the trial site which are relevant to the arrangements referred to in sub-paragraph (k); and (m) the arrangements for the recruitment of subjects.'

[46] The SOPs (p 24) follow the 2004 Regulations in defining 'Suspected Unexpected Serious Adverse Reaction' thus: An 'adverse reaction' is any untoward and unintended response in a subject to an investigational medicinal product which is related to any dose administered to that subject. An adverse reaction is 'serious' if it: (a) results in death; (b) is life-threatening; (c) requires hospitalisation or prolongation of existing hospitalisation; (d) results in persistent or significant disability or incapacity; (e) consists of a congenital anomaly or birth defect. An adverse reaction is 'unexpected' if its nature and severity are not consistent with the information about the medicinal product in question set out: (a) in the case of a product with a marketing authorisation, in the summary of product characteristics for that product; (b) in the case of any other investigational medicinal product; (c) in the investigator's brochure relating to the trial in question.

[47] For which see: http://eudract.emea.eu.int/document.html#guidance.

significant by the investigator. The Chief Investigator must inform the Committee of any such event within 15 days of it coming to his/her attention.

18.23   While as a strict matter of law the guidelines only carry weight in respect of CTIMPs by virtue of the 2004 Regulations, there are several reasons why the carrying out of medical research will be effectively impossible without following them and receiving the necessary approval. To begin with, it is not possible to use NHS patients or resources for an unapproved project.[48] Funding is also likely to be denied unless an ethics committee's imprimatur is obtained, and the results of unapproved research will not be accepted for publication by reputable scientific journals. There are also pragmatic grounds compelling compliance with the guidelines—which clearly represent 'good medical practice'; appeal to *Bolam* principles would be virtually unavailable in the event of misadventure associated with research undertaken without approval—the *Bolitho* limitations (see para 9.40 above) would almost certainly apply.

18.24   The decisions of ethics committees have been declared to be subject to judicial review;[49] in the same way, a researcher frustrated by a LREC could pursue a remedy by that route. Appeal mechanisms are also in place.[50] The aggrieved research subject may also seek redress, in his case most obviously through an action against the researcher.[51] Indeed, there is an obligation, as part of the ethical approval mechanism, to ensure that adequate compensation measures are available (see below). Beyond this, however, it could be argued that a relationship exists between the committee member and the research subject which is of sufficient proximity to give rise to a duty of care and that this might, in theory, lead to civil liability in a case where a committee member has failed to exercise due care in the scrutiny of a research proposal. This, however, has never been tested in court. Furthermore, the guidelines make it clear that the appointing Authority will take full responsibility for all the actions of members in the course of carrying out their duties other than those involving bad faith, wilful default or gross negligence (para 4.14). The precise meaning of the last term in the context of an indemnity is uncertain.[52]

[48] The body conducting research is encouraged to submit its proposals to a LREC even when there is no NHS involvement.

[49] *R v Ethical Committee of St Mary's Hospital (Manchester), ex p H (or Harriott)* [1988] 1 FLR 512.

[50] See SOPs, Section 5, n 39 above.

[51] Those injured in the course of pharmaceutical trials may be compensated by the company sponsoring the trial, as recommended by the Association of the British Pharmaceutical Industry in its *Clinical Trial Compensation Guidelines* (1991, as amended).

[52] Accountability prior to the recent guidelines was considered in a major review: J V McHale 'Guidelines for Medical Research—Some Ethical and Legal Problems' (1993) 1 Med L Rev 160.

RANDOMISED CONTROLLED TRIALS

18.25   Biomedical research almost inevitably involves a randomised controlled trial at some time.[53] Indeed, it was the ubiquity and particularity of this type of research that drove the European Union to adopt the Clinical Trials Directive in 2001. The principle of this form of research is simple—in order to decide whether a new drug or other treatment is better than an existing one, or is preferable to none at all, the new treatment is given to a group of patients or healthy volunteers and not given to as similar a group as can be obtained. The subtleties of experimental design are critical to the success of the project because, as should be abundantly self-evident, a badly conceived trial is fundamentally unethical. But even the best designed trial has its built-in moral problem—depending on how one looks at it, on the one hand, a relatively untried treatment which may do harm is being given to one group while, on the other, a treatment which may be of considerable benefit is being withheld from a similar group. In one view, this is ethically unacceptable, as there can be no grounds—other than, possibly, those of limited resources—for withholding a treatment which is believed to be beneficial. The doctor must do his best for patients but the problem is to know what is best and, in particular, to know whether the patient's recovery is being hindered by the restraints of the experimental protocol.[54] The first essential for any controlled trial is, therefore, that it must provide its answer as rapidly as possible and it must be terminable as soon as an adverse effect becomes apparent. Conflict may arise between statisticians and doctors, with the former possibly insisting on evidence from many more cases—and possibly observed for longer—than the latter may feel is necessary.

18.26   When, then, should randomised trials stop? At what point does the clinician say that enough is enough and that the evidence of benefit is sufficient to justify the conclusion that a treatment does, indeed, do good? Conversely, at what point does the apparent emergence of an adverse effect dictate that the project be abandoned? The patient involved in such a trial will have been informed that he is possibly being denied a potential benefit—yet his consent will have been based on his trust that there is genuine scientific uncertainty. Once this uncertainty is resolved to the extent of a belief—on, say, a balance of probabilities—that the treatment offers clinical benefit, then it becomes questionable whether it can still be denied to some in a continuing

---

[53] Other forms of trial, which are beyond the scope of this book, can be used and may be preferable on ethical grounds. For a very full and useful description, see A L Avins 'Can Unequal Be More Fair? Ethics, Subject Allocation, and Randomised Clinical Trials' (1998) 24 J Med Ethics 401.

[54] The practical anxiety is outlined in simple terms in F Verdú-Pascual and A Castelló-Ponce 'Randomised Clinical Trials: A Source of Ethical Dilemmas' (2001) 27 J Med Ethics 177—and the statisticians put the counter-argument: J Hilden and A Gammelgaard 'Premature Stopping and Informed Consent in AMI Trials' (2002) 28 J Med Ethics 188.

quest for statistical significance.[55] In deciding this question, it is important that the researcher bears in mind the fundamental precept which governs ethical medical research—that one does not use patients as a means to a scientific end but treats them as an end in themselves. Even so, the practical dilemma remains—the clinically-orientated researcher stands to see his subsequent report criticised for want of scientific support while the more scientifically minded one sleeps uneasily because he worries that his research has reached an inadequate conclusion. Well designed trials should include plans for periodic analysis; there is also a good case to be made for an independent observer, or the ethical committee itself, being responsible for monitoring the trial from this angle.[56]

18.27   While in previous editions of this book we could only speculate as to the possible legal position in respect of clinical trials by extrapolating from ethical principles, we now have the 2004 Regulations which we can test against those ethical parameters. We have already seen, for example, that before initiating a CTIMP, the sponsor(s) must obtain both a positive endorsement from an ethics committee[57] as well as Clinical Trial Authorisation (CTA) from the Medicines and Healthcare Products Regulatory Agency (MHRA).[58] It is a criminal offence to do otherwise.[59] Monitoring of research sites is now also part of the review process[60] but, in general, a REC is not responsible in law for proactively monitoring research.[61] It does, however, have a duty to keep its favourable ethical opinion under review throughout the trial, especially in light of progress reports provided by the researchers. In particular, there is a statutory obligation of quarterly safety reporting by the sponsor(s) to the ethics committee and to the MHRA where one or more SUSARs (see above for definition) have occurred in the prior relevant quarterly period.[62] An REC can review its favourable ethical opinion of a research project at any time. The SOPs state that:

A favourable ethical opinion may be suspended or terminated due to serious concern about one of the following:

(a) The scientific validity of the study

(b) The health or safety of subjects

(c) The competence or conduct of the investigator(s)

[55] For an analysis, see N Johnson, R J Lilford and W Brazier 'At what Level of Collective Equipoise Does a Clinical Trial Become Ethical?' (1991) 17 J Med Ethics 30. The standards of proof have been compared to the different standards applied in the civil and criminal courts: The Lancet 'On Stopping a Trial before its Time' (1993) 342 Lancet 1311.

[56] E Pickworth 'Should Local Research Ethics Committees Monitor Research They Have Approved?' (2000) 26 J Med Ethics 330. The author thinks not—mainly on the practical grounds that they could not accommodate the extra work-load but also because it would introduce an element of policing into what is an advisory role. The Declaration of Helsinki, however, acknowledges a Committee's right to do so (at para 13).

[57] The Regulations require that ethical review must normally occur within 60 days of receipt of an application to conduct a CTIMP, n 11 above, reg 15.

[58] See SOP, n 39 above, p 74. The 2005 version of the Research Governance Framework, n 38 above, also now requires independent expert review of research protocols.

[59] 2004 Regulations, n 11 above, reg 49.   [60] See SOP, n 39, above, section 4.

[61] See SOP, n 39, above, section 9 for operational policy on research monitoring.   [62] Ibid.

(d) Serious or repeated breach of approval conditions

(e) A delay of at least 2 years in the commencement of the study

(f) The adequacy of the site or facilities.

18.28   Only a quorate meeting of the full ethics committee can suspend or terminate its own prior favourable ethical opinion and the SOPs are clear that, before taking this course, 'the REC should weigh carefully the implications for any research participants already recruited'.[63]

18.29   The principle of randomisation lies at the core of clinical trials and of the ethical problems associated with their conduct. It is almost impossible for health professionals not to have some preference when there is a choice of treatments.[64] For this reason, if for no other, many doctors having care—and especially primary care—of patients distrust the randomised clinical trial. Most do so for fear that the doctor-patient relationship will be jeopardised; a significant number are, however, concerned with the problems of informed consent.[65] This is discussed in greater detail later,[66] but here it can be said that it also has a profound effect on the patient's acceptance of a trialist status. Refusal may be on simple utilitarian grounds but is equally liable to stem from confusion. No randomised therapeutic trial can be ethical unless the professionals genuinely cannot agree as to which treatment yields the best results. Given that the doctors are unsure, it may be difficult for the patient to solve what appears to him to be an insoluble problem. The result of the cumulative adverse factors is that accrual rates to important trials can be low—it has been reported, for example, that a fundamental research project intended to identify the best treatment for early breast cancer had to be closed after a very low recruitment because the insistence on full informed consent frightened off both surgeons and patients.[67] Researchers therefore seek devices which will circumvent the confrontation between clinicians and patient and most of these involve some form of pre-selection—or 'pre-randomisation'—prior to discussion of treatment.[68] There are specific ethical and practical objections to such manoeuvres but, in general, it seems morally doubtful to use what is essentially a ruse in order to obviate an agreed ethical practice which is an

---

[63] Ibid, paras 9.52–9.55.

[64] True 'equipoise', or indifference, may be impossible to attain for many reasons; at best, it will be unusual. Perhaps we should be looking for genuine disagreement among experts rather than genuine uncertainty. See Avins, n 53 above.

[65] Edwards et al (n 13 above) refer to three trials in which 47% of doctors concerned thought that few patients knew they were taking part in a controlled experiment, even though they had given written consent. The problem of consent may be particularly acute where the participants in a randomised trial are illiterate or where they do not share the scientific view of the researcher: see M Barry and M Molyneux 'Ethical Dilemmas in Malaria Drug and Vaccine Trials: a Bioethical Perspective' (1992) 18 J Med Ethics 189. See also, M Angell 'Investigators' Responsibilities for Human Subjects in Developing Countries' (2000) 342 New Engl J Med 967.

[66] See para 18.48 below.

[67] M Baum, K Zilkha and J Houghton 'Ethics of Clinical Research: Lessons for the Future' (1989) 299 BMJ 251.

[68] For a simple explanation of pre-randomisation, see D J Torgerson and M Roland 'What Is Zelen's Design?' (1998) 316 BMJ 606.

integral part of the basic principles not only of the Declaration of Helsinki but also of all modern directives and guidelines. One does well, however, not to lose sight of the view from the other side. One perfectly arguable school of thought will hold that this is the penalty we have to accept: 'unless we wish to return to the dark ages when treatment was determined by conceptual rationalism rather than scientific method'.[69]

18.30   One further feature deserves mention before we leave the subject of randomisation—that is the 'double-blind' technique. This form of research, which is virtually confined to drug trials, attempts to reduce subjectivity in assessment by keeping the assigned therapeutic groups secret not only from the patients but also from the physicians involved. This clearly dictates that the patient's doctor cannot be the researcher; it also makes it implicit that the ethical justification of the trial is agreed by the 'caring' physicians involved, for they must have perfect equipoise if they are to join in the trial and, at the same time, provide what is, to their mind, the 'best treatment' for their patients. This, further, leads to some form of conscious pre-selection in that it may be, for example, necessary to exclude patients on the grounds of the severity of their disease; the trial then becomes limited to establishing the effectiveness of a treatment for the milder forms of the disease and loses much of its validity. We find it hard to justify many aspects of the ethics of the 'double-blind' trial and the regulatory authorities also take a cautious approach; while the European Commission recommends that *normally* reports of SUSARs should mean that trials then be unblinded, the UK position is stricter still in requiring that *all* reports of adverse reactions in double-blinded trials *must* be unblinded.[70]

GROUPS OF SUBJECTS

18.31   There may be clear advantages in using healthy volunteers as experimental subjects—the Declaration of Helsinki does not preclude their use (para 16) but, by definition, it must be limited to non-therapeutic research. Medical research may be combined with medical care (para 28) but we doubt if this could be extended to using patients as if they were healthy; we believe that the use of a group of persons who are already under stress, and who probably have a sense of obligation to the doctors, simply because of their accessibility, must bring such research close to unethical practice; non-therapeutic research in patients should be confined to a type which adds no extra burden—for example, through the use of existing blood samples as is discussed below.[71] As already suggested, it can be argued that the use of healthy volunteers is, a priori, unjustifiable but we prefer the view that people have a right to exercise altruistic impulses, particularly in a society in which the benefits of free health care are

---

[69] Baum et al (1989) 299 BMJ 251. For a passionate defence of 'scientific medicine' see, recently, R Tallis *Hippocratic Oaths* (2004).

[70] SOPs, n 39 above, paras 8.6 and 9.32.

[71] See para 18.77. For what is, perhaps, the all time greatest example of the dangers of using patients in this way, see *Hyman v Jewish Chronic Disease Hospital* 206 NE 2d 338 (1965) where a group of hospital patients were injected with cancer cells as an active control for a group of cancer patients who were similarly treated.

extended to all. None the less, considerable caution is needed, particularly as to the repetitive volunteer who is particularly prone to exploitation even if the researchers are unconscious of this. Motivation of the ever-ready volunteer takes several forms, some good and others less so, and, among these, the problem of recompense looms large. Both the Declaration of Helsinki and the authoritative Directive 2001/20/EC are silent on this aspect[72] but it is probable that, in the conditions of present-day society, few suitable volunteers would come forward in the absence of some inducement; large payments would, however, be clearly unethical and a reasonable balance must be set— if for no other reason than to satisfy the needs of randomisation. It might be noted that the Royal College of Physicians Report *Research Involving Patients* described payments to patients as 'generally undesirable' but occasionally acceptable in the case of long and tedious studies.[73] Even in such cases, 'payments should not be for undergoing risk, and payments should not be such as to persuade patients to volunteer against their better judgement'.

18.32   The topic of inducement does, however, bring us to the problems of the use of specific populations who are special because of their easy access, malleability and the like. Students, and particularly medical students, provide an example about whom there is little difficulty; they are of an age to make legally valid decisions, they may well have an active interest in the trial and most, if not all, educational establishments have very stringently controlling ethics committees to protect against, say, repetitive use. Much the same could be said for the armed forces, who may be particularly vulnerable to improper research in war or when war threatens—even in 1990, non-consensual trials were allowed on American troops engaged in the Gulf War[74] and we have mentioned the use of experimental vaccines above (see para 18.11). The use of prisoners, however, exposes many ethical issues that are based, essentially, on the argument that some advantage, even if only imagined, must accrue to the prisoner participating in a trial; that advantage may be so great as to induce the prisoner to volunteer for research which involves greater discomfort or risk than would be accepted by a free man and, in particular, it may compromise his inalienable right to withdraw from the trial. The arguments are not, however, entirely one way—it is always possible to be paternalistic in an attempt to preserve other peoples' autonomy. Thus, prisoners could well resent protective attitudes on the grounds that it is their right to dispose of their bodies and to take such risks as they please that is being compromised. This could be the subject of lengthy debate but we suggest that the conditions in today's prisons are such that any process which provides some relief deserves, at least, a sympathetic evaluation and, secondly, that many prisoners might

---

[72] The latter proscribes incentives and financial inducements other than compensation but only in respect of minors (Article 4(d)) and incapacitated adults (Article 5(d)), and these are repeated in Parts 4 and 5 of Schedule 1 to the 2004 Regulations. Otherwise, the matter would be considered by the responsible ethics committee.

[73] Royal College of Physicians *Research Involving Patients* (1990).

[74] G J Annas and M A Grodin 'Treating the Troops: Commentary' (1991) 21 Hastings Center Rep (2) 24.

be benefited therapeutically through helping society.[75] But it is also felt that experiments on prisoners should be particularly rigidly controlled by ethical committees which should always contain lay members with experience in criminology. Nowhere is it more important to observe the maxim 'the aims do not justify the method—the method must be judged in its own right'.[76]

18.33   When comparing treatments, however, the use of patients is axiomatic. This is what the Declaration of Helsinki means by medical research combined with professional care which is admissible 'only to the extent that the research is justified by its potential prophylactic, diagnostic or therapeutic value' (para 28).

18.34   A clinical trial is rarely undertaken unless there is good reason to suppose that one therapy will show an advantage over others and particularly over those currently accepted as the best available. The advantage need not be direct; it could, for example, be collateral in that the results of the method were not better but were achieved with less disfigurement or with fewer side effects. Anticipation of advantage can, in general, only be based on laboratory or, where appropriate, animal experimentation[77] and, while the view is occasionally expressed that the latter is less moral than is human biomedical research, it is, still, generally acceptable given that the conditions are controlled. The corollary, as we have already emphasised, is that an untried method must be immediately withdrawn if it is found to be positively deleterious and the patients involved must be transferred, whenever possible, to an alternative regime. There is a legal obligation to report early terminations of clinical trials to both the REC and the MHRA with full explanation for the decision.[78]

18.35   The results of trials involving innovative therapies may, however, take a considerable time to filter through and, by then, there may be no turning back. A typical example was provided by the study of the use of folic acid supplements in order to reduce the incidence of neural tube defects in infants. Two pilot studies were undertaken; both showed an apparent marked reduction in recurrence rates in affected families but neither stood up to statistical analysis. The problem then arose as to whether the study should be continued and, if so, whether the clinical impression was sufficient to render the use of placebos unethical. It was decided that the matter was so important that a major randomised trial was indicated, the intent being to study at least 2,000 pregnancies. In the event, after more than seven years, sufficient

---

[75] The Council of Europe Additional Protocol on Biomedical Research (2005), n 10 above, states in Article 20: 'Where the law allows research on persons deprived of liberty, such persons may participate in a research project in which the results do not have the potential to produce direct benefit to their health only if the following additional conditions are met: (a) research of comparable effectiveness cannot be carried out without the participation of persons deprived of liberty; (b) the research has the aim of contributing to the ultimate attainment of results capable of conferring benefit to persons deprived of liberty, and (c) the research entails only minimal risk and minimal burden'.

[76] Specific governmental arrangements are in place for ethical review of research on prisoners: *Governance Arrangements for NHS Research Ethics Committees* (2001), Section B.

[77] The view is occasionally expressed that the latter is at least as, if not more, objectionable than is research on humans. The 2000 version of the Declaration is noticeably more sensitive in this respect than was its predecessors.

[78] See, 2004 Regulations, n 11 above, regs 30–31.

information had been gained from 1,195 informative pregnancies. Thus, the trial could then be ended, it being clear that folic acid supplements had no adverse effects but had a significant protective effect as regards fetal neural tube defect.[79]

THE USE OF PLACEBOS

18.36   A placebo is an inert substance without pharmacological action. But in humans the mere taking of a substance in a clinical or quasi-clinical setting may lead to subjective, or symptomatic, improvement; this is the 'placebo effect', which must be considered whenever a new drug or procedure is on trial. On the other hand, the trial drug may do more harm than inactivity; but, for psychological reasons, inactivity must involve apparent activity if the two regimens are to be properly compared. In either case, the controlled giving of a placebo necessarily involves the deception of patients and this raises some complex issues.

18.37   The extreme position is that placebos offend against the fundamental rightness of fidelity.[80] If, as is often the case, there is patient resistance to the use of such controls, this should not be regarded as an excuse for further deception but rather as an indication that such experiments are unacceptable to society. To which one could reply that a poor experiment is a worse affront to society and that the simple expedient is to leave out those who object—little is lost, other than, perhaps, absolute numbers, and, as previously discussed, experimental volunteers are, by nature, already a selected group.

18.38   More practical objections are based on the effect of the experiment on patient care; the circumstances in which it is ethical to deprive a patient of treatment must be strictly regulated. It would, for example, be improper to use placebo controls when pain was a feature of the condition under treatment, despite the fact that some patients might derive benefit; many pain killers are available and can be used as reference substances. The basic circumstances in which placebo trials are ethical and, perhaps, necessary include, first, and perhaps foremost, when there is no alternative to the experimental treatment available. Such a situation might arise in the treatment of degenerative neural disease—though, even here, *some* form of pharmacologically active substance might well be thought preferable. Second, the use of a placebo could be justified when the effect of adding a new treatment to an established one is under study. In the majority of instances, however, the purpose of their use is to analyse the effect of a treatment on subjective symptoms rather than on organic disease.[81]

[79] MRC Vitamin Study Research Group 'Prevention of Neural Tube Defects: Results of the Medical Research Council Vitamin Study' (1991) 338 Lancet 131.

[80] For a seminal analysis, see B Simmons 'Problems in Deceptive Medical Procedures: An Ethical and Legal Analysis of the Administration of Placebos' (1978) 4 J Med Ethics 172.

[81] For further criticism, see K J Rothman and K B Michels 'The Continuing Unethical Use of Placebo Controls' (1994) 331 New Engl J Med 384. A cautious but relatively benign attitude, which, to an extent, parallels our views, is adopted by P P De Deyn and R D'Hooge 'Placebos in Clinical Practice and Research' (1996) 22 J Med Ethics 140.

18.39   The most recent version of the Declaration of Helsinki has raised some interesting additional points as to the use of placebos. Para 29 states:

The benefits, risks, burdens and effectiveness of a new method should be tested against those of the best current prophylactic, diagnostic, and therapeutic methods. This does not exclude the use of placebo, or no treatment, in studies where no proven prophylactic, diagnostic or therapeutic method exists.

18.40   The European Agency for the Evaluation of Medical Products criticised this in 2001 on the grounds that the use of placebos is ruled out whenever an alternative exists. The Agency believes that comparison of a new method with an active control does not always give the same scientific satisfaction as does comparison with a passive control;[82] the argument, although not stated in precise terms, seems to be that an ideal trial might require the use of placebo as a comparator to both the old and the new alternatives. One can see why this might be so but it presupposes considerable understanding on the part of the research subjects. Perhaps more significantly in the ethical context, it has been pointed out that, although the clause is there to prohibit exploitation of vulnerable communities, the use of an established method as a control may be beyond the socio-economic means of many developing countries.[83]

18.41   The World Medical Association then added a Note of Clarification to the Declaration in respect of para 29 in 2002 which is worth repeating in full:

The WMA hereby reaffirms its position that extreme care must be taken in making use of a placebo-controlled trial and that in general this methodology should only be used in the absence of existing proven therapy. However, a placebo-controlled trial may be ethically acceptable, even if proven therapy is available, under the following circumstances: (a) Where for compelling and scientifically sound methodological reasons its use is necessary to determine the efficacy or safety of a prophylactic, diagnostic or therapeutic method; or (b) Where a prophylactic, diagnostic or therapeutic method is being investigated for a minor condition and the patients who receive placebo will not be subject to any additional risk of serious or irreversible harm. All other provisions of the Declaration of Helsinki must be adhered to, especially the need for appropriate ethical and scientific review.[84]

18.42   All of which may seem trite and fairly easily accommodated within an ethical spectrum. But times move on, and in the last few years we have been confronted with the extension of the placebo concept into surgery—and especially, although not exclusively, into the surgery of those conditions in which symptoms and signs become intermingled; the paradigmatic example is in the use of fetal brain implants in the

---

[82] See, European Agency for the Evaluation of Medicinal Products/Committee for Proprietary Medicinal Products *Position Statement on the Use of Placebo in Clinical Trials with regard to the Revised Declaration of Helsinki* (2001), available at: www.emea.eu.int/pdfs/human/press/pos/1742401en.pdf.

[83] S M Tollman 'Fair Partnerships Support Ethical Research' (2001) 323 BMJ 1417.

[84] In similar vein, Article 23(3) of the Additional Protocol on Biomedical Research (2005) to the Council of Europe Biomedicine and Human Rights Convention (1997) states: 'The use of placebo is permissible where there are no methods of proven effectiveness, or where withdrawal or withholding of such methods does not present an unacceptable risk or burden'.

treatment of Parkinsonism (see para 14.76 above).[85] Essentially, we have here a ran-domised controlled trial in which some patients are implanted but in which the control group's brains are untouched. Space does not admit of further discussion. Suffice it to point out that, on top of the philosophical difficulties involved in the acceptance of medicinal placebo therapy, we must now impose deceptive target imaging by way of magnetic resonance imaging, an anaesthetic, a scalp incision and at least a token hole in the skull on a person who is to receive no additional therapy. Justification of the programme on utilitarian grounds is possible but certainly not easy.

EXPERIMENTAL TREATMENT

18.43   Early in the chapter, we distinguished between research and experimentation—the latter being regarded as involving ad hoc and relatively—or entirely—untried treat-ment applied to an individual with little more scientific basis other than expediency. It follows that we see medical experiments—as opposed to research—on human beings as being morally justified only in extreme conditions.

18.44   The status of the experimental therapist has always been uncertain since 1797 when the unfortunate Dr Baker was pilloried in court for introducing what still remains the standard treatment for fractures of the limb bones.[86] The innovative doctor cannot depend upon *Bolam* if things go wrong since, by definition, no supportive body of medical opinion is available—the pioneer therefore seems alone in more senses than one. Perhaps a more accurate measure of how the pioneer will be judged, however, is to be found in the earlier Scottish case of *Hunter v Hanley*[87] which, it must be remembered, was accepted in *Bolam* as laying down the correct test for assessing medical conduct which departs from the norm. As Lord Clyde stated, a mere devi-ation from ordinary professional practice is not necessarily evidence of negligence; indeed, '. . . it would be disastrous if this were so, for all inducement to progress in medical science would then be destroyed'. Moreover, he went so far as to remark that '[e]ven a substantial deviation from normal practice may be warranted by the particu-lar circumstances'. Where there *is* to be liability for deviation this is to be judged by a three-fold test: (1) it must be shown that there is a usual and normal practice, (2) it must be proved that this practice was not adopted, and (3) it must be established that

[85] For which see: W Dekkers and G Boer 'Sham Neurosurgery in Patients with Parkinson's Disease: Is it Morally Acceptable?' (2001) 27 J Med Ethics 151. For uncompromising criticism, see P A Clark 'Placebo Surgery for Parkinson's Disease: Do the Benefits Outweigh the Risks?' (2002) 30 J Law Med Ethics 58. These papers particularly contrast and analyse those by T Freeman et al 'Use of Placebo Surgery in Controlled Trials of a Cellular-based Therapy for Parkinson's Disease' (1999) 341 New Engl J Med 988 and R Macklin 'The Ethical Problems with Sham Surgery in Clinical Research' (1999) 341 New Engl J Med 992.

[86] *Slater v Baker and Stapleton* (1797) 95 ER 860.   [87] 1955 SC 200, 1955 SLT 213.

the course the doctor adopted was one which no professional man of ordinary skill would have taken if he had been acting with ordinary care. This is nothing more than an alternative formulation of the reasonableness test, and the sum and substance of the legal position of the experimentalist, then, is that it will be for the court to ask in the circumstances of each and every case—drawing on medical opinion as it thinks fit—whether the deviation from established practice was a reasonable course of conduct for the patient at hand.[88]

18.45   Thus, the patient who has no other hope is surely entitled to grasp an outside chance and, given the fact that he believes it to be a genuine chance, the doctor is entitled, and perhaps ought, to provide it. He must, however, believe that there is a chance—he cannot provide, nor can the patient consent to, treatment that is certain to result in serious bodily harm or death.[89] In this respect, the ruling in *Bolitho* (see para 9.40 above) may be greatly to the doctor's advantage; given the conditions envisaged, it could be relatively easy in the event of an action in negligence to convince a court that his decision was logical *in all the circumstances* of the case. In practice, the Declaration of Helsinki supports the concept of experimental treatment:

In the treatment of a patient, where proven prophylactic, diagnostic and therapeutic methods do not exist or have been ineffective, the physician, with informed consent from the patient, must be free to use unproven or new . . . measures, if in the physician's judgement it offers hope of saving life, re-establishing health or alleviating suffering.[90]

18.46   Clearly, the informed consent of the patient is of paramount importance, not only in the current context of experimentation but for all forms of research, and we return to this universally accepted precept in due course. But even where informed consent is not possible, highly experimental treatment may be legal in the right circumstances. As we have already seen many times, in the absence of consent, the law in the United Kingdom falls back on 'best interests', and we have also noted the tendency of the courts to rely on the *Bolam* standard to help determine what a patient's best interests might be. Each of these elements came together in the case of *Simms v Simms* to demonstrate how far the concept of best interests can extend beyond proven treatment into the realm of unproven experiment.

18.47   The joined cases of *Simms v Simms; A v A and Another*[91] concerned the circumstances of two desperately ill teenagers in the advanced stages of variant Creutzfeldt-Jakob disease (vCJD): a degenerative, incurable, and terminal brain condition. Both sets of parents sought declaratory relief to confirm that it would be lawful to undertake a highly experimental course of 'treatment' which had never been tested in

---

[88] An excellent illustration is provided by the little-known case of *Hepworth v Kerr* [1995] 6 Med LR 139 in which an anaesthetist was found negligent in using an unnecessary and unvalidated hypotensive technique to provide a blood-free operating area. The patient sustained neurological damage.

[89] *A-G's Reference (No. 6 of 1980)*, n 23 above.

[90] Para 32. The paragraph adds that the case should be included in a structured research project whenever possible.

[91] [2003] 2 WLR 1465, [2003] 1 All ER 669, [2003] 1 FCR 361.

humans, about which the risks and benefits were unknown, but which had shown some marginal varying success in mice, rats and dogs in Japan (although higher doses in dogs often caused severe reactions and death). The evident 'last chance' nature of the case permeates the judgment—it was accepted by all that the children would not recover. Notwithstanding, the President of the Family Division sought to apply the best interests test and held that this justified the attempt in light of medical evidence whereby no witness was willing to rule of the *possibility* that some benefit might accrue. Moreover, Lady Butler-Sloss added further qualifiers, namely, that since the disease was progressive and fatal, and because there was no alternative treatment, and so long as there were no significant risks of increasing the suffering of the patient, then it would not be unlawful to try (even when the risks and benefits were largely unknown). Finally, the President held that because there was some medical evidence that did not rule out a chance of benefit, she was content to assume that the *Bolam* test had been complied with. Tellingly, and echoing the words of Lord Clyde (above), she stressed that the *Bolam* test 'ought not to be allowed to inhibit medical progress';[92] in the circumstances there was a responsible body of sufficient expertise to satisfy its terms. The balance, then, between progress and patient interests remains a fine one. Beyond this, however, it is difficult to tell what sort of precedent, if any, is set by this case. The extreme nature of the circumstances alone means that similar facts are likely to arise only rarely, and one cannot but have tremendous sympathy for both the parents and the President who must all have felt that 'doing something' was far better than 'doing nothing'. While we may wish to dress this up in legalese, we should at the same time recognise it as a perfectly natural and understandable human response to tragic circumstances.[93]

INFORMED CONSENT AND THE (IN)COMPETENT RESEARCH SUBJECT

18.48   On one view, research (and experimentation) involving incapacitated persons should not be ruled out entirely because to do so would not only deprive them of an opportunity to engage in community-oriented beneficial activities to which they might have consented if able, but it would also mean that much research into the conditions from which these people suffer would simply be impossible.[94] In both circumstances, it is strongly arguable that a complete ban is unethical. By the same token, the extreme vulnerability of members of this group of research subjects

---

[92] *Ibid*, para 48. Note that the President followed her own ruling in similar cases: *An NHS Trust v HM* [2004] Lloyd's Rep Med 207; *EP v Trusts A, B, & C* [2004] Lloyd's Rep Med 211.

[93] Something of an interesting contrast is to be seen in the case of *Re MM (a child) (medical treatment)* [2000] 1 FLR 224 in which the court upheld the decision of a child's doctors to abandon what they regarded as experimental foreign treatment in favour of their own approach. See further chapter 19.

[94] This was expressly recognised in *Simms v Simms*, above, para 57.

requires that special care is taken to protect them and their interests. Beyond this, it is undeniable that the 'ideal' ethical research programme is one that can be based on free, autonomous participation by the subject and this, in turn, depends upon 'informed consent', the nature of which has been discussed in chapter 10.

18.49   The principles in relation to research and experimentation are similar to those governing therapy; most commentators would, however, hold that the patient's rights are, if anything, greater in the former situation than they are in the sphere of pure patient management. The standard of information provided must certainly be that of the 'reasonable subject'—if not that of the actual subject—rather than that of the 'reasonable doctor'.[95] Even so, there are many and varied difficulties which make it almost impossible to lay down hard and fast rules—these include the essential need for some measure of ignorance in the trial, the seriousness of the condition being treated, the psychology of individual patients and the like. The complexity is such that some confrontation between the back-room and the coal-face is almost inevitable:

> The central dogma [of professional medical ethicists] seems to be that whatever is done for the sake of medical science is alien to the treatment of the individual, and should therefore be labelled an 'experiment', necessitating informed consent by the patient and adjudication by an ethics committee.[96]

18.50   Such general problems are amplified in practice. It is widely agreed that the subject's consent must be based on four main lines of explanation: the purpose of the experiment; the benefits to the subject and society; the risks involved; and the alternatives open to the subject. Who is to impart the information—the subject's physician or the researcher? Should the subject have the benefit of a 'friend' to interpret for him? Should there be confirmation of the consent procedure? It has been fairly widely mooted that, in fact, informed consent is a double-edged weapon—token consent may take the place of the genuine and relieve the researcher of responsibility. Might it not be better to burden the investigator with full responsibility rather than provide such a shield? Many of the states of the United States have enacted 'informed consent statutes', some of which lay down specific disclosure requirements for particular procedures. In the same spirit, United States courts, dealing with claims that inadequate information has been given to research subjects, have tended to stress the requirement that there be a considerably higher burden of disclosure in cases involving non-therapeutic research than in therapeutic cases,[97] a view shared by a

---

[95] For a short resumé of the debate, see L Doyal and J S Tobias 'Informed Consent in Medical Research' (1998) 316 BMJ 1000. Much of the current discussion centres on the ethics of publication; this is inevitable as research without publication is so much wasted effort.

[96] Lancet 'Medical Ethics: Should Medicine Turn the Other Cheek?' (1990) 336 Lancet 846. But can one wonder at this when one reads of Dr Milhaud who seemingly used, and caused the death of, a patient in the permanent vegetative state in research on hypovolaemic shock: G Maio 'The Cultural Specificity of Research Ethics—or Why Ethical Debate in France is Different' (2002) 28 J Med Ethics 147. The author points to the difficulties in harmonising differing national cultures within an international framework.

[97] E.g. *Whitlock v Duke University* 637 F Supp 1463 (NC, 1986); affd 829 F 2d 1340 (1987).

Canadian court in the well-known case of *Halushka v University of Saskatchewan*.[98] Here the court said: 'There can be no exceptions to the ordinary requirements of disclosure in the case of research as there may well be in ordinary medical practice'.

18.51   These difficulties are highlighted in 'care associated' research when, effectively, the doctrine of informed consent implies that the subject has to choose for him or herself whether to accept an experimental treatment or to be randomised in a comparative therapeutic trial. The philosophical basis of personal autonomy is perfectly clear, but is the ideal end attainable in practice? Ought a patient to be told of a 'last chance' effort? Is the medically naive subject capable of giving consent as required? Can he or she be expected to understand the risks when the medical profession itself is so divided?

18.52   A real problem here is that doubts as to subjects' ability to understand complex medical information can very easily result in the striking of an unacceptably paternalistic attitude—sometimes with shocking consequences. Such a situation arose in New Zealand in the course of the Auckland cervical cancer campaign.[99] Here, a senior doctor, believing that cancer in situ would not spread, was strongly of the view that some women with abnormal cervical smear tests were best left untreated. These patients were denied treatment over a period of 15–20 years without being told that they were, in effect, involved in a therapeutic experiment. The doctor in charge of the experimental research believed honestly and firmly in his hypothesis, but his failure to obtain consent was severely criticised both by medical colleagues and by the judicial inquiry which was established to investigate the matter; the impact on medicine in New Zealand and, hopefully, elsewhere, has been profound.[100]

18.53   Many of these ethical concerns have now been addressed by law in the guise of the 2001 Directive, the UK's 2004 implementing Regulations, and guidance from COREC on their interpretation.[101] Schedule 1, Part 3 of the Regulations provide, for example, that (a) the subject must have an interview with the investigator (or a member of his team) and be given the opportunity to understand the nature, objectives, risks and inconveniences of the trial; (b) the subject must be informed of his right to withdraw from the trial at any time without detriment; (c) he must be provided with a contact point where he can obtain more information about the trial; and, most crucially, (d) he must give his informed consent. On this last point, the Regulations state:

a person gives informed consent to take part . . . in a clinical trial only if his decision—

[98] (1965) 53 DLR (2d) 436: K Morin 'The Standard of Disclosure in Human Subject Experimentation' (1998) 19 J Leg Med 157.

[99] Judge S Cartwright *The Report of the Cervical Cancer Enquiry* (1988); discussed by A V Campbell 'An "Unfortunate Experiment" ' (1989) 3 Bioethics 59.

[100] C Paul 'The New Zealand Cancer Study: Could it Happen Again' (1988) 297 BMJ 533; P McNeill 'The Implications for Australia of the New Zealand Report of the Cervical Cancer Inquiry: No Cause for Complacency' (1989) 150 Med J Austral 264; G Gillett 'NZ Medicine after Cartwright' (1990) 300 BMJ 893.

[101] COREC, *Medicines for Human Use (Clinical Trials Regulations) 2004: Informed Consent in Clinical Trials* (2005), available at: www.corec.org.uk.

    (a) is given freely after that person is informed of the nature, significance, implications and risks of the trial; and

    (b) either—

        (i)   is evidenced in writing, dated and signed, or otherwise marked, by that person so as to indicate his consent, or

        (ii) if the person is unable to sign or to mark a document so as to indicate his consent, is given orally in the presence of at least one witness and recorded in writing.

18.54   An inherent limitation in these provisions is that, at best, a subject is to be given 'the opportunity to understand' what they are consenting to. There is no further obligation on the part of investigators to inquire as to whether any degree of actual understanding has been reached.

RESEARCH AND THE INCOMPETENT

18.55   Particularly difficult ethical and legal problems arise in respect of those patients who cannot give a valid consent to participation in clinical research by virtue of their mental condition. Such patients must be excluded automatically if informed consent is an absolute prerequisite for involvement in research, yet this would have the effect of halting valuable lines of inquiry into serious and debilitating diseases. One way round this difficulty is to accept that there are special groups of patients who cannot consent but whose involvement is vital if research into a condition from which they suffer is to make progress. Such patients might be used in research provided that certain safeguards were erected; these would be designed so as to ensure that they are not subjected to appreciable risk or inconvenience and would include the agreement of relatives and/or that of some independent supervisory party. The required approval of an independent authority would cover those instances in which it was suspected that uncaring relatives had been thoughtless. Almost precisely the same arguments can be made in respect of minors, but we deal with their particular circumstances in the following chapter.

18.56   The Additional Protocol to the Convention on Human Rights and Biomedicine has addressed the matter of the incompetent research subject directly and proposes that research on a person without the capacity to consent to research may be undertaken if:

    (i)   the results of the research have the potential to produce real and direct benefit to his or her health;

    (ii) research of comparable effectiveness cannot be carried out on individuals capable of giving consent;

    (iii) the person undergoing research has been informed of his or her rights and the safeguards prescribed by law for his or her protection, unless this person is not in a state to receive the information;

    (iv) the necessary authorisation has been given specifically and in writing by the legal representative or an authority, person or body provided for by law, and . . . taking into account the person's previously expressed wishes or objections . . .

(v)   the person concerned does not object.[102]

18.57   Exceptionally, where condition (i) above is not satisfied, research may be authorised if it has the aim of contributing 'to the ultimate attainment of results capable of conferring benefit to the person concerned or to other persons in the same age category or afflicted with the same disease or disorder or having the same condition' provided, at the same time, that the research entails only minimal risk and minimal burden for the individual concerned. It is this latter criterion, not the ultimate value of the research, that constitutes the benchmark.

18.58   While the United Kingdom has not yet ratified the Council of Europe Biomedicine Convention nor signed the Additional Protocol, the requirements of the EC Directive and the 2004 Regulations are in effect and reflect many of the terms of the Protocol. Moreover, they seek to apply both a principled and pragmatic approach to clinical trials research involving incapacitated persons. As to principles, the Regulations provide in Schedule 1, Part 5 that the following underpin research involving the incompetent: (1) informed consent given by a legal representative to an incapacitated adult in a clinical trial shall represent that adult's presumed will, (2) the clinical trial has been designed to minimise pain, discomfort, fear and any other foreseeable risk in relation to the disease and the cognitive abilities of the patient, (3) the risk threshold and the degree of distress have to be specially defined and constantly monitored and, (4) the interests of the patient always prevail over those of science and society.

18.59   The Regulations also lay down some eleven conditions for lawful research. In these, the subject's legal representative is central, and the same provisions regarding research involving competent persons apply equally to the representative of the incapax.

18.60   The provisions of the Mental Capacity Act 2005 also consider research involving incapable adults but these explicitly exclude subjects involved in clinical trials (governed by the 2004 Regulations above).[103] Briefly, the approach taken is that the intrusive research is illegal unless the elements of the Act are complied with. The requirements are very similar save that, specifically, non-paid carers must be consulted as to the incapax's past (and likely present) views or wishes in respect of the research. Any indication, past or present, from the subject himself that he does not wish to participate must be respected. Importantly, however, and in contrast to the 2004 Regulations, the role of the carer is not to give or withhold their consent but rather 'to advise' on whether the incapacitated person should take part in the research. The ethics committee is the final approval authority.

18.61   While the 2004 Regulations now also apply to Scotland for clinical trials, the situation there in respect of all forms of research has been clear for the last few years where research on incompetent adults has been regulated by primary legislation.[104] The necessary conditions almost exactly parallel those laid down in the Additional Protocol to the Council of Europe Convention save that, in addition, authority for surrogate consent is specifically vested in a person appointed as the incapax's

---

[102] N 10 above, Article 15. See also the general agreement with the Declaration of Helsinki, para 24.
[103] Mental Capacity Act 2005, ss 30–34.   [104] Adults with Incapacity (Scotland) Act 2000, s 51.

guardian or welfare attorney; where there is no appointed guardian welfare attorney, power to consent lies with the subject's nearest relative.[105]

18.62 The Scottish legislation provides a list of relatives who have authority to act for the incapacity in the order that they appear in the list;[106] the position south of the border can be discerned from the COREC Guidance on Consent in Clinical Trials which similarly details a 'hierarchy of consent' for legal representatives.[107]

THE UNETHICAL RESEARCHER

18.63 All that has gone before has assumed that the researcher is acting in good faith with the interests of the profession and of the public at heart. Occasionally, however, concern arises both as to non-intentional conduct of researchers which falls short of acceptable ethical standards as well as to intentionally fraudulent behaviour[108] and/or the publication of frankly fraudulent studies.[109] An international survey of biostatisticians working closely with medical researchers revealed in 2000, for example, that 51 per cent of respondents were aware of fraudulent projects, extending from the fabrication or falsification of data through deceptive research design and reporting and on to the deliberate suppression of 'unfavourable' results.[110]

18.64 Doctors are under some pressure in this area. The competitive spirit may have a lamentable effect on high-profile research. The temptation to falsify results or to suppress the truth may be too much for some scientists, particularly when there is a prospect of high earnings from commercial deals. Even in the more mundane reaches of medicine, the senior academic who publishes frequently is likely to attract more funding than his colleague who does not, and the advantage of 'being first' encourages premature reporting. More importantly, advancement in hierarchical medicine now depends heavily on the number of publications to the junior's credit. Such influences can lead to 'sloppy science' which is, perhaps, understandable. There is, however, no excuse for the deliberate falsification of results.[111] The danger in these cases is that the

---

[105] In the 2000 Act the reader is referred to the Mental Health (Scotland) Act 1984, ss 53–57 for a definition of the term 'nearest relative' but this Act was repealed by the Mental Health (Care and Treatment) (Scotland) Act 2003, s 254 of which now defines the term.

[106] *Ibid*, s 254(1)(b).

[107] The COREC Guidance on Consent in Clinical Trials, n 101 above, para 18.

[108] Ten cases of scientific fraud were processed through the disciplinary committee of the GMC between 1987 and 1993: S Kingman 'GMC may not pay legal costs for investigating Fraud' (1993) 307 BMJ 403. The penalties for scientific fraud are severe, and include that of being struck off the register for misconduct: C Dyer 'Doctor Admits Research Fraud' (1998) 316 BMJ 647.

[109] See generally, S Lock, F Wells and M Farthing (eds) *Fraud and Misconduct in Biomedical Research*, 3rd edn (2001).

[110] J Ranstain, M Bayse, S L George et al 'Fraud in Medical Research: An International Survey of Biostatisticians' (2000) 21 Controlled Trials 415.

[111] A number of high-profile examples were reported in the late 1980s and early 1990s: J Smith 'Preventing Fraud' (1991) 302 BMJ 362.

public, often prompted by the news media, may be led to believe in therapeutic claims which are unsupported by the available data or that, as a result, they may be subjected to valueless or dangerous treatment schedules. The issue is also, understandably, of great interest to pharmaceutical companies, who may be wrongly deprived of profits if a drug is withdrawn from the market on the basis of fraudulent results.[112]

18.65   This happened in the case of Debendox, which was withdrawn after claims by the Australian gynaecologist, William McBride, that the drug could cause deformities in a small proportion of the children of those women to whom it was administered. An inquiry by the New South Wales Medical Tribunal subsequently concluded that McBride claimed statistically significant results where none, in fact, existed.[113] McBride is reported as saying that he had changed his data in 'the long-term interests of humanity'.[114] A more recent example is the controversy surrounding the claim that the MMR vaccine is linked to autism in children.[115] The initial publication in *The Lancet*[116] has been subject to strong challenges on both scientific[117] and ethical grounds.[118] The main ethical allegation is that of conflict of interest whereby the principal investigator in the MMR study, Dr Andrew Wakefield, had not disclosed that at the time of the research he had been paid £55,000 by the Legal Aid Board to advise on whether the families of some of the children in the study might be able to sue for vaccine damage.

18.66   The fraudulent researcher, of course, faces a variety of sanctions. He may be criminally liable for fraudulently obtaining research funds, and he could, also, face civil action for any loss incurred by drug manufacturers. In addition, there are powerful professional disciplinary procedures that can effectively end a scientific career. Indeed, as we go to press the General Medical Council has announced a public hearing scheduled for late 2005/early 2006 to determine Dr Wakefield's fitness to practise medicine in light of the allegations surrounding his MMR study.

18.67   The problem of the unethical researcher has concerned the medical and publishing world for some time.[119] The Committee on Publication Ethics (COPE) was founded

[112] The effect of publication of results—genuine as well as fraudulent—on the stock-market has also to be considered. Researchers who also trade in the relevant pharmaceutical shares may find themselves in breach of the Company Securities (Insider Dealing) Act 1985: see D S Freestone and H Mitchell 'Inappropriate Publication of Trial Results and Potential for Allegations of Illegal Share Dealing' (1993) 306 BMJ 1112.

[113] M Ragg 'Australia: McBride Guilty of Scientific Fraud' (1993) 341 Lancet 550.

[114] N Swan 'Australian Doctor Admits Fraud' (1991) 302 BMJ 1421.

[115] This is discussed from a public health perspective in chapter 2.

[116] A Wakefield et al 'Ileal-lymphoid-nodular Hyperplasia, Non-specific Colitis, and Pervasive Development Disorder in Children' (1998) 351 The Lancet 637.

[117] See, for example, K M Madsen et al 'A Population-Based Study of Measles, Mumps and Rubella Vaccination and Autism' (2002) 347 New Eng J Med 1477.

[118] See, for example the Medico-Legal Investigations Newsletter (March 2004): www.medicolegal-investigations.com/news8.htm and the on-going campaign by Sunday Times journalist Brian Deer: http://briandeer.com/mmr-lancet.htm.

[119] Medico-Legal Investigations Ltd was set up in 1996 to investigate allegations of fraud and research misconduct and to assist in the bring of criminal and professional disciplinary proceedings: www.medicolegal-investigations.com/. A succinct leading editorial article is to be found in M J Tobin 'Reporting Research, Retraction of Results and Responsibility' (2000) 162 Amer J Respir Crit Care Med 773.

in 1997 by medical journal editors to address their growing concern about the number of breaches of research and publication ethics they were witnessing in their work.[120] Fifty-one cases of major research misconduct were reported to COPE in 2001 with a further 23 in 2002 and 30 in 2003. Numerous others were being investigated by the Association of British Pharmaceutical Industries and the General Medical Council during this period.[121] The US Office for Research Integrity has seen a marked rise in allegations of research misconduct in recent years—38 new cases in 1998, 51 in 1999, 59 in 2000, jumping to 274 in 2004 (being 50 per cent higher than 2003).[122] Although it has been pointed out that 70 per cent of cases prove to be innocent on investigation,[123] the figures remain alarming. Yet, while the United States and many other countries have established bodies to tackle this issue, the same has not been true in the United Kingdom. No less than a former editor of the BMJ has accused Britain of institutional complacency and arrogant inaction in respect of addressing research misconduct[124] and, despite the efforts of various august bodies to prompt some sort of consolidated response,[125] nothing that attracted governmental support happened until early 2005 when Universities UK (UUK) announced the creation of the UK Panel for Health and Biomedical Research Integrity, to commence work in October 2005.[126] The extent of governmental support remains unclear at the time of writing: funding for the body is expected to come from the Department of Health but contributions from the pharmaceutical industry have also not been ruled out thereby shrouding the Panel in controversy before it has even begun its work.[127] The remit of the Panel would be to promote good research practices, to prevent research misconduct and to develop nationwide codes of practice on optimal standards for all research in Universities and the NHS. The Panel would not have the power to investigate alleged misconduct itself but, rather, would advise other bodies on such investigations. This is at odds with the function of similar bodies elsewhere, such as in the US or Denmark, where an investigatory remit imbues the watchdog with considerable regulatory power.

18.68   It is an offence to provide a research ethics committee with false or misleading

---

[120] www.publicationethics.org.uk. The website offers an excellent resource whereby case studies detailing research and publication dilemmas are outlined together with advice on how they should be addressed.

[121] R Jones 'Research Misconduct' (2002) 19 Fam Pract 123.

[122] Office of Research Integrity Newsletter, March 2005, available at: http://ori.dhhs.gov.

[123] C Martyn 'Fabrication, Falsification and Plagarism' (2003) 96 Q J Med 243.

[124] S Lock 'Britain Prefers Talk to Action: Which is Why it has Failed to Tackle Research Misconduct' (2003) 327 BMJ 940, and from another former editor see R Smith 'The Need for a National Body for Research Misconduct' (1998) 316 BMJ 1686.

[125] See, for example, Royal College of Physicians of Edinburgh, *Consensus Statement on Misconduct in Biomedical Research* (1999), available at: www.rcpe.ac.uk/esd/consensus/misconduct_99.html, and P Stonier, GDO Lowe, G McInnes, J Murie, J Petrie, and F Wells, 'A National Panel for Research Integrity: A Proposed Blueprint for the Prevention and Investigation of Misconduct in Biomedical Research' (2001) 31 *Proc R Coll Physicians Edin* 253.

[126] C White 'UK Agency to Combat Research Misconduct' (2005) 330 BMJ 616.

[127] See, J Giles 'Plans for Research Watchdog Praised, But it May Lack Teeth' (2005) 434 (7031) Nature 263.

information in a research application relating to a CTIMP.[128] Furthermore, the Standard Operating Procedures for ethics committees make it clear that a committee must report evidence of fraud or misconduct to its appointing authority and COREC, as well as to the MHRA when the research relates to clinical trials.[129] These bodies then decide on what further action to pursue; ethics committees should not undertake their own investigations, but they can review and suspend their prior favourable opinion in light of an allegation of misconduct.

18.69   The public-spirited objective of research, as we have said, is to produce generalisable knowledge to improve human health. But private interests are invariably also at stake for those involved in conducting the research, not all of which can be reconciled with the greater public good; this, then, can lead to unethical practice. In this respect, we must differentiate between two sets of actors: the researchers and their funders. Researchers must publish, again as we have seen, and to this extent there need be no conflict with the public interest: society must know one way or another whether new innovations are better or worse for us. But funders may at times have an interest in keeping unfavourable results out of the public domain. While this may not amount to outright public deception, there may be many reasons for a commercial enterprise to wish to protect its financial interests by questioning or disputing the value of research that goes against those interests. The dilemma is no better illustrated than by the Olivieri affair which attracted such attention as to merit an entire edition of the *Journal of Medical Ethics*.[130]

18.70   In brief, the affair concerned a triangular relationship between Dr Olivieri, expert in haematology and professor at the University of Toronto, the University as her employer, and Apotex Inc., which agreed to fund trials on a new treatment of thalassemia to be conducted by Dr Olivieri. Importantly, Apotex also entered discussions with the University around this time involving multi-million dollar supportive donations by the company. When Dr Olivieri became concerned about some trial results and for the safety of her patients, and wanted to act on these concerns (inter alia, by informing the patients), she received warnings from Apotex alleging a potential breach of the confidentiality clause of her contract should she do so. Moreover, Olivieri received little support from the University and, it is alleged, was at one point constructively dismissed by the Institution over the dispute. The outcome was the establishment of a Task Force to examine the issues of conflict of interests and freedom of research in Canada, and Dr Olivieri has since published numerous articles disputing the claims of Apotex as to the safety of their treatment. But the affair highlights the fundamental importance of publishing all kinds of results—both the positive and the negative—as well as drawing attention to the need to address the dangers of public/private partnerships in research whereby the interests of the

---

[128] SOPs, n 39 above, para 9.60 and 2004 Regulations, reg 49.
[129] SOPs, *ibid*, para 9.58.
[130] 'The Olivieri Symposium' (2004) 30(1) J Med Ethics.

partners may come into conflict with those of the researchers and the wider public.[131] There cannot, however, be any doubt as the hierarchy of values in this context (as the Additional Protocol and the EU Directive make clear): (1) the interests of the patient always prevail over those of science and society and (2) freedom of research must be preserved.

18.71   The considerable increase in research regulation activity—and bureaucracy—in Europe and the rest of the Western world has driven some researchers to pursue their work elsewhere—most notably to developing countries where research populations may be more accessible and programmes are subject to less intense scrutiny.[132] Notwithstanding this, the ethical imperatives surrounding research involving human beings remain more or less universal; the lack of local regulation is no excuse for not respecting the ethical fundamentals at stake.[133]

QUESTIONABLE EXPERIMENTATION

18.72   We have already referred to the closely allied problem of experimental treatment where the difficulty may lie in distinguishing courageous innovation from unethical experimentation—and, human nature being what it is, the answer often depends on the outcome. The case which remains most vividly in the memory is that in which a baboon's heart was transplanted into a neonate with congenital heart disease.[134] The parents of the child were unmarried minors and doubts have been expressed as to whether they could give 'informed consent' in the true sense. A consultant summed up the procedure:

I think this xenograft is premature because I am not aware of any finding in the clinical literature that suggests anything but the prevailing rule—the human body will reject a transplanted animal organ. Baby Fae will reject her baboon heart within the next week or two, and cyclosporine will not prevent it.[135]

18.73   Most would agree with this assessment—Baby Fae actually survived for two and a half weeks—but the procedure had been approved by the university's institutional research board and there was some further professional support for the operation. Nevertheless, it does appear to be an example of premature experimental treatment which fails the test of a reasonable chance.

18.74   We are left with the complex problem of whether or not information gained from

---

[131] For a notable British example, consider the case of Nottingham University which accepted almost £4m from British American Tobacco to fund its International Centre for Corporate Social Responsibility. For strong critique see S Chapman and S Shatenstein 'The Ethics of the Cash Register: Taking Tobacco Research Dollars' (2001) 10 Tob Control 1.

[132] D Cyranoski 'Chinese Clinical Trials: Consenting Adults? Not Necessarily . . .' (2005) 435 Nature 138.

[133] See, Nuffield Council on Bioethics The Ethics of Research Relating to Healthcare in Developing Countries (2002) and the follow-up discussion paper from March 2005, both available at: www.nuffieldbioethics.org.

[134] L L Hubband 'The Baby Fae Case' (1987) 6 Med Law 385.

[135] Details taken from H S Schwartz 'Bioethical and Legal Considerations in Increasing the Supply of Transplantable Organs: From UAGA to "Baby Fae" ' (1985) 10 Amer J Law Med 397.

frankly immoral research should be used for the general good—the classic, and ultimate, examples being data obtained in the concentration camps of the Second World War. The arguments are finely balanced. In the end, we subscribe to the view that the fact that children do not, say, now die from certain forms of hypothermia is best regarded as a monument to those who suffered and died to make it possible; if the material is used, they will, at least, not have done so in vain.

COMPENSATION FOR PERSONAL INJURY IN RESEARCH

18.75   The research volunteer who is injured in the course of medical research may resort to a claim for compensation under the law of tort. Such a route, of course, may prove to be difficult: researchers may have taken every precaution to avoid injury and there may therefore be no evidence of negligence. A few years ago, one would have said that an action based on inadequate provision of information would be unlikely to succeed unless the failure of disclosure was of an obviously material nature; now, one would not be so sure. Lord Woolf's move towards increased attention to the expectations of the reasonable patient, expressed in *Pearce*,[136] has yet to work its way through the courts and consent in the context of research would be expected to attract particularly harsh inquiry. Nevertheless, although the odds against a plaintiff in such actions may not be as long as they were, the research subject could still be in a somewhat uncertain situation and it is, no doubt, for this reason that all modern guidelines or directives as to the management of research projects emphasise the importance of compulsory protection of subjects against the possibility of mishap. Thus, as already noted, the EC Directive states unequivocally that a clinical trial may be undertaken only if, inter alia, provision has been made for insurance or indemnity to cover the liability of the investigator and sponsor (Article 3(2)(f)) while, before approving a proposal, a REC in the United Kingdom must, currently, be adequately reassured as to the insurance and indemnity arrangements for treatment and compensation in the event of injury, disablement or death of a research participant attributable to participation in the research.[137]

18.76   As to what constitutes reassurance, the SOPs state that, in the case of NHS-sponsored research, NHS indemnity will be conferred after a favourable ethical opinion from the REC and once final management permission is given for the research.[138] Non-NHS sponsors must provide evidence of adequate insurance cover with details of the extent of cover and the source of funds.[139] When the research relates to commercially-sponsored CTIMPs or new medical devices, compensation

---

[136] *Pearce v United Bristol Healthcare NHS Trust* (1999) 48 BMLR 118 at 124.
[137] Guidelines, para 9.15(l) and SOPs paras 3.39–3.43.   [138] SOPs, para 3.41.
[139] *Ibid*, para 3.40.

may be available under the schemes administered by the Association of British Pharmaceutical Industry (ABPI) or Association of British Health-Care Industry (ABHI). If so, the REC should receive sufficient details of the form of indemnity to be deployed.[140] None of this, of course, guarantees the research subject adequate compensation should anything go wrong. We suspect that most commentators would favour a form of no-fault compensation but the answer lies in the hands of government.

RESEARCH INVOLVING HUMAN TISSUE AND PERSONAL DATA

18.77　The discussion thus far has proceeded on the assumption that research or experimentation will involve some direct intrusion of the physical integrity of the research subject, i.e. some form of bodily touching. This, of course, is by no means necessary for many forms of research, particularly of epidemiological type, which can be conducted quite happily without any need to involve the subject directly. Patient data and samples taken or given previously for unrelated purposes (such as treatment) are, in fact, the source of potentially very valuable medical research. On one view, the use of data in patient records or archived samples subjects the patient to no further discomfort and it could be thought reasonable to pursue research in the name of the 'public good'. By the same token, there is a clear element of potential invasion of the patient's privacy in 'finding out things' about him without his consent, not to mention the sense of indignation, or even outrage, that can be generated at the idea of using these 'personal' rudiments—again, without the proper authority to do so. It was precisely this reaction that provoked the investigations at Bristol and Alder Hey into the retention of body parts for 'research purposes' that we have discussed already in chapter 15.

18.78　The problems here are manifold, not least because the 'call for consent' is not always realisable, nor is it necessarily desirable in some cases. For example, if a researcher wishes to examine tissue samples gathered many decades previously, is it reasonable to expect him to attempt to obtain consent from all the persons from whom the samples were taken—persons who may have moved, married or died years before? The cost implications alone may make any such study non-viable *ab initio*.[141] Another example relates to longitudinal studies, i.e. those that propose to study subjects over many years and usually by on-going review of their medical records. Given that, by its very nature research generates new knowledge, is it reasonable to require

---

[140]　*Ibid*, para 3.42.

[141]　P N Furness and M L Nicholson 'Obtaining Explicit Consent for the Use of Archival Tissue Samples: Practical Issues' (2004) 30 J Med Ethics 561.

researchers to revisit subjects on a regular basis in order to obtain re-consent in the light of developments in the research?

18.79   A crude analysis of these examples might cast the core issue as one of pitting cost and convenience against consent. This, however, would be to misconstrue the dilemma which, in fact, arises from trying to force the issues into the consent paradigm—that is, from the belief that consent is 'the' answer to (all) ethical concerns.[142] It must be remembered, however, that consent itself is a means to an end and that the real aim is to respect persons and their interests. Consent is but one means by which to achieve this. In this vein, then, we have the Medical Research Council (MRC) opining that 'existing holdings' of tissue samples can be used for research even in the absence of consent if: (a) the samples are anonymised, (b) there is no potential harm to the donors through the research use, (c) the researchers are satisfied that the samples were not obtained unethically and, in particular, that there was valid consent to the 'taking', and (d) when a research ethics committee agrees that the research can proceed.[143] By the same token, the MRC's guidance re-inforces the point that, in future, the possibility of later research should be explained and appropriate consent obtained. But this still leaves the problem of what is meant by 'appropriate consent', especially in the context of long-term studies. Here the MRC has stated more recently that 'broad consent' is an acceptable concept whereby it is consent to 'future medical research projects which would have to be approved by a properly constituted research ethics committee'.[144] Thus we can see how the protectionist role of the ethics committee can be employed to circumvent some of the thornier issues surrounding specific consent.

18.80   Nevertheless, it is undeniable that consent remains the primary policy device in legitimating medical research. This is seen in both pieces of legislation governing research on personal data and samples, being respectively, the Data Protection Act 1998 and the Human Tissue Act 2004. Having said this, it is to be noted that neither Act requires consent in all circumstances, and both fall back on anonymisation as a way of permitting research to continue in the absence of consent.[145] Anonymisation here is essentially a means to protect research subjects' privacy interests[146] and justification, once again, lies in the ill-defined notion of the public interest.[147] But the

---

[142] See further O Corrigan 'Empty Ethics: The Problem with Informed Consent' (2003) 25 Sociology of Health and Illness 768.

[143] Medical Research Council, *Human Tissue and Biological Samples for Use in Research* (2001), para 10.2, and see also now: *MRC Operational and Ethical Guidelines: Human Tissue and Biological Samples for Use in Research—Clarification Following Passage of the Human Tissue Act 2004* (2005), both available at: www.mrc.ac.uk.

[144] *Ibid*, Guidelines (2005), para 4.4.

[145] The provisions of the 1998 Act do not apply to anonymised data; the Human Tissue Act 2004, s 1(9) is authority for conducting research on anonymised samples without consent (although suitable ethical approval is required). In neither case must the data or sample be 'irrreversibly anonymised', that is, that a link between the data and a person can never again be made.

[146] For a discussion of anonymisation in the common law context the reader is referred to chapter 7 and the case of *R v Department of Health, ex p Source Informatics Ltd* [2001] QB 424, [2000] 1 All ER 786, CA.

[147] Further guidance is available from the Information Commissioner's Office *Use and Disclosure of Health Data* (2002), especially chapters 3 and 4.

problems continue because of the not infrequent loss of useful data that accompanies anonymisation. Some forms of research simply cannot succeed in the absence of access to data from which individual subjects can be identified. Sections 60–61 of the Health and Social Care Act 2001 seek to address this in England and Wales. These provisions allow the Secretary of State to make regulations permitting uses of (identifiable) patient data, inter alia, in the public interest and provide for the establishment of the Patient Information Advisory Group (PIAG) to oversee any applications for such uses. PIAG's 2004 Report reveals the extensive work that the Group has undertaken since its establishment, including the development of clear guidelines as to when s 60 can be used. For example, the Group will only entertain an application when it is demonstrated that 'there is no other reasonably practicable way . . . of carrying out activities that require the use of patient identifiable information'. Moreover, it continues '. . . it must be shown that the activity cannot practicably rely upon patient consent or the use of anonymised data in the near future'.[148] A similar, yet more ad hoc, approval system operates in Scotland through the Privacy Advisory Committee set up by the Chief Medical Officer for Scotland.[149]

NEW APPROACHES TO RESEARCH GOVERNANCE

18.81   We end this chapter with a brief discussion of emerging, more holistic, approaches to research governance. The plethora of legal instruments and official guidance which has so recently invaded the sphere of medical research sadly does little to improve the most important relationship in the entire research enterprise—namely, that between researcher and research subject. For the researcher, the foregoing discussion must seem like a bureaucratic nightmare from which he can only hope to wake up unaffected,[150] while the research subject may find that the net result of all this additional protection may simply be that there is more paperwork to read and sign. But, as the complexities of conducting research have increased, so too sensitivity to the related ethical and social issues has heightened in many quarters. There are now numerous examples of research endeavours which are not content simply to follow the prescribed regulatory path but which, rather, seek to adopt a 'Regulation-Plus' approach that engages more directly and more fully with the ethical, legal, and social issues at stake. Two related examples illustrate the point.

18.82   UK Biobank is funded by the Wellcome Trust and the Medical Research Council in order to develop a resource from which to facilitate research into the relationship

---

[148] Patient Information Advisory Group *Annual Report July 2003-June 2004* (2004), para 4.3.

[149] Privacy Advisory Committee website: www.show.scot.nhs.uk/confidentiality/externalresources/pac.htm.

[150] See, as an example, J Peto, O Fletcher and C Gilham 'Data Protection, Informed Consent, and Research' (2004) 328 BMJ 1029.

between genetics and environment in the development of human disease.[151] The project seeks to recruit 500,000 healthy participants aged between 40–69 years and to follow them and their health status through the final stages of their lives. It will involve taking blood samples from participants and securing on-going access to and scrutiny of their medical records. The 'up-front' approach adopted by the funders towards the attendant ethical, legal and social (ELSA) issues is of interest from the regulatory perspective. An Interim Advisory Group on Ethics and Governance was established at the same time as the research protocol was being developed to advise the funders on *how* UK Biobank should be set up and operate. All aspects of the project were considered—from consent through confidentiality and on to commercialisation. The recommendations were then put out to public consultation and a final framework was agreed in light of the response. Central to that framework is the establishment of a permanent Ethics and Governance Council to act as a 'mirror' to UK Biobank in respect of its activities and its relationship with participants. The important point to note is that all of this has been done *in addition* to the ethical regulatory requirements we have outlined and discussed above. Moreover, the fact that the ELSA discussion took place while the research protocol was being developed left open the possibility that one might influence the other and vice versa. It is an example of a genuine attempt to make ethics and science work in tandem so as to optimise the operation of the research project from all viewpoints.

18.83   A very similar project called Generation Scotland is being developed north of the border.[152] It too will explore the relationship between genes and environment although the recruitment base will be Scottish families of all ages, including those with family members who are ill. Generation Scotland has also adopted a similar up-front ELSA approach with a very strong programme of research into public engagement. The aim is to respond as far as is possible to public views and concerns about the project; this extends from design of the project itself to issues such as the commercialisation of the outputs of research.[153] Ultimately, the exercise serves to re-enforce one of the most crucial lessons in this field: human biomedical research is impossible without the participation and the support of the public.

[151] UK Biobank website: www.ukbiobank.ac.uk.

[152] Generation Scotland website: www.generationscotland.org/.

[153] See G Haddow, G Laurie, S Cunningham-Burley and K G Hunter 'Tackling Community Concerns about Commercialisation and Genetic Research: A M Interdisciplinary Proposal', forthcoming.

19

RESEARCH ON CHILDREN, FETUSES AND EMBRYOS

19.1 A child is by no means a miniature version of an adult. Children respond differently to drugs, as they do to a number of other treatments, and it is impossible to say that the effect of a particular therapy on an adult will be mirrored when applied to a child. Medical research on children is, therefore, necessary before a treatment can be approved for paediatric use. As in adults, such research may entail not only therapeutic research on sick children but also essential non-therapeutic research on normal control groups; it is this non-therapeutic research which poses the most controversial ethical and legal problems.[1] These should, however, be kept in perspective. Research involving children has lowered the rate of infant mortality considerably; for example, research on vitamin A deficiency in children in developing countries has made it possible to lower mortality rates among those affected by measles.[2] Similarly, research on mother/child transmission of HIV has reduced the incidence of infection in the children of infected mothers—an important matter in the control of the global pandemic. At the same time, numerous surveys also indicate that there is a worrying dearth of well-conducted research involving children.[3] One study by community paediatricians, for example, found that quality research to support their clinical decisions only existed in 40 per cent of cases.[4]

19.2   Such research as there is involves a variety of procedures, ranging from the completely benign—such as studies of weight and height—to those which are frankly invasive. As an example of the latter, the Institute of Medical Ethics cited a French project which involved lumbar punctures on newborn infants for non-therapeutic reasons.[5] There is also evidence that other dangerous procedures have been used with

[1] For general discussion of the issue, see J K Mason *Medico-Legal Aspects of Reproduction and Parenthood* (2nd edn, 1998) p 319 et seq.

[2] Working Group on Women and Child Health, F Dabis, J Orne-Gliemann, F Perez et al 'Improving Child Health: the Role of Research' (2002) 324 BMJ 1444.

[3] R L Smyth, 'Research with Children' (2001) 322 BMJ 1377.

[4] M Rudolf et al 'A Search for the Evidence Supporting Community Paediatric Practice' (1999) 80 Arch Dis Child 257.

[5] See R H Nicholson (ed) *Medical Research with Children: Ethics, Law and Practice* (1990) p 19.

children being exposed to radiation and unproved vaccines.[6] Such investigations would not be approved by research ethics committees today, but the conclusions of the Alder Hey Inquiry into the post-mortem retention of children's organs remind us of the fact that research might still be conducted with scant regard to the rights and sensitivities of others.[7] The Court of Appeals of Maryland recently identified the kernel of the issue thus:

It is not in the best interest of a specific child, in a non-therapeutic research project, to be placed in a research environment, which might possibly be, or which proves to be, hazardous to the health of the child. We have long stressed that the 'best interests of the child' is the overriding concern of this Court in matters relating to children. Whatever the interests of a parent, and whatever the interests of the general public in fostering research that might, according to a researcher's hypothesis, be for the good of all children, this Court's concern for the particular child and particular case, over-arches all other interests.[8]

19.3   We suggest that the same sentiment underlies the legal framework in the United Kingdom; notwithstanding this, there has been little judicial treatment of the topic, as we will see.

NON-THERAPEUTIC RESEARCH ON CHILDREN

19.4   The essential difficulty with non-therapeutic research on children lies, as we have noted in the previous chapter, in the question of consent. An adult may be able to give an informed, and therefore valid, consent to participation in research—but can the same be said of a child? If a child can consent for him or herself—that is, if his or her autonomy is sufficiently developed—then it may be acceptable, ethically at least, to allow the child to consent on his or her own behalf.[9] Indeed, the child should be consulted in any circumstances involving his or her personal integrity and, if the child's capacity is found to be such that he or she *can* consent, then the child's wishes should always be respected; but would that be enough on its own to authorise research? We come to the legal position below, simply noting for present purposes that this is another example of where one may legitimately argue as to the role of the

---

[6] The *Final Report of the Advisory Committee on Human Radiation Experiments* (Washington, 2000) contains a valuable account of the history of experimentation on children, as well as extensive information on radiation experiments: http://tis.eh.doe.gov/ohre/roadmap/achre/report.html.

[7] H Bauchner and R Vinci 'What Have We Learnt from the Alder Hey Affair?' (2001) 322 BMJ 309 and S Dewar and P Boddington 'Returning to the Alder Hey Report and its Reporting: Addressing Confusions and Improving Inquiries' (2004) 30 J Med Ethics 463.

[8] *Grimes v Kennedy-Krieger Institute; Higgins v Kennedy-Krieger Institute* 782 A2d 807 (2001). For critical comment, see V Hassner Sharav 'Children in Clinical Research: A Conflict of Moral Values' (2003) 3 Am J Bioethics W12.

[9] For a range of views on the child and consent in the research context see: American Journal of Bioethics (2003) vol. 3(4), especially D Wendler and S Shah 'Should Children Decide Whether They Are Enrolled in Non-Beneficial Research?' (2003) 3 Am J Bioethics 1.

law in respect of the mature minor: should the law respect a child's developing autonomy in respect of *any* decision, or should it remain protective and restrictive of the child's autonomy until such time as legal adulthood is attained?[10]

19.5 And what of the child who is clearly unable to exercise his or her self-determination? The Declaration of Helsinki specifically mentions the 'legally incompetent' participant in research, stating that the consent of the guardian should be procured;[11] this approach was also adopted in the guidelines on research issued by the Royal College of Paediatrics and Child Health,[12] the Medical Research Council,[13] the British Medical Association[14] and, in the United States, by the National Institutes of Health.[15] All of these influential bodies accept that non-therapeutic research on children is justified when it is intended to benefit other children—although it should not be carried out if it can be done equally well using adults.

19.6 Parental consent will not be sufficient if proposed non-therapeutic research involves more than a minimal risk to the child—a condition which, inevitably, raises the issue of what risks are minimal. Federal Regulations in the United States have held that the risk is minimal where 'the probability and magnitude of harm or discomfort anticipated in the research are not greater in and of themselves than those ordinarily encountered in daily life or during the performance of routine physical or psychological examinations or tests.'[16] The Institute of Medical Ethics, which studied the question in-depth in the 1980s,[17] defined a minimal risk as one which carried a risk of death lower than 1:1,000,000, a risk of major complications less than 1:100,000 and a risk of minor complications of less than 1:1,000.[18] The American approach uses language; this approach uses figures. Both convey the same general message: a risk has ceased to be minimal where there is a risk that makes one stop and think.[19] In

---

[10] The Additional Protocol on Biomedical Research (2005) to the Council of Europe Convention on Biomedicine and Human Rights (1997) states specifically in Article 15(1)(iv) that: 'The opinion of a minor shall be taken into consideration as an increasingly determining factor in proportion to age and degree of maturity'.

[11] World Medical Association *Ethical Principles for Medical Research Involving Human Subjects* (Revised, 2000), para 25. The Declaration is reproduced in Appendix D.

[12] Royal College of Paediatrics and Child Health: Ethics Advisory Committee 'Guidelines for the Ethical Conduct of Medical Research Involving Children' (2000) 82 Arch Dis Child 177.

[13] Medical Research Council *Medical Research Involving Children* (2004). For exceptional circumstances where guardians might not be involved see para 5.5.4.

[14] British Medical Association *Consent, Rights and Choice in Healthcare for Children and Young People* (2001).

[15] National Institutes of Health *Policy and Guidelines on the Inclusion of Children as Participants in Research Involving Human Subjects* (1998).

[16] 45 CFR Sec 46 (102.i) (1997).

[17] Institute of Medical Ethics 'Medical Research with Children: Ethics, Law and Practice' (1986) Bull no. 14, p 8. For discussion of the recommendations, see R J Robinson 'Ethics Committees and Research on Children' (1987) 294 BMJ 1243. See also M A Grodin, L H Glantz and A M Dellinger 'Children as Research Subjects: Science, Ethics and Law' (1996) 21 J Hlth Politics Policy Law 159.

[18] For a more recent discussion of assessment of risk, see D B Resnik 'Eliminating the Daily Life Risks Standard from the Definition of Minimal Risk' (2005) 31 J Med Ethics 35.

[19] For guidance on minimising risks, see National Academy of the Sciences *Ethical Conduct of Clinical Research Involving Children* (2004).

addition, the Institute thought that a child's consent should be obtained after the age of seven years. The recent MRC guidelines place considerable emphasise on evidence of child refusal, stating that: 'A child's refusal to participate or continue in research should always be respected . . . [i]f a child becomes upset by a procedure, researchers must accept this as a valid refusal'.[20] No age limit seems to be applied.

19.7   Obtaining parental consent is clearly important, but the fact that it has been given does not, of itself, justify carrying out research on children. Our first concern here must be with the welfare of the child, and it need hardly be said that parental consent to something which is obviously to the detriment of the child is unacceptable.[21] Parents do not have an absolute, unfettered right to regulate their children's lives; it is implicit in the modern concept of parenthood that the aim of such parental powers as there are is to protect and enhance the status of the child.[22] It follows that the researcher cannot simply say: 'The parents have consented and this means that I can go ahead'; parental consent may justify the involvement of children in non-therapeutic research but it will do so only when it points to the acceptability of the research in terms of some interest of the child.

19.8   One way of assessing parental consent is to see it as a substitute for the child's own judgment which cannot, as yet, be expressed. Under this theory, parental consent does no more than voice what the child would be expected to state, had he the ability to do so. Acceptance of this approach salves any qualms the researcher might have—in effect, the child consents to what is done, the only complication being that this cannot be expressed personally. Critics of theories of proxy consent point out that this involves a blatant fiction. It would be more honest, they argue, to accept that this constitutes non-consensual research and to admit the need to justify it on other grounds. The difficulty cannot be avoided by attempting to justify the child's involvement in terms of his 'future identification' with the decision made on his behalf.[23] It is difficult to see any distinction between 'identification' and 'consent' and, whatever terms one uses to imply future assent, there is no certainty that the child will, in fact, later endorse what his parents have decided. We have already noted, however, that the substituted judgment test has no role in UK law in respect of treatment and care; there is no reason why it should or would be any different in the context of research.

19.9   The matter may, none the less, be approached from an entirely different perspective

---

[20] MRC n 13 above, p 6.

[21] The converse is also true, namely, that parental objection to interventions which are deemed to be in the child's interests do not necessarily hold sway. See *Re MM (medical treatment)* [2000] 1 FLR 224, [2000] Fam Law 92 which, although dealing with treatment and not research per se, involved a dispute over the acceptability of risk in experimental circumstances. The court declared itself willing to override the parental objection if necessary.

[22] See B M Dickens 'The Modern Function and Limits of Parental Rights' (1981) 97 LQR 462; also A McCall Smith 'Is There Anything left of Parental Rights' in E Sutherland and A McCall Smith (eds) *Family Rights* (1991) ch 1.

[23] R B Redmon 'How Children Can Be Respected as Ends yet Still Be Used as Subjects in Non-therapeutic Research' (1986) 12 J Med Ethics 77.

— one which focuses not on any imagined consent of the child but on what is in that child's best interests. This test would allow the parents to involve the child in that which is in—or, alternatively, that which is not manifestly against—the child's best interests. The first of these would require that the non-therapeutic research secures some benefit for the child—a difficult, though not impossible, case to make. A child is a member of a class within the community—the class of children—and the individual can be said to be a potential beneficiary if research will benefit the class as a whole. It is also possible to extrapolate the reasoning used to justify organ donation (see chapter 14) and to argue that participation in research related to a disease from which, for example, a sibling is suffering will benefit the normal child—it being in his interests that his sibling should recover.

19.10   An allied benefit-based theory focuses on the altruistic nature of participation in non-therapeutic research.[24] Here, the issue is, at base, whether or not parents have the right to involve their children in projects by way of imposed selflessness. Such co-operation is undoubtedly good for the subject, but this would apply only if the child were sufficiently mature to understand the philanthropic nature of what he was doing. An older child may later derive satisfaction from the fact that he helped others when younger, but the same objection applies here as to proxy consent—how can we be sure that this is what he would feel?

19.11   The alternative interpretation of the best interests test, which allows for measures which are not to the actual detriment of the child—or not against its interests—clearly licenses the child's involvement in non-therapeutic research so long as the risks involved are negligible.[25] This assessment gives a wider discretion to the parent, who may choose to interpret his duty to society as including a duty to engage his children in pro-social activities. Such parents act within their rights, and cannot be regarded as abusing their position until such time as the child suffers actual harm or runs an appreciable risk of harm or demonstrates an unwillingness to proceed.[26]

19.12   It is now established beyond doubt that the best interests test is the legal determinant of acceptable treatment with respect to children. We have discussed this at length at various junctures so far.[27] The extension of the test in the context of research along the lines suggested above, however, would be a matter for judicial discretion; there is no ruling to date on whether the test would admit of such a generous reading. Certainly, the courts have been unsparing in recent years in fleshing out the test in respect of care, and the concept of *overall* interests has been employed time and again. We suggest that it would not be too much of a stretch of our imaginations to adopt a similar approach to child research—an approach that reflects the child's interests in

[24] See A McCall Smith 'Research and Experimentation Involving Children' in J K Mason (ed) *Paediatric Forensic Medicine and Pathology* (1989) p 469.

[25] For further discussion, see the wide-ranging recent analysis by A Plomer 'Participation of Children in Clinical Trials: UK, European and International Perspectives on Consent' (2000) 5 Med L Internat 1.

[26] The test of acceptability then becomes one of the 'reasonable parent': see J K Mason *Medico-legal Aspects of Reproduction and Parenthood* (2nd edn, 1998) p 324 et seq.

[27] See, for example, paras 16.13 and 16.33.

his broader relationships with the community; this would be subject always, and of course, to a minimal, negligible or non-existent risk to the child in question. The closest authority we have is the case of *Simms v Simms; A v A and Another*[28] which we discuss more fully in chapter 18. It will be recalled that the case related to a 16-year-old and an 18-year-old, both suffering from the incurable brain disease variant Creut-zfeldt-Jakob disease (vCJD). The patients could not consent for themselves and the President of the High Court applied the best interests test to authorise the application of a highly experimental treatment on the children—never before tested on humans—as a last chance therapeutic effort. The legal basis for doing so was the presence of medical evidence which agreed that there was at least a possibility that benefit might accrue. While this case was not concerned with non-therapeutic interventions as such, the extreme, untried nature of the intervention—the risks of which were unknown—blurs considerably the line between the two categories of research. We suspect that best interests may yet be deployed in the non-therapeutic context.

19.13   Thus far, we have assumed that the child in question is not of an age to give any meaningful consent. Even so, we have already made the point (at 19.4) that many children of relatively tender age will be able to understand the issues involved and the question then arises as to the weight to be given to any agreement they might give. The age at which a child can appreciate the implications of what he is doing will obviously vary, but some generalisations may be made.[29] Children under the age of seven are usually considered to be incapable of that degree of morally sophisticated thought required to make consistent altruistic decisions but, above that age, a child may be perfectly able to understand that he is helping doctors to cure others by taking part in the research programme.[30] A child who was not able to grasp the general idea of medical research by the age of 14 would probably be an exception today. This view is supported by a study which was designed to assess the ability of groups of nine- and 14-year-olds to make decisions relating to medical treatment. The 14-year-olds were shown to have the same general level of capacity to make this sort of decision as did adults and a surprising degree of competence was shown in the nine-year-old group.[31] The age of 14 has also been supported more recently as an acceptable cut-off for determining the ethics of research with children involving their own consent.[32]

---

[28] [2003] 2 WLR 1465, [2003] 1 All ER 669, [2003] 1 FCR 361.

[29] See J Berryman 'Discussing the Ethics of Research on Children' in J van Eys (ed) *Research on Children* (1978) p 85. See discussion by P Alderson and J Montgomery *Health Care Choices: Making Decisions with Children* (1996); M Paul 'Informed Consent in Medical Research. Children from the Age of 5 should be Presumed Competent' (1997) 314 BMJ 1480.

[30] Cf, N Ondrusek et al 'Empirical Examination of the Ability of Children to Consent to Clinical Research' (1998) 24 J Med Ethics 158.

[31] L A Weithorn and S B Campbell 'The Competency of Children and Adolescents to make Informed Treatment Decisions' (1982) 53 Child Develop 285. For discussion, see R H Nicholson (ed) *Medical Research with Children* (1986) p 146.

[32] K Toner and R Schwartz, 'Why a Teenager over Age 14 Should Be Able to Consent, Rather than Merely Assent, to Participation as a Human Subject of Research' (2003) 3 Am J Bioethics 38. Cf, R Ashcroft, T Goodenough, J Kent and E Williamson 'Children's Consent to Research Participation: Social Context and Personal Experience Invalidate Fixed Cutoff Rules' (2003) 3 Am J Bioethics 16.

19.14   The ethical issues might be clarified to an extent if the law could give a clear answer to this question. Unfortunately, the law itself is uncertain in this area and this has not eased the difficulties of those involved in paediatric research. As long ago as 1962 the Medical Research Council stated that:

> in the strict view of the law, parents and guardians of minors cannot give consent on their behalf to any procedures which are of no particular benefit to them and which may carry some risk of harm.[33]

19.15   This was followed by a Department of Health circular which confirmed that interpretation in a negative way:

> Health authorities are advised that they ought not to infer [from a Royal College of Physicians' recommendation that children can be used in certain forms of research provided the consent of the guardian has been obtained] that the fact that consent has been given by the parent or guardian and that the risk involved is considered negligible will be sufficient to bring such clinical research investigation within the law as it stands.[34]

19.16   The advice of the Department of Health was roundly attacked by doctors. Lawyers were also critical of this strict view of the law, pointing out the paucity of authority on the point.[35] The position remains more or less the same to this day. In these conditions—almost amounting to a legal vacuum—the proper way of approaching the issue is to look at general legal principles governing the parent/child relationship and to infer from these what a court might decide if the matter were to come before it.[36]

19.17   The judgment of the House of Lords in *Gillick v West Norfolk and Wisbech Area Health Authority*[37] confirmed the view that the consent of a minor to medical treatment may be adequate even without parental ratification provided that the child has sufficient understanding and intelligence to appreciate what is involved. 'Parental rights', said Lord Scarman, 'exist only so long they are needed for the protection of the person and property of the child'. It is not certain, however, whether the *Gillick* principle, which is concerned with consent to treatment, would be applied to cases of non-therapeutic experimentation. Much would, of course, depend on the severity of the procedure—this being one of the factors to be balanced in the assessment of '*Gillick*-competence'. As to statute, it is clear that the Family Law Reform Act 1969, s 8 refers only to diagnosis and treatment[38]—the statutory age of 16 years has, therefore,

---

[33] *Report of the Medical Research Council for 1962–3* (Cmnd 2382) pp 21–25.

[34] *Supervision of the Ethics of Clinical Research Investigations and Fetal Research* HSC (5) 153.

[35] See e.g. discussion by G Dworkin 'Law and Medical Experimentation: Of Embryos, Children and Others with Limited Legal Capacity' (1987) 13 Monash Univ LR 189.

[36] It must be said, however, that more guidance is now available on how to deal with children in this context. See, for example, Department of Health *Seeking Consent: Working with Children* (2001); the Central Office for Research Ethics Committees (COREC) has also developed templates to help with the design of patient information sheets and consent forms relating to research involving children, see www.corec.org.uk.

[37] [1986] AC 112, [1985] 3 All ER 402, HL.

[38] It is problematic as to whether this limitation applies in Scotland in so far as the Age of Legal Capacity (Scotland) Act 1991, s 2(4) refers to consent by the understanding minor to 'any surgical, medical or dental *procedure* or treatment' (our emphasis).

no relevance as to consent to research or experimentation. To infer from this that consent to non-therapeutic investigations is impossible below the age of majority would be, again, to accept a total embargo on paediatric research. It is not unreasonable to extrapolate Lord Donaldson's interpretation of the law in *Re R*[39] and to infer that anyone who can legally do so may give consent but that demurral by the minor would be a very important consideration in judging whether to carry out the research. Moreover, this would be even more significant than it would be in relation to treatment—to such an extent that it would be improbable in the extreme that a responsible doctor would ignore the minor's negative attitude.[40] The problem then becomes that of deciding whether there is any age below which a person is deemed incapable of consent and, while there is no law on the point, it would be unwise, in our opinion, for a researcher to accept the unendorsed consent of a child under the age of 16; indeed, the circumstances in which such a consent would be acceptable would be exceptional. Hazardous experimentation authorised by the consent of a minor alone might, in fact, be unlawful.[41]

19.18   To say that a procedure is legal is not to say that it is necessarily morally acceptable; furthermore, there is no reason to assume that the court, if asked, would approve an action which was unethical. The position is, therefore, still delicately balanced. Anticipating a judicial reaction is a matter for ethical committees who may assume that the court would act as a wise parent would act—giving first consideration to the child but being, at the same time, hospitable to good research.[42] Thus, the essential measure is the 'risk-benefit ratio' of the investigation—but, within this, the 'risk' factor must, without doubt, retain primary control. We also suggest that, notwithstanding what the true legal position may be, it would be, in practice, improper to proceed with research involving a child against the wishes of its parents. The only exception might be when that refusal was clearly unreasonable and was jeopardising an otherwise essential trial to which a child who was capable of understanding—the 'mature minor' of *Gillick*—had already consented. Such conditions must be extremely rare; in the event of their materialising, a decision to go ahead should be taken only after very careful consideration—and, probably, not even then.

19.19   It must not be thought that an ethical assessment of a project is always clear cut. A most apposite, albeit now historic, example was an experiment in preventive medicine which entailed the deliberate infection with the virus of hepatitis of children in a home for the subnormal. Although the chances of the children being infected naturally within six months of admission were as high as 60%, the project was castigated by

---

[39] *Re R (a minor) (wardship: medical treatment)* [1992] Fam 11, (1991) 7 BMLR 147.

[40] Relevant to the assessment of competence to take one's own decisions would also be the test laid down in *Re C (adult: refusal of medical treatment)* [1994] 1 All ER 819, [1994] 1 WLR 290, for which see chapter 10.

[41] Lord Donaldson distinguished between medical treatment and a severely damaging operation which gave no benefit to the subject: *Re W (a minor) (medical treatment)* [1992] 4 All ER 627 at 635, 639, (1992) 9 BMLR 22 at 31, 35.

[42] For an interesting comparative analysis, see C Lenk et al 'Non-therapeutic Research with Minors: How Do Chairpersons of German Research Ethics Committees Decide?' (2004) 30 J Med Ethics 85.

some writers.[43] Others disagreed with such an analysis—one of Britain's most respected paediatricians at the time described the experiment as: 'a small, carefully controlled trial for which the director also deserves a great deal of credit for his scrupulous care in securing the truly informed consent of the children's parents'.[44] The legal implications of using children as research subjects have been aired more recently in the United States in *Grimes v Kennedy Krieger Inst Inc*,[45] a decision of the Maryland Court of Appeals. The facts of this case make disturbing reading. Families with children were encouraged to move into houses in which only partial lead-pollution controls had been implemented. The level of lead contamination in the blood of the children living in such houses was then measured against levels in a control group living in less polluted conditions. The court held that it would not be left to the researchers to determine what is an acceptable risk to the health of children, and that the consent of parents would not be sufficient where there was a real risk of harming the health of children.[46]

THERAPEUTIC RESEARCH ON CHILDREN

19.20   And that is an appropriate comment by which to lead us to a brief discussion of therapeutic research on children which, it might be thought, raises no more issues than does non-therapeutic research as we have discussed above.

19.21   A moment's thought, however, shows us that this is not true. To begin with, we cannot apply a substituted judgment test of any sort. We can make a reasonable assumption that a child would want to be cured of a disease or disability if that were possible. What we cannot know is *how* he or she would want to be cured—and we certainly cannot know if he or she would want to take a chance on a lottery choice of treatments.

19.22   As in the case of non-therapeutic research, we can appeal to the principle of respect for autonomy when the child is old enough to be capable of making a decision—although the assessment of capacity would surely have to be exceptionally rigorous in the conditions envisaged—but we have no such fall-back position in the case of the neonate or young child. The onus of consent falls squarely on the parents and we must ask if it is ever possible—or ever fair—to expect a fully informed consent as to therapeutic research from parents who are confronted by a sick, possibly dying, child. The issue thus presents starkly as one of the child's welfare or 'best interests'. The

---

[43] See, for a good review at the time, L Golman 'The Willowbrook Debate' (1973) 9 World Med (1)(79).

[44] A W Franklin 'Research Investigation on Children' (1973) 1 BMJ 402 at 405.

[45] 782 A 2d 807 (2001).

[46] For discussion, see G Johnson, 'Recent Development: *Grimes v Kennedy Krieger Inst Inc*' (2001) 9 U Balt J Environ Law 72. And for a spirited defence: L F Ross 'In Defense of the Hopkins Lead Abatement Studies' (2002) 30 J Law Med Ethics 50. See too, M Spriggs 'Canaries in the Mines: Children, Risk, Non-Therapeutic Research, and Justice' (2004) 30 J Med Ethics 176.

evident nature of forced choices to try almost anything in desperate circumstances is illustrated all too well in the case of *Simms v Simms* discussed above (para 19.12).

19.23   But the application of the best interests test does still not necessarily resolve the dilemma. By definition, the doctor does not know which of the treatments on offer is the 'best' for the child—the research programme would be fundamentally unethical if he did; it follows that there is a 50 per cent chance of the decision *not* being in the child's best interests whichever choice is made—indeed, there is a 50 per cent chance of it failing a 'no detriment' test. Following this one step further, it becomes easy to conclude that therapeutic research on children can *never* be justified—or, at best, can be justified only in exceptional circumstances. Yet we all know that it must be done or paediatrics will become a static subject. Allmark et al have argued that every infant has a 'global' interest in medical progress and it is this which tips the scales in favour of ethical justification for participation in therapeutic research on children.[47] Admittedly, this carries the stamp of the advocate's last card—and it is scarcely a high trump card; nevertheless, it may well provide the escape from what is, essentially, a cul-de-sac for the utilitarian.

19.24   These problems, taken together, are sufficient to explain why paediatricians may be loath to seek parental consent to their children being involved in a dedicated programme of therapeutic research. Failure to do so, however, involves following a dangerous road—consent is now accepted as providing both the key and the lock to medical interventions of any sort.[48] An example of the difficulties in defining the ethical limits of research in children was provided by the long-running investigation into the randomised controlled trial of the treatment of premature infants with breathing difficulties conducted in North Staffordshire.[49] Eighteen parents of babies involved in the study complained to the General Medical Council that they had not been informed of the experimental nature of the treatment,[50] and as a result an official inquiry was established which was severely critical of the study from many aspects.[51] An interesting feature of this incident was the attention that it drew not only to the ethical conduct of a research project—as, for example, in obtaining informed consent—but also to the ethical component lodged in the *design* of a research project—is the design such that it will provide valid results? Clearly, this will often be controversial[52] and a main, and widely agreed, recommendation of the Griffith Report

[47] P Allmark, S Mason, A B Gill and C Megone 'Is it in a Neonate's Best Interest to Enter a Randomised Controlled Trial?' (2001) 27 J Med Ethics 110.

[48] Further complications arise when 'incentives' are involved: R Dobson 'Lump Sums for Children Taking Part in Research May Distort Parents' Judgment' (2002) 325 BMJ 796.

[49] M P Samuels, J Raine, T Wright et al 'Continuous Negative Extrathoracic Pressure in Neonatal Respiratory Failure' (1996) 98 Pediatrics 1154.

[50] J Jones 'Doctors Suspended in Child Health Inquiry' (2000) 320 BMJ.

[51] NHS Executive *Report of a Review of the Research Framework in North Staffordshire Hospital NHS Trust* (R Griffiths, chair) (2000) (www.doh.gov.uk/wmro/northstaffs.htm, updated 08/05/00).

[52] Compare, for example, E Hey and I Chalmers 'Investigating Allegations of Research Misconduct: the Vital Need for Due Process' (2000) 321 BMJ 752 with Anonymous 'North Staffs – a Progress (?) Report' (2001) Bull Med Ethics, no. 172, p 3. The conclusions are at startling variance.

was to the effect that a new governance framework should be elaborated to cover research undertaken in the NHS. This, as we have seen in chapter 18, has now been instituted. It remains to be seen whether it will improve conditions for research on children or, indeed, subjects of any age.

19.25 The importance of research of all kinds is now widely accepted and incorporate into legal instruments at both the national and international levels. Thus, as we have already noted in the preceding chapter, we have the Additional Protocol on Bio-medical Research (2005) to the Council of Europe Convention on Biomedicine and Human Rights (1997) stating:

Exceptionally and under the protective conditions prescribed by law, where the research has not the potential to produce results of direct benefit to the health of the person concerned, such research may be authorised subject to the conditions laid down in [this Article] and to the following additional conditions:

(i)   the research has the aim of contributing, through significant improvement in the scientific understanding of the individual's condition, disease or disorder, to the ultimate attainment of results capable of conferring benefit to the person concerned or to other persons in the same age category or afflicted with the same disease or disorder or having the same condition;

(ii)   the research entails only minimal risk and minimal burden for the individual concerned; and any consideration of additional potential benefits of the research shall not be used to justify an increased level of risk or burden.

19.26 In the context of clinical trials, the 2001 EC Directive[53] makes specific provision for research involving minors and this has now been translated into domestic law by virtue of the 2004 Clinical Trials Regulations.[54] Briefly, these provide that the research must be governed first and foremost be four key principles, being (1) the interests of the patient always prevail over those of science and society, (2) informed consent should be given by a person with parental responsibility or a legal representative to a minor taking part in a clinical trial and that this shall represent the minor's presumed will, (3) the clinical trial has been designed to minimise pain, discomfort, fear and any other foreseeable risk in relation to the disease and the minor's stage of development, and (4) the risk threshold and the degree of distress have to be specially defined and constantly monitored.[55]

19.27 Schedule 1, Part 4 of the Regulations contain further safeguards for the minor, including: (a) the need for a guardian or legal representative to have an interview with a member of the research team and to be given the opportunity to understand the nature and scope of the study, (b) that this person is apprised of the right to withdraw

---

[53] European Parliament and the Council of Europe Directive 2001/20/EC of 4 April 2001 relating to the implementation of good clinical practice in the conduct of clinical trials on medicinal products for human use.

[54] The Directive was implemented in the United Kingdom by the Medicines for Human Use (Clinical Trials) Regulations 2004, SI 2004/1031.

[55] See too, Association of the British Pharmaceutical Industry Current Issues in Paediatric Clinical Trials (2005).

at any time without reason or risk of this affecting future care, (c) that this person gives informed consent, (d) that the minor is involved to the extend that his capacity allows and that his wishes are respected, and (e) the clinical trial relates directly to a clinical condition from which the minor suffers or is of such a nature that it can only be carried out on minors.[56]

19.28   We cannot leave the subject of research involving children without some discussion of examples of good practice. Our focus in this chapter is clearly medical research but it is important to bear in mind that children can be involved in many different kinds of investigation and, often, the ethical and legal issues will be the same or very similar.[57] Indeed, medical and social science research may well overlap, thus further complicating the governance exercise. The Children of the 90s project (aka ALSPAC) is a long-term study designed to unravel how the physical and social environments interact with genetic inheritance to affect children's health, behaviour and development.[58] The aim is to follow the children into adulthood. The study is particularly interesting for its active involvement of parents and children in the research design, leading to very high retention rates among family participants. It will be interesting to see, however, whether this continues when the children reach decisional maturity and the question of their voluntary, continued participation arises. This will be an excellent testing ground both to explore notions of emerging autonomy and to examine how well researchers approach these sensitive issues.

FETAL RESEARCH AND EXPERIMENTATION

19.29   Several of the legal and moral attitudes to fetal life have already been discussed. The possibilities of fetal research and experimentation, which are repugnant to many, extend the area of debate and merit further discussion. Research on the fetus is of considerable importance: just as children are, medically, more than little adults so, or rather more so, are fetuses not just immature children; the environment in which they exist is wholly different and, as has already been discussed, it is within that environment that something in the region of half the morbidity and mortality of infancy is fashioned.[59] Major areas of disease will never be properly understood in the absence of fetal research. Nor will the outstanding dilemma of drug therapy during pregnancy be fully resolved.

[56] The COREC Guidance on Informed Consent in Clinical Trials (2005) details a 'hierarchy of consent' to determine which legal representatives should be approached, para 15.

[57] See, for example, F C Manga, 'Protecting Children's Rights in Social Science Research in Botswana: Some Ethical and Legal Dilemmas' (2005) 19 Int J Law Policy Fam 102.

[58] www.alspac.bris.ac.uk.

[59] The Peel Committee, reporting in 1972, listed 53 ways in which fetal research could be valuable: *Report of the Committee on the Use of Fetuses and Fetal Material for Research* (1972).

SOURCES OF FETAL MATERIAL AND THE PROBLEMS OF CONSENT

19.30   Other than those which are born alive prematurely and with which we are not currently concerned, fetuses become available for research either through spontaneous miscarriage or as a result of therapeutic abortion. It is axiomatic that any necessary consent to their use can only be given by the mother and both her attitude and that of her physicians may be different in the two scenarios.

19.31   The position seems clear in the case of miscarriage. The mother is distressed and, normally, wants everything possible done for her offspring. It seems unlikely in the circumstances that a research project will be contemplated but, were it so, the informed consent of the mother would be required. The therapeutic abortion situation is rather different. In the majority of cases, the mother will have requested termination and it could be held that, in so doing, she has effectively abandoned her fetus. The Peel Committee made the following recommendation:

> There is no legal requirement to obtain the patient's consent for research but, equally, there is no statutory right to ignore the parent's wishes—the parent must be offered the opportunity to declare any special directions about the fetus.[60]

19.32   This recommendation would now be considered inadequate. The very strict rules as to consent to research on the abandoned embryo should, in theory, be extrapolated to the abandoned fetus.[61] Moreover, the Peel Report has been overtaken by that of the Polkinghorne Committee[62] which detected no material distinction between the results of therapeutic or spontaneous miscarriage.[63] It was firmly recommended that positive consent be obtained from the mother before fetal tissue is used for research or treatment in either circumstance[64]—for it was thought to be too harsh a judgment to infer that she has no special relationship with her fetus that has been aborted under the terms of the Abortion Act 1967;[65] the mother was entitled, at least, to counselling on the point. The Committee also recommended that her consent should include the relinquishing of any property rights—a recommendation which has been discussed in greater detail above.[66] Interestingly, the Committee rejected the notion of any control by the father over the disposal of his child—this being on the grounds that paternal consent was not required for an abortion and that his relationship to the fetus is less intimate than is that of the mother.[67] We have already referred to the general denial of paternal interests in the fetus which we see as unreasonable;[68] this seems to be a further questionable extension of the principle of the woman's right to self-determination, at least from a moral, communitarian perspective.

19.33   The Polkinghorne Committee was established mainly in response to concerns over

---

[60] At para 42.   [61] Human Fertilisation and Embryology Act 1990, Sch 3.

[62] *Review of the Guidance on the Research Use of Fetuses and Fetal Material* (Cmnd 762).

[63] At para 2.9.   [64] At para 3.10.   [65] At para 2.8.   [66] See para 15.9.

[67] At para 6.7. For this and several other criticisms of the recommendations, see J Keown 'The Polkinghorne Report on Fetal Research: Nice Recommendations, Shame about the Reasoning' (1993) 19 J Med Ethics 114.

[68] See para 5.110 above.

fetal brain implants (which we discuss as a separate issue above)[69], and, as a consequence, one of its main concerns was that the research worker seeking consent should be wholly independent of the caring gynaecologist—every moral and public policy principle dictates that it be made absolutely clear that abortions are not being performed in order to provide research or therapeutic material; the timing of a therapeutic abortion should be subject only to considerations of care for the pregnant woman.

19.34 The recommendations of the Polkinghorne Committee were re-examined in the wake of the Bristol and Alder Hey reports into organ retention (see chapter 15). The Government's subsequent consultation report[70] then examined all aspects of the use of human tissue and endorsed the Polkinghorne principles. It suggested, however, that in certain areas the climate of opinion has altered sufficiently to merit changes in approach. In relation to maternal consent, for example, a possible revised system was set out which would give the woman the right to information about anonymisation and about the circumstances in which tissue might be used in future for purposes other than those originally explained to her. The report also considered a role for the father and set out a possible approach which would give the him a role in consenting to research on fetal materials—provided that the woman was prepared to identify him for the purposes of obtaining his views. In those circumstances, any objection which he raised to the proposed research would be respected. It is important to note that in a case where the proposed research would be conducted on identifiable tissue, and where this could have personal implications for both the man and the woman, the proposal would require the consent of both. The Human Tissue Act 2004 followed upon the government's consultation exercise and, as we have explained elsewhere, it is an ambitious piece of legislation which tries to juggle with many balls in the air at once. There are no specific provisions relating to fetal material, yet it must be assumed that the provisions extend to such matter since the exclusions of 'relevant material' relate only to embryos outside the human body and hair and nails from the body of a living person. The new Human Tissue Authority will have the power and responsibility to produce Codes of Practice in respect of the Act and doubtless these will extend to uses of fetal material. In the interim, the Department of Health has issued guidance on the disposal of fetal material, stressing the need at all times for a sensitive approach to the issue.[71]

THE STATUS OF THE FETUS

19.35 The Polkinghorne Committee was fully alert to the fact that conditions for fetal research are not uniform and, in particular, that the fetal subject may be alive or

---

[69] See paras 14.76 et seq above.

[70] Department of Health and Welsh Assembly Government, *Human Bodies, Human Choices: The Law on Human Organs and Human Tissue in England and Wales* (2002).

[71] Department of Health *Question and Answer on Disposal Following Pregnancy Loss Before 24 Weeks Gestation* (2004), available at: www.dh.gov.uk.

dead—or it may be killed during the process of abortion. The living human fetus should be accorded a profound respect—a conclusion which is based upon its potential for development into a fully formed human being.[72] In so saying, the Committee clearly differentiated the dead fetus but still thought that this commanded respect. Research on the living fetus should be considered in a way broadly similar to that pertaining to children and adults and it was, therefore, recommended that it should not be undertaken if the risk to the fetus was more than minimal; research or experimentation carrying a greater risk should be limited to that which was of direct benefit to the subject. Respect for the dead fetus was recognised by the belief that research in that area should also be considered by ethics committees.[73]

19.36   Somewhat surprisingly, the Committee did not seek that the law be used to impose their restrictions. Rather, fetal research was to be overseen by local ethical research committees[74] and the general ethical and legal principles involved still merit discussion.

19.37   Some useful research is non-invasive and may be coupled with patient care but even then there is no simple answer. Thus, the experimental use of X-rays, at least in the first trimester, would be unethical; ultrasonic investigations seem, by contrast, to be wholly safe—but we cannot yet know, for example, whether fetal ultrasonic investigations will affect the subject at retiring age. Our more immediate concern is with invasive investigations and these, once again, focus attention on the uncertainties surrounding the legal status of the unborn child (see chapter 5).

19.38   It is now clear that 'wrongful death' in utero of the fetus that is incapable of being born alive gives rise to no action in the United Kingdom; neither the dead non-viable fetus nor the stillbirth has any right of action of itself and the only redress available to the parents for the loss of the fetus as a result of negligence rests on the grounds of distress, inconvenience and the like.[75] If the fetus were born deformed, it would clearly have right of action against a research worker whose defence, assuming causation to have been proved, would depend on a standard of reasonable care having been observed (see further chapter 9). The matter of consent to subsequent research then becomes paramount and must be judged in the same light as has been discussed in relation to children.

19.39   But what if the fetus should die? The fetus not being a legal person, there is no offence of feticide as such; but, should the fetus die prior to or during a resultant miscarriage, an offence may lie under the Offences Against the Person Act 1861, s 58 or under the Infant Life (Preservation) Act 1929, s 1 if the subject were capable of being born alive. Both these sections, however, include a requirement of intent, in the former to procure a miscarriage and in the second to destroy life. To prove an offence, it would then be necessary to show that the action amounted to constructive intent—

[72] At para 2.4.   [73] At para 7.3.   [74] At para 2.3.
[75] See eg *Bagley v North Herts Health Authority* [1986] NLJ Rep 1014; *Grieve v Salford Health Authority* (1991) 2 Med LR 295. Actions for wrongful death of the fetus have, however, succeeded in the United States where the large majority of states recognise an action for the death of a viable fetus: see *Santana v Zilog Inc* 95 F 3d 780 (1996).

that is, something was done when it was known that fetal death was a very high probability—and this seems a very doubtful proposition. It is, however, quite clear that intentional or reckless intra-uterine injury which results in neonatal death can attract a charge of manslaughter or of culpable homicide;[76] it is at least likely that disregard of the recommendations of the Polkinghorne Committee would give rise to an inference of recklessness. We do, however, see such eventualities as being extremely rare.

THE PRE-VIABLE FETUS

19.40   Perhaps it is the pre-viable fetus which attracts most emotion in the general issue of fetal research. Pre-viability implies that the fetus as a whole is incapable of a separate existence but that, nevertheless, there are signs of life in some organs. There can be no doubt that this is the fetal state which offers the greatest research potential; it is also true that the time available for such research is limited and so, therefore, is the opportunity for abuse. But, again, one must ask—is this, morally speaking, an ensouled human being with the rights of a human being? And, moreover, do we know that it has no feeling and is incapable of experiencing pain and suffering?[77] The Polkinghorne Committee was unable to discern any relevant ethical distinction between the pre-viable and the viable fetus—thereby diverging from the Peel Report. None the less, the status of the pre-viable fetus in relation to the criminal law needs consideration and the door is not quite closed on the moral concerns of the researcher.

19.41   We suggest that the criminal law is inadequate in this area. To destroy a fetus outside the terms of the Abortion Act is certainly a destruction of life, but what offence, if any, is being committed? No charge of murder or manslaughter can be raised in respect of a fetus absent its survival after birth;[78] the discussion may, therefore, seem sterile in present conditions. It is doubtful whether the Abortion Act 1967 would be an adequate safeguard in the event of an extension of techniques being coupled with a deterioration in professional standards; it might then be necessary to invent an offence of feticide.[79] The moral dilemma is clear from the questions posed above and, equally, turns on the definition of 'life'. We suggest that the moral problem may be resolved by considering, first, whether or not a placenta is present and whether there is or is not a competent fetal-maternal connection. If there is, the fetus is, subject

[76] *Kwok Chak Ming v R* [1963] HKLR 349; *McCluskey v HM Advocate* 1989 SLT 175; *A-G's Reference (No. 3 of 1994)* [1996] QB 581, [1996] 2 All ER 10.

[77] The problem of fetal experience of pain seems unresolved and one wonders if it is capable of resolution: Z Kmietowicz 'Antiabortionists Hijack Fetal Pain Argument' (1996) 313 BMJ 188; I Murray 'Guidelines Will Ensure Foetuses Feel no Pain' *The Times*, 25 October 1997, p 2. The majority opinion seems to be that fetuses of less than 24 weeks' gestation feel no pain.

[78] Para 19.39 above.

[79] Although the attitude of the European Court of Human Rights to the staggering clinical lapses demonstrated in *Vo v France* [2004] 2 FCR 577, (2004) 79 BMLR 71 makes this unlikely—even allowing for a distinction between clinical practice and research.

to normality, alive and destructive research or experimentation would be morally unacceptable; they should be disallowed on these grounds alone. If, however, the pre-viable fetus is separated from its mother, it is no longer capable of an existence; it is, therefore, possible to argue that its state is one of somatic death. Experiments or research conducted on the body are, by this reasoning, conducted during the interval between somatic and ultimate cellular death which has been described in chapter 13. Accordingly, we suggest that the processes involve neither moral nor legal culpability—although the opportunities for research within these parameters seem limited.

THE DEAD FETUS AND FETAL MATERIALS

19.42 Much useful research can be done on fetuses which are clearly dead or are incomplete; the major debate as to the morality of such research depends on how the fetus came to be dead—any objection on principle to the use of tissue from dead fetuses is almost certainly grounded on an overall objection to abortion.[80] Disposal of the dead fetus and fetal materials[81] must, ultimately, be subject to the mother's discretion but the extent of her authority is currently a matter of legal debate. Despite the strong reservations expressed by the Polkinghorne Committee, it is possible that property rights in respect of such tissues might arise, but case law and the terms of the Human Tissue Act 2004 indicates that such rights would vest in the researchers rather than the mother (and only in circumstances when 'work' had been done on the material to covert it into an 'ownable' thing). We discuss this further in chapter 15. The Polkinghorne Committee condemned out of hand the sale of fetal tissues and materials for commercial purposes; this sentiment certainly persists in Article 21 of the European Convention on Human Rights and Biomedicine, which prohibits commerce in 'the human body and its parts, as such',[82] although this makes no specific mention of the placenta, in which, there *is* a recognised commercial value.

19.43   The rules concerning certification and disposal of stillbirths and of babies who die after birth do not apply to the fetus which is born dead at or before twenty four weeks' gestation. Under Department of Health guidelines, such fetuses are normally incinerated unless any contrary wishes are expressed by parents.[83] Comparable guidelines have also been issued by the Royal College of Nursing, which has expressed concerns as to the practical difficulties involved in providing for their sensitive disposal which is

[80] For discussion of attitudes and practices in relation to fetal tissue research in various countries, see 'Fetal Tissue Research around the World' (1992) 304 BMJ 591.

[81] I.e., those parts of the products of conception which are discarded by both the mother and the fetus— the placenta and its membranes and the umbilical cord. The Polkinghorne Committee preferred the term 'other contents of the uterus'.

[82] See also, *Human Bodies, Human Choices*, n 70 above, which raises the possibility of legislation specifically excluding property rights in the body of a fetus or fetal tissue. This has not happened under the Human Tissues Act 2004, instead see s 32(9).

[83] For a recent update see n 71 above.

envisaged in official recommendations.[84] Hospital incineration is, after all, a functional process which is not easily modified.

EMBRYOS AND EMBRYONIC STEM CELL RESEARCH

19.44   There are two quite distinct forms of research involving human embryos. The moral debate which preceded the passage of the Human Fertilisation and Embryology Act 1990 was concerned with research on the embryo with a view to understanding embryo development, reproductive issues, and genetic disease. In the final years of the twentieth century this form of research was somewhat eclipsed by strong enthusiasm for research into the therapeutic use of stem cells taken from embryos. In this form of research, the embryo is a potential source of material for use on others; it is not the embryo itself which is the object of interest. In this section we will consider the two forms of research separately because of their important moral and scientific distinction and despite the fact that there are, of course, moral issues which are common to both.

EMBRYONIC RESEARCH

19.45   Research into human infertility and an understanding of embryonic development and implantation are inseparable. Embryonic research is also essential to the study and conquest of genetic disease. Systematic study in both these fields depends upon a supply of human embryos, for there always comes a time when animal models are inadequate for human research purposes. Essentially, there are two adoptable attitudes: either one can be totally opposed to research and experimentation on what are considered to be living human beings who cannot refuse consent to manipulation, or one can hold that the benefits to mankind are likely to be so great that the opportunity for study must be grasped if it is presented. Given that the case for human research is agreed—and we believe that it must be—the problem then arises as to how the necessary material is to be obtained and used within an acceptable moral framework. There are, again, two possibilities which are by no means mutually exclusive—either one can use the inevitable surplus of embryos that are produced for infertility treatments, or one can go one stage further and create embryos in vitro for the explicit purpose of using them for research. It is first necessary to look at the general proposition.

19.46   Arguments against a policy which prohibits embryo research rely, ultimately, on the view that, although the embryo may have human properties, it is not a human being invested with the same moral rights to respect as are due to other living members of

---

[84] Royal College of Nursing *Sensitive Disposal of All Fetal Remains—Guidance for Nurses and Midwives* (2001).

the human community.[85] This approach has a familiar ring to it; indeed, it introduces the same concepts of personhood that have been so much a part of the abortion debate. There is, however, a crucial distinction to be made between lethal embryo research and abortion. The life of the aborted fetus is extinguished because its interests are outweighed by a more powerful and tangible set of interests—namely, those of the pregnant woman. The embryo subjected to experimentation, by contrast, dies because of the far less obvious interests of society in the pursuit of medical knowledge. The justification of feticide in abortion does not necessarily license the taking of in vitro embryonic life—and the legislative concern for the latter in the face of a liberal abortion policy may not be as unreasonable as is sometimes argued.[86]

19.47   Yet, if we consider, first, the surplus embryo, we have to ask: 'what is the alternative to embryocide?' The techniques in IVF and the welfare of the patient demand that more embryos are created than are strictly necessary; to say that all must be implanted would be to fly in the face of the reality that there are insufficient wombs available for the purpose. The alternatives then lie between embryocide and reduction of multiple pregnancy—of which the former is clearly the less objectionable in so far as it involves the destruction of organisms which, left to themselves, have no future. We have discussed elsewhere[87] the ethics of obtaining good from a morally poor or doubtful *fait accompli*. It is only the innate public fear of the 'scientist'[88] which stands against the acceptance of such a principle—one which we believe to be valid, perhaps particularly so in respect of the undifferentiated embryo.

19.48   But this can only hold so long as the basic tenet of the doctrine of double effect—that the good result must not be achieved by means of the ill-effect—is observed and it is this that distinguishes research on the surplus embryo from that undertaken on the embryo that has been created for the purpose; it follows that the latter needs further justification. The proponents of unrestricted research would reply that it is acceptable not only because the embryo fails to satisfy the requirements of personhood (which the fetus, also, fails to satisfy) but also because, at least in its earlier stages,[89] its cells are totipotential. In other words, in the early days of development, the conceptus is not a single, identifiable individual; any of its cells can develop along a number of lines, into a placenta, a hydatidiform mole, a human being or, indeed,

---

[85] For a statement of this position, see J Harris 'Embryos and Hedgehogs: On the Moral Status of the Embryo' in A Dyson and J Harris (eds) *Experiments on Embryos* (1990) p 65. The issue of the status of the embryo, and in particular the ethical and religious implications of using the embryo for research, are fully and clearly canvassed in the report of the US National Bioethics Advisory Commission *Ethical Issues in Human Stem Cell Research* (1999).

[86] See e.g. Mason at n 1 p 471.   [87] See chapter 18.

[88] M Warnock *A Question of Life* (1985) p xiii.

[89] The use of the term 'pre-embryo' is suggested for this stage of development. We feel, however, that this smacks of changing words to establish a moral bolt-hole.

several human beings. The early embryo thus lacks the essential qualities which go to make the human individual unique and worthy of moral respect.[90]

19.49   The counter-assertion is, of course, that the embryo is the first stage of the human being that is born at the end of pregnancy—and that this holds from the moment of syngamy. It has been pointed out that the embryo stage is an essential part of life and that it makes no sense to argue that a person's life begins only with the appearance of the primitive streak on about the fourteenth day after conception.[91] It follows that the use of an embryo for any purpose that does not bear upon its future good constitutes a wrong; the embryo is, otherwise, being treated as a means to an end rather than as an end in itself—a process which offends a fundamental principle governing the way in which we treat other persons. To create human life in the full knowledge that it can have only the most limited future is seen by many opponents of embryo experimentation as an example of amoral exploitation and a fairly firm step on yet another slippery slope.

19.50   Between the two 'extreme' positions—that of a total rejection of embryo research on the grounds of its inescapable immorality and that of its acceptance in the case of any embryo, however derived—lies the middle view that, whereas research on surplus embryos is acceptable, the creation of embryos for that purpose is not. This latter is, in fact, expressly prohibited by Article 18 of the Council of Europe Convention on Biomedicine and Human Rights. It is a view which is held by many and one with which we have very great empathy. Even so, it is not easy to establish a valid moral basis for the claim—because, in so far as the ultimate outcome is their destruction, the harm done to the embryos is the same in each case. A possible philosophical solution depends on distinguishing harm from wrong. No *wrong* is done to the embryo at the time it is formed with a view to implantation; a later failure to achieve that goal is due to circumstances which are, to a large extent, beyond the control of the person who has brought it into being. By contrast, the embryo which is developed with the express intention of harming it is clearly *wronged* at the moment of its formation. Thus, while the harm done to each is the same, the wrong done is of a different quality. But do those who take the middle road adopt such reasoning in reality? It seems more probable that they accept instinctively that a utilitarian argument which holds that the benefit to mankind exceeds the harm done to what are the unfortunate rejects of a legitimate therapeutic activity cannot be substantiated in the case of specially created research subjects. This problem has raised what has been, perhaps, the most difficult hurdle for the world's legislatures[92]—and the United Kingdom Parliament is a world 'leader', if that is not an inappropriate use of the term, in having opted in favour of

---

[90] For other recent scientific arguments on the status of the embryo see E Russo 'Stem Cells Without Embryos? New Methods of Generating Pluripotent Cells may Placate Critics, but may not Work, Say Scientists' *The Scientist*, 25 March 2005, available at: www.biomedcentral.com/news/20050325/01.

[91] A Holland 'A Fortnight of My Life is Missing: A Discussion of the Status of the Pre-embryo' (1990) 7 J Appl Philos 25.

[92] The UK debate is well summarised in R G Lee and D Morgan *Human Fertilisation and Embryology* (2001).

the similar moral status of in vitro embryos whether they be surplus or purposeful creations. The UK stands alone in Europe, save for Belgium, in allowing the creation of embryos for the specific purpose of performing research on them.

THE LEGAL RESPONSE

19.51   The legal regulation of embryo research in the United Kingdom is embodied in the Human Fertilisation and Embryology Act 1990, by virtue of which, it is illegal to conduct any research on human embryos except under licence from the Authority. The Authority can only issue such a licence if the project is thought to be desirable for the purposes of advancing the treatment of infertility, for increasing knowledge of the causes of congenital disease, for studying the causes of miscarriage, for developing methods of contraception, or for developing methods of detecting the presence of genetic or chromosomal abnormalities in embryos before implantation; other reasons may be added by regulation.[93] In the absence of further regulation, no licence may authorise altering the genetic structure of a cell while it is part of an embryo[94] and, while the hamster test for the normality of human sperm is allowed, all products of such research must be destroyed not later than the two-cell stage. There are strict regulations as to the maintenance of experimental records.[95] Overall, licences cannot authorise keeping or using an embryo after the appearance of the primitive streak— taken as being not later than 14 days after the gametes were mixed—nor may any embryo be placed in any animal.[96] Most importantly, in decreeing that research may be carried out, Parliament placed no restrictions on the source of the embryos used; the Authority has no mandate to impose an overall embargo on the creation of embryos for that specific purpose.[97] Importantly, the HFEA granted its first licence to create human embryonic stem cells using cell nuclear transfer in August 2004 and it is to a consideration of this topic that we now turn.

EMBRYONIC STEM CELL RESEARCH

19.52   The framers of the 1990 legislation may have imagined that the issue of embryo research would no longer be controversial once Parliament had answered the funda-mental moral question and a system of tight regulation was in place. If so, they were to be proved right, but only for a relatively short time. The successful production of stable cell lines from human embryonic stem cells in 1998 provoked major interest in the possible use of such cells in transplantation therapy.[98] The adult human body is

[93] Schedule 2, para 3(2).
[94] An organism formed by cell nuclear replacement is considered to be an embryo: *R (on the application of Quintavalle) v Secretary of State for Health* [2003] 2 AC 687.
[95] Section 15.   [96] Section 3.
[97] An update on guidance and licences granted is available at the HFEA website: www.hfea.gov.uk.
[98] J A Thomson et al 'Embryonic Stem Cell Lines Derived from Human Blastocysts' (1998) 282 *Science* 1145.

composed of 50 trillion cells of around 200 different kinds, each with a particular function, be it an eye cell, a muscle cell, a blood cell etc. In the beginning, however, it is not so complicated. Over a matter of hours from the initial creation of the zygote, this entity divides again and again but the cells that are created at this stage have no dedicated function—they are said to be *undifferentiated*. Indeed, within this initial period of division—which lasts no more than 3–4 days—these undifferentiated stem cells are *totipotent*—that is, each has the capacity to become a complete and separate embryo. This quality is soon lost, however, and by days 5–7 the organism has become a *blastocyst*, a ball of around 100 cells each of which is now *pluripotent*—that is, each has the capacity to develop into any of the 200 cell types that make up the human body, but it is no longer possible for them to develop into separate embryos. As time passes, the organism—which we might now wish to call an *embryo*—will continue to grow so long as it is furnished with an appropriate environment and nutrition. These are provided by implantation in the lining of the womb from which a blood supply can be drawn (occurring around day 8 of development). It is arguable that it is not until this point that the organism achieves the potential for 'human life'—a distinction which is very important when considering the status of the embryo in the petrie dish. Thereafter, the embryo will continue to develop, with the first signs of a nervous system appearing at days 14–15 (the primitive streak). As the embryo grows, its cells slowly become more task-orientated (*differentiated*) and begin to assume their eventual role within the body. While there is no hard and fast rule, an embryo is generally referred to as a *fetus* from week eight of its development onwards.[99] Clearly one would be holding an immensely powerful research and therapeutic resource if one could produce a pluripotent cell line—that is, a self-perpetuating line of cells that can be replicated indefinitely in the laboratory. As things stand, only a handful of embryonic stem cell lines is currently in existence, with the UK announcing its first success in August 2003.[100]

19.53   Stem cells can also be derived from aborted fetal germ cells—that is, the cells that would have become the sperm or egg cells. These germ cells can be cultivated into stem cells in the same way as can occur naturally in the case of embryos. They were first developed in 1998 and they can now be differentiated into an increasingly broad range of dedicated cells.[101] A final and further source of stem cells can be found in adults, but in the main these tend to be *multipotent*—that is, they can only evolve into particular kinds of cell, or *progenitor cells*, which, although they are clearly destined for a particular end, are as yet undifferentiated. Even so, it now appears that adult

---

[99] Although it saves a lot of misconception if one reserves the term embryo for the pre-implantation stage of human development.

[100] S Pickering et al 'Preimplantation Genetic Diagnosis as a Novel Source of Embryos for Stem Cell Research' (2003) 7(3) *Reproductive BioMedicine Online*, available at www.rbmonline.com/Article/1074.

[101] D Graham-Rowe 'Regenerating the Retina' 177 (2380) *New Scientist*, 1 February 2003, 14.

stem cells can differentiate into a far broader range of cells than was originally thought.[102]

19.54   The value of stem cells of whatever origin is two-fold. First, they can divide and multiply more or less indefinitely without differentiation and, second, they can be manipulated so as to differentiate into particular specialised cells. These qualities mean that scientists have both a potentially endless supply of raw research material and also the means to develop a number of therapeutic applications. These range from gene therapy (for which, see chapter 7) to developments in so-called regenerative medicine whereby diseased or damaged cells can be replaced in conditions such as diabetes, Parkinson's disease, chronic heart failure and injuries to, or degenerative disease of, the spinal cord. As we have already discussed, one of the main drawbacks in transplantation therapy is the rejection by the body of the implanted foreign tissue. Stem cell biology has developed its own way round this problem whereby the nucleus of an embryonic cell is replaced with a nucleus taken from the cell of the prospective patient. Stem cells are then taken from the resulting embryo and tissue is grown from them which can be transplanted back to the patient without risk of rejection. The process of creating such an embryo is known as therapeutic cloning. This is quite distinct from reproductive cloning, because the embryo is not allowed to develop beyond an early point and is not implanted in a uterus.[103]

19.55   But, as should by now be clear, not all stem cells can differentiate into all kinds of cells. Presently, most promise of this lies with embryonic stem cells that are extracted from the blastocyst when they have pluripotent qualities. It is important to re-emphasise that no embryo can be derived from such cells. Equally importantly, however, is the fact that the blastocyst is destroyed in this process. If one views this organism as embryonic life at this stage we have, then, the makings of a classic ethical controversy.[104]

19.56   The ethical and legal issues surrounding human stem cell research of this nature differ from those addressed in the earlier debate on embryo research in that, whereas other forms of embryo research may be intended to assist reproductive medicine and future embryos, this type involves using embryos for the benefit of persons in general. This has invigorated the opposition of those who have a principled objection to any form of embryo research.[105] At the same time, arguments in favour of such research have been forcefully advanced, often on the grounds that the benefit to humanity of

---

[102] Y Jiang et al 'Pluripotency of Mesenchymal Stem Cells Derived from Adult Marrow', 418 *Nature*, 4 July 2002, 41–49, and R Nowak 'Do Nose Cells Know How to Bridge the Spinal Gap?', 175(2351), *New Scientist*, 13 July 2002, 18.

[103] See European Commission Staff Working Paper *Report on Human Embryonic Stem Cell Research* (2003) for a good account of the science and promise of stem cells.

[104] A comparative study of the diversity of governmental responses is provided by B Gratton 'Survey on the National Regulations in the European Union Regarding Research on Human Embryos' (July 2002), prepared for the European Group on Ethics in Science and New Technologies to the European Commission, available at: http://europa.eu.int/comm/european_group_ethics/docs/nat_reg.pdf.

[105] See C Tollefsen 'Embryos, Individuals, and Persons: An Argument Against Embryo Creation and Research' (2001) 18 J Appl Philosoph 65 for an expression of ethical opposition to embryo research.

the resulting therapies outweighs the interests of the embryos, particularly if use is made of cells derived from embryos which were rendered surplus within the accepted IVF treatment programme.[106]

19.57   Scientific interest in the possibilities opened by embryonic stem cell research was accompanied by intense bioethical debate in Western Europe and the United States. Although the Human Fertilisation and Embryology Act 1990 allowed for research on human embryos in the United Kingdom, the purposes for which such research could be carried out were, as we have seen, limited by the conditions of Sch 2, para 3(2); the list of permitted projects does not embrace research on embryos with a view to using embryonic stem cells for therapeutic purposes; moreover, replacement of the cells of an embryo was specifically disallowed under s 3(3)(d) of the 1990 Act. Fresh regulations were, therefore, needed before any such work could be carried out in the United Kingdom. Public debate on the issue was initiated by the appointment by the Government of an expert group to advise on the ethical and scientific aspects of stem cell research. This group recommended that embryonic stem cell research should be permitted and that therapeutic cloning involving cell nuclear replacement should be allowed.[107] A similar conclusion was reached at about the same time by a group set up by the Nuffield Council on Bioethics.[108]

19.58   The parliamentary airing of the issue resulted in the approval of additions to the regulations in Schedule 2. These additions permit embryonic research for the purpose of increasing knowledge about the development of embryos, increasing knowledge about serious disease and enabling such knowledge to be applied in developing treatments for serious disease. The Government, however, agreed to a review of these regulations by a select committee of the House of Lords which, in due course, reported in favour of the proposed additions.[109] Embryonic stem cell research for therapeutic purposes is thus now legal in the United Kingdom, provided a licence is obtained from the Human Fertilisation and Embryology Authority, the first of which, as we have seen, was granted in 2004. The UK Stem Cell Bank—the world's first—was established in 2003 in order to provide quality research materials under optimal governance restrictions in this field.[110] It, together with other stem cell and tissue collections, will soon be subject to the provisions of the EU Tissue and Cells Directive, adopted in March 2004.[111] While the final version of this instrument is largely concerned with matters of storage and safety, it is important to point out that earlier versions were subject to intense lobbying in the European Parliament in an attempt to

---

[106] For an argument that the surplus status of the embryo does not necessarily make stem cell research more acceptable, see J-E S Hansen 'Embryonic Stem Cell Production through Therapeutic Cloning has Fewer Ethical Problems than Stem Cell Harvest from Surplus IVF Embryos' (2002) 28 J Med Ethics 86.

[107] Department of Health *Stem Cell Research: Medical Progress with Responsibility* (2000).

[108] Nuffield Council on Bioethics *Stem Cell Therapy: A Discussion Paper* (2000).

[109] House of Lords *Stem Cell Research* (HL Paper 83(i) 2002).

[110] www.ukstemcellbank.org.uk/.

[111] European Directive 2004/23/EC on setting standards of quality and safety for the donation, procurement, testing, processing, preservation, storage and distribution of human tissues and cells, came into effect on 8 April 2004. Member states must implement the terms of the Directive by 7 April 2006.

use the Directive to outlaw embryo and stem cell research entirely. These attempts did not succeed—there is, in fact, probably no legal authority for the Union to so legislate—but the attempt demonstrates well the continuing controversial nature of the research.

19.59   While the United Kingdom has proved ready to facilitate stem cell research, other countries have been either more cautious or, in some cases, frankly hostile to the process.[112] There is an outright ban on all forms of embryo research in some jurisdictions; a compromise has been reached in others. There has been a particularly prolonged debate in Germany, both within and outside Parliament, and the resulting compromise allows the importation, for research purposes, of embryonic stem cell lines established prior to the date of passage of the legislation. A similar compromise had been suggested in the United States, where there has been strong political hostility to the use of Federal funds for this purpose. Federal funding controls, however, do not preclude the carrying out of research in a strictly privately-funded setting and it is, therefore, theoretically possible to carry out even more extensive embryo research in the United States than may be undertaken under the seemingly more liberal regimes of the United Kingdom or Belgium. In practice, however, major institutions will be severely inhibited by federal funding restrictions. It seems to us to be rather difficult—if not impossible—to maintain a consistent ethical stance in these circumstances. It cannot be the case that the ethics of embryonic stem cell research can fundamentally change depending on who funds the work.[113]

---

[112] L Matthiesen-Guyader (ed) *Survey on Opinion of National Ethics Committees or Similar Bodies, Public Debate and National Legislation in Relation to Human Embryonic Stem Cell Research and Use in EU Member States* (2004).

[113] See most recently, President's Council on Bioethics *Monitoring Stem Cell Research* (2004) and *White Paper: Alternative Sources of Human Pluripotent Stem Cells* (2005).

20

MENTAL HEALTH AND HUMAN RIGHTS

20.1   The practice of psychiatry is one of the most controversial areas of medicine, the subject of endless public debate and of frequent political intervention. The reasons for this are complex; one factor, however, stands out: while treatment for physical conditions almost always depends upon the consent of the patient, the psychiatrist may be called upon to treat the unwilling. The associated powers may involve detention for a considerable time, something which is usually reserved to the judiciary in a state governed by law. In addition, psychiatric treatment is likely to be aimed at ameliorating a disturbance of mood or behaviour. In so doing, it sets out to alter the functioning of the human mind and this can be seen as an interference with human autonomy which will be justified only in the most exceptional circumstances. Thus, in the view of some critics,[1] the powers accorded to psychiatric medicine give rise to unnecessary and unwanted intervention in the lives of persons whose situation, although unusual, may be tolerable from their own point of view. Others have taken a quite different stand, and have argued that society has not been ready enough to intervene in this area, particularly where issues of public safety are involved. The tension between these positions has led to shifts in psychiatric and legal policy, as governments have wrestled with conflicting demands.

THE EVOLUTION OF MENTAL HEALTH LAW

20.2   In the earlier part of the twentieth century, society favoured the institutional or asylum approach to the management of mental illness. Those diagnosed as suffering from a psychiatric illness were usually sent to 'mental hospitals' where in-patient treatment would be provided. This system was inevitably both stigmatising and coercive, and, in the late 1950s, a fundamental change in emphasis was signalled in the

---

[1] For classic examples of radical views of mental illness and society's response to it, see T S Szasz *The Myth of Mental Illness* (1972) and R D Laing *The Divided Self* (1965). A more recent critique is contained in C Unsworth *The Politics of Mental Health* (1987); see also T Mason and L Jennings 'The Mental Health Act and Professional Hostage Taking' (1997) 37 Med Sci & Law 58.

United Kingdom with the publication of the Percy Commission Report, which advocated the treatment of psychiatric patients as far as possible on a voluntary basis. The legislation which followed from this, the Mental Health Act 1959 and its Scottish counterpart, were seen as a liberalising measures but, over the following two decades, concern grew up over the extent to which detained patients could be compulsorily treated without any possibility of review or without any safeguards against the abuse of medical power. The mental health legislation which was introduced at the beginning of the 1980s, the Mental Health Act 1983 and the Mental Health (Scotland) Act 1984, was intended to boost patient rights while at the same time allowing for compulsory detention and treatment of those who were unable or unwilling to consent. Safeguards were also introduced to ensure that certain forms of treatment, such as electroconvulsive therapy, could not be given without further consultation (see para 20.60 below).

20.3   Greater sensitivity to the rights of the mentally ill was accompanied by an enthusiasm for returning psychiatric patients to the community. This policy, which was founded on concern for patients and a desire to allow their re-integration, was welcomed by governments which were keen to contain hospital costs. The closure of psychiatric wards, however, had the effect of limiting opportunities for care and treatment, and was seen by many to be incompatible with patient welfare. At the same time, inadequate provision was made for treatment and supervision in the community, and this was exacerbated by the public's concern over its own safety. Against this background, the United Kingdom entered into a further period of legislative review at the turn of the twentieth century, resulting in the publication in 2000 of a major White Paper, *Reforming the Mental Health Act.* This document set out the shape of the third great reform of mental health law undertaken within 50 years. Like its predecessors, it demonstrated how mental health policy involves the balancing of public protection, patient welfare, and human rights considerations.[2] The human rights elements in this equation are now more important than ever, and any legislative response or judicial interpretation has to take full account of the implications of the Convention rights which have been incorporated in our domestic law by way of the Human Rights Act 1998. Several articles of the European Convention have a direct bearing on mental health law—in particular, on the issues of detention and compulsory treatment. The most important of these is Article 5, which sets out the right to liberty in the following terms:

Everyone has the right to liberty and security of person. No one shall be deprived of his liberty save in the following cases and in accordance with a procedure prescribed by law.

20.4   There then follow six exceptions, the relevant one in this context being: (e) the

---

[2] The resulting Bill was subject to severe criticism, for a useful précis of which see L Birmingham 'Detaining Dangerous People with Mental Disorders' (2002) 325 BMJ 2. Ultimately, it was withdrawn and we now have a further draft Mental Health Bill 2004. Somewhat ironically, this has resulted in successive editions of our text being presented with uncertainties as to the true position.

lawful detention of persons for the prevention of the spreading of infectious diseases, of persons of unsound mind, alcoholics or drug addicts or vagrants.

20.5   The leading case on the interpretation of Article 5 as it applies to psychiatric treatment is *Winterwerp v Netherlands*,[3] in which the European Court of Human Rights set out certain minimum conditions which must be satisfied if detention under mental health legislation is to be justified. These are:

- the patient must be 'reliably shown' by 'objective medical expertise' to be of 'unsound mind';

- the disorder must be of a nature to justify detention; and

- the disorder must persist throughout the period in which the patient is detained.

20.6   These requirements are framed in broad terms, and there is obviously some leeway in which states may interpret them. Importantly, however, the jurisprudence of the European Court of Human Rights has established that patients should not be detained if nothing can be done for them medically. In *Aerts v Belgium*,[4] for example, the Court held it was a breach of Article 5 to detain a mentally disordered patient in a prison, without treatment, because a hospital bed was not available. Article 5 has also been found to require timely release on recovery (even if it is reasonable to stage release in the interests of the patient or the community),[5] and to require reasonably early and frequent reviews of detention decisions.[6] Closer to home, it has now been laid down that a patient cannot be detained simply on the grounds of medical necessity.[7] This is largely on the grounds of Article 8 which recognises that: 'Everyone has the right to respect for his private and family life, his home and his correspondence.' This establishes a prima facie presumption of non-interference with the person—and it requires strong justification to set that presumption aside. Moreover, when Article 8(1) is taken along with Article 3 ('no one should be subjected to torture or to inhuman or degrading treatment or punishment') there are very strong human rights grounds on which to question the legitimacy of *any* compulsory treatment for mental disorder. Article 8(2) allows for exceptions to Article 8(1) on the grounds, amongst others, of the protection of health[8] but it is no longer sufficient for professionals merely to appeal to what they see as the patient's 'clinical' best interests to justify compulsory treatment; broader welfare matters must also be brought into the assessment.

20.7   The 'therapeutic' protection afforded to psychiatric patients by the Human Rights Act 1998 was considered by the Court of Appeal in *R (on the application of Wilkinson) v RMO, Broadmoor Hospital Authority*.[9] The patient in this case had been detained in a high security hospital for over 30 years, having been convicted of the rape of a young

---

[3] (1979) 2 EHRR 387.   [4] (1998) 29 EHRR 50, (1998) 53 BMLR 79.
[5] *Johnson v United Kingdom* (1999) 27 EHRR 440.   [6] *E v Norway* (1994) 17 EHRR 30.
[7] *HL v United Kingdom* (2004) 81 BMLR 131. See para 20.32 below for further discussion.
[8] *Herczegfalvy v Austria* (1992) 15 EHRR 437, (1992) 18 BMLR 48.
[9] [2001] EWCA Civ 1545, [2002] 1 WLR 419, (2002) 65 BMLR 15.

girl. There was a difference of psychiatric opinion as to the diagnosis, most of the psychiatrists who had examined him over the years having diagnosed psychopathic personality disorder. Latterly the doctor in charge of his case had decided that treatment would be appropriate for psychotic symptoms—treatment which the patient was determined to resist. The issue then arose as to whether treatment by way of ss 63 and 58(3)(b) of the Mental Health Act 1983, which justifies non-consensual treatment in such circumstances, was compatible in this case with the patient's Convention rights. It was argued for the patient that the Convention permitted treatment in the face of refusal by a capacitated patient only where this was necessary to protect others from serious harm or possibly to ensure the safety of the patient himself. Such an interpretation would seriously limit the grounds of medical intervention in the circumstances and, in the result, it was not accepted by the court, although it was agreed that judicial review of treatment decisions was appropriate where differences of psychiatric opinion emerged.[10] However, the judgment of Simon Brown LJ contained obiter remarks which suggested that it is 'increasingly difficult to justify' any exception to the proposition that a patient, voluntary or otherwise, should be entitled to refuse medical treatment. These remarks caused some concern amongst psychiatrists, and this was well-founded. Indeed, a strong case can be made out that not treating a treatable and sufficiently serious mental disorder in the face of patient unwillingness to consent itself amounts to inhuman or degrading treatment under Article 3 of the Convention.[11]

20.8　　The proposition was examined extensively in *R (on the application of N) v M*,[12] a case which, again, concerned refusal of anti-psychotic treatment. Interestingly, N claimed that she was suffering from an untreatable personality disorder and that a body of responsible opinion would support her contention that 'treatment' would be ineffective.[13] In, this respect, the Court of Appeal reinforced the growing opposition to the *Bolam* test, pointing out that the medical construct of *Bolam* was necessary but insufficient evidence on which to base a treatment decision. More general conditions had to be taken into consideration—in particular, whether it was *convincingly* shown, first, that the claimant suffered from a treatable illness and, second, that the proposed medical treatment was necessary, this being the standard laid down in *Herczegfalvy v Austria*[14] by which to ensure that non-consensual treatment did not engage Article 3 of the European Convention on Human Rights. That test having been satisfied, there was no case for judicial review of the medical decision.

[10] The courts appear very reluctant to apply Article 8 in cases such as this, generally holding that non-consensual treatment for serious disease is proportionate when it is necessary for the protection of health under Article 8(2): *R (on the application of PS) v G (Responsible Medical Officer)* [2003] EWHC 2335, *R (on the application of B) v SS* [2005] EWHC 86.

[11] Shortly after *Wilkinson*, Lord Eassie in the Court of Session also held that non-consensual treatment under s 26 of the Mental Health (Scotland) Act 1984 did not infringe Articles 6 and 8 of the Convention. The treatment concerned was not, however, a treatment requiring a second opinion (see para 20.63 below): *M, Petitioner* 2003 SC 52, 2002 SCLR 1001, OH.

[12] [2003] 1 WLR 562, (2003) 72 BMLR 81.

[13] Thus, applying the *Bolam* test, which we have discussed extensively in chapter 10, in reverse.

[14] N 8 above.

THE GROUNDS FOR INTERVENTION

20.9 The mere presence of a psychiatric condition will not, of itself, be sufficient to justify compulsory treatment. As we have seen above, a person may suffer from psychiatric illness and yet still be able to reach a reasoned decision as to whether or not to undergo therapy. Moreover, compulsory treatment of mental disorder is justified only if the disorder is sufficiently serious to warrant treatment and if the person's remaining untreated poses a threat to his own health or safety or to the safety of others.[15]

DANGER TO OTHERS

20.10 The detention of mentally disordered persons who pose a threat to others is a widely accepted practice and has become an increasingly important issue in mental health policy. The proportion of psychiatrically disturbed people likely to commit violent acts is actually very small, but such persons engender substantial concern. It is politically difficult for governments to resist pressure to make this form of detention easier, and yet there are serious civil libertarian concerns over the too-ready use of powers provided by mental health laws by which persons may be deprived of their freedom. It would contribute little to the overall welfare of mentally disordered persons if exaggerated concerns as to the risk of violence by them were to reverse progress made in allowing psychiatric patients to lead their lives in as normal as possible conditions within the community.[16] It is salutary to ask why public safety considerations justify the detention of those who are mentally disordered and thought to be potentially dangerous, when those who seek to do so will not allow the preventive detention of persons who are not mentally disordered but are, perhaps, equally dangerous—or are reckoned to be so on the basis of their past conduct or their disclosed intentions for the future.[17] Attempts may be made to justify the distinction on the grounds that those in the former group are both less predictable and less amenable to deterrence—and, therefore, inherently more of a risk to others than are the latter; alternatively, the presence of mental disorder may have a quite opposite result and make the risk of harm to others much more quantifiable. Whatever justification is preferred, the

---

[15] Draft Mental Health Bill 2004 (hereafter 'the draft Bill') c 9. In addition, the treatment available must be appropriate to the individual case—all of which is, essentially, a statutory expression of the *Herczeg-falvy* decision.

[16] P J Taylor and J Gunn 'Homicides by People with Mental Illness: Myth and Reality' (1999) 174 Brit J Psychiat 174. The contribution of mental illness to the overall level of violence within society is thought to be small: E Walsh, A Buchanan and T Fahy 'Violence and Schizophrenia: Examining the Evidence' (2002) 180 Brit J Psychiat 490.

[17] One might wonder if the introduction of antisocial behaviour orders (Crime and Disorder Act 1988; Antisocial Behaviour (Scotland) Act 2004) might be the first step on the road to doing just that.

prediction of dangerousness is an imprecise—and, perhaps, fruitless—exercise.[18] Many attempts have been made to determine an objective concept of dangerousness but none has succeeded sufficiently in allaying doubts as to the strong element of subjectivity that is inherent in such judgments.[19] Disparities are frequently detected; in one such study, 60 per cent agreement between a group of assessors was achieved in only four out of 16 case appraisals.[20] Psychiatric assessment of dangerousness must not, therefore, be considered an exact science—although the fact remains that reliable prediction is exactly what courts, parole boards and tribunals may expect. It is, indeed, possible that dangerousness is best established retrospectively by way of a history of recidivism; the problem then becomes one for the criminologist rather than the psychiatrist.[21]

20.11   It is not easy to second guess the Government's policy in this field. The 2000 White Paper, *Reforming the Mental Health Act,* signalled an intention to deal with the dangerously mentally disordered as a separate group within the category of those requiring compulsory treatment; such patients were to have a care and treatment plan which would be primarily designed to 'manage and reduce high risk behaviours which pose a significant risk to others'.[22] Over the last decade, however, Parliament has trodden a rocky path between the twin pillars of public safety and individual freedom and, in the event, the Mental Health Bill of 2001 was withdrawn in the face of considerable opposition to its public safety orientation. As a result, the tone of the follow-up draft Bill of 2004 is significantly different; the protection of patients' rights is now the predominant theme and 'dangerous people with a severe personality disorder' are not described as such in the draft.[23] The definition of mental disorder is, however, now broadened (see para 20.38 below) so that such persons are by no means excluded from the potential legislation—indeed, it could be claimed that sexual deviants and drug dependents, who are currently dealt with as separate categories, could also find

[18] For a discussion of the potential effect of risk assessments on the prevention of homicide, see E Munro and J Rumgay 'Role of Risk Assessments in Reducing Homicides by People with Mental Illnesses' (2000) 176 Brit J Psychiat 116.

[19] P E Mullen 'A Reassessment of the Link between Mental Disorder and Violent Behaviour' (1997) 31 Austral NZ J Psychiat 3. Opinions differ amongst psychiatrists as to the ethical implications of making predictions of dangerousness. Not all psychiatrists are reluctant to do so; see e.g. T Grisso and P S Applebaum 'Is it Unethical to Offer Predictions of Future Violence?' (1992) 16 Law and Hum Behav 621. Legislators might prove ready to act on such predictions: M A Bochnewich 'Prediction of Dangerousness and Washington's Sexually Violent Predator Statute' (1992) 29 Cal West Law R 277.

[20] G Montadon and T Harding 'The Reliability of Dangerousness Assessments: A Decision-making Exercise' (1984) 144 Brit J Psychiat 149. This study is now rather old and some commentators believe that prognostic possibilities are improving: G T Harris ad M E Rice 'Risk Appraisal and Management of Violent Behavior' (1997) 48 Psychiat Serv 1168.

[21] See, in general, J K Mason 'The Legal Aspects and Implications of Risk Assessment' (2000) 8 Med L Rev 69 and, more specifically, J R McMillan 'Dangerousness, Mental Disorder and Responsibility' (2003) 29 J Med Ethics 232.

[22] *Reforming the Mental Health Act,* Part 2, 1.4.

[23] This is the currently preferred term for those commonly known as psychopaths or persons with psychopathic personality.

themselves in the ranks of those subject to statutory compulsory treatment.[24] The main management plan for those who have been remanded for medical treatment by the courts will now rest on the preparation and application of care plans under the aegis of clinical supervisors (draft Bill, c 99), and this is essential whether the person concerned is remanded (c 93) or committed (c 94) for medical treatment or is subject to a mental health order (c 116).[25] The way is, therefore, still open to managing potentially dangerous persons by way of the widely canvassed option of placing them in institutions which are neither part of the mainstream health nor prison services. The intention is that stress should be laid on the therapeutic benefit of care plans for individual patients but, where it is necessary, 'treatment' may be confined to managing behaviour that might lead to serious harm to other people.

20.12   Human rights considerations are addressed by way of procedural proposals. These include the constitution of a new Mental Health Tribunal and Mental Health Appeal Tribunal (draft Bill, cc 4, 8, see below para 20.29) which will deal with applications by or in respect of all patients who will come under the auspices of the Act as well as those who have come to the attention of the courts. The lower courts will not be able to remand a person for medical treatment which continues for longer than 28 days (c 90(4)). The Court of Appeal may do so but, in such circumstances, the person's clinical supervisor must apply to the Mental Health Tribunal for an order approving the plan.[26]

20.13   Compulsory treatment imposed by the criminal courts is, currently, dictated by diagnosis and is limited to treatment of the condition which justified the hospital order and, where appropriate, a restriction order—a limitation which may cause considerable difficulty when the patient is considered to be suffering from more than one mental disorder or when, as so often happens in criminal cases, the diagnosis is changed following observation.[27]

20.14   The problem of continued hospitalisation of the mentally disordered criminal was, in fact, first directly addressed by statute in Scotland with the passing of the Mental Health (Public Safety and Appeals) (Scotland) Act 1999.[28] This Act empowered the

[24] Birmingham, n 2 above.

[25] A mental health order, which can be made before sentencing, may or may not be accompanied by a restriction order (c 125). A hospital direction, which can be imposed after sentencing, is always backed by a restriction order (c 130). A restriction direction may be imposed on a person who has been transferred from prison to hospital (c 139). For Scotland, see the insertions to the Criminal Procedure (Scotland) Act 1995, s 52 inserted by the Mental Health (Care and Treatment) (Scotland) Act 2003, s 130. We do, however, emphasise that we are not attempting to describe the practical aspects of the interplay between the criminal law and the Mental Health legislation.

[26] As already intimated, much of the fine tuning of the draft Bill owes its origin to the severe criticism meted out to the previous Green and White Papers: see P E Mullen 'Dangerous People with Severe Personality Disorder' (1999) 319 BMJ 1146.

[27] This is particularly so when distinguishing schizophrenia from psychopathy. See, for example, *W v Egdell* [1990] Ch 359; [1990] 1 All ER 835 discussed above at para 8.17; *Reid v Secretary of State for Scotland* [1999] 2 AC 512, [1999] 1 All ER 481.

[28] In addition, the Scottish Executive published its own document of intent *Renewing Mental Health Law* (2001).

Sheriff to refuse an appeal for discharge from hospital by a patient who is subject to a restriction order[29] if he is satisfied that the patient is suffering from a mental disorder 'the effect of which is such that it is necessary, *in order to protect the public from serious harm,* that the patient continue to be detained in hospital, *whether for medical treatment or not'* (authors' emphasis). The 1999 Act, which was always intended to be an interim measure has now been repealed, but the power to detain a person in hospital whether or not for treatment is retained by the Scottish Ministers by way of the Mental Health (Care and Treatment) (Scotland) Act 2003, Part 10, Chapter 2 and this whether the detainee is subject to a compulsion order, a restriction order or to a hospital direction.[30]

20.15 The complicating factor here has always lain in the problem of whether or not psychopathy is treatable—a question which still remains open to debate.[31] The significance of this lies—and still does pending enactment of the new Bill—in the wording of the Mental Health Act 1983, ss 3 and 73[32] the first of which, in effect, states that a person cannot be compulsorily admitted to a mental hospital for treatment unless the mental condition is treatable—which means that treatment is likely to alleviate or prevent a deterioration of his condition; the latter section, which applies to the discharge of a person subject to a restriction order, holds that an appeal for discharge will be accepted if, at the time, the patient is not suffering from a psychopathic disorder which makes it appropriate for him to be detained in hospital. The House of Lords considered the relationship of the two sections in *Reid v Secretary of State for Scotland*[33] and held that the conditions determining an order for discharge were to be interpreted by reference to the statutory criteria for detention in hospital—in other words, an order for discharge was inevitable once it was established that the psychopathic condition was unlikely to respond to treatment.[34] Just such a situation occurred shortly after this ruling when a dangerous psychopath (Ruddle) was declared to be untreatable and, therefore, had to be discharged from a secure hospital.[35] The public furore which followed resulted in the 1999 Act which was passed as an emergency measure. It was, in fact, the first act to be passed by the newly reconstituted Scottish Parliament.

20.16 A challenge to the terms of the 1999 Act by way of the Human Rights Act 1998 was virtually inevitable—particularly in view of the fact that the relevant sections in the

---

[29] See Criminal Procedure (Scotland) Act 1995, s 59 or Mental Health Act 1983, s 41.

[30] The order, which is to be reviewed annually, is, however, still conditional upon the patient having a mental disorder which dictates detention in order to protect any other person from serious harm.

[31] G Adshead 'Murmurs of Discontent: Treatment and Treatability of Personality Disorder' (2001) 7 Adv Psychiat Treatment 407 gives a good up-to-date review.

[32] Mirrored in the Scottish Act of 1984, ss 17 and 64.

[33] N 27 above.

[34] Thus, the House of Lords overturned the contrary judgment of the English Court of Appeal in *R v Canons Park Mental Review Tribunal, ex p A* [1995] QB 60, [1994] 2 All ER 659. Both courts, however, ruled that the hospital environment did, of itself, alleviate the condition and that the patient could be detained legitimately.

[35] *Ruddle v Secretary of State for Scotland* 1999 GWD 29–1395.

Mental Health Acts were designed for the protection of the individual. When *A v The Scottish Ministers*[36] was heard in the Inner House, the Court, essentially, undertook a balancing exercise between, on the one hand, the Government's duty under Article 2 to protect the lives of its citizens and, on the other, the individual's right to liberty embodied in Article 5. In addition to giving high priority to Article 2, the House depended heavily on the derogations permitted in Article 5(1)(e)[37]—that the detention of persons is lawful for reasons which we have already noted above and which, if used to their limits, allow the state a remarkably wide margin of appreciation.

20.17   *A* and its associated cases were then taken to the Privy Council[38] where, again, the safety of the public was considered paramount and the appeal was dismissed unanimously—the dictum of Lord Clyde sums up the position well:

In principle, it cannot be right that the public peace and safety should be subordinated to the liberty of persons whose mental states render them dangerous to society.

Indeed, *A v The Scottish Ministers* appears to confirm a general impression that, in interpreting the Human Rights Act 1998, the United Kingdom courts tend not to use the rights of the individual as their benchmark but will, rather, concentrate on the reasonableness or unreasonableness of their infringement by the state. In the event, the 'Scottish saga' was brought to an end in the European Court of Human Rights where Mr Reid made his final sally.[39] The UK was certainly rapped over the knuckles—largely on account of its procrastination—but, most importantly, the court held that, given the high risk of the applicant reoffending, his continued detention was justified under Article 5(1)(e) of the Convention; there was no requirement under that Article that detention in a mental hospital was contingent upon his mental condition being amenable to treatment.

20.18   Clearly, government and executive on both sides of the border were now anxious to avoid a repeat of the *Ruddle* case and it may be for this reason that 'treatability' has no part in the 2004 draft Bill; it is, in any case, now a tautology in view of the very wide definition of 'medical treatment' that is likely to be adopted throughout the United Kingdom.[40] Paradoxically, this may contribute to the cumulative antipathy to the draft Bill in so far as it seems to open the door to compulsory 'hospitalisation' of many whose liberty is, currently, uncompromised.[41]

---

[36] 2001 SC 1, [2000] UKHRR 439. The Inner House decision is considered and criticised by one of us— G T Laurie 'Medical Law and Human Rights: Passing the Parcel Back to the Profession?' in A Boyle et al (eds) *Human Rights and Scots Law* (2002).

[37] Following, in particular, the European Court of Human Rights in *Litwa v Poland* (2001) 33 EHRR 53.

[38] [2003] 2 AC 602, 2002 SC 63.

[39] *Hutchison Reid v United Kingdom* (2003) 37 EHRR 9, (2003) *The Times*, 26 February.

[40] In Scotland, medical treatment for mental disorder is now defined in statute so as to include nursing, care, psychological intervention, habilitation and rehabilitation: Mental Health (Care and Treatment) (Scotland) Act 2003, s 329. This is followed in the English draft Bill at c 2(7).

[41] J Coid and T Maden 'Should Psychiatrists Protect the Public?' (2003) 326 BMJ 406. For a major modern review of the problem, see P Bartlett 'The Test of Compulsion in Mental Health Law: Capacity, Therapeutic Benefit and Dangerousness as Possible Criteria' (2003) 11 Med LR 326. See also the debate led by T Szasz

Liability for premature release

20.19 Nevertheless, it is clear that the threat of harm to others as a result of premature release from hospital detention of persons with a tendency to violence is very real and is likely to influence the medical officers who are responsible for the clinical decisions; yet it is equally clear that excessive caution may cause injustice to the patients themselves. This issue has provoked litigation in the United States where the courts have imposed civil liability upon psychiatrists when patients have been released and have subsequently harmed others.[42] Undoubtedly, *Tarasoff v Regents of the University of California*[43] remains the most significant case in this context. Here, a patient had confessed to a therapist that he intended to harm a woman who had rejected his advances. The therapist failed to act so as to protect her from the danger and she was later killed by the patient; her family then sued the therapist's employers successfully.

20.20 The important feature of *Tarasoff*—which has been both rejected and extended in later US cases—is to be found not so much in the failure to warn as in the failure to take preventive action which was available to the therapist by way of the unique power to control his patient that he held. In fact, there is evidence of increasing acceptance in the US that the psychotherapist is fully entitled to disclose the facts of a 'dangerous patient' if 'disclosure to the authorities is the only means of averting the threatened harm'.[44] Absent such a rule, it would be unsurprising if psychiatrists' judgments were to be clouded by the possible consequences of releasing a patient who might re-offend.[45]

20.21 Considerable strains could be forced on a national health system if it had to bear the costs of harm caused by mentally disordered persons and it is interesting to speculate on how the United Kingdom courts are likely to react in similar circumstances. There have been a number of cases concerning the comparable responsibility of the police which provide pointers; the most important of these, in so far as it has gone to the European Court of Human Rights, is *Osman v Ferguson*.[46] Here, a known paedophile 'stalker' admitted that he might well do violence; the police took no action and he later injured a child and killed one of its parents. An action in negligence was dismissed, mainly on the grounds that it would not be just, fair or reasonable to hold that the general duty laid on the police to suppress crime included liability to unpredictable victims of crime.

'Psychiatry and the Control of Dangerousness: On the Apotropaic Function of the Term "Mental Illness" '(2003) 29 J Med Ethics 227.

[42] See, for example, *Perreira v State* 768 P 2d 1198 (Colo, 1989).

[43] 529 P 2d 55 (Cal, 1974); on appeal 551 P 2d 334 (Cal, 1976).

[44] *United States v Chase* 301 F 3d 11019 (9th Circuit, 2002)

[45] *Estates of Morgan v Fairfield Family Counselling Center* 673 NE 2d 1311 (Ohio, 1997). See T E Gammon and J K Hulston 'The Duty of Mental Health Care Providers to Restrain their Patients or Warn Third Parties' (1995) 60 Mo L Rev 749.

[46] [1993] 4 All ER 344; *Osman v United Kingdom* [1999] 1 FLR 193. The ECtHR confirmed the findings of the Court of Appeal save as to freedom of access to the courts which it was thought had been compromised. See, now, *Barrett v Enfield London Borough Council* [2001] 2 AC 550, [1999] 3 All ER 193, HL.

20.22   The same issue arose in a medical context in *Palmer v Tees Health Authority*,[47] in which damages were sought by the mother of a child who had been abducted and murdered by a psychiatric out-patient under the defendant's care. The court was reluctant to impose a duty of care on the basis that the relationship of proximity between plaintiff and defendant had not been established. Not only was the identity of the potential victim unknown to the defendant, thus ruling out proximity—and, as Stuart-Smith LJ put it in the Court of Appeal, the possibility of issuing a warning— but it was also suggested that to impose liability could lead to the practice of defensive medicine and could divert the attention of health authorities away from their primary function. In fact, it is fast becoming clear that liability for damage occasioned to another's person is the exception, not the rule, where there is a third agency which constitutes the immediate cause of the damage.[48]

20.23   *Palmer*, however, did not tell us what would happen in the event of a prospective victim being identifiable. For this, we can find some, albeit rather indirect, evidence from *Clunis v Camden and Islington Health Authority*.[49] In this case, the plaintiff, a psychiatric patient suffering from a schizo-affective disorder, had been discharged into community care but had missed four appointments made for him by the doctor who was responsible for his care. He was convicted of manslaughter on the grounds of diminished responsibility after he had attacked and killed an innocent stranger. He then sued the health authority responsible for his care,[50] arguing that the authority's negligent failure to assess his mental state had resulted in his suffering losses resulting from conviction and imprisonment. The Court of Appeal upheld the authority's argument that to impose liability in this case would be to allow the plaintiff to profit from his own illegal act, which is contrary to the ex turpi causa rule preventing a wrongdoer from claiming damages in such circumstances. More importantly in the present context, it was held that, in this instance, the psychiatrist who certified that Clunis was fit for discharge was not liable to him by way of a duty of care. The arguments were, however, largely based on the liability for after-care imposed on the Health Authority and the local social services authority under the Mental Health Act 1983, s 117;[51] significantly, it was stated that the principle of a common law duty in such conditions was undecided—and it remains open for consideration in appropriate cases.[52]

---

[47] (1998) 45 BMLR 88, QBD; [1999] Lloyd's Rep Med 151, CA.

[48] Paraphrasing Laws LJ in *K v Secretary of State for the Home Office* [2002] EWCA Civ 775—a very similar case to that of Mrs Palmer.

[49] [1998] QB 978, [1998] 3 All ER 180.

[50] The limitations on liability provided by the Mental Health Act 1983, s 139(1) do not apply to health authorities and National Health Service Trusts (s 139(4)).

[51] The local authority can only be expected to use its 'best endeavours' to meet the conditions imposed: *R (on the application of W) v Doncaster Metropolitan Borough Council* [2004] EWCA Civ 378, (2004) *The Times*, 13 May.

[52] A patient for whom aftercare is essential should not, however, be discharged unless the provision of such care is assured: *R (on the application of H) v Ashworth Hospital Authority* [2003] 1 WLR 127, (2003) 70 BMLR 40.

20.24   These actions were taken in negligence and, following the success of Ms Akenzua,[53] who won a very similar case against the police but, on this occasion, taken as one of misfeasance in public office, we have debated the possibility of success were an action to be raised against a NHS Trust on these grounds;[54] we conclude, however, that the chances would be negligible. Indeed, the evidence from various sources strongly suggests to us that public policy considerations, of themselves, would inhibit a *Tarasoff*-like decision in the United Kingdom. It is probable that a duty of care to a third party would only be established if there was some pre-existing relationship between the health care professional and the ultimate victim.

CONTROLLING TREATMENT

PATERNALISM AND MENTAL HEALTH

20.25   Non-voluntary treatment of the dangerous person can, as we have seen, be justified to an extent by concern for the safety of third parties. By contrast, the compulsory treatment of mental illness in those who pose no threat to others is based on the notion of justified paternalism.[55] A paternalistic act is one which is not sought by the patient but which is provided with the intention of protecting him or her from harm. Ordinarily, paternalistic action will be suspect because it offends the principle of autonomy. It may be justified, however, when the person for whose benefit the act is performed is unable to make an informed choice for himself. The intellectually impaired and the mentally ill may well fit into this category in that their ability to understand the reality of their situation is compromised by their mental state. The absence of rationality in such cases then warrants action directed towards preventing their being harmed. In such circumstances, it may be appropriate to take the frankly paternalistic route to management and apply a 'best interests' test.[56] However, it cannot be denied that legitimising paternalism in this way carries the danger of licensing excessive interference in the lives of those afflicted by mental illness. There must, therefore, be limits both as to the determination of incompetence and the extent of treatment.

20.26   These problems of the incapacitated have been addressed recently by the United Kingdom legislatures—in England and Wales by way of the Mental Capacity Act 2005 and in Scotland by the Adults with Incapacity (Scotland) Act 2000 which have been

[53] *Akenzua and Coy v Secretary of State for the Home Department* [2003] 1 All ER 35, [2003] 1 WLR 741.

[54] J K Mason and G T Laurie 'Misfeasance in Public Office: An Emerging Medical Law Tort?' (2003) 11 Med L Rev 194.

[55] For an extensive survey of paternalism, see A E Buchanan and D W Brock *Deciding for Others: The Ethics of Surrogate Decision Making* (1990) esp ch 7.

[56] C W van Staden and C Kruger 'Incapacity to Give Informed Consent owing to Mental Disorder' (2003) 29 J Med Ethics 41.

discussed to some extent in chapter 12. The two Acts reach much the same conclusions but, whereas the English Act perpetuates the theme of 'best interests',[57] the Scottish Parliament was at some pains to distance itself from the concept which was considered to have unacceptable paternalistic overtones. As a result, the Scottish legislation leans towards adopting the doctrine of 'substituted judgment'—for discussion of which, see chapter 16. We have to admit, however, to the somewhat cynical view that the debate does little more than confirm that, save in exceptional circumstances, adherence to either principle achieves the same result.

20.27   At the same time, just as it might be wrong in certain circumstances to force treatment upon an unwilling patient, so too might it be wrong in some cases to deny treatment out of misplaced respect for the patient's rights. Both incapacitated patients and, especially, those who are frankly mentally ill may be subject to prolonged and avoidable suffering if legislation goes too far in protecting them from unwanted treatment. In Canada, considerations of civil liberty have significantly eroded the paternalistic claim of society to treat those who are suffering from mental disorder. In *Fleming v Reid*,[58] the appellants, who had committed crimes of violence, had been diagnosed as suffering from schizophrenia. Their doctor had decided that they were incompetent and proposed to treat them with neuroleptic drugs, a proposal which was vetoed by the patients' substitute decision-maker. The latter pointed out that the patients had had previous experience of this form of treatment and had objected to it at a time when they were competent. Under the relevant mental health legislation, the Ontario Mental Health Act, the substitute decision-maker's refusal to consent could be overridden by a review board and it was the decision by a review board to do just this that led to the legal challenge. In due course, the Ontario Court of Appeal held that this decision contravened Article 7 of the Charter of Rights and Freedoms, which protects the right to bodily integrity and personal autonomy. It was only in the absence of any indication of the patient's previously expressed, competent rejection of treatment, that a best interest argument might be used to justify imposing involuntary treatment on an incompetent person. Psychiatric treatment is, thus, put on the same footing as the treatment of physical illness.[59]

STATUTORY CONTROL OF TREATMENT

20.28   A distinction must be made in law, however, between those who have simply lost capacity to handle their own affairs and those who are suffering from a recognisable mental disorder. The latter, by reason of their illness, may be a danger to themselves and, hence, require the protection of the State. This is bound to involve a measure of control, the need for which may not be appreciated by those suffering from the disorder. This, in turn, leads inevitably to compulsion which exaggerates the element

---

[57] S 4.   [58] (1991) 82 DLR 4th 298.

[59] No distinction is made as to the refusal of treatment under the Mental Capacity Act 2005, s 26. It is a condition of a valid advance directive that the person had the capacity to make it (s 24).

of coercion in the treatment of mental disorder—and finding the correct level of compromise is the function of mental health legislation. As has been noted already, the English mental health legislation remains, for the time being, governed by the Mental Health Act 1983 pending the possible passage of the draft Mental Health Bill 2004; legislation comparable to the latter is now, however, in force in Scotland[60] where the natural sister to the 1983 Act—the Mental Health (Scotland) Act 1984—has been repealed. The current state of mental health law is, therefore, in transition. As a result, we have been thrust into something of an editorial dilemma in that we approached this chapter on the assumption that the 2004 Bill would have been enacted by the time this edition reached the booksellers' shelves. Readers will, however, be well aware that this has not come to pass due to the intervention of the dissolution of Parliament while the manuscript was with the publishers. It is true that there was considerable opposition even to the 2004 draft Bill from supporters of human rights and the Bill itself was destined for a stormy passage;[61] even so, the new government announced in the Queen's speech that it intended to press on with the new legislation. It is our view that this will come to pass fairly rapidly and we have taken the decision to continue on this assumption and to refer, in the main, to the 2004 Bill which contains what are undoubtedly the more apt expressions of modern mental health law. At the same time it must be appreciated that what follows could never be regarded as a substitute for a book dedicated to mental health law—in general, we are concerned mainly with those aspects of the Bill and Statute[62] which may impact on the ethical practice of medicine or on the human rights of the mental patient. The reader who seeks the precise wording of the Mental Health Act 1983 is referred to our previous edition or to a major standard work.

20.29   State paternalism begins with administration and a Mental Welfare Commission[63]—the general remit of which is to promote the best practice as to the functioning of the Act and to advise the Authorities proactively as respects the general and individual welfare of persons with mental disorder—has long been, and remains, a major feature of the Scottish system. The duties of the similar English body will, in future, be undertaken by the Commission for Healthcare Audit and Inspection and both jurisdictions are introducing Mental Health Tribunals,[64] the function of which is to deal with applications made by or on behalf of—or, sometimes, in respect of—patients in accordance with the legislation. Appeals against the decisions of a Tribunal will be made to newly established Mental Health Appeal Tribunals in England and Wales or to the Sheriff Principal in Scotland;[65] further appeals to the Court of Appeal or the Court of Session will be available as applicable. In addition, a new Patient Advocacy Service will be established in both jurisdictions and will provide access to

---

[60] Mental Health (Care and Treatment) (Scotland) Act 2003.

[61] Z Kmietowicz 'Rip up Draft Mental Health Bill, Says BMA' (2005) 330 BMJ 326.

[62] The '2004 Bill' and the '2003 Act'. Note that the greater part of the Mental Health (Patients in the Community) Act 1995 is repealed in Scotland and the conditions are absorbed in the 2003 Act.

[63] Continued in existence by the 2003 Act, s 4.

[64] 2004 Bill, c 4; 2003 Act, s 21.   [65] 2004 Bill, cc 8, 249; 2003 Act, ss 320, 322.

information and legal representation (2004 Bill, c 247; 2003 Act, s 259). There are, thus, wide provisions to protect the rights of both compulsorily detained and informal mental patients as defined in Article 5 of the European Convention on Human Rights although it is clearly a matter for argument as to whether these are adequate—at least in England and Wales.

20.30   We confess to some difficulty in endorsing the degree of antipathy that the publication of the draft Bill—and its now defunct predecessor[66]—has provoked, particularly among the medical profession.[67] Certainly, it suggests that a wider group of persons than was previously possible could now be subject to compulsory regulation—and this could include those who are, basically, anti-social. Most would agree, however, that we are witnessing major social changes and it is difficult for the law to ignore these. Moreover, where the Bill appears from its tone to be delimiting human rights, it is, at most, permissive—there is no compulsion to extend the catchment area of the legislation. Finally, the Bill, together with the Scottish Act, follows the pattern of much modern social statute law in establishing a Code of Practice as a base on which it should be applied. How the new Acts operate will, therefore, be as much in the hands of the coal-face workers as in those of the bureaucrats of Westminster and Holyrood. If there is to be criticism, it seems that it is more properly aimed at yet another increase in the administrative burden that is being forced on the medical profession.

Informal treatment

20.31   Treatment for mental illness is provided on either a voluntary or an involuntary basis. Informal—that is, voluntary—treatment may be provided by any registered medical practitioner or, indeed, by any layman provided that the provisions of the Medical Act 1983 as to impersonation are observed. The proportion of informal patients has increased markedly over the last three decades and the majority of treatments are now given under this heading; current intentions in both England and Scotland are that voluntary treatment should continue to be the ideal.

20.32   Thus, many seriously incapacitated psychiatric patients are looked after in nursing homes and other institutions without having any formal order made in respect of their care. In *R v Bournewood Community and Mental Health NHS Trust, ex p L*[68] the House of Lords considered the position of informal patients who lack the capacity to give a proper consent to treatment but who are, none the less, compliant. In this case, a profoundly autistic adult was admitted for in-patient treatment following an outburst of disturbed, self-harming behaviour. He was not detained compulsorily under the provisions of the Mental Health Act as he did not resist admission. Relations between the hospital and the plaintiff's carers deteriorated, with the result that an

---

[66] Z Kmietowicz 'Organisations Unite against Draft Mental Health Bill' (2002) 325 BMJ 9.

[67] And politicians. As we write, the Bill has been condemned on human rights grounds by the scrutinising Parliamentary Committee: C Dyer 'Draft Mental Health Bill Needs Major Overhaul, Says Committee' (2005) 330 BMJ 747.

[68] [1998] 3 All ER 289, [1998] 3 WLR 107.

action was brought against the health trust for damages for unlawful detention. The Court of Appeal allowed recovery but the House of Lords overturned this decision after hearing argument that requiring such patients to be detained under the Act—rather than admitted informally—would pose an immense burden on existing arrangements. In effect, compulsorily detaining such patients would be a luxury which the system simply could not afford at current levels of funding. In the result, the House of Lords ruled that informal treatment of compliant patients who were, nevertheless, incapable of consenting was justified on the principle of necessity and was in accordance with the Mental Health Act's objective of facilitating informal treatment; the Act, it was held, does not exclude the application of common law powers in the provision of treatment to psychiatric patients.

20.33   As pointed out by Lord Steyn, patients in this category who are detained—and both Lord Nolan and Lord Steyn, in particular, emphasised that they *are* detained—are denied the statutory protections afforded those who are treated under compulsion. These were undoubtedly unfortunate legacies of the House of Lords' decision and it was largely on these grounds that informal detention was ultimately declared contrary to Article 5.1 of the Convention by the European Court of Human Rights[69]—where it was held that, under the existing system, the hospital's health care professionals assumed full control of the liberty and treatment of a vulnerable incapacitated individual solely on the basis of their own clinical assessments; Article 5.4 was also violated in that there was no opportunity for the detainee to have his case heard speedily by a court.

20.34   A rather similar situation has arisen even more recently concerning a Down's syndrome adult aged 32 whose behaviour was becoming increasingly aggressive and who was admitted for assessment under the Mental Health Act 1983, s 2.[70] The statutory limit of 28 days' detention became prolonged as a result of various administrative difficulties and legal manoeuvring—including a contested application to replace the patient's mother as her nearest relative under s 29 of the Act; an application for judicial review of the situation was rejected at first instance. The Court of Appeal, however, found that the Act was incompatible with Article 5(4) of the European Convention on the grounds that s 2 does not provide adequately for a reference of the case to a court in the event, as in the instant case, that the patient was incapable of expressing her rights on her own initiative. Section 29 was also found to be incompatible in that there is no provision for reference to a court of a case in which the reason for extended detention lay in s 29 itself.

20.35   The effect of these judgments on the psychiatric services has yet to emerge.[71] It serves to emphasise the need for incorporating both flexibility and uniform protection of the patients' interests in any system. The avowed intention of the

---

[69] *L v United Kingdom* (2004) Application no. 45508/99, *sub nom HL v UK* (2005) 81 BMLR 131.

[70] *R (on the application of MH) v Secretary of State for the Department of Health* [2004] EWCA Civ 1690, (2005) 82 BMLR 168.

[71] And the Government has issued an urgent consultation paper: Department of Health *Bournewood Consultation* (2005) www.dh.gov.uk/assetRoot/04/10/69/47/04106947.pdf.

legislation proposed in the 2002 Bill was to focus on the needs and characteristics of individual patients. That part which set out to clarify the rights of the informal patient has, however, been withdrawn from the 2004 Bill[72] and appears to be superseded by the provisions of the Mental Capacity Act (see chapter 12). The proposed legislation, thus, embodies two distinct jurisdictional concepts. On the one hand governed by mental health legislation, we have compulsory treatment based on a rigid set of checks and balances with the patient's ultimate fate placed in the hands of the Mental Health Tribunal; on the other, concerned with mental capacity simpliciter, we have informal treatment governed by a far looser code, the operation of which is determined by the best interests of the individual patient[73] and which is, at the end of the day, subject to the aegis of the Court of Protection.[74] It remains to be seen how, in the latter case, the extensive powers vested in the donee of a lasting power of attorney—and based on the ephemeral concept of 'best interests'—will stand up in practice. It may well be that managing an incapacitated person by way of a relatively uncontrolled care system will be preferred to the use of the unbending, yet clearly more protective, terms of the Mental Health Acts which, by their very nature, carry the risk of stigmatising the patient. On the other hand, the existing and proposed legislation predates the European Court of Human Rights' decision in the *Bournewood* case,[75] the effect of which is yet to be seen Our suspicion is that the Government may now be forced to locate the informal patient under the umbrella of the mental health legislation—to which we now return.

Compulsory admission

20.36   A major civil rights concern in this area is that the boundaries of mental illness should not be drawn so widely as to embrace forms of behaviour that are no more than non-conformist and, indeed, any new legislation must be compatible with the Human Rights Act 1998. Compulsory admission must be limited to conditions which amount to an illness that can be said to compromise the mental health of the sufferer.

20.37   In seeking this position, both the English draft Bill of 2004 and the Scottish Act of 2003 follow much the same pattern. Perhaps the most glaring potential administrative divergence lies in the retention of the Mental Welfare Commission, which is responsible to the Ministers overall in respect of mental disorder, in Scotland and its abolition in England (c 257). The difference may be more apparent than real as the functions of the English Commission still persist within the Commission for Healthcare Audit and Inspection. There are, however, those who feel that mental health involves responsibilities that are too specific and extensive to be subsumed under the aegis of a non-specialised organisation; on such a view, the Scottish position is to be

---

[72] Save as related to patients below the age of 18 (Part 6).

[73] 'In determining for the purposes of this Act what is in a person's best interests, the person making the determination . . . must consider all the relevant circumstances' (Mental Capacity Act 2005, s 4).

[74] A rather complex system of appeals by way of the hierarchy of the judges of the Court of Protection and, exceptionally, to the Court of Appeal, is envisaged (Mental Capacity Act 2005, s 53).

[75] N 69 above.

preferred and that in England may yet be retained. Ultimate responsibility for the day-to-day practice of the services will be vested in Mental Health Tribunals for England, Scotland and Wales; the main functions of the Tribunals will become apparent in the following paragraphs.

20.38   A possibly more important distinction for those who must apply the legislation lies in the definition of mental disorder. This is defined in England and Wales as:

An impairment or a disturbance in the functioning of the mind or brain resulting from any disability or disorder of the mind or brain.[76]

The Scottish Act is rather more specific in that mental disorder means:

(a) any mental illness;

(b) personality disorder; or

(c) learning disability

however caused or manifested.[77] Since both definitions appear all embracing, we are, again, presented with a distinction without a difference. But it is in the realm of exclusions that we see some possible real differences. While the Scottish Act excludes sexual orientation, sexual deviancy, transsexualism, transvestism, dependence on or use of drugs or alcohol, alarming or distressful behaviour and imprudent activity as lying outside the diagnosis when present without any other evidence of mental disorder,[78] similar specific exclusions that are present in the Mental Health Act 1983 have disappeared from the 2004 Bill. The two jurisdictions are, nonetheless, united in defining what constitutes treatment for mental disorder. This includes nursing, care, psychological intervention, habilitation and rehabilitation.[79] We have seen, however, that, in terms of human rights, this may be something of a two edged sword. It may well be there for the benefit of the individual; at the same time it may be used as a sophistic means by which to detain a person whose underlying disability is, effectively, untreatable.[80]

20.39   Other specific points to which we draw attention include the recognition of the current emphasis on medical validation by way of establishment of 'approved medical practitioners' in Scotland and 'approved clinicians' in England and Wales—both being defined as persons who have satisfied the appropriate authority as having special experience in the diagnosis or treatment of mental disorder.[81]

20.40   Basically, compulsory treatment in the absence of criminality is considered in the 2004 draft Bill in three phases—examination, assessment and treatment. All three are subject to a greater or lesser extent to fulfilment of the relevant conditions which can be summarised thus:

---

[76] C 2(5)   [77] S 328.   [78] 2003 Act, s 328(2).   [79] 2004 Bill, c 2; 2003 Act, s 329.
[80] See, for example, *A v The Scottish Ministers*, n 36 above.
[81] The appropriate authority in England is the Secretary of State; in Scotland, it is the appropriate Health Board. Clause 2 of the 2004 Bill also allows for the appointment of approved mental health professionals who will be approved by the relevant social services authority.

- that the patient is suffering from a mental disorder;
- that the mental disorder warrants the provision of medical treatment;
- that the treatment is necessary for the protection of the patient or of others;
- that the treatment cannot be given lawfully other than subject to the Act;
- that treatment is available which is appropriate given all the circumstances of the case.

(a) *Examination.* Once these criteria are met—and the importance of their being so cannot be overemphasised—it is the duty of the appropriate authority, on request,[82] to arrange for the examination of a patient by two registered medical practitioners— one being an approved specialist—and an approved mental health practitioner. The essential purpose of the examination will be to determine whether the patient should be admitted to hospital for assessment or whether this can be done on an out-patient basis. In the event that the patient is found liable to assessment, there are intricate arrangements for notification of the determination; the approved mental health practitioner is also responsible for appointing a nominated person to represent the patient and also for ensuring that advocacy services are available.

(b) *Assessment.* Compulsory admission, or restriction, for assessment depends, initially, on registration—and any consequent action must be started within 7 days of registration. Subsequently, a clinical supervisor, who will determine the management of the patient, must be appointed; the assessment must be concluded within 28 days. Perhaps the most important feature for the detainee is that his or her clinical supervisor must prepare a care plan for any registered patient—and, in doing so, the patient, his or her nominated person, and any carer of the patient, must be consulted. The plan itself, however, is confidential between the supervisor and the patient unless the latter's wishes otherwise (c 32). An application for discharge of liability to assessment may be made to the Tribunal at any time.

(c) *Treatment.* Once a decision has been made confirming that these criteria have been satisfied, the clinical supervisor must make an application to the Tribunal for an order authorising the patient's treatment (c 38) and the Tribunal must determine the issue within 28 days. The application must include the care plan and state whether the patient is to be managed as a resident or non-resident patient. As might be expected, any changes in respect of assessment or treatment must be covered by a further order from the Tribunal. It is noteworthy that stringent conditions may be laid down if the patient is to be treated on a non-residential basis. These include specified attendances at specified places and specifications as to residence making him- or herself available for treatment; the Tribunal may also make recommendations as to what action should be taken in the event of non-compliance (c 46). The original treatment order and the

---

[82] The request may well result from removal of a person to a place of safety under emergency regulations (cc 227–230). It is to be noted that the second doctor can be dispensed with if his or her participation involves undesirable delay (c 17).

first further order may not remain in force for more than 6 months; orders after this may extend to 12 months (c 47). Even so, this licence is subject to the strict interpretation of statute and, in particular, it was assumed under the 1983 Act that authority to treat is limited to treatment of the condition for which the patient was admitted. This seems to be perpetuated in the 2004 Bill under which a fresh application will have to be made to the Tribunal before additional treatment can be instituted if the diagnosis is changed, or the patient develops an additional mental disorder, whilst subject to compulsory admission for a condition that, as a result of treatment, no longer justifies detention (c 58). The proposition is, however, now uncertain. In *R (on the application of B) v Ashworth Hospital Authority*,[83] the patient was detained under s 37 of the 1983 Act by reason of mental illness—one of the four forms of mental disorder which justify admission for compulsory treatment.[84] He was, however, treated for psychopathic disorder in a personality disorder ward; the Court of Appeal held that treatment without consent under s 63 would be unlawful until such time as he was reclassified.[85] Even so, *B v Ashworth Hospital* was again overturned in the House of Lords where it was agreed unanimously that, on an ordinary interpretation of the words, the 1983 Act, s 63 indicates that a person compulsorily admitted to hospital can be treated without consent for any mental disorder for which he or she is suffering—not just the specific disorder which justified admission to hospital.[86] This interpretation would certainly be consistent with statute were the wide definition of mental disorder proposed in the 2004 draft Bill (see para 20.38 above) to be adopted.

20.41   The Scottish legislation is broadly in line with that proposed for England in distinguishing:

20.42   (a) *Emergency detention.* which can be initiated by a single medical practitioner, following positive consultation with a mental health officer, given that, if the patient were not detained in hospital, there would be a significant risk to the health, safety or welfare of the patient or others.[87] A patient admitted to hospital under an emergency detention certificate must be examined by an approved medical practitioner as soon as is practicable. The certificate is valid for 72 hours during which time the approved medical practitioner may issue a short term detention certificate.

20.43   (b) *Short term detention certificate.* which enables the detention of the patient in

---

[83] [2002] EWHC 1442, QBD; [2003] 4 All ER 319, (2003) 74 BMLR 58, CA—yet another case which demonstrates the difficulty of distinguishing schizophrenia from personality disorder.

[84] The others being severe mental impairment, psychopathic disorder and mental impairment (s 38).

[85] Again, however, the precise conditions are important. In a later case involving recall for treatment, it was held that a person detained under the Criminal Procedure (Insanity) Act 1964, s 5(1)(a) (which does not require specification of the mental disorder) could be recalled irrespective of the diagnosis: *R (on the application of L) v S of S for the Home Department* (2005) *The Times*, 27 January.

[86] *R (on the application of B) v Ashworth Hospital Authority* [2005] 2 All ER 289, [2005] 2 WLR 695.

[87] 2003 Act, s 36. Mental Health Officers are appointed by local authorities essentially to ensure that their duties under the Act are fulfilled (s 32). The local authority may initiate inquiries ab initio in suitable cases of suspected mental disorder (s 33).

hospital for up to 28 days subject to the consent of the mental health officer who must, where practicable, consult with the patient's named person. An extension certificate valid for 3 days can be issued[88] pending application to the Tribunal for a compulsory treatment order.

20.44   (c) *Compulsory treatment order.*   which can only be made by a mental health officer. Subject to giving the opportunity to large numbers of interested parties to make representations, and if satisfied that the necessary conditions are fulfilled, the Tribunal may authorise such treatments as are thought necessary for 6 months. Alternatively, the Tribunal can make an interim compulsory treatment order on the application of any person having an interest in the proceedings—this lasts for 28 days, and the total of such orders must not exceed 56 days. Compulsory treatment orders are, as can be imagined, subject to mandatory review by the responsible medical officer.

20.45   Both the draft English bill and the Scottish Act of 2003 maintain the move to a community care philosophy in psychiatric treatment that was expressed in the Mental Health (Patients in the Community) Act 1995[89] and compulsory treatment orders allow for the requirement that patients will attend for out-patient treatment or for assistance from the social services.[90] This must mean that there is a number of relatively seriously ill patients living outside psychiatric hospitals and it has been suggested that the existing measures of supervision, such as guardianship, provide inadequate protection for the patient and the public. The difficulty, once again, is to accommodate adequate preventive medicine while, at the same time, preserving the rights of the individual patient. Thus, the practice of granting leave from hospital (permissible under the Act) and revoking the leave if the patient became non-compliant was expressly declared to be unlawful under the existing legislation.[91] We have already noted above that lack of supervision has resulted in a number of crimes of violence which have contributed to a general sense of dissatisfaction with the existing system. As a result, the proposed English legislation and the 2003 Act both provide statutory authority not only for the application of care and treatment orders to patients outside hospital but also for the authorisation of measures to ensure compliance with their terms.[92] Perhaps the most important generalisation in respect of the new legislation is that compulsory treatment must be subject to an approved care plan and that, while the responsible clinicians may initiate changes to that plan, the ultimate authority for approving such changes rests with the Tribunals in all UK

---

[88] The patient may apply to the Mental Health Tribunal for revocation of either a short-term detention or an extension certificate (s 50). The Commission may also revoke such orders if it appears that the conditions are no longer satisfied.

[89] The 2003 Act repeals the 1995 Act in respect of Scotland but retains its purpose.

[90] 2003 Act s 66; Draft Bill c 46(4) which also states that the order must protect the patient and the public from the risks that justified compulsory treatment.

[91] *R v Hallstrom, ex p W; R v Gardner, ex p L* [1986] QB 1090, [1986] 2 All ER 306.

[92] Thus, in the event of non-compliance, the responsible medical officer can arrange for the patient to be taken into custody (2003 Act, ss 112, 113; Draft Bill cc 80, 81).

jurisdictions; the vulnerable patient is, therefore, at least partially protected against excessive medical paternalism.

20.46   At the same time, it is clear that emergency powers must be available in conditions where strict adherence to the rules outlined above would be impracticable. Thus, section 243 of the 2003 Act authorises urgent treatment of a patient detained in hospital when it is to the patient's advantage; significantly, however, it also empowers urgent treatment to prevent the patient behaving violently or being a danger to others.[93] Possibly more Draconian are those sections which authorise entry to premises and removal to a place of safety of a person who has a mental disorder, who is living alone and is unable to look after him- or herself (ss 292, 293).[94] In addition, a constable can remove a person to a place of safety who he reasonably suspects to be suffering from a mental disorder and is in immediate need of care (s 297); this containment is valid for a maximum of 24 hours or until the person is seen by a medical practitioner.[95]

20.47   Persons without physical illness who are compulsorily detained in hospital—and particularly those who are mentally disturbed—are likely to see themselves as victims of paternalistic injustice. The strong possibility exists that they may institute proceedings against those responsible for their committal to and/or detention in hospital. This was foreseen in s 139 of the Mental Health Act 1983 and is reiterated in c 298 of the draft Bill, which states:

> In any civil proceedings against an individual in respect of any act purporting to be done under or in pursuance of this Act . . . it is a defence that the act was done in good faith and with reasonable care.[96]

20.48   Moreover, no civil proceedings may be brought against any person without the leave of the High Court. In this respect, the Court of Appeal in *Winch*[97] overturned the trial judge's ruling that leave to proceed depended upon there being a prima facie case to bring. The court was no longer required to establish that there were substantial grounds for the patient's contention; the issue was simply whether or not the complaint appeared to be such that it deserved the fuller investigation which would be possible if the applicant was allowed to proceed—in Miss Winch's case, the court went so far as to deny any suggestion that the proceedings were likely to succeed. In passing, it will be remembered that the relevant section relates only to actions against individuals. No such protection is afforded, for instance, to a Health Authority.

---

[93] In certain well-defined circumstances, a nurse may detain a patient for 2 hours pending medical examination (s 299).

[94] The relationship between these powers and those provided under the National Assistance Act 1948, s 47 is discussed at para 12.18. Similar powers exist if the person is being ill-treated or neglected.

[95] Similar provisions are made in the draft Bill at cc 227–229.

[96] The Secretary of State is specifically excluded as an individual as is the manager of an independent hospital or care home when acting in that capacity.

[97] *Winch v Jones, Winch v Hayward* [1986] QB 296, [1985] 3 All ER 97, CA.

Application for judicial review does not constitute 'civil proceedings' for the purposes of the Act and remains open to an aggrieved patient.[98]

CONDITIONS JUSTIFYING COMPULSORY ADMISSION

20.49   Thus, the legislators are in something of a quandary as to how and why to limit compulsory treatment for abnormal mental states. As we have already intimated, the concept of 'treatability' has been banished from the English Bill which, it seems, is making provision for the compulsory treatment of those who are likely to benefit from no more than their environment.

20.50   The 2004 draft Bill now defines mental disorder as an impairment of or a disturbance in the functioning of the mind or brain resulting from any disability or disorder of the mind or brain[99]—a definition which, at first glance, seems to be as wide and as circular as it is possible to get; for the purposes of the application of the resulting Act, however, it must be of such a nature or degree as to warrant the provision of medical treatment. The Scottish Act of 2003, as we have seen, retains three categories of mental disorder: mental illness, learning disability and personality disorder. The meaning of some of these terms is, therefore, worthy of brief consideration.[100]

20.51   There is a wide consensus that psychoses such as schizophrenia—and also anorexia nervosa—are included within mental illness but neurotic conditions (essentially, reactions to stress of various types) may well be considered as being unlikely to warrant hospital detention and, therefore, to be beyond the scope of the Act.[101] Sexual deviancy is specifically excluded as a sole ground for intervention under the 2003 Act but such a provision, which was included in the 1983 Act, appears to have been dismissed from the English draft Bill. Whether this means that a person who engages in outrageous sexual practices will, for that reason alone, be liable to compulsory treatment in England—but will not be so liable in Scotland unless he also manifests one of the other qualifying mental disorders—remains uncertain.

20.52   Personality disorders may be distinguished from mental illness, as the Scottish Executive intends, on a variety of grounds. The role of organic factors in the former is controversial;[102] moreover, if one of the criteria of illness is that it 'overlays' the normal self, this cannot be said of a personality disorder which lies at the core of 'self'. The condition of psychopathy, which was identified by psychiatrists of the nineteenth

---

[98] *Ex p Waldron* [1986] QB 824, sub nom *R v Hallstrom, ex p W* [1985] 3 All ER 775, CA. Discussed by Legal Correspondent 'Actions by Psychotic Patients' (1986) 292 BMJ 128.

[99] And ' "mentally disordered" is to be read accordingly': draft Bill c 2(5).

[100] In fact, the only legal definition of mental illness within the UK jurisdiction is to be found in Mental Health (Northern Ireland) Order 1986, SI 1986/595 (NI 4), Article 3(1).

[101] Interestingly, psychiatric harm is not 'bodily injury'—at least within the terms of the Warsaw Convention. *King v Bristow Helicopters Ltd* [2002] 2 AC 628, [2002] 2 All ER 565.

[102] See M Dolan 'Psychopathy: a Neuro-biological Perspective' (1994) 165 Brit J Psychiat 151. A genetic factor may, however, be operating: M Roth 'Psychopathic (Sociopathic) Personality' in R Bluglass and P Bowden (eds) *Principles and Practice of Forensic Psychiatry* (1990). Roth also cites research revealing EEG abnormalities in psychopaths.

century,[103] is listed as a mental disorder in the American Psychiatric Association's DSM-IV. Yet its precise defining criteria are unclear[104] and there is some concern that the tendency to label a wide range of anti-social conduct as psychopathic may lead to an undue medicalisation of deviant behaviour. One Scottish judge, having listened to a description of its symptomatology, remarked:

It is, to my mind, descriptive rather of a typical criminal than of a person . . . regarded as being possessed of diminished responsibility.[105]

This is an unscientific view but, in a sense, it points to the difficulty which many people have with the concept—namely, how is psychopathy to be distinguished, if at all, from uncomplicated sociopathic conduct?[106]

CONSENT TO TREATMENT

20.53   Previous legislation made no direct reference to the conditions under which a person compulsorily admitted could be given hospital treatment. It is important to note that 'compulsory treatment' under the existing Mental Health Act 1983 refers only to treatment given for the mental condition itself. It is probable, however, that the back-up provided by the Mental Capacity Act 2005, to which, together with the Adults with Incapacity (Scotland) Act 2000, we refer in chapter 12, will clarify the situation under statute rather than common law; in Scotland, s 243 of the 2003 Act specifically allows for the responsible medical officer to provide urgent treatment in the absence of consent that is designed to save the patient's life, prevent deterioration in his of her condition or alleviate serious suffering on the part of the patient.[107] The need to distinguish between mental and physical disease, such as is apparent in cases, say, of anorexia nervosa, seems to be largely eliminated.[108]

---

[103] The historical background was well discussed in N Walker and S McCabe *Crime and Insanity in England and Wales* (1973) at II, p 205. See also P Pichot 'Psychopathic Behaviour: A Historical Overview' in R D Hare and D Schalling (eds) *Psychopathic Behaviour: Approaches to Research* (1978).

[104] The category of personality disorder is now more differentiated—and refined. For a survey of advances in the diagnosis of conditions of this nature, see P Tyrer, P Carey and B Ferguson 'Personality Disorder in Perspective' (1991) 159 Brit J Psychiat 463.

[105] *Carraher v HM Advocate* 1946 JC 108 at 117, per Lord Normand.

[106] The third category, learning disability, is defined by the US National Institute of Neurological Disorders and Stroke as disorders that affect the ability to understand spoken or written language, do mathematical calculations, co-ordinate movements or direct attention. Being a disability rather than a disease, there is no treatment. There may be no obvious cause but learning disorder associated with chromosomal abnormality is probably the circumstance of most practical importance in medical ethics.

[107] This applies whether the patient is detained under the 2003 Act or the Criminal Procedure (Scotland) Act 1995.

[108] For reminder of the arguments deployed, the interested reader is referred to the salient cases: *Re W (a minor) (medical treatment: court's jurisdiction)* [1993] Fam 64, [1992] 4 All ER 627; *Riverside Mental Health NHS Trust v Fox* [1994] 1 FLR 614, sub nom *F v Riverside Health Trust* (1993) 20 BMLR 1; *Re KB (adult) (mental patient: medical treatment)* (1994) 19 BMLR 144; *B v Croydon Health Authority* [1995] Fam 133,

Forced feeding of prisoners

20.54   The complexities of paternalistic intervention in the face of potential mental disorder are, however, perhaps maximised in the case of compulsory feeding of prisoners, many of whom in which the situation arises will have a background of personality disorder, but as many of whom will be acting from political or other non-medical motives. As a consequence of this mix, the position of the doctor who wishes to save the life of a subject who is actively resisting sustenance demands particularly careful assessment.

20.55   Current policy is that the doctor's role is to advise the prisoner of the dangers of starvation, to have treatment and hospital facilities available but, otherwise, to refrain from interference. While this policy accords with the Declaration of Tokyo,[109] the doctor must, at times, be concerned as to whether the prisoner can, in truth, form an unimpaired and rational judgment. Voluntary starvation leads to severe metabolic dysfunction and, consequently, to mental impairment. A major ethical dilemma then arises as to whether the doctor can or should adjust his attitude according to the subject's current mental state.

20.56   This clearly smacks of 'cat-and-mouse' treatment which would by today's ethical standards be deemed improper; moreover, re-feeding after some three weeks of starvation carries a serious risk of cardiac failure.[110] One would, in fact, have thought that the question had been solved in *Secretary of State for the Home Department v Robb*[111] in which Thorpe J firmly held that the right of the defendant to determine his future was plain. That right was not diminished by his status as a detained prisoner and there was no countervailing state interest to be set in the balance. However, Kennedy, in a closely argued analysis,[112] has pointed out, first, that it was unusual for the case, which concerned a prisoner rather than a patient, to be considered on the basis of medical law rather than of human rights and, secondly, that the tenor of the judgment was permissive rather than obligatory—the authorities *need* not feed, not *may* not feed. In short, *Robb* rested on its own merits—the principle of respect for personal autonomy was maintained because the prisoner was fully competent.

20.57   This point was raised in the later case of *R v Collins, ex p Brady*[113] in which the prisoner, Brady, went on hunger strike, ostensibly in protest at an attempt to move him from his protected environment. His responsible medical officer decided to force feed him and Brady was granted judicial review of that decision. The court approached the question as one of human rights which was to be judged by way of reasonableness.[114] It was adjudged that Brady's going on hunger strike was a symptom

---

[1995] 1 All ER 683, CA. We wonder if the adult cases would stand up today now that the courts are so imbued with the concept of patient autonomy.

[109] See Appendix C.   [110] M Peel 'Hunger Strikes' (1997) 315 BMJ 829.

[111] [1995] Fam 127, [1995] 1 All ER 677.

[112] I Kennedy 'Consent: Force-feeding of Prisoners' (1995) 3 Med L Rev 189.

[113] (2001) 58 BMLR 173, [2000] Lloyd's Rep Med 355.

[114] In its turn, to be based on the principles laid down in *R v Ministry of Defence, ex p Smith* [1996] QB 517, [1996] 1 All ER 257—a particularly high standard of 'reasonableness' is needed in cases involving fundamental human rights.

of his admitted personality disorder and that, as a result, treatment of starvation was treatment of the underlying psychopathy; the decision to treat was perfectly reasonable. In addition, in so far as he was unable to weigh the contending issues as to risks and needs in his own mind,[115] he was incapacitated in relation to all his decisions about food; the doctors were legally entitled to supply medical treatment in his best interests. As an addendum, in an obiter statement, Kay J had this to say:

> It would seem to me to be a matter for deep regret if the law has developed to a point in this area where the rights of a patient count for everything and other ethical values and institutional integrity count for nothing.[116]

20.58 We have every sympathy with Kay J who was forced to concede that it was beyond the compass of a first instance judge to decide the point in the absence of a need to do so.

Limitations as to treatment of mental disorder

20.59 The extent to which treatment can be given for mental disorder itself is limited by the conditions imposed by ss 57 and 58 of the existing 1983 Act and are continued in cc 177–197 of the draft Bill (and ss 234–241 of the 2003 Act).

20.60 Clauses 177–190 refer to electro-convulsive therapy (ECT) and deal with registered adults and children under 16 who are either capable or incapable of giving consent. Broadly, a patient's clinical supervisor may certify ECT treatment if the patient is capable of consenting, has been appraised of the purpose and likely effects of the treatment, and understands its nature and likely effects; there are, of course, a number of safeguards including withdrawal of consent. In the event that the Mental Health Tribunal is satisfied that the patient is incapable of understanding the procedure, the Tribunal may authorise a specified course of treatment; this, however, is subject to approval by a member of the expert medical panel who must, him- or herself have examined the patient and consulted a registered nurse and one other person who is not a nurse or a doctor (c 181). In the case of a patient under the age of 16, authority for treatment may be given by the High Court or the Mental Health Tribunal. The latter must, again, appoint an expert who must consult with a nurse and another layperson and also any person with parental responsibility—provided it is not inappropriate to do so. He may also be required to consult another registered medical practitioner (c 187).

20.61 Clause 191 considers what are generally known as Type A medical treatments which, pending further regulations, consist of surgical operations the primary purpose of which is the destruction of brain tissue or of its function.[117] It applies to the treatment of both voluntary and involuntary patients but Type A treatments cannot be given to persons under the age of 16. Consent by the patient is needed before such

---

[115] *Re C (adult: refusal of medical treatment)* [1994] 1 All ER 819, (1993) 15 BMLR 77.

[116] (2001) 58 BMLR 173 at 193.

[117] The current limitations under the 1983 Act are laid out in the Mental Health (Hospital, Guardianship and Consent to Treatment) Regulations 1983, SI 1983/893.

treatment can be given under the 1983 Act but the draft Bill allows for non-consensual treatment (c 193); the door to treatment of severely affected patients which was previously closed is, thus, to be opened. Before seeking authority for Type A medical treatment, the clinical supervisor must notify the patient's nominated person; the appropriate authority must appoint a medical member of the expert panel and two other non-medical members of the panel as assessors. Again the experts must consult with a nurse and another person who is not a nurse both of whom must have been professionally involved with the patient—the 1983 Act also requires consultation with two lay persons who have been professionally involved with the patient and these may not be easy to find. In addition, the experts must consult the patient's nominated person and may consult his or her carer. Non-consensual Type A treatment will have to be authorised by the High Court following similar consultations.[118]

20.62   The Bill also allows for Type B treatments, yet to be defined by regulations, which must be authorised before they are given but these will be nominated in regulations that are, of course, yet to come. The process of authorisation is less stringent than that for ECT and Type A treatments so they will, presumably, include less hazardous treatments. It is to be noted that long-term treatments and the surgical implantation of hormones for the suppression of the male sex drive, which are subject to authorisation under the 1983 Act, are not specifically mentioned in the draft Bill.

20.63   The Scottish Act of 2003, as is to be expected of the model for the draft Bill, follows much the same lines. Designated medical practitioners play the same role as the medical expert panel though, in the case of the assessment of a child, the certifier must be a child specialist. In the case of surgical operations, two persons who are not medical practitioners, must certify as to the patient's capacity and, if he or she is found to be incapable of consent, treatment may only be authorised by the Court of Session. Electroconvulsive therapy (s 237) and long term therapy—that is, treatment given for longer than 2 months (s 240)—can be given to a consenting patient on the certificate of his or her responsible medical officer. Treatment may be given to a patient incapable of consenting on the authority of a designated medical practitioner who is not the patient's responsible medical officer—subject, as we have said, to the certifier being a child specialist in the case of a child patient. Otherwise, treatment for the mental condition can be given when the responsible medical officer deems it to be in the patient's best interests.[119]

Behaviour modification

20.64   The focus of our discussion so far has been on treatment, the main purpose of which is to restore the patient—as far as is possible—to the pre-morbid state. Psychiatry and psychology may, however, make rather broader claims and offer to alter undesirable

---

[118] An average of 4–5 patients receive surgery for mental disorder (see para 20.64 below) per year in Scotland: Scottish Association in Mental Health *Looking at Psychosurgery* (1999) www.samh.org.uk.

[119] Interestingly, the 'best interests' test, which was abandoned in the 2000 Act, seems to have crept back into that of 2003.

behaviour. The methods used to achieve this may be non-intrusive, in the sense that they involve no physical intervention, or they may be very invasive—brain surgery, commonly referred to as neurosurgery for mental disorder (NMD)—being the most extreme example. Several ethical problems arise in either case. Are coercive techniques *ever* acceptable? To what extent has the therapist the right to impose his model of desirable behaviour on the patient?[120] Can consent ever be given to such treatments if they are offered in the form of an inducement—for example, as an alternative to punishment? These questions are posed most dramatically in relation to neurosurgery for mental disorder, which, as a result, merits separate discussion.

20.65   The essential claim of NMD is that it can change behaviour patterns in reasonably predictable ways. Modern techniques involve localised stereotactic interference with parts of the brain which influence feelings and sexuality—a process which results in destruction of brain tissue approximating in size to that of a garden pea. NMD has, in the past, been offered for a variety of conditions, most frequently for affective illnesses; other indications have included aggressive behaviour, intractable pain and unacceptable sexual urges but these last are not now considered to be legitimate indications for surgical intervention—modern practice virtually confines the procedure to the treatment of depression, obsessive compulsive disorders and bi-polar affective disorder.[121] Any discussion of the effectiveness of the procedure raises, of course, the question of the standpoint from which success is measured. It is important to distinguish the concept of therapeutic success—removal of symptoms without incurring unacceptable side-effects—from that of manageability. It is hardly proper to regard a treatment as successful if its main effect is merely to render the patient passive and compliant. In one sense, this constitutes little more than the 'neutralising' of the patient and psychosurgery lies open to the challenge that it is primarily a method of social control. As one writer has put it, 'Life in "Brave New World" may be more pleasant for all, but only John the Savage is fully human'.[122] It is, therefore, important to appreciate that, although successful surgery for mental disorder might result in significant behavioural changes, the primary aim is 'to engender a release of adaptive behaviour, not a suppression of an "undesirable" or "unwanted" behavioural repertoire'.[123]

20.66   The Assembly of the United Nations has resolved that NMD should never be imposed on an involuntary patient and that, otherwise, its use should be subject to informed consent by the patient.[124] But, even if one accepts that the patient is capable

---

[120] A McCall Smith 'Changing the Offender: Ethical Issues in Behaviour Modification' (1988) Acta Juridica 169; J Holmes and R Linley *The Values of Psychotherapy* (1989).

[121] Royal College of Psychiatrists Working Group *Neurosurgery for Mental Disorder* (2000) www.rcpsych.ac.uk/publications/cr/council/cr89.pdf. Neurosurgery is also offered for non-obsessive-compulsive anxiety disorders in Sweden.

[122] J Kleinig *Ethical Issues in Psychosurgery* (1985).

[123] D Christmas, C Morrison, M S Eljamel and K Matthews 'Neurosurgery for Mental Disorder' (2004) 10 Adv Psychiat Treatment 189, to which we are indebted for much of the detail in this discussion.

[124] General Assembly of the United Nations *Resolution A/RES/46/119* of 17 December 1991, principle 11(14).

of giving a consent which is valid, in that it is informed and uncoerced, that fact alone may not be sufficient to justify the treatment—a maiming and irreversible operation which achieves only a doubtful therapeutic purpose could well be seen as a procedure which is unacceptable on grounds of public policy. The alternative view might well be that there is no reason why patients should be denied a potentially effective treatment purely because it is open to abuse or is hazardous. Such treatments should, of course, be subjected to control—preferably control which embodies an element of outside, lay opinion—but they should not be excluded from the range of those available by virtue only of their nature. It is for this reason that the Mental Health (Care and Treatment) (Scotland) Act 2003 has taken the rather bold step, in view of the surrounding controversy, of allowing non-consensual NMD subject to approval of each individual case by the Court of Session.[125]

20.67   There are, in fact, only two centres in the United Kingdom now offering neuro-surgery for mental disorder—one in Wales and the other in Scotland. Surgery is only considered in the case of severe, chronic illness that has defied less radical treat-ment.[126] As a result, 33 procedures were performed in Scotland between 1990 and 2001, together with 39 between 1994 and 2000 in Wales.[127]

20.68   Controversy of almost equal intensity surrounds the use of chemical methods to control the behaviour of actual or potential sex offenders. Opponents of these pro-cedures have described them in such terms as 'chemical castration' and have been especially concerned as to their inherently coercive nature. On the other hand, it is perfectly possible to see behaviour modification of this type in a properly therapeutic light. The person troubled by sexual inclinations which he cannot control may look upon drug treatment as his only hope of a normal life in the community.[128] On this analysis, the refusal of such treatment to someone who genuinely seeks it can amount to unacceptable paternalism—and this may well be behind this deletion from the category of treatments to which special safeguards apply in the draft Bill.

20.69   Just such an instance arose in *R v Mental Health Commission, ex p X*.[129] X was a compulsive paedophile who sought medical help. Standard antiandrogen treatment was unsuccessful and he was transferred to a new and relatively untried synthetic compound with the proprietary name of Goserelin; this was administered monthly by the subcutaneous insertion of a thin cylindrical implant. A satisfactory response was obtained with three insertions; however, the Mental Health Commission was now concerned as to the validity of his consent and withdrew its approval of the relevant certificates. X applied for judicial review—as a result of which, the Commission's

[125] Ss 234–236. Note that the position in England and Wales is still controlled by the rigid conditions of the Mental Health Act 1983, s 57.

[126] See Scottish Office Working Group on Mental Illness *Neurosurgery for Mental Disorder* (1996) for a particularly useful overview.

[127] Christmas et al, n 123 above.

[128] For early consideration of the issues which remains valid, see S L Halleck 'The Ethics of Antiandrogen Therapy' (1981) 138 Am J Psychiat 642.

[129] (1988) 9 BMLR 77.

decision was quashed. Once again, some of the observations made may be seen as bordering on the casuistic; nevertheless, we feel that the case demonstrates that, if it is possible to do so, the courts will disapprove a bureaucratic attempt to separate a patient from the treatment he genuinely seeks and that they will support the doctors who are supplying it in good faith. We have, in fact, commented on such a symbiosis throughout this book and it seems an appropriate note on which to finish the work.

APPENDIX A

The Hippocratic Oath

I swear by Apollo the physician, by Aesculapius, Hygiea and Panacea, and I take to witness all the gods, all the goddesses, to keep according to my ability and my judgement the following Oath:

'To consider dear to me as my parents him who taught me this art; to live in common with him and if necessary to share my goods with him; to look upon his children as my own brothers, to teach them this art if they so desire without fee or written promise; to impart to my sons and the sons of the master who taught me and the disciples who have enrolled themselves and have agreed to the rules of the profession, but to these alone, the precepts and the instruction. I will prescribe regimen for the good of my patients according to my ability and my judgement and never do harm to anyone. To please no one will I prescribe a deadly drug, nor give advice which may cause his death. Nor will I give a woman a pessary to procure abortion. But I will preserve the purity of my life and my art. I will not cut for stone, even for patients in whom the disease is manifest; I will leave this operation to be performed by practitioners (specialists in this art). In every house where I come I will enter only for the good of my patients, keeping myself far from all intentional ill-doing and all seduction, and especially from the pleasures of love with women or with men, be they free or slaves. All that may come to my knowledge in the exercise of my profession or outside of my profession or in daily commerce with men, which ought not to spread abroad, I will keep secret and will never reveal. If I keep this oath faithfully, may I enjoy my life and practice my art, respected by all men and in all times; but if I swerve from it or violate it, may the reverse by my lot.'

APPENDIX B

Declaration of Geneva
(As amended at Stockholm, 1994)*

At the time of being admitted as a member of the medical profession:

I solemnly pledge myself to consecrate my life to the service of humanity;
I will give to my teachers the respect and gratitude which is their due;
I will practice my profession with conscience and dignity;
The health of my patient will be my first consideration;
I will respect the secrets which are confided in me, even after the patient has died;
I will maintain by all means in my power, the honour and the noble traditions of
the medical profession;
My colleagues will be my sisters and brothers;
I will not permit consideration of age, disease or disability, creed, ethnic origin,
gender, nationality, political affiliation, race, sexual orientation, or social standing
to intervene between my duty and my patient;
I will maintain the utmost respect for human life from its beginning even under
threat, and I will not use my medical knowledge contrary to the laws of humanity.
I make these promises solemnly, freely and upon my honour.

* The authors are grateful to the Medical Ethics Department of the British Medical Association for
providing the current updated texts of Appendices B-D. Additional clauses to Appendices B and C are
anticipated in 2006.

APPENDIX C

Declaration of Tokyo, 1975

Statement on torture and other cruel, inhuman or degrading treatment or punishment.

Preamble

It is the privilege of the medical doctor to practise medicine in the service of humanity, to preserve and restore bodily and mental health without distinction as to persons, to comfort and to ease the suffering of his or her patients. The utmost respect for human life is to be maintained even under threat, and no use made of any medical knowledge contrary to the laws of humanity.

For the purpose of this Declaration, torture is defined as the deliberate, systematic or wanton infliction of physical or mental suffering by one or more persons acting along or on the orders of any authority, to force another person to yield information, to make a confession, or for any other reason.

Declaration

1. The doctor shall not countenance, condone or participate in the practice of torture or other forms of cruel, inhuman or degrading procedures, whatever the offence of which the victim of such procedures is suspected, accused or guilty, and whatever the victim's beliefs or motives, and in all situations, including armed conflict and civil strife.
2. The doctor shall not provide any premises, instruments, substances or knowledge to facilitate the practice of torture or other forms of cruel, inhuman or degrading treatment or to diminish the ability of the victim to resist such treatment.
3. The doctor shall not be present during any procedure during which torture or other forms of cruel, inhuman or degrading treatment is used or threatened.
4. A doctor must have complete clinical independence in deciding upon the care of a person for whom he or she is medically responsible. The doctor's fundamental role is to alleviate the distress of his or her fellow men, and no motive whether personal, collective or political shall prevail against this higher purpose.
5. Where a prisoner refuses nourishment and is considered by the doctor as capable of forming an unimpaired and rational judgement concerning the consequences of such a voluntary refusal of nourishment, he or she shall not be fed artificially. The decision as to the capacity of the prisoner to form such a judgement should be confirmed by at least one other independent doctor. The consequences of the refusal of nourishment shall be explained by the doctor to the prisoner.

6. The World Medical Association will support and should encourage the international community, the national medical association and fellow doctors to support the doctor and his or her family in the face of threats or reprisals resulting from a refusal to condone the use of torture or other forms of cruel, inhuman or degrading treatment.

Declaration of Helsinki
(Last revised at Edinburgh, 2000)

Ethical Principles for medical research involving human subjects

A. Introduction

1. The World Medical Association has developed the Declaration of Helsinki as a statement of ethical principles to provide guidance to physicians and other participants in medical research involving human subjects. Medical research involving human subjects includes research on identifiable human material or identifiable data.
2. It is the duty of the physician to promote and safeguard the health of the people. The physician's knowledge and conscience are dedicated to the fulfilment of this duty.
3. The Declaration of the Geneva of the World Medical Association binds the physician with the words, 'The health of my patient will be my first consideration,' and the International Code of Medical Ethics declares that, 'A physician shall act only in the patients interest when providing medical care which might have the effect of weakening the physical and mental condition of the patient.'
4. Medical progress is based on research which ultimately must rest in part on experimentation involving human subjects.
5. In medical research on human subjects, considerations related to the well-being of the human subject should take precedence over the interests of science and society.
6. The primary purpose of medical research involving human subjects is to improve prophylactic, diagnostic and therapeutic procedures and the understanding of the aetiology and pathogenesis of disease. Even the best proven prophylactic, diagnostic and therapeutic methods must continuously be challenged through research for their effectiveness, efficiency, accessibility and quality.
7. In current medical practice and in medical research, most prophylactic, diagnostic and therapeutic procedures involve risks and burdens.
8. Medical research is subject to ethical standards that promote respect for all human beings and protect their health and rights. Some research populations are vulnerable and need special protection. The particular needs of the economically and medically disadvantaged must be recognized. Special attention is also

required for those who cannot give or refuse consent for themselves, for those who may be subject to giving consent under duress, for those who will not benefit personally from the research and for those for whom the research is combined with care.

9. Research investigators should be aware of the ethical, legal and regulatory requirements for research on human subjects in their own countries as well as applicable international requirements. No national ethical, legal or regulatory requirement should be allowed to reduce or eliminate any of the protections for human subjects set forth in this Declaration.

B. Basic Principles for all medical research

10. It is the duty of the physician in medical research to protect life, health, privacy, and dignity of the human subject.

11. Medical research involving human subjects must conform to generally accepted scientific principles, be based on a through knowledge of the scientific literature, other relevant sources of information, and on adequate laboratory and, where appropriate, animal experimentation.

12. Appropriate caution must be exercised in the conduct of research which may affect the environment, and the welfare of animals used for research must be respected.

13. The design and performance of each experimental procedure involving human subjects should be clearly formulated in an experimental protocol. This protocol should be submitted for consideration, comment, guidance, and where appropriate, approval to a specially appointed ethical review committee, which must be independent of the investigator, the sponsor or any other kind of undue influence. This independent committee should be in conformity with the laws and regulations of the country in which the research experiment is performed. The committee has the right to monitor ongoing trials. The researcher has the obligation to provide monitoring information to the committee, especially any serious adverse events. The researcher should also submit to the committee, for review, information regarding funding, sponsors, institutional affiliations, other potential conflicts of interest and incentives for subjects.

14. The research protocol should always contain a statement of the ethical considerations involved and should indicate that there is compliance with the principles enunciated in this Declaration.

15. Medical research involving human subjects should be conducted only by scientifically qualified persons and under the supervision of a clinically competent medical person. The responsibility for the human subject must always rest with a medically qualified person and never rest on the subject of the research, even though the subject has given consent.

16. Every medical research project involving human subjects should be preceded by careful assessment of predictable risks and burdens in comparison with foreseeable benefits to the subjects or to others. This does not preclude the participation of healthy volunteers in medical research. The design of all studies should be publicly available.

17. Physicians should abstain from engaging in research projects involving human subjects unless they are confident that the risks involved have been adequately assessed and can be satisfactorily managed. Physicians should cease any investigation if the risks are found to outweigh the potential benefits or if there is conclusive proof of positive and beneficial results.

18. Medical research involving human subjects should only be conducted if the importance of the objective outweighs the inherent risks and burdens to the subject. This is especially important when the human subjects are healthy volunteers.

19. Medical research is only justified if there is a reasonable likelihood that the populations in which the research is carried out stand to benefit from the results of the research.

20. The subjects must be volunteers and informed participants in the research project.

21. The rights of research subjects to safeguard their integrity must always be respected. Every precaution should be taken to respect the privacy of the subject, the confidentiality of the patient's information and to minimize the impact of the study on the subject's physical and mental integrity and on the personality of the subject.

22. In any research on human beings, each potential subject must be adequately informed of the aims, methods, sources of funding, any possible conflicts of interest, institutional affiliations of the researcher, the anticipated benefits and potential risks of the study and the discomfort it may entail. The subject should be informed of the right to abstain from participation in the study or to withdraw consent to participate at any time without reprisal. After ensuring that the subject has understood the information, the physician should then obtain the subject's freely-given informed consent, preferably in writing. If the consent cannot be obtained in writing, the non-written consent must be formally documented and witnessed.

23. When obtaining informed consent for the research project the physician should be particularly cautious if the subject is in a dependent relationship with the physician or may consent under duress. In that case the informed consent should be obtained by a well-informed physician who is not engaged in the investigation and who is completely independent of this relationship.

24. For a research subject who is legally incompetent, physically or mentally incapable of giving consent or is a legally incompetent minor, the investigator must obtain informed consent from the legally authorized representative in accordance with applicable law. These groups should not be included in research unless the

research is necessary to promote the health of the population represented and this research cannot instead be performed on legally competent persons.

25. When a subject deemed legally incompetent, such as a minor child, is able to give assent to decisions about participation in research, the investigator must obtain that assent in addition to the consent of the legally authorized representative.

26. Research on individuals from whom it is not possible to obtain consent, including proxy or advance consent, should be done only if the physical/mental condition that prevents obtaining informed consent is a necessary characteristic of the research population. The specific reasons for involving research subjects with a condition that renders them unable to given informed consent should be stated in the experimental protocol for consideration and approval of the review committee. The protocol should state that consent to remain in the research should be obtained as soon as possible from the individual or a legally authorized surrogate.

27. Both authors and publishers have ethical obligations. In publication of the results of research, the investigators are obliged to preserve the accuracy of the results. Negative as well as positive results should be published or otherwise publicly available. Sources of funding, institutional affiliations and any possible conflicts of interests should be declared in the publication. Reports of experimentation not in accordance with the principles laid down in this Declaration should not be accepted for publication.

C. Additional principles for medical research combined with medical care

28. The physician may combine medical research with medical care, only to the extent that the research is justified by its potential prophylactic, diagnostic or therapeutic value. When medical research is combined with medical care, additional standards apply to protect the patients who are research objects.

29. The benefits, risks, burdens and effectiveness of a new method should be tested against those of the best current prophylactic, diagnostic or therapeutic methods. This does not exclude the use of placebo, or no treatment, in studies where no proven methods exists.

30. At the conclusion of the study, every patient entered into the study should be assured of access to the best proven prophylactic, diagnostic or therapeutic methods identified by the study.

31. The physician should fully inform the patient which aspects of the care are related to the research. The refusal of a patient to participate in a study must never interfere with the patient-physician relationship.

32. In the treatment of a patient, where proven prophylactic, diagnostic and therapeutic methods do not exist or have been ineffective, the physician, with

informed consent from the patient, must be free to use unproven or new prophylactic, diagnostic and therapeutic measures, if in the physician's judgement it offers hope of saving life, re-establishing health or alleviating suffering. Where possible, these measures should be made the object of research, designed to evaluate their safety and efficacy. In all cases, new information should be recorded and, where appropriate, published. The other relevant guidelines of this Declaration should be followed.

Clarification of paragraph 29

The WMA hereby reaffirms its position that extreme care must be taken in making use of a placebo-controlled trial and that in general this methodology should only be used in the absence of existing proven therapy. However, a placebo-controlled trial may be ethically acceptable, even if proven therapy is available, under the following circumstances:

- Where for compelling and scientifically sound methodological reasons its use is necessary to determine the efficacy or safety of a prophylactic, diagnostic or therapeutic method; or
- Where a prophylactic, diagnostic or therapeutic method is being investigated for a minor condition and the patients who receive placebo will not be subject to any additional risk of serious or irreversible harm.

All other provisions of the Declaration of Helsinki must be adhered to, especially the need for appropriate ethical and scientific review.

Clarification of paragraph 30

The WMA hereby reaffirms its position that it is necessary during the study planning process to identify post-trial access by study participants to prophylactic, diagnostic and therapeutic procedures identified as beneficial in the study or access to other appropriate care. Post-trial access arrangements or other care must be described in the study protocol so the ehtical review committee may consider such arrangements during its review.

INDEX